Tuttle

Chinese-
English
Dictionary

Tuttle

Chinese-English Dictionary

LI Dong 李冬

TUTTLE PUBLISHING
Tokyo • Rutland, Vermont • Singapore

Published by Tuttle Publishing, an imprint of Periplus Editions (HK) Ltd., with editorial offices at 364 Innovation Drive, North Clarendon, VT 05759 U.S.A. and at 61 Tai Seng Avenue #02-12, Singapore 534167.

Library of Congress Control Number: 2008938337
ISBN 978-0-8048-3991-4

North America, Latin America and Europe
Tuttle Publishing
364 Innovation Drive, North Clarendon,
VT 05759-9436 USA.
Tel: 1(802) 773-8930
Fax: 1(802) 773-6993
info@tuttlepublishing.com
www.tuttlepublishing.com

Asia Pacific
Berkeley Books Pte. Ltd.
61 Tai Seng Avenue #02-12, Singapore 534167
Tel: (65) 6280-1330
Fax: (65) 6280-6290
inquiries@periplus.com.sg
www.periplus.com

12 11 10 09
6 5 4 3 2 1

Printed in Singapore

Contents

Introducing Chinese

1 PRONUNCIATION

1.1 Vowels

SINGLE VOWELS

There are seven basic single vowels:

a similar to *a* in *ah*
e similar to *a* in *ago*
ê similar to *e* in *ebb* (this sound never occurs alone and is transcribed as **e**, as in **ei**, **ie**, **ue**)
i similar to *ee* in *cheese* (spelled **y** when not preceded by a consonant)
o similar to *oe* in *toe*
u similar to *oo* in *boot* (spelled **w** when not preceded by a consonant)
ü similar to German **ü** in *über* or French **u** in *tu*; or you can get **ü** by saying **i** and rounding your lips at the same time (spelled **u** after **j**, **q**, **x**; spelled **yu** when not preceded by a consonant)

VOWEL COMBINATIONS

These single vowels combine with each other or with the consonants of **n** or **ng** to form what are technically known as *diphthongs*. These combinations are pronounced as a single sound, with a little more emphasis on the first part of the sound.

You can learn these combinations in four groups:

Group 1: diphthongs starting with **a/e/ê**
    ai   similar to *y* in *my*
    ao   similar to *ow* in *how*
    an
    ang
    en
    eng
    ei   similar to *ay* in *may*

Group 2: diphthongs starting with **i**
    ia
    ie   similar to *ye* in *yes*
    iao
    iou   similar to *you* (spelled **iu** when preceded by a consonant)
    ian
    ien   similar to *in* (spelled **in** when preceded by a consonant)
    ieng   similar to *En* in *English* (spelled **ing** when preceded by a consonant)
    iang   similar to *young*
    iong

Group 3: diphthongs starting with **u/o**
    ua
    uo
    uai   similar to *why* in British English

uei	similar to *way* (spelled **ui** when preceded by a consonant)
uan	
uen	(spelled **un** when preceded by a consonant)
ueng	
uang	
ong	

Group 4: diphthongs starting with **ü**

üe	used only after **j, q, x**; spelled **ue**
üen	used only after **j, q, x**; spelled **un**
üan	used only after **j, q, x**; spelled **uan**

1.2 Consonants

Consonants may be grouped in the following ways.

Group 1: These consonants are almost the same in Chinese and English.

CHINESE	ENGLISH
m	*m*
n	*n*
f	*f*
l	*l*
s	*s*
r	*r*
b	pronounced as hard *p* (as in *speak*)
p	*p* (as in *peak*)
g	pronounced as hard *k* (as in *ski*)
k	*k* (as in *key)*
d	pronounced as hard *t* (as in *star*)
t	*t* (as in *tar*)

Group 2: Some modification is needed to get these Chinese sounds from English.

CHINESE	ENGLISH
j	as *j* in *jeep* (but unvoiced, not round-lipped)
q	as *ch* in *cheese* (but not round-lipped)
x	as *sh* in *sheep* (but not round-lipped)
c	as *ts* as in *cats* (make it long)
z	as *ds* as in *beds* (but unvoiced, and make it long)

Group 3: No English counterparts

Chinese **zh**, **ch**, and **sh** have no English counterparts. You can learn to say **zh**, **ch** and **sh** starting from **z**, **c** and **s**. For example, say **s** (which is almost the same as the English *s* in *sesame*) and then roll up your tongue to touch the roof of your mouth. You get **sh**.

TONES

Chinese is a tonal language, i.e. a sound pronounced in different tones is understood as different words. So the tone is an indispensable component of the pronunciation of a word.

1.3 Basic tones

There are four basic tones. The following five-level pitch graph shows the values of the four tones:

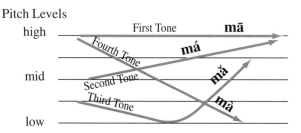

- The First Tone is a high, level tone and is represented as ¯, e.g. 妈 **mā** (meaning *mother*, *mom*).

- The Second Tone is a high, rising tone and is represented by the tone mark ´, e.g. 麻 **má** (*hemp* or *sesame*).

- The Third Tone is a falling, then rising tone. As you can see from the pitch graph it falls from below the middle of the voice range to nearly the bottom and then rises to a point near the top. It is represented by the tone mark ˇ, e.g. 马 **mǎ** (*horse*).

- The Fourth Tone is a falling tone. It falls from high to low and is represented by the tone mark ` , e.g. 骂 **mà** (*curse*).

In Chinese speech, as in English speech, some sounds are unstressed, i.e. pronounced short and soft. They do not have any of the four tones. Such sounds are said to have Neutral Tone. Sounds with the neutral tone are not marked. For example in 爸爸 **bàba** (*daddy*) the first syllable is pronounced in the fourth tone and the second syllable in the neutral tone, i.e. unstressed.

TONE CHANGES

Tones may undergo changes in actual speech ("tone sandhi"). The third tone, when followed by a first, second, fourth or neutral tone sound, loses its final rise and stops at the low pitch. Followed by another third tone sound, it becomes the second tone. This is a general rule and the notation of third tone sounds remains unchanged.

For example, in 所以 **suǒyǐ** (*therefore*, *so*), notation remains the third tone for both syllables, but the word is actually pronounced like **suóyǐ**.

Two important words 不 **bù** (*no*) and 一 **yī** (*one*) also undergo tone changes. You will find the details of their tone changes under these entries.

1.4 Syllables: Distinct units

Normally a consonant and a vowel, said in a particular tone, merge to form a syllable in Chinese. Every syllable is a distinct unit in speech. Learners should say each syllable clearly and give full value to most syllables in speech. The general impression of Chinese speech, described in musical terms, is staccato rather than legato (which could be used to describe English).

1.5 *Pinyin:* the romanization scheme to show pronunciation

As Chinese writing normally does not indicate pronunciation, a romanization scheme, known as *pinyin*, is used to represent the sounds and tones of Chinese, as in this dictionary. *Pinyin* is useful for learning the phonetics of Mandarin.

2   WRITING CHINESE: 汉字 Hànzi

Chinese is not phonetic like most European languages (in varying degrees). Chinese is written in logograms, known as 汉字 (**Hànzi**) and generally referred to as "Chinese characters", or "Sinograms."

2.1 Chinese characters as syllables

Each Chinese character is pronounced as a syllable. It is of course important to be able to read a character with the correct pronunciation.

2.2 The composition of Chinese characters: Meaningful components

Chinese characters can be analyzed into components. It is acknowledged that there are three kinds of components. Of the three, the most interesting to learners of Chinese is a group of components that convey certain meanings. The presence of such a component in a character gives you some clue to its meaning of the character. Hence, learning the meaning of these component parts will deepen your understanding of characters you know, and help you guess the meaning of unfamiliar characters. See List 1 on page xv.

2.3 The writing of Chinese characters

STROKES

Each Chinese character is composed of strokes. The table below shows the basic strokes. Recognizing the strokes in a character is helpful for finding a character or radical in the Stroke Index, List of Radicals and Radical Index. Each of the strokes shown in the table is counted as one stroke.

Stroke	Writing the stroke	Examples
Héng	left to right 一	千 主 女
Shù	top to bottom 丨	千 山 北
Piě	top (right) to bottom (left) 丿	千 人 厶

Stroke	Writing the stroke	Examples
Nà	top (left) to bottom (right) ╲	人 木 又
Diǎn	top to bottom ╲	主 心 习
Tí	bottom (left) to top (right) ╱	习 打 北
Stroke with hook	left to right, top to bottom ⟶亅丿亅乚	买打以心
Stroke with turn(s)	㇄㇆㇊㇆	山马女么又
Stroke with turn(s) and hook	㇄㇉㇂㇠乙	北习认马

STROKE ORDER

For the character to look correct, its strokes should be written in the correct order. Knowing the order will also help you remember characters. The general rules of stroke order are as shown below.

Rule	Example	Stroke order
Top before bottom	三	一 二 三
Left before right	什	丿 亻 仁 什
Horizontal before vertical/downward	天	一 二 于 天
"Enter the room, then close the door"	日	丨 冂 月 日
Vertical stroke before sides/bottom	小	亅 小 小

SIMPLIFIED AND TRADITIONAL CHARACTERS

The Chinese government simplified hundreds of Chinese characters in mid-1950 by reducing the numbers of their strokes. Such simplified characters are called 简体字 **jiǎntǐzì**. This dictionary uses **jiantizi**. Traditional versions (also known as complicated characters) are still used in Taiwan and Hong Kong, and they are shown after "Trad" where applicable, e.g.:

学 xué Trad 學

3 VOCABULARY: Word-formation

Chinese words are either of one syllable or more than one syllable (mostly two syllables). When they are made up of two or more syllables, their meanings are usually transparent; that is, the way a word is formed tells you a lot about its meaning. Therefore it is very helpful to know the meanings of the components in a word and the way the word is formed, and it also makes understanding the word easier and more interesting.

There are six basic word-formation methods:

- **Compounding:** the components of a word are complementary to each other in meaning and are of the same status. For example:

    重 once again + 复 repeat → 重复 *repeat*

- **Modification:** one component modifies the other. For example:

    外 outside + 国 country → 外国 *foreign country*

- **Verb+object:** the word has a verb-and-object relationship. For example:

    发 develop + 烧 burning, fever → 发烧 *to run a fever*

- **Verb+complementation:** the word has a verb-and-complement relationship, that is, the first component is a verb or an adjective and the second one modifies it. For example:

    提 raise + 高 high → 提高 *raise*

- **Suffixation:** the word contains a suffix. For example:

    本 a book + 子 nominal suffix → 本子 *notebook*

- **Idioms:** the word is an idiomatic expression. For example:

    马上 → *at once, immediately*

4 GRAMMAR

4.1 Main features of Chinese grammar

TOPIC+COMMENT STRUCTURE

The basic principle in making Chinese sentences is to follow the "topic+comment" structure. "Topic" means the subject matter you want to talk about, and "comment" is the information you give about the subject matter. To make a Chinese sentence, you simply first mention the subject matter you want to talk about, and then say what you have to say about it. For example, you can say 那本书 **nà běn shū** (that book) first as the "topic" and then add "comment":

那本书 **Nà běn shū** (that book) + 很有意思 **hěn yǒu yìsi** (very interesting) → *That book is very interesting.*

那本书 **Nà běn shū** (that book) + 卖完了 **mài wán le** (sold out) → *That book has been sold.*

那本书 **Nà běn shū** (that book) + 你有吗 **nǐ yǒu ma** (do you have) → *Do you have that book?*

那本书 **Nà běn shū** (that book) + 语言很优美 **yǔyán hěn yōuměi** (language is beautiful) → *The language of that book is beautiful.*

ELLIPSIS OF SENTENCE ELEMENTS

Chinese speakers may leave out words that are supposed to be understood, and therefore need not be spoken. Subjects and conjunctions are often omitted. For example, you may translate the English sentence *If you like it, you may buy it, but if you don't like it, you don't have to*, into the Chinese sentence 喜欢就买, 不喜欢就别买。**Xǐhuan jiùmǎi, bù xǐhuan jiù bié mǎi.** Literally, it means "Like it, and buy, don't like then don't buy." Compare the two sentences, and you will find that some English words, such as *if*, *you*, *it*, and *but* are not translated.

WORD CLASSES: FLEXIBILITY, NO INFLECTION

Chinese words do not have inflections, i.e. they do not change to indicate grammatical categories. For example, the verb 去 **qù** (*to go*) is invariably 去 **qù**; there is no past form or any other inflected form of this verb. Neither do Chinese words normally have formal markers of word class. Consequently it is rather easy for a word to be used in more than one word class. This relative flexibility in word classes, however, does not mean that Chinese does not have word classes (see Section 4.2).

MEASURE WORDS AND PARTICLES

Measure words (量词 **liàngcí**) and particles (助词 **zhùcí**) are two word classes found in Chinese but not in English and most other languages.

Measure words are usually required when a noun is modified by a numeral. For example, 两书 **liǎng shū** is unacceptable; you must use the measure word 本 **běn** between the numeral and the noun: 两本书 **liǎng běn shū** (*two books*). Furthermore, Chinese nouns require specific measure words to go with them. For example, the noun 书 **shū** (*book*) must be used with the measure word 本 **běn**. See List 2 on pages xvi–xvii for the common measure words.

In Chinese grammar, particles are words attached to other words or at the end of a sentence to indicate grammatical concepts or to express emotions. For example, the particles 了 **le**, 着 **zhe**,

过 **guo** are attached to verbs to indicate, respectively, whether the actions denoted are completed, in progress or past experiences.

4.2 Word classes

Following are brief explanations of the basic terms in Chinese grammar used in this dictionary. (A word of warning: it is a rather complicated matter to define grammatical terms accurately. Here we will be content with some general but useful ideas.)

ADJECTIVE	a describing word, a word that describes people, things or actions, typically used before a noun
ADVERB	a word that modifies a verb, an adjective or another adverb
CONJUNCTION	a word used to link two words, phrases or sentences, indicating certain relationships between them
IDIOM	a set phrase, the meaning of which cannot be readily derived from its components
INTERJECTION	a word that expresses strong emotions
MEASURE WORD	a word that connects a numeral to a noun. Measure words are a special feature of Chinese; a list of measure words is given in List 2
MODAL VERB	a word used before a verb to indicate necessity, possibility, willingness, etc.
NOUN	a naming word, a word that names people, animals, plants, things, ideas, etc.
NUMERAL	a word that represents a number, typically used with a noun
ONOMATOPOEIA	a word that imitates the sounds of a thing or an action
PARTICLE	a word used with another word, phrase, or sentence to indicate certain grammatical meanings or to express strong emotions
PREPOSITION	a word used before a noun or pronoun to indicate time, place, direction, manner, reason of an action, etc.
PRONOUN	a word that is used in the place of a noun, a verb, an adjective, etc.
VERB	an action word, a word that indicates what somebody does or feels

4.3 Other grammar terms

ATTRIBUTE	the element that modifies the subject or object of a sentence; or, in word-formation analysis, a word that modifies a noun
ADVERBIAL	the element that is used before the predicate of a sentence and modifies it; or, in word-formation analysis, a word that precedes a verb or an adjective to modify it
COMPLEMENT	the element that is used after the predicate of a sentence and modifies it; or, in word-formation analysis, a word that follows a verb or an adjective to modify it
IMPERATIVE SENTENCE	a command or a request
OBJECT	the element that follows a predicative verb, typically to indicate the target of an action
PREDICATE	the comment or information about the subject, typically a verb or an adjective
PREFIX	an additional element that immediately precedes the word it is attached to
SUBJECT	the topic of a sentence, what the speaker wants to talk about, typically a noun or pronoun
SUFFIX	an additional element that closely follows the word it is attached to

List 1
Meaningful Character Components

冫 = freezing, ice (e.g. 冰 **bīng**, 冷 **lěng**, 寒 **hán**)

讠, 言 = word (e.g. 语 **yǔ**, 词 **cí**)

八 = dividing (e.g. 分 **fēn**, 半 **bàn**)

亻, 人 = man, person (e.g. 他 **tā**, 信 **xìn**)

刂, 刀 = knife (e.g. 利 **lì**, 剩 **shèng**)

力 = muscle, strength (e.g. 男 **nán**, 办 **bàn**)

阝 (on the left) = mound, steps (e.g. 院 **yuàn**, 附 **fù**)

阝 (on the right) = city, region (e.g. 部 **bù**, 邮 **yóu**)

氵, 水 = water (e.g. 河 **hé**, 海 **hǎi**)

忄, 心 = the heart, emotions (e.g. 情 **qíng**, 怕 **pà**, 感 **gǎn**)

宀 = roof, house (e.g. 家 **jiā**, 室 **shì**)

广 = roof, hut (e.g. 庭 **tíng**, 店 **diàn**)

门 = door, gate (e.g. 闻 **wén**, 间 **jiān**)

土 = earth (e.g. 场 **chǎng**, 城 **chéng**)

女 = woman (e.g. 妇 **fù**, 妈 **mā**)

饣, 食 = food (e.g. 饭 **fàn**, 饱 **bǎo**)

口 = the mouth, speech, eating (e.g. 问 **wèn**, 吃 **chī**)

囗 = boundary (e.g. 围 **wéi**, 园 **yuán**)

子, 孑 = child (e.g. 孩 **hái**, 学 **xué**)

艹 = plant, vegetation (e.g. 草 **cǎo**, 菜 **cài**)

纟 = silk, texture (e.g. 组 **zǔ**, 纸 **zhǐ**)

辶 = walking (e.g. 道 **dào**, 过 **guò**)

彳 = path, walking (e.g. 行 **xíng**, 往 **wǎng**)

巾 = cloth (e.g. 布 **bù**, 带 **dài**)

马 = horse (e.g. 骑 **qí**)

扌, 手, 攵 = the hand, action (e.g. 拿 **ná**, 擦 **cā**)

灬, 火 = fire, heat (e.g. 烧 **shāo**, 热 **rè**)

礻, 示 = spirit (e.g. 神 **shén**, 祖 **zǔ**)

户 = door, window (e.g. 房 **fáng**)

父 = father (e.g. 爸 **bà**)

日 = the sun (e.g. 晴 **qíng**, 暖 **nuǎn**)

月 = the moon (e.g. 阴 **yīn**, 明 **míng**)

月, 肉 = flesh, human organ (e.g. 脸 **liǎn**, 脚 **jiǎo**)

贝 = shell, treasure (e.g. 贵 **guì**)

止 = toe (e.g. 步 **bù**)

木 = tree, timber (e.g. 树 **shù**, 板 **bǎn**)

王, 玉 = jade (e.g. 理 **lǐ**, 球 **qiú**)

见 = seeing (e.g. 视 **shì**, 现 **xiàn**)

气 = vapor (e.g. 汽 **qì**)

车 = vehicle (e.g. 辆 **liàng**)

疒 = disease, ailment (e.g. 病 **bìng**, 疼 **téng**)

立 = standing (e.g. 站 **zhàn**, 位 **wèi**)

穴 = cave, hole (e.g. 空 **kōng**, 窗 **chuāng**)

衤, 衣 = clothing (e.g. 裤 **kù**, 袜 **wà**)

钅, 金 = metal (e.g. 银 **yín**, 钱 **qián**)

石 = stone, rock (e.g. 碗 **wǎn**, 磁 **cí**)

目 = the eye (e.g. 眼 **yǎn**, 睡 **shuì**)

田 = farm, field (e.g. 界 **jiè**, 里 **lǐ**)

瓜 = melon, gourd (e.g. 瓢 **piáo**, 瓣 **bàn**)

禾 = seedling, crop (e.g. 种 **zhǒng**, 秋 **qiū**)

鸟 = bird (e.g. 鸡 **jī**)

米 = rice (e.g. 糖 **táng**, 精 **jīng**)

竹 = bamboo (e.g. 筷 **kuài**, 笔 **bǐ**)

舌 = the tongue (e.g. 话 **huà**, 活 **huó**)

舟 = boat (e.g. 船 **chuán**)

酉 = fermentation (e.g. 酒 **jiǔ**)

走 = walking (e.g. 起 **qǐ**)

足 = the foot (e.g. 跳 **tiào**, 踢 **tì**)

List 2
Measure Words

Measure words are a special feature of Chinese. A particular measure word, or set of measure words, occurs with each noun whenever one is speaking of numbers. The measure word may function like a collective noun (like a *pride* [of lions] or a *school* [of fish]) or may be related to the shape of the object. Noun phrases using measure words often have the structure "number + measure word + noun," e.g.

- 一把刀 **yì bǎ dāo** *a knife*
- 两道难题 **liǎng dào nántí** *two difficult questions*

Some measure words occur with verbs, and may be related to the frequency or duration of the action. For verbs, the expression may have the structure "verb + number + measure word," e.g.

- 看了三遍 **kànle sān biàn** *read three times*
- 去过两次 **qùguo liǎng cì** *have been ... twice*

bǎ 把 for objects with handles; a handful

bān 班 class (in school)

bèi 倍 fold, time

běn 本 for books

bǐ 笔 for a sum of money

biàn 遍 times, indicating the frequency of an action done in its complete duration from the beginning to the end

cè 册 volume (books)

céng 层 story, floor

chǎng 场 for movies, sport events

chǐ 尺 a traditional Chinese unit of length (equal to ⅓ meter)

cì 次 time, expressing frequency of an act

cùn 寸 a traditional Chinese unit of length (equal to ⅟₃₀ meter)

dào 道 for questions in a school exercise, examination, etc.; for things in the shape of a line

dī 滴 drop (of liquid)

diǎn 点 o'clock

dù 度 degree (of temperature, longitude, latitude, etc.)

duàn 段 section of something long

dùn 顿 for meals

duǒ 朵 for flowers

fēn 分 Chinese currency (1 分 **fēn** = 0.1 角 **jiǎo** = 0.01 元 **yuán**), cent

fèn 份 for a set of things or newspapers, documents, etc.

fēng 封 for letters

fú 幅 for pictures, poster, maps, etc.

gè 个 the most commonly used measure word for nouns that do not take special measure words, or in default of any other measure word

gēn 根 for long, thin things

gōngchǐ 公尺 meter (formal)

gōngjīn 公斤 kilogram

gōnglǐ 公里 kilometer

háng 行 used with nouns that are formed in lines; line, row, queue

hù 户 used with nouns denoting households and families

huí 回 number of times

jiā 家 for families or businesses

jiān 间 for rooms

jiàn 件 for things, affairs, clothes or furniture

jiǎo 角 Chinese currency (0.1 **yuán** or 10 **fēn**), ten cents, a dime

jié 节 a period of time

jīn 斤 a Chinese unit of weight equivalent to half a kilogram

jù 句 for sentences

kē 棵 for trees

kè 克 gram

kè 刻 quarter of an hour

kǒu 口 for members of a family

kuài 块 for things that can be broken into lumps or chunks; for money; yuan, dollar

lǐ 里 a Chinese unit of length, equivalent to 0.5 kilometers

lì 粒 for rice, pearls

liǎng 两 a traditional Chinese unit of weight, equivalent to 50 grams; ounce

liàng 辆 for vehicles

liè 列 for trains

máo 毛 a Chinese money unit, colloquialism for 角 **jiǎo** (= 0.1 元 **yuán** or 10 分 **fēn**)

mén 门 for school subjects, languages, etc.

mǐ 米 meter (colloquial)

miàn 面 for flat objects

miǎo 秒 second (of time)

míng 名 for people, especially for those with a specific position or occupation

mǔ 亩 a traditional Chinese unit of area, especially in farming (equal to $1/15$ hectare or 667 square meters)

pái 排 for things arranged in a row

pī 批 for a batch of goods, and for things/ people arriving at the same time

pǐ 匹 for horses

piān 篇 for a piece of writing

piàn 片 for a thin and flat piece, slice

píng 瓶 a bottle of

qún 群 a crowd/group of

shēn 身 for clothes

shǒu 首 for songs and poems

shuāng 双 a pair of (shoes, chopsticks, etc.)

suì 岁 year (of age)

suǒ 所 for houses, or institutions housed in a building

tái 台 for machines, big instruments, etc.

tàng 趟 for trips

tào 套 a set of

tiáo 条 for things with a long, narrow shape

tóu 头 for cattle or sheep

wèi 位 a polite measure word for people

xià 下 used with certain verbs to indicate the number of times the action is done

xiàng 项 item, component

yè 页 for pages (of a book)

yīngchǐ 英尺 foot (as a measurement of length)

yīngcùn 英寸 inch

yuán 元 the basic unit of Chinese currency (1 元 **yuán** = 10 角 **jiǎo**/毛 **máo** = 100 分 **fēn**), dollar

zhāng 张 for paper, beds, tables, desks

zhèn 阵 for an action or event that lasts for some time

zhī 支 for stick-like things

zhī 只 for animals, utensils, or objects

zhǒng 种 kind, sort

zuò 座 for large and solid objects, such as a large building

Using the Dictionary

Note: You are recommended to read *Introducing Chinese* (pp.vii–xiv) before using the dictionary.

1 Pronunciation

The pronunciation of Chinese words as transcribed in this dictionary uses the *pinyin* scheme, which is the official, internationally recognized Chinese romanization system. Every Chinese character in this dictionary is accompanied by its *pinyin* spelling so that you will know how to pronounce every word and say every sentence.

2 Word-formation

Word-formation methods of Chinese headwords are indicated, whenever it is practical to do so. The information is shown immediately after the headword, e.g.

爱护 àihù [comp: 爱 love + 护 protect]

3 Word class

The word class of each headword is indicated after the word-formation or immediately after the head word, e.g.

爱护 àihù [comp: 爱 love + 护 protect] *v*

阿姨 āyí *n* mother's sister

When a headword may be used in different word classes, they are shown by I, II, and so on, e.g.

爱好 àihào **I** *v* like, be interested in, have as a hobby

   II *n* hobby, interest

4 Traditional characters

If a character has a traditional version (传统字 **chuántǒng zì**, also known as 繁体字 **fántǐzì** "complicated character"), it is shown as part of the headword, preceded by Trad, e.g.:

爱 ài Trad 愛

5 Definitions

For Chinese headwords English equivalents or near equivalents are given, in most cases, as definitions, e.g.

高兴 gāoxìng *adj* joyful, delighted, willing

For grammatical words that have no English equivalents, concise explanations are given in brackets, e.g.

的 de *particle* (attached to a word, phrase or clause to indicate that it is an attribute. 的 **de** is normally followed by a noun.)

When a headword has more than one meaning under the same word class, the different meanings are indicated by 1, 2, etc. For example:

月 yuè *n* 1 month 2 the moon

Homonyms (words pronounced and written the same but with different, unrelated meanings) are treated as separate words, e.g.

代¹ **dài** *n* **1** generation

代² **dài** *v* take the place of, perform on behalf of

6 Measure Words

After the definition of a Chinese noun, the specific measure word used with the noun is shown, if it is one of the headwords in the dictionary, e.g.

书 **shū** book (本 **běn**)

When the specific measure word is not within the scope of this dictionary and therefore is not shown, you can often use the default measure word 个 **ge**.

7 Antonyms

Antonyms (words of opposite meaning) are shown after the definition of most Chinese adjectives and some nouns, if they are headwords of the Chinese-English dictionary, e.g.

短 **duǎn** *adj* (of length, time) short (antonym 长 **cháng**)

8 Common Collocations

Collocations are words habitually juxtaposed with each other. This dictionary shows common collocations related to the headwords, with clear definitions and necessary sample sentences. For example:

包 **bāo** *n* parcel, bag

钱包 **qiánbāo** wallet, purse

书包 **shūbāo** schoolbag

邮包 **yóubāo** mailbag, parcel for posting

9 Example Sentences

Words become really meaningful only when used in sentences. That is why a host of example sentences are supplied for almost each and every headword in the dictionary. All the sentences are carefully constructed to be idiomatic and communicatively useful. For example, the headword **bàozhǐ** 报纸 has two example sentences:

报纸 **bàozhǐ** □ 我很少看报纸。**Wǒ hěn shǎo kàn bàozhǐ.** *I seldom read newspapers.* □ 这份报纸广告比新闻多。**Zhè fèn bàozhǐ guǎnggào bǐ xīnwén duō.** *There are more advertisements than news in this newspaper.*

In the first example sentence the headword 报纸 **bàozhǐ** functions as an object after the common verb 看 **kàn**. In the second example sentence 报纸 **bàozhǐ** is used in the subject position and is collocated with the measure word 份 **fèn**.

Studying the sentences carefully will help you learn how to use Chinese words in everyday communication.

The example sentences in the Chinese-English sentences are all composed of the Chinese words that are treated as headwords in the dictionary. This means that this dictionary is self-contained.

10 English Translation of Chinese Sentences

All Chinese example sentences are accompanied by an English translation. In some cases a second translation is provided in brackets to aid comprehension and idiomatic expression. → indicates a freer, more idiomatic translation and ←, a more literal translation. For example:

> 让 ràng □ 你应该让那辆车先行。**Nǐ yīnggāi ràng nà liàng chē xiānxíng.** *You should let that vehicle go first.* (→ *You should give way to that vehicle.*)

11 Note

The Note presented in a color box gives essential information on cultural context, pronunciation, grammar and usage. These help you use the language in a socially acceptable and idiomatic way. For example:

> 肥 féi...

> NOTE: 肥 **féi** is normally used to describe animals. It is insulting to use it to describe humans.

12 How to find Chinese words

BY PINYIN SPELLING

Headwords are arranged alphabetically according to their *pinyin* spelling. So if you know how a word is pronounced, you can find it easily, just like the way you will look up an English word in an English dictionary.

If you do not know the pronunciation of a word you can find it either by its radical or the number of its strokes.

BY RADICALS

Radicals (部首 **bùshǒu**) are certain component parts of characters that have been used in Chinese dictionary-making for nearly 2,000 years. Characters sharing a radical are grouped together under the heading of that radical. To find a character in a dictionary, follow these steps:

(i)   In the List of Radicals, look up the character's radical according to the number of strokes in the radical. This gives a Radical Index number.

(ii) Turn to the number in the Radical Index.

(iii) Locate the character according to the number of remaining strokes needed to write the character (i.e. number of total strokes minus radical strokes = remaining strokes). You will find the *pinyin* by the character.

For example, to find 活 by Radical Index:

(i)   The radical group of 活 is 氵, which has three strokes. In the List of Radicals, look up 氵 in the section marked "3 strokes":

3 strokes

氵   34

(ii) Turn to number 34 in the Radical Index.

(iii) As there are nine strokes in 活, and the radical has three strokes, six strokes remain to complete the character 活 (9 − 3 = 6). Look in the section "6 strokes" and locate 活:

6 strokes

活　**huó**

(iv) Turn to **huó** in the dictionary.

huó 活 ...

BY STROKE NUMBERS

Unfortunately, looking for a character by its radical is not an entirely satisfactory method as learners may not always know which part of the character is the radical. Therefore, this section includes a Stroke Index to aid the learner further. Simply look for the character according to the number of its strokes, and then locate the character by its first stroke.

For example, to find 活 by Stroke Index:

(i)　There are nine strokes in 活. Go to the section of nine strokes.

9 strokes

(ii)　As the first stroke of 活 is "、", locate 活 under "、".

丶

活　**huó**

(iii) Turn to **huó** in the dictionary.

huó 活 ...

List of Radicals

Radical Index

All characters are listed here under their radical plus the number of additional strokes needed to write them.

1 、

举	jǔ
叛	pàn
为	wéi, wèi
永	yǒng
之	zhī
州	zhōu
主	zhǔ

2 一

一	yī, yí, yì

1–2 strokes

才	cái
丁	dīng
七	qī
三	sān
万	wàn
下	xià
于	yú
与	yǔ
丈	zhàng

3 strokes

不	bú, bù
丰	fēng
互	hù
世	shì
屯	tún
无	wú
五	wǔ
牙	yá
尤	yóu
专	zhuān

4 strokes

丙	bǐng
册	cè
东	dōng
甘	gān
可	kě
平	píng
正	zhēng, zhèng

5 strokes

而	ér
亚	yà
再	zài

6 strokes

辰	chén
更	gēng, gèng
来	lái
丽	lì
两	liǎng
求	qiú
巫	wū
严	yán

7–21 strokes

甫	béng
奉	fèng
哥	gē
耕	gēng
恭	gōng
柬	jiǎn
赖	lài
面	miàn
囊	náng
融	róng
甚	shèn
事	shì
爽	shuǎng
泰	tài
夏	xià
艳	yàn
枣	zǎo
奏	zòu

3 丨

承	chéng
刁	diāo
了	le, liǎo
买	mǎi
司	sī
习	xí
也	yě

4 乙

乙	yǐ

2–8 strokes

巴	bā
丑	chǒu
飞	fēi
幻	huàn
君	jūn
矛	máo
民	mín
乡	xiāng
予	yú
昼	zhòu

5 丨

串	chuàn
临	lín
且	qiě
申	shēn
师	shī
书	shū
央	yāng
由	yóu
中	zhōng

6 丿

1–2 strokes

川	chuān
瓜	guā
及	jí
九	jiǔ
久	jiǔ
么	me
乞	qǐ
千	qiān
丸	wán
义	yì

3–4 strokes

长	cháng, zhǎng
丹	dān
乏	fá

瓜	guā
乎	hū
乐	lè, yuè
丘	qiū
升	shēng
生	shēng
失	shī
氏	shì
甩	shuǎi
乌	wū

5 strokes

丢	diū
年	nián
乔	qiáo
向	xiàng
兆	zhào

6–14 strokes

重	chóng, zhòng
垂	chuí
囱	cōng
够	gòu
乖	guāi
甥	shēng
舞	wǔ
周	zhōu

7 亠

2–3 strokes

亢	kàng
六	liù
市	shì
亡	wáng

4–5 strokes

充	chōng
交	jiāo
亩	mǔ
齐	qí
弃	qì

6–7 strokes

哀	āi
帝	dì

京	jīng
亮	liàng
氓	máng
亭	tíng
弯	wān
享	xiǎng

8–9 strokes

高	gāo
竟	jìng
离	lí
率	lǜ, shuài
商	shāng

10–15 strokes

膏	gāo
豪	háo
就	jiù
敲	qiāo
衰	shuāi
童	tóng
赢	yíng
衷	zhōng

8 冫

2–4 strokes

冰	bīng
冲	chōng, chòng
次	cì
决	jué

5–6 strokes

冻	dòng
净	jìng
况	kuàng
冷	lěng
冶	yě

8-14 strokes

凑	còu
减	jiǎn
凉	liáng
凌	líng
凝	níng
凄	qī

准	zhǔn	诬	wū	支	zhī	**15 卜**		冤	yuān
9 讠		误	wù	**5–10 strokes**		卜	bó, bǔ	**18 冂**	
2–3 strokes		诱	yòu	卑	bēi	**3–6 strokes**		内	nèi
订	dìng	语	yǔ	博	bó	卡	kǎ	肉	ròu
讥	jī	**8 strokes**		辜	gū	占	zhàn	同	tóng
计	jì	调	diào, tiáo	卖	mài	卓	zhuó	网	wǎng
记	jì	读	dú	南	nán	**16 刂**		**19 勹**	
让	ràng	诽	fěi	丧	sāng, sàng	**3–5 strokes**		包	bāo
认	rèn	课	kè	真	zhēn	别	bié, biè	匆	cōng
讨	tǎo	谅	liàng	直	zhí	创	chuàng	勾	gōu
训	xùn	请	qǐng	**12 厂**		刚	gāng	句	jù
议	yì	谁	shéi, shuí	厂	chǎng	划	huá, huà	勺	sháo
4 strokes		谈	tán	**2–3 strokes**		刊	kān	勿	wù
讹	é	谊	yì	历	lì	利	lì	旬	xún
访	fǎng	诸	zhū	厉	lì	列	liè	匀	yún
讽	fěng	**9–12 strokes**		厅	tīng	判	pàn	**20 刀**	
讲	jiǎng	谤	bàng	**4–10 strokes**		刨	páo	刀	dāo
论	lùn	谎	huǎng	厕	cè	删	shān	**1–5 strokes**	
设	shè	谨	jǐn	厨	chú	刑	xíng	负	fù
讼	sòng	谜	mí	后	hòu	则	zé	龟	guī
许	xǔ	谬	miù	厚	hòu	**6–8 strokes**		免	miǎn
讯	xùn	谋	móu	厘	lí	剥	bāo, bō	切	qiè
讶	yà	谱	pǔ	戚	qī	刺	cì	刃	rèn
5 strokes		谦	qiān	厦	shà	到	dào	韧	rèn
词	cí	谴	qiǎn	咸	xián	刮	guā	色	sè
评	píng	谓	wèi	厢	xiāng	剂	jì	危	wēi
识	shí	谐	xié	压	yā	剑	jiàn	召	zhào
诉	sù	谢	xiè	厌	yàn	剧	jù	争	zhēng
译	yì	谣	yáo	雁	yàn	刻	kè	**6–14 strokes**	
诈	zhà	**10 二**		原	yuán	剖	pōu	剪	jiǎn
诊	zhěn	二	èr	**13 匚**		刹	shā	劈	pī
证	zhèng	**1–6 strokes**		臣	chén	刷	shuā	券	quàn
6 strokes		井	jǐng	匪	fěi	剃	tì	兔	tù
诧	chà	亏	kuī	匠	jiàng	削	xiāo, xuē	象	xiàng
诚	chéng	些	xiē	巨	jù	制	zhì	豫	yù
该	gāi	元	yuán	匹	pǐ	**9–10 strokes**		**21 力**	
话	huà	云	yún	区	qū	副	fù	力	lì
诗	shī	**11 十**		卧	wò	割	gē	**2–4 strokes**	
试	shì	十	shí	医	yī	剩	shèng	办	bàn
详	xiáng	**2–4 strokes**		**14 匕**		**17 冖**		动	dòng
询	xún	古	gǔ	**3 strokes**		冠	guàn	加	jiā
7 strokes		华	huá	北	běi	罕	hǎn	劣	liè
诞	dàn	克	kè	**12 strokes**		军	jūn	劝	quàn
诫	jiè	午	wǔ	疑	yí	农	nóng		
说	shuō	协	xié			写	xiě		
诵	sòng								

幼	yòu	**23 亻**		伸	shēn	倚	yǐ	拿	ná

幼 yòu

5 strokes

劫 jié
劲 jìn
劳 láo
励 lì
努 nǔ

6–11 strokes

勃 bó
舅 jiù
勘 kān
勉 miǎn
勤 qín
势 shì
勇 yǒng
助 zhù

22 八

八 bā

2–4 strokes

半 bàn
并 bìng
分 fēn, fèn
公 gōng
共 gòng
关 guān
兰 lán
兴 xīng, xìng

5–6 strokes

兵 bīng
单 dān
弟 dì
典 diǎn
兑 duì
谷 gǔ
具 jù
其 qí

7–9 strokes

兼 jiān
前 qián
首 shǒu
兽 shòu
养 yǎng
益 yì

23 亻

1–2 strokes

仇 chóu
化 huà
仅 jǐn
仆 pú
仁 rén
仍 réng
什 shén
亿 yì

3 strokes

代 dài
付 fù
们 men
他 tā
仙 xiān
仪 yí
仔 zǐ

4 strokes

传 chuán, zhuàn
伐 fá
仿 fǎng
份 fèn
伏 fú
伙 huǒ
价 jià
件 jiàn
任 rèn
伤 shāng
似 sì
伟 wěi
伪 wěi
伍 wǔ
休 xiū
仰 yǎng
伊 yī
优 yōu

5 strokes

伴 bàn
伯 bó
伺 cì, sì
但 dàn
低 dī
佛 fó, fú
估 gū
何 hé
你 nǐ

伸 shēn
体 tǐ
位 wèi
佣 yōng
住 zhù
作 zuò

6 strokes

侧 cè
侈 chǐ
供 gōng, gòng
佳 jiā
例 lì
侣 lǚ
佩 pèi
侨 qiáo
使 shǐ
侍 shì
修 xiū
依 yī
侦 zhēn
侄 zhí

7 strokes

保 bǎo
便 biàn, pián
促 cù
俄 é
俘 fú
俭 jiǎn
俊 jùn
俩 liǎ
俏 qiào
侵 qīn
俗 sú
侮 wǔ
信 xìn

8 strokes

倍 bèi
倡 chàng
倒 dǎo, dào
俯 fǔ
候 hòu
健 jiàn
借 jiè
俱 jù
倦 juàn
倾 qīng
倘 tǎng

倚 yǐ
债 zhài
值 zhí

9–10 strokes

傲 ào
傍 bàng
偿 cháng
储 chǔ
傅 fù
假 jiǎ, jià
偶 ǒu
偏 piān
停 tíng
偷 tōu
做 zuò

11–13 strokes

催 cuī
僵 jiāng
僚 liáo
僻 pì
傻 shǎ
像 xiàng

24 人

人 rén
入 rù

1–2 strokes

仓 cāng
从 cóng
个 gè
介 jiè
今 jīn
以 yǐ

3–4 strokes

从 cóng
合 hé
会 huì, kuài
令 lìng
企 qǐ
全 quán
伞 sǎn
众 zhòng

5–10 strokes

含 hán
盒 hé
金 jīn
命 mìng

拿 ná
禽 qín
舍 shě, shè
舒 shū
余 yú

25 儿

儿 ér

4–9 strokes

兜 dōu
先 xiān

26 几

几 jī, jǐ

1–12 strokes

凳 dèng
凡 fán
凤 fèng
凰 huáng
凭 píng

27 又

又 yòu

1–2 strokes

叉 chā
反 fǎn
双 shuāng
友 yǒu

3–11 strokes

变 biàn
叠 dié
对 duì
发 fā
欢 huān
艰 jiān
难 nán, nàn
叔 shū
叙 xù

28 凵

凹 āo
出 chū
函 hán
画 huà
击 jī
凸 tū
凶 xiōng

29 厶

参	cān
能	néng
去	qù
叁	sān
台	tái
县	xiàn
允	yǔn

30 廴

建	jiàn
延	yán

31 卩

即	jí
卷	juǎn
卵	luǎn
却	què
卫	wèi
卸	xiè
印	yìn

32 阝 (on left)

2–5 strokes

阿	ā
陈	Chén
队	duì
防	fáng
附	fù
际	jì
阶	jiē
陆	lù
阳	yáng
阴	yīn
阵	zhèn
阻	zǔ

6–8 strokes

除	chú
陡	dǒu
降	jiàng
隆	lóng
陋	lòu
陌	mò
陪	péi
陶	táo
险	xiǎn

陷	xiàn
限	xiàn
院	yuàn

9–12 strokes

隘	ài
隔	gé
随	suí
隧	suì
隙	xì
隐	yǐn
障	zhàng

33 阝 (on right)

邦	bāng
鄙	bǐ
部	bù
都	dōu, dū
郊	jiāo
郎	láng
邻	lín
那	nà, nèi
邪	xié
邮	yóu
郁	yù
郑	zhèng

34 氵

2–4 strokes

沉	chén
池	chí
泛	fàn
沟	gōu
汗	hàn
汉	hàn
沪	hù
汇	huì
江	jiāng
沥	lì
没	méi
沏	qī
汽	qì
沙	shā
汰	tài
汤	tāng
汪	wāng
沃	wò

污	wū
汹	xiōng
汁	zhī

5 strokes

波	bō
泊	bó
法	fǎ
沸	fèi
河	hé
泪	lèi
泌	mì
沫	mò
泥	ní
泞	níng
泡	pào
沛	pèi
泼	pō
泣	qì
浅	qiǎn
泄	xiè
泻	xiè
沿	yán
泳	yǒng
油	yóu
泽	zé
沾	zhān
沼	zhǎo
治	zhì
注	zhù

6 strokes

测	cè
洞	dòng
洪	hóng
浑	hún
活	huó
济	jì
浇	jiāo
洁	jié
津	jīn
浓	nóng
派	pài
洽	qià
洒	sǎ
洗	xǐ
洋	yáng
洲	zhōu

浊	zhuó

7 strokes

涤	dí
浮	fú
海	hǎi
浩	hào
浸	jìn
酒	jiǔ
浪	làng
涝	lào
流	liú
润	rùn
涉	shè
涛	tāo
涕	tì
涂	tú
消	xiāo
浴	yù
涨	zhǎng

8 strokes

淡	dàn
淀	diàn
混	hùn
渐	jiàn
淋	lín
清	qīng
渠	qú
深	shēn
渗	shèn
淘	táo
添	tiān
淆	xiáo
淹	yān
液	yè
淫	yín
涌	yǒng
渔	yú

9 strokes

渡	dù
溉	gài
港	gǎng
湖	hú
滑	huá
溅	jiàn
渴	kě
溜	liú

湿	shī
湾	wān
温	wēn
游	yóu
渣	zhā
滞	zhì
滋	zī

10–11 strokes

滨	bīn
滴	dī
滚	gǔn
滥	làn
溜	liū
漏	lòu
滤	lǜ
满	mǎn
漫	màn
漠	mò
漂	piào
漆	qī
溶	róng
滩	tān
滔	tāo
演	yǎn
源	yuán

12–17 strokes

澳	ào
潮	cháo
澄	chéng
灌	guàn
激	jī
潦	liáo
瀑	pù
潜	qián
潭	tán
溪	xī
澡	zǎo

35 忄

1–5 strokes

怖	bù
怪	guài
怀	huái
快	kuài
怜	lián
忙	máng

怕	pà	光	guāng	寇	kòu	廊	láng	近	jìn
怯	qiè	尖	jiān	宽	kuān	廉	lián	连	lián
性	xìng	少	shǎo, shào	容	róng	鹿	lù	迫	pò
忆	yì		**4–9 strokes**	宿	sù	磨	mó	违	wéi
忧	yōu	尝	cháng	宵	xiāo	唐	táng	迎	yíng
	6–8 strokes	党	dǎng	宴	yàn	席	xí	远	yuǎn
惭	cán	辉	huī	宰	zǎi	鹰	yīng	运	yùn
惨	cǎn	尚	shàng		**9–11 strokes**	庸	yōng	这	zhè, zhèi
悼	dào	省	shěng	察	chá	座	zuò		**5–6 strokes**
惦	diàn	肖	xiào	富	fù			迪	dí
惯	guàn			寡	guǎ		**40 门**	迹	jì
恨	hèn		**37 宀**	寒	hán	门	mén	迷	mí
恒	héng		**2–4 strokes**	蜜	mì		**2–4 strokes**	逆	nì
恢	huī	安	ān	寞	mò	闭	bì	适	shì
悔	huǐ	宏	hóng	塞	sāi	闯	chuǎng	述	shù
惊	jīng	牢	láo	寓	yù	间	jiān, jiàn	送	sòng
惧	jù	宁	níng, nìng	寨	zhài	闷	mēn, mèn	逃	táo
恼	nǎo	守	shǒu			闪	shǎn	退	tuì
恰	qià	它	tā		**38 丬**	问	wèn	选	xuǎn
悄	qiāo	完	wán	鉴	jiàn	闲	xián	逊	xùn
情	qíng	宇	yǔ	将	jiāng		**5–9 strokes**	追	zhuī
惋	wǎn	灾	zāi	妆	zhuāng	阐	chǎn		**7–8 strokes**
悟	wù	宅	zhái	壮	zhuàng	阀	fá	逮	dài
惜	xī	字	zì	状	zhuàng	闺	guī	递	dì
悦	yuè		**5–6 strokes**		**39 广**	阂	hé	逗	dòu
	9–13 strokes	宝	bǎo	广	guǎng	阔	kuò	逢	féng
懂	dǒng	宠	chǒng		**3–4 strokes**	闹	nào	逛	guàng
惰	duò	定	dìng	床	chuáng	闻	wén	逻	luó
愤	fèn	宫	gōng	库	kù	阅	yuè	逝	shì
憾	hàn	官	guān	庆	qìng	闸	zhá	速	sù
慌	huāng	客	kè	序	xù			通	tōng
慨	kǎi	审	shěn	应	yīng, yìng		**41 辶**	透	tòu
慷	kāng	实	shí	庄	zhuāng		**2–3 strokes**	途	tú
愧	kuì	室	shì		**5–6 strokes**	边	biān	造	zào
懒	lǎn	宪	xiàn	底	dǐ	达	dá	逐	zhú
愣	lèng	宣	xuān	店	diàn	过	guò, guo		**9–12 strokes**
慢	màn	宜	yí	度	dù	辽	liáo	逼	bī
慎	shèn	宙	zhòu	废	fèi	迈	mài	避	bì
惕	tì	宗	zōng	府	fǔ	迁	qiān	遍	biàn
愉	yú		**7–8 strokes**	庙	miào	巡	xún	道	dào
		案	àn	庞	páng	迅	xùn	遣	qiǎn
	36 小	宾	bīn	庭	tíng		**4 strokes**	邀	yāo
小	xiǎo	害	hài		**7–16 strokes**	迟	chí	遥	yáo
	1–3 strokes	寂	jì	腐	fǔ	返	fǎn	遗	yí
尘	chén	寄	jì	康	kāng	还	hái, huán	遇	yù
当	dāng, dàng	家	jiā			进	jìn	遭	zāo

遮	zhē	垄	lǒng	志	zhì	获	huò	**48 廾**	
遵	zūn	坡	pō			菊	jú	弊	bì
		坛	tán	**46 上**		菌	jūn	开	kāi
42 工		坦	tǎn	上	shàng	莲	lián	弄	nòng
工	gōng	型	xíng			萝	luó	异	yì
2–6 strokes		幸	xìng	**47 ⺿**		萌	méng		
功	gōng	址	zhǐ	1–4 strokes		莫	mò	**49 大**	
攻	gōng	坐	zuò	艾	ài	萍	píng	大	dà, dài
汞	gǒng	7–8 strokes		芭	bā	萨	sà	1–3 strokes	
巩	gǒng	埠	bù	苍	cāng	萄	táo	夺	duó
贡	gòng	堵	dǔ	芳	fāng	营	yíng	夫	fū
巧	qiǎo	堆	duī	芬	fēn	著	zhù	夹	jiā
式	shì	基	jī	花	huā	9–12 strokes		夸	kuā
项	xiàng	埋	mái, mán	节	jié	蔼	ǎi	太	tài
左	zuǒ	培	péi	芹	qín	蔽	bì	头	tóu
		堂	táng	苏	sū	葱	cōng	5–9 strokes	
43 干		域	yù	芽	yá	董	dǒng	奥	ào
干	gān, gàn	9–17 strokes		艺	yì	葫	hú	奔	bēn
刊	kān	堡	bǎo	芝	zhī	蕉	jiāo	奋	fèn
		壁	bì	5–6 strokes		葵	kuí	奖	jiǎng
44 土		堤	dī	草	cǎo	落	là, luò	奇	qí
土	tǔ	堕	duò	茶	chá	蓝	lán	牵	qiān
2–3 strokes		赫	hè	荡	dàng	蔓	màn	奢	shē
场	chǎng	境	jìng	范	fàn	蒙	méng	套	tào
地	de, dì	堪	kān	荒	huāng	蔑	miè		
坑	kēng	墙	qiáng	茧	jiǎn	幕	mù	**50 寸**	
圣	shèng	壤	rǎng	荐	jiàn	墓	mù	寸	cùn
寺	sì	塑	sù	茎	jīng	慕	mù	4–9 strokes	
在	zài	塌	tā	苦	kǔ	葡	pú	封	fēng
至	zhì	塔	tǎ	荔	lì	蔬	shū	耐	nài
4–6 strokes		塘	táng	茫	máng	蒜	suàn	辱	rǔ
坝	bà	填	tián	茅	máo	蓄	xù	寿	shòu
城	chéng	墟	xū	茂	mào	蕴	yùn	尊	zūn
赤	chì	增	zēng	苗	miáo	葬	zàng		
垫	diàn			苹	píng	蔗	zhè	**51 扌**	
坊	fāng	**45 士**		茄	qié	蒸	zhēng	2–3 strokes	
坟	fén	士	shì	荣	róng	13–16 strokes		扒	bá
坏	huài	3–11 strokes		若	ruò	薄	báo, bó	打	dǎ
圾	jī	鼓	gǔ	药	yào	藏	cáng	扣	kòu
坚	jiān	壶	hú	英	yīng	蕾	lěi	扩	kuò
均	jūn	吉	jí	7–8 strokes		蘑	mó	扑	pū
垦	kěn	嘉	jiā	菠	bō	薯	shǔ	扔	rēng
垮	kuǎ	壳	ké	菜	cài	藤	téng	扫	sǎo, sào
块	kuài	声	shēng	菇	gū	薪	xīn	托	tuō
垃	lā	喜	xǐ	荷	hé			扬	yáng
垒	lěi	壹	yī	黄	huáng			扎	zhā

4 strokes		拍	pāi	损	sǔn	10 strokes		吐	tǔ, tù
把	bǎ	披	pī	捅	tǒng	摆	bǎi	吸	xī
扳	bān	抬	tái	挽	wǎn	搬	bān	吓	xià
扮	bàn	拖	tuō	振	zhèn	搏	bó	吁	yù
报	bào	拓	tuò	捉	zhuō	搞	gǎo	4 strokes	
抄	chāo	押	yā	8 strokes		摸	mō	吧	ba
扯	chě	拥	yōng	捶	chuí	摄	shè	吵	chǎo
抖	dǒu	择	zé	措	cuò	摊	tān	呈	chéng
扶	fú	招	zhāo	掂	diàn	携	xié	吹	chuī
抚	fǔ	拙	zhuō	掉	diào	摇	yáo	呆	dāi
护	hù	6 strokes		接	jiē	11–16 strokes		吨	dūn
技	jì	按	àn	捷	jié	播	bō	吩	fēn
拒	jù	持	chí	据	jù	擦	cā	否	fǒu
抗	kàng	挡	dǎng	掘	jué	操	cāo	告	gào
抠	kōu	拱	gǒng	控	kòng	撤	chè	吼	hǒu
抡	lūn	挂	guà	掠	lüè	撑	chēng	呕	ǒu
拟	nǐ	挥	huī	描	miáo	摧	cuī	听	tīng
拧	níng, nǐng	挤	jǐ	捻	niǎn	撵	niǎn	吞	tūn
扭	niǔ	挎	kuà	排	pái	撇	piē	吻	wěn
抛	pāo	括	kuò	捧	pěng	撒	sā	呜	wū
批	pī	挠	náo	掐	qiā	擅	shàn	呀	yā, ya
抢	qiǎng	挪	nuó	授	shòu	摔	shuāi	员	yuán
扰	rǎo	拼	pīn	探	tàn	撕	sī	5 strokes	
投	tóu	拾	shí	掏	tāo	攒	zǎn	哎	āi
抑	yì	拴	shuān	推	tuī	摘	zhāi	咐	fù
折	zhē, zhé	挑	tiāo, tiǎo	掀	xiān	撞	zhuàng	呵	hē
找	zhǎo	挺	tǐng	掩	yǎn			呼	hū
执	zhí	挖	wā	掷	zhì	**52 口**		咖	kā
抓	zhuā	挟	xié	9 strokes		口	kǒu	咙	lóng
5 strokes		挣	zhēng, zhèng	插	chā	2 strokes		呢	ne
拔	bá	指	zhǐ	搀	chān	叭	bā	味	wèi
拌	bàn	拽	zhuài	搓	cuō	叼	diāo	咏	yǒng
抱	bào	7 strokes		搭	dā	叮	dīng	咋	zǎ
拨	bō	挨	ái	搁	gē	号	hào	6 strokes	
拆	chāi	捌	bā	搅	jiǎo	叫	jiào	哆	duō
抽	chōu	捕	bǔ	揭	jiē	另	lìng	哈	hā
担	dàn	挫	cuò	揪	jiū	史	shǐ	哄	hǒng, hòng
抵	dǐ	捣	dǎo	揽	lǎn	叹	tàn	哗	huá
拐	guǎi	捍	hàn	搂	lǒu	兄	xiōng	咳	ké
拣	jiǎn	换	huàn	揉	róu	叶	yè	鸣	míng
拘	jū	捡	jiǎn	搜	sōu	右	yòu	哪	nǎ
拉	lā	捐	juān	提	tí	只	zhī, zhǐ	品	pǐn
拦	lán	捆	kǔn	握	wò	3 strokes		呻	shēn
拢	lǒng	捞	lāo	援	yuán	吃	chī	虽	suī
抹	mā, mǒ	捏	niē	揍	zòu	吊	diào	哇	wā
拇	mǔ	捎	shāo			吗	ma	响	xiǎng

哑	yǎ	嗽	sòu	**3–9 strokes**		衍	yǎn	狸	lí

哑 yǎ
咽 yàn
咬 yǎo
咱 zán
咨 zī

7–9 strokes

啊 ā
唉 āi
唱 chàng
喘 chuǎn
唇 chún
啡 fēi
喊 hǎn
喝 hē
哼 hēng
喉 hóu
唤 huàn
啃 kěn
喇 lǎ
啦 la
唠 láo
啰 luō
哦 ǒ
喷 pēn
啤 pí
啥 shà
哨 shào
唆 suō
唾 tuò
唯 wéi
喂 wèi
啸 xiào
喧 xuān
喻 yù
哲 zhé
啄 zhuó

10–17 strokes

嘲 cháo
嘿 hēi
嚼 jiáo
嘛 ma
嗯 ng
噢 ō
器 qì
嚷 rǎng
嗓 sǎng

嗽 sòu
嗦 suo
嗡 wēng
嗅 xiù
噪 zào
嘱 zhǔ
嘴 zuǐ

53 口

2–3 strokes

回 huí
团 tuán
因 yīn

4–5 strokes

固 gù
国 guó
困 kùn
图 tú
围 wéi
园 yuán

7–8 strokes

圈 quān
圆 yuán

54 巾

巾 jīn

2–6 strokes

帮 bāng
币 bì
布 bù
带 dài
帆 fān
帅 shuài
帖 tiě
希 xī
帐 zhàng
帜 zhì

7–12 strokes

常 cháng
幅 fú
帽 mào
幢 zhuàng

55 山

山 shān

3–9 strokes

岸 àn
崩 bēng
岔 chà
崇 chóng
岛 dǎo
峰 fēng
岗 gāng
峻 jùn
凯 kǎi
岭 lǐng
岂 qǐ
嵌 qiàn
岁 suì
炭 tàn
峡 xiá
崖 yá
岩 yán
幽 yōu
屿 yǔ
崭 zhǎn

56 彳

3–5 strokes

彼 bǐ
彻 chè
行 háng, xíng
径 jìng
往 wǎng
役 yì
征 zhēng

6–14 strokes

待 dāi, dài
得 dé, de, děi
德 dé
很 hěn
衡 héng
徊 huái
徽 huī
街 jiē
律 lù
徘 pái
徒 tú
微 wēi
衔 xián
循 xún

衍 yǎn

57 彡

彩 cǎi
形 xíng
须 xū
影 yǐng
彰 zhāng

58 夕

夕 xī

2–8 strokes

多 duō
梦 mèng
名 míng
外 wài
夜 yè

59 夂

备 bèi
处 chǔ, chù
冬 dōng
复 fù
各 gè
务 wù

60 犭

3–6 strokes

狈 bèi
独 dú
犯 fàn
狗 gǒu
狠 hěn
狐 hú
狡 jiǎo
狂 kuáng
狮 shī
狭 xiá
犹 yóu
狱 yù

7–10 strokes

猜 cāi
猖 chāng
猴 hóu
猾 huá
狼 láng

狸 lí
猎 liè
猫 māo
猛 měng
猿 yuán
猪 zhū

61 饣

2–4 strokes

饭 fàn
饥 jī
饪 rèn
饮 yǐn

5–10 strokes

饱 bǎo
饼 bǐng
馋 chán
饿 è
馆 guǎn
饺 jiǎo
馒 mán
饶 ráo
蚀 shí
饰 shì
饲 sì
馅 xiàn

62 彐

归 guī
录 lù
寻 xún

63 尸

尸 shī

1–5 strokes

层 céng
尺 chǐ
届 jiè
尽 jǐn, jìn
居 jū
局 jú
尼 ní
尿 niào
屁 pì
屈 qū
屉 tì

尾	wěi	奴	nú	学	xué	编	biān

6–11 strokes

屡	lǚ	如	rú	孕	yùn	缠	chán
履	lǚ	她	tā			绸	chóu
屏	píng	妥	tuǒ	**70 纟**		锻	duàn
屎	shǐ	妄	wàng			缝	féng, fèng
属	shǔ	妖	yāo	**2–4 strokes**		缚	fù
屠	tú	**5 strokes**		纯	chún	缓	huǎn
屋	wū	姑	gū	纺	fǎng	继	jì
屑	xiè	姐	jiě	纷	fēn	绩	jì
展	zhǎn	妹	mèi	纲	gāng	缴	jiǎo
		姆	mǔ	红	hóng	绢	juàn
64 已		妻	qī	级	jí	绿	lǜ
已	yǐ	始	shǐ	纪	jì	绵	mián
		姓	xìng	纠	jiū	渺	miǎo
65 己		**6–12 strokes**		纳	nà	绳	shéng
己	jǐ	婚	hūn	纽	niǔ	缩	suō
		嫉	jí	纱	shā	维	wéi
66 巳		嫁	jià	丝	sī	绣	xiù
导	dǎo	姜	jiāng	纹	wén	续	xù
卷	juǎn	娇	jiāo	纤	xiān	绪	xù
巷	xiàng	姥	lǎo	约	yuē	缘	yuán
		媒	méi	纸	zhǐ	缀	zhuì
67 弓		嫩	nèn	纵	zòng	综	zōng
弓	gōng	娘	niáng	**5 strokes**			
1–13 strokes		娶	qǔ	练	liàn	**71 马**	
弹	dàn	嫂	sǎo	络	luò	马	mǎ
疆	jiāng	婶	shěn	绍	shào	**3–14 strokes**	
弥	mí	耍	shuǎ	绅	shēn	驳	bó
强	qiáng	娃	wá	细	xì	驰	chí
弱	ruò	媳	xí	线	xiàn	驾	jià
弦	xián	嫌	xián	织	zhī	骄	jiāo
引	yǐn	姨	yí	终	zhōng	驴	lú
张	zhāng	姻	yīn	组	zǔ	骡	luó
		婴	yīng	**6 strokes**		骆	luò
68 女		娱	yú	绑	bǎng	骂	mà
女	nǚ	姿	zī	给	gěi, jǐ	骗	piàn
2–4 strokes				绘	huì	骑	qí
妒	dù	**69 子**		绞	jiǎo	驱	qū
妨	fáng	子	zǐ, zi	结	jiē, jié	骚	sāo
妇	fù	**1–6 strokes**		经	jīng	驶	shǐ
好	hǎo, hào	存	cún	绝	jué	驼	tuó
奸	jiān	孤	gū	络	luò	验	yàn
妈	mā	孩	hái	绕	rào	骤	zhòu
妙	miào	孔	kǒng	绒	róng	驻	zhù
奶	nǎi	孙	sūn	统	tǒng		
		孝	xiào	**7–13 strokes**			
				绷	bēng		

72 灬	
4–6 strokes	
点	diǎn
杰	jié
烈	liè
烹	pēng
热	rè
8–10 strokes	
熬	áo
煎	jiān
焦	jiāo
然	rán
熟	shú
熊	xióng
熏	xūn
燕	yàn
照	zhào
煮	zhǔ

73 文	
文	wén

74 方	
方	fāng
4–10 strokes	
放	fàng
旅	lǚ
旁	páng
旗	qí
施	shī
旋	xuán
族	zú

75 心	
心	xīn
1–4 strokes	
必	bì
忽	hū
忌	jì
念	niàn
忍	rěn
态	tài
忘	wàng
忠	zhōng
5–6 strokes	
怠	dài

7–12 strokes		晒	shài	贱	jiàn	致	zhì	**4–8 strokes**	
辈	bèi	晓	xiǎo	贸	mào	**8–11 strokes**		版	bǎn
辐	fú	星	xīng	贴	tiē	敞	chǎng	牌	pái
辅	fú	映	yìng	**6–12 strokes**		敷	fū		
辑	jí	晕	yùn	赌	dǔ	敬	jìng	**96 斤**	
辆	liàng	昨	zuó	贿	huì	散	sǎn, sàn	斤	jīn
输	shū	**7–11 strokes**		赖	lài	数	shǔ, shù	**1–9 strokes**	
辖	xiá	暗	àn	赂	lù			斥	chì
舆	yú	暴	bào	赔	péi	**91 牛**		断	duàn
		曾	céng	赛	sài	牛	niú	斯	sī
84 比		晨	chén	赏	shǎng	**4–7 strokes**		所	suǒ
比	bǐ	晶	jīng	赞	zàn	犁	lí	欣	xīn
2 strokes		景	jǐng	贼	zéi	牧	mù	新	xīn
毕	bì	晾	liàng	赠	zèng	牲	shēng		
		暮	mù	赚	zhuàn	特	tè	**97 爪**	
85 日		暖	nuǎn	资	zī	物	wù	爪	zhuǎ
晋	jìn	普	pǔ			牺	xī	**4–6 strokes**	
量	liáng, liàng	晴	qíng	**88 见**				爱	ài
曲	qū, qǔ	暑	shǔ	见	jiàn	**92 手**		采	cǎi
替	tì	晚	wǎn	**2–5 strokes**		手	shǒu	爬	pá
显	xiǎn	晤	wù	观	guān	**5–15 strokes**		乳	rǔ
暂	zàn	晰	xī	规	guī	掰	bāi	受	shòu
最	zuì	智	zhì	觉	jiào, jué	拜	bài		
				览	lǎn	攀	pān	**98 月**	
86 日		**87 贝**				拳	quán	月	yuè
日	rì	贝	bèi	**89 父**		掌	zhǎng	**2–3 strokes**	
1–4 strokes		**2–3 strokes**		父	fù	挚	zhì	肠	cháng
昂	áng	财	cái	**2–6 strokes**				肚	dù
昌	chāng	贞	zhēn	爸	bà	**93 毛**		肝	gān
旦	dàn	**4 strokes**		爹	diē	毛	máo	肌	jī
旱	hàn	败	bài	斧	fǔ	**6–10 strokes**		有	yǒu
昏	hūn	贬	biǎn	爷	yé	毫	háo	**4 strokes**	
旧	jiù	贩	fàn			耗	hào	肪	fáng
旷	kuàng	贯	guàn	**90 攵**		髦	máo	肥	féi
昆	kūn	购	gòu	**2–5 strokes**		毯	tǎn	肤	fū
明	míng	货	huò	改	gǎi			服	fú
时	shí	贫	pín	故	gù	**94 气**		股	gǔ
旺	wàng	贪	tān	收	shōu	气	qì	肩	jiān
易	yì	贤	xián	政	zhèng	**4–8 strokes**		朋	péng
早	zǎo	责	zé	**6–7 strokes**		氮	dàn	肾	shèn
者	zhě	质	zhì	敌	dí	氛	fēn	胁	xié
旨	zhǐ	**5 strokes**		敢	gǎn	氢	qīng	育	yù
5–6 strokes		贷	dài	教	jiāo, jiào	氧	yǎng	胀	zhàng
春	chūn	费	fèi	救	jiù			肢	zhī
晃	huǎng	贵	guì	敏	mǐn	**95 片**		肿	zhǒng
昧	mèi	贺	hè	效	xiào	片	piàn		

5 strokes		腰	yāo	炎	yán	**106 水**		碟	dié
胞	bāo			灶	zào	水	shuǐ	硅	guī
背	bēi, bèi	**99 欠**		炸	zhá	**5–6 strokes**		碱	jiǎn
胆	dǎn	欠	qiàn	**6–14 strokes**		浆	jiāng	磕	kē
肺	fèi	**4–10 strokes**		爆	bào	泉	quán	磷	lín
骨	gǔ	歌	gē	烦	fán			硫	liú
胡	hú	款	kuǎn	焊	hàn	**107 聿**		碌	lù
脉	mài	欧	ōu	烘	hōng	隶	lì	碰	pèng
胖	pàng	欺	qī	煌	huáng	肆	sì	确	què
胜	shèng	歉	qiàn	烤	kǎo	肃	sù	硕	shuò
胃	wèi	软	ruǎn	煤	méi			碎	suì
6 strokes		歇	xiē	燃	rán	**108 止**		碳	tàn
脆	cuì	欲	yù	熔	róng	止	zhǐ	碗	wǎn
胳	gē			烧	shāo	**2–4 strokes**		硬	yìng
脊	jǐ	**100 天**		烫	tàng	步	bù		
胶	jiāo	天	tiān	熄	xī	此	cǐ	**111 业**	
朗	lǎng			烟	yān	肯	kěn	业	yè
脑	nǎo	**101 风**		焰	yàn	歧	qí	**7 strokes**	
胸	xiōng	风	fēng	烛	zhú	歪	wāi	凿	záo
脏	zāng, zàng	**11 strokes**							
脂	zhī	飘	piāo	**104 礻**		**109 龙**		**112 目**	
7–8 strokes				福	fú	龙	lóng	目	mù
脖	bó	**102 殳**		祸	huò	**6 strokes**		**2–4 strokes**	
朝	cháo	殿	diàn	礼	lǐ	聋	lóng	盯	dīng
脚	jiǎo	段	duàn	社	shè	袭	xí	盾	dùn
腊	là	毁	huǐ	神	shén			看	kān, kàn
脸	liǎn	殴	ōu	视	shì	**110 石**		盲	máng
脾	pí	毅	yì	祥	xiáng	石	shí	冒	mào
期	qī			祝	zhù	**3–5 strokes**		眉	méi
腔	qiāng	**103 火**		祖	zǔ	础	chǔ	盼	pàn
脱	tuō	火	huǒ			砍	kǎn	眨	zhǎ
望	wàng	**2–5 strokes**		**105 戈**		矿	kuàng	**5–13 strokes**	
朝	zhāo	灿	càn	裁	cái	码	mǎ	睬	cǎi
9–16 strokes		炒	chǎo	成	chéng	破	pò	瞪	dèng
膀	bǎng	炊	chuī	戴	dài	砌	qì	督	dū
臂	bì	灯	dēng	或	huò	砂	shā	睛	jīng
膊	bó	灰	huī	截	jié	研	yán	瞒	mán
腹	fù	灸	jiǔ	戒	jiè	砸	zá	眯	mí
膜	mó	炕	kàng	威	wēi	砖	zhuān	眠	mián
膨	péng	烂	làn	我	wǒ	**6–12 strokes**		睦	mù
腮	sāi	炼	liàn	武	wǔ	碍	ài	瞥	piē
膛	táng	灵	líng	戏	xì	磅	bàng	瞧	qiáo
腾	téng	炉	lú	栽	zāi	碑	bēi	睡	shuì
腿	tuǐ	灭	miè	战	zhàn	碧	bì	瞎	xiā
膝	xī	炮	pào			磁	cí	眼	yǎn
腥	xīng	烁	shuò			磋	cuō	瞻	zhān

睁 zhēng

113 田

田 tián
2–7 strokes
畅 chàng
电 diàn
番 fān
甲 jiǎ
界 jiè
累 lèi
留 liú
略 lüè
男 nán
畔 pàn
畏 wèi
畜 xù
野 yě

114 四

四 sì
4–8 strokes
罢 bà
罚 fá
暑 shǔ
罩 zhào
置 zhì
罪 zuì

115 皿

盗 dào
监 jiān
盟 méng
盘 pán
盆 pén
盛 shèng
血 xiě, xuè
衅 xìn
盐 yán
盈 yíng
盏 zhǎn

116 钅

2–4 strokes
钞 chāo
钓 diào

钉 dīng, dìng
钙 gài
钢 gāng
钩 gōu
钦 qīn
钥 yào
针 zhēn
钟 zhōng
5–6 strokes
铲 chǎn
铃 líng
铝 lǚ
铅 qiān
钱 qián
钳 qián
铁 tiě
铜 tóng
银 yín
铀 yóu
钻 zuān, zuàn
7 strokes
锄 chú
锋 fēng
锅 guō
链 liàn
铺 pū
锐 ruì
锁 suǒ
销 xiāo
锌 xīn
锈 xiù
铸 zhù
8–17 strokes
锤 chuí
错 cuò
镀 dù
锻 duàn
键 jiàn
锦 jǐn
镜 jìng
锯 jù
镰 lián
锣 luó
镁 měi
锹 qiāo
锡 xī

镶 xiāng
镇 zhèn
镯 zhuó

117 矢

矮 ǎi
短 duǎn
矩 jǔ
知 zhī

118 禾

禾 hé
2–4 strokes
秉 bǐng
和 hé
季 jì
科 kē
秒 miǎo
秋 qiū
私 sī
秃 tū
委 wěi
香 xiāng
秀 xiù
种 zhǒng, zhòng
5–6 strokes
称 chèn, chēng
乘 chéng
秤 chèng
积 jī
秘 mì
税 shuì
秧 yāng
移 yí
秩 zhì
租 zū
7–12 strokes
程 chéng
稠 chóu
稻 dào
稿 gǎo
稼 jià
穆 mù
稍 shāo
穗 suì
稳 wěn

稀 xī
稚 zhì

119 白

白 bái
1–9 strokes
百 bǎi
的 de, dí
皇 huáng
皆 jiē
魄 pò
皂 zào

120 用

用 yòng

121 鸟

鸟 niǎo
2–7 strokes
鹅 é
鸽 gē
鸡 jī
鹊 què
鸦 yā
鸭 yā

122 疒

2–5 strokes
疤 bā
病 bìng
疮 chuāng
疯 fēng
疾 jí
疗 liáo
疲 pí
疼 téng
疫 yì
症 zhèng
6–12 strokes
癌 ái
痹 bì
痴 chī
痕 hén
痪 huàn
瘤 liú
瘸 qué

瘦 shòu
瘫 tān
痰 tán
痛 tòng
瘟 wēn
痒 yǎng

123 立

立 lì
1–9 strokes
产 chǎn
端 duān
竭 jié
竞 jìng
亲 qīn
竖 shù
站 zhàn
章 zhāng

124 穴

穴 xué
2–11 strokes
穿 chuān
窗 chuāng
窜 cuàn
窖 jiào
究 jiū
空 kōng, kòng
窟 kū
帘 lián
窿 lóng
窃 qiè
穷 qióng
突 tū
窝 wō
窑 yáo
窄 zhǎi

125 衤

2–3 strokes
补 bǔ
衬 chèn
初 chū
衫 shān
4–7 strokes
袄 ǎo

145 艮

既	jì
良	liáng

146 羽

羽	yǔ

4–12 strokes

翅	chì
翠	cuì
翻	fān
翘	qiào
翁	wēng
翼	yì

147 糸

繁	fán
紧	jǐn
素	sù
索	suǒ
絮	xù
紫	zǐ

148 麦

麦	mài

149 走

走	zǒu

3–8 strokes

超	chāo
趁	chèn
赴	fù
赶	gǎn
起	qǐ
趋	qū
趣	qù
趟	tàng
越	yuè

150 里

里	lǐ

4 strokes

野	yě

151 足

足	zú

3–6 strokes

跌	diē
跺	duò
跟	gēn
跪	guì
践	jiàn
距	jù
跨	kuà
路	lù
趴	pā
跑	pǎo
跳	tiào
跃	yuè

7–13 strokes

蹦	bèng
踩	cǎi
蹈	dǎo
蹲	dūn
踏	tā, tà
蹋	tà
踢	tī
蹄	tí
躁	zào
踪	zōng

152 采

释	shì

153 豸

貌	mào

154 身

身	shēn

3–8 strokes

躲	duǒ
射	shè
躺	tǎng

155 角

角	jiǎo

6 strokes

触	chù
解	jiě

156 言

言	yán

6–13 strokes

警	jǐng
譬	pì
誓	shì
誉	yù

157 辛

辛	xīn

6–12 strokes

瓣	bàn
辨	biàn
辩	biàn
辫	biàn
辣	là
辟	pì

158 系

系	xì

159 束

束	shù

9 strokes

整	zhěng

160 非

非	fēi

7 strokes

靠	kào

161 酉

酬	chóu
醋	cù
酱	jiàng
酷	kù
酶	méi
酿	niàng
配	pèi
酸	suān
醒	xǐng
酗	xù
酝	yùn
酌	zhuó
醉	zuì

162 豆

豆	dòu

163 隹

雌	cí
雕	diāo
集	jí
雀	què
售	shòu
雄	xióng
雅	yǎ
耀	yào

164 青

青	qīng

6 strokes

静	jìng

165 鱼

鱼	yú

4–8 strokes

鲸	jīng
鲁	lǔ
鲜	xiān

166 雨

雨	yǔ

3–13 strokes

霸	bà
雹	báo
霍	huò
雷	léi
零	líng
露	lù
霉	méi
霜	shuāng
雾	wù
霞	xiá
需	xū
雪	xuě
震	zhèn

167 齿

齿	chǐ

5 strokes

龄	líng

168 革

革	gé

2–9 strokes

鞭	biān
鞠	jū
勒	lè
鞋	xié
靴	xuē

169 是

是	shì

2–6 strokes

匙	chí, shi
题	tí

170 食

食	shí

7 strokes

餐	cān

171 鬼

鬼	guǐ

4 strokes

魂	hún

172 音

音	yīn

4 strokes

韵	yùn

173 麻

麻	má

4–9 strokes

摩	mó
魔	mó

174 黑

黑	hēi

3–4 strokes

墨	mò
默	mò

175 鼠

鼠	shǔ

Stroke Index

This index lists all characters in this dictionary according to the number of strokes used to write them. Characters with the same number of strokes are grouped together according to the first stroke used. These groups are listed in the following order:

1. 一 (including ⼁ ⺄)
2. 丨 (including 亅丿)
3. 丿 (including 丿一亅)
4. 丶 (including 丶 ⟍)
5. ⇁ (including フ乛⻊乙⻊乙⻊)
6. ⼃ (including ⼃⼃⼃⼃⼃)

Within each group, characters are arranged alphabetically according to *pinyin*.

1–2 strokes	工 gōng	亡 wáng	区 qū	仓 cāng	勿 wù	⼃
一	亏 kuī	之 zhī	犬 quǎn	长 cháng,	凶 xiōng	比 bǐ
厂 chǎng	三 sān	⇁	市 shì	zhǎng	月 yuè	幻 huàn
丁 dīng	尸 shī	叉 chā	世 shì	仇 chóu	勾 yún	以 yǐ
二 èr	士 shì	飞 fēi	太 tài	从 cóng		允 yǔn
弓 gōng	土 tǔ	己 jǐ	天 tiān	丹 dān	丶	
七 qī	万 wàn	马 mǎ	厅 tīng	乏 fá	订 dìng	**5 strokes**
十 shí	下 xià	刃 rèn	屯 tún	反 fǎn	斗 dòu	一
一 yī, yí, yì	于 yú	卫 wèi	瓦 wǎ	分 fēn, fèn	方 fāng	艾 ài
丨	丈 zhàng	习 xí	王 wáng	风 fēng	户 hù	扒 bá
卜 bó, bǔ	丨	也 yě	无 wú	凤 fèng	火 huǒ	本 běn
丿	巾 jīn	已 yǐ	五 wǔ	父 fù	讥 jī	丙 bǐng
八 bā	口 kǒu	子 zǐ, zi	牙 yá	公 gōng	计 jì	布 bù
儿 ér	山 shān	⼃	艺 yì	勾 gōu	亢 kàng	打 dǎ
几 jī, jǐ	上 shàng	女 nǚ	尤 yóu	化 huà	六 liù	东 dōng
九 jiǔ	小 xiǎo	乡 xiāng	友 yǒu	介 jiè	认 rèn	甘 gān
人 rén	丿	与 yǔ	元 yuán	斤 jīn	为 wéi, wèi	功 gōng
入 rù	川 chuān		云 yún	今 jīn	文 wén	古 gǔ
⇁	凡 fán	**4 strokes**	扎 zhā	仅 jǐn	心 xīn	击 jī
刀 dāo	个 gè	一	支 zhī	毛 máo	忆 yì	节 jié
刁 diāo	及 jí	不 bú, bù	专 zhuān	牛 niú	⇁	刊 kān
了 le, liǎo	久 jiǔ	车 chē	丨	片 piàn	巴 bā	可 kě
力 lì	么 me	歹 dǎi	贝 bèi	仆 pú	办 bàn	厉 lì
乙 yǐ	乞 qǐ	丰 fēng	见 jiàn	气 qì	尺 chǐ	龙 lóng
又 yòu	千 qiān	夫 fū	内 nèi	欠 qiàn	丑 chǒu	灭 miè
	勺 sháo	戈 gē	日 rì	仁 rén	队 duì	末 mò
3 strokes	丸 wán	互 hù	少 shǎo,	仍 réng	孔 kǒng	平 píng
一	夕 xī	井 jǐng	shào	什 shén	劝 quàn	扑 pū
才 cái	义 yì	巨 jù	水 shuǐ	升 shēng	书 shū	巧 qiǎo
寸 cùn	亿 yì	开 kāi	止 zhǐ	氏 shì	双 shuāng	切 qiè
大 dà, dài	丶	历 lì	中 zhōng	手 shǒu	引 yǐn	去 qù
干 gān, gàn	广 guǎng	木 mù	丿	乌 wū	予 yú	扔 rēng
	门 mén	匹 pǐ	币 bì	午 wǔ		石 shí

宇 yǔ	把 bǎ	坑 kēng	址 zhǐ	兵 bīng	秀 xiù	沏 qī
宅 zhái	坝 bà	抠 kōu	志 zhì	伯 bó	役 yì	柴 qī
舟 zhōu	扳 bān	块 kuài	抓 zhuā	岔 chà	饮 yǐn	启 qǐ
州 zhōu	扮 bàn	来 lái	走 zǒu	肠 cháng	佣 yōng	弃 qì
庄 zhuāng	报 bào	劳 láo		彻 chè	犹 yóu	汽 qì
字 zì	材 cái	李 lǐ	吧 ba	伺 cì, sì	余 yú	穷 qióng
	苍 cāng	丽 lì	别 bié	囱 cōng	皂 zào	饪 rèn
驰 chí	抄 chāo	励 lì	步 bù	但 dàn	针 zhēn	沙 shā
导 dǎo	扯 chě	连 lián	财 cái	岛 dǎo	住 zhù	社 shè
防 fáng	辰 chén	两 liǎng	吵 chǎo	低 dī	作 zuò	识 shí
观 guān	赤 chì	抡 lūn	呈 chéng	钉 dìng	坐 zuò	诉 sù
欢 huān	村 cūn	麦 mài	串 chuàn	肚 dù		汰 tài
阶 jiē	抖 dǒu	拟 nǐ	吹 chuī	返 fǎn	补 bǔ	完 wán
尽 jǐn, jìn	豆 dòu	尿 niào	呆 dāi	饭 fàn	灿 càn	汪 wāng
买 mǎi	坊 fāng	扭 niǔ	盯 dīng,	佛 fó, fú	沉 chén	忘 wàng
那 nà, nèi	芳 fāng	弄 nòng	dìng	肝 gān	初 chū	沃 wò
孙 sūn	芬 fēn	抛 pāo	吨 dūn	告 gào	床 chuáng	闲 xián
驼 tuó	坟 fén	批 pī	吩 fēn	估 gū	词 cí	辛 xīn
戏 xì	否 fǒu	抢 qiǎng	岗 gāng	龟 guī	冻 dòng	汹 xiōng
寻 xún	扶 fú	芹 qín	旱 hàn	含 hán	弟 dì	序 xù
阳 yáng	抚 fǔ	求 qiú	吼 hǒu	何 hé	兑 duì	言 yán
异 yì	杆 gān, gǎn	却 què	坚 jiān	角 jiǎo	泛 fàn	冶 yě
阴 yīn	杠 gàng	扰 rǎo	旷 kuàng	近 jìn	沟 gōu	译 yì
羽 yǔ	更 gēng,	韧 rèn	困 kùn	灸 jiǔ	罕 hǎn	应 yīng,
阵 zhèn	gèng	声 shēng	里 lǐ	狂 kuáng	宏 hóng	yìng
	攻 gōng	寿 shòu	男 nán	利 lì	沪 hù	忧 yōu
毕 bì	汞 gǒng	束 shù	呕 ǒu	邻 lín	怀 huái	灾 zāi
妇 fù	贡 gòng	苏 sū	时 shí	卵 luǎn	间 jiān,	灶 zào
好 hǎo, hào	还 hái,	坛 tán	听 tīng	乱 luàn	jiàn	诈 zhà
红 hóng	huán	投 tóu	围 wéi	每 měi	究 jiū	这 zhè, zhèi
级 jí	护 hù	吞 tūn	吻 wěn	免 miǎn	库 kù	诊 zhěn
纪 jì	花 huā	违 wéi	呜 wū	你 nǐ	快 kuài	证 zhèng
奸 jiān	坏 huài	巫 wū	县 xiàn	刨 páo	况 kuàng	
妈 mā	极 jí	孝 xiào	肖 xiào	伸 shēn	牢 láo	阿 ā
如 rú	技 jì	形 xíng	呀 yā, ya	身 shēn	冷 lěng	驳 bó
收 shōu	歼 jiān	杏 xìng	邮 yóu	私 sī	沥 lì	层 céng
她 tā	劫 jié	芽 yá	员 yuán	体 tǐ	疗 liáo	陈 chén
纤 xiān	戒 jiè	严 yán	园 yuán	条 tiáo	没 méi	迟 chí
巡 xún	进 jìn	杨 yáng	帐 zhàng	秃 tū	闷 mēn,	附 fù
约 yuē	玖 jiǔ	医 yī	助 zhù	妥 tuǒ	mèn	改 gǎi
旨 zhǐ	拒 jù	抑 yì	状 zhuàng	位 wèi	亩 mǔ	鸡 jī
	均 jūn	远 yuǎn	足 zú	我 wǒ	判 pàn	即 jí
	抗 kàng	运 yùn		希 xī	沛 pèi	忌 jì
7 strokes	壳 ké	找 zhǎo	伴 bàn	系 xì	评 píng	际 jì
	克 kè	折 zhē, zhé	狈 bèi	仙 xiān		劲 jìn
芭 bā						

券 quàn	屈 qū	荡 dàng	柿 shì	将 jiāng	便 biàn,	秋 qiū
衫 shān	刷 shuā	垫 diàn	树 shù	界 jiè	pián	泉 quán
审 shěn	肃 sù	栋 dòng	耍 shuǎ	咳 ké	饼 bǐng	饶 ráo
诗 shī	弦 xián	毒 dú	拴 shuān	览 lǎn	钞 chāo	牲 shēng
实 shí	限 xiàn	封 fēng	挑 tiāo,	临 lín	重 chóng,	胜 shèng
试 shì	驻 zhù	赴 fù	tiǎo	蚂 mǎ	zhòng	狮 shī
视 shì		革 gé	挺 tǐng	骂 mà	促 cù	食 shí
祥 xiáng	参 cān	拱 gǒng	挖 wā	冒 mào	待 dāi, dài	蚀 shí
享 xiǎng	姑 gū	故 gù	歪 wāi	昧 mèi	贷 dài	适 shì
泄 xiè	贯 guàn	挂 guà	威 wēi	哪 nǎ	胆 dǎn	顺 shùn
泻 xiè	姐 jiě	厚 hòu	咸 xián	趴 pā	独 dú	俗 sú
性 xìng	练 liàn	胡 hú	相 xiāng	盼 pàn	段 duàn	逃 táo
学 xué	妹 mèi	荒 huāng	项 xiàng	品 pǐn	俄 é	侮 wǔ
询 xún	姆 mǔ	挥 huī	巷 xiàng	省 shěng	俘 fú	狭 xiá
沿 yán	叁 sān	挤 jǐ	挟 xié	是 shì	复 fù	香 xiāng
炎 yán	绍 shào	茧 jiǎn	型 xíng	竖 shù	钙 gài	卸 xiè
夜 yè	绅 shēn	柬 jiǎn	鸦 yā	思 sī	竿 gān	信 xìn
宜 yí	始 shǐ	荐 jiàn	研 yán	虽 suī	缸 gāng	修 xiū
泳 yǒng	细 xì	砍 kǎn	殃 yāng	炭 tàn	钢 gāng	须 xū
油 yóu	线 xiàn	枯 kū	要 yāo, yào	贴 tiē	钩 gōu	叙 xù
育 yù	姓 xìng	垮 kuǎ	药 yào	哇 wā	鬼 guǐ	选 xuǎn
泽 zé	织 zhī	挎 kuà	珍 zhēn	畏 wèi	很 hěn	衍 yǎn
闸 zhá	终 zhōng	括 kuò	挣 zhēng,	胃 wèi	狠 hěn	钥 yào
沾 zhān	纵 zòng	栏 lán	zhèng	虾 xiā	徊 huái	盈 yíng
沼 zhǎo	组 zǔ	厘 lí	政 zhèng	峡 xiá	皇 huáng	狱 yù
郑 zhèng		荔 lì	指 zhǐ	显 xiǎn	急 jí	怨 yuàn
治 zhì	**9 strokes**	玲 líng	柱 zhù	响 xiǎng	剑 jiàn	怎 zěn
宙 zhòu		珑 lóng	拽 zhuài	削 xiāo,	饺 jiǎo	钟 zhōng
注 zhù	按 àn	茫 máng	砖 zhuān	xuē	狡 jiǎo	种 zhǒng,
宗 zōng	柏 bǎi	面 miàn	奏 zòu	星 xīng	矩 jǔ	zhòng
	帮 bāng	某 mǒu		哑 yǎ	俊 jùn	追 zhuī
承 chéng	甭 béng	耐 nài	唉 āi	咽 yàn	看 kān, kàn	
孤 gū	标 biāo	南 nán	背 bēi, bèi	咬 yǎo	科 kē	哀 āi
函 hán	柄 bǐng	挠 náo	尝 cháng	蚁 yǐ	俩 liǎ	袄 ǎo
驾 jià	玻 bō	柠 níng	点 diǎn	映 yìng	铃 líng	疤 bā
艰 jiān	勃 bó	挪 nuó	哆 duō	哟 yō	律 lǜ	扁 biǎn
建 jiàn	残 cán	拼 pīn	罚 fá	幽 yōu	脉 mài	测 cè
降 jiàng	草 cǎo	砌 qì	骨 gǔ	咱 zán	贸 mào	差 chā, chà
届 jiè	茶 chá	牵 qiān	贵 guì	眨 zhǎ	勉 miǎn	穿 chuān
居 jū	查 chá	轻 qīng	哈 hā	战 zhàn	秒 miǎo	疮 chuāng
隶 lì	城 chéng	荣 róng	虹 hóng	昨 zuó	胖 pàng	帝 dì
陋 lòu	持 chí	砂 shā	哄 hǒng,		盆 pén	洞 dòng
录 lù	春 chūn	珊 shān	hòng	拜 bài	俏 qiào	度 dù
弥 mí	带 dài	甚 shèn	哗 huá	胞 bāo	钦 qīn	阀 fá
陌 mò	挡 dǎng	拾 shí	贱 jiàn	保 bǎo	氢 qīng	疯 fēng

宫 gōng	施 shī	眉 méi	耽 dān	热 rè	哼 hēng	俯 fǔ
冠 guàn	室 shì	屏 píng	档 dàng	辱 rǔ	唤 huàn	胳 gē
闺 guī	首 shǒu	柔 róu	捣 dǎo	捎 shāo	晃 huǎng	逛 guàng
阂 hé	说 shuō	屎 shǐ	都 dōu, dū	逝 shì	贿 huì	航 háng
恨 hèn	烁 shuò	退 tuì	逗 dòu	殊 shū	监 jiān	候 hòu
恒 héng	送 sòng	屋 wū	顿 dùn	素 sù	浆 jiāng	脊 jǐ
洪 hóng	诵 sòng	险 xiǎn	恶 ě, è, wù	速 sù	桨 jiǎng	舰 jiàn
恢 huī	剃 tì	逊 xùn	匪 fěi	损 sǔn	紧 jǐn	健 jiàn
浑 hún	庭 tíng	勇 yǒng	赶 gǎn	索 suǒ	峻 jùn	胶 jiāo
活 huó	亭 tíng	院 yuàn	哥 gē	泰 tài	哭 kū	借 jiè
迹 jì	突 tū	昼 zhòu	格 gé	桃 táo	唠 láo	俱 jù
济 jì	弯 wān		根 gēn	套 tào	赂 lù	倦 juàn
姜 jiāng	闻 wén	⎿	耕 gēng	捅 tǒng	虑 lù	狼 láng
将 jiāng	诬 wū	绑 bǎng	恭 gōng	顽 wán	眠 mián	狸 lí
奖 jiǎng	误 wù	怠 dài	顾 gù	挽 wǎn	哦 ǒ	铃 líng
浇 jiāo	洗 xǐ	给 gěi, jǐ	桂 guì	桅 wéi	畔 pàn	留 liú
觉 jiào, jué	宪 xiàn	绘 huì	捍 hàn	夏 xià	晒 shài	秘 mì
洁 jié	宣 xuān	娇 jiāo	耗 hào	校 xiào	哨 shào	拿 ná
诫 jiè	洋 yáng	绞 jiǎo	荷 hé	盐 yán	嗦 suō	脑 nǎo
津 jīn	养 yǎng	结 jiē, jié	核 hé	艳 yàn	蚊 wén	铅 qiān
举 jǔ	疫 yì	皆 jiē	壶 hú	样 yàng	晓 xiǎo	钱 qián
烤 kǎo	音 yīn	经 jīng	换 huàn	原 yuán	圆 yuán	钳 qián
客 kè	诱 yòu	绝 jué	获 huò	砸 zá	晕 yùn	倾 qīng
烂 làn	语 yǔ	姥 lǎo	捡 jiǎn	栽 zāi	贼 zéi	缺 quē
类 lèi	炸 zhá	垒 lěi	轿 jiào	载 zài	啄 zhuó	耸 sǒng
炼 liàn	洲 zhōu	络 luò	较 jiào	盏 zhǎn	桌 zhuó	颂 sòng
亮 liàng	祝 zhù	怒 nù	晋 jìn	哲 zhé		笋 sǔn
浏 liú	浊 zhuó	绕 rào	捐 juān	真 zhēn	⌐	倘 tǎng
美 měi	咨 zī	绒 róng	恐 kǒng	振 zhèn	爱 ài	特 tè
迷 mí	姿 zī	统 tǒng	捆 kǔn	挚 zhì	笆 bā	铁 tiě
恼 nǎo	籽 zǐ	娃 wá	捞 lāo	致 zhì	颁 bān	透 tòu
逆 nì	总 zǒng	姨 yí	栗 lì	珠 zhū	般 bān	途 tú
浓 nóng	祖 zǔ	姻 yīn	莲 lián	株 zhū	倍 bèi	徒 tú
派 pài			烈 liè	逐 zhú	笔 bǐ	翁 wēng
叛 pàn	⌐	**10 strokes**	柳 liǔ	捉 zhuō	舱 cāng	息 xī
炮 pào	除 chú		珑 lóng	酌 zhuó	倡 chàng	牺 xī
柒 qī	陡 dǒu	⌐	埋 mái,		称 chèn,	笑 xiào
恰 qià	盾 dùn	挨 ái	mán	啊 ā	chēng	胸 xiōng
洽 qià	费 fèi	捌 bā	莫 mò	唉 āi	乘 chéng	秧 yāng
前 qián	孩 hái	班 bān	难 nán, nàn	罢 bà	秤 chèng	氧 yǎng
窃 qiè	贺 hé	捕 bǔ	捏 niē	柴 chái	臭 chòu	倚 yǐ
亲 qīn	既 jì	蚕 cán	配 pèi	党 dǎng	脆 cuì	铀 yóu
染 rǎn	架 jià	耻 chǐ	破 pò	恩 ēn	倒 dǎo, dào	脏 zāng,
洒 sǎ	骄 jiāo	翅 chì	起 qǐ	峰 fēng	敌 dí	zàng
神 shén	垦 kěn	础 chǔ	桥 qiáo	跟 gēn	爹 diē	
	骆 luò	唇 chún			逢 féng	
		挫 cuò				

造 zào	凉 liáng	冤 yuān	掉 diào	梢 shāo	雀 què	犁 lí
债 zhài	谅 liàng	悦 yuè	堵 dǔ	奢 shē	蛇 shé	脸 liǎn
脂 zhī	料 liào	阅 yuè	堆 duī	盛 shèng	梳 shū	领 lǐng
值 zhí	凌 líng	宰 zǎi	辅 fú	授 shòu	堂 táng	笼 lóng
秩 zhì	流 liú	窄 zhǎi	副 fù	爽 shuǎng	唾 tuò	铝 lǚ
皱 zhòu	旅 lǚ	站 zhàn	梗 gěng	硕 shuò	晚 wǎn	猫 māo
租 zū	旁 páng	涨 zhǎng	菇 gū	探 tàn	唯 wéi	猛 měng
钻 zuān,	袍 páo	症 zhèng	硅 guī	掏 tāo	晤 wù	敏 mǐn
zuàn	疲 pí	衷 zhōng	黄 huáng	萄 tao	虚 xū	您 nín
	瓶 píng	诸 zhū	基 jī	梯 tī	悬 xuán	偶 ǒu
案 àn	剖 pōu	烛 zhú	检 jiǎn	桶 tǒng	鸭 yā	徘 pái
被 bèi	凄 qī	准 zhǔn	教 jiāo,	推 tuī	崖 yá	盘 pán
宾 bīn	悄 qiāo	资 zī	jiào	袭 xí	眼 yǎn	偏 piān
病 bìng	请 qǐng	座 zuò	接 jiē	掀 xiān	野 yě	售 shòu
部 bù	拳 quán		捷 jié	厢 xiāng	婴 yīng	停 tíng
瓷 cí	容 róng	剥 bāo, bō	救 jiù	械 xiè	跃 yuè	铜 tóng
递 dì	润 rùn	剧 jù	菊 jú	酗 xù	崭 zhǎn	偷 tōu
涤 dí	扇 shàn	恳 kěn	据 jú	雪 xuě	睁 zhēng	脱 tuō
调 diào,	烧 shāo	陪 péi	掘 jué	掩 yǎn	蛀 zhù	悉 xī
tiáo	涉 shè	弱 ruò	菌 jūn	营 yíng		衔 xián
读 dú	谁 shéi,	桑 sāng	勘 kān	域 yù	笨 bèn	馅 xiàn
饿 è	shuí	陶 táo	控 kòng	酝 yùn	舶 bó	象 xiàng
烦 fán	衰 shuāi	通 tōng	勒 lè	职 zhí	脖 bó	斜 xié
诽 fěi	谈 tán	陷 xiàn	理 lǐ	掷 zhì	猜 cāi	衅 xìn
粉 fěn	唐 táng	屑 xiè	辆 liàng	著 zhù	彩 cǎi	移 yí
浮 fú	烫 tàng	验 yàn	聊 liáo		铲 chǎn	银 yín
高 gāo	涛 tāo	预 yù	聋 lóng	崩 bēng	猖 chāng	悠 yōu
海 hǎi	疼 téng	展 zhǎn	掠 lüè	蝉 chán	偿 cháng	猪 zhū
害 hài	涕 tì		啰 luō	常 cháng	船 chuán	做 zuò
浩 hào	涂 tú	继 jì	萝 luó	唱 chàng	袋 dài	
烘 hōng	袜 wà	绢 juàn	梅 méi	晨 chén	得 dé, de,	惭 cán
悔 huǐ	悟 wù	能 néng	萌 méng	匙 chí, shi	děi	惨 cǎn
疾 jí	席 xí	娘 niáng	梦 mèng	崇 chóng	笛 dí	阐 chǎn
家 jiā	消 xiāo	射 shè	描 miáo	啡 fēi	第 dì	凑 còu
兼 jiān	宵 xiāo	绣 xiù	捻 niǎn	患 huàn	舵 duò	粗 cū
浸 jìn	效 xiào	娱 yú	排 pái	距 jù	符 fú	淡 dàn
竞 jìng	羞 xiū		培 péi	啃 kěn	竿 gān	盗 dào
酒 jiǔ	袖 xiù	**11 strokes**	捧 pěng	啦 la	鸽 gē	悼 dào
课 kè	畜 xù		票 piào	累 lèi	够 gòu	惦 diàn
宽 kuān	烟 yān	菠 bō	萍 píng	略 lüè	馆 guǎn	淀 diàn
朗 lǎng	宴 yàn	埠 bù	戚 qī	啰 luō	盒 hé	断 duàn
浪 làng	谊 yì	菜 cài	掐 qiā	逻 luó	凰 huáng	袱 fú
涝 lào	益 yì	捶 chuí	球 qiú	眯 mí	假 jiǎ, jià	盖 gài
离 lí	涌 yǒng	措 cuò	娶 qǔ	啤 pí	脚 jiǎo	惯 guàn
恋 liàn	浴 yù	掂 diān	啥 shà	圈 quān	梨 lí	焊 hàn

毫 háo	窑 yáo	棒 bàng	翘 qiáo	喉 hóu	短 duǎn	曾 céng
痕 hén	液 yè	逼 bī	琴 qín	辉 huī	鹅 é	窗 chuāng
谎 huǎng	淫 yín	博 bó	趋 qū	践 jiàn	番 fān	窜 cuàn
祸 huò	庸 yōng	裁 cái	确 què	晶 jīng	锋 fēng	道 dào
混 hùn	渔 yú	插 chā	惹 rě	景 jǐng	傅 fù	渡 dù
寄 jì	欲 yù	搀 chān	揉 róu	喇 lǎ	猴 hóu	惰 duò
寂 jì	章 zhāng	超 chāo	萨 sà	量 liáng,	猾 huá	愤 fèn
剪 jiǎn	着 zháo,	朝 cháo	散 sǎn, sàn	liàng	集 jí	粪 fèn
减 jiǎn	zhe,	趁 chèn	森 sēn	晾 liàng	焦 jiāo	富 fù
渐 jiàn	zhuó	厨 chú	斯 sī	帽 mào	街 jiē	溉 gài
惊 jīng	逐 zhuó	葱 cōng	搜 sōu	跑 pǎo	筋 jīn	港 gǎng
竟 jìng	族 zú	搓 cuō	塔 tǎ	赔 péi	腊 là	割 gē
惧 jù		搭 dā	提 tí	喷 pēn	链 liàn	雇 gù
康 kāng	逮 dài	堤 dī	替 tì	嵌 qiàn	猎 liè	寒 hán
寇 kòu	蛋 dàn	董 dǒng	椭 tuǒ	晴 qíng	鲁 lǔ	湖 hú
廊 láng	弹 dàn	搁 gē	握 wò	啥 shá	牌 pái	滑 huá
粒 lì	兜 dōu	辜 gū	喜 xǐ	赏 shǎng	脾 pí	痪 huàn
梁 liáng	堕 duò	棺 guān	雄 xióng	暑 shǔ	铺 pū	慌 huāng
淋 lín	敢 gǎn	棍 gùn	雅 yǎ	蛙 wā	腔 qiāng	溅 jiàn
鹿 lù	颈 jǐng	葫 hú	雁 yàn	喂 wèi	禽 qín	就 jiù
率 lǜ, shuài	隆 lóng	惠 huì	壹 yī	晰 xī	然 rán	慨 kǎi
麻 má	颇 pō	惑 huò	椅 yǐ	啸 xiào	锐 ruì	渴 kě
谜 mí	骑 qí	颊 jiá	硬 yìng	喧 xuān	筛 shāi	裤 kù
密 mì	随 suí	椒 jiāo	援 yuán	遗 yí	稍 shāo	愧 kuì
谋 móu	屠 tú	搅 jiǎo	越 yuè	喻 yù	甥 shēng	阔 kuò
烹 pēng	隐 yǐn	揭 jiē	暂 zàn	遇 yù	剩 shèng	愣 lèng
清 qīng		敬 jìng	葬 zàng	凿 záo	释 shì	蛮 mán
情 qíng	绷 bēng	揪 jiū	朝 zhāo	装 zhuāng	舒 shū	渺 miǎo
渠 qú	毙 bì	堪 kān	植 zhí	紫 zǐ	税 shuì	普 pǔ
商 shāng	绸 chóu	棵 kē	殖 zhí	最 zuì	锁 suǒ	谦 qiān
深 shēn	婚 hūn	款 kuǎn	煮 zhǔ		毯 tǎn	裙 qún
渗 shèn	绩 jì	葵 kuí	棕 zōng	傲 ào	艇 tǐng	善 shàn
兽 shòu	绿 lù	落 là, luò	揍 zòu	奥 ào	筒 tǒng	湿 shī
宿 sù	绵 mián	揽 lǎn	琢 zuó	掰 bāi	稀 xī	惕 tì
淘 táo	婶 shěn	棱 léng		傍 bàng	销 xiāo	童 tóng
添 tiān	绳 shéng	联 lián	悲 bēi	惫 bèi	锌 xīn	痛 tòng
惋 wǎn	维 wéi	裂 liè	辈 bèi	策 cè	锈 xiù	湾 wān
望 wàng	续 xù	硫 liú	敞 chǎng	馋 chán	循 xún	温 wēn
谓 wèi	绪 xù	搂 lǒu	喘 chuǎn	程 chéng	粤 yuè	窝 wō
惜 xī	缀 zhuì	棉 mián	跌 diē	惩 chéng	智 zhì	羡 xiàn
淆 xiáo	综 zōng	棚 péng	赌 dǔ	锄 chú	筑 zhù	翔 xiáng
谐 xié		葡 pú	幅 fú	储 chǔ	铸 zhù	谢 xiè
旋 xuán	**12 strokes**	期 qī	喊 hǎn	答 dā, dá	谤 bàng	焰 yàn
淹 yān		欺 qī	喝 hē	氮 dàn	遍 biàn	谣 yáo
痒 yǎng	斑 bān	棋 qí	黑 hēi	等 děng		游 yóu

愉 yú	鼓 gǔ	督 dū	键 jiàn	塞 sāi	嘉 jiā	ノ
寓 yù	瑰 guī	跺 duò	解 jiě	慎 shèn	碱 jiǎn	膀 bǎng
裕 yù	瑚 hú	蛾 é	锦 jǐn	数 shǔ, shù	截 jié	鼻 bí
渣 zhā	槐 huái	蜂 fēng	锯 jù	塑 sù	境 jìng	膊 bó
掌 zhǎng	魂 hún	跪 guì	筷 kuài	滩 tān	静 jìng	镀 dù
筝 zhēng	辑 jí	鉴 jiàn	锣 luó	痰 tán	聚 jù	锻 duàn
滞 zhì	禁 jìn	酱 jiàng	镁 měi	滔 tāo	酷 kù	管 guǎn
滋 zī	赖 lài	睛 jīng	签 qiān	溪 xī	璃 lí	僚 liáo
尊 zūn	蓝 lán	窟 kū	腮 sāi	新 xīn	榴 liú	箩 luó
	雷 léi	跨 kuà	傻 shǎ	意 yì	蔓 màn	馒 mán
隘 ài	零 líng	龄 líng	鼠 shǔ	愈 yù	髦 máo	貌 mào
登 dēng	楼 lóu	路 lù	腾 téng	誉 yù	酶 méi	膜 mó
隔 gé	碌 lù	盟 méng	腿 tuǐ	源 yuán	蔑 miè	魄 pò
屡 lǚ	蒙 méng	嗯 ng	微 wéi	韵 yùn	模 mó, mú	锹 qiāo
骗 piàn	摸 mǒ	暖 nuǎn	像 xiàng		慕 mù	算 suàn
强 qiáng	幕 mù	频 pín	腥 xīng	殿 diàn	暮 mù	稳 wěn
骚 sāo	墓 mù	遣 qiǎn	腰 yāo	叠 dié	酿 niàng	舞 wǔ
疏 shū	碰 pèng	嗓 sǎng	遥 yáo	辟 pì	撇 piē	鲜 xiān
属 shǔ	聘 pìn	署 shǔ	猿 yuán	群 qún	墙 qiáng	熏 xūn
隙 xì	勤 qín	睡 shuì	稚 zhì	障 zhàng	榷 què	舆 yú
粥 zhōu	鹊 què	跳 tiào			誓 shì	
	瑞 ruì	嗡 wēng		缠 chán	摔 shuāi	察 chá
编 biān	厦 shà	歇 xiē	痹 bì	缝 féng,	酸 suān	粹 cuì
缎 duàn	摄 shè	嗅 xiù	滨 bīn	fèng	碳 tàn	滴 dī
缓 huǎn	输 shū	愚 yú	痴 chī	缚 fù	辖 xiá	端 duān
媒 méi	肆 sì	照 zhào	慈 cí	嫉 jí	墟 xū	腐 fǔ
渺 miǎo	蒜 suàn	罩 zhào	福 fú	嫁 jià	需 xū	膏 gāo
嫂 sǎo	碎 suì	置 zhì	滚 gǔn	舅 jiù	愿 yuàn	寡 guǎ
絮 xù	塌 tā	罪 zuì	煌 huáng	媳 xí	遭 zāo	豪 háo
缘 yuán	摊 tān		煎 jiān	嫌 xián	榨 zhà	竭 jié
	塘 táng	ノ	窖 jiào	颖 yǐng	摘 zhāi	精 jīng
13 strokes	填 tián	矮 ǎi	谨 jǐn		蔗 zhè	慷 kāng
	碗 wǎn	堡 bǎo	窟 kū	**14 strokes**		辣 là
碍 ài	雾 wù	愁 chóu	滥 làn		弊 bì	漏 lòu
摆 bǎi	献 xiàn	稠 chóu	廉 lián	蔼 ǎi	雌 cí	慢 màn
搬 bān	想 xiǎng	筹 chóu	粮 liáng	熬 áo	裳 cháng	漫 màn
雹 báo	携 xié	触 chù	溜 liū	榜 bǎng	颗 kē	蜜 mì
碑 bēi	蓄 xù	锤 chuí	滤 lù	碧 bì	蜡 là	漂 piào
搏 bó	靴 xuē	辞 cí	满 mǎn	蔽 bì	嘛 ma	谱 pǔ
酬 chóu	摇 yáo	催 cuī	煤 méi	磁 cí	睦 mù	漆 qī
楚 chǔ	蒸 zhēng	错 cuò	谬 miù	摧 cuī	蜻 qīng	旗 qí
辅 fú	丨	躲 duǒ	漠 mò	磋 cuō	嗽 sòu	歉 qiàn
概 gài	暗 àn	腹 fù	寞 mò	碟 dié	蝇 yíng	敲 qiāo
感 gǎn	鄙 bǐ	锅 guō	熔 róng	歌 gē	蜘 zhī	熔 róng
搞 gǎo	睬 cǎi	毁 huǐ	溶 róng	赫 hè	赚 zhuàn	赛 sài

裳 shàng
瘦 shòu
瘟 wēn
熄 xī
演 yǎn
寨 zhài
彰 zhāng
遮 zhē

翠 cuì
凳 dèng
骡 luó
隧 suì

嫩 nèn
缩 suǒ
熊 xióng
疑 yí

15 strokes

磅 bàng
播 bō
槽 cáo
撤 chè
撑 chēng
聪 cōng
醋 cù
敷 fū
横 héng
慧 huì
蕉 jiāo
磕 kē

霉 méi
撵 niǎn
飘 piāo
趣 qù
撒 sā
蔬 shū
撕 sī
趟 tàng
豌 wān
橡 xiàng
鞋 xié
薪 xīn
樱 yīng
蕴 yùn
增 zēng
震 zhèn
撞 zhuàng
醉 zuì

暴 bào
憋 biē
踩 cǎi
嘲 cháo
蝶 dié
嘿 hēi
蝴 hú
蝗 huáng
瞒 mán
墨 mò
噢 ō
器 qì
遣 qiǎn
踏 tā, tà

踢 tī
题 tí
瞎 xiā
影 yǐng
嘱 zhǔ
幢 zhuàng
踪 zōng

稻 dào
德 dé
稿 gǎo
稼 jià
箭 jiàn
靠 kào
黎 lí
僻 pì
篇 piān
艘 sōu
膛 táng
躺 tǎng
膝 xī
箱 xiāng
镇 zhèn

澳 ào
潮 cháo
澄 chéng
懂 dǒng
额 é
糊 hú
潦 liáo
瘤 liú
摩 mó

潜 qián
熟 shú
瘫 tān
潭 tán
颜 yán
毅 yì
遵 zūn

履 lǚ
劈 pī
慰 wèi
豫 yù

16 strokes

薄 báo, bó
操 cāo
颠 diān
霍 huò
橘 jú
蕾 lěi
融 róng
擅 shàn
薯 shǔ
醒 xǐng
燕 yàn
整 zhěng

餐 cān
默 mò
瞥 piē
蹄 tí
噪 zào

赠 zèng
嘴 zuǐ

雕 diāo
衡 héng
僵 jiāng
鲸 jīng
镜 jìng
篮 lán
篱 lí
穆 mù
膨 péng
邀 yāo
赞 zàn

辨 biàn
辩 biàn
糕 gāo
憾 hàn
激 jī
懒 lǎn
窿 lóng
磨 mó
凝 níng
瘸 qué
糖 táng
澡 zǎo

壁 bì
避 bì

缴 jiǎo

17-23 strokes

霸 bà
鞭 biān
擦 cā
蠢 chǔn
戴 dài
覆 fù
警 jǐng
鞠 jū
磷 lín
露 lù
檬 méng
磨 mó
攀 pān
壤 rǎng
霜 shuāng
藤 téng
霞 xiá
攒 zǎn

蹦 bèng
蹈 dǎo
瞪 dèng
蹲 dūn
嚼 jiáo
螺 luó
瞧 qiáo
嚷 rǎng
蹋 tà
耀 yào
躁 zào
瞻 zhān

簸 bǒ
翻 fān
繁 fán
罐 guàn
徽 huī
籍 jī
镰 lián
穗 suì
镶 xiān
镯 zhuó

癌 ái
瓣 bàn
爆 bào
辫 biàn
颤 chàn
灌 guàn
糠 kāng
魔 mó
囊 náng
瀑 pù
燃 rán
鹰 yīng
赢 yíng
糟 zāo
燥 zào

臂 bì
疆 jiāng
譬 pì
翼 yì
骤 zhòu

A

阿 **ā** *prefix* (used to address certain relatives or friends to convey sentiment of intimacy)
　阿爸 **ā bà** daddy
　阿婆 **ā pó** (maternal) granny

阿拉伯文 **Ālābówén** *n* the Arabic language (especially the writing) □ 阿拉伯文是从右向左写。 **Ālābówén shì cóng yòu xiàng zuǒ xiě.** *Arabic is written from right to left.*

阿拉伯语 **Ālābóyǔ** *n* the Arabic language □ 阿拉伯语是一种古老而优美的语言。 **Ālābóyǔ shì yì zhǒng gǔlǎo ér yōuměi de yǔyán.** *Arabic is an ancient and beautiful language.*

阿姨 **āyí** *n* mother's sister □ 我妈妈有一个姐姐, 一个妹妹, 所以我有两个阿姨。 **Wǒ māma yǒu yí ge jiějie, yí ge mèimei, suǒyǐ wǒ yǒu liǎng ge āyí.** *My mother has an elder sister and a younger sister, so I have two aunts.*

NOTES: (1) 阿姨 **āyí** is a form of address used by a child for a woman about his/her mother's age. It is also common to put a family name before 阿姨 **āyí**, e.g. 张阿姨 **Zhāng āyí**. (2) 阿姨 **āyí** is also used by adults and children for domestic helpers and female nursery staff.

啊 **ā** **I** *interj* (used to express strong emotions such as surprise, admiration, regret etc.) oh, ah □ 啊, 海风多么凉爽! **Ā, hǎifēng duōme liángshuǎng!** *How refreshing the sea breeze is!* **II** *particle* (attached to a sentence to express strong emotions such as surprise, admiration, regret etc.) □ 海风真凉爽啊! **Hǎifēng zhēn liángshuǎng a!** *How refreshing the sea breeze is!* □ 北京的冬天真冷啊! **Běijīng de dōngtiān zhēn lěng a!** *How cold the winter in Beijing is!*

哎 **āi** *interj* (used to attract attention or express surprise) □ 哎, 你还在玩电子游戏? **Āi, nǐ hái zài wán diànzǐ yóuxì?** *Oh, you're still playing computer games?*

哎呀 **āiyā** *interj* (used to express surprise or annoyance) □ 哎呀, 我说了半天, 你怎么还不明白? **Āiyā, wǒ shuōle bàntiān, nǐ zěnme hái bù míngbai?** *Goodness, I've been explaining for ages, how come you still don't see the point?*

哎哟 **āiyō** *interj* (used to express surprise or pain)

唉 **āi** *interj* **1** (as a sigh) alas □ 唉, 孩子又病了。 **Āi, háizi yòu bìng le.** *Alas, the child is sick again.* **2** (as a response) yes, right □ 唉, 我来了! **Āi, wǒ lái le!** *Yes, I'm coming!*

哀 **āi** **I** *v* mourn **II** *adj* grieved
　哀悼 **āidào** *v* mourn
　哀求 **āiqiú** *v* entreat, implore

挨 **ái** *v* undergo (some painful or unpleasant experience) □ 那个小偷挨了一顿打。 **Nàge xiǎotōu ái le yí dùn dǎ.** *That thief was beaten up.*

癌 **ái** *n* cancer □ 他爸爸得了癌, 正在进行治疗。 **Tā bàba déle ái, zhèngzài jìnxíng zhìliáo.** *His father has got cancer and is undergoing therapy.*
　肺癌 **fèi'ái** lung cancer
　胃癌 **wèi'ái** stomach cancer

蔼 **ǎi** Trad 藹 *adj* amiable, friendly (See 和蔼 **hé'ǎi**)

矮 **ǎi** *adj* (of a person or plant) of short stature, short (antonym 高 **gāo**) □ 他虽然长得矮, 但是篮球打得挺好。 **Tā suīrán zhǎng de ǎi, dànshì lánqiú dǎ de tǐng hǎo.** *Although he's short, he's a good basketball player.* □ 妹妹比我矮一点儿。 **Mèimei bǐ wǒ ǎi yìdiǎnr.** *My younger sister is a bit shorter than me.*

爱 **ài** Trad 愛 *v* **1** love □ 我爱爸爸妈妈, 爸爸妈妈也爱我。 **Wǒ ài bàba māma, bàba māma yě ài wǒ.** *I love my mom and dad, and they love me too.* **2** like, be fond of □ 她爱表现自己。 **Tā ài biǎoxiàn zìjǐ.** *She likes to show off.*

爱戴 **àidài** *v* love and esteem

爱好 **àihào** [comp: 爱 love + 好 like, be fond of] **I** *v* like, be interested in, have as a hobby □ 我爱好旅行, 爱好了解世界各地人民的风俗习惯。 **Wǒ àihào lǚxíng, àihào liáojiě shìjiè gèdì rénmín de fēngsú xíguàn.** *I like traveling; I like getting to know the social customs and practices of peoples everywhere.* **II** *n* hobby, interest □ "你有什么爱好?" "我的爱好比较广泛, 不过我最大的爱好是玩电子游戏。" **"Nǐ yǒu shénme àihào?" "Wǒde àihào bǐjiào guǎngfàn, búguò wǒ zuìdà de àihào shì wán diànzǐ yóuxì."** *"What's your hobby?" "I have many hobbies, but my favorite is playing computer games."*

爱护 **àihù** [comp: 爱 love + 护 protect] *v* care for and protect, cherish □ 父母都爱护自己的孩子。 **Fùmǔ dōu àihù zìjǐ de háizi.** *All parents care for and protect their children.* □ 我们应该爱护我们之间的友谊。 **Wǒmen yīnggāi àihù wǒmen zhī jiān de yǒuyì.** *We should cherish our friendship.*

爱面子 **ài miànzi** *v* be overly concerned about one's image

爱情 **àiqíng** [comp: 爱 love + 情 feeling, affection] *n* romantic love □ 年轻人都希望获得爱情。 **Niánqīngrén dōu xīwàng huòdé àiqíng.** *Young people all yearn for love.* □ 婚姻一定要建立在爱情的基础上。 **Hūnyīn yídìng yào jiànlì zài àiqíng de jīchǔ shang.** *Marriage must be based on love.*
　爱情小说 **àiqíng xiǎoshuō** love story, romance fiction

爱人 **àirén** [modif: 爱 love + 人 person] *n* husband or wife □ 我和爱人结婚十年了。 **Wǒ hé àirén jiéhūn shí nián le.** *My husband (or wife) and I have been married for ten years.*

NOTE: 爱人 **àirén** as *husband* or *wife* is only used in Mainland China as a colloquialism. On formal occasions 丈夫 **zhàngfu** (husband) and 妻子 **qīzi** (wife) are used instead. Now there is a decreasing tendency to use 爱人 **àirén** in China. In its place 先生 **xiānsheng** and 太太 **tàitai** are used to refer to *husband* and *wife*, a long established practice in Taiwan, Hong Kong and overseas Chinese communities. For example: □ 你先生近来忙吗? **Nǐ xiānsheng jìnlái máng ma?** *Is your husband busy these days?* □ 我太太要我下班回家的路上买些菜。 **Wǒ tàitai yào wǒ xiàbān huíjiā de lù shang mǎi xiē cài.** *My wife wants me to buy some vegetables on my way home after work.*

爱惜 **àixī** *v* cherish, value highly
　爱惜自己的名誉 **àixī zìjǐ de míngyù** treasure one's reputation

碍 **ài** Trad 礙 *v* hinder
　碍事 **àishì** *v* be in one's way

艾 **ài** *n* mugwort
艾滋病 **àizībìng** *n* AIDS

NOTE: 艾滋病 is a transliteration, i.e. reproducing the sounds of the English word AIDS.

隘 **ài** *adj* narrow (See 狭隘 **xiá'ài**)

安 **ān** *adj* peaceful, safe
安定 **āndìng** [comp: 安 peace + 定 settled, stable] *adj* peaceful and stable □ 这个社会表面上安定，其实矛盾很多。**Zhège shèhuì biǎomiànshàng āndìng, qíshí máodùn hěn duō.** *This society seems to be stable on the surface; actually there are many contradictions within.*
安静 **ānjìng** [comp: 安 peace + 静 quiet] *adj* quiet, peaceful, serene □ 这里很少有车开过，环境很安静。**Zhèli hěn shǎo yǒu chē kāiguò, huánjìng hěn ānjìng.** *There is very little traffic here. The environment is very peaceful.* □ 请大家安静! **Qǐng dàjiā ānjìng!** *Please be quiet, everyone!* □ 这位老人只想过安静的生活。**Zhè wèi lǎorén zhǐ xiǎng guò ānjìng de shēnghuó.** *This old man only wants to live a quiet life.*
安乐死 **ānlèsǐ** [modif: 安乐 peaceful and happy + 死 death] *n* euthanasia
安宁 **ānníng** *adj* calm, composed
安排 **ānpái** [comp: 安 to settle, to arrange + 排 to arrange, to put in order] *v* arrange, make arrangements, plan □ 大学生一般都很忙，因此必须安排好时间。**Dàxuéshēng yìbān dōu hěn máng, yīncǐ bìxū ānpái hǎo shíjiān.** *University students are generally busy people, so they must plan their time well.* □ 董事长下个月去中国旅行，请你安排一下。**Dǒngshìzhǎng xià ge yuè qù Zhōngguó lǚxíng, qǐng nǐ ānpái yíxià.** *The chairman of the board is going to China for a trip next month. Please make the arrangements.*
安全 **ānquán** [comp: 安 peace + 全 complete, all-around] **I** *n* security, safety □ 开车安全第一。**Kāichē ānquán dì yī.** *When you are driving, safety is the most important thing.*
　安全带 **ānquándài** safety belt
　安全帽 **ānquánmào** safety helmet
II *adj* safe, secure □ 在这里夜里一个人在街上走，安全吗? **Zài zhèli yèlǐ yí ge rén zài jiē shang zǒu, ānquán ma?** *Is it safe to walk alone in the streets here at night?*
安慰 **ānwèi** [comp: 安 make peace + 慰 comfort] *v* comfort, console □ 他们失去了心爱的女儿，心情悲痛，朋友们都来安慰他们。**Tāmen shīqùle xīn'ài de nǚ'ér, xīnqíng bēitòng, péngyoumen dōu lái ānwèi tāmen.** *They are in deep sorrow as they have lost their beloved daughter. Their friends have all come to comfort them.*
安稳 **ānwěn** [comp: 安 peace + 稳 steady, secure] *adj* safe and secure
安详 **ānxiáng** [comp: 安 peace + 详 calm] *adj* (of facial expression) serene, composed
安心 **ānxīn** [v+obj: 安 make peace + 心 the heart] *adj* be relaxed and content □ 她不安心在小学教书，她想当电影演员。**Tā bù ānxīn zài xiǎoxué jiāoshū, tā xiǎng dāng diànyǐng yǎnyuán.** *She is not content to be a primary school teacher; she wants to be a movie star.*

安置 **ānzhì** [modif: 安 safely + 置 to place] *v* find an appropriate place (for people)
安装 **ānzhuāng** [modif: 安 safely + 装 to install] *v* install, fix
　安装空调设备 **ānzhuāng kōngtiáo shèbèi** install an air-conditioner

岸 **àn** *n* bank or shore (of a river, lake, or sea) □ 河的两岸是一个个小村子。**Hé de liǎng àn shì yí gège xiǎo cūnzi.** *The river is flanked by small villages.*
　海岸 **hǎi àn** coast
　河岸 **hé'àn** river bank
　上岸 **shàng àn** go ashore

按 **àn** *prep* according to, in accordance with □ 按计划，这座工厂将在明年四月建成。**Àn jìhuà, zhè zuò gōngchǎng jiāng zài míngnián Sìyuè jiànchéng.** *According to our plan, the factory will be built by April next year.* □ 我一定按你说的做。**Wǒ yídìng àn nǐ shuō de zuò.** *I will definitely do as you say.*
按揭 **ànjiē** *n* mortgage
按期 **ànqī** [v+obj: 按 according to + 期 scheduled time] *adv* according to schedule
按时 **ànshí** [v+obj: 按 according to + 时 time] *adv* according to a fixed time, on time □ 学生要按时完成作业。**Xuéshēng yào ànshí wánchéng zuòyè.** *Students must finish their assignments on time.* □ 你得按时吃药，病才会好。**Nǐ děi ànshí chī yào, bìng cái huì hǎo.** *You've got to take the medicine at the specified times, or you won't get well.*
按照 **ànzhào** *prep* according to, in accordance with (same as 按 **àn**)

案 **àn** *n* case, plan
案件 **ànjiàn** *n* case, legal case
　民事案件 **mínshì ànjiàn** civil case
　刑事案件 **xíngshì ànjiàn** criminal case
　调查案件 **diàochá ànjiàn** investigate a (police) case

暗 **àn** *adj* **1** dark, dim □ 房间里太暗了，你要看书得开灯。**Fángjiān li tài àn le, nǐ yào kàn shū děi kāi dēng.** *The room is dim. Turn on the light if you want to read.*
暗暗 **àn'àn** *adv* secretly
　暗暗得意 **àn'àn déyì** secretly very pleased with oneself
暗淡 **àndàn** [comp: 暗 dark + 淡 of light color] *adj* dim, gloomy
　光线暗淡的房间 **guāngxiàn àndàn de fángjiān** a dimly-lit room
暗杀 **ànshā** [modif: 暗 secretly + 杀 kill] *v* assassinate
暗示 **ànshì** [modif: 暗 secretly + 示 show, indicate] **I** *v* drop a hint **II** *n* hint
暗室 **ànshì** [modif: 暗 dark + 室 room] *n* darkroom (for developing films)
暗中 **ànzhōng** *adv* in the dark, in secret
　暗中帮忙 **ànzhōng bāngmáng** secretly help

昂 **áng** *v* hold (the head) high
昂起头 **ángqǐ tóu** hold the head high
昂贵 **ángguì** [comp: 昂 holding high + 贵 expensive] *adj* very expensive, costly □ 物价昂贵。**Wùjià ángguì.** *The prices are exhorbitant.*
昂扬 **ángyáng** *adj* in high spirits

凹 **āo** *adj* concave, sunken, dented (antonym 凸 **tū**)
　凹凸不平 **āotū bùpíng** rugged, full of bumps and holes

熬 **áo** *v* stew, boil
熬汤 áo tāng prepare soup by simmering

袄 **ǎo** Trad 襖 *n* a Chinese-style coat or jacket
棉袄 mián'ǎo padded coat

傲 **ào** *adj* arrogant (See 骄傲 **jiāo'ào**)

奥 **ào** *adj* deep, profound
奥秘 àomì [comp: 奥 deep + 秘 secret] *n* deep secret, profound mystery
探索奥秘 tànsuǒ àomì explore a mystery

澳 **ào** *n* deep waters
澳大利亚 Àodàlìyà *n* Australia

B

八 **bā** *num* eight □ 八八六十四。**Bā bā liùshísì.** *Eight times eight is sixty-four.*

捌 **bā** *num* Same as 八 **bā**

扒 **bā** *v* 1 strip off, take off (clothes, etc.) 2 hold on to, cling to

叭 **bā** *onomatopeia* crack

巴 **bā** *n* cheek
巴结 bājie *v* flatter, fawn on

芭 **bā** *n* flower
芭蕾舞 bāléiwǔ *n* ballet

笆 **bā** *n* bamboo fence (See 篱笆 **líbā**)

疤 **bā** *n* scar (See 伤疤 **shāngbā**)

吧 **bā** *n* bar
酒吧 jiǔbā wine bar, bar, pub
网吧 wǎngbā Internet café

拔 **bá** *v* pull out, pull up
拔苗助长 bá miáo zhù zhǎng pull up a young plant to help it grow (→ spoil things by excessive enthusiasm)

把 1 **bǎ** *prep* (used before a noun or pronoun to indicate it is the object of the sentence) □ 哥哥把自行车修好了。**Gēge bǎ zìxíngchē xiūhǎo le.** *My elder brother has fixed the bike.* □ 请你把这封信交给李先生。**Qǐng nǐ bǎ zhè fēng xìn jiāogěi Lǐ xiānsheng.** *Please deliver this letter to Mr Li.* □ 我可以把车停在这里吗? **Wǒ kěyǐ bǎ chē tíng zài zhèli ma?** *May I park my car here?*

把 2 **bǎ** I *n* handle II *measure wd* 1 (for objects with handles) 2 a handful of
一把刀 yì bǎ dāo a knife
一把米 yì bǎ mǐ a handful of rice
把柄 bǎbǐng [comp: 把 handle + 柄 handle] *n* 1 handle 2 something that may be used against someone
抓住了他的把柄 zhuāzhùle tāde bǎbǐng have got evidence that may be used against him
把关 bǎguān *v* check on
把手 bǎshǒu *n* handle, handrail
把握 bǎwò I *n* being certain and assured, confidence □ 你有成功的把握吗? **Nǐ yǒu chēnggōng de bǎwò ma?**

Are you sure of success? II *v* seize (an opportunity)
把握时机 bǎwò shíjī seize an opportunity
把戏 bǎxì *n* trick
玩把戏 wán bǎxi play a trick

爸 **bà** *n* dad, daddy, papa
爸爸 bàba *n* daddy, papa □ 我爸爸工作很努力。**Wǒ bàba gōngzuò hěn nǔlì.** *My father works hard.* □ 爸爸, 这个星期五晚上我想用一下你的车, 行不行? **Bàba, zhège Xīngqīwǔ wǎnshang wǒ xiǎng yòng yíxià nǐ de chē, xíng bu xíng?** *Daddy, I'd like to use your car this Friday evening. Is it all right?*

坝 **bà** Trad 壩 *n* dam, embankment
大坝 dàbà big dam

霸 **bà** I *n* tyrant II *v* dominate, rule by might
恶霸 èbà local tyrant
霸道 bàdào [modif: 霸 tyrant + 道 way] *adj* overbearing, high-handed
霸权 bàquán [modif: 霸 tyrant + 权 power] *n* hegemony
霸权主义 bàquán zhǔyì hegemonism
霸占 bàzhàn [modif: 霸 tyrant + 占 occupy, possess] *v* occupy or possess by force
霸占民房 bàzhàn mínfáng seize possession of private property by force

罢 **bà** Trad 罷 *v* stop
罢工 bàgōng [v+obj: 罢 stop + 工 work] *v* stage a strike, down tools

吧 **ba** *particle* 1 (used to make a suggestion) □ 我们一块儿去吃中饭吧。**Wǒmen yíkuàir qù chī zhōng-fàn ba.** *Let's go and have lunch together.* □ 今天太冷了, 别去游泳吧! **Jīntiān tài lěng le, bié qù yóuyǒng ba!** *It's too cold today. Don't go swimming, OK?* 2 (used to indicate supposition) □ 你是新加坡来的张先生吧? **Nǐ shì Xīnjiāpō lái de Zhāng xiānsheng ba?** *Aren't you Mr Zhang from Singapore?* □ 你对这个地方很熟悉吧? **Nǐ duì zhège dìfang hěn shúxi ba?** *You're familiar with this place, aren't you?*

掰 **bāi** *v* break off with hands

白 **bái** I *adj* white □ 下雪以后, 路上一片白。**Xiàxuě yǐhòu, lù shang yí piàn bái.** *The road was all white after the snowfall.* □ 她穿白衣服特别好看。**Tā chuān bái yīfu tèbié hǎokàn.** *She looks especially beautiful in white.* II *adv* in vain, without any result □ 他根本不思改进, 你说了也白说。**Tā gēnběn bù sī gǎijìn, shuōle yě bái shuō.** *He does not want to improve his work at all. You said all that in vain.* □ 我忘了在电脑里保存文件, 一个晚上的工作白做了。**Wǒ wàngle zài diànnǎo li bǎocún wénjiàn, yí ge wǎnshang de gōngzuò dōu bái zuò le.** *I forgot to save my document in the computer. An evening's work all came to nothing.* III *adv* for free □ 世界上没有白吃的午餐。**Shìjiè shang méiyǒu bái chī de wǔcān.** *There is no free lunch in the world.* (→ *There's no such thing as a free lunch.*)

NOTE: In Chinese tradition, white symbolizes death and is the color for funerals.

白白 báibái [comp: 白 in vain + 白 in vain] *adv* in vain, for nothing
白菜 báicài [modif: 白 white + 菜 vegetable] *n* cabbage (棵 kē) □ 在中国北方, 白菜是冬天最便宜、最普通

的蔬菜。 **Zài Zhōngguó běifāng, báicài shì dōngtiān zuì piányi, zuì pǔtōng de shūcài.** *In North China, cabbage is the cheapest, most ordinary vegetable in winter.*

白酒 **báijiǔ** [modif: 白 white + 酒 alcoholic drink] *n* spirits usually distilled from sorghum or rice, white spirits

白开水 **báikāishuǐ** *n* plain boiled water □ 感冒了要喝白开水。 **Gǎnmào le yào hē báikāishuǐ.** *You should drink a lot of boiled water when you've got a cold.*

白领 **báilǐng** [modif: 白 white + 领 collar] *n* white-collar worker

白人 **báirén** [modif: 白 white + 人 person, people] *n* Caucasian person, Caucasian people

白天 **báitiān** [modif: 白 white + 天 day] *n* daytime □ 春天来了，白天越来越长了。 **Chūntiān lái le, báitiān yuèláiyuè cháng le.** *Spring has come. Days become longer and longer.* □ 他家白天一般没有人，你还是晚上去吧。 **Tā jiā báitiān yìbān méiyǒu rén, nǐ háishì wǎnshang qù ba.** *There is usually no one at his home during the day. You should go there in the evening.*

百 **bǎi** *num* hundred
三百元 **sānbǎi yuán** three hundred yuan/dollars

NOTE: 百 **bǎi** may have the abstract sense of *a great deal of* and *a multitude of*. This sense can be found in many expressions, e.g. 百闻不如一见 **Bǎi wén bùrú yí jiàn**, which literally means *A hundred sounds are not as good as one sight* and may be translated as *Seeing is believing*. Another example is 百忙 **bǎi máng**, meaning *very busy*. For example: □ 你百忙中还来看我，太好了。 **Nǐ bǎi máng zhōng hái lái kàn wǒ, tài hǎo le.** *It's very kind of you to come to see me when you're so busy.*

百货 **bǎihuò** [modif: 百 hundred + 货 goods] *n* general merchandise
百货商店 **bǎihuò shāngdiàn** department store

百日咳 **bǎirìké** [modif: 百 hundred + 日 day + 咳 cough] *n* whooping cough

百姓 **bǎixìng** [modif: 百 hundred + 姓 family name] *n* common people

NOTE: 老百姓 **lǎobǎixìng** is also used to mean "common people".

柏 **bǎi** *n* cypress
柏树 **bǎishù** cypress tree, cypress

摆 **bǎi** Trad 擺 *v* put, place, arrange □ 桌子上摆着一只大花瓶。 **Zhuōzi shang bǎizhe yì zhī dà huāpíng.** *On the table is placed a big vase.* □ 吃饭了，你把碗筷摆好吧！ **Chīfàn le, nǐ bǎ wǎnkuài bǎihǎo ba!** *It's mealtime, will you please set the table?*

摆动 **bǎidòng** *v* sway, swing
摆脱 **bǎituō** *v* break away from, shake off

败 **bài** Trad 敗 *v* be defeated (antonym 胜 **shèng**) □ 我们球队又败了，得研究一下原因。 **Wǒmen qiúduì yòu bài le, děi yánjiū yíxià yuányīn.** *Our (ball) team was defeated again. We've got to look into the reason.*

败坏 **bàihuài** *v* ruin, corrupt
道德败坏 **dàodé bàihuài** rotten morals

拜 **bài** *v* do obeisance, pay respect to
拜访 **bàifǎng** [comp: 拜 pay respect + 访 visit]

v pay a visit (to a senior person), make a courtesy call

拜会 **bàihuì** [comp: 拜 pay respect + 会 meet] *v* make an official call

拜年 **bài nián** *v* pay a New Year's call, wish someone a Happy New Year

班 **bān** *n* **1** class (in school) □ 我们班有十二个男生，十四个女生。 **Wǒmen bān yǒu shí'èr ge nánshēng, shísì ge nǔshēng.** *Our class has twelve male students and fourteen female students.* **2** shift (in a workplace)
加班 **jiābān** work overtime
上班 **shàngbān** go to work
下班 **xiàbān** finish work
□ 这位护士上个星期上白天班，这个星期上夜班。 **Zhè wèi hùshi shàng ge xīngqī shàng báitiān bān, zhègè xīngqī shàng yèbān.** *This nurse was on day shift last week, and is on night shift this week.* □ 我妈妈每天九点上班，五点下班。 **Wǒ māma měi tiān jiǔ diǎn shàngbān, wǔ diǎn xiàbān.** *My mother goes to work at nine o'clock and finishes work at five o'clock.*

班机 **bānjī** [modif: 班 shift + 机 airplane] *n* airliner, flight □ 我乘560班机去新加坡。 **Wǒ chéng wǔ-liù-líng bānjī qù Xīnjiāpō.** *I'll go to Singapore by flight 560.*

班长 **bānzhǎng** [modif: 班 class, squad + 长 leader] *n* leader (of a class in school, a squad in the army, etc.) □ 你打算选谁当班长？ **Nǐ dǎsuàn xuǎn shéi dāng bānzhǎng?** *Whom are you going to elect as class monitor?*

斑 **bān** *n* spot, speck
斑点 **bāndiǎn** spot, stain

斑马 **bānmǎ** [modif: 斑 spot + 马 horse] *n* zebra

般 **bān** *n* kind, sort (See 一般 **yìbān**)

搬 **bān** *v* move (heavy objects) □ 我们把这张桌子搬到房间外面去吧。 **Wǒmen bǎ zhè zhāng zhuōzi bān dào fángjiān wàimiàn qù ba.** *Let's move this table out of the room.*
搬不动 **bān bu dòng** cannot move/cannot be moved
搬得动 **bān de dòng** can move/can be moved

搬家 **bānjiā** [comp: 搬 move + 家 home] *v* move (house) □ 我们这个周末搬家，有几位朋友来帮忙。 **Wǒmen zhège zhōumò bānjiā, yǒu jǐ wèi péngyou lái bāngmáng.** *We're moving house this weekend. Some friends will come to help.*

搬运 **bānyùn** [comp: 搬 move + 运 transport] *v* transport, move
搬运工人 **bānyùn gōngrén** mover

颁 **bān** *v* issue, confer on
颁布 **bānbù** [comp: 颁 issue + 布 promulgate] *v* promulgate, proclaim

颁发 **bānfā** [comp: 颁 issue + 发 issue] *v* issue, distribute
颁发奖状 **bānfā jiǎngzhuàng** issue a certificate of merit

扳 **bān** *v* pull, turn
扳手 **bānshǒu** *n* spanner, wrench

板 **bǎn** *n* board
木板 **mùbǎn** wooden plank

版 **bǎn** *n* printing plate
第一版 **dìyī bǎn** the first edition

办 **bàn** Trad 辦 *v* handle, manage □ 这件事不容易办。 **Zhè jiàn shì bù róngyì bàn.** *This matter is*

not easy to handle. □ 你办事我很放心。 **Nǐ bànshì wǒ hěn fàngxīn.** *I feel reassured when you're handling a matter.* (→ *I have confidence in you when you're in charge.*) □ 这件事我来办。 **Zhè jiàn shì wǒ lai bàn.** *Let me handle this matter.*

办法 bànfǎ [modif: 办 handle, manage + 法 method] *n* **1** way of doing things □ 这些老办法都不行。 **Zhèxie lǎo bànfǎ dōu bùxíng.** *All these old methods won't work.* □ 你试试我的办法。 **Nǐ shìshi wǒ de bànfǎ.** *Do try my method.* **2** method
想办法 xiǎng bànfǎ think up a plan, find a way of doing things
有办法 yǒu bànfǎ have a way with ..., be resourceful
没有办法 méiyǒu bànfǎ there's nothing we can do □ 飞机票全卖完了，我们明天不能走，没有办法。 **Fēijī piào quán màiwán le, wǒmen míngtiān bù néng zǒu, méiyǒu bànfǎ.** *All the air tickets are sold out. We won't be able to leave tomorrow. There's nothing we can do.*

办公 bàngōng [comp: 办 handle + 公 public, public office] *v* work (as a white-collar worker, usually in an office) □ 王经理在办公，你有事可以给他留个话。 **Wáng jīnglǐ zài bàngōng, nǐ yǒushì kěyǐ gěi tā liú ge huà.** *Mr Wang, the manager, is working in his office. You can leave him a message, if you've any business.*
办公时间 bàngōng shíjiān office hours, working hours
办公大楼 bàngōng dàlóu office building

办公室 bàngōngshì [comp: 办 handle + 公 public, public office + 室 room] *n* office (间 **jiān**) □ 大华公司的办公室在十四楼。 **Dàhuá gōngsī de bàngōngshì zài shísì lóu.** *The office of Dahua Company is on the fourteenth floor.* □ 请你到我办公室来一下。 **Qǐng nǐ dào wǒ bàngōngshì lái yíxià.** *Please come to my office.*

办理 bànlǐ [comp: 办 handle, manage + 理 manage, run] *v* deal with, go through □ 我正在办理到中国去的签证。 **Wǒ zhèngzài bànlǐ dào Zhōngguó qù de qiānzhèng.** *I'm in the process of obtaining a visa for China.*

办事 bànshì [v+obj: 办 handle, manage + 事 affairs, business] *v* conduct affairs, manage affairs □ 他很会办事。 **Tā hěn huì bànshì.** *He is very good at getting things done.*

办学 bànxué [comp: 办 manage + 学 education, school] *v* run a school

半 bàn *measure wd* half □ 我等她等了一个半小时。 **Wǒ děng tā děngle yí ge bàn xiǎoshí.** *I waited one and a half hours for her.*

半岛 bàndǎo [modif: 半 half + 岛 island] *n* peninsula
九龙半岛 Jiǔlóng bàndǎo Kowloon Peninsula (in Hong Kong)

半径 bànjìng [modif: 半 half + 径 diameter] *n* radius

半路 bànlù [modif: 半 half + 路 way] *n* halfway, midway

半数 bànshù [modif: 半 half + 数 number] *n* half the number, half

半天 bàntiān [modif: 半 half + 天 day] *n* **1** half a day **2** a period of time felt to be very long; a very long time □ 我等你等了半天了。 **Wǒ děng nǐ děngle bàntiān le.** *I've been waiting for you for a long time.* □ 那本书我找了半天，还没找到。 **Nà běn shū wǒ zhǎole bàntiān, hái méi zhǎodào.** *I've been looking for the book for a long time but I still haven't found it.*

半途而废 bàntú ér fèi *idiom* give up halfway

半夜 bànyè [modif: 半 half + 夜 night] *n* midnight, at midnight □ 他经常工作到半夜才睡。 **Tā jīngcháng gōngzuò dào bànyè cái shuì.** *He often works till midnight before going to bed.*

拌 bàn *v* mix

伴 bàn *n* companion
同伴 tóngbàn companion

伴侣 bànlǚ [comp: 伴 companion + 侣 companion] *n* companion (especially husband or wife)
终身伴侣 zhōngshēn bànlǚ life-long companion, husband and wife

伴随 bànsuí *v* go along with, keep company

伴奏 bànzòu *v* accompany with musical instrument

扮 bàn *v* disguise as
扮演 bànyǎn *v* play the role (of a character in a play, movie, etc.)

瓣 bàn *n* petal, segment
花瓣 huābàn petal, flower petal

帮 bāng Trad 幫 *v* help, assist □ 上个周末，很多朋友来帮他搬家。 **Shàng ge zhōumò, hěn duō péngyou lái bāng tā bānjiā.** *Last weekend, many friends came to help him move house.* □ 你能帮我找一下这本书吗？ **Nǐ néng bāng wǒ zhǎo yíxià zhè běn shū ma?** *Can you help me find this book?*

NOTES: 帮 **bāng**, 帮忙 **bāngmáng** and 帮助 **bāngzhù** are synonyms. Their differences are: (1) 帮忙 **bāngmáng** is a verb that takes no object, while 帮 **bāng** and 帮助 **bāngzhù** are usually followed by an object. (2) As verbs, 帮 **bāng** and 帮助 **bāngzhù** are interchangeable, but 帮 **bāng** is more colloquial than 帮助 **bāngzhù**. (3) 帮助 **bāngzhù** can also be used as a noun.

帮忙 bāngmáng *v* help, help out □ 上个周末，他搬家，很多朋友来帮忙。 **Shàng ge zhōumò tā bānjiā, hěn duō péngyou lái bāngmáng.** *Last weekend, he moved house. Many friends came to help out.*

NOTE: See note on 帮 **bāng**.

帮助 bāngzhù [comp: 帮 help + 助 assist] **I** *v* help, assist □ 富国应该帮助穷国。 **Fùguó yīnggāi bāngzhù qióngguó.** *Rich countries should help poor countries.* □ 李先生帮助我们解决了很多困难。 **Lǐ xiānsheng bāngzhù wǒmen jiějuéle hěn duō kùnnan.** *Mr Li helped us overcome many difficulties.* **II** *n* help, assistance □ 非常感谢你的帮助。 **Fēicháng gǎnxiè nǐ de bāngzhù.** *Thank you very much for your help.* □ 没有你的帮助，我们不可能及时完成任务。 **Méiyǒu nǐ de bāngzhù, wǒmen bù kěnéng jíshí wánchéng rènwù.** *Without your help we couldn't have accomplished the task in time.*

NOTE: See note on 帮 **bāng**.

邦 bāng *n* country

绑 bāng Trad 綁 *v* tie, bind (with a rope)
绑架 bǎngjià *v* kidnap

榜 bǎng *n* list of names, honor roll
榜样 bǎngyàng *n* (positive) example, role model

□ 我们的老师是美国人, 说一口标准中文, 真是我们的好榜样! **Wǒmen de lǎoshī shì Měiguórén, shuō yì kǒu biāozhǔn Zhōngwén, zhēn shì wǒmen de hǎo bǎngyàng!** *Our teacher is an American and speaks standard Chinese. He really is a good role model for us.*

膀 **bǎng** *n* upper arm
　翅膀 chìbǎng wing

傍 **bàng** *v* be close to
　傍晚 bàngwǎn [modif: 傍 towards, close to + 晚 evening] *n* dusk, at dusk □ 他们傍晚的时候才走出树林, 不一会天就黑了。 **Tāmen bàngwǎn de shíhòu cái zǒuchū shùlín, bú yíhuì tiān jiù hēi le.** *They came out of the woods at dusk, and soon it was dark.*

磅 **bàng** *n* (measurement for weight) pound
　两磅牛肉 liǎng bàng niúròu two pounds of beef

谤 **bàng** Trad 謗 *v* slander
　诽谤 fěibàng slander

棒 **bàng** **I** *n* stick, club (根 **gēn**)
　铁棒 tiěbàng iron bar
　II *adj* strong, very good □ 这个小伙子很棒。 **Zhège xiǎohuǒzi hěn bàng.** *This young man is very strong.* □ 他篮球打得真棒。 **Tā lánqiú dǎ de zhēn bàng.** *He really plays basketball very well.* (→ *He is a wonderful basketball player.*)

棒球 **bàngqiú** [modif: 棒 club + 球 ball] *n* baseball
　棒球场 bàngqiúchǎng baseball court
　棒球运动员 bàngqiú yùndòngyuán baseball player

包 **bāo** **I** *n* parcel, bag □ 他在路边拣到一个包, 马上交给警察。 **Tā zài lùbiān jiǎn dào yíge bāo, mǎshàng jiāo gei jǐngchá.** *He picked up a parcel by the roadside and immediately handed it over to the police.*
　钱包 qiánbāo wallet, purse
　书包 shūbāo schoolbag
　邮包 yóubāo mailbag, parcel for posting
　II *v* wrap up □ 顾客: "请你把这只花瓶好好包起来。" **Gùkè: "Qǐng nǐ bǎ zhè zhī huāpíng hǎohǎo bāo qǐlai."** *Customer: "Could you please wrap up this vase carefully?"*

包办 **bāobàn** *v* assume full responsibility for, do entirely by oneself
　包办宴席 bāobàn yànxí (of a restaurant) take care of everything for banquets

包袱 **bāofu** *n* a bundle wrapped in a cloth-wrapper

包裹 **bāoguǒ** *n* parcel, package

包含 **bāohán** [comp: 包 wrap up + 含 contain] *v* contain, have as ingredients

包括 **bāokuò** [comp: 包 embrace + 括 include] *v* include, embrace □ 旅行团包括一名翻译, 一共十五人。 **Lǚxíngtuán bāokuò yì míng fānyì, yígòng shíwǔ rén.** *There are fifteen people in the tour group, including an interpreter.*

包围 **bāowéi** [comp: 包 wrap up + 围 surround] *v* surround, encircle, lay siege

包装 **bāozhuāng** *n* package, packaging
　包装材料 bāozhuāng cáiliào packaging material

包子 **bāozi** [suffix: 包 bun + 子 nominal suffix] *n* steamed bun with filling □ 我早饭吃了两个包子。 **Wǒ zǎofàn chīle liǎng ge bāozi.** *I had two steamed buns for breakfast.*

胞 **bāo** *n* the placenta
　细胞 xìbāo cell

剥 **bāo** *v* peel, peel off

薄 **báo** *adj* thin, flimsy (antonym 厚 **hòu**) □ 天冷了, 这条被子太薄, 要换一条厚一点儿的。 **Tiān lěng le, zhè tiáo bèizi tài báo, yào huàn yì tiáo hòu yìdiǎn de.** *It's getting cold. This blanket is too thin. You need a thicker one.*

NOTE: See note on 薄 **bó**.

雹 **báo** *n* hail
　雹子 báozi hail

宝 **bǎo** Trad 寶 *n* treasure
　宝岛 bǎodǎo treasure island
　宝库 bǎokù treasure house

宝贝 **bǎobèi** [comp: 宝 treasure + 贝 shellfish] *n* treasured object, treasure
　小宝贝 xiǎo bǎobèi (endearment for children) darling, dear

宝贵 **bǎoguì** [comp: 宝 precious + 贵 valuable] *adj* valuable, precious □ 世界上什么最宝贵? **Shìjiè shang shénme zuì bǎoguì?** *What is the most valuable thing in the world?* □ 我不想浪费你们的宝贵时间, 就直话直说了。 **Wǒ bù xiǎng làngfèi nǐmen de bǎoguì shíjiān, jiù zhí huà zhí shuō le.** *I don't want to waste your precious time, and will say what I have to say without mincing words.*

宝剑 **bǎojiàn** [modif: 宝 precious + 剑 sword] *n* double-edged sword (把 **bǎ**)

宝石 **bǎoshí** [modif: 宝 precious + 石 stone] *n* precious stone

保 **bǎo** *v* conserve, protect □ 这房子用了新材料, 特别保暖。 **Zhè fángzi yòngle xīn cáiliào, tèbié bǎo nuǎn.** *This house uses a new type of material that is particularly good at keeping the house warm.*

保安 **bǎo'ān** [v+obj: 保 protect + 安 security] *n* security guard

保持 **bǎochí** [comp: 保 conserve + 持 maintain] *v* keep, maintain □ 他去年在学校运动会上得了长跑冠军, 今年能保持吗? **Tā qùnián zài xuéxiào yùndònghuì shang déle chángpǎo guànjūn, jīnnián néng bǎochí ma?** *He was the champion in long-distance running at the school sports meet last year. Can he maintain it this year?* (→ *Can he defend his position this year?*)

保存 **bǎocún** [comp: 保 conserve + 存 keep] *v* keep, save □ 这个文件很重要, 你打好以后, 千万别忘了保存。 **Zhège wénjiàn hěn zhòngyào, nǐ dǎhǎo yǐhòu, qiānwàn bié wàngle bǎocún.** *This is an important document. After you've done (← typed) it, do remember to save it.*

保管 **bǎoguǎn** [comp: 保 conserve + 管 take charge of] *v* take charge of
　保管员 bǎoguǎnyuán storekeeper

保护 **bǎohù** [comp: 保 conserve + 护 protect] *v* protect, safeguard, conserve □ 这片大森林一定要保护好, 不能开发为旅游区。 **Zhè piàn dà sēnlín yídìng yào bǎohù hǎo, bù néng kāifā wéi lǚyóuqū.** *This vast forest must be conserved and mustn't be developed into a tourist area.*

保健 **bǎojiàn** [v+compl: 保 conserve + 健 healthy] *n* health care, health protection
　保健食品 bǎojiàn shípǐn health food

妇幼保健 fùyòu bǎojiàn maternity and child care

保龄球 **bǎolíngqiú** [modif: 保龄 bowling + 球 ball] *n* bowling

保留 **bǎoliú** [comp: 保 conserve + 留 retain] *v* retain, reserve □ 这张飞机票我们给你保留三天。 **Zhè zhāng fēijīpiào wǒmen gěi nǐ bǎoliú sān tiān.** *We'll reserve this air ticket for you for three days.* □ 你可以保留自己的意见，但是大家的决定不能违反。 **Nǐ kěyǐ bǎoliú zìjǐ de yìjiàn, dànshì dàjiā de juédìng bù néng wéifǎn.** *You can have your personal opinions, but the collective decision must not be opposed.*

保密 **bǎomì** [v+compl: 保 conserve + 密 secret, confidential] *v* keep...secret □ 这件事一定要保密。 **Zhè jiàn shì yídìng yào bǎomì.** *This matter must be kept secret.*

保密文件 bǎomì wénjiàn classified document

保姆 **bǎomǔ** [modif: 保 protect + 姆 woman] *n* (children's) nurse, nanny

当保姆 dāng bǎomǔ work as a nanny

保守 **bǎoshǒu** [comp: 保 protect + 守 observe, abide by] **I** *v* guard, keep □ 你能保守一个秘密吗？ **Nǐ néng bǎoshǒu yí ge mìmì ma?** *Can you keep a secret?* **II** *adj* conservative □ 一个人年纪大了，往往会保守。 **Yí ge rén niánjì dà le, wǎngwǎng huì bǎoshǒu.** *As one gets old, one tends to be conservative.*

保卫 **bǎowèi** [comp: 保 protect + 卫 defend] *v* defend □ 当外敌入侵时，每个人都应该保卫自己的国家。 **Dāng wài dí rùqīn shí, měi ge rén dōu yīnggāi bǎowèi zìjǐ de guójiā.** *When an enemy invades our country, everybody should defend it.*

保温 **bǎowēn** [v+compl: 保 keep + 温 warm] *v* preserve heat

保险 **bǎoxiǎn** [comp: 保 protect + 险 risk] **I** *adj* safe, risk-free **II** *v* insure **III** *n* insurance

保险单 bǎoxiǎndān insurance policy

保险费 bǎoxiǎnfèi insurance premium

保险公司 bǎoxiǎn gōngsī insurance company

保养 **bǎoyǎng** [comp: 保 protect + 养 maintain] *v* 1 take good care of one's health

(人)保养得很好 (rén) bǎoyǎng de hěn hǎo (of people) well preserved

2 maintain (automobiles, machines, etc.), keep in good state

车辆保养 chēliàng bǎoyǎng vehicle maintenance

保障 **bǎozhàng** [comp: 保 protect + 障 defense] *v* secure, insure, guarantee

社会保障 shèhuì bǎozhàng social security

保证 **bǎozhèng** [comp: 保 protect + 证 evidence] **I** *v* guarantee, pledge □ 我保证以后不犯这样的错误。 **Wǒ bǎozhèng yǐhòu bú fàn zhèyàng de cuòwù.** *I guarantee that I won't repeat this mistake.* □ 本公司保证产品质量。 **Běn gōngsī bǎozhèng chǎnpǐn zhìliàng.** *This company guarantees the quality of its products.* **II** *n* guarantee □ 你们能为产品提供保证吗？ **Nǐmen néng wèi chǎnpǐn tígōng bǎozhèng ma?** *Can you provide a guarantee for your products?*

产品保证书 chǎnpǐn bǎozhèngshū (product) quality guarantee

保重 **bǎozhòng** *v* take good care of oneself □ 您退休以后，多多保重身体。 **Nín tuìxiū yǐhòu, duōduō bǎozhòng shēntǐ.** *(I hope) you will take good care of your health after retirement.*

堡 **bǎo** *n* fortress, castle

堡垒 **bǎolěi** [comp: 堡 fortress + 垒 bastion] *n* fort, fortress

饱 **bǎo** Trad 飽 *adj* having eaten one's fill, full (antonym 饿 è)

饱吃一顿 bǎo chī yídùn have a square meal, eat to one's fill

吃得饱 chī de bǎo have enough to eat

吃不饱 chī bu bǎo not have enough to eat (→ not have enough food) □ 谢谢，我饱了。 **Xièxie, wǒ bǎo le.** *Thank you. I'm full.* □ 您吃饱了吗？ **Nín chī bǎo le ma?** *Have you had (← eaten) enough?*

NOTE: It is customary for a Chinese host to ask a guest who seems to have finished the meal: 您吃饱了吗？ **Nín chī bǎo le ma?** *Have you had (eaten) enough?* The guest is expected to reply: 吃饱了。多谢。您慢慢吃。 **Chī bǎo le. Duō xiè. Nín mànman chī.** *Yes, I have. Thank you. Please take your time to eat.*

饱和 **bǎohé** *adj* saturated

饱满 **bǎomǎn** [comp: 饱 full + 满 full] *adj* full, plump

报 **bào** Trad 報 **I** *n* newspaper (same as 报纸 **bàozhǐ**)

看报 kànbào read a newspaper

II *v* respond, reciprocate

报仇 **bàochóu** [v+obj: 报 reciprocate + 仇 enmity] *v* avenge, revenge

报酬 **bàochou** [comp: 报 respond + 酬 reward] *n* renumeration, reward

报酬很高 bàochou hěn gāo well-paid

报到 **bàodào** *v* report for duty, register □ 学校九月一日开学，学生从八月二十五日起报到。 **Xuéxiào Jiǔyuè yīrì kāixué, xuésheng cóng Bāyuè èrshíwǔ rì qǐ bàodào.** *The academic year begins on September 1, and students start registration on August 25.*

报道 **bàodào** (or 报导 **bàodǎo**) **I** *v* report (news), cover □ 今天城里各家报纸都报道了昨天的交通事故。 **Jīntiān chéng li gè jiā bàozhǐ dōu bàodàole zuótiān de jiāotōng shìgù.** *Today all the newspapers in the city covered yesterday's road accident.* **II** *n* news story □ 你看了关于昨天交通事故的报道没有？ **Nǐ kànle guānyú zuótiān jiāotōng shìgù de bàodào méiyǒu?** *Have you read the news story about yesterday's road accident?*

独家报道 dújiā bàodào exclusive report

深入报道 shēnrù bàodào in-depth report

现场报道 xiànchǎng bàodào on-the-spot ("alive") report

报恩 **bào'ēn** [v+obj: 报 respond to + 恩 kindness] *v* pay a debt of gratitude

报复 **bàofù** *v* retaliate, revenge □ 谁得罪了她，她一定要报复。 **Shéi dézuìle tā, tā yídìng yào bàofù.** *She will retaliate against whoever has offended her.*

报告 **bàogào** **I** *v* report, make known □ 播音员："现在报告新闻。" **Bōyīnyuán: "Xiànzài bàogào xīnwén."** *Newscaster: "Now the news."* □ 医院发现这种病的病人，没有立即向卫生局报告。 **Yīyuàn fāxiàn shēng zhè zhǒng bìng de bìngrén, méiyǒu lìjí xiàng wèishēngjú bàogào.** *The hospital failed to report to the Bureau of Health immediately after finding a case of this disease.* **II** *n* report, talk (at a large-

scale meeting) (份 **fèn**) □ 董事会收到了一份重要报告。**Dǒngshìhuì shōudàole yí fèn zhòngyào bàogào.** *The Board of Directors received an important report.*
财务报告 cáiwù bàogào financial report
秘密报告 mìmì bàogào confidential report
报刊 **bàokān** [comp: 报 newspapers + 刊 periodicals] *n* newspapers and periodicals, the press
报考 **bàokǎo** *v* enter oneself for an examination
报名 **bàomíng** *v* enter one's name, sign up, apply for (a place in school) □ 我已经向一所大学报名。**Wǒ yǐjīng xiàng yì suǒ dàxué bàomíng.** *I have applied for a place in a university.* □ 有六百多人报名参加星期天的长跑。**Yǒu liùbǎi duō rén bàomíng cānjiā Xīngqītiān de chángpǎo.** *Over 600 people have signed up for Sunday's long-distance run.*
报社 **bàoshè** [modif: 报 newspaper + 社 association] *n* newspaper office
报销 **bàoxiāo** *v* submit an expense account, get reimbursement
报纸 **bàozhǐ** [modif: 报 reporting + 纸 paper] *n* newspaper (张 **zhāng**, 份 **fèn**) □ 今天报纸上有什么重要消息？**Jīntiān bàozhǐ shang yǒu shénme zhòngyào xiāoxi?** *What important news is there in today's paper?* □ 我很少看报纸。**Wǒ hěn shǎo kàn bàozhǐ.** *I seldom read newspapers.* □ 这份报纸广告比新闻多。**Zhè fèn bàozhǐ guǎnggào bǐ xīnwén duō.** *There are more advertisements than news in this newspaper.*

NOTE: In colloquial Chinese, 报 **bào** is often used instead of 报纸 **bàozhǐ**, e.g.□ 你看得懂中文报吗？**Nǐ kàndedǒng Zhōngwén bào ma?** *Can you understand Chinese newspapers?*

抱 **bào** *v* hold ... in arms, embrace, hug □ 妈妈抱着孩子。**Māma bàozhe háizi.** *The mother is holding her baby in her arms.* □ 让我抱抱你。**Ràng wǒ bàobao nǐ.** *Let me hug you.*
抱负 **bàofù** *n* aspiration, ambition
抱歉 **bàoqiàn** *adj* apologetic, be sorry, regretful □ 很抱歉，今天我不能加班。**Hěn bàoqiàn, jīntiān wǒ bù néng jiābān.** *I'm sorry, but I won't be able to work overtime today.* □ 我忘了昨天的会议，实在抱歉! **Wǒ wàngle zuótiān de huìyì, shízài bàoqiàn!** *I'm awfully sorry that I forgot the meeting yesterday.*
抱怨 **bàoyuàn** *v* complain, grumble
暴 **bào** *adj* fierce and brutal
暴动 **bàodòng** [modif: 暴 violent + 动 action] *n* rebellion, insurrection
暴力 **bàolì** [modif: 暴 violent + 力 force] *n* violence, brutal force
暴力电影 bàolì diànyǐng violent movie
有暴力倾向 yǒu bàolì qīngxiàng have a tendency to violence
暴露 **bàolù** [comp: 暴 expose + 露 show, reveal] *v* expose, lay bare
暴雨 **bàoyǔ** [modif: 暴 violent + 雨 rain] *n* rainstorm, torrential rain
爆 **bào** *v* explode
爆发 **bàofā** *v* break out, burst out □ 火山爆发。**Huǒshān bàofā.** *A volcano erupted.* □ 第二次世界大战是哪一年爆发的? **Dì'èrcì Shìjiè Dàzhàn shì nǎ yì nián bàofā de?** *In which year did World War II break out?*

爆破 **bàopò** *v* demolish with dynamite
爆炸 **bàozhà** [comp: 爆 explode + 炸 bomb, explode] **I** *v* explode **II** *n* explosion
自杀炸弹爆炸 zìshā zhàdàn bàozhà the explosion of a suicide bomb
杯 **bēi** *n* cup, mug, glass (只 **zhī**) □ 这些杯子要洗一下。**Zhèxiē bēizi yào xǐ yíxià.** *These cups/mugs/glasses need washing.*
杯子 bēizi cup, mug, glass
茶杯 chábēi teacup
酒杯 jiǔbēi wine glass
一杯茶/酒 yì bēi chá/jiǔ a cup of tea, a glass of wine

NOTE: 杯 **bēi** may denote either *cup*, *mug*, or *glass*. 杯 **bēi** is seldom used alone. It is usually suffixed with 子 **zi**: 杯子 **bēizi**, or combined with 茶 **chá** or 酒 **jiǔ**: 茶杯 **chábēi**, 酒杯 **jiǔbēi**.

背 **bēi** *v* carry...on the back □ 孩子每天高高兴兴背着书包上学校。**Háizi měi tiān gāo-gāo-xìng-xìng bēizhe shūbāo shàng xuéxiào.** *Every day the child goes to school happily, his schoolbag on his back.*
背包 bēibāo [v+obj: 背 carry on the back + 包 parcel, bag] *n* backpack, knapsack
卑 **bēi** *adj* 1 low and humble 2 mean, contemptible
卑鄙 bēibǐ [comp: 卑 mean + 鄙 low, base] *adj* contemptible, despicable
卑鄙小人 bēibǐ xiǎorén despicable person/people
碑 **bēi** *n* stone tablet
纪念碑 jìniànbēi monument
悲 **bēi** *n* grieved
悲哀 bēi'āi [comp: 悲 grieved + 哀 grieved] *adj* deeply grieved
悲惨 bēicǎn [comp: 悲 grieved + 惨 miserable] *adj* miserable, tragic
悲愤 bēifèn [comp: 悲 grieved + 愤 angry] *adj* very sad and angry, filled with grief and indignation
悲观 bēiguān [modif: 悲 grieved, sad + 观 view] *adj* pessimistic (antonym 乐观 **lèguān**) □ 你太悲观了，情况不会这么坏吧。**Nǐ tài bēiguān le, qíngkuàng bú huì zhème huài ba.** *You're too pessimistic. Things can't be that bad.*
悲观主义 bēiguānzhǔyì pessimism
悲观者 bēiguānzhě pessimist
悲剧 bēijù [modif: 悲 grieved, sad + 剧 drama] *n* tragedy
悲伤 bēishāng [comp: 悲 grieved, sad + 伤 hurt] *adj* deeply sorrowful
悲痛 bēitòng [comp: 悲 grieved, sad + 痛 agony] *adj* deeply grieved, agonized, with deep sorrow □ 他在交通事故中失去了妻子、女儿，悲痛极了。**Tā zài jiāotōng shìgù zhōng shīqùle qīzi, nǚ'ér, bēitòng jíle.** *He lost his wife and daughter in a road accident and is deeply grieved.*
北 **běi** *n* north, northern
北极 běijí the North Pole (← the north extreme) □ 在北半球，刮北风，天就冷。**Zài běi bànqiú, guā běifēng, tiān jiù lěng.** *In the northern hemisphere, the weather becomes cold when a north wind blows.*
北极星 běijíxīng the North Star, Polaris
北边 běibian [modif: 北 north + 边 side] *n* north side, to the north, in the north □ 山的北边是一大片

原。**Shān de běibian shì yí dà piàn cǎoyuán.** *North of the mountains is a vast pasture.* □ 加拿大在美国的北边。**Jiānádà zài Měiguó de běibian.** *Canada is to the north of U.S.A.*

北方 **běifāng** [modif: 北 north + 方 region] *n* northern region □ 中国南方和北方以长江为界。**Zhōngguó nánfāng hé běifāng yǐ Chángjiāng wéi jiè.** *South China and North China are demarcated by the Yangtze River.*

北京 **Běijīng** *n* Beijing (Peking) (the capital of the People's Republic of China)

北面 **běimiàn** *n* Same as 北边 **běibian**

辈 **bèi** Trad 輩 *n* generation, lifetime

贝 **bèi** Trad 貝 *n* shellfish
贝壳 **bèiké** *n* shell

狈 **bèi** Trad 狽 *n* a legendary beast, similar to the wolf

备 **bèi** Trad 備 *v* prepare
备忘录 **bèiwànglù** [modif: 备 prepare + 忘 forget + 录 record] *n* memorandum, memo
备用 **bèiyòng** *v* reserve, spare
备用轮胎 **bèiyòng lúntāi** spare tire

惫 **bèi** Trad 憊 *adj* fatigued

背 **bèi** I *v* 1 turn away, leave, go away 2 learn by heart II *n* back
背面 **bèimiàn** [modif: 背 reverse + 面 side] *n* reverse side, the back of an object
背叛 **bèipàn** *v* betray
背叛…的信任 **bèipàn...de xìnrèn** betray the trust of ...
背诵 **bèisòng** [comp: 背 learn by heart + 诵 recite] *v* repeat from memory □ 他们六岁的孩子能背诵好几首唐诗。**Tāmen liù suì de háizi néng bèisòng hǎojǐ shǒu Táng shī.** *Their six-year-old child can recite quite a few Tang poems.*
背心 **bèixīn** *n* vest, waistcoat

被 **bèi** *prep* by (introducing the doer of an action) □ 花瓶被小明打破了。**Huāpíng bèi Xiǎo Míng dǎpò le.** *The vase was broken by Xiao Ming.* □ 他被人欺负了。**Tā bèi rén qīfu le.** *He was bullied by somebody.*
被动 **bèidòng** *adj* passive
被动式 **bèidòngshì** (in grammar) the passive voice
被动吸烟 **bèidòng xīyān** passive smoking
被告(人) **bèigào(rén)** *n* defendant
被迫 **bèipò** *v* be forced to, be compelled to
被子 **bèizi** *n* quilt, blanket (条 **tiáo**) □ 冬天出太阳的时候，很多中国人喜欢晒被子。**Dōngtiān chū tàiyang de shíhou, hěn duo Zhōngguórén xǐhuan shài bèizi.** *Many Chinese like to sun quilts when it's sunny in winter.* (→ *On sunny winter days, many Chinese like to air their quilts.*)

倍 **bèi** *measure word* (-fold, times) □ 这个学校的学生人数比我们学校多一倍。(这个学校的学生人数是我们学校的两倍。)**Zhège xuéxiào de xuésheng rénshù bǐ wǒmen xuéxiào duō yí bèi. (Zhège xuéxiào de xuésheng rénshù shì wǒmen xuéxiào de liǎng bèi.)** *The number of students in this school is twice as many as that of our school.* (→ *The student population of this school is twice of ours.*)
倍数 **bèishù** *n* (in math) multiple

奔 **bēn** *v* run fast
奔驰 **bēnchí** [comp: 奔 run fast + 驰 run, gallop] *v* (of animals and vehicles) run fast, speed
奔跑 **bēnpǎo** [comp: 奔 run fast + 跑 run] *v* run fast, whizz
奔腾 **bēnténg** *v* gallop

本 **běn** I *n* principal, capital
赔本 **péi běn** lose one's capital in investments or other business dealings
II *measure wd* (for books, magazines, etc.)
一本书 **yì běn shū** a book
III *adj* this one, one's own □ 本店春节照常营业。**Běn diàn chūnjié zhàocháng yíngyè.** *This store will do business as usual during the Spring Festival.* (→ *We'll be open during the Chinese New Year.*)

NOTE: 本 **běn** in the sense of *this one* is only used on formal occasions.

本地 **běndì** [modif: 本 this + 地 place] *n* this locality □ 我向你介绍一个本地的名菜。**Wǒ xiàng nǐ jièshao yí ge běndì de míngcài.** *I'll recommend you a famous dish of this town.*
本来 **běnlái** *adv* originally, at first □ 这个旅馆本来是一个富商的家。**Zhège lǚguǎn běnlái shì yí ge fù shāng de jiā.** *This hotel was originally a rich merchant's residence.* □ 我本来不想去看电影，他一定要我去，我就去了。**Wǒ běnlái bù xiǎng qù kàn diànyǐng, tā yídìng yào wǒ qù, wǒ jiù qù le.** *At first I did not want to go to the movie, but he insisted I should go, so I went with him.*
本领 **běnlǐng** *n* skill, ability, capability □ 他已经二十多岁了，还没有本领独立生活。**Tā yǐjīng èrshí duō suì le, hái méiyǒu běnlǐng dúlì shēnghuó.** *He is over twenty, but still lacks the skills to live independently.*
本能 **běnnéng** [modif: 本 original + 能 ability] *n* instinct, intuition
求生的本能 **qiúshēng de běnnéng** the instinct to survive
本钱 **běnqián** [modif: 本 capital + 钱 money] *n* the money with which one makes investments or conducts other business dealings, capital
本事 **běnshì** *n* ability, capability □ 他自以为本事很大，其实什么都做不好。**Tā zì yǐwéi běnshì hěn dà, qíshí shénme dōu zuò bu hǎo.** *He thinks himself very capable; actually he can't get anything done properly.*

NOTE: 本领 **běnlǐng** and 本事 **běnshì** are synonyms, but 本领 **běnlǐng** emphasizes skills while 本事 **běnshì** has a more general sense of "the ability to get things done" and may be used with negative connotations.

本性 **běnxìng** [modif: 本 original + 性 nature] *n* natural character, inherent quality □ 本性难改。**Běnxìng nán gǎi.** *It's difficult to change one's nature.* (→ *A leopard will not change its spots.*)
本质 **běnzhì** [comp: 本 origin + 质 nature] *n* innate character, true nature □ 研究问题我们要透过表面现象看到本质。**Yánjiū wèntí, wǒmen yào tòuguo biǎomiàn xiànxiàng kàndào běnzhì.** *When studying a problem we should see beyond appearances and get to its essence.*

本子 **běnzi** [suffix: 本 a book + 子 nominal suffix] *n* notebook (本 **běn**) □ 他丢了一个很重要的本子。**Tā diūle yí ge hěn zhòngyào de běnzi.** *He's lost an important notebook.* □ 这本本子记了朋友的电话号码，传真号码和电子邮件地址。**Zhè běn běnzi jìle péngyou de diànhuà hàomǎ, chuánzhēn hàomǎ hé diànzǐ yóujiàn dìzhǐ.** *In this notebook are recorded his friends' telephone numbers, fax numbers and e-mail addresses.*

笨 **bèn** *adj* dumb, stupid □ 他不善于言词，其实一点都不笨。**Tā bú shànyú yáncí, qíshí yìdiǎn dōu bú bèn.** *He is not good at expressing himself, but he is by no means stupid.* □ 千万不能对孩子说 "你真笨!" 这样的话。**Qiānwàn bù néng duì háizi shuō "Nǐ zhēn bèn!" zhèyàng de huà.** *Never, ever say to a child such things as "How stupid you are!"*

笨蛋 **bèndàn** [modif: 笨 stupid + 蛋 egg] *n* fool, idiot □ 你这个笨蛋! **Nǐ zhège bèndàn!** *You idiot!*

笨重 **bènzhòng** [comp: 笨 dumb + 重 heavy] *adj* heavy and cumbersome

笨拙 **bènzhuō** [comp: 笨 dumb + 拙 clumsy] *adj* clumsy

崩 **bēng** *v* collapse
崩溃 **bēngkuì** [comp: 崩 collapse + 溃 decay] *v* collapse, crumble

绷 **bēng** Trad 繃 *v* stretch tight
绷带 **bēngdài** [modif: 绷 stretch tight + 带 band] *n* bandage

甭 **béng** *adv* (contraction of 不用 **búyòng**) don't □ 甭客气! **Béng kèqi!** *Don't stand on ceremony! It's OK.*

蹦 **bèng** *v* jump
蹦床 **bèngchuáng** trampoline
蹦极跳 **bèngjítiào** bungee jump

逼 **bī** *v* 1 force, compel 2 get close to, press on towards
逼近 **bījìn** [comp: 逼 get close on + 近 get near to] *v* close in on, gain on
逼迫 **bīpò** [comp: 逼 force + 迫 force] *v* force, coerce

鼻 **bí** *n* nose
鼻子 **bízi** the nose □ 有些中国人叫西方人 "大鼻子"，这是不礼貌的。**Yǒuxiē Zhōngguórén jiào Xīfāngrén "dà bízi", zhè shì bù lǐmào de.** *Some Chinese call Westerners "Big Noses"; this is impolite.*
鼻涕 **bítì** *n* nasal mucus

比 **bǐ** I *prep* (introducing the object that is compared with the subject of a sentence), than □ 你比他高一点。**Nǐ bǐ tā gāo yìdiǎn.** *You're a bit taller than he is.* □ 今天比昨天冷得多。**Jīntiān bǐ zuótiān lěng de duō.** *Today is much colder than yesterday.* □ 我跑得比你快。**Wǒ pǎo de bǐ nǐ kuài.** *I run faster than you.* □ 你写汉字没有我写得快，但是写得比我好看。**Nǐ xiě Hànzì méiyǒu wǒ xiě de kuài, dànshì xiě de bǐ wǒ hǎokàn.** *You write Chinese characters more slowly, but more beautifully than I do.* II *v* compete, compare, contrast □ 你们俩谁跑得快? 比一比! **Nǐmen liǎ shuí pǎo de kuài? Bǐ yì bǐ!** *Of you two, who runs faster? Let's see!*

比方 **bǐfang** *n* example, analogy
打比方 **dǎ bǐfang** make an analogy, draw an analogy
比分 **bǐfēn** *n* score (of a game or sporting competition)
比价 **bǐjià** *n* 1 price ratio 2 exchange rate □ 人民币和美元的比价是多少? **Rénmínbì hé Měiyuán de bǐjià**

shì duōshǎo? *What is the exchange rate between Renminbi and U.S. dollar?*

比较 **bǐjiào** I *v* compare □ 这两种方法哪个好，我们要比较一下。**Zhè liǎng zhǒng fāngfǎ nǎge hǎo, wǒmen yào bǐjiào yíxià.** *Which of the two approaches is the better one? We need to compare them.*
和…比较 **hé…bǐjiào** compare ... with □ 和农村比较，城市的生活方便得多。**Hé nóngcūn bǐjiào, chéngshì de shēnghuó fāngbiàn de duō.** *Compared to living on a farm, city life is much more convenient.*
II *adv* relatively, quite, to some degree □ 这两天天气比较好。**Zhè liǎng tiān tiānqì bǐjiào hǎo.** *The weather these days is not bad.* □ 李先生在海外生活多年了，但还是比较喜欢吃中国菜。**Lǐ xiānsheng zài hǎiwài shēnghuó duō nián le, dàn háishì bǐjiào xǐhuan chī Zhōngguócài.** *Mr Li has been living overseas for quite a few years, but he still prefers Chinese food.*

比例 **bǐlì** *n* percentage □ 这个学校海外留学生在学生人数中占多少比例? **Zhège xuéxiào hǎiwài liúxuésheng zài xuéshéng rénshù zhōng zhàn duōshǎo bǐlì?** *What percentage of this school's enrolment is from overseas students?*

比如 **bǐrú** *conj* for example □ 今年我们都取得了很大进步，比如约翰，现在已经会用中文写电子邮件了。**Jīnnián wǒmen dōu qǔdéle hěn dà jìnbù, bǐrú Yuēhàn, xiànzài yǐjīng huì yòng Zhōngwén xiě diànzǐ yóujiàn le.** *We have all made good progress this year. Take John for example, now he can write e-mails in Chinese.*

NOTE: In spoken Chinese you can also use 比如说 **bǐrúshuō.**

比赛 **bǐsài** [comp: 比 compare + 赛 compete] I *v* compete, have a match □ 我们比赛一下，看谁打字打得又快又好。**Wǒmen bǐsài yíxià, kàn shéi dǎ zì dǎ de yòu kuài yòu hǎo.** *Let's have a contest to see who types quickly and accurately. (→ Let's compete and see who types better.)* □ 今天晚上我们和他们比赛篮球。**Jīntiān wǎnshang wǒmen hé tāmen bǐsài lánqiú.** *This evening we'll have a basketball match with them.* II *n* competition, match, game □ 昨天晚上的篮球比赛精彩极了! **Zuótiān wǎnshang de lánqiú bǐsài jīngcǎi jíle.** *The basketball match yesterday evening was wonderful!* □ 下个月北京举行中国武术比赛。**Xià ge yuè Běijīng jǔxíng Zhōngguó wǔshù bǐsài.** *There will be a Chinese martial arts contest in Beijing next month.*
比赛项目 **bǐsài xiàngmù** event (of a sports meet)
参加比赛 **cānjiā bǐsài** participate in a game (or sports event)
和/跟...比赛 **hé/gēn...bǐsài** have a match/race with
看比赛 **kàn bǐsài** watch a game (or sports event)
比喻 **bǐyù** [comp: 比 comparison + 喻 analogy] *n* metaphor
比重 **bǐzhòng** *n* 1 specific gravity 2 proportion

鄙 **bǐ** *adj* low, base (See 卑鄙 **bēibǐ**)

笔 **bǐ** Trad 筆 *n* writing instrument, pen, pencil (支 **zhī**) □ 这支笔很好写。**Zhè zhī bǐ hěn hǎoxiě.** *This pen writes well.* □ 我可以借用你的笔吗? **Wǒ kěyǐ jièyòng nǐ de bǐ ma?** *May I borrow your pen?*

钢笔 gāngbǐ fountain pen
画笔 huàbǐ paintbrush (for art)
毛笔 máobǐ Chinese writing brush
圆珠笔 yuánzhūbǐ ballpen
笔记 bǐjì *n* notes (taken in class or while reading) □ 我昨天没来上课，你的笔记能借我看一下吗? **Wǒ zuótiān méi lái shàngkè, nǐ de bǐjì néng jiè wǒ kàn yíxià ma?** *I was absent from class yesterday. Could you let me have a look at your notes?*
记笔记 jì bǐjì take notes (in class, at a lecture, etc.)
做笔记 zuò bǐjì make notes (while reading).
笔记本 bǐjìběn *n* notebook
　笔记本电脑 bǐjìběn diànnǎo notebook computer
笔迹 bǐjì [modif: 笔 pen + 迹 mark] *n* handwriting
　辨认笔迹 biànrèn bǐjì decipher someone's handwriting
笔试 bǐshì [modif: 笔 pen + 试 test] *n* written test, written examination
笔直 bǐzhí *adj* perfectly straight
彼 bǐ *pron* that, the other
　彼此 bǐcǐ [comp: 彼 that + 此 this] *pron* each other
碧 bì *adj* green
　碧绿 bìlǜ [comp: 碧 green + 绿 green] *adj* green, dark green
蔽 bì *v* cover, conceal (See 隐蔽 yǐnbì)
毙 bì Trad 斃 *v* die (See 枪毙 qiāngbì)
币 bì Trad 幣 *n* currency (See 人民币 Rénmínbì)
痹 bì *n* paralysis (See 麻痹 mábì)
必 bì I *adv* certainly, inevitably II *modal v* must
必定 bìdìng [comp: 必 certainly + 定 definitely] *adv* certainly, definitely
必将 bìjiāng *adv* will surely
必然 bìrán *adj* inevitable, be bound to □ 他因为骄傲而失败，这是必然的。 **Tā yīnwèi jiāo'ào ér shībài, zhè shì bìrán de.** *He failed because he was conceited. This was inevitable.*
必胜客 Bìshèngkè *n* Pizza Hut (Restaurant)
必修 bìxiū [modif: 必 must + 修 study] *adj* compulsory (courses, subjects of study)
　必修课 bìxiūkè compulsory subject, required course
必须 bìxū [comp: 必 must + 须 need, have to] *modal v* must □ 每个公民都必须遵守法律。 **Měi ge gōngmín dōu bìxū zūnshǒu fǎlǜ.** *Every citizen must abide by the law.* □ 你要在那个大学学习，必须在半年前报名。 **Nǐ yào zài nàge dàxué xuéxí, bìxū zài bànnián qián bàomíng.** *You must apply for enrolment half a year earlier if you want to study in that university.*
必需 bìxū [comp: 必 must + 需 need] *v* must have
　必需品 bìxūpǐn daily necessities
必要 bìyào [comp: 必 must + 要 require] *adj* necessary □ 你不必要送这么贵的礼物。 **Nǐ bú bìyào sòng zhème guì de lǐwù.** *You don't have to give such an expensive present.* □ 你外出旅行两天，带这么多衣服，必要吗? **Nǐ wàichū lǚxíng liǎngtiān, dài zhème duō yīfu, bìyào ma?** *Is it necessary to take so many clothes with you for a trip of two days?*

必要条件 bìyào tiáojiàn necessary condition
毕 bì Trad 畢 *v* finish
毕竟 bìjìng *adv* after all, anyway
毕业 bìyè [v+obj: 毕 finish + 业 course of study] *v* graduate from school □ 你哪一年毕业? **Nǐ nǎ yì nián bìyè?** *When will you graduate?* □ 我父亲二十多年前从一所著名大学毕业。 **Wǒ fùqin èrshí duō nián qián cóng yì suǒ zhùmíng dàxué bìyè.** *My father graduated from a famous university over twenty years ago.*
闭 bì Trad 閉 *v* close, shut up □ 老人看报看累了，闭上眼睛休息一会。 **Lǎorén kàn bào kàn lèi le, bìshang yǎnjing xiūxi yíhuìr.** *The old man was tired from reading the newspapers. He closed his eyes to rest for a while.* □ 她愤怒地喊: "闭嘴!" **Tā fènnù de hǎn: "Bì zuǐ!"** *She shouted angrily, "Shut up!"*

NOTE: 闭嘴! **Bìzuǐ!** *Shut your mouth!* is a very impolite expression to tell people to stop talking. You can also say 闭上你的嘴! **Bì shang nǐ de zuǐ!** *Shut your mouth!*

闭幕 bìmù [v+obj: 闭 close + 幕 curtain] *v* the curtain falls (of a theatrical performance, an event, etc.), close
闭幕式 bìmùshì [modif: 闭幕 the curtain falls + 式 ceremony] *n* closing ceremony
闭塞 bìsè [comp: 闭 closed + 塞 blocked] *adj* cut off from the outside world, secluded
弊 bì *n* fraud, corrupt practice
作弊 zuòbì cheat (especially in examinations)
舞弊 wǔbì be engaged in fraud, misconduct or malpractice
弊病 bìbìng [comp: 弊 corrupt practice + 病 sickness] *n* malpractice, disadvantage
避 bì *v* evade, avoid □ 很多人在商场里避雨。 **Hěn duō rén zài shāngchǎng li bì yǔ.** *Many people are in the shopping mall to shelter from the rain.*
避免 bìmiǎn [comp: 避 evade + 免 be free from] *v* avoid, avert □ 她避免和以前的男朋友见面。 **Tā bìmiǎn hé yǐqián de nánpéngyou jiànmiàn.** *She avoids meeting her ex-boyfriend.* □ 自然灾害是无法避免的。 **Zìrán zāihài shì wúfǎ bìmiǎn de.** *Natural disasters cannot be avoided.*
避孕 bìyùn [v+obj: 避 avoid + 孕 pregnancy] *n* contraception, birth control
避孕套 bìyùntào condom
避孕药 bìyùnyào contraceptive pill
壁 bì *n* wall (See 隔壁 gébì)
臂 bì *n* arm
一臂之力 yí bì zhì lì a helping hand
鞭 biān *n* whip
鞭子 biānzi whip (条 tiáo)
鞭策 biāncè *v* spur on, urge on
鞭炮 biānpào *n* firecracker
放鞭炮 fàng biānpào set off firecrackers
边 biān Trad 邊 *n* side, border □ 山的这一边有很多树，那一边没有树。 **Shān de zhè yì biān yǒu hěn duō shù, nà yì biān méiyǒu shù.** *On this side of the hill there are lots of trees, and on the other side there are no trees.*

NOTE: The most frequent use of 边 biān is to form "com-

pound location nouns": 东边 **dōngbian** *east side*, 南边 **nánbian** *south side*, 西边 **xībian** *west side*, 北边 **běibian** *north side*, 里边 **lǐbian** *inside*, 外边 **wàibian** *outside*. 边 **biān** in such cases is often pronounced in the neutral tone.

边…边 **biān...biān** *conj* (used with verbs to indicate simultaneous actions) □ 他们边走边谈, 不一会儿就到市中心了。 **Tāmen biān zǒu biān tán, bùyíhuìr jiù dào shì zhōngxīn le.** *They chatted while walking, and soon reached the city center.*

边防 **biānfáng** [modif: 边 border + 防 defense] *n* frontier defense

边防部队 **biānfáng bùduì** frontier guards

边防检查站 **biānfáng jiǎncházhàn** frontier checkpoint

边疆 **biānjiāng** [comp: 边 border+ 疆 frontier] *n* border area

边疆地区 **biānjiāng dìqū** border area

边界 **biānjiè** [comp: 边 side, border + 界 realm] *n* border (between two countries)

边界线 **biānjiè xiàn** boundary (between two countries)

边境 **biānjìng** [modif: 边 side, border + 境 place] *n* frontier, border

边缘 **biānyuán** [comp: 边 side, border + 缘 edge] *n* edge, periphery

边缘状态 **biānyuán zhuàngtài** borderline case

编 **biān** Trad 編 *v* compile, compose □ 那本词典是一位有丰富教学经验的老教授编的。 **Nà běn cídiǎn shì yí wèi yǒu fēngfù jiàoxuè jīngyàn de lǎo jiàoshòu biān de.** *That dictionary was compiled by an old professor with rich teaching experience.*

编号 **biānhào** [modif: 编 compile + 号 number] *n* serial number

护照编号 **hùzhào biānhào** passport's serial number

编辑 **biānjí** [comp: 编 compile, compose + 辑 compile] **I** *v* edit, compile **II** *n* editor □ 报纸编辑每天收到很多读者来信。 **Bàozhǐ biānjí měitiān shōudào hěn duō dúzhě lái xìn.** *The newpaper editor receives a large number of readers' letters.*

财经编辑 **cáijīng biānjí** finance editor

特约编辑 **tèyuē biānjí** contributing editor

总编辑 **zǒngbiānjí** chief editor

编制 **biānzhì** *v* 1 weave, braid 2 draw up (a plan, a computer programme, etc.)

贬 **biǎn** *v* reduce, derogate

贬低 **biǎndī** [v+compl: 贬 derogate + 低 low] *v* belittle, play down

贬低别人的成绩 **biǎndī biéren de chéngjì** belittle someone's achievements

贬值 **biǎnzhí** [v+obj: 贬 reduce + 值 value] *v* devalue, depreciate

货币贬值 **huòbì biǎnzhí** currency devaluation

扁 **biǎn** *adj* flat □ 面包放在这么多菜的下面, 都压扁了。 **Miànbāo fàng zài zhème duō cài de xiàmiàn, dōu yā biǎn le.** *Placed under so many groceries, the bread was crushed flat.*

变 **biàn** Trad 變 *v* transform, change □ 世界上任何事情都在变。 **Shìjiè shang rènhé shìqing dōu zài biàn.** *Everything in the world is changing.*

变成 **biànchéng** [v+compl: 变 change + 成 into]

v change into □ 几年不见, 小女孩变成了大姑娘。 **Jǐnián bújiàn, xiǎo nǚhái biànchéngle yí ge dà gūniang.** *I hadn't seen her for several years and the little girl had changed into a young lady.*

变动 **biàndòng** [comp: 变 change + 动 move] *v* 1 alter, change 2 (of organizations) reshuffle, reorganize

人事变动 **rénshì biàndòng** reshuffle of personnel

变革 **biàngé** [comp: 变 change + 革 change] *v* transform, change

变更 **biàngēng** [comp: 变 change + 更 alter] *v* alter, modify

变更旅行路线 **biàngēng lǚxíng lùxiàn** change one's itinerary

变化 **biànhuà** [comp: 变 change + 化 transform] **I** *v* transform, change □ 情况变化了, 不能仍然用老办法。 **Qíngkuàng biànhuà le, bù néng réngrán yòng lǎo bànfǎ.** *Things have changed. We cannot use old ways of doing things as before.* (→ *We cannot continue doing things the old way.*)

千变万化 **qiānbiàn wànhuà** always in a state of flux, everchanging

II *n* transfomation, change □ 几年没来, 我觉得这里变化很明显。 **Jǐnián méi lái, wǒ juéde zhèli biànhuà hěn míngxiǎn.** *After a few years' absence, I find obvious changes in this place.* □ 这些年来这个城市没有多大变化。 **Zhèxiē nián lái zhège chéngshì méiyǒu duō dà biànhuà.** *This city has not had much change over these years.*

巨大变化 **jùdà biànhuà** tremendous changes

NOTE: As a verb 变化 **biànhuà** is interchangeable with 变 **biàn**, 变化 **biànhuà** being a little more formal than 变 **biàn**.

变换 **biànhuàn** [comp: 变 change + 换 exchange] *v* vary, alternate

变迁 **biànqiān** [comp: 变 change + 迁 move] *v* change, evolve

变形 **biànxíng** [v+obj: 变 change + 形 shape] *v* deform, transfigure

变形金刚 **biànxíng jīn'gāng** transformer (a toy)

变质 **biànzhì** [v+obj: 变 change + 质 quality] *v* change the nature of, deteriorate □ 这些过期食品变质了。 **Zhèxiē guòqī shípǐn biànzhì le.** *These foodstuffs are past their sell-by dates and have gone bad.*

便 **biàn** *adv* Same as 就 **jiù3** *adv*. Used only in written Chinese.

便道 **biàndào** [modif: 便 convenient + 道 path] *n* shortcut

便利 **biànlì** [comp: 便 convenient + 利 benefit] *adj* convenient, easy □ 住在市中心, 交通很便利。 **Zhù zài shìzhōngxīn, jiāotōng hěn biànlì.** *Transport is easy if you live in the city center.* (→ *If you live in the city center, it's easy to go places.*)

便条 **biàntiáo** [modif: 便 handy + 条 note] *n* informal written message □ 老王给我留了一张便条, 说他明天下午三点半来看我。 **Lǎo Wáng gěi wǒ liúle yì zhāng biàntiáo, shuō tā míngtiān xiàwǔ sān diǎn bàn lái kàn wǒ.** *Lao Wang left a note for me, saying that he would come to see me at 3:30 tomorrow afternoon.*

留便条 **liú biàntiáo** leave a note

便于 **biànyú** *v* be easy to, be convenient for

辩 biàn Trad 辯 *v* argue, debate
辩个明白 biàn ge míngbai debate until the truth is out
辩护 biànhù [comp: 辩 argue + 护 defend] *v* speak in defense of
辩护律师 biànhù lǜshī defense lawyer, defense counsel
辩解 biànjiě [comp: 辩 argue + 解 explain] *v* try to defend oneself
无力的辩解 wúlì de biànjiě feeble excuses
辩论 biànlùn [comp: 辩 argue + 论 discuss] **I** *v* debate □ 我不想和任何人辩论有关宗教的问题。**Wǒ bùxiǎng he rènhé rén biànlùn yǒuguān zōngjiào de wèntí.** *I don't want to debate with anyone on matters of religion.* **II** *n* debate (场 **chǎng**)
举行一场辩论 jǔxíng yì chǎng biànlùn hold a debate

辨 biàn *v* distinguish, discriminate
辨别 biànbié [comp: 辨 distinguish + 别 difference] *v* distinguish, tell ... from ...
辨别是非 biànbié shìfēi distinguish what is right from what is wrong
辨认 biànrèn [comp: 辨 distinguish + 认 recognize] *v* identify, recognize
辨认罪犯 biànrèn zuìfàn identify a criminal

辫 biàn Trad 辮 *n* pigtail, braid
辫子 biànzi pigtail, braid (条 **tiáo**)

遍 biàn *measure wd* (for frequency of an action done in its complete duration from beginning to end) □ 这本书我看了三遍。**Zhè běn shū wǒ kànle sān biàn.** *I've read this book three times.* □ 上个月我看了三个电影, 其中一个看了两遍。**Shàng ge yuè wǒ kànle sān ge diànyǐng, qízhōng yí ge kànle liǎng biàn.** *I saw three movies last month, one of which I saw twice.*
遍地 biàndì *n* everywhere

标 biāo Trad 標 *v* mark
标本 biāoběn *n* sample, specimen
采集标本 cǎijí biāoběn collect samples or specimen
标点 biāodiǎn [comp: 标 mark + 点 point] *n* punctuation mark
标点符号 biāodiǎn fúhào punctuation marks □ 你这个标点用得不对。**Nǐ zhège biāodiǎn yòng de bú duì.** *The punctuation mark you used is not correct.* (→ *You used a wrong punctuation mark.*) □ 我这里应该用什么标点? **Wǒ zhèlǐ yīnggāi yòng shénme biāodiǎn?** *Which punctuation mark should I use here?*
标题 biāotí [comp: 标 mark + 题 title] *n* title, heading
大标题 dà biāotí banner headline
标语 biāoyǔ [modif: 标 mark + 语 words] *n* slogan
标志 biāozhì [comp: 标 mark + 志 record] *n* sign, mark
社会地位的标志 shèhuì dìwèi de biāozhì status symbol
标准 biāozhǔn [comp: 标 standard + 准 accuracy] **I** *n* standard, criterion
符合标准 fúhé biāozhǔn conform to the standard □ 这些产品不符合标准, 不能出厂。**Zhèxiē chǎnpǐn bù fúhé biāozhǔn, bù néng chūchǎng.** *These products do not conform to the standard and cannot leave the factory.* (→ *These products do not meet the standard and cannot be shipped.*)
达到标准 dádào biāozhǔn reach the standard □ 你们的汉语水平达到什么标准? **Nǐmen de Hànyǔ shuǐpíng**

dádào shénme biāozhǔn? *What proficiency level has your Chinese reached?*
II *adj* standard, perfect □ 外国人说汉语发音不太标准, 问题不大; 在中国, 又有多少人说标准的普通话呢? **Wàiguórén shuō Hànyǔ fāyīn bú tài biāozhǔn, wèntí bú dà; zài Zhōngguó, yòu yǒu duōshǎo rén shuō biāozhǔn de Pǔtōnghuà ne?** *It doesn't matter if a foreigner doesn't speak Chinese with perfect pronunciation. After all, how many (mainland) Chinese speak perfect Putonghua?*

表 1 biǎo Trad 錶 *n* watch (块 **kuài**, 只 **zhī**) □ 我的表慢了一点。**Wǒ de biǎo màn le yìdiǎn.** *My watch is a bit slow.* □ 我的表停了, 你的表几点? **Wǒ de biǎo tíng le, nǐ de biǎo jǐ diǎn?** *My watch has stopped. What time is it by your watch?* □ 他戴了一块新表。**Tā dàile yí kuài xīn biǎo.** *He wears a new watch.*
男表 nán biǎo men's watch
女表 nǚ biǎo ladies' watch

表 2 biǎo *n* form (张 **zhāng**, 份 **fèn**) □ 这张表我不会填, 你能帮帮我吗? **Zhè zhāng biǎo wǒ bú huì tián, nǐ néng bāngbang wǒ ma?** *I don't know how to fill in this form. Could you help me?*

表 3 biǎo *v* express, show
表表心意 biǎobiǎo xīnyì show one's goodwill (or gratitude)
表达 biǎodá [comp: 表 express + 达 reach] *v* express (thoughts or emotions) □ 你能不能用简单的中文把意思表达清楚? **Nǐ néng bu néng yòng jiǎndān de Zhōngwén bǎ yìsi biǎodá qīngchu?** *Can you express the meaning clearly in simple Chinese?* □ 我当时的心情很复杂, 很难表达清楚。**Wǒ dāngshí de xīnqíng hěn fùzá, hěn nán biǎodá qīngchu.** *I had mixed feelings at that moment, it was difficult to express them clearly.*
表面 biǎomiàn [modif: 表 surface + 面 face] *n* surface □ 他表面上很友好, 其实完全不是这样。**Tā biǎomiàn shang hěn yǒuhǎo, qíshí wánquán búshì zhèyàng.** *He appears to be very friendly; actually he is not friendly at all.*
表面文章 biǎomiàn wénzhāng something done just for the show, pay lip service
表明 biǎomíng [v+compl: 表 express + 明 clear] *v* make clear, demonstrate □ 她一直不说话, 表明她其实不赞成。**Tā yìzhí bù shuōhuà, biǎomíng tā qíshí bú zànchéng.** *She was silent all the way, showing that actually she disapproved.* □ 我向他清楚地表明, 我们公司完全保证产品质量。**Wǒ xiàng tā qīngchu de biǎomíng, wǒmen gōngsī wánquán bǎozhèng chǎnpǐn zhìliàng.** *I made it very clear to him that our company completely guarantees the quality of our products.*
表情 biǎoqíng [modif: 表 surface + 情 feelings] *n* facial expression □ 从她的表情可以看出她的内心的感情吗? **Cóng tāde biǎoqíng kěyǐ kànchū tāde nèixīn de gǎnqíng ma?** *Can you tell the feelings in her heart from her facial expression?*
一付严肃的表情 yífù yánsù de biǎoqíng with a serious expression
表示 biǎoshì [comp: 表 show, express + 示 indicate] *v* express, show □ 一般点头表示同意, 摇头表示不同意。**Yìbān diǎntóu biǎoshì tóngyì, yáotóu biǎoshì bù tóngyì.** *Generally, nodding indicates agreement and shaking one's head indicates disagreement.* □ 他一

句话也没说, 表示不高兴。**Tā yí jù huà yě méi shuō, biǎoshì bù gāoxìng.** *He did not say a word, showing his displeasure.*

表现 **biǎoxiàn** [comp: 表 show, express + 现 display] *v* 1 display, show □ 他表现得很热情。**Tā biǎoxiàn de hěn rèqíng.** *He showed great enthusiasm.* 2 perform □ 新工人表现很好, 老板决定增加他的工资。**Xīn gōngrén biǎoxiàn hěn hǎo, lǎobǎn juédìng zēngjiā tā de gōngzī.** *The new worker performed well, and the boss decided to raise his wages.*

表演 **biǎoyǎn** [comp: 表 show + 演 act] **I** *v* put on (a show), perform, demonstrate □ 他们星期六在这里表演歌舞。**Tāmen Xīngqīliù zài zhèli biǎoyǎn gēwǔ.** *They perform singing and dancing here on Saturday.* **II** *n* performance, show (场 **cháng**)
参加表演 cānjiā biǎoyǎn participate in a performance/demonstration
看表演 kàn biǎoyǎn watch a performance □ 他们的表演很精彩。**Tāmen de biǎoyǎn hěn jīngcǎi.** *Their performance was wonderful.*

表扬 **biǎoyáng** [comp: 表 display + 扬 raise, make known] *v* praise, commend (antonym 批评 **pīpíng**) □ 他学习进步很大, 老师在班上表扬了他。**Tā xuéxí jìnbù hěn dà, lǎoshī zài bān shang biǎoyángle tā.** *He made great progress in his studies and the teacher praised him in class.*

表彰 **biǎozhāng** *v* commend, honor

憋 **biē** *v* suppress resentment with effort, contain oneself
憋不住 biē bu zhù cannot contain oneself, unable to hold oneself back

别 1 **bié** *adv* don't □ 别说话了, 电影开始了。**Bié shuōhuà le, diànyǐng kāishǐ le.** *Don't talk. (→ Stop talking.) The movie has started.* □ 你不愿意去, 就别去了。**Nǐ bú yuànyì qù, jiù bié qù le.** *If you don't want to go, then don't go.*

NOTE: 别 **bié** is a contraction of 不要 **búyào** in an imperative sentence. It is only used colloquially.

别 2 **bié** *pron* other, the other
别处 biéchù [modif: 别 other + 处 place] *n* other place(s), elsewhere
别的 biéde *pron* other □ 他大学毕业以后一直在教书, 没有做过别的工作。**Tā dàxué bìyè yǐhòu yìzhí zài jiāoshū, méiyǒu zuòguo biéde gōngzuò.** *He has been teaching since graduating from university and has not held any other job (← done any other work).*
别人 biérén [modif: 别 other + 人 person, people] *pron* other people, others □ 别人怎么说我不管, 只要你喜欢就行。**Biérén zěnme shuō wǒ bù guǎn, zhǐyào nǐ xǐhuan jiù xíng.** *I don't mind what others may say. It's OK as long as you like it.*
别字 biézì [modif: 别 other + 字 character, word] *n* a character which is not written or pronounced correctly

别 3 **bié** *n* farewell
告别 gàobié bid farewell

别 **biè** See 别扭 **bièniu**
别扭 bièniu *adj* awkward, uncomfortable □ 我感到挺别扭。**Wǒ gǎndao tǐng bièniu.** *I feel awkward. (→ I find the situation uncomfortable.)*

闹别扭 nào bièniu to be at odds with someone, to be difficult with someone; make difficulties for someone

宾 **bīn** Trad 賓 *n* guest
嘉宾 jiābīn distinguished guest, guest speaker
宾馆 bīnguǎn [modif: 宾 guest + 馆 house] *n* guesthouse □ 这是政府宾馆, 不对外开放。**Zhè shì zhèngfǔ bīnguǎn, bú duì wài kāifàng.** *This is a government guesthouse. It is not open to the public.*

滨 **bīn** Trad 濱 *n* shore, bank
海滨 hǎibīn seashore

冰 **bīng** *n* ice □ 水到零度就结成冰。**Shuǐ dào líng dù jiù jiéchéng bīng.** *Water freezes to ice at 0°C.*
冰棍儿 bīnggùnr [modif: 冰 ice + 棍儿 stick] *n* flavored popsicle
冰淇淋 bīngqílín [modif: 冰 ice + 淇淋 cream (transliteration)] *n* ice cream
冰箱 bīngxiāng [modif: 冰 ice + 箱 box] *n* refrigerator □ 冰箱里没有什么东西, 看来得出去吃晚饭了。**Bīngxiāng lǐ méiyǒu shénme dōngxi, kànlái děi chūqu chī wǎnfàn le.** *There isn't much in the fridge. Looks like we'll have to dine out.*
电冰箱 diàn bīngxiāng refrigerator

兵 **bīng** *n* soldier
当兵 dāng bīng be a soldier, serve in the armed forces □ 她哥哥在部队当兵。**Tā gēge zài bùduì dāng bīng.** *Her brother is serving in the armed forces.*

饼 **bǐng** Trad 餅 *n* cake (只 **zhī**)
大饼 dàbǐng sesame cake (a breakfast food)
烙饼 làobǐng pancake
月饼 yuèbǐng mooncake (for the Mid-Autumn Festival)
饼干 bǐnggān [modif: 饼 cake + 干 dried food] *n* cookie(s), biscuit(s) (片 **piàn**, 包 **bāo**) □ 他肚子饿了, 就吃饼干。**Tā dùzi è le, jiù chī bǐnggān.** *He ate some biscuits when he was hungry.*
一包饼干 yì bāo bǐnggān a package of cookies
一片饼干 yí piàn bǐnggān a cookie

丙 **bǐng** *n* the third of the "Celestial Stems," the third

柄 **bǐng** *n* handle, stem

秉 **bǐng** *v* hold in hand

并 **bìng** Trad 並 **I** *adv* (used before a negative word for emphasis) □ 事情并不像你想象的那么简单。**Shìqing bìng bú xiàng nǐ xiǎngxiàng de nàme jiǎndān.** *Things are not at all as simple as you imagine.* □ 他并不是没有试过, 但是不成功。**Tā bìng bú shì méiyǒu shìguò, dànshì bù chénggōng.** *It was not the case that he never tried, but that he was not successful.* **II** *conj* Same as 并且 **bìngqiě**. Used only in written Chinese. **III** *v* combine, incorporate

NOTE: 并 **bìng** is used to emphasize the negation. It is not grammatically essential; without 并 **bìng** the sentences still stand. The following is perfectly acceptable: □ 事情不象你想象的那么简单。**Shìqing bú xiàng nǐ xiǎngxiàng de nàme jiǎndān.** *Things are not as simple as you imagine.*

并存 **bìngcún** [modif: 并 combine + 存 exist] *v* co-exist

并非 bìngfēi *adv* not, not at all
并非如此 bìngfēi rúcǐ not like that
并排 bìngpái *v* be side by side, be abreast with
并且 bìngqiě *conj* moreover, what's more, and □ 技术员发现并且解决了问题。**Jìshùyuán fāxiàn bìngqiě jiějué wèntí.** *The technician discovered the problem and solved it.* (← *The technician discovered the problem; what's more, he solved it.*) □ 他去机场接朋友, 并且带他游览市区。**Tā qù jīchǎng jiē péngyou, bìngqiě dài tā yóulǎn shìqū.** *He met his friend at the airport and took him on a sightseeing trip of the city.*

病 bìng I *v* fall ill, be ill □ 我爸爸病了, 在家休息。**Wǒ bàba bìng le, zài jiā xiūxi.** *My father's ill and is taking a rest at home.* □ 他病得很重, 得住院。**Tā bìng de hěn zhòng, děi zhùyuàn.** *He is seriously ill and needs to be hospitalized.* II *n* illness, disease
肺病 fèibìng lung disease, tuberculosis
急性病 jíxìngbìng acute disease
慢性病 mànxìngbìng chronic disease
生病 shēng bìng to fall ill □ 他生什么病? **Tā shēng shénme bìng?** *What is he ill with?* (→ *What's wrong with him?*) □ 这一点儿小病, 没关系。**Zhè yìdiǎnr xiǎo bìng, méi guānxi.** *This is a mild case (of illness); it doesn't matter.*
病床 bìngchuáng [modif: 病 sick + 床 bed] *n* hospital bed
病虫害 bìngchónghài [modif: 病 disease + 虫 insect + 害 disaster] *n* plant diseases and insect pests
病毒 bìngdù [modif: 病 disease + 毒 poison] *n* virus
电脑病毒 diànnǎo bìngdù computer virus
病房 bìngfáng [modif: 病 sickness + 房 room] *n* (hospital) ward □ 医生每天上午十点查病房。**Yīshēng měitiān shàngwǔ shí diǎn chá bìngfáng.** *The doctors make their rounds of the wards at ten o'clock every morning.*
小儿科病房 xiǎo'érkē bìngfáng pediatrics ward
重病房 zhòngbìngfáng intensive care ward
病假 bìng jià sick leave
请病假 qǐng bìngjià ask for/apply for sick leave □ 她请了三天病假。**Tā qǐngle sāntiān bìngjià.** *She asked for three days' sick leave.*
病菌 bìngjūn [modif: 病 disease + 菌 germ] *n* pathogenic bacteria
病情 bìngqíng [modif: 病 disease + 情 situation] *n* patient's conditions
病人 bìngrén [modif: 病 sick + 人 person] *n* patient □ 病人要听医生的嘱咐。**Bìngrén yào tīng yīshēng de zhǔfu.** *Patients should take their doctors' advice.*
门诊病人 ménzhěn bìngrén outpatient
住院病人 zhùyuàn bìngrén inpatient (warded patient)
病史 bìngshǐ [modif: 病 sick + 史 history] *n* medical record
剥 bō *v* peel, strip
波 bō *n* ripple, wave
波动 bōdòng *v* fluctuate (like a wave)
情绪波动 qíngxù bōdòng constantly changing moods
波浪 bōlàng [comp: 波 ripple + 浪 wave] *n* wave
波涛 bōtāo [comp: 波 wave + 涛 billow] *n* high wave
汹涌波涛 xiōngyǒng bōtāo roaring waves
玻 bō *n* glass
玻璃 bōli *n* glass □ 大楼的正面全部是玻璃。**Dàlóu**

de zhèngmiàn quánbù shì bōli. *The front of the big building is all covered by glass.*
玻璃杯 bōlibēi glass
玻璃窗 bōlichuāng glass window, glass pane

菠 bō *n* spinach
菠菜 bōcài spinach

播 bō *v* 1 sow 2 broadcast
播放 bōfàng [comp: 播 sow + 放 release] *v* broadcast (radio or TV programs)
播送 bōsòng [comp: 播 sow + 送 deliver] *v* broadcast (radio programs)
播音 bōyīn [v+obj: 播 sow + 音 sound] *v* broadcast (radio programs)
播音员 bōyīnyuán newsreader
播种 bōzhòng [comp: 播 sow + 种 plant] *v* sow seeds

拨 bō Trad 撥 *v* 1 stir with a finger or stick 2 allocate
拨款 bōkuǎn [v+obj: 拨 allocate + 款 funds] *v* allocate funds, appropriate (money)

伯 bó *n* Same as 伯父 bófù
伯父 bófù *n* father's elder brother □ 伯父只比爸爸大两岁, 但是看来比爸爸老得多。**Bófù zhǐ bǐ bàba dà liǎng suì, dànshì kànlái bǐ bàba lǎo de duō.** *My father's elder brother is only two years older than he, but looks much older.*

NOTE: 伯父 **bófù** is also a form of address for men older than your father but not old enough to be your grandfather. The colloquialism for 伯父 **bófù** is 伯伯 **bóbo**.

伯母 bómǔ *n* father's elder brother's wife □ 我的伯父伯母住在香港。**Wǒ de bófù bómǔ zhù zài Xiānggǎng.** *My uncle* (← *father's elder brother*) *and aunt* (*his wife*) *live in Hong Kong.*

NOTE: 伯母 **bómǔ** is also a form of address for women older than your mother but not old enough to be your grandmother. It is generally used by well-educated urban Chinese.

勃 bó *adj* vigorous
舶 bó *n* ship
泊 bó *v* (of ships) anchor, moor
驳 bó Trad 駁 *v* refute
驳斥 bóchì [comp: 驳 refute + 斥 tongue-lash] *v* refute, rebut
脖 bó *n* neck
脖子 bózi neck □ 我的脖子扭伤了。**Wǒ de bózi niǔ shāng le.** *My neck was sprained.*
博 bó *adj* 1 plentiful, abundant 2 wide, extensive
博客 bókè *n* blogger
博客论坛 bókè lùntán blog

NOTE: 博客 **bókè** is a transliteration of *blogger*. To blog, i.e. write as a blogger, is 写博 **xiě bó**.

博览会 bólǎnhuì [modif: 博 plentiful, extensive + 览 view + 会 meeting] *n* exposition, exhibition, fair

世界博览会 shìjiè bólǎnhuì World Exposition, World Expo

博士 bóshì [modif: 博 erudite + 士 scholar] *n* doctor, Ph.D. □ 张博士是一位中国著名的生物化学家。**Zhāng bóshì shì yíwèi Zhōngguó zhùmíng de shēngwùhuàxuéjiā.** *Dr Zhang is a well-known biochemist in China.*

博士生 bóshìshēng Ph.D. candidate
博士生导师 bóshìshēng dǎoshī Ph.D. supervisor
博士后 bóshìhòu post-doctorate
博士学位 bóshì xuéwèi Ph.D. degree

博物馆 bówùguǎn [modif: 博物 natural science + 馆 building] *n* museum
历史博物馆 lìshǐ bówùguǎn museum of history

膊 bó *n* arm (See 胳膊 **gēbo**)

搏 bó *v* be engaged in a hand-to-hand combat, fight
搏斗 bódòu [comp: 搏 fight + 斗 fight] *v* battle, wrestle

薄 bó *adj* meager, small (antonym 厚 **hòu**)
一份薄礼 yí fèn bó lǐ an insignificant gift

NOTE: The character 薄 has two pronunciations: **báo** and **bó**. While 薄 **báo** is used to describe material "thin-ness," (eg. 一条薄被子 **yì tiáo báo bèizi** *a thin blanket*), 薄 **bó** is used in a figurative sense. See 薄 **báo** for examples.

薄膜 bómó [modif: 薄 thin + 膜 membrane, film] *n* membrane, film
薄弱 bóruò [comp: 薄 thin + 弱 weak] *adj* frail, weak

簸 bǒ *v* jerk (See 颠簸 **diānbǒ**)

卜 bo Trad 蔔 (See 萝卜 **luóbo**)

捕 bǔ *v* catch, arrest
捕捞 bǔlāo [comp: 捕 catch + 捞 fish for] *v* catch (fish)

卜 bǔ *v* divine, predict
未卜先知 wèi bǔ xiān zhī have foresight, foresee

补 bǔ Trad 補 *v* mend, patch □ 衣服破了, 补一下还能穿。**Yīfu pò le, bǔ yíxià hái néng chuān.** *The coat is torn, but mend it and it can still be worn.*

补偿 bǔcháng [comp: 补 mend + 偿 compensate] *v* compensate, make up
补充 bǔchōng [comp: 补 supplement + 充 fill up] *v* make up, supplement □ 刚才小李谈了这个问题, 我想补充几句。**Gāngcái Xiǎo Lǐ tánle zhège wèntí, wǒ xiǎng bǔchōng jǐ jù.** *Just now Xiao Li spoke of this problem. I'd like to add a few points.*
补救 bǔjiù [comp: 补 mend + 救 rescue] *v* remedy
补救办法 bǔjiù bànfǎ corrective measure, remedial measure
补课 bǔkè [v+obj: 补 make up + 课 lessons] *v* make up for missed lessons □ 上星期一王老师开会, 没有上课, 今天下午补课。**Shàng Xīngqīyī Wáng lǎoshī kāihuì, méiyǒu shàngkè, jīntiān xiàwǔ bǔkè.** *Last Monday Teacher Wang had a meeting and missed a class. He will make up for it this afternoon.*
补贴 bǔtiē [comp: 补 patch + 贴 paste] **I** *n* subsidy **II** *v* subsidize

补习 bǔxí *v* take or give supplementary lessons □ 他英文不行, 妈妈给他请家庭教师补习。**Tā Yīngwén bù xíng, māma gěi tā qǐng jiātíng jiàoshī bǔxí.** *He is poor at English, and his mother hired a home tutor to give him extra lessons.*
补习班 bǔxíbān (after school) class
补助 bǔzhù [comp: 补 mend + 助 aid] *n* subsidy, grant-in-aid

不 bù *adv* no, not □ 今天不冷。**Jīntiān bù lěng.** *It's not cold today.* □ 你说得不对。**Nǐ shuō de bú duì.** *You're not correct.* □ "你是美国人吗?" "不, 我是加拿大人。" **"Nǐ shì Měiguórén ma?" "Bù, wǒ shì Jiānádàrén."** *"Are you an American?" "No, I'm a Canadian."*

NOTE: When followed by a syllable in the fourth (falling) tone, 不 undergoes tone change (tone sandhi) from the normal fourth tone to the second (rising) tone, e.g. 不对 **búduì**, 不是 **búshì**.

不必 búbì [modif: 不 not + 必 necessary] *adv* need not, not have to, unnecessarily □ 你不必送这么贵重的礼物。**Nǐ búbì sòng zhème guìzhòng de lǐwù.** *You don't have to give such an expensive gift.* □ 孩子会很快恢复健康的, 你完全不必担心。**Háizi huì hěn kuài huīfù jiànkāng de, nǐ wánquán búbì dānxīn.** *The child will recover very soon. You really don't have to worry.*
不比 bùbǐ *v* unlike
不辞而别 bù cí ér bié *idiom* leave without saying good-bye, take French leave
不错 búcuò [modif: 不 not + 错 wrong] *adj* **1** not wrong □ 你告诉我的电话号码不错。**Nǐ gàosu wǒ de diànhuà hàomǎ bú cuò.** *The telephone number you gave (←told) me is correct.* **2** quite right, not bad, quite good □ 这个电影不错。**Zhè ge diànyǐng búcuò.** *This movie is rather good.* □ 这孩子画得真不错。**Zhè háizi huà de zhēn búcuò.** *This child really doesn't draw badly.* (→ *This child draws quite well.*)

NOTE: …得不错 ...de búcuò is ambiguous. It may mean either ... *correctly* or ... *rather well.* For example, the sentence 你说得不错。**Nǐ shuō de búcuò.** may mean either *You spoke correctly.* (→ *You're right.*) or *You spoke quite well.* (→ *Well said.*)

不大 búdà *adv* not very, not much □ 今天不大热。**Jīntiān búdà rè.** *Today is not very hot.* □ 我不大喜欢吃日本菜。**Wǒ búdà xǐhuan chī Rìběncài.** *I'm not very fond of Japanese food.*
不但 búdàn *conj* not only ... (but also)
…不但…, 而且 ...búdàn..., érqiě *conj* not only ..., but also ... □ 我爸爸不但会开车, 而且会修车。**Wǒ bàba búdàn huì kāi chē, érqiě huì xiū chē.** *My daddy can not only drive but also fix cars.* □ 这个电脑游戏不但小孩爱玩, 而且大人也爱玩。**Zhège diànnǎo yóuxì búdàn xiǎohái ài wán, érqiě dàren yě ài wán.** *Not only children but also grownups like to play this electronic game.* □ 这家饭店的菜不但好吃, 而且好看。**Zhè jiā fàndiàn de cài búdàn hǎochī, érqiě hǎokàn.** *The dishes in this restaurant are not only delicious but also beautiful.* □ 她不但唱歌唱得好听, 而且跳舞跳得好看。**Tā búdàn chànggē chàng de hǎotīng, érqiě tiàowǔ tiào de**

de hǎokàn. *She not only sings beautifully, but also dances gracefully.*

不当 **búdàng** [modif: 不 not + 当 appropriate] *adj* improper, unsuitable

不得不 **bùdébù** *adv* have to, have no choice but □ 我做错了题目，不得不重做。 **Wǒ zuòcuòle tímù, bùdébù chóng zuò.** *I did the wrong question [for a school assignment] and had to do it all over again.* □ 这个星期去上海的飞机票全部卖完了，我们不得不改到下星期去。 **Zhège xīngqī qù Shànghǎi de fēijīpiào quánbù màiwán le, wǒmen bùdébù gǎi dào xià xīngqī qù.** *This week's air tickets to Shanghai are sold out, so we have no choice but to change our departure date to next week.*

不得了 **bùdéliǎo** I *adj* horrible, extremely serious □ 不得了了，对面房子着火了! **Bùdéliǎo le, duìmiàn fángzi zháohuǒ le!** *How terrible, the house opposite is on fire!* □ 你没有什么不得了的事，就别麻烦朋友了。 **Nǐ méiyǒu shénme bùdéliǎo de shì, jiù bié máfan péngyou le.** *If it isn't anything really serious, don't bother your friends.* II *adv* extremely (used after an adjective and introduced by 得 **de**) □ 昨天热得不得了。 **Zuótiān rè de bùdéliǎo.** *It was extremely hot yesterday.* □ 爬那座雪山危险得不得了，你们非充分准备不可。 **Pá nà zuò xuěshān wēixiǎn de bùdéliǎo, nǐmen fēi chōngfèn zhǔnbèi bùkě.** *It is extremely dangerous to climb that snowy mountain. You must be well prepared.*

不得已 **bùdéyǐ** *adj* having no alternative but to ..., acting against one's will □ 非到不得已的时候，不能用这笔钱。 **Fēidào bùdéyǐ de shíhou, bú néng yòng zhè bi qián.** *You're not allowed to use this money, unless you really have to.*

不等 **bùděng** [modif: 不 not + 等 equal] *v* vary, differ

不定 **búdìng** [modif: 不 not + 定 definite] *adj* indefinite, not sure

不断 **búduàn** [modif: 不 not + 断 interrupt] *adv* without interruption, continuously, incessantly □ 只有不断努力，才能永远进步。 **Zhǐyǒu búduàn nǔlì, cái néng yǒngyuǎn jìnbù.** *Only by continuous efforts can one make progress forever.*

不法 **bùfǎ** [modif: 不 not + 法 legal] *adj* illegal, lawless

不法分子 **bùfǎ fènzi** criminal

不法行为 **bùfǎ xíngwei** illegal act, illegal practice

不妨 **bùfáng** *adv* might as well □ 你不妨试试针灸，看看有没有效果。 **Nǐ bùfáng shìshi zhēnjiǔ, kànkan yóuméiyǒu xiàoguǒ.** *You might as well try acupuncture to see if it is efficacious.*

不敢当 **bùgǎndāng** *idiom* Thank you, I don't dare to accept (a polite/modest reply to a compliment) □ "您中文说得很标准。" "不敢当，还要不断练习。" **"Nín Zhōngwén shuō de hěn biāozhǔn." "Bùgǎndāng, háiyào búduàn liànxí."** *"You speak standard Chinese. (→ Your Chinese is perfect.)" "Thank you very much. I still need constant practice."* □ "您对这个问题分析得极其深刻。" "不敢当，您对这个问题有什么看法?" **"Nín duì zhège wèntí fēnxī de jíqí shēnkè." "Bùgǎndāng, nín duì zhège wèntí yǒu shénme kànfǎ?"** *"You've made a penetrating analysis of this problem." "I don't deserve such praise. What's your view on this matter?"*

不公 **bùgōng** [modif: 不 not + 公 fair] *adj* unfair, unjust

不够 **búgòu** [modif: 不 not + 够 enough] *adj* not enough, insufficient

不顾 **búgù** [modif: 不 not + 顾 attend to] I *v* disregard II *prep* in spite of

不管 **bùguǎn** *conj* no matter (what, who, how, etc.) □ 不管你在那里看到他，他都带着他的小狗。 **Bùguǎn nǐ zài nǎlǐ kàndào tā, tā dōu dàizhe tā de xiǎo gǒu.** *No matter where you see him, he is with his puppy.* □ 不管你明天来不来，都给我一个电话。 **Bùguǎn nǐ míngtiān lái bu lái, dōu gěi wǒ yí ge diànhuà.** *Whether you come or not tomorrow, give me a call.* □ 不管他多么忙，他总是每天给妈妈发一份电子邮件。 **Bùguǎn tā duōme máng, tā zǒngshì měi tiān gěi māma fā yí fèn diànzǐ yóujiàn.** *No matter how busy he is, he always sends his mother a daily e-mail.*

NOTE: 不管 **bùguǎn** may be replaced by 不论 **búlùn** or 无论 **wúlùn**, but 不管 **bùguǎn** is more colloquial.

不过 **búguò** *conj* Same as 但是 **dànshì**. Used colloquially.

不好意思 **bù hǎoyìsi** *idiom* I'm embarrassed (a polite phrase used when you are offering an apology, giving a gift, or receiving a gift or other acts of kindness) □ 不好意思，我又迟到了。 **Bù hǎoyìsi, wǒ yòu chídào le.** *I'm sorry I'm late again.* □ 又让你送我礼物，真不好意思。 **Yòu ràng nǐ sòng wǒ lǐwù, zhēn bù hǎoyìsi.** *Oh, you gave me a gift again, it's embarrassing.* □ 这点小礼物，请您收下，不好意思。 **Zhè diǎn xiǎo lǐwù, qǐng nín shōuxià, bù hǎoyìsi.** *Please accept this little present.*

NOTE: 不好意思 **bù hǎoyìsi** literally means *I'm embarrassed*. It is easy to understand why you say it when you are apologizing or receiving a gift. When you are giving a gift, however, you also say it to imply that the gift is so insignificant that you feel embarrassed about it.

不见 **bújiàn** [modif: 不 not + 见 see] *v* disappear, be lost

不见得 **bú jiàndé** *adv* not necessarily, unlikely □ 这位医生的诊断不见得对，你最好再看另一位医生。 **Zhè wèi yīshēng de zhěnduàn bújiàndé duì, nǐ zuìhǎo zài kàn lìngyí wèi yīshēng.** *This doctor's diagnosis is not necessarily correct, you've better see another one.*

不禁 **bùjīn** *adv* cannot help oneself from, cannot refrain from

不仅 **bùjǐn** *conj* Same as 不但 **búdàn**. Tends to be used in writing.

不久 **bùjiǔ** *adv* not long afterwards, in the near future, soon □ 他们不久就要回国了。 **Tāmen bùjiǔ jiù yào huíguó le.** *They're returning to their country soon.*

不堪 **bùkān** I *v* cannot bear, cannot stand

不堪设想 **bùkān shèxiǎng** (of consequences) too serious to face, very bad II *adv* (used after an adjective) utterly

混乱不堪 **hùnluàn bùkān** in utter chaos

不愧 **búkuì** [modif: 不 not + 愧 be ashamed] *v* be worthy of, deserve to be called

不利 **búlì** [modif: 不 not + 利 beneficial] *adj* unfavorable, disadvantageous

不料 **búliào** *adv* unexpectedly □ 公司以为这个新产品会很受欢迎，不料销路很差。 **Gōngsī yǐwéi zhège**

xīnchǎnpǐn huì hěn shòu huānyíng, búliào xiāolù hěn chà. *The company thought the new product would be popular; unexpectedly sales were poor.*

不论 búlùn *conj* Same as 不管 **bùguǎn**. Used more in writing.

不满 bùmǎn [modif: 不 not + 满 satisfied] *adj* Same as 不满意 **bùmǎnyì** dissatisfied

不免 bùmiǎn *adv* unavoidable, inevitable, would only be natural

不平 bùpíng [modif: 不 not + 平 fair] *n* injustice, resentment □ 不平则鸣 **Bù píng zé míng** *Where there is injustice, there will be an outcry.*

不然 bùrán *conj* otherwise, or □ 你别说了，不然我真要生气了。**Nǐ bié shuō le, bùrán wǒ zhēn yào shēngqì le.** *Don't say any more, or I'll really be angry.* □ 他一定遇到了非常麻烦的事，不然情绪不会这么坏。**Tā yídìng yùdàole fēicháng máfan de shì, bùrán qíngxù bú huì zhème huài.** *He must have gotten into big trouble, otherwise he wouldn't be in such a bad mood.*

NOTE: To be more emphatic, you can use 不然的话 **bùrán de huà** instead of 不然 **bùrán**.

不容 bùróng [modif: 不 not + 容 tolerate] *v* not tolerate, not allow

不如 bùrú *v* be not as good as, not as ... as □ 走路不如骑车快。**Zǒulù bùrú qíchē kuài.** *Walking is not as fast as riding a bicycle.* □ 我体育不如你，但是你功课不如我。**Wǒ tǐyù bùrú nǐ, dànshì nǐ gōngkè bùrú wǒ.** *I'm not as good as you are in sports, but you're not as good as me in academic work.*

不少 bùshǎo [modif: 不 not + 少 few, little] *adj* quite a few □ 我在这个城市有不少好朋友。**Wǒ zài zhège chéngshì yǒu bùshǎo hǎo péngyou.** *I have quite a few good friends in this city.* □ 我做了不少解释，她还是不原谅我。**Wǒ zuòle bùshǎo jiěshì, tā háishì bù yuánliàng wǒ.** *I have given many explanations, but she still won't forgive me.*

不是 búshì *n* fault, blame □ 那是我的不是，不能怪你。**Nàshì wǒde bú shì, bùnéng guài nǐ.** *It's my fault; you're not to blame.*

不是…而是… bú shì...ér shì... *conj* not ... but ... □ 他不是美国人，而是加拿大人。**Tā bú shì Měiguórén, ér shì Jiānádàrén.** *He is not an American, but a Canadian.*

不是…就是… bú shì...jiùshì... *conj* either ... or ... □ 他不是美国人，就是加拿大人。**Tā bú shì Měiguórén, jiùshì Jiānádàrén.** *He is either an American or a Canadian.*

不时 bùshí *adv* now and then, from time to time

不停 bùtíng [modif: 不 not + 停 stop] *adv* without letup, incessantly □ 雨不停地下了两天。**Yǔ bùtíng de xiàle liǎng tiān.** *It rained for two days without any letup.*

不同 bùtóng [modif: 不 not + 同 same] *adj* not the same, different □ 人和人不同，不能比较。**Rén hé rén bùtóng, bù néng bǐjiào.** *People are different and cannot be compared.* □ 这两个字发音相同，写法不同，意思也不同。**Zhè liǎng ge zì fāyīn xiāngtóng, xiěfǎ bùtóng, yìsi yě bùtóng.** *These two characters have the same pronunciation but they are different in writing and meaning.*

…和/跟…不同 **...hé/gēn...bùtóng ...** is/are different from .... □ 我的意见跟他的意见不同。**Wǒ de yìjiàn gēn tā de yìjiàn bùtóng.** *My opinion is different from his.*

不惜 bù xī [modif: 不 not + 惜 grudge] *v* not hesitate, not spare

不惜工本 **bù xī gōngběn** spare neither labor or money, spare no expense

不像话 búxiànghuà *adj* totally unreasonable, outrageous

不相上下 bù xiāng shàng xià *idiom* equally matched, be as good as

不幸 búxìng [modif: 不 not + 幸 fortunate] *adj* unfortunate □ 这次交通事故死了一人，伤了三人，真是一件不幸的事。**Zhè cì jiāotōng shìgù sǐle yì rén, shāngle sān rén, zhēn shì yí jiàn búxìng de shì.** *One person died and three others were injured in this road accident, which is indeed an unfortunate event.*

NOTE: 不幸 **búxìng** is used to describe serious events or matters, often involving death. Do not use 不幸 **búxìng** for trivial matters. For example, even though in English it is acceptable to say, "Unfortunately, I haven't seen the film," in Chinese it would be wrong to say 我不幸没有看过那个电影。**Wǒ búxìng méiyǒu kànguo nàge diànyǐng.**

不行 bùxíng *adj* 1 will not do, not allowed □ "妈妈，这个周末我带十几个同学来家里玩，行不行？" "不行。" **"Māma, zhège zhōumò wǒ dài shí jǐ ge tóngxué lái jiālǐ wán, xíng bu xíng?" "Bù xíng."** *"Mom, may I bring a dozen classmates home for a party this weekend?" "No, you may not."* 2 not (be) good (at ...) □ 我的中文不行，请你多多帮助。**Wǒ de Zhōngwén bù xíng, qǐng nǐ duōduō bāngzhù.** *My Chinese is not good. Please help me.* □ 他体育很好，但是功课不行。**Tā tǐyù hěn hǎo, dànshì gōngkè bùxíng.** *He is good at sports, but poor at schoolwork.*

不朽 bùxiǔ [modif: 不 not + 朽 rot] *adj* immortal

不许 bùxǔ *v* not permitted, not allowed □ 不许逃学。**Bùxǔ táo xué.** *Truancy is not allowed.* □ 爸爸不许她和那个男孩出去玩。**Bàba bùxǔ tā hé nèi ge nán hái chūqu wán.** *Father does not allow her to go out with that boy.*

不言而喻 bù yán ér yù *idiom* it goes without saying it is self-evident

不要 búyào *adv* (used in an imperative sentence or as advice) do not □ 你们不要说话了，电影开始了。**Nǐmen búyào shuōhuà le, diànyǐng kāishǐ le.** *Please don't talk any more. The movie has started.* □ 你不要着急，你孩子的病很快会好的。**Nǐ búyào zháojí, nǐ háizi de bìng hěnkuài huì hǎo de.** *Don't you worry, your child will recover soon.*

NOTE: See note on 别 **bié**.

不宜 bùyí [modif: 不 not + 宜 suitable] *adv* unsuitable □ 这部电影儿童不宜。**Zhè bù diànyǐng értóng bùyí.** *This film is not suitable for chidren.* (→ This is an adult movie.)

不用 búyòng *adv* no need, there's no need, don't have to □ 如果你明天不舒服，就不用来了。**Rúguǒ nǐ míngtiān bù shūfu, jiù búyòng lái le.** *If you're not well*

tomorrow, you don't have to come. □ 不用麻烦了，我们一会儿就走。**Búyòng máfan le, wǒmen yíhuìr jiù zǒu.** *Don't bother. We'll be leaving soon.*

不由得 **bù yóude** *adv* cannot but, cannot help

不在乎 **búzàihu** *v* not mind, not care

满不在乎 **mǎn búzàihu** not care at all, couldn't care less □ 他这个学期考试门门不及格，但是他还是满不在乎。**Tā zhège xuéqī kǎoshì ménmén bù jígé, dànshì tā háishi mǎnbúzàihu.** *He failed in every subject this semester, but he couldn't care less.*

不怎么样 **bù zěnmeyàng** *adv* not up to too much, not very

不止 **bùzhǐ** *adv* more than, not limited to

不只 **bùzhǐ** *adv* not only

不至于 **búzhìyú** *adv* not as far as, not so bad as

不足 **bùzú** [modif: 不 not + 足 sufficient] *adj* inadequate, insufficient

资金不足 zījīn bùzú insufficient funds

布 1 **bù** *n* cotton or linen cloth (块 **kuài**, 片 **piàn**) □ 这块布很好看，做裙子正合适。**Zhè kuài bù hěn hǎokàn, zuò qúnzi zhèng héshì.** *This piece of cotton cloth looks good, it is just right for a skirt.*

棉布 **miánbù** cotton cloth, cotton material

布 2 **bù** Trad 佈 *v* arrange, deploy

布告 **bùgào** [comp: 布 deploy + 告 announce] **I** *v* announce publicly **II** *n* public announcement, bulletin

布局 **bùjú** layout, overall arrangement

布置 **bùzhì** *v* decorate, furnish □ 他们马上要结婚了，这几天正在布置新房。**Tāmen mǎshàng yào jiēhūn le, zhè jǐ tiān zhèngzài bùzhì xīnfáng.** *They're getting married soon and are decorating their new home these days.*

埠 **bù** *n* dock, port

步 **bù** *n* step, pace □ 走几步就到了，不用开车。**Zǒu jǐ bù jiù dào le, bú yòng kāi chē.** *It's just a few steps away. There's no need to drive.*

步子 **bùzi** step, pace

下一步 xià yí bù the next step, the next stage

步兵 **bùbīng** [modif: 步 step + 兵 soldier] *n* infantry, infantryman

步伐 **bùfá** *n* step, pace

步骤 **bùzhòu** *n* procedure, steps □ 她没有按照步骤关电脑，结果死机了。**Tā méiyǒu ànzhào bùzhòu guān diànnǎo, jiéguǒ sǐjī le.** *She didn't follow the procedures to shut down the computer and, as a result, it crashed.*

怖 **bù** *v* fear (See 恐怖 **kǒngbù**)

部 **bù** *n* part, unit

部队 **bùduì** *n* troops, the army □ 部队是锻炼年轻人的好地方。**Bùduì shì duànliàn niánqīngrén de hǎo dìfang.** *The army is a good place to toughen up young people.*

部分 **bùfen** [comp: 部 part + 分 division] *n* portion, part □ 中国的中学分初中和高中两部分。**Zhōngguó de zhōngxué fēn chūzhōng hé gāozhōng liǎng bùfen.** *Chinese high schools consist of junior high and senior high schools.*

大部分 dà bùfen most of ..., the majority of ...

部件 **bùjiàn** *n* component, part

部门 **bùmén** [comp: 部 department + 门 gate, door] *n* department □ 他们虽然都在市政府工作，但是在不同的部门，相互不熟悉。**Tāmen suīrán dōu zài shì zhèngfǔ gōngzuò, dànshì zài bùtóng de bùmén, xiānghù bù shúxi.** *Although they both work in the city government, they work in different departments and do not know each other well.*

部署 **bùshǔ** **I** *v* map out, deploy **II** *n* plan

部位 **bùwèi** *n* in position, location

部长 **bùzhǎng** [modif: 部 ministry + 长 chief, the person in charge] *n* (government) minister

教育部长 jiàoyù bùzhǎng minister of education

外交部长 wàijiāo bùzhǎng minister of foreign affairs, foreign minister

C

擦 **cā** *v* clean or erase by wiping or rubbing □ 窗户脏了，要擦一下。**Chuānghu zāng le, yào cā yíxià.** *The window is dirty and needs cleaning.* □ 每个星期一他去公司上班前，总要把皮鞋擦得很亮。**Měi ge Xīngqīyī tā qù gōngsī shàngbān qián, zǒngyào ba píxié cā de hěn liàng.** *Every Monday before he goes to work in his company, he will polish his shoes.* □ 我的自行车太脏了，我要把它擦干净。**Wǒ de zìxíngchē tài zāng le, wǒ yào ba tā cā gānjing.** *My bike is dirty. I'll wipe it clean.*

猜 **cāi** *v* guess □ "谁来了？你猜猜看。" "我猜不着。告诉我吧。" **"Shéi lái le? Nǐ cāicai kàn." "Wǒ cāi bu zháo. Gàosu wǒ ba."** *"Guess who's come?" "I can't. Just tell me."*

猜测 **cāicè** [comp: 猜 guess + 测 measure] *v* guess, conjecture

猜想 **cāixiǎng** [comp: 猜 guess + 想 think] *v* suppose, conjecture

才 1 **cái** Trad 纔 *adv* 1 (before a verb) a short time ago, just □ 我才来，不知道这件事。**Wǒ cái lái, bù zhīdào zhè jiàn shì.** *I've just arrived and don't know anything about this matter.* □ 我才认识他，对他还不了解。**Wǒ cái rènshi tā, duì tā hái bù liǎojiě.** *I came to know him not long ago, and I don't know him very well.* 2 (used before a word of time or quantity to indicate that the speaker feels the time is too early, too short or the quantity is too little), only, as early as, as few/little as □ 我学中文才一年，说得不好。**Wǒ xué Zhōngwén cái yì nián, shuō de bù hǎo.** *I've learned Chinese for only one year, and can't speak it very well.* □ 这本书才十块钱，太便宜了。**Zhè běn shū cái shí kuài qián, tài piányi le.** *This book is only ten dollars. It's really cheap.* 3 (used after a word of time to indicate that the speaker feels the time is too late or there is too much delay) as late as □ 这个小孩三岁才会走。**Zhège xiǎo hái sānsuì cái huì zǒu.** *This child learned to walk as late as three years old.* □ 妈妈等到孩子都回来了才睡觉。**Māma děngdào háizi dōu huílai le, cái shuìjiào.** *Mother did not go to bed until all her children came home.*

才 2 **cái** *n* talent, remarkable ability

才干 **cáigàn** *n* talent, competence

有才干 yǒu cáigàn capable and talented

才能 **cáinéng** [comp: 才 talent + 能 ability] *n* talent, ability

才智 **cáizhì** [comp: 才 talent + 智 intelligence] *n* talent and high intelligence, ability and wisdom

财 **cái** Trad 財 *n* wealth, property

财产 **cáichǎn** [comp: 财 property, fortune + 产 property] *n* property, belongings

个人财产 gèrén cáichǎn private property, personal belongings

财富 **cáifù** [comp: 财 property, fortune + 富 riches] *n* wealth, fortune

财经 **cáijīng** [comp: 财 finance + 经 economy] *n* finance and economy

财会 **cáikuài** [comp: 财 finance + 会 accounting] *n* finance and accounting

财会专业 cáikuài zhuānyè the profession (or department) of finance and accounting

NOTE: 会 is pronounced **kuài** here, not **huì**.

财力 **cáilì** [modif: 财 finance, wealth + 力 strength] *n* financial capacity

财务 **cáiwù** [modif: 财 finance, wealth + 务 affair] *n* financial affairs, finance

财务部门 cáiwù bùmén department(s) of finance (in a company or an institution)

财务主任 cáiwù zhǔrèn director of finance (in a company or an institution)

财政 **cáizhèng** [modif: 财 finance, wealth + 政 governance] *n* public finance

财政部 cáizhèngbù the Ministry of Finance
财政年度 cáizhèng niándù fiscal year

材 **cái** *n* material

材料 **cáiliào** *n* **1** materials, e.g. steel, timber, plastic □ 建筑材料越来越贵, 房子的造价也就越来越贵。 **Jiànzhù cáiliào yuèláiyuè guì, fángzi de zàojià yě jiù yuèláiyuè guì.** *As building materials become more and more expensive, building houses also becomes more and more expensive.* **2** data (for a thesis, a report, etc.) □ 报上提供的材料对我写文章很有帮助。 **Bào shang tígōng de cáiliào duì wǒ xiě wénzhāng hěn yǒu bāngzhù.** *The data provided in the newspapers are very helpful to my writing.*

裁 **cái** *v* **1** cut into parts, cut down **2** judge, decide

裁缝 **cáifeng** [comp: 裁 cut + 缝 sew] *n* tailor, dressmaker

裁减 **cáijiǎn** [comp: 裁 cut down + 减 reduce] *v* cut down, reduce

裁决 **cáijué** [comp: 裁 judge + 决 decide] *v* judge, rule

裁判 **cáipàn** [comp: 裁 arbitrate + 判 judge] **I** *v* **1** (in law) judge **2** (in sports) act as referee or umpire **II** *n* referee, umpire (位 wèi, 名 míng) □ 裁判不公平, 引起观众不满。 **Cáipàn bùgōngpíng, yǐnqǐ guānzhòng bùmǎn.** *The referee was unfair and it made the spectators unhappy.*

当裁判 dāng cáipàn act as a referee

裁判员 **cáipànyuán** *n* Same as 裁判 **cáipàn II**

裁员 **cáiyuán** [v+obj: 裁 cut down + 员 staff] *v* reduce staff

采 **cǎi** Trad 採 *v* pick, gather □ 公园里的花, 是给大家看的, 任何人都不采。 **Gōngyuán li de huā shì gěi**

dàjiā kàn de, rènhé rén bù néng cǎi. *The flowers in the park are for everyone to admire. Nobody is allowed to pick them.*

采访 **cǎifǎng** [comp: 采 gather + 访 visit] *v* (of mass media) interview

采购 **cǎigòu** [comp: 采 pick + 购 purchase] *v* (corporate) purchase

采购员 cǎigòuyuán purchasing agent

采集 **cǎijí** [comp: 采 gather + 集 gather] *v* gather, collect

采集标本 cǎijí biāoběn collect (plant, insect, etc.) specimen

采纳 **cǎinà** [comp: 采 gather + 纳 take] *v* accept, adopt

采纳建议 cǎinà jiànyì accept a proposal

采取 **cǎiqǔ** [comp: 采 pick + 取 take] *v* adopt (a policy, a measure, an attitude, etc.) □ 对这个重大的经济问题, 政府准备采取什么措施? **Duì zhège zhòngdà de jīngjì wèntí, zhèngfǔ zhǔnbèi cǎiqǔ shénme cuòshī?** *What measures is the government prepared to adopt to deal with this major economic problem?*

采用 **cǎiyòng** [comp: 采 pick + 用 use] *v* use, employ

采用新技术 cǎiyòng xīn jìshù adopt a new technique

彩 **cǎi** *adj* colorful, multi-colored

彩票 **cǎipiào** [modif: 彩 multi-colored + 票 ticket] lottery, lottery ticket □ 我赢彩票啦! **Wǒ yíng cǎipiào la!** *I've won the lottery!*

彩色 **cǎisè** [modif: 彩 multi-colored + 色 color] *adj* multi-colored □ 现在大部分人家都有彩色电视机, 谁还看黑白电视机? **Xiànzài dà bùfen rénjiā dōu yǒu cǎisè diànshìjī, shéi hái kàn hēibái diànshìjī?** *Now that most families have color TV sets, who wants to watch black-and-white TV?*

踩 **cǎi** *v* step on, tread on □ 你们在花园里玩球, 可别踩了花。 **Nǐmen zài huāyuán li wán qiú, kě bié cǎile huā.** *When you play ball in the garden, don't step on the flowers.*

睬 **cǎi** *v* pay attention to

菜 **cài** *n* **1** vegetables □ 一个人既要吃肉, 又要吃菜, 才能健康。 **Yí ge rén jì yào chī ròu, yòu yào chī cài, cái néng jiànkāng.** *One should eat both meat and vegetables in order to be healthy.*

种菜 zhòng cài grow vegetables □ 这菜是我们自己种的, 你尝尝。 **Zhè cài shì wǒmen zìjǐ zhòng de. Nǐ chángchang.** *We grew this vegetable ourselves. Do try some.* **2** any non-staple food such as vegetables, meat, fish, eggs etc

买菜 mǎi cài buy non-staple food, do grocery shopping □ 妈妈每个星期五都要买很多菜, 有鱼、有肉、还有蔬菜。 **Māma měi ge Xīngqīwǔ dōu yào mǎi hěn dōu cài, yǒu yú, yǒu ròu, háiyǒu shūcài.** *Every Friday, mother buys lots of food: fish, meat and vegetables.* **3** cooked dish □ 这个菜又好看又好吃, 是谁做的? **Zhège cài yòu hǎokàn yòu hǎochī, shì shuí zuò de?** *This dish is both beautiful and delicious. Who cooked it?* □ 请别客气, 多吃点菜! **Qǐng bié kèqi, duō chī diǎn cài!** *Please don't be too polite. Eat more food!*

点菜 diǎn cài order a dish (in a restaurant) □ 我们每个人点一个菜, 好吗? **Wǒmen měi ge rén diǎn yí ge cài, hǎo ma?** *Shall we each order a dish?*

中国菜 Zhōngguócài Chinese dishes, Chinese food

菜单 càidān *n* menu

参 **cān** Trad 參 *v* call, enter

参观 cānguān [comp: 参 call + 观 watch, see] *v* visit (a place) □ 这个古迹十分有名, 每天有很多人来参观。 **Zhège gǔjì shífēn yǒumíng, měitiān yǒu hěn duō rén lái cānguān.** *This historical site is well-known. Many people come to visit it every day.* □ 我在中国的时候, 参观了很多学校。 **Wǒ zài Zhōngguó de shíhou, cānguānle hěn duō xuéxiào.** *I visited many schools when I was in China.*

参加 cānjiā [v+compl: 参 enter + 加 add] *v* **1** join □ 我可以参加中文班吗? **Wǒ kěyǐ cānjiā Zhōngwén bān ma?** *May I join the Chinese class?* □ 欢迎你参加我们的俱乐部。 **Huānyíng nǐ cānjiā wǒmen de jùlèbù.** *You're welcome to join our club.* **2** participate, attend □ 我们出版社有兴趣参加这个书展。 **Wǒmen chūbǎnshè yǒu xìngqù cānjiā zhège shūzhǎn.** *Our publishing house is interested in participating in this book fair.* □ 欢迎您来参加我们的晚会。 **Huānyíng nín lái cānjiā wǒmen de wǎnhuì.** *You're welcome to our evening party.*

参考 cānkǎo *v* consult, refer to

参考书 cānkǎo shū reference book(s)

仅供参考 jǐn gōng cānkǎo for reference only

参谋 cānmóu [comp: 参 participate + 谋 scheme, plan] **I** *v* offer advice **II** *n* **1** staff officer

参谋长 cānmóuzhǎng chief of staff

2 advice

给我当参谋 gěi wǒ dāng cānmóu give me advice

参议员 cānyìyuán [suffix: 参 participate + 议 discuss, comment + 员 personal suffix] *n* senator

参议院 cānyìyuàn [modif: 参 participate + 议 discuss, comment + 院 place] *n* senate, the Senate

参与 cāiyú *v* participate, involve

参阅 cānyuè *v* consult (a book, a periodical, etc.) □ 请参阅下文。 **Qǐng cānyuè xiàwén.** *Please also read the next article.*

参照 cānzhào *v* use as reference, refer to

餐 **cān** *n* meal

一日三餐 yīrì sāncān three meals a day

餐车 cānchē [modif: 餐 meal + 车 carriage] *n* dining car (on a train)

餐厅 cāntīng [modif: 餐 meal + 厅 hall] *n* restaurant □ 旅馆的餐厅在十二楼。 **Lǚguǎn de cāntīng zài shí'èr lóu.** *The restaurant in the hotel is on the twelfth floor.*

残 **cán** Trad 殘 *adj* damaged, savage

残暴 cánbào [comp: 残 savage + 暴 violent] *adj* ferocious, brutal

残暴的独裁统治 cánbào de dúcái tǒngzhì tyrannical dictatorship

残疾 cánjí [comp: 残 damaged + 疾 disease] *adj* disabled

残疾人 cánjírén disabled person(s) □ 这个车位是残疾人专用的, 你的车不能停在这里。 **Zhège chēwèi shì cánjírén zhuānyòng de, nǐ de chē bùnéng tíng zài zhèlǐ.** *This parking lot is only for the disabled; you can't park your car here.*

残酷 cánkù *adj* cruel, brutal

残忍 cánrěn *adj* cruel, merciless

使用残忍的手段 shǐyòng cánrěnde shǒuduàn with most cruel means

残余 cányú *adj* remnants, survivors

残障 cánzhàng Same as 残疾 cánjí

惭 **cán** Trad 慚 *n* shame

惭愧 cánkuì [comp: 惭 shame + 愧 sense of guilt] *adj* be ashamed □ 由于我的错误, 给你带来了不便, 我深感惭愧。 **Yóuyú wǒ de cuòwù, gěi nǐ dàiláile búbiàn, wǒ shēn gǎn cánkuì.** *My error has caused you inconvenience. I feel deeply ashamed.*

蚕 **cán** Trad 蠶 *n* silkworm (条 tiáo)

惨 **cán** Trad 慘 *adj* miserable, tragic

灿 **càn** Trad 燦 *adj* brilliant

灿烂 cànlàn *adj* magnificent, splendid

仓 **cāng** Trad 倉 *n* storage

仓促 cāngcù *adj* hasty, hurried

仓促离去 cāngcù líqù leave in a hurry

仓库 cāngkù [comp: 仓 storage + 库 warehouse] *n* warehouse

苍 **cāng** Trad 蒼 *n* dark green

苍白 cāngbái [comp: 苍 dark green + 白 white] *adj* pallid, pale

苍蝇 cāngying *n* housefly □ 那里有一只苍蝇, 拍死它。 **Nàli yǒu yì zhī cāngying, pāi sǐ tā!** *There's a fly, kill it!*

苍蝇拍 cāngying pāi flyswatter

舱 **cāng** Trad 艙 *n* cabin (in a ship or an airplane)

经济舱 jīngjìcāng economy class (on a plane)

商务舱 shāngwùcāng business class (on a plane)

头等舱 tóuděngcāng first class (on a plane)

藏 **cáng** *v* hide, conceal □ 他把玩具藏在床下, 不让妈妈看见。 **Tā bǎ wánjù cáng zài chuáng xia, bú ràng māma kànjiàn.** *He hid the toy under the bed so his mother wouldn't see.*

捉迷藏 zhuō mícáng hide-and-seek

操 **cāo** *n* drill, exercise

操场 cāochǎng [modif: 操 drill, exercise + 场 ground] *n* sports ground, playground □ 我们学校的操场很大。 **Wǒmen xuéxiào de cānchǎng hěn dà.** *Our school sports ground is very big.*

(在)操场上(zài) cāochǎng shang on the sports ground □ 很多学生在操场上玩。 **Hěn duō xuésheng zài cāochǎng shang wán.** *Many students are playing on the sports ground.*

操劳 cāoláo *v* toil, work very hard

操练 cāoliàn [comp: 操 drill + 练 practice] *v* drill, practice, train

操心 cāoxīn [v+obj: 操 exercise + 心 the heart] *v* deeply concern, be at pains

操纵 cāozòng *v* control, operate

操作 cāozuò [comp: 操 operate + 作] *v* operate □ 你会操作这台机器吗? **Nǐ huì cāozuò zhè tái jīqì ma?** *Do you know how to operate this machine?*

操作手册 cāozuò shǒucè operating manual

操作系统 cāozuò xìtǒng operating system

槽 **cáo** *n* trough

跳槽 tiàocáo abandon one's job in favor of another, get a new job

草 **cǎo** *n* grass, weed (棵 kē) □ 你们每天给马喂几次草? **Nǐmen měi tiān gěi mǎ wèi jǐ cì cǎo?** *How many times a day do you feed the horses?* (← *How many times a day do you feed the horses grass?*)

野草 yěcǎo weed

草案 **cǎo'àn** [modif: 草 rough + 案 document] *n*
draft (of a plan, proposal, a document, etc.)

草地 **cǎodì** [modif: 草 grass + 地 land] *n* **1** lawn
□ 我家房前有一片草地。**Wǒ jiā fáng qián yǒu yí piàn
cǎodì.** *There is a lawn in front of our house.*
2 meadow

草率 **cǎoshuài** *adj* careless, sloppy

草原 **cǎoyuán** [modif: 草 grass + 原 flat land] *n*
grassland, steppe, pasture □ "你见过真正的草原吗?"
"没有, 我一直住在大城市里。" **"Nǐ jiànguo zhēnzhèng
de cǎoyuán ma?" "Méiyǒu, wǒ yìzhí zhù zài dà chéngshì li."** *"Have you ever seen real grasslands?" "No,
I've been living in a big city all along."*

册 **cè** *measure wd* (used for books) volume
两千册图书 **liǎngqiān cè túshū** two thousand
[volumes of] books

厕 **cè** Trad 廁 *n* toilet
厕所 **cèsuǒ** *n* toilet □ 请问, 厕所在哪里? **Qǐngwèn,
cèsuǒ zài nǎli?** *Excuse me, where is the toilet?*
公共厕所 **gōnggòng cèsuǒ** public toilet
男厕所 **náncèsuǒ** men's toilet
女厕所 **nǚcèsuǒ** women's toilet

NOTE: See note on 洗手间 **xǐshǒujiān** (in 洗 **xǐ**).

测 **cè** Trad 測 *v* measure, gauge
测定 **cèdìng** [comp: 测 measure + 定 deter-
mine] *v* determine (the position, speed, etc.) by
measuring
测量 **cèliáng** [comp: 测 measure + 量 measure,
gauge] *v* survey, measure
测试 **cèshì** [comp: 测 measure + 试 test] *v* test
测算 **cèsuàn** [comp: 测 measure + 算 calculate]
v measure and calculate
测算有害气体排放量 **cèsuàn yǒuhài qìtǐ páifàng-
liáng** calculate the emission of harmful gases
测验 **cèyàn** [comp: 测 measure + 验 test] **I** *v* test
(in a school) □ 明天数学测验, 请同学们好好准备。
**Míngtiān shùxué cèyàn, qǐng tóngxuémen hǎohǎo
zhǔnbèi.** *There will be a mathematics test tomorrow.
Be well prepared, everyone.* **II** *n* test, examination
□ 这个学期一共有四次测验。**Zhège xuéqī yígòng yǒu
sì cì cèyàn.** *There will be four tests this semester.*
测验题目 **cèyàn tímù** test questions

侧 **cè** **I** *n* side
大楼的右侧 **dàlóu de yòucè** the right side of the
building
II *v* incline, lean
侧面 **cèmiàn** [comp: 侧 incline + 面 face, side] *n*
side, flank

策 **cè** *n* plan (See 政策 **zhèngcè**)
策划 **cèhuà** [comp: 策 plan + 划 plan] *v* plan
(an event, a theatrical performance, etc.)
策划人 **cèhuàrén** planner
策略 **cèlüè** [comp: 策 plan + 略 strategy] *n* tactics
有策略的 **yǒu cèlüè de** tactful

层 **céng** Trad 層 *measure wd* story (storey), level,
floor □ 这座大楼一共有二十层。**Zhè zuò dàlóu
yígòng yǒu èrshí céng.** *This building has twenty levels.*
□ "你住在第几层?" "我住在第三层。" **"Nǐ zhù zài dì jǐ
céng?" "Wǒ zhù zài dì sān céng."** *"Which floor do you
live on?" "I live on the third floor."*

NOTE: See note on 楼 **lóu**.

层次 **céngcì** *n* **1** administrative or educational level
2 arrangement of ideas in writing or colors in
painting

曾 **céng** *adv* Same as 曾经 **céngjīng**. Used more in
writing.

曾经 **céngjīng** *adv* once, formerly □ 我曾经在那个
城市里住过两年。**Wǒ céngjīng zài nàge chéngshì li
zhùguo liǎng nián.** *I once lived in that city for two
years.* □ 这位老人曾经是一位著名的科学家。**Zhè wèi
lǎorén céngjīng shì yí wèi zhùmíng de kēxuéjiā.** *That
old gentleman was once a famous scientist.*

NOTE: 曾经 **céngjīng** is used to emphasize that an action
or situation took place in the past.

叉 **chā** *n* fork (把 **bǎ**)
叉子 **chāzi** fork (把 **bǎ**)

差 **chā** *n* **1** difference, discrepancy
时差 **shíchā** time difference (between time
zones)
2 mistake, error
差别 **chābié** [comp: 差 difference + 别 other] *n*
disparity, gap
城乡差别 **chéngxiāng chābié** the urban-rural gap
差错 **chācuò** [comp: 差 mistake + 错 mistake] *n*
error, fault
没有差错 **méiyǒu chācuò** error-free
差距 **chājù** [comp: 差 difference + 距 distance]
n gap, disparity
贫富差距 **pín-fù chājù** the gap between rich and
poor
差异 **chāyì** [comp: 差 difference + 异 difference]
n diversity, difference

插 **chā** *v* insert, stick in □ 花瓶里要插一些花才好。
Huāpíng li yào chā yìxiē huā cái hǎo. *It would be
good to have some flowers in the vase.*
插花艺术 **chāhuā yìshù** the art of flower arrangement
插秧 **chāyāng** [v+obj: 插 stick in + 秧 rice seedling]
v transplant rice seedlings
插嘴 **chāzuǐ** [v+obj: 插 insert + 嘴 the mouth] *v*
interrupt by saying something

茶 **chá** *n* tea □ 茶凉了, 快喝吧。**Chá liáng le, kuài hē
ba.** *The tea is no longer hot. Please drink it.* □ 您喝
红茶还是绿茶? **Nín hē hóngchá háishì lǜchá?** *Do you
drink black tea or green tea?* □ 经常喝茶, 特别是绿茶
对身体很有好处。**Jīngcháng hē chá, tèbié shì lǜchá,
duì shēntǐ hěn yǒu hǎochù.** *Drinking tea regularly,
especially green tea, is very beneficial to health.*
茶杯 **chá bēi** teacup
茶袋 **chá dài** teabag
茶壶 **chá hú** teapot
茶叶 **cháyè** tea leaf
红茶 **hóngchá** black tea
绿茶 **lǜchá** green tea
喝茶 **hē chá** drink tea
茶馆 **chāguǎn** [modif: 茶 tea + 馆 house] *n* teahouse
茶话会 **chāhuà huì** [modif: 茶 tea + 话 speech + 会
meeting] *n* tea party

查 chá v check, investigate, look up □ 我可以用一下你的词典吗? 我要查一个字。 **Wǒ kěyǐ yòng yíxià nǐ de cídiǎn ma? Wǒ yào chá yí ge zì.** *May I use your dictionary? I want to look up a word.* □ 请你查查, 你们学校有没有这个学生? **Qǐng nǐ chácha, nǐmen xuéxiào yǒu méiyǒu zhège xuésheng?** *Please find out if your school has this student.*

查词典 **chá cídiǎn** look up words in a dictionary

查办 **chábàn** [comp: 查 investigate + 办 punish] v investigate and punish

查获 **cháhuò** [comp: 查 investigate + 获 obtain] v hunt down and seize (stolen goods, criminals, etc.)

查明 **chámíng** [v+compl: 查 investigate + 明 clear] v investigate and clarify, prove after an investigation

查询 **cháxún** [comp: 查 check + 询 inquire] v inquire about

电话号码查询服务 **diànhuà hàomǎ cháxún fúwù** telephone directory service

查阅 **cháyuè** [comp: 查 check + 阅 read] v search (reference books, documents, etc.)

查阅五年前的统计数字 **cháyuè wǔ nián qián de tǒngjì shùzì** search the statistics from five years ago

察 chá v examine, look over closely (See 观察 **guānchá**, 警察 **jǐngchá**)

岔 chà I n branching off

岔路 **chàlù** fork (in a road)

II v change the subject

打岔 **dǎchà** interrupt and change the subject (of a talk)

差 chà I v be short of, lack in □ 我还差二十块钱, 你可以借给我吗? **Wǒ hái chà èrshí kuài qián, nǐ kěyǐ jiè gěi wǒ ma?** *I'm still short of twenty dollars. Can you give me a loan?* □ 现在是十一点差五分。 **Xiànzài shì shíyī diǎn chà wǔ fēn.** *It's five to eleven now.*

II adj poor, not up to standard □ 这种电冰箱不但价格贵, 而且质量差。 **Zhè zhǒng diànbīngxiāng búdàn jiàgé guì, érqiě zhìliàng chà.** *This refrigerator is not only expensive but also of poor quality.* □ 他身体很差, 经常生病。 **Tā shēntǐ hěn chà, jīngcháng shēngbìng.** *He is in poor health and often falls ill.*

差不多 **chàbuduō** adv 1 more or less the same □ 他们俩年龄差不多, 经历也差不多, 很快成了好朋友。 **Tāmen liǎ niánlíng chàbuduō, jīnglì yě chàbuduō, hěn kuài chéngle hǎo péngyou.** *They were more or less of the same age and had more or less the same experiences, and soon became good friends.* 2 almost □ "你报告写完了吗?" "差不多了。" **"Nǐ bàogào xiěwánle ma?" "Chàbuduō le."** *"Have you finished writing the report?" "Almost."* □ 我们晚饭吃得差不多了, 弟弟才回来。 **Wǒmen wǎnfàn chī de chàbuduō le, dìdi cái huílai.** *We had almost finished dinner when my younger brother came home.* □ 差不多十二点了, 她怎么还不来上班? **Chàbuduō shí'èr diǎn le, tā zěnme hái bù lái shàngbān?** *It's almost twelve o'clock. Why hasn't she turned up for work?*

差点儿 **chàdiǎnr** adv almost, nearly □ 今天是妻子的生日, 陈先生差点儿忘了。 **Jīntiān shì qīzi de shēngrì, Chén xiānsheng chàdiǎnr wàngle.** *Today is his wife's birthday. Mr Chen almost forgot it.* (→ *Mr Chen nearly forgot it is his wife's birthday today.*) □ 去年他几次犯错误, 差点儿丢了饭碗。 **Qùnián tā jǐ cì fàn**

cuòwù, chàdiǎnr diūle fànwǎn. *Last year he made several mistakes and nearly lost his job.*

诧 chà Trad 詫 v be surprised

诧异 **chàyì** v be surprised, be amazed

拆 chāi v take apart, demolish □ 小孩把玩具拆开了, 可是不知道怎样再装起来。 **Xiǎohái bǎ wánjù chāikāi le, kěshì bù zhīdào zěnyàng zài zhuāng qǐlai.** *The child took the toy apart, but did not know how to reassemble it.*

拆除 **chāichú** v demolish and remove

拆穿 **chāichuān** v expose (a lie, a plot, etc.)

拆迁 **chāiqiān** [comp: 拆 demolish + 迁 move] v demolish (a dwelling) and relocate (inhabitants)

柴 chái n firewood (See 火柴 **huǒchái**)

柴油 **cháiyóu** n diesel oil

搀 chān Trad 攙 v 1 help by the arm 2 mix, mingle

蝉 chán Trad 蟬 n cicada

馋 chán Trad 饞 adj too fond of eating, gluttonous

嘴馋 **zuǐchán** too fond of eating

缠 chán Trad 纏 v 1 wind, twine 2 pester

产 chǎn Trad 產 v produce

产地 **chǎndì** [modif: 产 produce + 地 place] n origin of manufacturing

产量 **chǎnliàng** [modif: 产 product + 量 quantity] n (production) output, yield □ 仅仅增加产量是没有意义的。 **Jǐnjǐn zēngjiā chǎnliàng shì méiyǒu yìyì de.** *Increasing output alone is meaningless.* □ 你们工厂去年的产量是多少? **Nǐmen gōngchǎng qùnián de chǎnliàng shì duōshǎo?** *What was the output of your factory last year?*

产品 **chǎnpǐn** [modif: 产 production + 品 goods] n product □ 我们必须不断研究和开发新产品。 **Wǒmen bìxū búduàn yánjiū hé kāifā xīn chǎnpǐn.** *We continually research and develop new products.* □ 产品质量是企业的生命。 **Chǎnpǐn zhìliàng shì qǐyè de shēngmìng.** *The quality of its products is the lifeblood of an enterprise.*

产生 **chǎnshēng** [comp: 产 produce + 生 grow] v produce, give rise to, lead to □ 新科技的应用产生了一些新的社会现象。 **Xīn kējì de yìngyòng chǎnshēngle yìxiē xīn de shèhuì xiànxiàng.** *The use of new technology has given rise to some new social phenomena.*

产物 **chǎnwù** [modif: 产 produced + 物 thing] n outcome, result

产业 **chǎnyè** n property, estate

产值 **chǎnzhí** [modif: 产 produced + 值 value, worth] n output value

铲 chǎn Trad 鏟 n spade

铲子 **chǎnzi** spade

阐 chǎn Trad 闡 v explain

阐明 **chǎnmíng** [v+compl: 阐 explain + 明 clear] v explain clearly, clarify

阐述 **chǎnshù** [comp: 阐 explain + 述 narrate] v elaborate, explain

颤 chàn Trad 顫 v quiver, vibrate

颤动 **chàndòng** [comp: 颤 quiver + 动 move] v quiver, shake

颤抖 **chàndǒu** [comp: 颤 quiver + 抖 shake] v (of people) tremble, shake

昌 chāng *v* prosper
昌盛 **chāngshèng** [comp: 昌 propser + 盛 flourish] *adj* prosperous, flourishing

猖 chāng *adj* ferocious
猖狂 **chāngkuáng** [comp: 猖 ferocious + 狂 mad] *adj* ferocious, savage

长 cháng Trad 長 *adj* long (antonym 短 **duǎn**) □ 中国的历史很长。**Zhōngguó de lìshǐ hěn cháng.** *China has a long history.* □ 你还年轻, 生活道路还长着呢。**Nǐ hái niánqīng, shēnghuó dàolù hái chángzhe ne.** *You're still young, and have a long way to go in life.*
长城 **Chángchéng** *n* the Great Wall (a historic landmark in Northern China)
长处 **chángchu** [modif: 长 long + 处 place] *n* strong point, merit, strength
长度 **chángdù** [modif: 长 length + 度 degree, measurement] *n* length
长短 **chángduǎn** [comp: 长 long + 短 short] *n* 1 length 2 right and wrong 3 mishap, accident

NOTE: See note on 大小 **dàxiǎo.**

长江 **Chángjiāng** *n* the Yangtze River (China's longest river)
长跑 **chángpǎo** *n* long-distance running
长跑运动员 **chángpǎo yùndòngyuán** long-distance runner
长期 **chángqī** [modif: 长 long + 期 period] *n* a long period of time □ 他长期研究汉语语法, 发表过很多文章。**Tā chángqī yánjiū Hànyǔ yǔfǎ, fābiǎoguo hěn duō wénzhāng.** *He has studied Chinese grammar for a long time, and has published many essays.* □ 农民问题长期没有受到重视。**Nóngmín wèntí chángqī méiyǒu shòudào zhòngshì.** *For a long time the peasants' problem has not been given attention.*
长寿 **chángshòu** [modif: 长 long + 寿 longevity] *adj* enjoying longevity □ 祝您健康长寿! **Zhù nín jiànkāng chángshòu!** *Wishing you good health and longevity!* (said to an old person)
长途 **chángtú** [modif: 长 long + 途 way] *n* long distance □ 我要打一个国际长途电话到纽约。**Wǒ yào dǎ yí ge guójì chángtú diànhuà dào Niǔyuē.** *I want to make an international call to New York.*
长途电话 **chángtú diànhuà** long-distance telephone call
国际长途电话 **guójì chángtú diànhuà** international telephone call
长途汽车 **chángtú qìchē** long-distance bus, coach
长远 **chángyuǎn** [comp: 长 long + 远 far] *adj* long-term, long-range
长远打算 **chángyuǎn dǎsuàn** long-term plan

尝 cháng Trad 嘗 *v* taste □ 这种水果我没有吃过, 想尝尝。**Zhè zhǒng shuǐguǒ wǒ méiyǒu chīguo, xiǎng chángchang.** *I've never eaten this fruit. I'd like to taste it.*
尝试 **chángshì** [comp: 尝 taste + 试 try] *v* try

偿 cháng Trad 償 *v* make up, compensate
偿还 **chánghuán** [comp: 偿 compensate + 还 return] *v* pay back (a debt)

常 cháng I *adv* often
常常 **chángcháng** often □ 我常(常)去市图书馆

借书。**Wǒ cháng (cháng) qù shì túshūguǎn jiè shū.** *I often go to the city library to borrow books.*

NOTE: Colloquially, 常常 **chángcháng** is often used instead of 常 **cháng.**

不常 **bù cháng** not often, seldom □ 他住在乡下, 不常进城。**Tā zhù zài xiāngxia, bù cháng jìn chéng.** *He lives in the countryside and seldom goes to town.*
II *adj* 1 common, regular 2 normal
常规 **chángguī** [modif: 常 normal + 规 regular] *adj* regular, conventional
常规武器 **chángguī wǔqì** conventional weapon
常年 **chángnián** *adv* all year round
常识 **chángshí** [modif: 常 common + 识 knowledge] *n* 1 common sense □ 孩子从生活中学会很多常识。**Háizi cóng shēnghuó zhōng xuéhuì hěn duō chángshí.** *Children learn a lot of common sense from life.* 2 basic knowledge □ 我不是计算机专家, 我只知道计算机的常识。**Wǒ bú shì jìsuànjī zhuānjiā, wǒ zhǐ zhīdào jìsuànjī de chángshí.** *I'm not a computer expert; I've only got some basic knowledge.*
常务 **chángwù** [modif: 常 regular + 务 affair] *adj* day-to-day
常务委员 **chángwù wěiyuán** member of a standing committee
常务委员会 **chángwù wěiyuánhuì** standing committee

肠 cháng Trad 腸 *n* intestine
大肠 **dàcháng** large intestine
小肠 **xiǎocháng** small intestine
肠胃病 **chángwèibìng** [modif: 肠 intestine + 胃 stomach + 病 disease] *n* gastrointestinal disease
肠炎 **chángyán** [modif: 肠 intestine + 炎 inflammation] *n* enteritis

厂 chǎng Trad 廠 *n* factory, works, mill
钢铁厂 **gāngtiěchǎng** iron and steelworks
造纸厂 **zàozhǐchǎng** paper mill
厂房 **chǎngfáng** [modif: 厂 factory + 房 house] *n* factory building
厂商 **chǎngshāng** [comp: 厂 factory + 商 business] *n* 1 factory, firm 2 factory owner
厂长 **chǎngzhǎng** [modif: 厂 factory + 长 chief] *n* factory manager

敞 chǎng *v* open
敞开 **chǎngkāi** [comp: 敞 open + 开 open] open wide

场 chǎng Trad 場 I *n* ground, field
体育场 **tǐyùchǎng** stadium
飞机场 **fēijīchǎng** airport
市场 **shìchǎng** market
II *measure wd* (for movies, sport events, etc.)
一场电影 **yì chǎng diànyǐng** a show of film □ 这个电影院一天放六场电影。**Zhège diànyǐngyuàn yìtiān fàng liù chǎng diànyǐng.** *This cinema has six film shows a day.*
一场球赛 **yì chǎng qiúsài** a ball game, a ball match
场地 **chǎngdì** [comp: 场 ground + 地 ground] *n* venue (especially for sports)
场合 **chǎnghé** *n* occasion, situation
场面 **chǎngmiàn** *n* scene (in a play, movie, novel, etc.
场所 **chǎngsuǒ** *n* place (for public activity)

公共场所 gōnggòng chǎngsuǒ public place(s)

倡 chàng v initiate
倡议 chàngyì [v+obj: 倡 initiate + 议 proposal]
I v propose **II** n proposal, suggestion (项 **xiàng**)

唱 chàng v sing
唱歌 chànggē sing songs, sing □ 你唱歌唱得真好
听! **Nǐ chànggē chàng de zhēn hǎotīng!** *You really sing
well!* □ 你会唱中文歌吗? **Nǐ huì chàng Zhōngwén gē
ma?** *Can you sing Chinese songs?*

畅 chàng Trad 暢 adj uninhibited, unimpeded
畅快 chàngkuài adj carefree
畅谈 chàngtán [modif: 畅 freely + 谈 talk] v talk
freely and openly
畅通 chàngtōng [comp: 畅 unimpeded + 通 through]
adj unimpeded, flowing freely and smoothly
畅销 chàngxiāo [modif: 畅 freely + 销 sell] v sell well
畅销书 chàngxiāoshū bestseller

抄 chāo v copy by hand □ 这些数字很重要, 我要抄下
来。**Zhèxiē shùzì hěn zhòngyào, wǒ yào chāo xiàlai.**
These are important numbers. I'll write them down.
抄写 chāoxiě v Same as 抄 chāo

超 chāo v go beyond, exceed
超产 chāochǎn [v+obj: 超 exceed + 产 produc-
tion] v exceed production quota
超出 chāochū [comp: 超 exceed + 出 out] v go
beyond, exceed
超额 chāo'é [v+obj: 超 exceed + 额 quota] v exceed
quotas
超过 chāoguò v 1 overtake □ 我前面的车开得太慢, 我
要超过它。**Wǒ qiánmiàn de chē kāi de tài màn, wǒ yào
chāoguò tā.** *The car in front of me is moving too
slowly. I want to overtake it.* **2** exceed □ 去年到这个国
家的旅游者超过了三百万。**Qùnián dào zhège guójiā de
lǚyóuzhě chāoguòle sānbǎiwàn.** *The number of tourists
visiting this country last year exceeded three million.*
超级 chāojí [modif: 超 exceed + 级 grade] adj super
超级大国 chāojí dàguó superpower
超级公路 chāojí gōnglù super-highway, motorway
超级市场 chāojí shìchǎng supermarket □ 你经常
去哪一家超级市场? **Nǐ jīngcháng qù nǎ yì jiā chāojí
shìchǎng?** *Which supermarket do you often go to?*
超声波 chāoshēngbō [modif: 超 exceed + 声 sound
+ 波 wave] n ultrasonic wave, supersonic wave
超越 chāoyuè [comp: 超 exceed + 越 go beyond] v
transcend, surpass

钞 chāo Trad 鈔 n paper money
现钞 xiànchāo cash, ready money
钞票 chāopiào [modif: 钞 paper money + 票 ticket]
n paper money, banknotes (张 **zhāng**)

朝 cháo **I** v face □ 中国人的房子大多朝南。
Zhōngguórén de fángzi dàduō cháo nán. *Chinese
people's houses mostly face the south.* (→ *Most Chinese houses face south.*) **II** prep towards, to □ 你一
直朝前走十分钟左右, 就到公园了。**Nǐ yìzhí cháo qián
zǒu shí fēnzhōng zuǒyòu, jiù dào gōngyuán le.** *Walk
straight ahead for about ten minutes and you'll reach
the park.* **III** n dynasty
朝代 cháodài [comp: 朝 dynasty + 代 generation]
n dynasty

潮 cháo adj wet
潮湿 cháoshī [comp: 潮 wet + 湿 damp] adj
damp, humid

潮水 cháoshuǐ n tidewater

嘲 cháo v jeer, mock
嘲笑 cháoxiào [comp: 嘲 jeer + 笑 laugh] v
ridicule, sneer at

吵 chǎo **I** v (Same as 吵架 **chǎojià**) quarrel □ 他
们夫妻俩又吵了。**Tāmen fūqī liǎ yòu chǎo le.**
The couple quarreled again. **II** adj (Same as 吵闹
chǎonào II) noisy □ 这间房间对大街, 太吵了。**Zhè
jiān fáng miàn duì dàjiē, tài chǎo le.** *This room faces a
main street. It's too noisy.*
吵架 chǎojià v quarrel

NOTE: For "quarrel," 吵架 **chǎojià** is more commonly used
than 吵 **chǎo**, for example □ 他们夫妻俩又吵架了。**Tāmen
fūqī liǎ yòu chǎojià le.** *The couple quarreled again.*

吵闹 chǎonào [modif: 吵 make a big noise + 闹
make a loud noise] **I** v wrangle, raise hell **II** adj
noisy, hustle and bustle
吵嘴 chǎozuǐ v bicker, quarrel

炒 chǎo v 1 stir-fry, roast **2** sensationalize, create
a commotion
炒股票 chǎo gǔpiào speculate on the stock
exchange
炒鱿鱼 chǎo yóuyú fire (an employee), send ...
packing

车 chē Trad 車 n vehicle, traffic (辆 **liàng**) □ 我的
车坏了。**Wǒ de chē huài le.** *My car (or bicycle) has
broken down.* □ 路上车很多。**Lùshang chē hěn duō.**
There is lots of traffic on the road. □ 我可以借用你的
车吗? **Wǒ kěyǐ jièyòng nǐ de chē ma?** *May I borrow
your car (or bicycle)?*
车牌 chē pái (vehicle) license plate
车牌号 chē pái hào (vehicle) license plate number
开车 kāi chē drive an automobile
骑车 qí chē ride a bicycle
停车场 tíngchēchǎng parking lot, carpark
修车 xiū chē repair a car/bicycle
修车行 xiūchēháng motor vehicle repair and servic-
ing shop
学车 xué chē learn to drive (or to ride a bicycle)
车床 chēchuáng n machine tool
车间 chējiān n workshop (in a factory) □ 这个车间有
多少工人? **Zhège chējiān yǒu duōshǎo gōngrén?** *How
many workers work in this workshop?*
车辆 chēliàng n vehicles, traffic □ 街上车辆很多。
Jiēshang chēliàng hěn duō. *There is heavy traffic in
the street.*
车辆管理 chēliàng guǎnlǐ vehicle administration
车厢 chēxiāng n carriage (in a train)
车站 chēzhàn [modif: 车 vehicle + 站 station] n
bus stop, coach station, railway station □ "车站离
这里远不远?" "不远, 开车只要十分钟。" **"Chēzhàn lí
zhèlǐ yuán bù yuán?" "Bù yuǎn, kāi chē zhǐyào shí
fēnzhōng."** *"Is the railway (or bus) station far from
here?" "No, it's only ten minutes' drive."* □ 王先生
去车站接朋友了。**Wáng xiānsheng qù chēzhàn jiē
péngyou le.** *Mr Wang's gone to the railway (or coach)
station to meet a friend.*
长途汽车站 chángtú qìchēzhàn coach station
出租汽车站 chūzū qìchēzhàn taxi stand
火车站 huǒchēzhàn railway station

扯 chě *v* **1** pull **2** tear **3** chat

撤 chè *v* **1** remove **2** withdraw, retreat

撤退 **chètuì** [comp: 撤 withdraw + 退 move back] *v* retreat

撤销 **chèxiāo** *v* cancel, revoke

彻 chè Trad 徹 *adj* thorough

彻底 **chèdǐ** [comp: 彻 thorough + 底 end, bottom] *adj* thorough, complete □ 经过彻底调查，确定这个地区没有这种病。 **Jīngguò chèdǐ diàochá, quèdìng zhège dìqū méiyǒu zhè zhǒng bìng.** *After a thorough investigation it is confirmed that this region is free from this disease.*

臣 chén *n* (in ancient times) minister, official

辰 chén *n* **1** celestial body **2** time

沉 chén **I** *v* sink □ 一公斤铁在水里会沉，一公斤棉花沉吗？ **Yì gōngjīn tiě zài shuǐ li huì chén, yì gōng jīn miánhuā huì chén ma?** *While a kilogram of iron will sink in water, will a kilogram of cotton?* **II** *adj* **1** deep, profound **2** heavy

沉淀 **chédiàn** **I** *v* (of a substance) precipitate, settle **II** *n* sediment

沉静 **chénjìng** [comp: 沉 heavy + 静 quiet] *adj* serene, placid

沉闷 **chénmèn** [comp: 沉 heavy + 闷 depressed] *adj* **1** (of weather) depressing, oppressive **2** (of moods) in low spirit **3** (of ambiance, atmosphere) dull, boring

沉默 **chénmò** [comp: 沉 deep + 默 silent] *adj* silent, reticent □ 他总是很沉默，没人知道他到底在想什么。 **Tā zǒngshì hěn chénmò, méi rén zhīdào tā dàodǐ zài xiǎng shénme.** *He is always reticent, and nobody knows what he is thinking.*

沉思 **chénsī** [modif: 沉 deep + 思 think] *v* ponder, be lost in thought

沉痛 **chéntòng** [modif: 沉 heavy + 痛 agonized] *adj* deeply grieved, in deep sorrow

沉重 **chénzhòng** [comp: 沉 heavy + 重 heavy] *adj* heavy, serious

沉着 **chénzhuó** *adj* cool-headed, composed

陈 chén Trad 陳 **I** *adj* old, stale **II** *v* display

陈酒 **chénjiǔ** [modif: 陈 old + 酒 wine] *n* vintage wine

陈旧 **chénjiù** [comp: 陈 old + 旧 old] *adj* old-fashioned, outdated

陈列 **chénliè** [comp: 陈 display + 列 line up] *v* display, exhibit □ 商店里陈列着最新的电子产品。 **Shāngdiàn li chénliè zhe zuìxīn de diànzǐ chǎnpǐn.** *Latest electronic products are displayed in the store.*

陈列橱窗 **chénliè chúchuāng** showcase

陈列厅 **chénliètīng** exhibition hall, showroom

陈述 **chenshù** *v* state (one's views, reasons, etc.)

晨 chén *n* early morning (See 早晨 **zǎochén**)

尘 chén Trad 塵 *n* dust (See 灰尘 **huīchén**)

尘土 **chéntǔ** dust, dirt

衬 chèn Trad 襯 *n* (clothes) lining, underwear

衬衫 **chènshān** *n* shirt (件 **jiàn**) □ 你去公司上班，当然要每天换衬衫。 **Nǐ qù gōngsī shàngbān, dāngrán yào měitiān huàn chènshān.** *If you work*

in a company, of course you should change shirts every day.

衬衣 **chènyī** *n* shirt or similar underwear (件 **jiàn**) □ 他拿着干净的衬衣短裤，进浴室去洗澡。 **Tā názhe gānjìng de chènyī duǎnkù, jìn yùshì qu xǐzǎo.** *Carrying clean underwear, he went into the bathroom to take a bath.*

趁 chèn *prep* taking advantage of, while, when □ 我想趁这个机会，向大家说几句话。 **Wǒ xiǎng chèn zhège jīhuì, xiàng dàjiā shuō jǐ jù huà.** *I'd like to take this opportunity to say a few words to you.* □ 趁王董事长也在这里，我想报告一下最近的营业情况。 **Chèn Wáng dǒngshìzhǎng yě zài zhèli, wǒ xiǎng bàogào yíxià zuìjìn de yíngyè qíngkuàng.** *Now that Chairman Wang is here, I'd like to report our recent business situation.*

称 chèn Trad 稱 *v* suit, fit well

称心 **chènxīn** [v+obj: 称 suit + 心 one's heart] *adj* very much to one's liking, find ... satisfactory

称 chēng Trad 稱 *v* **1** call, be known as, address ... as □ 电脑又称计算机。 **Diànnǎo yòu chēng jìsuànjī.** *"Diannao" is also known as "jisuanji."* □ 比我们都大一点，我们都称他"李大哥"。 **Tā bǐ wǒmen dōu dà yìdiǎn, wǒmen dōu chēng tā "Lǐ dàgē".** *As he is older than us, we all call him "Elder Brother Li."* **2** weigh □ 他去飞机场之前，称了一下行李，看看有没有超重。 **Tā qù fēijīchǎng zhī qián, chēngle yíxià xíngli, kànkan yǒu méi yǒu chāozhòng.** *He weighed his luggage before leaving for the airport to make sure it was not overweight.*

称号 **chēnghào** *n* honorific title

称呼 **chēnghu** [comp: 称 call, name + 呼 call] **I** *v* call, address □ 我见了你的父母，该怎么称呼他们？ **Wǒ jiàn le nǐ de fùmǔ, gāi zěnme chēnghu tāmen?** *How should I address your parents when I meet them?* **II** *n* form of address □ 使用正确的称呼是很重要的。 **Shǐyòng zhèngquè de chēnghu shì hěn zhòngyào de.** *It is very important to use correct forms of address.*

称赞 **chēngzàn** [comp: 称 praise + 赞 praise] *v* compliment, praise □ 老板称赞他工作努力，成绩优秀。 **Lǎobǎn chēngzàn tā gōngzuò nǔlì, chéngjì yōuxiù.** *The boss praised him as a hardworking high achiever.*

撑 chēng *v* prop up, support

成 chéng *v* become, turn into □ 几年没见，她成了一个漂亮的大姑娘了。 **Jǐnián méi jiàn, tā chéngle yí ge piàoliang de dàgūniang le.** *After several years' absence, she had become a pretty young lady.* □ 他是我小学时的同学，没想到成了一位大人物。 **Tā shì wǒ xiǎoxué shí de tóngxué, méi xiǎngdào chéngle yí wèi dàrénwù.** *He was my primary school classmate and, unexpectedly, has become a big shot.*

成本 **chéngběn** *n* (in business) cost □ 生产厂家必须降低成本才能生存。 **Shēngchǎn chǎngjiā bìxū jiàngdī chéngběn cái néng shēngcún.** *Manufacturers must reduce cost if they are to survive.*

生产成本 **shēngchǎn chéngběn** production cost

成分 **chéngfèn** [comp: 成 percentage + 分 element] *n* component part, ingredient (种 **zhǒng**) □ 这种中药有哪些成分？ **Zhè zhǒng Zhōngyào yǒu nǎxiē chéngfèn?** *What are the ingredients in this Chinese medicine?*

成功 **chénggōng** [v+obj: 成 accomplish + 功 merits, feat] **I** *v* succeed □ 经过无数次的试验, 科学家们终于成功了。 **Jīngguò wúshù cì de shìyàn, kēxuéjiāmen zhōngyú chénggōng le.** *After numerous experiments, the scientists finally succeeded.* □ 祝你成功! **Zhù nǐ chénggōng!** *I wish you success!* **II** *adj* successful □ 在一个成功的男人背后, 总有一位好妻子。 **Zài yí ge chénggōng de nánrén bèihou, zǒng yǒu yí wèi hǎo qīzi.** *Behind a successful man, there stands a good wife.* □ 这次会谈十分成功。 **Zhè cì huìtán shífēn chénggōng.** *This formal talk was a success.*

成果 **chéngguǒ** [comp: 成 achievement + 果 fruit, good result] *n* positive result, achievement (项 **xiàng**) □ 我们中文学习进步这么大, 都是老师辛苦工作的成果。 **Wǒmen Zhōngwén xuéxí jìnbù zhème dà, dōu shì lǎoshī xīnkǔ gōngzuò de chéngguǒ.** *The rapid progress we have made in our Chinese studies is the result of our teachers' hard work.*

成绩 **chéngjì** [comp: 成 accomplish + 绩 result] *n* achievement, examination result □ 他去年的考试成绩非常好。 **Tā qùnián de kǎoshì chéngjì fēicháng hǎo.** *His examination results last year were very good.* □ 你的工作成绩不理想, 必须努力改进。 **Nǐ de gōngzuò chéngjì bù lǐxiǎng, bìxū nǔlì gǎijìn.** *Your work results are not good enough. You must work harder to improve them.*
考试成绩 **kǎoshì chéngjì** examination result
取得成绩 **qǔdé chéngjì** make an achievement, get (positive, good) results

成见 **chéngjiàn** *n* prejudice

成交 **chéng jiāo** *v* complete a business deal

成就 **chéngjiù** [comp: 成 achievement + 就 achievement] *n* great achievement (项 **xiàng**) □ 我们在经济发展方面取得了很大成就。 **Wǒmen zài jīngjì fāzhǎn fāngmiàn qǔdéle hěn dà chéngjiù.** *We have won great achievements in economic development.*

成立 **chénglì** [comp: 成 accomplish + 立 establish] *v* establish, set up □ 你们公司是哪一年成立的? **Nǐmen gōngsī shì nǎ yì nián chénglì de?** *When was your company set up?*

成名 **chéng míng** *v* become famous □ 她写了那本小说, 几乎一夜成名。 **Tā xiěle nà běn xiǎoshuō, jīhū yí yè chéng míng.** *She wrote that novel and became famous almost overnight.*

成品 **chéngpǐn** *n* end product, finished product

成千上万 **chéng qiān shàng wàn** *idiom* thousands of, a large number of

成人 **chéngrén** *n* adult
成人教育 **chéngrén jiàoyù** adult education
成人电影 **chéngrén diànyǐng** adult movie

成熟 **chéngshú** [comp: 成 accomplish + 熟 mature] **I** *v* mature □ 秋天是很多水果成熟的季节。 **Qiūtiān shì hěn duō shuǐguǒ chéngshú de jìjié.** *Autumn is the season when many fruits ripen.* **II** *adj* ripe, mature □ 他虽然二十多岁了, 但是还不够成熟。 **Tā suīrán èrshí duō suì le, dànshì hái bú gòu chéngshú.** *Although he is over twenty, he is not mature enough.*

成套 **chéngtào** *adj* in a complete set
成套设备 **chéngtào shèbèi** complete set of equipment (or machinery)

成天 **chéngtiān** *adv* all day long, all the time

成为 **chéngwéi** [comp: 成 become + 为 be] *v* become □ 这个小城已经成为著名的大学城。 **Zhège xiǎo chéng yǐjīng chéngwéi zhùmíng de dàxué chéng.** *This town has become a well-known university town.* □ 她想为一名电影演员。 **Tā xiǎng chéngwéi yì míng diànyǐng yǎnyuán.** *She wants to become a film star.*

成效 **chéngxiào** *n* desired effect, beneficial effect

成心 **chéngxīn** *adv* intentionally, purposely

成语 **chéngyǔ** *n* idiom, set phrase

成员 **chéngyuán** *n* member

成长 **chéngzhǎng** [comp: 成 become + 长 grow] *v* grow up □ 他已经成长为一名优秀青年。 **Tā yǐjīng chéngzhǎng wéi yìmíng yōuxiù qīngnián.** *He has grown into a fine young man.*

城 **chéng** *n* city, town (座 **zuò**)
城里 **chénglǐ** in town, downtown
城外 **chéngwài** out of town, suburban area
进城 **jìn chéng** go to town, go to the city center □ 我今天下午进城, 有什么事要我办吗? **Wǒ jīntiān xiàwǔ jìn chéng, yǒu shénme shì yào wǒ bàn ma?** *I'm going to town this afternoon. Is there anything you want me to do for you?*

城市 **chéngshì** [comp: 城 city wall, city + 市 market] *n* city, urban area (as opposed to rural area) (座 **zuò**) □ 城市的中心是商业区, 东面是工业区。 **Chéngshì de zhōngxīn shì shāngyè qū, dōngmiàn shì gōngyè qū.** *The city center is a business district and the eastern part is an industrial area.* □ 这个城市不大, 但是很漂亮。 **Zhège chéngshì bú dà, dànshì hěn piàoliang.** *This city is not big, but it's quite beautiful.* □ 我喜欢住在大城市里。 **Wǒ xǐhuan zhù zài dà chéngshì li.** *I like to live in big cities.*
城市生活 **chéngshì shēnghuó** city life
城市规划 **chéngshì guīhuà** city planning
大城市 **dà chéngshì** big city, metropolis
国际城市 **guójì chéngshì** cosmopolis

城镇 **chéngzhèn** [comp: 城 city + 镇 town] *n* cities and towns, urban area
城镇人口 **chéngzhèn rénkǒu** urban population

诚 **chéng** Trad 誠 *adj* sincere
以诚待人 **yǐ chéng dài rén** treat people with sincerity

诚恳 **chéngkěn** [comp: 诚 sincere + 恳 sincere] *adj* sincere □ 我们诚恳地希望你提出批评建议。 **Wǒmen chéngkěn de xīwàng nǐ tíchū pīpíng jiànyì.** *We sincerely hope you will give us your criticism and suggestions.*

诚实 **chéngshí** [comp: 诚 sincere + 实 true] *adj* honest, simple □ 爸爸从小教育我做人要诚实。 **Bàba cóng xiǎo jiàoyù wǒ zuòrén yào chéngshí.** *Since my childhood, father has taught me to be an honest person.*

诚心诚意 **chéngxīn chéngyì** *adj* very sincerely

诚信 **chéngxìn** *n* sincerity and trust, trust

诚意 **chéngyì** [modif: 诚 sincere + 意 intent] *n* good faith, sincerity

诚挚 **chéngzhì** *adj* sincere, cordial

承 **chéng** *v* bear, undertake
承办 **chéngbàn** *v* undertake

承包 **chéngbāo** *v* contract □ 我们公司承包了这项工程。 (or 这项工程承包给我们公司了。) **Wǒmen gōngsī chéngbāo le zhè xiàng gōngchéng. (or Zhè xiàng gōngchéng chéngbāo gěi wǒmen gōngsī le.)** *This project is contracted to our company.*
承包商 **chéngbāoshāng** contractor

承认 chéngrèn *v* **1** acknowledge, recognize □ 大家都承认他是一位有成就的科学家。**Dàjiā dōu chéngrèn tā shì yí wèi yǒu chéngjiù de kēxuéjiā.** *Everyone acknowledges that he is a scientist who has made great achievements.* **2** admit (mistake, error, etc.) □ 他错了，还不承认。**Tā cuò le, hái bù chéngrèn.** *He is wrong, but he still doesn't admit it.* □ 我承认自己不了解情况，批评错了。**Wǒ chéngrèn zìjǐ bù liǎojiě qíngkuàng, pīpíng cuò le.** *I admit that I did not know the situation well and made a wrong criticism.*

承受 chéngshòu *v* endure, bear
承受力 chéngshòulì endurance

乘¹ chéng *v* **1** use (a means of transport), travel (by car, train, plane, etc.) □ 爸爸每天乘公共汽车上班。**Bàba měi tiān chéng gōnggòng qìchē shàngbān.** *Father goes to work by bus every day.* □ 你打算乘火车，还是乘飞机到北京去？**Nǐ dǎsuàn chéng huǒchē, háishì chéng fēijī qù Běijīng?** *Do you plan to go to Beijing by train or by plane?* **2** take advantage of
乘人之危 chéng rén zhì wēi take advantage of the misfortune (or weakness) of others

乘² chéng *v* multiply □ 二乘三等于六。(2 x 3 = 6) **Èr chéng sān děngyú liù.** *Two multiplied by three is six.*

乘客 chéngkè [乘 travel by vehicle + 客 guest] *n* passenger

乘机 chéngjī [v+obj: 乘 take advantage of + 机 opportunity] *v* seize an opportunity

乘务员 chéngwùyuán *n* attendant (on a train, coach, etc.)

呈 chéng *v* **1** appear, assume **2** present
呈现 chéngxiàn *v* appear, show

程 chéng *n* regulation, procedure
程度 chéngdù *n* level, degree □ 汽车坏到这种程度，已经修不好了。**Qìchē huài dao zhè zhǒng chéngdù, yǐjīng xiū bù hǎo le.** *The car is damaged to such a degree that it cannot be repaired.*

程序 chéngxù [comp: 程 regulation + 序 order] *n* procedure
计算机程序 jìsuànjī chéngxù computer program

惩 chéng Trad 懲 *v* punish
惩办 chéngbàn [comp: 惩 punish + 办 deal with] *v* (of the authorities) punish
惩罚 chéngfá [comp: 惩 punish + 罚 penalize] *v* punish, penalize

澄 chéng *adj* (of water) clear, clean
澄清 chéngqīng *v* clarify
澄清事实 chéngqīng shìshí clarify a matter

秤 chèng *n* scale(s)

吃 chī *v* eat □ "你吃过早饭没有？" "吃过了。" "**Nǐ chī guo zǎofàn méiyǒu?**" "**Chī guo le.**" *"Have you had breakfast?" "Yes, I have."*

吃惊 chījīng *v* be shocked, be startled, be alarmed □ 股票跌得这么快，王先生很吃惊。**Gǔpiào diē de zhème kuài, Wáng xiānsheng hěn chījīng.** *Mr Wang was shocked that the share prices fell so quickly.*
大吃一惊 dà chī yì jīng greatly shocked, have the fright of one's life □ 他回家时，发现家门大开，大吃一惊。**Tā huíjiā shí, fāxiàn jiā mén dà kāi, dà chī yì jīng.** *When he got home, he had the fright of his life when he saw the door wide open.*

吃苦 chīkǔ [v+obj: 吃 eat + 苦 bitterness] *v* endure hardships, suffer
吃了很多苦 chī le hěn duō kǔ have suffered a lot

吃亏 chīkuī [v+obj: 吃 eat + 亏 loss] *v* suffer losses, be at a disadvantage □ 不了解市场情况，就要吃亏。**Bù liǎojiě shìchǎng qíngkuàng, jiùyào chīkuī.** *If you don't know the market, you'll suffer losses.*

吃力 chīlì *adj* making or requiring great efforts

痴 chī *adj* foolish, stupid
白痴 báichī idiot

池 chí *n* pool, pond
游泳池 yóuyǒngchí swimming pool

池塘 chítáng [comp: 池 pool + 塘 pond] *n* pond

迟 chí Trad 遲 *adj* late

迟到 chídào [modif: 迟 late + 到 arrive] *v* come late, be late (for work, school, etc.) □ 对不起，我迟到了。**Duìbuqǐ, wǒ chídào le.** *I'm sorry I'm late.* □ 我今天早上差点儿迟到。**Wǒ jīntiān zǎoshang chàdiǎnr chídào.** *I was almost late this morning.* □ "你今天迟到了二十分钟，明天不要再迟到了。" "请您原谅，我明天一定不迟到。" "**Nǐ jīntiān chídàole èrshí fēnzhōng, míngtiān bú yào zài chídào le.**" "**Qǐng nín yuánliàng, Wǒ míngtiān yídìng bù chídào.**" *"You were late twenty minutes today. Don't be late tomorrow." "My apologies. I'll definitely not be late tomorrow."*

迟缓 chíhuǎn [comp: 迟 late + 缓 delayed] *adj* (of movement) slow, sluggish

迟疑 chíyí [comp: 迟 late + 疑 doubtful] *v* hesitate, waver

持 chí *v* persevere
持久 chíjiǔ [comp: 持 persevere + 久 a long time] *adj* enduring, lasting
持续 chíxù [comp: 持 persevere + 续 continue] *v* continue, sustain, persist
可持续发展 kě chíxù fāzhǎn sustainable development

匙 chí *n* spoon
汤匙 tāngchí soup spoon

驰 chí Trad 馳 *v* move quickly, gallop

尺 chǐ **I** *n* ruler (把 bǎ)
尺子 chǐzi ruler □ 要划直线，就要有一把尺。**Yào huà zhí xiàn, jiù yào yǒu yì bǎ chǐ.** *You need a ruler if you want to draw a straight line.*
II *measure wd* a traditional Chinese unit of length (equal to ⅓ meter)
公尺 gōngchǐ meter
英尺 yīngchǐ foot (as a measurement of length) □ 三尺等于一公尺，也就是说一尺等于三分之一公尺。**Sān chǐ děngyú yī gōngchǐ, yě jiù shì shuō yì chǐ děngyú sān fēnzhī yī gōngchǐ.** *Three chi make a meter; that is to say, one chi is a third of a meter.*

尺寸 chǐcun [comp: 尺 foot + 寸 inch] *n* size, measurements □ 你做衣服以前，要量一下尺寸。**Nǐ zuò yīfu yǐqián, yào liáng yíxià chǐcun.** *Before a garment is made for you, measurements should be taken.*

尺码 chǐmǎ *n* size (of shoes, shirts, ready-made clothing, etc.) □ 我们有各种尺码的裙子，保证您满意。**Wǒmen yǒu gè zhǒng chǐmǎ de qúnzi, bǎozhèng nín mǎnyì.** *We have skirts of various sizes. Your satisfaction is guaranteed.*

侈 chǐ *adj* wasteful (See 奢侈 shēchǐ)

齿 chǐ Trad 齒 *n* tooth, teeth
齿轮 chǐlún [modif: 齿 tooth + 轮 wheel] *n* gear wheel, gear

耻 chǐ Trad 恥 *n* shame
可耻 kěchǐ shameful, disgraceful
耻辱 chǐrǔ [comp: 耻 shame + 辱 insult] *n* deep shame, humiliation

赤 chì *adj* red
赤道 chìdào [modif: 赤 red + 道 zone] *n* the equator
赤字 chìzì [modif: 赤 red + 字 character, word] *n* the number in red, deficit

翅 chì *n* wing
翅膀 chìbǎng *n* wing (of a bird) □ 这只鸟翅膀受伤了，不能飞了。**Zhè zhī niǎo chìbǎng shòu shāng le, bù néng fēi le.** *This bird's wing is injured, it can't fly.*

斥 chì *v* scold, shout at

冲 chōng Trad 衝 *v* 1 clash 2 charge, rush, dash
冲锋 chōngfēng *v* (of troops) charge, assault
冲浪 chōnglàng [comp: 冲 charge + 浪 waves] *v* surf
冲破 chōngpò *v* break through, breach
冲突 chōngtū I *v* clash II *n* conflict, clash □ 警察和抗议者在市政府大楼前发生了冲突。**Jǐngchá hé kàngyìzhě zài shìzhèngfǔ dàlóu qián fāshēngle chōngtū.** *The police and protesters clashed in front of the municipal government building.*
利益冲突 lìyì chōngtū conflict of interest

充 chōng *adj* sufficient, full
充分 chōngfèn *adj* abundant, ample, adequate □ 对明天的会谈双方都做了充分的准备。**Duì míngtiān de huìtán shuāngfāng dōu zuòle chōngfèn de zhǔnbèi.** *Both parties made ample preparations for the talk tomorrow.*
充满 chōngmǎn [comp: 充 filled + 满 full] *adj* full of, be filled with □ 他充满了信心，一定能完成公司的任务。**Tā chōngmǎnle xìnxīn, yídìng néng wánchéng gōngsī de rènwù.** *He is full of confidence that he will complete the task set by the company.*
充沛 chōngpèi *adj* abundant, plentiful
精力充沛 jīnglì chōngpèi full of vigor and vitality, very energetic
充实 chōngshí I *adj* substantial II *v* strengthen, enrich
充足 chōngzú [comp: 充 filled + 足 enough] *adj* sufficient, adequate, enough □ 我有充足的理由相信，这次试验能成功。**Wǒ yǒu chōngzú de lǐyóu xiāngxìn, zhè cì shìyàn néng chénggōng.** *I have enough reason to believe that the experiment will succeed this time.* □ 他们有充足的资金研究和开发这项新技术。**Tāmen yǒu chōngzú de zījīn yánjiū hé kāifā zhè xiàng xīn jìshù.** *They have sufficient funds to research and develop this new technology.*

虫 chóng Trad 蟲 *n* insect, worm
虫子 chóngzi [suffix: 虫 insect + 子 nominal suffix] *n* insect, worm (只 zhī) □ 有一只虫子在你背上爬。**Yǒu yì zhī chóngzi zài nǐ bèi shang pá.** *There's an insect crawling on your back.*

重 chóng *adv* again, once again □ 我在电脑上做的文件没有保存，只好重做。**Wǒ zài diànnǎo shang zuò de wénjiàn méiyǒu bǎocún, zhǐ hǎo chóng zuò.** *I failed to save the file in the computer, and had to redo [the work].*

重叠 chóngdié *v* overlap
重复 chóngfù [comp: 重 once again + 复 repeat] *v* repeat □ 我离家前，妈妈又把话重复了一遍。**Wǒ lí jiā qián, māma yòu bǎ huà chóngfùle yí biàn.** *Before I left home, mother repeated what she had said.*
重新 chóngxīn [comp: 重 once again + 新 renew] *adv* Same as 重 chóng

崇 chóng *adj* high, lofty
崇拜 chóngbài [modif: 崇 lofty + 拜 bow down] *v* worship, adore
崇高 chónggāo [comp: 崇 high, lofty + 高 high] *adj* lofty, sublime □ 不少人不相信世界上有什么崇高的东西。**Bùshǎo rén bù xiāngxìn shìjiè shang yǒu shénme chónggāo de dōngxi.** *Quite a few people do not believe there is anything lofty in the world.*
崇敬 chóngjìng [comp: 崇 lofty + 敬 respect] *v* hold in high esteem, revere

宠 chǒng Trad 寵 *v* pamper, indulge
宠物 chǒngwù [modif: 宠 pamper + 物 object] *n* pet

冲 chòng *adj* strong, forceful

抽 chōu *v* take out (from in-between)
抽空 chōukòng *v* manage to find time
抽水机 chōushuǐjī [modif: 抽 draw + 水 water + 机 machine] *n* water pump
抽屉 chōuti *n* drawer
抽象 chōuxiàng *adj* abstract □ 这么抽象的道理，有多少人听得懂？**Zhème chōuxiàng de dàolǐ, yǒu duōshǎo rén tīng de dǒng?** *How many people understand such abstract concepts?*
抽烟 chōuyān [v+obj: 抽 suck + 烟 smoke] *v* smoke a cigarette (cigar), smoke

绸 chóu Trad 綢 *n* silk (See 丝绸 sīchóu)

愁 chóu *v* worry □ 你别愁，大伙儿会帮助你的。**Nǐ bié chóu, dàhuǒr huì bāngzhù nǐ de.** *Don't worry. We'll all help you.*

酬 chóu *v* reward

稠 chóu *adj* thick, dense
稠密 chóumì [comp: 稠 dense + 密 dense] *adj* dense
人口稠密 rénkǒu chóumì densely populated

筹 chóu Trad 籌 *v* prepare
筹备 chóubèi [comp: 筹 prepare + 备 prepare] *v* prepare (a conference, an event, etc.)
筹建 chóujiàn [comp: 筹 prepare + 建 build] *v* prepare to construct (a factory, a school, etc.)

仇 chóu *n* deep hatred
仇恨 chóuhèn intense hatred

丑 chǒu Trad 醜 *adj* ugly □ 他很丑，但是他很温柔。**Tā hěn chǒu, dànshì tā hěn wēnróu.** *He's ugly, but he's gentle and sweet.*
丑恶 chǒu'è [comp: 丑 ugly + 恶 evil] *adj* ugly, hideous
丑闻 chǒuwén [modif: 丑 ugly + 闻 news] *n* scandal □ 丑闻暴露后，市长只能辞职。**Chǒuwén bàolù hòu, shìzhǎng zhǐ néng cízhí.** *When the scandal was exposed, the mayor had to resign.*

臭 chòu *adj* smelly, stinking (antonym 香 xiāng) □ 他的脚爱出汗，一脱鞋就闻到臭味。**Tā de jiǎo ài chūhàn, yì tuō xié jiù wéndào chòu wèi.** *He has sweaty*

feet. *The moment he takes off his shoes, you smell the foul smell.* □ 臭豆腐，闻闻臭，吃起来香。**Chòu dòufu, wénwen chòu, chī qǐlai xiāng.** *The preserved beancurd smells bad but tastes delicious.*

出 chū *v* emerge from, go out, exit

出版 **chūbǎn** *v* publish □ 这本词典由一家国际出版公司出版。**Zhè běn cídiǎn yóu yì jiā guójì chūbǎn gōngsī chūbǎn.** *This dictionary is published by an international publishing house.* □ 老教授又出版了一本书。**Lǎo jiàoshòu yòu chūbǎnle yì běn shū.** *The old professor has published another book.*

出差 **chūchāi** *v* be on a business trip, leave town on business

出产 **chūchǎn** [comp: 出 out + 产 produce] *v* produce, manufacture

出动 **chūdòng** [comp: 出 out + 动 move] *v* set out, go into action

出发 **chūfā** [comp: 出 depart + 发 discharge] *v* set off (on a journey), start (a journey) □ 他们天不亮就出发了。**Tāmen tiān bú liàng jiù chūfā le.** *They set off before dawn.* □ "我们明天什么时候出发？" "早上八点。" **"Wǒmen míngtiān shénme shíhou chūfā?" "Zǎoshang bā diǎn."** *"When do we set off tomorrow?" "Eight o'clock in the morning."*

出发点 **chūfādiǎn** starting point, point of departure

出国 **chūguó** *v* go abroad, go overseas □ 我爸爸每年都要出国开会。**Wǒ bàba měi nián dōu yào chūguó kāihuì.** *My father goes abroad for conferences every year.*

出境 **chūjìng** [v+obj: 出 out of + 境 border] *v* leave the country, exit

办理出境手续 **bànlǐ chūjìng shǒuxù** go through exit formalities

出口 **chūkǒu** [v+obj: 出 leave + 口 mouth, port] **I** *v* 1 export (antonym 进口 **jìnkǒu**) □ 这个国家出口大量工业品到世界各地。**Zhège guójiā chūkǒu dàliàng gōngyèpǐn dào shìjiè gè dì.** *This country exports large amounts of industrial products to various places in the world.*

出口公司 **chūkǒu gōngsī** export company

出口贸易 **chūkǒu màoyì** export business in foreign trade

2 speak, utter **II** *n* exit □ 这是停车场的出口，不能从这里进。**Zhè shì tíngchēchǎng de chūkǒu, bù néng cóng zhèlǐ jìn.** *This is the carpark exit. You can't enter from here.*

出来 **chūlai** [v+compl: 出 exit + 来 come] *v* come out □ 请你出来一下。**Qǐng nǐ chūlai yíxià.** *Would you please step out for a while?*

出路 **chūlù** [modif: 出 out + 路 path] *n* outlet, way out

出卖 **chūmài** *v* 1 sell, be for sale □ 工厂倒闭以后，出卖机器还债。**Gōngchǎng dǎobì yǐhòu, chūmài jīqì huán zhài.** *After the factory went bankrupt, the machines were sold to pay back debts.* 2 betray, sell out □ 犹大为了三十块金币出卖耶稣。**Yóudà wèile sānshí kuài jīnbì chūmài Yēsū.** *Judas sold out Jesus for 30 pieces of gold.*

出门 **chūmén** [v+obj: 出 leave + 门 door] *v* leave home, go out

出面 **chūmiàn** *v* act in the name of

出名 **chūmíng** *adj* famous, well-known □ 他出名了。**Tā chūmíng le.** *He's become famous.*

出纳 **chūnà** *n* Same as 出纳员 **chūnà yuán**

出纳员 **chūnàyuán** *n* cashier

出品 **chūpǐn** *n* product

出去 **chūqu** [v + comp: 出 exit + 去 go] *v* go out □ 请你出去一下。**Qǐng nǐ chūqu yíxià.** *Please go out for a while.* (→ *Please leave us for a while.*)

出入 **chūrù** [comp: 出 out + 入 in] **I** *v* go in and come out **II** *n* inconsistency, discrepancy

出色 **chūsè** *adj* outstanding, remarkable

出身 **chūshēn** *n* family background, (a person's) social origin

出神 **chūshén** *v* be lost in thought, be spellbound

出生 **chūshēng** [comp: 出 come out + 生 be born] *v* be born □ 他出生在1980年。**Tā chūshēng zài yījiǔ-bā-líng nián.** *He was born in 1980.* □ 他于1980年出生在中国。**Tā yú yī-jiǔ-bā-líng nián chūshēng zài Zhōngguó.** *He was born in China in the year 1980.*

出生地 **chūshēng dì** place of birth

出生日期 **chūshēng rìqī** date of birth

出生证 **chūshēng zhèng** birth certificate

出事 **chūshì** *v* (an accident) take place

出事地点 **chūshìdìdiǎn** the scene of an accident

出席 **chūxí** *v* attend (a meeting, a court trial, etc.) □ 你出席明天的会议吗？**Nǐ chūxí míngtiān de huìyì ma?** *Are you going to attend the meeting tomorrow?*

出息 **chūxi** *n* (a person's) future

有出息 **yǒu chūxi** (especially of a young person) have a bright future, promising

出现 **chūxiàn** [comp: 出 emerge + 现 appear] *v* come into view, appear, emerge □ 开车两小时，一座漂亮的小山城出现在我们面前。**Kāichē liǎng xiǎoshí, yí zuò piàoliang de xiǎo shānchéng chūxiàn zài wǒmen miànqián.** *After two hours' drive, a beautiful small mountain town appeared before us.* □ 最近社会上出现了一些奇怪的现象。**Zuìjìn shèhuì shang chūxiànle yìxiē qíguài de xiànxiàng.** *Unusual phenomena have emerged in society recently.*

出洋相 **chūyángxiàng** [v+obj: 出 present + 洋相 foreign appearance] *v* make a fool of oneself, cut a ridiculous figure

出院 **chūyuàn** *v* be discharged from hospital □ 医生，我什么时候可以出院？**Yīshēng, wǒ shénme shíhou kěyǐ chūyuán?** *When can I be discharged, doctor?*

出租 **chūzū** [comp: 出 out + 租 rent] *v* have ... for hire, rent □ 这家商店出租电视机。**Zhè jiā shāngdiàn chūzū diànshìjī.** *This store has TV sets for hire.*

房屋出租 **fángwū chūzū** house for rent, house to let

出租汽车 **chūzū qìchē** *n* taxi □ 我要一辆出租汽车去飞机场。**Wǒ yào yí liàng chūzū qìchē qù fēijīchǎng.** *I need a taxi to go to the airport.*

NOTE: The slang expression 打的 **dǎdī**, which means *to call a taxi* or *to travel by taxi*, is very popular in everyday Chinese.

初 chū **I** *n* beginning

月初 **yuèchū** at the beginning of a month

年初 **niánchū** at the beginning of a year

II *adj* at the beginning, for the first time □ 我初来贵国，情况还不熟悉。**Wǒ chū lái guì guó, qíngkuàng hái bù shúxī.** *I have just arrived in your country, and do*

not know much about it. **III** *prefix* (used for the first ten days of a lunar month), the first

初一 chū yī the first day (of a lunar month)

五月初八 Wǔyuè chū bā the eighth day of the fifth lunar month

年初一/大年初一 nián chū yī/dà nián chū yī the first day of the first lunar month (Chinese New Year's Day)

初步 **chūbù** [modif: 初 initial + 步 step] *adj* initial, tentative □ 这仅仅是我们的初步打算。**Zhè jǐnjǐn shì wǒmen de chūbù dǎsuàn.** *This is but our tentative plan.*

初级 **chūjí** [modif: 初 initial + 级 grade] *adj* elementary, initial

初级小学/初小 chūjí xiǎoxué/chūxiǎo elementary school (from Grade 1 to Grade 4 of a primary school)

初级中学/初中 chūjí zhōngxué/chūzhōng junior high school

初期 **chūqī** [modif: 初 initial + 期 period] *n* initial stage

除 chú **I** *v* get rid of **II** *prep* except, apart from
除草 **chú cǎo** [v+obj: 除 get rid of + 草 weeds] *v* to weed

除草剂 chúcǎojì weed killer, herbicide

除虫 **chú chóng** [v+obj: 除 get rid of + 虫 insect] **I** *v* to kill insects **II** *n* insecticide

除此以外 chúcǐ yǐwài *prep* apart from this, besides

除非 **chúfēi** *conj* unless, only if □ 除非他们正式邀请我，否则我是不会去参加他们的婚礼的。**Chúfēi tāmen zhèngshì yāoqǐng wǒ, fǒuzé wǒ shì bú huì qù cānjiā tāmen de hūnlǐ de.** *I'm not going to attend their wedding, unless they send me a formal invitation.*

除了…(以外) **chúle … (yǐwài)** *prep* except, besides □ 这个动物园除了圣诞节每天开放。**Zhège dòngwùyuán chúle Shèngdànjié měitiān kāifàng.** *This zoo is open to the public all year round except on Christmas Day.* □ 我除了英文以外，还会说一点儿中文。**Wǒ chúle Yīngwén yǐwài, hái huì shuō yìdiǎnr Zhōngwén.** *Besides English I speak a little Chinese.*

NOTES: (1) While *except* and *besides* are two distinct words in English, 除了…以外, **chúle…yǐwài** may mean either *except* or *besides*, as is shown in the examples. (2) 以外 **yǐwài** may be omitted, i.e. 除了…以外 **chúle… (yǐwài)** and 除了… **chúle** are the same.

除夕 **chúxī** *n* New Year's eve

NOTE: In colloquial Chinese, the Chinese New Year's eve is called 大年夜 **dàniányè.** The dinner on the Chinese New Year's eve is 年夜饭 **niányèfàn**, or 团圆饭 **tuányuánfàn**, a family reunion dinner.

厨 chú Trad 廚 *n* kitchen
厨房 **chúfáng** [modif: 厨 kitchen + 房 room] *n* kitchen □ 厨房又乱又脏，要收拾一下。**Chúfáng yòu luàn yòu zāng, yào shōushi yíxia.** *The kitchen is dirty and messy. It needs tidying up.* □ 她在厨房里忙了好久了。**Tā zài chúfángli mángle hǎojiǔ le.** *She has been busy working in the kitchen for a long time.*

厨房设备 chúfáng shèbèi kitchen equipment

厨房用具 chúfáng yòngjù kitchen utensils

厨师 **chúshī** [modif: 厨 kitchen + 师 master] *n* chef

大厨师 dàchúshī master chef

锄 chú Trad 鋤 **I** *n* hoe
锄头 chútóu hoe (把 **bǎ**)
II *v* do hoeing

处 chǔ Trad 處 *v* handle, deal with
处罚 **chǔfá** [comp: 处 deal with + 罚 punish] *v* penalize, discipline

处方 **chǔfāng** *n* (doctor's) prescription

处方药 chǔfāng yào prescribed medicine

非处方药 fēi chǔfāng yào over-the-counter medicine

开处方 kāi chǔfāng write out a prescription

处分 **chǔfèn** **I** *n* disciplinary action □ 十名官员因接受贵重礼物受到处分。**Shí míng guānyuán yīn jiēshòu guìzhòng lǐwù shòudào chǔfèn.** *Disciplinary action was taken against the ten officials who had accepted expensive gifts.*

警告处分 jǐnggào chǔfèn disciplinary warning
II *v* take disciplinary action □ 处分这名学生是为了教育全校所有的学生。**Chǔfèn zhè míng xuésheng shì wèile jiàoyù quán xiào suǒyǒu de xuésheng.** *The purpose of taking disciplinary action against this student is to educate all the students of the school.*

处分服用兴奋剂的运动员 chǔfèn fúyòng xīngfènjì de yùndòngyuán take disciplinary action against athletes who have taken stimulants

处境 **chǔjìng** *n* (usually) bad situation, plight

处境危险 chǔjìng wēixiǎn in a dangerous situation

处决 **chǔjué** *v* put to death, execute

处理 **chǔlǐ** *v* **1** handle, deal with □ 对于顾客提出的意见，我们都会认真处理。**Duìyú gùkè tíchū de yìjiàn, wǒmen dōu huì rènzhēn chǔlǐ.** *We deal with customers' suggestions seriously.* □ 这种关系很难处理。**Zhè zhǒng guānxi hěn nán chǔlǐ.** *This kind of relationship is difficult to handle.* **2** sell at reduced prices

处理品 chǔlǐpǐn goods sold at reduced prices
3 take disciplinary action

处理违反校纪的学生 chǔlǐ wéifǎn xiào jì de xuésheng take disciplinary action against students who have violated school regulations

处于 **chǔyú** *v* be in state of, be situated at

处置 **chǔzhì** *v* dispose of, handle, deal with

础 chǔ Trad 礎 *n* plinth (See 基础 **jīchǔ**)

楚 chǔ *adj* clear, neat (See 清楚 **qīngchu**)

储 chǔ Trad 儲 *v* store
储备 **chǔbèi** [comp: 储 store + 备 prepare] *v* store away

储存 **chǔcún** [comp: 储 store + 存 preserve] *v* **1** store away, keep in reserve **2** (in computing) save a file

储蓄 **chǔxù** [comp: 储 store + 蓄 save up] *v* save (money), deposit (money)

定期储蓄 dìngqī chǔxù fixed deposits, term deposit

活期储蓄 huóqī chǔxù checking account

处 chù Trad 處 *n* place, location □ 你知道他现在的住处吗？**Nǐ zhīdào tā xiànzài de zhùchù ma?** *Do you know where he lives now?*

处处 **chùchù** *adv* everywhere

触 **chù** Trad 觸 v touch, contact
触电 **chùdiàn** v get an electric shock □ 小心触电!
Xiǎoxīn chùdiàn! *Danger! Electricity!*
触犯 **chùfàn** [comp: 触 touch + 犯 violate] v violate
(law), offend (a person)

穿 **chuān** v 1 wear (clothes, shoes), be dressed
in □ 你穿黑衣服去参加中国人的婚礼, 不合适。**Nǐ
chuān hēi yīfu qù cānjiā Zhōngguórén de hūnlǐ, bù
héshì.** *It is not appropriate for you to go to a Chinese
wedding in black.*
穿着 **chuānzhe** be dressed in □ 那个穿着红衣服的女
孩子是我哥哥的女朋友。**Nàge chuānzhe hóng yīfu de
nǚháizi shì wǒ gēge de nǚpéngyou.** *The girl in red is
my elder brother's girlfriend.*
2 put on (clothes, shoes) □ 这个小孩会穿衣服了, 可
是还不会穿鞋子。**Zhège xiǎohái huì chuān yīfu le,
kěshì hái bú huì chuān xiézi.** *This child can put on his
clothes, but still can't put on his shoes.*

川 **chuān** n river

船 **chuán** n boat, ship □ 从香港坐船到上海去, 只要
两天。**Cóng Xiānggǎng zuòchuán dào Shànghǎi qù,
zhǐ yào liǎng tiān.** *It takes only two days to travel from
Hong Kong to Shanghai by sea.*
划船 **huá chuán** row a boat
坐船 **zuò chuán** travel by boat/ship
船舶 **chuánbó** [comp: 船 ship + 舶 ship] n boats
and ships
船舶公司 **chuánbó gōngsī** shipping company

传 **chuán** Trad 傳 v 1 pass (something) on,
transmit □ 你看完这份文件后, 请按照名单传给下一
个人。**Nǐ kàn wán zhè fèn wénjiàn hòu, qǐng ànzhào
míngdān chuán gěi xià yí ge rén.** *After reading this
document, please pass it onto the next person on the
list.* **2** spread (news, rumor) □ 好事不出门, 坏事传
千里。**Hǎo shì bù chūmén, huài shì chuán qiān lǐ.**
*Good news stays at home, but bad news travels far
and wide.*
传播 **chuánbō** [comp: 传 spread + 播 sow] v
propagate, disseminate □ 学校不仅仅是传播知识的地
方。**Xuéxiào bù jǐnjǐn shì chuánbō zhīshi de dìfang.** *A
school is more than a place to disseminate knowledge.*
□ 这种病传得很快。**Zhè zhǒng bìng chuánbō de hěn
kuài.** *This disease spreads fast.*
传达 **chuándá** [comp: 传 transmit + 达 arrive] v
pass on, relay, transmit
传达室 **chuándá shì** reception office
传达总公司的指令 **chuándá zǒnggōngsī de zhǐlìng**
pass on instructions from the company's HQ
传递 **chuándì** [comp: 传 transmit + 递 deliver] v
transmit, deliver
传媒 **chuánméi** n media, mass media
大众传媒 **dàzhòng chuánméi** mass media
传染 **chuánrǎn** [comp: 传 spread + 染 contact] v
infect □ 验血表明, 他被传染上艾滋病毒了。**Yànxuè
biǎomíng, tā bèi chuánrǎn shàng àizībìngdú le.** *Blood
tests indicate that he is infected with the AIDS virus.*
传染病 **chuánrǎnbìng** infectious (contagious) disease
传授 **chuánshòu** [comp: 传 transmit + 授 teach] v
teach, pass on (knowledge, skill, etc.)
传说 **chuánshuō** [comp: 传 transmit + 说 saying] **I** n
legend, folklore

民间传说 **mínjiān chuánshuō** folktale
II v it is said, they say
传送 **chuánsòng** v convey, deliver
传送带 **chuánsòngdài** conveyor belt
传统 **chuántǒng** n tradition, heritage □ 每个民族都有
自己的传统。**Měi ge mínzú dōu yǒu zìjǐ de chuántǒng.**
Every ethnic group has its own traditions. □ 中医、
武术、国画都是中国人的传统文化。**Zhōngyī, wǔshù,
guóhuà dōu shì Zhōngguórén de chuántǒng wénhuà.**
*Chinese medicine, martial arts and Chinese painting
are all part of traditional Chinese culture.*
传统服装 **chuántǒng fúzhuāng** traditional costume
传销 **chuánxiāo** [comp: 传 spread + 销 sale] n
pyramid selling
传真 **chuánzhēn** [v+obj: 传 transmit + 真 true] n
fax □ 我的传真号码和电话号码是一样的。**Wǒ de
chuánzhēn hàomǎ hé diànhuà hàomǎ shì yíyàng de.**
My fax number is the same as my telephone number.
□ 我发了一份传真给他。**Wǒ fāle yí fèn chuánzhēn gei
tā.** *I sent him a fax.*

喘 **chuǎn** v breathe with difficulty, pant

串 **chuàn** v string together

疮 **chuāng** n sore, open sore
冻疮 **dòngchuāng** chilblain
疮疤 **chuāngbā** [comp: 疮 sore + 疤 scar] n scar

窗 **chuāng** n window (扇 **shàn**)
玻璃窗 **bōlichuāng** glass window
窗户 **chuānghu** [comp: 窗 window + 户 door] n
window (扇 **shàn**) □ 我房间的窗户朝东。**Wǒ fángjiān
de chuānghu cháo dōng.** *The window in my room
faces east.* □ 马上要下雨了, 把窗户关上吧。**Mǎshang
yào xià yǔ le, bǎ chuānghu guānshang ba.** *It's going to
rain soon. Let's close the window.*
打开窗户 **dǎkāi chuānghu** open a window
关上窗户 **guānshang chuānghu** close a window
窗口 **chuāngkǒu** n window
窗帘 **chuānglián** [modif: 窗 window + 帘 curtain] n
(window) curtain (块 **kuài**) □ 天黑了, 把窗帘拉上吧。
Tiān hēi le, bǎ chuānglián lā shàng ba. *It's getting
dark. Let's close the curtains.*
窗台 **chuāngtái** n window sill

床 **chuáng** n bed (张 **zhāng**) □ 这张床很舒服。**Zhè
zhāng chuáng hěn shūfu.** *This bed is very comfortable.* □ 这个房间很小, 放了一张大床, 就剩下不多地方
了。**Zhè ge fángjiān hěn xiǎo, fàngle yì zhāng dà chuáng
jiù shèngxia bù duō dìfang le.** *This room is small. With
a big bed in it, there is not much space left.*
单人床 **dānrénchuáng** single bed
双人床 **shuāngrénchuáng** double bed
床单 **chuángdān** n bedsheet (条 **tiáo**)
床铺 **chuángpù** n bed (in school dormitories, army
barracks, etc.) (张 **zhāng**)
床位 **chuángwèi** n bed (in a hospital, ship, train,
etc.) (张 **zhāng**)

闯 **chuǎng** Trad 闖 v charge, rush
闯祸 **chuǎnghuò** [v+obj: 闯 rush into + 祸 dis-
aster] v cause disasters, get into trouble

创 **chuàng** Trad 創 v create
创建 **chuàngjiàn** [comp: 创 create + 建 build] v
found (a company, an institution, etc.)

创立 chuànglì [comp: 创 establish + 立 stand] v set up, found

创业 chuàngyè [comp: 创 establish + 业 undertaking] v start an undertaking
创业精神 chuàngyè jīngshen pioneering spirit

创造 chuàngzào [comp: 创 create + 造 build, make] v create □ 有人说神创造了天地。 **Yǒurén shuō shén chuàngzàole tiān-dì.** *Some people say God created the universe.*

创造性 chuàngzàoxìng n creativity □ 创造性是艺术作品的生命。 **Chuàngzàoxìng shì yìshù zuòpǐn de shēngmìng.** *Creativity is the life of a work of art.*

创作 chuàngzuò [comp: 创 create + 作 make] I v create (works of art and literature) □ 这位作家创作了反映农民生活的小说。 **Zhè wèi zuòjiā chuàngzuòle fǎnyìng nóngmín shēnghuó de xiǎoshuō.** *This author wrote novels about peasant lives.* II n work of art or literature □ 这位作家的新创作是中国文学的伟大成就。 **Zhè wèi zuòjiā de xīn chuàngzuò shì Zhōngguó wénxué de wěidà chéngjiù.** *This author's new work is a great achievement in Chinese literature.*

吹 chuī v blow, puff □ 风吹草动。 **Fēng chuī cǎo dòng.** *Winds blow and the grass stirs.* (→ *There are signs of disturbance/trouble.*)
吹牛 chuīniú v brag, boast □ 你别相信他, 他在吹牛。 **Nǐ bié xiāngxìn tā, tā zài chuīniú.** *Don't believe him. He's bragging.*
吹牛大王 chuīniú dàwáng braggart
吹捧 chuīpěng v lavish praise on, flatter
相互吹捧 xiānghù chuīpěng flatter each other

炊 chuī v cook
炊事员 chuīshìyuán [modif: 炊 cooking + 事 affair + 员 person] n cook, kitchen staff (in a school, a factory, etc.)

垂 chuí v hang down
垂直 chuízhí adj vertical
垂直线 chuízhíxiàn vertical line

锤 chuí v hammer
锤子 chuízi hammer (把 **bǎ**)

捶 chuí v beat with a fist or stick

春 chūn n spring
春季 chūnjì spring (season)
春节 Chūnjié [modif: 春 spring + 节 festival] n Spring Festival (the Chinese New Year) □ 春节是中国人最重要的节日。 **Chūnjié shì Zhōngguórén zuì zhòngyào de jiérì.** *The Spring Festival is the most important festival for the Chinese.* □ 小明的哥哥, 姐姐都要回家过春节。 **Xiǎo Míng de gēge, jiějie dōu yào huí jiā guò Chūnjié.** *Xiao Ming's elder brothers and sisters will be coming home for the Spring Festival.*
春天 chūntiān [modif: 春 spring + 天 days] n spring □ 春天来了, 花园里的花都开了。 **Chūntiān lái le, huāyuán lǐ de huā dōu kāi le.** *Spring is here. The flowers in the garden are in full bloom.* □ 我最喜欢春天, 不太冷, 也不太热。 **Wǒ zuì xǐhuan chūntiān, bú tài lěng, yě bú tài rè.** *I like spring best; it's neither too cold nor too hot.*

纯 chún Trad 純 adj pure
纯粹 chúncuì adj unadulterated, pure and simple □ 这纯粹是谎言! **Zhè chúncuì shì huǎngyán!** *This is a lie, pure and simple!*

纯洁 chúnjié [comp: 纯 pure + 洁 clean] adj pure, ingenuous

唇 chún Trad 脣 n lip
嘴唇 zuǐchún (mouth) lip
嘴唇皮儿 zuǐchúnpír (mouth) lip

蠢 chǔn adj stupid, foolish
蠢事 chǔnshì an act of folly
干蠢事 gān chǔnshì do a stupid thing, commit a folly

雌 cí adj (of animals) female (antonym 雄 **xióng**) □ 我不知道家里的狗是雌的还是雄的。 **Wǒ bù zhīdào jiālǐ de gǒu shì cí de háishì xióng de.** *I don't know whether our family dog is female or male.*

词 cí Trad 詞 n word □ 现代汉语的词一般是由两个字组成。 **Xiàndài Hànyǔ de cí yìbān shì yóu liǎng ge zì zǔchéng.** *Modern Chinese words generally consist of two characters.* □ 我没有听说过这个词。 **Wǒ méiyǒu tīngshuōguo zhè ge cí.** *I haven't heard of this word.*
词典 cídiǎn n dictionary (本 **běn**) □ 这本词典对我们很有帮助。 **Zhè běn cídiǎn duì wǒmen hěn yǒu bāngzhù.** *This dictionary is very helpful to us.* □ 你看, 我买了一本新词典。 **Nǐ kàn, wǒ mǎile yì běn xīn cídiǎn.** *Look, I've bought a new dictionary.*
查词典 chá cídiǎn consult a dictionary

瓷 cí n porcelain
瓷器 cíqì [modif: 瓷 porcelain + 器 ware] n porcelain

磁 cí n magnetism
磁带 cídài [modif: 磁 magnetic + 带 tape] n magnetic tape, audio tape (盘 **pán**) □ 这一盘磁带是我爷爷最喜欢的, 几乎每天都听。 **Zhè yì pán cídài shì wǒ yéye zuì xǐhuan de, jīhū měi tiān dōu tīng.** *This is my granddad's favorite tape. I listen to it almost every day.*
磁卡 cíkǎ [modif: 磁 magnetic + 卡 card] n magnetic card (for making telephone calls, etc.)
磁盘 cípán [modif: 磁 magnetic + 盘 disk] n magnetic disc

慈 cí adj kind and loving
慈爱 cí'ài [comp: 慈 kind and loving + 爱 affectionate] n love and affection (from an elderly person, e.g. a grandmother)
慈祥 cíxiáng [comp: 慈 kind and loving + 祥 serene] adj (of an elderly person's countenance) kindly

辞 cí Trad 辭 v take leave
辞职 cízhí [v+obj: 辞 take leave + 职 position] v resign (from job, position)

此 cǐ pron 1 this □ 此路不通。 **Cǐ lù bù tōng.** *This road is blocked.* (→ *No through road.*)
此时此地 cǐshícǐdì here and now
2 here □ 会议到此结束。 **Huìyì dào cǐ jiéshù.** *The meeting ends here/at this point.* (→ *This is the end of the meeting.*)
此后 cǐhòu conj after this, ever after
此刻 cǐkè n this moment
此时 cǐshí adv right now
此外 cǐwài conj besides, apart from (that), as well □ 他买了一台新电脑, 此外, 还买了一些软件。 **Tā mǎile yì tái xīn diànnǎo, cǐwài, hái mǎile yìxiē ruǎnjiàn.** *He bought a new computer and some software as well.*

次 1 cì measure wd time (expressing frequency of an act) □ 我去过他家两次。 **Wǒ qùguo tā jiā liǎng**

liǎng cì. *I've been to his home twice.* □ 这是我第一次
出国旅行。**Zhè shì wǒ dì-yī cì chūguó lǚxíng.** *This is
my first trip abroad.*

下次 xiàcì next time

次数 cìshù *n* number of times

次 2 **cì** *adj* inferior
次品 cìpǐn [modif: 次 inferior + 品 article, prod-
uct] *n* substandard product, seconds (used goods)

次要 cìyào *adj* next in importance, of secondary
importance

次 3 **cì** *n* order, sequence
次序 cìxù [comp: 次 order + 序 order] *n* order,
sequence

伺 **cì** *v* wait on
伺候 cìhou *v* wait on, serve

刺 **cì** **I** *v* prick □ 花儿很美，但是会刺人。**Huār hěn
měi, dànshì huì cì rén.** *The flower is beautiful, but it
may prick you.* **II** *n* thorn

刺激 cìjī [comp: 刺 prick + 激 excite] *v* **1** irritate □ 强
烈的阳光刺激我的眼睛，很不舒服。**Qiángliè de yángguāng
cìjī wǒ de yǎnjing, hěn bù shūfu.** *The strong sunlight
irritates my eyes; it's very uncomfortable.* **2** stimulate,
give incentive to □ 公司决定增加加班费，来刺激工人
的积极性。**Gōngsī juédìng zēngjiā jiābānfèi, lái cìjī
gōngrén de jījíxìng.** *The company decided to increase
overtime pay in order to arouse workers' enthusiasm.*

囱 **cōng** *n* chimney (See 烟囱 **yāncōng**)

聪 **cōng** Trad 聰 *n* acute hearing
聪明 cōngmíng [comp: 聪 acute hearing + 明
keen eyesight] *adj* clever, bright, intelligent □ 他
不但聪明，而且用功，所以考试总是第一名。**Tā búdàn
cōngmíng, érqiě yònggōng, suǒyǐ kǎoshì zǒngshi dì-yī
míng.** *He is not only clever, but also hardworking, so
he always comes out first in the exams.*

匆 **cōng** Trad 忽 *adj* hurriedly
匆匆 cōngcōng *adj* hurriedly, in a rush
匆忙 cōngmáng [comp: 匆 hurriedly + 忙 busy] *adj*
in a hurry, in haste

葱 **cōng** *n* onion, scallion
大葱 dàcōng green Chinese onion
洋葱 yángcōng onion
小葱 xiǎocōng spring onion

从 **cóng** Trad 從 *prep* following, from □ "你从哪
里来？" "我从很远的地方来。" **"Nǐ cóng nǎlǐ lái?"**
"Wǒ cóng hěn yuǎn de dìfang lái." *"Where did you
come from?" "I came from a faraway place."*
从…出发 cóng...chūfā set out from ...
从不 cóngbù *adv* never □ 我从不吸烟。**Wǒ cóngbù
xīyān.** *I never smoke.*
从此 cóngcǐ *conj* since then, from then on □ 我上次
跟他开玩笑，他竟生气了，从此我不跟他开玩笑了。**Wǒ
shàng cì gēn tā kāi wánxiào, tā jìng shēngqì le, cóngcǐ
wǒ bù gēn tā kāi wánxiào le.** *He got angry when I
joked with him the last time. Since then I have never
joked with him.*
从…到… cóng...dào... *prep* from ... to ..., from ...
till ... □ 我从上午九点到下午三点都要上课。**Wǒ cóng
shàngwǔ jiǔ diǎn dào xiàwǔ sān diǎn dōu yào shàngkè.** *I've classes from nine o'clock in the morning till
three o'clock in the afternoon.* □ 从中国到英国要经过
许多国家。**Cóng Zhōngguó dào Yīngguó yào jīngguò**

xǔduō guójiā. *Traveling from China to England, one
has to pass through many countries.*
从早到晚 cóng-zǎo-dào-wǎn from morning till
night, many hours in a day □ 夏天他从早到晚都
在农场工作。**Xiàtiān tā cóng-zǎo-dào-wǎn dōu zài
nóngchǎng gōngzuò.** *In summer he works on the farm
from morning till night.*
从古到今 cóng-gǔ-dào-jīn from the remote past till
now □ 从古到今，出现过多少英雄人物! **Cóng-gǔ-dào-jīn
chūxiànguo duōshǎo yīngxióng rénwù!** *From the remote
past to now, history has produced so many heroes!*
从而 cóng'ér *conj* thus, thereby □ 我要认真学好
中文，从而了解中华文化。**Wǒ yào rènzhēn xué hǎo
Zhōngwén, cóng'ér liǎojiě Zhōnghuá wénhuà.** *I will
study the Chinese language earnestly, thereby gaining
an understanding of Chinese culture.*
从来 cónglái *adv* always, ever
从来不 cónglái bù never □ 我从来不喝酒。**Wǒ
cónglái bù hē jiǔ.** *I never drink wine.* □ 有钱的越来
越有钱，没钱的越来越没钱，从来如此。**Yǒuqiánde
yuèláiyuè yǒu qián, méiqiánde yuèláiyuè méi qián,
cónglái rúcǐ.** *The rich get richer and the poor get
poorer—it has always been this way.*
从…起 cóng...qǐ *prep* starting from ... □ 我决定
从明年一月一日起每天早上跑步。**Wǒ juédìng cóng
míngnián Yīyuè yírì qǐ měi tiān zǎoshang pǎobù.** *I've
decided to jog every morning starting from January 1
next year.*
从前 cóngqián *n* **1** past, in the past □ 我从前不
知道学中文多么有意思。**Wǒ cóngqián bù zhīdao
xué Zhōngwén duōme yǒu yìsi.** *I did not know how
interesting it is to learn Chinese.* **2** once upon a time
(used in story-telling) □ 从前有个农民，他… **Cóng-
qián yǒu ge nóngmín, tā...** *Once upon a time there was
a farmer, who...*
从容 cóngróng *adj* unhurried, leisurely
从事 cóngshì *v* be engaged in (business, education,
law, etc.)
从未 cóngwèi *adv* never in the past

从 **cóng** Trad 叢 *n* shrub, thicket
丛书 cóngshū *n* a series of books on a specific
topic

凑 **còu** *v* put together, pool
凑钱 còu qián pool money
凑合 còuhe *v* make do, make do with
凑巧 còuqiǎo *adj* luckily, as luck would have it

粗 **cū** *adj* thick (antonym 细 **xì**), crude □ 这根绳
子太细了，要粗点儿的。**Zhè gēn shéngzi tài xì le,
yào cū diǎnr de.** *This rope is too thin. We need a
thicker one.*
粗暴 cūbào [comp: 粗 crude + 暴 violent] *adj*
rough, brutal
粗鲁 cūlǔ [comp: 粗 crude + 鲁 rash] *adj* rude,
boorish
粗细 cūxì [comp: 粗 thick + 细 thin] *n* degree of
thickness

NOTE: See note on 大小 **dàxiǎo**.

粗心 cūxīn [modif: 粗 thick + 心 the heart] *adj*
careless (antonym 细心 **xìxīn**) □ 她太粗心了，考试
的时候竟然漏了一道题目。**Tā tài cūxīn le, kǎoshì de**

shíhou jìngrán lòule yí dào tímù. *She was so careless she missed a question in the exam.*

促 **cù** *v* urge

促进 **cùjìn** [v+obj: 促 promote + 进 progress] *v* promote, advance □ 工会的目的是促进工人的利益。**Gōnghuì de mùdì shì cùjìn gōngrén de lìyì.** *The purpose of the trade union is to advance workers' interests.* □ 让我们为促进友谊努力。**Ràng wǒmen wèi cùjìn yǒuyì nǔlì.** *Let's work hard to promote our friendship.*

促使 **cùshǐ** *v* impel, urge

醋 **cù** *n* vinegar □ 他喜欢吃酸的，什么东西都放醋。**Tā xǐhuan chī suān de, shénme dōngxi dōu fàng cù.** *He is fond of sour flavors, and adds vinegar to whatever he eats.*

窜 **cuàn** Trad 竄 *v* 1 rush about 2 falsify, fabricate

催 **cuī** *v* urge, hurry □ 他催我还钱。**Tā cuī wǒ huán qián.** *He urged me to pay him back.* □ 别催她，时间还早。**Bié cuī tā, shíjiān hái zǎo.** *Don't hurry her. There's enough time.*

摧 **cuī** *v* break, destroy

摧残 **cuīcán** *v* devastate, wreck

摧毁 **cuīhuǐ** *v* destroy completely

脆 **cuì** *adj* crisp

脆弱 **cuìruò** [comp: 脆 crispy + 弱 weak] *adj* fragile, frail

粹 **cuì** *adj* pure

翠 **cuì** *n* green, bluish green

村 **cūn** *n* village

村庄 **cūnzhuāng** [comp: 村 village + 庄 village] *n* village

村子 **cūnzi** [suffix: 村 village + 子 nominal suffix] *n* village (座 **zuò**) □ 你们村子有多少户人家? **Nǐmen cūnzi yǒu duōshǎo hù rénjiā?** *How many households are there in your village?*

存 **cún** *v* store, keep □ 她一有钱就存在银行里。**Tā yì yǒu qián jiù cún zài yínháng lǐ.** *As soon as she gets some money, she deposits it in the bank.* □ 他出国前把一些东西存在姐姐家。**Tā chū guó qián bǎ yìxiē dōngxi cún zài jiějie jiā.** *Before going abroad he stored some stuff at his sister's home.*

存储 **cúnchǔ** *v* 1 save a file (in computing) 2 store

存放 **cúnfàng** [comp: 存 store + 放 put] *v* leave in someone's care

存款 **cúnkuǎn** *n* savings □ 她从银行取出一些存款, 给女儿办婚礼。**Tā cóng yínháng qǔchū yìxiē cúnkuǎn, gěi nǚ'ér bàn hūnlǐ.** *She withdrew some money from her savings in the bank for her daughter's wedding.*

存盘 **cún pán** *v* save (a computer file)

存在 **cúnzài** *v* exist □ 这家公司存在严重问题。**Zhè jiā gōngsī cúnzài yánzhòng wèntí.** *There are serious problems with this company.*

寸 **cùn** *measure wd* a traditional Chinese unit of length (equal to $\frac{1}{30}$ meter)

英寸 **yīngcùn** inch

磋 **cuō** *v* consult

磋商 **cuōshāng** [comp: 磋 consult + 商 discuss] *v* consult, discuss

搓 **cuō** *v* rub with the hands

错 **cuò** Trad 錯 *adj* wrong (antonym 对 **duì**) □ 我错了, 我不应该那么做。**Wǒ cuò le, wǒ bù yīnggāi nàme zuò.** *I was wrong. I shouldn't have done that.* □ 你这个字写错了。**Nǐ zhège zì xiě cuò le.** *You've written this character wrongly.*

错字 **cuòzì** wrong character

错误 **cuòwù** [comp: 错 wrong + 误 miss] I *n* mistake, error □ 你这次作业有很多错误。**Nǐ zhè cì zuòyè yǒu hěn duō cuòwù.** *You've made many mistakes in this assignment.*

犯错误 **fàn cuòwù** make a mistake □ 人人都会犯错误。**Rénrén dōu huì fàn cuòwù.** *Everybody makes mistakes.*

纠正错误 **jiūzhèng cuòwù** correct a mistake

II *adj* wrong, erroneous □ 这是一个错误的决定。**Zhè shì yí ge cuòwù de juédìng.** *This is a wrong decision.*

措 **cuò** *v* arrange, handle

措施 **cuòshī** *n* measure, step □ 我们必须迅速采取有效措施。**Wǒmen bìxū xùnsù cǎiqǔ yǒuxiào cuòshī.** *We must take immediate and effective measures.* □ 由于措施不当, 问题更加严重了。**Yóuyú cuòshī bú dàng, wèntí gèngjiā yánzhòng le.** *Owing to inappropriate measures, the problem became even more serious.*

挫 **cuò** *v* frustrate, defeat

受挫 **shòucuò** be frustrated, be defeated

挫折 **cuòzhé** [comp: 挫 frustrate + 折 break] *n* setback, frustration

D

答 **dā** *v* answer

答应 **dāying** [comp: 答 reply + 应 respond] *v* 1 answer, reply □ 我按了半天门铃, 也没人答应。**Wǒ ànle bàntiān ménlíng, yě méi rén dāying.** *I pressed the doorbell for a long time, but nobody answered.* 2 promise □ 爸爸答应给他买一台笔记本电脑。**Bàba dāying gěi tā mǎi yì tái bǐjìběn diànnǎo.** *Father has promised to buy him a notebook computer.*

搭 **dā** *v* put up, build

搭配 **dāpèi** I *v* arrange in pairs or groups II *n* (word) collocation

达 **dá** Trad 達 *v* reach, attain

达成 **dáchéng** *v* reach (an agreement, an understanding, a business deal, etc.)

达到 **dádào** [comp: 达 reach + 到 reach] *v* reach, achieve □ 需要学几年才能达到高等汉语水平? **Xūyào xué jǐ nián cái néng dádào gāoděng Hànyǔ shuǐpíng?** *How many years do I have to study to reach the Advanced Level of Chinese proficiency?* □ 他的要求太高, 很难达到。**Tā de yāoqiú tài gāo, hěn nán dádào.** *His demands are too high. It is difficult to meet them.* □ 不能为了达到目的, 而不择手段。**Bù néng wèile dádào mùdì, ér bù zé shǒuduàn.** *One shouldn't stop at nothing in order to achieve one's aim. (→ The end doesn't always justify the means.)*

答 **dá** *v* answer, reply □ 这个问题我不会答。**Zhège wèntí wǒ bú huì dá.** *I can't answer this question.*

答案 **dá'àn** [modif: 答 anwer + 案 file] *n* answer (to a list of questions) □ 测验以后, 老师发给学生标准答案。**Cèyàn yǐhòu, lǎoshī fā gěi xuésheng biāozhǔn**

dá'àn. *After the test, the teacher distributed standardized answers to students.* □ 关于这个问题, 还是没有答案。**Guānyú zhège wèntí, háishì méiyǒu dá'àn.** *There is still no answer to this question.*

答辩 **dábiàn** [comp: 答 reply + 辩 defense] *v* speak in self-defense

论文答辩 **lùnwén dábiàn** (postgraduate students') oral examination in defense of a thesis

答复 **dáfù** I *v* (formally) reply II *n* (formal) reply

答卷 **dájuàn** *n* answer sheet

打 **dǎ** *v* 1 strike, hit □ 不能打人。**Bù néng dǎ rén.** *You can't hit people.* 2 play (certain games)

打棒球 **dǎ bàngqiú** play baseball

打高尔夫球 **dǎ gāo'ěrfūqiú** play golf

打篮球 **dǎ lánqiú** play basketball

打台球 **dǎ táiqiú** play pool

打败 **dǎbài** *v* defeat, beat

打扮 **dǎbàn** *v* dress up, make up □ 新娘打扮得很漂亮。**Xīnniáng dǎbàn de hěn piàoliang.** *The bride was beautifully dressed.* □ 她每天要花很多时间打扮。**Tā měi tiān yào huā hěn duō shíjiān dǎbàn.** *Every day she spends lots of time putting on makeup.*

打车 **dǎ chē** *v* call a taxi □ 时间很紧了, 我们得打车。**Shíjiān hěn jǐn le, wǒmen děi dǎ chē.** *We don't have much time now; we've got to call a taxi.*

打倒 **dǎdǎo** [v+compl: 打 strike + 倒 down] *v* strike down, overthrow, down with ...

打的 **dǎ dī** *v* Same as 打车 **dǎ chē**

打电话 **dǎ diànhuà** *v* make a telephone call

打发 **dǎfa** *v* dispatch, send away

打工 **dǎgōng** *v* work (especially as a manual laborer) □ 我希望在暑假里有机会打工, 付明年的学费。**Wǒ xīwàng zài shǔjià lǐ yǒu jīhuì dǎgōng, fù míngnián de xuéfèi.** *I hope I'll have an opportunity to work in the summer vacation to pay for my tuition fee next year.*

打击 **dǎjī** [comp: 打 strike + 击 strike] *v* strike a blow against (a crime, a bad tendency, etc.), deal with and punish severely

打击盗版 **dǎjī dàobǎn** attack the crime of piracy (of intellectual products)

打架 **dǎjià** *v* fight (between people), come to blows

打交道 **dǎ jiāodao** *v* to have dealings with, negotiate with

和各式各样的人打交道 **hé gèshìgèyàng de rén dǎ jiāodao** deal with all kinds of people. □ 他很会和政府部门打交道。**Tā hěn huì hé zhèngfǔ bùmén dǎ jiāodao.** *He is very good at dealing with government departments.*

打卡 **dǎkǎ** *v* punch a card, record attendance at work by punching a time machine

打瞌睡 **dǎ kēshuì** *v* doze, doze off

打一会儿瞌睡 **dǎ yíhuìr kēshuì** have a doze-off

打量 **dǎliang** *v* measure with the eye, size up

打猎 **dǎliè** *v* hunt

打破 **dǎpò** *v* break

打破花瓶 **dǎpò huāpíng** break a vase

打破世界纪录 **dǎpò shìjiè jìlù** break a world record

打球 **dǎ qiú** *v* play baseball/basketball/volleyball, etc.

打扰 **dǎrǎo** *v* disturb, interrupt □ 爸爸在写一份重要的报告, 你别去打扰他。**Bàba zài xiě yí fèn zhòngyào de bàogào, nǐ bié qù dǎrǎo tā.** *Daddy is working on an important report. Don't disturb him.*

NOTE: You can use 打搅 **dǎjiǎo** instead of 打扰 **dǎrǎo**, with the same meaning. When you call on someone, especially at their home, you can say 打扰你们了 **Dǎrǎo nǐmen le** as a polite expression.

打扫 **dǎsǎo** *v* clean up □ 中国人在过春节前, 要打扫屋子。**Zhōngguórén zài guò chūnjié qián, yào dǎsǎo wūzi.** *Before the Spring Festival, Chinese people clean up their houses.*

打算 **dǎsuàn** [comp: 打 act + 算 calculate] *v* plan, contemplate □ 你打算毕业以后做什么？**Nǐ dǎsuàn bìyè yǐhòu zuò shénme?** *What do you plan to do after graduation?* □ 我不打算买什么。**Wǒ bù dǎsuàn mǎi shénme.** *I don't intend to buy anything.*

打听 **dǎtīng** *v* inquire, ask □ 您从北京大学来, 我想跟您打听一位教授。**Nín cóng Běijīng Dàxué lái. Wǒ xiǎng gēn nín dǎtīng yí wèi jiàoshòu.** *As you're from Beijing University, I'd like to ask you about a professor.* □ 你到了那里打听一下就知道了。**Nǐ dàole nàli dǎtīng yíxià jiù zhīdào le.** *When you're there, just make some inquiries and you'll find out.*

打压 **dǎyā** [comp: 打 strike + 压 oppress] *v* press hard, oppress

打仗 **dǎzhàng** *v* go to war, fight in a war

打招呼 **dǎ zhāohu** *v* 1 greet, say hello to 2 let know, notify

打针 **dǎzhēn** *v* give (or get) an injection □ 病人每天要打针吃药。**Bìngrén měi tiān yào dǎzhēn chīyào.** *The patient must get injections and take medicine every day.*

打字 **dǎzì** *v* type □ 他打字打得又快又好。**Tā dǎzì dǎ de yòu kuài yòu hǎo.** *He types fast and well.* (→ He has excellent keyboard skills.)

大 **dà** *adj* big, large (antonym 小 **xiǎo**) □ 中国实在很大。**Zhōngguó shízài hěn dà.** *China is indeed big.* □ 我爷爷种的树都长大了。**Wǒ yéye zhòng de shù dōu zhǎngdà le.** *The trees that my grandfather planted have all matured.*

大半 **dàbàn** *adv* more than half

大便 **dàbiàn** [modif: 大 big, major + 便 convenience] I *n* solid waste from the body, stool II *v* move the bowels

大臣 **dàchén** *n* official (in a royal court), minister

大大 **dàdà** *adv* greatly, enormously

大胆 **dàdǎn** [modif: 大 big + 胆 gallbladder] *adj* bold, courageous □ 你可以大胆地试验, 失败了不要紧。**Nǐ kěyǐ dàdǎn de shìyàn, shībàile búyàojǐn.** *You can experiment boldly. It doesn't matter if you fail.*

NOTE: See note on 胆 **dǎn**.

大道 **dàdào** [modif: 大 big + 道 road] *n* main road, thoroughfare

大地 **dàdì** *n* land, the earth

大都 **dàdōu** Same as 大多 **dàduō**

大多 **dàduō** [modif: 大 big + 多 many] *adv* mostly □ 这个国家的人大多会说一点儿英文。**Zhège guójiā de rén dàduō huì shuō yìdiǎnr Yīngwén.** *Most people in this country can speak a little English.* □ 商场里卖的衣服大多是中国制造的。**Shāngchǎng li mài de yīfu dàduō shì Zhōngguó zhìzào de.** *Most of the garments sold in shopping malls are made in China.*

大多数 dàduōshù [modif: 大 big + 多数 majority] *n* great majority, overwhelming majority □ 大多数人支持新政府。**Dàduōshù rén zhīchí xīn zhèngfǔ.** *Most of the people support the new government.* □ 大多数时间这位科学家都在实验室工作。**Dàduōshù shíjiān zhè wèi kēxuéjiā dōu zài shíyànshì gōngzuò.** *Most of the time this scientist works in the lab.*

大方 dàfang *adj* 1 generous, liberal
出手大方 chūshǒu dàfang spend money freely, very generous
2 elegant and natural
式样大方 shìyàng dàfang elegant style

大概 dàgài I *adj* general, more or less □ 他的话我没听清楚，但是大概的意思还是懂的。**Tā de huà wǒ méi tīng qīngchu, dànshì dàgài de yìsi háishì dǒng de.** *I did not catch his words clearly, but I understood the general idea.* II *adv* probably □ 商店大概已经关门了，你明天去吧。**Shāngdiàn dàgài yǐjīng guānmén le, nǐ míngtiān qù ba.** *The shop is probably closed. You should go tomorrow.*

大锅饭 dàguōfàn [modif: 大 big + 锅 pot + 饭 rice] *n* food prepared in a big pot
吃大锅饭 chī dàguōfàn *idiom* everyone getting the same reward regardless of different functions and contributions

大后天 dàhòutiān *n* three days from now

大会 dàhuì [modif: 大 big + 会 meeting] *n* assembly, congress, rally □ 全国人民代表大会每年三月在北京举行会议。**Quánguó Rénmín Dàibiǎo Dàhuì měi nián Sānyuè zài Běijīng jǔxíng huìyì.** *The National People's Congress [of China] holds meetings in Beijing in March every year.*

大伙儿 dàhuǒr *pron* everybody, all the people □ 大伙儿都说他是个好小伙子。**Dàhuǒr dōu shuō tā shì ge hǎo xiǎohuǒzi.** *Everybody says he is a good lad.* □ 我们大伙儿一条心，一定能把事办好。**Wǒmen dàhuǒr yìtiáoxīn, yídìng néng bǎ shì bàn hǎo.** *All of us are united and we're sure to do a good job.*

NOTE: 大伙儿 **dàhuǒr** is a very colloquial word. For general use, 大家 **dàjiā** is preferred.

大家 dàjiā *pron* all, everybody □ 请大家安静一下，我有一件重要的事跟大家说。**Qǐng dàjiā ānjìng yíxià, wǒ yǒu yí jiàn zhòngyào de shì gen dàjiā shuō.** *Please be quiet, everybody. I've something important to say to you all.* □ 既然大家都赞成这个计划，那么就执行吧。**Jìrán dàjiā dōu zànchéng zhège jìhua, nàme jiù zhíxíng ba.** *As everybody is for this plan, let's carry it out.*
我们大家 wǒmen dàjiā all of us □ 我们大家都想去参观那个展览会。**Wǒmen dàjiā dōu xiǎng qù cānguān nàge zhǎnlǎnhuì.** *We all want to visit that exhibition.*
你们大家 nǐmen dàjiā all of you
他们大家 tāmen dàjiā all of them

大街 dàjiē [modif: 大 big + 街 street] *n* main street □ 大街两旁是大大小小的商店。**Dàjiē liǎng páng shì dà-dà-xiǎo-xiǎo de shāngdiàn.** *On both sides of the street are stores big and small.*
逛大街 guàng dàjiē take a stroll in the streets, do window-shopping

大局 dàjú *n* overall public interest

大理石 dàlǐshí [modif: 大理 a place in Yunnan Province + 石 stone] *n* marble

大力 dàlì [modif: 大 great + 力 strength] *adj* vigorous, energetic

大量 dàliàng *adj* a large amount of, a large number of □ 每年夏季大量大学毕业生进入人才市场。**Měi nián xiàjì dàliàng dàxué bìyèsheng jìnrù réncái shìchǎng.** *In summer every year, large numbers of graduates enter the labor market.* □ 人们可以从英特网获取大量信息。**Rénmen kěyǐ cóng yīngtèwǎng huòqǔ dàliàng xìnxī.** *People can obtain a great deal of information from the Internet.*

大陆 dàlù [modif: 大 big + 陆 land] *n* continent, mainland □ 亚洲大陆是世界上人口最多的地方。**Yàzhōu dàlù shì shìjiè shang rénkǒu zuì duō de dìfang.** *The Asian continent is the most populated place in the world.*
中国大陆 Zhōngguó dàlù mainland China

大米 dàmǐ [modif: 大 big + 米 rice] *n* rice □ 日本每年消费大量大米。**Rìběn měi nián xiāofèi dàliàng dàmǐ.** *Japan consumes a large quantity of rice every year.*

大拇指 dàmǔzhǐ *n* the thumb

NOTE: 拇指 **mǔzhǐ** can also be used to denote *the thumb*. In Chinese the thumb is considered one of the fingers—手指 **shǒuzhǐ**.

大脑 dànǎo [modif: 大 big, major + 脑 brain] *n* cerebrum, brain

大牌 dàpái [modif: 大 big + 牌 poster] *n* celebrity, hotshot
大牌明星 dàpái míngxīng celebrity movie star

大炮 dàpào [modif: 大 big + 炮 gun, cannon] *n* cannon

大批 dàpī [modif: 大 big + 批 batch] *adj* a large quantity of, lots of □ 大批农民离开农村，到城市找工作。**Dàpī nóngmín líkāi nóngcūn, dào chéngshì zhǎo gōngzuò.** *Large numbers of peasants leave their villages to seek jobs in cities.*

大片 dàpiān [modif: 大 big + 片 film] *n* blockbuster
好莱坞大片 Hǎoláiwù dàpiān Hollywood blockbuster

大气 dàqì *n* atmosphere

大人 dàren [modif: 大 big + 人 person] *n* adult, grown-up (antonym 小孩儿 xiǎoháir) □ 小孩儿都希望很快变成大人。**Xiǎoháir dōu xīwàng hěn kuài biànchéng dàren.** *Children all hope to become adults very soon.* (→ *All children hope to grow up quickly.*) □ 你已经是大人了，怎么还和孩子一样? **Nǐ yǐjīng shì dàren le, zěnme hái hé háizi yíyàng?** *You're a grown-up. How can you behave like a child?*

NOTE: 大人 **dàren** is a colloquialism. The general word for *adult* is 成年人 **chéngnián rén**.

大人物 dà rénwù great personage, big shot, very important person (VIP)

大厦 dàshà *n* super-big, imposing building (座 zuò)

大声 dàshēng [modif: 大 big + 声 sound, voice] *adj* in a loud voice □ 请你大声点，我听不清。**Qǐng nǐ dàshēng diǎn, wǒ tīng bu qīng.** *Speak up, please. I can hardly hear you.*

大师 dàshī [modif: 大 great + 师 master] *n* master (of art or scholarship)
国画大师 guóhuà dàshī master of traditional Chinese art

大使 dàshǐ [modif: 大 big + 使 envoy] *n* ambassador
中国驻美国大使 Zhōngguó zhù Měiguó dàshǐ Chinese ambassador in the U.S.

大使馆 dàshǐguǎn [modif: 大 big + 使 envoy + 馆 house] *n* embassy □ 你有英国大使馆的电话号码吗? **Nǐ yǒu Yīngguó dàshǐguǎn de diànhuà hàomǎ ma?** *Do you have the telephone number of the British embassy?*

大事 dàshì *n* matter of importance

大肆 dàsì *adv* wantonly, without restraint

大体 dàtǐ *n* on the whole, in the main
大体来说 dàtǐ láishuō on the whole

大小 dàxiǎo [comp: 大 big + 小 small] *n* size □ 你知道那间房间的大小吗? **Nǐ zhīdào nà jiān fángjiān de dàxiǎo ma?** *Do you know the size of that room?*

NOTE: 大 dà and 小 xiǎo are opposites. Put together, 大小 dàxiǎo means *size*. There are other Chinese nouns made up of antonyms e.g. 长短 chángduǎn *length*, 粗细 cūxì *thickness*, 好坏 hǎohuài *quality*, 高低 gāodī *height*.

大型 dàxíng [modif: 大 big + 型 model] *adj* large-scale, large-sized □ 今年十月这个城市要举行一个大型汽车展览会。**Jīnnián Shíyuè zhège chéngshì yào jǔxíng yí ge dàxíng qìchē zhǎnlǎnhuì.** *In October this year a large-scale auto show will be held in this city.*

大学 dàxué [modif: 大 big + 学 school] *n* university (座 zuò, 所 suǒ) □ 这座大学很有名。**Zhè zuò dàxué hěn yǒumíng.** *This university is well-known.* □ 你们国家有多少所大学? **Nǐmen guójiā yǒu duōshǎo suǒ dàxué?** *How many universities are there in your country?*
考大学 kǎo dàxué sit for the university entrance examination
考上大学 kǎo shàng dàxué pass the university entrance examination □ 我今年一定要考上大学。**Wǒ jīnnián yídìng yào kǎo shàng dàxué.** *I'm determined to pass the university entrance examination this year.*
上大学 shàng dàxué go to university, study in a university

大洋洲 Dàyángzhōu [modif: 大 big + 洋 ocean + 洲 continent] *n* Oceania □ 新西兰在大洋洲。**Xīnxīlán zài Dàyángzhōu.** *New Zealand is in Oceania.*

大衣 dàyī [modif: 大 big + 衣 clothes, coat] *n* overcoat □ 今天很冷，外出要穿大衣，戴帽子。**Jīntiān hěn lěng, wàichū yào chuān dàyī, dài màozi.** *It's cold today. You need to wear an overcoat and a hat when going out.*

大意 dàyì [modif: 大 major + 意 meaning] *n* rough idea

大约 dàyuē *adj, adv* approximate, approximately, about, nearly □ 昨天下午大约四点钟有人给你打电话。**Zuótiān xiàwǔ dàyuē sì diǎnzhōng yǒu rén gěi nǐ dǎ diànhuà.** *Someone telephoned you at about four o'clock yesterday afternoon.*

大致 dàzhì *adj* rough, general

大众 dàzhòng [modif: 大 big + 众 multitude] *n* the masses
大众媒体 dàzhòng méitǐ mass media

大自然 dàzìrán *n* Nature, Mother Nature

呆 dāi I *adj* foolish, stupid □ 她很呆, 竟会相信这个广告。**Tā hěn dāi, jìng huì xiāngxìn zhège guǎnggào.** *I[t] is foolish of her to believe the commercial.*
呆子 dāizi idiot
II *v* Same as 待 dāi

待 dāi *v* stay □ 我这次来只待两三天。**Wǒ zhè cì lái zhǐ dāi liǎng-sān tiān.** *For this visit I'll stay only a couple of days.*

NOTE: 待 dāi in the sense of *stay* may be replaced by 呆 dāi.

歹 dǎi *adj* bad, evil (antonym 好 hǎo)
歹徒 dǎitú [modif: 歹 bad + 徒 man] *n* bad guy, criminal

大 dài as in 丈夫 dàifu.

大夫 dàifu *n* doctor (位 wèi). Same as 医生 yīshēng, used more as a colloquialism.

代1 dài *n* 1 generation □ 李家在这个村子里住了好几代了。**Lǐ jiā zài zhège cūnzi li zhùle hǎo jǐ dài le.** *The Lis have been living in this village for generations.* 2 dynasty □ 唐代中国是当时世界上最强大的国家。**Táng dài Zhōngguó shì dāngshí shìjiè shang zuì qiángdà de guójiā.** *China during the Tang Dynasty wa[s] the most powerful country in the world at that time.*

NOTE: The major Chinese dynasties are 秦 Qín, 汉 Hàn, 唐 Táng, 宋 Sòng, 元 Yuán, 明 Míng, 清 Qīng.

代2 dài *v* take the place of, perform on behalf of □ 这件事你得亲自做, 别人不能代你做。**Zhè jiàn shì nǐ děi qīnzì zuò, biérén bù néng dài nǐ zuò.** *You mus[t] do it by yourself; nobody can do it on your behalf.*
代课老师 dàikè lǎoshī relief teacher
代校长 dài xiàozhǎng acting principal
代部长 dài bùzhǎng acting minister

代办 dàibàn I *v* do or act for another II *n* charge d'affaires

代表 dàibiǎo [comp: 代 substitute + 表 manifest] I *n* representative, delegate □ 工会代表拒绝了公司的方案。**Gōnghuì dàibiǎo jùjuéle gōngsī de fāng'àn.** *The trade union representative has rejected the company's proposal.* □ 谁是你们的代表? **Shuí shì nǐmen de dàibiǎo?** *Who is your representative?* II *v* represent, indicate □ 这只是他个人的意见, 不代表公司的立场。**Zhè zhǐ shì tā gèrén de yìjiàn, bú dàibiǎo gōngsī de lìchǎng.** *This is only his personal opinion, which does[.] not represent the view of the company.*

代表团 dàibiǎotuán [modif: 代表 delegate + 团 team] *n* delegation, mission
美国商业代表团 Měiguó shāngyè dàibiǎotuán U.S. trade mission

代词 dàicí [modif: 代 substitute + 词 word] *n* pronoun
人称代词 rénchēng dàicí personal pronoun

代号 dàihào *n* code name

代价 dàijià [modif: 代 substitute + 价 price] *n* price (for achieving something), cost □ 她为了实现自己的抱负, 付出了很大的代价。**Tā wèile shíxiàn zìjǐ de bàofù, fùchūle hěn dà de dàijià.** *She paid a high price for achieving her ambition.*

代理 **dàilǐ** [modif: 代 perform on behalf of + 理 manage] act on behalf of, act as agent
代理人 **dàilǐrén** agent

代数 **dàishù** [v+obj: 代 substitute + 数 numbers] *n* algebra
代数方程式 **dàishù fāngchéngshì** algebraic formula

代替 **dàitì** *v* substitute for, replace □ 这次家长会你爸爸妈妈一定要出席，不能请人代替。**Zhè cì jiāzhǎnghuì nǐ bàba māma yídìng yào chūxí, bù néng qǐng rén dàitì.** *Your parents must attend this parents' meeting and nobody can go on their behalf.*

贷 **dài** Trad 貸 *v* loan

贷款 **dàikuǎn** [modif: 贷 loan + 款 fund] **I** *n* loan
无息贷款 **wúxī dàikuǎn** interest-free loan
II *v* loan money to, borrow money from
贷款给一家小企业 **dàikuǎn gěi yì jiā xiǎo qǐyè** loan money to a small business
向银行贷款 **xiàng yínháng dàikuǎn** ask the bank for a loan

带 1 **dài** Trad 帶 *v* bring, take □ 出去旅游，别忘了带照相机。**Chūqù lǚyóu, bié wàngle dài zhàoxiàngjī.** *Don't forget to bring along your camera when you go sightseeing.*

带动 **dàidòng** *v* spur on

带劲 **dàijìn** *adj* **1** interesting, exciting **2** energetic, forceful

带来/带…来 **dàilai/dài...lái** *v* bring ... □ 明天上课的时候，把词典带来。**Míngtiān shàngkè de shíhou, bǎ cídiǎn dàilai.** *Please bring your dictionary with you when you come to class tomorrow.*

带领 **dàilǐng** [comp: 带 lead, head + 领 lead, head] *v* lead, guide □ 教授要带领学生去非洲作野外调查。**Jiàoshòu yào dàilǐng xuésheng qù Fēizhōu zuò yěwài diàochá.** *The professor will take his students to Africa to do a field study.*

带去/带…去 **dàiqu/dài...qù** *v* take □ 你不知道图书馆在哪儿? 我带你去。**Nǐ bù zhīdào túshūguǎn zài nǎr? Wǒ dài nǐ qù.** *You don't know where the library is? I'll take you there.*

带头 **dàitóu** *v* take the lead, be the first
带头发言 **dàitóu fāyán** be the first to speak (at a meeting), set the ball rolling

带 2 **dài** Trad 帶 *n* belt, ribbon, band
安全带 **ānquándài** safety belt
皮带 **pídài** leather belt
丝带 **sīdài** silk ribbon

带 3 **dài** Trad 帶 *n* zone, area
寒带 **hándài** frigid zone
热带 **rèdài** tropical zone, tropics
温带 **wēndài** temperate zone

待 **dài** *v* **1** treat, deal with □ 他待朋友很热心。**Tā dài péngyou hěn rèxīn.** *He is warmhearted in dealing with friends.* □ 人家怎么待我，我就怎么待人家。**Rénjiā zěnme dài wǒ, wǒ jiù zěnme dài rénjiā.** *I treat people the way they treat me.* **2** wait for
待业 **dài yè** wait for a job opportunity

待遇 **dàiyù** *n* **1** treatment □ 代表团受到了贵宾待遇。**Dàibiǎotuán shòudàole guì bīn dàiyù.** *The delegation was given VIP treatment.* **2** remuneration □ 这个职务责任非常重，但是待遇很好。**Zhège zhíwù zérèn fēicháng zhòng, dànshì dàiyù hěn hǎo.** *This position carries heavy responsibilities, but pays well.*

逮 **dài** *v* catch

逮捕 **dàibǔ** [comp: 逮 arrest + 捕 capture] *v* arrest, take into custody □ 已经有两名高级官员因受贿被逮捕。**Yǐjing yǒu liǎng míng gāojí guānyuán yīn shòuhuì bèi dàibǔ.** *Two senior officials have already been arrested for taking bribes.*

袋 **dài** *n* sack, bag (只 **zhī**)
口袋 **kǒudài** pocket □ 他带了一个大袋子来装书。**Tā dàile yí ge dà dàizi lái zhuāng shū.** *He brought a big bag for his books.*

NOTE: 袋 **dài** *is* seldom used alone. It is either used with the nominal suffix 子 **zi** to form 袋子 **dài zi**, or with another noun to form a compound word, e.g. 口袋 **kǒudài** (pocket).

戴 **dài** *v* wear, put on □ 外面很冷，戴上帽子吧! **Wàimiàn hěn lěng, dàishang màozi ba!** *It's cold outside. Do put on your cap.*
戴手套儿 **dài shǒutàor** wear gloves
戴眼镜 **dài yǎnjìng** wear spectacles

怠 **dài** *adj* idle, slack

怠工 **dàigōng** [modif: 怠 slack + 工 work] *n* slowdown (as workers' protest)

怠慢 **dàimàn** [comp: 怠 slight + 慢 slight] *v* slight, give the cold shoulder to

单 **dān** Trad 單 *adj* single, separate □ 他不习惯和别人合住，一定要单住一个房间。**Tā bù xíguàn hé biérén hé zhù, yídìng yào dān zhù yí ge fángjiān.** *He is not used to sharing a room with another person and insists on having a room to himself.*
单人床 **dānrénchuáng** single bed
单人房间 **dānrén fángjiān** (hotel) room for a single person
单数 **dānshù** odd number

单纯 **dānchún** [comp: 单 single + 纯 pure] *adj* simple-minded, ingenuous

单词 **dāncí** [modif: 单 single + 词 word] *n* word □ 光学单词用处不大，一定要把单词放在句子中学。**Guāng xué dāncí yòngchu bú dà, yídìng yào bǎ dāncí fàng zài jùzi zhōng xué.** *Learning words in insolation is not very useful. You must learn words in sentences.*

单调 **dāndiào** [modif: 单 single + 调 tone] *adj* monotonous

单独 **dāndú** [comp: 单 single + 独 alone] *adj* alone, on one's own □ 经过半年培训，她能单独工作了。**Jīngguò bànnián péixùn, tā néng dāndú gōngzuò le.** *After six months' training, she can now work all by herself.*

单亲家庭 **dānqīn jiātíng** *n* single-parent family

单身贵族 **dānshēn guìzú** [modif: 单身 single, not attached + 贵族 aristocrat] *n* a single person with lots of money to spend, yuppy

单位 **dānwèi** *n* work unit, e.g. a factory, a school, a government department □ 你是哪个单位的? **Nǐ shì nǎge dānwèi de?** *Which work unit do you belong to?*

单元 **dānyuán** *n* unit (in an apartment house), apartment, flat

丹 **dān** *n* red color

担 **dān** Trad 擔 *v* carry on the shoulder, take on (responsibility, burden etc)

担保 **dānbǎo** [comp: 担 shoulder + 保 guarantee]
v guarantee, vouch for
　担保人 dānbǎorén guarantor
担负 **dānfù** [comp: 担 carry on the shoulder + 负
carry on the back] *v* take on (responsibility), meet
(expenditure), hold (a position)
　担负使命 dānfù shǐmìng undertake a mission
　担负子女的教育费 dānfù zǐnǚ de jiàoyùfèi meet
　children's educational costs
担任 **dānrèn** [comp: 担 shoulder + 任 act as] *v*
assume the office of, act in the capacity of □ 今年
谁担任我们的中文老师？ **Jīnnián shuí dānrèn wǒmen
de Zhōngwén lǎoshī?** *Who'll be our Chinese teacher
this year?* □ 政府邀请这位大学校长担任教育部长。
**Zhèngfǔ yāoqǐng zhè wèi dàxué xiàozhǎng dānrèn
jiàoyù bùzhǎng.** *The government has invited this university president to be the Minister of Education.*
担心 **dānxīn** *v* worry, fret □ 他担心考试不及格。 **Tā
dānxīn kǎoshì bù jígé.** *He is worried that he may fail
the exam.* □ 我为爸爸的身体担心。 **Wǒ wèi bàba de
shēntǐ dānxīn.** *I'm worried about daddy's health.*
担忧 **dānyōu** [comp: 担 worry + 忧 worry] *v* worry
耽 **dān** *v* delay
　耽误 **dānwù** [comp: 耽 delay + 误 miss] *v* delay
□ 你们没有按时交货，耽误了我们的生产。 **Nǐmen
méiyǒu ànshí jiāohuò, dānwùle wǒmen de shēngchǎn.**
*Your failure to deliver the goods on time has delayed
our production.* □ 有病得马上看，不要耽误。 **Yǒubìng
děi mǎshàng kàn, búyào dānwù.** *If you are sick you
should go to see a doctor immediately. Don't delay.*
　耽误时间 dānwù shíjiān waste time
胆 **dǎn** Trad 膽 *n* 1 gallbladder 2 courage
　胆子 dǎnzi courage
　胆子大 dǎnzi dà be brave, be bold
　胆子小 dǎnzi xiǎo be timid, be cowardly

NOTE: The ancient Chinese believed that the gallbladder
was the organ of courage—if one had a big gallbladder
it meant that the person was endowed with courage and
daring, and if one was timid it was because he had a
small gallbladder. Therefore, 他胆子很大 **Tā dǎnzi hěn dà**
and 他很大胆 **Tā hěn dàdǎn** means *He is bold*; 他胆子很
小 **Tā dǎnzi hěn xiǎo** and 他很胆小 **Tā hěn dǎnxiǎo** means
He is timid.

胆量 **dǎnliàng** [modif: 胆 courage + 量 amount] *n*
courage, guts
　试试他的胆量 shìshi tāde dǎnliàng test his courage,
　see how brave he is
胆怯 **dǎnqiè** *adj* timid, cowardly
旦 **dàn** *n* dawn (See 元旦 yuándàn)
但 **dàn** *conj* Same as 但是 **dànshì**. Used in writing.
　但是 **dànshì** *conj* but, yet □ 这种产品价格很
低，但是质量不好。 **Zhè zhǒng chǎnpǐn jiàgé hěn dī,
dànshì zhìliàng bù hǎo.** *This product is cheap but its
is of low quality.* □ 虽然他星期天不上班，但是好象比哪
一天都忙。 **Suīrán tā Xīngqītiān bú shàngbān, dànshì
hǎoxiàng bǐ nǎ yì tiān dōu máng.** *He does not go to
work on Sundays, but seems to be busier than on any
other day.* □ 这个女孩子长得很漂亮，但是大家都不喜
欢她。 **Zhège nǚháizi zhǎng de hěn piàoliang, dànshì

dàjiā dōu bù xǐhuan tā.** *This girl is quite pretty, but
nobody likes her.*
担 **dàn** Trad 擔 *n* load, burden
　担子 dànzi load, burden
　担子重 dànzi zhòng great burden, heavy responsibility
淡 **dàn** *adj* 1 not salty, tasteless, bland □ 汤太淡
了，得放些盐。 **Tāng tài dàn le, děi fàng xiē yán.**
The soup is tasteless. Put some salt in it. 2 (of tea,
coffee) weak (antonym 浓 **nóng**) □ 茶淡一点儿好，我
喝浓茶睡不着。 **Chá dàn yìdiǎnr hǎo, wǒ hē nóngchá
shuì bu zháo.** *I prefer weak tea. I can't fall asleep
after drinking strong tea.*
氮 **dàn** nitrogen
　氮肥 dànféi nitrogenous fertilizer
蛋 **dàn** *n* egg (especially chicken egg) □ 他每天早
上吃一个蛋。 **Tā měitiān zǎoshàng chī yí ge dàn.** *He
eats an egg every morning.* □ 鸡蛋营养丰富。 **Jīdàn
yíngyǎng fēngfù.** *Eggs are very nutritious.*
蛋白质 **dànbáizhì** [modif: 蛋白 egg white + 质 sub-
stance] *n* protein
蛋糕 **dàngāo** [modif: 蛋 egg + 糕 cake] *n* (western-style) cake □ 你饿吗？先吃点蛋糕当点心吧。 **Nǐ è
ma? Xiān chī diǎn dàngāo dàng diǎnxīn ba.** *Are you
hungry? Have some cake for a snack.*
诞 **dàn** Trad 誕 *v* be born
诞辰 **dànchén** [modif: 诞 be born + 辰 time]
n birthday □ 十二月二十五日是耶稣基督的诞辰。
Shí'èryuè èrshí wǔ rì shì Yēsū Jīdū de dànchén. *December 25th is the birthday of Jesus Christ.*
诞生 **dànshēng** [comp: 诞 be born + 生 be born]
v be born
弹 **dàn** Trad 彈 *n* bullet
弹药 **dànyào** [comp: 弹 bullets + 药 gunpowder]
n ammunition
　弹药库 dànyàokù arms depot
当 **1 dāng** Trad 當 *prep* at the time of, when
□ 当他赶到火车站，火车已经开走了。 **Dāng tā
gǎndào huǒchēzhàn, huǒchē yǐjīng kāizǒu le.** *When he
hurried to the railway station, the train had already
left.*
当…的时候 **dāng...de shíhou** *conj* when ... □ 当
我在工作的时候，不希望别人来打扰我。 **Dāng wǒ zài
gōngzuò de shíhou, bù xīwàng biérén lái dǎrǎo wǒ.**
When I am working, I don't want to be disturbed.
□ 当我认识她的时候，她正在一家医院当护士。 **Dāng
wǒ rènshi tā de shíhou, tā zhèngzài yì jiā yīyuàn dāng
hùshi.** *When I first knew her, she was working as a
nurse in a hospital.*

NOTE: 当 **dāng** may be omitted, especially colloquially,
e.g. 我在工作的时候，不希望别人来打扰我。 **Wǒ zài
gōngzuò de shíhou, bù xīwàng biérén lái dǎrǎo wǒ.**

当 **2 dāng** Trad 當 *v* work as, serve as □ "你长大
了想当什么？" "我想当医生。" **"Nǐ zhǎngdàle xiǎng
dāng shénme?" "Wǒ xiǎng dāng yīshēng."** *"What do
you want to be when you grow up?" "I'd like to be a
doctor."*
当场 **dāngchǎng** *n* on the spot
　当场抓获 dāngchǎng zhuāhuò catch red-handed
当初 **dāngchū** *n* originally, at the outset

当代 **dāngdài** *adj* contemporary, present-day
当地 **dāngdì** *n* at the place in question, local
　当地人 dāngdì rén a local □ 他来自一个小城市，当地没有大学。**Tā láizi yí ge xiǎo chéngshì, dāngdì méiyǒu dàxué.** *He came from a small city, where there was no university.*
　当地时间 dāngdì shíjiān local time
当局 **dāngjú** *n* the authorities
当面 **dāngmiàn** *adv* to someone's face, in the very presence of
　当面撒谎 dāngmiàn sāhuǎng tell a barefaced lie
当年 **dāngnián** *n* in those years, then □ 想当年，亲戚朋友之间主要靠写信联系。哪有什么电子邮件？**Xiǎng dāngnián, qīnqi péngyou zhī jiān zhǔyào kào xiě xìn liánxì. Nǎyǒu shénme diànzǐ yóujiàn?** *In those years, relatives and friends mainly relied on letter-writing to keep in touch with each other. How could there be e-mails?* (→ *There was no such thing as e-mails.*)
当前 **dāngqián** *n* at present, now □ 王经理向我们介绍了当前市场情况。**Wáng jīnglǐ xiàng wǒmen jièshàole dāngqián shìchǎng qíngkuàng.** *Mr Wang, the manager, briefed us on the current marketing situation.*
当然 **dāngrán** *adv* of course □ 他们受到这么热情的招待，当然很高兴。**Tāmen shòudào zhème rèqíng de zhāodài, dāngrán hěn gāoxìng.** *They were of course delighted to be received so warmly.* □ "你到了北京别忘了给我发一份电子邮件。" "那当然，忘不了。" **"Nǐ dàole Běijīng bié wàngle gěi wǒ fā yí fèn diànzǐ yóujiàn." "Nà dāngrán, wàng bu liǎo."** *"Don't forget to send me an e-mail when you arrive in Beijing." "Of course, I won't forget."*
当时 **dāngshí** *n* at that time, then □ 当时我没有想到这一点。**Dāngshí wǒ méiyǒu xiǎngdào zhè yìdiǎn.** *At that time I missed this point.*
当事人 **dāngshìrén** *n* person/people concerned, party (to a lawsuit)
当心 **dāngxīn** *v* be cautious, take care
当选 **dāngxuǎn** *v* be elected
　当选为代表 dāngxuǎn wéi dàibiǎo be elected a delegate
当中 **dāngzhōng** *n* right in the middle, in the center
挡 **dǎng** Trad 擋 *v* block, keep off □ 记者被挡在门外。**Jìzhě bèi dǎng zài ménwài.** *The reporters were barred from the house.*
党 **dǎng** Trad 黨 *n* political party □ 他不参加任何党。**Tā bù cānjiā rènhé dǎng.** *He does not join any party.*

NOTE: As China is under a one-party rule, when people mention 党 dǎng in China, they usually refer to 中国共产党 **Zhōngguó Gòngchǎn Dǎng** the Chinese Communist Party.

党派 **dǎngpài** [comp: 党 party + 派 faction] *n* political party, political group
党委 **dǎngwěi** *n* (Chinese Communist) Party committee
　党委书记 dǎngwěi shūjì (Chinese Communist) Party committee secretary, (Chinese Communist) Party chief

NOTE: The Chinese Communist Party Committee in a province is called 省委 **shěngwěi**, and that in a city 市委 **shìwěi**. These are the most powerful organs in a Chinese province or city (not the local governments—政府 **zhèngfǔ**).

党员 **dǎngyuán** [modif: 党 party + 员 member] *n* party member □ 在中国重要官员几乎都是中国共产党党员。**Zài Zhōngguó zhòngyào guānyuán jīhū dōu shì Zhōngguó Gòngchǎn Dǎng dǎngyuán.** *In China almost all important officials are members of the Chinese Communist Party.*
荡 **dàng** Trad 蕩 *v* swing, sway
　荡秋千 dàng qiūqiān play on the swings
当 **dàng** Trad 當 *v* 1 treat as, regard as □ 他非常节省，一块钱当两块钱用。**Tā fēicháng jiéshěng, yí kuài qián dàng liǎng kuài qián yòng.** *He is very thrifty and wishes he could make one dollar go twice as far.* 2 think □ 你中文说得这么好，我还当你是中国人呢! **Nǐ Zhōngwén shuōde zhème hǎo, wǒ hái dàng nǐ shì Zhōngguórén ne!** *You speak Chinese so well that I thought you were a Chinese!*
当天 **dàngtiān** *n* the same day
当做 **dàngzuò** *v* treat as, regard as □ 我一直把他当做好朋友。**Wǒ yìzhí bǎ tā dàngzuò hǎo péngyou.** *I always regard him as a good friend.*
档 **dàng** Trad 檔 *n* 1 shelf, cabin 2 grade, class
　档案 dàng'àn (份 fèn) file, archive
档次 **dàngcì** *n* standard or level of quality, grade, class
刀 **dāo** *n* knife (把 bǎ) □ "我可以借用一下你的刀吗？" "可以。" **"Wǒ kěyǐ jièyòng yíxià nǐ de dāo ma?" "Kěyǐ."** *"May I use your knife?" "Yes."*
　刀子 dāozi a small knife
　铅笔刀 qiānbǐ dāo pencil sharpener
　水果刀 shuǐguǒ dāo penknife
刀刃 **dāorèn** *n* edge of a knife
岛 **dǎo** Trad 島 *n* island □ 新西兰有两个大岛：南岛和北岛。**Xīnxīlán yǒu liǎng ge dà dǎo: nán dǎo hé běi dǎo.** *New Zealand has two big islands: South Island and North Island.*
岛屿 **dǎoyǔ** [comp: 岛 island + 屿 small island] *n* island, islet
捣 **dǎo** Trad 搗 *v* beat, smash
　捣蛋 dǎodàn *v* make trouble (in a mischievous way)
　故意捣蛋 gùyì dǎodàn be deliberately mischievous
捣乱 **dǎoluàn** *v* make trouble, sabotage
　捣乱公共秩序 dǎoluàn gōnggòng zhixù disrupt public order
蹈 **dǎo** *v* dance (See 舞蹈 **wúdǎo**)
导 **dǎo** Trad 導 *v* lead, guide (See 辅导 **fǔdǎo**, 领导 **lǐngdǎo**, 指导 **zhǐdǎo**)
导弹 **dǎodàn** [modif: 导 guided + 弹 bullet] *n* guided missile (枚 méi)
导航 **dǎoháng** [modif: 导 guided + 航 navigation] *n* navigation (by electronic devices)
导师 **dǎoshī** [modif: 导 guiding + 师 teacher] *n* supervior (for postgraduate students)
导演 **dǎoyǎn** [modif: 导 guiding + 演 acting] **I** *n* director (for films or play)

名导演 **míng dǎoyǎn** famous director
II *v* direct (a film or play) □ 这部电影是谁导演的? **Zhè bù diànyǐng shì shéi dǎoyǎn de?** *Who directed this movie?*

导游 **dǎoyóu** [modif: 导 guide + 游 tourism] *n* tourist guide

导致 **dǎozhì** *v* lead to, cause

倒 **dǎo** *v* fall, topple □ 风大极了, 把很多树都刮倒了。 **Fēng dà jíle, bǎ hěn duō shù dōu guā dǎole.** *The winds were so strong that many trees were blown down.*

倒闭 **dǎobì** [comp: 倒 go bust + 闭 close down] go bust, cease operations

倒卖 **dǎomài** *v* resell at a profit

倒霉 **dǎoméi** *v* have bad luck, be out of luck

到 **dào** *v* arrive, come to, up to □ 北京来的飞机什么时候到? **Běijīng lái de fēijī shénme shíhou dào?** *When will the flight from Beijing arrive?* □ 陈经理下个月要到香港去。 **Chén jīnglǐ xià ge yuè yào dào Xiānggǎng qù.** *Mr Chen, the manager, will go to Hong Kong next month.* □ 我们已经学到第十八课了。 **Wǒmen yǐjīng xué dào dì-shíbā kè le.** *We've studied up to Lesson 18.*

到处 **dàochù** *adv* everywhere □ 坏人到处都有, 好人也到处都有。 **Huàirén dàochù dōu yǒu, hǎorén yě dàochù dōu yǒu.** *There are villains everywhere but there are good people everywhere, too.* □ 王老师家里到处都是书。 **Wáng lǎoshī jiā li dàochù dōu shì shū.** *There are books everywhere in Teacher Wang's home.* □ 他到处游览名胜古迹。 **Tā dàochù yóulǎn míngshèng gǔjì.** *He visits well-known scenic spots and historical sites everywhere.*

NOTE: 到处 **dàochù** is always placed before a verbal phrase, and is often followed by 都 **dōu**.

到达 **dàodá** [comp: 到 get to + 达 reach] *v* arrive, reach □ 张部长乘坐的飞机将在晚上六点三刻到达北京机场。 **Zhāng bùzhǎng chéngzuò de fēijī jiāng zài wǎnshang liù diǎn sān kè dàodá Běijīng jīchǎng.** *The airplane Minister Zhang is traveling in will arrive at Beijing Airport at 6:45 p.m.*

到底 **dàodǐ** [v+obj: 到 get to + 底 bottom] *adv* **1** in the end, finally □ 她到底还是找到了理想的丈夫。 **Tā dàodǐ háishì zhǎodàole lǐxiǎng de zhàngfu.** *Finally she found her ideal husband.* **2** after all (used in a question) □ 你到底去不去啊? **Nǐ dàodǐ qù bu qù a?** *Are you going or not?* □ 他到底想要什么? **Tā dàodǐ xiǎng yào shénme?** *What does he want after all?*

到来 **dàolái** [comp: 到 arrive + 来 come] *v* arrive

到期 **dàoqī** *v* become due, expire □ 签证月底到期。 **Qiānzhèng yuèdǐ dàoqī.** *The visa will expire at the end of the month.*

到…为止 **dào...wéizhǐ** *prep* until, by, up to □ 到上个月底为止, 公司今年的收入已经超过八百万。 **Dào shànggè yuè dǐ wéizhǐ, gōngsī jīnnián de shōurù yǐjing chāoguò bābǎiwàn.** *By the end of last month, the company revenue this year has exceeded eight million yuan.*

倒 **dào** **I** *v* **1** put upside down □ 他把画挂倒了。 **Tā bǎ huà guà dào le.** *He hung the picture upside down.* **2** pour (water), make (tea) □ 她给客人倒了一杯水。 **Tā gěi kèrén dàole yì bēi shuǐ.** *She gave the visitor a glass of water.* **II** *adv* contrary to what may be expected (used before a verb or an adjective to indicate an unexpected action or state) □ 弟弟倒比哥哥高。 **Dìdi dào bǐ gēge gāo.** *The younger brother is unexpectedly taller than his elder brother.* □ 用了电脑人们倒好像更忙了。 **Yòngle diànnǎo rénmen dào hǎoxiàng gèng máng le.** *With the use of computers people seem to be busier.*

倒计时 **dàojìshí** *n* countdown

倒退 **dàotuì** [comp: 倒 reverse + 退 step back] *v* go backward, regress

悼 **dào** *v* mourn

悼念 **dàoniàn** [comp: 悼 mourn + 念 think of] *v* mourn, grieve over

盗 **dào** *n* robber, bandit (See 强盗 **qiángdào**, 盗版 **dàobǎn**)

盗版 **dàobǎn** [modif: 盗 robber + 版 edition] **I** *n* pirated edition, pirated copy

盗版书 **dàobǎn shū** pirated edition of a book

盗版电影 **dàobǎn diànyǐng** pirated movie

II *v* make pirated copies

盗窃 **dàoqiè** [comp: 盗 rob + 窃 steal] *v* steal, embezzle, commit larceny

盗窃犯 **dàoqièfàn** thief, one who commits larceny

道 **I dào** *n* way, path

道德 **dàodé** [modif: 道 the way + 德 virtue] *n* morals, ethics □ 赚钱也要讲道德。 **Zhuànqián yě yào jiǎng dàodé.** *When making money you should also pay attention to ethics.*

不道德 **bú dàodé** immoral □ 这样做是不道德的。 **Zhèyàng zuò shì bú dàodé de.** *Such conduct is immoral.*

道理 **dàoli** [comp: 道 way, principle + 理 pattern, reason] *n* principle, reason, hows and whys □ 这个道理人人都懂。 **Zhège dàoli rénrén dōu dǒng.** *Everybody understands this principle.* (→ *Everybody understands why this is true/correct.*) □ 他说得很好听, 其实没有什么道理。 **Tā shuō de hěn hǎotīng, qíshí méiyǒu shénme dàoli.** *He mouthed fine words but in fact was not quite right.*

讲道理 **jiǎng dàoli** (of a person) be reasonable □ 他这个人很不讲道理。 **Tā zhège rén hěn bù jiǎng dàoli.** *This man is very unreasonable.*

有道理 **yǒu dàoli** reasonable, true □ 你说的话很有道理。 **Nǐ shuō de huà hěn yǒu dàoli.** *What you said is reasonable/true.*

NOTE: 道 **dào** and 理 **lǐ** are two important concepts in Chinese thought. The original meaning of 道 **dào** is *path, way*. By extension it denotes "the fundamental principle of the universe." 理 **lǐ** originally meant *the grain of a piece of jade* and came to mean "the underlying logic of things."

道路 **dàolù** [comp: 道 way + 路 road] *n* road, path □ 盖房子之前, 先要修道路。 **Gài fángzi zhīqián, xiān yào xiū dàolù.** *Before putting up houses, roads must be built.* □ 车辆把前面的道路堵住了。 **Chēliàng bǎ qiánmiàn de dàolù dǔzhù le.** *Traffic has blocked the road ahead.*

道 **2 dào** *measure wd* **1** (for things in the shape of a line)

一道光线 **yí dào guāngxiàn** a ray of sunshine

2 (for questions in a school exercise, examinations, etc.)

两道难题 liǎng dào nántí two difficult questions

道 3 **dào** v Same as 说 **shuō**, used only in old-fashioned writing

能说会道 néng shuō huì dào eloquent, glib

道歉 **dàoqiàn** [v+obj: 道 say + 歉 apology] v apologize, say sorry □ 你应该向他们道歉。**Nǐ yīnggāi xiàng tāmen dàoqiàn.** *You should apologize to them.*

稻 **dào** n rice, paddy

稻子 dàozi rice, paddy rice

得 **dé** v get, obtain □ 她去年英文考试得了A。**Tā qùnián Yīngwén kǎoshì déle A.** *She got an A for the English examination last year.*

得到 dédào succeed in getting/obtaining □ 他得到一个去中国学汉语的机会。**Tā dédào yí ge qù Zhōngguó xué Hànyǔ de jīhuì.** *He got a chance to go to China to study Chinese.* □ 我得到他们很大帮助。**Wǒ dédào tāmen hěn dà bāngzhù.** *I was greatly helped by them.*

NOTE: The verb 得 **dé** is seldom used alone. It is often followed by 到 **dào**, grammatically a complement, to mean *get* or *obtain*.

得病 **débìng** [v+obj: 得 get + 病 illness] v fall ill, contract a disease

得力 **délì** adj competent and efficient, very capable

得力助手 délìzhùshǒu very capable assistant, indispensable right-hand assistant

得失 **déshī** [comp: 得 obtain + 失 lose] n gain and loss, success and failure

得以 **déyǐ** modal v so that, can

得意 **déyì** adj complacent, deeply pleased with oneself

得意忘形 déyì wàng xíng be dizzy with success

得意洋洋 déyì yángyáng show extreme self-complacency, be elated

得罪 **dézuì** v offend, incur displeasure of ...

得罪不起 dézuì bùqǐ can't afford to offend

德 **dé** n virtue

德国 **Déguó** n Germany

德文 **Déwén** n the German language (especially the writing)

德语 **Déyǔ** n the German language

地 **de** particle (attached to a word or phrase to indicate that it is an adverb. 地 **de** is normally followed by a verb or an adjective.)

慢慢地说 mànman de shuō speak slowly

愉快地旅行 yúkuài de lǚxíng travel pleasantly

NOTE: See note on 的 **de**.

得 **de** particle (introducing a word, phrase or clause to indicate that it is a complement. 得 **de** is normally preceded by a verb or an adjective.)

说得大家都笑了起来 shuō de dàjiā dōu xiàole qǐlái talk in such a way that everybody starts laughing

贵得很 guì de hěn very expensive

来得很早 lái de hěn zǎo come early

NOTE: See note on 的 **de**.

的 **de** particle (attached to a word or phrase to indicate that it is an attribute. 的 **de** is normally followed by a noun.)

我的电脑 wǒ de diànnǎo my computer

最新型的电脑 zuì xīnxíng de diànnǎo the latest computer model

学校刚买来的电脑 xuéxiào gāng mǎilai de diànnǎo the computer that the school just bought

NOTE: 的, 得, 地 have different functions and are three distinct words. However, as they are pronounced the same (**de**) in everyday speech, some Chinese speakers do not distinguish them.

...的话 ...**de huà** conj if □ 明天下雨的话，就改期举行。**Míngtiān xià yǔ de huà, jiù gǎiqī jǔxíng.** *If it rains tomorrow, we'll change the date for the meeting.*

NOTE: See note on 要是 **yàoshì**.

得 **děi** modal v have to □ 时间不早了，我们得走了。**Shíjiān bù zǎo le, wǒmen děi zǒu le.** *It's quite late. We've got to go.* □ 这件事怎么办，我们还得想个办法。**Zhè jiàn shì zěnme bàn, wǒmen hái děi xiǎng ge bànfǎ.** *We've got to find a way of dealing with this matter.*

灯 **dēng** Trad 燈 n lamp, lighting □ 这个房间的灯坏了。**Zhège fángjiān de dēng huài le.** *The light in this room is out of order.* □ 最后一个离开办公室的人，别忘了关灯。**Zuìhòu yí ge líkāi bàngōngshì de rén, bié wàngle guān dēng.** *The last one to leave the office, please remember to turn off the light.*

电灯 diàndēng light, electric light

关灯 guān dēng turn off the light

开灯 kāi dēng turn on the light

日光灯 rìguāngdēng fluorescent lamp

台灯 táidēng desk lamp

灯火 **dēnghuǒ** [comp: 灯 light + 火 fire] n lights

灯火通明 dēnghuǒ tōngmíng (of a building) brightly lit

灯笼 **dēnglóng** n lantern

灯泡 **dēngpào** n light bulb (只 **zhī**)

登 **dēng** v 1 publish (in a newspaper, a journal, etc.) □ 今天各大报纸都登了这条新闻。**Jīntiān gè dà bàozhǐ dōu dēngle zhè tiáo xīnwén.** *This news is published in all the major newspapers today.*

登广告 dēng guǎnggào place an advertisement, advertise

2 go up, ascend

登机 **dēngjī** [v+obj: 登 go up + 机 plane] v board a plane

登机卡 dēngjīkǎ boarding card

登记 **dēngjì** v register, check in □ 在旅馆里住，都要登记。**Zài lǚguǎn li zhù, dōu yào dēngjì.** *To stay in a hotel, one has to register.*

登陆 **dēnglù** [v+obj: 登 go up + 陆 land] v land (from waters, especially by troops)

登山 **dēngshān** [v+obj: 登 ascend + 山 mountain, hill] v climb a mountain or hill

登山运动 dēngshān yùndòng mountaineering

登山运动员 dēngshān yùndòngyuán mountaineer

等 1 **děng** v wait, wait for □ 她在等一个重要的电话。**Tā zài děng yí ge zhòngyào de diànhuà.** *She is waiting for an important telephone call.* □ 我昨天等你等了半小时。**Wǒ zuótiān děng nǐ děngle bàn xiǎoshí.** *I waited for you for half an hour yesterday.*

等一下 **děng yíxià** wait a minute □ 等一下，我马上就来。**Děng yíxià, wǒ mǎshang jiù lái.** *Wait a minute, I'll come soon.*

等待 **děngdài** [comp: 等 wait + 待 await, anticipate] *v* wait (usually used in writing) □ 你不能总是等待机会，要主动寻找机会。**Nǐ bù néng zǒngshì děngdài jīhuì, yào zhǔdòng xúnzhǎo jīhuì.** *You mustn't always wait for an opportunity; you should proactively search for it.*

等到 **děngdào** *conj* by the time, as late as □ 等到发现问题，已经太晚了。**Děngdào fāxiàn yǒu wèntí, yǐjīng tài wǎn le.** *It was too late by the time the problem was identified.*

等候 **děnghòu** *v* Same as 等待 **děngdài**

等 2 **děng** *n* grade, rank, class □ 我们商店只卖一等品。**Wǒmen shāngdiàn zhǐ mài yì-děng pǐn.** *Our store sells first-class goods only.* (→ *We sell only the best here.*)

等级 **děngjí** [comp: 等 rank + 级 grade] *n* grade, rank 确定（商品的）等级 **quèdìng (shāngpǐn de) děngjí** determine the grades (of a commodity)

等于 **děngyú** *v* be equal to, equal, amount to □ 一加二等于三。**Yī jiā èr děngyú sān.** *One plus two equals three.*

等 3 **děng** *particle* **1** and so on and so forth, et cetera □ 我们在中国参观了北京、上海、西安等地。**Wǒmen zài Zhōngguó cānguānle Běijīng, Shànghǎi, Xī'ān děng dì.** *In China we visited Beijing, Shanghai, Xi'an and other places.* **2** (used at the end of a list) □ 我们在中国游览了北京、上海、西安等三个大城市。**Wǒmen zài Zhōngguó yóulǎn le Běijīng, Shànghǎi, Xī'ān děng sān ge dà chéngshì.** *We toured the three major cities of Beijing, Shanghai and Xi'an.*

瞪 **dèng** *v* open one's eyes wide, stare, glare

凳 **dèng** *n* stool (low chair) 凳子 **dèngzi** stool (个 **gè**)

低 **dī** **I** *adj* low (antonym 高 **gāo**) □ 这把椅子太低了，坐着不舒服。**Zhè ba yǐzi tài dī le, zuòzhe bù shūfu.** *This chair is too low, it's uncomfortable to sit in.* □ 她说话声音很低，你得仔细听才行。**Tā shuōhuà shēngyīn hěn dī, nǐ děi zǐxì tīng cái xíng.** *She speaks in a low voice. You've got to listen attentively.* **II** *v* lower □ 他低着头，离开校长办公室。**Tā dīzhe tóu, líkāi xiàozhǎng bàngōngshì.** *He left the principal's office with his head hung low.*

低调 **dīdiào** [modif: 低 low + 调 tone, tune] *adj* low key

低估 **dīgū** [modif: 低 low + 估 estimate] *v* underestimate

低级 **dījí** [modif: 低 low + 级 grade] *adj* **1** elementary **2** vulgar 低级趣味 **dījí qùwèi** vulgar interests, base taste

低劣 **dīliè** [comp: 低 low + 劣 inferior] *adj* inferior

堤 **dī** *n* dike, embankment

滴 **dī** *measure word* drop (used for liquids) □ 节约每一滴水。**Jiéyuē měi yì dī shuǐ.** *Save every drop of water.*

敌 **dí** Trad 敵 *n* enemy 敌对 **díduì** [comp: 敌 enemy + 对 opposite] *adj* hostile, antagonistic

敌对的态度 **díduì de tàidu** hostile attitude

敌人 **dírén** [modif: 敌 enemy + 人 person, people] *n* enemy □ 我想我在公司里没有敌人。**Wǒ xiǎng wǒ zài gōngsī li méiyǒu dírén.** *I don't think I have any enemies in the company.* □ 吸烟是健康的敌人。**Xīyān shì jiànkāng de dírén.** *Smoking is an enemy of health.*

敌视 **díshì** [modif: 敌 enemy + 视 view] *v* be hostile to

笛 **dí** *n* flute 笛子 **dízi** flute 吹笛子 **chuī dízi** play the flute

涤 **dí** Trad 滌 *v* wash, wash away

的 **dí** as in 的确 **díquè** 的确 **díquè** *adv* really, truly □ 这个名胜的确美丽。**Zhège míngshèng díquè měilì.** *This well-known scenic spot is truly beautiful.*

的士 **díshì** *n* taxi

迪 **dí** *v* enlighten 迪斯科 **dísīkē** *n* disco

底 **dǐ** *n* base, bottom 底片 **dǐpiàn** *n* (film) negative

底下 **dǐxia** [comp: 底 bottom + 下 under] *n* underneath, under □ 床底下有一双拖鞋。**Chuáng dǐxia yǒu yì shuāng tuōxié.** *There's a pair of slippers under the bed.* □ 孩子躲在桌子底下。**Háizi duǒ zài zhuōzi dǐxia.** *The child hid under the table.*

底线 **dǐxiàn** [modif: bottom 底 + line 线] *n* bottom line

抵 **dǐ** *v* **1** arrive **2** resist 抵偿 **dǐcháng** *v* compensate for 抵达 **dǐdá** [comp: 抵 arrive + 达 reach] *v* arrive at

抵抗 **dǐkàng** [comp: 抵 arrive + 抗 resist] *v* resist

抵押 **dǐyā** *v* pledge ... as security for a loan, mortgage 抵押品 **dǐyāpǐn** security (for a loan)

抵制 **dǐzhì** *v* boycott, reject

地 **dì** *n* earth, ground 地板 **dìbǎn** [modif: 地 ground + 板 plank] *n* floor, timber floor

地步 **dìbù** *n* **1** extent **2** (poor) condition

地带 **dìdài** *n* region, zone

地道 **dìdào** [modif: 地 ground + 道 way] **I** *n* tunnel, underpass (条 **tiáo**) □ 请走地道。**Qǐng zǒu dìdào.** *Please use the underpass.*

地道 **dìdao** *adj* genuine, authentic 地道的中国菜 **dìdao de Zhōngguócài** authentic Chinese cuisine

地点 **dìdiǎn** [comp: 地 place + 点 point] *n* the place for an event or activity, venue □ 会议的地点还没有定。**Huìyì de dìdiǎn hái méiyǒu dìng.** *The venue of the meeting has not been decided on.* □ 展览会的时间和地点决定以后，我会立即通知你。**Zhǎnlǎnhuì de shíjiān hé dìdiǎn juédìng yǐhòu, wǒ huì lìjí tōngzhī nǐ.** *After the time and venue of the exhibition are decided on, I will inform you immediately.*

地方 **dìfang** [comp: 地 earth + 方 place] *n* **1** place, location, area (个 **gè**) □ 你住在什么地方？**Nǐ zhù zài shénme dìfang?** *Where do you live?* □ 他们正在找开会的地方。**Tāmen zhèngzài zhǎo kāihuì de dìfang.** *They're looking for a venue for their conference.* **2** part of, aspect □ 这本书我有些地方不大明白。Zhè

běn shū wǒ yǒuxie dìfang búdà míngbai. *I'm not quite clear about parts of this book.*

NOTE: 地方 **dìfang** is a word of wide application. It has both concrete, specific senses and abstract, general senses, as in the following examples: □ 医生: 你什么地方不舒服? **Yīshēng: Nǐ shénme dìfang bù shūfu?** *Doctor: What spot ails you? (→ What's wrong with you?)* □ 照顾不到的地方, 请多多原谅。 **Zhàogù búdào de dìfang, qǐng duōduō yuánliàng.** *If there's anything not well attended to, please accept my sincere apology.*

地理 **dìlǐ** *n* geography
地理学家 dìlǐxuéjiā geographer
国家地理学会 Guójiā Dìlǐ Xuéhuì National Geographic Society
地面 **dìmiàn** [modif: 地 ground + 面 face] *n* the earth's surface, ground □ 这里的地面比海平面高出二百公尺。 **Zhèli de dìmiàn bǐ hǎipíngmiàn gāochū èrbǎi gōngchǐ.** *The ground here is 200 meters above sea level.*
地球 **dìqiú** [modif: 地 ground + 球 ball] *n* the earth □ 人类只有一个家园—地球。 **Rénlèi zhǐ yǒu yí ge jiāyuán—dìqiú.** *Mankind has only one home—the earth.*
地球科学 dìqiú kēxué earth science
地区 **dìqū** [modif: 地 place + 区 region] *n* region, area □ 这个国家东部地区比西部地区发达。 **Zhège guójiā dōngbù dìqū bǐ xībù dìqū fādá.** *In this country, the eastern regions are more developed than the western regions.*
地势 **dìshì** *n* physical features of a place, terrain
地毯 **dìtǎn** [modif: 地 ground + 毯 blanket] *n* carpet (张 **zhāng**)
地铁 **dìtiě** *n* underground railway, subway
地图 **dìtú** *n* map (张 **zhāng**) □ 这张地图太旧了, 没多大用处。 **Zhè zhāng dìtú tài jiù le, méi duō dà yòngchu.** *This map is too old and is not of much use.*
地图册 dìtúcè atlas
地位 **dìwèi** [comp: 地 place + 位 seat] *n* status, position □ 他在公司里有很高的地位。 **Tā zài gōngsī li yǒu hěn gāo de dìwèi.** *He holds a high position in the company.*
地下 **dìxià** [modif: 地 ground + 下 under] *n* underground
地下商场 dìxià shāngchǎng underground shopping center
地下铁路 (地铁) dìxià tiělù (dìtiě) underground railway, subway
地下停车场 dìxià tíngchēchǎng parking garage, underground carpark
地形 **dìxíng** *n* topography, terrain
地震 **dìzhèn** [modif: 地 earth + 震 quake] *n* earthquake, seism (场 **cháng**) □ 在南太平洋发生了里氏六级地震。 **Zài nán Tàipíngyáng fāshēng le Lǐ shì liù jí dìzhèn.** *An earthquake, measuring 6 on the Richter scale, occurred in the South Pacific Ocean.*
地址 **dìzhǐ** *n* address □ 这是我的地址和电话号码, 请你记一下。 **Zhè shi wǒ de dìzhǐ he diànhuà hàomǎ, qǐng nǐ jì yíxià.** *Here are my address and telephone number. Please write them down.*
地质 **dìzhì** *n* geology

地质调查 dìzhì diàochá geological survey
地质学家 dìzhìxuéjiā geologist
帝 **dì** *n* the Supreme Being
帝国 **dìguó** *n* empire
帝国主义 dìguózhǔyì imperialism
弟 **dì** *n* younger brother
弟弟 **dìdi** younger brother □ 我弟弟比我小两岁。 **Wǒ dìdi bǐ wǒ xiǎo liǎng suì.** *My younger brother is two years younger than me.* □ "你有没有弟弟?" "没有, 我只有一个哥哥。" "**Nǐ yǒu méiyǒu dìdi?**" "**Méiyǒu, wǒ zhǐ yǒu yí ge gēge.**" *"Do you have a younger brother?" "No, I only have an older brother."* □ 她弟弟还在念小学。 **Tā dìdi hái zài niàn xiǎoxué.** *Her younger brother is still studying in a primary school.*
弟妹 **dìmèi** *n* 1 younger brother and younger sister 2 younger brother's wife
弟兄 **dìxiōng** [comp: 弟 younger brother + 兄 elder brother] *n* brothers
递 **dì** Trad 遞 *v* hand over, pass on □ 请你把那本词典递给我。 **Qǐng nǐ bǎ nà běn cídiǎn dì gěi wǒ.** *Please pass me that dictionary.*
快递 kuàidì fast delivery (of mail)
快递服务 kuài dì fúwù fast delivery service
递交 **dìjiāo** [comp: 递 hand over + 交 hand in] *v* hand over, present
递增 **dìzēng** *v* increase progressively
第 **dì** *prefix* (used before a number to form an ordinal number)
第一 dì-yī the first
第一天 dì-yī tiān the first day
第十 dì-shí the tenth
第十课 dì-shí kè the tenth lesson, Lesson 10
第三者 **dì-sānzhě** *n* third party, one who has an affair with a married person
颠 **diān** Trad 顛 *v* bump, jolt
颠簸 **diānbǒ** [comp: 颠 bump + 簸 jerk] *v* bump, bump along
颠倒 **diāndǎo** *v* turn upside down, reverse
颠倒黑白 diāndǎo hēibái confound black and white, confuse right and wrong
颠覆 **diānfù** *v* subvert or overturn in an illegal way
掂 **diān** Trad 戡 *v* weigh in the hand
点 **diǎn** Trad 點 **I** *n* 1 drop, point, dot □ 雨点打在窗户上。 **Yǔdiǎn dǎ zài chuānghu shang.** *Raindrops beat on the window pane.* □ "点" 字下面有四点。 "**Diǎn**" zì xiàmian yǒu sì diǎn. *There're four dots at the bottom of the 点 character.*
墨点 mò diǎn ink stain
水点 shuǐ diǎn water stain
2 (indicating decimal)
三点四 sān diǎn sì 3.4 (three point four)
十二点三五 shí'èr diǎn sān wǔ 12.35 (twelve point three five)
II *measure wd* 1 a little, a bit
有(一)点儿… yǒu (yì) diǎnr... a bit ..., a little ... (used before nouns and adjectives) □ 我有一点儿累, 想休息一会儿。 **Wǒ yǒu yìdiǎnr lèi, xiǎng xiūxi yíhuìr.** *I'm a bit tired. I want to take a little break.* □ 他喜欢在睡觉前喝一点儿酒。 **Tā xǐhuan zài shuìjiào qián hē yìdiǎnr jiǔ.** *He likes to drink a little wine before going to bed.* □ 我去商店买一点儿东西, 很快就回来。 **Wǒ qù**

shāngdiàn mǎi yìdiǎnr dōngxi, hěn kuài jiù huílai. *I'll go to the store to do a little shopping and will be back soon.* **2 o'clock** □ "现在几点?" "三点正." **"Xiànzài jǐdiǎn?" "Sān diǎn zhèng."** *"What time is it?" "Three o'clock sharp."* □ 现在才八点一刻, 还早呢. **Xiànzài cái bā diǎn yí kè, hái zǎo ne.** *It's only a quarter past eight. It's still early.* **III** *v* drip, put a dot, touch □ 你给我点眼药水, 行吗? **Nǐ gěi wǒ diǎn yǎnyàoshuǐ, xíng ma?** *Could you please put my eye drops in for me?*

点火 **diǎnhuǒ** *v* light a fire
点名 **diǎnmíng** *v* call the roll, do roll-call
点燃 **diǎnrán** *v* kindle, ignite
点心 **diǎnxīn** *n* snack, light refreshments □ 有点儿饿了吧? 吃一点儿点心吧. **Yǒu diǎn è le ba? Chī yìdiǎn diǎnxīn ba.** *Aren't you a bit hungry? Have a snack!*

NOTE: The Cantonese pronunciation of 点心 is "dim sum." Many Chinese restaurants overseas sell Cantonese-style refreshments or snack known as "dim sum." To have such refreshments for a meal is "yum cha," the Cantonese pronunciation of 饮茶 **yǐnchá**, which literally means *drink tea.*

点钟 **diǎnzhōng** *n* o'clock □ "现在几点钟?" "三点钟." **"Xiànzài jǐ diǎnzhōng?" "Sān diǎnzhōng."** *"What time is it?" "Three o'clock."* □ 我每天十点钟睡觉, 七点钟起床. **Wǒ měi tiān shí diǎnzhōng shuìjiào, qī diǎnzhōng qǐchuáng.** *Every day, I go to bed at ten o'clock and get up at seven o'clock.*

NOTE: In colloquial Chinese 点钟 **diǎnzhōng** can be shortened to 点 **diǎn**, e.g. "现在几点?" "三点." **"Xiànzài jǐ diǎn?" "Sān diǎn."** *"What time is it?" "Three o'clock."*

点缀 **diǎnzhuì** [comp: 点 touch + 缀 decorate] *v* embellish, decorate
点子 **diǎnzi** *n* idea
鬼点子 **guǐdiǎnzi** wicked idea, trick
出点子 **chū diǎnzi** come up with ideas
典 **diǎn** *n* standard, law
典礼 **diǎnlǐ** [modif: 典 standard + 礼 rite] *n* ceremony □ 王先生, 王太太要到美国来参加他们女儿的大学毕业典礼. **Wáng xiānsheng, Wáng tàitai yào dào Měiguó lái cānjiā tāmen nǚ'ér de dàxué bìyè diǎnlǐ.** *Mr and Mrs Wang are coming to the States to attend their daughter's commencement.*
结婚典礼 jiéhūn diǎnlǐ wedding ceremony
典型 **diǎnxíng** *adj* typical, representative
典型事例 diǎnxíng shìlì typical case
电 **diàn** Trad 電 *n* electricity, power, electronics □ 我们这里电比较便宜. **Wǒmen zhèlǐ diàn bǐjiào piányi.** *Power is rather cheap here.* □ 今天停电. **Jīntiān tíng diàn.** *No power today.* (→ *There's a blackout/power failure today.*)
电报 **diànbào** [modif: 电 electric + 报 report] *n* telegram, cable (份 **fèn**) □ 现在还有人打电报吗? **Xiànzài háiyǒu rén dǎ diànbào ma?** *Do people still send telegrams?*
电车 **diànchē** [modif: 电 electricity + 车 vehicle] *n* trolley bus, streetcar (辆 **liàng**) □ 这辆电车去哪

儿? 这辆电车去哪儿? **Zhè liàng diànchē qù nǎr?** *Where does this trolley bus go?* □ 他每天坐电车上班. **Tā měitiān zuò diànchē shàngbān.** *He goes to work by trolley bus every day.*
电池 **diànchí** [comp: 电 electricity + 池 pool] *n* battery, electrical cell (节 **jié**)
可充电电池 kě chōngdiàn diànchí rechargeable battery
电灯 **diàndēng** [modif: 电 electricity + 灯 lamp] *n* electric light (个 **gè**) □ 这个房间的电灯坏了. **Zhège fángjiān de diàndēng huài le.** *The lights in this room are out of order.* □ 你会装电灯吗? **Nǐ huì zhuāng diàndēng ma?** *Do you know how to install an electric light?*
关电灯 guān diàndēng turn off the light
开电灯 kāi diàndēng turn on the light
电动机 **diàndòngjī** *n* (electric) motor (台 **tái**)
电风扇 **diànfēngshàn** *n* Same as 电扇 **diàn shàn**
电话 **diànhuà** [modif: 电 electricity + 话 speech] *n* telephone, telephone call (个 **gè**) □ "电话在哪里?" "在桌子上." **"Diànhuà zài nǎlǐ?" "Zài zhuōzi shang."** *"Where's the telephone?" "It's on the table."* □ "我可以用一下你的电话吗?" "当然可以." **"Wǒ kěyǐ yòng yíxia nǐ de diànhuà ma?" "Dāngrán kěyǐ."** *"May I use your telephone?" "Sure."*
无绳电话 wú shéng diànhuà cordless telephone
移动电话 yídòng diànhuà mobile phone
打电话 dǎ diànhuà use the telephone, be on the phone. □ 王先生在打电话. **Wáng xiānsheng zài dǎ diànhuà.** *Mr Wang is on the phone.*
给…打电话 gěi...dǎ diànhuà call ... on the telephone, ring ... □ "你常常给你妈妈打电话吗?" "常常打." **"Nǐ chángcháng gěi nǐ māma dǎ diànhuà ma?" "Chángcháng dǎ."** *"Do you often ring your mother?" "Yes."*
听电话 tīng diànhuà answer a telephone call □ 李小姐, 请你听电话. **Lǐ xiǎojiě, qǐng nǐ tīng diànhuà.** *Miss Li, you're wanted on the phone.*
电缆 **diànlán** *n* (electric) cable (条 **tiáo**)
电力 **diànlì** [modif: 电 electricity + 力 power] *n* electric power, power
电铃 **diànlíng** *n* electric bell
电炉 **diànlú** *n* electric stove, hot plate
电路 **diànlù** [modif: 电 electric + 路 path] *n* electric circuit
电脑 **diànnǎo** [modif: 电 electricity + 脑 brain] *n* computer (台 **tái**) □ 我会用电脑写汉字. **Wǒ huì yòng diànnǎo xiě Hànzì.** *I can input Chinese characters on a computer.* □ 这个机器是由电脑控制的. **Zhège jīqì shì yóu diànnǎo kòngzhì de.** *This machine is controlled by a computer.*
笔记本电脑 bǐjìběn diànnǎo notebook computer
电钮 **diànniǔ** *n* switch (on an electrical appliance)
电器 **diànqì** [modif: 电 electrical + 器 utensil] *n* electrical appliance
电器商店 diànqì shāngdiàn electrical appliances store
电扇 **diànshàn** [modif: 电 electricity + 扇 fan] *n* electric fan (台 **tái**) □ 夜里热极了, 我得开着电扇睡觉. **Yèlǐ rè jíle, wǒ děi kāizhe diànshàn shuìjiào.** *It's so hot at night that I have to sleep with the electric fan on.*

电视 **diànshì** [modif: 电 electricity + 视 view] *n* television □ "今天晚上的电视有没有好节目？" "没有。" **"Jīntiān wǎnshang de diànshì yǒu méiyǒu hǎo jiémù?" "Méiyǒu."** *"Are there any good programs on TV tonight?" "No."*
电视机 **diànshìjī** TV set (台 **tái**)
电视台 **diànshìtái** TV station
有线电视 **yǒuxiàn diànshì** cable TV
看电视 **kàn diànshì** watch TV □ 我很少看电视。**Wǒ hěn shǎo kàn diànshì.** *I seldom watch TV.*

电台 **diàntái** [modif: 电 electricity + 台 station] *n* radio station □ 我常常听这个电台。**Wǒ chángcháng tīng zhège diàntái.** *I often listen to this radio station.*

电梯 **diàntī** [modif: 电 electricity + 梯 stairs] *n* elevator, lift (部 **bù**) □ 大楼着火的时候，千万不能用电梯。**Dàlóu zháohuǒ de shíhou, qiānwàn bù néng yòng diàntī.** *Do not use the elevator when there is a fire in the building.*
乘电梯 **chéng diàntī** go up/down by elevator

电影 **diànyǐng** [modif: 电 electricity + 影 shadow] *n* movie, film (场 **chǎng**, 部 **bù**, 个 **gè**) □ 我昨天看的电影很有意思。**Wǒ zuótiān kàn de diànyǐng hěn yǒu yìsi.** *The film I saw yesterday was very interesting.*
电影票 **diànyǐngpiào** film ticket
电影院 **diànyǐngyuàn** cinema, cinema complex, movie theater (座 **zuò**) □ 这座新建的电影院有五个电影场。**Zhè zuò xīn jiàn de diànyǐngyuàn yǒu wǔ ge diànyǐngchǎng.** *This newly-built cinema complex has five cinemas.*
看电影 **kàn diànyǐng** watch a film, go to the movies. □ 他常常和女朋友一起看电影。**Tā chángcháng hé nǚpéngyou yìqǐ kàn diànyǐng.** *He often goes to the movies with his girlfriend.*

电源 **diànyuán** [modif: 电 power + 源 source] *n* power supply, mains

电子 **diànzǐ** [suffix: 电 electricity, electron + 子 nominal suffix] *n* electron
电子工业 **diànzǐ gōngyè** electronics industry
电子贺卡 **diànzǐ hèkǎ** e-card
电子邮件 **diànzǐ yóujiàn** e-mail □ 我今天收到两个电子邮件，发了三个电子邮件。**Wǒ jīntiān shōudào liǎng ge diànzǐ yóujiàn, fāle sān ge diànzǐ yóujiàn.** *I received two e-mail messages and sent three today.*
电子游戏 **diànzǐ yóuxì** electronic game

垫 **diàn** Trad 墊 **I** *v* put something under something else to raise it or make it level **II** *n* mat, pad, cushion
垫子 **diànzi** mat, pad, cushion

店 **diàn** *n* Same as 商店 **shāngdiàn**
店员 **diànyuán** *n* sales clerk, shop assistant

惦 **diàn** *v* keep thinking about, remember with concern
惦记 **diànji** [comp: 惦 keep thinking about + 记 remember] *v* keep thinking about, remember with concern

淀 **diàn** as in 淀粉 **diànfěn**
淀粉 **diànfěn** *n* starch, amylum

殿 **diàn** *n* hall (in a palace, temple, etc.)

雕 **diāo** *v* carve
浮雕 **fúdiāo** relief (sculpture)
石雕 **shídiāo** stone carving

雕刻 **diāokè** [comp: 雕 carve + 刻 carve] *v* carve, engrave (a work of art)
雕塑 **diàosù** *n* sculpture
雕像 **diàoxiàng** [modif: 雕 carved + 像 image] *n* statue

刁 **diāo** *adj* sly, tricky
刁难 **diāonàn** make things unnecessarily difficult in order to harrass

叼 **diāo** *v* hold in the mouth

掉 **diào** *v* fall, drop □ 杯子从桌子上掉到地上。**Bēizi cóng zhuōzi shang diàodao dì shang.** *The cup fell from the table to the floor.*

NOTE: 掉 diào is often used after a verb, as a complement to mean *finish (doing ...)*, e.g.
吃掉 **chīdiao** eat up □ 水果都吃掉了。**Shuǐguǒ dōu chīdiao le.** *The fruit is all eaten up.*
卖掉 **màidiao** sell out □ 那些书还没有卖掉。*Nà xiē shū hái méiyǒu màidiao. Those books aren't sold out yet.*
扔掉 **rēngdiao** throw away, discard □ 这件衣服太小了，不能穿了，你扔掉吧！**Zhè jiàn yīfu tài xiǎo le, bù néng chuān le, nǐ rēngdiao ba!** *This dress is too small for you. You'd better throw it away.*
忘掉 **wàngdiao** forget □ 这件事我怎么也忘不掉。**Zhè jiàn shì wǒ zěnme yě wàng bu diao.** *I can't forget this incident, no matter how hard I try.*
用掉 **yòngdiao** use up □ 我上个月用掉了一千块钱。**Wǒ shàng ge yuè yòngdiaole yìqiān kuài qián.** *I used up one thousand dollars last month. (→ I spent a thousand dollars last month.)*

钓 **diào** Trad 釣 *v* to fish with hook and line, angle □ 你钓到几条鱼？**Nǐ diàodao jǐ tiáo yú?** *How many fish have you caught [with hook and line]?*

调 **diào** Trad 調 *v* **1** exchange, swap □ 你想和我调一下座位吗？**Nǐ xiǎng hé wǒ diào yíxià zuòwèi ma?** *Would you like to swap seats with me?* **2** transfer □ 他调到总公司去工作了。**Tā diàodào zǒnggōngsī qù gōngzuò le.** *He has been transferred to the company headquarters.*

调查 **diàochá** **I** *v* investigate □ 政府有关部门正在调查这家公司的商业活动。**Zhèngfǔ yǒuguān bùmén zhèngzài diàochá zhè jiā gōngsī de shāngyè huódòng.** *The relevant government departments are investigating this company's commercial activities.* **II** *n* investigation □ 经过半年调查，发现这家公司违反了法律。**Jīngguò bàn nián diàochá, fāxiàn zhè jiā gōngsī wéifǎnle fǎlù.** *After six months of investigation the company was found to have violated the law.* □ 关于这个事件，警察正在进行调查。**Guānyú zhège shìjiàn, jǐngchá zhèngzài jìnxíng diàochá.** *The police are conducting an investigation of this incident.*
调查团 **diàochátuán** investigation team
调查人员 **diàochá rényuán** investigator
调动 **diàodòng** *v* transfer to another post
申请调动工作 **shēnqǐng diàodòng gōngzuò** apply for a job transfer
调度 **diàodù** *v* dispatch (vehicles or workers)
调换 **diàohuàn** *v* exchange (a purchase, a seat, etc.)

吊 **diào** Trad 弔 *v* hang, suspend
上吊 **shàngdiào** hang oneself (to commit suicide)

吊车 **diàochē** *n* crane (a heavy machine)

吊环 **diàohuán** *n* rings (in gymnastics)

吊销 **diàoxiāo** *v* revoke (a license, a permit, a certificate, etc.)
吊销营业执照 **diàoxiāo yíngyè zhízhào** revoke a business permit

跌 **diē** *v* 1 fall, tumble □ 老人跌了一交，摔断了左腿。**Lǎorén diēle yì jiāo, shuāiduànle zuǒ tuǐ.** *The old man (woman) fell down and broke his (her) left leg.* 2 (prices) fall, drop □ 昨天股票跌了，还是升了？**Zuótián gǔpiào diē le, háishì shēng le?** *Did the shares fall or rise yesterday?*

爹 **diē** *n* dad, daddy
爹爹 **diēdie** dad, daddy

碟 **dié** *n* small dish, small plate
碟子 **diézi** small dish
茶碟 **chádié** saucer

蝶 **dié** *n* butterfly

叠 **dié** Trad 疊 *v* pile up

丁 **dīng** *n* small cube
肉丁 **ròudīng** diced meat

钉 **dīng** Trad 釘 *n* (metal) nail

叮 **dīng** *v* 1 (of mosquitos) bite 2 remind repeatedly
叮嘱 **dīngzhǔ** *v* urge repeatedly, exhort

盯 **dīng** *v* gaze, stare □ 你别老盯着人家看，多不礼貌！**Nǐ bié lǎo dīngzhe rénjiā kàn, duō bù lǐmào!** *You shouldn't stare at people. How rude!*

顶 **dīng** Trad 頂 **I** *n* top (of the head), peak, summit
山顶 **shāndǐng** peak □ 今天我们能爬到山顶吗？**Jīntiān wǒmen néng pádào shāndǐng ma?** *Can we reach the mountain top today?*
头顶 **tóudǐng** crown of the head
屋顶 **wūdǐng** roof
II *v* carry on the head, hit with the head □ 九号队员顶球入门。**Jiǔhào duìyuán dǐng qiú rù mén.** *No. 9 headed the ball into the goal.*

顶点 **dīngdiǎn** [modif: 顶 top + 点 point] *n* zenith, apex

顶端 **dīngduān** [modif: 顶 top + 端 end] *n* top, peak

订 **dìng** Trad 訂 *v* book
订房间 **dìng fángjiān** reserve a hotel/motel room □ 我想订一个双人房间。**Wǒ xiǎng dìng yí ge shuāngrén fángjiān.** *I'd like to book a double room.*
订票 **dìng piào** book tickets □ 我现在订机票，万一有事能退吗？**Wǒ xiànzài dìng jī piào, wànyī yǒushì néng tuì ma?** *If I book an air ticket now, can I cancel it in case of emergency?*
订座 **dìng zuò** book a table (at a restaurant), book a seat (in a theater)

NOTE: 定 **dìng** can also be used in this sense, e.g. 定房间 = 订房间.

订购 **dìnggòu** [comp: 订 book+ 购 buy] *v* place an order

订户 **dìnghù** [modif: 订 book + 户 household] *n* subscriber (to a newspaper or magazine)

订婚 **dìnghūn** [v+obj: 订 book + 婚 marriage] *v* be engaged (for marriage)
订婚戒指 **dìnghūn jièzhǐ** engagement ring (枚 **méi**, 只 **zhī**)
和…订婚 **hé...dìnghūn** be engaged to ...

订货 **dìnghuò** [v+obj: 订 book + 货 goods] *v* order goods (in bulk), order
订货单 **dìnghuòdān** (written) order (份 **fèn**)

订阅 **dìngyuè** [comp: 订 book + 阅 read] *v* subscribe (a newspaper or magazine)

钉 **dìng** Trad 釘 *v* drive a nail into

定 **dìng** **I** *v* fix, set, determine □ 你去北京的日期定了吗？**Nǐ qù Běijīng de rìqī dìngle ma?** *Have you decided on the date to leave for Beijing?* **II** *adj* fixed, set, decided

定额 **dìng'é** [v+obj: 定 fix +额 quota] *n* quota (for sales, production, etc.)
完成销售定额 **wánchéng xiāoshòu dìng'é** fill a sales quota

定价 **dìngjià** [modif: 定 fix + 价 price] *n* fixed price, price

定居 **dìngjū** [modif: 定 fix + 居 inhabit] *v* start living in a place, settle down

定理 **dìnglǐ** [modif: 定 fixed + 理 reason] *n* theorem (条 **tiáo**)

定量 **dìngliàng** [v+obj: 定 determine + 量 quantity] *v* determine the quantity of
定量分析 **dìngliàng fēnxī** quantitative analysis

定律 **dìnglǜ** [modif: 定 fixed + 律 law] *n* (scientific law

定期 **dìngqī** [modif: 定 fixed + 期 period] *adv* at regular intervals
定期维修车辆 **dìngqī wéixiū chēliàng** regular maintenance of vehicles

定位 **dìngwèi** [v+obj: 定 determine + 位 position] *v* determine the position of
定位仪 **dìngwèiyí** GPS navigation system, GPS

定性 **dìngxìng** [v+obj: 定 determine + 性 nature, quality] *v* determine the quality of
定性分析 **dìngxìng fēnxī** qualitative analysis

定义 **dìngyì** [modif: 定 fixed + 义 meaning] *n* definition
下定义 **xià dìngyì** give a definition

丢 **diū** *v* lose, throw away □ 我的表丢了。**Wǒ de biǎo diū le.** *I've lost my watch.*

丢脸 **diūliǎn** lose face, be disgraced □ 他考试门门不及格，真丢脸！**Tā kǎoshì ménmen bù jígé, zhēn diūliǎn!** *It was disgraceful of him to fail every subject in the exam.*

丢三落四 **diū-sān-là-sì** *v* be forgetful, be scatterbrained □ 年纪大了，容易丢三落四的。**Niánjì dà le, róngyì diū-sān-là-sì de.** *When one gets old, one tends to be more forgetful.*

NOTE: 落 here is pronounced as **là**, not its usual **luò**.

丢失 **diūshī** [comp: 丢 lose + 失 lose] *v* lose

东 **dōng** Trad 東 *n* east, eastern □ 我在体育馆东门等你。**Wǒ zài tǐyùguǎn dōng mén děng nǐ.** *I'll be waiting for you at the east gate of the gymnasium.* □ 一直往东走，就是我们的学校。**Yìzhí wàng dōng zǒu**

jiùshì wǒmen de xuéxiào. *Walk straight towards the east and you'll come to our school.*

东北 **dōngběi** [comp: 东 east + 北 north] *n* northeast, the Northeast □ 中国东北天气非常冷。 **Zhōngguó Dōngběi tiānqì fēicháng lěng.** *It's very cold in Northeast China.*

NOTE: 东北 **dōngběi** as a specific geographical term refers to the northeastern part of China, which used to be known in the West as Manchuria.

东边 **dōngbian** *n* the east side, to the east, in the east □ 我们学校的东边是一座公园。 **Wǒmen xuéxiào de dōngbian shì yí zuò gōngyuán.** *To the east of our school is a park.* □ 日本在中国的东边。 **Rìběn zài Zhōngguó de dōngbian.** *Japan lies to the east of China.*

东道 **dōngdào** *n* host
东道国 **dōngdàoguó** host country
东道主 **dōngdàozhǔ** host (usually for an official function)

东方 **dōngfāng** [modif: 东 east + 方 direction, part] *n* the East, the Orient □ 东方文化和西方文化有很大的不同。 **Dōngfāng wénhuà hé xīfāng wénhuà yǒu hěn dà de bùtóng.** *There are major differences between the cultures of East and West.*

东面 **dōngmiàn** *n* Same as 东边 **dōngbian**

东南 **dōngnán** [comp: 东 east + 南 south] *n* southeast □ 中国东南地区经济发达, 人口很多。 **Zhōngguó dōngnán dìqū jīngjì fādá, rénkǒu hěn duō.** *The southeastern regions in China are economically well-developed and densely populated.*

东西 **dōngxi** *n* **1** thing, things (个 **gè**, 件 **jiàn**, 种 **zhǒng**) □ 这些东西都是小明的。 **Zhèxiē dōngxi dōu shì Xiǎo Míng de.** *All these things are Xiao Ming's.* □ 我没有看到过这种东西。 **Wǒ méiyǒu kàndàoguo zhè zhǒng dōngxi.** *I've never seen such a thing.* **2** a person or animal (used affectionately or disapprovingly in colloquial Chinese) □ 这小东西真可爱。 **Zhè xiǎo dōngxi zhēn kě'ài.** *What a cute little thing!* (referring to a baby or kitten) □ 你这个坏东西又在骗人了。 **Nǐ zhè ge huài dōngxi yòu zài piànrén le.** *You rascal! You're trying to deceive me again.*

NOTE: 东西 **dōngxi**, which literally means *east and west*, is an extremely common "all-purpose" noun that can denote any object or objects in Chinese. More examples: □ 妈妈出去买东西了。 **Māma chūqu mǎi dōngxi le.** *Mother's gone shopping.* □ 图书馆里不能吃东西。 **Túshūguǎn lǐ bù néng chī dōngxi.** *No food in the library.* □ 我想喝点儿东西。 **Wǒ xiǎng hē diǎnr dōngxi.** *I'd like to have a drink.*

冬 **dōng** *n* winter
冬季 **dōngjì** winter season
冬天 **dōngtiān** [modif: 冬 winter + 天 days] *n* winter □ 今年的冬天比去年冷。 **Jīnnián de dōngtiān bǐ qùnián lěng.** *This year's winter is colder than last year's.* □ 这一对老人喜欢在暖和的地方过冬天。 **Zhè yí duì lǎorén xǐhuan zài nuǎnhuo de dìfang guò dōngtiān.** *This old couple likes to spend winter in a warm region.* □ 我妈妈冬天常常生病。 **Wǒ māma**

dōngtiān chángcháng shēngbìng. *My mother is often sick in winter.*

董 **dǒng** as in 董事 **dǒngshì**
董事 **dǒngshì** *n* director (of a company), trustee
董事长 **dǒngshìzhǎng** chairman of the board of directors □ 大华公司王董事长在记者招待会上宣布了重大消息。 **Dàhuá Gōngsī Wáng dǒngshìzhǎng zài jìzhě zhāodàihuì shang xuānbùle zhòngdà xiāoxi.** *Mr Wang, chairman of the board of Da Hua Company, announced important news at the press conference.*

懂 **dǒng** *v* comprehend, understand □ 我不懂你的意思。 **Wǒ bù dǒng nǐ de yìsi.** *I don't understand what you mean.* □ 这首歌的意思你懂不懂? **Zhè shǒu gē de yìsi nǐ dǒng bu dǒng?** *Do you understand the meaning of this song?*

NOTE: 懂 is often used after another verb as a complement, e.g.
读懂 **dúdǒng** read and understand □ 这本书我读了两遍才读懂。 **Zhè běn shū wǒ dúle liǎng biàn cái dúdǒng.** *I understood this book only after reading it twice.*
看懂 **kàndǒng** see (or read) and understand □ 这个电影我没有看懂。 **Zhège diànyǐng wǒ méiyǒu kàndǒng.** *I didn't understand that movie.*
听懂 **tīngdǒng** listen and understand □ 我听得懂一些简单的中文。 **Wǒ tīng de dǒng yìxiē jiǎndān de Zhōngwén.** *I can understand a little simple spoken Chinese.*

懂事 **dǒngshì** [modif: 懂 understand + 事 things, matters] *adj* be sensible

动 **dòng** Trad 動 *v* move, act (antonym 静 **jìng**) □ 别动, 我给你照张像。 **Bié dòng, wǒ gěi nǐ zhào zhāng xiàng.** *Stay put, I'll take your picture.*

动工 **dònggōng** [v+obj: 动 act + 工 work] *v* begin construction □ 计算机房什么时候动工? **Jìsuànjī fáng shénme shíhòu dònggōng?** *When will the building of the computer lab start?*

动机 **dòngjī** *n* motive, intention □ 他的动机是好的, 可惜效果不那么好。 **Tā de dòngjī shì hǎo de, kěxī xiàoguǒ bù nàme hǎo.** *His intention was good; it's a shame the effect was not so good.*
动机不纯 **dòngjī bùchún** with hidden motives

动静 **dòngjing** [comp: 动 movement + 静 quietness] *n* signs of activity

动力 **dònglì** [modif: 动 movement + 力 power] *n* **1** source of power, power **2** driving force (to do something), motivation

动乱 **dòngluàn** [comp: 动 movement + 乱 chaos] *n* (social) turmoil, upheaval

动脉 **dòngmài** [modif: 动 movement + 脉 artery] *n* artery
主动脉 **zhǔ dòngmài** main artery

动人 **dòngrén** [modif: 动 moving + 人 people] *adj* moving, touching □ 这个电影的故事十分动人。 **Zhège diànyǐng de gùshi shífēn dòngrén.** *This film has a moving storyline.*

动身 **dòngshēn** [v+obj: 动 act + 身 the body] *v* start (a journey), set off (on a journey) □ 你如果要在天黑前到达, 就得早上动身。 **Nǐ rúguǒ yào zài tiān hēi qián dàodá, jiù děi zǎoshang dòngshēn.** *If you want to arrive before dark, you've got to set off early in the morning.*

动手 dòngshǒu [v+obj: 动 act + 手 hand] v start work □ 我们现在动手，一定能在七点前完成任务。**Wǒmen xiànzài dòngshǒu, yídìng néng zài qī diǎn qián wánchéng rènwù.** *If we start work now we're sure to be able to finish the job before seven o'clock.*

动态 dòngtài [modif: 动 movement + 态 condition] n general tendency of affairs, developments 科技动态 kējì dòngtài developments in science and technology, what's new in science and technology

动物 dòngwù [modif: 动 moving + 物 object] n animal (只 zhī) □ 这些小动物真可爱! **Zhèxiē xiǎo dòngwù zhēn kě'ài!** *These little animals are really adorable!* □ 小孩子特别喜欢动物。**Xiǎo háizi tèbié xǐhuan dòngwù.** *Children are particularly fond of animals.*
动物学 dòngwùxué zoology
动物园 dòngwùyuán zoo □ 下星期五我们班参观动物园。**Xià Xīngqīwǔ wǒmen bān cānguān dòngwùyuán.** *Our class will visit the zoo next Friday afternoon.*

动摇 dòngyáo [comp: 动 move + 摇 shake] v waver, vacillate
决不动摇 jué bù dòngyáo will not waver, be very firm and determined

动用 dòngyòng [comp: 动 move + 用 use] v put to use, draw on
动用预备金 dòngyòng yùbèi jīn draw on reserve fund

动员 dòngyuán [v+obj: 动 move + 员 staff, people] v mobilize

动作 dòngzuò [comp: 动 act + 作 do] n movement (of the body) □ 你跳舞的动作真优美! **Nǐ tiàowǔ de dòngzuò zhēn yōuměi!** *The movements of your dance are really beautiful! (→ You're a graceful dancer!)*

冻 dòng Trad 凍 v freeze □ 天这么冷，我真冻坏了。**Tiān zhème lěng, wǒ zhēn dòng huài le.** *It's so cold. I'm frozen to death.*
冻肉 dòngròu frozen meat
肉冻 ròudòng jellied meat
水果冻 shuǐguǒdòng fruit jelly

冻结 dòngjié v freeze
工资冻结 gōngzī dòngjié wage freeze

栋 dòng Trad 棟 measure wd (for buildings)
一栋古典风格的小楼 yí dòng gǔdiǎn fēnggé de xiǎo lóu a nice house in classical style

洞 dòng n hole, cave, cavity □ 你敢进这个山洞吗? **Nǐ gǎn jìn zhège shāndòng ma?** *Do you dare to enter this mountain cave?*

都 dōu adv all, both, without exception □ 学生们都喜欢上中文课。**Xuéshengmen dōu xǐhuan shàng Zhōngwén kè.** *All the students like having Chinese classes.* □ 我每天都跑步。**Wǒ měitiān dōu pǎobù.** *I jog every day.* □ 我所有的朋友都来了。**Wǒ suǒyǒu de péngyou dōu lái le.** *All my friends have come.*

NOTE: When words like 每天 měitiān (every day), 每个 měi ge (every one), 大家 dàjiā (everybody) or 所有的 suǒyǒu de (all) are used, they usually occur with the adverb 都 dōu.

兜 dōu I n pocket, bag II v 1 wrap up 2 move around 3 canvass, solicit

抖 dǒu v shake, tremble

陡 dǒu adj steep, precipitous

斗 dòu Trad 鬥 v fight
斗争 dòuzhēng [comp: 斗 fight + 争 strive] I v struggle, fight □ 为世界和平而斗争! **Wèi shìjiè hépíng ér dòuzhēng!** *Struggle for world peace!* II n struggle, fight □ 你们的斗争一定会胜利。**Nǐmen de dòuzhēng yídìng huì shènglì.** *Your struggle will definitely be victorious.*
斗志 dòuzhì [modif: 斗 fighting + 志 will] n will to fight, militancy

豆 dòu n bean, pea
豆子 dòuzi bean, pea

豆腐 dòufu [modif: 豆 soybean + 腐 curd] n bean curd, tofu □ 豆腐价格便宜，营养丰富。**Dòufu jiàgé piányi, yíngyǎng fēngfù.** *Bean curd is cheap and nutritious.*

豆浆 dòujiāng [modif: 豆 bean + 浆 liquid] n soybean milk

逗 dòu v play with, tease □ 他下班以后，最爱逗孩子玩。**Tā xiàbān yǐhòu, zuì ài dòu háizi wán.** *After work, the thing he likes to do best is play with the baby.*
逗留 dòuliú v stay briefly

都 dū n big city, metropolis
首都 shǒudū capital city, capital
都市 dūshì [comp: 都 metropolis + 市 city] n big city, metropolis

督 dū v supervise
督促 dūcù [comp: 督 supervise + 促 urge] v supervise and urge

毒 dú n 1 poison, toxin
毒蛇 dúshé poisonous snake
蛇毒 shédú snake's venom
有毒 yǒudú poisonous, venomous
2 narcotic drug (e.g. heroin, cocaine, etc.)
贩毒 fàndú drug trafficking
吸毒 xīdú drug taking

毒害 dúhài [comp: 毒 poison + 害 harm] v poison
毒害青少年 dúhài qīng shàonián poison the minds of young people

毒品 dúpǐn Same as 毒 dú 2

毒药 dúyào [modif: 毒 poison + 药 drug] n poison, toxicant

独 dú Trad 獨 adj solitary, alone
独裁 dúcái v establish a dictatorship, rule arbitrarily
独裁者 dúcáizhě dictator
独裁政权 dúcái zhèngquán dictatorial regime

独唱 dúchàng [modif: 独 solitary + 唱 singing] n (singing) solo
男高音独唱 nángāoyīn dúchàng tenor solo

独立 dúlì [modif: 独 solitary + 立 stand] v be independent □ 孩子大了都想独立，父母不用太担心。**Háizi dàle dōu xiǎng dúlì, fùmǔ búyòng tài dānxīn.** *When children grow up, they all want to be independent. Parents should not be too worried.*

独特 dútè [comp: 独 solitary + 特 unique] adj unique, distinctive
独特的风格 dútè de fēnggé unique style

独自 dùzì [comp: 独 solitary + 自 self] adv all by oneself, alone

独自旅游 dúzì lǚyóu have a holiday all by oneself

独奏 dùzòu [modif: 独 solitary + 奏 play an instrument] *n* solo performance on an musical instrument

萨克斯管独奏 sà kè sī guǎn dúzòu saxophone solo

读 dú Trad 讀 *v* 1 read, read aloud □ 他正在读一份重要文件。**Tā zhèng zài dú yí fèn zhòngyào wénjiàn.** *He is reading an important document.* 2 attend (a school), study (in a school)

读小学/中学/大学 dú xiǎoxué/ zhōngxué/ dàxué attend a primary school/high school/university □ 他们的大儿子在读中学, 小女儿在读小学。**Tāmen de dà érzi zài dú zhōngxué, xiǎo nǚ'er zài dú xiǎoxué.** *Their elder son is studying in a high school and their young daughter in a primary school.*

NOTE: (1) In colloquial Chinese, 读 **dú** may be replaced by 看 **kàn** when used in the sense of *read*, e.g. 看书 **kàn shū**, 看报 **kàn bào**. (2) When used in the sense of *attend (school)* or *study (in a school)* 读 **dú** may be replaced by 念 **niàn** to become 念小学/中学/大学 **niàn xiǎoxué/ zhōngxué/dàxué**, which is more colloquial.

读书 dúshū [v+obj: 读 read + 书 book] *v* 1 read □ 这孩子喜欢读书, 他爸爸妈妈看了真高兴。**Zhè háizi xǐhuan dúshū, tā bàba māma kànle zhēn gāoxìng.** *The child likes reading, much to the delight of his parents.* 2 be a student, study (in a school) □ 我姐姐工作了, 可是我妹妹还在读书。**Wǒ jiějie gōngzuò le, kěshì wó mèimei háizài dúshū.** *My elder sister is working but my younger sister is still a student.*

读物 dùwù [modif: 读 reading + 物 things] *n* reading material

儿童读物 értóng dúwù children's books

读者 dúzhě [suffix 读 read + 者 nominal suffix] *n* reader □ 今天报上登了很多读者来信, 对这个问题发表意见。**Jīntiān bào shang dēng le hěn duō dúzhě láixìn, duì zhège wèntí fābiǎo yìjian.** *Today's newspaper publishes many readers' letters airing views on this issue.*

堵 dǔ *v* block □ 什么东西堵住了下水道? **Shénme dōngxi dǔzhùle xiàshuǐdào?** *What is blocking the sewer?*

堵塞 dǔsè [comp: 堵 block + 塞 block] *v* block □ 水管堵塞了。**Shuǐguǎn dǔsè le.** *There is a blockage in the waterpipe.*

交通堵塞 jiāotōng dǔsè traffic jam

赌 dǔ *v* gamble

赌博 dǔbó [comp: 赌 gamble + 博 gamble] *v* gamble

赌场 dǔchǎng [modif: 赌 gamble + 场 place] *n* gambling house, casino

肚 dù *n* stomach

肚子 dùzi abdomen, stomach, belly □ 我肚子痛。**Wǒ dùzi tòng.** *I have a stomachache.* (← *My stomach hurts.*)

度 dù I *n* limit, extent

难度 nándù degree of difficulty □ 这篇课文难度太高。**Zhè piān kèwén nándù tài gāo.** *This text is too difficult.* II *measure wd* degree (of temperature, longitude, latitude, etc.) □ 今天最高气温是二十五度。**Jīntiān zuì gāo qìwēn shì èrshíwǔ dù.** *The highest temperature today is 25 degrees.*

度过 dùguò *v* spend (a period of time) □ 孩子们在爷爷奶奶家度过了愉快的暑假。**Háizimen zài yéye nǎinai jiā dùguòle yí ge yúkuài de shǔjià.** *The children spent a pleasant summer vacation with their grandpa and grandma.*

渡 dù *v* cross (a body of water, e.g. a river, a strait, etc.) □ 我们怎么渡江呢? **Wǒmen zěnme dù jiāng ne?** *How are we going to cross the river?*

渡船 dùchuán [modif: 渡 crossing + 船 ship, boat] *n* ferry boat, ferry (条 tiáo)

渡口 dùkǒu [modif: 渡 crossing + 口 mouth] *n* a place where people or things are carried across, ferry landing

渡轮 dùlún [modif: 渡 crossing + 轮 ship] *n* ferry boat, ferry (艘 sōu)

镀 dù Trad 鍍 *v* plate

镀金 dùjīn *v* get gilded

妒 dù *v* be jealous

妒忌 dùjì [comp: 妒 jealous + 忌 jealous] *v* be jealous of

妒忌别人的财富/成就 dùjì biéren de cáifù/chéngjiù be jealous of someone's wealth/achievements

妒忌心 dùjìxīn *n* jealousy □ 他的妒忌心很重。**Tā de dùjì xīn hěn zhòng.** *He is prone to jealousy.*

端 duān *v* carry ... level with one or both hands □ 她端了一大盘水果走了进来。**Tā duānle yí dà pán shuǐguǒ zǒule jìnlai.** *She came in, carrying a big plate of fruit.*

端正 duānzhèng *adj* upright, proper

短 duǎn *adj* (of length, time) short (antonym 长 cháng) □ 这条街很短, 只有十几座房子。**Zhè tiáo jiē hěn duǎn, zhǐ yǒu shíjǐ zuò fángzi.** *This is a short street, with only a dozen houses.* □ 我在上海的时间很短, 没有好好玩。**Wǒ zài Shànghǎi de shíjiān hěn duǎn, méiyǒu hǎohǎo wán.** *I only stayed in Shanghai for a short time and did not have much time for fun (e.g. sightseeing, etc.)*

短处 duǎnchù [modif: 短 short + 处 place] *n* shortcoming, defect (antonym 长处 chángchu)

短促 duǎncù [comp: 短 short + 促 hurried] *adj* very brief

短期 duǎnqī [modif: 短 short + 期 period] *n* short-term □ 她要去北京参加一个短期汉语口语训练班。**Tā yào qù Běijīng cānjiā yí ge duǎnqī Hànyǔ kǒuyǔ xùnliànbān.** *She is going to Beijing to attend a short training course in spoken Chinese.* □ 这个目标不可能在短期内达到。**Zhège mùbiāo bù kěnéng zài duǎnqī nèi dádào.** *This goal cannot be reached in a short time.*

短信 duǎnxìn [modif: 短 short + 信 letter] *n* text message (by cell phone), text

短信息服务 duǎnxìnxī fúwù short message service (SMS) □ 我昨天才收到他发来的两份短信。**Wǒ zuótiān shōudao tā fālái de liǎng fèn duǎnxìn.** *I received two text messages from him yesterday.*

短暂 duǎnzàn [comp: 短 short + 暂 temporory] *adj* short and temporary, momentary

段 duàn *measure wd* section (for something long)

一段经历 yí duàn jīnglì an experience [in life]

一段路 yí duàn lù a section of a road/street, part of a journey □ 这段路不平, 开车要特别小心。**Zhè duàn**

lù bù píng, kāi chē yào tèbié xiǎoxīn. *This section of the road is quite rough. One should be particularly careful when driving.*

断 duàn Trad 斷 *v* **1** break, snap □ 把电线剪断。**Bǎ diànxiàn jiǎn duàn.** *Cut the electric wire.* □ 我和她的联系断了，我不知道她在哪里。**Wǒ hé tā de liánxì duàn le, wǒ bù zhīdào tā zài nǎlǐ.** *I have lost contact with her. I do not know where she is.* **2** break off, cut off

断电 duàn diàn cut off electricity □ 一场大雪使这个地区断电三天。**Yì chǎng dà xuě shǐ zhège dìqū duàn diàn sān tiān.** *A heavy snow cut off electricity supply to this region for three days.*

断奶 duàn nǎi wean (a child)

断水 duàn shuǐ cut off water supply

断定 **duàndìng** *v* conclude

断断续续 **duàn-duàn-xù-xù** [comp: 断断 stop and stop + 续续 continue and continue] *adv* off and on, intermittently

断绝 **duànjué** *v* break off, sever

断绝贸易关系 duànjué màoyì guānxì break off trade relations

锻 duàn Trad 鍛 *v* forge, shape metal

锻炼 **duànliàn** [comp: 锻 shape metal + 炼 smelt] *v* undergo physical training, do physical exercises □ 你要成为一名好运动员，就得天天锻炼。**Nǐ yào chéngwéi yì míng hǎo yùndòngyuán, jiù děi tiāntiān duànliàn.** *If you want to become a good athlete, you have to train every day.*

缎 duàn Trad 緞 See 绸缎 **chóuduàn** satin, 缎子 **duànzi** satin

堆 duī *v* heap up, pile up □ 你要扔的东西都堆在墙角，明天打扫出去。**Nǐ yào rēng de dōngxi dōu duī zài qiángjiǎo, míngtiān dǎsǎo chūqu.** *Pile up whatever you want to dump in the corner. Tomorrow we'll get rid of it.*

堆积 **duījī** *v* pile up

对 1 duì Trad 對 *v* treat, deal with □ 她对我很好。**Tā duì wǒ hěn hǎo.** *She treats me well.* (→ *She is nice to me.*) □ 我的批评是对事不对人。**Wǒ de pīpíng shì duì shì bú duì rén.** *My criticism concerns the issue, not the person.*

对 2 duì Trad 對 *prep* **1** opposite **2** Same as 对于 **duìyú**

对岸 **duì'àn** [modif: 对 opposite + 岸 bank] *n* the other side of the river, lake or sea

对比 **duìbǐ** [comp: 对 check + 比 compare, contrast] *v* compare and contrast □ 你对比一下中文和英文，就会发现很多有趣的问题。**Nǐ duìbǐ yíxià Zhōngwén hé Yīngwén, jiù huì fāxiàn hěn duō yǒuqù de wèntí.** *If you compare and contrast Chinese and English, you will find many interesting issues.*

对不起 **duìbuqǐ** *idiom* I'm sorry, I beg your pardon □ 对不起，打错电话了。**Duìbuqǐ, dǎ cuò diànhuà le.** *Sorry, I've dialed a wrong number.* □ 对不起，我迟到了。**Duìbuqǐ, wǒ chídào le.** *Sorry, I'm late.* □ 对不起，我没听清楚，请你再说一遍。**Duìbuqǐ, wǒ méi tīng qīngchu, qǐng nǐ zài shuō yíbiàn.** *I'm sorry, I didn't catch it. Could you please repeat?*

NOTE: 对不起 **duìbuqǐ** is a very useful idiomatic expression in colloquial Chinese. It is used when you've

done something wrong or caused some inconvenience to others. For more formal occasions, use 请原谅 **qǐng yuánliàng** *please forgive me.*

对策 **duìcè** [modif: 对 deal with + 策 strategy] *n* countermeasure

对称 **duìchèn** *adj* symmetrical

不对称 búduìchèn asymmetrical

对待 **duìdài** [comp: 对 deal with + 待 treat] *v* treat (people), approach (matters)

对得起 **duìdeqǐ** *v* be worthy of, not let down

对得起良心 duìdeqǐ liángxīn be at peace with one's conscience

对方 **duìfāng** [modif: 对 the opposite side + 方 side] *n* the other side, the other party □ 你必须清楚地了解对方的企图。**Nǐ bìxū qīngchu de liǎojiě duìfāng de qìtú.** *You must have a clear idea of the other party's intention.*

对付 **duìfu** *v* cope with, deal with □ 这种不讲道理的人，实在难对付。**Zhè zhǒng bù jiǎng dàoli de rén, shízài nán duìfu.** *It is indeed difficult to deal with such unreasonable people.* □ 我不知道怎么样对付这种情况。**Wǒ bù zhīdào zēnmeyàng duìfu zhè zhǒng qíngkuàng.** *I don't know how to cope with such a situation.*

对话 **duìhuà** **I** *v* have a dialogue □ 他能够流利地用中文对话。**Tā nénggòu liúlì de yòng Zhōngwén duìhuà.** *He is able to have a dialogue in fluent Chinese.* **II** *n* dialogue □ 工人已经和老板进行了两次对话。**Gōngrén yǐjīng he lǎobǎn jìnxíng le liǎng cì duìhuà.** *Workers have conducted two rounds of talks with the boss.*

对抗 **duìkàng** [comp: 对 opposite + 抗 resist] antagonize, oppose vigorously

对立 **duìlì** [modif: 对 opposite + 立 stand] *v* oppose be hostile

对联 **duìlián** *n* antithetical couplet written on scrolls

对面 **duìmiàn** *n* opposite, the opposite side □ 学校的对面是一座公园。**Xuéxiào de duìmiàn shì yí zuò gōngyuán.** *Opposite the school is a park.*

对手 **duìshǒu** [modif: 对 opposite + 手 hand] *n* opponent

竞争对手 jìngzhēng duìshǒu opponent in a competition, rival

对象 **duìxiàng** *n* **1** person or thing to which action or feeling is directed, object □ 她研究的对象是学前儿童。**Tā yánjiū de duìxiàng shì xuéqián értóng.** *Preschool children are the object of her study.* **2** marriage partner, fiancé(e) □ 他已经三十多岁了，还没有对象。**Tā yǐjīng sānshí duō suì le, hái méiyǒu duìxiàng.** *He is over thirty, but still has no fiancée.*

找对象 zhǎo duìxiàng look for a marriage partner

对应 **duìyìng** *adj* corresponding

对应词 duìyìng cí corresponding word □ 这个英文词在中文里几乎没有对应词。**Zhège Yīngwén cí zài Zhōngwén lǐ jīhū méiyǒu duìyìng cí.** *You can hardly find a word in Chinese that corresponds to this English word.*

对照 **duìzhào** *v* contrast and compare, refer to

对于 **duìyú** *prep* **1** (introducing the object of an action) regarding □ 我对于这个理论还没有完全理解。

Wǒ duìyú zhège lǐlùn hái méiyǒu wánquán lǐjiě. *I still haven't fully understood this theory.* □ 对于产品质量，工厂十分重视。**Duìyú chǎnpǐn zhìliàng gōngchǎng shífēn zhòngshì.** *The factory attaches great importance to the quality of its products.* **2** (indicating a certain relationship) to, towards □ 学习中文对于了解中国人和中国文化很有帮助。**Xuéxí Zhōngwén duìyú liǎojiě Zhōngguórén he Zhōngguó wénhuà hěn yǒu bāngzhù.** *Learning Chinese is very helpful towards understanding the Chinese people and Chinese culture.*

对 **3 duì** Trad 對 *adj* correct, true (antonym 错 **cuò**) □ 你的话很对。**Nǐ de huà hěn duì.** *Your words are correct.* (→ *You're right.*) □ 你说得很对。**Nǐ shuō de hěn duì.** *You spoke correctly.* (→ *You're right.*)

NOTE: 对不对 **duì bu duì** is used at the end of a sentence to form a question, e.g. □ 他回答得对不对? **Tā huídá de duì bu duì?** *Did he answer correctly?* □ 你是英国人，对不对? **Nǐ shì Yīngguórén, duì bu duì?** *You're from the UK, aren't you?* □ 中华文明是世界上最古老的文明，对不对? **Zhōnghuá wénmíng shì shìjiè shang zuì gǔlǎo de wénmíng, duì bu duì?** *Chinese civilization is the oldest in the world, isn't it?*

对头 **duìtóu** *adj* correct, on the right track
不对头 **búduìtóu** wrong, not right □ 你的想法不对头。**Nǐde xiǎngfǎ búduìtóu.** *Your ideas are not quite right.*

对 **4 duì** Trad 對 *measure wd* pair, two (matching people or things)
一对花瓶 **yí duì huāpíng** two matching vases □ 他们结婚的时候，我送了一对花瓶。**Tāmen jiéhūn de shíhuo, wǒ sòngle yí duì huāpíng.** *I gave them two matching vases when they married.*
一对夫妻 **yí duì fūqī** a couple (husband and wife)

队 **duì** Trad 隊 *n* team
篮球队 **lánqiúduì** basketball team
足球队 **zúqiúduì** soccer team
队伍 **duìwu** *n* troops □ 队伍天黑后进了村。**Duìwu tiānhēi hòu jìnle cūn.** *The troops entered the village after dark.*
队员 **duìyuán** [modif: 队 team + 员 member] *n* member of a team
队长 **duìzhǎng** [modif: 队 team + 长 chief] *n* team leader □ 队员都服从队长。**Duìyuán dōu fúcóng duìzhǎng.** *All the team members submit to the team leader.*

兑 **duì** *v* exchange, convert
兑换 **duìhuàn** [comp: 兑 convert + 换 exchange] *v* (of currency) exchange, convert □ 把1,000美元兑换成人民币。**Bǎ yìqiān Měiyuán duìhuàn chéng Rénmínbì.** *Convert 1,000 U.S. dollars to Renminbi (Chinese yuan).*
兑换率 **duìhuànlǜ** exchange rate
兑现 **duìxiàn** *v* cash (a check)

屯 **dūn** Trad 噸 *measure wd* ton □ 一吨等于一千公斤。**Yí dūn děngyú yìqiān gōngjīn.** *One ton equals 1,000 kilograms.*

蹲 **dūn** *v* squat

盾 **dùn** *n* shield (See 矛盾 **máodùn**)

顿 **dùn** Trad 頓 *measure wd* (for meals) □ 我们一天吃三顿饭：早饭、午饭、晚饭。**Wǒmen yì tiān chī sān dùn fàn: zǎofàn, wǔfàn, wǎnfàn.** *We have three meals a day: breakfast, lunch and supper (or dinner).* □ 她好好地吃了一顿晚饭。**Tā hǎohǎo de chīle yí dùn wǎnfàn.** *She had a good meal for supper.* (→ *She had a good supper.*)
顿时 **dùnshí** *adv* immediately, at once

多 **duō** **I** *adj* many, much (antonym 少 **shǎo**) □ 今天的作业不多。**Jīntiān de zuòyè bù duō.** *There isn't much homework today.* □ 他有很多中国朋友。**Tā yǒu hěn duō Zhōngguó péngyou.** *He has many Chinese friends.*
比…得多 **bǐ...de duō** much more ... than □ 今天比昨天热得多。**Jīntiān bǐ zuótiān rè de duō.** *Today is much hotter than yesterday.* □ 他昨天酒喝得太多，今天头疼。**Tā zuótiān jiǔ hē de tài duō, jīntiān tóu téng.** *He drank too much last night. Today he has a headache.* **II** *num* more, over □ 我们学了五百多个汉字。**Wǒmen xuéle wǔbǎi duō ge Hànzì.** *We've learned more than five hundred Chinese characters.* □ 他在台湾住了八个多月。**Tā zài Táiwān zhùle bā ge duō yuè.** *He lived in Taiwan for over eight months.* **III** *adv* how ...! □ 要是我能去北京学中文，多好啊! **Yàoshì wǒ néng qù Běijīng xué Zhōngwén, duō hǎo a!** *How nice it would be if I could go to Beijing to study Chinese!* □ 老先生，您多大了? **Lǎo xiānsheng, nín duō dà le?** *How old are you, sir?* (to an elderly man)
多半 **duōbàn** [modif: 多 more than + 半 half] *adv* probably, most likely
多亏 **duōkuī** *adv* luckily, fortunately
多么 **duōme** *adv* Same as 多 III *adv*. Used in colloquial Chinese.
多媒体 **duōméitǐ** *n* multimedia
多少 **duōshǎo** [comp: 多 many, much + 少 few, little] *pron* how many, how much □ 你们班多少人学中文? **Nǐmen bān duōshǎo rén xué Zhōngwén?** *How many in your class are studying Chinese?*
…多少钱 **...duōshǎo qián** How much is ...? □ 这本书多少钱? **Zhè běn shū duōshǎo qián?** *How much is this book?*
没有多少 **méiyǒu duōshǎo** not many, not much □ 他没有多少钱，可是要装出很有钱的样子。**Tā méiyǒu duōshǎo qián, kěshì yào zhuāngchū hěn yǒuqián de yàngzi.** *He hasn't got much money, but he pretends to be rich.*

NOTE: See note on 几 **jǐ**.

多数 **duōshù** [modif: 多 many + 数 number] *n* majority □ 世界上多数国家都实行民主制度。**Shìjiè shang duōshù guójiā dōu shíxíng mínzhǔ zhìdù.** *The majority of countries in the world practice democracy.*
多余 **duōyú** [comp: 多 + 余 spare] *adj* surplus

哆 **duō** as in 哆嗦 **duōsuo**
哆嗦 **duōsuo** *v* tremble, shiver

夺 **duó** Trad 奪 *v* take by force, win □ 我们队夺得了冠军。**Wǒmen duì duódéle guànjūn.** *Our team has won the championship.*

夺取 duóqǔ [comp: 夺 take by force + 取 take] *v* capture, seize

朵 duǒ *measure wd* (for flowers) □ 送给你一朵花。**Sòng gei nǐ yì duǒ huā.** *I'll give you a flower.*

躲 duǒ *v* hide (oneself) □ 他躲在门背后。**Tā duǒ zài mén bèihòu.** *He hid behind the door.*

躲避 duǒbì [comp: 躲 hide + 避 avoid] *v* hide, avoid, keep away from
躲避债主 duǒbì zhàizhǔ hide from the creditor

躲藏 duǒcáng [comp: 躲 hide + 藏 hide] *v* go into hiding

跺 duò *v* stamp (one's foot)

舵 duò *n* rudder, helm

惰 duò *adj* be lazy □ 教不严, 师之惰。**Jiào bù yán, shī zhī duò.** *If the teaching is not rigorous, it's because the teacher is lazy.*

堕 duò Trad 墮 *v* fall
堕落 duòluò [comp: 堕 fall + 落 fall] *v* (of one's morals or behavior) become worse, degenerate

E

俄 é *n* (a shortened form of 俄国 Russia or 俄语 Russian)

俄国 Éguó *n* Russia

俄文 Éwén [comp: 俄 Russian + 文 writing] *n* the Russian language (especially the writing)

俄语 Éyǔ [comp: 俄 Russia + 语 speech] *n* the Russian language □ 俄语的语法很复杂。**Éyǔ de yǔfǎ hěn fùzá.** *Russian grammar is complicated.*

鹅 é Trad 鵝 *n* goose (只 zhī)
天鹅 tiān'é swan

蛾 é *n* moth
蛾子 ézi moth (个 gè)

额 é Trad 額 *n* forehead
额外 éwài *adj* additional, extra
额外的开支 éwài de kāizhī extra expenditure

讹 é Trad 訛 *v* extort, blackmail
讹诈 ézhà [comp: 讹 blackmail + 诈 extort] *v* extort, blackmail

恶 ě Trad 惡 *v* vomit
恶心 ěxīn *v* 1 feel sick, be sickened □ 我看到那种食物, 就感到恶心。**Wǒ kàndào nà zhǒng shíwù, jiù gǎndào ěxīn.** *I feel sick at the sight of the food.* 2 feel disgusted, be nauseated □ 她拍老板马屁的样子, 真叫人恶心! **Tā pāi lǎobǎn mǎpì de yàngzi, zhēn jiào rén ěxīn!** *The way she fawns over the boss is really nauseating!*

恶 è Trad 惡 *adj* bad, wicked (antonym 善 shàn) □ 人性是善, 还是恶? **Rénxìng shì shàn, háishi è?** *Is human nature good or bad?*

恶毒 èdú [comp: 恶 evil + 毒 poisonous] *adj* vicious, malicious

恶化 èhuà *v* get worse, aggravate

恶劣 èliè [comp: 恶 bad + 劣 inferior] *adj* very bad, abominable

恶性 èxìng [modif: 恶 malicious + 性 nature] *adj* malicious

恶性肿瘤 èxìng zhǒngliú malignant tumor, cancer
恶性事件 èxìng shìjiàn vicious crime

饿 è Trad 餓 *adj* hungry (antonym 饱 bǎo) □ 我饿了, 我们去吃饭吧! **Wǒ è le, wǒmen qù chī fàn ba!** *I'm hungry. Let's go and eat.* □ 看到这么多好吃的东西, 我感到饿了。**Kàndào zhème duō hǎochī de dōngxi, wǒ gǎndào è le.** *At the sight of so much delicious food, I feel hungry.*

恩 ēn *n* kindness, grace
恩爱 ēn'ài *adj* (between husband and wife) deep, caring love

恩惠 ēnhuì [comp: 恩 kindness + 惠 benefit] *n* kindness that brings about great benefits

恩情 ēnqíng [modif: 恩 kindness + 情 emotion] *n* lovingkindness

恩人 ēnrén [modif: 恩 kindness + 人 person] *n* benefactor

儿 ér Trad 兒 *n* child, son
儿女 érnǚ [comp: 儿 son + 女 daughter] *n* son(s) and daughter(s), children

儿童 értóng [comp: 儿 child + 童 child] *n* child(ren) □ 这种电影不适合儿童看。**Zhè zhǒng diànyǐng bù shìhé értóng kàn.** *This kind of film is not suitable for children.*
儿童时代 értóng shídài childhood

儿子 érzi [suffix: 儿 son + 子 nominal suffix] *n* son (个 gè) □ 他们有两个儿子, 大儿子工作了, 小儿子还在念大学。**Tāmen yǒu liǎng ge érzi, dà érzi gōngzuò le, xiǎo érzi háizài niàn dàxué.** *They have two sons. While the elder son has started working, the younger son is still studying in a university.* □ 他希望妻子生一个儿子。**Tā xīwàng qīzi shēng yí ge érzi.** *He hopes that his wife will give birth to a son.*

而 ér *conj* (indicating a contrast) but, yet, on the other hand □ 学而不用, 等于没学。**Xué ér bú yòng, děngyú méi xué.** *If you learn skills but do not use them, it is tantamount to not having learned them at all.* □ 他姐姐功课很好, 而他呢, 去年考试三门不及格。**Tā jiějie gōngkè hěn hǎo, ér tā ne, qùnián kǎoshì sān mén bù jígé.** *His sister's schoolwork is excellent, but he failed in three subjects last year.*

而且 érqiě *conj* moreover, what's more □ 这件衣服大了一点儿, 而且比较贵, 还是不买吧。**Zhè jiàn yīfu dàle yìdiǎnr, érqiě bǐjiào guì, háishì bù mǎi ba.** *This dress is a bit too big and also expensive. You shouldn't buy it.*

耳 ěr *n* ear
耳朵 ěrduo *n* the ear (只 zhī) □ 人有两只耳朵, 说明应该听不同的声音。**Rén yǒu liǎng zhī ěrduo, jiù shuōmíng yīnggāi tīng bùtóng de shēngyīn.** *A man has two ears, which means he should listen to different voices.* (→ *A man has two ears, which means he should hear out different opinions.*)

二 èr *num* second, two □ 我二哥去年结婚了。**Wǒ èrgē qùnián jiéhūn le.** *My second elder brother got married last year.*
二千二百二十二 èrqiān èrbǎi èrshí'èr two thousand, two hundred and twenty-two (2,222)

NOTE: See note on **两 liǎng**.

二奶 èr-nǎi [modif: 二 second + 奶 lady] *n* mistress, concubine, kept woman

包二奶 bāo èr-nǎi keep a woman as mistress
二手 èrshǒu [modif: 二 second + 手 hand] *adj*
second-hand, used
二手车 èrshǒu chē used car
二手房 èrshǒu fáng second-hand housing
二氧化碳 èryǎnghuàtàn *n* carbon dioxide

F

发 fā Trad 發 *v* 1 send out, release □ 我上个星期给
他发了一封信, 今天上午又发了一个传真。**Wǒ shàng
ge xīngqī gei tā fāle yì fēng xìn, jīntiān shàngwǔ yòu
fāle yí ge chuánzhēn.** *I sent him a letter last week and
a fax this morning.*
发传真 fā chuánzhēn send a fax
发电子邮件 fā diànzǐ yóujiàn send an e-mail message
发 (手机) 短信 fā (shǒujī) duǎnxìn send a text message (by cell phone)
2 develop (into a state)
发表 fābiǎo [comp: 发 release + 表 express] *v*
publicize, make known, publish □ 请您发表对目前
经济形势的看法。**Qǐng nín fābiǎo duì mùqián jīngjì
xíngshì de kànfǎ.** *Please express your views on the
current economic situation.*
发布 fābù *v* release, issue
发布通告 fābù tōnggào release an announcement
发布新闻 fābù xīnwén release news
发财 fācái [v+obj: 发 develop + 财 wealth] *v* make
a fortune, become prosperous
发出 fāchū [comp: 发 release + 出 out] *v* 1 produce,
emit, give off □ 水果成熟会发出特殊的香味。**Shuǐguǒ
chéngshú huì fāchū tèshū de xiāngwèi.** *Ripe fruit gives
off a special fragrance.* 2 send out □ 学校已经向新
生发出通知。**Xuéxiào yǐjīng xiàng xīnshēng fāchū
tōngzhī.** *The school has sent out notifications to the
new students.*
发达 fādá *adj* developed, well-developed □ 这个国家
制造业很发达。**Zhège guójiā zhìzàoyè hěn fādá.** *This
country has a well-developed manufacturing industry.*
发电 fādiàn [v+obj: 发 generate + 电 electricity] *v*
generate electricity
发电厂 fādiànchǎng power plant
发电机 fādiànjī generator
火力发电 huǒlì fādiàn thermal power
水力发电 shuǐlì fādiàn hydro power
发动 fādòng *v* launch (a massive campaign) □ 毛泽
东在1966年发动了文化大革命。**Máo Zédōng zài yī-jiǔ-
liù-liù nián fādòngle Wénhuà Dà Gémìng.** *The Cultural
Revolution was launched by Mao Zedong in 1966.*
发抖 fādǒu *v* tremble □ 她冷得发抖。**Tā lěng de
fādǒu.** *She trembled with cold.*
发挥 fāhuī *v* allow display, give free rein to □ 这
项工作能够充分发挥他在这方面的能力。**Zhè xiàng
gōngzuò nénggòu chōngfèn fāhuī tā zài zhè fāngmiàn
de nénglì.** *This job allows him to display his ability in
this area fully.*
发火 fāhuǒ [v+obj: 发 send out + 火 fire] *v* lose
temper, get angry
发觉 fājué *v* find, find out, become aware of
发明 fāmíng I *v* invent □ 飞机是谁发明的? **Fēijī shì

shuí fāmíng de?** *Who invented the airplane?* II *n*
invention (项 **xiàng**) □ 这项新发明会给公司带来巨大
的利益。**Zhè xiàng xīn fāmíng huì gěi gōngsī dàilái
jùdà de lìyì.** *This new invention will bring tremendous
benefits to the company.*
发脾气 fā píqi [v+obj: 发 send out + 脾气 temper] *v*
lose one's temper, flare up □ 千万别发脾气! **Qiānwàn
bié fā píqi!** *Never lose your temper!*
发票 fāpiào *n* receipt (张 **zhāng**)
发起 fāqǐ *v* launch, initiate
发热 fārè [v+obj: 发 develop + 热 heat] *v* Same as
发烧 fāshāo
发烧 fāshāo [v+obj: 发 develop + 烧 burning, fever]
v run a fever □ 她昨天着凉了, 夜里就发烧了。**Tā
zuótiān zháoliáng le, yèlǐ jiù fāshāo le.** *She caught a
cold yesterday and began to run a fever at night.*
发高烧 fā gāoshāo run a high fever
发射 fāshè [comp: 发 send out + 射 shoot] *v* shoot,
launch
发射嫦娥一号探月卫星 fāshè Cháng'é yíhào tànyuè
wèixīng launch Chang'e No. 1 Lunar Orbiting
Spacecraft
发生 fāshēng [comp: 发 develop + 生 grow] *v* take
place, happen □ 这里发生了什么事? **Zhèlǐ fāshēngle
shénme shì?** *What happened here?* □ 前面发生了交
通事故, 车辆必须绕道。**Qiánmiàn fāshēngle jiāotōng
shìgù, chēliàng bìxū ràodào.** *A road accident happened up ahead. Traffic must detour.*
发誓 fāshì *v* pledge, vow
发誓不再抽烟 fāshì búzài chōuyān vow not to
smoke again
发现 fāxiàn [comp: 发 develop + 现 show] *v*
discover, find, find out □ 谁先发现新西兰的? **Shuí
xiān fāxiàn Xīnxīlán de?** *Who first discovered New
Zealand?* □ 我发现他爱打扮了, 是不是有女朋友了? **Wǒ
fāxiàn tā ài dǎbàn le, shì bu shì yǒu nǚpéngyou le?** *I
notice that he is paying more attention to his groom-
ing. Has he gotten a girlfriend?*
发行 fāxíng *v* issue (books, stamps, etc.), publish
发言 fāyán [v+obj: 发 release + 言 words] I *v* speak
(at a meeting), make a speech □ 代表们在会上纷纷发
言。**Dàibiǎomen zài huìshang fēnfēn fāyán.** *The delegates spoke at the meeting, one after another.* II *n*
speech □ 他在会上的发言引起了代表们的争论。**Tā zài
huìshang de fāyán yǐnqǐle dàibiǎomen de zhēnglùn.**
*His speech at the meeting gave rise to a debate among
the delegates.*
发言人 fāyánrén spokesperson
发炎 fāyán [v+obj: 发 develop + 炎 inflammation]
v become inflamed
发扬 fāyáng [comp: 发 develop + 扬 unfold] *v* develop, carry forward □ 希望你发扬优点, 克服缺点。
Xīwàng nǐ fāyáng yōudiǎn, kèfú quēdiǎn. *I hope you
will develop your strong points and overcome your
shortcomings.*
发音 fāyīn [v+obj: 发 send out + 音 sound] *n* pronunciation □ 我这个字发音对不对? **Wǒ zhège zì fāyīn
duì bu duì?** *Did I pronounce this character correctly?*
□ 他中文说得很流利, 虽然发音不太好。**Tā Zhōngwén
shuō de hěn liúlì, suīrán fāyīn bú tài hǎo.** *He speaks
Chinese fluently, though his pronunciation is not too
good.*

发育 **fāyù** [comp: 发 develop + 育 cultivate] *v* (of humans) develop physically

发展 **fāzhǎn** [comp: 发 develop + 展 unfold] *v* develop □ 经济要发展, 政治要民主。**Jīngjì yào fāzhǎn, zhèngzhì yào mínzhǔ.** *The economy should be developed, and politics democratized.* □ 公司决定发展在这个地区的业务。**Gōngsī juédìng fāzhǎn zài zhè ge dìqū de yèwù.** *The company has decided to develop its business in this region.*

发展中国家 **fāzhǎnzhōng guójiā** developing country

乏 **fá** *v* lack (See 缺乏 **quēfá**.)

罚 **fá** Trad 罰 *v* punish, penalize □ 他因为超速驾车, 被罚了两百块。**Tā yīnwéi chāosù jiàchē, bèi fále liǎngbǎi kuài.** *He was fined 200 yuan for speeding.*

罚款 **fákuǎn** I *v* fine □ 超速要罚款。**Chāosù yào fákuǎn.** *Speeding will be fined.* II *n* fine

罚款单 **fákuǎndān** fine notice

缴罚款 **jiǎo fákuǎn** pay a fine

伐 **fá** *v* fell, cut down

伐木 **fámù** fell trees, do logging

伐木工人 **fámù gōngrén** lumberjack

阀 **fá** Trad 閥 *n* valve

阀门 **fámén** valve

法 **fǎ** *n* method, law

法定 **fǎdìng** *adj* required by law, legal

法定年龄 **fǎdìng niánlíng** legal age (for certain rights)

法定人数 **fǎdìng rénshù** quorum

法官 **fǎguān** [modif: 法 law + 官 official] *n* judge

法规 **fǎguī** [modif: 法 law + 规 regulation] *n* laws and regulations

法律 **fǎlǜ** [comp: 法 law + 律 rule] *n* law □ 他哥哥在读法律, 他想当律师。**Tā gēge zài dú fǎlǜ, tā xiǎng dāng lǜshī.** *His older brother is studying law; he wants to be a lawyer.* □ 每一个公民都必须遵守法律。**Měi yí ge gōngmín dōu bìxū zūnshǒu fǎlǜ.** *Every citizen must obey the law.*

违反法律 **wéifǎn fǎlǜ** violate the law

修改法律 **xiūgǎi fǎlǜ** amend a law

法人 **fǎrén** [modif: 法 legal + 人 person] *n* legal person

法庭 **fǎtíng** [modif: 法 law + 庭 courtyard] *n* law court, court

法文 **Fǎwén** [comp: 法 France + 文 writing] *n* the French language (especially the writing)

法西斯 **Fǎxīsī** *n* Fascism

法语 **Fǎyǔ** [comp: 法 France + 语 speech] *n* the French language □ 她法语说得很漂亮。**Tā Fǎyǔ shuō de hěn piàoliang.** *She speaks French beautifully.*

法院 **fǎyuàn** [modif: 法 law + 院 house] *n* law court, court

高级人民法院 **gāojí rénmín fǎyuàn** supreme people's court

中级人民法院 **zhōngjí rénmín fǎyuàn** intermediate people's court

法则 **fǎzé** [modif: 法 law + 则 principle] *n* rule, law

自然法则 **zìrán fǎzé** law of nature

法治 **fǎzhì** *n* rule of law

法制 **fǎzhì** [modif: 法 law + 制 system] *n* legal system, rule by law

法子 **fǎzi** *n* way of doing things, method

没法子 **méifǎzi** no way, there's nothing I can do

翻 **fān** *v* 1 turn, turn over □ 请把书翻到二十页。**Qǐng bǎ shū fāndào èrshí yè.** *Please turn your books to page 20.* 2 translate, interpret

翻译 **fānyì** I *v* translate, interpret □ 这本小说已被翻译成八种语言。**Zhè běn xiǎoshuō yǐjīng bèi fānyì chéng bā zhǒng yǔyán.** *This novel has been translated into eight languages.*

把…翻译成… **bǎ...fānyì chéng...** translate ... into ... □ 你能不能把这封信翻译成中文? **Nǐ néng bu néng bǎ zhè fēng xìn fānyì chéng Zhōngwén?** *Can you translate this letter into Chinese?*

II *n* translator, interpreter □ 这位翻译中文英文都好极了。**Zhè wèi fānyì Zhōngwén Yīngwén dōu hǎo jíle.** *This translator (or interpreter) has very good command of both Chinese and English.*

当翻译 **dāng fānyì** to work as a translator (or interpreter) □ 明天有中国朋友来参观我们工厂, 请你当翻译。**Míngtiān yǒu Zhōngguó péngyou lái cānguān wǒmen gōngchǎng, qǐng nǐ dāng fānyì.** *Tomorrow some Chinese friends will come to visit our factory. I'll ask you to act as interpreter.*

帆 **fān** *n* sail

帆船 **fānchuán** *n* sailboat (艘 **sōu**)

番 **fān** *adj* foreign, outlandish

番茄 **fānqié** [modif: 番 foreign + 茄 eggplant] *n* tomato (只 **zhī**)

凡 **fán** *adv* every

凡是 **fánshì** *adv* every, all □ 凡是我姐姐的朋友, 我都认识。**Fánshì wǒ jiějie de péngyou, wǒ dōu rènshi.** *I know every one of my sister's friends.* □ 凡是违反法律的事, 都不能做。**Fánshì wéifǎn fǎlǜ de shì, dōu bù néng zuò.** *You must not do anything that violates the law.*

NOTE: 凡是 **fánshì** is used before a noun phrase to emphasize that what is referred to is all-embracing, without a single exception. The phrase introduced by 凡是 **fánshì** usually occurs at the beginning of a sentence, and 都 **dōu** is used in the second half of the sentence.

烦 **fán** Trad 煩 *adj* annoyed

烦闷 **fánmèn** [comp: 烦 annoyed + 闷 stuffy] *adj* worried and unhappy

烦恼 **fánnǎo** [comp: 烦 annoyed + 恼 angry] *adj* annoyed and angry, vexed

烦躁 **fánzào** [comp: 烦 annoyed + 躁 restless] *adj* annoyed and impatient, fidgety

繁 **fán** *adj* numerous, abundant, complicated

繁多 **fánduō** [comp: 繁 numerous + 多 many] *adj* numerous, various

品种繁多 **pǐnzhǒng fánduō** many kinds of, a great variety of

繁华 **fánhuá** *adj* flourishing, booming, bustling

繁忙 **fánmáng** *adj* busy, fully occupied

繁荣 **fánróng** [comp: 繁 abundant + 荣 flourishing] *adj* prosperous, thriving □ 由于经济繁荣, 人民的生活水平不断提高。**Yóuyú jīngjì fánróng, rénmín de shēnghuó shuǐpíng búduàn tígāo.** *With a prosperous economy, the people's standard of living keeps rising.*

繁体字 **fántǐzì** [modif: 繁 complicated + 体 style + 字 character] *n* old-styled, unsimplified Chinese character, e.g. 門 for 门。

NOTE: As 繁体字 literally means *complicated style character*, some people don't like the negative implication, and prefer to use the term 传统字 *traditional character*. 繁体字 or 传统字 are used in Taiwan, Hong Kong and overseas Chinese communities.

繁殖 fánzhí *v* reproduce, breed

繁重 fánzhòng [comp: 繁 complicated + 重 heavy] *adj* strenuous, onerous

反 fǎn I *adj* reverse, opposite (antonym 正 zhèng) □ 请看反面。**Qǐng kàn fǎnmiàn.** *Please read the reverse side.* **II** *v* oppose

反驳 fǎnbó [comp: 反 oppose + 驳 refute] *v* argue against, refute, retort

反常 fǎncháng [modif: 反 reverse + 常 normal] *adj* abnormal, unusual □ 情况反常。**Qíngkuàng fǎncháng.** *We have an unusual situation here.*

反倒 fǎndào *adv* Same as 反而 fǎn'ér

反动 fǎndòng [modif: 反 reverse + 动 action] *adj* reactionary □ 反对民主就是反动。**Fǎnduì mínzhǔ jiù shì fǎndòng.** *Whoever opposes democracy is a reactionary.*

反动派 fǎndòngpài reactionaries

反对 fǎnduì [modif: 反 opposing + 对 deal with] *v* oppose, object to (antonym 同意 tóngyì) □ 我不反对你的计划，但是我觉得很难做到。**Wǒ bù fǎnduì nǐ de jìhuà, dànshì wǒ juéde hěn nán zuòdào.** *I don't object to your plan, but I think it'll be difficult to implement.*

反对意见 fǎnduì yìjiàn opposing opinion

反对党 fǎnduìdǎng the Opposition (party)

反而 fǎn'ér *adv* on the contrary (to expectations), instead □ 他吃了药，病情反而恶化了。**Tā chīle yào, bìngqíng fǎn'ér èhuà le.** *Contrary to expectations his conditions worsened after he took the medicine.*

反复 fǎnfù [comp: 反 reverse + 复 duplicate] *adv* repeatedly, over and over again □ 董事长反复强调市场调查的重要性。**Dǒngshìzhǎng fǎnfù qiángdiào shìchǎng diàochá de zhòngyàoxìng.** *The chairman of the board emphasized over and over again the importance of market surveys.*

反感 fǎngǎn [modif: 反 oppose + 感 feelings] *adj* feel disgusted, be averse to

对他的行为很反感 duì tāde xíngwéi hěn fǎngǎn feel disgusted with his behavior

反攻 fǎngōng [modif: 反 oppose + 攻 attack] **I** *n* counterattack, counteroffensive **II** *v* launch a counterattack

反抗 fǎnkàng [comp: 反 oppose + 抗 resist] *v* resist, fight back, rebel □ 当父母的如果管得太多，孩子会反抗。**Dāng fùmǔ de rúguǒ guǎn de tài duō, háizi huì fǎnkàng.** *If a parent is too bossy, the child will rebel.*

反馈 fǎnkuì [modif: 反 reverse + 馈 feed] *n* feedback

反射 fǎnshè [modif: 反 reverse + 射 shoot] *v* reflect

条件反射 tiáojiàn fǎnshè conditional reflection

反思 fǎnsī [modif: 反 reverse + 思 think] *v* think from a new angle, reflect on

反问 fǎnwèn [modif: 反 reverse + 问 ask] *v* ask a question as a reply □ 她反问我："你说呢?" **Tā fǎnwèn wǒ: "Nǐ shuō ne?"** *She replied, "What do you think?"*

反问句 fǎnwènjù *n* rhetorical question (e.g. 你难道不知道吗？**Nǐ nándào bùzhīdào ma?** *Don't you know?*)

反应 fǎnyìng [comp: 反 opposite + 应 reply, respond] *n* response, reaction □ 病人还在昏迷中，医生问他话，没有反应。**Bìngrén háizài hūnmí zhōng, yīshēng wèn tā huà, méiyǒu fǎnyìng.** *The patient is still in a coma and gives no response to the doctor's questions.* □ 对于这个新产品，市场反应非常好。**Duìyú zhège xīn chǎnpǐn, shìchǎng fǎnyìng fēicháng hǎo.** *There is excellent market response to this new product.*

反映 fǎnyìng *v* **1** reflect, mirror □ 这本小说反映了当代大学生的生活。**Zhè běn xiǎoshuō fǎnyìngle dāngdài dàxuéshēng de shēnghuó.** *This novel reflects the life of contemporary university students.* **2** report, make known, convey □ 我要把你们的意见反映给领导。**Wǒ yào bǎ nǐmen de yìjiàn fǎnyìng gěi lǐngdǎo.** *I will convey your views to the leadership.*

反正 fǎnzhèng [comp: 反 reverse + 正 front] *adv* anyway, at any rate □ 你同意也好，不同意也好，我反正决定这么办了。**Nǐ tóngyì yěhǎo, bùtóngyì yěhǎo, wǒ fǎnzhèng juédìng zhème bàn le.** *Whether you approve or not, I have decided to do it anyway.*

返 fǎn *v* return

返回 fǎnhuí return to, come back to

返回主页 fǎnhuí zhǔyè return to the homepage

犯 fàn *v* violate, offend

犯错误 fàn cuòwù make a mistake, commit an offense □ 他犯了一个严重错误，心里很难过。**Tā fànle yí ge yánzhòng cuòwù, xīnli hěn nánguò.** *He is very troubled that he made a serious mistake.*

犯法 fàn fǎ [v+obj: 犯 violate + 法 law] *v* break the law □ 打自己的孩子犯法吗？**Dǎ zìjǐ de háizi fànfǎ ma?** *Does it break the law to beat one's own children?*

犯规 fàn guī [v+obj: 犯 violate + 规 rule] *v* foul (in sports), break a rule

犯人 fànrén [modif: 犯 violate (law) + 人 person] *n* convict

犯罪 fànzuì [v+obj: 犯 commit + 罪 crime] *v* commit a crime, be engaged in criminal activites □ 这家贸易公司犯了逃税罪。**Zhè jiā màoyì gōngsī fànle táoshuìzuì.** *This trading company has committed the crime of tax evasion.*

犯罪分子 fànzuì fènzi criminal

犯罪现场 fànzuì xiànchǎng crime scene

范 1 fàn Trad 範 *n* model (See 模范 mófàn)

范 2 fàn Trad 範 *n* border, mould

范围 fànwéi [comp: 范 border + 围 boundary] *n* scope, range, limits □ 这不属于我的工作范围。**Zhè bù shǔyú wǒ de gōngzuò fànwéi.** *This is outside my job description.* □ 这家公司的营业范围很广。**Zhè jiā gōngsī de yíngyè fànwéi hěn guǎng.** *The business scope of this company is very wide. (→ This company has diverse business interests.)*

饭 fàn Trad 飯 *n* **1** cooked rice □ 小王每顿吃两碗饭。**Xiǎo Wáng měi dùn chī liǎng wǎn fàn.** *Xiao Wang eats two bowls of rice every meal.* □ 他是南方人，爱吃米饭，不爱吃馒头和面条儿。**Tā shì nánfāngrén, ài chī mǐfàn, bú ài chī mántou hé miàntiáor.** *He is a Southerner. He loves rice and doesn't like steamed buns or noodles.* **2** meal (顿 dùn) □ 他们常常在外面吃饭。**Tāmen chángcháng zài wàimiàn chīfàn.** *They often have their meals outside. (→ They often dine*

out.) □ 我请你吃饭。**Wǒ qǐng nǐ chīfàn.** *I'll treat you to a meal.*

饭店 **fàndiàn** [modif: 饭 meal + 店 shop, store] *n* **1** restaurant (家 **jiā**) □ 这家饭店饭菜好吃，价钱也便宜。**Zhè jiā fàndiàn fàncài hǎochī, jiàqián yě piányi.** *The dishes in this restaurant are delicious and affordable.* □ 市中心新开了一家饭店，听说不错。**Shìzhōngxīn xīn kāile yì jiā fàndiàn, tīng shuō búcuò.** *A new restaurant opened downtown recently, and everyone says it's good.* **2** hotel (家 **jiā**) □ 他住在一家五星饭店里。**Tā zhù zài yì jiā wǔxīng fàndiàn lǐ.** *He stays in a five-star hotel.*

NOTE: The original meaning of 饭店 **fàndiàn** is *restaurant*, but 饭店 is also used to denote *a hotel.* For example, 北京饭店 **Běijīng fàndiàn** may mean *Beijing Restaurant* or *Beijing Hotel.*

饭碗 **fànwǎn** [modif: 饭 rice + 碗 bowl] *n* rice bowl, way of making a living, job

贩 **fàn** *v* buy to resell
贩卖 **fànmài** [comp: 贩 buy + 卖 sell] *v* buy and sell for a profit (usually in an illegal way)
贩卖毒品 **fànmài dúpǐn** drug trafficking
贩卖人口 **fànmài rénkǒu** human trafficking

泛 **fàn I** *v* **1** float **2** flood **II** *adj* general, extensive
泛滥 **fànlàn** *v* overflow, flood, go rampant □ 假货泛滥市场。**Jiǎhuò fànlàn shìchǎng.** *The market is flooded with counterfeit goods.*

方 **fāng** *adj* square □ 中国人传统在方桌或者圆桌上吃饭，不用长桌吃饭。**Zhōngguórén chuántǒng zài fāngzhuō huòzhě yuánzhuō shang chīfàn, bú yòng chángzhuō chīfàn.** *Traditionally, the Chinese use a square or round table, not at an oblong one, for their meals.*
长方 **chángfāng** oblong, rectangular
正方 **zhèngfāng** square
方案 **fāng'àn** [comp: 方 method + 案 file] *n* plan, program (for a major project) □ 经过反复讨论，委员会通过了这个方案。**Jīngguò fǎnfù tǎolùn, wěiyuánhuì tōngguòle zhège fāng'àn.** *After repeated discussions the committee approved the program.*
方便 **fāngbiàn** *adj* convenient, handy (antonym 麻烦 **máfan**) □ 住在城里买东西很方便。**Zhù zài chénglǐ mǎi dōngxi hěn fāngbiàn.** *With city living, shopping is convenient.* □ 你方便的话，请帮我找一下这本书。**Nǐ fāngbiàn de huà, qǐng bāng wǒ zhǎo yíxià zhè běn shū.** *If it's not too much trouble, please help me locate this book.*
方便面 **fāngbiàn miàn** instant noodles

NOTE: A euphemism for "going to the toilet" is 方便一下 **fāngbiàn yíxià**, e.g. □ 我要方便一下。**Wǒ yào fāngbiàn yíxià.** *I'm going to use the restroom.*

方程 **fāngchéng** *n* equation
方程式 **fāngchéngshì** *n* Same as 方程 **fāngchéng**
方程式赛车 **fāngchéngshì sàichē** formula racing car
方法 **fāngfǎ** [comp: 方 method, way of doing things + 法 method] *n* method □ 这个方法不行，要另想办法。**Zhège fāngfǎ bùxíng, yào lìng xiǎng bànfǎ.** *This method won't do. We'll have to find another way.* □ 学中文有没有什么好方法？**Xué Zhōngwén yǒu méiyǒu**

shénme hǎo fāngfǎ? *Are there any good methods of learning Chinese?*

方面 **fāngmiàn** [comp: 方 side + 面 face, surface] *n* side, aspect □ 政府应该考虑社会各方面的意见。**Zhèngfǔ yīnggāi kǎolǜ shèhuì gè fāngmiàn de yìjiàn.** *The government should consider viewpoints from various aspects of society.* □ 大量生产这种产品，在技术方面还有些问题。**Dàliàng shēngchǎn zhèzhǒng chǎnpǐn, zài jìshù fāngmiàn hái yǒu xiē wèntí.** *There are still some technological problems if this new product is to be mass-produced.*
方式 **fāngshì** [comp: 方 method + 式 manner] *n* manner, way □ 说话的内容很重要，说话的方式同样重要。**Shuōhuà de nèiróng hěn zhòngyào, shuōhuà de fāngshì tóngyàng zhòngyào.** *What you say is important, and how you say it is equally important.*
生活方式 **shēnghuó fāngshì** way of life, lifestyle
方向 **fāngxiàng** *n* direction, orientation □ 你的方向错了。**Nǐ de fāngxiàng cuò le.** *You're in the wrong direction.* □ 汽车朝飞机场方向开去。**Qìchē cháo fēijīchǎng fāngxiàng kāiqu.** *The car headed in the direction of the airport.*
方针 **fāngzhēn** *n* guiding principle, policy □ 你们国家的教育方针是什么？**Nǐmen guójiā de jiàoyù fāngzhēn shì shénme?** *What are the guiding principles of education in your country?*

坊 **fāng** *n* side street, lane

芳 **fāng** *adj* fragrant
芳香 **fāngxiāng** sweet-smelling, fragrant
芳香的玫瑰 **fāngxiāng de méigui** fragrant roses

肪 **fáng** *n* fat (See 脂肪 **zhīfáng**)

防 **fáng** *v* prevent, guard against
防火 **fánghuǒ** fire prevention
防火墙 **fánghuǒqiáng** firewall
防病 **fángbìng** disease prevention □ 防火比救火重要，防病比治病重要。**Fánghuǒ bǐ jiùhuǒ zhòngyào, fángbìng bǐ zhìbìng zhòngyào.** *Preventing fires is more important than fire fighting; preventing diseases is more important than curing diseases.*
防盗 **fángdào** anti-burglary measures
防护 **fánghù** [comp: 防 prevent + 护 protect] *v* protect, shelter
防护林 **fánghùlín** shelter forest
防守 **fángshǒu** [comp: 防 prevent + 守 defend] *v* defend, guard
防线 **fángxiàn** [modif: 防 defense + 线 line] *n* defense line
防汛 **fángxùn** [v+obj: 防 prevent + 汛 flood] *n* flood prevention
防疫 **fángyì** [v+obj: 防 prevent + 疫 epidemic disease] *n* epidemic prevention
防疫针 **fángyìzhēn** inoculation
打防疫针 **dǎ fángyìzhēn** be inoculated (against)
防御 **fángyù** [comp: 防 prevent + 御 defend] *v* defend (usually in wars)
防止 **fángzhǐ** [comp: 防 prevent + 止 stop] *v* prevent, guard against □ 政府将采取措施防止人才外流。**Zhèngfǔ jiāng cǎiqǔ cuòshī fángzhǐ réncái wàiliú.** *The government will adopt measures to prevent brain drain.* □ 我们取得了优秀成绩，要防止骄傲情绪。

Wǒmen qǔdéle yōuxiù chéngjì, yào fángzhǐ jiāo'ào qíngxù. *After achieving excellent results we should guard against conceit.*

防治 **fángzhì** [comp: 防 prevent + 治 treat] *v* prevent and treat (diseases)
防治病虫害 **fángzhì bìngchónghài** prevention and treatment of plant diseases and elimination of pests

妨 **fáng** *v* hinder, impede
妨碍 **fáng'ài** [comp: 妨 hinder + 碍 hinder] *v* hinder, hamper, disturb □ 你们把车停在这里, 会妨碍交通。 **Nǐmen bǎ chē tíng zài zhèli, huì fáng'ài jiāotōng.** *If you park your car here, it will block traffic.*

房 **fáng** *n* 1 house (幢 **chuáng**) □ 他们现在租房住, 打算明年买房。 **Tāmen xiànzài zū fáng zhù, dǎsuàn míngnián mǎi fáng.** *They now live in a rented house and are planning to buy a house next year.*
草房 **cǎofáng** thatched cottage
楼房 **lóufáng** house of two or more levels
平房 **píngfáng** single-story house, bungalow
2 room (间 **jiān**)
病房 **bìngfáng** sickroom, hospital ward
客房 **kèfáng** guestroom, spare room □ 楼上有三间房。 **Lóu shang yǒu sān jiān fáng.** *There are three bedrooms upstairs.*
房产 **fángchǎn** [comp: 房 house + 产 property] real estate, property
房产商 **fángchǎnshāng** real estate agent, housing developer
房贷 **fángdài** [modif: 房 home + 贷 loan] *n* home loan, mortgage
房东 **fángdōng** *n* landlord, landlady
房间 **fángjiān** [comp: 房 room, home + 间 space] *n* room (间 **jiān**) □ 这间房间不大, 但是挺舒服。 **Zhè jiān fángjiān bú dà, dànshì tǐng shūfu.** *This room is not big, but it's very comfortable.*
房屋 **fángwū** [comp: 房 house + 屋 house] *n* houses, buildings
房子 **fángzi** [suffix: 房 house + 子 nominal suffix] *n* house, housing □ 他们有了钱就买房子。 **Tāmen yǒule qián jiù mǎi fángzi.** *They will buy a house once they have the money.*
房租 **fángzū** [modif: 房 housing + 租 rent] *n* rent (for housing)

仿 **fáng** *v* imitate
仿佛 **fǎngfú** *v* be like, be alike □ 他们俩年龄相仿佛, 经历也差不多。 **Tāmen liǎ niánlíng xiāng fǎngfú, jīnglì yě chàbuduō.** *The two of them are of similar age and share similar life experiences.*

纺 **fǎng** Trad 紡 *v* spin (into thread/yarn)
纺织 **fǎngzhī** [comp: 纺 spin + 织 weave] *v* spin and weave □ 在这个山村里, 还有老人会纺织土布。 **Zài zhège shāncūn li háiyǒu lǎorén huì fǎngzhī tǔbù.** *In this mountain village there are old people who still make homespun cloth.*
纺织工业 **fǎngzhī gōngyè** textile industry
纺织品 **fǎngzhīpǐn** textile goods

访 **fǎng** Trad 訪 *v* visit
访问 **fǎngwèn** [comp: 访 visit + 问 ask, ask after] *v* visit, interview □ 这位老人很有名, 经常有人来访问他。 **Zhè wéi lǎorén hěn yǒumíng, jīngcháng yǒu rén lái fǎngwèn tā.** *This old man is famous. People often come to visit him.* □ 已经有一百多万人访问过这

个网站。 **Yǐjīng yǒu yìbǎi duō wàn rén fǎngwènguo zhège wǎngzhàn.** *Over a million people have visited this website.*

放 **fàng** *v* put, put in □ 请你不要把你的书放在我的桌子上。 **Qǐng nǐ bú yào bǎ nǐ de shū fàng zài wǒ de zhuōzi shang.** *Please don't put your books on my desk.* □ 你的咖啡里要不要放糖? **Nǐ de kāfēi li yào bú yào fàng táng?** *Shall I put sugar in your coffee?*
放大 **fàngdà** [comp: 放 expand + 大 large] *v* enlarge, magnify □ 这张照片请放大。 **Zhè zhāng zhàopiàn qǐng fàngdà.** *Please enlarge this photo.*
放大镜 **fàngdàjìng** magnifying glass
放假 **fàngjià** [v+obj: 放 release + 假 holiday] *v* be on holiday, have the day off □ 我们学校从十二月十五日到一月二十日放假。 **Wǒmen xuéxiào cóng Shí'èr yuè shíwǔ rì dào Yíyuè èrshí rì fàngjià.** *We have school holidays from December 15 to January 20.* □ 明日停电, 学校放假一天。 **Míngrì tíngdiàn, xuéxiào fàngjià yì tiān.** *School's closed tomorrow due to a power cut.*
放弃 **fàngqì** [comp: 放 release + 弃 abandon] *v* abandon, give up □ 这个机会十分难得, 你不要放弃。 **Zhège jīhuì shífēn nándé, nǐ bú yào fàngqì.** *This is a very rare opportunity. Don't pass it up.* □ 我们已经放弃了原来的计划。 **Wǒmen yǐjīng fàngqìle yuánlái de jìhuà.** *We have abandoned our original plan.*
放射 **fàngshè** *v* radiate
放射科 **fàngshèkē** department of radiology (in a hospital)
放射科治疗 **fàngshèkē zhìliáo** radiotherapy (= 放射疗法 **fàngshè liáofǎ**)
放松 **fàngsōng** [comp: 放 release + 松 loose] *v* relax, rest and relax □ 这星期工作太紧张了, 周末我要好好放松放松。 **Zhè xīngqī gōngzuò tài jǐnzhāng le, zhōumò wǒ yào hǎohǎo fàngsōng fàngsōng.** *This week I've been really stressed out with work; I'll rest and relax over the weekend.*
放心 **fàngxīn** [v+obj: 放 set in place + 心 the heart] *v* set one's mind at ease, be at ease (antonym 担心 **dānxīn**) □ 你办事, 我放心。 **Nǐ bànshì, wǒ fàngxīn.** *With you in charge, my mind's at ease.* □ 才十几岁的孩子出国留学, 父母怎么会放心呢? **Cái shí jǐ suì de háizi chūguó liúxué, fùmǔ zénme huì fàngxīn ne?** *How can parents not worry when their teenage children go overseas to study?*
放学 **fàngxué** *v* 1 (of schools) be over □ 今天学校四点半放学。 **Jīntiān xuéxiào sì diǎn bàn fàngxué.** *Today school will be over at half past four.* 2 (of pupils) return home after school □ 你每天放学以后做什么? **Nǐ měitiān fàngxué yǐhòu zuò shénme?** *What do you do after school every day?*
放映 **fàngyìng** *v* show (a movie) □ 这个周末电影院放映什么影片? **Zhège zhōumò diànyǐngyuàn fàngyìng shénme yǐngpiàn?** *What movies will the cinema show this weekend?* (→ *What's on at the cinema this weekend?*)

飞 **fēi** Trad 飛 *v* fly □ 小鸟飞走了。 **Xiǎo niǎo fēi zǒule.** *The little bird flew away.*
飞机 **fēijī** [modif: 飞 flying + 机 machine] *n* airplane (架 **jià**) □ 从北京来的飞机什么时候到? **Cóng Běijīng lái de fēijī shénme shíhou dào?** *When does the plane from Beijing arrive?*
飞机票 **fēijīpiào** air ticket
飞机场 **fēijīchǎng** airport

开飞机 kāi fēijī pilot a plane

坐/乘飞机 zuò/chéng fēijī travel by plane □ 我们全家明天坐飞机去上海。**Wǒmen quán jiā míngtiān zuò fēijī qù Shànghǎi.** *My family will be going to Shanghai tomorrow by air.*

飞快 **fēikuài** *adj* with the speed of a flying object, very fast

飞翔 **fēixiáng** [comp: 飞 fly + 翔 fly] *v* circle in the air (like an eagle), hover

飞行 **fēixíng** [comp: 飞 fly + 行 travel] *v* (of aircraft) fly

飞行员 **fēixíngyuán** [suffix: 飞行 fly + 员 nominal suffix] *n* aircraft pilot

飞跃 **fēiyuè** [comp: 飞 fly + 跃 leap] **I** *v* go forward in leaps and bounds **II** *n* sudden and rapid development

非 **fēi** *adv* not, do not

非⋯不可 **fēi...bùkě** *adv* have no choice but to ..., simply must ... □ 我今天非写完这个报告不可。**Wǒ jīntiān fēi xiěwán zhège bàogào bùkě.** *I simply must finish writing this report today.*

NOTE: 非⋯不可⋯ **fēi...bùkě** is used to emphasize the verb after 非 **fēi**. 不可 **bùkě** may be omitted, e.g. 我今天非写完这个报告。**Wǒ jīntiān fēi xiěwán zhège bàogào.** *I simply must finish writing this report today.* Instead of 非, we can also use 非得 **fēiděi** 得⋯不可⋯, e.g. 我今天非得写完这个报告(不可)。**Wǒ jīntiān fēiděi xiěwán zhège bàogào (bùkě).**

非常 **fēicháng** [modif: 非 not + 常 usual] **I** *adv* unusually, very □ 中国非常大。**Zhōngguó fēicháng dà.** *China is very big.* □ 我非常想去新加坡旅行。**Wǒ fēicháng xiǎng qù Xīnjiāpō lǚxíng.** *I very much want to take a trip to Singapore.* **II** *adj* unusual, out of the ordinary

非常事件 fēicháng shìjiàn unusual incident

非常措施 fēicháng cuòshī emergency measures

非但 **fēidàn** Same as 不但 **bùdàn**

非法 **fēifǎ** [modif: 非 not + 法 legal] *adj* illegal, unlawful

非法同居 fēifǎ tóngjū illegal cohabitation

非洲 **Fēizhōu** [modif: 非 Africa + 洲 continent] *n* Africa

啡 **fēi** as in 咖啡 **kāfēi**

肥 **féi** *adj* fat, fattened □ 这头猪真肥! **Zhè tóu zhū zhēn féi!** *What a fat pig!*

NOTE: 肥 **féi** is normally used to describe animals. It is insulting to use it to describe humans.

肥料 **féiliào** [modif: 肥 fat, fatten + 料 material] *n* fertilizer

有机肥料 yǒujī féiliào organic fertilizer

肥沃 **féiwò** [comp: 肥 fat + 沃 fertile] *adj* (of soil) fertile

肥皂 **féizào** *n* soap (块 **kuài**)

肥皂粉 féizàofěn detergent powder

匪 **fēi** *n* bandit

匪帮 fēibāng gang of bandits, criminal gang

匪徒 fěitú bandit, criminal gangster

诽 **fěi** Trad 誹 *v* slander

诽谤 **fěibàng** [comp: 诽 slander + 谤 slander] *v* slander, libel

肺 **fèi** *n* the lungs □ 吸烟伤害肺。**Xīyān shānghài fèi.** *Smoking harms the lungs.*

肺气肿 fèiqìzhǒng pulmonary emphysema

肺炎 fèiyán pneumonia

费 **fèi** Trad 費 **I** *n* fee, charge □ 我一个月要花很多钱交各种各样的费。**Wǒ yí ge yuè yào huā hěnduō qián jiāo gè-zhǒng-gè-yàng de fèi.** *I spend a lot of money on various fees every month.*

管理费 guǎnlǐfèi administration charge

机场费 jīchǎngfèi airport tax

水电费 shuǐdiànfèi water and electricity bill

学费 xuéfèi tuition fee

交费 jiāofèi pay fees, a charge, etc

II *v* cost, spend □ 他费了很多钱才把车修好。**Tā fèile hěn duō qián cái bǎ chē xiūhǎo.** *Only after spending a small fortune did he get his car repaired.*

费了九牛二虎之力 **fèile jiǔ-niú-èr-hǔ zhī lì** spend the strength of nine bulls and two tigers, make tremendous efforts □ 我费了九牛二虎之力才完成这个任务。**Wǒ fèile jiǔ-niú-èr-hǔ zhī lì cái wánchéng zhège rènwù.** *It was with tremendous effort that I accomplished the task.*

费力 **fèilì** [v+obj: 费 cost + 力 strength] *adj* requiring great effort, painstaking

费力不讨好 fèilì bù tǎohǎo do a thankless job

费用 **fèiyòng** *n* expense, costs □ 在这个国家念大学, 一年的费用是多少? **Zài zhège guójiā niàn dàxué, yìnián de fèiyòng shì duōshǎo?** *How much is the annual cost of studying in a university in this country?*

生活费用 shēnghuó fèiyòng living expenses, cost of living

办公费用 bàngōng fèiyòng administration cost, overheads

废 **fèi** Trad 廢 *adj* useless

废除 fèichú *v* abolish, abrogate

废话 **fèihuà** [modif: 废 useless + 话 words] *n* nonsense, rubbish

废品 **fèipǐn** [modif: 废 useless + 品 article] *n* **1** reject, useless product **2** junk

废品回收 fèipǐnhuíshōu collecting junk, recycling

废气 **fèiqì** *n* waste gas

减少废气排放 jiǎnshǎo fèiqì páifàng reduce waste gas emission

废物 **fèiwù** [modif: 废 useless + 物 object] *n* **1** waste material □ 这些录音带、录像带都是废物了。**Zhè xiē lùyīndài, lùxiàngdài dōu shì fèiwù le.** *All these audiotapes and videotapes are waste materials now.* **2** good-for-nothing □ 她连这么简单的事都做不好, 真是个废物! **Tā lián zhème jiǎndan de shì dōu zuò buhǎo, zhēnshi gè fèiwù!** *She can't even do well such simple jobs. What a good-for-nothing!*

废墟 fèixū *n* ruins, debris

沸 **fèi** *v* boil

沸腾 **fèiténg** [comp: 沸 boil + 腾 gallop] *v* **1** boil **2** seethe with excitement

分 **fēn** **I** *v* **1** divide □ 今天是你的生日, 你来分生日蛋糕。**Jīntiān shì nǐ de shēngrì, nǐ lái fēn shēngrì dàngāo.** *Today's your birthday, come and cut your birthday cake.* **2** distribute **3** distinguish **II** *n* **1**

point, mark □ 你去年中文考试得了多少分? **Nǐ qùnián Zhōngwén kǎoshì dé le duōshǎo fēn?** *What marks did you get for the Chinese examination last year?* **2** minute □ 现在是十点二十分。**Xiànzài shì shí diǎn èrshí fēn.** *It's 10:20 now.* **III** *measure wd* (Chinese currency: 1 分 **fēn** = 0.1 角 **jiǎo** = 0.01 元 **yuán**), cent

···分之··· **...fēnzhī...** *num* (indicating fraction)
三分之二 sān fēnzhī èr two thirds
八分之一 bā fēnzhī yī one eighth
···百分之··· ...bǎi fēnzhī ... percent
百分之七十 bǎi fēnzhī qīshí seventy percent
百分之四十五 bǎi fēnzhī sìshíwǔ forty-five percent

分辨 **fēnbiàn** [comp: 分 divide + 辨 distinguish] *v* distinguish, differentiate
分辨不同的声调 fēnbiàn bùtóng de shēngdiào differentiate different tones (of Chinese syllables)

分辩 **fēnbiàn** [comp: 分 distinguish + 辩 speak in self-defense] *v* defend oneself (against a charge), make excuses

分别 **fēnbié** *v* **1** part with, be separated from □ 我和姐姐分别三年了, 今天见面, 多高兴啊! **Wǒ hé jiějie fēnbié sānnián le, jīntiān jiànmiàn, duō gāoxìng a!** *I'm meeting my older sister today after three years' separation. How happy I am!* **2** distinguish □ 对于犯错误的人, 我们要分别情况, 不同对待。**Duìyú fàn cuòwù de rén, wǒmen yào fēnbié qíngkuàng, bùtóng duìdài.** *Regarding those who have made mistakes, we should distinguish between circumstances and deal with them accordingly.*

分布 **fēnbù** *v* be distributed (over an area) □ 这家连锁餐馆分布在全国各地。**Zhè jiā liánsuǒ cānguǎn fēnbù zài quánguó gèdì.** *This chain of restaurants is spread out in various cities of the country.*

分寸 **fēncùn** [comp: 分 point + 寸 inch] *n* proper limits for speech or action, sense of propriety

分割 **fēngē** [comp: 分 divide + 割 carve up] *v* carve up, cut into pieces

分工 **fēngōng** [v+obj: 分 distribute + 工 work] *v* have a division of labor

分红 **fēnhóng** *v* pay or receive dividends

分化 **fēnhuà** *v* split up, break up

分解 **fēnjiě** *v* resolve, decompose

分类 **fēnlèi** [v+obj: 分 divide into + 类 kinds] *v* classify
分类账 fēnlèizhàng ledger
把文件分类存档 bǎ wénjiàn fēnlèi cúndàng classify and file documents

分离 **fēnlí** [comp: 分 divide + 离 depart] *v* separate, sever

分裂 **fēnliè** [comp: 分 divide + 裂 break up] *v* split, break up

分泌 **fēnmì** *v* secrete
分泌胃液 fēnmì wèiyè secrete gastric juice

分明 **fēnmíng** *adj* **1** sharply contoured **2** distinct □ 我的家乡四季分明。**Wǒ de jiāxiāng sìjì fēnmíng.** *My hometown has four distinct seasons.*

分母 **fēnmǔ** *n* denominator (in a fraction, e.g. "3" in $^2/_3$)

分配 **fēnpèi** [comp: 分 distribute + 配 ration] *n* distribute, allocate □ 根据各人的能力, 分配不同的工作。**Gēnjù gèrén de nénglì, fēnpèi bùtóng de gōngzuò.** *Different jobs are allocated according to the abilities of individuals.*

分批 **fēnpī** [v+obj: 分 divide into + 批 batches, groups] *adv* in batches, in groups
分批送货 fēnpī sònghuò deliver goods in batches

分期 **fēnqī** [v+obj: 分 divide into + 期 periods] *adv* by stages, in instalments
分期付款 fēnqī fùkuǎn pay (a bill) in instalments

分歧 **fēnqí** *n* difference (in opinions), divergence
消除分歧 xiāochú fēnqí settle differences

分清 **fēnqīng** [v+compl: 分 distinguish + 清 clear] *v* distinguish
分清主次 fēnqīng zhǔcì distinguish what is important from what is less so, prioritize

分散 **fēnsàn** **I** *v* disperse, scatter
分散投资 fēnsàn tóuzī diversify one's investments
II *adj* scattered

分数 **fēnshù** *n* **1** grade, point **2** fraction

分析 **fēnxī** [comp: 分 divide + 析 analyze] **I** *v* analyze □ 我们要仔细分析这两件事之间的关系。**Wǒmen yào zǐxì fēnxī zhè liǎng jiàn shì zhī jiān de guānxi.** *We should analyze the relationship between these two events carefully.* **II** *n* analysis □ 经过分析他们知道了这个药的化学成分。**Jīngguò fēnxī tāmen zhīdàole zhège yào de huàxué chéngfēn.** *After an analysis, they learned the drug's chemical components.*

分享 **fēnxiǎng** *v* share (joy, benefits, etc.)

分钟 **fēnzhōng** *n* minute (of an hour) □ 五分钟不是一段很长的时间。**Wǔ fēnzhōng bú shì yí duàn hěn cháng de shíjiān.** *Five minutes is not a long time.* □ 我等你等了四十多分钟。**Wǒ děng nǐ děngle sìshí duō fēnzhōng.** *I waited for you for over forty minutes.* □ 打长途电话, 以每分钟计费。**Dǎ chángtú diànhuà, yǐ měi fēnzhōng jìfèi.** *The cost of long-distance telephone calls is calculated by the minute.*

分子 **fēnzǐ** *n* numerator (in a fraction, e.g. "2" in $^2/_3$)

芬 **fēn** *n* fragrance, sweet smell
芬芳 **fēnfāng** [comp: 芬 fragrant + 芳 fragrant] *adj* fragrant, sweet-smelling

吩 **fēn** *v* instruct
吩咐 **fēnfù** *v* instruct, tell (what to do) □ 她吩咐旅馆服务员把晚饭送到房间来。**Tā fēnfù lǚguǎn fúwùyuán bǎ wǎnfàn sòngdào fángjiān lái.** *She instructed the hotel attendant to deliver the dinner to her room.*

纷 **fēn** Trad 紛 *adj* **1** numerous, varied **2** disorderly, confused
纷纷 **fēnfēn** *adj* numerous and disorderly □ 对于这个处分, 大家议论纷纷, 有人说太重, 有人说太轻。**Duìyú zhège chǔfen, dàjiā yìlùn fēnfēn, yǒurén shuō tài zhòng, yǒurén shuō tài qīng.** *There is great controversy over this disciplinary action; some say it is too severe, others say it is too light.*

氛 **fēn** *n* fog, atmosphere

坟 **fén** *n* tomb
坟墓 **fénmù** [comp: 坟 tomb + 墓 graveyard] *n* grave, tomb (座 **zuò**)

粉 **fěn** *n* powder
面粉 miànfěn wheat flour
奶粉 nǎifěn milk powder
药粉 yàofěn (medicinal) powder

粉笔 **fěnbǐ** [modif: 粉 powder + 笔 pen] *n* chalk (支 **zhī**) □ 约翰，请你到办公室去给我拿几支粉笔来。 **Yuēhàn, qǐng nǐ dào bàngōngshì qu gěi wǒ ná jǐ zhī fěnbǐ lái.** *John, please go to the office and get me a few pieces of chalk.*

粉末 **fěnmò** *n* powder, dust

粉碎 **fěnsuì** *v* smash, crush

分 **fèn** *n* **1** component **2** limit

糖分 **tángfèn** sugar content

分量 **fènliàng** *n* weight □ 你们这批货物分量不足。 **Nǐmen zhè pī huòwù fènliàng bù zú.** *This batch of your goods is short weight.* □ 他在公司里工作了二十多年了，说话很有分量。 **Tā zài gōngsī li gōngzuòle èrshí duō nián le, shuōhuà hěn yǒu fènliàng.** *He has been working in the company for over twenty years and what he says carries a lot of weight.*

分外 **fènwài** *adv* especially, unusually

分子 **fènzi** *n* member or element (of a social group)

犯罪分子 **fànzuìfènzi** criminal element, criminal

份 **fèn** *measure wd* (for a set of things or newspapers, documents, etc.)

一份礼物 **yí fèn lǐwù** a present

一份晚报 **yí fèn wǎnbào** a copy of the evening paper

一份报告 **yí fèn bàogào** a report

奋 **fèn** Trad 奮 *v* exert oneself

奋斗 **fèndòu** [modif: 奋 exert oneself + 斗 fight] *v* fight, struggle, strive □ 要成功就要奋斗。 **Yào chénggōng jiù yào fèndòu.** *If you want to succeed, you must fight for it.*

奋勇 **fènyǒng** *adj* courageous, brave, fearless

粪 **fèn** Trad 糞 *n* excrement, feces

愤 **fèn** Trad 憤 *n* anger

愤恨 **fènhèn** [comp: 愤 be angry + 恨 hate] *v* be angry and bitter, be very resentful

愤怒 **fènnù** [comp: 愤 angry + 怒 enraged] *adj* enraged, angry □ 她发现又受了欺骗，十分愤怒。 **Tā fāxiàn yòu shòule qīpiàn, shífēn fènnù.** *She was enraged to discover that she had been cheated again.*

丰 **fēng** Trad 豐 *adj* abundant, plentiful

丰富 **fēngfù** [comp: 丰 abundance + 富 wealth] *adj* abundant, rich, plenty □ 我们的生活很丰富。 **Wǒmen de shēnghuó hěn fēngfù.** *Our life is very rich.* (→ *We live a full life.*) □ 这位老师有丰富的经验。 **Zhè wèi lǎoshī yǒu fēngfù de jīngyàn.** *This teacher has rich experiences.* □ 这本书的内容非常丰富，值得反复阅读。 **Zhè běn shū de nèiróng fēicháng fēngfù, zhídé fǎnfù yuèdú.** *This book has very rich content and is worth repeated reading.*

丰满 **fēngmǎn** [comp: 丰 plentiful + 满 full] *adj* **1** plump **2** plentiful

身材丰满 **shēncái fēngmǎn** with a full (and attractive) figure

羽毛丰满 **yǔmáo fēngmǎn** full-fledged, developed well enough to be independent

丰收 **fēngshōu** [modif: 丰 abundant + 收 harvest] *n* bumper harvest

封 **fēng** **I** *measure wd* (for letters) □ 王先生，有你一封信。 **Wáng xiānsheng, yǒu nǐ yì fēng xìn.** *Mr Wang, here's a letter for you.* **II** *v* seal, block □ 大雪封山。 **Dà xuě fēng shān.** *The heavy snow has blocked up all roads to the mountains.*

封闭 **fēngbì** [comp: 封 seal + 闭 close] *v* close, seal

封建 **fēngjiàn** *adj* **1** feudal **2** traditional (in a bad sense)

封锁 **fēngsuǒ** [comp: 封 seal + 锁 lock] *v* block, seal off

封锁消息 **fēngsuǒ xiāoxī** news blackout

风 **fēng** Trad 風 *n* wind □ 今天风很大。 **Jīntiān fēng hěn dà.** *It's very windy today.* □ 冬天中国常常刮西北风。 **Dōngtiān Zhōngguó chángcháng guā xīběi fēng.** *In winter a northwestern wind prevails in China.*

风向 **fēngxiàng** wind direction

风暴 **fēngbào** *n* windstorm (场 **chǎng**)

风度 **fēngdù** *n* bearing, (elegant) demeanor

很有风度 **hěn yǒu fēngdù** with elegant demeanor

风格 **fēnggé** *n* style (of doing things)

管理风格 **guǎnlǐ fēnggé** managerial style

建筑风格 **jiànzhù fēnggé** architectural style

风光 **fēngguāng** *n* scenery, sight

风景 **fēngjǐng** *n* landscape, scenery □ 山顶上的风景特别优美。 **Shāndǐng shang de fēngjǐng tèbié yōuměi.** *The scenery at the top of the mountain is particularly beautiful.*

风浪 **fēnglàng** [comp: 风 wind + 浪 wave] **I** *n* high winds and big waves **II** *adj* stormy

风力 **fēnglì** [modif: 风 wind + 力 force] *n* wind force, wind power □ 今天风力很大，不能划船。 **Jīntiān fēnglì hěn dà, bù néng huáchuán.** *Today the wind is too strong for us to go boating.*

NOTE: In talking about the Beaufort wind scale, Chinese simply uses 一级 **yìjí**, 二级 **èrjí**, 三级 **sānjí**: 风力一级 **fēnglì yìjí** *light air*; 风力二级 **fēnglì èr jí** *light breeze*; 风力三级 **fēnglì sān jí** *gentle breeze*; 风力四级 **fēnglì sì jí** *moderate breeze*; 风力五级 **fēnglì wǔ jí** *fresh breeze*; 风力六级 **fēnglì liù jí** *strong breeze*; 风力七级 **fēnglì qī jí** *near gale*; 风力八级 **fēnglì bā jí** *gale*; 风力九级 **fēnglì jiǔ jí** *severe gale*; 风力十级 **fēnglì shí jí** *storm*; 风力十一级 **fēnglì shíyī jí** *violent storm*; 风力十二级 **fēnglì shí'èr jí** *hurricane*.

风气 **fēngqì** [comp: 风 winds + 气 atmosphere] *n* general mood and common practice (of a society, a locality or an organization)

风趣 **fēngqù** *n* humor, wit

有风趣 **yǒu fēngqù** witty, humorous

风沙 **fēngshā** [comp: 风 wind + 沙 sand] *n* sand blown up by winds

风尚 **fēngshàng** *n* prevailing norm or practice (in a positive sense)

风俗 **fēngsú** *n* custom, social customs □ 他每到一个地方就了解当地的风俗。 **Tā měi dào yí ge dìfang jiù liǎojiě dāngdì de fēngsú.** *Wherever he goes he will learn the local customs.* □ 有些旧风俗正在渐渐消失。 **Yǒuxiē jiù fēngsú zhèngzài jiànjiàn xiāoshī.** *Some old customs are gradually disappearing.*

风味 **fēngwèi** *n* special flavor, local color

风险 **fēngxiǎn** *n* risk

冒风险 **mào fēngxiǎn** run a risk

风筝 **fēngzheng** *n* kite (只 **zhī**)

放风筝 **fàngfēngzheng** fly a kite

疯 **fēng** Trad 瘋 *adj* insane, crazy □ 你疯啦？ **Nǐ fēng la?** *Are you crazy?*

疯狂 **fēngkuáng** [comp: 疯 insane + 狂 mad] *adj* insane, frenzied

疯子 **fēngzi** [suffix: 疯 insane + 子 nominal suffix] *n* lunatic, a crazy guy

蜂 **fēng** *n* wasp, bee

蜂蜜 **fēngmì** [modif: 蜂 bee + 蜜 honey] *n* honey

峰 **fēng** *n* mountain peak, peak (See 山峰 **shānfēng**)

锋 **fēng** Trad 鋒 *n* sharp point of a knife

锋利 **fēnglì** *adj* sharp

逢 **féng** *v* come upon, meet □ 每逢结婚纪念日, 他们夫妻总要庆祝一下。 **Měi féng jiéhūn jìniànrì, tāmen fūqī zǒngyào qìngzhù yíxià.** *Every time their wedding anniversary comes around, that couple will celebrate it.*

逢年过节 **féng-nián-guò-jié** *adv* on festival days and the New Year's Day, on festive occasions

缝 **féng** Trad 縫 *v* sew □ 现在很少人自己缝衣服了。 **Xiànzài hěn shǎo rén zìjǐ féng yīfu le.** *Very few people make their own clothes nowadays.*

讽 **fěng** Trad 諷 *v* satirize

讽刺 **fěngcì** [comp: 讽 mock + 刺 prick] **I** *n* satire **II** *v* use satire, satirize

奉 **fèng** *v* offer, obey, believe in

奉献 **fèngxiàn** [comp: 奉 offer + 献 offer] *v* offer as a tribute, present with respect

奉行 **fèngxíng** [comp: 奉 believe in + 行 act, do] *v* believe in and act upon, pursue (a policy, principle, etc.)

凤 **fèng** Trad 鳳 *n* as in 凤凰 **fènghuáng**

凤凰 **fènghuáng** *n* a mythical bird symbolic of peace and prosperity, phoenix

缝 **fèng** Trad 縫 *n* seam

见缝插针 **jiànfèng chāzhēn** stick a needle in a seam (→ make full use of every minute available)

佛 **Fó** *n* Buddha

佛教 **Fójiào** *n* Buddhism

否 **fǒu** *v* negate

否定 **fǒudìng** *v* negate, deny (antonym 肯定 **kěndìng**) □ 我不想否定你们的成绩。 **Wǒ bù xiǎng fǒudìng nǐmen de chéngjì.** *I don't want to deny your achievements.*

否决 **fǒujué** [modif: 否 negative + 决 decide] *v* vote down, veto, overrule

否认 **fǒurèn** *v* deny, repudiate (antonym 承认 **chéngrèn**)

否则 **fǒuzé** *conj* otherwise, or □ 这个问题必须尽快解决, 否则会危害整个工程。 **Zhège wèntí bìxū jìnkuài jiějué, fǒuzé huì wēihài zhěngge gōngchéng.** *This problem must be solved as soon as possible; otherwise it will jeopardize the entire project.* □ 你们一定要在十天内付清电费, 否则要断电。 **Nǐmen yídìng yào zài shí tiān nèi fùqīng diànfèi, fǒuzé yào duàndiàn.** *You must pay the electricity bill in ten days or face an electricity cutoff.*

夫 **fū** *n* man, husband

夫妇 **fūfù** [comp: 夫 man + 妇 woman] *n* Same as 夫妻 **fūqī**

夫妻 **fūqī** [comp: 夫 husband + 妻 wife] *n* husband and wife

夫妻关系 **fūqī guānxi** marital relationship

夫人 **fūrén** *n* (formal term for another person's) wife

□ 王董事长和夫人将出席宴会。 **Wáng dǒngshìzhǎng hé fūrén jiāng chūxí yànhuì.** *Chairman Wang and his wife will attend the dinner party.*

肤 **fū** Trad 膚 *n* skin (See 皮肤 **pífū**)

敷 **fū** *v* apply

敷药 **fū yào** apply medicine (to a wound)

敷衍 **fūyǎn** *v* go through the motions, be perfunctory

扶 **fú** *v* support with the hand

扶着老人过马路 **fúzhe lǎorén guò mǎlù** help an old person walk across the street

佛 **fú** (only used in 仿佛 **fǎngfú**)

服 **fú** **I** *v* obey **II** *n* clothing

服从 **fúcóng** [comp: 服 obey + 从 follow] *v* obey, submit to □ 少数服从多数。 **Shǎoshù fúcóng duōshù.** *The minority submits to the majority.* □ 我服从总公司的决定。 **Wǒ fúcóng zǒnggōngsī de juédìng.** *I will defer to the decision of the company headquarters.*

服气 **fúqì** *v* be convinced

服务 **fúwù** [comp: 服 obey + 务 work] *v* serve, work for

为…服务 **wèi...fúwù** serve ..., work for .... □ 我能为大家服务, 感到很高兴。 **Wǒ néng wèi dàjiā fúwù, gǎndào hěn gāoxìng.** *I'm happy to be able to serve you all.*

服务器 **fúwùqì** *n* (of computer) server

服务业 **fúwùyè** [modif: 服务 service + 业 industry] *n* service industry

服务员 **fúwùyuán** [suffix: 服务 serve + 员 person] *n* attendant, waiter/waitress □ 这位服务员态度不大好。 **Zhè wèi fúwùyuán tàidu bú dà hǎo.** *This attendant's work attitude is not very good.* □ 请你叫一下服务员。 **Qǐng nǐ jiào yíxià fúwùyuán.** *Please call the attendant.* □ 要付服务员小费吗? **Yào fù fúwùyuán xiǎofèi ma?** *Do we tip the attendants?*

NOTE: Though 服务员 **fúwùyuán** is used to refer to or address an attendant, a waiter or waitress, in everyday usage 小姐 **xiǎojiě** is more common (if the attendant is a woman).

服装 **fúzhuāng** [comp: 服 clothing + 装 clothing] *n* garments, apparel

服装工业 **fúzhuāng gōngyè** garment industry

服装商店 **fúzhuāng shāngdiàn** clothes store

浮 **fú** *v* float □ 你说说铁做的大轮船为什么会浮在水上? **Nǐ shuōshuo tiě zuò de dà lúnchuán wèishénme huì fú zài shuǐ shang?** *Can you tell me why a big ship made of iron can float on water?*

浮雕 **fúdiāo** *n* relief sculpture

浮动 **fúdòng** [comp: 浮 float + 动 move] *v* float, fluctuate

浮动汇率 **fúdòng huìlǜ** floating exchange rate

俘 **fú** *v* capture

战俘 **zhànfú** prisoner of war

俘虏 **fúlǔ** *n* captive, prisoner of war

幅 **fú** *measure wd* (for pictures, posters, maps, etc.)

一幅中国画 **yì fú Zhōngguó huà** a Chinese painting

幅度 **fúdù** *n* range, extent

福 **fú** *n* blessing, happiness
福利 **fúlì** [comp: 福 blessing + 利 benefit] *n* welfare, well-being
为职工谋福利 wéi zhígōng móu fúlì work for the welfare of the staff
福气 **fúqì** *n* good fortune
有福气 yǒu fúqì have good fortune, be very lucky

辐 **fú** Trad 輻 *n* (of a wheel) spoke
辐射 **fúshè** *v* radiate, spread out

符 **fú** *v* be in accord
符号 **fúhào** *n* symbol, mark
符合 **fúhé** [comp: 符 conform to + 合 accord with] *v* conform to, accord with □ 这种产品的质量不符合要求。 Zhè zhǒng chǎnpǐn de zhìliàng bù fúhé yāoqiú. *The quality of this product does not meet the requirements.* □ 政府的政策必须符合多数人的利益。 Zhèngfǔ de zhèngcè bìxū fúhé duōshùrén de lìyì. *Government policies must meet the interest of the majority of people.*

伏 **fú** *v* bend over

袱 **fú** Trad 襆 *n* cloth-wrapper

抚 **fǔ** Trad 撫 *v* 1 touch softly 2 foster (a child)
抚养 **fǔyǎng** [comp: 抚 foster + 养 provide for] *v* bring up (a child), provide for (a child)
抚育 **fǔyù** [comp: 抚 foster + 育 educate] *v* bring up (a child), educate (a child)

府 **fǔ** *n* government office (See 政府 zhèngfǔ)

俯 **fǔ** *v* bow one's head, bend down

斧 **fǔ** *n* hatchet, ax
斧子 **fǔzi** hatchet, ax

辅 **fǔ** Trad 輔 *v* assist, supplement
辅导 **fǔdǎo** *v* coach, tutor □ 王小姐辅导我们学中文。 Wáng xiǎojiě fǔdǎo wǒmen xué Zhōngwén. *Miss Wang tutors us in Chinese.* □ 王老师，您的辅导对我们很有帮助。 Wáng lǎoshī, nín de fǔdǎo duì wǒmen hěn yǒu bāngzhù. *Teacher Wang, your tutorial is helpful to us.*
辅导课 **fǔdǎokè** tutorial class, tutorial
辅导老师 **fǔdǎo lǎoshī** tutor, teaching assistant
辅助 **fǔzhù** [comp: 辅 assist + 助 help] *v* assist, play an auxiliary role

腐 **fǔ** *adj* rotten, decayed
腐败 **fǔbài** [comp: 腐 rotten + 败 collapse] **I** *adj* 1 badly decayed
腐败食品 fǔbài shípǐn food that has gone bad
2 corrupt □ 腐败的官员人人恨。 Fǔbài de guānyuán rénrén hèn. *Everyone hates corrupt officials.* **II** *n* corruption
腐化 **fǔhuà** [suffix: 腐 corrupt + 化 to become] *adj* degenerate, corrupt
腐烂 **fǔlàn** [comp: 腐 corrupt + 烂 rotten] *adj* decomposed, putrid
腐蚀 **fǔshí** *v* 1 corrode, etch 2 make (people) corrupt
腐朽 **fǔxiǔ** [comp: 腐 decomposed + 朽 decayed] *adj* decayed, rotten

父 **fù** *n* father
父亲 **fùqin** [modif: 父 father + 亲 parent] *n* father □ 您父亲作什么工作？ Nín fùqin zuò shénme gōngzuò? *What does your father do?* □ 我爱我父亲。 Wǒ ài wǒ fùqin. *I love my father.* □ 父亲的话，有的有道理，有的没有什么道理。 Fùqin de huà, yǒude yǒudàoli, yǒude méiyǒu shénme dàoli. *Some of my father's words are reasonable; others are not so reasonable.*

NOTE: 爸爸 **bàba** and 父亲 **fùqin** denote the same person. While 爸爸 **bàba** is colloquial, like *daddy*, 父亲 **fùqin** is formal, equivalent to *father*. When referring to another person's father, 父亲 **fùqin** is preferred. As a form of address to your own father, only 爸爸 **bàba** is normally used.

赴 **fù** *v* go to, attend

负 **fù** Trad 負 *v* 1 carry on the back 2 shoulder, bear
负担 **fùdān** [comp: 负 carry on the back + 担 carry on the shoulder] **I** *v* bear (costs)
负担旅费 fùdān lǚfèi bear travel expenses
II *n* burden, load
负伤 **fùshāng** *v* get wounded, get injured
负责 **fùzé** [v+obj: 负 carry on back + 责 responsibility] **I** *v* be responsible, be in charge □ 这件事我负责。 Zhè jiàn shì wǒ fùzé. *I'm responsible for this matter.* (or *I'm in charge of this matter.*) □ 你现在负责哪一方面的工作？ Nǐ xiànzài fùzé nǎ yì fāngmiàn de gōngzuò? *Which part of the job are you responsible for?*
负责人 fùzérén the person-in-charge □ 我很不满意，我要见你们的负责人。 Wǒ hěn bù mǎnyì, wǒ yào jiàn nǐmen de fùzérén. *I'm very dissatisfied (or disappointed). I want to see the person-in-charge here.*
II *adj* responsible □ 他做事非常负责。 Tā zuòshì fēicháng fùzé. *He has a strong sense of responsibility.*

妇 **fù** Trad 婦 *n* woman
妇女 **fùnǚ** [comp: 妇 woman + 女 woman] *n* woman, womankind □ 妇女的地位有了很大提高。 Fùnǚ de dìwèi yǒule hěn dà tígāo. *The social status of women has risen remarkably.*

付 **fù** *v* pay □ 提供服务后请立即付费。 Tígōng fúwù hòu qǐng lìjí fù fèi. *You are expected to pay as soon as a service is provided.* (→ *Pay promptly for services rendered.*) □ 我已经付给眼镜店百分之二十的定金。 Wǒ yǐjīng fù gěi yǎnjìngdiàn bǎifēn zhī èrshí de dìngjīn. *I have paid the optician a deposit of twenty percent.*
付出 **fùchū** [v+compl: 付 pay + 出 out] *v* pay out, contribute
付款 **fùkuǎn** [v+obj: 付 pay + 款 fund] *n* pay a sum of money □ 收到货后请马上付款。 Shōudào huò hòu qǐng mǎshàng fùkuǎn. *Please pay promptly after receiving the goods.*

附 **fù** *v* 1 be close to 2 attach, add
附带 **fùdài** *adj* additional
附带条件 fùdài tiáojiàn additional condition
附和 **fùhè** *v* chime in with, echo
附加 **fùjiā** [comp: 附 attach + 加 add] *adj* extra
增值附加税 zēngzhí fùjiāshuì value-added tax
附近 **fùjìn** [comp: 附 close to + 近 close by] *n* the area nearby □ 附近有没有邮局？ Fùjìn yǒu méiyǒu yóujú? *Is there a post office nearby?* □ 李先生就住

在附近。**Lǐ xiānshēng jiù zhù zài fùjìn.** *Mr Li lives near here.* □ 附近的学校都很好。**Fùjìn de xuéxiào dōu hěn hǎo.** *The schools nearby (or in this area) are all very good.*

附属 fùshǔ [comp: 附 attach + 属 belong to] *v* attach, affiliate
北京师范大学附属中学 Běijīng Shīfàn Dàxué Fùshǔ Zhōngxué *a middle school affiliated to Beijing Normal University*

附 **fù** *v* instruct (See 吩咐 **fēnfù**, 嘱咐 **zhǔfu**)

复 **fù** Trad 復 *adj* repeat, complex, compound
复合 **fùhé** *v* compound
复活节 **Fùhuójié** [modif: 复活 resurrection + 节 festival, day] *n* Easter
复述 **fùshù** [modif: 复 repeat + 述 narrate] *v* retell, repeat □ 请你把她的话一个一个字地复述一下。**Qǐng nǐ bǎ tā huà yí ge yí ge zì de fùshù yíxià.** *Please repeat what she says verbatim.*
复习 **fùxí** [modif: 复 repeat + 习 study] *v* review (one's lesson) □ 下星期要考试, 这几天我在复习。**Xià xīngqī yào kǎoshì, zhè jǐ tiān wǒ zài fùxí.** *I'll be having an examination next week. I'm reviewing my lesson these days.*
复兴 **fùxīng** [comp: 复 revive + 兴 flourish] *v* revive, rejuvenate
复印 **fùyìn** [modif: 复 double + 印 print] *v* photocopy
复印机 **fùyìnjī** photocopier
复杂 **fùzá** [comp: 复 multiple + 杂 miscellaneous] *adj* complicated, complex (antonym 简单 **jiǎndān**) □ 这件事很复杂, 我说不清楚。**Zhè jiàn shì hěn fùzá, wǒ shuō bu qīngchu.** *This is a complicated matter. I can't explain it clearly.* □ 这么复杂的中文句子, 我不会说。**Zhème fùzá de Zhōngwén jùzi, wǒ bú huì shuō.** *I can't say such a complicated sentence in Chinese.* □ 他把这件事搞得很复杂。**Tā bǎ zhè jiàn shì gǎo de hěn fùzá.** *He has complicated the matter.*
复制 **fùzhì** [modif: 复 double + 制 make] *n* copy, clone

覆 **fù** *v* cover
覆盖 **fùgài** *v* cover, cover up

复 **fù** *n* abdomen, belly

副 1 **fù** *measure wd* (for objects in pairs or sets) pair, set
一副手套儿 yí fù shǒutàor a pair of gloves
一副眼镜 yí fù yǎnjìng a pair of spectacles

副 2 **fù** *adj* 1 deputy, vice- ... □ 这几天校长生病, 有事可以找副校长。**Zhè jǐtiān xiàozhǎng shēngbìng, yǒu shì kěyǐ zhǎo fù xiàozhǎng.** *The principal is ill these days. You can go and talk to the deputy principal if there are any problems.* 2 secondary
副食 **fùshí** [modif: 副 secondary + 食 food] *n* non-staple foodstuffs
副业 **fùyè** [modif: 副 secondary + 业 industry] *n* side occupation, sideline
副作用 **fùzuòyòng** [modif: 副 secondary + 作用 function] *n* side effect

富 **fù** *adj* rich, wealthy (antonym 穷 **qióng**) □ 这个地区很富, 房子都很漂亮。**Zhège dìqū hěn fù, fángzi dōu hěn piàoliang.** *This is a wealthy area with beautiful houses.*

富人 fùrén rich person, rich people

NOTE: In everyday Chinese, 富 **fù** is not used as much as 有钱 **yǒuqián** to mean *rich*.

富强 **fùqiáng** [comp: 富 rich + 强 strong] *adj* (of a country) rich and powerful
富有 **fùyǒu** [comp: 富 rich + 有 having] *adj* rich, affluent
富裕 **fùyù** [comp: 富 rich + 裕 abundant] *adj* rich, well-to-do
富余 **fùyu** *v* have more and to spare

傅 **fù** *n* teacher, advisor (See 师傅 **shīfu**)

缚 **fù** Trad 縛 *v* bind, tie up

G

该 1 **gāi** Trad 該 *modal v* should, ought to □ 你不该常常迟到。**Nǐ bù gāi chángcháng chídào.** *You shouldn't be late so often.* □ 他不该答应了你, 又不去办。**Tā bù gāi dāyìngle nǐ, yòu bú qù bàn.** *He shouldn't have made you a promise and then done nothing.* □ 你该快毕业了吧。**Nǐ gāi kuài bìyè le ba.** *You should be graduating soon, I suppose.*

该 2 **gāi** Trad 該 *v* 1 be somebody's turn to do something □ 今天该你洗碗。**Jīntiān gāi nǐ xǐ wǎn.** *It's your turn to wash the dishes today.* 2 deserve □ 活该! **Huógāi!** *Serve you (or him/her/them) right!*

该 3 **gāi** Trad 該 *pron* that, the said, the above-mentioned □ 该校学生人数在五年内增加一倍。**Gāi xiào xuésheng rénshù zài wǔ nián nèi zēngjiā yí bèi.** *The student population of that school has doubled in five years.*

NOTE: 该 **gāi** in this sense is used only in formal writing.

改 **gǎi** *v* alter, change, correct □ 你这个字写错了, 要改一下。**Nǐ zhège zì xiě cuò le, yào gǎi yíxià.** *You've written a wrong character. You should correct it.* □ 你这个坏习惯一定要改。**Nǐ zhège huài xíguàn yídìng yào gǎi.** *You must break this bad habit.*
改行 **gǎiháng** change one's profession (or trade)
改期 **gǎiqī** change a scheduled time, change the date (of an event)
改变 **gǎibiàn** [comp: 改 alter + 变 change] **I** *v* transform, change □ 我想改变一下我们的旅行路线。**Wǒ xiǎng gǎibiàn yíxià wǒmende lǚxíng lùxiàn.** *I'd like to change our itinerary.* □ 青年人要改变世界, 老年人知道得改变自己。**Qīngniánrén yào gǎibiàn shìjiè, lǎoniánrén zhīdào děi gǎibiàn zìjǐ.** *Young people want to change the world, and old people know they have to change themselves.* **II** *n* change, transformation □ 你明年的计划有没有什么改变? **Nǐ míngnián de jìhuà yǒu méiyǒu shénme gǎibiàn?** *Are there any changes in your plan for the next year?*
改革 **gǎigé** [comp: 改 change + 革 remove] **I** *v* reform □ 大学考试制度应该改革。**Dàxué kǎoshì zhìdù**

yīnggāi gǎigé. *The university entrance examination system should be reformed.* □ 只有不断改革，才能跟上时代。**Zhǐyǒu búduàn gǎigé, cáinéng gēnshàng shídài.** *Only by constant reform can we keep abreast with the times.* **II** *n* reform □ 改革开放是中国八十年代以来的两项重大政策。**Gǎigé, kāifàng shì Zhōngguó bāshí niándài yǐlai de liǎng xiàng zhòngdà zhèngcè.** *Reform and opening-up have been two major policies in China since the 80s.*

改建 **gǎijiàn** [comp: 改 change + 建 build] *v* rebuild

改进 **gǎijìn** [v+compl: 改 change + 进 progress] **I** *v* improve, make ... more advanced/sophisticated □ 这个方法有一些问题，需要改进。**Zhège fāngfǎ yǒu yìxiē wèntí, xūyào gǎijìn.** *There are some problems with this method. It needs improving.* □ 怎么样改进我们的服务？请您多提意见。**Zěnmeyàng gǎijìn wǒmen de fúwù? Qǐng nín duō tí yìjiàn.** *What should we do to improve our service? Please feel free to make suggestions.* **II** *n* improvement (项 **xiàng**) □ 这项技术改进使产量大大增加。**Zhè xiàng jìshù gǎijìn shǐ chǎnliàng dàdà zēngjiā.** *This technological improvement greatly increased production.*

改良 **gǎiliáng** [v+compl: 改 change + 良 better] *v* improve, reform

改善 **gǎishàn** [v+compl: 改 change + 善 good] **I** *v* ameliorate, make ... better/more favorable □ 人人都想改善生活条件。**Rénrén dōu xiǎng gǎishàn shēnghuó tiáojiàn.** *Everybody wants to improve their living conditions.* □ 我们要改善和邻居的关系。**Wǒmen yào gǎishàn hé línjū de guānxi.** *We should improve our relationship with our neighbors.* **II** *n* improvement, amelioration □ 人们的居住条件得到了改善。**Rénmen de jūzhù tiáojiàn dédàole gǎishàn.** *People's housing conditions have been improved.*

改邪归正 **gǎi-xié-guī-zhèng** *idiom* give up evil and return to good, turn over a new leaf

改造 **gǎizào** [comp: 改 change + 造 build up] **I** *v* remold, rebuild, reform □ 这个城区要全面改造。**Zhège chéngqū yào quánmiàn gǎizào.** *This urban district will undergo comprehensive rebuilding.* **II** *n* remolding, rebuilding □ 这个城区的改造需要大量资金。**Zhège chéngqū de gǎizào xūyào dàliàng zījīn.** *The rebuilding of this urban district needs a large amount of funding.*

改正 **gǎizhèng** [v+compl: 改 change + 正 correct] *v* put ... right, rectify □ 改正下面句子中的错误。**Gǎizhèng xiàmiàn jùzi zhōng de cuòwù.** *Correct the errors in the following sentences.*

改组 **gǎizǔ** *v* re-organize

盖 1 **gài** Trad 蓋 *v* build □ 我们学校明年要盖一座电脑中心。**Wǒmen xuéxiào míngnián yào gài yí zuo diànnǎo zhōngxīn.** *Our school is going to build a computer center next year.*

盖 2 **gài** Trad 蓋 *n* cover, lid
盖子 **gàizi** cover, lid

概 **gài** *adj* broadly, general
概况 **gàikuàng** [modif: 概 general + 况 situation] *n* general situation, basic facts
中国概况 **Zhōngguó gàikuàng** basic facts about China, a profile of China
概括 **gàikuò** [comp: 概 total + 括 include] *v* summarize □ 你能不能把这份报告概括成五百个字左右的

短文？**Nǐ néng bu néng bǎ zhè fèn bàogào gàikuò chéng wǔbǎi ge zì zuǒyòu de duǎn wén?** *Can you summarize this report in about 500 Chinese characters?*

概念 **gàiniàn** [modif: 概 total + 念 idea] *n* concept, notion □ 你用老概念解释不了新现象。**Nǐ yòng lǎo gàiniàn jiěshì bù liǎo xīn xiànxiàng.** *You cannot explain fresh phenomena with outdated concepts.*
概念车 **gàiniànchē** concept car

溉 **gài** *v* irrigate (See 灌溉 **guàngài**)

钙 **gài** *n* calcium
钙片 **gàipiàn** calcium tablet

甘 **gān** **I** *v* be willing, be convinced
甘拜下风 **gānbài xiàfēng** *idiom* accept willingly defeat or inferiority
不甘失败 **bùgān shībài** not be reconciled to defeat, not accept defeat
II *adj* sweet, pleasant
甘心 **gānxīn** [modif: 甘 willing + 心 the heart] *v* be willing to, be ready to
甘蔗 **gānzhe** *n* sugar cane

干 **gān** Trad 乾 *adj* dry □ 衣服干了，收进来吧。**Yīfu gān le, shōu jìnlái ba.** *The clothes are dry. Let's take them in.*

干杯 **gānbēi** [v+obj: 干 to dry + 杯 cup] *v* drink a toast, "Bottoms up!" □ 为我们的友谊，干杯！**Wèi wǒmen de yǒuyì, gānbēi!** *To our friendship!*

干脆 **gāncuì** [comp: 干 dry + 脆 crisp] **I** *adj* decisive, not hesitant, straight to the point □ 做事要干脆，别犹犹豫豫。**Zuò shì yào gāncuì, bié yóu-yóu-yù-yù.** *Be decisive in action, don't be hesitant.* □ 行就行，不行就不行，就干脆地说吧！**Xíng jiù xíng, bù xíng jiù bù xíng, jiù gāncuì de shuō ba!** *Whether it's OK or not, just say it directly without mincing words.* **II** *adv* just, simply □ 你既然这么讨厌男朋友，干脆不要他了。**Nǐ jìrán zhème tǎoyàn nánpéngyou, gāncuì bú yào tā le!** *Since you dislike your boyfriend so much, just dump him!*

干旱 **gānhàn** [comp: 干 dry + 旱 drought] *n* drought, dry spell

干红 **gānhóng** *n* dry red wine
干红葡萄酒 **gān hóng pútaojiǔ** dry red wine

干净 **gānjìng** [comp: 干 dry + 净 clean] *adj* clean (antonym 脏 **zāng**) □ 这些衣服很干净，不用洗。**Zhèxiē yīfu hěn gānjìng, bú yòng xǐ.** *These clothes are clean. They don't need washing.* □ 这些是干净的衣服。**Zhèxiē shì gānjìng de yīfu.** *These are clean clothes.* □ 这件衣服洗不干净了。**Zhè jiàn yīfu xǐ bu gānjìng le.** *This dress cannot be washed clean.*

干涉 **gānshè** *v* intervene, interfere
干涉内政 **gānshè nèizhèng** interfere with the internal affairs (of a country)

干预 **gānyù** *v* intervene, meddle with
干预子女的婚姻 **gānyù zǐnǚ de hūnyīn** meddle in the marriage of (one's adult child)

干燥 **gānzào** [comp: 干 dry + 燥 arid] *adj* dry, arid □ 沙漠上天气干燥。**Shāmò shang tiānqì gānzào.** *In the desert, the weather is dry.*

杆 **gān** *n* pole
电线杆 **diànxiàn gān** electric pole, telephone/utility pole

肝 **gān** *n* the liver □ 他有肝病, 不能喝酒。**Tā yǒu gānbìng, bù néng hē jiǔ.** *He has liver trouble and cannot drink alcohol.*

竿 **gān** *n* pole, rod
钓鱼竿 diàoyúgān fishing rod

杆 **gān** *n* stick
枪杆 qiānggǎn the barrel of a rifle

赶 **gǎn** Trad 趕 *v* 1 catch up with 2 hurry up, rush for, try to catch □ 我得马上走, 去赶最后一班公共汽车。**Wǒ děi mǎshàng zǒu, qù gǎn zuì hòu yìbān gōnggòng qìchē.** *I've got to go right now to catch the last bus.*
赶上 gǎnshang catch up, catch up with
赶得上 gǎn de shàng can catch up □ 他跑得这么快, 我怎么赶得上? **Tā pǎo de zhème kuài, wǒ zénme gǎn de shàng?** *How can I catch up with him when he is running so fast?*
赶不上 gǎn bu shàng cannot catch up
没赶上 méi gǎn shàng fail to catch up

赶紧 **gǎnjǐn** *adv* hasten (to do something) □ 他母亲生重病住院了, 他得赶紧回家。**Tā mǔqin shēng zhòngbìng zhùyuàn le, tā děi gǎnjǐn huíjiā.** *His mother is hospitalized owing to a severe illness and he has to rush back home.*
赶快 **gǎnkuài** *adv* Same as 赶紧 **gǎnjǐn**
赶忙 **gǎnmáng** *adv* hurriedly, hastily

敢 **gǎn** *modal v* dare □ 这么多人, 我不敢讲话。**Zhème duō rén, wǒ bù gǎn jiǎnghuà.** *There're so many people here, I don't dare to speak.*
敢于 **gǎnyú** *v* dare to, have the courage to

感 **gǎn** *v* feel
感到 **gǎndào** [v+compl: 感 feel + 到 arrive (as a complement)] *v* feel □ 我有机会访问你们的国家, 感到很高兴。**Wǒ yǒu jīhuì fǎngwèn nǐmen de guójiā, gǎndào hěn gāoxìng.** *I feel very happy to have the opportunity to visit your country.* □ 听了他的不幸经历, 我感到很难过。**Tīngle tā de búxìng jīnglì, wǒ gǎndào hěn nánguò.** *After hearing about his unfortunate experience, I felt very sad.*

感动 **gǎndòng** [comp: 感 feel + 动 move] *v* move, touch emotionally □ 这个电影很感动人, 不少观众动得哭了。**Zhège diànyǐng hěn gǎndòng rén, bùshǎo guānzhòng gǎndòng de kū le.** *This film was so moving that many in the audience wept.*

感化 **gǎnhuà** *v* reform ... through gentle persuasion and/or by setting a good example

感激 **gǎnjī** [comp: 感 feel + 激 excite] *v* feel deeply grateful □ 你在我最困难的时候帮助我, 我十分感激。**Nǐ zài wǒ zuì kùnnán de shíhou bāngzhù wǒ, wǒ shífēn gǎnjī.** *I'm very grateful to you as you helped me in my most difficult times.*

感觉 **gǎnjué** [comp: 感 feel + 觉 be conscious of] I *v* feel □ 我感觉他对我们不大友好。**Wǒ gǎnjué tā duì wǒmen bú dà yǒuhǎo.** *I feel that he is not very friendly to us.* II *n* feeling, impression □ 她相信自己的感觉, 常常跟着感觉走。**Tā xiāngxìn zìjǐ de gǎnjué, chángcháng gēnzhe gǎnjué zǒu.** *She believes her instinct and often follows it.*

感慨 **gǎnkǎi** *v* sigh with deep inner feelings (over a revelation, an experience, etc.)

感冒 **gǎnmào** *v* catch a cold □ 突然变冷, 很多人感冒了。**Tūrán biàn lěng, hěn duō rén gǎnmào le.** *It suddenly became cold, so quite a few people caught colds.* □ 穿上衣服吧, 当心感冒! **Chuān shang yīfu ba, dāngxīn gǎnmào!** *Put on your clothes. Take care not to catch a cold.*

感情 **gǎnqíng** [comp: 感 feeling + 情 emotion, affection] *n* 1 feelings, emotion □ 你要理解她的感情。**Nǐ yào lǐjiě tā de gǎnqíng.** *You should understand her feelings.* 2 affection, love □ 他们在一起工作多年, 渐渐产生了感情。**Tāmen zài yìqǐ gōngzuò duō nián, jiànjiàn chǎnshēng le gǎnqíng.** *Having worked together for quite a few years, they have gradually become fond of each other.*

感染 **gǎnrǎn** *v* 1 (of a wound) become infected 2 (of a movie, a story, music, etc.) affect

感受 **gǎnshòu** *n* impression or lesson learned from personal experiences

感想 **gǎnxiǎng** [comp: 感 feeling + 想 thoughts] *n* impressions, reflections □ 请问, 您参观了这个学校, 有什么感想? **Qǐngwèn, nín cānguānle zhège xuéxiào, yǒu shénme gǎnxiǎng?** *Could you please tell us your impressions of the school you've just visited?*

感谢 **gǎnxiè** [v+obj: 感 feel + 谢 grateful] *v* be grateful, thank □ 我感谢你对我的帮助。**Wǒ gǎnxiè nǐ duì wǒ de bāngzhù.** *I'm grateful for your help.* □ 我真不知道怎么样感谢你才好。**Wǒ zhēn bù zhīdào zénmeyàng gǎnxiè nǐ cái hǎo.** *I really don't know how to thank you enough.*

感兴趣 **gǎn xìngqù** *v* be interested (in) □ 我对小说不感兴趣。**Wǒ duì xiǎoshuō bù gǎn xìngqù.** *I'm not interested in fiction.*

干 **gàn** Trad 幹 *v* do, work □ 你干了一下午了, 该休息休息了。**Nǐ gànle yíxiàwǔ le, gāi xiūxi xiūxi le.** *You've been working for the entire afternoon. You should take a break.* □ 这活儿我干不了。**Zhè huór wǒ gàn bu liǎo.** *I can't do this job.*

干部 **gànbù** *n* cadre, official (位 **wèi**)

NOTE: 干部 **gànbù** is a communist party term, denoting party (or government) officials. It is not commonly used today. In its stead, 官员 **guānyuán** is the word for government officials.

干劲 **gànjìn** *n* drive and enthusiasm (for a job)
干劲不足 gànjìn bùzú lack of enthusiasm
干劲十足 gànjìn shízú with enormous enthusiasm

干吗 **gànmá** *adv* 1 why □ 他干吗生气? **Tā gànmá shēngqì?** *Why is he angry?* 2 Same as 做什么 **zuò shénme** □ 咱们明天干吗? **Zánmen míngtiān gànmá?** *What are we going to do tomorrow?*

NOTE: 干吗 **gànmá** is a highly colloquial expression, used in casual conversational style.

缸 **gāng** *n* vat, jar (只 **zhī**)

刚 **gāng** Trad 剛 *adv* just, barely □ 他去年考试刚及格。**Tā qùnián kǎoshì gāng jígé.** *He barely passed the exam last year.*

刚才 **gāngcái** [comp: 刚 just + 才 only] *n* a short while ago, just □ 刚才王先生来电话, 说明天的会见要改期。**Gāngcái Wáng xiānsheng lái diànhuà, shuō míngtiān de huìjiàn yào gǎiqī.** *Mr Wang called*

just now, saying that tomorrow's meeting would be rescheduled. □ 我刚才看见小明到图书馆去, 你去那儿一定能找到他。 **Wǒ gāngcái kànjiàn Xiǎo Míng dào túshūguǎn qù, nǐ qù nàr yídìng néng zhǎodào tā.** *I saw Xiao Ming going to the library a short while ago. You're sure to find him there.*

刚刚 **gānggāng** *adv* Same as 刚 **gāng**, but more emphatic

钢 **gāng** Trad 鋼 *n* steel
钢笔 **gāngbǐ** [modif: 钢 steel + 笔 pen] *n* fountain pen (支 **zhī**) □ 你的钢笔我用一下, 行吗? **Nǐ de gāngbǐ wǒ yòng yíxià, xíng ma?** *I'll use your fountain pen for a while, is it OK?* (→ *May I use your fountain pen for a while?*) □ 现在有各种各样的笔, 很少人用钢笔。 **Xiànzài yǒu gè-zhǒng-gè-yàng de bǐ, hěn shǎo rén yòng gāngbǐ.** *Now that there are many varieties of pens, very few people use fountain pens.*
钢材 **gāngcái** [modif: 钢 steel + 材 material] *n* steel products, rolled steel
钢琴 **gāngqín** *n* piano (架 **jià**)
弹钢琴 **tán gāngqín** play the piano
钢铁 **gāngtiě** [comp: 钢 steel + 铁 iron] *n* iron and steel, steel □ 钢铁制造是基础工业。 **Gāngtiě zhìzào shì jīchǔ gōngyè.** *Steel and iron manufacturing is a basic (or primary) industry.*

纲 **gāng** Trad 綱 *n* guiding principle, outline
纲领 **gānglǐng** *n* fundamental principle, guideline
纲要 **gāngyào** *n* outline, essentials

岗 **gǎng** Trad 崗 *n* sentry post
岗位 **gǎngwèi** [comp: 岗 sentry post + 位 seat] *n* post (as a job)
脱离工作岗位 **tuōlí gōngzuò gǎngwèi** leave one's job

港 **gǎng** *n* port, harbor
海港 **hǎigǎng** seaport □ 上海港是中国最重要的海港之一。 **Shànghǎi gǎng shì Zhōngguó zuì zhòngyào de hǎigǎng zhī yī.** *The Port of Shanghai is one of the most important seaports in China.*
港口 **gǎngkǒu** port, harbor

杠 **gàng** *n* big, thick stick, bar
杠杆 **gànggǎn** *n* lever

高 **gāo** *adj* 1 tall, high (antonym 矮 **ǎi**, 低 **dī**) □ 我哥哥比我高。 **Wǒ gēge bǐ wǒ gāo.** *My elder brother is taller than I am.* □ 那座高高的楼房是一座新医院。 **Nà zuò gāogāo de lóufáng shì yí zuò xīn yīyuàn.** *That tall building is a new hospital.* □ 一年不见, 那孩子长高了不少。 **Yì nián bú jiàn, nà háizi zhǎnggāole bùshǎo.** *I haven't seen the child for a year. He's grown much taller.* 2 above average, superior
高超 **gāochāo** [comp: 高 superior + 超 super] *adj* (of skills) superior, consummate
高潮 **gāocháo** [modif: 高 high + 潮 tide] *n* high tide, high water
高大 **gāodà** [comp: 高 tall + 大 big] *adj* tall and big (antonym 矮小 **ǎixiǎo**) □ 他们有三个儿子, 都长得很高大。 **Tāmen yǒu sān ge érzi, dōu zhǎng de hěn gāodà.** *They have three sons who are all tall and big.*
高档 **gāodàng** [modif: 高 high + 档 grade] *adj* top grade, high quality
高档家具 **gāodàng jiājù** fine furniture
高等 **gāoděng** [modif: 高 high + 等 class] *adj* advanced, higher
高等教育 **gāoděng jiàoyù** higher education

高等学校 **gāoděng xuéxiào** institution of higher education, colleges and universities
高低 **gāodī** [comp: 高 high + 低 low] *n* 1 height 2 difference in quality, skills, etc. □ 比一比高低。 **Bǐyibǐ gāodī.** *Compete to see which one is better.*

NOTE: See note on 大小 **dàxiǎo**.

高度 **gāodù** [comp: 高 high + 度 degree] I *n* altitude, height □ 从三十公尺的高度往下跳, 当然很危险。 **Cóng sānshí gōngchǐ de gāodù wàng xià tiào, dāngrán hěn wēixiǎn.** *Jumping from a height of thirty meters is certainly very risky.* II *adj* a high degree □ 日本的汽车制造工业高度发达。 **Rìběn de qìchē zhìzào gōngyè gāodù fādá.** *Japan has a highly developed car manufacturing industry.*
高峰 **gāofēng** [modif: 高 high + 峰 peak] *n* peak, summit
高峰会议 **gāofēng huìyì** summit meeting
高贵 **gāoguì** [comp: 高 high + 贵 noble] *adj* 1 (of moral) noble, admirable 2 (of people) aristocratic, elitist
出身高贵 **chūshēn gāoguì** of an aristocratic or elitist family background
高级 **gāojí** [modif: 高 advanced, senior + 级 grade] *adj* advanced, high-level
高级小学 (高小) **gāojí xiǎoxué (gāoxiǎo)** higher primary school (Grades 5 and 6)
高级中学 (高中) **gāojí zhōngxué (gāozhōng)** senior high school
高级旅馆 **gāojí lǚguǎn** exclusive hotel
高考 **gāokǎo** *n* university entrance examinations

NOTE: 高考 **gāokǎo** is the shortened form of 高等学校入学考试 **gāoděng xuéxiào rùxué kǎoshì**. In everyday use of the language the Chinese have a tendency to shorten a long-winding term into a two-character word, e.g. 股市 **gǔshì** from 股票市场 **gǔpiào shìchǎng** *share market*; 人大 **Réndà** from 人民代表大会 **Rénmín Dàibiǎo Dàhuì** *the People's Congress.*

高空 **gāokōng** [modif: 高 high + 空 sky] *n* high altitude
高粱 **gāoliang** *n* sorghum
高明 **gāomíng** [comp: 高 advanced + 明 enlightened] *adj* (of ideas or skills) brilliant, consummate
高尚 **gāoshàng** *adj* (of moral, behavior, etc.) noble, lofty
高烧 **gāoshāo** [modif: 高 high + 烧 burning, fever] *n* high fever
发高烧 **fā gāoshāo** run a high fever
高深 **gāoshēn** [comp: 高 high + 深 deep] *adj* (of learning) profound, recondite, obscure
高速 **gāosù** [modif: 高 high + 速 speed] *adj* high-speed
高速公路 **gāosù gōnglù** superhighway, motorway
高兴 **gāoxìng** [comp: 高 high + 兴 excited] *adj* joyful, delighted, willing □ 见到你, 我很高兴。 **Jiàndào nǐ, wǒ hěn gāoxìng.** *I'm delighted to see you.* □ 我可不高兴给他送什么生日贺卡。 **Wǒ kě bù gāoxìng gěi tā sòng shénme shēngrì hèkǎ.** *I'm unwilling to send him any kind of birthday card.*

高血压 **gāoxuèyā** [modif: 高 high + 血 blood + 压 pressure] *n* high blood pressure

高压 **gāoyā** [modif: 高 high + 压 pressure] *n* high pressure

高压手段 gāoyā shǒuduàn high-handed measure

高雅 **gāoyǎ** [comp: 高 high + 雅 elegant] *adj* elegant, refined

高原 **gāoyuán** [modif: 高 high + 原 plain] *n* highland, plateau □ 高原的阳光特别强烈。**Gāoyuán de yángguāng tèbié qiángliè.** *Sunshine is particularly intense on a plateau.*

高涨 **gāozhàng** *v* upsurge, rise

高中 **gāozhōng** *n* See 高级 **gāojí.**

膏 **gāo** *n* paste, ointment (See 牙膏 **yágāo.**)

糕 **gāo** *n* cake (See 蛋糕 **dàngāo,** 糟糕 **zāogāo.**)

搞 **gǎo** *v* do, be engaged in (a trade, profession, etc.) □ "你父亲搞什么工作？" "他搞软件设计。" **"Nǐ fùqin gǎo shénme gōngzuò?" "Tā gǎo ruǎnjiàn shèjì."** *"What does your father do?" "He's engaged in software design."* □ 搞了半天，你原来不是我要找的人。 **Gǎole bàntiān, nǐ yuánlái bú shì wǒ yào zhǎo de rén.** *After so much ado, you turn out to be the person I'm looking for.*

搞鬼 **gǎoguǐ** [v+obj: 搞 be engage with + 鬼 ghost] *v* play dirty tricks on the sly □ 你在搞什么鬼？ **Nǐ zài gǎo shénme guǐ?** *What tricks are you up to?*

搞活 **gǎohuó** [v+compl: 搞 make + 活 alive] *v* vitalize, invigorate

稿 **gǎo** *n* draft (of an essay, a painting, etc.)

稿子 gǎozi draft

打稿子 dǎgǎozi draw up a draft

初稿 chūgǎo initial draft

稿件 **gǎojiàn** *n* manuscript, contribution (to a magazine, a publisher, etc.)

告 **gào** *v* 1 tell, inform □ 我告你一件事，你别对别人说。 **Wǒ gào nǐ yí jiàn shì, nǐ bié duì biérén shuō.** *I'll tell you something. Don't tell others.* 2 sue, bring a legal action against □ 有人告他偷东西。 **Yǒurén gào tā tōu dōngxi.** *He was charged with theft.*

告别 **gàobié** *v* bid farewell to, part with □ 我告别父母到中国来学汉语，已经八个月了。 **Wǒ gàobié fùmǔ dào Zhōngguó lái xué Hànyǔ, yǐjīng bā ge yuè le.** *It is eight months since I bade my parents farewell and came to China to study Chinese.*

告辞 **gàocí** *v* bid farewell formally

告诫 **gàojiè** *v* warn sternly, exhort, admonish

告诉 **gàosu** [comp: 告 tell + 诉 inform] *v* tell, inform □ 他告诉我一个重要消息。 **Tā gàosu wǒ yí ge zhòngyào xiāoxi.** *He told me an important piece of news.* □ 这件事千万别告诉他。 **Zhè jiàn shì qiānwàn bié gàosu tā.** *You mustn't tell him about this matter.*

告状 **gàozhuàng** *v* 1 file a lawsuit 2 bring a complaint (with someone's superior), report someone's wrongdoing

哥 **gē** *n* elder brother

哥哥 **gēge** *n* elder brother □ 我哥哥踢足球踢得很好。 **Wǒ gēge tī zúqiú tī de hěn hǎo.** *My elder brother plays soccer very well.* □ 她把哥哥介绍给自己最好的朋友。 **Tā bǎ gēge jièshào gěi zìjǐ zuìhǎo de péngyou.** *She introduced her elder brother to her best friend.*

歌 **gē** *n* song (首 **shǒu**) □ 这首歌很好听，我想再听一遍。 **Zhè shǒu gē hěn hǎotīng, wǒ xiǎng zài tīng yí biàn.** *This song is beautiful. I want to hear it once more.* 唱歌 chànggē sing a song □ 你会唱中文歌吗？ **Nǐ huì chàng Zhōngwén gē ma?** *Can you sing Chinese songs?*

歌词 **gēcí** *n* words of a song

歌剧 **gējù** [modif: 歌 song + 剧 theater] *n* opera

歌剧院 gējù yuàn opera house

歌曲 **gēqǔ** [comp: 歌 song + 曲 melody] *n* song

流行歌曲 liúxíng gēqǔ pop song

歌手 **gēshǒu** [modif: 歌 song + 手 hand] *n* singer

歌颂 **gēsòng** [歌 sing + 颂 praise] *v* sing the praise of, eulogize

歌星 **gēxīng** [modif: 歌 song + 星 star] *n* pop star

歌咏 **gēyǒng** *n* singing

歌咏队 gēyǒngduì singing group, chorus

胳 **gē** *n* arm

胳膊 **gēbo** *n* arm (只 **zhī**) □ 这位举重运动员胳膊特别粗。 **Zhè wèi jǔzhòng yùndòngyuán gēbo tèbié cū.** *This weightlifter has unusually thick arms.*

搁 **gē** *v* put, place □ 你先把脏衣服搁在洗衣机里。 **Nǐ xiān bǎ zāng yīfu gē zài xǐyījī li.** *You put the dirty clothes in the washing machine first.*

割 **gē** *v* cut □ 夏天割草，冬天可以喂牛羊。 **Xiàtiān gē cǎo, dōngtiān kěyǐ wèi niúyáng.** *Grass is cut in summer to feed cattle and sheep in winter.*

鸽 **gē** *n* dove (只 **zhī**)

鸽子 **gēzi** dove

革 **gé** *v* 1 expel, remove 2 transform, change

革命 **gémìng** *n* revolution (场 **chǎng**) □ 在那场革命中牺牲了很多人。 **Zài nà chǎng gémìng zhōng xīshēngle hěn duō rén.** *Many people died in that revolution.*

革新 **géxīn** *v* innovate, reform

技术革新 jìshù géxīn technological innovation

格 **gé** *n* pattern, standard

格格不入 **gé-gé-bú-rù** *idiom* like a square peg in a round hole, incompatible

格局 **géjú** [comp: 格 pattern + 局 situation] *n* arrangement pattern, layout

格式 **géshi** [comp: 格 pattern + 式 manner] *n* format, form

格外 **géwài** *adv* exceptionally, unusually

隔 **gé** *v* separate, partition □ 隔一条江就是另一个国家。 **Gé yì tiáo jiāng jiù shì lìng yí ge guójiā.** *Beyond the river is another country.*

隔壁 **gébì** *n* next door □ 我们家隔壁住着一对老夫妻。 **Wǒmen jiā gébì zhùzhe yí duì lǎo fūqī.** *Next door to our home lives an old couple.*

隔阂 **géhé** *n* feelings of alienation or estrangement, often caused by misunderstanding

消除隔阂 xiāochú géhé banish feelings of estrangement by clearing up a misunderstanding

隔绝 **géjué** *v* be completely cut off, be isolated

与世隔绝 yǔ shì géjué be isolated from the outside world

隔离 **gélí** *v* isolate (a patient, a criminal), quarantine

隔离病房 gélí bìngfáng isolation ward

个 **gè** Trad 個 *measure wd* (the most common measure word)

一个人 yí ge rén a person

两个苹果 liǎng ge píngguǒ two apples
三个工厂 sān ge gōngchǎng three factories

NOTE: 个 gè can be used as a "default" measure word, i.e. if you do not know the correct measure word to go with a noun, you can use this one. It is normally pronounced in the neutral tone.

个别 gèbié *adj* **1** very few, exceptional □ 这是个别现象。 *Zhè shì gèbié xiànxiàng. This is an isolated case.* **2** individual, one-to-one □ 对学习特别困难的学生, 老师个别辅导。 *Duì xuéxí tèbié kùnnán de xuésheng, lǎoshī gèbié fǔdǎo. The teacher gives individual tutoring to students with special difficulties.*

个儿 gèr *n* size (of a person)
高个儿 gāogèr tall guy □ 他个不高, 劲儿很大。 *Tā gèr bùgāo, jìnr hěn dà. He's short, but strong.*

NOTE: 个儿 gèr is only used in an informal situation.

个人 gèrén [modif: 个 individual + 人 person] *n* **1** individual (antonym 集体 jítǐ) □ 个人利益和集体利益产生矛盾时, 怎么处理? *Gèrén lìyì hé jítǐ lìyì chǎnshēng máodùn shí, zénme chùlǐ? How should we handle cases where there is a conflict between an individual's interest and the collective interest?* **2** personal □ 这是我个人的意见, 不代表公司。 *Zhè shì wǒ gèrén de yìjiàn, bú dàibiǎo gōngsī. This is my personal opinion and it does not represent that of the company.*
个人所得税 gèrénsuǒdé shuì personal income tax
个人隐私 gèrén yǐnsī personal and confidential matter, privacy

个体 gètǐ *n* individual

个性 gèxìng [modif: 个 personal + 性 nature] *n* personality
个性开朗 gèxìng kāilǎng an outgoing personality

个子 gèzi *n* height and size (of a person), build □ 他因为营养不良, 个子很小。 *Tā yīnwèi yíngyǎng bùliáng, gèzi hěn xiǎo. Due to malnutrition, he is of small build.*

各 gè *pron* each, every □ 各人的事, 各人自己负责。 *Gè rén de shì, gè rén zìjǐ fùzé. Everyone should be responsible for his own affairs.* □ 爸爸妈妈各有主张, 他不知道该听谁的。 *Bàba māma gè yǒu zhǔzhāng, tā bù zhīdào gāi tīng shuí de. Dad and mom each have their own views. He doesn't know whom to listen to.*

各别 gèbié *adv* individually
各别会见 gèbié huìjiàn meet individually
各别情况 gèbié qíngkuàng isolated case

各行各业 gè-háng-gè-yè *n* every trade and profession

各式各样 gè-shì-gè-yàng *adj* all kinds of, of every description
各式各样的电子产品 gèshì gèyàng de diànzǐ chǎnpǐn all kinds of electronic products

各种 gè zhǒng *adj* all kinds of □ 我各种水果都喜欢吃。 *Wǒ gè zhǒng shuǐguǒ dōu xǐhuan chī. I like to eat all kinds of fruit.*

各自 gèzì *pron* each
各自为政 gè zì wéi zhèng each doing things in his/her/their own way, administer autonomously

给 gěi Trad 給 **I** *v* give, provide □ 妈妈每两个星期给小明五十块钱。 *Māma měi liǎng ge xīngqī gěi Xiǎo Míng wǔshí kuài qián. Mom gives Xiao Ming fifty dollars every fortnight.* □ 在我写论文的过程中, 王老师给了我很多指导。 *Zài wǒ xiě lùnwén de guòchéng zhōng, Wáng lǎoshī gěile wǒ hěn duō zhǐdǎo. In the course of writing this thesis, Teacher Wang gave me a great deal of guidance.* **II** *prep* for, to □ 她给我们做了一顿很好吃的中国饭。 *Tā gěi wǒmen zuòle yí dùn hěn hǎochī de Zhōngguó fàn. She cooked us a delicious Chinese meal.* □ 今天晚上你们去看电影吧, 我给你们照顾孩子。 *Jīntiān wǎnshang nǐmen qù kàn diànyǐng ba, wǒ gěi nǐmen zhàogù háizi. You go and watch the film tonight. I'll take care of your child for you (→ I'll babysit your child).*

给以 gěiyǐ *v* be given
给以支持 gěiyǐ zhīchí be given support

根 gēn **I** *n* root □ 这棵树非常大, 根一定很深。 *Zhè kē shù fēicháng dà, gēn yídìng hěn shēn. This tree is very big. Its roots must be deep.* **II** *measure wd* (for long, thin things)
一根筷子 yì gēn kuàizi a chopstick

根本 gēnběn [comp: 根 root + 本 root] **I** *n* essence, what is fundamental □ 问题的根本在于产品的质量不合格。 *Wèntí de gēnběn zàiyú chǎnpǐn de zhìliàng bù hégé. The essence of the problem is that product quality is not up to standard.* **II** *adj* essential, fundamental, basic □ 我们不能头痛医头, 脚痛医脚, 而必须找到一个根本的解决方法。 *Wǒmen bù néng tóutòng yī tóu, jiǎotòng yī jiǎo, ér bìxū zhǎodào yí gè gēnběn de jiějué fāngfǎ. We cannot just take temporary and cosmetic measures, but must find a fundamental solution.*

根据 gēnjù **I** *v* do according to, on the basis of □ 我们根据最新情况, 对计划作了修改。 *Wǒmen gēnjù zuìxīn qíngkuàng, duì jìhuà zuòle xiūgǎi. We have amended our plan according to the latest situation.* **II** *n* grounds, basis □ 你对我的批评没有根据。 *Nǐ duì wǒ de pīpíng méiyǒu gēnjù. Your criticism of me is groundless.*

根深蒂固 gēnshēn dìgù *idiom* deep-rooted, ingrained
根深蒂固的种族偏见 gēnshēn dìgùde zhǒngzú piānjiàn deep-rooted racial prejudice

根源 gēnyuán [comp: 根 root + 源 source] *n* root cause, origin
宗教的根源 zōngjiào de gēnyuán the root cause of religion

跟 gēn **I** *v* follow □ 我在前面走, 我的小狗在后面跟。 *Wǒ zài qiánmiàn zǒu, wǒ de xiǎogǒu zài hòumiàn gēn. I walked in front and my puppy followed behind.* **II** *prep* with □ 老师: "请大家跟我念。" *Lǎoshī: "Qǐng dàjiā gēn wǒ niàn." Teacher: "Read after me, please."*

跟上 gēnshàng *v* catch up with, keep abreast with

跟前 gēnqián *n* near, nearby

跟随 gēnsuí *v* Same as 跟 gēn (= follow)

跟头 gēntou *n* **1** fall
跌跟头 diēgēntou have a fall, fall down
2 somersault
翻跟头 fāngēntou do a somersault

跟···一起 gēn...yìqǐ *prep* together with ... □ 我常常跟爸爸一起去看足球赛。 *Wǒ chángcháng gēn bàba yìqǐ qù kàn zúqiú sài. I often go to watch soccer games with my father.*

跟踪 gēnzōng [v+obj: 跟 follow + 踪 trace] v follow the tracks of, trail, shadow, stalk
发现被人跟踪 fāxiàn bèi rén gēnzōng find oneself be followed

耕 gēng v plough
耕地 gēngdì I [v+obj: 耕 plough + 地 land] v plough the field II n farmland
可耕地 kěgēngdì arable land
耕种 gēngzhòng [comp: 耕 plough + 种 plant] v farm, raise crops

更 gēng v change
更改 gēnggǎi [comp: 更 change + 改 change] v change, alter
更换 gēnghuàn [comp: 更 change + 换 replace] v replace
更换旧电脑 gēnghuàn jiù diànnǎo replace old computer(s)
更新 gēngxīn [v+compl: 更 change + 新 new] v renew, replace
设备更新 shèbèi gēngxīn renewal of equipment
更正 gēngzhèng [v+compl: 更 change + 正 correct] v make corrections
更正错误的数据 gēngzhèng cuòwù de shùjù correct wrong data

梗 gěng n stem, stalk

更 gèng adv still more, even more □ 美国很大, 加拿大更大。Měiguó hěn dà, Jiānádà gèng dà. America is big and Canada is even bigger. □ 我爱我的老师, 但我更爱真理。Wǒ ài wǒ de lǎoshī, dàn wǒ gèng ài zhēnlǐ. I love my teacher, but I love truth more.
更加 gèngjiā adv Same as 更 gèng

工 gōng n 1 work 2 worker
汽车修理工 qìchē xiūlǐ gōng automobile repairman (→ mechanic)
工厂 gōngchǎng [modif: 工 work + 厂 factory] n factory, works (座 zuò, 家 jiā) □ 这座工厂生产什么? Zhè zuò gōngchǎng shēngchǎn shénme? What does this factory make? □ 他在中国参观了三家工厂。Tā zài Zhōngguó cānguānle sān jiā gōngchǎng. He visited three factories in China.
办工厂 bàn gōngchǎng run a factory
建工厂 jiàn gōngchǎng build a factory
开工厂 kāi gōngchǎng set up a factory
工程 gōngchéng [modif: 工 work + 程 course] n 1 project, construction work (项 xiàng) □ 这项工程从设计, 施工到完成一共花了三年半时间。Zhè xiàng gōngchéng cóng shèjì, shīgōng dào wánchéng yígòng huāle sānnián bàn shíjiān. From design, construction till completion, this project took three and a half years. 2 engineering
土木工程 tǔmù gōngchéng civil engineering
水利工程 shuǐlì gōngchéng water conservancy project
工程师 gōngchéngshī [modif: 工程 engineering + 师 master] n engineer (位 wèi) □ 这座著名的大学培养了大批工程师。Zhè zuò zhùmíng de dàxué péiyǎngle dàpī gōngchéngshī. This well-known university has trained a large number of engineers.
总工程师 zǒnggōngchéngshī chief engineer
工地 gōngdì [modif: 工 work + 地 place] n worksite, construction site

工夫 gōngfu n 1 time □ 他用了一个晚上的工夫把报告修改了一遍。Tā yòngle yí ge wǎnshang de gōngfu bǎ bàogào xiūgǎile yí biàn. He spent an entire evening revising this report. 2 efforts □ 王老师每天花很大工夫备课。Wáng lǎoshī měitiān huā hěn dà gōngfu bèikè. Teacher Wang makes great efforts to prepare his lessons every day.
工会 gōnghuì [modif: 工 workers + 会 association] n labor union, trade union □ 工会代表工人要求增加工资, 改善工作条件。Gōnghuì dàibiǎo gōngrén yāoqiú zēngjiā gōngzī, gǎishàn gōngzuò tiáojiàn. On behalf of the workers, the trade union demanded a wage increase and improvement in working conditions.
工具 gōngjù [modif: 工 work + 具 implement] n tool (件 jiàn) □ 没有合适的工具, 这活儿没法干。Méiyǒu héshì de gōngjù, zhè huór méifǎ gàn. This job can't be done without the proper tools.
工具箱 gōngjùxiāng tool box
工龄 gōnglíng [modif: 工 work + 龄 age] n length of service
工钱 gōngqián [modif: 工 work + 钱 money] n Same as 工资 gōngzī
工人 gōngrén [modif: 工 work + 人 person] n workman, worker □ 工人在建一座新学校。Gōngrén zài jiàn yí zuò xīn xuéxiào. Workers are building a new school. □ 大批农民离开农村, 到城市当工人。Dàpī nóngmín líkāi nóngcūn, dào chéngshì dāng gōngrén. Large numbers of peasants leave rural areas to be workers in cities. □ 这道门坏了, 要请工人来修一下。Zhè dào mén huài le, yào qǐng gōngrén lái xiū yíxià. Something is wrong with this door. We should ask a worker to fix it.
当工人 dāng gōngrén be a worker
工伤 gōngshāng [modif: 工 worker + 伤 injury] n industrial injury
工伤事故 gōngshāng shìgù industrial injury, industrial accident
工事 gōngshì [modif: 工 work + 事 work] n defense works
工薪阶层 gōngxīn jiēcéng n wage or salary earners
工序 gōngxù [modif: 工 work + 序 order] n industrial procedure
工业 gōngyè [modif: 工 work + 业 industry] n (manufacturing) industry □ 工业发展了, 国家才能富。Gōngyè fāzhǎn le, guójiā cái néng fù. Only when industry is developed, can a country be rich. □ 这个国家没有汽车工业。Zhège guójiā méiyǒu qìchē gōngyè. This country does not have an automobile industry.
轻工业 qīnggōngyè light industry
新兴工业 xīnxīng gōngyè sunrise industry
重工业 zhònggōngyè heavy industry
工艺品 gōngyìpǐn [modif: 工艺 craft + 品 article] n handicraft (件 jiàn) □ 约翰打算买一些中国工艺品带回国送人。Yuēhàn dǎsuàn mǎi yìxiē Zhōngguó gōngyìpǐn dàihuí guó sòng rén. John planned to buy some Chinese handicrafts and bring them home as gifts.
工资 gōngzī [modif: 工 work + 资 fund] n wages, salary □ 你们是每月发工资, 还是每两个星期发工资? Nǐmen shì měi yuè fā gōngzī, háishì měi liǎng ge xīngqī fā gōngzī? Do you pay wages every month or every fortnight?

工作 **gōngzuò** [comp: 工 work + 作 do] **I** *v* work
□ 我们一星期工作五天。**Wǒmen yì xīngqī gōngzuò wǔ
tiān.** *We work five days in a week.* □ 她在一家跨国公司
工作。**Tā zài yì jiā kuàguó gōngsī gōngzuò.** *She works
in a multinational company.* **II** *n* work, job (件 **jiàn**)
□ 这件工作不太难。**Zhè jiàn gōngzuò bú tài nán.** *This
job is not too difficult.* □ 他找工作找了两个月了。**Tā
zhǎo gōngzuò zhǎole liǎng ge yuè le.** *He's been looking
for a job for two months.*

工作餐 **gōngzuò cān** *n* staff meal

功 **gōng** *n* **1** skill **2** achievement, merit

功夫 **gōngfu** *n* **1** Same as 工夫 **gōngfu** (= efforts)
2 martial arts

功夫片 **gōngfu piàn** martial arts film

练功夫 **liàn gōngfu** practice martial arts □ 每天一大
早他就起来练功夫。**Měitiān yí dà zǎo tā jiù qǐlái liàn
gōngfu.** *Every day he gets up in the early morning and
practices martial arts.*

功绩 **gōngjì** [comp: 功 merit + 绩 achievement] *n*
merits and achievements

功课 **gōngkè** *n* **1** schoolwork □ 他功课不错，考试成绩
总是很好。**Tā gōngkè búcuò, kǎoshì chéngjì zǒngshì
hěn hǎo.** *His schoolwork is quite good, and his examination results are always very good.* **2** homework
做功课 **zuò gōngkè** do homework.

功劳 **gōngláo** [功 merit + 劳 labor] *n* contribution,
credit □ 没有功劳，也有苦劳。**Méiyǒu gōngláo, yě yǒu
kǔláo.** *I've worked hard, even if my contributions are
not great.*

功能 **gōngnéng** *n* function

功能键 **gōngnéngjiàn** function key(s)

功效 **gōngxiào** *n* effect, efficacy

攻 **gōng** *v* attack

攻读 **gōngdú** [comp: 攻 attack + 读 read] *v*
study hard, specialize

攻读博士学位 **gōngdúbóshì xuéwèi** work hard to
gain a Ph.D. degree

攻克 **gōngkè** *v* attack and capture (a city, a fortress,
etc.)

攻心 **gōngxīn** [v+obj: 攻 attack + 心 the heart] *v*
win the hearts and minds of □ 攻心为上。**Gōngxīn
wéi shàng.** *To win the hearts and minds is of primary
importance.*

攻心战 **gōngxīnzhàn** psychological warfare

公 1 **gōng** *adj* male (of certain animals) (antonym
母 **mǔ**) □ 公牛脾气很大，你千万别惹它。**Gōngniú
píqì hěn dà. Nǐ qiānwàn bié rě tā.** *Bulls have a fierce
temper. Never provoke one.*

公 2 **gōng** *adj* **1** public (antonym 私 **sī**) □ 天下
为公。**Tiānxià wéi gōng.** *The world is for public
interests.* (→ *The world is for the people.*) **2** open,
public **3** fair

公安 **gōng'ān** [modif: 公 public + 安 security] *n*
public security

公安局 **gōng'ān jú** public security bureau (police
bureau)

公安人员 **gōng'ān rényuán** public security personnel, policeman

NOTE: See note on 警察 **jǐngchá**.

公报 **gōngbào** *n* communiqué, bulletin

公布 **gōngbù** *v* make a public announcement,
publish

公尺 **gōngchǐ** [modif: 公 metric + 尺 a traditional
Chinese measurement of length] *measure wd*
meter □ 这个游泳池长二十五公尺，宽十公尺。**Zhège
yóuyǒngchí cháng èrshíwǔ gōngchǐ, kuān shí gōngchǐ.**
This swimming pool is 25 by 10 meters.

公道 **gōngdào** [comp: 公 fair + 道 reasonable] *adj*
fair, just, impartial

公费 **gōngfèi** [modif: 公 public + 费 expenditure] *n*
(at) public expense

公费医疗 **gōngfèi yīliáo** medical care paid by the
government (→ free medical care for government
officials and others)

公分 **gōngfēn** [modif: 公 metric + 分 a traditional
Chinese measurement of length] *measure wd*
centimeter

公告 **gōnggào** [modif: 公 public + 告 announce-
ment] announcement (by a government agency)

公共 **gōnggòng** [comp: 公 public + 共 shared] *adj*
public, communal □ 这是一座公共图书馆，任何人都
可以进去看书。**Zhè shì yí zuò gōnggòng túshūguǎn,
rènhé rén dōu kěyǐ jìnqù kàn shū.** *This is a public
library. Anybody can go in and read.*

公共关系 **gōnggòng guānxi** *n* public relations

公共汽车 **gōnggòng qìchē** bus □ 我的车卖了，我现
在坐公共汽车上班。**Wǒ de chē mài le, wǒ xiànzài zuò
gōnggòng qìchē shàngbān.** *I've sold my car. Now I go
to work by bus.*

NOTE: The word for *bus* in Taiwan is 公车 **gōngchē**. In
Hong Kong, *bus* is 巴士 **bāshì**, obviously a transliteration of the English word *bus*.

公斤 **gōngjīn** [modif: 公 metric + 斤 a traditional
Chinese measurement of weight] *measure wd*
kilogram □ 这里有五公斤苹果，我送给你。**Zhèli yǒu
wǔ gōngjīn píngguǒ, wǒ sòng gei nǐ.** *Here are five
kilograms of apples, my gift to you.*

公关 **gōngguān** *n* (shortening of 公共关系 **gōnggòng
guānxi**) public relations

公开 **gōngkāi** [comp: 公 open + 开 open] **I** *adj*
open, public (antonym 秘密 **mìmì**) □ 他发表公开
谈话，反对政府的计划。**Tā fābiǎo gōngkāi tánhuà,
fǎnduì zhèngfǔ de jìhuà.** *He gave a public talk opposing the government plan.* **II** *v* make public, reveal
□ 希望你能公开自己的观点。**Xīwàng nǐ néng gōngkāi
zìjǐ de guāndiǎn.** *I hope you will make your views
known.*

公里 **gōnglǐ** [modif: 公 metric + 里 a traditional Chinese measurement of distance] *n* kilometer □ 从城
里到飞机场大概有十公里。**Cóng chénglǐ dào fēijīchǎng
dàgài yǒu shí gōnglǐ.** *It's about ten kilometers from
town to the airport.*

公路 **gōnglù** [modif: 公 public + 路 road] *n* public
road, highway (条 **tiáo**) □ 全国公路四通八达。**Quán
guó gōnglù sì-tōng-bā-dá.** *Public roads reach every
corner of the country.*

高速公路 **gāosù gōnglù** motorway, expressway

公民 **gōngmín** [modif: 公 public + 民 people, per-
son] *n* citizen □ 你拿哪个国家的护照，你就是那个国家
的公民。**Nǐ ná nǎge guójiā de hùzhào, nǐ jiù shì nàge**

guójiā de gōngmín. *You are a citizen of the country whose passport you hold.*

公平 **gōngpíng** [comp: 公 fair + 平 equal] *adj* fair, impartial
买卖公平 mǎimai gōngpíng fair trade

公顷 **gōngqīng** *n* hectare (= 10,000 square meters)

公然 **gōngrán** *adv* brazenly, openly
公然撒谎 gōngrán sāhuǎng tell a bare-faced lie

公认 **gōngrèn** [modif: 公 publicly + 认 acknowledge] *v* generally acknowledge, universally accept

公社 **gōngshè** *n* commune

公式 **gōngshì** *n* formula
数学公式 shùxué gōngshì mathematics formula

公司 **gōngsī** *n* commercial firm, company, corporation (家 jiā) □ 我们公司的营业范围很广泛。**Wǒmen gōngsī de yíngyè fànwéi hěn guǎngfàn.** *Our company has an extensive range of business activities.* □ 贵公司是哪一年成立的? **Guì gōngsī shì nǎ yì nián chénglì de?** *In which year was your company founded?*
分公司 fēn gōngsī branch of a company
总公司 zǒng gōngsī company headquarters

公务 **gōngwù** *n* public affairs, official duty

公务员 **gōngwùyuán** [suffix: 公务 public affair + 员 personal nominal suffix] *n* civil servant, government office holders

公用 **gōngyòng** *adj* for public use

公用电话 **gōngyòng diànhuà** [modif: 公用 public use + 电话 telephone] *n* public telephone, payphone □ 现在很多人都有手机, 公用电话不象从前那样重要了。**Xiànzài hěn duō rén dōu yǒu shǒujī, gōngyòng diànhuà búxiàng yǐqián nàyàng zhòngyào le.** *Nowadays many people have cell phones, so public telephones are not as important as before.*

公元 **gōngyuán** *n* of the Christian/common era, AD (Anno Domini)
公元前 gōngyuán qián BC (before Christ), BCE (before the Christian/common era) □ 他生于公元前二十五年, 死于公元三十一年。**Tā shēng yú gōngyuán qián èrshíwǔ nián, sǐ yú gōngyuán sānshíyī nián.** *He was born in 25 BC and died in AD 31.*

公园 **gōngyuán** [modif: 公 public + 园 garden] *n* public garden, park (座 zuò) □ 这个公园春天特别美。**Zhège gōngyuán chūntiān tèbié měi.** *This park is especially beautiful in spring.* □ 早上很多人在公园里跑步。**Zǎoshang hěn duō rén zài gōngyuán li pǎobù.** *Many people jog in the park early in the morning.*

公约 **gōngyuē** [modif: 公 public + 约 agreement] *n* 1 agreement, convention, pact 2 pledge
服务公约 fúwù gōngyuē service pledge

公债 **gōng zhài** [modif: 公 public + 债 debt] *n* government bonds
公债券 gōngzhài quàn bond

公证 **gōngzhèng** [modif: 公 public + 证 testify] *v* notarize
公证处 gōngzhèngchù notary office
公证人 gōngzhèngrén notary public, notary

恭 **gōng** *adj* deferential, reverent
恭敬 **gōngjìng** [comp: 恭 deferential + 敬 respectful] *adj* very respectful, deferential

供 **gōng** *v* supply □ 大风期间, 城市供水供电正常。**Dàfēng qījiān, chéngshì gōngshuǐ gōngdiàn zhèngcháng.** *During the storm, the city's water and electricity supply was maintained.* □ 供大于求。**Gōng dà yú qiú.** *Supply exceeds demand.* □ 供不应求。**Gōng bú yìng qiú.** *Supply falls short of demand.*

供给 **gōngjǐ** [comp: 供 supply + 给 provide] *v* supply, provide □ 对于经济特别困难的学生, 政府供给生活费。**Duìyú jīngjì tèbié kùnnan de xuésheng, zhèngfǔ gōngjǐ shēnghuófèi.** *The government provided a living stipend to students with special financial difficulties.*

NOTE: 给 in 供给 is pronounced as **jǐ**, not its usual **gěi**.

宫 **gōng** *n* palace
宫殿 gōngdiàn palace
王宫 wánggōng royal palace

弓 **gōng** I *n* bow II *v* bend, arch
弓箭 gōngjiàn bow and arrows

汞 **gǒng** *n* mercury

巩 **gǒng** Trad 鞏 *v* consolidate
巩固 **gǒnggù** [comp: 巩 consolidate + 固 reinforce] I *v* consolidate, strengthen □ 我们这次会谈是为了巩固和发展我们之间的合作关系。**Wǒmen zhè cì huìtán shì wèile gǒnggù hé fāzhǎn wǒmen zhī jiān de hézuò guānxi.** *The purpose of our talks is to strengthen and develop cooperation.* II *adj* solid, firm □ 他们夫妻之间关系很巩固。**Tāmen fūqī zhī jiān guānxi hěn gǒnggù.** *Their marital relationship has a solid foundation.*

拱 **gǒng** *n* arch
拱门 gǒngmén arched gate, arched door

共 **gòng** *adv* 1 altogether, in total □ 那座大学共有学生一万三千五百四十名。**Nà zuò dàxué gòng yǒu xuésheng yíwàn sānqiān wǔbǎi sìshí míng.** *That university has a total student population of 13,540.* 2 jointly, together (used only in writing) □ 两家公司的董事长将共进午餐。**Liǎng jiā gōngsī de dǒngshìzhǎng jiāng gòngjìn wǔcān.** *The chairmen of the two companies will have luncheon together.*

共产党 **gòngchǎndǎng** [modif: 共 to share + 产 property + 党 party] *n* communist party □ 你是中国共产党党员吗? **Nǐ shì Zhōngguó Gòngchǎndǎng dǎngyuán ma?** *Are you a member of the Chinese Communist Party?*

共和国 **gònghéguó** *n* republic □ 中国的全称是中华人民共和国。**Zhōngguó de quánchēng shì Zhōnghuá Rénmín Gònghéguó.** *China's full name is the People's Republic of China.* □ 什么样的国家才是真正的共和国? **Shénmeyàng de guójiā cái shì zhēnzhèng de gònghéguó?** *What kind of country is a genuine republic?*

共计 **gòngjì** [modif: 共 total + 计 calculate] *v* total, add up to

共鸣 **gòngmíng** [modif: 共 jointly+ 鸣 chirp] *n* 1 resonance 2 sympathetic response
引起共鸣 yǐnqǐ gòngmíng find a ready echo

共青团 **Gòngqīngtuán** *n* (shortening from 中国共产主义青年团 Zhōngguó gòngchǎnzhǔyì qīngniántuán) The Chinese Communist Youth League

共识 **gòngshì** [modif: 共 shared + 识 understanding] *n* common understanding
达成共识 dáchéng gòngshí achieve common undersatnding

共同 **gòngtóng** [comp: 共 together + 同 shared]

I *adj* common, shared **II** *adv* together, jointly □ 我们共同努力，保护我们共同的家园—地球。**Wǒmen gòngtóng nǔlì, bǎohù wǒmen gòngtóng de jiāyuán—dìqiú.** *Let's work together to protect our common homeland—the Earth.* □ 我们之间缺乏共同语言，就不必多谈了。**Wǒmen zhī jiān quēfá gòngtóng yǔyán, jiù bú bì duō tán le.** *As we do not have a common language, there is no need for fur-ther conversation.*

共性 **gòngxìng** [modif: 共 common + 性 nature] *n* generality, common characteristics

供 **gòng** *v* **1** confess, own up
口供 kǒugòng (criminal) confession
2 lay (offerings)

贡 **gòng** Trad 貢 *n* tribute
贡献 **gòngxiàn** [comp: 贡 tribute + 献 offer] **I** *v* contribute, dedicate **II** *n* contribution, devotion, dedication
为…作出贡献 **wèi…zuòchu gòngxiàn** make a contri-bution to …. □ 这位科学家为环境保护贡献了自己的一生。**Zhè wèi kēxuéjiā wèi huánjìng bǎohù gòngxiàn le zìjǐ de yìshēng.** *This scientist dedicated his life to environmental protection.* □ 在过去的一年中全体职工为公司的繁荣作出了贡献。**Zài guòqù de yì nián zhōng quántǐ zhígōng wèi gōngsī de fánróng zuòchūle gòngxiàn.** *In the past year, all the staff have contributed to the prosperity of the company.*

勾 **gōu** *v* **1** strike out with a pen **2** delineate (the outline of a drawing) **3** induce, evoke
勾结 **gōujié** *v* collaborate secretly with (on criminal matters)

沟 **gōu** Trad 溝 *n* ditch, trench (条 **tiáo**)
沟通 **gōutōng** *v* link up, connect
沟通意见 gōutōng yìjiàn exchange ideas

钩 **gōu** Trad 鈎 *n* hook (只 **zhī**)
钩子 gōuzi hook

狗 **gǒu** *n* dog (只 **zhī**, 条 **tiáo**) □ 我喜欢狗，但是不会象有些人那样让狗睡在我的床上。**Wǒ xǐhuan gǒu, dànshì bú huì xiàng yǒuxiē rén nàyàng ràng gǒu shuì zai wǒ de chuáng shang.** *I like dogs but, unlike some people, I won't let a dog sleep on my bed.*
母狗 mǔ gǒu bitch
小狗 xiǎo gǒu puppy

构 **gòu** Trad 構 *v* construct, form
构成 **gòuchéng** *v* make up, form □ 远山近水构成了美丽的风景。**Yuǎn-shān-jìn-shuǐ gòngchéngle měilì de fēngjǐng.** *Hills in the background and a lake in the foreground make up a beautiful landscape.*
构件 **gòujiàn** *n* component, part
构思 **gòusī** [v+obj: 构 construct + 思 thoughts] *v* (of writers or artists) work out the plot of a story or composition of a picture
构造 **gòuzào** *n* structure □ 小小的手机构造极其复杂。**Xiǎoxiǎo de shǒujī gòuzào jíqí fùzá.** *The cell phone, small as it is, has an extremely complex structure.*

购 **gòu** *v* purchase
购买 **gòumǎi** [comp: 购 purchase + 买 buy] *v* purchase
购买采矿设备 gòumǎi cǎi kuàng shèbèi purchase mining equipment
购买力 gòumǎilì purchasing power

够 **gòu** *adj* enough, sufficient □ 够了，够了，谢谢你！**Gòu le, gòu le, xièxie nǐ!** *That's enough. Thank*

you! □ 我们的汽油不够了，得加满才能开到目的地。**Wǒmen de qìyóu bú gòu le, děi jiā mǎn cái néng kāi dào mùdìdì.** *Our petrol is not enough. We've got to fill up to reach our destination.*

孤 **gū** *adj* lonely
孤儿 **gū'ér** [modif: 孤 lonely + 儿 child] *n* orphan
孤儿院 gū'éryuàn orphanage
孤立 **gūlì** [modif: 孤 lonely + 立 stand] *adj* isolated, without support or sympathy

辜 **gū** *v* (as in 辜负 **gūfù**)
辜负 **gūfù** *v* fail to live up to, let down
辜负父母的期望 gūfù fùmǔ de qīwàng fail to live up to parents' expectations

估 **gū** *v* estimate
估计 **gūjì** [comp: 估 estimate + 计 calculate] **I** *v* estimate, reckon, size up □ 我估计整个工程要花三百万元。**Wǒ gūjì zhěngge gōngchéng yào huā sānbǎiwàn yuán.** *I estimate the entire project will cost three mil-lion yuan.* □ 你估计他什么时候到？**Nǐ gūjì tā shénme shíhou dào?** *When do you reckon he will arrive?* **II** *n* estimate, approximate calculation, appraisal □ 根据专家估计，今年经济增长可达百分之五。**Gēnjù zhuānjiā gūjì, jīnnián jīngjì zēngzhǎng kě dá bǎifēn zhī wǔ.** *According to expert estimates, economic growth will reach five percent this year.*

姑 **gū** *n* aunt, woman
姑姑 **gūgu** *n* Same as 姑妈 **gūmā**, especially as a colloquialism
姑妈 **gūmā** *n* father's sister, aunt □ 我姑妈一直没有结婚，把我当做自己的孩子。**Wǒ gūmā yìzhí méiyǒu jiéhūn, bǎ wǒ dāngzuò zìjǐ de háizi.** *My father's sister never married and treats me as her own child.*
姑母 **gūmǔ** *n* Same as 姑妈 **gūmā**, especially used in writing.
姑娘 **gūniang** *n* unmarried young woman, girl, lass □ 那个姑娘是谁家的孩子？**Nàge gūniang shì shuí jiā de háizi?** *Whose child is that girl?*
大姑娘 dàgūniang young woman (usually unmar-ried), lass
小姑娘 xiǎo gūniang little girl

NOTE: 姑娘 **gūniang** is a colloquial word. When used to mean *unmarried young lady*, 姑娘 **gūniang** is used to-gether with the word 小伙子 **xiǎohuǒzi** (young man), e.g. □ 姑娘小伙子都爱热闹。**Gūniang xiǎohuǒzi dōu ài rènao.** *Young people all like having fun.*

姑且 **gūqiě** *adv* tentatively, for the time being

菇 **gū** *n* mushroom
香菇 xiānggū dried mushroom

古 **gǔ** *adj* ancient □ 中国是一个文明古国，有很多古建筑。**Zhōngguó shì yí ge wénmíng gǔguó, yǒu hěnduō gǔ jiànzhù.** *China is a country of ancient civilization and boasts a large number of ancient buildings.*
古代 **gǔdài** [modif: 古 ancient + 代 generation, time] *n* ancient times □ 古代中国创造了伟大的文明。**Gǔdài Zhōngguó chuàngzàole wěidà de wénmíng.** *Ancient China created a great civilization.*
古典 **gǔdiǎn** *adj* classical
古典音乐 gǔdiǎn yīnyuè classical music

古董 **gǔdǒng** *n* antique, old curio (件 **jiàn**)
老古董 **lǎogǔdǒng** old fogey (个 **gè**)

古怪 **gǔguài** *adj* weird, queer
行为古怪 **xíngwéi gǔguài** behave strangely

古迹 **gǔjì** [modif: 古 ancient + 迹 footprints] *n* historic site, place of historic interest □ 这个古迹每年吸引几万人参观。**Zhège gǔjì měi nián xīyǐn jǐ wàn rén cānguān.** *This historic site attracts tens of thousands of visitors every year.* □ 有些古迹没有得到有效保护,多么可惜! **Yǒuxiē gǔjì méiyǒu dédào yǒuxiào bǎohù, duōme kěxǐ!** *What a shame it is that some places of historic interest have not been protected effectively.*

古老 **gǔlǎo** [comp: 古 ancient + 老 old] *adj* ancient, time-honored □ 中国的苏州有两千五百多年的历史,真是一座古老的城市。**Zhōngguó de Sūzhōu yǒu liǎngqiān wǔbǎi duō nián de lìshǐ, zhēn shì yí zuò gǔlǎo de chéngshì.** *The city of Suzhou in China has a history of over 2,500 years. It is indeed an ancient city.*

鼓 **gǔ** *n* drum
鼓吹 **gǔchuī** *v* advocate, preach (usually wrong and harmful ideas)

鼓励 **gǔlì** *v* encourage □ 新加坡政府鼓励华人说华语。**Xīnjiāpō zhèngfǔ gǔlì Huárén shuō Huáyǔ.** *The Singapore government encourages ethnic Chinese to speak Mandarin.*
物质鼓励 **wùzhì gǔlì** material incentive
精神鼓励 **jīngshén gǔlì** moral incentive, moral encouragement

鼓舞 **gǔwǔ** [comp: 鼓 drum up + 舞 dance] *v* inspire, fire up … with enthusiasm, hearten □ 这个消息真是鼓舞人心! **Zhège xiāoxi zhēn shì gǔwǔ rénxīn!** *This news is really inspiring!*

鼓掌 **gǔzhǎng** [v+obj: 鼓 drum + 掌 palm] *v* applaud □ 小明要给大家唱一首中国歌曲, 让我们鼓掌欢迎。**Xiǎo Míng yào gěi dàjiā chàng yì shǒu Zhōngguó gēqǔ, ràng wǒmen gǔzhǎng huānyíng.** *Xiao Ming is going to sing us a Chinese song. Let's give him a big hand.*

骨 **gǔ** *n* bone
骨头 **gǔtou** *n* bone (根 **gēn**) □ 他扔给小狗一根骨头。**Tā rēng gěi xiǎogǒu yì gēn gǔtou.** *He threw the puppy a bone.*

骨干 **gǔgàn** *n* backbone (denoting people)
公司的骨干 **gōngsī de gǔgàn** the backbone (most important staff) of a company

骨肉 **gǔròu** [comp: 骨 bone + 肉 flesh] *n* one's flesh and blood

骨折 **gǔzhé** *v* fracture a bone

股 **gǔ** *n* share, stock (in a company)
股东 **gǔdōng** *n* shareholder, stockholder

股份 **gǔfèn** *n* share, stock

股票 **gǔpiào** [modif: 股 share + 票 ticket] *n* share, stock (份 **fèn**) □ 他上个月买了这家公司十万股票。**Tā shàngge yuè mǎile zhè jiā gōngsī shíwàn gǔpiào.** *He bought 10,000 shares of the company last month.*

股市 **gǔshì** [modif: 股 share + 市 market] *n* share market

谷 **gǔ** Trad 穀 *n* grain, cereal
谷子 **gǔzi** grain (粒 **lì**)

谷物 **gǔwù** *n* grain, cereal (collectively)
谷物价格 **gǔwù jiàgé** grain prices

雇 **gù** Trad 僱 *v* employ, hire
雇佣 **gùyōng** *v* hire, employ

NOTE: 雇佣 **gùyōng** is used when hiring low-rank employees, e.g. unskilled workers. To employ a professional, the verb to use is 聘用 **pìnyòng**.

雇员 **gùyuán** [suffix: 雇 employ + 员 suffix] *n* employee, staff member (antonym 雇主 **gùzhǔ**)

故 **gù** I *adj* old, former II *adv* on purpose, deliberately

故事 **gùshi** [modif: 故 old, past + 事 happening, event] *n* story, tale □ 这是一个真实的故事。**Zhè shì yí ge zhēnshí de gùshi.** *This is a true story.*
讲故事 **jiǎng gùshi** tell a story □ 他每天晚上都给孩子讲一个故事。**Tā měitiān wǎnshang dōu gěi háizi jiǎng yí ge gùshi.** *He tells his child a story every evening.*
听故事 **tīng gùshi** listen to a story

故乡 **gùxiāng** [modif: 故 former years + 乡 village, homeland] *n* native place, hometown, home village □ 他退休以后, 要回故乡定居。**Tā tuìxiū yǐhòu yào huí gùxiāng dìngjū.** *After retirement he will return to his hometown to live.*

故意 **gùyì** [modif: 故 on purpose + 意 intention] *adv* deliberately, intentionally, on purpose (antonym 无意 **wúyì**) □ 他犯的错误是无意的, 不是故意的。**Tā fàn de cuòwù shì wúyì de, búshì gùyì de.** *He did not commit this mistake deliberately, but by accident.*

故障 **gùzhàng** *n* breakdown (of a machine)
排除故障 **páichú gùzhàng** troubleshooting

顾 **gù** Trad 顧 *v* attend to, care for □ 你不能只顾自己, 不管别人。**Nǐ bù néng zhǐ gù zìjǐ, bù guǎn biérén.** *You shouldn't care for only yourself and nobody else.* □ 他忙得顾不上吃饭。**Tā máng de gù bu shàng chīfàn.** *He was so busy that he did not have time for meals.*

顾此失彼 **gùcǐ shībǐ** *idiom* pay too much attention to one thing at the expense of another

顾客 **gùkè** *n* customer, client (位 **wèi**) □ 我们尽量满足顾客的要求。**Wǒmen jìnliàng mǎnzú gùkè de yāoqiú.** *We try our best to meet customers' demands.*

顾虑 **gùlù** *v* have misgivings, worry
顾虑重重 **gùlù chóngchóng** be filled with misgivings

顾问 **gùwèn** *n* advisor, consultant (位 **wèi**)

固 **gù** I *adj* secure, solid II *v* secure, consolidate, strengthen

固定 **gùdìng** [comp: 固 secure + 定 fix] *v* fix, make immovable
固定资产 **gùdìng zīchǎn** fixed assets

固然 **gùrán** *conj* granted (that), although

固体 **gùtǐ** *n* solid matter, solid

固有 **gùyǒu** *adj* inherent, innate

固执 **gùzhí** *adj* obstinate, stubborn
固执己见 **gùzhí jǐjiàn** stubbornly stick to one's opinions, pigheaded

瓜 **guā** *n* melon, gourd (只 **zhī**)
瓜子 **guāzǐ** *n* melon seeds (颗 **kē**)

刮 **guā** *v* (of a wind) blow □ 这儿冬天经常刮西北风。**Zhèr dōngtiān jīngcháng guā xīběi fēng.** *A northwestern wind often blows here in winter.*

寡 **guǎ** *adj* 1 few, insufficient 2 widowed
孤儿寡母 **gū'ér guǎmǔ** orphan and widow
寡妇 **guǎfu** *n* widow

挂 **guà** Trad 掛 *v* hang □ 墙上挂着一幅世界地图。**Qiáng shang guàzhe yì fú shìjiè dìtú.** *A map of the world hung on the wall.*

挂钩 **guàgōu** *v* hook up, couple together

挂号 **guàhào** *v* register (at a hospital) □ 在中国看病的第一件事就是挂号。**Zài Zhōngguó kànbìng de dì-yī jiàn shì jiù shì guàhào.** *In China, when you go to see a doctor the first thing to do is to register.*

挂号费 **guàhào fèi** registration fee, doctor's consultation fee

挂号处 **guàhào chù** registration office

NOTE: In China if you are sick you go to a hospital where doctors work in their specialist departments, e.g. internal medicine, gynecology and dermatology. 挂号 **guàhào** means *to tell a receptionist which department you want to go to and pay the consultation fee.* Dentistry is usually one of the departments and a dentist is generally considered just another doctor.

挂念 **guàniàn** *v* miss and worry about (a person)

乖 **guāi** *adj* (of children) be good, be well-behaved

乖孩子 **guāi háizi** a well-behaved child

拐 **guǎi** *v* turn, make a turn □ 往前走，再向左拐，就是火车站。**Wàng qián zǒu, zài xiàng zuǒ guǎi, jiù shì huǒchēzhàn.** *Walk straight on, then turn left, and you will find the railway station.*

拐弯 **guǎiwān** *v* turn a corner

拐弯抹角 **guǎiwān mòjiǎo** *idiom* talk in a roundabout way, beat around the bush

怪 **guài** I *adj* strange, odd, queer □ 我刚才放在这儿的书怎么一会儿就不见了，真怪! **Wǒ gāngcái fàng zài zhèr de shū zěnme yíhuìr jiù bú jiàn le, zhēn guài!** *I left a book here just now and it's vanished. How odd!* □ 昨天我碰到了怪事。**Zuótiān wǒ pèngdàole guài shì.** *Something strange happened to me yesterday.* II *v* blame □ 都怪我，没讲清楚。**Dōu guài wǒ, méi jiǎng qīngchu.** *It was all my fault. I did not make it clear.* □ 你们别怪来怪去的，看看该怎么办吧。**Nǐmen bié guài-lái-guài-qù de, kànkan gāi zénme bàn ba.** *Don't blame each other. Try to find out what should be done.*

怪不得 **guàibudé** *adv* no wonder, so that's why

关 **guān** Trad 關 *v* 1 close □ 学校晚上十一点半关大门。**Xuéxiào wǎnshang shíyī diǎn bàn guān dàmén.** *The school gate closes at 11:30 p.m.* □ 把门/窗关上。**Bǎ mén/chuāng guānshang.** *Close the door/window.* □ 你离开的时候，请把灯关掉，把门关上。**Nǐ líkāi de shíhou, qǐng bǎ dēng guāndiào, bǎ mén guānshàng.** *When you leave, please turn off the lights and close the door.* 2 turn off, switch off

把电灯/电视机/录音机/机器关掉 **bǎ diàndēng/diànshì jī/lùyīnjī/jīqì guāndiào** turn off the lights/TV/recorder/machine

3 *v* concern, involve

关闭 **guānbì** [comp: 关 close + 闭 close] *v* close down, shut down

关闭机场 **guānbì jīchǎng** shut down the airport

关怀 **guānhuái** *v* be kindly concerned about, show loving care to

关键 **guānjiàn** [comp: 关 pass + 键 key] *n* what is crucial or critical □ 一家公司的成功，关键在于人力资源。**Yì jiā gōngsì de chénggōng, guānjiàn zàiyú rénlì zīyuán.** *The success of a company lies in its human resources.* □ 他踢进了关键的一球。**Tā tījìnle guānjiàn de yī qiú.** *He scored the crucial goal.*

关键词 **guānjiàncí** keyword

关节炎 **guānjiéyán** *n* arthritis

风湿性关节炎 **fēngshīxìng guānjiéyán** rheumatic arthritis

关切 **guānqiè** *v* be deeply concerned

关头 **guāntóu** *n* juncture, moment

在紧要关头 **zài jǐnyào guāntóu** at a critical juncture, at a crucial moment

关系 **guānxi** [comp: 关 related + 系 connected] I *n* connection, relation □ 我和他只是一般朋友关系。我希望保持这种关系。**Wǒ hé tā zhǐ shì yìbān péngyou guānxi. Wǒ xīwàng bǎochí zhè zhǒng guānxi.** *He and I are merely ordinary friends, and I intend to keep it that way.*

和…有关系 **hé...yǒu guānxi** have something to do with □ 这件事和大家都有关系。**Zhè jiàn shì hé dàjiā dōu yǒu guānxi.** *This matter concerns everybody.*

没(有)关系 **méi(yǒu)guānxi** it doesn't matter, it's OK □ "对不起。" "没关系。" **"Duìbuqǐ." "Méiguānxi."** [said when you have unintentionally hurt somebody] *"I'm sorry." "It's OK."* □ 这两件事有没有关系? **Zhè liǎng jiàn shì yǒu méiyǒu guānxi?** *Is there any connection between these two matters? (→ Are these two matters related?)*

II *v* affect, have bearing on □ 睡得好不好，关系到你的健康。**Shuì de hǎo bù hǎo, guānxi dào nǐ de jiànkāng.** *Whether you sleep well or not affects your health.* □ 能不能考上大学，关系到青年人的前途。**Néng bù néng kǎoshàng dàxué, guānxi dào qīngniánrén de qiántú.** *Whether a young person passes the university entrance examination or not has bearing on his/her future.*

关心 **guānxīn** [v + obj: 关 connected + 心 the heart] *v* be concerned about, care for □ 妈妈总是关心孩子的健康。**Māma zǒngshì guānxīn háizi de jiànkāng.** *Mothers are always concerned about their children's health.* □ 对公司的业务情况，每个职工都很关心。**Duì gōngsī de yèwù qíngkuàng, měi ge zhígōng dōu hěn guānxīn.** *Every employee is deeply concerned about the business of the company.*

关于 **guānyú** *prep* about, on □ 我很久没有听到关于他的消息了。**Wǒ hěn jiǔ méiyǒu tīngdào guānyú tā de xiāoxi le.** *I haven't heard about him for a long time.* □ 关于这个月的营业情况，你问问王经理。**Guānyú zhège yuè de yíngyè qíngkuàng, nǐ děi wèn Wáng jīnglǐ.** *You should ask Mr Wang, the manager, about business this month.*

关照 **guānzhào** [comp: 关 concerned + 照 look after] *v* 1 look after, take care of □ 这里的工作请你关照一下。**Zhèlǐ de gōngzuò qǐng nǐ guānzhào yíxia.** *Please keep an eye on the work here.* 2 notify, inform □ 我已经关照服务员叫出租汽车了。**Wǒ yǐjīng guānzhào fúwùyuán jiào chūzū qìchē le.** *I've already asked the attendant to call a taxi.*

NOTE: "请你多关照。" **"Qǐng nǐ duō guānzhào."** is often said

by someone who has just arrived or started working in a place, to someone who has been working there longer. It is a polite expression meaning something to the effect of "I'd appreciate your guidance."

观 **guān** Trad 觀 **I** v look at, observe **II** n view, outlook

观测 **guāncè** [comp: 观 observe + 测 measure] v observe
观测市场动向 guāncè shìchǎng dòngxiàng pay close attention to the market trend

观察 **guānchá** [comp: 观 see + 察 examine] v observe, watch □ 这个人是否可靠, 还需进一步观察。 **Zhège rén shìfǒu kěkào, hái xū jìnyíbù guānchá.** *Further observation is needed to determine whether this man is reliable or not.* □ 对于市场情况, 他观察得很仔细。 **Duìyú shìchǎng qíngkuàng, tā guānchá de hěn zǐxì.** *He watches the market very carefully.*

观察员 guāncháyuán observer (at a conference, especially an international conference)

观点 **guāndiǎn** [modif: 观 observe + 点 point] n viewpoint, view □ 对问题有不同的观点, 是很正常的。 **Duì wèntí yǒu bù tóng de guāndiǎn, shì hěn zhèngcháng de.** *It is normal to have different views on an issue.*

观光 **guānguāng** [v+obj: 观 observe + 光 view] v go sightseeing, visit and observe

观看 **guānkàn** [comp: 观 observe + 看 see] v watch (a theatrical performance, sports event)

观念 **guānniàn** n concept, sense
是非观念 shìfēi guānniàn the sense of what is right and what is wrong

观赏 **guānshǎng** [comp: 观 observe + 赏 admire] v view and admire (beautiful flowers, rare animals, etc.)
观赏野生动物 guānshǎng yěshēng dòngwù observe wild animals

观众 **guānzhòng** [modif: 观 watch + 众 crowd] n audience (in a theater, on TV, etc.), spectator □ 观众对这个戏反映很好。 **Guānzhòng duì zhège xì fǎnyìng hěn hǎo.** *The audience responded very well to this play.* □ 很多观众起立鼓掌。 **Hěn duō guānzhòng qǐlì gǔzhǎng.** *Many people in the audience stood up to applaud.*

官 **guān** n (government) official □ 很多中国人想当官。 **Hěn duō Zhōngguórén xiǎng dāng guān.** *Many Chinese want to be officials.*

NOTE: 官 **guān** is a colloquial word. For more formal occasions, use 官员 **guānyuán**.

官方 **guānfāng** [modif: 官 official + 方 side] adj official
官方消息 guānfāng xiāoxi official news, news released by the authorities

官僚 **guānliáo** n bureaucrat
官僚主义 guānliáozhǔyì bureaucracy

官员 **guānyuán** [suffix: 官 official + 员 nominal suffix] n official (位 **wèi**) □ 这位官员很负责。 **Zhè wèi guānyuán hěn fùzérèn.** *This official has a strong sense of responsibility.* □ 我想见一下这里的负责官员。 **Wǒ**

xiǎng jiàn yíxià zhèlǐ de fùzé guānyuán. *I want to see the official in charge here.*

NOTE: See note on 干部 **gànbù**.

棺 **guān** n coffin
棺材 guāncái coffin (口 **kǒu**)

管 **I guǎn** v be in charge, take care (of) □ 王老师管一年级的教学。 **Wáng lǎoshī guǎn yī-niánjí de jiàoxué.** *Teacher Wang is in charge of the first-year courses.* □ 你们公司谁管人力资源? **Nǐmen gōngsī shéi guǎn rénlì zīyuán?** *Who is in charge of human resources in your company?* □ 别管我! **Bié guǎn wǒ!** *Leave me alone!*

管理 **guǎnlǐ** [comp: 管 be in charge + 理 put in order] v manage, administer □ 他管理工厂很有办法。 **Tā guǎnlǐ gōngchǎng hěn yǒu bànfǎ.** *He is resourceful and efficient in managing the factory.* □ 这些图书资料管理得很好。 **Zhèxiē túshū zīliào guǎnlǐ de hěn hǎo.** *These books and files are well taken care of.*
商业管理 shāngyè guǎnlǐ business administration

管辖 **guǎnxiá** v have jurisdiction over

管 2 **guǎn** n tube, pipe
管子 guǎnzi tube, pipe (根 **gēn**)

管道 **guǎndào** [comp: 管 pipe + 道 path] n pipeline, conduit

馆 **guǎn** Trad 館 n building (for a specific purpose)
饭馆 fànguǎn restaurant
体育馆 tǐyùguǎn gymnasium
图书馆 túshūguǎn library
馆子 guǎnzi n restaurant (colloquial) (家 **jiā**)

冠 **guàn** n the best
冠军 guànjūn n champion, championship □ 我们学校获得了全市中学生篮球邀请赛冠军。 **Wǒmen xuéxiào huòdéle quán shì zhōngxuéshēng lánqiú yāoqǐngsài guànjūn.** *Our school has won the city high school basketball invitational tournament championship.*

贯 **guàn** v pass through
贯彻 guànchè v implement, carry out □ 贯彻这项新政策, 大约要半年时间。 **Guànchè zhè xiàng xīn zhèngcè, dàyuē yào bànnián shíjiān.** *Implementing the new policy will take about half a year.*

惯 **guàn** **I** adj accustomed to **II** n custom, convention
惯例 guànlì n usual practice, convention
打破惯例 dǎpò guànlì break with convention
惯用语 guànyòngyǔ n idiomatic expression
惯于 guànyú v be used to, habitually
惯于撒谎 guànyú sāhuǎng be a habitual liar

灌 **guàn** v fill (water, air), pour
灌溉 guàngài v irrigate
灌木 guànmù n bush

罐 **guàn** n tin, jar
罐头 guàntou [suffix: 罐 tin, can + 头 nominal suffix] n can, tin □ 这个罐头里面是什么呀? **Zhège guàntou lǐmiàn shì shénme ya?** *What's in this can?*
罐头食品 guàntou shípǐn canned food

光 **I guāng** **I** n light □ 发光的不一定是金子。 **Fā guāng de bù yídìng shì jīnzi.** *All that glitters is not gold.*
灯光 dēngguāng lamplight

阳光 yángguāng sunlight

月光 yuèguāng moonlight

II *adj* smooth, shiny

光彩 **guāngcǎi** [comp: 光 light + 彩 color] **I** *n* luster, splendor **II** *adj* honorable

觉得光彩 juéde guāngcǎi feel proud

光碟 **guāngdié** [modif: 光 light, laser + 碟 disk] *n* compact disk (CD) (盘 **pán**)

光滑 **guānghuá** [comp: 光 smooth + 滑 smooth] smooth, glossy

光辉 **guānghuī** [comp: 光 light + 辉 splendor] **I** *n* brilliance, radiance □ 云挡不住太阳的光辉。**Yún dǎng bu zhù tàiyang de guānghuī.** *The clouds cannot shut out the brilliance of the sunlight.* **II** *adj* brilliant, splendid □ 他在医学研究上取得了光辉的成绩。**Tā zài yīxué yánjiū shang qǔdéle guānghuī de chéngjì.** *He achieved brilliant results in medical research.*

光亮 **guāngliàng** *adj* bright, shiny

光临 **guānglín** *v* (a polite expression) be present, come

欢迎光临! **Huānyíng guānglín!** You're cordially welcome! We welcome you.

光明 **guāngmíng** [comp: 光 light + 明 bright] *adj* bright, promising □ 只要努力就会有光明的前途。**Zhǐyào nǔlì jiùhuì yǒu guāngmíng de qiántú.** *If only you work hard, you will have a bright future.*

光荣 **guāngróng** [comp: 光 light + 荣 glory] *adj* glorious, honorable □ 他代表全校参加这次比赛, 是很光荣的。**Tā dàibiǎo quánxiào cānjiā zhè cì bǐsài, shì hěn guāngróng de.** *He represented the school in the competition, which was a great honor.*

光线 **guāngxiàn** [comp: 光 light + 线 string] *n* light, ray (道 **dào**) □ 这个房间光线太暗。**Zhège fángjiān guāngxiàn tài àn.** *This room is not bright enough.*

光 2 **guāng** *adv* only, sole □ 光有钱就能幸福吗? **Guāng yǒu qián jiù néng xìngfú ma?** *Can money alone make you happy?* □ 她光练口语, 不写汉字, 可不行。**Tā guāng liàn kǒuyǔ, bù xiě Hànzì, kě bù xíng.** *She only practices oral Chinese and does not write characters. This won't do.*

光棍儿 **guānggùnr** *n* unmarried man, bachelor

打光棍儿 dǎ guānggùnr remain unmarried, be a bachelor

广 **guāng** Trad 廣 *adj* extensive, wide

广播 **guǎngbō** [modif: 广 extensive, wide + 播 sow, spread] **I** *v* broadcast □ 今天早上广播了一条重要新闻。**Jīntiān zǎoshang guǎngbōle yì tiáo zhòngyào xīnwén.** *A piece of important news was broadcast early this morning.* **II** *n* broadcasting □ 这位老人每天都听新闻广播。**Zhè wèi lǎorén měitiān dōu tīng xīnwén guǎngbō.** *This old man listens to the news broadcast every day.*

广播电台 guǎngbō diàntái radio station

广播公司 guǎngbō gōngsī broadcasting company

英国广播公司 Yīngguó Guǎngbō Gōngsī the British Broadcasting Company (BBC)

广播员 guǎngbōyuán newsreader

广场 **guǎngchǎng** [modif: 广 broad + 场 ground] *n* square □ 中国最著名的广场是天安门广场。**Zhōngguó zuì zhùmíng de guǎngchǎng shì Tiān'ānmén Guǎngchǎng.** *The best-known square in China is Tiananmen Square.*

广大 **guǎngdà** [comp: 广 broad + 大 big] *adj* vast, extensive □ 中国西北广大地区还没有充分开发。**Zhōngguó xīběi guǎngdà dìqū hái méiyǒu chōngfèn kāifā.** *The vast area of China's northwest is yet to be fully developed.*

广泛 **guǎngfàn** [comp: 广 broad + 泛 extensive] *adj* widespread, wide-ranging, extensive □ 他们对市场进行了广泛的调查。**Tāmen duì shìchǎng jìnxíngle guǎngfàn de diàochá.** *They conducted an extensive market investigation.*

广告 **guǎnggào** [modif: 广 broad + 告 inform] *n* advertisement □ 一般电视观众都讨厌电视广告。**Yìbān diànshì guānzhòng dōu tǎoyàn diànshì guǎnggào.** *TV viewers generally hate commercials.* □ 开店以前, 他们先在报上登了大广告。**Kāidiàn yǐqián, tāmen xiān zài bào shang dēngle dà guǎnggào.** *Before the store opened, they ran a huge advertisement in the newspaper.*

广阔 **guǎngkuò** [comp: 广 broad + 阔 wide] *adj* vast, wide □ 中国东北有一片广阔的平原。**Zhōngguó dōngběi yǒu yí piàn guǎngkuò de píngyuán.** *China's northeast boasts a vast plain.*

逛 **guàng** *v* stroll, take a random walk

逛公园 guàng gōngyuán stroll in the park

逛街 guàng jiē stroll around the streets, do window shopping □ 我这么忙, 哪有时间陪你逛街? **Wǒ zhème máng, nǎ yǒu shíjiān péi nǐ guàng jiē?** *I'm so busy. How can I find time to go window-shopping with you?*

瑰 **guī** as in 玫瑰 **méigui**

规 **guī** Trad 規 *n* compass, regulation, rule

规定 **guīdìng** [comp: 规 stipulate + 定 decide] **I** *v* stipulate, prescribe □ 政府规定, 珍贵文物不能带出国。**Zhèngfǔ guīdìng, zhēnguì wénwù bù néng dàichū guó.** *The government stipulates that precious cultural relics may not be taken out of the country.* **II** *n* regulation □ 必须遵守海关的规定。**Bìxū zūnshǒu hǎiguān de guīdìng.** *Customs regulations must be obeyed.*

规范 **guīfàn** *n* standard, norm

符合规范 fúhé guīfàn meet the standard

规格 **guīgé** *n* specifications (of a product), norm

规划 **guīhuà** **1** long-term program

五年发展规划 wǔ nián fāzhǎn guīhuà five-year development plan

2 draw up a long-term program

规矩 **guīju** [comp: 规 compass + 矩 ruler] **I** *n* rule, established practice

老规矩 lǎoguīju well-established practice

II *adj* well behaved, behave within the norm

规律 **guīlǜ** [comp: 规 regulation + 律 law] *n* law, regular pattern □ 经济活动十分复杂, 但是还是有规律的。**Jīngjì huódòng shífēn fùzá, dànshì háishì yǒu guīlǜ de.** *Economic activities are very complicated, but they also follow regular patterns.*

规模 **guīmó** *n* scale □ 这次航空展览会规模很大。**Zhè cì hángkōng zhǎnlǎnhuì guīmó hěn dà.** *This is a large-scale air show.*

规则 **guīzé** *n* rule, regulation

交通规则 jiāotōng guīzé traffic regulations

游戏规则 yóuxì guīzé game rules

规章 **guīzhāng** *n* rules, regulations

规章制度 guīzhāng zhìdù rules and regulations (of an organization, an institution, etc.)

归 **guī** Trad 歸 *v* return, go back to
归根结底 **guī-gēn-jié-dǐ** in the final analysis
归还 **guīhuán** [comp: 归 return + 还 return] *v*
return, revert
归还原主 **guīhuán yuánzhǔ** be returned to the
original owner
归结 **guījié** *v* sum up, put in a nutshell
归纳 **guīnà** *v* sum up, induce
归纳法 **guīnàfǎ** inductive method

硅 **guī** *n* silicon
硅谷 **guīgǔ** silicon valley

龟 **guī** *n* turtle
海龟 **hǎiguī** sea turtle

闺 **guī** *n* boudoir, a lady's chamber
闺女 **guīnǚ** *n* **1** girl, maiden **2** daughter

鬼 **guǐ** *n* ghost □ "你怕鬼吗?" "不怕, 我根本不相
信有鬼。" "**Nǐ pà guǐ ma?**" "**Bú pà, wǒ gēnběn bù
xiāngxìn yǒu guǐ.**" *Are you afraid of ghosts?" "No, I
don't believe in ghosts at all."*
鬼故事 **guǐ gùshi** ghost story
鬼屋 **guǐ wū** haunted house
鬼话 **guǐhuà** [modif: 鬼 ghost + 话 talk] *n* wild and
ridiculous talk, nonsense (aimed to deceive)
鬼话连篇 **guǐhuà liánpiān** a pack of lies

轨 **guǐ** *n* rail
出轨 **chūguǐ** (of a train) derail
轨道 **guǐdào** *n* track, orbit
上了轨道 **shàng le guǐdào** settle into normal routine

桂 **guì** *n* cassia, bay tree, sweet-scented asmanthus
桂冠 **guìguān** *n* laurel (emblem of victory or
success)

柜 **guì** Trad 櫃 *n* cupboard, cabinet
柜台 **guìtái** *n* counter, bar

贵 **guì** Trad 貴 *adj* **1** expensive, of great value (antonym 便宜 **piányi**) □ 这家商店的东西很贵。**Zhè jiā
shāngdiàn de dōngxi hěn guì.** *The goods in this shop
are all very expensive.* □ 什么? 要一千块钱? 太贵了!
Shénme? Yào yìqiān kuài qián? Tài guì le. *What? One
thousand dollars? It's too expensive.* **2** extremely
valuable, precious
贵金属 **guìjīnshǔ** rare metal, precious metal
3 of noble birth, high-ranking
贵宾 **guìbīn** [modif: 贵 valuable + 宾 guest] *n*
distinguished guest (位 **wèi**)
贵姓 **guìxìng** [modif: 贵 valuable + 姓 family name]
idiom your family name □ "请问, 您贵姓?" "我姓
王。" "**Qǐng wèn, nín guìxìng?**" "**Wǒ xìng Wáng.**"
"What's your family name?" "Wang." □ "您大名
是…?" "我叫宝华。" "**Nín dàmíng shì...?**" "**Wǒ jiào
Bǎohuá.**" *"And your given name is…?" "It's Baohua."* □ "您是王宝华先生吗?" "是, 是。" "**Nín shì Wáng
Bǎohuá xiānsheng?**" "**Shì, shì.**" *"Oh, you're Mr Wang
Baohua?" "That's right."*

NOTE: (1) While 贵姓 **guìxìng** is the polite form when ask-
ing about somebody's family name, the polite way to ask
somebody's given name is "请问, 您大名是…?" "**Qingwèn,
nín dàmíng shì...?**" 大名 literally means *big name*. The answer to this question is "我叫XX。" "**Wǒ jiào XX.**" (2) The
word 贵 **guì** in the sense of *valuable* is added to certain
nouns to mean *your ...*, e.g. 贵姓 **guìxìng** *your family*

name, 贵国 **guìguó** *your country*, 贵校 **guìxiào** *your school.*
They are only used in formal and polite contexts.

贵重 **guìzhòng** [comp: 贵 valuable + 重 important]
adj valuable, precious □ 贵重物品, 各自保管。
Guìzhòng wùpǐn, gèzì bǎoguǎn. *Take care of your
own valuables.*
贵族 **guìzú** *n* aristocrat, aristocracy

跪 **guì** *v* kneel
跪下去 **guìxià qù** kneel down

滚 **gǔn** *v* roll □ 球滚到沙发下面去了。**Qiú gǔn dào
shāfā xiàmiàn qù le.** *The ball rolled under the
armchair.*

NOTE: 滚 **gǔn** is used to tell somebody "get out of here"
or "beat it," e.g. □ 滚! 滚出去! **Gǔn! Gǔn chūqu!** *Get lost!
Get out of here!* □ 滚开! **Gǔn kāi!** *Beat it!* These are
highly offensive.

滚动 **gǔndòng** [comp: 滚 roll + 动 move] *v* roll

棍 **gùn** *n* stick, rod
棍子 **gùnzi** stick, rod (根 **gēn**)

锅 **guō** Trad 鍋 *n* pot, pan, wok □ 做好菜, 要把锅
洗干净。**Zuòhao cài, yào bǎ guō xǐ gānjìng.** *After
cooking, you should wash clean the pot.*
锅炉 **guōlú** *n* boiler

国 **guó** Trad 國 *n* country, nation □ 国与国之间
应该是平等的。**Guó yú guó zhī jiān yīnggāi shì
píngděng de.** *There should be equality among nations.*
德国 **Déguó** Germany
俄国 **Éguó** Russia
法国 **Fǎguó** France
美国 **Měiguó** the United States of America
英国 **Yīngguó** England, the United Kingdom
中国 **Zhōngguó** China
国法 **guófǎ** [modif: 国 country + 法 law] *n* the law
of a country
国防 **guófáng** [modif: 国 nation + 防 defense] *n*
national defense
国防部 **guófángbù** Ministry of National Defense
国会 **guóhuì** [modif: 国 the state + 会 conference]
n (the U.S.) Congress, Parliament
国会议员 **guóhuì yìyuán** Congressman, member of
Parliament (MP)
国籍 **guójí** *n* nationality
加入美国国籍 **jiārù Měiguó guójí** be naturalized as a
U.S. citizen
国际 **guójì** *adj* international □ 反对恐怖活动已经
成为一个国际问题。**Fǎnduì kǒngbù huódòng yǐjīng
chéngwéi yí ge guójì wèntí.** *Anti-terrorism has become
an international issue.* □ 打国际长途电话越来越便宜
了。**Dǎ guójì chángtú diànhuà yuèláiyuè piányi le.**
*International long-distance calls have become less
and less expensive.*
国家 **guójiā** [comp: 国 country + 家 family] *n* country, state □ 这个国家历史很长。**Zhège guójiā lìshǐ hěn
cháng.** *This country has a long history.* □ 他代表国家
参加运动会。**Tā dàibiǎo guójiā cānjiā yùndònghuì.**
He represented his country in the sports meet. □ "你
去过几个国家?" "**Nǐ qùguo jǐ ge guójiā?**" *"How many
countries have you been to?"*

NOTE: It is significant that the Chinese word meaning *country*—国家 **guójiā**—is composed of the word 国 **guó** (country) and the word 家 **jiā** (family). In traditional Chinese thought, China was one big family and the country was ruled as such, with the emperor as the patriarch.

国库 **guókù** [modif: 国 country + 库 warehouse] *n* national treasury

国民 **guómín** *n* national (of a country)

国民党 **Guómíndǎng** *n* the Kuomintang (KMT, the political party which ruled China before 1949 and is now a major party in Taiwan.)

国旗 **guóqí** *n* national flag (面 **miàn**)

国情 **guóqíng** [modif: 国 country + 情 conditions] *n* the conditions of a country

国庆节 **guóqìngjié** [modif: 国 nation + 庆 celebration + 节 festival] *n* National Day (October 1st in the People's Republic of China)

国王 **guówáng** [modif: 国 the country + 王 king] *n* king, monarch

国务卿 **guówùqīng** *n* (the U.S.) Secretary of State

国务院 **guówùyuàn** [modif: 国 the state + 务 affairs + 院 institution] *n* (Chinese) State Council, (the U.S.) State Department

国务院总理 **Guówùyuàn Zǒnglǐ** *n* (Chinese) Premier

国营 **guóyíng** [modif: 国 the state + 营 operate] *adj* state-operated

国有 **guóyǒu** [modif: 国 the state + 有 own] *adj* state-owned

果 **guǒ** *n* fruit

果断 **guǒduàn** *adj* resolute
采取果断措施 **cǎiqǔ guǒduàn cuòshī** take decisive measures

果然 **guǒrán** *adv* sure enough, as expected

果实 **guǒshí** *n* fruit

果树 **guǒshù** [modif: 果 fruit + 树 tree] *n* fruit tree (棵 **kē**)

果园 **guǒyuán** [modif: 果 fruit + 园 garden] *n* orchard (座 **zuò**)

过 **guò** Trad 過 *v* 1 pass, cross □ 过马路, 一定要小心。**Guò mǎlù, yídìng yào xiǎoxīn.** *You must be very careful when crossing the street.*

过来 **guòlai** come over, come across (towards the speaker) □ 他正从马路那边过来。**Tā zhèng cóng mǎlù nàbian guòlai.** *He's coming over from the other side of the street.* □ 公共汽车开过来了。**Gōnggòng qìchē kāi guòlai le.** *A bus is coming over.*

过去 **guòqu** go over, go across (away from the speaker) □ 街上车太多, 很难过去。**Jiē shang chē tài duō, hěn nán guòqu.** *Traffic in the street is too heavy. It's very difficult to go across.* □ 河水很急, 我游不过去。**Héshuǐ hěn jí, wǒ yóu bù guòqu.** *The river runs swiftly. I can't swim across it.*

2 spend (time), live (a life), observe (a festival) □ 他在国外过了这么多年, 生活习惯有些改变了。**Tā zài guówài guòle zhème duō nián, shēnghuó xíguàn yǒu xiē gǎibiàn le.** *He has spent so many years overseas that some of his habits have changed.* □ 从此以后, 他们俩过得很幸福。**Cóngcǐ yǐhòu, tāmen liǎ guò de hěn xìngfú.** *They lived happily ever after.*

过日子 **guò rìzi** live a life

过年 **guò nián** observe New Year's Day

过节 **guò jié** observe a festival

过程 **guòchéng** *n* process, course □ 从葡萄变成酒, 是一个又长又复杂的过程。**Cóng pútao biànchéng jiǔ, shì yí ge yòu cháng yòu fùzá de guòchéng.** *The process by which grapes become wine is a long and complicated one.*

过度 **guòdù** *adj* excessive, over-
饮酒过度 **yǐnjiǔ guò dù** drink excessively

过渡 **guòdù** [comp: 过 cross + 渡 ferry] *n* transition

过分 **guòfèn** [v+obj: 过 pass + 分 limit] *adj* excessive, going overboard
过分的要求 **guòfèn de yāoqiú** excessive demands

过后 **guòhòu** *adv* afterwards, later

过劳死 **guòláosǐ** *n* death from overwork

过滤 **guòlǜ** *v* filter

过去 **guòqù** [comp: 过 pass + 去 gone] *n* (something) in the past □ 过去的事, 不要多想了。**Guòqù de shì, bú yào duō xiǎng le.** *Don't keep thinking about what's past. (→ Let bygones be bygones.)* □ 他过去常常生病, 现在身体好多了。**Tā guòqù chángcháng shēngbìng, xiànzài shēntǐ hǎo duō le.** *He was often sick in the past. Now he is in much better health.*

过失 **guòshī** *n* fault, error

过问 **guòwèn** *v* take an interest in, concern oneself with

过于 **guòyú** *adv* too, excessively

过 **guo** Trad 過 *particle* (used after a verb or an adjective to emphasize a past experience) □ "你去过中国没有?" "去过, 我去过中国很多地方。" **"Nǐ qùguo Zhōngguó méiyǒu?" "Qùguo, wǒ qùguo Zhōngguó hěn duō dìfang."** *"Have you been to China?" "Yes, I've been to many parts of China."*

H

哈 **hā** *onomatopoeia* (sound of loud laughter)

哈哈 **hāhā** *onomatopoeia* (representing loud laughter) □ 听了孩子天真的话, 老人哈哈大笑起来。**Tīngle háizi tiānzhēn de huà, lǎorén hāhā dàxiào qǐlai.** *Hearing the child's naïve words, the old man burst into laughter.*

哈欠 **hāqian** *v* yawn
打哈欠 **dǎhāqian** give a yawn

还 **hái** Trad 還 *adv* still, as before □ 时间还早, 我还想看一会儿书再睡。**Shíjiān hái zǎo, wǒ xiǎng kàn yíhuìr shū zài shuì.** *It's still early. I want to do a little reading before going to bed.* □ 已经上午十点钟了, 我还没有吃早饭呢。**Yǐjīng shàngwǔ shí diǎnzhōng le, wǒ hái méiyǒu chī zǎofàn ne.** *It's already ten o'clock, and I still haven't had my breakfast.*

还是 **háishi** I *adv* still, as before □ 老师说了两遍, 我还是不大懂。**Lǎoshī shuōle liǎng biàn, wǒ háishi bú dà dǒng.** *The teacher has explained twice, but I still don't quite understand.* II *conj* or □ 你喝茶还是喝咖啡? **Nǐ hē chá háishi hē kāfēi?** *Would you like tea or coffee?* □ 我们今天去看电影还是明天去? **Wǒmen jīntiān qù kàn diànyǐng háishi míngtiān qù?** *Shall we go and see the movie today or tomorrow?*

孩 hái *n* child, children
孩子 háizi child, children □ 这个孩子真聪明! **Zhège háizi zhēn cōngmíng!** *This child is really smart!* (→ *What a bright child!*) □ 他们有一个男孩子, 两个女孩子。 **Tāmen yǒu yí ge nánháizi, liǎng ge nǚháizi.** *They have a son and two daughters.*

海 hǎi *n* sea □ 没有风, 海很平静。 **Méiyǒu fēng, hǎi hěn píngjìng.** *There's no wind. The sea is calm.* □ 这个国家任何地方都离海很近。 **Zhège guójiā rènhé dìfang dōu lí hǎi hěn jìn.** *Anywhere in this country is close to the sea.* □ 海水冷吗? 可以游泳吗? **Hǎi shuǐ lěng ma? Kěyǐ yóuyǒng ma?** *Is the seawater cold? Can we swim?*

海岸 hǎi'àn [modif: 海 sea + 岸 bank] *n* seashore, sea coast
海岸线 hǎi'ànxiàn coastline
海拔 hǎibá *n* height above sea level, elevation
海拔一百米 hǎibá yìbái mǐ 100 meters from sea level
海报 hǎibào *n* playbill, poster
贴海报 tiē hǎibào put up a poster
海滨 hǎibīn *n* seaside
海带 hǎidài [modif: 海 sea + 带 ribbon] *n* seaweed, kelp
海港 hǎigǎng [modif: 海 sea + 港 port] *n* seaport (座 zuò)
海关 hǎiguān [modif: 海 sea + 关 pass] *n* customs, customs house □ 通过海关的时候, 要检查护照。 **Tōngguò hǎiguān de shíhou, yào jiǎnchá hùzhào.** *Your passport will be examined when you pass through customs.*
海关检查 hǎiguān jiǎnchá customs inspection, customs examination
海关手续 hǎiguān shǒuxù customs formalities
海关人员 hǎiguān rényuán customs officer
海军 hǎijūn [modif: 海 sea, ocean + 军 troops] *n* navy
海面 hǎimiàn *n* sea/ocean surface
海鸥 hǎi'ōu *n* seagull (只 zhī)
海外 hǎiwài *adj* overseas
海外华侨 hǎiwài Huáqiáo overseas Chinese
海峡 hǎixiá [modif: 海 sea + 峡 gorge] *n* straits, channel
台湾海峡 Táiwān hǎixiá Taiwan Straits
海鲜 hǎixiān *n* seafood
海鲜馆 hǎixiān guǎn seafood restaurant
海啸 hǎixiào *n* tsunami
海洋 hǎiyáng [comp: 海 sea + 洋 ocean] *n* seas, ocean □ 地球表面十分之七是海洋。 **Dìqiú biǎomiàn shí fēnzhī qī shì hǎiyáng.** *Seven-tenths of the Earth's surface is covered by seas and oceans.*
海洋生物 hǎiyáng shēngwù marine creatures
海员 hǎiyuán *n* seaman, sailor
海运 hǎiyùn [modif: 海 sea + 运 transport] *n* sea transportation, ocean shipping
海蜇 hǎizhé *n* jellyfish

害 hài **I** *v* harm, cause harm to □ 吸烟不但害自己, 而且害别人。 **Xīyān búdàn hài zìjǐ, érqiě hài biérén.** *Smoking not only harms the smoker, it harms others too.* **II** *n* harm
有害 yǒuhài harmful □ 吸烟有害健康。 **Xīyān yǒuhài jiànkāng.** *Smoking is harmful to health.*

害虫 hàichóng [modif: 害 harmful + 虫 insect] *n* pest (insect)
害处 hàichu [modif: 害 harmful + 处 place] *n* harm (antonym 好处 hǎochu) □ 大家都知道吸烟的害处。 **Dàjiā dōu zhīdào xīyān de hàichu.** *Everybody knows the harm that smoking causes.* □ 对孩子严格一点, 只有好处, 没有害处。 **Duì háizi yángé yìdiǎn, zhǐyǒu hǎochu, méiyǒu hàichu.** *To be strict with children has only benefits, and will cause no harm.*
害怕 hàipà *v* fear, be fearful □ 她夜里一个人走回家, 心里有点害怕。 **Tā yèli yí ge rén zǒu huí jiā, xīnli yǒudiǎn hàipà.** *She was fearful of walking home alone at night.*
害羞 hàixiū *adj* be bashful, be shy

含 hán *v* **1** hold in the mouth □ 孩子嘴里含着一块糖, 说不清话。 **Háizi zuǐ li hánzhe yí kuài táng, shuō bu qīng huà.** *The child had a piece of candy in his (or her) mouth and couldn't speak clearly.* **2** contain, have … as ingredient
含糊 hánhu *adj* vague, ambiguous
含量 hánliàng [modif: 含 contain + 量 quantity] *n* amount of ingredient, content
含义 hányì *n* implied meaning, meaning

寒 hán *adj* cold
寒带 hándài [modif: 寒 cold + 带 band] *n* frigid zone
寒假 hánjià [modif: 寒 cold + 假 holiday] *n* winter vacation □ 中国的学校一般在一月开始放寒假。 **Zhōngguó de xuéxiào yìbān zài Yīyuè kāishǐ fàng hánjià.** *In China, schools generally begin their winter holidays in January.*
寒冷 hánlěng [comp: 寒 freezing + 冷 cold] *adj* freezing cold, frigid □ 世界上最寒冷的地方在南极。 **Shìjiè shang zuì hánlěng de dìfang zài Nánjí.** *The coldest place on earth is in the Antarctic.* □ 加拿大北部天气寒冷, 一年中有半年多下雪。 **Jiānádà běibù tiānqì hánlěng, yì nián zhōng yǒu bànnián duō xià xuě.** *North Canada is very cold; it snows over six months in a year.*
寒流 hánliú [modif: 寒 cold + 流 current] *n* cold current
寒暄 hánxuān *v* exchange greetings (at the beginning of a meeting)

函 hán *n* letter
公函 gōnghán official letter
函授 hánshòu *v* teach by correspondence
函授学校 hánshòu xuéxiào correspondence school

喊 hǎn *v* shout □ 有人在外面喊你。 **Yǒu rén zài wàimiàn hǎn nǐ.** *Someone is calling for you outside.*
喊叫 hǎnjiào [comp: 喊 shout + 叫 call] *v* cry out, shout

罕 hǎn *adv* rarely, seldom
罕见 hǎnjiàn [modif: 罕 seldom + 见 seen] *adj* rare

汗 hàn *n* sweat, perspiration
出汗 chūhàn to sweat, to perspire □ 这个房间热得我出汗。 **Zhège fángjiān rè de wǒ chūhàn.** *The room was so hot that I perspired.*

汉 Hàn Trad 漢 *n* the Han people (the main ethnic group among the Chinese)
汉奸 hànjiān [modif: 汉 Han Chinese + 奸 traitor] *n* traitor (to China), Chinese collaborator (with a foreign country)

汉人 **Hànrén** *n* a Han Chinese, Han Chinese people

汉学 **Hànxué** [modif: 汉 Chinese + 学 studies] *n* Sinology
汉学家 **Hànxuéjiā** sinologist

汉语 **Hànyǔ** [modif: 汉 the Han people + 语 speech] *n* the language of the Han people, the Chinese language □ 你学了几年汉语了? **Nǐ xuéle jǐ nián Hànyǔ le?** *How many years have you been learning Chinese?* □ 我会说一点汉语。**Wǒ huì shuō yìdiǎn Hànyǔ.** *I speak a little Chinese.*

NOTE: In Chinese there are a number of words denoting "the Chinese language." 汉语 **Hànyǔ** literally means *the language of the Han Chinese people*, in contrast with the languages of the non-Han peoples in China. 汉语 **Hànyǔ** is therefore the accurate, scientific term for the language. However, the most popular term for the Chinese language is 中文 **Zhōngwén**. In Singapore and other Southeast Asian countries, the standard Chinese language is often referred to as 华语 **Huáyǔ** in contrast to the various Chinese dialects spoken there. Also see note on 普通话 **Pǔtōnghuà**.

汉字 **Hànzì** [modif: 汉 the Han people + 字 word, character] *n* Chinese character, sinogram □ 这个汉字我不认识。**Zhège Hànzì wǒ bú rènshi.** *I don't know this Chinese character.* □ 你会写多少汉字? **Nǐ huì xiě duōshǎo Hànzì?** *How many Chinese characters can you write?*
常用汉字 **chángyòng Hànzì** frequently used Chinese characters, common Chinese characters

汉族 **Hànzú** [modif: 汉 Han + 族 race] *n* the Han nationality, Han Chinese people

旱 **hàn** *adj* (of climate) dry
旱冰场 **hànbīngchǎng** *n* roller-skating rink

旱灾 **hànzāi** [modif: 旱 dry + 灾 calamity] *n* drought

焊 **hàn** *v* weld
电焊工 **diànhàngōng** welder

捍 **hàn** *v* defend, guard
捍卫 **hànwèi** [modif: 捍 defend + 卫 defend] *v* defend, protect
捍卫公司的利益 **hànwèi gōngsī de lìyì** defend the interests of a company

憾 **hàn** *n* regret (See 遗憾 **yíhàn**)

行 **háng** I *measure wd* line, row, queue (used with nouns that are formed in lines)
第四页第二行 **dì-sì yè dì-èr háng** line two on page 4
十四行诗 **shísì háng shī** sonnet
II *n* profession, trade
行情 **hángqíng** *n* price quotations □ 黄金的行情看涨。**Huángjīn de hángqíng kànzhǎng.** *The price for gold is expected to rise.*
行业 **hángyè** [comp: 行 line, occupation + 业 industry] *n* trade and profession, industry
各行各业 **gè-háng-gè-yè** every trade and profession

航 **háng** *v* navigate
航班 **hángbān** *n* flight, flight number
105 航班 **yāo-líng-wǔ hángbān** Flight No 105
飞往广州的航班 **fēiwǎng Guǎngzhōu de hángbān** the flight to Guangzhou

航道 **hángdào** *n* waterway, channel
航海 **hánghǎi** *n* (ocean) navigation
航海家 **hánghǎijiā** (great) navigator
航空 **hángkōng** *n* aviation
航空公司 **hángkōng gōngsī** aviation company, airline
航空信 **hángkōngxìn** airmail letter
航空学校 **hángkōng xuéxiào** aviation school
航天 **hángtiān** *n* spaceflight
航天飞机 **hángtiān fēijī** space shuttle, spaceship
航线 **hángxiàn** *n* ocean or air route
航行 **hángxíng** *v* (of a ship) sail, (of an aircraft) fly
航运 **hángyùn** *n* shipping
航运公司 **hángyùn gōngsī** shipping company

豪 **háo** *adj* bold and unrestrained
豪华 **háohuá** [comp: 豪 bold and unrestrained + 华 brilliant] *adj* luxurious, sumptuous

毫 **háo** *n* fine long hair
毫不 **háo bù** *adv* not in the least, not at all □ 他读书不用功, 考试成绩不好毫不奇怪。**Tā dúshū bú yònggōng, kǎoshì chéngjì bù hǎo háo bù qíguài.** *He didn't study hard, so it's no wonder he got very poor grades at the exams.*

NOTE: 毫不 **háo bù** is an adverb used before an adjective of two or more syllables. For example, you can say 毫不奇怪 **háo bù qíguài** *not at all strange*, but you cannot say 毫不怪 **háo bú guài**.

毫米 **háomǐ** *n* millimeter
毫无 **háo wú** *v* have no … at all, be in total absence of □ 他心很硬, 对不幸的人毫无同情心。**Tā xīn hěn yìng, duì búxìng de rén háo wú tóngqíngxīn.** *He is hardhearted, and has no sympathy at all for less fortunate people.*

NOTE: The object of 毫无 **háo wú** usually takes a word of two or more syllables, and usually refers to something abstract, like 同情心 **tóngqíngxīn** *sympathy*.

好 1 **hǎo** *adj* good, all right (antonym 坏 **huài**, 差 **chà**) □ 他总是愿意帮助学生, 他是个好老师。**Tā zǒngshì yuànyì bāngzhù xuésheng, tā shì ge hǎo lǎoshī.** *He is always ready to help his students. He is a good teacher.* □ 我爸爸身体很好。**Wǒ bàba shēntǐ hěn hǎo.** *My father is in good health.* □ 你中文说得很好。**Nǐ Zhōngwén shuō de hěn hǎo.** *You speak Chinese very well.*
好比 **hǎobǐ** *v* may be compared as, be like, same as
好吃 **hǎochī** *adj* delicious (antonym 难吃 **nánchī**) □ 这种水果我没有尝试, 好吃不好吃? **Zhè zhǒng shuǐguǒ wǒ méiyǒu chángguo, hǎochī bu hǎochī?** *I've never tried this fruit before, is it good?* □ 王太太做的这个菜, 好吃极了! **Wáng tàitai zuò de zhège cài, hǎochī jíle!** *This dish cooked by Mrs Wang is really delicious*
好处 **hǎochu** *n* benefit, advantage (antonyms 坏处 **huàichu**, 害处 **hàichu**) □ 经常锻炼对身体有很多好处。**Jīngcháng duànliàn duì shēntǐ yǒu hěnduō hǎochu.** *Regular physical exercise is very beneficial to health.* □ 你惹爸爸生气, 有什么好处呢? **Nǐ rě bàba shēngqì, yǒu shénme hǎochu ne?** *What is the good of offending daddy?*

对…有好处 duì…yǒu hǎochu be beneficial to

好感 hǎogǎn [modif: 好 good + 感 feeling] *n* favorable impression, fondness (for somebody)

对他有好感 duì tā yǒu hǎogǎn be fond of him, have a soft spot for him

好汉 hǎohàn [modif: 好 good + 汉 man, guy] *n* brave man, hero □ 不到长城非好汉。**Búdào Chángchéng fēi hǎohàn.** *You're not a hero until you've been to the Great Wall.*

好好儿 hǎohǎor *adj* normal, nothing wrong □ 她昨天还好好儿的, 今天怎么病了呢? **Tā zuótiān hái hǎohǎor de, jīntiān zēnme bìng le ne?** *She was quite well yesterday. How come she should fall ill today?*

好坏 hǎohuài [comp: 好 good + 坏 bad] *n* what is good and what is bad (for somebody)

不知好坏 bùzhī hǎohuài don't know what is good and what is bad for oneself, be insensible

好久 hǎojiǔ *adv* a long time □ 我好久没玩得这么痛快了。**Wǒ hǎojiǔ méi wán de zhème tòngkuai le.** *I haven't had such fun for a long time.* □ 他等了她好久, 她才来。**Tā dēngle tā hǎojiǔ, tā cái lái.** *He waited for her for a long time before she came.*

好看 hǎokàn *adj* 1 pleasant to the eye, good-looking, pretty (antonym 难看 nánkàn) □ 她妈妈年轻的时候很好看。**Tā māma niánqīng de shíhou hěn hǎokàn.** *Her mother was beautiful when young.* **2** interesting, absorbing □ 这本小说好看不好看? **Zhè běn xiǎoshuō hǎokàn bu hǎokàn?** *Is this novel interesting?*

好容易 hǎo róngyì *adv* with great difficulty □ 我好容易找到他家, 他偏不在。**Wǒ hǎo róngyì zhǎodào tā jiā, tā piān bú zài.** *I found his home with great difficulty, and he had to be out.*

NOTE: 好容易 **hǎo róngyì** is an idiomatic expression. You can also say 好不容易 **hǎo bù róngyì**, with exactly the same meaning, e.g. □ 我好不容易找到他家, 他偏不在。**Wǒ hǎo bù róngyì zhǎodào tā jiā, tā piān bú zài.** *I found his home with great difficulty, and he had to be out.*

好听 hǎotīng *adj* pleasant to the ear, melodious (antonym 难听 nántīng) □ 这首歌真好听, 我越听越想听。**Zhè shǒu gē zhēn hǎotīng, wǒ yuè tīng yuè xiǎng tīng.** *This song is beautiful. The more I listen, the more I want to hear it.* □ 他说话的声音很好听。**Tā shuōhuà de shēngyīn hěn hǎotīng.** *The voice he speaks in is pleasant.* (→ *He has a pleasant voice.*)

好玩儿 hǎowánr *adj* great fun □ 这个游戏很好玩儿。**Zhège yóuxì hěn hǎowánr.** *This game is great fun.*

好像 hǎoxiàng *v* be like, similar to □ 天边的白云好像一座雪山。**Tiānbiān de bái yún hǎoxiàng yí zuò xuěshān.** *The white cloud on the horizon looks like a snow mountain.* □ 他今天好像不大高兴, 你知道为什么吗? **Tā jīntiān hǎoxiàng bú dà gāoxìng, nǐ zhīdào wèishénme ma?** *He looks unhappy today. Do you know why?* □ 你好像对这个地方很熟悉。**Nǐ hǎoxiàng duì zhège dìfang hěn shúxi.** *You seem to be familiar with this place.*

好心 hǎoxīn *adj* kindhearted □ 她是个好心人。**Tā shì ge hǎoxīn rén.** *She is a kindhearted person.*

好在 hǎozài *adv* fortunately, luckily

好转 hǎozhuǎn *v* take a turn for the better, improve

好 2 hǎo *adv* **1** very, very much **2** How…!□ 你这件新衣服好漂亮! **Nǐ zhè jiàn xīn yīfu hǎo piàoliang!** *How pretty your new dress is!*

好多 hǎo duō *adj* a good many, many, much □ 我生日那天, 好多朋友都送给我贺卡和礼物。**Wǒ shēngrì nà tiān, hǎo duō péngyou dōu sòng gei wǒ hèkǎ hé lǐwù.** *Many friends gave me greeting cards and gifts on my birthday.*

好些 hǎoxiē *adj* a good many, a large number of, lots of □ 我有好些日子没见到他了。**Wǒ yǒu hǎoxiē rìzi méi jiàndao tā le.** *I haven't seen him for a long time.*

NOTE: 好些 **hǎoxiē** is a colloquial word, only used in casual, familiar styles.

好 hào *v* be fond of

好吃 hào chī [v+obj: 好 be fond of + 吃 eating] *adj* fond of eating, gluttonous

好动 hào dòng [v+obj: 好 be fond of, like + 动 movement] *adj* hyperactive

好客 hàokè [v+obj: 好 be fond of + 客 guest] *adj* hospitable

热情好客 rèqíng hàokè warm and hospitable

好奇 hào qí *adj* be curious, inquisitive □ 这个孩子对什么都好奇。**Zhège háizi duì shénme dōu hàoqí.** *This child is curious about everything.*

好色 hào sè [v+obj: 好 be fond of, like + 色 sex] *adj* oversexed, lewd

好学 hào xué [v+obj: 好 be fond of + 学 study] *adj* fond of learning, thirsty for knowledge □ 这个学生虚心好学, 进步很快。**Zhège xuésheng xūxīn hào xué, jìnbù hěn kuài.** *This student is modest and fond of learning. He is making rapid progress.*

耗 hào *v* consume

耗费 hàofèi [comp: 耗 consume + 费 cost] *v* consume (especially in a wasteful way), cost (a large amount of money, time, etc.)

号 hào Trad 號 *n* **1** order of sequence □ 小王住在三号楼五号房间。**Xiǎo Wáng zhù zài sān hào lóu, wǔ hào fángjiān.** *Xiao Wang lives in Building 3, Room 5.* **2** date of month □ 今天几号? **Jīntiān jǐ hào?** □ 今天二十号, 九月二十号。**Jīntiān èrshí hào, Jiǔyuè èrshí hào.** *"What is the date today?" "It's the 20th, September 20th."*

NOTE: See note on 日 **rì**.

号称 hàochēng *v* be known as (something great), claim to be

号码 hàomǎ [comp: 号 order of sequence + 码 size] *n* serial number, size □ 你知道张先生的电话号码吗? **Nǐ zhīdào Zhāng xiānsheng de diànhuà hàomǎ ma?** *Do you know Mr Zhang's telephone number?* □ "你穿多大号码的衬衫?" "我穿四十码。" **"Nǐ chuān duō dà hàomǎ de chènshān?" "Wǒ chuān sìshí mǎ."** *"What size shirt do you wear?" "Size 40."* □ 这双鞋小了一点, 有没有大一号码的? **Zhè shuāng xié xiǎo le yìdiǎn, yǒu méiyǒu dà yī hàomǎ de?** *This pair of shoes is a bit too small. Do you have a bigger size?*

号召 hàozhào *v* call upon, appeal □ 中国政府号召一对夫妻只生一个孩子。**Zhōngguó zhèngfǔ hàozhào yí**

duì fūqī zhǐ shēng yí ge háizi. *The Chinese government appeals to each couple to have only one child.*

浩 **hào** *adj* vast, numerous

浩大 **hàodà** [comp: 浩 vast + 大 big] *adj* huge, gigantic
浩大的工程 **hàodà de gōngchéng** a huge engineering project

呵 **hē** *v* blow a puff of breath, exhale through the mouth

喝 **hē** *v* drink □ 我口渴, 我想喝点水。 **Wǒ kǒu kě, wǒ xiǎng hē diǎn shuǐ.** *I'm thirsty. I'd like to drink some water.* □ 中国人一般先吃饭后喝汤, 或者边吃饭边喝汤。 **Zhōngguórén yìbān xiān chī fàn hòu hē tāng, huòzhě biān chī fàn biān hē tāng.** *The Chinese usually have the main course before soup, or have the main course and soup at the same time.*

NOTE: 喝 **hē** (drink) and 渴 **kě** (thirsty) look similar. Be careful not to confuse the two characters.

合 **hé** *v* 1 close □ 他太累了, 一合上眼就睡着了。 **Tā tài lèi le, yì hé shang yǎn jiù shuìzháo le.** *He was so tired that he fell asleep the moment he closed his eyes.* 2 co-operate, do in partnership
合办企业 **hébàn qǐyè** run an enterprise in partnership 3 conform with
不合我的口味 **bùhé wǒde kǒuwèi** not to my taste 4 be equal to
合法 **héfǎ** [v+obj: 合 conform to + 法 the law] *adj* legal, legitimate □ 他是个有妇之夫, 和另一个女人同居是不合法的。 **Tā shì ge yǒu fù zhī fū, hé lìng yī ge nǚrén tóngjū shì bùhé fǎ de.** *He is a married man, and it is not legal for him to live with another woman.*
合格 **hégé** [v+obj: 合 conform to + 格 standard] *adj* qualified, up to standard
合乎 **héhū** *v* conform with, correspond to
合乎惯例 **héhū guànlì** conform with normal practice
合伙 **héhuǒ** *v* form a partnership, work in a partnership
和老同学合伙开公司 **hé lǎo tóngxué héhuǒ kāi gōngsī** set up a company in partnership with an old classmate
合金 **héjīn** *n* alloy
合理 **hélǐ** [v+obj: 合 conform + 理 reason] *adj* conforming to reason, reasonable, logical □ 你这个建议十分合理。 **Nǐ zhège jiànyì shífēn hélǐ.** *Your proposal is very reasonable.* □ 对于你们的合理要求, 我们会尽力满足。 **Duìyú nǐmen de hélǐ yāoqiú, wǒmen huì jìnlì mǎnzú.** *We will do our best to meet your reasonable demands.*
合适 **héshì** [comp: 合 harmony + 适 fit] *adj* suitable, appropriate □ 他做这个工作非常合适。 **Tā zuò zhège gōngzuò fēicháng héshì.** *He is very suitable for this job.* □ 他比你年纪大, 你叫他小张不合适。 **Tā bǐ nǐ niánjì dà, nǐ jiào tā Xiǎo Zhāng bù héshì.** *He is older than you. It's inappropriate for you to call him "Little Zhang."* □ 这个工作对他不合适。 **Zhège gōngzuò duì tā bù héshì.** *This job is not right for him.*
合算 **hésuàn** *adj* worthwhile paying □ 这笔生意做得不合算。 **Zhè bǐ shēngyì zuò de bù hésuàn.** *This business deal didn't pay.*
合同 **hétóng** *n* contract, agreement (份 **fèn**) □ 我们公

司已经和市政府签订合同, 在新区建一座小学。 **Wǒmen gōngsī yǐjīng hé shì zhèngfǔ qiāndìng hétóng, zài xīn qū jiàn yí zuò xiǎoxué.** *Our company has signed a contract with the city government to build a primary school in the new district.*
合资 **hézī** *v* pool capital to run a business
合资企业 **hézī qǐyè** joint venture
合作 **hézuò** [modif: 合 jointly + 作 operate] I *v* co-operate, work together □ 我们非常高兴和你们合作。 **Wǒmen fēicháng gāoxìng hé nǐmen hézuò.** *We're very happy to cooperate with you.* □ 两国正在合作研究开发新能源。 **Liǎng guó zhèngzài hézuò yánjiū kāifā xīn néngyuán.** *The two countries are cooperating in the development of new energy sources.* II *n* cooperation □ 我们应该加强合作。 **Wǒmen yīnggāi jiāqiáng hézuò.** *We should enhance our cooperation.* □ 王董事长对我们两家公司之间的合作十分满意。 **Wáng dǒngshìzhǎng duì wǒmen liǎng jiā gōngsī zhī jiān de hézuò shífēn mǎnyì.** *Chairman Wang is very pleased with the co-operation between our two companies.*

盒 **hé** *n* box □ 她的铅笔盒子里有四支铅笔。 **Tāde qiānbǐ hézi li yǒu sì zhī qiānbǐ.** *There are four pencils in her pencil box.*
盒子 **hézi** box (只 **zhī**)

何 **hé** *pron* which, what
何等 **héděng** I *adj* what kind II *adv* how, what
何况 **hékuàng** *conj* 1 what's more, moreover 2 let alone

荷 **hé** *n* lotus
荷花 **héhuā** lotus flower

河 **hé** *n* river (条 **tiáo**) □ 这条河太宽, 我游不过去。 **Zhè tiáo hé tài kuān, wǒ yóu bu guòqu.** *This river is too broad. I can't swim across it.*

NOTE: In modern Chinese, 江 **jiāng** and 河 **hé** both mean *river*. Usually (not always) rivers in the south are known as 江 **jiāng** and rivers in the north are 河 **hé**.

河道 **hédào** *n* river course
河流 **héliú** *n* rivers
阂 **hé** *v* hinder, obstruct

禾 **hé** *n* seedling, (especially) rice seedling
禾苗 **hémiáo** *n* seedling (of cereal crops)

和 **hé** I *conj* and □ 我和你都在学中文。 **Wǒ hé nǐ dōu zài xué Zhōngwén.** *You and I are both learning Chinese.* II *prep* with
和⋯⋯一起 **hé...yìqǐ** together with... □ 昨天我和朋友一起吃中饭。 **Zuótiān wǒ hé péngyou yìqǐ chī zhōngfàn.** *Yesterday I had lunch with a friend of mine.* □ 我想和你谈谈。 **Wǒ xiǎng hé nǐ tántan.** *I'd like to have a word with you.*

核 **hé** *n* kernel, core, pit
核电站 **hédiànzhàn** *n* nuclear power plant
核桃 **hétao** *n* walnut (颗 **kē**)
核武器 **héwǔqì** *n* nuclear weapon
核心 **héxīn** [comp: 核 core + 心 the heart] *n* core, kernel

贺 **hè** Trad 賀 *v* congratulate
贺词 **hècí** *n* speech of congratulations
贺卡 **hèkǎ** [modif: 贺 greeting + 卡 card] *n* greeting card (张 **zhāng**) □ 去年圣诞节你收到多少贺卡? **Qùnián**

shèngdànjié nǐ shōudao duōshǎo hèkǎ? *How many cards did you get last Christmas?* □ 明天是小王生日，我们送他一张生日贺卡吧。 **Míngtiān shì Xiǎo Wáng shēngrì, wǒmen sòng tā yì zhāng hèkǎ ba.** *Tomorrow is Xiao Wang's birthday. Let's give him a card.*

赫 **hè** *adj* conspicuous, grand
  显赫 xiǎnhè distinguished and influential, illustrious

赫赫 **hèhè** *adj* illustrious, impressive
  赫赫有名 hèhè yǒumíng very famous, illustrious

黑 **hēi** *adj* black, dark □ 我不喜欢穿黑颜色的衣服。 **Wǒ bù xǐhuan chuān hēi yánsè de yīfu.** *I don't like to wear black.* □ 天快黑了，他们还在踢球。 **Tiān kuài hēi le, tāmen hái zài tīqiú.** *It's almost dark, but they're still playing soccer.*

黑暗 **hēi'àn** [comp: 黑 black, dark + 暗 dim] *adj* dark (antonym 光明 **guāngmíng**) □ 他很天真，不知道社会的黑暗面。 **Tā hěn tiānzhēn, bù zhīdào shèhuì de hēi'àn miàn.** *He is naïve, and is unaware of the seamy side of society.*

黑板 **hēibǎn** *n* blackboard □ 我们现在不用黑板，用白板。 **Wǒmen xiànzài bú yòng hēibǎn, yòng báibǎn.** *Now we don't use the blackboard; we use the whiteboard.*

黑夜 **hēiyè** *n* night
  白天黑夜 báitiān hēiyè day and night

嘿 **hēi** *interj* 1 (used to attract someone's attention in a casual or impolite manner) □ 嘿，这里不准吸烟。 **Hēi, zhèli bùzhǔn xīyān.** *Hey! You can't smoke here.* 2 (used to indicate admiration) □ 嘿，昨天的球赛咱们队打得真棒! **Hēi, zuótiān de qiúsài zánmen duì dǎ de zhēn bàng!** *Hey, our team played marvelously in yesterday's match!*

痕 **hén** *n* trace
  伤痕 shānghén scar

痕迹 **hénjì** [comp: 痕 trace + 迹 footprint] *n* trace, mark, stain

狠 **hěn** *adj* 1 cruel, relentless
  心毒手狠 xīndú shǒuhěn with a vicious mind and cruel means
2 severe, stern
  狠狠地批评 hěnhěnde pīpíng criticize severely

狠毒 **hěndú** [comp: 狠 cruel + 毒 poisonous] *adj* cruel and vicious

狠心 **hěnxīn** I *adj* ruthless 2 *v* make a painful decision
  下狠心 xià hěnxīn make a tough decision resolutely

很 **hěn** *adv* very, quite □ 见到你，我很高兴。 **Jiàndào nǐ, wǒ hěn gāoxìng.** *I'm glad to meet you.* □ 我很讨厌下雨天。 **Wǒ hěn tǎoyàn xià yǔ tiān.** *I hate rainy days.*

NOTE: When used as predicates, Chinese adjectives normally require an adverb. For example, 我高兴 **Wǒ gāoxìng** sounds unnatural, while 我很高兴 **Wǒ hěn gāoxìng** (I'm [very] happy), 我不高兴 **Wǒ bù gāoxìng** (I'm not happy) or 我非常高兴 **Wǒ fēicháng gāoxìng** (I'm very happy) are normal sentences. The adverb 很 **hěn** is often used as a default adverb before an adjective. In such cases the meaning of 很 **hěn** is very weak.

恨 **hèn** *v* 1 hate, be angry with (antonym 爱 **ài**) □ 她恨男朋友欺骗了她。 **Tā hèn nánpéngyou qīpiàn**

le tā. *She hates her boyfriend for cheating on her.* 2 regret deeply □ 他恨自己念书不用功，但是太晚了。 **Tā hèn zìjǐ niànshū bú yònggōng, dànshì tài wǎn le.** *He deeply regrets not having studied hard, but it's too late.*

恨不得 **hènbude** *adv* how … wish to □ 他恨不得马上回家过年。 **Hā hènbude mǎshàng huíjiā guònián.** *How he wishes he could go home right now for the spring festival.*

NOTE: We use 恨不得 to express a wish that is very strong but cannot be fulfilled. If we say 他恨不得马上回家过年。 **Hā hènbude mǎshàng huíjiā guònián,** it means *it is quite impossible for him to go back home right now.*

哼 **hēng** *v* 1 snort □ 他哼了一声，翻过身去，又睡了。 **Tā hēngle yìshēng, fānguo shēn qù, yòu shuì le.** *He gave a snort, turned over and fell asleep again.* 2 hum □ 她一边做饭，一边哼着歌。 **Tā yìbiān zuòfàn, yìbiān hēngzhe gē.** *While she cooked, she hummed a song.*

衡 **héng** I *n* weighing instrument II *v* weigh, measure

衡量 **héngliáng** [comp: 衡 weigh + 量 measure] *v* judge, consider
  衡量利弊 héngliáng lìbì consider the pros and cons

恒 **héng** I *adj* permanent, forever II *n* perseverance

恒心 **héngxīn** *n* perseverance

恒星 **héngxīng** *n* star (颗 kē) □ 太阳是一颗恒星，地球是一颗行星。 **Tàiyáng shì yìkē héngxīng, dìqiú shì yìkē xíngxīng.** *While the sun is a star, the earth is a planet.*

横 **héng** *adj* 1 horizontal 2 violent, fierce
  横行 héngxíng *v* play the tyrant, run amok

轰 **hōng** Trad 轟 *v* rumble, explode

轰动 **hōngdòng** [comp: 轰 rumble + 动 move] *v* cause a sensation

轰炸 **hōngzhà** *v* bomb
  轰炸机 hōngzhàjī bomber

烘 **hōng** *v* dry or warm by the fire, roast
  烘干机 hōnggānjī (clothes) dryer

红 **hóng** Trad 紅 *adj* 1 red □ 中国人传统上喜欢红颜色。 **Zhōngguórén chuántǒng shang xǐhuan hóng yánsè.** *Traditionally the Chinese love the color red.* □ 红花绿树，你的花园真好看。 **Hóng huā, lǜ shù, nǐ de huāyuán zhēn hǎokàn.** *With red flowers and green trees, your garden is really beautiful.* 2 popular, favored

红包 **hóngbāo** *n* a red envelope (containing money), bribe □ 在那里办事，要送红包。 **Zài nàli bànshì, yào sòng hóngbāo.** *To get things done there, bribes must be given.*
  收红包 shōu hóngbāo take bribes

红茶 **hóngchá** [modif: 红 red + 茶 tea] *n* black tea □ 中国人喝红茶，不放糖和牛奶。 **Zhōngguórén hē hóngchá, bú fàng táng hé niúnǎi.** *The Chinese don't put sugar or milk in their black tea.*

红绿灯 **hónglǜdēng** *n* traffic lights, stoplights

红人 **hóngrén** *n* a trusted and favored employee or member of an organization

红外线 **hóngwàixiàn** *n* infrared ray

红血球 **hóngxuèqiú** *n* red blood cell, erythrocyte

红眼病 **hóngyǎnbìng** *n* 1 conjunctivitis (eye disease) 2 envy, jealousy

虹 **hóng** *n* rainbow
彩虹 **cǎihóng** rainbow (道 **dào**)

宏 **hóng** *adj* grand, magnificent
宏大 **hóngdà** *adj* great, grand
宏观 **hóngguān** *adj* macroscopic
宏观经济学 **hóngguān jīngjìxué** macroeconomics
宏伟 **hóngwěi** *adj* magnificent, grand

洪 **hóng** *n* big
洪水 **hóngshuǐ** flood

哄 **hǒng** *v* 1 coax 2 cheat, hoodwink
哄骗 **hǒngpiàn** [comp: 哄 cheat + 骗 deceive] *v* lie in order to cheat

哄 **hòng** *n* horseplay
起哄 **qǐhòng** start a horseplay

喉 **hóu** *n* throat
喉咙 **hóulóng** *n* throat, larynx
喉咙疼 **hóulóng téng** have a sore throat

猴 **hóu** *n* monkey
猴子 **hóuzi** *n* monkey (只 **zhī**) □ 动物园里的猴子每天吸引很多小朋友。**Dòngwùyuán li de hóuzi měi tiān xīyǐn hén duō xiǎo péngyou.** *The monkeys in the zoo attract many children every day.*

吼 **hǒu** *v* roar, howl

后 **hòu** Trad 後 *n* back, rear (antonyms 前 **qián**, 先 **xiān**) □ 请用后门。**Qǐng yòng hòumén.** *Please use the back door.*
后边 **hòubian** [modif: 后 back, rear + 边 side] *n* back, rear, (antonym 前边 **qiánbian**) □ 我家的后边有一条小河。**Wǒ jiā de hòubian yǒu yì tiáo xiǎo hé.** *There is a stream behind our house.* □ 听课的时候我喜欢坐在前边, 不喜欢坐在后边。**Tīng kè de shíhou, wǒ xǐhuan zuò zài qiánbian, bù xǐhuan zuò zài hòubian.** *When attending lectures, I like to sit in the front row, not the back row.*
后代 **hòudài** [modif: 后 rear + 代 generation] *n* succeeding generations, posterity
后方 **hòufāng** *n* rear, behind (antonyms 前方 **qiánfāng**, 前线 **qiánxiàn**)
后果 **hòuguǒ** [modif: 后 later + 果 result] *n* consequences □ 你愿意承受这一行动的后果吗? **Nǐ yuànyì chéngshòu zhè yī xíngdòng de hòuguǒ ma?** *Are you willing to bear the consequences of this action?*
后悔 **hòuhuǐ** [modif: 后 afterwards + 悔 regret, repent] *v* regret, feel sorry (for having done something) □ 我真后悔, 没听爸爸的话。**Wǒ zhēn hòuhuǐ, méi tīng bàba de huà.** *I really regret not taking father's advice.* □ 你放弃这么好的机会, 以后会后悔的。**Nǐ fàngqì zhème hǎo de jīhuì, yǐhòu huì hòuhuǐ de.** *You'll regret giving up such a good opportunity.*
后来 **hòulái** [modif: 后 late + 来 come] *n* afterwards, later on □ 他刚到北京的时候, 不爱吃中国菜, 后来就慢慢习惯了。**Tā gāng dào Běijīng de shíhou, bú ài chī Zhōngguó cài, hòulái mànman xíguàn le.** *When he first came to Beijing he did not like Chinese food, but later on he gradually got used to it.*
后面 **hòumian** *n* Same as 后边 **hòubian**
后年 **hòunián** [modif: 后 late + 年 year] *n* the year after next □ 我今年十九岁, 后年就二十一岁了。**Wǒ jīnnián shíjiǔ suì, hòunián jiù èrshíyī suì le.** *I'm nineteen this year, and I'll be twenty-one the year after next.*

后期 **hòuqī** *n* later stage, later periods
后勤 **hòuqín** *n* logistics, support services
后台 **hòutái** *n* 1 backstage 2 behind-the-scenes supporter
后天 **hòutiān** [modif: 后 late + 天 day] *n* the day after tomorrow □ 今天刚星期三, 后天才星期五呢。**Jīntiān gāng Xīngqīsān, hòutiān cái Xīngqīwǔ ne.** *It's only Wednesday today. Friday will be the day after tomorrow.*
后头 **hòutou** *n* Same as 后面 **hòumian** or 后边 **hòubian**, used colloquially.
后退 **hòutuì** *v* retreat, draw back

厚 **hòu** *adj* thick (antonym 薄 **báo**) □ 这么厚的小说, 她两天就看完了。**Zhème hòu de xiǎoshuō, tā liǎng tiān jiù kànwán le.** *It took her only two days to finish reading such a thick novel.*
厚度 **hòudù** [modif: 厚 thick + 度 degree] *n* thickness

候 **hòu** *v* wait
候补 **hòubǔ** *v* be a candidate (for a position)
候补委员 **hòubǔ wěiyuán** alternative member of a committee
候选人 **hòuxuǎnrén** *n* candidate (for an election or selection)

乎 **hū** *particle* (added to another word to express strong emotions) (See 几乎 **jīhū**, 似乎 **sìhū**.)

呼 **hū** *v* 1 exhale 2 shout, cry out
呼声 **hūshēng** [modif: 呼 shouting + 声 voice] *n* 1 call, crying 2 public voice, expression of public opinion
呼吸 **hūxī** [comp: 呼 exhale + 吸 inhale] *v* breathe □ 我刚才不大舒服, 在花园里呼吸了新鲜空气, 感到好多了。**Wǒ gāngcái búdà shūfu, zài huāyuán li hūxīle xīnxiān kōngqì, gǎndào hǎo duō le.** *I didn't feel well just now. I'm feeling much better now that I've had some fresh air in the garden.*
呼吁 **hūyù** *v* appeal, call on

忽 **hū** *adv* suddenly
忽然 **hūrán** *adv* suddenly □ 刚才天气还好好儿的, 忽然下起大雨来了。**Gāngcái tiānqì hái hǎohǎor de, hūrán xià qǐ dà yǔ lái le.** *Just now the weather was still fine. Suddenly it's raining hard.*
忽视 **hūshì** *v* overlook, neglect □ 他们忽视了一个细节, 使计划失败。**Tāmen hūshì le yī ge xìjié, shǐ jìhuà shībài.** *They overlooked a detail, which doomed the plan.*

胡 1 **hú** Trad 鬍 *n* beard, mustache
胡子 **húzi** beard, whiskers
刮胡子 **guā húzi** shave (beard, whiskers) □ 你的胡子长了, 要刮一下。**Nǐ de húzi cháng le, yào guā yíxià.** *You've grown quite a beard. You need a shave.*

胡 2 **hú** *adj* foreign, outlandish

NOTE: In ancient China, 胡 **hú** was used to refer to foreigners, especially the nomadic tribesmen from Central Asia. A number of words with 胡 **hú** were created to denote objects introduced to China by or through these people. Words with 胡 **hú** may also have derogatory meanings.

胡来 **húlái** *v* fool with, mess up
胡乱 **húluàn** *adv* rashly, carelessly

胡萝卜 **húluóbo** [modif: 胡 foreign + 萝卜 turnip]
　n carrot

胡闹 **húnào** *v* act noisily and willfully, create a scene

胡琴 **húqin** *n* a traditional musical instrument with
　two strings, also called 二胡 **èrhú** (把 **bǎ**)
　拉胡琴 (二胡) lā húqín (èrhú) play the *erhu*

胡说 **húshuō** [modif: 胡 foreign + 说 talking] **I** *v*
　talk nonsense □ 你别胡说, 我和她只是朋友关系。
　Nǐ bié húshuō, wǒ hé tā zhǐ shì péngyou guānxi.
　Don't talk nonsense, she and I are only friends. **II** *n*
　nonsense
　胡说八道 húshuō bādào pure nonsense

胡同 **hútòng** *n* narrow lane in Beijing

瑚 **hú** as in 珊瑚 **shānhú**

葫 **hú** as in 葫芦 **húlu**
　葫芦 **húlu** *n* bottle gourd, calabash

糊 **hú** **I** *v* paste **II** *n* mush, gruel

糊涂 **hútu** [comp: 糊 muddled + 涂 mire] *adj*
　muddle-headed, muddled, confused (antonym 明
　白 **míngbai**) □ 你真糊涂, 怎么又忘了把钥匙放在哪儿
　了? **Nǐ zhēn hútu, zēnme yòu wàngle bǎ yàoshi fàng
　zài nǎ'er le?** *You're really muddle-headed. How is
　it that you've forgotten where you've left the keys
　again?* □ 你越解释, 我越糊涂, 还是让我自己再看一遍
　书吧。**Nǐ yuè jiěshì, wǒ yuè hútu, háishì ràng wǒ zìjǐ
　zài kàn yí biàn shū ba.** *The more you explain, the
　more confused I am. I'd better read the book once
　more by myself.*
　糊涂虫 **hútu chóng** [modif: 糊涂 muddle-headed +
　虫 bug] *n* muddle-headed person, bungler

湖 **hú** *n* lake □ 中国最大的湖是青海省的青海湖。
　**Zhōngguó zuì dà de hú shì Qīnghǎi Shěng de
　Qīnghǎi Hú.** *China's biggest lake is Qinghai Lake in
　Qinghai Province.*
　湖泊 **húpō** *n* lakes

蝴 **hú** as in 蝴蝶 **húdié**
　蝴蝶 **húdié** *n* butterfly

壶 **hú** Trad 壺 *n* kettle (把 **bǎ**)
　水壶 shuǐhú kettle □ 壶里还有水吗? **Hú li hái yǒu
　shuǐ ma?** *Is there any water left in the kettle?*

狐 **hú** *n* fox
　狐狸 húli fox

虎 **hǔ** *n* tiger (See 老虎 **lǎohǔ**, 马虎 **mǎhu**)

互 **hù** **I** *adj* reciprocal **II** *adv* mutually, each other
　互利 **hùlì** *adj* of mutual benefit

互联网 **hùliánwǎng** [modif: 互 each other + 联
　linked + 网 net] *n* the Internet, the World Wide
　Web □ 有了互联网, 信息交流方便多了。**Yǒule
　hùliánwǎng, xìnxī jiāoliú fāngbiàn duōle.** *With the
　Internet, information exchange is so much more
　convenient.* □ 我每天都上互联网, 看新闻, 找资料。**Wǒ
　měitiān dōu shàng hùliánwǎng, kàn xīnwén, zhǎo
　zīliào.** *I get on the Internet every day to read news or
　search for data.*

互相 **hùxiāng** *adv* each other, one another □ 我
　们是好朋友, 应当互相关心, 互相帮助。**Wǒmen shì
　hǎo péngyou, yīngdāng hùxiāng guānxīn, hùxiāng
　bāngzhù.** *We're good friends, so we should care for
　each other and help each other.*

互助 **hùzhù** *v* help each other

户 **hù** *measure wd* (used with nouns denoting
　households and families) □ 这条街上有三十几户人
　家。**Zhè tiáo jiē shang yǒu sānshí jǐ hù rénjiā.** *There
　are over 30 households [living] along this street.*

户口 **hùkǒu** [comp: 户 household + 口 mouth] *n*
　registered permanent residence
　城镇户口 chéngzhèn hùkǒu urban residence
　农村户口 nóngcūn hùkǒu rural residence

护 **hù** Trad 護 *v* protect
　护士 **hùshi** *n* nurse □ 护士按照医生的嘱咐给病人
　吃药。**Hùshi ànzhào yīshēng de zhǔfu gěi bìngrén chī
　yào.** *Nurses administer medicine to patients according
　to doctors' instructions.*

NOTE: In China nurses are almost exclusively women. To
address a nurse politely, use 护士小姐 **hùshì xiǎojiě**, e.g.
□ 护士小姐, 我还需要吃这个药吗? **Hùshì xiǎojiě, wǒ hái
xūyào chī zhè ge yào ma?** *Nurse, do I still need to take
this medicine?* or you can put her family name before 护
士 **hùshì**, e.g. 张护士 **Zhāng hùshì**, 李护士 **Lǐ hùshì**.

护照 **hùzhào** *n* passport (份 **fèn**) □ 约翰在北京旅行
　的时候, 发现护照丢了, 就马上和大使馆联系。**Yuēhàn
　zài Běijīng lǚxíng de shíhou, fāxiàn hùzhào diū le,
　jiù mǎshang hé dàshǐguǎn liánxì.** *While traveling in
　Beijing, John found that he had lost his passport and
　immediately contacted the embassy.*
　申请护照 shēnqǐng hùzhào apply for a passport

沪 **hù** Trad 滬 *n* a shortened form for the metropo-
　lis of Shanghai
　沪东 Hù-Dōng East Shanghai

花 1 **huā** *n* flower (朵 **duǒ**) □ 去医院看病人, 可以带
　一些花。**Qù yīyuàn kàn bìngrén, kěyǐ dài yìxiē
　huā.** *You can take some flowers with you when you
　visit a patient in the hospital.*
　种花 zhòng huā plant flowers, do gardening

NOTE: In colloquial Chinese 花儿 **huār** may be used
instead of 花 **huā**, e.g. □ 去医院看病人, 可以带一些花
儿。**Qù yīyuàn kàn bìngrén, kěyǐ dài yìxiē huār.** *You can
take some flowers with you when you visit a patient in
the hospital.*

花朵 **huāduǒ** *n* flowers

花瓶 **huāpíng** *n* vase (只 **zhī**) □ 花瓶里插了几朵美丽
　的花。**Huāpíng li chāle jǐ duǒ měilì de huā.** *Some
　beautiful flowers were placed in the vase.*
　瓷器花瓶 cíqì huāpíng porcelain vase

花儿 **huār** **I** *n* Same as 花 **huā** **II** *adj* full of colors,
　mottled, loud □ 这条裙子太花儿了, 你穿不合适。**Zhè
　tiáo qúnzi tài huār le, nǐ chuān bù héshì.** *This skirt is
　too flashy. It's unsuitable for you to wear.*

花色 **huāsè** *n* **1** (of fabric) design and color **2** (of a
　commodity) variety of designs, colors, sizes, etc.

花生 **huāshēng** *n* peanut
　花生酱 huāshēngjiàng peanut butter

花纹 **huāwén** *n* decorative pattern, pattern

花样 **huāyàng** *n* **1** pattern, variety
　花样溜冰 huāyàngliūbīng figure skate
　2 trick
　和我玩花样 hé wǒ wán huāyang play tricks on me

花园 **huāyuán** [modif: 花 flower + 园 garden] *n*

garden (座 **zuò**) □ 这里几乎每座房子都有一个小花园。
Zhèli jīhū měi zuò fángzi dōu yǒu yí ge xiǎo huāyuán. *Almost every house here has a small garden.*

花2 **huā** *v* 1 spend □ 去年我花了两百元买书。　　**Qùnián wǒ huāle liǎngbǎi yuán mǎi shū.** *Last year I spent 200 yuan on books.* □ 你每天花多少时间做作业? **Nǐ měitiān huā duōshǎo shíjiān zuò zuòyè?** *How much time do you spend on assignments every day?* 2 cost (money) □ 这次旅行花了我三千块钱。**Zhè cì lǚxíng huāle wǒ sānqiān kuài qián.** *This trip cost me 3,000 yuan.* □ 在英国留学一年要花多少钱? **Zài Yīngguó liúxué yì nián yào huā duōshǎo qián?** *How much would it cost to study in the UK for a year?* 3 take (time) □ 写这篇文章花了我整整两天。**Xiě zhè piān wénzhāng huāle wǒ zhěngzhěng liǎng tiān.** *It took me two full days to write this essay.*

NOTE: In writing, the character 化 **huà** can be used instead of 花 **huā** as a verb meaning *spend, cost,* etc.

花费 **huāfèi** I *v* consume, spend
花费大量心血 **huāfèi dàliàng xīnxuè** put in a great deal of effort
II *n* money spent, expenses

划 **huá** Trad 劃 *v* 1 row, paddle
划船 **huáchuán** row a boat
2 scratch or scrape with a sharp object □ 我的手划破了, 不能在花园里干活了。**Wǒ de shǒu huá pò le, bù néng zài huāyuán li gànhuó le.** *I've scratched my hand. I can't work in the garden any more.* 3 be worth the money spent
划算 **huásuàn** *adj* worth it, getting money's worth

滑 **huá** *adj* slippery □ 下雪以后, 路上很滑。**Xià xuě yǐhòu, lù shang hěn huá.** *After a snowfall, roads are slippery.*
滑冰 **huábīng** *v* skate (on ice), ice-skating
滑头 **huátóu** I *adj* crafty, shifty II *n* a crafty, shifty person
滑雪 **huáxuě** I *v* ski II *n* skiing

猾 **huá** as in 狡猾 **jiǎohuá**

华 **huá** Trad 華 I *n* China II *adj* magnificent, gorgeous
华丽 **huálì** [comp: 华 magnificent + 丽 beautiful] *adj* gorgeous, magnificent
华侨 **huáqiáo** *n* overseas Chinese
华人 **huárén** *n* ethnic Chinese
华氏 **huáshì** *n* Fahrenheit scale
华氏温度计 **huáshì wēndùjì** Fahrenheit thermometer

NOTE: The Fahrenheit scale is not used in China. Instead the Celsius (Centigrade) scale, which is 摄氏 **shèshì**, is used.

哗 **huá** Trad 嘩 *n* noise

化 **huà** I *v* 1 melt □ 太阳出来, 雪很快化了。**Tàiyang chūlai, xuě hěn kuài huà le.** *When the sun came out, the snow melted very quickly.* 2 transform II *n* chemistry
化肥 **huàféi** [modif: 化 chemical + 肥 fertilizer] *n* chemical fertilizer

化工 **huàgōng** [modif: 化 chemical + 工 industry] *n* chemical industry
化工厂 **huàgōngchǎng** chemical plant
化合 **huàhé** *n* chemical combination
化石 **huàshí** *n* fossil
化纤 **huàxiān** [modif: 化 chemical + 纤 fiber] *n* chemical fiber
化学 **huàxué** [modif: 化 change, transform + 学 study] *n* chemistry □ 他对化学感兴趣, 以后想当化学工程师。**Tā duì huàxué gǎn xìngqu, yǐhòu xiǎng dāng huàxué gōngchéngshī.** *He is interested in chemistry, and hopes to become a chemical engineer.*
化学家 **huàxuéjiā** chemist
化学工业(化工) **huàxué gōngyè (huàgōng)** chemical industry
化验 **huàyàn** [modif: 化 chemical + 验 test] *n* chemical test, laboratory test □ 你必须化验一下血。**Nǐ bìxū huàyàn yíxià xuè.** *You must have your blood tested.*
化验报告 **huàyàn bàogào** laboratory test report
化验单 **huàyàn dān** laboratory test application (a form signed by a doctor for the patient to have a test done in a laboratory)
化验室 **huàyàn shì** laboratory
化验员 **huàyàn yuán** laboratory assistant, laboratory technician
化妆 **huàzhuāng** *v* put on make-up
化妆品 **huàzhuāngpǐn** cosmetics

划 **huà** Trad 劃 *v* 1 plan 2 delimit
划分 **huàfēn** *v* divide, differentiate

画 **huà** Trad 畫 *v* 1 draw, paint □ 这个小孩喜欢画各种动物, 而且画得挺好。**Zhège xiǎohái xǐhuan huà gè zhǒng dòngwù, érqiě huà de tǐng hǎo.** *This child likes to draw animals, and is very good at it.*
国画 **guóhuà** traditional Chinese painting
铅笔画 **qiānbǐ huà** pencil drawing
水彩画 **shuǐcǎi huà** watercolor (painting)
油画 **yóuhuà** oil painting
中国画 **Zhōngguóhuà** Same as 国画 **guóhuà**
画儿 **huàr** *n* picture, drawing (张 **zhāng**, 幅 **fú**) □ 这张画儿画得真好! **Zhè zhāng huàr huà de zhēn hǎo!** *This picture is so well done!*

NOTE: You can use 画 **huà** instead of 画儿 **huàr**, e.g. □ 这张画画得真好! **Zhè zhāng huà huà de zhēn hǎo!** *This picture is so well done!*

画报 **huàbào** [modif: 画 picture + 报 paper] *n* illustrated magazine, pictorial (份 **fèn**, 本 **běn**) □ 星期天的报纸大多有一份画报。**Xīngqītiān de bàozhǐ dàduō yǒu yí fèn huàbào.** *Most Sunday newspapers carry a pictorial (or color) supplement.*
画家 **huàjiā** [suffix: 画 paint + 家 nominal suffix denoting an expert] *n* painter, artist (位 **wèi**) □ 这位画家画风景画得特别好。**Zhè wèi huàjiā huà fēngjǐng huà de tèbié hǎo.** *This artist is particularly good at landscapes.*
画面 **huàmiàn** *n* image on the screen or the canvas
画蛇添足 **huà shé tiān zú** *idiom* add legs to a snake (→ do superfluous things, thus causing damage or attracting ridicule)

话 **huà** Trad 話 *n* speech, what is said, words (句 **jù**) □ 你这句话很有道理。**Nǐ zhè jù huà hěn yǒu**

dàolǐ . *Your words are very reasonable.* (→ *You're quite right there.*) □ 他说的话没有一句是真的。**Tā shuō de huà méiyǒu yí jù shì zhēn de.** *Nothing that he said is true.* □ 别忘了我的话。**Bié wàngle wǒ de huà.** *Don't forget what I said.*

话剧 **huàjù** [modif: 话 speech + 剧 drama] *n* stage play (as opposed to opera)

话题 **huàtí** [modif: 话 speech + 题 theme] *n* topic of conversation, subject of a talk, theme

槐 **huái** *n* Chinese scholar tree

槐树 **huáishù** Chinese scholar tree (棵 **kē**)

徊 **huái** *v* walk to and fro (See 徘徊 **páihuái**)

怀 **huái** Trad 懷 **I** *n* bosom **II** *v* **1** keep in mind **2** miss, think of

怀念 **huáiniàn** [comp: 怀 miss + 念 think of] *v* think of tenderly

怀疑 **huáiyí** [v+obj: 怀 harbor + 疑 doubt] *v* **1** disbelieve, doubt □ 我怀疑他说的话是不是真的。**Wǒ huáiyí tā shuōde huà shìbushì zhēn de.** *I doubt if he was telling the truth.* **2** think something is unlikely, suspect □ 我怀疑他在撒谎。**Wǒ huáiyí tā zài sāhuǎng.** *I suspect that he was lying.*

NOTE: 怀疑 **huáiyí** has two seemingly contradictory meanings – *disbelieve* and *think something is unlikely*, but the context will make the meaning clear.

怀孕 **huáiyùn** *v* be pregnant

坏 **huài** Trad 壞 **I** *adj* bad (antonym 好 **hǎo**) □ 小孩子看电影，总爱问谁是好人，谁是坏人。**Xiǎoháizi kàn diànyǐng, zǒng ài wèn shéi shì hǎorén, shéi shì huàirén.** *When children watch movies, they like to ask who the good guy is and who the bad guy is.* **II** *v* break down, be out of order □ 这台电脑已经用坏了，得买台新的。**Zhè tái diànnǎo yǐjīng yòng huài le, děi mǎi yì tái xīn de.** *This computer has already broken down, you need to buy a new one.* □ 电视机坏了，今天没法看电视新闻了。**Diànshìjī huài le, jīntiān méi fǎ kàn diànshì xīnwén le.** *The TV set has broken down. There's no way we can watch the TV news today.* □ 他们的车半路上坏了。**Tāmen de chē bànlù shang huài le.** *Their car broke down halfway.*

坏处 **huàichu** [modif: 坏 bad + 处 place] *n* negative effect, disadvantage (antonym 好处 **hǎochu**) □ 这样做坏处很多，但是也有不少坏处。**Zhèyàng zuò hǎochu hěn duō, dànshì yě yǒu bù shǎo huàichu.** *This way of doing things has many advantages, but it also has quite a few disadvantages.*

NOTE: 坏处 **huàichu** and 害处 **hàichu** both refer to the undesirable effects of an action or actions. 坏处 **huàichu** connotes general negativity while 害处 **hàichu** emphasizes the harm that results.

坏蛋 **huàidàn** [modif: 坏 bad + 蛋 egg] *n* bad person, villain, rascal

欢 **huān** Trad 歡 *adj* joyful

欢呼 **huānhū** [modif: 欢 joyfully + 呼 shout] *v* cheer, hail

欢乐 **huānlè** [comp: 欢 joyful + 乐 happy] *adj* joyful, happy

欢送 **huānsòng** [modif: 欢 joyfully + 送 send off] *v* send off □ 我们明天到机场去欢送中国公司的代表。**Wǒmen míngtiān dào jīchǎng qù huānsòng Zhōngguó gōngsī de dàibiǎo.** *We're going to the airport tomorrow to send off the representative from the Chinese company.*

欢送会 **huānsònghuì** a send-off party (e.g. a farewell tea party)

欢喜 **huānxǐ** [comp: 欢 joyful + 喜 happy] *adj* joyful, happy, delighted

欢笑 **huānxiào** *v* laugh heartily

欢迎 **huānyíng** [modif: 欢 joyfully + 迎 meet] *v* welcome □ 热烈欢迎您! **Rèliè huānyíng nín!** *A warm welcome to you!* □ 怎样改进我们的服务? 欢迎顾客们提建议。**Zěnyàng gǎijìn wǒmen de fúwù? Huānyíng gùkèmen tí jiànyì.** *What can we do to improve our service? Customers are welcome to give us their suggestions.*

还 **huán** Trad 還 *v* return, pay back □ 他向银行借了十万元，要在五年内还清。**Tā xiàng yínháng jièle shíwàn yuán, yào zài wǔ nián nèi huán qīng.** *He borrowed 100,000 yuan from a bank and must repay the loan within five years.* □ 这本书在这个星期一定要还给图书馆。**Zhè běn shū zài zhège xīngqī yídìng yào huán gei túshūguǎn.** *This book must be returned to the library within this week.* □ 有借有还, 再借不难。**Yǒu jiè yǒu huán, zài jiè bù nán.** *Return what you borrowed, and it won't be difficult to borrow again.*

还原 **huányuán** [v+obj: 还 return to + 原 the original] *v* return to the original, restore

环 **huán** Trad 環 *n* circle, ring

环节 **huánjié** *n* link

重要环节 **zhòngyào huánjié** important link

环境 **huánjìng** [comp: 环 surroundings + 境 boundary, area] *n* environment □ 这座大学在城外，三面环山，环境安静美丽。**Zhè zuò dàxué zài chéngwài, sān miàn huán shān, huánjìng ānjìng měilì.** *This university is outside the city, surrounded by hills on three sides. The environment is peaceful, quiet, and beautiful.* □ 这家造纸厂污染环境，引起当地居民的强烈不满。**Zhè jiā zàozhǐ chǎng wūrǎn huánjìng, yǐnqǐ dāngdì jūmín de qiángliè bùmǎn.** *This paper mill pollutes the environment, arousing the local people's great displeasure.*

环境保护 **huánjìng bǎohù** environmental protection

缓 **huǎn** Trad 緩 *adv* leisurely

缓和 **huǎnhé** **I** *v* ease up, alleviate (antonym 紧张 **jǐnzhāng**) □ 她说了一个笑话，让会场上的紧张气氛缓和下来。**Tā shuōle yí ge xiàohua, ràng huìchǎng shàng de jǐnzhāng qìfen huǎnhé xiàlai.** *She told a joke, which defused tension at the meeting.* **II** *adj* relaxed, gentle

口气缓和 **kǒuqì huǎnhé** with a gentle, mild tone

缓慢 **huǎnmàn** [comp: 缓 relaxed + 慢 slow] *adj* slow, unhurried

换 **huàn** Trad 換 *v* change, replace □ 她的地址换了，我不知道她的新地址。**Tā de dìzhǐ huàn le, wǒ bù zhīdào tā de xīn dìzhǐ.** *She has changed her address. I don't have her new one.* □ 这双鞋太小了，我想换大一号的。**Zhè shuāng xié tài xiǎo le, wǒ xiǎng huàn dà yí hào de.** *This pair of shoes is too small. I'd like to replace it with a bigger size.*

换取 **huànqǔ** *v* exchange for, get in return

唤 **huàn** *v* call out

痪 **huàn** *n* paralysis (See 瘫痪 **tānhuàn**)

幻 **huàn** *adj* illusory
幻灯 **huàndēng** *n* slide show
幻灯机 **huàndēngjī** slide projector
幻灯片 **huàndēngpiàn** slide, lantern slide (张 **zhāng**)
幻想 **huànxiǎng** [modif: 幻 illusory + 想 think] *v* fantasize, have illusions

患 **huàn** *v* suffer (from a disease)
患者 **huànzhě** *n* patient
精神病患者 **jīngshénbìng huànzhě** one who suffers from a mental disorder

荒 **huāng** I *adj* barren, desolate II *n* crop falure, famine
荒地 **huāngdì** [modif: 荒 barren + 地 land] *n* uncultivated land, wasteland,
荒凉 **huāngliáng** [comp: 荒 barren + 凉 cold] *adj* bleak, desolate
荒谬 **huāngmiù** *adj* absurd, preposterous
荒谬之极 **huāngmiù zhìjí** absolutely absurd
荒唐 **huāngtáng** *adj* preposterous, way off the mark
荒唐透顶 **huāngtáng tòudǐng** incredibly silly, totally unreasonable

慌 **huāng** *adj* flustered, panic-stricken □ 他考试要迟到了, 慌得坐错了车。**Tā kǎoshì yào chídào le, huāng de zuòcuòle chē.** *As he was about to be late for the examination, he was so flustered that he took the wrong bus.*
慌了手脚 **huāngle shǒu jiǎo** be so flustered as to not know what to do, be at a loss as to what to do
慌乱 **huāngluàn** [comp: 慌 flustered + 乱 chaotic] *adj* panic-stricken, flustered
慌张 **huāngzhāng** *adj* in frantic haste, flustered

皇 **huáng** *n* emperor
皇帝 **huángdì** *n* emperor □ 中国历史上第一个皇帝是秦始皇。**Zhōngguó lìshǐ shang dì yī ge huángdì shì Qín Shǐ Huángdì.** *The first emperor in Chinese history was Qin Shi Huangdi.*
皇后 **huánghòu** *n* wife of an emperor, empress

蝗 **huáng** *n* locust
蝗虫 **huángchóng** locust
蝗灾 **huángzāi** locust disaster

凰 **huáng** *n* female phoenix

煌 **huáng** *adj* intensely bright

黄 **huáng** *adj* yellow □ 香蕉和桔子都是黄的。**Xiāngjiāo hé júzi dōu shì huáng de.** *Bananas and tangerines are yellow.*
黄瓜 **huángguā** *n* cucumber (根 **gēn**) □ 我夏天爱吃新鲜黄瓜。**Wǒ xiàtiān ài chī xīnxiān huángguā.** *I love to eat fresh cucumber in summer.*
黄色 **huángsè** I *n* the yellow color II *adj* pornographic
黄色电影 **huángsè diànyǐng** pornographic movie
黄色网站 **huángsè wǎngzhàn** pornographic website
黄油 **huángyóu** *n* butter □ 在新鲜面包上涂一层黄油, 可好吃了! **Zài xīnxiān miànbāo shang tú yì céng huángyóu, kě hǎo chī le!** *If you spread a thin layer of butter on freshly baked bread, how delicious it is!*

晃 **huǎng** *v* sway, shake

谎 **huǎng** *n* lie
谎话 **huǎnghuà** lie (especially used in speech)
谎言 **huǎngyán** lie (especially used in writing)

徽 **huī** *n* emblem, sign
国徽 **guóhuī** national emblem
校徽 **xiàohuī** school badge

灰 **huī** I *adj* gray □ 这个城市污染很严重, 天空总是灰灰的。**Zhège chéngshì wūrǎn hěn yánzhòng, tiānkōng zǒng shì huīhuī de.** *This city has a serious pollution problem. Its sky is always gray.* II *n* ash, dust
灰尘 **huīchén** *n* dust
灰心 **huīxīn** *adj* disheartened, discouraged □ 他虽然遭到失败, 但是没有灰心。**Tā suīrán zāodào shībài, dànshì méiyǒu huīxīn.** *Although he failed, he was not disheartened.*

恢 **huī** *adj* extensive, vast
恢复 **huīfù** *v* recover, restore □ 祝你早日恢复健康! **Zhù nǐ zǎorì huīfù jiànkāng!** *I wish you a speedy recovery of health!* □ 经过十几天的圣诞和新年假期, 城市生活又恢复正常了。**Jīngguò shí jǐ tiān de shèngdàn hé xīnnián jiàqī, chéngshì shēnghuó yòu huīfù zhèngcháng le.** *After a dozen days of Christmas and New Year holidays, city life returned to normal.*

挥 **huī** Trad 揮 *v* 1 wave (See 发挥 **fāhuī**.) 2 scatter, disperse
挥霍 **huīhuò** *v* spend money carelessly, be a spendthrift, squander

辉 **huī** Trad 輝 *n* splendor
辉煌 **huīhuáng** [comp: 辉 splendid + 煌 bright] *adj* brilliant, splendid

回 I **huí** 1 *v* return (to a place), go back □ 时间不早了, 我们回家吧。**Shíjiān bù zǎo le, wǒmen huí jiā ba.** *It's quite late. Let's go back home.* □ 小陈在英国大学毕业以后, 就回中国找工作。**Xiǎo Chén zài Yīngguó dàxué bìyè yǐhòu, jiù huí Zhōngguó zhǎo gōngzuò.** *After graduating from university in the UK, Xiao Chen returned to China to look for a job.* 2 reply, answer
回电话 **huí diànhuà** call back
回避 **huíbì** *v* evade, dodge
回避问题 **huíbì wèntí** evade a question
回答 **huídá** [comp: 回 reply + 答 answer] *v* reply, answer □ 警察说: "我问你几个问题, 你要老实回答。" **Jǐngchá shuō: "Wǒ wèn nǐ jǐ ge wèntí, nǐ yào lǎoshí huídá."** *The policeman said, "I'm going to ask you some questions. You must answer truthfully."* □ 他上个周末向女朋友求婚, 女朋友说要考虑考虑再回答。**Tā shàng ge zhōumò xiàng nǚpéngyou qiúhūn, nǚpéngyou shuō yào kǎolǜ kǎolǜ zài huídá.** *Last weekend he asked his girlfriend to marry him, but she said she needed to think it over before replying.*
回顾 **huígù** *v* look back, review
回国 **huíguó** *v* return to one's home country □ 每年在美国的留学生大学毕业后, 有多少人回国? **Měi nián zài Měiguó de liúxuéshēng dàxué bìyè hòu, yǒu duōshǎo rén huí guó?** *How many foreign students in the USA return to their home countries after graduation every year?*
回击 **huíjī** *v* counterattack

回来 **huílai** *v* return to a place (coming towards the speaker) □ 哥哥要从国外回来过圣诞节。**Gēge yào cóng guówài huílai guò shèngdànjié.** *My elder brother is coming home from abroad for Christmas.* □ 妈, 我回来了! **Mā, wǒ huílai le!** *Mom, I'm home!*

回去 **huíqu** *v* return to a place (away from the speaker) □ 你回去以后, 要常常给我们发电子邮件, 保持联系。**Nǐ huíqu yǐhòu, yào chángcháng gěi wǒmen fā diànzǐ yóujiàn, bǎochí liánxì.** *After you've returned home, you should send us e-mail often to keep in touch.*

回收 **huíshōu** *v* reclaim, recover
废品回收 fèipǐn huíshōu collect junk for recycling

回头 **huítóu** *adv* later □ 回头见! **Huítóu jiàn!** *See you later!* □ 回头再说。**Huítóu zài shuō.** *I'll talk to you later.*

NOTE: 回头 **huítóu** is a colloquialism, used only in very informal styles.

回想 **huíxiǎng** *v* recall, recollect
回信 **huíxìn** [modif: 回 reply + 信 message] *n* reply (either spoken or written) □ 我们上个月送去了报价, 还没有收到他们回信。**Wǒmen shàng ge yuè sòngqule bàojià, hái méiyǒu shōudào tāmen huíxìn.** *We sent them quotes last month, and still haven't gotten a reply from them.*

回忆 **huíyì** I *v* recall, recollect □ 你回忆一下, 最后一次是在哪里用那把钥匙的。**Nǐ huíyì yíxià, zuìhòu yí cì shì zài nǎli yòng nà bǎ yàoshi de.** *Try to remember where you used that key for the last time.* II *n* recollection, memory □ 根据被害人的回忆, 事故发生在夜里十一点钟左右。**Gēnjù bèihàirén de huíyì, shìgù fāshēng zài yèlǐ shíyī diǎnzhōng zuǒyòu.** *According to the victim's recollection, the accident took place around eleven o'clock at night.*

回 2 **huí** *measure wd* number of times (of doing something) □ 我去看了他们两回了, 他们一次都没有来过。**Wǒ qù kànle tāmen liǎng huí le, tāmen yí cì dōu méiyǒu láiguo.** *I've visited them twice, but they haven't come to see me even once.*

毁 **huǐ** *v* destroy
毁坏 **huǐhuài** [comp: 毁 destroy + 坏 damage] *v* do irreparable damage
毁坏名誉 huǐhuài míngyù destroy one's reputation

毁灭 **huǐmiè** [comp: 毁 destroy + 灭 annihilate] *v* exterminate
毁灭罪证 huǐmiè zuìzhèng destroy incriminating evidence

悔 **huǐ** *v* repent, regret
悔改 **huǐgǎi** [comp: 悔 regret + 改 change] *v* repent and mend one's way
悔恨 **huǐhèn** [comp: 悔 regret + 恨 hate] *v* repent bitterly

惠 **huì** *n* benefits, kindness (See 恩惠 **ēnhuì**)

慧 **huì** *adj* wise, intelligent (See 智慧 **zhìhuì**)

贿 **huì** Trad 賄 *v* bribe
贿赂 **huìlù** I *v* bribe □ 在这个国家, 贿赂官员是常见的事吗? **Zài zhège guójiā, huìlù guānyuán shì chángjiàn de shì ma?** *Is it commonplace to bribe of-*

ficials in this country? II *n* bribery □ 这家公司通过贿赂和政府部门保持良好关系。**Zhè jiā gōngsī tōngguò huìlù hé zhèngfǔ bùmén bǎochí liánghǎo guānxi.** *This company maintains good relationships with government departments by bribery.*

汇 **huì** Trad 匯 *v* 1 converge, gather 2 remit
汇报 **huìbào** *v* report (to one's superior)
汇集 **huìjí** [comp: 汇 converge + 集 gather] *v* compile, collect, gather
汇集有关的文件 huìjí yǒuguān de wénjiàn compile relevant documents

汇款 **huìkuǎn** [v+obj: 汇 remit + 款 money] *v* remit money, send remittance
汇率 **huìlǜ** *n* (currency) exchange rate

会 1 **huì** Trad 會 I *modal v* 1 know how to, can □ 我会游泳, 但是今天不能去游泳, 因为我感冒了。**Wǒ huì yóuyǒng, dànshì jīntiān bù néng qù yóuyǒng, yīnwèi wǒ gǎnmào le.** *I can swim, but I'm not able to today because I've got a cold.* 2 probably, will □ 我看夜里会下雨。**Wǒ kàn yèlǐ huì xiàyǔ.** *I think it will rain tonight.* □ 只要努力工作, 就会取得满意的成绩。**Zhǐyào nǔlì gōngzuò, jiù huì qǔdé mǎnyì de chéngjì.** *Provided you work hard, you will achieve satisfactory results.* II *v* have the ability or knowledge □ 你会日文吗? **Nǐ huì Rìwén ma?** *Do you speak (or write) Japanese?* □ 这道题目我不会。**Zhè dào tímù wǒ bú huì.** *I don't know how to do this question.*

NOTE: 会 **huì** as a full verb meaning *have the ability* or *knowledge* is used with a limited range of nouns, such as nouns denoting languages. Using 会 **huì** in this way is colloquial.

会 2 **huì** Trad 會 *n* 1 meeting, conference
大会 dàhuì an assembly, a rally
开会 kāi huì have a meeting □ 我去开会了, 这里请你照顾一下。**Wǒ qù kāi huì le, zhèli qǐng nǐ zhàogù yíxià.** *I'm going to a meeting. Please keep an eye on things here.* □ 明天的会非常重要, 请您一定参加。**Míngtiān de huì fēicháng zhòngyào, qǐng nín yídìng cānjiā.** *The meeting tomorrow is very important. Please be sure to attend it.*
2 association
读书会 dúshū huì book club
工会 gōnghuì labor union
学生会 xuéshenghuì students union
会场 **huìchǎng** [modif: 会 meeting, conference + 场 venue] *n* venue for a meeting, conference, assembly or rally □ 大会会场布置得很庄严。**Dàhuì huìchǎng bùzhì de hěn zhuāngyán.** *The assembly hall was solemnly decorated.*
会话 **huìhuà** I *v* talk, hold a conversation □ 我和她一天用中文会话, 一天用英文会话。**Wǒ hé tā yìtiān yòng Zhōngwén huìhuà, yìtiān yòng Yīngwén huìhuà.** *She and I talk in Chinese one day, and in English the next day.* II *n* conversation □ 中文会话不太难, 难的是写汉字。**Zhōngwén huìhuà bú tài nán, nán de shì xiě hànzì.** *Chinese conversation is not too difficult. What is difficult is writing Chinese characters.*
会见 **huìjiàn** [comp: 会 meet + 见 see] *v* (formal) meet □ 明天上午商业部长会见我们公司的王董事长。**Míngtiān shàngwǔ Shāngyè Bùzhǎng huìjiàn wǒmen**

gōngsī de Wáng dǒngshìzhǎng. *The Minister of Commerce will meet Chairman Wang from our company tomorrow morning.*

会客 **huìkè** [v+obj: 会 meet + 客 guest] *v* receive visitors □ 今天市长有重要会议，不能会客。**Jīntiān shìzhǎng yǒu zhòngyào huìyì, bù néng huì kè.** *Today the mayor is at an important conference and is not able to receive visitors.*

会谈 **huìtán** [comp: 会 meet + 谈 talk] *v* hold (formal) talks □ 两个大学的校长将举行会谈，讨论怎样加强合作。**Liǎng ge dàxué de xiàozhǎng jiāng jǔxíng huìtán, tǎolùn zěnyàng jiāqiáng hézuò.** *The presidents of the two universities will hold a talk to discuss how to strengthen cooperation.*

会晤 **huìwù** [comp: 会 meet + 晤 meet] *v* meet (formally)

会议 **huìyì** [comp: 会 meet + 议 discuss] *n* meeting, conference □ 这次会议讨论什么问题？**Zhè cì huìyì tǎolùn shénme wèntí?** *What questions will be discussed at the conference? (→ What is on the conference agenda?)*

参加会议 cānjiā huìyì participate in a meeting or conference □ 参加会议的还有全国各地的中学校长代表。**Cānjiā huìyì de háiyǒu quán guó gè dì de zhōngxué xiàozhǎng dàibiǎo.** *Representatives of high school principals from various parts of the country also attended the conference.*

出席会议 chūxí huìyì attend a meeting or conference □ 教育部长和几位重要人物出席了会议。**Jiàoyù bùzhǎng hé jǐ wèi zhòngyào rénwù chūxíle huìyì.** *The Minister of Education and several other VIPs attended this conference.*

举行会议 jǔxíng huìyì hold a meeting or conference □ 下个月这个城市要举行一个国际会议。**Xià ge yuè zhège chéngshì yào jǔxíng yí ge guójì huìyì.** *An international conference will be held in this city next month.*

取消会议 qǔxiāo huìyì cancel a meeting or conference □ 你知道为什么取消这次会议吗？**Nǐ zhīdào wèishénme qǔxiāo zhè cì huìyì ma?** *Do you know why this meeting was canceled?*

召开会议 zhàokāi huìyì convene a meeting or conference □ 校长召开全体教师会议，讨论学生纪律问题。**Xiàozhǎng zhàokāi quántǐ jiàoshī huìyì, tǎolùn xuésheng jìlù wèntí.** *The principal convened a teachers' meeting to discuss the issue of student discipline.*

会员 **huìyuán** *n* member of an asspciation

会员证 huìyuánzhèng membership card
工会会员 gōnghuì huìyuán labor union member
俱乐部会员 jùlèbù huìyuán club member

绘 **huì** *v* paint, draw

绘画 **huìhuà** *n* painting, drawing

昏 **hūn** *v* faint

昏迷 **hūnmí** [comp: 昏 faint + 迷 coma] *v* fall into a coma □ 他在交通事故中受伤，昏迷了一天一夜才醒来。**Tā zài jiāotōng shìgù zhōng shòule shāng, hūnmíle yì-tiān-yí-yè cái xǐnglai.** *He was injured in a traffic accident and was unconscious for twenty-four hours.*

婚 **hūn** *n* marriage

婚姻 **hūnyīn** [comp: 婚 marriage + 姻 marriage] *n* marriage □ 婚姻是人生大事。**Hūnyīn shì rénshēng dà shì.** *Marriage is an important event in one's life.*

魂 **hún** *n* soul (See 灵魂 línghún)

浑 **hún** *adj* 1 muddy 2 whole, all over

浑身 **húnshēn** [modif: 浑 all over + 身 body] *adj* from head to foot, all over the body

浑身疼痛 húnshēn téngtòng ache all over

混 **hùn** *v* 1 mix up □ 这两个词发音相同，意思不同，你别把它们混起来。**Zhè liǎng ge cí fāyīn xiāngtóng, yìsi bù tóng, nǐ bié bǎ tāmen hùn qǐlai.** *These two words have the same pronunciation, but different meanings. Do not mix them up.*

混为一谈 hùn wéi yì tán lump different things together, fail to make distinction between different things 2 pass for, pass off as 3 get along, get along with

混合 **hùnhé** [comp: 混 mix up + 合 combine] *v* mix, blend, mingle

混乱 **hùnluàn** [comp: 混 mix up + 乱 chaos] *adj* chaotic, confused

混凝土 **hùnníngtǔ** *n* cement, concrete

混淆 **hùnxiáo** *v* eliminate differences in order to confuse, mix up

混淆是非 hùnxiáo shìfēi confuse right and wrong

混浊 **hùnzhuó** *adj* murky, turbid

活 **huó** I *v* 1 be alive 2 work II *adj* alive, living □ 很多中国人只吃活鱼，不吃死鱼。**Hěn duō Zhōngguórén zhǐ chī huó yú, bù chī sǐ yú.** *Many Chinese only eat live (→ freshly caught) fish, not dead ones.*

活动 **huódòng** [comp: 活 alive + 动 move] I *v* do physical exercise □ 他每天起床后，先在花园里活动，再吃早饭。**Tā měi tiān qǐchuáng hòu, xiān zài huāyuán li huódòng, zài chī zǎofàn.** *Every day after getting up he does a bit of exercise in the garden before having breakfast.* II *n* activity

参加活动 cānjiā huódòng participate in an activity □ 您退休以后，最好参加一些活动，别老待在家里。**Nín tuìxiū yǐhòu, zuìhǎo cānjiā yìxiē huódòng, bié lǎo dāi zài jiā li.** *After retirement it's best that you participate in some activities. Don't stay at home all the time.*

活该 **huógāi** *v* serve one right, deserve □ 他活该！**Tā huógāi!** *Serves him right!*

活力 **huólì** [modif: 活 alive + 力 force] *n* vitality, vigor

活泼 **huópo** *adj* lively, vivacious □ 她性格活泼，爱交朋友，到处受欢迎。**Tā xìnggé huópo, ài jiāo péngyou, dàochù shòu huānyíng.** *She is vivacious by nature and likes to make friends, so she is popular wherever she goes.*

活儿 **huór** *n* work, job

干活儿 gàn huór work, do a job □ 这活儿不容易，你干得了吗？**Zhè huór bù róngyì, nǐ gàn de liǎo ma?** *This job is not easy. Can you manage it?* □ 没有适当的工具，这活儿没法干。**Méiyǒu shìdàng de gōngjù, zhè huór méi fǎ gàn.** *This job can't be done without the proper tools.*

NOTE: 活儿 **huór** and 干活儿 **gàn huór** are very colloquial, and usually refer to manual work.

活跃 **huóyuè** [comp: 活 alive + 跃 leap, jump] *adj* active, brisk □ 这两天股票市场十分活跃。**Zhè liǎng tiān gǔpiào shìchǎng shífēn huóyuè.** *The share market is very brisk these days.*

火 huǒ *n* fire □ 生了火，房间里就暖和了。**Shēngle huǒ, fángjiān li jiù nuǎnhuo le.** *After a fire was lit, the room became warm.*
着火 zháo huǒ catch fire, be caught on fire □ 着火了! 着火了! **Zháo huǒ le! Zháo huǒ le!** *Fire! Fire!*

火柴 huǒchái [modif: 火 fire + 柴 wood] *n* match (根 **gēn**, 盒 **hé**) □ "你有火柴吗？" "没有，我有打火机。" **"Nǐ yǒu huǒchái ma?" "Méiyǒu, wǒ yǒu dǎhuǒjī."** *"Have you got a match?" "No, but I've got a cigarette lighter."*
火柴盒 huǒchái hé a matchbox
划火柴 huá huǒchái strike a match

火车 huǒchē [modif: 火 fire + 车 vehicle] *n* train (辆 **liàng**, 列 **liè**) □ 我们坐火车到北京去。**Wǒmen zuò huǒchē dào Běijīng qù.** *We'll go to Beijing by train.* □ 上海来的火车晚上八点二十五分到达。**Shànghǎi lái de huǒchē wǎnshang bā diǎn èrshíwǔ fēn dàodá.** *The train from Shanghai arrives at 8:25 in the evening.*
火车站 huǒchē zhàn railway station
火车票 huǒchē piào train ticket
火车时刻表 huǒchē shíkè biǎo railway timetable

火箭 huǒjiàn [modif: 火 fire + 箭 arrow] *n* rocket (枚 **méi**)
发射火箭 fāshè huǒjiàn launch a rocket

火力 huǒlì [modif: 火 fire + 力 power] *n* 1 fire power 2 thermal energy
火力发电 huǒlì fādiàn thermal power

火山 huǒshān [modif: 火 fire + 山 mountain] *n* volcano (座 **zuò**)
火山爆发 huǒshān bàofā the eruption of a volcano
活火山 huó huǒshān active volcano
死火山 sǐ huǒshān dormant volcano

火焰 huǒyàn *n* flame
熊熊火焰 xióngxióng huǒyàn raging flames

火药 huǒyào [modif: 火 fire + 药 drug] *n* gunpowder

火灾 huǒzāi [modif: 火 fire + 灾 disaster] *n* fire disaster, fire (场 **cháng**)

伙 huǒ Trad 夥 *n* partner
伙伴 huǒbàn [comp: 伙 partner + 伴 companion] *n* partner, mate

伙食 huǒshí *n* meals (provided by a school, a factory, etc.) □ 部队里的伙食很好。**Bùduì li de huǒshí hěn hǎo.** *The army canteens provide good meals.*

霍 huò as in 霍乱 **huòluàn**
霍乱 huòluàn *n* cholera

祸 huò Trad 禍 *n* disaster, calamity
祸害 huòhài [comp: 祸 disaster + 害 harm] I *n* disaster, scourge II *v* bring disaster to, ruin

或 huò *conj* Same as 或者 **huòzhě**. Used more in writing.

或多或少 huòduō huòshǎo *adv* more or less, somehow

或许 huòxǔ *adv* perhaps, maybe

或者 huòzhě *conj* or, either ... or □ 你明天一定要给我回信，可以打电话，或者发电子邮件。**Nǐ míngtiān yídìng yào gěi wǒ huíxìn, kěyǐ dǎ diànhuà, huòzhě fā diànzǐ yóujiàn.** *You must give me a reply tomorrow, either by phone or by email.*

惑 huò *v* confuse (See 迷惑 **míhuò**)

货 huò Trad 貨 *n* goods □ 暂时没有货，过两天再来问吧。**Zànshí méiyǒu huò, guò liǎng tiān zài**

lái wèn ba. *We're out of stock for the time being. Do come and inquire after a couple of days.*

货币 huòbì *n* currency
货币贬值 huòbì biǎnzhí currency devaluation
货币升值 huòbìshēngzhí currency appreciation

货物 huòwù [comp: 货 goods + 物 things] *n* goods, commodities, merchandise

获 huò Trad 獲 *v* gain, win
获得 huòdé [comp: 获 gain, win + 得 get] *v* win, obtain, get □ 他工作努力，获得了优秀成绩。**Tā gōngzuò nǔlì, huòdéle yōuxiù chéngjì.** *He works hard and has won excellent achievements.*

获取 huòqǔ [comp: 获 gain + 取 abtain] *v* gain, obtain

J

击 jī Trad 擊 *v* strike (See 打击 **dǎjī**)

几 jī Trad 幾 *adv* nearly
几乎 jīhū *adv* almost, nearly □ 这个国家的人几乎都会说一点英语。**Zhège guójiā de rén jīhū dōu huì shuō yìdiǎn Yīngyǔ.** *Almost everyone in this country speaks some English.* □ 她的工资几乎全用来买新衣服。**Tā de gōngzī jīhū quán yònglai mǎi xīn yīfu.** *She spends nearly all her salary on new clothes.*

饥 jī Trad 飢 *adj* starved
饥饿 jī'è [comp: 饥 starved + 饿 hungry] *adj* starved, hungry

机 jī Trad 機 *n* 1 machine 2 opportunity
机场 jīchǎng [modif: 机 airplane + 场 ground, field] *n* airport □ "机场离这里远不远？" "不远，大概十公里。" **"Jīchǎng lí zhèli yuǎn bu yuǎn?" "Bù yuǎn, dàgài shí gōnglǐ."** *"Is the airport far from here?" "Not very far. About ten kilometers."* □ 下午我要去机场接一个朋友。**Xiàwǔ wǒ yào qù jīchǎng jiē yí ge péngyou.** *I'm going to the airport this afternoon to receive a friend.*

机车 jīchē *n* locomotive (辆 **liàng**)

机床 jīchuáng *n* machine tool (台 **tái**) □ 这一台机床是从国外进口的。**Zhè yí tái jīchuáng shì cóng guówài jìnkǒu de.** *This machine tool was imported from overseas.*

机动 jīdòng *adj* 1 flexible
机动资金 jīdòng zījīn emergency fund, reserve fund 2 motorized, machine-powdered
机动车 jīdòngchē motorized vehicle (e.g. automobiles, motorcycles)

机构 jīgòu *n* government agency, organization

机关 jīguān *n* government office, state organ □ 这一地区有很多重要的政府机关。**Zhè yí dìqū yǒu hěn duō zhòngyào de zhèngfǔ jīguān.** *There are many important government offices in this district.*

机会 jīhuì [comp: 机 situation, opportunity + 会 by chance] *n* opportunity, chance □ 你有没有机会去北京学中文？**Nǐ yǒu méiyǒu jīhuì qù Běijīng xué Zhōngwén?** *Do you have any chance of going to Beijing to learn Chinese?*
放弃机会 fàngqì jīhuì give up an opportunity
抓住机会 zhuāzhù jīhuì grasp an opportunity
错过机会 cuòguò jīhuì miss an opportunity □ 这个

机会很难得，不要错过。**Zhège jīhuì hěn nándé, bú yào cuòguo.** *This is a rare opportunity. Don't miss it.*

机灵 **jīling** *adj* quick-witted

机密 **jīmì** *adj* secret, classified, confidential
机密文件 **jīmìwénjiàn** classified document

机器 **jīqì** [comp: 机 device, machine + 器 utensil] *n* machine (台 **tái**)
使用机器 **shǐyòng jīqì** operate a machine □ 你会不会使用这台机器? **Nǐ huì bu huì shǐyòng zhè tái jīqì?** *Do you know how to use this machine?*
修理机器 **xiūlǐ jīqì** repair a machine

机器人 **jīqì rén** [modif: 机器 machine + 人 man, person] *n* robot

机体 **jītǐ** *n* organism

机械 **jīxiè** [comp: 机 machinery + 械 tool] *n* machine, machinery □ 建筑机械已经进入工地，马上要开工了。**Jiànzhù jīxiè yǐjīng jìnrù gōngdì, mǎshàng yào kāigōng le.** *Construction machinery has entered the construction site. (→ Construction machinery is on the site now.) Work will begin soon.*

机遇 **jīyù** *n* rare opportunity, favorable situation

机智 **jīzhì** **I** *n* wit **II** *adj* sharp-witted

肌 **jī** *n* muscle, flesh
肌肉 **jīròu** [comp: 肌 muscle + 肉 flesh] *n* muscle

讥 **jī** Trad 譏 *v* sneer, mock
讥笑 **jīxiào** [comp: 讥 sneer + 笑 laugh] *v* sneer at, laugh at, ridicule

鸡 **jī** Trad 雞 *n* chicken (只 **zhī**) □ 我们晚饭吃鸡，好吗? **Wǒmen wǎnfàn chī jī, hǎo ma?** *We'll have chicken tonight, OK?* □ 我最爱喝鸡汤。**Wǒ zuì ài hē jītāng.** *Chicken soup is my favorite food.*
公鸡 **gōngjī** rooster
母鸡 **mǔjī** hen
小鸡 **xiǎojī** chick
肯德基烤鸡 **Kěn dé jī kǎojī** Kentucky Fried Chicken (KFC)

NOTE: 鸡 **jī**, as a general term, may denote either a *hen*, a *rooster* or *chick*, though they may be specified by 公鸡 **gōngjī** *cock*, 母鸡 **mǔjī** *hen* and 小鸡 **xiǎojī** *chicken*. As food, it is always 鸡 **jī**.

鸡蛋 **jīdàn** [modif: 鸡 hen + 蛋 egg] *n* hen's egg (只 **zhī**, 个 **gè**) □ 妈妈每星期买两公斤鸡蛋。**Māma měi xīngqī mǎi liǎng gōngjīn jīdàn.** *Mom buys two kilograms of eggs every week.* □ 新鲜鸡蛋营养丰富。**Xīnxiān jīdàn yíngyǎng fēngfù.** *Fresh eggs are very nutritious.*

积 **jī** Trad 積 *v* accumulate, amass
积极 **jījí** *adj* **1** enthusiastic, active (antonym 消极 **xiāojí**) □ 王老师积极推广普通话。**Wáng lǎoshī jījí tuīguǎng Pǔtōnghuà.** *Teacher Wang is very enthusiastic about popularizing Putonghua.* □ 我对这件事不积极; 我觉得没多大意思。**Wǒ duì zhè jiàn shì bù jījí; wǒ juéde méi duōdà yìsi.** *I'm not enthusiastic about this matter; I don't think it makes much sense.* **2** positive □ 对于困难，我们应该采取积极的态度。**Duìyú kùnnán, wǒmen yīnggāi cǎiqǔ jījí de tàidu.** *We should adopt a positive attitude towards difficulties.*

积极性 **jījíxìng** *n* initiative, enthusiasm, zeal □ 要使我们的公司成功，每一名职工必须发挥积极性。**Yào shǐ wǒmen de gōngsī chénggōng, měi yì míng zhígōng bìxū fāhuī jījíxìng.** *To make our company a success, every staff member must exercise initiative.*

积累 **jīlěi** [comp: 积 accumulate + 累 pile up] *v* accumulate, build up □ 他在三十年工作中积累了丰富的经验。**Tā zài sānshí nián gōngzuò zhōng jīlěile fēngfù de jīngyàn.** *He accumulated rich experience in the course of his career of over thirty years.*

积压 **jīyā** *v* keep too long in store, overstock
积压物资 **jīyā wùzī** overstocked supplies

基 **jī** *n* (earthen) foundation

基本 **jīběn** [comp: 基 (earthen) foundation + 本 root] *adj* fundamental, basic □ 这件事的基本情况我已经知道了。**Zhè jiàn shì de jīběn qíngkuàng wǒ yǐjīng zhīdào le.** *I've learned the basic facts of this matter (or event).*
基本上 **jīběn shang** basically, on the whole □ 我基本上同意你的计划。**Wǒ jīběn shang tóngyì nǐ de jìhuà** *I basically approve of your plan.*

基层 **jīcéng** *n* primary level, grass-roots

基础 **jīchǔ** [comp: 基 foundation + 础 plinth, base] *n* foundation, basis □ 你想建高楼，就要先打好基础。**Nǐ xiǎng jiàn gāolóu, jiù yào xiān dǎhao jīchǔ.** *If you want to erect a high building, you must first of all lay a good foundation.* □ 学中文，第一年是打基础。**Xué Zhōngwén, dì-yī nián shì dǎ jīchǔ.** *The first year of your Chinese studies lays the foundation.*

基地 **jīdì** [modif: 基 base + 地 place] *n* base

基金 **jījīn** [modif: 基 foundation + 金 money] *n* fund
教育基金 **jiàoyù jījīn** educational fund

基金会 **jījīnhuì** [modif: 基金 fund + 会 society] *n* foundation
儿童福利基金会 **értóng fúlì jījīnhuì** Foundation for Children's Welfare

基因 **jīyīn** [comp: 基 base + 因 cause] *n* gene

激 **jī** **I** *v* arouse, excite **II** *adj* violent, fervent
激动 **jīdòng** [comp: 激 arouse emotion + 动 move] **I** *v* arouse, excite □ 比赛结束前两分钟，他踢进一球，真是激动人心! **Bǐsài jiéshù qián liǎng fēnzhōng, tā tījìn yì qiú, zhēnshì jīdòng rénxīn!** *Two minutes before the end of the match he scored a goal. How exciting!* **II** *adj* excited, very emotional □ 我妹妹听了这个消息激动得一夜没睡。**Wǒ mèimei tīngle zhège xiāoxi jīdòng de yíyè méi shuì.** *After hearing the news my sister was so excited that she didn't sleep the entire night.*

激发 **jīfā** [comp: 激 excite + 发 release] *v* arouse, stir up
激发爱国主义 **jīfā àiguózhǔyì** arouse patriotism

激光 **jīguāng** *n* laser
激光打印机 **jīguāng dǎyìnjī** laser printer

激励 **jīlì** [comp: 激 excite + 励 encourage] *v* excite and urge, strongly encourage

激烈 **jīliè** [comp: 激 exciting + 烈 fierce] *adj* fierce, intense □ 运动会上运动员之间的竞赛十分激烈。**Yùndònghuì shang yùndòngyuán zhī jiān de jìngsài shífēn jīliè.** *At the sports meet competition between athletes was very fierce.*

激情 **jīqíng** [modif: 激 exciting + 情 emotion] *n* intense emotion, passion

激素 **jīsù** *n* hormone

圾 **jī** *n* garbage (See 垃圾 **lājī**.)

及 **jí** I *conj* and, with □ 他父亲、伯父、及祖父都是商人。 *Tā fùqin, bófù, jí zǔfù dōu shì shāngrén. His father, uncle and grandfather were all businessmen.* II *v* reach, come up to III *adv* in time for

及格 **jígé** [comp: 及 reach + 格 grade] *v* pass (a test, an examination etc.) □ "王老师，我这次测验及格吗？" "你不但及格，而且取得优秀成绩。" *"Wáng lǎoshī, wǒ zhè cì cèyàn jígé ma?" "Nǐ búdàn jígé, érqiě qǔdé yōuxiù chéngjì." "Teacher Wang, did I pass the test?" "Yes, you did, and you also got an excellent grade."*

及时 **jíshí** [v+obj: 及 reach + 时 time] I *adj* timely, at the proper time □ 这场雨下得真及时，农民高兴极了。 *Zhè cháng yǔ xià de zhēn jíshí, nóngmín gāoxìng jíle. This rain came at the right time. Farmers are delighted.* II *adv* immediately, promptly, without delay □ 感谢您及时回复我们的信。 *Gǎnxiè nín jíshí huífù wǒmen de xìn. Thank you for replying promptly to our letter.*

及早 **jízǎo** *adv* as soon as possible, promptly

籍 **jí** *n* 1 registration 2 membership
会籍 **huìjí** membership of an association

籍贯 **jíguàn** *n* place of one's birth or origin

级 **jí** Trad 級 *n* grade, rank □ 他是一级教师。 *Tā shì yì-jí jiàoshī. He is a first-class teacher.*

级别 **jíbié** *n* grade, scale
工资级别 **gōngzījíbié** wage/salary scale

极 **jí** Trad 極 *adv* extremely, highly □ 今天天气极好。 *Jīntiān tiānqì jí hǎo. The weather is extremely good today.*

极端 **jíduān** [comp: 极 extreme + 端 extreme] *adv* extremely
走极端 **zǒu jíduān** go to extremes

极了 **jíle** *adv* extremely, very □ 这两天我忙极了。 *Zhè liǎng tiān wǒ máng jíle. I'm extremely busy these days.*

NOTE: 极了 **jíle** is used after adjectives or some verbs to mean *extremely ...* or *very ...* For example: □ 忙极了 **máng jíle** *extremely busy* □ 高兴极了 **gāoxìng jíle** *very happy, delighted*

极力 **jílì** *adv* to one's utmost
极力劝他戒烟 **jílì quàn tā jiè yān** try all one can to persuade him to give up smoking

极其 **jíqí** *adv* extremely, highly □ 我们极其重视产品质量。 *Wǒmen jíqí zhòngshì chǎnpǐn zhìliàng. We attach great importance to the quality of our products.* □ 顾客对这样的服务态度极其不满。 *Gùkè duì zhèyàng de fúwù tàidu jíqí bùmǎn. Customers are extremely unhappy with such service.*

极限 **jíxiàn** [comp: 极 extreme + 限 limit] *n* the ultimate, the limit

吉 **jí** *adj* lucky, fortunate, auspicious
吉普车 **jípǔchē** *n* jeep (辆 **liàng**)

吉祥 **jíxiáng** [comp: 吉 lucky + 祥 auspicious] *adj* lucky, auspicious

吉祥物 **jíxiángwù** [modif: 吉祥 lucky + 物 thing] *n* mascot

辑 **jí** *v* compile, edit (See 编辑 **biānjí**)

疾 **jí** *n* disease
疾病 **jíbìng** [comp: 疾 disease + 病 illness] *n* disease, illness

嫉 **jí** *v* be jealous
嫉妒 **jídù** [comp: 嫉 be jealous + 妒 be jealous] *v* be jealous
嫉妒她妹妹的美貌 **jídù tā mèimei de měimào** be jealous of her younger sister's beauty

即 **jí** *v* be, mean
非此即彼 **fēicǐ jíbǐ** if it is not this one, it must be that one

即便 **jíbiàn** *conj* even if, even though

即将 **jíjiāng** *adv* soon

即使 **jíshǐ** *conj* even if, even though □ 他即使非常忙，也要抽工夫学中文。 *Tā jíshǐ fēicháng máng, yě yào chōu gōngfu xué Zhōngwén. Even though he is very busy, he will try and find time to learn Chinese.*

急 **jí** *adj* 1 anxious □ 他心里很急。 *Tā xīnlǐ hěn jí. He's very anxious.* 2 urgent □ 这件事很急。 *Zhè jiàn shì hěn jí. This is an urgent matter.* □ 他家里有急事，今天没来上班。 *Tā jiāli yǒu jíshì, jīntiān méi lái shàngbān. He has an urgent family matter [to attend to] and did not come to work today.*

急剧 **jíjù** *adj* sudden and intense, abrupt

急忙 **jímáng** [comp: 急 hurried + 忙 hastened] *adj* hurried, hasty □ 听说孩子病了，她急忙赶回家。 *Tīngshuō háizi bìng le, tā jímáng gǎn huíjiā. Hearing that her child was sick, she rushed back home.*

急切 **jíqiè** *adj* eager and impatient, urgent

急性子 **jíxìngzi** *n* an impatient or impetuous person □ 我妈妈是个急性子，爸爸是个慢性子，但是他们俩好像很合得来。 *Wǒ māma shì ge jíxìngzi, bàba shì ge mànxìngzi, dànshì tāmen liǎ hǎoxiàng hěn hé de lái. My mother is an impatient person while my father moves slowly. However, they seem to get along quite well.*

急于 **jíyú** *v* be eager to, be anxious to
急于求成 **jí yú qiú chéng** eager to have immediate success

急躁 **jízào** [comp: 急 hurried + 躁 impetuous] *adj* impetuous, impatient □ 他有一个缺点，就是性情急躁。 *Tā yǒu yí ge quēdiǎn, jiùshì xìngqíng jízào. He has a shortcoming; that is, he is rather impatient.*

集 **jí** *v* gather
集合 **jíhé** [comp: 集 assemble + 合 combine] *v* gather together, assemble □ 我们明天上午十点钟在火车站集合。 *Wǒmen míngtiān shàngwǔ shí diǎnzhōng zài huǒchēzhàn jíhé. We'll assemble at the railway station at ten o'clock tomorrow morning.*

集会 **jíhuì** [comp: 集 gather + 会 meet] *n* meeting, assembly

集市 **jíshì** *n* country fair, market

集体 **jítǐ** [modif: 集 collective + 体 body] *adj* collective (antonym 个人 **gèrén**) □ 这是董事会集体的决定。 *Zhè shì dǒngshìhuì jítǐ de juédìng. This is the collective decision of the board of directors.*

集团 **jítuán** *n* group, grouping

集邮 **jíyóu** [v+obj: 集 gather + 邮 stamps] *n* stamp collecting, philately

集中 **jízhōng** I *v* concentrate, focus □ 这个国家的重工业集中在一个很小的地区。 *Zhège guójiā de zhònggōngyè jízhōng zài yí ge hěn xiǎo de dìqū. The heavy industry of this country is concentrated in a*

small region. □ 我要集中精力, 学好中文。 **Wǒ yào jízhōng jīnglì, xuéhao Zhōngwén.** *I will concentrate my energy on gaining a good command of the Chinese language.* **II** *adj* concentrated, focused □ 这个学生上课时注意力不集中。 **Zhège xuésheng shàngkè shí zhùyìlì bù jízhōng.** *This student's attention is not focused in class.* (→ *This student doesn't pay attention in class.*)

集资 jízī [v+obj: 集 gather + 资 funds] *v* raise funds

几 jǐ Trad 幾 *pron* 1 several, some □ 我上星期买了几本书。 **Wǒ shàng xīngqī mǎile jǐ běn shū.** *I bought several books last week.* 2 how many □ 你上星期买了几本书? **Nǐ shàng xīngqī mǎile jǐ běn shū?** *How many books did you buy last week?*

NOTE: When 几 **jǐ** is used in a question to mean *how many*, it is presumed that the answer will be a number less than ten. Otherwise 多少 **duōshǎo** should be used instead. Compare: □ 你有几个哥哥? **Nǐ yǒu jǐ ge gēge?** *How many elder brothers do you have?* □ 你们学校有多少学生? **Nǐmen xuéxiào yǒu duōshǎo xuéshēng?** *How many students are there in your school?*

几何 jǐhé *n* geometry

脊 jǐ *n* spine, backbone
　脊梁 jǐliang *n* spine, backbone
脊椎 jǐzhuī *n* vertebra

己 jǐ *pron* self (See 自己 **zìjǐ**.)

挤 jǐ Trad 擠 **I** *v* squeeze, crowd □ 你会挤牛奶吗? **Nǐ huì jǐ niúnǎi ma?** *Do you know how to milk cows?* □ 他再忙也要挤出时间和孩子玩玩。 **Tā zài máng yě yào jǐchu shíjiān hé háizi wánwan.** *No matter how busy he is, he always finds time to play with his children.* □ 这间房间挤不下这么多人。 **Zhè jiān fángjiān jǐ bú xià zhème duō rén.** *It is impossible to pack so many people in this room.* **II** *adj* crowded □ 圣诞节前几天商店很挤。 **Shèngdànjié qián jǐ tiān shāngdiàn hěn jǐ.** *Stores are crowded days before Christmas.*

给 jǐ Trad 給 *v* provide (See 供给 **gōngjǐ**)

计 jì Trad 計 *v* 1 plan 2 calculate
计划 jìhuà [comp: 计 plan + 划 plan] **I** *n* plan □ 这个计划不可行。 **Zhè ge jìhuà bù kěxíng.** *This plan is not feasible.* □ 他们还在制定明年的计划。 **Tāmen hái zài zhìdìng míngnián de jìhuà.** *They are still working on their plan for next year.* □ 你明年有什么计划? **Nǐ míngnián yǒu shénme jìhuà?** *What's your plan for next year?* **II** *v* plan □ 我计划明年去美国旅游。 **Wǒ jìhuà míngnián qù Měiguó lǚyóu.** *I plan to tour the States next year.*
　制定计划 zhìdìng jìhuà draw up a plan
　执行计划 zhíxíng jìhuà implement a plan
计较 jìjiào [comp: 计 calculate + 较 compare] *v* 1 be fussy, haggle over 2 argue, dispute
　斤斤计较 jīnjīn jìjiào haggle over insignificant things, quibble over trivia
计算 jìsuàn [comp: 计 calculate + 算 calculate] *v* calculate □ 请你计算一下这个班去年考试的平均成绩。 **Qǐng nǐ jìsuàn yíxià zhège bān qùnián kǎoshì de píngjūn chéngjì.** *Please calculate the average marks of this class for last year's examination.*

计算机 jìsuànjī Same as 电脑 **diànnǎo**. Used as a more formal term.

记 jì Trad 記 *v* 1 remember, recall □ 那条街叫什么, 我记不清了。 **Nà tiáo jiē jiào shénme, wǒ jì bu qīng le.** *I don't remember clearly the name of that street.* (→ *I can't quite recall that street.*) 2 record (usually by writing down), bear in mind □ 你说得慢一点儿, 我把它记下来。 **Nǐ shuō de màn yìdiǎnr, wǒ bǎ tā jì xiàlai.** *Speak slowly. I'll write it down.* □ 我把她要我买的东西记下来了。 **Wǒ bǎ tā yào wǒ mǎi de dōngxi dōu jì xiàlai le.** *I've written down the things she wants me to buy.*
记得 jìde *v* can remember, can recall □ 我们第一次在什么地方见面的, 你还记得吗? **Wǒmen dì-yī cì shì zài shénme dìfang jiànmiàn de, nǐ hái jìde ma?** *Do you still remember where we first met?*
　记不得 jì bu de cannot remember, cannot recall □ 我记不得了。 **Wǒ jìbude le.** *I can't remember.*
记笔记 jì bǐjì *v* take notes
记号 jìhao *n* mark, sign
　做记号 zuò jìhao put a mark
　留下记号 liúxià jìhao leave a mark
记录 jìlù [comp: 记 record + 录 record] **I** *v* record □ 护士把病人的体温记录下来。 **Hùshi bǎ bìngrén de tǐwēn jìlù xiàlai.** *The nurse recorded the patient's temperature.* **II** *n* record □ 这位运动员打破了世界记录。 **Zhè wèi yùndòngyuán dǎpòle shìjiè jìlù.** *This athlete broke the world record.*
　会议记录 huìyì jìlù minutes (of a meeting)
记性 jìxing *n* ability to memorize things, memory □ 我弟弟记性很好。 **Wǒ dìdi jìxing hěn hǎo.** *My younger bother has a very good memory.*
记忆 jìyì [comp: 记 remember + 忆 recall] **I** *v* remember, memorize □ 童年的经历老人还记忆犹新。 **Tóngnián de jīnglì lǎorén hái jìyì yóuxīn.** *The old man still vividly remembers his childhood experiences.* **II** *n* memory □ 他们俩在海边共度的夏天, 成了他难忘的记忆。 **Tāmen liǎ zài hǎibiān gòngdù de xiàtiān, chéngle tā nánwàng de jìyì.** *The summer they spent together by the seaside has become an indelible memory for him.*
记载 jìzǎi *n* written record
记者 jìzhě [suffix: 记 record + 者 nominal suffix] *n* correspondent, reporter □ 记者及时报导了那次交通事故。 **Jìzhě jíshí bàodàole nà cì jiāotōng shìgù.** *Journalists reported the road accident promptly.*
　记者招待会 jìzhě zhāodàihuì press conference, news conference
　新闻记者 xīnwén jìzhě news reporter, journalist
记住 jìzhù *v* learn by heart, bear in mind □ 你要记住我的话, 别忘了! **Nǐ yào jìzhù wǒ de huà, bié wàng le!** *You should bear in mind what I said. Don't forget it.*

纪 jì Trad 紀 *n* 1 discipline 2 record
纪律 jìlǜ [comp: 纪 discipline + 律 rule] *n* discipline (条 tiáo) □ 军队的纪律很严格。 **Jūnduì de jìlǜ hěn yángé.** *Discipline in the army is very strict.* □ 他违反学校纪律, 受到了批评。 **Tā wéifǎn xuéxiào jìlǜ, shòudàole pīpíng.** *He violated school discipline and was reprimanded.*
纪念 jìniàn [comp: 纪 record + 念 remember] *v* commemorate □ 中国的端午节纪念一位伟大的爱国诗人。 **Zhōngguó de Duānwǔ jié jìniàn yí wèi wěidà**

de **àiguó shīrén**. *The Chinese boat festival commemorates a great patriotic poet.*

纪要 **jìyào** *n* major points, summary, digest

技 **jì** *n* skill, ability

技能 **jìnéng** [comp: 技 skill + 能 ability] *n* skill, technical skill

技巧 **jìqiǎo** *n* skill, craftsmanship

写作技巧 **xiězuòjìqiǎo** writing skills

技术 **jìshù** [comp: 技 skill + 术 craft] *n* technique, technology, skill □ 由于新技术的应用, 产品质量有了很大提高。**Yóuyú xīn jìshù de yìngyòng, chǎnpǐn zhìliàng yǒule hěn dà tígāo.** *Thanks to the application of the new technology, the product quality has been greatly improved.* □ 你得学点技术, 走到哪儿都有用。**Nǐ děi xué diǎn jìshù, zǒu dào nǎr dōu yǒuyòng.** *You've got to learn some skills, which will be useful wherever you go.*

技术工人 **jìshù gōngrén** skilled worker

技术员 **jìshùyuán** [modif: 技术 technique, technology + 员 person] *n* technician (位 **wèi**) □ 车床出问题了, 要请技术员来看一下。**Chēchuáng chū wèntí le, yào qǐng jìshùyuán lái kàn yíxià.** *Something has gone wrong with the machine tool. Please send for the technician.*

际 **jì** Trad 際 *n* boundary, border (See 国际 **guójì**, 实际 **shíjì**.)

季 **jì** *n* season

季度 **jìdù** *n* quarter (of a year)

季节 **jìjié** [comp: 季 season + 节 solar term] *n* season □ 春夏秋冬, 你最喜欢哪个季节? **Chūn-xià-qiū-dōng, nǐ zuì xǐhuan nǎge jìjié?** *Spring, summer, autumn and winter—which season do you like best?*

济 **jì** Trad 濟 *v* aid (See 经济 **jīngjì**.)

剂 **jì** Trad 劑 *n* medicine

剂量 **jìliàng** [modif: 剂 medicine + 量 amount] *n* dose, dosage

迹 **jì** *n* remains, trace (See 古迹 **gǔjì**.)

迹象 **jìxiàng** *n* sign, indication

地震的迹象 **dìzhèn de jìxiàng** signs of a (forthcoming) earthquake

既 **jì** *conj* **1** same as 既然 **jìrán**. Used more in writing. **2** both ... and ...

既...又... **jì...yòu...** both ... and .... □ 她既要上班, 又要管孩子。**Tā jì yào shàngbān, yòu yào guǎn háizi.** *She has to both work and care for the children.*

既...也... **jì...yě...** both ... and .... □ 你既要看到一个人的优点, 也要看到一个人的缺点。**Nǐ jì yào kàndao yí ge rén de yōudiǎn, yěyào kàndao yí ge rén de quēdiǎn.** *You should see both the merits and shortcomings of a person.*

既然 **jìrán** *conj* now that, since, as □ 他既然已经决定, 你就不必多说了。**Tā jìrán yǐjīng juédìng, nǐ jiù búbì duō shuō le.** *Now that he's made up his mind, you needn't say anything more.* □ 既然你不喜欢他, 为什么还要和他一起出去玩呢? **Jìrán nǐ bù xǐhuan tā, wèishénme háiyào hé tā yìqǐ chūqu wán ne?** *Since you don't like him, why do you still go out with him?*

忌 **jì** *v* **1** avoid, shun **2** be jealous

忌酒 **jìjiǔ** avoid wine, refrain from drinking wines

忌妒 **jìdu** Same as 嫉妒 **jídù**

绩 **jì** Trad 績 *n* accomplishment (See 成绩 **chéngjì**.)

继 **jì** Trad 繼 *v* continue

继承 **jìchéng** [comp: 继 continue + 承 inherit] *v* inherit, carry on

继承人 **jìchéngrén** [modif: 继承 inherit + 人 person] *n* heir, successor

继续 **jìxù** [comp: 继 continue + 续 keep on] *v* continue □ 我们吃午饭吧, 下午继续开会。**Wǒmen chī wǔfàn ba, xiàwǔ jìxù kāihuì.** *Let's have lunch. The meeting will continue in the afternoon.* □ 这种情况不能再继续下去了。**Zhè zhǒng qíngkuàng bùnéng zài jìxù xiàqu le.** *This situation must not be allowed to go on.*

寂 **jì** *adj* lonely

寂静 **jìjìng** [comp: 寂 lonely + 静 silent] *adj* peaceful and quiet, still

寂寞 **jìmò** *adj* lonely

寄 **jì** *v* **1** send by mail, post □ 请你马上把这些书寄给王先生。**Qǐng nǐ mǎshàng bǎ zhèxiē shū jìgei Wáng xiānsheng.** *Please post these books to Mr Wang immediately.* □ 我要寄这封信去香港。**Wǒ yào jì zhè fēng xìn qù Xiānggǎng.** *I want to post this letter to Hong Kong.*

寄快件 **jì kuàijiàn** send by express mail

2 entrust

寄托 **jìtuō** *v* entrust

寄托希望 **jìtuō xīwàng** place one's hope on

加 **jiā** *v* **1** add, plus □ 一加二等于三。**Yì jiā èr děngyú sān.** *One plus two equals three.* **2** increase

加班 **jiābān** [modif: 加 add + 班 shift] *v* work overtime

加班费 **jiābān fèi** overtime pay

加工 **jiāgōng** [v+obj: 加 add + 工 work] *v* process (unfinished products) □ 这个工厂主要做来料加工。**Zhège gōngchǎng zhǔyào zuò láiliào jiāgōng.** *This factory mainly processes supplied materials.*

来料加工 **láiliào jiāgōng** processing of supplied materials

食品加工 **shípǐn jiāgōng** food processing

加紧 **jiājǐn** *v* intensify, speed up

加紧准备 **jiājǐn zhǔnbèi** speed up preparations

加剧 **jiājù** *v* aggravate, exacerbate

加拿大 **Jiānádà** *n* Canada

加强 **jiāqiáng** [comp: 加 add + 强 strong] *v* strengthen, reinforce □ 我们要加强研究开发工作。**Wǒmen yào jiāqiáng yánjiū kāifā gōngzuò.** *We should strengthen research and development work.*

加热 **jiārè** [v+obj: 加 add + 热 heat] *v* heat, heat up

加入 **jiārù** [comp: 加 add + 入 enter] *v* **1** become a member of, join **2** add in

加入网球俱乐部 **jiārù wǎngqiú jùlèbù** join a tennis club

加深 **jiāshēn** *v* deepen

加深两国之间的相互理解 **jiāshēn liǎngguó zhījiān de xiānghù lǐjiě** deepen mutual understanding between the two countries

加速 **jiāsù** [v+obj: 加 add + 速 speed] *v* accelerate, quicken

加速器 **jiāsù qì** accelerator

加以 **jiāyǐ** **I** *v* (used before a verb to indicate what should be done) □ 这个问题应及时加以解决。**Zhège wèntí yīng jíshí jiāyǐ jiějué.** *This problem should be solved promptly.* □ 对违反纪律的学生必须加以严肃处理。**Duì wéifǎn jìlǜ de xuésheng bìxū jiāyǐ yánsù**

chǔlǐ. *Students who have violated discipline must be dealt with seriously.* **II** *conj* in addition, moreover □ 他身体很差，加以工作太辛苦，终于病倒在床上。 **Tā shēntǐ hěn chà, jiāyǐ gōngzuò tài xīnkǔ, zhōngyú bìngdǎo zài chuáng shang.** *He was in poor health; moreover, he worked too hard and was finally bed-ridden with illness.*

NOTE: 加以 **jiāyǐ** as a verb smacks of officialese and is chiefly used in writing. The sentence still stands when 加以 **jiāyǐ** is omitted, e.g. □ 这个问题应及时解决。**Zhège wèntí yīng jíshí jiějué.** *This problem should be solved promptly.*

加油 **jiāyóu** *v* **1** add fuel, fuel up
　加油站 jiāyóuzhàn gas station, service station
2 make extra efforts
　加油干 jiāyóugàn double one's efforts, put more effort into one's work

NOTE: 加油 **jiāyóu** is the colloquial expression used to cheer on a sportsperson or a sporting team in a competition, equivalent to *Come on!*, or *Go! Go!*

加重 **jiāzhòng** [v+obj: 加 add + 重 weight] *v* increase the amount, aggravate
　加重负担 jiāzhòng fùdān increase the burden

嘉 **jiā** *adj* good, fine
　嘉宾 jiābīn honored guest
嘉奖 **jiājiǎng** *v* commend, cite

佳 **jiā** *adj* good, fine, beautiful
　佳节 jiājié joyous festival

夹 **jiā** *v* pinch, squeeze, wedge between, sandwich □ 你会不会用筷子夹一个蛋？ **Nǐ huì bu huì yòng kuàizi jiā yí ge dàn?** *Can you use chopsticks to pick up an egg?*
夹杂 **jiāzá** *v* be mixed up with
夹子 **jiāzi** *n* tong, clip
　衣服夹子 yīfu jiāzi clothes pin

家 **jiā** **I** *n* **1** family, household □ 我家有四口人：父亲、母亲，姐姐和我。**Wǒ jiā yǒu sì kǒu rén: fùqin, mǔqin, jiějie hé wǒ.** *There're four people in my family: my father, my mother, my sister and I.* **2** home □ 下课以后我就回家。**Xià kè yǐhòu wǒ jiù huíjiā.** *I go home as soon as school is over.* **II** *measure wd* (for families or businesses)
　四家人家 sì jiā rénjiā four families
　一家商店 yì jiā shāngdiàn a store
　两家工厂 liǎng jiā gōngchǎng two factories
III *suffix* (denoting an accomplished expert)
　画家 huàjiā painter, artist
　教育家 jiàoyùjiā educator
　科学家 kēxuéjiā scientist
家常 **jiācháng** *adj* everyday life, commonplace
　淡家常 tán jiācháng have a chitchat
　家常便饭 jiācháng biànfàn simple meal, usually home-cooked
家畜 **jiāchù** *n* domesticated animal (头 **tóu**)
家教 **jiājiào** [modif: 家 home, at home + 教 teach] *n* **1** private tutor □ 他们的女儿数学不行，他们要给她找一位家教。**Tāmen de nǚ'ér shùxué bùxíng, tāmen yào gěi tā zhǎo yí wèi jiājiào.** *Their daughter is not good*

at math, so they're going to find a private tutor for her. **2** family upbringing
家具 **jiājù** [modif: 家 home + 具 implements] *n* furniture (套 **tào**, 件 **jiàn**) □ 他们结婚时买了一套漂亮而实用的家具，后来又添了几件小家具。**Tāmen jiéhūn shí mǎile yí tào piàoliang ér shíyòng de jiājù, hòulái yòu tiānle jǐ jiàn xiǎo jiājù.** *When they got married, they bought a beautiful and practical set of household furniture, and later on added several pieces of occasional furniture.*
家属 **jiāshǔ** *n* family member, one's dependent (名 **míng**)
家庭 **jiātíng** [comp: 家 home, family + 庭 courtyard] *n* family (个 **gè**) □ 他的家庭很幸福。**Tā de jiātíng hěn xìngfú.** *He has a happy family.* □ 她在这里没有家庭，也没有朋友。**Tā zài zhèlǐ méiyǒu jiātíng, yě méiyou péngyou.** *She has neither family nor friends here.* □ 中国人比较重视家庭。**Zhōngguórén bǐjiào zhòngshì jiātíng.** *The Chinese attach much importance to the family.*

NOTE: 家 **jiā** has more meanings than 家庭 **jiātíng**. While 家庭 **jiātíng** means only *family*, 家 **jiā** may mean *family*, *household* or *home*.

家务 **jiāwù** [modif: 家 family, home + 务 work, duty] *n* household chores, housework (件 **jiàn**) □ 你帮太太做家务吗？**Nǐ bāng tàitai zuò jiāwù ma?** *Do you help your wife with household chores?*
家乡 **jiāxiāng** [modif: 家 home + 乡 village] *n* hometown, home village □ 这几年家乡发生了巨大变化。**Zhè jǐ nián, jiāxiāng fāshēngle jùdà biànhuà.** *In the past few years great changes have taken place in my hometown.*
家喻户晓 **jiā yù hù xiǎo** *idiom* be a household name, widely known
家长 **jiāzhǎng** [modif: 家 family + 长 head] *n* **1** head of a family **2** parent

颊 **jiá** *n* cheek

甲 **jiǎ** *n* first

甲 **jiǎ** *n* shell, nail
　指甲 zhǐjia fingernail
甲板 **jiǎbǎn** *n* deck (of a ship)

假 **jiǎ** *adj* **1** false, untrue □ 他说的这些话都是假的。**Tā shuō de zhèxiē huà dōu shì jiǎ de.** *All he said was untrue.* **2** artificial
假定 **jiǎdìng** *v* Same as 假设 **jiǎshè**
假话 **jiǎhuà** [modif: 假 false + 话 word] *n* falsehood, lie
假货 **jiǎhuò** [modif: 假 false + 货 commodity] *n* fake (goods), forgery, counterfeit
假冒 **jiǎmào** *v* pass off as genuine
假如 **jiǎrú** *conj* supposing, if
假若 **jiǎruò** *conj* Same as 假如 **jiǎrú**
假设 **jiǎshè** *v* suppose, assume
假腿 **jiǎtuǐ** [modif: 假 artificial + 腿 leg] *n* artificial leg
假牙 **jiǎyá** [modif: 假 artificial + 牙 tooth] *n* denture
假装 **jiǎzhuāng** [comp: 假 false + 装 disguise] *v* pretend, feign

稼 **jià** *n* crops (See 庄稼 **zhuāngjià**.)

价 **jià** Trad 價 *n* price, value

价格 **jiàgé** *n* price □ 新汽车价格合理，卖得很快。**Xīn qìchē jiàgé hélǐ, màide hěn kuài.** *The new car is reasonably priced and sells quickly.*

价钱 **jiàqian** [comp: 价 price + 钱 money] *n* price □ 价钱太贵，还是不要买吧。**Jiàqian tài guì, háishì bú yào mǎi ba.** *The price is too high. Don't buy it.* □ 他只是问一下价钱，没打算买。**Tā zhǐshì wèn yíxià jiàqian, méi dǎsuàn mǎi.** *He only asked the price and didn't intend to buy it.*

价值 **jiàzhí** [comp: 价 price + 值 worth] *n* value □ 这些书太旧了，没有多大价值。**Zhèxiē shū tài jiù le, méiyǒu duō dà jiàzhí.** *These books are too old and do not have much value.*

价值观 **jiàzhíguān** [modif: 价值 value + 观 view] *n* values □ 对不起，我的价值观和你不一样。**Duìbuqǐ, wǒ de jiàzhíguān hé nǐ bù yíyàng.** *Sorry, my values are different from yours.*

驾 **jià** Trad 駕 *v* drive, pilot

驾驶 **jiàshǐ** *v* drive, pilot
驾驶轮船 **jiàshǐ lúnchuan** pilot a ship
驾驶飞机 **jiàshǐ fēijī** pilot a plane
驾驶汽车 **jiàshǐ qìchē** drive an automobile
驾驶员 **jiàshǐyuán** [suffix: 驾驶 drive, pilot + 员 nominal suffix] *n* driver, pilot

架 1 **jià** *measure wd* (used for machines, aircraft etc.)
一架客机 **yí jià kèjī** a passenger plane

架 2 **jià** *n* shelf, stand
书架 **shūjià** bookshelf

嫁 **jià** *v* (of a woman) marry □ 他们的女儿嫁给了一个美国人。**Tāmen de nǚér jiàgeile yí ge Měiguórén.** *Their daughter married an American.* □ 嫁鸡随鸡，嫁狗随狗。**Jià jī suí jī, jià gǒu suí gǒu.** *Marry a rooster and you follow a rooster; marry a dog and you follow a dog. (An old saying meaning that a woman complies with whoever she marries.)*

NOTE: 嫁 **jià** means specifically *(for a woman) to marry*, while *(for a man) to marry* is 娶 **qǔ**. However more and more people simply use the verb 和…结婚 **hé...jiéhūn** to mean *marry*, e.g. 他们的女儿和一个美国人结婚。**Tāmen de nǚér he yí ge Měiguórén jiéhūn.** *Their daughter married an American.*

假 **jià** *n* holiday, leave

假期 **jiàqī** [modif: 假 holiday + 期 period] *n* holiday period, leave □ 假期你打算做什么? **Jiàqī nǐ dǎsuàn zuò shénme?** *What do you plan to do during the holidays?* □ 假期的时候，火车飞机都很挤。**Jiàqī de shíhou, huǒchē fēijī dōu hěn jǐ.** *During the holiday period, trains and planes are all crowded.*

假条 **jiàtiáo** [comp: 假 leave + 条 slip] *n* an application for leave, a leave form □ 明天家里有重要的事不能来上课，这是假条。**Míngtiān jiāli yǒu zhòngyào de shì, bù néng lái shàngkè, zhè shì jiàtiáo.** *I can't come to class tomorrow as there's important family business to attend to. Here's my leave application.*
病假条 **bìngjiàtiáo** an application for sick leave, a doctor's certificate of illness, a medical certifi-

cate □ 医生给他开了病假条。**Yīshēng gěi tā kāile bìngjiàtiáo.** *The doctor gave him a medical certificate.*

尖 **jiān** *adj* sharp, pointed □ 这孩子耳朵尖，我们这么小声说话她都听见了。**Zhè háizi ěrduo jiān, wǒmen zhème xiǎoshēng shuōhuà tā dōu tīngjiànle.** *This child has sharp ears. We talked in such low voices but she heard us.*

尖端 **jiānduān** [modif: 尖 sharp, pointed + 端 end] **I** *n* pointed end **II** *adj* sophisticated
尖端产品 **jiānduān chǎnpǐn** technologically advanced product
尖端科学 **jiānduānkēxué** sophisticated science
尖端技术 **jiānduān jìshù** most advanced technology

尖锐 **jiānruì** [comp: 尖 pointed + 锐 sharp] *adj* **1** very sharp, penetrating □ 多家报纸对政府提出尖锐批评。**Duō jiā bàozhǐ duì zhèngfǔ tíchū jiānruì pīpíng.** *Several newspapers made biting criticism of the government.* **2** fierce, uncompromising □ 他们之间的矛盾很尖锐。**Tāmen zhī jiān de máodùn hěn jiānruì.** *There is bitter conflict between them.*

尖子 **jiānzi** *n* the pick (of a group), top student

坚 **jiān** Trad 堅 *adj* hard, firm

坚持 **jiānchí** [modif: 坚 firm, firmly + 持 hold] *v* uphold, persist (in) □ 不管刮风下雨，他坚持每天跑步。**Bùguǎn guāfēng xià yǔ, tā jiānchí měi tiān pǎobù.** *He persists in jogging every day no matter how wet or windy it is.* □ 尽管大家都不同意，他仍然坚持自己的观点。**Jǐnguǎn dàjiā dōu bù tóngyì, tā réngrán jiānchí zìjǐ de guāndiǎn.** *Despite everyone's disagreement, he still holds on to his views.*

坚定 **jiāndìng** [comp: 坚 solid + 定 fixed] *adj* firm □ 我坚定地相信公司的决定是正确的。**Wǒ jiāndìng de xiāngxìn gōngsī de juédìng shì zhèngquè de.** *I'm firmly convinced that the company's decision is correct.*

坚固 **jiāngù** [comp: 坚 solid + 固 solid] *adj* solid, sturdy

坚决 **jiānjué** [comp: 坚 solid + 决 determined] *adj* resolute, determined □ 我坚决执行公司的决定。**Wǒ jiānjué zhíxíng gōngsī de juédìng.** *I will resolutely carry out the company's decision.*

坚强 **jiānqiáng** [comp: 坚 solid+ 强 strong] *adj* strong, staunch
性格坚强 **xìnggé jiānqiáng** strong character

坚实 **jiānshí** [comp: 坚 solid + 实 substantial] *adj* solid, substantial
打下坚实的基础 **dǎxià jiānshí de jīchǔ** lay a solid foundation

坚硬 **jiānyìng** [comp: 坚 solid + 硬 hard] *adj* solid and hard □ 大门是用坚硬的木头做的。**Dàmén shì yòng jiānyìng de mùtou zuò de.** *The gate is made from very hard timber.*

间 **jiān** Trad 間 **I** *n* room (for a special purpose)
洗澡间 **xǐzǎo jiān** bathroom
手术间 **shǒushù jiān** operating theater, surgical room **II** *measure wd* (for rooms)
一间教室 **yì jiān jiàoshì** a classroom
两间办公室 **liǎng jiān bàngōngshì** two offices

肩 **jiān** *n* the shoulder □ 我左肩疼。**Wǒ zuǒ jiān téng.** *My left shoulder hurts.*

艰 **jiān** Trad 艱 *adj* difficult

艰巨 **jiānjù** [comp: 艰 difficult + 巨 gigantic] *adj* (of a big and important task) very difficult,

strenuous □ 他们要到外国去开辟市场, 这是一项艰巨的任务。**Tāmen yào dào wàiguó qù kāipì shìchǎng, zhè shì yí xiàng jiānjù de rènwu.** *They are going overseas to open up a new market, which is a difficult and immense undertaking.*

艰苦 **jiānkǔ** [comp: 艰 difficult + 苦 bitter, harsh] *adj* difficult, hard, tough □ 城里人往往不了解很多农民的艰苦生活。**Chénglírén wǎngwǎng bù liáojiě hěnduō nóngmín de jiānkǔ shēnghuó.** *People in the city usually do not know the hard life many peasants live.*

艰难 **jiānnán** [comp: 艰 difficult + 难 difficult] *adj* arduous, hard
　艰难的任务 jiānnán de rènwu arduous task

艰险 **jiānxiǎn** [comp: 艰 difficult + 险 perilous] *adj* hard and difficult, perilous

兼 **jiān** *adv* concurrently □ 他是这家公司的董事长兼总经理。**Tā shì zhè jiā gōngsī de dǒngshìzhǎng jiān zǒngjīnglǐ.** *He is chairman of the board and concurrently CEO of the company.*

监 **jiān** Trad 監 **I** *v* supervise, inspect **II** *n* prison, jail

监察 **jiānchá** [comp: 监 supervise + 察 inspect] *v* supervise, monitor

监督 **jiāndū** [comp: 监 supervise + 督 superintend] *v* 1 supervise, superintend 2 have under surveillance, watch over

监视 **jiānshì** [comp: 监 supervise + 视 view] *v* keep under surveillance, monitor □ 在入口处安装了摄像机, 来监视进出人员。**Zài rùkǒuchù ānzhuāngle shèxiàngjī, lái jiānshì jìnchū rényuán.** *A camera has been installed at the entrance to keep a watch on the people coming and going.*

监狱 **jiānyù** *n* jail, prison (座 **zuò**)

歼 **jiān** *v* wipe out
　歼击机 jiānjījī *n* fighter plane
歼灭 **jiānmiè** *v* annihilate, wipe out

奸 **jiān** **I** *adj* wicked and treacherous **II** *n* traitor
　汉奸 hànjiān traitor to the Han people, traitor to the Chinese people

煎 **jiān** *v* fry, shallow-fry

剪 **jiān** *v* cut (with scissors), shear □ 剪羊毛是很辛苦的, 不过工资挺高。**Jiǎn yángmáo shì hěn xīnkǔ de, búguò gōngzī tǐng gāo.** *Sheep shearing is a hard job, but pays well.*

剪彩 **jiǎncǎi** *v* cut the ribbon at an opening ceremony
剪刀 **jiǎndāo** *n* scissors, shears (把 **bǎ**)

茧 **jiǎn** Trad 繭 *n* 1 callus 2 cocoon
　老茧 lǎojiǎn callus

柬 **jiǎn** *n* letter
　请柬 qǐngjiǎn letter of invitation, invitation

检 **jiǎn** Trad 檢 *v* examine
检测 **jiǎncè** [comp: 检 examine + 测 test] *v* check and measure, verify

检查 **jiǎnchá** [comp: 检 examine + 查 inspect, check] *v* examine, inspect, check □ 先生, 我要检查一下你的行李。**Xiānsheng, wǒ yào jiǎnchá yíxià nǐ de xíngli.** *I need to inspect your luggage, sir.* □ 他每年检查一次身体。**Tā měi nián jiǎnchá yí cì shēntǐ.** *He has a physical examination (or medical checkup) once a year.* □ 下个月总公司要派人来检查我们的工作。**Xià**

ge yuè zǒnggōngsī yào pài rén lái jiǎnchá wǒmen de gōngzuò.** *Next month the head office will send people to inspect our work.*

检察 **jiǎnchá** [comp: 检 examine + 察 examine] *n* procuratorial work
检察员 jiǎncháyuán procurator
检察院 jiǎncháyuàn procuratorate
最高人民检察院 Zuìgāo Rénmín Jiǎncháyuàn the Supreme People's Procuratorate

检讨 **jiǎntǎo** **I** *v* 1 examine 2 review **II** *n* self-criticism
书面检讨 shūmiàn jiǎntǎo written self-criticism
做检讨 zuò jiǎntǎo make a self-criticism

检修 **jiǎnxiū** [comp: 检 examine + 修 repair] *v* examine and repair (a machine), maintain
大检修 dàjiǎnxiū overhaul
汽车检修工 qìchē jiǎnxiū gōng car mechanic

检验 **jiǎnyàn** [comp: 检 examine + 验 test] **I** *v* examine, test **II** *n* examination, testing □ 我们的产品都是经过严格的质量检验的。**Wǒmen de chǎnpǐn dōu jīngguò yángé de zhìliàng jiǎnyàn de.** *All our products undergo strict quality control.*

捡 **jiǎn** Trad 撿 *v* pick up □ 把垃圾捡起来。**Bǎ lājī jiǎn qǐlái.** *Pick up the litter.*

俭 **jiǎn** Trad 儉 *adj* thrifty (See 勤俭 qínjiǎn)

拣 **jiǎn** Trad 揀 *v* 1 choose, select □ 这么多漂亮衣服, 她不知道拣哪一件好。**Zhème duō piàoliang yīfu, tā bù zhīdào jiǎn nǎ yí jiàn hǎo.** *There were so many pretty dresses, she did not know which to choose.* 2 Same as 捡 **jiǎn**

减 **jiǎn** *v* 1 subtract, deduct □ 三百六十七减二百八十六是多少? **Sānbǎi liùshíqī jiǎn èrbǎi bāshíliù shì duōshǎo?** *How much is 367 minus 268?*
减数 jiǎnshù subtrahend (e.g. 268 in the example)
被减数 bèi jiǎnshù minuend (e.g. 367 in the example)
2 reduce, lighten

减轻 **jiǎnqīng** [v+compl: 减 subtract + 轻 light] *v* lighten, alleviate □ 使用电脑以后, 人们的工作量并没有减轻。**Shǐyòng diànnǎo yǐhòu, rénmen de gōngzuò liàng bìng méiyǒu jiǎnqīng.** *With the use of the computer, people's workload has not in fact been lightened.*

减弱 **jiǎnruò** [v+compl: 减 subtract + 弱 weak] *v* weaken, reduce in force

减少 **jiǎnshǎo** [v+compl: 减 subtract + 少 few, little] *v* make fewer, make less, reduce □ 在过去三年中, 这个学校的学生人数减少了百分之二十。**Zài guòqù sān nián zhōng, zhège xuéxiào de xuésheng rénshù jiǎnshǎole bǎifēn zhī èrshí.** *In the past three years, the student population of this school has been reduced by twenty percent.*

简 **jiǎn** Trad 簡 *adj* simple

简便 **jiǎnbiàn** [comp: 简 simple + 便 convenient] *adj* simple and convenient, handy

简称 **jiǎnchēng** [modif: 简 simple + 称 call] **I** *v* be called ... for short, be abbreviated as **II** *n* shortened form, shortening

简单 **jiǎndān** [comp: 简 simple + 单 single] *adj* simple, uncomplicated (antonym 复杂 **fùzá**) □ 这个问题不简单, 要好好想一想。**Zhège wèntí bù jiǎndān, yào hǎohǎo xiǎng yi xiǎng.** *This question is not a simple one. It needs careful consideration.* □ 中饭吃得简单些, 不要搞这么多菜。**Zhōngfàn chī de jiǎndān**

xie, búyào gǎo zhème duō cài. *Let's just have a simple lunch and not have so many dishes.*

简短 jiǎnduǎn [comp: 简 simple + 短 short] *adj* simple and short, brief
简短的发言 jiǎnduǎn de fāyán a brief speech, a short talk

简化 jiǎnhuà [suffix: 简 simple + 化 v suffix] *v* simplify
简化手续 jiǎnhuà shǒuxù simplify formalities

简陋 jiǎnlòu *adj* simple and crude

简明 jiǎnmíng [comp: 简 simple + 明 lucid] *adj* simple and clear, concise

简体字 jiǎntǐzì [modif: 简 simple + 体 style + 字 character] *n* simplified Chinese character

NOTE: See note on 繁体字 **fántǐzì**.

简讯 jiǎnxùn [modif: 简 simple + 讯 information] *n* news in brief, bulletin

简要 jiǎnyào *adj* brief and to the point
简要提纲 jiǎnyào tígāng brief outline

简易 jiǎnyì [comp: 简 simple + 易 easy] *adj* simple and easy □ 这台机器操作简易。**Zhètái jīqí cāozuò jiǎnyì.** *The operartion of the machine is easy.*

简直 jiǎnzhí *adv* simply, virtually
简直叫人不敢相信 jiǎnzhí jiào rén bùgǎn xiāngxìn simply unbelievable

碱 **jiǎn** *n* alkali, soda

件 **jiàn** *measure wd* (for things, affairs, clothes or furniture)
一件东西 yí jiàn dōngxi a thing, something □ 我有一件东西忘在机场了。**Wǒ yǒu yí jiàn dōngxi wàng zài jīchǎng le.** *I've [inadvertently] left something in the airport.*
一件事情 yí jiàn shìqing a matter □ 我有几件事情要跟你说。**Wǒ yǒu jǐ jiàn shìqing yào gēn nǐ shuō.** *I've something to discuss with you.*
一件衣服 yí jiàn yīfu a piece of clothing (e.g. a jacket, dress) □ 他上星期买了三件衣服。**Tā shàng xīngqī mǎile sān jiàn yīfu.** *He bought three pieces of clothing last week.*

见 **jiàn** Trad 見 *v* see, perceive □ 我能不能见一下王先生？**Wǒ néng bu néng jiàn yíxià Wáng xiānsheng?** *May I see Mr Wang?* □ 经理, 有一位小姐要见你。**Jīnglǐ, yǒu yí wèi xiàojiě yào jiàn nǐ.** *There's a young lady here who wants to see you, sir (← manager).*

见解 jiànjiě *n* opinion, view
提出见解 tíchū jiànjiě voice one's opinion

见面 jiànmiàn [v+obj: 见 see + 面 face] *v* meet, see (a person) □ "我们以前见过面吗？" "见过一次。" **"Wǒmen yǐqián jiànguo miàn ma?" "Jiànguo yí cì."** *"Have we met before?" "Yes, once."* □ 这个周末她要带男朋友回家和父母见面。**Zhège zhōumò tā yào dài nánpéngyou huíjiā hé fùmǔ jiànmiàn.** *This weekend she will bring her boyfriend home to meet her parents.*

见识 jiànshi *n* knowledge, experience

见效 jiànxiào *v* produce the desired result, be effective

舰 **jiàn** Trad 艦 *n* warship (艘 **sōu**)
航空母舰 hángkōng mǔjiàn aircraft carrier

驱逐舰 qūzhújiàn destroyer
巡洋舰 xúnyángjiàn cruiser

舰队 jiànduì *n* fleet of warships

剑 **jiàn** Trad 劍 *n* sword (把 **bǎ**)

建 **jiàn** *v* 1 build, construct □ 在新区里要建两座学校。**Zài xīnqū li yào jiàn liǎng zuò xuéxiào.** *Two schools will be built in the new district.* 2 found, set up □ 这座大学建于1950年。**Zhè zuò dàxué jiàn yu yījiǔwǔlíng nián.** *This university was founded in 1950.*

建交 jiànjiāo *v* establish diplomatic relations

建立 jiànlì [comp: 建 found + 立 establish] *v* 1 establish, set up □ 我们希望和你们建立友好合作关系。**Wǒmen xīwàng hé nǐmen jiànlì yǒuhǎo hézuò guānxi.** *We hope to establish a relationship of friendly cooperation with you.* 2 Same as 建 **jiàn** (= build, construct)

建设 jiànshè [comp: 建 build + 设 install] *v* build, construct □ 我们努力工作, 建设自己的国家。**Wǒmen nǔlì gōngzuò, jiànshè zìjǐ de guójiā.** *We work hard to build our country.* □ 真难想象, 在一片沙漠上建设起这样一座城市。**Zhēn nán xiǎngxiàng, zài yí piàn shāmò shang jiànshèqǐ zhèyàng yí zuò chéngshì.** *It's hard to imagine that such a city could have been built in the desert.* □ 国家的建设靠全体人民的长期努力。**Guójiā de jiànshè kào quántǐ rénmín de chángqī nǔlì.** *Building a country depends on the long-term hard work of all the people.*

建议 jiànyì *v* suggest, propose □ 他建议用电脑系统控制生产过程。**Tā jiànyì yòng diànnǎo xìtǒng kòngzhì shēngchǎn guòchéng.** *He suggests that the production process be controlled by a computer system.* □ 他的建议没有被采用, 甚至没有被考虑。**Tā de jiànyì méiyǒu bèi cǎiyòng, shènzhì méiyǒu bèi kǎolǜ.** *His suggestion was not adopted; it was not even considered.*

建造 jiànzào [comp: 建 build + 造 build] *v* construct, build
建造一座大水库 jiànzào yízuò dà shuǐkù build a big reservoir

建筑 jiànzhù [comp: 建 build + 筑 build] *n* 1 building, edifice (座 **zuò**) □ 这座古代建筑具有很高的艺术价值。**Zhè zuò gǔdài jiànzhù jùyǒu hěn gāo de yìshù jiàzhí.** *This ancient building has high artistic value.* 2 architecture □ 他写过一本关于当代美国建筑的书。**Tā xiěguo yì běn guānyú dāngdài Měiguó jiànzhù de shū.** *He has written a book on contemporary American architecture.*

建筑师 jiànzhùshī [modif: 建筑 architecture + 师 master] *n* architect

建筑物 jiànzhùwù *n* architectural structure, building

建筑学 jiànzhùxué [modif: 建筑 architecture + 学 studies] *n* (the discipline of) architecture

健 **jiàn** *adj* strong

健儿 jiàn'ér [modif: 健 healthy + 儿 child] *n* athlete (as a term of approbation) (位 **wèi**)

健康 jiànkāng [comp: 健 energetic + 康 good health] **I** *n* health □ 母亲很关心孩子的健康。**Mǔqin hěn guānxīn háizi de jiànkāng.** *Mothers are very concerned for their children's health.* □ 生了病才知道健康多么宝贵。**Shēngle bìng cái zhīdào jiànkāng duōme bǎoguì.** *You don't know how precious good health is until you are ill.* **II** *adj* healthy, in good health □ 这位老人身体很健康。**Zhè wèi lǎorén shēntǐ hěn**

jiànkāng. *This old person is in good health.* □ 祝您健康! /祝您身体健康! **Zhù nín jiànkāng! / Zhù nín shēntǐ jiànkāng!** *I wish you good health.*

健美 jiànměi [comp: 健 healthy + 美 beautiful] *adj* vigorous and graceful, of athletic beauty

健美操 jiànměicāo *n* calisthenics

健全 jiànquán [comp: 健 healthy + 全 whole] **I** *adj* sound, perfect
身心健全 shēn-xīn jiànquán a healthy body and a sound mind
健全的税收制度 jiànquán de shuìshōu zhìdù a sound tax system
II *v* make perfect, improve

健身 jiànshēn [v+obj: 健 invigorate + 身 the body] *v* do physical exercises, have a work-out

健身房 jiànshēnfáng *n* gymnasium, health club

健壮 jiànzhuàng [comp: 健 healthy + 壮 robust] *adj* healthy and strong, robust

键 **jiàn** *n* key (See 关键 guānjiàn.)
键盘 jiànpán *n* keyboard

荐 **jiàn** Trad 薦 *v* recommend (See 推荐 tuījiàn.)

鉴 **jiàn** Trad 鑒 **I** *n* mirror
以史为鉴 yǐ shǐ wéi jiàn take history as a mirror (→ learn from history)
II *v* inspect, examine
鉴别 jiànbié *v* distinguish, discern
鉴别古画 jiànbié gǔhuà appraise an ancient painting, study an ancient painting to determine its authenticity and/or value
鉴于 jiànyú *prep* in view of, considering

贱 **jiàn** Trad 賤 *adj* cheap

溅 **jiàn** Trad 濺 *v* splash, spatter

践 **jiàn** Trad 踐 *v* trample
践踏 jiàntà [comp: 践 stample + 踏 step on] *v* trample underfoot
践踏公民权利 jiàntà gōngmín quánlì trample on civil rights

渐 **jiàn** Trad 漸 *adv* Same as 渐渐 jiànjiàn
渐渐 jiànjiàn *adv* gradually, by and by □ 他渐渐习惯了那里的生活。 **Tā jiànjiàn xíguànle nàli de shēnghuó.** *He gradually grew accustomed to the life there.*

箭 **jiàn** *n* arrow □ 你会射箭吗? **Nǐ huì shè jiàn ma?** *Do you know how to shoot an arrow?*
箭头 jiàntóu *n* **1** arrow head **2** sign of an arrow to show direction

间 **jiàn** Trad 間 *v* separate
间隔 jiàngé [comp: 间 separate + 隔 separate] **I** *n* interval, space between **II** *v* have intervals
间接 jiànjiē *adj* indirect

江 **jiāng** *n* river (条 tiáo) □ 这条江从西向东流。 **Zhè tiáo jiāng cóng xī xiàng dōng liú.** *This river flows from west to east.* □ 你能游过江吗? **Nǐ néng yóuguo jiāng ma?** *Can you swim across the river?*

NOTE: The most famous 江 **jiāng** in China is 长江 **Cháng jiāng**, the longest river in China. 长江 **Cháng jiāng**, which literally means *long river*, is also known as the Yangtze River. See note on 河 **hé**.

疆 **jiāng** *n* border, boundary

僵 **jiāng** *adj* stiff and numb, deadlocked
冻僵 dòngjiāng frozen stiff

姜 **jiāng** Trad 薑 *n* ginger

将 1 **jiāng** Trad 將 *prep* Same as 把 bǎ, but only used in writing.

将 2 **jiāng** Trad 將 *adv* will, shall, be going to, be about to □ 张部长将在下周二出席会议, 并发表重要讲话。 **Zhāng bùzhǎng jiāng zài xià zhōuèr chūxí huìyì, bìng fābiǎo zhòngyào jiǎnghuà.** *Minister Zhang will attend the conference next Tuesday and deliver an important speech.*
将近 jiāngjìn *adv* be close to, near
将军 jiāngjūn *n* (armed forces) general
将来 jiānglái [modif: 将 shall, will + 来 come] *n* future □ 我现在看不懂中文报纸, 将来一定看得懂。 **Wǒ xiànzài kàn bu dǒng Zhōngwén bàozhǐ, jiānglái yídìng kàn de dǒng.** *I can't read Chinese newspapers now, but I'll certainly be able to in the future.* □ 将来的世界会怎么样? 谁也不知道。 **Jiānglái de shìjiè huì zěnmeyàng? Shéi yě bù zhīdào.** *What will the world be like in the future? Nobody knows.*
将要 jiāngyào *adv* Same as 将 jiāng 2 adv

浆 **jiāng** Trad 漿 *n* thick liquid
豆浆 dòujiāng soybean milk, soy milk

讲 **jiǎng** Trad 講 *v* **1** talk □ 别讲了, 这些事我知道。 **Bié jiǎng le, zhè xiē shì wǒ zhīdào.** *Say no more. I know all about these matters.* □ 他讲得多, 做得少。 **Tā jiǎng de duō, zuò de shǎo.** *He talks a lot but does little.* **2** tell
讲故事 jiǎng gùshi tell a story
3 pay attention to, attach importance to
讲卫生 jiǎng wèishēng pay attention to personal hygiene
讲话 jiǎnghuà [comp: 讲 speak + 话 speak] *n* speech, talk □ 我的讲话只是代表我个人的意见, 不代表公司立场。 **Wǒ de jiǎnghuà zhǐshì dàibiǎo wǒ gèrén de yìjiàn, bú dàibiǎo gōngsī lìchǎng.** *My talk expresses only my personal opinion, and does not reflect the stand of the company.*
讲解 jiǎngjiě [comp: 讲 talk + 解 explain] *v* explain orally
讲究 jiǎngjiu **I** *v* be particular about, pay much attention to □ 她十分讲究穿着。 **Tā shífēn jiǎngjiu chuānzhuó.** *She pays much attention to clothes.* **II** *adj* exquisite, of very high standard
讲课 jiǎngkè [v+obj: 讲 talk + 课 lesson] *v* lecture, teach
讲理 jiǎnglǐ *v* Same as 讲道理 jiǎng dàoli
讲述 jiǎngshù [comp: 讲 talk + 述 narrate] *v* give an account of, narrate, tell about
讲演 jiǎngyǎn *v* deliver a speech
讲义 jiǎngyì *n* lecture notes, teaching materials
讲座 jiǎngzuò *n* lecture, course of lectures □ 李教授在下学期要做当代中国经济讲座, 共分十二讲。 **Lǐ jiàoshòu zài xià xuéqí yào zuò dāngdài Zhōngguó jīngjì jiǎngzuò, gòng fēn shí'èr jiǎng.** *Next semester, Professor Li will offer a course in Contemporary Chinese Economy, which will be given in twelve lectures.*

奖 jiǎng Trad 獎 **I** *n* prize, award □ 这个电影得过奖，不过一点也不好看。**Zhège diànyǐng déguo jiǎng, búguò yìdiǎn yě bù hǎokàn.** *This film has won an award, but isn't at all interesting.* **II** *v* award □ 这首诗怎么翻译成中文? 谁翻译得好, 就奖给谁一本词典。**Zhè shǒu shī zěnme fānyì chéng Zhōngwén? Shéi fānde hǎo, jiù jiǎnggei shéi yì běn cídiǎn.** *How may this poem be translated into Chinese? Whoever gives the best translation will be awarded a dictionary.*

奖杯 jiǎngbēi [modif: 奖 prize, award + 杯 cup] *n* trophy, cup (given as a prize)

奖金 jiǎngjīn [modif: 奖 prize, award + 金 money] *n* **1** prize money (笔 **bǐ**) **2** bonus (笔 **bǐ**) □ 到年底, 公司里的职工每人多发一个月的工资作为奖金。**Dào niándǐ, gōngsī lǐ de zhígōng měirén duō fā yí gè yuè de gōngzī zuòwéi jiǎngjīn.** *At the end of the year, every staff member in the company is paid one extra month wages as bonus.*

奖励 jiǎnglì [comp: 奖 reward + 励 encourage] *v* reward in order to encourage
奖励助人为乐者 jiǎnglì zhù-rén-wéi-lè zhě reward and encourage a good Samaritan

奖品 jiǎngpǐn [modif: 奖 prize, award + 品 thing] *n* prize, award (份 **fèn**, 件 **jiàn**)
颁发奖品 bānfā jiǎngpǐn present a prize/an award
领取奖品 lǐngqǔ jiǎngpǐn receive a prize/an award

奖学金 jiǎngxuéjīn [modif: 奖 award + 学 study + 金 gold, money] *n* scholarship □ 他获得了教育部奖学金, 去英国进修一年。**Tā huòdéle jiàoyùbù jiǎngxuéjīn, qù Yīngguó jìnxiū yì nián.** *He was granted a Ministry of Education scholarship for a year of advanced studies in the UK.*

奖状 jiǎngzhuàng *n* certificate of award, certificate of merit (张 **zhāng**)

桨 jiǎng Trad 槳 *n* oar

降 jiàng *v* fall, lower (antonym 升 **shēng**) □ 一天中气温降了十度。**Yì tiān zhōng qìwēn jiàngle shí dù.** *The temperature fell by ten degrees within a day.*

降低 jiàngdī [comp: 降 fall + 低 lower] (antonym 升高 **shēnggāo**) *v* lower, cut down, reduce □ 顾客很少, 他们只能降低价格。**Gùkè hěn shǎo, tāmen zhǐnéng jiàngdī jiàgé.** *As there were few customers, they had to reduce prices.* □ 很多老年人觉得社会道德水平降低了。**Hěn duō lǎoniánrén juéde shèhuì dàodé shuǐpíng jiàngdī le.** *Quite a few elderly people feel that the level of morality in society has declined.*

降价 jiàngjià [v+obj: 降 reduce + 价 price] *v* reduce prices

降临 jiànglín *v* befall, arrive

酱 jiàng Trad 醬 *n* soy paste
　酱油 jiàngyóu [comp: 酱 soybean + 油 oil, sauce] *n* soy sauce □ 做中国菜怎么少得了酱油呢? **Zuò Zhōngguó cài zěnme shǎodeliǎo jiàngyóu ne?** *How can one cook Chinese dishes without soy sauce?*

匠 jiàng *n* craftsman

交 jiāo *v* **1** hand over, pay (bills, fees) □ 这件事交给我办吧。**Zhè jiàn shì jiāogei wǒ bàn ba.** *Hand this matter over for me to deal with.* □ 这个月的电费你交了吗? **Zhè ge yuè de diànfèi nǐ jiāole ma?** *Have you paid this month's electricity bill?* **2** cross, intersect

交叉 jiāochā *v* intersect, cross

交叉点 jiāochādiǎn Same as 交点 **jiāodiǎn**

交错 jiāocuò *v* crisscross, interlock

交代 jiāodài *v* **1** leave word, hand over
交代任务 jiāodài rènwu give information about a job, brief on a task
2 confess (a wrongdoing)

交待 jiāodài Same as 交代 **jiāodài**

交点 jiāodiǎn (modif: 交 cross + 点 point) *n* point of intersection

交付 jiāofù *v* pay, hand over

交换 jiāohuàn [comp: 交 transfer + 换 exchange] *v* exchange □ 主客交换了礼物。**Zhǔ-kè jiāohuànle lǐwù.** *The host and the guest exchanged gifts.* □ 这两个大学每年交换五名学生。**Zhè liǎng ge dàxué měi nián jiāohuàn wǔmíng xuésheng.** *The two universities exchange five students every year.*

交际 jiāojì **I** *n* social contact, social intercourse, communication □ 她和外人没有什么交际。**Tā hé wàirén méiyǒu shénme jiāojì.** *She doesn't have many social contacts.* **II** *v* make social contacts □ 他善于交际, 朋友很多。**Tā shànyú jiāojì, péngyou hěn duō.** *He is good at making social contacts and has numerous friends.* □ 和不同的人交际要用不同的方法。**Hé bùtóng de rén jiāojì yào yòng bùtóng de fāngfǎ.** *You should use different ways to maintain social contact with different people.*

交际费 jiāojìfèi *n* entertainment expense

交际花 jiāojìhuā *n* social butterfly

交际舞 jiāojìwǔ *n* ballroom dancing

交流 jiāoliú [comp: 交 associate with + 流 flow] *v* exchange, communicate □ 老师们常常在一起交流教学经验。**Lǎoshīmen chángcháng zài yìqǐ jiāoliú jiàoxué jīngyàn.** *Teachers often get together to exchange teaching experiences.*

交涉 jiāoshè *v* negotiate

交手 jiāoshǒu [v+obj: 交 cross + 手 hand] *v* fight hand to hand, cross swords with

交谈 jiāotán *v* have a conversation, talk with
用中文交谈 yòng Zhōngwén jiāotán have a conversation in Chinese

交替 jiāotì *v* **1** replace **2** alternate

交通 jiāotōng [comp: 交 transfer + 通 open, through] *n* transport, transportation, traffic □ 火车仍然是中国最主要的交通工具。**Huǒchē réngrán shì Zhōngguó zuì zhǔyào de jiāotōng gōngjù.** *The railway remains China's chief means of transport.* □ 住在市中心, 交通很方便。**Zhù zài shìzhōngxīn, jiāotōng hěn fāngbiàn.** *Transportation is convenient for those living in the city center.*
交通事故 jiāotōng shìgù traffic accident, road accident
交通警察 jiāotōng jǐngchá traffic policeman, traffic police

交往 jiāowǎng *v* associate with, be in contact with

交易 jiāoyì *n* business transaction, business deal (笔 **bǐ**)
做一笔交易 zuò yìbǐ jiāoyì do a business deal

胶 jiāo Trad 膠 *n* rubber
　胶卷 jiāojuǎn *n* roll of film

胶片 jiāopiàn *n* film (for a camera)

郊 jiāo *n* outskirts, suburbs

郊区 jiāoqū *n* suburbs, outskirts (of a city) □ 在

西方人们一般都喜欢居住在郊区。**Zài Xīfāng rénmen yìbān dōu xǐhuan jūzhù zài jiāoqū.** *In the West, people generally prefer to live in the suburbs.*

浇 jiāo Trad 澆 v water
浇花 jiāohuā water flowers
浇水 jiāoshuǐ supply water to plants or crops
浇灌 jiāoguàn v irrigate, water

教 jiāo v teach □ 张小姐教我们中文。**Zhāng xiǎojiē jiāo wǒmen Zhōngwén.** *Miss Zhang teaches us Chinese.* □ 请你教我怎么使用这台新电脑。**Qǐng nǐ jiāojiao wǒ zěnme shǐyòng zhè tái xīn diànnǎo.** *Please teach me how to use this new computer.*

骄 jiāo Trad 驕 adj conceited
骄傲 jiāo'ào [comp: 骄 conceited, proud + 傲 arrogant] adj proud, conceited, arrogant □ 他为自己的孩子感到骄傲。**Tā wèi zìjǐ de háizi gǎndào jiāo'ào.** *He is proud of his children.* □ 你能力很强，但也不能骄傲啊! **Nǐ nénglì hěn qiáng, dàn yě bù néng jiāo'ào a!** *You're very capable, but you mustn't be conceited.*

娇 jiāo adj 1 tender and beautiful 2 Same as 娇气 jiāoqi
娇惯 jiāoguàn v pamper, spoil
娇气 jiāoqì adj 1 finicky, squeamish 2 fragile, delicate

焦 jiāo adj 1 scorched, burnt 2 anxious, worried
焦点 jiāodiǎn n focus
焦急 jiāojí adj anxious, very worried
焦急地等待 jiāojí de děngdài wait anxiously

蕉 jiāo n banana (See 香蕉 xiāngjiāo)

椒 jiāo n hot spice plant (See 辣椒 làjiāo)

嚼 jiáo v chew, munch

角 1 jiǎo n corner □ 不少人常常在公园的一角练习英语口语，那地点就成了 "英语角"。**Bùshǎo rén chángcháng zài gōngyuán de yì jiǎo liànxí Yīngyǔ kǒuyǔ, nà dìdiǎn jiù chéngle "Yīngyǔ Jiǎo".** *Many people often practice oral English in a corner of the park, and that spot becomes the "English Corner."*
角度 jiǎodù n angle, point of view
角落 jiǎoluò n corner, nook

角 2 jiǎo measure wd (Chinese currency: 1 角 jiǎo = 0.1 元 yuán = 10 分 fēn) ten cents, a dime
两角钱 liǎng jiǎo qián two *jiao*, twenty cents
八块九角五分 bā kuài jiǔ jiǎo wǔ fēn eight *yuan* nine *jiao* and five *fen* = eight dollars and ninety-five cents

NOTE: In colloquial Chinese 毛 **máo** is often used instead of 角 jiǎo, e.g. 两毛钱 **liǎng máo qián** is equivalent to two *jiao* twenty cents

饺 jiǎo Trad 餃 n Same as 饺子 jiǎozi
饺子 jiǎozi [suffix: 饺 dumpling + 子 nominal suffix] n stuffed dumpling, *jiaozi* □ 你晚饭吃了多少个饺子? **Nǐ wǎnfàn chīle duōshǎo ge jiǎozi?** *How many dumplings did you eat for supper?*
包饺子 bāo jiǎozi make *jiaozi*

狡 jiǎo adj sly, cunning
狡猾 jiǎohuá [comp: 狡 sly, cunning + 猾 sleek] adj cunning, crafty

脚 jiǎo n foot (只 zhī) □ 我的脚很大，穿不下这双鞋。**Wǒ de jiǎo hěn dà, chuān bú xià zhè shuāng xié.** *My feet are big. This pair of shoes doesn't fit.* □ 他的左脚受伤了。**Tā de zuǒ jiǎo shòushāng le.** *His left foot is injured.*
脚步 jiǎobù [modif: 脚 foot + 步 step] n footstep, step

搅 jiǎo Trad 攪 v 1 mix 2 confuse, disturb
搅拌 jiǎobàn [comp: 搅 mix + 拌 mix] v stir, mix

缴 jiǎo v 1 pay, hand in 2 capture
缴纳 jiǎonà v pay, hand in
缴纳罚款 jiǎonà fákuǎn pay a fine

绞 jiǎo v wring, twist
把毛巾绞干 bǎ máojīn jiǎo gān wring a towel dry

轿 jiào Trad 轎 n sedan chair
轿车 jiàochē n sedan car, car

叫 1 jiào v call, address, shout, cry out □ 大家都叫他小王。**Dàjiā dōu jiào tā Xiǎo Wáng.** *Everybody calls him Xiao Wang.* □ 我见了你的父母，应该叫什么? **Wǒ jiànle nǐ de fùmǔ, yīnggāi jiào shénme?** *How should I address your parents when I meet them?*
叫喊 jiàohǎn [comp: 叫 call + 喊 shout] v shout, call out
叫唤 jiàohuan [comp: 叫 call + 唤 call] v cry out, call out
叫嚷 jiàorǎng [comp: 叫 call + 嚷 yell] v yell, howl
叫做 jiàozuò v be called, be known as, be referred to as □ 这种病叫做百日咳。**Zhè zhǒng bìng jiàozuò bǎirìké.** *This illness is called the "hundred-day cough" (or whooping cough).*

叫 2 jiào prep Same as 被 bèi. Used more in colloquialisms.

教 jiào n teaching
教材 jiàocái [modif: 教 teaching + 材 material] n teaching material, textbook, coursebook (份 fèn, 本 běn) □ "你们上中文课用什么教材?" "用我们老师自己编的教材。" **"Nǐmen shàng Zhōngwén kè yòng shénme jiàocái?" "Yòng wǒmen lǎoshī zìjǐ biān de jiàocái."** *"What textbook do you use for Chinese?" "The one written by our teacher."*
教导 jiàodǎo [comp: 教 teach + 导 guide] v instruct, give moral guidance
教会 jiàohuì [modif: 教 religious + 会 association] n organized religious group, church
天主教会 Tiānzhǔ jiàohuì the Catholic Church
教练 jiàoliàn [comp: 教 teach + 练 train] n (sports) coach
教师 jiàoshī [modif: 教 teaching + 师 teacher, master] n teacher (位 wèi, 名 míng) □ 在中国人的传统中，严格的教师才是好教师。**Zài Zhōngguórén de chuántǒng zhōng, yángé de jiàoshī cái shì hǎo jiàoshī.** *In the Chinese tradition, only a strict teacher was a good teacher.*
教室 jiàoshì [modif: 教 teaching + 室 room] n classroom (间 jiān) □ "你们的教室在哪里?" "在二楼，二二三房间。" **"Nǐmen de jiàoshì zài nǎlǐ?" "Zài èrlóu, èr-èr-sān fángjiān."** *"Where is your classroom?" "It's on the second floor, Room 223."* □ 我们在那间教室上数学课。**Wǒmen zài nà jiān jiàoshì shàng shùxué kè.** *We have our mathematics class in that classroom.*
教室大楼 jiàoshì dàlóu classroom block

教授 **jiàoshòu** [comp: 教 teach + 授 teach] *n* university professor □ 李教授既要教学，又要研究。**Lǐ jiàoshòu jìyào jiàoxué, yòu yào yánjiū.** *Professor Li is engaged in both teaching and research.*
副教授 **fùjiàoshòu** associate professor

教唆 **jiàosuō** *v* instigate and abet

教堂 **jiàotáng** [modif: 教 religion + 堂 hall] *n* church building, church
大教堂 **dàjiàotáng** cathedral
上教堂 **shàng jiàotáng** go to church (for worship)

教条 **jiàotiáo** *n* dogma

教学 **jiàoxué** *n* teaching, education □ 老师们每月开会，讨论教学中出现的问题。**Lǎoshīmen měi yuè kāihuì, tǎolùn jiàoxué zhong chūxiàn de wèntí.** *The teachers have a monthly meeting to discuss problems encountered in teaching.*

教训 **jiàoxun** [comp: 教 teach + 训 lecture] **I** *v* lecture, talk down to □ 你可以不同意别人的意见，可别老是教训别人。**Nǐ kěyǐ bù tóngyì biérén de yìjiàn, kě bié lǎoshì jiàoxun biérén.** *You may hold different opinions from others, but you shouldn't always talk down to them.* **II** *n* lesson (learnt from mistakes or experience), moral □ 犯错误不要紧，重要的是接受教训。**Fàn cuòwù bú yàojǐn, zhòngyào de shì jiēshòu jiàoxùn.** *Making mistakes doesn't matter, what's important is to learn your lesson.*

教养 **jiàoyǎng** *n* upbringing, education
有教养 **yǒu jiàoyǎng** well brought up, well-bred

教育 **jiàoyù** [modif: 教 teach + 育 nurture] **I** *v* educate, teach □ 父母应该教育自己的孩子。**Fùmǔ yīnggāi jiàoyù zìjǐ de háizi.** *Parents should educate their children.* **II** *n* education □ 教育关系到国家的将来。**Jiàoyù guānxi dào guójiā de jiānglái.** *Education has an important bearing on the future of a country.* □ 我姐姐在大学念教育。**Wǒ jiějie zài dàxué niàn jiàoyù.** *My elder sister studies education at the university.*

教员 **jiàoyuán** [modif: 教 teaching + 员 staff] *n* teacher (in a particular school) □ 这个学校有二十四名教员。**Zhège xuéxiào yǒu èrshísì míng jiàoyuán.** *This school has twenty-four teachers.*

觉 **jiào** Trad 覺 See 睡觉 **shuìjiào**

较 **jiào** Trad 較 **I** *prep* Same as 比 **bǐ** 1 *prep*. Used only in writing. **II** *adv* Same as 比较 **bǐjiào** 2 *adv*. Used only in writing.
较量 **jiàoliàng** *v* test the strength of, compete

窖 **jiào** *n* cellar
地窖 **dìjiào** cellar, pit

阶 **jiē** Trad 階 *n* steps, grade
阶段 **jiēduàn** [comp: 阶 steps, stair + 段 section] *n* period, stage □ 这项工程正处在开始阶段。**Zhè xiàng gōngchéng zhèng chù zài kāishǐ jiēduàn.** *This project is just at an initial stage.*
阶级 **jiējí** [comp: 阶 steps, stair + 级 grade] *n* social class □ 今天的中国社会有哪些阶级? **Jīntiān de Zhōngguó shèhuì yǒu nǎxiē jiējí?** *What classes does today's Chinese society have?*

揭 **jiē** *v* take off, reveal
揭发 **jiēfā** *v* expose, uncover
揭发一起逃税案 **jiēfā yìqǐ táoshuì àn** expose a case of tax evasion
揭露 **jiēlù** *v* uncover, reveal

揭露阴谋 **jiēlù yīnmóu** uncover a conspiracy
揭示 **jiēshì** [comp: 揭 reveal + 示 show] *v* bring to light, reveal
揭示真相 **jiēshì zhēnxiàng** reveal the truth

皆 **jiē** *pron* all, both □ 人人皆知。**Rénrén jiē zhī.** *Everyone knows.*

结 **jiē** Trad 結 *v* bear (fruit)
结实 **jiēshi** *adj* sturdy, strong, robust □ 他们做的家具都很结实。**Tāmen zuò de jiājù dōu hěn jiēshi.** *The furniture they make is very sturdy.* □ 他身体很结实。**Tā shēntǐ hěn jiēshi.** *He has a robust body.*

接 **jiē** *v* **1** receive (a letter, a telephone call) □ 我昨天接到一封信，两个传真和八个电子邮件。**Wǒ zuótiān jiēdao yì fēng xìn, liǎng ge chuánzhēn hé bā ge diànzǐ yóujiàn.** *Yesterday I received a letter, two faxes and eight e-mail messages.* □ 我要休息一会儿，谁的电话都不接。**Wǒ yào xiūxi yíhuìr, shuí de diànhuà dōu bù jiē.** *I'll have a rest and take no calls.* **2** meet and greet (a visitor) □ 王先生是第一次到这里来，你应该去机场接他。**Wáng xiānsheng shì dì-yī cì dào zhèlǐ lái, nǐ yīnggāi qù jīchǎng jiē tā.** *This is the first time that Mr Wang's coming here. You should go and meet him at the airport.*

接班 **jiēbān** *v* take over from, carry on
接触 **jiēchù** [comp: 接 join + 触 touch] *v* get in touch (with) □ 我先和他们初步接触一下，了解他们的想法。**Wǒ xiān hé tāmen chūbù jiēchù yíxià, liǎojiě tāmen de xiǎngfǎ.** *I'll first get in touch with them tentatively to find out their thoughts.*
接待 **jiēdài** [comp: 接 receive + 待 entertain] *v* receive (a visitor) □ 今天市长不接待。**Jīntiān shìzhǎng bù jiēdài.** *The mayor is not receiving visitors today.*
接到 **jiēdao** [v+compl: 接 receive + 到 arrive] *v* have received □ 我还没有接到会议邀请信。**Wǒ hái méiyǒu jiēdao huìyì yāoqǐngxìn.** *I have not yet received a letter of invitation to the conference.*
接见 **jiējiàn** [comp: 接 receive + 见 see] *v* receive (somebody), meet (somebody), give an audience □ 教育部长昨天接见了中学教师代表。**Jiàoyù bùzhǎng zuótiān jiējiànle zhōngxué jiàoshī dàibiǎo.** *The Minister of Education received representatives of secondary school teachers yesterday.*

NOTE: 接见 **jiējiàn** meaning *receive* or *meet* is only used for formal or official occasions. It implies that the receiving party is superior in status to the one being received.

接近 **jiējìn** *v* be close to, be near □ 她接近董事会，很了解内情。**Tā jiējìn dǒngshìhuì, hěn liǎojiě nèiqíng.** *She is close to the board of directors and knows the inside information.* □ 已经接近下班时间了，工作只作了一半。**Yǐjīng jiējìn xiàbān shíjiān le, gōngzuò zhǐ zuòle yí bàn.** *It is close to the time to get off work, but the job is only half done.*
接连 **jiēlián** *adv* successively, one after another □ 我接连收到公司三个电子邮件，催我马上付款。**Wǒ jiēlián shōu dào gōngsī sān gè diànzǐ yóujiàn, cuī wǒ mǎshàng fùkuǎn.** *I received three e-mail messages from the company in a row, urging me to pay the bill immediately.*
接洽 **jiēqià** *v* arrange with
接受 **jiēshòu** [comp: 接 receive + 受 accept] *v* ac-

cept □ 我们不接受礼物。**Wǒmen bù jiēshòu lǐwù.** *We do not accept gifts.*

接受批评 jiēshòu pīpíng accept criticism, take criticism

接着 jiēzhe *conj* and immediately, then, at the heels of (a previous action or event) □ 我先听到有人叫我，接着小王跑了进来。**Wǒ xiān tīngdao yǒu rén jiào wǒ, jiēzhe Xiǎo Wáng pǎole jìnlai.** *I first heard someone calling me, and then Xiao Wang ran into the room.*

街 **jiē** *n* street (条 **tiáo**) □ 我家前边的那条街总是很安静。**Wǒ jiā qiánbian de nà tiáo jiē zǒngshì hěn ānjìng.** *The street in front of my home is always quiet.*

街上 jiē shang on the street □ 街上人很多。**Jiē shang rén hěn duō.** *There are many people in the street.*

步行街 bùxíng jiē pedestrian street

逛大街 guàng dàjiē stroll the streets, do window shopping

街道 **jiēdào** [comp: 街 street + 道 way] *n* street (条 **tiáo**) □ 这里的街道很安静。**Zhèli de jiēdào hěn ānjìng.** *The streets in this area are quiet.*

街道委员会 jiēdào wěiyuánhuì neighborhood committee

街坊 **jiēfang** *n* neighbor

街头 **jiētóu** *n* street

街头流浪汉 jiētóu liúlànghàn a homeless being in the street

节 **jié** Trad 節 **I** *n* 1 festival □ 这个节我过得很愉快。**Zhège jié wǒ guò de hěn yúkuài.** *I had a very happy festival.* □ 这个地方一年有好几个节。**Zhège dìfang yì nián yǒu hǎo jǐ ge jié.** *There're quite a number of festivals in this area.*

过节 guò jié observe a festival, celebrate a festival

中秋节 zhōngqiūjié Mid-Autumn Festival (the Moon Festival, on the fifteenth day of the eighth lunar month)

2 section, division **II** *measure wd* a period of time

一节课 yì jié kè a period of class

III *v* save, economize

节目 **jiémù** [comp: 节 section + 目 item] *n* program □ 昨天的电视节目很精彩。**Zuótiān de diànshì jiémù hěn jīngcǎi.** *The TV program yesterday was wonderful!* □ 这个节目是谁编的? 谁演的? **Zhège jiémù shì shuí biān de? Shuí yǎn de?** *Who wrote this program? Who acted it?*

儿童节目 értóng jiémù children's program

体育节目 tǐyù jiémù sports program

文艺节目 wényì jiémù theatrical program

新闻节目 xīnwén jiémù news program (on TV or radio)

节日 **jiérì** [modif: 节 festival + 目 day] *n* festival day □ 中国人最重要的节日是春节，也就是中国人的新年。**Zhōngguórén zuì zhòngyào de jiérì shì chūnjié, yě jiùshì Zhōngguórén de xīnnián.** *The most important festival for the Chinese is the Spring Festival, which is the Chinese New Year.*

节省 **jiéshěng** *v* save, be frugal with (antonym 浪费 **làngfèi**) □ 你平时节省一点钱，几年下来就可能有一大笔钱。**Nǐ píngshí jiéshěng yìdiǎn qián, jǐ nián xiàlai jiù kěnéng yǒu yídà bǐ qián.** *If you save a little money routinely, after several years you may have a substantial sum of money.*

节约 **jiéyuē** *v* economize, save, practice thrift (antonym 浪费 **làngfèi**) □ 我们应当节约用电，节约用水。**Wǒmen yīngdāng jiéyuē yòngdiàn, jiéyuē yòngshuǐ.** *We should cut down electricity and water consumption.*

节约能源 (节能) jiéyuē néngyuán (jiénéng) conserve energy

节制 **jiézhì** *v* control, be moderate in

节制生育 (节育) jiézhì shēngyù (jiéyù) birth control, family planning

节奏 **jiézòu** *n* rhythm, tempo

结 **jié** Trad 結 *v* 1 tie, end 2 form, congeal

结构 **jiégòu** *n* structure, construction □ 这座古代建筑是木结构的。**Zhèzuò gǔdài jiànzhù shì mù jiégòu de.** *This ancient building is a timber structure.*

结果 **jiéguǒ** [v+obj: 结 form + 果 fruit] **I** *n* result, consequence □ 这次试验的结果很鼓舞人心。**Zhè cì shìyàn de jiéguǒ hěn gǔwǔ rénxīn.** *The result of this test is heartening.* **II** *adv* as a result, consequently, finally □ 我们找了他半天，结果在图书馆找到了他。**Wǒmen zhǎole tā bàntiān, jiéguǒ zài túshūguǎn zhǎodàole tā.** *We looked for him for a long time and finally found him in the library.* □ 他们讨论了半天，结果取得了一致意见。**Tāmen tǎolùnle bàntiān, jiéguǒ qǔdéle yízhì yìjiàn.** *They discussed it for a long time, and finally reached a unanimous agreement.* □ 技术员连续工作二十小时，结果解决了问题。**Jìshùyuán liánxù gōngzuò èrshí xiǎoshí, jiéguǒ jiějuéle wèntí.** *Technicians worked for twenty hours continuously, and finally solved the problem.*

结合 **jiéhé** [comp: 结 tie + 合 merge] *v* combine, integrate □ 热情的态度要和冷静的头脑相结合。**Rèqíng de tàidu yào hé lěngjìng de tóunǎo xiāng jiéhé.** *Enthusiasm should be combined with a cool head.* □ 他们俩终于结合为一对幸福的夫妻。**Tāmen liǎ zhōngyú jiéhéwéi yí duì xìngfú de fūqī.** *They were finally joined as a happy couple.*

结婚 **jiéhūn** [v+obj: 结 tie + 婚 marriage] *v* marry (antonym 离婚 **líhūn**) □ 他和中学时的女朋友结婚。**Tā hé zhōngxué shí de nǚpéngyou jiéhūn.** *He married his high school sweetheart.* □ 他结过两次婚，下个月又要结婚了。**Tā jiéguo liǎng cì hūn, xià ge yuè yòu yào jiéhūn le.** *He has been married twice and will marry again next month.*

结晶 **jiéjīng** *n* 1 crystallization 2 fruit, result

多年努力的结晶 duōnián nǔlì de jiéjīng the fruit of many years' painstaking efforts

结局 **jiéjú** *n* outcome, final result

结论 **jiélùn** [modif: 结 end + 论 view, treatise] *n* verdict, conclusion □ 经过调查，我们的结论如下。**Jīngguò diàochá, wǒmen de jiélùn rú xià.** *As a result of the investigation, our conclusions are as follows.* □ 我不同意你的结论。**Wǒ bù tóngyì nǐ de jiélùn.** *I don't agree with your conclusion.*

结束 **jiéshù** [comp: 结 tie + 束 knot] *v* end, terminate (antonym 开始 **kāishǐ**) □ 电影什么时候结束? **Diànyǐng shénme shíhou jiéshù?** *When does the movie end?* □ 第二次世界大战是哪一年开始，哪一年结束的? **Dì-èr ci shìjiè dàzhàn shì nǎ yì nián kāishǐ, nǎ yì nián jiéshù de?** *In which year did World War II begin, and in which year did it end?*

结算 **jiésuàn** [modif: 结 tie + 算 calculation] *v* settle an account, close an account

结业 jiéyè [v+obj: 结 end + 业 study] *v* complete a course of study, graduate

洁 jié Trad 潔 *adj* clean
洁白 jiébái [comp: 洁 clean + 白 white] *adj* pure white, spotless

截 jié *v* intercept, stop
截止 jiézhǐ *v* end, up to □ 招标日期本星期五截止。**Zhāobiāo rìqī běn Xīngqīwǔ jiézhǐ.** *Invitation to public bidding will end by this Friday.*

劫 jié *v* rob, raid
劫持 jiéchí *v* kidnap, hijack

杰 jié Trad 傑 *adj* outstanding, excellent
杰出 jiéchū [comp: 杰 excellent + 出 out] *adj* outstanding, distinguished
杰作 jiézuò [modif: 杰 outstanding + 作 work] *n* outstanding work (of art, music or literature)

捷 jié *adj* quick (See 敏捷 mǐnjié)

竭 jié *v* exhaust
竭力 jiélì [v+obj: 竭 exhaust + 力 strength, power] *v* do one's utmost, do everything within one's power
竭力满足顾客 jiélì mǎnzú gùkè do all one can to satisfy customers

姐 jiě *n* Same as 姐姐 jiějie
姐姐 jiějie *n* elder sister □ 我姐姐对我很好。**Wǒ jiějie duì wǒ hěn hǎo.** *My elder sister is very nice to me.*

解 jiě *v* untie, undo □ 医生：请你把上衣解开，我要听听你的心肺。**Yīshēng: Qǐng nǐ bǎ shàngyī jiě kāi, wǒ yào tīngtīng nǐ de xīnfèi.** *Doctor: Please undo your jacket. I want to listen to your heart and lungs.*
解答 jiědá [comp: 解 untie + 答 reply] *v* provide an answer, give an explanation □ 这个问题谁会解答？**Zhè ge wèntí shuí huì jiědá?** *Who can answer this question?*
解放 jiěfàng [comp: 解 untie + 放 release] **I** *v* set free, liberate, emancipate □ 美国南北战争解放了南方的黑人。**Měiguó nánběi zhànzhēng jiěfàngle nánfāng de hēirén.** *The American South-North War (→ the American Civil War) emancipated Black people in the South.* **II** *n* liberation, emancipation □ 民族解放需要伟大的民族领袖。**Mínzú de jiěfàng xūyào wěidà de mínzú lǐngxiù.** *The emancipation of a nation calls for great national leaders.*
解雇 jiěgù [v+obj: 解 release + 雇 employment] *v* dismiss (an employee), discharge
解决 jiějué [comp: 解 dissect + 决 finalize] *v* solve (a problem), settle (an issue) □ 这个问题还没有解决。**Zhè ge wèntí hái méiyǒu jiějué.** *This problem has not been resolved.* □ 要解决目前的困难，必须和各方面合作。**Yào jiějué mùqián de kùnnan, bìxū hé gè fāngmiàn hézuò.** *We must cooperate with all parties if the present difficulties are to be overcome.*
解剖 jiěpōu [comp: 解 dissect + 剖 cut open] *v* **1** dissect **2** analyse, probe
解散 jiěsàn *v* dismiss, disband
解释 jiěshì [comp: 解 untie + 释 clarify] **I** *v* explain, account for □ 请你解释一下这个句子。**Qǐng nǐ jiěshì yíxià zhè ge jùzi.** *Please explain this sentence to me.* □ 科学家无法解释这种现象。**Kēxuéjiā wú fǎ jiěshì zhè zhǒng xiànxiàng.** *Scientists cannot account for this phenomenon.* **II** *n* explanation, interpretation □ 对

这种现象，我有一个解释。**Duì zhè zhǒng xiànxiàng, wǒ yǒu yí ge jiěshì.** *I have an explanation for this phenomenon.*

介 jiè *v* lie between, interpose
介绍 jièshào [comp: 介 intervene + 绍 connect] *v* **1** introduce □ 我来介绍一下，这位是李先生，这位是王小姐。**Wǒ lái jièshào yíxià, zhè wèi shì Lǐ xiānsheng, zhè wèi shì Wáng xiǎojiě.** *Let me introduce [the people here]. This is Mr. Li. This is Miss Wang.* **2** provide information, brief □ 你刚从中国回来，请你介绍一下中国的情况。**Nǐ gāng cóng Zhōngguó huílai, qǐng nǐ jièshào yíxià Zhōngguó de qíngkuàng.** *As you've just come back from China, please tell us something about the current situation in China.*
介绍人 jièshào rén matchmaker, sponsor (for membership in a club, a political party, an association etc.)
介绍信 jièshàoxìn letter of recommendation

届 jiè *measure wd* (used for a conference or congress held at regular intervals, for graduating classes) □ 我是那个中学九九届的毕业生。**Wǒ shì nà ge zhōngxué jiǔjiǔ jiè de bìyèshēng.** *I was a graduate of the class of '99 of that high school.* □ 第十届国际生物学大会将于十二月在新加坡举行。**Dì-shí jiè guójì shēngwùxué dàhuì jiāng yú Shí'èr yuè zài Xīnjiāpō jǔxíng.** *The 10th International Conference on Biology will be held in Singapore in December.*

界 jiè *n* **1** border, boundary **2** realm, circle
商业界 shāngyè jiè business circle
体育界 tǐyù jiè sporting circle
界限 jièxiàn [comp: 界 boundary + 限 limit] *n* dividing line, limits
界线 jièxiàn [modif: 界 boundary + 线 line] *n* boundary line, demarcation line
把球打出界线 bǎ qiú dǎchū jièxiàn send the ball outside (the court)

借 jiè *v* borrow, lend □ 他借给我一百元。**Tā jiègei wǒ yìbǎi yuán.** *He lent me one hundred dollars.* □ 我向他借了一百元。**Wǒ xiàng tā jièle yìbǎi yuán.** *I borrowed one hundred dollars from him.* □ 借东西要还。**Jiè dōngxi yào huán.** *If you borrow something, you must return it.*

NOTE: This verb may mean either *borrow* or *lend*, depending on the patterns in which it occurs: □ A借给 B... **A jiègei B...** *A lends B ...* □ A向B借… **A xiàng B jiè...** *A borrows ... from B*

借鉴 jièjiàn [v+obj: 借 borrow + 鉴 mirror] *v* use for reference, learn (lessons) from
借口 jièkǒu [v+obj: 借 borrow + 口 mouth] **I** *v* use as an excuse
借口身体不好不上班 jièkǒu shēntǐ bùhǎo bù shàngbān use poor health as an excuse for not going to work
II excuse, pretext
找借口 zhǎo jièkǒu make up an excuse, invent an excuse
借助 jièzhù [v+obj: 借 borrow + 助 help] *v* have the aid of, make use of

戒 jiè *v* guard against
戒严 jièyán **1** *n* curfew, martial law **2** *v* enforce martial law, impose a curfew

诚 **jiè** Trad 誡 *v* admonish, warn (See 告诫 **gàojiè**)

巾 **jīn** *n* towel (See 毛巾 **máojīn**.)

今 **jīn** *n* now, the present
今后 **jīnhòu** *n* from today, from now on □ 我保证今后不迟到，不早退。**Wǒ bǎozhèng jīnhòu bù chídào, bù zǎotuì.** *I assure you that from now on I will not be late for work or leave work earlier than is allowed.*
今年 **jīnnián** [modif: 今 now + 年 year] *n* this year □ 今年是二零零九年。**Jīnnián shì èrlínglíngjiǔ nián.** *This year is the year 2009.* □ 我祖父今年八十岁了。**Wǒ zǔfù jīnnián bāshí suì le.** *My grandfather is eighty years old this year.*
今天 **jīntiān** [modif: 今 now + 天 day] *n* today □ 今天天气很好。**Jīntiān tiānqì hěn hǎo.** *The weather's fine today.* □ 我今天要上五节课。**Wǒ jīntiān yào shàng wǔ jié kè.** *I have five classes today.*

筋 **jīn** *n* tendon, vein

津 **jīn** *v* ferry
津贴 **jīntiē** *n* subsidy, stipend

斤 **jīn** *n* jin (a traditional Chinese unit of weight equal to half a kilogram) □ 这条鱼重八斤。**Zhè tiáo yú zhòng bā jīn.** *This fish weighs eight jin.* □ 妈妈买了两斤肉。**Māma mǎile liǎng jīn ròu.** *Mom bought two jin of meat.*

金 **jīn** *n* 1 gold (两 **liǎng** *ounce*) □ 这块金表价值极高，你要好好保存。**Zhè kuài jīn biǎo jiàzhí jí gāo, nǐ yào hǎohǎo bǎocún.** *This gold watch is very valuable. You must keep it well.*
金子 **jīnzi** gold
2 money □ 他每两周拿五百块退休金。**Tā měi liǎng zhōu ná wǔbǎi kuài tuìxiū jīn.** *He gets five hundred dollars as pension money every fortnight.*
金额 **jīn'é** [modif: 金 money + 额 sum] *n* sum of money (笔 **bǐ**)
一大笔金额 yí dàbǐ jīn'é a large sum of money
金黄 **jīnhuáng** *adj* golden (color)
金牌 **jīnpái** *n* gold medal
金牌获得者/金牌得主 jīnpái huòdézhě/ jīnpái dezhǔ gold medalist
金钱 **jīnqián** [comp: 金 gold + 钱 money] *n* money
金融 **jīnróng** *n* finance, banking □ 香港是重要的国际金融中心。**Xiānggǎng shì zhòngyào de guójì jīnróng zhōngxīn.** *Hong Kong is an important international financial center.*
金属 **jīnshǔ** *n* metal □ 金、银、铜、铁都是金属。**Jīn, yín, tóng, tiě dōu shì jīnshǔ.** *Gold, silver, copper and iron are all metals.*
金鱼 **jīnyú** *n* goldfish (条 **tiáo**)
金鱼缸 jīnyúgāng goldfish bowl
养金鱼 yǎng jīnyú keep goldfish
金字塔 **jīnzìtǎ** [modif: 金字 the character 金 + 塔 tower] *n* the pyramid

仅 **jǐn** Trad 僅 *adv* only, merely □ 她一个月的工资仅够付房租和吃饭。**Tā yí ge yuè de gōngzī jǐn gòu fù fángzū hé chīfàn.** *Her monthly wages are only enough for rent and food.* □ 小王是我在这个城市里仅有的朋友。**Xiǎo Wáng shì wǒ zài zhège chéngshì li jǐn yǒu de péngyou.** *Xiao Wang is my only friend in this city.*

仅仅 **jǐnjǐn** *adv* Same as 仅 **jǐn**, but more emphatic.

尽 **jǐn** Trad 盡 *v* to the greatest extent □ 这事要尽快办。**Zhè shì yào jǐnkuài bàn.** *This matter must be handled as soon as possible.*
尽管 **jǐnguǎn** I *adv* feel free to, not hesitate □ 有什么问题，尽管和我联系。**Yǒu shénme wèntí, jǐnguǎn hé wǒ liánxì.** *If you have any questions, do not hesitate to contact me.* □ 你尽管吃，菜还多着呢! **Nǐ jǐnguǎn chī, cài hái duōzhe ne!** *Eat to your heart's content. More dishes are coming.* II *conj* even though □ 尽管她很聪明，但是念书不用功，结果成绩不好。**Jǐnguǎn tā hěn cōngmíng, dànshì niànshū bú yònggōng, jiéguǒ chéngjì bùhǎo.** *Even though she is quite intelligent, she does not study hard and consequently fails to get good results in exams.*
尽量 **jǐnliàng** [modif: 尽 to the greatest extent + 量 amount] *adv* to the best of one's capacity, to the greatest extent
尽量快一点 jǐnliàng kuài yìdiǎn as fast as possible, as soon as possible □ 对孩子你要尽量耐心一点。**Duì háizi nǐ yào jǐnliàng nàixīn yìdiǎn.** *In dealing with children you should try your best to be patient.* □ 你们多商量商量，尽量取得一致的意见。**Nǐmen duō shāngliang-shāngliang, jǐnliàng qǔdé yízhì de yìjiàn.** *You all should discuss the matter more and try your best to reach a unanimous view.*

锦 **jǐn** *n* brocade
锦绣 **jǐnxiù** *adj* splendid, beautiful

谨 **jǐn** *adj* cautious
谨慎 **jǐnshèn** [comp: 谨 cautious + 慎 cautious] *adj* cautious, careful
谨慎驾驶 jǐnshèn jiàshǐ drive carefully

紧 **jǐn** Trad 緊 *adj* 1 tight, taut □ 今天的活动安排得比较紧。**Jīntiān de huódòng ānpái de bǐjiào jǐn.** *Today's activities are scheduled rather tightly.* □ 这件衣肩部紧了一点。**Zhè jiàn shàngyī jiānbù jǐnle yìdiǎn.** *The shoulders of the coat are a bit tight.* 2 urgent, tense
握紧方向盘 wòjǐn fāngxiàngpán grip the steering wheel firmly
3 be close to
紧靠着地铁站 jǐn kàozhe dìtiězhàn very close to a subway station
4 in short supply □ 时间很紧。**Shíjiān hěn jǐn.** *Time is in short supply.* (→ *We're pressed for time.*)
5 pressing, urgent
紧急 **jǐnjí** [comp: 紧 pressing + 急 urgent] *adj* urgent, pressing
紧急任务 jǐnjírènwu urgent task
紧急状况 jǐnjí zhuàngkuàng emergency situation, contingency
紧密 **jǐnmì** [comp: 紧 close + 密 dense] *adj* very close, intimate
紧密配合 jǐnmì pèihé in close coordination
紧缩 **jǐnsuō** [comp: 紧 taut + 缩 shrink] *v* tighten, reduce
紧缩开支 jǐnsuō kāizhī cut back expenditure
紧张 **jǐnzhāng** [comp: 紧 tight + 张 tense] *adj* tense, nervous □ 明天要考试了，我没有很好准备，心里很紧张。**Míngtiān yào kǎoshì le, wǒ méiyǒu hěn hǎo zhǔnbèi, xīnli hěn jǐnzhāng.** *We're having an examination tomorrow. I'm not well prepared, and*

feel really nervous. □ 这个电影很紧张, 看得我心直跳。 **Zhège diànyǐng hěn jǐnzhāng, kàn de wǒ xīn zhí tiào.** *This film was so nerve-racking that my heart beat violently.*

晋 **jìn** *v* go forward, advance

晋升 **jìnshēng** [comp: 晋 advance + 升 rise] *v* promote (to a higher position)

晋升为教授 jìnshēng wéi jiàoshòu be promoted to professorship level

尽 **jìn** Trad 盡 *v* exhaust, use up □ 我已经尽了最 大努力。 **Wǒ yǐjīng jìnle zuì dà nǔlì.** *I've already exhausted my energies [on this]. (→ I've done my very best.)*

尽力 **jìnlì** [v+obj: 尽 exhaust + 力 effort] *v* do all one can □ 我已经尽力了。 **Wǒ yǐjīng jìnlì le.** *I've done my very best.*

进 **jìn** Trad 進 *v* move forward, enter □ 请进! **Qǐng jìn!** *Please come in! (or Please go in!)*

进步 **jìnbù** I *adj* progressive (antonym 落后 luòhòu) □ 社会上的进步力量一定会取胜。 **Shèhuì shang de jìnbù lìliàng yídìng huì qǔshèng.** *The progressive forces in society will surely prevail.* II *n* progress □ 你们的中文学习有了很大进步。 **Nǐmen de Zhōngwén xuéxí yǒule hěn dà jìnbù.** *You have made very good progress in your Chinese studies.*

进程 **jìnchéng** *n* course (of progress), process

进而 **jìn' ér** *adv* and then, subsequently

进攻 **jìngōng** [comp: 进 advance + 攻 attack] *v* advance and attack, attack □ 部队出发进攻敌人。 **Bùduì chūfā jìngōng dírén.** *The troops set out to attack the enemy forces.*

进化 **jìnhuà** [comp: 进 advance + 化 change, transform] *v* evolve, develop □ 人是从猴子进化来的, 你信 不信? **Rén shì cóng hóuzi jìnhuà lái de, nǐ xìn bú xìn?** *Man evolved from the monkey. Do you believe this?*

进化论 **jìnhuàlùn** *n* (Charles Darwin's) theory of evolution

进军 **jìnjūn** *v* march, advance

进口 **jìnkǒu** [v+obj: 进 enter + 口 the mouth] I *v* import (antonym 出口 chūkǒu) □ 这台机床是从德国 进口的。 **Zhè tái jīchuáng shì cóng Déguó jìnkǒu de.** *This machine tool was imported from Germany.* □ 这 个国家每年进口大量农产品。 **Zhège guójiā měi nián jìnkǒu dàliàng nóngchǎnpǐn.** *This country imports large quantities of farm produce every year.* II *n* entry, entrance

进来 **jìnlai** [v+compl: 进 enter + 来 come] *v* come in, come into □ 进来吧, 我们在等你呢! **Jìnlai ba, wǒmen zài děng nǐ ne!** *Please come in. We've been waiting for you.*

进取 **jìnqǔ** *v* be enterprising, be aggressive and ambitious

进取心 jìnqǔxīn enterprising spirit

进去 **jìnqu** [v+compl: 进 enter+ 去 go] *v* go in, go into □ 他们在开会, 请不要进去。 **Tāmen zài kāihuì, qǐng bú yào jìnqu.** *They're having a meeting. Please don't go in.*

进入 **jìnrù** [comp: 进 enter + 入 enter] *v* enter, enter into □ 狗不得进入商场。 **Gǒu bùdé jìnrù shāngchǎng.** *Dogs are not allowed to enter the shopping center.* □ 工程进入最后阶段。 **Gōngchéng jìnrù zuìhòu jiēduàn.** *The project has entered into its last stage.*

进行 **jìnxíng** [comp: 进 enter + 行 walk] *v* conduct, carry out □ 孩子做错了事, 应该进行教育。 **Háizi zuò cuòle shì, yīnggāi jìnxíng jiàoyù.** *When a child makes a mistake, he should be educated.*

NOTE: The object that 进行 **jìnxíng** takes must be a noun of two or more syllables. 进行 **jìnxíng** is used only in formal Chinese.

进修 **jìnxiū** *v* do advanced studies, undergo in-service advanced training □ 我们的中文老师要去北京进 修半年。 **Wǒmen de Zhōngwén lǎoshī yào qù Běijīng jìnxiū bànnián.** *Our Chinese teacher will go to Beijing for half a year's advanced studies.*

进一步 **jìnyíbù** [v+obj: 进 advance + 一步 one (more) step] *adv* advancing a step further, further, more deeply □ 对于这个问题, 我们还要进一步研究。 **Duìyú zhège wèntí, wǒmen hái yào jìnyíbù yánjiū.** *We need to study this problem further.* □ 他们进一步提出 了要求。 **Tāmen jìnyíbù tíchūle yāoqiú.** *They made further demands.*

近 **jìn** *adj* close to, close by (antonym 远 yuǎn) □ 商店很近, 不用开车去。 **Shāngdiàn hěn jìn, búyòng kāichē qù.** *The store is close by. There is no need to drive.*

离…近 lí...jìn be close to □ 爸爸的办公室离家很近。 **Bàba de bàngōngshì lí jiā hěn jìn.** *Father's office is close to home.*

近代 **jìndài** [modif: 近 close to + 代 generations] *n* modern times (usually from the year 1840)

近来 **jìnlái** *adv* recently, nowadays, these days □ 他 近来好事连连。 **Tā jìnlái hǎoshì liánlián.** *These days good things are happening to him, one after another.* □ 近来天气反常。 **Jìnlái tiānqì fǎncháng.** *The weather has been rather abnormal recently.*

近年 **jìnnián** [modif: 近 close to + 年 year] *n* recent years

近期 **jìnqī** [modif: 近 close to + 期 period] *n* in the near future

近视 **jìnshi** [modif: 近 close to + 视 sight] *n* nearsightedness, shortsightedness

近视眼镜 jìnshi yǎnjing spectacles for nearsightedness

近似 **jìnsì** [comp: 近 close to + 似 similar] *adj* similar, approximate

近似值 jìnsì zhí approximate value, approximation

劲 **jìn** Trad 勁 *n* physical strength □ 这位举重运动 员真有劲! **Zhè wèi jǔzhòng yùndòngyuán zhēn yǒu jìn!** *This weight lifter is really powerful!*

没劲 méijìn dull, boring, bored □ 这日子过得真没劲! **Zhè rìzi guòde zhēn méijìn!** *Life is so boring!*

劲头 **jìntóu** *n* 1 strength, energy 2 zeal, vigor

劲头十足 jìntóu shízú full of vigor, in high spirits

浸 **jìn** *v* soak, steep

禁 **jìn** *v* forbid

禁区 **jìnqū** [modif: 禁 forbidden + 区 area] *n* forbidden zone

军事禁区 jūnshì jìnqū military zone

禁止 **jìnzhǐ** [comp: 禁 forbid + 止 stop] *v* forbid, prohibit □ 电影院内严格禁止使用手机。 **Diànyǐngyuàn nèi yángé jìnzhǐ shǐyòng shǒujī.** *Using the cell phone*

is strictly forbidden in the cinema. □ 外国人禁止入内。**Wàiguórén jìnzhǐ rùnèi.** *Out of bounds to foreigners.* □ 禁止吸烟。**Jìnzhǐ xīyān.** *No smoking.*

京 **jīng** n 1 capital city 2 (shortened for) Beijing
京剧 **jīngjù** [modif: 京 Beijing (Peking) + 剧 opera] n Beijing (Peking) opera □ 京剧有歌有舞, 还有武术, 真精彩! **Jīngjù yǒu gē yǒu wǔ, háiyǒu wǔshù, zhēn jīngcǎi!** *Beijing opera contains singing, dancing and martial arts as well. It's really brilliant!*

鲸 **jīng** n whale
鲸鱼 **jīngyú** whale (条 **tiáo**)

晶 **jīng** n crystal (See 结晶 **jiéjīng**)

茎 **jīng** n stem or stalk (of a plant)

经 **jīng** Trad 經 v pass through, experience
经常 **jīngcháng** [comp: 经 constant + 常 often] adv often □ 你经常迟到, 这样不好。**Nǐ jīngcháng chídào, zhèyàng bù hǎo.** *You're often late, which is not good.* □ 他们夫妻俩都讨厌做饭, 所以经常在外面吃。**Tāmen fūqī liǎ dōu tǎoyàn zuòfàn, suǒyǐ jīngcháng zài wài-mian chī.** *Both husband and wife hate cooking, so they often eat out.*
经典 **jīngdiǎn** n classic
经费 **jīngfèi** n outlay, fund (for a specific purpose or the regular running of an organization)
经过 **jīngguò** [comp: 经 go through + 过 pass] I v go through, pass □ 我去学校的路上, 要经过一座公园。**Wǒ qù xuéxiào de lùshang, yào jīngguò yí zuò gōngyuán.** *I pass by a park on my way to school.* □ 没有亲自经过, 就不知道多难。**Méiyǒu qīnzì jīngguò, jiù bù zhīdào duō nán.** *Without experiencing it personally, you wouldn't know how difficult it is.* II prep through, after □ 经过这件事, 他变得聪明了。**Jīngguò zhè jiàn shì, tā biàn de cōngmíng le.** *He was more sensible after this incident.*
经济 **jīngjì** [comp: 经 govern + 济 bring relief to] n economy □ 这个国家的经济不太好。**Zhège guójiā de jīngjì bú tài hǎo.** *This country's economy is not in very good shape.* □ 每个国家都在发展自己的经济。**Měi ge guójiā dōu zài fāzhǎn zìjǐ de jīngjì.** *Every country is working hard to develop its economy.*
经济学 **jīngjìxué** economics
经济学家 **jīngjìxuéjiā** economist
市场经济 **shìchǎng jīngjì** market economy
经纪人 **jīngjìrén** [modif: 经纪 manage + 人 person] n agent, manager
经理 **jīnglǐ** [comp: 经 manage + 理 administrate] n manager (位 **wèi**) □ 他是管人力资源的经理。**Tā shì guǎn rénlì zīyuán de jīnglǐ.** *He is the manager in charge of human resources.*
副经理 **fùjīnglǐ** deputy manager
市场经理 **shìchǎng jīnglǐ** marketing manager
总经理 **zǒngjīnglǐ** general manager, chief executive officer (CEO)
经历 **jīnglì** 1 v experience, undergo □ 这位老人经历了很多困难, 才获得幸福的晚年。**Zhè wèi lǎorén jīnglìle hěn duō kùnnan, cái huòdé xìngfú de wǎnnián.** *This old man has experienced many troubles before enjoying a blissful old age.* 2 n personal experience □ 请你谈谈在美国学习和工作的经历。**Qǐng nǐ tántan zài Měiguó xuéxí hé gōngzuò de jīnglì.** *Please tell us*

about your experience studying and working in the States.

经商 **jīngshāng** v engage in business, be a businessman
经受 **jīngshòu** v undergo, withstand
经受考验 **jīngshòu kǎoyàn** face a test, undergo a test
经销 **jīngxiāo** v sell, deal with
经销豪华汽车 **jīngxiāo háohuá qìchē** deal with luxury cars
经验 **jīngyàn** [comp: 经 go through + 验 test] n experience, lesson (learnt from experiences) □ 这个经验对我很有价值。**Zhège jīngyàn duì wǒ hěn yǒu jiàzhí.** *This experience is very valuable to me.*
取得经验 **qǔdé jīngyàn** acquire experience
有经验 **yǒu jīngyàn** experienced □ 她是一位有经验的老师。**Tā shì yí wèi yǒu jīngyàn de lǎoshī.** *She's an experienced teacher.*
经营 **jīngyíng** v operate (a business)

惊 **jīng** Trad 驚 v startle, surprise
惊动 **jīngdòng** [v+compl: 惊 startle + 动 move] v disturb, alarm
惊慌 **jīnghuāng** [comp: 惊 be startled + 慌 confused] adj panic-stricken, alarmed
惊慌失措 **jīnghuāng shīcuò** be panic-stricken
惊奇 **jīngqí** v be surprised and incredulous, be amazed
惊讶 **jīngyà** v be astonished, be surprised
惊异 **jīngyì** v be astounded and puzzled

睛 **jīng** n the pupil of the eye (See 眼睛 **yǎnjing**.)

精 **jīng** adj choice, refined
精彩 **jīngcǎi** [comp: 精 choice + 彩 colorful, brilliant] adj (of a theatrical performance or sports event) brilliant, thrilling, wonderful □ 昨天的足球比赛真精彩啊! **Zuótiān de zúqiú bǐsài zhēn jīngcǎi a!** *The football match yesterday was really wonderful!* □ 他在会上的发言十分精彩, 赢得了热烈的掌声。**Tā zài huì shang de fāyán shífēn jīngcǎi, yíngdéle rèliè de zhǎngshēng.** *He made a stirring speech at the meeting and earned warm applause.*
精打细算 **jīngdǎ xìsuàn** idiom be very careful in budgeting to save every cent
精华 **jīnghuá** n the cream of the crop, the very best
精简 **jīngjiǎn** v trim and prune (an organization), reduce staffing
精力 **jīnglì** [comp: 精 energy + 力 strength] n energy, vigor □ 我父亲年纪大了, 精力不如以前了。**Wǒ fùqin niánjì dà le, jīnglì bùrú yǐqián le.** *My father is getting old and is not so energetic as before.*
精美 **jīngměi** [comp: 精 refined + 美 beautiful] adj exquisite and beautiful
精密 **jīngmì** adj precise
精密仪器 **jīngmì yíqì** precision instrument
精确 **jīngquè** adj accurate, precise
精神 **jīngshén** [comp: 精 essence + 神 spirit] n 1 vigor, vitality □ 这位老人八十多岁了, 但是精神很好。**Zhè wèi lǎorén bāshí duō suì le, dànshì jīngshén hěn hǎo.** *This old man (or woman) is over eighty, but is energetic and alert.* □ 不知道为什么, 我今天没有精神。**Bù zhīdào wèishénme, wǒ jīntiān méiyǒu jīngshén.** *I don't know why, but I'm in low spirits today.* 2 spirit, the mind

精神病 jīngshénbìng [modif: 精神 the mind + 病 disease] *n* mental illness

精神病院 jīngshénbìngyuàn mental institution

精神病医生 jīngshénbìng yīshēng psychiatrist

精通 jīngtōng *adj* having great proficiency in, be master of

精细 jīngxì *adj* paying attention to details, meticulous

精益求精 jīng yì qiú jīng *v* seek perfection

精致 jīngzhì *adj* exquisite, fine

景 jǐng *n* view, scenery

景色 jǐngsè [comp: 景 view + 色 color] *n* view, scenery

景象 jǐngxiàng *n* sight, scene

警 jǐng I *v* alert II *n* 1 police 2 alarm

警车 jǐngchē police car

火警 huǒjǐng fire alarm

警察 jǐngchá *n* policeman, police □ 这里发生了交通事故，快叫警察! Zhèlǐ fāshēngle jiāotōng shìgù, kuài jiào jǐngchá! *A traffic accident has happened here. Call the police quickly!*

NOTE: In China the police bureau is called 公安局 gōng'ānjú *Public Security Bureau*, which should be distinguished from 国安局 guó'ānjú *Bureau of National Security*.

警告 jǐnggào [comp: 警 warn + 告 tell] I *v* warn, caution □ 路旁有牌子警告，前面是弯曲山路，必须减速。Lùpáng yǒu páizi jǐnggào, qiánmian shì wānqū shānlù, bìxū jiǎnsù. *A poster by the roadside warns motorists to reduce speed as the road ahead is zigzagging and hilly.* II *n* warning

警戒 jǐngjiè *v* guard against, be on alert

警惕 jǐngtì *v* be vigilant

警卫 jǐngwèi *v* guard and defend (a military installation, a VIP, etc.)

井 jǐng *n* well, (water) well

水井 shuǐjǐng water well

油井 yóujǐng oil well

颈 jǐng Trad 頸 *n* neck

头颈 tóujǐng the neck

长颈鹿 (long-neck-deer) chángjǐnglù giraffe

竞 jìng Trad 競 *v* compete

竞赛 jìngsài [comp: 竞 compete + 赛 contest] *v* contest, compete □ 他们兄弟俩一直竞赛，看谁学习成绩好。Tāmen xiōngdì liǎ yìzhí jìngsài, kàn shuí xuéxí chéngjì hǎo. *The two brothers have always been competing with each other to see who the better student is.*

竞选 jìngxuǎn [v+obj: 竞 compete for + 选 election] *v* run for office

竞争 jìngzhēng [comp: 竞 compete + 争 strive] I *v* compete □ 在这个市场上有好几个公司和我们竞争。Zài zhège shìchǎngshang yǒu hǎo jǐ gè gōngsī hé wǒmen jìngzhēng. *Quite a few companies are competing with us in this market.* II *n* competition □ 我们相信公平竞争。Wǒmen xiāngxìn gōngpíng jìngzhēng. *We believe in fair competition.*

竟 jìng *adv* unexpectedly

竟然 jìngrán *adv* unexpectedly, contrary to expectation □ 这个小孩下棋竟然胜了他爸爸。Zhège xiǎohái xiàqí jìngrán shèngle tā bàba. *Quite unexpectedly the child should beat his father in chess.*

境 jìng *n* boundary, place

国境 guójìng territory (of a country), border

国境线 guójìngxiàn national boundary line

境地 jìngdì *n* situation, plight

危险的境地 wēixiǎn de jìngdì dangerous position

镜 jìng Trad 鏡 *n* mirror

镜子 jìngzi mirror (面 miàn)

照镜子 zhào jìngzi look at oneself in a mirror

镜头 jìngtóu *n* 1 camera lens 2 shot, scene

径 jìng Trad 徑 *n* track (See 田径 tiánjìng)

敬 jìng *v* respect

敬爱 jìng'ài [comp: 敬 respect + 爱 love] *v* respect and love □ 有多少孩子敬爱自己的父母? Yǒu duōshǎo háizi jìng'ài zìjǐ de fùmǔ? *How many children respect and love their parents?*

敬而远之 jìng-ér-yuǎn-zhī *idiom* keep a respectful distance from, give a wide berth to

敬酒 jìngjiǔ *v* propose a toast □ 我提议向我们的主人敬酒。Wǒ tíyì xiàng wǒmende zhǔrén jìngjiǔ. *I'd like to propose a toast to our host.*

敬礼 jìnglǐ *v* salute

静 jìng *adj* quiet, peaceful, silent □ 阅览室里很静，针掉在地上都听得见。Yuèlǎnshì li hěn jìng, zhēn diào zài dìshang dōu tīng de jiàn. *The reading room is so quiet that one can hear a pin drop.* □ 别管我，让我在这里静静地坐一会。Bié guǎn wǒ, ràng wǒ zài zhèlǐ jìngjìng de zuò yíhuì. *Please leave me alone and let me sit here quietly for a while.* □ 请大家静一静，我要宣布一件事。Qǐng dàjiā jìng yi jìng, wǒ yào xuānbù yí jiàn shì. *Be quiet, everybody. I have an announcement to make.*

静悄悄 jìngqiāoqiāo *adj* perfectly quiet and hushed

静坐 jìngzuò [modif: 静 quietly + 坐 sit] *v* 1 meditate

静坐养生 jìngzuò yǎngshēng meditate to keep in good health

2 stage a sit-in

净 jìng *adj* clean (See 干净 gānjing.)

净化 jìnghuà [suffix: 净 clean + 化 verb suffix] *v* purify

净化废水 jìnghuà fèishuǐ purify waste water

究 jiū *v* investigate, probe

究竟 jiūjìng *adv* Same as 到底 dàodǐ

纠 jiū Trad 糾 *v* rectify

纠纷 jiūfēn *n* dispute

纠正 jiūzhèng [v+compl: 纠 rectify + 正 correct] *v* rectify, correct □ 我们应该及时纠正错误。Wǒmen yīnggāi jíshí jiūzhèng cuòwù. *We should rectify our mistakes promptly.*

揪 jiū Trad 揫 *v* hold tight, seize

九 jiǔ *num* nine □ 九九八十一。Jiǔjiǔ bāshíyī. *Nine times nine is eighty-one.*

九一一 jiǔ-yāo-yāo 9/11 September 11

九千九百九十九 jiǔqiān jiǔbǎi jiǔshíjiǔ 9,999

NOTE: See note on 一 yī regarding pronunciation of 一 as yāo.

玖 jiǔ *num* nine

久 jiǔ *adv* for a long time □ 时间太久了，我记不清了。**Shíjiān tài jiǔle, wǒ jìbuqīng le.** *It was too long ago. I can't remember it clearly.* □ 我等你等了很久了。**Wǒ děng nǐ děngle hěn jiǔle.** *I've been waiting for you for a long time.* □ 日久见人心。**Rì jiǔ jiàn rénxīn.** *As time goes on, you will know a person's nature.*

灸 jiǔ *n* moxibustion (See 针灸 **zhēnjiǔ**.)

酒 jiǔ *n* alcoholic beverage (种 **zhǒng**, 瓶 **píng**) □ 这种酒，我不喜欢喝。**Zhè zhǒng jiǔ, wǒ bù xǐhuan hē.** *I don't like this kind of alcoholic drink.* □ 我不喝酒，我还要开车。**Wǒ bù hē jiǔ, wǒ háiyào kāichē.** *No alcoholic drinks for me. I'll be driving.*
白酒 **bái jiǔ** colorless spirit distilled from grains
葡萄酒 **pútaojiǔ** (grape) wine
黄酒 **huáng jiǔ** yellow rice wine
酒吧 **jiǔ bā** [modif: 酒 wine + 吧 bar] (wine) bar, pub
酒店 **jiǔ diàn** *n* 1 wine shop 2 restaurant 3 hotel

NOTE: Although 酒店 **jiǔ diàn** literally means *wine shop*, it is sometimes used to mean *a hotel*, usually a luxury one. This usage is especially common in Hong Kong, e.g. 香港半岛酒店 **Xiānggǎng bàndǎo jiǔdiàn** *The Peninsula Hong Kong Hotel.* Also see note on 饭店 **fàndiàn**.

酒会 **jiǔhuì** *n* cocktail party, reception
酒精 **jiǔjīng** *n* alcohol

旧 jiù Trad 舊 *adj* (of things) old, second-hand (antonym 新 **xīn**) □ 这件衣服不太旧，还可以穿。**Zhè jiàn yīfu bú tài jiù, hái kěyǐ chuān.** *This jacket is not too old. It can still be worn.* □ 他把旧车卖了一千块钱。**Tā bá jiù chē màile yìqiān kuài qián.** *He sold his old car for one thousand dollars.* □ 旧的不去，新的不来。**Jiù de bú qù, xīn de bù lái.** *If the old doesn't go, the new won't come.* (→ *If you don't discard old stuff, you won't have new things.*)

舅 jiù *n* mother's brother, uncle
舅父 **jiùfù** mother's brother, uncle
舅舅 **jiùjiù** Same as 舅父 **jiùfù**, used as a form of address
舅妈 **jiùmā** Same as 舅母 **jiùmǔ**, used as a form of address
舅母 **jiùmǔ** mother's brother's wife, aunt

救 jiù *v* save, rescue □ 王医生及时动手术，救了他的命。**Wáng yīshēng jíshí dòng shǒushù, jiùle tā de mìng.** *Dr Wang operated on him immediately and saved his life.* □ 他在河中大叫，"救命! 救命!" **Tā zài hé zhong dà jiào, "Jiù mìng! Jiù mìng!"** *He cried out in the river, "Help! Help!"*
救火 **jiùhuǒ** put out a fire, fire fighting
救火车 **jiùhuǒchē** fire engine
救护车 **jiùhùchē** ambulance
救济 **jiùjì** *v* provide relief

就¹ jiù *prep* 1 with regard to, concerning □ 商业部长就物价问题发表谈话。**Shāngyè bùzhǎng jiù wùjià wèntí fābiǎo tánhuà.** *The Minister of Commerce delivered a talk on prices.* 2 as far as ... is concerned, in terms of □ 就人口来说，中国是世界上

第一大国。**Jiù rénkǒu láishuō, Zhōngguó shì shìjiè shang dì-yī dà guó.** *In terms of population, China is the biggest country in the world.*

就² jiù *adv* as early as ..., as soon as ... (used before a verb to emphasize that the action takes place very early, very quickly or only for a very short period of time) □ 他今天早上六点钟就起床了。**Tā jīntiān zǎoshang liù diǎnzhōng jiù qǐchuáng le.** *He got up as early as six o'clock this morning.* □ 我马上就来。**Wǒ mǎshàng jiù lái.** *I'll come immediately.* (→ *I'm coming.*)
一…就… **yī...jiù...** as soon as ... □ 妈妈一下班就做晚饭。**Māma yí xiàbān jiù zuò wǎnfàn.** *Mom prepared supper as soon as she got off work.*
就餐 **jiùcān** *v* take a meal
就地 **jiùdì** *adv* on the spot
就近 **jiùjìn** *adv* nearby
就是 **jiùshì** *conj* even if □ 我就是不睡觉，也要做完这个作业。**Wǒ jiùshì bú shuìjiào, yě yào zuòwán zhège zuòyè.** *Even if I don't sleep, I must finish this assignment.* □ 他们就是借钱，也要供儿子上大学。**Tāmen jiùshì jièqián, yě yào gòng érzi shàng dàxué.** *They are determined to put their son through university even if they have to borrow money.*
就算 **jiùsuàn** *conj* even if, even though
就业 **jiùyè** *v* obtain employment
就职 **jiuzhí** *v* take office

居 jū *v* 1 occupy (See 邻居 **línjū**, 居民 **jūmín**, 居住 **jūzhù**.) 2 inhabit, dwell
居留 **jūliú** [comp: 居 reside + 留 stay] *v* reside, live
居留权 **jūliúquán** right of residency, residency
居留证 **jūliúzhèng** residency permit
居民 **jūmín** [modif: 居 occupy + 民 people] *n* resident, inhabitant
居民委员会 **jūmín wěiyuánhuì** neighborhood committee

NOTE: 居民委员会 **jūmín wěiyuánhuì** is the grassroot organization in Chinese cities, under government supervision. In colloquial Chinese it is shortened to 居委会 **jūwěihuì**.

居然 **jūrán** *adv* unexpectedly
居室 **jūshì** [modif: 居 reside + 室 room] *n* bedroom
一套三居室的公寓 **yítào sān jūshì de gōngyù** a three-bedroom apartment
居住 **jūzhù** [comp: 居 occupy + 住 live] *v* reside, inhabit, live

拘 jū *v* 1 detain, arrest 2 limit
拘留 **jūliú** [comp: 拘 detain + 留 make stay] *v* detain by the police
拘留所 **jūliúsuǒ** detention center, detention camp
拘束 **jūshù** [comp: 拘 limit + 束 restrain] *adj* restrained, ill at ease

鞠 jū *v* as in 鞠躬 **jūgōng**
鞠躬 **jūgōng** *v* bow, take a bow

菊 jú *n* chrysanthemum
菊花 **júhuā** chrysanthemum
菊花展览 **júhuā zhǎnlǎn** chrysanthemum show
秋菊 **qiū jú** chrysanthemum

局 jú *n* office
局部 **júbù** *adj* part (not whole), local □ 今天本市

局部停电。 **Jīntiān běnshì júbù tíngdiàn.** *Today parts of this city will not have power supply.*

局面 **júmiàn** *n* situation, phase
打开局面 dǎkāi júmiàn usher in a new phase, make a breakthrough

局势 **júshì** *n* situation

局限 **júxiàn** *v* limit, confine

局长 **júzhǎng** [modif: 局 bureau + 长 chief] *n* director/chief of a bureau □ 一个部下面有几个局，所以一位部长下面有几位局长。 **Yí ge bù xiàmian yǒu jǐ ge jú, suǒyǐ yí wèi bùzhǎng xiàmian yǒu jǐ wèi júzhǎng.** *As there are several bureaus under a ministry, there are several bureau chiefs under a minister.*

矛 **jú** *n* tangerine
橘树 jú shù tangerine tree
橘子 júzi tangerine □ 苹果、香蕉、橘子，我都爱吃。 **Píngguǒ, xiāngjiāo, júzi, wǒ dōu ài chī.** *I like apples, bananas and tangerines.*

NOTE: 橘子 **júzi** can also be written as 桔子 **júzi.**

矩 **jǔ** *n* carpenter's square (See 规矩 **guīju**)

举 **jǔ** Trad 舉 *v* hold high, raise, lift □ 谁同意，请举手! **Shuí tóngyì, qǐng jǔ shǒu!** *Those in favor [of the motion], please raise your hands.* □ 举头望明月，低头思故乡 (李白) **Jǔ tóu wàng míng yuè, dī tóu sī gùxiāng (Lí Bái)** *I raise my head to gaze at the bright moon and hang my head yearning for my hometown (lines from a poem by Li Bai)*

举办 **jǔbàn** *v* conduct (a meeting, an event)

举动 **jǔdòng** *n* (body) movement, act
一举一动 yìjǔ yídòng every movement (of a person)

举世闻名 **jǔshì wénmíng** *idiom* world-renowned

举行 **jǔxíng** *v* hold (a meeting, a ceremony) □ 下个月将举行国际会议，讨论这个问题。 **Xiàge yuè jiāng jǔxíng guójì huìyì, tǎolùn zhège wèntí.** *An international conference will be held next month to discuss this issue.*

聚 **jù** *v* assemble, get together
聚会 júhuì [comp: 聚 get together + 会 meet] *n* social gathering, (social) party
举行生日聚会 jǔxíng shēngri júhuì throw a birthday party

NOTE: See note on 派对 **pàiduì.**

聚集 **jùjí** [comp: 聚 assemble + 集 collect] *v* gather, collect
聚集资金 (集资) jùjí zījīn (jízī) collect funds, raise funds
聚精会神 **jùjīng huìshén** *idiom* give undivided attention to

句 **jù** *measure wd* (for sentences)
一句话 yí jù huà one sentence
这句话 zhè jù huà this sentence
句子 jùzi [suffix: 句 sentence + 子 nominal suffix] *n* sentence (句 jù, 个 gè) □ 张老师，这句句子什么意思? 我看不懂。 **Zhāng lǎoshī, zhè jù jùzi shénme yìsi? Wǒ kàn bu dǒng.** *Teacher Zhang, what is the meaning of this sentence? I don't understand it.* □ 这句句子语法不对。 **Zhè jù jùzi yǔfǎ bú duì.** *The grammar of this sentence is wrong.*

拒 **jù** *v* resist, refuse
拒不认错 jù bù rèncuò refuse to admit to a mistake

具 **jù** *v* own, possess
具备 **jùbèi** *v* possess, be provided with □ 这个小城市不具备建立大学的条件。 **Zhège xiǎo chéngshì bú jùbèi jiànlì dàxué de tiáojiàn.** *This small city does not possess the conditions necessary for establishing a university.*
具体 **jùtǐ** *adj* specific, concrete □ 你说他这个人不好，能不能说得具体些? **Nǐ shuō tā zhège rén bù hǎo, néng bù néng shuōde jùtǐ xiē?** *You say he is not a good man. Can you be more specific?* □ 请你举两三个具体的例子。 **Qǐng nǐ jǔ liǎng-sān ge jùtǐ de lìzi.** *Please give two or three concrete examples.*
具有 **jùyǒu** *v* have, possess, be provided with □ 这一事件具有重大的历史意义。 **Zhè yí shìjiàn jùyǒu zhòngdà de lìshǐ yìyì.** *This incident has major historic significance.* □ 中国文化具有哪些特点? **Zhōngguó wénhuà jùyǒu nǎxiē tèdiǎn?** *What characteristic features does Chinese culture have?*

俱 **jù** *adv* together
俱乐部 **jùlèbù** [modif: 俱 together + 乐 joy + 部 department] *n* club □ 这个俱乐部每年要交多少会费? **Zhège jùlèbù měi nián yào jiāo duōshǎo huìfèi?** *What are the annual dues of this club?*

惧 **jù** Trad 懼 *v* fear
惧内 jùnèi fear one's wife, be henpecked

剧 **jù** Trad 劇 **I** *n* drama, play **II** *adj* severe, intense
剧本 **jùběn** [modif: 剧 play + 本 book] *n* script of a play
电影剧本 diànyǐng jùběn script of a film, scenario
剧场 **jùchǎng** [modif: 剧 drama + 场 site] *n* theater (座 zuò) □ 今晚在剧场里有精彩演出。 **Jīnwǎn zài jùchǎng li yǒu jīngcǎi yǎnchū.** *There will be a wonderful performance in the theater this evening.*
剧烈 **jùliè** *adj* fierce, severe
剧烈的疼痛 jùliè de téngtòng acute pain
剧团 **jùtuán** [modif: 剧 drama + 团 group] *n* theatrical company
剧院 **jùyuàn** [modif: 剧 drama + 院 courtyard] *n* playhouse, theater (座 zuò)

据 **jù** Trad 據 *prep* according to
据说 **jùshuō** *idiom* it is said, they say, rumor has it □ 据说王小姐现在在美国工作。 **Jùshuō Wáng xiǎojiě xiànzài zài Měiguó gōngzuò.** *It is said that Miss Wang is working in America.* □ 据说，一家外国公司就要买下我们工厂了。 **Jùshuō, yì jiā wàiguó gōngsī jiù yào mǎixia wǒmen gōngchǎng le.** *Rumor has it that a foreign company is going to buy our factory.*

锯 **jù** *n* saw
锯子 jùzi hand saw (把 bǎ)
电锯 diànjù chainsaw

巨 **jù** *adj* gigantic
巨大 **jùdà** [comp: 巨 gigantic + 大 big] *adj* huge, gigantic, tremendous □ 我们国家的经济发展取得了巨大的成绩。 **Wǒmen guójiā de jīngjì fāzhǎn qǔdéle jùdà de chéngjì.** *Our country has made tremendous achievements in economic development.*

拒 **jù** *v* repel, resist
拒绝 **jùjué** *v* refuse, reject □ 她拒绝了他的邀请

Tā jùjuéle tā de yāoqǐng. *She turned down his invitation.* □ 他拒绝承认错误。**Tā jùjué chéngrèn cuòwù.** *He refused to admit to any wrong.*

距 **jù** *n* a stretch of distance
距离 **jùlí** *n* distance □ 两地之间的距离有一百多公里。**Liǎngdì zhī jiān de jùlí yǒu yìbǎi duō gōnglǐ.** *The distance between the two places is over a hundred kilometers.* □ 她和谁都保持一定距离。**Tā hé shuí dōu bǎochí yídìng jùlí.** *She keeps a distance from everybody.* (→ *She gives everyone a wide berth.*)

捐 **juān** *v* donate, contribute
捐款 **juānkuǎn** [v+obj: 捐 donate + 款 fund] I *v* contribute money, make a cash donation II *n* cash donation, financial donation
捐献 **juānxiàn** [comp: 捐 donate + 献 offer] *v* donate (something of considerable value)
捐赠 **juānzèng** [comp: 捐 donate + 赠 gift] *v* contribute as a gift, donate

卷 **juǎn** *v* roll up □ 他把地图卷起来，放在书架上。**Tā bǎ dìtú juǎn qǐlai, fàng zài shūjià shang.** *He rolled the map up and placed it on the bookshelf.*

绢 **juàn** Trad 絹 *n* silk (See 手绢 **shǒujuàn**.)

倦 **juàn** *adj* tired (See 疲倦 **píjuàn**)

掘 **jué** *v* dig
掘土机 **juétǔjī** excavation machine, earth mover

决 ¹ **jué** *adv* definitely, under any circumstance (used before a negative word, e.g. 不 **bù**) □ 我决不做任何对社会有害的事。**Wǒ jué bú zuò rènhé duì shèhuì yǒuhài de shì.** *I would never, ever, do anything that is harmful to society.*

决 ² **jué** *v* decide, determine
决策 **juécè** [v+obj: 决 decide + 策 policy] I *v* decide on a policy, formulate strategy II *n* policy decision, strategic decision (项 **xiàng**)
决定 **juédìng** [comp: 决 determine + 定 decide] I *v* decide, determine, make up one's mind □ 你有没有决定买哪一辆汽车? **Nǐ yǒu méiyǒu juédìng mǎi nǎ yí liàng qìchē?** *Have you decided which car to buy?* □ 这件事实在很难决定。**Zhè jiàn shì shízài hěn nán juédìng.** *This really is a difficult matter to decide.* II *n* decision □ 你们的决定是错误的。**Nǐmen de juédìng shì cuòwù de.** *You've made a wrong decision.* □ 我希望你改变这个决定。**Wǒ xīwàng nǐ gǎibiàn zhège juédìng.** *I hope you will change this decision.* 做决定 zuò juédìng make a decision □ 买哪一座房子，他们还没有做决定。**Mǎi nǎ yí zuò fángzi, tāmen hái méiyǒu zuò juédìng.** *They haven't decided which house to buy.*
决赛 **juésài** [modif: 决 decisive + 赛 match] *n* final game, final round, finals
决心 **juéxīn** [modif: 决 determined + 心 heart] I *n* determination □ 他的决心很大。**Tā de juéxīn hěn dà.** *He is very determined.* □ 我们有决心，有信心，一定按时完成计划。**Wǒmen yǒu juéxīn, you xìnxīn, yídìng ànshí wánchéng jìhuà.** *We are determined, and we are confident, that we will fulfill the plan according to schedule.* 下决心 xià juéxīn make up one's mind, be determined II *v* be determined, make up one's mind □ 我们决心按时完成计划。**Wǒmen juéxīn ànshí wánchéng**

jìhuà. *We are determined to fulfill the plan according to schedule.*

决议 **juéyì** *n* resolution
提出决议 tíchū juéyì put forward a resolution
作出决议 zuòchū juéyì adopt a resolution
决战 **juézhàn** I *v* wage a decisive battle II *n* decisive battle

觉 **jué** Trad 覺 *v* feel, sense
觉察 **juéchá** [comp: 觉 feel + 察 observe] *v* detect, perceive
觉得 **juéde** *v* feel, find, think □ 我觉得你说的话很有道理。**Wǒ juéde nǐ shuō de huà hěn yǒu dàolǐ.** *I think what you said is quite true (or reasonable).* □ 你觉得他的想法行不行? **Nǐ juéde tā de xiǎngfǎ xíng bu xíng?** *Do you think his idea will work?*
觉悟 **juéwù** [comp: 觉 feel + 悟 realize] *v* gain understanding, become aware of
觉醒 **juéxǐng** [觉 feel + 醒 awake] *v* be awakened (to truth, reality, etc.)

绝 **jué** Trad 絕 I *adj* absolute II *v* cut off, sever
绝对 **juéduì** *adv* absolutely □ 我告诉你的消息绝对准确。**Wǒ gàosù nǐ de xiāoxi juéduì zhǔnquè.** *The news I told you is absolutely correct.*
绝对多数 juéduì duōshù absolute majority
绝望 **juéwàng** [v+obj: 绝 cut off + 望 hope] *v* despair, give up all hope
绝缘 **juéyuán** *v* (of electricity) insulate
绝症 **juézhèng** *n* terminal illness

军 **jūn** Trad 軍 *n* army, armed forces
海军 hǎijūn navy
空军 kōngjūn air force
陆军 lùjūn army
军备 **jūnbèi** [modif: 军 military + 备 preparations] *n* weapons and equipment, armaments
军队 **jūnduì** [modif: 军 army + 队 rows of people] armed forces, troops (支 **zhī**) □ 军队应该属于国家。**Jūnduì yīnggāi shǔyú guójiā.** *The armed forces should belong to the state.*
军官 **jūnguān** [modif: 军 military + 官 official] *n* military officer, officer (名 **míng**, 位 **wèi**)
军火 **jūnhuǒ** *n* arms and ammunition
军舰 **jūnjiàn** [modif: 军 military + 舰 warship] *n* warship (艘 **sōu**)
军人 **jūnrén** [modif: 军 military + 人 person] *n* serviceman, soldier (名 **míng**)
军事 **jūnshì** [modif: 军 army + 事 affair] *n* military affairs □ 军事上的事，我不大懂。**Jūnshì shang de shì, w bú dà dǒng.** *I don't know much about military affairs*
军需 **jūnxū** [modif: 军 military + 需 needs] *n* military supplies
军用 **jūnyòng** *adj* for military use
军装 **jūnzhuāng** [modif: 军 military + 装 garments] *n* army uniform

君 **jūn** *n* 1 monarch 2 gentleman
君主 **jūnzhǔ** *n* monarch
君主立宪 jūnzhǔ lìxiàn constitutional monarchy
君子 **jūnzǐ** *n* cultured and honorable man, gentlema

NOTE: In Confucianism 君子 **jūnzǐ** refers to *a cultured gentleman and a man of virtue.* 君子 **jūnzǐ** is in contrast with 小人 **xiǎorén,** *a mean person* or *an inferior being.*

匀 **jūn** *adj* equal
匀匀 **jūnyún** *adj* well distributed, evenly applied

菌 **jūn** *n* fungus, bacterium (See 细菌 **xìjūn**.)

峻 **jùn** *adj* harsh, stern (See 严峻 **yánjùn**)

俊 **jùn** *adj* handsome (See 英俊 **yīngjùn**)
美女俊男 **měinǚ jùnnán** beautiful women and handsome men

K

加 **kā** used in 咖啡 **kāfēi** only
咖啡 **kāfēi** *n* coffee (杯 **bēi**) □ 这种咖啡很好喝。 **Zhè zhǒng kāfēi hěn hǎohē.** *This kind of coffee tastes good.* □ 从厨房飘来咖啡的香味。 **Cóng chúfáng piāolái kāfēi de xiāngwèi.** *The aroma of coffee floated in from the kitchen.*
浓咖啡 nóng kāfēi espresso
速溶咖啡 sùróng kāfēi instant coffee
冲咖啡 chōng kāfēi make (instant) coffee
煮咖啡 zhǔ kāfēi brew coffee

NOTE: 咖啡 **kāfēi** is one of the few transliterations (音译词 **yīnyìcí**) in Chinese vocabulary, as it represents more or less the sound of "coffee."

卡 **kǎ** *n* card (张 **zhāng**) □ 这张卡很重要，你要放好了。 **Zhè zhāng kǎ hěn zhòngyào, nǐ yào fànghǎo le.** *This is a very important card. Keep it safely.*
贺卡 hèkǎ greeting card
借书卡 jièshū kǎ library card
信用卡 xìnyòng kǎ credit card
银行卡 yínháng kǎ banking card
卡车 **kǎchē** *n* lorry, truck (辆 **liàng**) □ 开过来一辆卡车。 **Kāi guòlái yí liàng kǎchē.** *A truck is coming.* □ 我叔叔是个卡车司机。 **Wǒ shūshu shì ge kǎchē sījī.** *My uncle is a truck driver.*

NOTE: The composition of 卡车 **kǎchē** is a semi-transliteration (半音译词 **bàn yīnyìcí**): 卡 **kǎ** represents the sound of the English word "car" and 车 **chē** means *vehicle*. See 咖啡 **kāfēi** for an example of transliteration.

卡片 **kǎpiàn** *n* card (张 **zhāng**)

开 **kāi** Trad 開 *v* **1** open, open up (antonym 关 **guān**) □ 开开门! **Kāikai mén!** *Open the door, please!* **2** turn on, switch on (antonym 关 **guān**) □ 天黑了，开灯吧。 **Tiān hēi le, kāi dēng ba.** *It's dark. Let's turn on the light.* **3** drive (a vehicle), pilot (a plane) □ 我会开汽车，不会开飞机。 **Wǒ huì kāi qìchē, bú huì kāi fēijī.** *I can drive a car, but I can't pilot a plane.* **4** start
开采 **kāicǎi** *v* mine, excavate
开除 **kāichú** *v* expel
被学校开除 bèi xuéxiào kāichú be expelled from the school
开刀 **kāidāo** *v* perform a medical operation
开发 **kāifā** [comp: 开 open + 发 develop] *v* develop (land, resources, products, etc.) □ 这个地区资源丰富，经济落后，需要开发。 **Zhège dìqū zīyuán fēngfù,**

jīngjì luòhòu, xūyào kāifā. *This region is rich in natural resources but is backward economically. It needs developing.* □ 我们公司花大量资金研究开发新产品。 **Wǒmen gōngsī huā dàliàng zījīn yánjiū kāifā xīn chǎnpǐn.** *Our company spends large amounts of funds on researching and developing new products.*
开发商 kāifāshāng (real estate, land) developer
开放 **kāifàng** [comp: 开 open + 放 release] *v* open, open up □ 这个展览会从下周起对外开放。 **Zhège zhǎnlǎnhuì cóng xià zhōu qǐ duìwài kāifàng.** *This exhibition will open to the public next week.*
开工 **kāigōng** [v+obj: 开 start + 工 work] *v* (of a factory) start production, (of a construction project) start building
开关 **kāiguān** [comp: 开 turn on + 关 trun off] *n* switch □ 这个机器的开关坏了。 **Zhège jīqì de kāiguān huài le.** *The switch of this machine is out of order.*
开会 **kāihuì** [v+obj: 开 open up + 会 meeting] *v* attend a meeting, hold a meeting □ 我们最好开个会，讨论一下这个问题。 **Wǒmen zuìhǎo kāi ge huì, tǎolùn yíxià zhège wèntí.** *We'd best have a meeting to discuss this issue.* □ 王老师在开会。 **Wáng lǎoshī zài kāihuì.** *Teacher Wang is at a meeting.*
开课 **kāikè** [v+obj: 开 start + 课 lesson] *v* introduce a course, teach a subject
开垦 **kāikěn** [comp: 开 open + 垦 reclaim] *v* reclaim (wasteland)
开口 **kāikǒu** [v+obj: 开 open + 口 the mouth] *v* start to talk
难以开口 nányǐ kāikǒu find it difficult to bring up a matter
开阔 **kāikuò** [comp: 开 open + 阔 wide] *adj* open and wide, expansive, spacious
开朗 **kāilǎng** *adj* broad-minded and outspoken, always cheerful
性格开朗 xìnggé kāilǎng of a cheerful disposition
开门 **kāimén** *v* open for business □ "这里的商店什么时候开门？" "九点钟开门。" **"Zhèlǐ de shāngdiàn shénme shíhou kāimén?" "Jiǔ diǎnzhōng kāimén."** *"When do stores here open for business?" "Nine o'clock."*
开明 **kāimíng** *adj* civilized, enlightened
开幕 **kāimù** [v+obj: 开 open + 幕 curtain] *v* (of a play, a ceremony, conference, etc.) open, start
开幕式 kāimùshì opening ceremony
开辟 **kāipì** [comp: 开 open up + 辟 open up] *v* open up, start □ 这里要开辟成特别经济区。 **Zhèlǐ yào kāipì chéng tèbié jīngjìqū.** *A special economic zone will be started here.*
开设 **kāishè** *v* **1** offer (a course in a college) **2** open (an office, a factory, etc.)
开始 **kāishǐ** [comp: 开 open + 始 begin] **I** *v* begin, commence (antonym 结束 **jiéshù**) □ 我从明年一月一日开始每天跑步半小时。 **Wǒ cóng míngnián Yíyuè yírì kāishǐ měi tiān pǎobù bàn xiǎoshí.** *I'll begin jogging half an hour every day from January 1 next year.* □ 我进电影院的时候，电影已经开始了。 **Wǒ jìn diànyǐngyuàn de shíhou, diànyǐng yǐjīng kāishǐ le.** *The film had started by the time I entered the cinema.* **II** *n* beginning, start □ 我开始觉得中文非常难，现在觉得不太难了。 **Wǒ kāishǐ juéde Zhōngwén fēicháng nán, xiànzài juéde bú tài nán le.** *At the beginning I*

found Chinese very difficult, but now I think it's not too difficult.

开头 kāitóu *n* Same as 开始 **kāishǐ**, used colloquially.

开拓 kāituō *v* open up

开玩笑 kāi wánxiào *v* joke □ 别开玩笑了! **Bié kāi wánxiào le!** *Stop kidding!* □ 这是很严肃的事, 你不要开玩笑。**Zhè shì hěn yánsù de shì, nǐ bú yào kāi wánxiào.** *This is a very serious matter. Don't joke about it.* (→ *This is no laughing matter.*)
跟/和…开玩笑 **gēn/hé…kāi wánxiào** joke with …, make fun of …. □ 他常常跟妹妹开玩笑。**Tā chángcháng gēn mèimei kāi wánxiào.** *He often jokes with his younger sister.*

开心 kāixīn *adj* feeling happy, delighted

开学 kāixué [v+obj: 开 open + 学 school] *v* start (school) □ 中国的学校一般九月一日开学。你们国家的学校哪一天开学? **Zhōngguó de xuéxiào yìbān Jiǔyuè yírì kāixué. Nǐmen guójiā de xuéxiào nǎ yì tiān kāixué?** *Schools in China usually start on September 1. On which day does school begin in your country?*

开演 kāiyǎn [v+obj: 开 open + 演 performance] *v* start (a performance, a film, etc.) □ 电影什么时候开演? **Diànyǐng shénme shíhou kāiyǎn?** *When does the film start?*

开夜车 kāi yèchē *v* burn the midnight oil □ 明天要交作业, 今天晚上我得开夜车。**Míngtiān yào jiāo zuòyè, jīntiān wǎnshang wǒ děi kāi yèchē.** *I must hand in my assignment tomorrow. I'll have to burn the midnight oil tonight.*

开展 kāizhǎn [comp: 开 open up + 展 fold] *v* launch, develop, expand □ 他一当上经理, 就积极开展业务。**Tā yì dāngshang jīnglǐ, jiù jījí kāizhǎn yèwù.** *As soon as he became manager, he actively expanded the business.*

开支 kāizhī **I** *v* pay (expenses) **II** *n* expenditure, expenses
日常家用开支 **rìcháng jiāyòng kāizhī** daily household expenses

凯 kǎi *adj* triumphant
凯旋 kǎixuán *v* return in triumph

慨 kǎi *adj* deeply touched (See 感慨 **gǎnkǎi**)

刊 kān *v* publish
刊登 kāndēng *v* publish (in a newspaper, magazine, etc.)
刊物 kānwù [modif: 刊 publish + 物 things] *n* periodical, journal, magazine

勘 kān *v* survey, investigate
勘探 kāntàn *n* prospecting, exploration
石油勘探队 **shíyóukāntàn duì** oil prospecting team

堪 kān *modal v* may, can

看 kān *v* look after, take care of
看孩子 **kān háizi** look after children, baby-sit

NOTE: This verb 看 is pronounced in the first tone when used in this sense.

砍 kǎn *v* chop, hack □ 这棵树要砍掉。**Zhè kē shù yào kǎndiào.** *This tree should be chopped down.*

看 kàn *v* 1 look, watch □ 我看看你的新衣服。**Wǒ kànkan nǐ de xīn yīfu.** *Let me have a look at your*

new dress. 2 read □ "你每天看报吗?" "我不每天看报。" **"Nǐ měi tiān kàn bào ma?" "Wǒ bù měi tiān kàn bào."** *"Do you read newspapers every day?" "No."*
看电视 **kàn diànshì** watch TV
看电影 **kàn diànyǐng** watch a film
看体育比赛 **kàn tǐyù bǐsài** watch a sport event

NOTE: See note on 看见 **kànjiàn**.

看病 kànbìng [v + obj: 看 see + 病 illness] *v* see a doctor □ 我下午要请半天假, 去看病。**Wǒ xiàwǔ yào qǐng bàn tiān jià, qù kànbìng.** *I'll ask for half a day leave to see a doctor this afternoon.*

看不起 kànbuqǐ *v* look down upon, despise □ 我看不起这种不老实的人。**Wǒ kànbuqǐ zhè zhǒng bù lǎoshí de rén.** *I despise such dishonest people.*
看得起 **kàndeqǐ** respect, hold in esteem

NOTE: In colloquial Chinese, 瞧不起 **qiáobuqǐ** can be used instead of 看不起 **kànbuqǐ**. Likewise 看得起 **kàndeqǐ** may be replaced by 瞧得起 **qiáodeqǐ**.

看待 kàndài *v* look upon, regard, treat □ 所有的职工都一律看待。**Suǒyǒu de zhígōng dōu yílù kàndài.** *All staff members are treated alike.*

看法 kànfǎ [modif: 看 view + 法 way, method] *n* 1 way of looking at things, view □ 你的看法不一定对。**Nǐ de kànfǎ bù yídìng duì.** *Your view is not necessarily correct.* 2 negative opinion □ 他对我有看法。**Tā duì wǒ yǒu kànfǎ.** *He has a negative opinion of me.*

看见 kànjiàn [v+comp: 看 look + 见 see] *v* see, get sight of □ 我朝山上看了很久, 才看见一个人在爬山。**Wǒ cháo shān shang kànle hěn jiǔ, cái kànjiàn yí ge rén zài pá shān.** *I looked at the hills for a long time before I saw a man climbing.*
看不见 **kàn bu jiàn** cannot see
看得见 **kàn de jiàn** can see □ "山上的人, 你看得见吗?" "看不见。" **"Shān shang de rén, nǐ kàn de jiàn ma?" "Kàn bu jiàn."** *"Can you see the man (or people) on the hill?" "No, I can't."*
没(有)看见 **méi (yǒu) kànjiàn** fail to see □ 我没看见他在图书馆里。**Wǒ méi kànjiàn tā zài túshūguǎn li.** *I did not see him in the library.*

NOTE: While 看 **kàn** is *to look* or *to look at*, 看见 **kànjiàn** is *to see* or *to catch sight of*. For example □ 我朝窗外看, 没有看见什么。**Wǒ cháo chuāng wài kàn, méiyǒu kànjiàn shénme.** *I looked out of the window and did not see anything.*

看来 kànlái *adv* it looks as if, it seems as if □ 看来要下大雨了。**Kànlái yào xià dà yǔ le.** *It seems that a downpour is coming our way.* □ 他看来很能干。**Tā kànlái hěn nénggàn.** *He looks like a very able man.*

看望 kànwàng [comp: 看 see + 望 look] *v* call on, pay a visit to □ 我每年过年都要看望中学时的老师。**Wǒ měi nián guònián dōu yào kànwàng zhōngxué shí de lǎoshī.** *I pay a visit to my high school teacher every New Year's Day.*

看样子 kànyàngzi *adv* Same as 看来 **kànlái**

看做 kànzuò *v* regard as, look upon as

把你看做我的好朋友 bǎ nǐ kàn zuò wǒde hǎo péngyou (I) regard you as my good friend, take you for my good friend

康 **kāng** *n* good health (See 健康 **jiànkāng**.)

慷 **kāng** as in 慷慨 **kāngkài**

慷慨 **kāngkài** *adj* generous, liberal

糠 **kāng** *n* husk, bran, chaff

抗 **kàng** *v* resist (See 反抗 **fǎnkàng**, 抗议 **kàngyì**.)

抗击 **kàngjī** [comp: 抗 resist + 击 strike] *v* beat back, resist by fighting

抗议 **kàngyì** I *v* protest □ 许多居民抗议建造新机场。**Xǔduō jūmín kàngyì jiànzào xīn jīchǎng.** *Many residents protested against the building of a new airport.* II *n* protest

亢 **kàng** *adj* high, haughty

炕 **kàng** *n* a heatable brick bed, *kang*

考 **kǎo** *v* examine, test □ 下星期二考中文。**Xià Xīngqī'èr kǎo Zhōngwén.** *There will be an examination on Chinese next Tuesday.* □ 他不是不知道怎么回答, 而是要考考你。**Tā bú shì bù zhīdào zěnme huídá, érshì yào kǎokao nǐ.** *It is not that he did not know how to answer the question, but that he wanted to test you.*

考察 **kǎochá** [comp: 考 examine + 察 investigate] *v* 1 inspect, make an on-the-spot investigation 2 test and judge (a person)

考古 **kǎogǔ** [v+obj: 考 examine + 古 ancient] *v* do archaeological studies

考古学 **kǎogǔxué** archaeology

考核 **kǎohé** [comp: 考 examine + 核 check] *v* examine and check

年终考核 **niánzhōng kǎohé** annual (staff) performance review

考虑 **kǎolǜ** *v* think over carefully, consider, contemplate □ 我要好好考虑一下你的建议, 明天给你回答。**Wǒ yào hǎohǎo kǎolǜ yíxià nǐ de jiànyì, míngtiān gěi nǐ huídá.** *I need to consider your suggestion carefully. I will give you a reply tomorrow.* □ 他正在考虑转到另一个学校去。**Tā zhèngzài kǎolǜ zhuǎndào lìng yí ge xuéxiào qu.** *He is contemplating transferring to another school.*

考取 **kǎoqǔ** *v* pass an examination for admission to employment or study

考取名牌大学 **kǎoqǔ míngpái dàxué** gain admission to a famous university by passing an examination

考试 **kǎoshì** [comp: 考 examine, inquire + 试 test] I *v* examine, test □ 我们明天考试。**Wǒmen míngtiān kiǎoshì.** *We're having an examination tomorrow.*

考得好 **kǎo de hǎo** do well in an examination

考得不好 **kǎo de bù hǎo** do poorly in an examination □ 我去年中文考得不好。**Wǒ qùnián Zhōngwén kǎo de bù hǎo.** *I did not do well in the Chinese examination last year.* II *n* examination, test (次 **cì**, 场 **cháng**) □ 这次考试太难了! **Zhè cì kǎoshì tài nán le!** *This test was really difficult!* □ "你怕考试吗?" "准备好了就不怕, 没准备好就怕。" **"Nǐ pà kǎoshì ma?" "Zhǔnbèi hǎole jiù bú pà, méi zhǔnbèihǎo jiù pà."** *"Are you afraid of examinations?" "Not when I'm prepared. If I weren't prepared, I'd be afraid."*

高等学校入学考试 (高考) **gāoděng xuéxiào rùxué kǎoshì (gāokǎo)** university entrance examination

汉语水平考试 **Hànyǔ Shuǐpíng Kǎoshì (HSK)** Chinese Proficiency Test

考验 **kǎoyàn** [comp: 考 test + 验 examine] I *v* test, put through rigorous testing II *n* rigorous test, trial

烤 **kǎo** *v* bake, roast □ 中国人很少吃烤牛肉。**Zhōngguórén hěn shǎo chī kǎo niúròu.** *The Chinese rarely eat roast beef.*

靠 **kào** *v* rely on, depend on □ 这事全靠你了。**Zhè shì quán kào nǐ le.** *This matter depends entirely on you.* □ 做事不能靠运气。**Zuòshì bù néng kào yùnqi.** *You cannot rely on luck to get things done.*

靠得住 **kàodezhù** trustworthy, reliable

靠不住 **kàobuzhù** untrustworthy, unreliable

靠近 **kàojìn** *v* close to, near

科 **kē** *n* 1 section (of an administration office)

财务科 **cáiwùkē** finance section

2 branch (of academic study)

工科 **gōngkē** faculty of engineering

理科 **lǐkē** faculty of (natural) sciences

文科 **wénkē** faculty of arts

3 shortening for 科学 **kēxué**

科技 **kējì** science and technology

科目 **kēmù** *n* (school) subject, course

科学 **kēxué** [modif: 科 classification + 学 study] *n* science □ 科学能解决世界上所有的问题吗? **Kēxué néng jiějué shìjiè shang suǒyǒu de wèntí ma?** *Can science solve all the problems in the world?* □ 我丈夫学科学, 我学语言。**Wǒ zhàngfu xué kēxué, wǒ xué yǔyán.** *My husband studies science, and I study languages.*

科学研究 (科研) **kēxué yánjiū (kēyán)** scientific research

科学家 **kēxuéjiā** [modif: 科学 science + 家 nominal suffix] *n* scientist (位 **wèi**) □ 这座大学有几位世界著名的科学家。**Zhè zuò dàxué yǒu jǐ wèi shìjiè zhùmíng de kēxuéjiā.** *This university has several world-renowned scientists.*

科学院 **kēxuéyuàn** *n* academy of science

科长 **kēzhǎng** [modif: 科 section + 长 head] *n* section head

棵 **kē** *measure wd* (for plants)

三棵树 **sān kē shù** three trees

一棵草 **yì kē cǎo** a blade of grass

颗 **kē** *measure wd* (for beans, pearl, etc.)

一颗黄豆 **yìkē huángdòu** a soybean

磕 **kē** *v* knock

磕头 **kētóu** [v+obj: 磕 knock + 头 (one's) head (on the ground)] *v* kowtow

咳 **ké** *v* cough

咳嗽 **késou** [comp: 咳 cough + 嗽 cough up] *v* cough □ 这个病人每天夜里都咳嗽。**Zhège bìngrén měi tiān yèli dōu késou.** *The patient coughs every night.* □ 你咳嗽很厉害, 得去看病。**Nǐ késou hěn lìhai, děi qù kànbìng.** *You've got a bad cough. You need to see a doctor.*

咳嗽药水 **késou yàoshuǐ** cough syrup

咳嗽糖 **késou táng** cough lozenge, cough drop

壳 **ké** *n* shell

鸡蛋壳 **jīdànké** egg shell

可 **kě** I *adv* 1 indeed (used before an adjective for emphasis) □ 当父母可不容易呢! **Dāng fùmǔ kě bù róngyì ne!** *Being a parent is indeed no easy job!* □ 她跳舞跳得可美啦。 **Tā tiàowǔ tiào de kě měi la.** *She dances really beautifully!* 2 after all (used before a verb for emphasis) □ 我可找到你了! **Wǒ kě zhǎodào nǐ le!** *I've found you after all.* □ 他可出院了。 **Tā kě chūyuàn le.** *He was discharged from the hospital after all.* 3 be sure to (used in an imperative sentence for emphasis) □ 可别忘了给他发一份电子邮件。 **Kě bié wàngle gěi tā fā yí fèn diànzǐ yóujiàn!** *Be sure not to forget to send him an e-mail.* (→ *Be sure to send him an e-mail.*) □ 考试的时候可要看懂题目。 **Kǎoshì de shíhou kě yào kàndǒng tímù.** *During an examination, make sure that you understand the questions.* II *modal v* can be, may be III *conj* Same as 可是 **kěshì**

NOTE: 可 **kě** is only used colloquially. When using 可 **kě** to emphasize an adjective or a verb, 啦 **la**, 呢 **ne** or 了 **le** is often used at the end of the sentence.

可爱 **kě'ài** *adj* lovable, lovely □ 这小女孩真可爱! **Zhè xiǎo nǚhái zhēn kě'ài!** *What a lovely little girl!*

NOTE: 可 in the sense of *can be*, *may be* plus a verb forms an adjective, similar to English adjectives of *v+ -able/ible*. For example, 可爱 **kě'ài** is similar to *lovable*. Quite a number of Chinese adjectives are formed in the same way as 可爱 **kě'ài**.

可耻 **kěchǐ** *adj* shameful, disgraceful
可观 **kěguān** *adj* considerable, sizeable
一笔可观的现金 yìbǐ kěguān de xiànjīn a considerable sum of cash
可贵 **kěguì** *adj* valuable, recommendable
可见 **kějiàn** *conj* it can be seen, it is thus clear
可靠 **kěkào** *v* reliable, trustworthy □ 很难找到可靠的人来管理秘密文件。 **Hěn nán zhǎodào kěkào de rén lái guǎnlǐ mìmìwénjiàn.** *It is difficult to find a trustworthy person to take care of confidential documents.* □ 你这个消息可靠吗? **Nǐ zhège xiāoxi kěkào ma?** *Is your news reliable?*
可口 **kěkǒu** *adj* palatable, tasty
可口可乐 **kěkǒukělè** *n* Coca-Cola (瓶 **píng**) □ 可口可乐有吗? **Kěkǒukělè yǒu ma?** *Do you have Coca-Cola?* □ 我很渴, 我想喝一瓶可口可乐。 **Wǒ hěn kě, wǒ xiǎng hē yì píng kěkǒukělè.** *I'm thirsty, I want to drink a bottle of Coca-Cola.*
百事可乐 **bǎishìkělè** Pepsi[-Cola]

NOTE: 可口可乐 **kěkǒukělè** is a transliteration of "Coca-Cola." It can be shortened into 可乐 **kělè**.

可怜 **kělián** *adj* pitiful, pitiable □ 这小孩的父母在交通事故中死了, 真可怜! **Zhè xiǎohái de fùmǔ zài jiāotōng shìgù zhong sǐ le, zhēn kělián!** *Both his parents died in a road accident, the poor child!*
可能 **kěnéng** [comp: 可 may + 能 can] I *modal v* may, possible, possibly □ 他两天没来上课, 可能病了。 **Tā liǎng tiān méi lái shàngkè, kěnéng bìng le.** *He's been absent from class for two days. He may be ill.* □ 他听了可能会生气。 **Tā tīngle kěnéng huì shēngqì.** *He may be*

offended when he hears this. II *n* possibility □ 这种可能是有的。 **Zhè zhǒng kěnéng shì yǒu de.** *This is possible* (没)有可能 (méi) yǒu kěnéng (im)possible, (im)possibly □ "这件事有解决的可能吗?" "有可能。" **"Zhè jiàn shì yǒu jiějué de kěnéng ma?" "Yǒu kěnéng."** *"Is it possible to solve this matter?" "Yes."*
可怕 **kěpà** *adj* fearsome, frightening □ 这种病很可怕, 还没有药治。 **Zhè zhǒng bìng hěn kěpà, hái méiyǒu yào zhì.** *This disease is frightening, as there is still no medicine for it.*
可是 **kěshì** *conj* Same as 但是 **dànshì**, used colloquially
可恶 **kěwù** *adj* detestable, hateful
可惜 **kěxī** *adj* be a pity, be a shame □ 真可惜! **Zhēn kěxī!** *What a shame!*
可喜 **kěxǐ** *adj* gratifying, heartening
可笑 **kěxiào** *adj* laughable, ridiculous
可行 **kěxíng** *adj* can be done, feasible
可行性 **kěxíngxìng** feasibility
可行性报告 **kěxíngxìng bàogào** feasibility report
可疑 **kěyí** *adj* suspicious
可疑分子 **kěyífènzǐ** a suspect
行为可疑 **xíngwéi kěyí** suspicious behavior
可以 **kěyǐ** *modal v* giving permission, may, can, be allowed □ "我可以走了吗?" "可以。" **"Wǒ kěyǐ zǒu le ma?" "Kěyǐ."** *"May I leave now?" "Yes, you may."* □ 你不可以把阅览室的书带回家。 **Nǐ bù kěyǐ bǎ yuèlǎnshì de shū dàihuí jiā.** *You are not allowed to take books home from the reading room.*

渴 **kě** *adj* thirsty □ 我渴了, 请给我一杯水。 **Wǒ kě le, qǐng gěi wǒ yì bēi shuǐ.** *I'm thirsty. Please give me a glass of water.*
口渴 **kǒukě** thirsty □ 你口渴吗? 这里有水。 **Nǐ kǒukě ma? Zhèli yǒu shuǐ.** *Are you thirsty? Here's some water.*

NOTE: See note on 喝 **hē**.

渴望 **kěwàng** [comp: 渴 thirsty + 望 hope] *v* thirst for, long for
克 **kè** *measure wd* gram
五百克 wǔbǎi kè 500 grams
克服 **kèfú** *v* overcome, conquer □ 我相信一定能克服这些暂时的困难。 **Wǒ xiāngxìn yídìng néng kèfú zhèxiē zànshí de kùnnan.** *I am convinced that we are surely able to overcome these temporary difficulties.*
刻 1 **kè** *v* carve □ 他在石头上刻上自己的名字。 **Tā zài shítou shang kè shang zìjǐ de míngzi.** *He carved his name on the rock.*
刻 2 **kè** *measure wd* quarter of an hour
一刻钟 yí kè zhōng a quarter of an hour, 15 minutes
三点一刻 sān diǎn yí kè a quarter past three
刻苦 **kèkǔ** *adj* hardworking, assiduous, painstaking □ 这位科学家刻苦研究十几年, 终于找到了答案。 **Zhè wèi kēxuéjiā kèkǔ yánjiū shí jǐ nián, zhōngyú zhǎodào le dá'àn.** *The scientist researched arduously for a dozen years and finally found the answer.*
客 **kè** *n* guest
客车 **kèchē** *n* 1 passenger train 2 coach
客观 **kèguān** *adj* objective
客观的报道 kèguān de bàodào objective report
客户 **kèhù** *n* client, buyer

客气 **kèqi** [modif: 客 guest + 气 manner] *adj* **1** polite, standing on ceremony □ 您跟我们一起吃午饭吧，别客气。**Nín gēn wǒmen yìqǐ chī wǔfàn ba, bié kèqi.** *Have lunch with us. Don't stand on ceremony.* □ 他要请你帮忙的时候，就很客气。**Tā yào qǐng nǐ bāngmáng de shíhou, jiù hěn kèqi.** *When he asks for your help, he's very polite.* **2** modest □ 你唱歌唱得这么好，还说不好，太客气了。**Nǐ chànggē chàng de zhème hǎo, hái shuō bù hǎo, tài kèqi le.** *You sing so well but you still say you don't sing well. You're too modest.*

客人 **kèrén** *n* guest, visitor □ 宴会八点钟开始，七点三刻客人陆续到来。**Yànhuì bā diǎnzhōng kāishǐ, qī diǎn sān kè kèrén lùxù dàolai.** *The banquet began at eight o'clock; guests arrived one after another at a quarter to eight.*

客厅 **kètīng** [modif: 客 guest + 厅 hall] *n* living room, sitting room

课 **kè** Trad 課 *n* lesson, class, lecture □ 今天的课你听懂没有？**Jīntiān de kè nǐ tīngdǒng méiyǒu?** *Do you understand today's lesson?*
上课 **shàng kè** go to class
下课 **xià kè** finish class

课本 **kèběn** [modif: 课 lesson + 本 book] n textbook, course book (本 **běn**) □ 你知不知道哪一本中文课本比较好？**Nǐ zhī bu zhīdào nǎ yì běn Zhōngwén kèběn bǐjiào hǎo?** *Do you know which Chinese textbook is relatively good?* (→ *Do you know of a good Chinese textbook?*) □ 王老师打算编一本适合日本学生学中文的课本。**Wáng lǎoshī dǎsuàn biān yì běn shìhé Rìběn xuésheng xué Zhōngwén de kèběn.** *Teacher Wang plans to compile a textbook suitable for Japanese students of Chinese.*

课程 **kèchéng** [modif: 课 lesson + 程 course] *n* course, a program of study □ 医学课程花的时间比其他课程长。**Yīxué kèchéng huā de shíjiān bǐ qítā kèchéng cháng.** *A course in medicine takes more time than other courses.* □ 我们的课程排得很满，没有多少时间搞课外活动。**Wǒmen de kèchéng pái de hěn mǎn, méiyǒu duōshǎo shíjiān gǎo kèwài huódòng.** *Our timetable is very crowded and leaves little time for extracurricular activities.*

课时 **kèshí** *n* class hour
课堂 **kètáng** *n* classroom
课题 **kètí** *n* research topic
课文 **kèwén** [modif: 课 lesson + 文 writing] *n* text (篇 **piān**) □ 这篇课文写得真好。**Zhè piān kèwén xiě de zhēn hǎo.** *This text is really well written.* □ 我要多念几遍课文。**Wǒ yào duō niàn jǐ biàn kèwén.** *I should read the text a few more times.*

肯 **kěn** *modal v* be willing to □ 你肯不肯帮我做一件事？**Nǐ kěn bu kěn bāng wǒ zuò yí jiàn shì?** *Are you willing to do something for me?* (→ *Would you do me a favor?*) □ 中国的父母一般肯为孩子作出牺牲。**Zhōngguó de fù-mǔ yìbān kěn wèi háizi zuòchu xīshēng.** *Generally speaking, Chinese parents are willing to make sacrifices for their children.*

肯定 **kěndìng** **I** *v* confirm, acknowledge (antonym 否定 **fǒudìng**) □ 总公司充分肯定你们的成绩。**Zǒnggōngsī chōngfèn kěndìng nǐmen de chéngjì.** *The company's head office fully acknowledges your achievements.* **II** *adj* affirmative, positive, definite (antonym 否定 **fǒudìng**) □ "你支持我们的计划吗？"

"我肯定支持。" "**Nǐ zhīchí wǒmen de jìhuà ma?**" "**Wǒ kěndìng zhīchí.**" *"Do you support our plan?" "I definitely support it."* □ 很抱歉，我不能给你一个肯定的回答。**Hěn bàoqiàn, wǒ bù néng gěi nǐ yí ge kěndìng de huídá.** *I'm sorry, but I'm not in a position to give you a definite reply.*

啃 **kěn** *v* gnaw, nibble

恳 **kěn** Trad 懇 *adj* sincere
恳切 **kěnqiè** *adj* earnest, sincere
恳求 **kěnqiú** [modif: 恳 sincere + 求 request] *v* implore, entreat

垦 **kěn** Trad 墾 *v* cultivate (land)
垦荒 **kěnhuāng** [v+obj: 垦 reclaim + 荒 wasteland] *v* reclaim wasteland

坑 **kēng** *n* pit, hollow

空 **kōng** **I** *adj* empty □ 箱子是空的，里面什么也没有。**Xiāngzi shì kōng de, lǐmiàn shénme yě méiyǒu.** *The suitcase is empty, there's nothing in it.* **II** n sky

空洞 **kōngdòng** [modif: 空 empty + 洞 cave] *adj* hollow, devoid of content
空洞的承诺 **kōngdòng de chéngnuò** hollow promise

空话 **kōnghuà** [modif: 空 empty + 话 word] *n* empty talk, hollow words

空间 **kōngjiān** *n* space, room □ 要给孩子留一些空间，让他做自己喜欢做的事。**Yào gěi háizi liú yìxiē kōngjiān, ràng tā zuò zìjǐ xǐhuan zuò de shì.** *Leave a child room (or time) to let him do what he enjoys doing.*

空军 **kōngjūn** [modif: 空 air + 军 force] *n* air force

空气 **kōngqì** [modif: 空 empty + 气 vapor] *n* air □ 这里的空气真好！**Zhèli de kōngqì zhēn hǎo!** *The air here is really fresh.* □ 空气是由什么组成的？**Kōngqì shì yóu shénme zǔchéng de?** *What is air composed of?*

空前 **kōngqián** *adj* unprecedented □ 这种经济增长的速度是空前的。**Zhè zhǒng jīngjì zēngzhǎng de sùdù shì kōngqián de.** *This kind of economic growth rate is unprecedented.*

空调 **kōngtiáo** *n* air conditioning
空调机 **kōngtiáojī** air conditioner
有空调的房间 **yǒu kòngtiáo de fángjiān** air-conditioned room

空想 **kōngxiǎng** [modif: 空 empty + 想 thinking] *n* pipe-dream, fantasy

空心 **kōngxīn** [modif: 空 empty + 心 heart] *adj* hollow

空虚 **kōngxū** [comp: 空 empty + 虚 void] *adj* void, empty
生活空虚 **shēnghuó kōngxū** live a life devoid of any meaning, a meaningless existence

空中 **kōngzhōng** *n* in the sky, in the air □ 他们在表演空中飞人的节目。**Tāmen zài biǎoyǎn kōngzhōng fēirén de jiémù.** *They are performing on the flying trapeze.*

恐 **kǒng** *v* fear

恐怖 **kǒngbù** [comp: 恐 fear + 怖 terrifying] *adj* horrible, terrifying □ 这个电影太恐怖了，小孩子不能看。**Zhège diànyǐng tài kǒngbù le, xiǎo háizi bù néng kàn.** *This film is too frightening for children to see.*

恐怖电影 kǒngbù diànyǐng horror movie
恐怖分子 kǒngbù fènzi terrorist
恐怖活动 kǒngbù huódòng terrorist activity
恐怖主义 kǒngbù zhǔyì terrorism
恐惧 **kǒngjù** [comp: 恐 fear + 惧 dread] *v* be in great fear of, dread
恐怕 **kǒngpà** [comp: 恐 fear, dread + 怕 fear] *adv* I'm afraid, perhaps □ 他的病恐怕两三天好不了。**Tā de bìng kǒngpà liǎng-sān tiān hǎobùliǎo.** *I'm afraid he won't recover in a couple of days.* □ 她恐怕已经回国了。**Tā kǒngpà yǐjīng huíguó le.** *She has perhaps gone back to her home country.*

NOTE: 恐怕 **kǒngpà** and 也许 **yěxǔ** may both mean *perhaps*, but 恐怕 **kǒngpà** implies that what might perhaps happen is undesirable.

孔 **kǒng** *n* aperture, hole □ 这座桥有三个孔。**Zhè zuò qiáo yǒu sān ge kǒng.** *The bridge has three arches.*
孔夫子 **Kǒngfūzǐ** *n* Confucius

NOTE: (1) 孔夫子 **Kǒngfūzǐ**, the most influential Chinese philosopher, is given a Europeanized name – *Confucius*. The great ancient philosopher 孟子 **Mèngzǐ** also has a Europeanized name, viz. *Mencius*. (2) 孔夫子 **Kǒngfūzǐ** is also called 孔子 **Kǒngzǐ** in Chinese. (3) His teachings are referred to as 孔子学说 **Kǒngzǐ xuéshuō** or 儒家学说 **Rújiā xuéshuō.**

孔雀 **kǒngquè** *n* peacock (只 **zhī**)
空 **kòng** I *adj* unoccupied, vacant
空房 kòngfáng vacant room
II *n* free time □ "你今天晚上有空吗？" "我今天晚上没有空, 明天晚上有空。" "**Nǐ jīntiān wǎnshang yǒukòng ma?**" "**Wǒ jīntiān wǎnshang méiyǒu kòng, míngtiān wǎnshang yǒu kòng.**" *"Are you free this evening?" "No, I'm not. I'll be free tomorrow evening."* □ 你有空常来玩。**Nǐ yǒu kòng cháng lái wán.** *Do come to visit us when you have time.*
空白 **kòngbái** [comp: 空 vacant + 白 white] *adj* blank space
空白支票 kòngbái zhīpiào blank check
空缺 **kòngquē** [comp: 空 vacant + 白 white] *n* vacant position
空隙 **kòngxì** [comp: 空 vacant + 隙 crack] *n* narrow gap, brief interval
空闲 **kòngxián** I *adj* be free II *n* free time, leisure
空子 **kòngzi** *n* loophole
钻空子 zuān kòngzi take advantage of a loophole
控 **kòng** *v* 1 control 2 accuse
控告 **kònggào** [comp: 控 accuse + 告 sue] *v* accuse, sue
控股公司 **kònggǔ gōngsī** *n* holding company
控制 **kòngzhì** [comp: 控 accuse + 制 restrain] *v* control, dominate □ 我们要控制人口的增长, 提高人口的质量。**Wǒmen yào kòngzhì rénkǒu de zēngzhǎng, tígāo rénkǒu de zhìliàng.** *We should control population growth and raise the quality of the population.* □ 她控制不住自己的感情, 大哭起来。**Tā kòngzhì bú zhù zìjǐ de gǎnqíng, dàkū qǐlai.** *She couldn't control her emotions and began to cry loudly.*

抠 **kōu** *v* dig with a finger

口 **kǒu** I *n* mouth □ 病从口入。**Bìng cóng kǒu rù.** *Disease enters your body by the mouth.* (→ *Bad food causes disease.*) II *measure wd* (for members of a family) □ 我家有四口人。**Wǒ jiā yǒu sì kǒu rén.** *There're four people in my family.*
口岸 **kǒu'àn** *n* port
口才 **kǒucái** [modif: 口 oral + 才 talent] I *n* the ability to speak well, gift of gab II *adj* eloquent
有口才 yǒu kǒucái be eloquent
口吃 **kǒuchī** *v* stammer, stutter
口齿 **kǒuchǐ** *n* the ability to pronounce sounds and words clearly
口齿清楚 kǒuchǐ qīngchǔ with clear enunciation
口袋 **kǒudài** *n* pocket (只 **zhī**) □ 他喜欢把手插在口袋里。**Tā xǐhuan bǎ shǒu chā zài kǒudài li.** *He likes to put his hands in his pockets.*
口号 **kǒuhào** *n* slogan (条 **tiáo**) □ 这种政治口号已经没有人喊了。**Zhè zhǒng zhèngzhì kǒuhào yǐjīng méiyǒu rén hǎn le.** *Nobody shouts such political slogans any more.*
口气 **kǒuqì** *n* 1 tone (of speech)
温和的口气 wēnhé de kǒuqì gentle tone
2 manner of speaking
听他的口气 tīng tāde kǒuqì judging by the way he spoke
口腔 **kǒuqiāng** *n* oral cavity
口试 **kǒushì** [modif: 口 oral + 试 test] *n* oral examination
口头 **kǒutóu** *adj* oral, spoken
口头协议 kǒutóu xiéyì oral agreement
口语 **kǒuyǔ** [modif: 口 the mouth + 语 speech] *n* spoken language, speech □ 我中文口语不行, 很多话不会说。**Wǒ Zhōngwén kǒuyǔ bù xíng, hěn duō huà bú huì shuō.** *My oral Chinese is rather poor. There are many things I can't express.* □ 要学好口语, 就要多听, 多说。**Yào xué hǎo kǒuyǔ, jiù yào duō tīng, duō shuō.** *To learn the spoken language well, one should listen a lot and speak a lot.* □ 他喜欢找中国人说话练口语。**Tā xǐhuan zhǎo Zhōngguórén shuōhuà liàn kǒuyǔ.** *He likes to talk with Chinese to practice his oral Chinese.*

扣 **kòu** I *n* 1 button
扣子 kòuzi button
2 knot
系个扣儿 xì gè kòur make a knot
II *v* 1 button up
扣扣子 kòu kòuzi do up the buttons
2 detain, arrest 3 deduct
扣除 **kòuchú** [comp: 扣 deduct + 除 divide] *v* deduct
扣留 **kòuliú** *v* detain, hold in custody
扣留驾驶执照 kòuliú jiàshǐ zhízhào suspend a driving license
扣押 **kòuyā** *v* distrain, detain
扣压 **kòuyā** *v* withhold, pigeonhole

寇 **kòu** *n* bandit

哭 **kū** *v* cry, weep, sob (antonym 笑 **xiào**) □ 别哭了, 有话好好说。**Bié kū le, yǒu huà hǎohǎo shuō.** *Don't cry. Speak up if you have something to say.* □ 她

难过得哭起来。**Tā nánguò de kū qǐlai.** *She was so sad that she cried.* □ 听了他的话，我哭笑不得。**Tīngle tā de huà, wǒ kū-xiào bù dé.** *Hearing what he said, I didn't know whether to laugh or cry.*

枯 **kū** *adj* withered
枯燥 **kūzào** [comp: 枯 withered + 燥 dry] *adj* dull and dry
枯燥乏味 **kūzào fáwèi** dull and insipid

窟 **kū** *n* cave, hole
窟窿 **kūlong** *n* hole, cavity

苦 **kǔ** *adj* 1 bitter □ 这杯咖啡太苦了，要放点儿糖。**Zhè bēi kāfēi tài kǔ le, yào fàng diǎnr táng.** *This coffee is too bitter. Put a bit of sugar in it.* 2 (of life) hard, miserable □ 经济不好，不少人生活很苦。**Jīngjì bù hǎo, bù shǎo rén shēnghuó hěn kǔ.** *As the economy is not in good shape, many people's lives are very hard.*
吃苦 **chīkǔ** suffer hardships, endure hardships
苦闷 **kǔmèn** *adj* depressed, dejected
苦难 **kǔnàn** [comp: 苦 bitter + 难 disaster] *n* great suffering, misery
苦恼 **kǔnǎo** *adj* vexed, troubled

库 **kù** Trad 庫 *n* warehouse (See 仓库 **cāngkù**)
库存 **kùcún** *n* stock, reserve

裤 **kù** Trad 褲 *n* trousers
裤子 **kùzi** [suffix: 裤 trousers + 子 nominal suffix] *n* trousers (条 **tiáo**) □ 这条裤子短了一点儿。**Zhè tiáo kùzi duǎnle yìdiǎnr.** *This pair of trousers is a bit too short.* □ 这个小孩会脱裤子，但还不会穿裤子。**Zhège xiǎohái huì tuō kùzi, dàn hái bú huì chuān kùzi.** *This child can take off his trousers, but still can't put them on.*

酷 **kù** *adj* 1 cruel
酷刑 **kùxíng** cruel torture, torture
2 cool □ 太酷了! **Tài kù le!** *It's really cool!*

夸 **kuā** *v* 1 exaggerate, boast 2 praise
夸大 **kuādà** *v* exaggerate
夸奖 **kuājiǎng** *v* praise, commend

垮 **kuǎ** *v* collapse, break down
打垮 **dǎkuǎ** defeat, rout, smash

跨 **kuà** *v* take big strides □ 他再向前跨一步，就要滚下楼梯了。**Tā zài xiàngqián kuà yí bù, jiùyào gǔnxia lóutī le.** *If he took another step forward he would tumble down the staircase.*
跨国公司 **kuàguó gōngsī** multinational company

挎 **kuà** *v* carry on the arm

快 **kuài** *adj* quick, fast (antonym 慢 **màn**) □ 快，公共汽车来了! **Kuài, gōnggòng qìchē lái le!** *Quick, the bus is coming!* □ 他跑得很快。**Tā pǎo de hěn kuài.** *He runs very fast.*
快餐 **kuàicān** [modif: 快 fast + 餐 meal] *n* fast food
快车 **kuài chē** [modif: 快 fast + 车 vehicle] *n* express train
快递 **kuàidì** [modif: 快 quick, fast + 递 delivery] *n* express delivery
快乐 **kuàilè** *adj* joyful, happy □ 祝你生日快乐! **Zhù nǐ shēngrì kuàilè!** *Happy birthday!* □ 在这个快乐的节日里，人们暂时忘了生活中种种不愉快的事。**Zài zhège kuàilè de jiérì li, rénmen zànshí wàngle shēnghuó zhōng zhǒng-zhǒng bù yúkuài de shì.** *At this happy festival, people forget for the time being the unpleasant things in life.*

快速 **kuàisù** [modif: 快 quick + 速 speed] *adj* high-speed

会 **kuài** as in 会计 **kuàijì**
会计 **kuàijì** *n* 1 accounting
会计年度 **kuàijì niándù** fiscal year
2 accountant
会计主任 **kuàijì zhǔrèn** chief accountant

块 **kuài** Trad 塊 *measure wd* 1 (for things that can be broken into lumps or chunks)
一块蛋糕 **yí kuài dàngāo** a piece/slice of cake
两块面包 **liǎng kuài miànbāo** two pieces of bread
2 (for money) yuan, dollar (only in spoken Chinese)
三块钱 **sān kuài qián** three yuan (or dollars)

NOTE: See note on 元 **yuán**.

筷 **kuài** *n* chopstick
筷子 **kuàizi** chopsitick, chopsticks
一双筷子 **yì shuāng kuàizi** a pair of chopsticks

宽 **kuān** Trad 寬 *adj* 1 wide, broad □ 江面很宽，我游不过去。**Jiāngmiàn hěn kuān, wǒ yóu bu guòqu.** *The river is too wide for me to swim across.* 2 lenient, generous 3 well-off
宽敞 **kuānchang** [comp: 宽 wide + 敞 open] *adj* spacious
宽大 **kuāndà** *adj* 1 roomy, spacious 2 lenient
宽带 **kuāndài** [modif: 宽 broad + 带 band] *n* broadband
宽广 **kuānguǎng** *adj* extensive, expansive
宽阔 **kuānkuò** *adj* broad, wide

款 **kuǎn** *n* sum of money (笔 **bǐ**) □ 你可以用这张卡取款，或者存款。**Nǐ kěyǐ yòng zhè zhāng kǎ qǔ kuǎn, huòzhě cún kuǎn.** *You can withdraw or deposit money with this card.*
款待 **kuǎndài** *v* entertain hospitably

狂 **kuáng** *adj* mad, wild
狂风 **kuángfēng** [modif: 狂 wild + 风 wind] *n* terrible wind, strong fast wind
狂人 **kuángrén** [modif: 狂 wild + 人 person] madman, maniac
狂妄 **kuángwàng** [comp: 狂 wild + 妄 preposterous] *adj* outrageously conceited

况 **kuàng** *n* situation (See 情况 **qíngkuàng**, 状况 **zhuàngkuàng**.)
况且 **kuàngqiě** *conj* moreover, besides

矿 **kuàng** Trad 礦 *n* (coal, gold, etc.) mine (座 **zuò**), mineral □ 这座矿已经开了一百多年了。**Zhè zuò kuàng yǐjīng kāile yìbǎi duō nián le.** *This coal mine has been mined for over a century.*
金矿 **jīnkuàng** gold mine
煤矿 **méikuàng** coal mine
油矿 **yóukuàng** oilfield
矿藏 **kuàngcáng** [modif: 矿 mineral + 藏 resources] *n* mineral resources
矿产 **kuàngchǎn** [modif: 矿 mineral + 产 product] *n* mineral products
矿工 **kuànggōng** *n* miner
矿区 **kuàngqū** *n* mining area
矿山 **kuàngshān** *n* mine
矿石 **kuàngshí** [modif: 矿 mineral + 石 rock] *n* mineral ore
矿物 **kuàngwù** *n* mineral

旷 kuàng *adj* free from worries
　旷工 **kuànggōng** *v* absent from work without leave
　旷课 **kuàngkè** *v* absent from school without leave

亏 kuī I *n* loss (antonym 盈 **yíng**)
　转亏为盈 **zhuǎn kuī wéi yíng** turn loss into gain
　II *v* 1 lose, be deficient 2 thank to
　亏待 **kuīdài** *v* treat shabbily
　亏损 **kuīsǔn** [comp: 亏 loss + 损 loss] *n* loss, deficiency

葵 kuí as in 葵花 **kuíhuā**
　葵花 **kuíhuā** *n* sunflower

愧 kuì *adj* ashamed (See 惭愧 **cánkuì**.)

昆 kūn as in 昆虫 **kūnchóng**
　昆虫 **kūnchóng** *n* insect (只 **zhī**)

捆 kǔn I *v* bundle up, tie II *measure wd* bundle

困 kùn I *v* be stranded, be in a tough spot □ 由于突然发大水，人们被困在那个小山村。**Yóuyú tūrán fā dàshuǐ, rénmen bèi kùn zài nàge xiǎo shāncūn.** *Because of a sudden flood, people were stranded in the small mountain village.* II *adj* sleepy
　困苦 **kùnkǔ** *adj* poverty-stricken, destitute
　困难 **kùnnan** [comp: 困 be stranded + 难 difficult] I *n* difficulty □ 困难是有的，但是没有关系。**Kùnnan shì yǒu de, dànshì méiyǒu guānxi.** *There are difficulties, but it doesn't matter.* □ 你不要怕困难，要想一想怎么办。**Nǐ bú yào pà kùnnan, yào xiǎng yi xiǎng zěnme bàn.** *You mustn't be afraid of difficulties. You should think of what to do.*
　克服困难 **kèfú kùnnan** overcome difficulty
　II *adj* difficult □ 我们现在的情况比较困难。**Wǒmen xiànzài de qíngkuàng bǐjiào kùnnan.** *Our situation is rather difficult.*

扩 kuò Trad 擴 *v* spread out
　扩充 **kuòchōng** *v* strengthen, reinforce
　扩大 **kuòdà** *v* expand, enlarge □ 这个城市的范围在不断扩大。**Zhège chéngshì de fànwéi zài búduàn kuòdà.** *The boundary of this city is constantly expanding.* □ 他们打算扩大生产规模。**Tāmen dǎsuàn kuòdà shēngchǎn guīmó.** *They plan to expand the scale of production.*
　扩散 **kuòsàn** *v* spread, proliferate
　扩张 **kuòzhāng** *v* expand, extend

括 kuò *v* include, embrace (See 概括 **gàikuò**.)

阔 kuò *adj* wide (See 广阔 **guǎngkuò**.)

L

拉 lā *v* pull □ 请你拉这个门，别推这个门。**Qǐng nǐ lā zhège mén, bié tuī zhège mén.** *Please pull this door, not push it.*

垃 lā as in 垃圾 **lājī**
　垃圾 **lājī** *n* rubbish, garbage □ 请不要乱扔垃圾。**Qǐng bú yào luàn rēng lājī.** *Please do not litter.*
　垃圾处理 **lājī chǔlǐ** rubbish disposal
　垃圾袋 **lājī dài** rubbish bag

垃圾箱 **lājī xiāng** rubbish bin
垃圾邮件 **lājī yóujiàn** *n* junk mail
　阻止垃圾邮件 **zǔzhǐ lājī yóujiàn** prevent junk mail

喇 lǎ as in 喇叭 **lǎba**
　喇叭 **lǎba** *n* 1 horn, trumpet 2 loudspeaker
　吹喇叭 **chuī lǎba** blow the horn, play the trumpet

蜡 là Trad 蠟 *n* wax
　蜡烛 **làzhú** *n* candle (支 **chī**)
　点蜡烛 **diǎn làzhú** light a candle

腊 là Trad 臘 *adj* 1 of the twelfth month of the lunar year 2 (of meat) salted and dried, cured
　腊肉 **làròu** *n* cured meat, ham
　腊月 **làyuè** *n* the twelfth (and last) month of the lunar year

落 là *v* 1 leave out 2 lag behind

NOTE: When used in these senses, 落 is pronounced as **là**, not as **luò**, which it usually is.

辣 là *adj* spicy hot, peppery
　辣椒 **làjiāo** *n* red pepper, chilli

啦 la *particle* (an exclamation indicating completion of an action and/or emergence of a new situation; 了 **le** + 啊 **a**) a) □ 我们赢啦! **Wǒmen yíng la!** *We've won!* □ 我做完作业啦! **Wǒ zuòwán zuòyè la!** *I've finished my assignment!*

NOTE: 啦 **la** is the combination of 了 **le** and 啊 **a**. It is only used at the end of a sentence. You can replace 啦 **la** with 了 **le** but then the strong emotive coloring of 啊 **a** is lost. Compare: 我赢啦! **Wǒ yíng la!** *I won!* and 我赢了。**Wǒ yíng le.** *I won.*

来 1 **lái** Trad 來 *v* come, come to, move towards to the speaker (antonym 去 **qù**) □ 王先生来了没有? **Wáng xiānsheng láile méiyǒu? ** *Has Mr Wang come?* □ 他是三年前来新西兰的。**Tā shì sān nián qián lái Xīnxīlán de.** *He came to New Zealand three years ago.*
　来宾 **láibīn** *n* guest, visitor
　来不及 **láibují** *v* not have enough time (to do something), there isn't enough time (to do something) □ 到那时候，哭都来不及。**Dào nà shíhou, kū dōu láibují.** *Should such a moment come, there would be no time even to cry (→ it would be too late to regret).* □ 来不及吃早饭了。**Láibují chī zǎofàn le.** *There is no time for breakfast.*

NOTE: The opposite to 来不及 **láibují** is 来得及 **láidejí**, e.g. □ 还来得及吃早饭。**Hái láidejí chī zǎofàn.** *There is still enough time to have breakfast.*

　来访 **láifǎng** *v* come to visit, come to call
　来回 **láihuí** *v* make a round trip, make a return journey
　来客 **láikè** *n* guest, customer (to a restaurant, hotel, etc.)
　来历 **láilì** *n* origin, background
　来历不明 **láilì bùmíng** of uncertain origin, of dubious background
　来临 **láilín** *v* arrive, approach

来年 **láinián** *n* the coming year

来往 **láiwang** [comp: 来 come + 往 return] *n* dealings, connection
和他们没有来往 hé tāmen méiyǒu láiwang have had no dealings with them

来信 **láixìn** [modif: 来 arriving + 信 letter] *n* letter received, incoming letter □ 来信早已收到。**Láixìn zǎo yǐ shōudào.** *I received your letter long ago.*

来源 **liáyuán** *n* source, origin
消息来源 xiāoxi láiyuán source of the news

来自 **láizì** *v* come from □ 这个中文班的学生来自世界各国。**Zhège Zhōngwén bān de xuésheng láizì shìjiè ge guó.** *The students of this Chinese class came from all over the world.*

来 2 **lái** Trad 來 *num* approximately, more or less, close to (used after the number 10 or a multiple of 10 to indicate approximation)
十来辆车 shí lái liàng chē about ten cars
五十来个学生 wǔshí lái ge xuésheng approximately fifty students
三百四十来块钱 sānbǎi sìshí lái kuài qián about 340 yuan

赖 **lài** Trad 賴 *v* rely (See 依赖 yīlài)

兰 **lán** Trad 蘭 *n* orchid
兰花 lánhuā orchid

栏 **lán** Trad 欄 *n* railing, fence
栏杆 lángān railing, banister, balustrade

拦 **lán** Trad 攔 *v* stop, block, hold back □ 你要去就去, 没人拦你。**Nǐ yào qù jiù qù, méi rén lán nǐ.** *If you want to go, go ahead. Nobody is trying to stop you.*

蓝 **lán** Trad 藍 *adj* blue □ 天很蓝, 因为空气很干净。**Tiān hěn lán, yīnwèi kōngqì hěn gānjìng.** *The sky is blue because the air is clean.* □ 蓝蓝的天上白云飘, 多好看啊! **Lánlán de tiān shang báiyún piāo, duō hǎokàn a!** *White clouds float in the blue sky. How beautiful!*

篮 **lán** Trad 籃 *n* basket
篮球 **lánqiú** [modif: 篮 basket + 球 ball] *n* basketball □ 他们在打篮球。**Tāmen zài dǎ lánqiú.** *They're playing basketball.*
篮球比赛 lánqiú bǐsài basketball match
篮球队 lánqiú duì basketball team
打篮球 dǎ lánqiú play basketball
篮子 **lánzi** [suffix: 篮 basket + 子 nominal suffix] *n* basket

览 **lǎn** Trad 覽 *v* view (See 游览 yóulǎn, 阅览室 yuèlǎnshì, 展览 zhǎnlǎn.)

揽 **lǎn** Trad 攬 *v* 1 pull into one's arms, take into one's arms 2 take on
揽生意 lǎn shēngyì canvass for business

懒 **lǎn** Trad 懶 *adj* lazy, indolent □ 你真太懒了, 收到他来信两个星期了, 还不回信。**Nǐ zhēn tài lǎn le, shōudào tā láixìn liǎng ge xīngqī le hái bù huíxìn.** *You're really lazy. It's two weeks since you received his letter and you still haven't replied.*
懒惰 **lǎnduò** [comp: 懒 lazy + 惰 inertial] *adj* lazy
懒骨头 **lǎn gútou** [modif: 懒 lazy + 骨头 bone] *n* lazybones

烂 **làn** Trad 爛 **I** *v* rot, go bad □ 水果容易烂, 运输是个问题。**Shuǐguǒ róngyì làn, yùnshū shì ge wèntí.** *Fruit rots easily, and its transport is a problem.* **II** *adj* rotten □ 这个苹果烂了, 扔了吧。**Zhège píngguǒ làn le, rēng le ba.** *This apple is rotten. Throw it away.*

滥 **làn** Trad 濫 **I** *v* overflow, flood (See 泛滥 fànlàn) **II** *adj* excessive, indiscriminate
滥用 **lànyòng** [modif: 滥 excessive + 用 use] *v* abuse, misuse
滥用职权 lànyòng zhíquán abuse one's power

狼 **láng** *n* wolf (只 zhī) □ 狼是羊群的大敌。**Láng shì yángqún de dàdí.** *Wolves are the great enemies of the sheep flock.*
披着羊皮的狼 pīzhe yángpí de láng a wolf in sheep's clothing
一群狼 yì qún láng a pack of wolves
狼狈 **lángbèi** *adj* in an awkward position
狼狈为奸 **lángbèi wéijiān** *v* act in collusion with each other

廊 **láng** *n* corridor

郎 **láng** *suffix* (for certain nouns of people)
放羊郎 fàng yángláng shepherd

朗 **lǎng** *adj* loud and clear
朗读 **lǎngdú** [modif: 朗 loud and clear + 读 read] *v* read in a loud and clear voice □ 学外语, 一定要朗读课文。**Xué wàiyǔ, yídìng yào lǎngdú kèwén.** *To learn a foreign language, one should read texts aloud.*
朗诵 **lǎngsòng** *v* recite (a poem) theatrically

浪 **làng** **I** *n* wave □ 风急浪高, 不能出海。**Fēng jí làng gāo, bù néng chūhǎi.** *The winds are strong and the waves high. We can't go out to sea.* **II** *adj* uncontrolled, dissolute
浪潮 **làngcháo** [comp: 浪 wave + 潮 tide] *n* tide, tidal wave
浪费 **làngfèi** *v* waste □ 浪费时间就是浪费生命。**Làngfèi shíjiān jiùshì làngfèi shēngmìng.** *To waste time is to waste life.*
浪漫 **làngmàn** *adj* romantic

捞 **lāo** Trad 撈 *v* pull or drag out of water □ 孩子们在小河里捞什么呢? **Háizimen zài xiǎo hé li lāo shénme ne?** *What are the children trying to scoop out of the stream?*
打捞 dǎlāo salvage (a sunken ship, etc.)

劳 **láo** Trad 勞 *v* toil
劳动 **láodòng** [comp: 劳 toil + 动 move] *v* do manual labor □ 他夏天在父亲的农场劳动。**Tā xiàtiān zài fùqin de nóngchǎng láodòng.** *In summer he works on his father's farm.*
脑力劳动 nǎolì láodòng mental work
体力劳动 tǐlì láodòng physical (manual) labor
劳动节 **láodòng jié** *n* Labor Day (on May 1)
劳动力 **láodònglì** *n* work force, manpower
劳动力不足 láodònglì bùzú short of manpower
劳驾 **láojià** *idiom* Excuse me, Would you mind (doing ... for me) □ 劳驾, 请您让一下。**Láojià, qǐng nín ràng yíxià.** *Excuse me, would you please make way?*

NOTE: 劳驾 **láojià** is a northern dialect expression. To say *Excuse me*, 对不起 **duìbuqǐ** is more widely used.

唠 **láo** as in 唠叨 **láodao**
唠叨 **láodao** *adj* be garrulous
唠唠叨叨说个没完 láoláo dāodāo shuō gè méiwán chatter on and on

牢 láo I *adj* firm, fast **II** *n* shortening for 牢房 **láofáng**

坐牢 zuòláo serve jail term

牢房 **láofáng** *n* Same as 监狱 **jiānyù**, used only informally.

牢固 **láogù** [comp: 牢 firm + 固 solid] *adj* firm, solid

牢骚 **láosāo** *n* discontent, grumbling

发牢骚 fāláosāo grumble

老 lǎo I *adj* **1** old, elderly □ 爸爸老了，不能在农场劳动了。**Bàba lǎo le, bù néng zài nóngchǎng láodòng le.** *Father is old and can't work on the farm.* □ 他在帮一位老太太过马路。**Tā zài bāng yí wèi lǎo tàitai guò mǎlù.** *He's helping an old lady cross the street.*

老太太 lǎo tàitai old lady, old woman

老先生 lǎo xiānsheng old gentleman, old man

2 long-standing □ 这个老问题一直没有办法解决。**Zhè ge lǎo wèntí yìzhí méiyǒu bànfǎ jiějué.** *This perennial problem has remained unsolved for a long time.*

老朋友 lǎopéngyou long-standing friend □ 我们在小学的时候就认识了，是老朋友。**Wǒmen zài xiǎoxué de shíhou jiù rènshi le, shì lǎo péngyou.** *We've known each other since primary school. We're old friends.* **II** *prefix* (added to numbers to indicate seniority among siblings)

老大 lǎo dà the eldest child

老二 lǎo èr the second child

NOTE: Chinese tradition values and respects old age. Today, people still attach 老 **lǎo** to a family name as a form of address to show respect and friendliness to an older person, e.g. 老李 **Lǎo Lǐ**, 老王 **Lǎo Wáng**. See note on 小 **xiǎo**.

老百姓 **lǎobǎixìng** [modif: 老 old + 百 hundred + 姓 family names] *n* common people, ordinary folk □ 老百姓对当官的有意见，怎么办呢？**Lǎobǎixìng duì dāngguānde yǒu yìjiàn, zénme bàn ne?** *What should common people do when they have a complaint against an official?*

老板 **lǎobǎn** *n* **1** boss □ 他是我的老板，他要我做什么我就做什么。**Tā shì wǒ de lǎobǎn, tā yào wǒ zuò shénme wǒ jiù zuò shénme.** *He is my boss; I do what he tells me to do.* **2** owner of a store, a business, etc. □ 老板不在，没人可以作主。**Lǎobǎn bú zài, méi rén kěyǐ zuòzhǔ.** *As the owner is away, nobody can make a decision.*

老成 **lǎochéng** *adj* (of a youngster) mature and experienced

老大娘 **lǎodàniáng** *n* (a respectful form of address or reference to an old woman) (位 **wèi**) □ 他把座位让给一位老大娘。**Tā bǎ zuòwèi rànggěi yí wèi lǎodàniáng.** *He offered his seat to an old woman.* □ 老大娘，您找谁？**Lǎodàniáng, nín zhǎo shuí?** *Who are you looking for, ma'am?*

NOTE: 老大娘 **lǎodàniáng** has a rustic flavor. It is normally not used in cities or among better-educated people. 老太太 **lǎotàitai** is a more appropriate word.

老大爷 **lǎodàye** *n* (a respectful form of address or reference to an old man) (位 **wèi**) □ 老大爷，请您让我看看您的票子。**Lǎodàye, qǐng nín ràng wǒ kànkan nín de piàozi.** *Please show me your ticket, sir.*

NOTE: 老大爷 **lǎodàye** has a rustic flavor. It is normally not used in cities or among better-educated people. 老先生 **lǎoxiānsheng** is a more appropriate word.

老汉 **lǎohàn** *n* old man, old fellow

老虎 **lǎohǔ** [prefix: 老 nominal prefix + 虎 tiger] *n* tiger (头 **tóu**, 只 **zhī**) □ 动物园里的老虎逃跑了! **Dòngwùyuán li de lǎohǔ táopǎo le!** *A tiger has escaped from the zoo!*

小老虎 xiǎo lǎohǔ tiger cub

老化 **lǎohuà** [suffix: 老 old + 化 verb suffix] *v* **1** becoming old

人口老化 rénkǒulǎohuà ageing of the population **2** becoming outdated

知识老化 zhīshi lǎohuà outdated knowledge

老家 **lǎojiā** *n* native place

老龄 **lǎolíng** *n* old age, people of old age

老年 **lǎonián** *n* old age

老年人 lǎoniánrén old person

老婆 **lǎopó** *n* (vulgarism) wife, old girl

老人 **lǎorén** [modif: 老 old + 人 person] *n* old person, elderly person (位 **wèi**) □ 这位老人人老心不老，还在学中文和武术。**Zhè wèi lǎorén rén lǎo xīn bù lǎo, háizài xué Zhōngwén hé wǔshù.** *This old person is young at heart. He/She is still learning Chinese and martial arts.*

老人家 **lǎorenjia** *n* (respectful form of address for an old person) □ 您老人家身体好吗？**Nín lǎorenjia shēntǐ hǎoma?** *Are you in good health, sir (or ma'am)?*

老师 **lǎoshī** [modif: 老 aged + 师 teacher, master] *n* teacher (位 **wèi**) □ 我的中文老师是北京人。**Wǒ de Zhōngwén lǎoshī shì Běijīngrén.** *My Chinese teacher is from Beijing.* □ 我要问老师几个问题。**Wǒ yào wèn lǎoshī jǐ ge wèntí.** *I want to ask the teacher some questions.*

NOTE: 老师 **lǎoshī**, usually prefixed by a family name, is the standard form of address to a teacher, e.g. 王老师 **Wáng Lǎoshī**. There is no equivalent of 王老师 **Wáng Lǎoshī** in English. This dictionary uses the literal translation *Teacher Wang*.

老是 **lǎoshi** *adv* always, constantly □ 你怎么老是这么晚回家？**Nǐ zěnme lǎoshi zhème wǎn huíjiā?** *Why do you always come home so late?* □ 他老是写错这个字。**Tā lǎoshi xiěcuò zhège zì.** *He always writes this character wrongly.*

老实 **lǎoshi** *adj* honest □ 说老实话，做老实人。**Shuō lǎoshi huà, zuò lǎoshi rén.** *Speak the truth and be an honest person.* □ 他太老实，容易受人欺骗。**Tā tài lǎoshi, róngyì shòurén qīpiàn.** *He is too honest and is prone to be deceived.*

老实话 lǎoshi huà plain truth

老实人 lǎoshi rén honest person

老实说 lǎoshi shuō to be frank, to tell the truth □ 老实说，你这种做法我并不赞成。**Lǎoshi shuō, nǐ zhè zhǒng zuòfǎ wǒ bìng bù zànchéng.** *To tell the truth, I don't approve of your way of doing things.*

老鼠 **lǎoshǔ** *n* mouse, mice, rat, rats (只 **zhī**)

老太婆 **lǎotàipó** *n* old woman

NOTE: See note on 老头儿 **lǎotóur**.

老太太 **lǎotàitai** *n* (a respectful form of address or reference to an old woman) (位 **wèi**) □ 老太太, 您找谁? **Lǎotàitai, nín zhǎo shuí?** *Who are you looking for, ma'am?* □ 他把座位让给一位老太太。**Tā bǎ zuòwèi rànggěi yí wèi lǎotàitai.** *He offered his seat to an old lady.*

老天爷 **lǎotiānyé** *n* the Old Lord of Heaven, Heaven, God □ 我的老天爷! **Wǒde lǎotiānyé!** *My God! Goodness gracious!*

老头儿 **lǎotóur** *n* old man (个 **gè**) □ 几个老头儿在树下打牌。**Jǐ ge lǎotóur zài shù xia dǎpái.** *Some old men were playing cards under the tree.*

NOTES: (1) 老头儿 **lǎotóur** is an impolite way of referring to *an old man*. As a form of address, 老头儿 **lǎotóur** is very rude. Instead, use the neutral term 老人 **lǎorén** or the polite terms 老先生 **lǎoxiānsheng** or 老大爷 **lǎodàyé**. (2) The corresponding impolite word for *an old woman* is 老太婆 **lǎotàipó**. Use 老太太 **lǎotàitai** or 老大娘 **lǎodàniáng** instead.

老外 **lǎowài** *n* foreigner

NOTE: 老外 **lǎowài** is a familiar term for *foreigner* in China. It is quite informal, but not really impolite. The formal term is 外国人 **wàiguórén**.

老先生 **lǎoxiānsheng** [modif: 老 old, elderly + 先生 gentleman] *n* (a respectful form of address or reference to an old man) (位 **wèi**) □ 先生, 请您让我看看您的票子。**Lǎoxiānsheng, qǐng nín ràng wǒ kànkan nín de piàozi.** *Please show me your ticket, sir.*

老爷 **lǎoye** *n* (old fashioned) lord, sir

姥 **lǎo** as in 姥姥 **lǎolao**
姥姥 **lǎolao** *n* (maternal) granny

涝 **lào** *n* waterlogging, flooding
旱涝保收 **hànlào bǎoshōu** (of crops) sure to reap a good harvest even if there is drought or flooding

乐 **lè** Trad 樂 *adj* happy, delighted, joyful
乐观 **lèguān** [modif: 乐 happy + 观 view] *adj* optimistic (antonym 悲观 **bēiguān**) □ 他很乐观, 相信世界会越变越好。**Tā hěn lèguān, xiāngxìn shìjiè huì yuè biàn yuè hǎo.** *He is optimistic, believing that the world is getting ever better.* □ 根据乐观的估计, 今年经济增长可以达到百分之五。**Gēnjù lèguān de gūjì, jīnnián jīngjì zēngzhǎng kěyǐ dádào bǎifēn zhī wǔ.** *According to an optimistic estimate, the economy will grow by five percent this year.*
乐观主义 **lèguān zhǔyì** optimism
乐观主义者 **lèguānzhǔyìzhě** optimist
乐趣 **lèqù** [comp: 乐 joy + 趣 interest] *n* pleasure, joy
乐意 **lèyì** [modif: 乐 happy + 意 will] *adj* be happy to, be willing to

勒 **lè** *v* rein in
勒索 **lèsuǒ** *v* extort, blackmail

了 **le** *particle* 1 (used after a verb to indicate the completion of an action) □ 我昨天写了三封信。**Wǒ zuótiān xiěle sān fēng xìn.** *I wrote three letters yesterday.* □ 他吃了晚饭就上网玩游戏。**Tā chīle**

wǎnfàn jiù shàngwǎng wán yóuxì. *As soon as he had eaten supper, he went online to play games.* 2 (used at the end of a sentence to indicate the emergence of a new situation) □ 秋天来了, 树叶黄了。**Qiūtiān lái le, shùyè huáng le.** *Autumn has come and leaves have turned yellow.* □ 我会说一点儿中文了。**Wǒ huì shuō yìdiǎnr Zhōngwén le.** *I can speak a bit of Chinese now.*

雷 **léi** *n* thunder □ 昨天又打雷, 又闪电, 挺吓人的。**Zuótiān yòu dǎ léi, yòu shǎndiàn, tǐng xiàrén de.** *There was thunder and lightning yesterday. It was rather frightening.*
打雷 **dǎléi** thunder
雷达 **léidá** *n* radar
雷雨 **léiyǔ** [comp: 雷 thunder + 雨 rain] *n* thunderstorm

蕾 **lěi** *n* (flower) bud

垒 **lěi** Trad 壘 *n* as in 垒球 **lěiqiú**
垒球 **lěiqiú** *n* softball
垒球棒 **lěiqiúbàng** softball bat (根 **gēn**)

泪 **lèi** Trad 淚 *n* teardrop, tear (See 眼泪 **yǎnlèi**.)

类 **lèi** Trad 類 *n* kind, category, class □ 这两类不同的情况, 不要混为一谈。**Zhè liǎng lèi bùtóng de qíngkuàng, bú yào hùnwéi yìtán.** *These are two different situations. Don't lump them together.*
类似 **lèisì** *adj* similar
类型 **lèixíng** [comp: 类 category + 型 type] *n* type (种 **zhǒng**)

累 **lèi** *adj* exhausted, tired □ "你劳动了半天, 累不累?" "不累, 一点都不累。" **"Nǐ láodòngle bàntiān, lèi bu lèi?" "Bú lèi, yìdiǎn dōu bú lèi."** *"Are you tired after doing manual labor for such a long time?" "No, I'm not the least tired."*

棱 **léng** *n* edge

冷 **lěng** *adj* cold (antonym 热 **rè**) □ 今天很冷。**Jīntiān hěn lěng.** *It's cold today.* □ 他每天都洗冷水澡。**Tā měi tiān dōu xǐ lěngshuǐ zǎo.** *He takes a cold bath every day.*
冷淡 **lěngdàn** [comp: 冷 cold + 淡 bland] *adj* cold, indifferent, apathetic □ 商业界对政府的新政策很冷淡。**Shāngyè jiè duì zhèngfǔ de Xīnzhèngcè hěn lěngdàn.** *The business circle is indifferent to the new policies of the government.*
冷静 **lěngjìng** [comp: 冷 cold + 静 quiet] *adj* calm, sober □ 你冷静一些, 别这么激动。**Nǐ lěngjìng yìxiē, bié zhème jīdòng.** *Calm down; don't be so agitated.*
冷却 **lěngquè** I *v* to make cool II *n* cooling
冷却剂 **lěngquèjì** coolant, cooler
冷饮 **lěngyǐn** [modif: 冷 cold + 饮 drink] *n* cold drink, ice-cream

愣 **lèng** *adj* stupefied, blank
发愣 **fālèng** look stupefied, stare blankly

厘 **lí** *measure wd* one thousandth of a foot
厘米 **límǐ** *measure wd* centimeter □ 他身高178厘米。**Tā shēngāo yìbǎi qīshí bā límǐ.** *He is 178 centimeters tall.*

离 **lí** Trad 離 I *v* depart, leave □ 他每天很早就离家, 很晚才回家。**Tā měitiān hěn zǎo jiù lí jiā, hěn wǎn cái huí jiā.** *He leaves home early and returns late*

every day. **II** *prep* (indicating distance in space or time) away from, from □ 加拿大离英国很远, 离美国很近。 **Jiānádà lí Yīngguó hěn yuǎn, lí Měiguó hěn jìn.** *Canada is far away from Britain, and close to the U.S.A.* □ 现在离寒假只有两个星期了。 **Xiànzài lí hánjià zhǐyǒu liǎngge xīngqī le.** *There are only two weeks before the winter holiday.*
离…近 lí…jìn close to
离…远 lí…yuǎn far away from
离别 líbié [comp: 离 leave + 别 depart] *v* leave, bid farewell
离婚 líhūn [v+obj: 离 separate + 婚 marriage] *v* divorce □ 他们终于离婚了。 **Tāmen zhōngyú líhūn le.** *They eventually divorced.* □ 她和丈夫离婚了。 **Tā hé zhàngfu líhūn le.** *She and her husband are divorced.*
离婚协议 líhūn xiéyì divorce settlement
申请离婚 shēnqǐng líhūn file a divorce, sue for a divorce
离开 líkāi [comp: 离 leave + 开 away from] *v* 1 depart, leave □ 他十八岁的时候离开父母, 到美国去念书。 **Tā shíbā suì de shíhou líkāi fùmǔ, dào Měiguó qù niànshū.** *When he was eighteen he left his parents and went to America to study.* □ 我离开一会儿, 马上就回来。 **Wǒ líkāi yíhuìr, mǎshàng jiù huílai.** *Excuse me for a minute. I'll be back soon.* 2 do without
离不开 líbukāi cannot do without □ 孩子还小, 离不开妈。 **Háizi hái xiǎo, líbukāi mā.** *The child is too young to be without his mother.*
离休 líxiū [comp: 离 leave + 休 rest] *v* (of officials) retire
篱 lí Trad 籬 *n* hedge, fence
篱笆 líba *n* bamboo fence, twig fence
黎 lí as in 黎明 límíng
黎明 límíng *n* dawn, daybreak
狸 lí *n* racoon dog
梨 lí *n* pear (只 zhī) □ 这梨很甜, 你尝尝。 **Zhè lí hěn tián, nǐ chángchang.** *This pear is very sweet. Try it.*
犁 lí *n* plough
璃 lí *n* glass (See 玻璃 bōli.)
李 Lǐ *n* (a family name)

礼 lǐ Trad 禮 *n* 1 rite, ceremony 2 gift
礼拜天 Lǐbàitiān [modif: 礼拜 worship + 天 day] *n* Same as 星期天 Xīngqītiān. A rather old-fashioned word.
礼节 lǐjié *n* etiquette, protocol
礼貌 lǐmào *adj* polite, courteous □ 礼貌待客。 **Lǐmào dài kè.** *Treat customers with courtesy.* □ 盯着人家看, 是不礼貌的。 **Dīngzhe rénjiā kàn, shì bù lǐmào de.** *It is impolite to stare at others.*
礼品 lǐpǐn [modif: 礼 gift + 品 thing] *n* gift (件 jiàn)
礼堂 lǐtáng [modif: 礼 ceremony, ritual + 堂 hall] *n* auditorium, assembly hall (座 zuò) □ 礼堂里正在举行一个大会。 **Lǐtáng li zhèngzài jǔxíng yí ge dàhuì.** *A rally is being held in the auditorium.*

礼物 lǐwù [modif: 礼 gift + 物 thing] *n* gift, present (件 jiàn) □ 这件小小的礼物, 请您收下。 **Zhè jiàn xiǎoxiǎo de lǐwù, qǐng nín shōuxia.** *Please accept this small present.* □ 今天是你的生日, 我送你一件小礼物。 **Jīntiān shì nǐ de shēngrì, wǒ sòng nǐ yí jiàn xiǎo lǐwù.** *Today's your birthday. I'll give you a little gift.*
结婚礼物 jiéhūn lǐwù wedding present
生日礼物 shēngrì lǐwù birthday present
新年礼物 xīnnián lǐwù New Year present

里 1 lǐ Trad 裏 *n* inside (antonym 外 wài) □ 房间里没有人。 **Fángjiān li méiyǒu rén.** *There is nobody in the room.* □ 生活里总会出现种种麻烦。 **Shēnghuó li zǒng huì chūxiàn zhǒng-zhǒng máfan.** *You are bound to encounter various troublesome situations in life.*
里边 lǐbian [modif: 里 inner + 边 side] *n* inside, in (antonym 外边 wàibian) □ 房子外边不好看, 里边很舒服。 **Fángzi wàibian bù hǎokàn, lǐbian hěn shūfu.** *The outside of the house is not very attractive, but inside is quite comfortable.* □ 箱子里边有什么? **Xiāngzi lǐbian yǒu shénme?** *What's inside the box?*
里面 lǐmiàn *n* Same as 里边 lǐbian
里 2 lǐ *measure wd* (a traditional Chinese unit of distance, equivalent to half a kilometer) □ 从市中心到飞机场有二十里, 也就是十公里。 **Cóng shìzhōngxīn dào fēijīchǎng yǒu èrshí li, yě jiù shì shí gōnglǐ.** *From the city center to the airport it's twenty li, or ten kilometers.*
理 lǐ *n* pattern, reason **II** *v* manage, handle
理睬 lǐcǎi *v* (usu. negative sense) show interest in, pay attention to
理发 lǐfà [v+obj: 理 tidy up + 发 hair] *v* have a haircut and shampoo, have one's hair done □ 我半个月理一次发。 **Wǒ bàn ge yuè lǐ yí cì fà.** *I have a haircut every half a month.*
理发店 lǐfàdiàn barbershop, hair salon
理发师 lǐfàshī barber, hairdresser, hairstylist

理会 lǐhuì *v* 1 comprehend, understand 2 take notice of
不理会 bùlǐhuì take no notice of, ignore
理解 lǐjiě [comp: 理 reason + 解 understand] *v* understand, comprehend □ 这首古诗我不理解。 **Zhè shǒu gǔ shī wǒ bù lǐjiě.** *I don't understand this classic poem.* □ 我理解你的心情。 **Wǒ lǐjiě nǐ de xīnqíng.** *I understand how you feel.*

理亏 lǐkuī *adj* be in the wrong
    自知理亏 zìzhī lǐkuī know oneself to be in the wrong, realize that justice is not on one's side
理论 lǐlùn [comp: 理 reason + 论 theory] *n* theory □ 你用什么理论来解释这一现象? **Nǐ yòng shénme lǐlùn lái jiěshì zhè yí xiànxiàng?** *What theory are you going to apply to interpret this phenomenon?*
理念 lǐniàn [comp: 理 ideal + 念 idea] *n* notion, ideal
理事 lǐshì *n* member of a council
理所当然 lǐsuǒdāngrán *adj* naturally, as should be expected
理想 lǐxiǎng [comp: 理 reason + 想 thought, wish] *n* ideal, aspiration □ 我小时候的理想是当个旅行家。 **Wǒ xiǎoshíhou de lǐxiǎng shì dāng ge lǚxíngjiā.** *When I was a child, I dreamed of being a traveler.*
    理想主义 lǐxiǎng zhǔyì idealism
    实现理想 shíxiàn lǐxiǎng realize an ideal
理由 lǐyóu [comp: 理 reason + 由 origin, cause] *n* reason, justification, ground, argument □ 我们有充分的理由处分他。 **Wǒmen yǒu chōngfèn de lǐyóu chǔfèn tā.** *We have sufficient reason to discipline him.* □ 你有什么理由不来上班? **Nǐ yǒu shénme lǐyóu bù lái shàngbān?** *What reason can you give for being absent from work?*
理直气壮 lǐzhíqìzhuàng *adj* bold and assured that justice is on one's side

力 lì *n* strength, force, might □ 他提出的理由很有力。 **Tā tíchū de lǐyóu hěn yǒulì.** *He put forward forceful arguments.* □ 我全身无力, 恐怕生病了。 **Wǒ quánshēn wú lì, kǒngpà shēngbìng le.** *I feel weak all over; I'm afraid I'm ill.*
力量 lìliang *n* **1** strength □ 人多力量大。 **Rén duō lìliang dà.** *Strength lies in numbers.* **2** efforts, ability □ 我们尽最大的力量克服当前的困难。 **Wǒmen jìn zuì dà de lìliang kèfú dāngqián de kùnnan.** *We are making maximum efforts to overcome the present difficulties.*
力气 lìqi *n* physical strength □ 没想到这个孩子力气这么大。 **Méi xiǎngdào zhège háizi lìqi zhème dà.** *I did not expect this child to be so strong.*
力求 lìqiú *v* strive for, do one's best for
    力求完美 lìqiú wánměi strive for perfection
力图 lìtú *v* try hard, try one's best to
    力图改善处境 lìtú gǎishàn chǔjìng try hard to improve one's situation
力争 lìzhēng *v* work hard for, do all one can to

历 lì Trad 歷 *n* past experience
    历代 lìdài *n* successive dynasties
历来 lìlái *adv* all through the ages, always, ever since
历史 lìshǐ [comp: 历 past experience + 史 recording] *n* history □ 中国的历史非常长, 有三千多年。 **Zhōngguó de lìshǐ fēicháng cháng, yǒu sānqiān duō nián.** *China has a very long history of over three thousand years.* □ 你知道这个城市的历史吗? **Nǐ zhīdào zhège chéngshì de lìshǐ ma?** *Do you know the history of this city?*
    历史学家 lìshǐxuéjiā historian

沥 lì Trad 瀝 *v* drip, trickle
    沥青 lìqīng *n* asphalt
荔 lì as in 荔枝 lìzhī
    荔枝 lìzhī *n* litchi, lichee
隶 lì *n* slave (See 奴隶 núlì)

栗 lì chestnut
    栗子 lìzi chestnut (颗 **kē**)
立 lì **I** *v* stand □ 你立在门口干什么? **Nǐ lì zài ménkǒu gàn shénme?** *Why are you standing by the door?*
    坐立不安 zuò-lì-bù-ān on pins and needles, on tenterhooks, anxious
    II *adv* immediately, at once
立场 lìchǎng *n* position, standpoint □ 站在公司的立场上, 你就会同意这个措施是必要的。 **Zhàn zài gōngsī de lìchǎng shang, nǐ jiù huì tóngyì zhège cuòshī shì bìyào de.** *From the company's standpoint, you would agree that this measure is necessary.*
立方 lìfāng *measure wd* (mathematics) cube
    三立方米/公尺 sān lìfāng mǐ/gōngchǐ 3 cubic meters
立即 lìjí *adv* immediately, without delay □ 王董事长要我立即飞往上海处理一件事。 **Wáng dǒngshìzhǎng yào wǒ lìjí fēiwǎng Shànghǎi chǔlǐ yí jiàn shì.** *Chairman Wang wants me to fly to Shanghai immediately to handle an emergency.*
立交桥 lìjiāoqiáo *n* flypast, flyover (座 **zuò**)
立刻 lìkè [comp: 立 immediately + 刻 a brief time] *adv* at once, immediately □ 我接到你的电话, 立刻就来了。 **Wǒ jiēdào nǐ de diànhuà, lìkè jiù lái le.** *I came immediately after getting your call.* □ 你要我立刻拿出这么多钱, 办不到。 **Nǐ yào wǒ lìkè náchū zhème duō qián, bàn bú dào.** *You want me to produce such a large amount of money right away. I can't do it.*
立体 lìtǐ *adj* three-dimensional

厉 lì Trad 厲 *adj* severe, strict
    厉害 lìhai *adj* severe, fierce, formidable □ 这个人说话很厉害。 **Zhège rén shuōhuà hěn lìhai.** *This person has a sharp tongue.* □ 她看样子厉害, 其实没有用。 **Tā kànyàngzi lìhai, qíshí méiyǒuyòng.** *She looks formidable but actually is rather useless.*

NOTES: (1) 厉害 lìhai is often used with 得 de to indicate a very high degree, e.g. □ 这两天热得厉害。 **Zhèliǎngtiān rède lìhai.** *These days are terribly hot.* □ 情人节花儿贵得厉害。 **Qíngrénjié huār guìde lìhai.** *Flowers are terribly expensive on Valentine's Day.* (2) 厉害 lìhai may be written as 利害 lìhai.

丽 lì Trad 麗 *adj* beautiful (See 美丽 měilì.)

励 lì Trad 勵 *v* encourage (See 鼓励 gǔlì.)

利 lì *n* **1** benefit, advantage **2** profit, interest
    利弊 lìbì [comp: 利 advantage + 弊 disadvantage] *n* pros and cons
利害 lìhai Same as 厉害 lìhai
利率 lìlǜ *n* interest rate □ 你看银行会在最近提高利率吗? **Nǐ kàn yínháng huì zài zuìjìn tígāo lìlǜ ma?** *Do you think the banks will raise interest rates soon?*
利润 lìrùn *n* profit □ 这家公司今年第一季度的利润下降了百分之十二。 **Zhè jiā gōngsī jīnnián dìyī jìdù de lìrùn xiàjiàngle bǎifēnzhī shí'èr.** *The company profits decreased by 12 percent in the first quarter this year.*
利息 lìxī *n* interest (on a loan)
利益 lìyì [comp: 利 benefit + 益 benefit] *n* benefit, interest □ 每个人都为了个人利益而工作, 但也要考虑社会的利益。 **Měi gè rén dōu wèile gèrén de lìyì ér gōngzuò, dàn yě yào kǎolǜ shèhuì de lìyì.** *Everybody*

works for their personal interest, but should also take into consideration the interests of society.

利用 **lìyòng** [comp: 利 benefit + 用 use] *v* make use of, benefit from □ 你应该好好利用时间。**Nǐ yīnggāi hǎohǎo lìyòng shíjiān.** *You should make good use of your time.* □ 我们要合理地利用自然资源。**Wǒmen yào hélǐ de lìyòng zìrán zīyuán.** *We should make use of natural resources in a rational way.*

例 **lì** *n* example
例子 **lìzi** [suffix: 例 example + 子 nominal suffix] *n* example (个 **gè**) □ 王老师举了很多例子, 说明这个词的用法。**Wáng lǎoshī jǔle hěn duō lìzi, shuōmíng zhège cí de yòngfǎ.** *Teacher Wang gave many examples to illustrate the way this word is used.*
举例子 **jǔ lìzi** give an example
例如 **lìrú** [comp: 例 example + 如 same as] *conj* for example, such as □ 有些汉字, 例如 "日"、"月"、"山", 是从图画变来的。**Yǒuxiē hànzì, lìrú "rì," "yuè," "shān," shì cóng túhuà biànlai de.** *Some Chinese characters, such as 日, 月, 山, are derived from pictures.*
例外 **lìwài** *n* exception

粒 **lì** *measure wd* (for rice, pearls, etc)
一粒米 **yí lì mǐ** a grain of rice

俩 **liǎ** Trad 倆 *num* two people □ 他们俩是好朋友, 经常在一起玩。**Tāmen liǎ shì hǎo péngyou, jīngcháng zài yìqǐ wán.** *The two of them are good friends. They often play together.* □ 这件事你们夫妻俩好好商量一下。**Zhè jiàn shì nǐmen fùqī liǎ hǎohǎo shāngliang yíxià.** *(To a couple) I hope you two will discuss this matter properly.*

连 **lián** Trad 連 **I** *v* connect, join □ 海洋把世界连成一片。**Hǎiyáng bǎ shìjiè lián chéng yípiàn.** *Oceans and seas connect the entire world.* **II** *adv* in succession, repeatedly □ 我连发了三份电子邮件给他, 他都没有回。**Wǒ lián fāle sān fèn diànzǐ yóujiàn gěi tā, tā dōu méiyǒu huí.** *I sent him three e-mail messages in succession but there has been no reply.* **III** *prep* even □ 你连中文报纸都会看了! **Nǐ lián Zhōngwén bàozhǐ dōu huì kàn le!** *You can even read Chinese language newspapers!*
连…都… **lián…dōu…** *idiom* even □ 连三岁小孩都知道。**Lián sān suì xiǎohái dōu zhīdào.** *Even a toddler (←a three-year-old) knows this.*

NOTES: (1) 连…都… **lián…dōu…** is an emphatic expression, stressing the word after 连 **lián**. (2) 都 **dōu** may be replaced by 也 **yě**, i.e. 连…也… **lián…yě…** is the same as 连…都… **lián…dōu…**, e.g. □ 连三岁小孩也知道。**Lián sān suì xiǎohái yě zhīdào.** *Even a toddler knows this.*

连队 **liánduì** *n* company (in the army)
连连 **liánlián** *adv* repeatedly, again and again
连忙 **liánmáng** *v* make haste, hasten without the slightest delay □ 他踩了一位小姐的脚, 连忙说 "对不起, 对不起。" **Tā cǎile yí wèi xiǎojiě de jiǎo, liánmáng shuō "duìbuqǐ, duìbuqǐ."** *Stepping on a young lady's toes, he hastened to say, "I'm sorry, I'm sorry."* □ 她听说老父亲跌倒了, 连忙回家。**Tā tīngshuō lǎo fùqin diēdǎo le, liánmáng huíjiā.** *Hearing that her old father had had a fall, she hastened back home.*
连绵 **liánmián** *v* continue, be continuous, be uninterrupted

连同 **liántóng** *conj* together with
连续 **liánxù** *v* be continuous, in succession, in a row □ 他连续四天开夜车。**Tā liánxù sì tiān kāi yèchē.** *He burned the midnight oil for four consecutive nights.* □ 他连续喝了八瓶啤酒, 终于醉倒了。**Tā liánxù hēle bā píng píjiǔ, zhōngyú zuìdǎo le.** *He drank eight bottles of beer in succession and finally became drunk.*
连续剧 **liánxùjù** [modif: 连续 continuous + 剧 play] *n* TV series
连夜 **liányè** *adv* that very night

莲 **lián** *n* lotus
莲子 **liánzǐ** lotus seed

廉 **lián** *adj* 1 inexpensive, cheap 2 morally clean
廉价 **liánjià** *adj* low-priced, inexpensive
廉价出售 **liánjià chūshòu** sell at low prices
廉洁 **liánjié** [comp: 廉 morally clean + 洁 clean] *adj* (of officials) honest and clean, not corrupt

镰 **lián** *n* sickle
镰刀 **liándāo** sickle (把 **bǎ**)

帘 **lián** *n* curtain (See 窗帘 **chuānglián**)

怜 **lián** Trad 憐 *v* pity (See 可怜 **kělián**.)

联 **lián** Trad 聯 *v* connect
联邦 **liánbāng** *n* federation, union
联合 **liánhé** [comp: 联 join + 合 merge] *v* unite, get together (to do something) □ 两国要联合开发海洋资源。**Liǎng guó yào liánhé kāifā hǎiyáng zīyuán.** *The two countries will jointly develop their ocean resources.*
联合国 **Liánhé Guó** the United Nations
联合国部队 **Liánhé Guó bùduì** United Nations troops
联欢 **liánhuān** [modif: 联 jointly + 欢 have a good time] *v* have a get-together, have a gala/party □ 明天中外学生联欢, 你表演什么节目? **Míngtiān zhōngwài xuésheng liánhuān, nǐ biǎoyǎn shénme jiémù?** *At the gala for Chinese and overseas students tomorrow, what item will you be performing?*
联络 **liánluò** *v* liaise, get in touch with
联络员 **liánluòyuán** liaison officer
联盟 **liánméng** *n* alliance, coalition
联系 **liánxì** [comp: 联 connect + 系 tie, knot] **1** *v* get in touch, contact □ 你有什么事, 可以用电子邮件和张小姐联系。**Nǐ yǒu shénme shì, kěyǐ yòng diànzǐ yóujiàn hé Zhāng xiǎojiě liánxì.** *You can contact Miss Zhang by e-mail if you've an issue.* □ 如感兴趣, 请与陈先生联系。**Rú gǎn xìngqù, qǐng yu Chén xiānsheng liánxì.** *If interested, please contact Mr Chen.* **2** *n* connection, relationship □ 这两件事有什么联系? **Zhè liǎng jiàn shì yǒu shénme liánxì?** *What do these two matters have to do with each other?*
联想 **liánxiǎng** *v* make a connection in the mind, associate with

脸 **liǎn** Trad 臉 *n* face (张 **zhāng**) □ 我每天早上用冷水洗脸。**Wǒ měitiān zǎoshang yòng lěngshuǐ xǐ liǎn.** *I wash my face in cold water every morning.* □ 顾客来了, 她总是笑脸相迎。**Gùkè lái le, tā zǒngshì xiào liǎn xiāngyíng.** *When a customer comes, she always smiles a welcome.* □ 出了这样的事, 他觉得没脸见人。**Chūle zhèyang de shì, tā juéde méi liǎn jiàn rén.** *After this event, he felt too ashamed to face anyone.*
丢脸 **diūliǎn** be disgraced, lose face
脸盆 **liǎnpén** *n* wash basin (只 **zhī**)

脸色 **liǎnsè** *n* **1** complexion
脸色苍白 **liǎnsè cāngbái** pale complexion
2 facial expression

链 **liàn** *n* chain

练 **liàn** Trad 練 *v* practice, drill □ 他早晨五点起床, 先练武术, 再练中文口语。 **Tā zǎochén wǔ diǎn qǐchuáng, xiān liàn wǔshù, zài liàn Zhōngwén kǒuyǔ.** *He gets up at five o'clock in the morning, practices martial arts first and then oral Chinese.*

练习 **liànxí** [comp: 练 drill, train + 习 practice] **I** *v* exercise, train, drill □ 你常常练习汉语口语吗? **Nǐ chángcháng liànxí Hànyǔ kǒuyǔ ma?** *Do you often practice oral Chinese?* **II** *n* exercise, drill □ 我数学练习做好了, 还有三道英文练习没有做。 **Wǒ shùxué liànxí zuò hǎo le, hái yǒu sān dào Yīngwén liànxí méiyǒu zuò.** *I've finished my mathematics exercises. I haven't done the three English exercises.*

炼 **liàn** Trad 煉 *v* smelt (See 锻炼 **duànliàn**, 训练 **xùnliàn**.)

恋 **liàn** Trad 戀 *n* infatuation, love
恋爱 **liàn'ài** [comp: 恋 infatuate + 爱 love] **I** *v* be in romantic love, be courting □ 他们俩恋爱了两年, 在上个月结婚了。 **Tāmen liǎ liàn'ài le liǎngnián, zài shàng ge yuè jiéhūn le.** *They courted for two years and got married last month.* **II** *n* romantic love □ 恋爱、婚姻是青年人的大事。 **Liàn'ài, hūnyīn shì qīngniánrén de dàshì.** *Falling in love and marriage are major events for young people.*
谈恋爱 **tán liàn'ài** be in courtship, in love

良 **liáng** *adj* good
良好 **liánghǎo** [comp: 良 good + 好 good] *adj* good, fine, commendable □ 这种药经过试验, 证明效果良好。 **Zhè zhǒng yào jīngguò shìyàn, zhèngmíng xiàoguǒ liánghǎo.** *After testing, this medicine proved to have good effects.*
良种 **liángzhǒng** *n* fine breed, improved variety

凉 **liáng** *adj* cool, chilly □ 尽管中午很热, 早上和夜里还是挺凉的。 **Jǐnguǎn zhōngwǔ hěn rè, zǎoshang hé yèli háishì tǐng liáng de.** *Even though it is hot at noon, it is still cool in the early morning and at night.*
凉菜 **liángcài** [modif: 凉 cold + 菜 dish] *n* cold dish, salad
凉快 **liángkuai** [comp: 凉 cool + 快 pleasant] *adj* pleasantly cool □ 今天很热, 但是树下挺凉快。 **Jīntiān hěn rè, dànshì shù xià tǐng liángkuai.** *It's hot today but it's rather cool under the tree.*

量 **liáng** *v* measure, take measurements □ 你量一量, 这个房间有多大。 **Nǐ liáng yi liáng, zhège fángjiān yǒu duō dà.** *Measure the room, find out how big it is.*

粮 **liáng** Trad 糧 *n* grain
粮食 **liángshi** [comp: 粮 grain + 食 food] *n* grain, cereal, staple food □ 大米和小麦是中国的主要粮食。 **Dàmǐ hé xiǎomài shì Zhōngguó de zhǔyào liángshi.** *Rice and wheat are China's staple food.*

梁 **liáng** Trad 樑 *n* beam (in structure) (See 桥梁 **qiáoliáng**.)

两 1 **liǎng** Trad 兩 *measure wd* (a traditional Chinese unit of weight equivalent to 50 grams), ounce □ 我买二两茶叶。 **Wǒ mǎi èr liǎng cháyè.** *I want two liang of tea.*

两 2 **liǎng** Trad 兩 *num* **1** two
两个人 **liǎng ge rén** two people
两本书 **liǎng běn shū** two books
2 (as an approximation) a couple of, a few □ 我来说两句话。 **Wǒ lái shuō liǎng jù huà.** *Let me say a few words.*

NOTE: Both 两 **liǎng** and 二 **èr** may mean *two*, but are used differently. 二 **èr** must be used in mathematics or when saying the number 2 in isolation, e.g. □ 一、二、三、四 …**yī, èr, sān, sì...** *1, 2, 3, 4 …* □ 二加三是五。 **Èr jiā sān shì wǔ.** *2 plus 3 is 5.* Use 两 **liǎng** when referring to "two something," e.g. □ 两张桌子 **liǎng zhāng zhuōzi** *two tables* □ 两个小时 **liǎng ge xiǎoshí** *two hours.* The ordinal number second is 第二 **dì-èr**.

亮 **liàng** *adj* bright □ 天亮了! **Tiān liàng le!** *Day is breaking!* □ 这个灯不太亮。 **Zhège dēng bú tài liàng.** *This lamp is not very bright.*
亮丽 **liànglì** [modif: 亮 bright + 丽 beautiful] *adj* spectacularly beautiful

谅 **liàng** Trad 諒 *v* forgive (See 原谅 **yuánliàng**.)

晾 **liàng** *v* dry in the sun, dry in the air

辆 **liàng** *measure wd* (for vehicles)
一辆汽车 **yí liàng qìchē** a car
两辆自行车 **liǎng liàng zìxíngchē** two bicycles

量 **liàng** *n* quantity, capacity
酒量 **jiǔliàng** capacity for liquor, how much wine one can hold
保质保量 **bǎozhì bǎoliàng** ensure both the quality and quantity (of products)

聊 **liáo** *v* chat
聊天 **liáotiān** *v* chat □ 奶奶常去邻居家聊天。 **Nǎinai cháng qù línjū jiā liáotiān.** *My granny often goes to her neighbor's home for a chat.* □ 我没空陪你聊天。 **Wǒ méi kòng péi nǐ liáotiān.** *I don't have the time to chat with you.*
聊天室 **liáotiānshì** *n* (Internet) chatroom

僚 **liáo** *n* official (See 官僚 **guānliáo**)

潦 **liáo** *adj* slovenly
潦草 **liáocǎo** *adj* (of handwriting) illegible, done hastily and carelessly

辽 **liáo** Trad 遼 *adj* vast
辽阔 **liáokuò** *adj* vast, extensive

疗 **liáo** Trad 療 *v* treat, cure
疗养 **liáoyǎng** *v* recuperate, convalesce
疗养院 **liáoyǎngyuàn** sanitorium

了 **liǎo** *v* finish, be done with □ 这么多工作, 一星期也做不了。 **Zhème duō gōngzuò, yì xīngqī yě zuò bu liǎo.** *So much work can't be finished even in a week.*

NOTE: 了 **liǎo**, together with 得 **de** or 不 **bu**, is often used after a verb as a complement to mean *can* ... or *cannot* ... e.g. □ 这件事我干得了, 那件事我干不了。 **Zhè jiàn shì wǒ gàn de liǎo, nà jiàn shì wǒ gàn bu liǎo.** *I can do this job, but I can't do that job.*

了不起 **liǎobuqǐ** *adj* wonderful, terrific □ 这个孩子门门功课第一名, 真了不起! **Zhège háizi ménmén gōngkè**

dì-yī míng, zhēn liǎobuqǐ! *This child came out first in all the subjects. How wonderful!* □ 你别自以为了不起。**Nǐ bié zì yǐwéi liǎobuqǐ.** *Don't think yourself so terrific. (→ Don't think you're so hot.)*

了解 **liǎojiě** [comp: 了 see through + 解 analyze, comprehend] *v* know, understand, find out □ 我和他是老朋友, 我很了解他。**Wǒ hé tā shì lǎo péngyou, wǒ hěn liǎojiě tā.** *He and I are old friends. I know him very well.* □ 我来是要了解这一地区的市场情况。**Wǒ lái shì yào liǎojiě zhè yí dìqū de shìchǎng qíngkuàng.** *I've come to find out the marketing situation in this region.*

料 1 **liào** *n* material (See 材料 **cáiliào**, 燃料 **ránliào**, 染料 **rǎnliào**, 塑料 **sùliào**, 饮料 **yǐnliào**, 原料 **yuánliào**, 资料 **zīliào**.)

料 2 **liào** *v* anticipate, expect
料事如神 **liàoshìrúshén** predict accurately as if one were a god

列 **liè** *measure wd* (for trains)
一列火车 yí liè huǒchē a train

烈 **liè** *adj* intense
烈火 **lièhuǒ** [modif: 烈 intense + 火 fire] *n* raging flame

烈士 **lièshì** *n* martyr (位 **wèi**)

裂 **liè** *v* crack, splint

猎 **liè** Trad 獵 *v* hunt
猎人 lièrén hunter
打猎 dǎliè go hunting, hunt

劣 **liè** *adj* inferior, bad (quality) (See 恶劣 **èliè**)

磷 **lín** *n* phosphorus (P)

邻 **lín** Trad 鄰 *n* neighbor
邻居 **línjū** [modif: 邻 neighboring + 居 residents] *n* neighbor □ 和邻居保持良好的关系, 很重要。**Hé línjū bǎochí liánghǎo de guānxi, hěn zhòngyào.** *It is important to maintain good relations with the neighbors.* □ 我家左面的邻居是一对老夫妻。**Wǒ jiā zuǒmiàn de línjū shì yí duì lǎo fūqī.** *My neighbors on the left are an old couple.*

林 **lín** *n* forest, woods
林场 **línchǎng** *n* forestry center
林区 **línqū** *n* forest, forest land
林业 **línyè** *n* forestry industry, timber industry

淋 **lín** *v* drench, pour
淋浴 **línyù** *n* shower (bath)
洗淋浴 xǐ línyù take a shower

临 **lín** Trad 臨 *v* arrive
临时 **línshí** *adj* tentative, provisional □ 这是临时措施, 正式办法还要研究制定。**Zhè shì línshí cuòshī, zhèngshì bànfǎ hái yào yánjiū zhìdìng.** *This is only a tentative measure. We need to study and devise formal measures.*

灵 **líng** Trad 靈 **I** *n* fairy **II** *adj* agile, quick
灵魂 **línghún** [comp: 灵 fairy + 魂 soul] *n* soul, spirit
灵活 **línghuó** [comp: 灵 agile + 活 alive] *adj* flexible, agile □ 他头脑灵活, 能迅速对付各种不同的情况。**Tā tóunǎo línghuó, néng xùnsù duìfù gè zhǒng bùtóng de qíngkuàng.** *He is quick-witted and can cope with various situations promptly.*

零 **líng** **I** *num* zero
一百零二 yìbǎi líng èr 102
四千零五 sìqiān líng wǔ 4005
II *adj* fractional, fragmentary

NOTES: (1) No matter how many zeros there are between digits, only one 零 **líng** is used. For example, 4005 is 四千零五 **sìqiān líng wǔ**, not 四千零零五 **sìqiān líng líng wǔ**. (2) 零 **líng** can also be written as 〇, e.g 四千〇五 **sìqiān líng wǔ** 4005.

零件 **língjiàn** *n* part, spare part
零钱 **língqián** [modif: 零 parts + 钱 money] *n* allowance, pocket money, small change □ 我身上没有零钱。**Wǒ shēnshang méiyǒu língqián.** *I don't have small change on me.* □ 一个月该给孩子多少零钱比较合适? **Yí ge yuè gāi gěi háizi duōshǎo língqián bǐjiào héshì?** *How much monthly allowance is appropriate for children?*

铃 **líng** Trad 鈴 *n* bell □ 门铃响了, 看看是谁来了。**Mén líng xiǎng le, kànkan shì shéi lái le.** *The doorbell is ringing. Go and see who's there.* □ 上课铃响了, 学生们陆续走进教室。**Shàngkè líng xiǎng le, xuésheng men lùxù zǒujìn jiàoshì.** *The bell rang for class and students entered the classroom one after another.*

玲 **líng** as in 玲珑 **línglóng**
玲珑 **línglóng** *adj* **1** (of things) exquisite **2** (of people) clever and nimble

龄 **líng** Trad 齡 *n* age (See 年龄 **niánlíng**.)

凌 **líng** *v* approach
凌晨 **língchén** *n* the time before dawn

岭 **líng** *n* mountain range, ridge

领 **lǐng** Trad 領 *v* lead, take □ 服务员领客人到他们预订的桌子。**Fúwùyuán lǐng kèrén dào tāmen yùdìng de zhuōzi.** *The waiter led the customers to the table they had reserved.*
领导 **lǐngdǎo** [comp: 领 lead + 导 guide] *v* **1** lead, provide leadership □ 政府领导人民发展经济。**Zhèngfǔ lǐngdǎo rénmín fāzhǎn jīngjì.** *The government provides leadership for the people to develop the economy.* **2** have jurisdiction over **II** *n* leader, the person in charge □ 领导不在, 你有什么事情请跟我说。**Lǐngdǎo bú zài, nǐ yǒu shénme shìqíng qǐng gēn wǒ shuō.** *The person in charge is not in. Please talk to me if you've any business.* □ 我要找你们的领导。**Wǒ yào zhǎo nǐmen de lǐngdǎo.** *I want to see the person in charge here.*

NOTES: (1) 领导 **lǐngdǎo** as a verb is somewhat pompous, appropriate only for grand occasions. (2) As a noun 领导 **lǐngdǎo** is no longer very popular in China and has never been very popular in other Chinese-speaking communities. To refer to "the person in charge," many Chinese use 老板 **lǎobǎn** (boss) or specific terms such as 厂长 **chǎngzhǎng** (factory manager) or 校长 **xiàozhǎng** (headmaster, school principal, university president).

领土 **lǐngtǔ** *n* territory
领袖 **lǐngxiù** *n* leader (位 **wèi**) □ 他是这个国家的一位重要政治领袖。**Tā shì zhège guójiā de yí wèi zhòngyà**

zhèngzhì lǐngxiù. *He is an important political leader of this country.*

令 **lìng** *v* command, cause to (See 命令 **mìnglìng**.)

另 **lìng** *adj* Same as 另外 **lìngwài**. Used before a monosyllabic verb.

另外 **lìngwài** *adj* other, another □ 这个方法不行, 得另外想办法。 **Zhège fāngfǎ bù xíng, děi lìngwài xiǎng bànfǎ.** *This method doesn't work. We've got to find another way.* □ 除了小王以外, 另外有没有人会用这台机器? **Chúle Xiǎo Wáng yǐwài, lìngwài yǒu méiyǒu rén huì yòng zhè tái jīqì?** *Is there anybody other than Xiao Wang who can operate this machine?*

溜 **liū** *v* **1** slide, glide **2** sneak off, slip away

留 **liú** *v* remain (in the same place), stay behind □ 你们先回家吧, 我再留一会儿做完这件事。 **Nǐmen xiān huíjiā ba, wǒ zài liú yíhuìr zuòwán zhè jiàn shì.** *You go home first. I'll stay behind for a while to finish this job.* □ 妈妈知道我爱吃鸡腿, 总是把鸡腿留给我吃。 **Māma zhīdào wǒ ài chī jītuǐ, zǒngshì bǎ jītuǐ liúgěi wǒ chī.** *Mom knows I like to eat chicken drumsticks. She always leaves them for me.* □ 我留他吃饭, 他说有事要办, 就走了。 **Wǒ liú tā chī fàn, tā shuō yǒu shì yào bàn, jiù zǒu le.** *I asked him to stay for a meal, but he said he had something to attend to, and left.*

留学 **liúxué** [comp: 留 stay + 学 study] *v* study abroad □ 很多亚洲学生在美国留学。 **Hěn duō Yàzhōu xuésheng zài Měiguó liúxué.** *Many Asian students are studying in America.*

留学生 **liúxuéshēng** international students (especially in a university) □ 不少留学生星期日也在图书馆学习。 **Bùshǎo liúxuéshēng Xīngqīrì yě zài túshūguǎn xuéxí.** *Even on Sundays quite a few international students study in the library.*

瘤 **liú** *n* tumor

榴 **liú** *n* pomegranate
石榴 shíliú pomegranate

硫 **liú** *n* sulfur
硫酸 liúsuān sulfuric acid

流 **liú** *v* flow □ 河水慢慢地向东流去。 **Hé shuǐ mànmàn de xiàng dōng liúqù.** *The river flows slowly to the east.*

流动 **liúdòng** [comp: 流 flow + 动 move] *v* flow, move from place to place
流动人口 liúdòng rénkǒu floating population, migrant population

流利 **liúlì** *adj* fluent □ 我什么时候才能流利地说中文呢? **Wǒ shénme shíhou cái néng liúlì de shuō Zhōngwén ne?** *When will I be able to speak Chinese fluently?*

流氓 **liúmáng** *n* hooligan, gangster

流行 **liúxíng** *v* be fashionable, be popular □ 今年流行绿色。 **Jīnnián liúxíng lǜsè.** *The green color is in fashion this year.*
流行歌手 liúxíng gēshǒu pop singer
流行音乐 liúxíng yīnyuè pop music
流行病 liúxíngbìng *n* epidemic
流行性感冒（流感）liúxíngxìng gǎnmào (liúgǎn) *n* influenza, flu

刘 **liú** as in 浏览 **liúlǎn**
浏览 liúlǎn *v* browse

浏览器 liúlǎnqì *n* (computer) browser

柳 **liǔ** *n* willow
杨柳 yángliǔ willow
柳树 liǔshù willow, willow tree (棵 **kē**)

六 **liù** *num* six
六十六 liùshí liù sixty-six
六十五岁 liùshí wǔ suì sixty-five years of age

龙 **lóng** Trad 龍 *n* dragon (条 **tiáo**) □ 中国人把自己称作 "龙的传人"。 **Zhōngguórén bǎ zìjǐ chēngzuò "lóng de chuánrén".** *The Chinese call themselves "descendants of the dragon."*

聋 **lóng** Trad 聾 *adj* deaf, hard of hearing
聋子 lóngzi deaf person
聋哑人 lóngyǎrén *n* deaf and dumb person, deaf mute

笼 **lóng** Trad 籠 *n* cage
笼子 lóngzi cage
鸟笼 niǎolóng bird cage

窿 **lóng** *n* pit, hole (See 窟窿 **kūlong**)

隆 **lóng** *adj* grand
隆重 lóngzhòng *adj* grand, ceremonious

咙 **lóng** Trad 嚨 *n* as in 喉咙 **hóulóng**

珑 **lóng** Trad 瓏 *adj* as in 玲珑 **línglóng**

垄 **lǒng** Trad 壟 *n* ridge
垄断 lǒngduàn *v* monopolize

拢 **lǒng** Trad 攏 *v* hold together

楼 **lóu** Trad 樓 *n* **1** building with two or more stories (座 **zuò**) □ 这座楼是去年建的。 **Zhè zuò lóu shì qùnián jiàn de.** *This building was built last year.* □ 她住在那座黄色的大楼里。 **Tā zhù zài nà zuò huángsè de dàlóu li.** *She lives in that yellow building.* **2** floor (层 **céng**) □ 这一层楼有多少房间? **Zhè yì céng lóu yǒu duōshǎo fángjiān?** *How many rooms are there on this floor?* □ 老师的办公室在三楼。 **Lǎoshī de bàngōngshì zài sān-lóu.** *Teachers' offices are on the third floor.*
楼上 lóushàng upstairs
楼下 lóuxià downstairs
大楼 dàlóu a big building (especially a high-rise building)
高楼 gāolóu high-rise

NOTE: In naming floors, the Chinese system is the same as the American system but different from the British one, i.e. 一楼 **yī-lóu** is the American first floor, and the British ground floor.

楼房 **lóufáng** *n* multi-storied building (cf. 平房 **píngfáng** one-story building, bungalow)

楼梯 **lóutī** [modif: 楼 floor, story + 梯 steps] *n* stairs, stairway, staircase □ 别站在楼梯上讲话, 会妨碍别人上下。 **Bié zhàn zài lóutī shang jiǎnghuà, huì fáng'ài biérén shàng-xià.** *Do not stand talking on the stairs. It'll obstruct people going up and down.*

搂 **lǒu** Trad 摟 *v* embrace, hold in arms

漏 **lòu** *v* **1** leak □ 屋顶漏了, 要找人修理。 **Wūdǐng lòu le, yào zhǎo rén xiūlǐ.** *The roof leaks. We'll have to find someone to fix it.* **2** leave out by mistake

漏洞 **lòudòng** *n* loophole, inconsistency (in argument)

漏税 **lòushuì** [v+obj: 漏 leave out + 税 tax] **I** *v* evade tax **II** *n* tax evasion

陋 **lòu** *adj* ugly (See 简陋 **jiǎnlòu**)

炉 **lú** Trad 爐 *n* stove, furnace
　炉子 lúzi stove, furnace

虏 **lǔ** Trad 虜 *n* captive (See 俘虏 **fúlǔ**)

鲁 **lǔ** *adj* rash (See 粗鲁 **cūlǔ**)

陆 **lù** Trad 陸 *n* land
　陆军 lùjūn [modif: 陆 land + 军 troops] *n* army
　陆续 lùxù *adv* one after another, in succession □ 开会的代表陆续到达。**Kāihuì de dàibiǎo lùxù dàodá.** *Congress delegates arrived one after another.*

录 **lù** Trad 錄 *v* record
　录取 lùqǔ *v* enroll (students), appoint (job applicants)
　录像 lùxiàng [v+obj: 录 record + 像 image] *v* record with a video camera or video recorder □ 他们的婚礼全录像了。**Tāmen de hūnlǐ quán lùxiàng le.** *Their wedding ceremony was videotaped.*
　　录像机 lùxiàngjī video recorder
　录音 lùyīn [v+obj: 录 record + 音 sound] *v* make a recording of sounds (e.g. music, reading) □ 这里在录音, 请安静! **Zhèli zài lùyīn, qǐng ānjìng!** *Recording is in progress. Please be quiet.* □ 你有没有听过王老师读这篇课文的录音? **Nǐ yǒu méiyǒu tīngguo Wáng lǎoshī dú zhè piān kèwén de lùyīn?** *Have you listened to the recording of Teacher Wang's reading of this text?*
　　录音机 lùyīnjī audio recorder, sound recorder
　录用 lùyòng *v* employ (staff)

碌 **lù** *adj* busy (See 忙碌 **mánglù**)

路 **lù** *n* road (条 **tiáo**) □ 这条路很长, 一直通到山里。**Zhè tiáo lù hěn cháng, yìzhí tōngdào shān li.** *This road is very long and leads all the way into the hills.* □ 你认识去大学的路吗? **Nǐ rènshì qù dàxué de lù ma?** *Do you know the way to the university?*
　马路 mǎlù road (in a city)
　路程 lùchéng [modif: 路 road + 程 course] *n* distance traveled, journey
　路过 lùguò *v* pass, pass by, pass through
　路口 lùkǒu [modif: 路 road + 口 mouth] *n* intersection, crossing
　路面 lùmiàn *n* road surface
　路上 lùshang *n* **1** on one's way (to) □ 她去学校的路上, 要经过一座公园。**Tā qù xuéxiào de lùshàng, yào jīngguò yí zuò gōngyuán.** *On her way to school, she passes by a park.* **2** on the road □ 路上车辆很多。**Lùshang chēliàng hěn duō.** *There is lots of traffic on the road.*
　路线 lùxiàn [modif: 路 road + 线 line] *n* route, itinerary □ 这是不是去那里最近的路线? **Zhè shì bu shì qù nàli zuì jìn de lùxiàn?** *Is this the shortest route to that place?*
　路子 lùzi *n* way and means of doing things
　　很有路子 hěn yǒu lùzi very resourceful

露 **lù** *v* show, reveal □ 她笑的时候, 露出雪白的牙齿。**Tā xiào de shíhou, lùchū xuěbái de yáchǐ.** *When she smiles, white teeth show.*

赂 **lù** Trad 賂 *v* bribe (See 贿赂 **huìlù**)

鹿 **lù** *n* deer

驴 **lǘ** *n* donkey
　驴子 lǘzi donkey

铝 **lǚ** *n* aluminum (Al)

侣 **lǚ** *n* companion (See 伴侣 **bànlǚ**)

旅 **lǚ** *v* travel
　旅馆 lǚguǎn [modif: 旅 travel + 馆 house] *n* hotel (座 **zuò**, 家 **jiā**) □ 我上个月在那家旅馆订了房间。**Wǒ shàng ge yuè zài nà jiā lǚguǎn dìngle fángjiān.** *I booked a room in that hotel last month.*
　　汽车旅馆 qìchē lǚguǎn motel
　　五星旅馆 wǔxīng lǚguǎn five-star hotel
　旅客 lǚkè [modif: 旅 traveling + 客 guest] *n* hotel guest, passenger (of coach, train, plane, etc.) □ 航空公司尽力保证旅客的安全。**Hángkōng gōngsī jìnlì bǎozhèng lǚkè de ānquán.** *The airline does all it can to guarantee the safety of the traveling public.* □ 旅客们, 欢迎你们乘坐本次列车。**Lǚkèmen, huānyíng nǐmen chéngzuò běn cì lièchē.** *Welcome aboard this train, everyone!*
　旅途 lǚtú [modif: 旅 travel + 途 journey] *n* journey, travels □ 祝你旅途愉快! **Zhù nǐ lǚtú yúkuài!** *Have a pleasant journey!* □ 他把旅途看到, 听到的都写下来。**Tā bǎ lǚtú kàndào, tīngdào de dōu xiě xiàlái.** *He wrote down all he saw and heard on his travels.*
　旅行 lǚxíng [comp: 旅 travel + 行 walk, go] *v* travel □ 我在中国旅行的时候, 学到不少知识。**Wǒ zài Zhōngguó lǚxíng de shíhou, xuédào bùshǎo zhīshi.** *I gained a lot of knowledge when I traveled in China.* □ 一个人在外国旅行, 千万要注意安全。**Yígerén zài wàiguó lǚxíng, qiānwàn yào zhùyì ānquán.** *When you are traveling alone in a foreign country, you must always be mindful of personal safety.*
　　旅行社 lǚxíngshè travel agency □ 我要去旅行社买去英国的飞机票。**Wǒ yào qù lǚxíngshè mǎi qù Yīngguó de fēijī piào.** *I'll go to the travel agency to buy an air ticket to Britain.*
　旅游 lǚyóu [comp: 旅 travel + 游 play, holiday] *v* travel for pleasure □ 我有了钱, 就到国外去旅游。**Wǒ yǒule qián, jiù dào guówài qù lǚyóu.** *I'll go overseas for a holiday when I've got the money.*
　　旅游车 lǚyóuchē tour bus
　　旅游公司 lǚyóu gōngsī travel company
　　旅游路线 lǚyóu lùxiàn tour itinerary
　　旅游团 lǚyóutuán tour group
　　旅游业 lǚyóuyè the tourism industry, tourism
　　旅游者 lǚyóuzhě tourist, holiday-maker

履 **lǚ** **I** *n* shoe **II** *v* carry out, fulfill
　履历 lǚlì *n* résumé
　履行 lǚxíng *v* fulfill (one's promise), perform (one's obligation)

屡 **lǚ** Trad 屢 *adv* repeatedly
　屡次 lǚcì *adv* repeatedly

率 **lǜ** *n* rate (See 效率 **xiàolǜ**.)

绿 **lǜ** Trad 綠 *adj* green □ 春天到了, 树木都绿了。**Chūntian dào le, shùmù dōu lǜ le.** *Spring has*

come; the trees are all green. □ 红花绿树, 美极了。 **Hónghuā lǜshù, měi jíle.** *Red flowers and green trees—they're so beautiful!*

绿党 **lǜdǎng** the Green Party

绿化 **lǜhuà** [suffix: 绿 green + 化 verb suffix] *v* make green by planting trees, afforest

绿卡 **lǜkǎ** *n* green card (permanent residency permit in the U.S.A. and some other countries)

律 **lǜ** *n* law

律师 **lǜshī** [modif: 律 law + 师 master] *n* lawyer

律师事务所 **lǜshī shìwùsuǒ** law firm

虑 **lǜ** Trad 慮 *v* ponder (See 考虑 kǎolǜ.)

滤 **lǜ** Trad 濾 *v* filter

卵 **luǎn** *n* egg (a cell)

卵子 **luǎnzǐ** egg

乱 **luàn** Trad 亂 *adj* **1** disorderly, chaotic (antonym 整齐 **zhěngqí**) □ 我的房间很乱, 要收拾一下。 **Wǒ de fángjiān hěn luàn, yào shōushi yíxià.** *My room is in a mess and needs tidying up.* **2** at will, random □ 他总是乱花钱。 **Tā zǒngshì luàn huā qián.** *He always spends money unwisely.* (→ *He always wastes his money.*) □ 你别乱说。 **Nǐ bié luànshuō.** *Do not talk irresponsibly.*

乱码 **luànmǎ** [modif: 乱 chaotic + 码 code] *n* crazy code, confusion code

乱七八糟 **luànqībāzāo** *idiom* in an awful mess, very messy

略 **lüè** *v* capture (See 侵略 **qīnlüè**.)

略微 **lüèwēi** *adj* slight

掠 **lüè** *v* plunder

掠夺 **lüèduó** [comp: 掠 plunder + 夺 grab] *v* plunder, rob

抡 **lūn** Trad 掄 *v* brandish, swing

轮 **lún** Trad 輪 **I** *n* wheel **II** *v* take turns

轮船 **lúnchuán** [modif: 轮 wheel + 船 boat, ship] *n* steamship, ship □ 现在很少人坐轮船旅行。 **Xiànzài hěn shǎo rén zuò lúnchuán lǚxíng.** *Few people travel by ship now.*

轮廓 **lúnkuò** *n* outline, contour

轮流 **lúnliú** *v* take turns

轮流值班 **lúnliú zhíbān** be on duty by turns

轮子 **lúnzi** [suffix: 轮 wheel + 子 nominal suffix] *n* wheel

论 **lùn** Trad 論 *v* discuss

论点 **lùndiǎn** [modif: 论 argument + 点 point] *n* argument, point of contest (个 **gè**)

提出两个论点 **tíchū liǎng gè lùndiǎn** put forward two arguments

论述 **lùnshù** [comp: 论 argue + 述 narrate] *v* explain (an argument), discuss

论文 **lùnwén** [comp: 论 treatise + 文 essay] *n* dissertation, thesis, essay (篇 **piān**) □ 张教授发表了多篇关于中国历史的论文。 **Zhāng jiàoshòu fābiǎole duō piān guānyú Zhōngguó lìshǐ de lùnwén.** *Professor Zhang has published several theses on Chinese history.*

论证 **lùnzhèng** [comp: 论 argue + 证 prove] *v* prove (an argument), demonstrate, discuss

啰 **luō** as in 啰唆 **luō suō**

啰唆 **luōsuō** *adj* long-winded, wordy, verbose

螺 **luó** *n* snail

螺丝 **luósī** screw

螺丝刀 **luósīdāo** *n* screwdriver (把 **bǎ**)

螺丝钉 **luósīdīng** *n* screw (颗 **kē**) □ 掉了一颗螺丝钉。 **Diàole yìkē luósīdīng.** *A screw is missing.*

骡 **luó** *n* mule

骡子 **luózi** mule (头 **tóu**)

锣 **luó** *n* gong (面 **miàn**)

箩 **luó** *n* bamboo basket

箩筐 **luókuāng** *n* large bamboo or wicker basket (只 **zhī**)

萝 **luó** Trad 蘿 *n* trailing plant

萝卜 **luóbo** *n* turnip, radish, carrot (根 **gēn**, 个 **gè**) □ 咱们做个萝卜汤吧。 **Zánmen zuò ge luóbo tāng ba.** *Let's prepare turnip soup.*

白萝卜 **bái luóbo** turnip

红萝卜 **hóng luóbo** radish

胡萝卜 **hú luóbo** carrot

逻 **luó** *v* petrol

逻辑 **luóji** *n* logic

骆 **luò** as in 骆驼 **luòtuo**

骆驼 **luòtuo** *n* camel (头 **tóu**)

络 **luò** Trad 絡 *n* net

络绎不绝 **luòyì bùjué** *adv, adj* in an endless stream, endless

落 **luò** *v* fall, drop □ 秋天, 树叶落了。 **Qiūtiān, shùyè luò le.** *In autumn, leaves fall.*

落成 **luòchéng** *v* (of a building or engineering project) be completed

落后 **luòhòu** *adj* backward, outdated □ 你这种观点太落后了。 **Nǐ zhè zhǒng guāndiǎn tài luòhòu le.** *Your views are outdated.*

落实 **luòshí** *v* (of a policy or idea) be implemented, be fulfilled

落选 **luòxuǎn** *v* lose an election, fail to be chosen

M

妈 **mā** Trad 媽 *n* ma, mom

妈妈 **māma** *n* mom, mommy □ 妈妈在辅导妹妹做作业。 **Māma zài fúdǎo mèimei zuò zuòyè.** *Mom is tutoring my younger sister in her homework.* □ 我想每个人都爱自己的妈妈。 **Wǒ xiǎng měi ge rén dōu ài zìjǐ de māma.** *I think everyone loves their mom.*

抹 **mā** *v* wipe, wipe off

抹桌子 **mā zhuōzi** wipe the table

抹布 **mābù** [modif: 抹 wipe + 布 cloth] *n* rag (块 **kuài**)

麻 **má** **I** *n* hemp

麻袋 **mádài** sack (只 **zhī**)

II *adj* numb

麻痹 **mábì** **I** *v* benumb, lull **II** *n* paralysis

小儿麻痹症 **xiǎoér mábìzhèng** infantile paralysis

麻烦 **máfan** [idiom] **I** *v* bother □ 这封信我能翻译, 不用麻烦陈先生了。 **Zhè fēng xìn wǒ néng fānyì, búyòng máfan Chén xiānsheng le.** *I can translate this letter. We don't have to bother Mr Chen.* □ 麻

烦你把这封信交给王经理。**Máfan nǐ bǎ zhè fēng xìn jiāo gei Wáng jīnglǐ.** *Would you mind delivering this letter to Mr Wang, the manager?* **II** *adj* troublesome, complicated □ 这件事很麻烦，我不一定能做好。**Zhè jiàn shì hěn máfan, wǒ bù yídìng néng zuò hǎo.** *This matter is complicated. I'm not sure I can get it done well.*

NOTE: 麻烦您 **máfan nín** is a polite expression to request somebody's service or to ask a favor. More examples: □ 麻烦您把盐递给我。**Máfan nín bǎ yán dì gei wǒ.** *Please pass the salt [to me].* □ 麻烦您查一下他的电话号码。**Máfan nín chá yíxià tā de diànhuà hàomǎ.** *Would you mind finding out his telephone number for me?*

麻将 **májiàng** *n* (the game) mahjong
打麻将 **dǎmájiàng** play mahjong □ 你不能每个星期天都打麻将啊! **Nǐ bù néng měi ge Xīngqītiān dōu dǎ májiàng a!** *You mustn't play mahjong every Sunday!* □ 打麻将好像挺有趣，你教教我，好吗? **Dǎ májiàng hǎoxiàng tǐng yǒuqù, nǐ jiāojiao wǒ, hǎoma?** *Mahjong seems an interesting game. Would you teach me please?*
麻木 **mámù** [comp: 麻 numb + 木 wooden] *adj* unable to feel anything, numb
麻雀 **máquè** *n* sparrow (只 **zhī**)
麻醉 **mázuì** [comp: 麻 numb + 醉 drunk] **I** *v* anesthetize **II** *n* anesthesia
麻醉师 **mázuìshī** anesthetist, anesthesiologist
局部麻醉 **júbù mázuì** localized anesthesia
全身麻醉 **quánshēnmázuì** general anesthesia

马 **mǎ** Trad 馬 *n* horse (匹 **pǐ**) □ 你会骑马吗? **Nǐ huì qí mǎ ma?** *Can you ride a horse?* □ 马跑得快，还是狗跑得快? **Mǎ pǎo de kuài, háishì gǒu pǎo de kuài?** *Which runs faster—the horse or the dog?*
马达 **mǎdá** *n* motor
马虎 **mǎhu** *adj* sloppy, careless □ 你这个作业作得太马虎了。**Nǐ zhège zuòyè zuò de tài mǎhu le.** *You did this assignment carelessly.*

NOTE: 马马虎虎 **mǎ-mǎ-hū-hū** is a common idiomatic expression meaning *so-so, not too bad* or *just managing.* For example □ "去年你考试成绩怎么样?" "马马虎虎。" **"Qùnián nǐ kǎoshì chéngjì zénmeyàng?" "Mǎ-mǎ-hū-hū."** *"How did you do in the exams last year?" "So-so."*

马力 **mǎlì** *n* horse power
马铃薯 **mǎlíngshǔ** *n* potato
马路 **mǎlù** [modif: 马 horse + 路 road] *n* street, avenue (条 **tiáo**) □ 这条马路从早到晚车很多。**Zhè tiáo mǎlù cóng-zǎo-dào-wǎn chē hěn duō.** *This street has lots of traffic from morning till night.*
马路上 **mǎlù shang** in the street, on the road □ 你不能把车停在马路上。**Nǐ bù néng bǎ chē tíng zài mǎlù shang.** *You can't park the car in the street.*
过马路 **guò mǎlù** walk across a street □ 过马路要特别小心。**Guò mǎlù yào tèbié xiǎoxīn.** *One should be especially careful when crossing the street.*
马上 **mǎshàng** [idiom] *adv* at once, immediately □ 好，我马上来! **Hǎo, wǒ mǎshàng lái!** *OK, I'm coming!* □ 他要我们马上回信。**Tā yào wǒmen mǎshàng huíxìn.** *He demands a prompt reply.*

马戏 **mǎxì** [modif: 马 horse + 戏 play] *n* circus performance (场 **cháng**)
马戏团 **mǎxìtuán** circus

码 **mǎ** Trad 碼 *v* stack up
码头 **mǎtóu** *n* dock, wharf □ 船马上要靠码头了。**Chuán mǎshàng yào kào mǎtóu le.** *The ship will soon anchor at the dock.*
码头工人 **mǎtóu gōngrén** docker, longshoreman

蚂 **mǎ** Trad 螞 as in 蚂蚁 **mǎyǐ**
蚂蚁 **mǎyǐ** ant (只 **zhī**)

骂 **mà** Trad 罵 *v* curse, swear □ 你怎么骂人? **Nǐ zěnme mà rén?** *How can you swear at people?*

嘛 **ma** *particle* surely, that goes without saying (used at the end of a sentence to indicate that the truth of the statement is obvious) □ 农村的空气就是比城市干净嘛! **Nóngcūn de kōngqì jiùshì bǐ chéngshì gānjìng ma!** *The air in rural areas is surely cleaner than that in cities.*

吗 **ma** Trad 嗎 *particle* (used at the end of a sentence to turn it into a yes-or-no question) □ 你说中文吗? **Nǐ huì shuō Zhōngwén ma?** *Do you speak Chinese?* □ 你去过香港吗? **Nǐ qùguo Xiānggǎng ma?** *Have you been to Hong Kong?* □ 这么简单的题目，你也不会做吗? **Zhème jiǎndān de tímù, nǐ yě bú huì zuò ma?** *Can't you do such a simple question?*

埋 **mái** *v* bury □ 他把死狗埋在树下。**Tā bǎ sǐ gǒu mái zài shù xia.** *He buried his dead dog under the tree.*
埋没 **máimò** [comp: 埋 bury + 没 annul] *v* stifle (talent)
埋头 **máitóu** [v+obj: 埋 bury + 头 one's head] *v* devote wholeheartedly to, be engrossed in
埋头苦干 **máitóukǔgàn** devote oneself to hard work without complaint and for a long time

买 **mǎi** Trad 買 *v* buy □ 我要买一双鞋。**Wǒ yào mǎi yì shuāng xié.** *I want to buy a pair of shoes.* □ 你这本书在哪儿买的? **Nǐ zhè běn shū zài nǎr mǎi de?** *Where did you buy this book?*
买卖 **mǎimai** [comp: 买 buy + 卖 sell] *n* trade, business □ 最近店里的买卖怎么样? **Zuìjìn diànlǐ de mǎimai zěnmeyàng?** *How is business at your shop recently?* □ 他在城里有个小卖买。**Tā zài chénglǐ yǒu ge xiǎo mǎimai.** *He has a small business in town.*
做买卖 **zuò mǎimai** do business, be engaged in business □ 几乎每一家大公司都想跟中国做买卖。**Jīhū měi yì jiā dà gōngsī dōu xiǎng gēn Zhōngguó zuò mǎimai.** *Almost every corporation wants to do business with China.* □ 他很会做买卖，几年工夫就发财了。**Tā hěn huì zuò mǎimai, jǐ nián gōngfu jiù fācái le.** *He is very good at doing business, and has become prosperous in just a few years.*

迈 **mài** Trad 邁 *v* step forward □ 完成了这项任务，我们就朝工厂自动化迈了一大步。**Wánchéngle zhè xiàng rènwù, wǒmen jiù cháo gōngchǎng zìdònghuà màile yí dà bù.** *After completing this project, we will have made a big stride towards automation of the factory.*

麦 **mài** Trad 麥 *n* wheat (See 小麦 **xiǎomài**.)

卖 **mài** Trad 賣 *v* sell □ 他把汽车卖了。**Tā bǎ qìchē mài le.** *He sold his car.* □ 你们这里卖水果吗? **Nǐmen zhèlǐ mài shuǐguǒ ma?** *Do you sell fruit here?*

脉 **mài** Trad 脈 *n* blood vessel

脉搏 **màibó** *n* pulse

埋 **mán** as in 埋怨 **mányuàn**

埋怨 **mányuàn** *v* blame, complain

瞒 **mán** Trad 瞞 *v* conceal truth from □ 这件事你不该瞒我。**Zhè jiàn shì nǐ bù gāi mán wǒ.** *You shouldn't have hidden this matter from me.*

馒 **mán** as in 馒头 **mántou**

馒头 **mántou** *n* steamed bun (只 **zhī**) □ 我早饭吃了两个馒头。**Wǒ zǎofàn chīle liǎng ge mántou.** *I ate two steamed buns for breakfast.*

蛮 **mán** Trad 蠻 *adj* unrestrained and wild

蛮不讲理 **mán bù jiǎnglǐ** totally unreasonable and behaving atrociously

满 **mǎn** Trad 滿 **I** *adj* 1 full, full to the brim □ 碗里的水满了。**Wǎn li de shuǐ mǎn le.** *The bowl is full of water.* □ 房间里挤得满满的。**Fángjiān li jǐ de mǎnmǎn de.** *The room is packed.* 2 satisfied **II** *v* reach the limit

满额 **mǎn'é** [modif: 满 full + 额 quota] *adj* reaching full quota

满意 **mǎnyì** [v+obj: 满 make full + 意 wish, desire] *adj* satisfied, pleased □ 我们要让顾客高兴地来，满意地走。**Wǒmen yào ràng gùkè gāoxìng de lái, mǎnyì de zǒu.** *We should ensure customers arrive happy and leave satisfied.* □ 我对你们的服务很不满意。**Wǒ duì nǐmen de fúwù hěn bù mǎnyì.** *I'm very dissatisfied with your service.*

对…满意 **duì...mǎnyì** be satisfied with

满月 **mǎnyuè** [modif: 满 full + 月 month] **I** *v* (of a newborn baby) be one month old

满月酒 **mǎnyuè jiǔ** dinner party in celebration of a baby's first month

II *n* full moon

满足 **mǎnzú** *v* meet the needs of, satisfy □ 老师尽量满足学生的要求。**Lǎoshī jǐnliàng mǎnzú xuésheng de yāoqiú.** *The teacher tries his best to meet the demands of his students.* □ 我们要增加产量，满足市场的需要。**Wǒmen yào zēngjiā chǎnliàng, mǎnzú shìchǎng de xūyào.** *We should increase output to satisfy the needs of the market.*

慢 **màn** *adj* slow (antonym 快 **kuài**) □ 我的表慢了五分钟。**Wǒ de biǎo mànle wǔ fēnzhōng.** *My watch is five minutes slow.* □ 别着急，慢慢地走。**Bié zháojí, mànman de zǒu.** *Don't be impatient. Walk slowly.* □ 你说得慢，我就听得懂。**Nǐ shuō de màn, wǒ jiù tīng de dǒng.** *If you speak slowly, I can understand you.*

慢性 **mànxìng** *adj* 1 (of diseases) chronic (antonym 急性 **jíxìng**)

慢性肝炎 **mànxìng gānyán** chronic hepatitis
2 Same as 慢性子 **mànxìngzi**

慢性子 **mànxìngzi** *adj* (of a person) slow or indolent

漫 **màn** *v* overflow

漫长 **máncháng** *adj* long, endless

蔓 **màn** as in 蔓延 **mànyán**

蔓延 **mànyán** *v* spread, extend

忙 **máng** *adj* busy □ 我最近很忙，没有空儿跟你去看电影。**Wǒ zuìjìn hěn máng, méiyǒu kòngr gēn nǐ qù kàn diànyǐng.** *I'm busy these days, and don't have time to go to the movies with you.* □ 你在忙什么？**Nǐ zài máng shénme?** *What are you busy with?*

NOTE: When friends meet in China, a common conversation opener is 你最近忙吗? **Nǐ zuìjìn máng ma?** *Have you been busy lately?*

忙碌 **mánglù** *adj* busy

忙忙碌碌 **mángmáng lùlù** very busy, always engaged in doing something

茫 **máng** *adj* boundless and indistinct

茫茫 **mángmáng** boundless and blurred, vast

茫然 **mángrán** *adj* knowing nothing about, ignorant, in the dark

盲 **máng** *adj* blind

盲从 **mángcóng** [modif: 盲 blindly + 从 follow] *v* follow blindly

盲人 **mángrén** [modif: 盲 blind + 人 person] *n* blind person

盲人学校 **mángrén xuéxiào** school for the blind

盲文 **mángwén** *n* braille

氓 **máng** *n* man (See 流氓 **liúmáng**)

猫 **māo** Trad 貓 *n* cat (只 **zhī**) □ 我家有一只小白猫。**Wǒ jiā yǒu yì zhī xiǎo bái māo.** *We keep a white kitten at home.*

猫头鹰 **māotóuyīng** [modif: 猫 cat + 头 head + 鹰 eagle] *n* owl (只 **zhī**)

毛 1 **máo** *n* hair

羊毛 **yángmáo** wool

毛笔 **máobǐ** [modif: 毛 hair + 笔 pen] *n* traditional Chinese writing brush (支 **zhī**, 管 **guǎn**)

毛病 **máobìng** *n* 1 illness □ 我什么毛病也没有，身体健康得很。**Wǒ shénme máobìng yě méiyǒu, shēntǐ jiànkāng de hěn.** *I have no complaints at all; I am in excellent health.* 2 trouble, breakdown □ 洗衣机出毛病了。**Xǐyījī chū máobìng le.** *The washing machine is out of order.*

毛巾 **máojīn** *n* towel (条 **tiáo**) □ 他拿着一条大毛巾进浴室洗澡。**Tā názhe yì tiáo dà máojīn jìn yùshì xǐzǎo.** *He went into the bathroom with a big towel to take a bath.*

毛衣 **máoyī** [modif: 毛 woolen + 衣 clothing] *n* woolen sweater, woolen pullover (件 **jiàn**) □ 她给对象织了一件毛衣。**Tā gěi duìxiàng zhīle yí jiàn máoyī.** *She knitted a woolen sweater for her fiancé.*

毛 2 **máo** measure wd Same as 角 **jiǎo** 2 *measure wd.* Used colloquially.

髦 **máo** long hair (See 时髦 **shímáo**)

矛 **máo** *n* spear, lance

矛盾 **máodùn** [comp: 矛 spear + 盾 shield] **I** *n* contradiction, conflict □ 他们之间有很大的矛盾。**Tāmen zhījiān yǒu hěn dà de máodùn.** *There is a big rift between them.* **II** *adj* contradictory, inconsistent

自相矛盾 **zìxiāng máodùn** self-contradictory, inconsistent □ 这篇文章前后自相矛盾。**Zhè piān wénzhāng qiánhòu zìxiāng máodùn.** *This article is inconsistent in its argument.*

NOTE: 矛盾 **máodùn** is a colorful word derived from an ancient Chinese fable. A man who sold spears (矛 **máo**) and shields (盾 **dùn**) boasted that his spears were so sharp

that they could penetrate any shield, and that his shields were so strong that no spear could ever penetrate them. As there seemed to be a contradiction there, 矛盾 **máodùn** came to mean *inconsistency* or *contradiction*.

茅 **máo** *n* cogongrass
茅屋 **máowū** *n* thatched cottage (间 **jiān**)

茂 **mào** *adj* luxuriant
茂密 **màomì** [comp: 茂 luxuriant + 密 dense] *adj* (of vegetation) luxuriant, thick, dense
茂盛 **màoshèng** [comp: 茂 luxuriant + 盛 thriving] *adj* (of vegetation) luxuriant, lush

冒 **mào** *v* 1 emit, send forth, give off □ 开水冒着热气。 **Kāishuǐ màozhe rè qì.** *Boiling water gives off steam.* 2 risk 3 make false claims
冒牌 **màopái** [v+obj: 冒 falsely claim + 牌 brand] *v* counterfeit, forge
冒牌货 **màopáihuò** (goods) counterfeit, fake, forgery
冒险 **màoxiǎn** [v+obj: 冒 risk + 险 danger] *v* risk, take a risk

帽 **mào** *n* hat, cap
帽子 **màozi** hat, cap (顶 **dǐng**)
戴帽子 **dài màozi** put on/wear a hat (or a cap) □ 今天外面很冷, 你要戴帽子。 **Jīntiān wàimiàn hěn lěng. Nǐ yào dài màozi.** *It's very cold outside. You'd better wear a hat.*
脱帽子 **tuō màozi** take off a hat (or a cap)

贸 **mào** Trad 貿 *n* trade
贸易 **màoyì** [comp: 贸 trade + 易 exchange] *n* trade, exchange □ 搞制造和搞贸易, 那个更赚钱? **Gǎo zhìzào hé gǎo màoyì, nǎge gèng zhuànqián?** *Manufacturing or trade, which is more profitable?*
贸易公司 **màoyì gōngsī** trading company
对外贸易 **duìwài màoyì** foreign trade
国际贸易 **guójì màoyì** international trade

貌 **mào** *n* appearance (See 礼貌 **lǐmào**, 面貌 **miànmào**.)

么 **me** Trad 麽 *particle* (used to form certain words) (See 多么 **duōme**, 那么 **nàme**, 什么 **shénme**, 为什么 **wèishénme**, 怎么 **zěnme**, 怎么样 **zěnmeyàng**, 这么 **zhème**.)

眉 **méi** *n* eyebrow
眉毛 **méimao** eyebrow

没 **méi** *adj* Same as 没有 **méiyǒu**, used colloquially.
没错 **méicuò** *adj* quite right
没关系 **méi guānxi** See 关系 **guānxi**.
没什么 **méishénme** *idiom* nothing serious, it doesn't matter □ "你不舒服吗?" "没什么, 就是有点儿头疼。" **"Nǐ bù shūfu ma?" "Méishénme, jiùshì yǒudiǎnr tóuténg."** *"Aren't you feeling well?" "Nothing serious, just a bit of headache."* □ "对不起, 我这么晚打电话给你。" "没什么, 有什么事吗?" **"Duìbuqǐ, wǒ zhème wǎn dǎ diànhuà gei nǐ." "Méishénme, yǒu shénme shì ma?"** *"I'm sorry for ringing you so late." "It doesn't matter. What can I do for you?"*
没说的 **méishuōde** *adj* above reproach, perfect
没意思 **méi yìsi** See 意思 **yìsi**.
没用 **méiyòng** *adj* useless □ 这本词典太旧, 没用了。 **Zhè běn cídiǎn tài jiù, méiyòng le.** *That dictionary is too old and is no longer useful.* □ 他这个人太没用了, 连一个小孩都对付不了。 **Tā zhège rén tài méiyòng le,**

连一个小孩都对付不了。 *That man is really useless. He can't even deal with a child.*
没有 **méiyǒu** I *v* 1 do not have □ 我没有这么多钱。 **Wǒ méiyǒu zhème duō qián.** *I don't have that much money.* □ 他没有兄弟, 只有一个姐姐。 **Tā méiyǒu xiōngdì, zhǐyǒu yí ge jiějie.** *He has no brothers, only an elder sister.* 2 there is/are no □ 房间里没有人。 **Fángjiān li méiyǒu rén.** *There is nobody in the room.* □ 这条街上没有饭店。 **Zhè tiáo jiē shang méiyǒu fàndiàn.** *There is no restaurant on this street.* II *adv* did not, have not (indicating negation of past experiences, usually used before a verb or at the end of a question) □ 我没有学过这个字。 **Wǒ méiyǒu xuéguo zhège zì.** *I haven't learned this Chinese character.*
还没有 **hái méiyǒu** not yet □ "你去过中国没有?" "还没有。" **"Nǐ qùguo Zhōngguó méiyǒu?" "Hái méiyǒu."** *"Have you ever been to China?" "Not yet."*

NOTE: In spoken Chinese, 没有 **méiyǒu** is often shortened to 没 **méi**. However, when 没有 **méiyǒu** is used at the end of a question, it cannot be replaced by 没 **méi**. For example, you can say: 你去过中国没有? **Nǐ qùguo Zhōngguó méiyǒu?** but not 你去过中国没? **Nǐ qùguo Zhōngguó méi?**

枚 **méi** *measure wd* (for small objects, such a coin)
一枚硬币 **yìméi yìngbì** a coin

玫 **méi** as in 玫瑰 **méigui**
玫瑰 **méigui** *n* rose (朵 **duǒ**)
两朵玫瑰花 **liǎng duǒ méiguihuā** two roses
一束玫瑰花 **yí shù méiguihuā** a bouquet of roses

煤 **méi** *n* coal □ 这个国家不产煤。 **Zhège guójiā bù chǎn méi.** *This country does not produce coal.*
煤矿 **méikuàng** coal mine
煤矿工 **méikuànggōng** coal miner, collier
煤气 **méiqì** coal gas
煤田 **méitián** coalfield

媒 **méi** *n* 1 matchmaking
媒人 **méirén** matchmaker 2 go-between, intermediary
媒介 **méijiè** *n* medium
媒体 **méitǐ** *n* medium
大众媒体 **dàzhòng méitǐ** mass media

梅 **méi** *n* plum tree
梅花 **méihuā** plum blossom

NOTE: 梅花 **méihuā** is unique to China, as you cannot find this flower in other parts of the world. Therefore, though conventionally translated as *plum*, it is actually not the same thing.

酶 **méi** *n* enzyme

霉 **méi** *n* mold, mildew
发霉 **fā méi** go moldy

每 **měi** I *adv* every, each □ 我每隔三天游一次泳。 **Wǒ měi gé sān tiān yóu yí cì yǒng.** *I swim once every three days.* □ 卡车司机每工作两天, 休息一天。 **Kǎchē sījī měi gōngzuò liǎng tiān, xiūxi yì tiān.** *The truck drivers have a day off after working for two days.* II *pron* every, each □ 你每天都看电视新闻吗? **Nǐ měitiān dōu kàn diànshì xīnwén ma?** *Do you watch*

TV news everyday? □ 这条街每座房子都不一样。**Zhè tiáo jiē měi zuò fángzi dōu bù yíyàng.** *Every house on this street is different from the other.*

NOTE: Usage in Chinese requires that 每 **měi** is followed by 都 **dōu** all, without exception.

美 **měi** *adj* beautiful □ 这里的风景真美! **Zhèli de fēngjǐng zhēn měi!** *The scenery here is truly beautiful!* □ 她从小就是个美人儿。**Tā cóngxiǎo jiù shì ge měirénr.** *She has been a beauty since childhood.*

美德 **měidé** [modif: 美 beautiful + 德 virtue] *n* virtue, moral excellence

美观 **měiguān** [modif: 美 beautiful + 观 looking] *adj* pleasing to the eye

美国 **Měiguó** *n* the U.S.A., America □ 中国和美国离得很远。**Zhōngguó hé Měiguó lí de hěn yuǎn.** *China and the U.S. are far apart.*

美好 **měihǎo** [comp: 美 beautiful + 好 fine] *adj* (of abstract things) fine, beautiful □ 我有一个美好的愿望。**Wǒ yǒu yí ge měihǎo de yuànwàng.** *I have a beautiful aspiration.* □ 世界上的事物并不都象人们希望的那样美好。**Shìjiè shang de shìwù bìng bù dōu xiàng rénmen xīwàng de nàyàng měihǎo.** *Things in the world are not all as fine as people wish them to be.*

美丽 **měilì** [comp: 美 beautiful + 丽 beautiful] *adj* beautiful □ 春天各种颜色的花儿都开放了, 花园真美丽。**Chūntiān gè zhǒng yánsè de huār dōu kāifàng le, huāyuán zhēn měilì.** *In spring with flowers of all colors in full bloom, the garden is beautiful.*

美满 **měimǎn** [comp: 美 beautiful + 满 full, totally satisfied] *adj* (of marriage, family, etc.) totally satisfactory, happy □ 她有美满的家庭、成功的事业, 真是太幸福了。**Tā yǒu měimǎn de jiātíng, chénggōng de shìyè, zhēnshì tài xìngfú le.** *She has a happy family and a successful career. What a fortunate woman!*

美妙 **měimiào** [comp: 美 beautiful + 妙 wonderful] *adj* wonderful, splendid

美容 **měiróng** I *v* make one's skin and face more beautiful II *n* comestics

美容师 **měiróngshī** beautician

美容院 **měiróngyuàn** beauty salon, beauty parlor

美术 **měishù** [modif: 美 beautiful + 术 craft] *n* fine arts □ 她对美术非常感兴趣。**Tā duì měishù fēicháng gǎn xìngqù.** *She has a great interest in the fine arts.*

美术馆 **měishùguǎn** gallery, art museum

美术家 **měishùjiā** artist

美元 **Měiyuán** [modif: 美 American + 元 dollar] *n* U.S. dollar, greenback □ 我想换一些美元。**Wǒ xiǎng huàn yìxiē Měiyuán.** *I want to change some money into American dollars.*

美中不足 **měizhōngbùzú** *idiom* a blemish in something otherwise perfect

美洲 **Měizhōu** [modif: 美 America + 洲 continent] *n* continent of America, America

镁 **měi** Trad 鎂 *n* magnesium (Mg)

妹 **mèi** *n* younger sister

妹妹 **mèimei** younger sister □ 我妹妹还在念小学呢。**Wǒ mèimei háizài niàn xiǎoxué ne.** *My younger sister is still in primary school.* □ 去年夏天我教妹妹游泳。**Qùnián xiàtiān wǒ jiāo mèimei yóuyǒng.** *Last summer I taught my younger sister to swim.*

昧 **mèi** *adj* ignorant (See 愚昧 **yúmèi**)

闷 **mēn** Trad 悶 *adj* stuffy, close

门 1 **mén** Trad 門 *n* door, gate (道 **dào**) □ 我们学校的大门正对汽车站。**Wǒmen xuéxiào de dàmén zhèng duì qìchē zhàn.** *There is a bus stop directly opposite the gate of our school.*

大门 **dàmén** gate

门口 **ménkǒu** [modif: 门 door/gate + 口 mouth] *n* doorway, by the door, by the gate □ 他站在门口等一个朋友。**Tā zhàn zài ménkǒu děng yí ge péngyou.** *He's standing by the door, waiting for a friend.*

门市部 **ménshìbù** *n* sales department

门诊 **ménzhěn** *n* outpatient service

门诊部 **ménzhěnbù** outpatient department (of a hospital)

门 2 **mén** Trad 門 *measure wd* (for school subjects, languages, etc.) □ 你今年念几门课? **Nǐ jīnnián niàn jǐ mén kè?** *How many subjects do you study this year?* □ 要学会一门语言, 非下功夫不可。**Yào xuéhuì yì mén yǔyán, fēi xià gōngfu bùkě.** *To learn a language, you simply must make great efforts.*

闷 **mèn** Trad 悶 *adj* in low spirits, lonely, depressed

们 **men** Trad 們 *suffix* (indicating plural number) □ 学生们都很喜欢这位新老师。**Xuéshengmen dōu hěn xǐhuan zhè wèi xīn lǎoshī.** *All the students like this new teacher.*

NOTE: As a plural number marker, 们 **men** is only used with nouns denoting people. It is not used when there are words indicating plurality, such as numbers or words like 一些 **yìxiē**, 很多 **hěn duō**. In many cases, the plural number of a personal noun is implicit without the use of 们 **men**. In the example sentence, 们 **men** is not obligatory, i.e. 学生都很喜欢这位新老师。**Xuésheng dōu hěn xǐhuan zhè wèi xīn lǎoshī.** *All the students like this new teacher.* is correct and idiomatic.

蒙 **méng** *v* cover

檬 **méng** as in 柠檬 **níngméng**

萌 **méng** *v* sprout

萌芽 **méngyá** *v* sprout, bud, shoot forth

盟 **méng** *n* alliance

结盟 **jiéméng** forge an alliance, form an alliance

盟国 **méngguó** *n* ally (country)

猛 **měng** *adj* fierce, violent

猛烈 **měngliè** *adj* fierce, furious

梦 **mèng** Trad 夢 I *n* dream □ 我昨天夜里做了一个奇怪的梦。**Wǒ zuótiān yèli zuòle yí ge qíguài de mèng.** *I had a strange dream last night.*

做梦 **zuòmèng** have a dream

II *v* dream, have a dream

梦想 **mèngxiǎng** [comp: 梦 dream + 想 think] *v* dream of, have a pipe dream

眯 **mī** *v* narrow one's eyes

迷 **mí** *v* be lost, be deluded
迷糊 **míhu** [comp: 迷 be lost + 糊 muddle] *adj* **1** (of vision) blurred **2** muddle-headed
迷惑 **míhuò** *v* **1** puzzle, be puzzled **2** delude, be deluded
迷失 **míshī** [迷 be lost + 失 be lost] *v* lose one's bearings
迷失方向 **míshī fāngxiàng** lose one's bearings
迷信 **míxìn** *n* superstition

谜 **mí** Trad 謎 *n* riddle
谜语 **míyǔ** *n* riddle
猜谜语 (猜谜) **cāi míyǔ (cāi mí)** guess a riddle □ 我给你猜一个谜语。**Wǒ gěi nǐ cāi yí ge míyǔ.** *Can you guess my riddle?*

弥 **mí** Trad 彌 *adj* full, overflowing
弥补 **míbǔ** *v* make up, remedy
弥漫 **mímàn** *adj* fill (the air)

米 1 **mǐ** *measure wd* meter (colloquial)
一米 **yì mǐ** one meter
三米半 **sān mǐ bàn** three and half meters.

NOTE: The formal word for meter is 公尺 **gōngchǐ**.

米 2 **mǐ** *n* rice, paddy rice (粒 **lì**) □ 在中国南方，很多农民种米。**Zài Zhōngguó nánfāng, hěn duō nóngmín zhòng mǐ.** *In South China many farmers grow rice.*
米饭 **mǐfàn** [comp: 米 rice + 饭 meal] *n* cooked rice (碗 **wǎn**) □ 米饭煮好了，菜还没有做好。**Mǐfàn zhǔ hǎo le, cài hái méiyǒu zuò hǎo.** *The rice is cooked, but the dishes are not ready yet.* □ 王家是南方人，每天都吃米饭。**Wáng jiā shì nánfāngrén, měitiān dōu chī mǐfàn.** *The Wangs are southerners. They eat rice every day.* □ 外国人煮的米饭，中国人往往不爱吃。**Wàiguórén zhǔ de mǐfàn, Zhōngguórén wǎngwǎng bú ài chī.** *A Chinese person usually does not like the cooked rice prepared by a foreigner.*

NOTE: The staple food for southern Chinese (Chinese living south of the Yangtze River) is 米饭 **mǐfàn**, while northern Chinese mainly eat 面食 **miànshí** (food made of wheat flour), such as 面条儿 **miàntiáor** (noodles) and 馒头 **mántou** (steamed buns).

米酒 **mǐjiǔ** *n* rice wine
秘 **mì** *adj* secret
秘密 **mìmì** [comp: 秘 secret + 密 confidential] **I** *n* secret □ "我告诉你一个秘密。" "要是你能告诉我，那就不是秘密。" **"Wǒ gàosù nǐ yí ge mìmì." "Yàoshi nǐ néng gàosù wǒ, nà jiù bú shì mìmì."** *"I'll tell you a secret." "If you can tell me, then it's not really a secret."* **II** *adj* secret, confidential □ 她有一个秘密信箱。**Tā yǒu yí ge mìmì xìnxiāng.** *She has a secret post office box.*
秘密警察 **mìmì jǐngchá** secret police
秘密文件 **mìmì wénjiàn** classified document
秘书 **mìshū** *n* secretary □ 要当秘书，一定要打字打得好。**Yào dāng mìshū, yídìng yào dǎzì dǎ de hǎo.** *To be a secretary, one must have good typing skills.* □ 他要秘书通知小王马上来见他。**Tā yào mìshū tōngzhī Xiǎo Wáng mǎshàng lái jiàn tā.** *He wants his secretary to inform Xiao Wang to come and see him immediately.*

私人秘书 **sīrén mìshū** private secretary

泌 **mì** *v* secrete (See 分泌 **fēnmì**)

密 **mì** *adj* close, dense
密度 **mìdù** [modif: 密 dense + 度 degree] *n* density, thickness
密封 **mìfēng** [modif: 密 dense + 封 seal] *v* seal, seal up
密切 **mìqiè** [comp: 密 close + 切 intimate] *adj* close, intimate □ 这家人家的兄弟姐妹关系很密切。**Zhè jiā rénjiā de xiōng-dì-jiě-mèi guānxi hěn mìqiè.** *The siblings in this family are very close to each other.* □ 公司各部门要密切配合，不能自行其是。**Gōngsī gè bùmén yào mìqiè pèihé, bù néng zì xíng qí shì.** *The departments in a company should be closely coordinated, and not act as they think fit.*

蜜 **mì** *n* honey
蜜蜂 **mìfēng** [modif: 蜜 honey + 蜂 wasp] *n* bee (只 **zhī**) □ 他养蜜蜂为生。**Tā yǎng mìfēng wéishēng.** *He makes a living by beekeeping.*

棉 **mián** *n* cotton
棉花 **miánhua** [modif: 棉 cotton + 花 bloom] *n* cotton □ 中国是棉花进口国，还是棉花出口国? **Zhōngguó shì miánhua jìnkǒuguó, háishì miánhua chūkǒuguó?** *Is China a cotton importer or cotton exporter?*
棉衣 **miányī** *n* cotton-padded jacket (件 **jiàn**)
棉大衣 **miándàyī** cotton-padded overcoat

绵 **mián** Trad 綿 *n* silk floss
绵羊 **miányáng** sheep (只 **zhī**)

眠 **mián** *v* sleep (See 睡眠 **shuìmián**)

免 **miǎn** *v* avoid, do without
免除 **miǎnchú** *v* be free from, be exempt from
免得 **miǎnde** *conj* so as not to, lest □ 你要早作准备，免得临时匆忙。**Nǐ yào zǎo zuò zhǔnbèi, miǎnde línshí cōngmáng.** *You should start preparing early, so as not to be in a hurry when the time comes.*
免费 **miǎnfèi** [v+obj: 免 do without + 费 fee, payment] *adj* free of charge, free □ 世界上没有免费的午餐。**Shìjièshang méiyǒu miǎnfèi de wǔcān.** *There is no free lunch in the world.*

勉 **miǎn** *v* **1** strive **2** encourage, exhort **3** force
勉励 **miǎnlì** *v* encourage, urge
勉强 **miǎnqiáng** **I** *adv* grudgingly, barely □ 他勉强应了我的要求。**Tā miǎnqiáng dāyìngle wǒ de yāoqiú.** *He yielded to my demand grudgingly.* □ 他的理由很勉强。**Tā de lǐyóu hěn miǎnqiáng.** *His justifications are not at all convincing.* **II** *v* force to do □ 他不愿去，你就别勉强他。**Tā bú yuàn qù, nǐ jiù bié miǎnqiáng tā.** *If he's unwilling to go, don't force him to.* □ 你真的不想学下去，就别勉强了。**Nǐ zhēnde bù xiǎng xuéxiàqu, jiù bié miǎnqiáng le.** *If you really don't want to go on studying, then don't force yourself to.*

面 1 **miàn** *n* **1** face **2** (maths) surface □ 你们俩有矛盾，还是面对面地谈一下吧。**Nǐmen liǎ yǒu máodùn, háishì miàn-duì-miàn de tán yíxià ba.** *If there is conflict between the two of you, you'd better discuss it face to face.*
面对 **miànduì** *v* be faced with
面对一个复杂的问题 **miànduì yí ge fùzá de wèntí** be faced with a complicated problem
面积 **miànjī** *n* (mathematics) area □ 这个房间的面积

是二十平方公尺。**Zhège fángjiān de miànjī shì èrshí píngfāng gōngchǐ.** *This room has an area of 20 square meters.*

面孔 miànkǒng *n* (human) face, facial features

面临 miànlín *v* be faced with, be up against
面临新的挑战 miànlín xīn de tiǎozhàn be up against a new challenge

面貌 miànmào [comp: 面 face + 貌 looks, appearance] *n* appearance, state (of things) □ 改革以来, 社会上出现了新面貌。**Gǎigé yǐlái, shèhuì shang chūxiànle xīn miànmào.** *Since the reform, society has taken on a new look.*

面面俱到 miànmiànjùdào *idiom* cover every aspect (of a matter)

面目 miànmù [comp: 面 face + 目 eye] *n* appearance, look

面前 miànqián *n* in the face of, in front of, before □ 在我们面前摆着两种选择。**Zài wǒmen miànqián bǎizhe liǎng zhǒng xuǎnzé.** *We are faced with two choices.*

面容 miànróng *n* facial features

面子 miànzi *n* face, honor
爱面子 ài miànzi be keen on face-saving
丢面子 diū miànzi lose face
给…留面子 gěi…liú miànzi save face (for somebody)

面 2 **miàn** Trad 麵 *n* 1 (面条儿 **miàntiáor**) noodle
方便面 fāngbiàn miàn instant noodles □ 他中饭常常只吃一碗方便面。**Tā zhōngfàn chángcháng zhǐ chī yì wǎn fāngbiànmiàn.** *He often only has a bowl of instant noodles for lunch.*
2 wheat flour
和面 huómiàn knead dough

面包 miànbāo [modif: 面 wheat flour + 包 lump] *n* bread (片 **piàn**, 只 **zhī**, 条 **tiáo**) □ 新做的面包特别香。**Xīn zuò de miànbāo tèbié xiāng.** *Freshly baked bread smells particularly good.*
一片面包 yípiàn miànbāo a slice of bread

面包车 miànbāochē [modif: 面包 bread + 车 vehicle] *n* minibus, van (辆 **liàng**)

面包房 miànbāo fáng bakery

面粉 miànfěn *n* flour

面条儿 miàntiáor *n* noodles (碗 **wǎn**) □ 面条儿要热的才好吃。**Miàntiáor yào rè de cái hǎochī.** *Noodles must be eaten hot.* □ 她是北方人, 面条儿做得好, 米饭做不好。**Tā shì běifāngrén, miàntiáor zuò de hǎo, mǐfàn zuò de bù hǎo.** *She's a northerner. She makes good noodle meals, but doesn't cook rice well.* □ 简单点, 做碗面条儿就行。**Jiǎndān diǎn, zuò wǎn miàntiáor jiù xíng.** *Let's keep it simple. Just a bowl of noodles will do.*

面 3 **miàn** *measure wd* (for flat objects)
一面镜子 yí miàn jìngzi a mirror
两面旗子 liǎng miàn qízi two flags

苗 miáo *n* seedling

描 miáo *v* trace, copy

描绘 miáohuì [comp: 描 trace + 绘 paint] *v* depict, describe

描述 miáoshù [comp: 描 trace + 述 narrate] *v* describe, give an account of

描写 miáoxiě [comp: 描 trace + 写 write] *v* describe (in writing) □ 她在信中描写了那里的美丽风景。**Tā**

zài xìn zhōng miáoxiěle nàli de měilì fēngjǐng. *In her letter she gives a description of the beautiful landscape there.*

秒 miǎo *measure wd* (of time) second □ 我跑一百公尺要十四秒, 你呢? **Wǒ pǎo yìbǎi gōngchǐ yào shísì miǎo, nǐ ne?** *It takes me 14 seconds to run 100 meters. How about you?*

渺 miǎo *adj* distant and indistinct
渺小 miǎoxiǎo *adj* tiny, insignificant

妙 miào *adj* wonderful, ingenious □ 你的主意真妙! **Nǐ de zhǔyi zhēn miào!** *What a wonderful idea!*
不妙 búmiào not good, unpromising □ 这两天情况不妙。**Zhè liǎngtiān qíngkuàng búmiào.** *Things are not good these days.*

妙不可言 miào bùkěyán *idiom* so wonderful as to beg description

庙 miào Trad 廟 *n* temple (座 **zuò**) □ 在中国的名胜, 常常有一座古庙。**Zài Zhōngguó de míngshèng, chángcháng yǒu yí zuò gǔ miào.** *Among the scenic spots in China, there is often an ancient temple.*

灭 miè Trad 滅 *v* extinguish, put out, go out □ 火灭了。**Huǒ miè le.** *The fire was extinguished.*

灭火器 mièhuǒqì *n* fire extinguisher

灭亡 mièwáng *v* exterminate, be exterminated, become extinct

蔑 miè *v* disdain, smear
蔑视 mièshì *v* look upon with contempt

民 mín *n* 1 people 2 civilian

民兵 mínbīng [comp: 民 people + 兵 soldier] *n* militia

民航 mínháng [modif: 民 civilian + 航 aviation] *n* civil aviation

民间 mínjiān *adj* 1 among common folks
民间故事 mínjiān gùshi folk tale
2 people-to-people
民间往来 mínjiān wǎnglái people-to-people exchange

民生 mínshēng [modif: 民 people's + 生 life, living] *n* the people's (economic) life, economy

民事 mínshì [modif: 民 people + 事 matter] *adj* (of law) civil
民事案件 mínshì ànjiàn civil case

民意 mínyì [modif: 民 people + 意 opinion] *n* the will of the masses
民意调查 mínyì diàochá opinion poll

民用 mínyòng *adj* for civilian use

民众 mínzhòng *n* the masses of the people

民主 mínzhǔ I *n* democracy □ 世界上发达国家都实行真正的政治民主。**Shìjiè shang fādá guójiā dōu shíxíng zhēnzhèng de zhèngzhì mínzhǔ.** *All the developed countries in the world practice genuine political democracy.* II *adj* democratic □ 没有民主的制度, 不可能长期稳定。**Méiyǒu mínzhǔ de zhìdù, bù kěnéng chángqī wěndìng.** *There can be no long-term stability without a democratic system.*

NOTE: 民主 mínzhǔ literally means *the people rule.* The word-formation is "subject + predicate," which is fairly uncommon.

民族 mínzú [comp: 民 people + 族 clan] *n* ethnic group, nationality (个 **gè**) □ 汉民族是中国最大的民族。**Hàn mínzú shì Zhōngguó zuì dà de mínzú.** *The*

Hans are the biggest ethnic group in China. □ 你们国家有多少个民族? **Nǐmen guójiā yǒu duōshǎo ge mínzú?** *How many ethnic groups are there in your country?*

少数民族 **shǎoshù mínzú** minority ethnic group

多民族文化 **duō mínzú wénhuà** multiculturalism

敏 **mǐn** *adj* quick, agile

敏感 **mǐngǎn** *adj* sensitive

敏捷 **mǐnjié** *adj* agile, nimble

敏锐 **mǐnruì** [comp: 敏 quick + 锐 sharp] *adj* alert, sharp-witted

名¹ **míng** *n* **1** name □ 你记得他家的那条街名吗? **Nǐ jìdé tā jiā de nà tiáo jiē míng ma?** *Do you remember the name of the street where his home is?* **2** (personal) given name □ 他们要给新生儿取个名。 **Tāmen yào gěi xīnshēngér qǔ ge míng.** *They're going to name their newborn baby.* □ 我姓张，名大华。 **Wǒ xìng Zhāng, míng Dàhuá.** *My family name is Zhang, and my given name Dahua.* **3** reputation

出名 **chūmíng** become famous

国名 **guómíng** name of a country

名² **míng** *measure wd* (used for people, especially those with a specific position or occupation)

一名军人 **yì míng jūnrén** a soldier

两名学生 **liǎng míng xuésheng** two students

名称 **míngchēng** *n* (non-personal) name

公司的名称 **gōngsī de míngchēng** company name

名单 **míngdān** [modif: 名 name + 单 list] *n* name list, roll (张 zhāng, 份 fèn)

学生名单 **xuésheng míngdān** class roll

名额 **míng'é** *n* the number of people assigned or allowed for a particular purpose, quota of people

大学招生名额 **dàxué zhāoshēng míng'é** university enrolment quota

名副其实 **míngfùqíshí** *idiom* be worthy of the name

名副其实的好老师 **míngfùqíshí de hǎo lǎoshī** a good teacher in every sense of the word

名贵 **míngguì** [comp: 名 famous + 贵 distinguished] *adj* precious, of great value

名牌 **míngpái** *n* famous brand, branded name

名人 **míngrén** *n* famous person, well-known personality

名声 **míngshēng** *n* reputation

破坏我们的名声 **pòhuài wǒmende míngshēng** smear our reputation

名胜 **míngshèng** *n* famous scenic spot □ 这个地区有很多名胜，每年吸引大批旅游者。 **Zhège dìqū yǒu hěn duō míngshèng, měi nián xīyǐn dàpī lǚyóuzhe.** *The area boasts many famous scenic spots and attracts large numbers of tourists every year.*

名义 **míngyì** *n* name, capacity

以我个人的名义 **yǐ wǒ gèrén de míngyì** in my own name

以总经理代表的名义 **yǐ zǒngjīnglǐ dàibiǎo de míngyì** in the capacity of the representative of the CEO

名誉 **míngyù** *n* reputation, honor

名誉博士 **míngyù bóshì** honorary doctorate

恢复名誉 **huīfù míngyù** restore one's honor

名字 **míngzi** [comp: 名 given name + 字 courtesy name] *n* name, given name □ 我的名字叫王小明。 **Wǒ de míngzi jiào Wáng Xiǎo Míng.** *My name is Wang Xiaoming.* □ "你知道他的名字吗?" "不知道。"

"**Nǐ zhīdào tā de míngzi ma?**" "**Bù zhīdào.**" *"Do you know his name?" "No."*

NOTE: To be exact, 名字 **míngzi** only means *given name*, but informally 名字 **míngzi** may also mean *full name* (family name + given name). The formal word for *full name* is 姓名 **xìngmíng**. See 姓 **xìng**.

明 **míng** *adj* bright

明白 **míngbai** [comp: 明 bright + 白 white] **I** *adj* clear, obvious □ 对不起，我没有说明白。 **Duìbuqǐ, wǒ méiyǒu shuō míngbai.** *Sorry, I didn't make it very clear.* **II** *v* understand, see the point □ 老师又解释了一遍，我才明白了。 **Lǎoshī yòu jiěshì yí biàn, wǒ cái míngbai le.** *I only understood after the teacher explained it again.* □ 我还不明白，能不能再说一遍。 **Wǒ hái bù míngbai, néng bu néng zài shuō yí biàn?** *I still don't understand. Could you say it again?*

明亮 **míngliàng** [comp: 明 bright + 亮 bright] *adj* bright, well-lit □ 这间房间很明亮，我很喜欢。 **Zhè jiān fángjiān hěn míngliàng, wǒ hěn xǐhuan.** *This room is very bright. I like it.*

明明 **míngmíng** *adv* clearly, obviously, as clear as day □ 你明明知道，为什么要说不知道? **Nǐ míngmíng zhīdào, wèishénme yàoshuō bùzhīdào?** *You obviously knew it, why did you say you didn't?*

明年 **míngnián** [modif: 明 (in this context) next + 年 year] *n* next year □ 明年我二十一岁了! **Míngnián wǒ èrshíyī suì le!** *I'll be twenty-one next year!*

NOTE: 明年 **míngnián** is next year relative only to this year 今年 **jīnnián**. For the year after another year, we use 第二年 **dì-èr nián** or 下一年 **xià yì nián**. For example □ 他们在2002年结婚，第二年生了一个儿子。 **Tāmen zài èr-líng-líng-èr nián jiéhūn, dì-èr nián shēngle yí ge érzi.** *They married in 2002 and had a son the following year.* It would be wrong to use 明年 **míngnián** in this example.

明确 **míngquè** [comp: 明 clear + 确 definite, specific] **I** *adj* definite and explicit □ 他说得很明确，本月十五日下午三点二十五分到达北京机场。 **Tā shuō de hěn míngquè, běnyuè shíwǔ rì xiàwǔ sān diǎn èrshíwǔ fēn dàodá Běijīng jīchǎng.** *He made it very clear—he will be arriving at Beijing Airport at 3:25 p.m. on the fifteenth of this month.* **II** *v* make definite and explicit □ 请你明确一下品种、数量和交货日期。 **Qǐng nǐ míngquè yíxià pǐnzhǒng, shùliàng hé jiāohuò rìqī.** *Please be definite about the product specifications, quantity and date of shipment.*

明天 **míngtiān** [modif: 明 (in this context) next + 天 day] *n* tomorrow □ "明天是几月几日?" "明天是六月二十一日。" "**Míngtiān shì jǐ yuè jǐ rì?**" "**Míngtiān shì Liùyuè èrshíyī rì.**" *"What date is tomorrow?" "It's June 21."* □ 我想睡觉了，这些作业明天再做吧。 **Wǒ xiǎng shuìjiào le, zhèxiē zuòyè míngtiān zài zuò ba.** *I want to go to bed. I'll do these assignments tomorrow.*

明显 **míngxiǎn** [comp: 明 clear + 显 showing] *adj* obvious, apparent, evident □ 你明显瘦了。 **Nǐ míngxiǎn shòu le.** *You've obviously lost weight.* □ 价格没有明显变化。 **Jiàgé méiyǒu míngxiǎn biànhuà.** *There has been no apparent change in prices.*

明信片 **míngxìnpiàn** *n* postcard (张 zhāng)

明星 míngxīng n movie star, star
体育明星 tǐyù míngxīng sports star
鸣 míng Trad 鳴 v (of bird) chirp, crow
耳鸣 ěrmíng ringing in the ears
命 mìng n 1 life 2 fate, destiny
命令 mìnglìng I n order □ 军人必须服从命令。 **Jūnrén bìxū fúcóng mìnglìng.** *A soldier must obey orders.* II v order □ 公司总部命令分公司立即关闭。 **Gōngsī zǒngbù mìnglìng fēngōngsī lìjí guānbì.** *The company's head office ordered immediate closure of the branch.*
命名 mìngmíng v give a name to, name
命题 mìngtí v set a question for an examination, assign a subject or topic for writing
命运 mìngyùn [comp: 命 destiny + 运 luck] n fate, destiny □ 他总是怪自己命运不好。 **Tā zǒngshì guài zìjǐ mìngyùn bù hǎo.** *He always blames his bad luck (← poor fate).* □ 有些传统的中国人相信出生的年、月、日、时决定一个人的命运。 **Yǒuxiē chuántǒng de Zhōngguórén xiāngxìn chūshēng de nián, yuè, rì, shí juédìng yí ge rén de mìngyùn.** *Some traditional Chinese believe that the year, month, date and hour of one's birth determines a person's fate.*
谬 miù adj mistaken, absurd
谬论 miùlùn [modif: 谬 mistaken + 论 theory] n fallacy, spurious argument
谬误 miùwù [modif: 谬 mistaken + 误 error] n mistake, error
摸 mō v 1 touch □ 请不要摸展览品。 **Qǐng bú yào mō zhǎnlǎnpǐn.** *Please do not touch the exhibits.* 2 grope
摸索 mōsuǒ [comp: 摸 grope + 索 search] v grope, search for, explore
模 mó I n model, copy II v imitate
模特儿（模特）mótèr (mótè) n (fashion) model
模范 mófàn n good example, model
模仿 mófǎng [comp: 模 mould + 仿 simulate] v imitate, ape, be a copycat □ 小明喜欢模仿爸爸讲话，而且模仿得很象。 **Xiǎo Míng xǐhuan mófǎng bàba jiǎnghuà, érqiě mófǎng de hěn xiàng.** *Xiao Ming likes to mimic his daddy, and he does it well.*
模型 móxíng n copy, model □ 我父亲在中学的时候喜欢装飞机模型。 **Wǒ fùqin zài zhōngxué de shíhou xǐhuan zhuāng fēijī móxíng.** *My father liked to assemble airplane models when he was a high school student.*
膜 mó n membrane
塑料薄膜 sùliào bómó plastic film
磨 mó v grind
磨刀 módāo sharpen a knife
2 rub, wear 3 waste time
磨时间 móshíjiān stall, kill time
磨洋工 móyánggōng idiom loaf during working hours, stage a slow-down
蘑 mó n mushroom
蘑菇 mógu mushroom
摩 mó v rub, scrape
摩擦 mócā [comp: 摩 rub + 擦 wipe] I v rub II n friction, clash
和同事发生摩擦 hé tóngshì fāshēng mócā generate friction among colleagues
摩托车 mótuōchē n motorcycle (辆 liàng) □ 开摩托车千万要小心，别开得太快。 **Kāi mótuōchē qiānwàn**

yào xiǎoxīn, bié kāi de tài kuài. *You should be very, very careful when riding a motorcycle. Don't ride too fast.*
魔 mó I n demon, monster II adj magic
魔鬼 móguǐ [comp: 魔 monster + 鬼 ghost] n monster, demon (个 gè)
魔术 móshù [modif: 魔 magic + 术 craft] n magic
魔术师 móshùshī magician
变魔术 biàn móshù do magic (as entertainment)
抹 mǒ v 1 apply by smearing 2 strike out, erase
抹杀 mǒshā v totally ignore (one's merit, achievement, etc.)
莫 mò v don't □ 莫谈国事。 **Mòtán guóshì.** *Do not talk about state affairs.* (→ *Do not talk about politics.*)
莫名其妙 mòmíng qímiào idiom be utterly baffled
漠 mò n desert (See 沙漠 shāmò.)
寞 mò adj silent, desolate (See 寂寞 jìmò)
末 mò n end (See 周末 zhōumò)
沫 mò n foam, froth
啤酒沫 píjiǔmò beer froth
肥皂沫 féizàomò soapsuds, lather
墨 mò n ink
墨水 mòshuǐ [modif: 墨 ink + 水 water] n ink □ 电脑打字很费墨水。 **Diànnǎo dǎzì hěn fèi mòshuǐ.** *Computer printing takes up lots of ink.*
默 mò adj silent
默默 mòmò adv quietly, silently
陌 mò adj path
陌生 mòshēng adj unfamiliar
陌生人 mòshēngrén stranger □ 很多小孩都知道不跟陌生人说话。 **Hěn duō xiǎohái dōu zhīdào bù gēn mòshēngrén shuōhuà.** *Many children know not to talk to a stranger.*
谋 móu Trad 謀 v plot, plan
谋害 móuhài v plot to murder
谋求 móuqiú [comp: 谋 plot + 求 seek] v seek, be in quest of
谋求最大利润 móuqiú zuìdà lìrùn seek the maximum profits
某 mǒu pron certain (used to denote an indefinite person or thing, usually in writing) □ 在该国某地发生森林大火。 **Zài gāiguó mǒu dì fāshēng sēnlín dàhuǒ.** *At a certain place in that country a forest fire broke out.*
某人 mǒurén n certain person, certain people, somebody
某事 mǒushì n certain thing or event, something
某些 mǒuxiē pron some, certain ones
模 mú n mould, matrix
模样 múyàng I n appearance, look II adv approximately, about
母 mǔ I adj 1 maternal, of a mother □ 孩子需要母爱。 **Háizi xūyào mǔ'ài.** *Children need maternal love.* 2 female (of certain animals) (antonym 公 gōng) □ 他们养了八只公鸡，二十多只母鸡。 **Tāmen yǎngle bā zhī gōngjī, èrshí duō zhī mǔ jī.** *They keep eight roosters and over twenty hens.* II n mother
母亲 mǔqin [modif: 母 mother + 亲 parent] n

mother □ 母亲在家照顾孩子。**Mǔqin zài jiā zhàogù háizi.** *Mother takes care of her children at home.* □ 你常常给母亲打电话吗? **Nǐ chángcháng gěi mǔqin dǎ diànhuà ma?** *Do you often give your mother a call?*
母亲节 **Mǔqinjié** Mother's Day
母性 **mǔxìng** *n* maternal instinct
母语 **mǔyǔ** *n* mother tongue □ 她英语说得这么好, 真让人不相信英语不是她的母语。**Tā Yīngyǔ shuō de zhème hǎo, zhēn ràng rén bù xiāngxìn Yīngyǔ bú shì tā de mǔyǔ.** *She speaks English so well that it's hard to believe that it isn't her mother tongue.*

姆 **mǔ** *n* woman tutor (See 保姆 **bǎomǔ**)

拇 **mǔ** *n* thumb
拇指 **mǔzhǐ** thumb

亩 **mǔ** Trad 畝 *measure wd* (a traditional Chinese unit of area, especially in farming: 1 *mu* is equivalent to 1/15 hectare, about 667 square meters)
十亩地 (田) **shí mǔ dì (tián)** 10 *mu* of ground (paddy fields/farmland)

木 **mù** *n* 1 Same as 木头 **mùtou** 2 tree □ 独木不成林。**Dú mù bù chéng lín.** *A single tree does not make a forest.* (→ *One swallow does not make a summer.*)
木材 **mùcái** *n* timber, wood
木匠 **mùjiang** *n* carpenter
木头 **mùtou** [suffix: 木 wood + 头 nominal suffix] *n* wood, timber □ 我喜欢木头家具。**Wǒ xǐhuan mùtou jiājù.** *I like wooden furniture.*

目 **mù** *n* eye
双目失明 **shuāngmù shīmíng** having lost sight in both eyes, be blind
目标 **mùbiāo** [modif: 目 eye + 标 target] *n* target, objective, goal □ 她的目标是五年内存十万元。**Tā de mùbiāo shì wǔ nián nèi cún shíwàn yuán.** *Her goal is to save a hundred thousand dollars in five years.*
目的 **mùdì** *n* aim, purpose □ 我们做市场调查的目的是更好地为顾客服务。**Wǒmen zuò shìchǎng diàochá de mùdì shì gèng hǎo de wèi gùkè fúwù.** *The purpose of our market investigation is to serve our customers more satisfactorily.*
目睹 **mùdǔ** *v* see with one's own eyes, witness
目光 **mùguāng** *n* sight, vision
目光远大 **mùguāng yuǎndà** farseeing, farsighted and ambitious
目录 **mùlù** *n* catalog
产品目录 **chǎnpǐn mùlù** product catalog
图书目录 **túshū mùlù** library catalog
目前 **mùqián** *n* at present □ 目前的困难是暂时的。**Mùqián de kùnnan shì zànshí de.** *The present difficulties are only temporary.*
目中无人 **mùzhōng wúrén** *idiom* believe no one is better than oneself; overweening, conceited and arrogant

暮 **mù** I *n* dusk, evening twilight II *adj* late
暮年 **mùnián** old age

慕 **mù** *v* admire
慕名 **mùmíng** *v* be attacted by somebody's reputation
慕名而来 **mùmíng érlái** come out of admiration

墓 **mù** *n* tomb
公墓 **gōngmù** cemetery

墓地 **mùdì** *n* graveyard

幕 **mù** *n* curtain, screen
谢幕 **xièmù** answer a curtain call

穆 **mù** *adj* solemn
穆斯林 **Mùsīlín** *n* Muslim

牧 **mù** I *v* herd (cattle, horses, etc.)
牧羊 **mùyáng** herd sheep
II *n* animal husbandry
牧场 **mùchǎng** [modif: 牧 herding + 场 ground] *n* grazing land, pastureland
牧民 **mùmín** *n* herdsmen
牧区 **mùqū** *n* pastoral area
牧业 **mùyè** *n* animal husbandry

睦 **mù** *adj* peaceful, harmonious
睦邻 **mùlín** *n* good neighborhood

N

拿 **ná** I *v* hold, carry in hand □ 我手里拿着很多书, 不能开门, 请你帮帮我。**Wǒ shǒu li názhe hěn duō shū, bù néng kāi mén, qǐng nǐ bāngbang wǒ.** *I'm holding lots of books and can't open the door. Please help me.* II *prep* regarding, as to
拿…来说 **ná...láishuō** *v* take … for example
拿手 **náshǒu** *adj* very good at, adept at
拿手好戏 **náshǒu hǎoxì** something that one is adept at, one's favorite game
拿主意 **ná zhǔyi** *v* make a decision □ 这件事你得自己拿主意。**Zhè jiàn shì nǐ děi zìjǐ ná zhǔyi.** *You've got to make a decision about this matter by yourself.*
拿走 **ná zǒu** *v* take away, remove □ 他已经不在这个办公室工作了, 不过东西还没拿走。**Tā yǐjīng bú zài zhège bàngōngshì gōngzuò le, búguò dōngxi hái méiyǒu názǒu.** *He no longer works in this office, but he has not removed his things.*

哪 **nǎ** *pron* 1 which □ 哪辆自行车是你的? **Nǎ liàng zìxíngchē shì nǐ de?** *Which bicycle is yours?* □ 这么多新车, 你说哪辆最漂亮? **Zhème duō xīn chē, nǐ shuō nǎ liàng zuì piàoliang?** *So many new cars, which do you think is the most attractive?* 2 whatever, whichever □ 这些鞋子, 我哪双都不喜欢。**Zhèxiē xiézi, wǒ nǎ shuāng dōu bù xǐhuan.** *I don't like any of the shoes here.* □ 下星期我都在家, 你哪天来都可以。**Xià xīngqī wǒ dōu zài jiā, nǐ nǎ tiān lái dōu kěyǐ.** *I'll be home all next week. You may come any day.*
哪里 **nǎli** [modif: 哪 which + 里 place] *adv* where □ 你住在哪里? **Nǐ zhù zài nǎli?** *Where do you live?*

NOTE: 哪里哪里 **nǎli nǎli** is an idiomatic expression used as a modest reply to a compliment, e.g. □ "你汉字写得真漂亮。" "哪里哪里。" **"Nǐ Hànzì xiě de zhēn piàoliang." "Nǎli, nǎli."** *"You write beautiful Chinese characters." "Thank you."*

哪怕 **nǎpà** *conj* even if, even though □ 哪怕卖掉房子, 王先生和王太太也要让孩子念大学。**Nǎpà màidiào fángzi, Wáng xiānsheng hé Wáng tàitai yěyào ràng háizi niàn dàxué.** *Even if they have to sell the house, Mr and Mrs Wang will put their child through uni-*

versity. □ 他总是完成每天的工作, 哪怕要开夜车。**Tā zǒngshì wánchéng měi tiān de gōngzuò, nǎpà yào kāi yèchē.** *He always finishes the day's work, even when he has to burn the midnight oil.*

NOTE: 哪怕 **nǎpà** introduces an exaggerated, rather unlikely situation to emphasize the statement of the sentence.

哪儿 **nǎr** *adv* Same as 哪里 **nǎli**. Used colloquially.

哪些 **nǎxiē** *pron* the plural form of 哪 **nǎ** □ 你想看哪些书? **Nǐ xiǎng kàn nǎxiē shū?** *Which books do you want to read?*

那 **nà** I *pron* that □ 这辆自行车是我的, 那辆自行车是我弟弟的。**Zhè liàng zìxíngchē shì wǒ de, nà liàng zìxíngchē shì wǒ dìdi de.** *This bike is mine. That one is my younger brother's.* □ "麻烦你帮我租一套房子。" "那不难。" **"Máfan nǐ bāng wǒ zū yí tào fángzi." "Nà bù nán."** *"Would you mind renting a house for me?" "That won't be a problem."* II Same as 那么 **nàme**

那个 **nàge** [modif: 那 that + 个 one] *pron* that one □ 那个不是我的, 我的在这里。**Nàge bú shì wǒ de, wǒ de zài zhèli.** *That one is not mine. Mine's here.*

那里 **nàli** [modif: 那 that + 里 place] *adv* there, over there □ 他在那里工作。**Tā zài nàli gōngzuò.** *He works there.* □ 那里就是图书馆。**Nàli jiù shì túshūguǎn.** *Over there is the library.*

NOTES: (1) 那里 **nàli** is used after a personal noun or pronoun to make it a place word, as a personal noun or pronoun cannot be used immediately after a preposition, e.g. 我从张小姐听到这个消息。**Wǒ cóng Zhāng xiǎojiě tīngdao zhège xiāoxi.** is incorrect. 那里 **nàli** must be added after 张小姐 **Zhāng xiǎojiě** (*Miss Zhang*): 我从张小姐那里听到这个消息。**Wǒ cóng Zhāng xiǎojiě nàli tīngdao zhège xiāoxi.** *I learned the news from Miss Zhang.* In this case 张小姐那里 **Zhāng xiǎojiě nàli** becomes a place word which can occur after the preposition 从 **cóng**. (2) Colloquially, 那儿 **nàr** may replace 那里 **nàli**.

那么 **nàme** I *adv* like that □ 上海没有北京那么冷。**Shànghǎi méiyǒu Běijīng nàme lěng.** *Shanghai is not as cold as Beijing.* □ 你那么做, 她会不高兴。**Nǐ nàme zuò, tā huì bù gāoxìng.** *If you behave like that, she'll be unhappy.* II *conj* in that case, then □ 你不喜欢吃米饭, 那么吃面包吧。**Nǐ bù xǐhuan chī mǐfàn, nàme chī miànbāo ba.** *You don't like rice; in that case eat bread.* (→ *Since you don't like rice, have bread instead.*) □ "去北京的飞机票全卖完了。" "那么, 我们就乘火车去吧。" **"Qù Běijīng de fēijī piào quán màiwán le." "Nàme, wǒmen jiù chéng huǒchē qù ba."** *"The air tickets to Beijing are sold out." "In that case, let's go by train."*

NOTE: Although 那么 **nàme** as a conjunction is glossed as *in that case, then*, Chinese speakers tend to use it much more than English speakers use "in that case" or "then." In colloquial Chinese 那么 **nàme** is often shortened to 那 **nà**, e.g. □ 你不喜欢吃米饭, 那吃面包吧。**Nǐ bù xǐhuan chī mǐfàn, nà chī miànbāo ba.** *You don't like rice; in that case eat bread.*

那儿 **nàr** *pron* Same as 那里 **nali**, used colloquially.

那些 **nàxiē** *pron* those □ 这些是中文书, 那些是英文书。**Zhèxiē shì Zhōngwén shū, nàxiē shì Yīngwén shū.** *These are Chinese books. Those are English books.*

那样 **nàyàng** *adv* Same as 那么 **nàme 1** *adv*

纳 **nà** *v* pay, offer
纳闷儿 **nàmènr** *v* be wondering (why, what, who, how, etc.), be perplexed
纳税 **nàshuì** *v* pay taxes
纳税人 **nàshuìrén** tax-payer

奶 **nǎi** *n* milk
奶粉 **nǎifěn** [modif: 奶 milk + 粉 powder] *n* milk powder
奶奶 **nǎinai** *n* paternal grandmother, granny □ 奶奶, 我上学去了! **Nǎinai, wǒ shàngxué qù le!** *Granny, I'm going to school!*

NOTE: The formal word for *paternal grandmother* is 祖母 **zǔmǔ** and that for *maternal grandmother* is 外祖母 **wàizǔmǔ**. While 奶奶 **nǎinai** is the colloquialism for 祖母 **zǔmǔ**, that for 外祖母 **wàizǔmǔ** is 姥姥 **lǎolao**, or 外婆 **wàipó**.

奶油 **nǎiyóu** [modif: 奶 milk + 油 oil] *n* cream
耐 **nài** *v* able to endure
耐烦 **nàifán** [v+obj: 耐 tolerate + 烦 irritation] *adj* patient □ 尽管顾客东挑西拣, 营业员也不能露出不耐烦的样子。**Jǐnguǎn gùkè dōng-tiāo-xī-jiǎn, yíngyèyuán yě bù néng lùchu bú nàifán de yàngzi.** *Even if the customer is very choosy, the shop assistant mustn't appear impatient.*

NOTE: 耐烦 **nàifán** is only used in its negative form, 不耐烦 **bú nàifán**.

耐力 **nàilì** [modif: 耐 endure + 力 strength] *n* endurance, staying power
耐心 **nàixīn** [modif: 耐 tolerate + 心 heart] I *adj* patient □ 他对孩子很有耐心。**Tā duì háizi hěn yǒu nàixīn.** *She is really patient with children.* □ 除了耐心地等待, 没有别的办法。**Chúle nàixīn de děngdài, méiyǒu biéde bànfǎ.** *There is nothing you can do except wait patiently.* II *n* patience □ 我看他快要没有耐心了。**Wǒ kàn tā kuài yào méiyǒu nàixīn le.** *I think he will soon run out of patience.*
耐用 **nàiyòng** *adj* durable □ 我们的产品很耐用。**Wǒmen de chǎnpǐn hěn nàiyòng.** *Our products are durable.* □ 这种牌子的手表很便宜, 但是不耐用。**Zhè zhǒng páizi de shǒubiǎo hěn piányi, dànshì bú nàiyòng.** *Watches of this brand are cheap but don't last long.*

男 **nán** *adj* (of humans) male (antonym 女 **nǔ**)
男孩子 **nán háizi** boy □ 那个男孩子是王先生的小儿子。**Nàge nán háizi shì Wáng xiānsheng de xiǎo érzi.** *That boy is Mr Wang's youngest son.*
男青年 **nán qīngnián** young man □ 昨天有一个男青年来找你。**Zuótiān yǒu yí ge nán qīngnián lái zhǎo nǐ.** *A young man came to see you yesterday.*
男人 **nánrén** man, men □ 男人能做的事, 女人也能做。**Nánrén néng zuò de shì, nǚrén yě néng zuò.** *What men can do, women also can.*
男生 **nánshēng** *n* male student/pupil

男性 **nánxìng** [modif: 男 male + 性 gender] *n* the male gender, male

男子 **nánzǐ** *n* male adult

大男子主义 **dànánzǐzhǔyì** male chauvinism

南 **nán** *n* south, southern (antonym 北 **běi**) □ 很多老年人喜欢住在南方。**Hěn duō lǎoniánrén xǐhuan zhù zài nánfāng.** *Many old people like to live in the south.*

南边 **nánbian** [modif: 南 south + 边 side] *n* south side, to the south, in the south □ "新西兰的南边还有什么国家吗？" "没有了。" **"Xīnxīlán de nánbian hái yǒu shénme guójiā ma?" "Méiyǒu le."** *"Is there any country to the south of New Zealand?" "No, there isn't."*

南部 **nánbù** [modif: 南 south + 部 part] *n* southern region (of a country)

南方 **nánfāng** *n* the southern part, the south of a country □ 中国的南方夏天一般很热。**Zhōngguó de nánfāng xiàtiān yìbān hěn rè.** *In southern China, summer is generally very hot.*

南方人 **nánfāngrén** southerner

南面 **nánmiàn** *n* Same as 南边 **nánbian**

难 **nán** Trad 難 *adj* difficult (antonym 容易 **róngyì**) □ 这道练习太难了，我不会做。**Zhè dào liànxí tài nán le, wǒ bú huì zuò.** *This exercise is too difficult. I can't do it.* □ 在这个政府部门，人难见，事难办。**Zài zhège zhèngfǔ bùmén, rén nán jiàn, shì nán bàn.** *In this government department, it is difficult to meet any officials or to get things done.*

难产 **nánchǎn** [modif: 难 difficult + 产 childbirth] difficult childbirth, difficult labor

难道 **nándào** *adv* (used at the beginning of a sentence or before a verb to make it a rhetorical question) □ 难道你不知道吗? **Nándào nǐ bù zhīdào ma?** *Didn't you know?* □ 他连旧车都买不起, 难道还买得起新车吗? **Tā lián jiù chē dōu mǎi bu qǐ, nándào hái mǎi de qǐ xīn chē ma?** *He can't even afford a second-hand car. How can he afford a new car?*

难得 **nándé** *adj* hard to come by, rare □ 这个机会很难得, 你别错过。**Zhège jīhuì hěn nándé, nǐ bié cuòguo.** *This is a rare opportunity; don't you miss it.*

难度 **nándù** [modif: 难 difficult + 度 degree] *n* degree of difficulty

难怪 **nánguài** *adv* no wonder

难关 **nánguān** [modif: 难 difficult + 关 pass] *n* critical moment, crisis

度过难关 **dùguò nán guān** go through a crisis

难过 **nánguò** *adj* sad, grieved (antonym 高兴 **gāoxìng**) □ 听到这个不幸的消息, 我们非常难过。**Tīngdào zhège búxìng de xiāoxi, wǒmen fēicháng nánguò.** *On hearing this unfortunate news, we were all very sad.*

NOTE: 难过 **nánguò** is usually used as a predicate, and seldom as an attribute.

难堪 **nánkān** *adj* embarrassed, embarrassing

难堪的局面 **nánkān de júmiàn** embarrassing situation, awkward plight

难看 **nánkàn** *adj* ugly (antonym 好看 **hǎokàn**) □ 他穿这件衣服真难看。**Tā chuān zhè jiàn yīfu zhēn nánkàn.** *He really looks ugly in that suit.*

难免 **nánmiǎn** *adj* hardly avoidable

难受 **nánshòu** *adj* 1 feeling ill, uncomfortable □ 他昨天晚上酒喝得太多, 今天早上头疼难受。**Tā zuótiān wǎnshang jiǔ hē de tài duō, jīntiān zǎoshang tóuténg nánshòu.** *He drank too much last night. This morning he had a headache and felt terrible (→ had a hangover).* □ 这双新鞋小了点儿, 穿着难受。**Zhè shuāng xīn xié xiǎole diǎnr, chuānzhe nánshòu.** *The new shoes are too small, and are uncomfortable to wear.* 2 feeling sorry, feeling bad/sad □ 我的错误给公司带来损失, 我心里很难受。**Wǒ de cuòwù gěi gōngsī dàilai sǔnshī, wǒ xīnlǐ hěn nánshòu.** *I feel bad that my mistake has caused loss to the company.*

难题 **nántí** *n* difficult issue, insoluble problem

难以 **nányǐ** *adv* difficult to

难以理解 **nányǐ lǐjiě** difficult to understand, incomprehensible

难 **nàn** Trad 難 *n* disaster, adversity

逃难 **táonàn** flee from war or natural disaster

难民 **nànmín** [modif: 难 disaster + 民 people] *n* refugee

难民营 **nànmínyíng** refugee camp

囊 **náng** *n* bag, pocket

挠 **náo** *v* scratch

挠痒痒 **náoyǎngyang** scratch at an itch

脑 **nǎo** Trad 腦 *n* brain

脑外科 **nǎo wàikē** brain surgery

脑袋 **nǎodai** [modif: 脑 brain + 袋 bag] *n* Same as 头 **tóu**. Used only colloquially and in a derogatory sense.

脑筋 **nǎojīn** *n* brains, mental capacity

动脑筋 **dòng nǎojīn** rack one's brains

脑力 **nǎolì** [modif: 脑 brain + 力 power] *n* brain power

脑力劳动 **nǎolì láodòng** mental work (antonym 体力劳动 **tǐlì láodòng** physical work, manual labor)

脑子 **nǎozi** [suffix: 脑 brain + 子 nominal suffix] *n* brain, mind □ 他怎么有这种想法? 脑子出问题了吧? **Tā zěnme yǒu zhè zhǒng xiǎngfǎ? Nǎozi chū wèntí le ba?** *How come he has such ideas? Something wrong with his mind?* (or *He must be out of his mind./He must be crazy.*)

动脑子 **dòng nǎozi** use brains □ 遇到难题, 要多动脑子, 总会找到解决的办法。**Yùdao nántí, yào duō dòng nǎozi, zǒnghuì zhǎodao jiějué de bànfǎ.** *When confronted with difficulties, use your brains and you will always find a solution.*

恼 **nǎo** *adj* irritated, vexed

恼火 **nǎohuǒ** *adj* annoyed, angry

闹 **nào** Trad 鬧 *v* make trouble, cause a disturbance □ 这几个孩子闹得我根本看不进书。**Zhè jǐ ge háizi nào de wǒ gēnběn kànbujìn shū.** *These kids raised such a ruckus that I could not concentrate on reading at all.* □ 别闹了, 邻居该来提意见了。**Bié nào le, línjū gāilái tí yìjiàn le.** *Stop making such a noise. The neighbors will come to complain.*

闹脾气 **nào píqi** *v* throw a tantrum

闹事 **nào shì** *v* make trouble, provoke a disturbance

闹笑话 **nào xiàohua** *v* make a fool of oneself, cut a ridiculous figure

呢 **ne** *particle* 1 (used at the end of a question to soften the tone of an enquiry) □ 你打算明年做

什么呢? **Nǐ dǎsuàn míngnián zuò shénme ne?** *What do you intend to do next year?* **2** How about ...? Where is (are) ...? □ 你们明天出去旅游, 孩子呢? **Nǐmen míngtiān chūqu lǚyóu, háizi ne?** *You're going on holiday tomorrow. How about the kids?* □ 小明, 你妈呢? **Xiǎo Míng, nǐ mā ne?** *Xiao Ming, where is your mom?*

邪 nèi Same as 那 **nà**. Used colloquially.

内 nèi *n* inside, within (antonym 外 **wài**) □ 房间内外都很干净。 **Fángjiān nèi wài dōu hěn gānjìng.** *The home is clean both inside and out.* □ 我一定在十天内还清借款。 **Wǒ yídìng zài shí tiān nèi huánqīng jièkuǎn.** *I will pay off the debt within ten days.*

内部 nèibù *n* interior, inside □ 展览会内部整理, 暂停对外开放。 **Zhǎnlǎnhuì nèibù zhěnglǐ, zàntíng duìwài kāifàng.** *The exhibition is temporarily closed for reorganization.*

内部资料 **nèibù zīliào** document for internal circulation (e.g. within a government department)

内地 nèidì [modif: 内 interior + 地 land] *n* the interior part (of a country), inland

内阁 nèigé *n* (government) cabinet

内行 nèiháng *n* expert, professional (antonym 外行 **wàiháng**)

内科 nèikē [modif: 内 inside + 科 department] *n* department of internal medicine (in a hospital)

内幕 nèimù *n* inside story

内容 nèiróng [modif: 内 inside + 容 contain] *n* content, substance □ 这本书的内容很丰富。 **Zhè běn shū de nèiróng hěn fēngfù.** *The book is rich in content.* □ 他说了半天, 但是没有什么内容。 **Tā shuōle bàntiān, dànshì méiyǒu shénme nèiróng.** *He talked for a long time but there wasn't much substance.* □ 王董事长讲话的主要内容是什么? **Wáng dǒngshìzhǎng jiǎnghuà de zhǔyào nèiróng shì shénme?** *What is the main idea behind Chairman Wang's talk?*

内心 nèixīn [modif: 内 inside + 心 the heart] *n* one's heart of hearts, one's inner world □ 她内心很矛盾。 **Tā nèixīn hěn máodùn.** *She suffers from conflicting thoughts.* (→ *She is torn by conflicting thoughts.*)

内在 nèizài [modif: 内 inner + 在 being] *adj* inherent, intrinsic (antonym 外在 **wàizài**)

内脏 nèizàng *n* internal organs

内战 nèizhàn *n* civil war

内政 nèizhèng *n* internal affairs, domestic affairs

干涉内政 **gānshè nèizhèng** interfere in the internal affairs (of another country)

嫩 nèn *adj* young and tender, tender □ 请你把牛肉做得嫩一点。 **Qǐng nǐ bǎ niúròu zuò de nèn yìdiǎn.** *Please make the beef tender.* (→ *Don't overcook the beef.*)

能 néng **I** *modal v* can, be able to □ 我今天不舒服, 不能去上班。 **Wǒ jīntiān bù shūfu, bù néng qù shàngbān.** *I'm unwell today and won't be able to go to work.* □ 这辆车加满汽油, 能跑多少公里? **Zhè liàng chē jiā mǎn qìyóu, néng pǎo duōshǎo gōnglǐ?** *How many kilometers can this car run on a full tank?* **II** *n* energy

NOTE: See note on 会 **huì** *modal verb*.

能干 nénggàn *adj* (of people) able, capable, efficient □ 他非常能干, 别人一星期做的工作, 他三天就完成了。 **Tā fēicháng nénggàn, biérén yì xīngqī zuò de gōngzuò, tā sān tiān jiù wánchéng le.** *He is very efficient. He can finish in three days what takes others a week to do.*

能歌善舞 nénggēshànwǔ *idiom* be good at singing and dancing

能够 nénggòu *modal v* Same as 能 **néng** *modal v*

能力 nénglì [comp: 能 ability + 力 strength] *n* ability □ 他能力比一般人强, 但是太骄傲了。 **Tā nénglì bǐ yìbān rén qiáng, dànshì tài jiāo'ào le.** *He is more capable than most people, but he is too conceited.* □ 我们要求职工有使用电脑的能力。 **Wǒmen yāoqiú zhígōng yǒu shǐyòng diànnǎo de nénglì.** *We require that our staff have computer competence.* (← *We require that our staff have the ability to use computers.*)

能量 néngliàng [modif: 能 ability + 量 amount] *n* energy, capabilities

能手 néngshǒu [modif: 能 able + 手 hand] *n* expert, dab hand

能源 néngyuán [modif: 能 energy + 源 source, resource] *n* energy resources □ 石油和煤总有用完的一天, 人类必须开发新能源。 **Shíyóu hé méi zǒngyǒu yòngwán de yìtiān, rénlèi bìxū kāifā xīn néngyuán.** *There will come a day when oil and coal are exhausted. Mankind must develop new energy resources.*

嗯 ng *interj* (used after a question to reinforce questioning) □ 你把自行车借给谁了, 嗯? **Nǐ bǎ zìxíngchē jiègei shuí le, ng?** *Who did you lend your bicycle to, eh?*

尼 ní *n* Buddhist nun

尼庵 **ní'ān** Buddhist nunnery

尼姑 **nígū** Buddhist nun

尼龙 **nílóng** *n* nylon

泥 ní *n* mud □ 他们在下雨天踢球, 搞得身上都是泥。 **Tāmen zài xiàyǔtiān tīqiú, gǎode shēnshang dōushì ní.** *They played soccer in the rain and got themselves all covered with mud.*

泥泞 nínìng *adj* muddy, miry

泥土 nítǔ *n* soil, earth, clay

拟 nǐ Trad 擬 *v* draw up, draft

拟订 **nǐdìng** *v* draw up, work out

拟订计划 **nǐdìng jìhuà** draw up a plan

你 nǐ *pron* you (singular) □ 你好! **Nǐ hǎo!** *How do you do? Hello!* □ 你好吗? **Nǐ hǎoma?** *How're you?* □ 你是谁? **Nǐ shì shuí?** *Who're you?*

你们 **nǐmen** [suffix: 你 you (singular) + 们 suffix denoting a plural number] *pron* you (plural) □ 你们都是我的朋友。 **Nǐmen dōu shì wǒ de péngyou.** *You all are my friends.* □ 我告诉你们一个好消息。 **Wǒ gàosu nǐmen yí ge hǎo xiāoxi.** *I'll tell you a piece of good news.*

逆 nì *adj* contrary, counter

逆流 **nìliú** [modif: 逆 contrary + 流 flow] *n* adverse current (of water)

年 nián *n* year (no measure word required) □ 一年有十二个月。 **Yì nián yǒu shí'èr ge yuè.** *There're twelve months in a year.* □ 我在美国住了两年。 **Wǒ zài Měiguó zhùle liǎng nián.** *I lived in the States for two years.*

今年 **jīnnián** this year

明年 **míngnián** next year

去年 **qùnián** last year

NOTE: No measure word is used with 年 **nián**, e.g. 一年 **yì nián** (one year), 两年 **liǎng nián** (two years), 三年 **sān nián** (three years).

年代 niándài [comp: 年 year + 代 age] *n* a decade of a century □ 我爸爸妈妈喜欢听〈二十世纪〉七十年代的歌。**Wǒ bàba māma xǐhuan tīng (èrshí shìjì) qīshí niándài de gē.** *My dad and mom enjoy listening to songs of the seventies (of the twentieth century).*

年度 niándù I *n* year
财务年度 **cáiwù niándù** fiscal year
II *adj* annual
年度报表 **niándù bàobiǎo** annual report

年级 niánjí [comp: 年 year + 级 grade] *n* grade (in school) □ 这个年级有多少学生？**Zhège niánjí yǒu duōshǎo xuésheng?** *How many students are there in this grade?* □ 他们的女儿刚念一年级。**Tāmen de nǚ'ér gāng niàn yì niánjí.** *Their daughter is only a first grade pupil.*

年纪 niánjì [comp: 年 year + 纪 number] *n* age □ 他虽然年纪小，但是很懂事。**Tā suīrán niánjì xiǎo, dànshì hěn dǒngshì.** *Although he's very young, he's quite sensible.* □ "老先生，您多大年纪了？" "七十了。" **"Lǎo xiānsheng, nín duōdà niánjì le?" "Qīshí le."** *"How old are you, sir?" "Seventy."*

NOTE: 您多大年纪了？**Nín duōdà niánjì le?** is an appropriate way to ask the age of an elderly person. To ask a young child his/her age, the question should be: 你几岁了？**Nǐ jǐ suì le?** For people who are neither children nor elderly, the question to use is: 你多大岁数？**Nǐ duō dà suìshù?**

年龄 niánlíng [comp: 年 year + 龄 age] *n* age (of a person or other living things) □ 你别问别人的年龄，尤其别问女士的年龄。**Nǐ bié wèn biérén de niánlíng, yóuqí bié wèn nǚshì de niánlíng.** *Do not ask about somebody's age, especially a lady's age.* □ 这棵树的年龄比我爷爷还大。**Zhè kē shù de niánlíng bǐ wǒ yéye hái dà.** *This tree is older than my grandpa.*

年轻 niánqīng [modif: 年 age + 轻 light] *adj* young □ 你还年轻，有些事你还不大懂。**Nǐ hái niánqīng, yǒuxiē shì nǐ hái bú dà dǒng.** *You're still too young to understand some matters.* □ 他年轻的时候可能干了！**Tā niánqīng de shíhou, kě nénggàn le!** *He was a very capable man when he was young.*
年轻人 **niánqīngrén** young person, youth

撵 niǎn Trad 攆 *v* drive away, oust

捻 niǎn *v* twist with the fingers

念 niàn I *v* **1** read, read aloud □ 你每天念中文课文吗？**Nǐ měi tiān niàn Zhōngwén kèwén ma?** *Do you read your Chinese lessons everyday?* **2** study (in a school) □ 他们的大儿子在英国念大学，他念数学。**Tāmen de dà érzi zài Yīngguó niàn dàxué, tā niàn shùxué.** *Their eldest son is studying in a university in the UK; he studies mathematics.* **II** idea, thought

NOTE: See note on 读 **dú**.

念头 niàntou *n* idea, thought

娘 niáng *n* **1** mom, ma (used in the northern dialect) **2** girl (See 姑娘 **gūniang**.)

酿 niàng Trad 釀 *v* brew, make (wine)
酿酒 **niàngjiǔ** make wine

鸟 niǎo Trad 鳥 *n* bird (只 **zhī**) □ 两只鸟在花园里飞来飞去。**Liǎng zhī niǎo zài huāyuán li fēi-lái-fēi-qù** *Two birds darted here and there in the garden.*

尿 niào *n* urine
撒尿 **sāniào** piss, pee, go pee

NOTE: 撒尿 **sāniào** is a vulgar or childish word for *urinate*. The formal word for *urinate* is 小便 **xiaopian**.

捏 niē *v* **1** mold, knead **2** make up, fabricate
捏造 **niēzào** [comp: 捏 mold + 造 make] *v* fabricate, make up

您 nín *pron* you (honorific)

NOTE: 您 **nín** is the honorific form of 你 **nǐ**. Use 您 **nín** when respect or deference is called for. Normally, 您 **nín** does not have a plural form. 您们 **nínmen** is absolutely unacceptable in spoken Chinese, and only marginally so in written Chinese. To address more than one person politely, you can say 您两位 **nín liǎng wèi** (two people), 您三位 **nín sān wèi** (three people), or 您几位 **nín jǐ wèi** (several people).

凝 níng *v* curdle, coagulate
凝结 **níngjié** [comp: 凝 coagulate + 结 coagulate] *v* (of gas or hot air) condense
凝视 **níngshì** [modif: 凝 freeze + 视 look] *v* look at steadily and for a long time, gaze fixedly, stare

宁 níng Trad 寧 *adj* peaceful, tranquil
宁静 **níngjìng** [comp: 宁 tranquil + 静 silent] *adj* tranquil and peaceful, serene

柠 níng Trad 檸 as in 柠檬 **níngméng**
柠檬 **níngméng** *n* lemon (只 **zhī**)

泞 níng Trad 濘 as in 泥泞 **nínìng**

拧 níng Trad 擰 *v* wring, twist
拧毛巾 **níng máojīn** wring a towel

拧 nǐng Trad 擰 *v* screw, wrench
拧螺丝 **nǐng luósī** turn a screw (to tighten or loosen it)

宁 nìng Trad 寧 *modal v* would rather
宁死不屈 **nìng sǐ bù qū** would rather die than succumb

宁可 nìngkě *modal v* Same as 宁肯 **nìngkěn**
宁肯 nìngkěn *modal v* would rather □ 她宁肯走去，也不搭他的车。**Tā nìngkěn zǒuqù, yě bù dā tāde chē.** *She would rather walk there than go in his car.*

NOTE: As is shown in the example sentence, 宁肯 **nìngkěn** is often used alongside with 也 **yě**: 宁肯⋯也⋯ **nìngkěn…yě…**

宁愿 nìngyuàn *modal v* Same as 宁肯 **nìngkěn**

牛 niú *v* ox, cow (头 **tóu**) □ 牛在草地上吃草。**Niú zài cǎodì shang chī cǎo.** *The cattle are grazing in the field.* □ 西方人用狗放羊放牛，所以他们说狗是人最好的朋友。**Xīfāngrén yòng gǒu fàng yáng**

fàng niú, suǒyǐ tāmen shuō gǒu shì rén zuì hǎo de péngyou. *People in the West use dogs to herd cattle and sheep; that's why they say the dog is man's best friend.*

牛奶 niúnǎi cow's milk, milk
牛肉 niúròu beef
公牛 gōng niú bull
黄牛 huángniú ox
奶牛 nǎiniú cow
水牛 shuǐniú water buffalo
小牛 xiǎo niú calf

NOTE: In the Chinese context, the ox (黄牛 **huángniú**) and the water buffalo (水牛 **shuǐniú**) are more important than the milk cow (奶牛 **nǎiniú**).

扭 niǔ *v* turn (one's head, back, etc.)
扭转 niǔzhuǎn *v* turn around, reverse
纽 niǔ Trad 紐 *n* knob, button
纽扣 niǔkòu *n* button (颗 **kē**, 个 **gè**)
农 nóng Trad 農 *n* farming
农产品 nóngchǎnpǐn *n* farm produce
农场 nóngchǎng [modif: 农 farming + 场 field, ground] *n* farm □ 这个农场真大! **Zhège nóngchǎng zhēn dà!** *How big this farm is!* □ 外国人可以在这里买农场吗? **Wàiguórén kěyǐ zài zhèli mǎi nóngchǎng ma?** *Can a foreigner buy a farm here?*
农场主 nóngchǎngzhǔ farmer
农村 nóngcūn [modif: 农 farming + 村 village] *n* farming area, rural area, countryside (antonym 城市 **chéngshì**) □ 农村人口比较少, 生活不太方便。**Nóngcūn rénkǒu bǐjiào shǎo, shēnghuó bú tài fāngbiàn.** *In rural areas, the population is small and life is not very convenient.* □ 在中国, 农村很多地区还比较落后。**Zài Zhōngguó, nóngcūn hěn duō dìqū hái bǐjiào luòhòu.** *Many regions in rural China are still rather backward.*
农户 nónghù [modif: 农 farming + 户 household] *n* rural household
农具 nóngjù [modif: 农 farming + 具 tool] *n* farm implements
农贸市场 nóngmào shìchǎng *n* farm produce market
农民 nóngmín [modif: 农 farming + 民 people] *n* peasant, farmer □ 农民都很关心天气。**Nóngmín dōu hěn guānxīn tiānqì.** *Farmers are all concerned about the weather.* □ 这个村子的农民生活相当困难。**Zhège cūnzi de nóngmín shēnghuó xiāngdāng kùnnan.** *The peasants in this village live a tough life.* □ 她十年前和一位农民结婚, 以后一直住在农村。**Tā shí nián qián hé yí wèi nóngmín jiéhūn, yǐhòu yìzhí zhù zài nóngcūn.** *She married a farmer ten years ago and has since lived in rural areas.*
农田 nóngtián [modif: 农 agriculture + 田 field] *n* farm land
农药 nóngyào *n* agricultural chemical, pesticide
农业 nóngyè [modif: 农 farming + 业 industry] *n* agriculture □ 农业十分重要。**Nóngyè shífēn zhòngyào.** *Agriculture is of great importance.* □ 我们必须努力发展农业。**Wǒmen bìxū nǔlì fāzhǎn nóngyè.** *We must work hard to develop agriculture.*
农作物 nóngzuòwù *n* agricultural crop

浓 nóng Trad 濃 *adj* (of gas or liquid) thick, dense (antonym 淡 **dàn**), concentrated □ 今天早上有浓雾。**Jīntiān zǎoshang yǒu nóng wù.** *There was dense fog this morning.* □ 我不喝浓咖啡, 不要冲得太浓。**Wǒ bù hē nóng kāfēi, bú yào chōng de tài nóng.** *I don't drink strong coffee. Don't make it too strong.*
浓厚 nónghòu [comp: 浓 thick + 厚 thick] *adj* 1 (of smoke, cloud, etc.) thick 2 (of atmosphere, interest, etc.) strong, heavy
弄 nòng *v* 1 do, manage, get … done □ 我弄饭, 你去买点儿酒。**Wǒ nòng fàn, nǐ qù mǎi diǎnr jiǔ.** *I'll do the cooking, you go and buy some wine.* □ 这么多事儿, 我今天弄不完。**Zhème duō shìr, wǒ jīntiān nòng bu wán.** *There're so many things to do, I can't finish them all today.* 2 fool with
弄虚作假 nòngxū zuòjiǎ *idiom* use deception, practice fraud
奴 nú *n* slave
奴隶 núlì *n* slave
奴役 núyì *v* enslave
努 nǔ *v* work hard
努力 nǔlì [comp: 努 physical effort + 力 strength] *adj* making great efforts □ 她是个很努力的学生, 考试一定能取得好成绩。**Tā shì ge hěn nǔlì de xuésheng, kǎoshì yídìng néng qǔdé hǎo chéngjì.** *She's a hard-working student, and will definitely get good results in the examinations.* □ 我们大家努力工作, 为了更好的明天。**Wǒmen dàjiā nǔlì gōngzuò, wèile gèng hǎo de míngtiān.** *We all work hard for a better tomorrow.* □ 他中文学习得很努力。**Tā Zhōngwén xuéxí de hěn nǔlì.** *He studies Chinese very diligently.*
怒 nù *adj* angry, outraged
怒吼 nùhǒu [modif: 怒 angry + 吼 roar] *n* angry roar
怒火 nùhuǒ [modif: 怒 angry + 火 flame] *n* fury
女 nǚ *adj* (of humans) female (antonym 男 **nán**) □ 请问, 女洗手间在哪里? **Qǐng wèn, nǚ xǐshǒujiān zài nǎlǐ?** *Excuse me, where is the women's toilet?*
女孩子 nǚ háizi girl
女青年 nǚ qīngnián young woman
女生 nǚshēng female student
女儿 nǚ'ér *n* daughter (个 **gè**) □ 他们的三个孩子都是女儿, 没有儿子。**Tāmen de sān ge háizi dōu shì nǚ'ér, méiyǒu érzi.** *All their three children are daughters; they don't have a son.*
女人 nǚrén [modif: 女 female human + 人 person] *n* woman, adult woman (antonym 男人 **nánrén**) □ 这条街都是卖女人穿的衣服, 所以叫 "女人街"。**Zhè tiáo jiē dōu shì mài nǚrén chuān de yīfu, suǒyǐ jiào "nǚrén jiē".** *The shops along this street all sell women's clothes, so it is known as "Women's Street".*
女士 nǚshì [modif: 女 female human + 士 gentleman, gentlewoman] *n* (respectful form of address or reference to a woman) Madam, Ms, lady □ 王女士是我们城市的教育局局长。**Wáng nǚshì shì wǒmen chéngshì de jiàoyùjú júzhǎng.** *Madam Wang is the director of our city's education bureau.* □ 女士们, 先生们, 请允许我代表市政府热烈欢迎大家。**Nǚshìmen, xiānshengmen, qǐng yúnxǔ wǒ dàibiǎo shì zhèngfǔ rèliè huānyíng dàjiā.** *Ladies and gentlemen, allow me to extend to you a warm welcome on behalf of the city government.*

女子 nǚzǐ *n* female adult

暖 **nuǎn** *adj* warm □ 在中国, 一到四月天就暖了。 **Zài Zhōngguó, yídào Sìyuè tiān jiù nuǎn le.** *In China the weather becomes warm when April comes.*

暖和 **nuǎnhuo** [comp: 暖 warm + 和 (in this context) mild] *adj* pleasantly warm □ 春天的太阳不太热, 很暖和。 *The sunshine in spring is not hot; it's warm.* □ 她的话说得我心里很暖和。 **Tā de huà shuō de wǒ xīnli hěn nuǎnhuo.** *What she said warmed my heart.*

暖瓶 **nuǎnpíng** [modif: 暖 warm + 瓶 bottle] *n* thermos bottle (只 **zhī**)

暖气 **nuǎnqì** [modif: 暖 warm + 气 air] *n* central heating

暖水瓶 **nuǎnshuǐpíng** *n* Same as 暖瓶 **nuǎnpíng**

挪 **nuó** *v* move, shift

挪用 **nuóyòng** [comp: 挪 move + 用 use] *v* divert (funds)

挪用公款 nuóyòng gōngkuǎn misappropriate public funds

O

噢 **ō** *interj* (used to indicate understanding or a promise) □ 噢, 我明白了。 **Ō, wǒ míngbai le.** *Oh, I see.* □ 噢, 我忘不了。 **Ō, wǒ wàng bu liǎo.** *Yes, I won't forget it.*

哦 **ǒ** *interj* (used to indicate doubt) □ 哦, 他还会说日本话? **Ǒ, tā hái huì shuō Rìběn huà?** *Well, he also speaks Japanese?*

欧 **ōu** Trad 歐 *n* Europe

欧元 **Ōuyuán** [modif: 欧 Europe + 元 dollar] *n* Euro □ 一百欧元可以换多少美元? **Yìbǎi Ōuyuán kěyǐ huàn duōshǎo Měiyuán?** *How many U.S. dollars can a hundred Euros be exchanged for?*

欧洲 **Ōuzhōu** [modif: 欧 Europe + 洲 continent] *n* Europe □ 我有了钱, 就去欧洲旅游。 **Wǒ yǒule qián, jiù qù Ōuzhōu lǚyóu.** *When I have the money, I'll go to Europe for a holiday.*

殴 **ōu** Trad 毆 *v* beat up (people)

殴打 **ōudǎ** [comp: 殴 beat + 打 beat] *v* beat up (people)

呕 **ǒu** Trad 嘔 *v* vomit

呕吐 **ǒutù** [comp: 呕 vomit + 吐 vomit] *v* vomit, be sick □ 我想呕吐。 **Wǒ xiǎng ǒutù.** *I feel sick.*

偶1 **ǒu** *adv* 1 occasionally

偶尔 ǒu'ěr occasionally, once in a while **2** accidentally

偶然 ǒurán accidentally, by chance

偶2 **ǒu** *n* even number

偶数 ǒushù even number (antonym 奇数 **jīshù**)

P

趴 **pā** *v* lie on one's stomach

爬 **pá** *v* crawl, climb □ 他们的儿子才一岁, 还不会走路, 只会在地上爬。 **Tāmen de érzi cái yí suì, hái bú huì zǒulù, zhǐ huì zài dì shang pá.** *Their son is only a year old, he still can't walk and can only crawl on the floor.*

爬行 **páxíng** *v* crawl, creep

爬行动物 **páxíng dòngwù** [modif: 爬行 crawling + 动物 animal] *n* reptile

扒 **pá** *v* rake up

扒手 **páshǒu** *n* pickpocket □ 火车站扒手很多; 要保管好自己的钱包。 **Huǒchēzhàn páshǒu hěn duō; yào bǎoguǎn hǎo zìjǐ de qiánbāo.** *There're many pickpockets at the railway station; take very good care of your wallets.*

怕 **pà** I *v* fear, be afraid □ 一个人住这么大的房子, 我有点儿怕。 **Yí ge rén zhù zhème dà de fángzi, wǒ yǒu diǎnr pà.** *I'm a bit afraid to live alone in such a big house.* □ 我怕他没接到我的信, 又打了电话。 **Wǒ pà tā méi jiēdao wǒ de xìn, yòu dǎle diànhuà.** *I was afraid he might not get my letter, so I rang him.* II *adv* Same as 恐怕 **kǒngpà**, but with less force.

拍 **pāi** *v* pat, clap

拍马屁 **pāi mǎpì** [modif: 拍 pat + 马屁 horse's behind] *v* flatter sickeningly, lick the boots of

拍卖 **pāimài** *v* auction, sell at a reduced price □ 这幢豪宅将在下星期拍卖。 **Zhè chuáng háo zhái jiāng zài xià xīngqī pāimài.** *This luxury mansion will be auctioned next week.*

拍摄 **pāishè** *v* take a photo, shoot (a movie)

拍手 **pāishǒu** *v* clap, applaud □ 孩子们拍手欢迎新老师。 **Háizimen pāishǒu huānyíng xīn lǎoshī.** *The children gave the new teacher a big hand.*

拍照 **pāizhào** *v* take photos, have one's photo taken □ 你的手机能拍照吗? **Nǐde shǒujī néng pāi zhào ma?** *Can your cell phone take photos?*

拍子 **pāizi** *n* 1 bat, racket

乒乓球拍子 pīngpāngqiú pāizi table tennis racket

羽毛球拍子 yǔmáoqiúpāi zi tennis racket **2** measurement of musical time, beat, time

打拍子 dǎpāizi beat time

排 **pái** I *v* 1 arrange in a definite order □ 旅客成一行, 等待登机前检查。 **Lǚkè pái chéng yì háng, děngdài dēngjī qián jiǎnchá.** *The travelers stood in a line for the preflight inspection.* **2** reject, rank II *n* 1 row, rank □ "你的票是几排几座?" "七排四座。" **"Nǐ de piào shì jǐ pái jǐ zuò?" "Qī pái sì zuò."** *"What is the seat and row in your ticket?" "Row 7, Seat 4."* □ 我要坐在前排, 后排听不清。 **Wǒ yào zuòzài qián pái, hòu pái tīng bu qīng.** *I want to sit in a front row. I can't hear clearly in the back seats.* **2** (army) platoon

排长 **páizhǎng** platoon leader III *measure wd* (for things arranged in a row) 一排椅子 yì pái yǐzi a row of chairs

排斥 **páichì** *v* expel, reject

排除 **páichú** [comp: 排 expel + 除 deduct] *v* rule out, eliminate

排除这种可能性 páichú zhè zhǒng kěnéngxing rule out this possibility

排除障碍 páichú zhàng'ài surmount an obstacle

排队 páiduì v form a line, line up, queue up

排挤 páijǐ [comp: 排 expel + 挤 squeeze] v elbow out, push aside, squeeze out

排列 páiliè v arrange, put in order

按字母顺序排列 àn zìmǔ shùnxù páiliè arrange in alphabetical order

排球 páiqiú [modif: 排 row + 球 ball] n volleyball (只 zhī) □ 夏天我们常常在海边打排球。**Xiàtiān wǒmen chángcháng zài hǎibiān dǎ páiqiú.** In summer we often play volleyball at the seaside.

徘 pái v as in 徘徊 páihuái

徘徊 páihuái v pace up and down, move hesitantly

牌1 pái n playing cards (张 zhāng, 副 fù) □ 他在火车上和别的旅客一起打牌。**Tā zài huǒchē shang hé biéde lǚkè yìqǐ dǎpái.** He played cards with fellow passengers on the train. □ 我不会打这种牌。**Wǒ bú huì dǎ zhè zhǒng pái.** I don't know how to play this card game.

打牌 dǎpái play cards
发牌 fāpái deal cards
洗牌 xǐpái shuffle cards

牌2 pái n brand name, brand □ 你买的汽车是什么牌的? **Nǐ mǎi de qìchē shì shénme pái de?** What brand of car did you buy?

名牌 míngpái famous brand, branded name

牌子 páizi [suffix: 牌 signboard + 子 nominal suffix] n 1 signboard (块 kuài) □ 他在门口放了一块牌子，"减价出售"。**Tā zài ménkǒu fàngle yí kuài páizi, "jiǎnjià chūshòu".** He put up a "Discount sale" signboard at the gate. 2 Same as 牌 **pái 2** □ 这种牌子的衣服特别贵。**Zhè zhǒng páizi de yīfu tèbié guì.** Clothes of this branded name are extremely expensive.

派1 pài 1 v 1 dispatch □ 公司派我到上海开发市场。**Gōngsī pài wǒ dào Shànghǎi kāifā shìchǎng.** The company sent me to Shanghai to develop the market. 2 assign (a job) □ 校长派我教三年级。**Xiàozhǎng pài wǒ jiāo sān-nián jí.** The principal assigned me to teach third grade.

派2 pài n faction, school (of thought) □ 在这个问题上有很多派。**Zài zhège wèntí shang yǒu hěn duō pài.** There are many schools of thought on this issue.

保守派 bǎoshǒupài the conservative faction, conservatives

派别 pàibié n faction, group, school (of thought)

派出所 pàichūsuǒ n police station

派对 pàiduì n (social) party □ 我们搬进新房子以后要开一个派对。**Wǒmen bānjìn xīnfángzi yǐhòu yào kāi yí ge pàiduì.** We'll give a party after moving into the new house.

NOTE: 派对 **pàiduì** is a transliteration of (social) party, used among urban fashionable people. 聚会 **jùhuì** is a more formal word.

派遣 pàiqiǎn v send, dispatch (troops, formal delegate, etc.)

攀 pān v climb

攀登 pāndēng [comp: 攀 climb + 登 ascend] v climb, scale

盘 pán Trad 盤 n dish, plate

盘子 pánzi plate, dish, tray (只 zhī) □ 她在饭店里端盘子。**Tā zài fàndiàn li duān pánzi.** She carries plates in a restaurant. (→ She is a waitress in a restaurant.)

盘旋 pánxuán v (of a bird or airplane) spiral, circle

判 pàn v judge, distinguish

判处 pànchǔ v (in a law court) sentence

判处无期徒刑 pànchǔ wúqī túxíng sentenced to life imprisonment

判定 pàndìng [comp: 判 judge + 定 decide] v decide, come to a conclusion

判断 pànduàn [comp: 判 judge + 断 reach a verdict] I v judge, decide □ 他说的话是真是假, 你怎么判断? **Tā shuō de huà shì zhēn shì jiǎ, nǐ zěnme pànduàn?** How do you judge whether his statement is true or false? □ 他判断是非的能力很强。**Tā pànduàn shì-fēi de nénglì hěn qiáng.** He is very good at telling right from wrong. II n judgment, verdict □ 我的判断是这批货都是假的。**Wǒ de pànduàn shì zhè pī huò dōu shì jiǎ de.** My judgment is that this batch of goods is counterfeit.

判决 pànjué n court decision, judgment

盼 pàn v expect, hope for

盼望 pànwàng [comp: 盼 expect + 望 look forward to] v look forward to, long for □ 母亲盼望孩子们都回家过春节。**Mǔqīn pànwàng háizimen dōu huíjiā guò chūnjié.** The mother longed for the homecoming of all her children for Chinese New Year. □ 我盼望不久就和你见面。**Wǒ pànwàng bùjiǔ jiù hé nǐ jiànmiàn.** I look forward to meeting you soon.

畔 pàn n (river, lake, etc.) side, bank

叛 pàn v betray, revolt

叛变 pànbiàn [comp: 叛 betray + 变 change] v turn traitor, become a turncoat

叛徒 pàntú n traitor, turncoat

旁 páng n side □ 路旁都摆着各种各样的小摊子。**Lùpáng dōu bǎizhe gè-zhǒng-gè-yàng de xiǎo tānzi.** By the roadside are all kinds of stalls.

旁边 pángbiān [modif: 旁 aside + 边 side] n side □ 王先生旁边那位先生是谁? **Wáng xiānsheng pángbiān nà wèi xiānsheng shì shéi?** Who is the man beside Mr Wang? □ 小河旁边有一个农场。**Xiǎo hé pángbiān yǒu yí ge nóngchǎng.** There's a farm by the small river.

旁观 pángguān v look on, observe □ 旁观者清。**Pángguānzhě qīng.** The onlooker sees most of the game.

庞 páng Trad 龐 adj huge

庞大 pángdà [comp: 庞 big + 大 big] adj huge, enormous

胖 pàng adj fat, plump □ 现在胖的人越来越多了。**Xiànzài pàng de rén yuèláiyuè duō le.** There are more and more fat people now.

胖子 pàngzi [suffix: 胖 fat + 子 nominal suffix] n fat person, "fatty"

抛 pāo v throw, hurl

抛弃 pāoqì [comp: 抛 throw + 弃 discard] v abandon, forsake

刨 páo v dig, unearth, excavate

袍 páo *n* gown, robe
袍子 páozi gown, robe

跑 pǎo *v* run □ 我们比一比，看谁跑得快。**Wǒmen bǐ yi bǐ, kàn shéi pǎo de kuài.** *Let's compete and see who runs faster.*

跑步 **pǎobù** [modif: 跑 run + 步 steps] *v* jog □ 每天早上很多人在公园里跑步。**Měi tiān zǎoshang hěn duō rén zài gōngyuán li pǎobù.** *Many people jog in the park early every morning.*

跑道 **pǎodào** *n* runway, track (in a sports ground)

炮 pào *n* cannon, gun (门 mén, 座 zuò) □ 山顶上放着一门古炮。**Shāndǐng shang fàngzhe yì mén gǔ pào.** *On top of the hill stands an old cannon.*

炮兵 **pàobīng** *n* artillery man

炮弹 **pàodàn** *n* artillery shell (发 fā, 颗 kē)

炮火 **pàohuǒ** *n* artillery fire

泡 pào **I** *n* **1** bubble
肥皂泡 féizàopào soap bubble
2 blister **II** *v* soak, steep

泡沫 **pàomò** [comp: 泡 bubble + 沫 foam] *n* foam, froth

泡沫塑料 **pàomò sùliào** [modif: 泡沫 foam + 塑料 plastic] *n* styrofoam

陪 péi *v* accompany □ 他妻子上街买衣服，他陪她去。**Tā qīzi shàngjiē mǎi yīfu, tā péi tā qù.** *His wife went out to buy clothes, and he went with her.* □ 我今天没有空陪你去看电影。**Wǒ jīntiān méiyǒu kòng péi nǐ qù kàn diànyǐng.** *I don't have time to go to the movies with you.*

陪同 **péitóng** *v* accompany

培 péi *v* cultivate

培训 **péixùn** [comp: 培 cultivate + 训 train] **I** *n* training □ 秘书们都要参加新电脑软件使用的培训。**Mìshūmen dōu yào cānjiā xīn diànnǎo ruǎnjiàn shǐyòng de péixùn.** *Secretaries will all have training in the use of a new computer software.*

培训班 péixùnbān training class, training course
培训生 péixùn shēng trainee
II *v* train
培训新职工 péixùn xīn zhígōng train new staff

培养 **péiyǎng** [comp: 培 cultivate + 养 provide for] *v* **1** train, develop **2** cultivate, breed

培育 **péiyù** [comp: 培 cultivate + 育 nurture] *v* bring up, nurture and educate
培育下一代 péiyù xià yídài bring up the next generation, bring up one's children

赔 péi Trad 賠 *v* compensate, pay for (damage, loss, etc.) □ 你借给我的书，我丢了。我赔你吧。**Nǐ jiè gei wǒ de shū, wǒ diū le. Wǒ péi nǐ ba.** *I've lost the book you lent me. Let me pay for it.*

赔偿 **péicháng** [comp: 赔 compensate + 偿 give back] *v* compensate

赔款 **péikuǎn** [modif: 赔 compensation + 款 fund] *n* reparation, indemnity

佩 pèi *v* **1** wear **2** admire
佩服 **pèifu** admire □ 我佩服自学成才的人。**Wǒ pèifu zì-xué-chéng-cái de rén.** *I admire those who become a success from being self-taught.*

achievement, e.g. □ "你五门功课都是一百分？佩服！佩服！" **"Nǐ wǔ mén gōngkè dōu shì yìbǎi fēn? Pèifu! Pèifu!"** *"You got full marks for all the five subjects? Wow!"*

配 pèi *v* **1** match, blend **2** be worthy of, deserve
配得上 pèi de shàng be worthy of, good enough to be
配不上 pèi bushàng not good enough to be, unworthy of

配备 **pèibèi** *v* allocate, provide with, be equipped with □ 每个教室配备一台电脑。**Měige jiàoshì pèibèi yìtái diànnǎo.** *Equip each classroom with a computer.*

配方 **pèifāng** *n* medical prescription, formula

配合 **pèihé** [comp: 配 match + 合 cooperate] *v* cooperate, coordinate □ 各个部门都要相互配合。**Gè ge bùmén dōu yào xiānghù pèihé.** *All the departments should cooperate with each other.* □ 病人要和医生密切配合，才能早日恢复健康。**Bìngrén yào hé yīshēng mìqiè pèihé, cáinéng zǎorì huīfù jiànkāng.** *A patient should cooperate closely with his doctor so as to achieve a speedy recovery.*

配偶 **pèi'ǒu** *n* spouse

配套 **pèitào** *v* make up a complete set

沛 pèi *adj* abundant (See 充沛 **chōngpèi**)

喷 pēn Trad 噴 *v* sprinkle, spray □ 这棵树上有虫子，要喷点儿药。**Zhè kē shù shang yǒu chóngzi, yào pēn diǎnr yào.** *This tree has insects on it and needs spraying.*

喷射 **pēnshè** *v* spurt, spray

喷水池 **pēnshuǐchí** *n* fountain

盆 pén *n* basin, pot (个 gè)
花盆 huāpén flower pot
洗脸盆 xǐliǎnpén washbasin

盆地 **péndì** *n* (in geography) basin

烹 pēng *v* boil, cook

烹饪 **pēngrèn** *n* cuisine, cooking

烹调 **pēngtiáo** *v* cook
烹调技术 pēngtiáo jìshù cooking skill
中华烹调 Zhōnghuá pēngtiáo Chinese cuisine

朋 péng *n* companion, friend
朋友 **péngyou** [comp: 朋 companion + 友 friend] *n* friend □ 朋友之间应该互相帮助。**Péngyou zhī jiān yīnggāi hùxiāng bāngzhù.** *Friends should help one another.* □ 他有很多朋友。**Tā yǒu hěn duō péngyou.** *He has many friends.*
跟/和…交朋友 gēn/hé…jiāo péngyou make friends with … □ 他在中学的时候交了不少朋友。**Tā zài zhōngxué de shíhou jiāole bù shǎo péngyou.** *He made quite a few friends in high school.*
男朋友 nánpéngyou boyfriend
女朋友 nǚpéngyou girlfriend

棚 péng *n* shed
棚子 péngzi shed

膨 péng *v* expand, inflate
膨胀 **péngzhàng** [comp: 膨 expand + 胀 swell] *v* expand, dilate

捧 pěng *v* **1** hold in both hands (with care, pride, etc.) □ 他捧着一盆花回家。**Tā pěngzhe yì pén huā huíjiā.** *He came home with a pot of flowers in his*

hands. **2** sing somebody's praise (especially insincerely), flatter □ 你别捧我, 我知道自己有几斤几两。 **Nǐ bié pěng wǒ, wǒ zhīdào zìjǐ yǒu jǐ jīn jǐ liǎng.** *Don't flatter me. I know my worth.*

碰 **pèng** *v* bump into, touch □ 别碰我, 我手里拿着水呢! **Bié pèng wǒ, wǒ shǒu li názhe shuǐ ne!** *Don't bump into me. I'm carrying water.*

碰到 **pèngdao** meet unexpectedly, run into □ 我昨天在城里碰到一个老同学。 **Wǒ zuótiān zài chénglǐ pèngdao yí ge lǎo tóngxué.** *I ran into an old classmate in town yesterday.*

碰钉子 **pèng dīngzi** [v+obj: 碰 meet + 钉子 a nail] *idiom* meet with a sharp rebuff, be given the cold shoulder □ 他向老板要求加薪, 可是碰了钉子。 **Tā xiàng lǎobǎn yāoqiú jiāxīn, kěshì pèngle dīngzi.** *She asked the boss for a raise, but met with a sharp rebuff.*

批 **pī** **I** *measure wd* (for a batch of goods, and for things/people arriving at the same time)
一批新书 **yì pī xīn shū** a batch of new books (published at about the same time)
两批旅游者 **liǎng pī lǚyóuzhě** two groups of tourists **II** *v* criticize, comment on, give instructions

批发 **pīfā** *v* sell wholesale (antonym 零售 **língshòu**)

批改 **pīgǎi** *v* correct and grade (students' exercises, essays, etc.)

批判 **pīpàn** *v* criticize

批评 **pīpíng** [comp: 批 criticism + 评 comment] **I** *v* criticize, scold (antonym 表扬 **biǎoyáng**) □ 老师批评他常常迟到。 **Lǎoshī pīpíng tā chángcháng chídào.** *The teacher criticized him for being often late for class.* **II** *n* criticism □ 你对他的批评很正确。 **Nǐ duì tā de pīpíng hěn zhèngquè.** *Your criticism of him is correct.* □ 我接受你对我的批评。 **Wǒ jiēshòu nǐ duì wǒ de pīpíng.** *I accept your criticism.*

批示 **pīshì** **I** *v* write comments on a document (e.g. report, request) submitted by subordinates **II** *n* comments on a document (e.g. report, request) submitted by subordinates

批准 **pīzhǔn** [comp: 批 express opinion + 准 approve, permit] *v* approve, ratify □ 你的申请已经批准了。 **Nǐ de shēnqǐng yǐjīng pīzhǔn le.** *Your application has been approved.*

劈 **pī** *v* chop to split

披 **pī** *v* drape over the shoulder □ 他披着大衣, 看孩子在雪地里玩。 **Tā pīzhe dàyī, kàn háizi zài xuědì li wán.** *With an overcoat draped over his shoulders, he watched the children play in the snow.*

皮 **pí** *n* **1** skin □ 她从自行车上摔下来, 擦破了点皮。 **Tā cóng zìxíngchē shang shuāi xiàlai, cāpòle diǎn pí.** *She fell off the bike and scraped her skin.* **2** leather, hide
牛皮 **niúpí** ox hide

皮带 **pídài** *n* leather belt
系上皮带 **xìshang pídài** buckle up one's belt

皮肤 **pífū** [comp: 皮 skin + 肤 skin] *n* skin (human) □ 她的皮肤又白又嫩。 **Tā de pífū yòu bái yòu nèn.** *Her skin is fair and tender.* □ 在海边住了一个夏天, 他的皮肤晒黑了。 **Zài hǎibiān zhùle yí ge xiàtiān, tā de pífū shài hēi le.** *After a summer day by the sea, he was tanned.*

皮革 **pígé** *n* leather, hide
皮革制品 **pígé zhìpǐn** leather product, leatherware

皮鞋 **píxié** *n* leather shoes

皮衣 **píyī** *n* fur coat, leather jacket

疲 **pí** *adj* fatigued

疲惫 **píbèi** *adj* physically and mentally exhausted

疲乏 **pífá** *adj* tired, weary

疲倦 **píjuàn** [comp: 疲 fatigued + 倦 tired] *adj* weary, tired

疲劳 **píláo** *adj* fatigued, tired □ 我连续工作了六小时, 实在疲劳。 **Wǒ liánxù gōngzuòle liù xiǎoshí, shízài píláo.** *I have been working nonstop for six hours. I am indeed tired.*

啤 **pí** *n* beer

啤酒 **píjiǔ** *n* beer (瓶 **píng**, 杯 **bēi**) □ 这种啤酒很好喝。 **Zhè zhǒng píjiǔ hěn hǎohē.** *This beer tastes good.* □ 爸爸每星期五买很多啤酒。 **Bàba měi Xīngqīwǔ mǎi hěn duō píjiǔ.** *Daddy buys lots of beer every Friday.*

NOTE: 啤酒 **píjiǔ** is an example of a semi-transliteration: 啤 **pí** represents the sound of English word *beer* and 酒 **jiǔ** means *alcoholic drink*.

脾 **pí** *n* spleen
脾气 **píqi** *n* disposition, temper □ 王医生脾气好, 很少生气。 **Wáng yīshēng píqi hǎo, hěn shǎo shēngqì.** *Dr Wang is good-tempered; he rarely gets angry.*
脾气坏 **píqi huài** have an irritable temper
发脾气 **fā píqi** throw a tantrum, lose one's temper □ 他为什么发脾气? **Tā wèishénme fā píqi?** *Why did he lose his temper?*

匹 **pǐ** *measure wd* (for horses)
一匹快马 **yì pǐ kuài mǎ** a fast horse

屁 **pì** *n* flatulence, fart
屁股 **pìgu** *n* bottom, buttocks

辟 **pì** Trad 闢 *v* open up (See 开辟 **kāipì**.)

僻 **pì** *adj* unusual, out-of-the-way (See 偏僻 **piānpì**.)

譬 **pì** *n* example
譬如 **pìrú** *conj* Same as 比如 **bǐrú**

偏 1 **piān** **I** *adj* not straight, slanting **II** *v* be prejudiced, show favoritism
偏爱 **piān'ài** [modif: 偏 impartial + 爱 love] *v* be partial, favor
偏爱他的小女儿 **piān'ài tāde xiǎonǚ'ér** favor one's youngest daughter

偏差 **piānchā** *n* deviation, error

偏见 **piānjiàn** [modif: 偏 impartial + 见 view] *n* prejudice, bias
对同性恋者有偏见 **duì tóngxìngliànzhě yǒu piānjiàn** hold prejudice against homosexuals

偏僻 **piānpì** *adj* remote, out-of-the-way

偏向 **piānxiàng** **I** *v* show favoritism **II** *n* erroneous tendency

偏 2 **piān** *adv* must (used to indicate that the action in question is contrary to one's expectation or wishes) □ 大家都要睡觉了, 他偏把收音机开得很响。 **Dàjiā dōu yào shuìjiào le, tā piān bǎ shōuyīnjī kāide hěn xiǎng.** *When everybody else wanted to sleep, he must turn up the radio.* □ 明天有一个重要的考试, 她偏今天病倒了。 **Míngtiān yǒu yí ge zhòngyào de kǎoshì, tā piān jīntiān bìngdǎo le.** *Just as there'll be an important exam tomorrow, what must she do*

but fall ill today? □ 我正在洗澡, 电话铃偏响了。 **Wǒ zhèngzài xǐzǎo, diànhuàlíng piān xiǎng le.** *The telephone must ring when I was taking a bath.*

NOTE: You can use 偏偏 **piānpian** instead of 偏 **piān**.

篇 **piān** *measure wd* (for a piece of writing)
一篇文章 yì piān wénzhāng an article/essay

便 **pián** as in 便宜 **piányi**
便宜 **piányi** *adj* inexpensive, cheap (antonym 贵 guì) □ 这家商店东西很便宜。 **Zhè jiā shāngdiàn dōngxi hěn piányi.** *Things are cheap in this store.* □ 我想买便宜一点儿的衣服。 **Wǒ xiǎng mǎi piányi yìdiǎnr de yīfu.** *I want to buy less expensive clothes.*
便宜货 piányi huò cheap goods, bargain

片 **piàn** **I** *n* thin and flat piece □ 王太太做的肉片特别好吃。 **Wáng tàitai zuò de ròupiàn tèbié hǎochī.** *The meat slices cooked by Mrs Wang are particularly delicious.* **II** *measure wd* (for thin, flat pieces)
一片面包 yí piàn miànbāo a slice of bread
片面 **piànmiàn** *adj* one-sided, unilateral (antonym 全面 **quánmiàn**) □ 我们应该全面考虑问题, 不要有片面的观点。 **Wǒmen yīnggāi quánmiàn de kǎolù wèntí, bú yào yǒu piànmiàn de guāndiǎn.** *We should approach an issue from all sides and not have a one-sided view.*

骗 **piàn** *v* deceive, fool □ 你受骗了! **Nǐ shòu piàn le!** *You've been duped!* □ 那个人骗我钱。 **Nàge rén piàn wǒ qián.** *That man cheated me out of my money.*
骗局 piànjú *n* hoax, fraud
揭穿一个骗局 jiēchuān yí ge piànjú expose a fraud
骗子 **piànzi** [suffix: 骗 cheat + 子 nominal suffix] *n* swindler, con-man

漂 **piāo** *v* float, drift

飘 **piāo** Trad 飄 *v* flutter □ 彩旗飘飘。 **Cǎiqí piāopiāo.** *Colorful banners fluttered in the breeze.*
飘扬 **piāoyáng** *v* (of banners, flags, etc.) flutter, wave

票 **piào** *n* ticket (张 **zhāng**) □ 这场电影票全卖完了。 **Zhè chǎng diànyǐng piào quán màiwán le.** *Tickets are all sold out for this movie.* □ 我买两张去香港的飞机票。 **Wǒ mǎi liǎng zhāng qù Xiānggǎng de fēijī piào.** *I want to buy two air tickets to Hong Kong.*
电影票 diànyǐng piào movie ticket
飞机票 fēijī piào air ticket
火车票 huǒchē piào train ticket
门票 ménpiào admission ticket (to a show, sporting event, etc.)
汽车票 qìchē piào bus/coach ticket

漂 **piào** as in 漂亮 **piàoliang**
漂亮 **piàoliang** [idiom] *adj* pretty, good-looking □ 这个小女孩真漂亮! **Zhège xiǎo nǚhái zhēn piàoliang!** *This little girl is really pretty.* (→ *What a pretty little girl!*) □ 她买了好几件漂亮衣服。 **Tā mǎile hǎo jǐ jiàn piàoliang yīfu.** *She bought some pretty clothes.* □ 你的汉字写得真漂亮。 **Nǐ de Hànzì xiě de zhēn piàoliang.** *Your Chinese characters are beautifully written.*

撇 **piē** *v* **1** discard, abandon **2** skim off from the surface of a liquid

瞥 **piē** **I** *v* take a glance at, shoot a glance at **II** *n* glimpse

拼 **pīn** *v* **1** fight bitterly, risk one's life **2** put together
拼搏 **pīnbó** [comp: 拼 fight bitterly + 搏 wrestle] *v* fight hard against a formidable adversary (often figuratively)
拼搏精神 pīnbó jīngshen fierce fighting spirit
拼命 **pīnmìng** [v+obj: 拼 fight bitterly + 命 one's life] *v* do all one can, risk one's life □ 他拼命赚钱, 都是为了什么呢? **Tā pīnmìng zhuànqián, dōushì wèile shénme ne?** *He does everything possible to earn money, but for what purpose?*
拼音 **pīnyīn** [v+obj: 拼 put together + 音 sound] **I** *v* spell, phonetize **II** *n* Romanized Chinese writing, pinyin □ 老师, 我不会写的汉字, 可以写拼音吗? **Lǎoshī, wǒ búhuì xiě de Hànzì, kěyǐ xiě pīnyīn ma?** *Teacher, can I use pinyin for those Chinese characters I can't write?*
拼音文字 pīnyīn wénzì phonetic writing
汉语拼音方案 Hànyǔ pīnyīn fāng'àn Scheme for the Chinese Phonetic Alphabet

频 **pín** Trad 頻 *adv* frequently
频道 **píndào** [modif: 频 frequency + 道 channel] *n* frequency channel, (TV) channel
频繁 **pínfán** *adj* frequent
频率 **pínlǜ** [modif: 频 frequent + 率 rate] *n* frequency

贫 **pín** Trad 貧 *adj* poor, lacking
贫乏 **pínfá** [comp: 贫 poor + 乏 lacking] *adj* lacking in, deficient
资源贫乏 zīyuán pínfá poor in natural resources
贫苦 **pínkǔ** [comp: 贫 poor + 苦 miserable] *adj* poor and miserable, poverty-stricken
贫困 **pínkùn** [comp: 贫 poor + 困 stranded] *adj* poor, destitute
贫民 **pínmín** [modif: 贫 poor + 民 people] *n* poor people, people living below the poverty line
贫穷 **pínqióng** [comp: 贫 poor + 穷 poor] *adj* poor, poverty-stricken

品 **pǐn** **I** *n* **1** article, product **2** quality, grade
上品 shàngpǐn superior quality, product of superior quality
II *v* savor
品尝 **pǐncháng** [comp: 品 savor + 尝 taste] *v* savor, taste
品德 **pǐndé** [comp: 品 quality + 德 virtue] *n* moral character
品德高尚 pǐndé gāoshàng of lofty (excellent) moral character
品行 **pǐnxíng** [comp: 品 quality + 行 behavior] *n* moral character and conduct, behavior
品行不良 pǐnxíng bùliáng of poor moral standard and behave badly
品质 **pǐnzhì** *n* **1** (of people) moral character, intrinsic quality □ 这个人很讨人喜欢, 但是品质不好。 **Zhège rén hěn tǎorén xǐhuan, dànshì pǐnzhì bù hǎo.** *This guy is quite pleasant, but has bad moral character.* **2** (of products) quality
品种 **pǐnzhǒng** [comp: 品 article + 种 kind] *n* variety, breed □ 超级市场里的水果品种多得不得了, 简直让人眼睛都看花了。 **Chāojíshìchǎng li de shuǐguǒ pǐnzhǒng duō de bùdeliǎo, jiǎnzhí ràng rén yǎnjing dōu kànhuā le.** *There is a huge variety of fruits in the supermarket. It is simply dazzling.*

聘 **pìn** *v* invite for service/employment
聘请 **pìnqǐng** [comp: 聘 invite for service + 请 invite] *v* invite for service, employ
聘任 **pìnrèn** *v* appoint (for a professional or managerial position)
聘书 **pìnshū** *n* letter of appointment (份 **fèn**)

乒 **pīng** *n* bang (sound)
乒乓球 **pīngpāngqiú** *n* table tennis, table tennis ball (只 **zhī**) □ 很多中国人乒乓球打得很好。**Hěn duō Zhōngguórén pīngpāngqiú dǎ de hěn hǎo.** *Many Chinese are good at table tennis.*

平 **píng** *adj* 1 flat, level, smooth □ 这张桌面不平。**Zhè zhāng zhuōmiàn bù píng.** *This table surface is not level.* 2 be on the same level, equal 3 average, common
平安 **píng'ān** [comp: 平 peace + 安 peace] *adj* safe and sound □ 祝你一路平安! **Zhù nǐ yílù píng'ān!** *I wish you a safe journey! (→ Bon voyage!)* □ 高高兴兴上班, 平平安安回家。**Gāo-gāo-xìng-xìng shàngbān, píng-píng-ān-ān huíjiā.** *Come to work in high spirits and return home safe and sound. (A Chinese slogan urging workers to observe occupational safety.)*
平常 **píngcháng** [comp: 平 flat + 常 usual] **I** *adj* ordinary, common □ 这位世界冠军的父母都是平平常常的人。**Zhè wèi shìjiè guànjūn de fùmǔ dōushì píng-píng-cháng-cháng de rén.** *The parents of this world champion are just ordinary people.* □ 那是我一生中最不平常的一天。**Nà shì wǒ yìshēng zhong zuì bù píngcháng de yì tiān.** *That was the most unusual day of my life.* **II** *adv* ordinarily, usually, normally □ 我平常不喝酒, 只有节日的时候喝一点儿。**Wǒ píngcháng bù hē jiǔ, zhǐyǒu jiérì de shíhou hē yìdiǎnr.** *I normally don't drink. I only drink a little on festive occasions.*
平等 **píngděng** [modif: 平 flat + 等 grade] **I** *adj* equal (in status) □ 法律面前人人平等。**Fǎlù miànqián rénren píngděng.** *Everyone is equal in the eyes of the law.* □ 尽管他是董事长, 也应该平等待人。**Jǐnguǎn tā shì dǒngshìzhǎng, yě yīnggāi píngděng dàirén.** *Even though he is the chairman of the board, he should treat people as equals.* □ 社会上还有很多不平等现象。**Shèhuì shang háiyǒu hěn duō bù píngděng xiànxiàng.** *There are still many cases of inequality in society.* **II** *n* equality □ 夫妻之间的平等是现代婚姻的基础。**Fūqī zhījiān de píngděng shì xiàndài hūnyīn de jīchǔ.** *Equality between husband and wife is the foundation of modern marriages.*
平凡 **píngfán** *adj* ordinary, common
平方 **píngfāng** *n* (in maths) square
三平方公尺 **sān píngfāng gōngchǐ** 3 square meters
平衡 **pínghéng** **I** *n* balance, equilibrium **II** *v* to keep in balance
平静 **píngjìng** [comp: 平 peace + 静 quiet] *adj* calm, quiet, uneventful □ 没有一点风, 大海十分平静。**Méiyǒu yìdiǎn fēng, dàhǎi shífēn píngjìng.** *It is windless. The sea is perfectly calm.* □ 老人平静的生活被这个消息打乱了。**Lǎorén píngjìng de shēnghuó bèi zhège xiāoxi dǎluàn le.** *The old man's peaceful life was shattered by this news.*
平均 **píngjūn** *adj* average □ 这个城市的人平均收入是一年一万元。**Zhège chéngshì de rén píngjūn shōurù shì yì nián yíwàn yuán.** *The average per capita income of this city is 10,000 yuan a year.*

平面 **píngmiàn** [modif: 平 flat + 面 face] *n* (in mathematics) plane
平面几何 **píngmiàn jǐhé** plane geometry
平民 **píngmín** [modif: 平 ordinary + 民 people] *n* the common people, civilian (个 **gè**, 名 **míng**)
平日 **píngrì** *adv* on an ordinary day (not a holiday or festival)
平时 **píngshí** [comp: 平 ordinary + 时 time] *adv* usually, under normal circumstances □ 我平时六点半起床, 周末八点多才起床。**Wǒ píngshí liù diǎnbàn qǐchuáng, zhōumò bā diǎn duō cái qǐchuáng.** *I usually get up at half past six, but on weekends I get up after eight o'clock.*
平坦 **píngtǎn** *adj* level and broad
平稳 **píngwěn** *adj* smooth and stable
平行 **píngxíng** *adj* parallel
平行线 **píngxíngxiàn** parallel lines
平庸 **píngyōng** *adj* mediocre, ordinary
平原 **píngyuán** *n* flatland, plain □ 中国东北地区是一个大平原。**Zhōngguó dōngběi dìqù shì yí ge dà píngyuán.** *The northeast region of China is a huge plain.*

评 **píng** Trad 評 *v* 1 comment 2 appraise
评比 **píngbǐ** [comp: 评 appraise + 比 compare] *v* appraise through comparison
年终评比 **niánzhōng píngbǐ** end-of-the-year appraisal (of performance of a number of people or groups)
评定 **píngdìng** [comp: 评 appraise + 定 decide] *v* evaluate, assess
评估 **pínggū** [comp: 评 appraise + 估 estimate] *v* assess, appraise
资产评估 **zīchǎn pínggū** assets appraisal
评价 **píngjià** [v+obj: 评 appraise + 价 value] **I** *v* appraise, evaluate **II** *n* evaluation
高度评价 **gāodù píngjià** place a high value on, speak highly of
评论 **pínglùn** [comp: 评 comment + 论 discuss] **I** *v* comment □ 我不想评论他们之间的矛盾。**Wǒ bù xiǎng pínglùn tāmen zhījiān de máodùn.** *I have no comment on the conflict between them.* **II** *n* comment, commentary
评选 **píngxuǎn** [comp: 评 appraise + 选 select] *v* appraise and select, select by public appraisal

苹 **píng** Trad 蘋 *n* apple
苹果 **píngguǒ** [modif: 苹 apple + 果 fruit] *n* apple (个 **gè**) □ 这种苹果多少钱一公斤? **Zhè zhǒng píngguǒ duōshǎo qián yì gōngjīn?** *How much does a kilo of these apples cost?* □ 这苹果太酸, 我不爱吃。**Zhè píngguǒ tài suān, wǒ bú ài chī.** *This apple is too sour. I don't like it.*
苹果园 **píngguǒ yuán** apple orchard

萍 **píng** *n* duckweed
萍水相逢 **píngshuǐ xiāngféng** *idiom* (of strangers) meet by chance like drifting duckweed

凭 **píng** Trad 憑 **I** *n* evidence, proof
真凭实据 **zhēnpíng shíjù** hard evidence **II** *v* go by, base on
凭票入场 **píngpiào rùchǎng** admission by tickets

屏 **píng** *n* screen
屏风 **píngfēng** *n* partition
屏幕 **píngmù** *n* (movie, TV, computer) screen

瓶 **píng** **I** *n* bottle (个 **gè**)
瓶子 **píngzi** bottle □ 给我一个空瓶子。**Gěi wǒ yí ge**

kōng píngzi. *Give me an empty bottle.*
II *measure wd* a bottle of
一瓶啤酒 yì píng píjiǔ a bottle of beer
两瓶可口可乐 liǎng píng kěkǒukělè two bottles of Coca-Cola.

坡 pō *n* slope □ 骑自行车上坡很累。**Qí zìxíngchē shàng pō hěn lèi.** *Cycling up a slope is very tiring.*

泼 pō Trad 潑 **I** *v* sprinkle **II** *adj* vigorous, bold (See 活泼 **huópo**.)

颇 pō *adv* quite, rather

迫 pò *v* compel, oppress
迫害 **pòhài** [comp: 迫 oppress + 害 harm] *v* persecute
迫切 **pòqiè** *adj* urgent, pressing □ 我们的迫切任务是了解市场情况。**Wǒmen de pòqiè rènwù shì liǎojiě shìchǎng qíngkuàng.** *Our urgent task is to understand the market situation.*
迫使 **pòshǐ** [comp: 迫 compel + 使 make] *v* compel, force

破 pò **I** *v* **1** break, damage **2** break, split □ 你的衣服破了。**Nǐ de yīfu pò le.** *Your clothes are torn.* **II** *adj* torn, damaged □ 这件破衣服不能穿了。**Zhè jiàn pò yīfu bù néng chuān le.** *This torn coat is no longer wearable.* □ 花瓶打破了。**Huāpíng dǎpò le.** *The vase is broken.*
破产 **pòchǎn** **I** *v* go bankrupt **II** *n* bankruptcy □ 没有想到，这家大公司会宣布破产。**Méiyǒu xiǎngdào, zhè jiā dà gōngsī huì xuānbù pòchǎn.** *It is quite unexpected that this big company should declare bankruptcy.*
破除 **pòchú** *v* do away with, eradicate
破坏 **pòhuài** [v+compl: 破 break + 坏 bad] *v* sabotage, damage □ 不准破坏公共财物。**Bù zhǔn pòhuài gōnggòng cáiwù.** *Vandalism of public property is not allowed.*
破获 **pòhuò** *v* solve (a criminal case), catch (criminals)
破旧 **pòjiù** [comp: 破 torn + 旧 old] *adj* old and worn-out, shabby
破旧的厂房 pòjiù de chǎngfáng run-down factory building
破烂 **pòlàn** [comp: 破 torn + 烂 rotten] *adj* worn-out, tattered
捡破烂 jiǎn pòlàn pick up what is valuable from among garbage, make a living by doing this
破裂 **pòliè** [comp: 破 break + 裂 crack] *v* split, break down
破碎 **pòsuì** [comp: 破 break + 碎 broken] **I** *v* break into pieces, smash **II** *adj* broken into pieces, smashed, crushed □ 他的梦想破碎了。**Tā de mèngxiǎng pòsuì le.** *His dream was shattered.*

魄 pò *n* **1** soul, spirit **2** vigor
魄力 **pòlì** [comp: 魄 vigor + 力 strength] *n* daring, resolution

剖 pōu *v* cut open
剖析 **pōuxī** [comp: 剖 cut open + 析 analyse] *v* dissect
剖析一个典型事例 pōuxī yí ge diǎnxíng shìlì study a typical case in great detail

扑 pū *v* **1** pounce on **2** flap
扑克 **pūkè** *n* playing cards
扑克牌 pūkèpái (张 **zhāng**, 副 **fù**)

NOTE: 扑克 **pūkè** is a transliteration of *poker*, to mean *playing cards*, not the card game. 扑克牌 **pūkèpái**, however, is more commonly used in everyday Chinese. We say 打扑克牌 **dǎ pūkè pái**, or 打牌 **dǎ pái** for the verb *to play cards*. See 牌 **pái** and the note on it.

扑灭 **pūmiè** [comp: 扑 beat + 灭 extinguish] *v* extinguish, put out

铺 pū *v* spread, unfold □ 桌子上铺着一块漂亮的桌布。**Zhuōzi shang pūzhe yí kuài piàoliang de zhuōbù.** *A beautiful tablecloth was spread over the table.*

葡 pú *n* as in 葡萄 **pútao**
葡萄 **pútao** *n* grape (颗 **kē**) □ 这里的葡萄又大又甜。**Zhèli de pútao yòu dà yòu tián.** *The grapes here are big and sweet.*
葡萄酒 pútaojiǔ grape wine
葡萄园 pútaoyuán vineyard

仆 pú Trad 僕 *n* servant
仆人 **púrén** (domestic) servant (个 **gè**, 名 **míng**)

NOTE: 仆人 **púrén** is an old-fashioned word for *servant*. Use 用人 **yòngrén** or 保姆 **bǎomǔ**.

菩 pú as in 菩萨 **Púsà**
菩萨 **Púsà** *n* Buddha, Bodhisattva

朴 pǔ Trad 樸 *adj* plain, simple
朴实 **pǔshí** *adj* **1** (of style) simple and plain, down-to-earth **2** (of people) sincere and honest
朴素 **pǔsù** *adj* simple and plain □ 她喜欢穿朴素的衣服。**Tā xǐhuan chuān pǔsù de yīfu.** *She likes to dress simply.*

普 pǔ *adj* common, universal
普遍 **pǔbiàn** [comp: 普 common + 遍 everywhere] *adj* widespread, commonplace □ 在那个地方，少女母亲的现象很普遍。**Zài nàge dìfang, shàonǚ mǔqin de xiànxiàng hěn pǔbiàn.** *In that area, teenage mothers are quite commonplace.* □ 人们普遍认为这种做法是不对的。**Rénmen pǔbiàn rènwéi zhè zhǒng zuòfǎ shì bú duì de.** *People generally think this kind of behavior is wrong.*
普查 **pǔchá** [modif: 普 general + 查 survey] *n* survey
人口普查 rénkǒu pǔchá census
普及 **pǔjí** *v* popularize, make commonplace □ 在这个地区电脑已经普及了，几乎每个家庭都有一台电脑。**Zài zhège dìqū diànnǎo yǐjīng pǔjí le, jīhū měi ge jiātíng dōu yǒu yì tái diànnǎo.** *In this region computers have become commonplace; almost every household has one.*
普通 **pǔtōng** *adj* common, commonplace, ordinary □ 在这个城市里一座普通的房子要多少钱？**Zài zhège chéngshìli yí zuò pǔtōng de fángzi yào duóshǎo qián?** *How much is an ordinary house in this city?*
普通话 **Pǔtōnghuà** [modif: 普通 common + 话 speech] *n* Standard Modern Chinese, Mandarin, Putonghua □ 大多数中国人都听得懂普通话。**Dàduōshù Zhōngguórén dōu tīng de dǒng Pǔtōnghuà.** *Most Chinese people understand Putonghua.* □ 你说普通话不太标准，也不要紧。**Nǐ shuō Pǔtōnghuà bú tài biāozhǔn, yě bú yàojǐn.** *It doesn't matter if you don't speak perfect Putonghua.*

NOTE: Modern Standard Chinese is known as 普通话 **Pǔtōnghuà** in China, 国语 **Guóyǔ** in Taiwan and 华语 **Huáyǔ** in Singapore and other Southeast Asian countries. They refer to the same language, though slight differences do exist among them.

谱 **pǔ** I *v* set to music II *n* musical score
乐谱 yuèpǔ musical score
钢琴谱 gāngqín pǔ piano score
谱曲 **pǔqǔ** *v* set music to words

瀑 **pù** *n* waterfall
瀑布 **pùbù** *n* waterfall

Q

七 **qī** *num* seven
七个小矮人 qī ge xiǎo ǎirén the seven dwarves
七百七十七 qībǎi qīshíqī seven hundred and seventy-seven

柒 **qī** *num* seven

沏 **qī** *v* infuse
沏茶 qīchá make tea

妻 **qī** *n* wife
妻子 qīzi wife □ 丈夫和妻子应当互相爱护, 互相尊重。 **Zhàngfu hé qīzi yīngdāng hùxiāng àihu, hùxiāng zūnzhòng.** *A couple should care for and respect each other.* □ 他对他妻子好吗? **Tā duì tā qīzi hǎo ma?** *Is he nice to his wife?*

凄 **qī** *adj* chilly, cold
凄惨 **qīcǎn** [comp: 凄 chilly + 惨 miserable] *adj* miserable, wretched
凄凉 **qīliáng** [comp: 凄 chilly + 凉 chilly] *adj* desolate, dreary, miserable

漆 **qī** *n* lacquer, paint
漆黑 **qīhēi** *adj* pitch dark, pitch black
漆黑一团 qīhēiyìtuán pitch dark

期 **qī** I *n* fixed time
按期 àn qī according to the schedule, on time □ 贵公司订购的货物我们一定按期送到。 **Guìgōngsī dìnggòu de huòwù wǒmen yídìng àn qī sòngdào.** *We will certainly deliver on time the goods your company ordered.*
到期 dàoqī expire, due
过期 guòqī overdue, expired
II *v* expect
期待 **qīdài** *v* expect, look forward to
期间 **qījiān** *n* period, time □ 春节期间饭店的生意特别好。 **Chūnjié qījiān fàndiàn de shēngyi tèbié hǎo.** *During the Chinese New Year holidays, restaurants have particularly good business.*
期刊 **qīkān** *n* periodical, journal (本 **běn**)
期望 **qīwàng** [comp: 期 expect + 望 look forward to] I *v* expect, hope II *n* expectations, hope
期望过高 qīwàng guògāo expect too much
期限 **qīxiàn** *n* deadline, time limit
超过期限 chāoguò qīxiàn exceed the time limit, become overdue
定一个期限 dìng yí ge qīxiàn set a deadline

戚 **qī** *n* relative (See 亲戚 **qīnqi**)

欺 **qī** *v* cheat, bully
欺负 **qīfu** *v* bully, take advantage of (someone) □ 他有了一点儿权, 就要欺负别人。 **Tā yǒu le yìdiǎnr quán, jiùyào qīfu biéren.** *He tried to bully others once he'd got some power.*
欺骗 **qīpiàn** [comp: 欺 cheat + 骗 deceive] *v* deceive □ 这件事我完全了解, 他无法欺骗我。 **Zhè jiàn shì wǒ wánquán liǎojiě, tā wúfǎ qīpiàn wǒ.** *I know this matter fully well. There is no way he can deceive me.*

歧 **qí** *adj* different, divergent
歧视 **qíshì** I *v* discriminate against
歧视残疾人士 qíshì cánjírénshì discriminate against the disabled
II *n* discrimination
种族歧视 zhǒngzú qíshì racial discrimination

齐 **qí** Trad 齊 I *adj* neat, in a straight line □ 书架上的书放得很齐。 **Shūjià shang de shū fàng de hěn qí.** *The books in the bookshelf are neatly arranged.* II *v* reaching to the same height □ 树长得齐屋顶了。 **Shù zhǎng de qí wūdǐng le.** *The trees have grown as tall as the roof.* III *adv* together, all ready
齐全 **qíquán** *adj* complete, all in readiness
品种齐全 pǐnzhǒng qíquán have a complete range of products (goods)

其 **qí** *pron* this, that
其次 **qícì** *adv* next, secondary, secondly □ 他们离婚的原因首先是性格不合, 其次是经济上有矛盾。 **Tāmen líhūn de yuányīn shǒuxiān shì xìnggé bù hé, qícì shì jīngjì shang yǒu máodùn.** *The first reason they gave for divorcing was incompatibility of disposition and the second reason was financial conflict.*
其实 **qíshí** *adv* actually, as a matter of fact □ 她说懂了, 其实她还是不明白。 **Tā shuō dǒng le, qíshí tā háishi bù míngbai.** *She said she understood, but actually she still didn't comprehend it.*
其他 **qítā** *pron* other, else □ 我只要买一台笔记本电脑, 其它什么都不要。 **Wǒ zhǐyào mǎi yì tái bǐjìběn diànnǎo, qítā shénme dōu bú yào.** *I only want to buy a notebook computer. I don't want anything else.*
其余 **qíyú** *pron* the rest, the remainder □ 我付了学费以后把其余的钱存进了银行。 **Wǒ fùle xuéfèi yǐhòu bǎ qíyú de qián cúnjìnle yínháng.** *After paying the tuition fee, I deposited the remainder of the money in the bank.*
其中 **qízhōng** *n* among them, in it □ 北京有很多名胜古迹, 故宫是其中之一。 **Běijīng yǒu hěn duō míngshèng gǔjì, gùgōng shì qízhōng zhī yī.** *There are many scenic spots and historical sites in Beijing. The Palace Museum is one of them.*

棋 **qí** *n* chess
下棋 xiàqí play chess
下一盘棋 xià yìpánqí play a game of chess
棋盘 **qípán** *n* chess board
棋子 **qízǐ** *n* chess piece

旗 **qí** *n* flag, banner (面 **miàn**)
旗杆 qígān flagstaff, flag pole
国旗 guóqí national flag
升旗 shēngqí hoist a flag
旗袍 **qípáo** *n* a woman's dress with high neck and slit skirt, cheongsam

旗帜 **qízhì** *n* banner (面 **miàn**)

旗子 **qízi** [suffix: 旗 flag, banner + 子 nominal suffix] *n* flag, banner (面 **miàn**) □ 国旗是代表国家的旗子。**Guóqí shì dàibiǎo guójiā de qízi.** *A national flag is one that symbolizes the country.*

奇 **qí** *adj* strange

奇怪 **qíguài** [comp: 奇 strange + 怪 unusual] *adj* strange, unusual, odd □ 他一年到头戴着一顶黄帽子，真奇怪。**Tā yì-nián-dào-tóu dàizhe yì dǐng huáng màozi, zhēn qíguài.** *It is really odd that he wears a yellow cap all year long.* □ 对这种奇怪的现象，我不能解释。**Duì zhè zhǒng qíguài de xiànxiàng, wǒ bù néng jiěshì.** *I cannot explain this strange phenomenon.*

奇花异草 **qíhuāyìcǎo** *n* rare, exotic flora

奇迹 **qíjì** *n* miracle, wonder

创造奇迹 **chuàngzào qíjì** perform a miracle, work wonders

奇妙 **qímiào** *adj* marvelous, intriguing

奇特 **qítè** *adj* peculiar, unique

骑 **qí** Trad 騎 *v* ride (a horse, bicycle etc.)

骑马 **qí mǎ** ride a horse

骑自行车 **qí zìxíngchē** ride a bicycle □ 我每天骑自行车去上学。**Wǒ měi tiān qí zìxíngchē qù shàngxué.** *I go to school by bike every day.*

岂 **qǐ** Trad 豈 *adv* (forming a rhetorical question)

岂不 **qǐbù** *adv* wouldn't it, doesn't it □ 岂不浪费钱财？**Qǐbù làngfèi qiáncái?** *Wouldn't it be a waste of money?*

岂有此理 **qǐyǒucǐlǐ** *idiom* preposterous, outrageous □ 真是岂有此理！**Zhēnshi qǐyǒucǐlǐ!** *How absurd! That's really outrageous!*

企 **qǐ** *v* hope, eagerly look forward to

企图 **qǐtú** I *v* attempt, try □ 恐怖分子企图破坏铁路和公路，制造大规模交通事故。**Kǒngbùfènzǐ qǐtú pòhuài tiělù hé gōnglù, zhìzào dà guīmó jiāotōng shìgù.** *Terrorists attempted to sabotage railways and highways to cause large-scale traffic accidents.* II *n* attempt □ 他们的企图失败了。**Tāmen de qǐtú shībài le.** *Their attempt failed.*

NOTE: 企图 **qǐtú** is usually used for negative situations. For example, we usually do not say 他企图帮助我。**Tā qǐtú bāngzhù wǒ.** *He tried to help me.* but 他企图欺骗我。**Tā qǐtú qīpiàn wǒ.** *He tried to deceive me.*

企业 **qǐyè** *n* enterprise (家 **jiā**)

企业家 **qǐyèjiā** entrepreneur

国有企业 **guóyǒu qǐyè** state-owned enterprise

私有企业 **sīyǒu qǐyè** private enterprise □ 管理一个大型企业是极其复杂的。**Guǎnlǐ yí ge dàxíng qǐyè shì jíqí fùzá de.** *To manage a large enterprise is an extremely complex undertaking.*

启 **qǐ** Trad 啟 *v* 1 open 2 start, initiate

启程 **qǐchéng** *v* start a journey, set out

启发 **qǐfā** [comp: 启 open + 发 release] I *v* enlighten, arouse □ 我们应该启发孩子的学习兴趣。**Wǒmen yīnggāi qǐfā háizi de xuéxí xìngqù.** *We should arouse an interest to learn in children.* II *n* enlightenment, inspiration □ 科学家常常从平常的自然现象得到启发。**Kēxuéjiā chángcháng cóng píngcháng de zìrán xiànxiàng dédào qǐfā.** *Scientists are often inspired by commonplace natural phenomena.*

启示 **qǐshì** [comp: 启 enlighten + 示 indicate] *n* revelation, inspiration, enlightenment

启事 **qǐshì** *n* public announcement

乞 **qǐ** *v* beg

乞丐 **qǐgài** *n* beggar

乞求 **qǐqiú** [comp: 乞 beg + 求 implore] *v* implore, beg for

乞求宽恕 **qǐqiú kuānshù** beg for mercy

起 **qǐ** *v* rise, get up □ 快十点钟了，他还没起呢！**Kuài shí diǎnzhōng le, tā hái méi qǐ ne!** *It's almost ten o'clock and he still isn't up!*

从…起 **cóng...qǐ** starting from ... □ 从晚上七点起，网吧就特别忙。**Cóng wǎnshang qī diǎn qǐ, wǎngbā jiù tèbié máng.** *Starting from seven o'clock in the evening, the Internet cafe is particularly busy.*

NOTE: 起 **qǐ** is seldom used alone. To express *to get up (out of bed)*, 起床 **qǐchuáng** is more common than 起 **qǐ**. One can very well say: 快十点钟了，他还没起床呢！**Kuài shí diǎnzhōng le, tā hái méi qǐchuáng ne!** *It's almost ten o'clock and he still isn't up!*

起草 **qǐcǎo** *v* make a draft of (a plan, a document, etc.)

起初 **qǐchū** *adv* at first, at the onset

起床 **qǐchuáng** *v* get up (out of bed) □ "你每天几点起床？" "平时七点，周末就晚一点。" **"Nǐ měi tiān jǐ diǎn qǐchuáng?" "Píngshí qī diǎn, zhōumò jiù wǎn yì diǎn."** *"When do you get up every day?" "Seven o'clock usually, but a bit later on weekends."*

起点 **qǐdiǎn** *n* starting point

起飞 **qǐfēi** *v* (of a plane) take off

起伏 **qǐfú** I *v* undulate, fluctuate II *n* fluctuation, setback

起哄 **qǐhòng** *v* set up a commotion in a light-hearted or mocking manner

起劲 **qǐjìn** *adv* enthusiastically, in high spirits

起来 **qǐlai** *v* get up (out of bed), stand up □ 校长走进教室，大家都站起来。**Xiàozhǎng zǒujin jiàoshì, dàjiā dōu zhàn qǐlai.** *When the principal entered the classroom, everybody stood up.*

NOTE: 起来 **qǐlai** is often used after a verb as a complement to express various meanings. Among other meanings, 起来 **qǐlai** may be used after a verb to mean *begin to ...*, e.g. □ 我们不等爸爸了，吃起来吧。**Wǒmen bù děng bàba le, chī qǐlai ba.** *We're not going to wait for daddy any longer. Let's start eating.*

起码 **qǐmǎ** *adj* the very least, minimum

起身 **qǐshēn** *v* 1 get up 2 set out, set off

起诉 **qǐsù** *v* sue, file a lawsuit against

起诉书 **qǐsùshū** indictment

起义 **qǐyì** I *v* stage an uprising, revolt II *n* uprising

农民起义 **nóngmín qǐyì** peasants' uprising

起源 **qǐyuán** [comp: 起 start + 源 source] I *n* origin □ 你知道人类的起源吗？**Nǐ zhīdào rénlèi de qǐyuán ma?** *Do you know the origin of humankind?* II *v* originate

砌 **qì** *v* lay (bricks), build by laying bricks

砌一堵墙 **qì yì dǔ qiáng** build a brick wall

泣 **qì** *v* sob, cry

哭泣 **kūqì** cry, weep and sob

气 1 **qì** Trad 氣 *n* 1 air, gas □ 车轮没有气了。**Chēlún méiyǒu qì le.** *The tire is flat.* 2 breath 3 spirit, morale

NOTE: Apart from its concrete meaning of *air, gas*, 气 **qì** is an important concept in traditional Chinese thought, meaning something like *vital force of life*.

气喘 **qìchuǎn** I *v* gasp for air II *n* asthma
　气喘病 **qìchuǎn bìng** asthma
气氛 **qìfēn** *n* atmosphere, ambiance □ 我喜欢这家酒吧友好的气氛。**Wǒ xǐhuan zhè jiā jiǔbā yǒuhǎo de qìfēn.** *I like the friendly ambiance of this bar.*
气概 **qìgài** *n* lofty spirit, (heroic) mettle
气功 **qìgōng** [modif: 气 breath + 功 skill] *n* a form of exercises involving deep breath, *qigong*
　练气功 **liàn qìgōng** practice exercises of deep breath, practice *qigong*
气候 **qìhòu** *n* climate □ 地球上的气候在渐渐变暖。**Dìqiú shang de qìhòu zài jiànjiàn biàn nuǎn.** *The climate on earth is gradually becoming warmer.*
气力 **qìlì** *n* strength, energy
　花很大气力 **huā hěn dà qìlì** make great efforts
气流 **qìliú** [modif: 气 air + 流 flow] *n* air current
气魄 **qìpò** *n* daring, boldness
气球 **qìqiú** *n* balloon
　热气球 **rèqìqiú** hot-air balloon
气势 **qìshì** *n* momentum
气体 **qìtǐ** *n* gas
气味 **qìwèi** *n* smell, odor □ 这个剩菜气味不对, 不能吃了。**Zhè ge shèngcài qìwèi búduì, bù néng chīle.** *The leftovers have a funny smell, and can't be eaten.*
气温 **qìwēn** [modif: 气 atmosphere + 温 temperature] *n* atmospheric temperature □ 今天最高气温十五度, 最低气温八度。**Jīntiān zuì gāo qìwēn shíwǔ dù, zuì dī qìwēn bā dù.** *Today's maximum temperature is 15 degrees, and the minimum is 8 degrees.* □ 受寒流影响, 今天夜里气温要下降十度左右。**Shòu hánliú yǐngxiǎng, jīntiān yèlǐ qìwēn yào xiàjiàng shí dù zuǒyòu.** *Owing to a cold current, the temperature will fall by about 10 degrees tonight.*

NOTE: See note on 温度 **wēndù**.

气息 **qìxī** *n* 1 breath, breathing 2 flavor
气象 **qìxiàng** *n* meteorological phenomena, weather
　气象台 **qìxiàngtái** meteorological observatory
　气象学 **qìxiàngxué** meteorology
　气象预报 **qìxiàng yùbào** weather forecast □ 你听今天的气象预报了吗? **Nǐ tīng jīntiān de qìxiàng yùbào le ma?** *Have you listened to today's weather forecast?*
气压 **qìyā** *n* atmospheric pressure, air pressure

气 2 **qì** Trad 氣 *v* be angry, make angry □ 知道他一直在骗我, 我气极了。**Zhīdào tā yìzhí zài piàn wǒ, wǒ qì jíle.** *When I found that he had been deceiving me all the time, I was very angry.* □ 你干吗说这种话气她? **Nǐ gànmá shuō zhè zhǒng huà qì tā?** *Why on earth did you say that and make her angry?*
气愤 **qìfèn** [comp: 气 angry + 愤 angry] *adj* very angry, fumingly mad
汽 **qì** *n* vapor, steam
汽车 **qìchē** [modif: 汽 vapor + 车 vehicle] *n*

automobile, car (辆 **liàng**) □ 我的汽车坏了。**Wǒde qìchē huài le.** *My car has broken down.*
开汽车 **kāi qìchē** drive a car □ 你会开汽车吗? **Nǐ huì kāi qìchē ma?** *Can you drive a car?*

NOTE: In everyday Chinese, 车 **chē** is often used instead of 汽车 **qìchē** to refer to *a car*, e.g. □ 我可以把车停在这里吗? **Wǒ kěyǐ bǎ chē tíng zài zhèli ma?** *May I park my car here?*

汽船 **qìchuán** *n* steamboat [艘 **sōu**]
汽水 **qìshuǐ** [modif: 汽 vapor + 水 water] *n* soda water, soft drink, soda, pop (瓶 **píng**, 杯 **bēi**) □ 这瓶汽水是给你的。**Zhè píng qìshuǐ shì gěi nǐ de.** *This bottle of soda water is for you.* □ 我不喝汽水, 我喝矿泉水。**Wǒ bù hē qìshuǐ, wǒ hē kuàngquánshuǐ.** *I don't drink soft drinks. I drink mineral water.*
汽油 **qìyóu** *n* gasoline, petroleum □ 我们的汽油快用完了, 到前面的加油站要停下加油。**Wǒmen de qìyóu kuài yòngwán le, dào qiánmiàn de jiāyóuzhàn yào tíngxia jiāyóu.** *We've almost run out of gas. We'll have to stop for gas at the next gas station.*
弃 **qì** Trad 棄 *v* abandon (See 放弃 **fàngqì**.)
器 **qì** *n* utensil
器材 **qìcái** [comp: 器 equipment + 材 material] *n* equipment, material
器官 **qìguān** *n* (human and animal) organ
器械 **qìxiè** *n* apparatus, instrument
　医疗器械 **yīliáo qìxiè** medical equipment
掐 **qiā** *v* pinch, nip
恰 **qià** *adv* just, exactly
恰当 **qiàdàng** *adj* appropriate, suitable, proper
恰到好处 **qiàdào hǎochù** *idiom* just right, hitting the spot □ 你说的话, 恰到好处。**Nǐ shuōde huà, qià dào hǎochu.** *What you said hit the nail on the head.*
恰好 **qiàhǎo** *adv* just right, in the nick of time
恰恰 **qiàqià** *adv* exactly, precisely
恰巧 **qiàqiǎo** *adv* as luck would have it, fortunately □ 恰巧大家都在。**Qiàqiǎo dàjiā dōu zài.** *Fortunately everyone happened to be there.*
恰如其分 **qiàrúqífèn** *idiom* no more no less, apt
洽 **qià** *v* consult, discuss
洽谈 **qiàtán** [comp: 洽 consult + 谈 talk] *v* hold a talk
　和他们公司洽谈合作项目 **hé tāmen gōngsī qiàtán hézuò xiàngmù** hold talks with their company over co-operation
牵 **qiān** *v* lead along by hand
牵扯 **qiānchě** *v* involve, implicate
牵引 **qiānyǐn** [comp: 牵 lead by hand + 引 lead] *v* tow, draw
牵制 **qiānzhì** *v* restrain, be bogged down
千 **qiān** *num* thousand
　一千零一夜 **yìqiān líng yí yè** a thousand and one nights
　四千五百八十 **sìqiān wǔbǎi bāshí** four thousand, five hundred and eighty, 4,580
千方百计 **qiānfāng bǎijì** [comp: 千方 a thousand methods + 百计 a hundred plans] *idiom* in a thousand and one ways, by every possible means

千克 **qiānkè** *n* kilogram (kg)

千瓦 **qiānwǎ** *n* kilowatt (kW)

千万 **qiānwàn** *adv* be sure to, must never (used in an imperative sentence for emphasis) □ 你开车千万要小心! *Nǐ kāichē qiānwàn yào xiǎoxīn! Be very, very careful while driving.* □ 明天的会你千万别迟到。 *Míngtiān de huì nǐ qiānwàn bié chídào. Be sure not to be late for tomorrow's meeting.*

迁 **qiān** Trad 遷 *v* move

迁就 **qiānjiù** *v* accommodate oneself to, yield to

签 **qiān** Trad 簽 *v* sign, autograph

签订 **qiāndìng** *v* sign (a treaty, an agreement, etc.) □ 那家建筑公司和市政府签订了两份合同。 **Nà jiā jiànzhù gōngsī hé shì zhèngfǔ qiāndìngle liǎng fèn hétóng.** *The construction company has signed two contracts with the city government.*

签发 **qiānfā** [comp: 签 sign + 发 issue] *v* (of an official) sign and issue (an document, certificate, etc.)

签名 **qiānmíng** [v+obj: 签 sign + 名 name] **I** *v* autograph, sign one's name **II** *n* autograph, signature 请歌星签名 qǐng gēxīng qiānmíng ask a singer for his/her autograph

签署 **qiānshǔ** *v* sign (a treaty, a contract, etc.)

签证 **qiānzhèng** *n* visa 签证处 qiānzhèngchù visa section (of a consulate or embassy) 入境签证 rùjìng qiānzhèng entry visa 申请签证 shēnqǐng qiānzhèng apply for a visa

签字 **qiānzì** **I** *v* sign (a document) 在支票上签字 zài zhīpiào shang qiānzì sign a check **II** *n* signature

铅 **qiān** Trad 鉛 *n* lead (Pb)

铅笔 **qiānbǐ** [modif: 铅 lead + 笔 pen] *n* pencil (支 zhī) □ 我的红铅笔哪里去了? **Wǒ de hóng qiānbǐ nǎlǐ qù le?** *Where's my red pencil?* □ 我可以用一下你的铅笔吗? **Wǒ kěyǐ yòng yíxià nǐ de qiānbǐ ma?** *May I use your pencil for a while?* 铅笔盒 qiānbǐ hé pencil box 铅笔刀 qiānbǐ dāo pencil sharpener

谦 **qiān** Trad 謙 *adj* modest

谦虚 **qiānxū** [comp: 谦 modest + 虚 empty] *adj* modest, self-effacing □ 他对自己的成绩非常谦虚。 **Tā duì zìjǐ de chéngjì fēicháng qiānxū.** *He is very modest about his achievements.*

谦逊 **qiānxùn** *adj* modest, unassuming

前 **qián** **I** *n* 1 front, in front of (antonym 后 **hòu**) □ 房子前有一块草地。 **Fángzi qián yǒu yí kuài cǎodì.** *In front of the house is a lawn.* □ 中国人的姓名,姓在前, 名在后。 **Zhōngguórén de xìngmíng, xìng zài qián, míng zài hòu.** *In a Chinese person's name, the family name comes before the given name.* **2** Same as 以前 **yǐqián** **II** *adv* forward

NOTE: In everyday Chinese, 前 **qián** is seldom used alone to mean *front* or *in front of*. Often it is better to use 前边 **qiánbian**.

前辈 **qiánbèi** [modif: 前 previous + 辈 generation] *n* the older generation, elders, trailblazer

前边 **qiánbian** [modif: 前 front + 边 side] *n* front (antonym 后边 **hòubian**) □ 房子前边有一块草地。

Fángzi qiánbian yǒu yí kuài cǎodì. *In front of the house is a lawn.* □ 中国人的姓名姓在前边, 名在后边。 **Zhōngguórén de xìngmíng, xìng zài qiánbian, míng zài hòubian.** *In a Chinese person's name, the family name comes before the given name.*

前程 **qiánchéng** [modif: 前 in front + 程 journey] *n* future, prospects 远大前程 yuǎndà qiánchéng bright future

前方 **qiánfāng** *n* (in war) front, frontline

前后 **qiánhòu** [comp: 前 front + 后 rear] *adv* (of time) around, about 在2000年前后 zài èr-líng-líng-líng nián qiánhòu around the year 2000

前进 **qiánjìn** [comp: 前 advance + 进 advance] *v* go forward, advance (antonym 后退 **hòutuì**) □ 我们的经济在过去一年又前进了一大步。 **Wǒmen de jīngjì zài guòqu yì nián yòu qiánjìn le yí dà bù.** *Last year our economy took a big stride forward.*

前景 **qiánjǐng** [modif: 前 front + 景 view] *n* prospect, vista □ 前景不妙。 **Qiánjǐng búmiào.** *The future doesn't look too promising.*

前列 **qiánliè** *n* front rank, forefront

前面 **qiánmian** *n* Same as 前边 **qiánbian**

前年 **qiánnián** *n* the year before last □ 今年是2009年前年是2007年。 **Jīnnián shì èr-líng-líng-jiǔ nián, qiánnián shì èr-líng-líng-qī nián.** *This year is 2009 and the year before last was 2007.* □ 前年我刚开始学中文。 **Qiánnián wǒ gāng kāishǐ xué Zhōngwén.** *I just began to learn Chinese the year before last.*

前期 **qiánqī** *n* early stage, early days 工程的前期 gōngchéng de qiánqī the early stage of an engineering project

前人 **qiánrén** *n* predecessor, forefather □ 前人栽树, 后人乘凉。 **Qiánrén zāishù, hòurén chéngliáng.** *The forefathers planted the trees, and their descendants enjoy the shade.* (→ *We all enjoy the fruit of labor of our predecessors.*)

前所未有 **qiánsuǒwèiyǒu** *idiom* unprecedented, hitherto unheard of

前提 **qiántí** *n* **1** prerequisite, the prime consideration **2** (in logic) premise

前天 **qiántiān** *n* the day before yesterday □ 他前天去中国, 今天我收到了他从中国发来的电子邮件。 **Tā qiántiān qù Zhōngguó, jīntiān wǒ shōudàole tā cóng Zhōngguó fālái de diànzǐ yóujiàn.** *He left for China the day before yesterday, and today I got an e-mail he sent from China.*

前头 **qiántou** Same as 前面 **qiánmian**, used colloquially.

前途 **qiántú** [modif: 前 in front + 途 journey] *n* future, prospects, future prospects □ 一个青年连中学都没有毕业, 不可能有什么前途。 **Yí ge qīngnián lián zhōngxué dōu méiyǒu bìyè, bù kěnéng yǒu shénme qiántú.** *A young man does not have much of future prospects if he does not even finish high school.* □ 这次计划的成败将决定公司的前途。 **Zhè cì jìhuà de chéngbài jiāng juédìng gōngsī de qiántú.** *The success or failure of this plan will determine the future prospects of the company.*

前往 **qiánwǎng** *v* go to, proceed

前线 **qiánxiàn** *n* (in war) front, frontline 上前线 shàng qiánxiàn go to the front, go to war

钳 **qián** Trad 鉗 *n* pincer, plier, forceps
  钳子 **qiánzi** pincer, plier, forceps (把 **bǎ**)
  老虎钳 **lǎohǔqián** plier, pincer

潜 **qián** Trad 潛 *adj* hidden, latent
  潜伏 **qiánfú** *v* hide, lie low
  潜伏期 **qiánfúqī** (in medicine) incubation period
  潜力 **qiánlì** [modif: 潜 hidden + 力 strength] *n* latent capacity, potential, potentiality
  潜水 **qiánshuǐ** *v* go under water, dive
    潜水员 **qiánshuǐyuán** diver
  潜水艇 **qiánshuǐtǐng** *n* submarine (艘 **sōu**)

钱 **qián** Trad 錢 *n* money (笔 **bǐ**) □ 钱很重要, 但不是万能的。 **Qián hěn zhòngyào, dàn bú shì wànnéng de.** *Money is important, but it is not all-powerful.* □ 他在银行里有一大笔钱。 **Tā zài yínháng li yǒu yí dà bǐ qián.** *He has a big sum of money in the bank.* □ 他从来不向人借钱, 也不借钱给别人。 **Tā cónglái bú xiàng rén jiè qián, yě bú jiè qián gei biéren.** *He never borrows money, nor does he lend money to others.*
  钱包 **qiánbāo** wallet, purse

浅 **qiǎn** Trad 淺 *adj* **1** shallow (antonym 深 **shēn**) □ 这条河很浅, 可以走过去。 **Zhè tiáo hé hěn qiǎn, kěyǐ zǒu guòqu.** *This river is shallow. You can wade across it.* **2** easy, of low standard □ 这本书太浅, 你不用看。 **Zhè běn shū tài qiǎn, nǐ bú yòng kàn.** *This book is too easy for you; you don't have to read it.*

遣 **qiǎn** *v* send, dispatch (See 派遣 **pàiqiǎn**)

谴 **qiǎn** Trad 譴 *v* as in 谴责 **qiǎnzé**
  谴责 **qiǎnzé** *v* condemn, denounce

嵌 **qiàn** *v* inlay, imbed

欠 **qiàn** *v* owe, be in debt to □ 他欠我一百元。 **Tā qiàn wǒ yìbǎi yuán.** *He owes me a hundred yuan.*
  欠人情 **qiàn rénqíng** [v+ obj: 欠 owe + 人情 human feelings] *v* owe a debt of gratitude

歉 **qiàn** *n* **1** apology **2** crop failure
  歉意 **qiànyì** *n* apology, regret
  深表歉意 **shēn biǎo qiànyì** offer one's profound apology

腔 **qiāng** *n* cavity
  口腔 **kǒuqiāng** oral cavity

枪 **qiāng** Trad 槍 *n* small arms, gun, pistol (支 **zhī**, 把 **bǎ**) □ 在我们国家, 老百姓有枪是犯法的。 **Zài wǒmen guójiā, lǎobǎixìng yǒu qiāng shì fànfǎ de.** *In our country, it's against the law for ordinary citizens to own guns.*
  手枪 **shǒuqiāng** handgun (revolver, pistol)
  枪毙 **qiāngbì** *v* execute by shooting

强 **qiáng** **I** *adj* strong (antonym 弱 **ruò**) □ 她中文口语很强, 但是写汉字的能力比较弱。 **Tā Zhōngwén kǒuyǔ hěn qiáng, dànshì xiě Hànzì de nénglì bǐjiào ruò.** *She is strong in oral Chinese, but weak in writing characters.* **II** *adv* by force
  强大 **qiángdà** [comp: 强 strong + 大 big] *adj* powerful (antonym 弱小 **ruòxiǎo**) □ 谁都希望自己的祖国强大。 **Shéi dōu xīwàng zìjǐ de zǔguó qiángdà.** *Everybody wants their motherland to be a powerful country.*
  强盗 **qiángdào** *n* bandit, robber □ 他十几岁的时候是个小偷, 现在二十多岁了一名强盗 **Tā shí jǐ suì de shíhou shì ge xiǎotōu, xiànzài èrshí duō suì**

chéngle yì míng qiángdào. *When he was a teenager he was a thief. Now in his twenties, he has become a robber.*
  强调 **qiángdiào** [modif: 强 strong + 调 tone] *v* emphasize, lay stress on □ 王老师强调语音准确的重要性。 **Wáng lǎoshī qiángdiào yǔyīn zhǔnquè de zhòngyàoxìng.** *Teacher Wang emphasized the importance of correct pronunciation.*
  强度 **qiángdù** [modif: 强 strong + 度 degree] *n* intensity, strength □ 这种材料的强度还不够。 **Zhè zhǒng cáiliào de qiángdù hái bú gòu.** *This material does not have enough strength.*
  强化 **qiánghuà** *v* strengthen, intensify
  强奸 **qiángjiān** *v* rape
    强奸幼女 **qiángjiān yòunǚ** rape an underage girl
  强烈 **qiángliè** [comp: 强 strong + 烈 raging] *adj* strong, intense, violent □ 顾客们强烈要求退货。 **Gùkèmen qiángliè yāoqiú tuìhuò.** *The customers firmly demanded a refund.*
  强盛 **qiángshèng** [comp: 强 strong + 盛 prosperous] *adj* (of a country) strong and prosperous, powerful and wealthy
  强制 **qiángzhì** *v* coerce, force

墙 **qiáng** Trad 牆 *n* wall (道 **dào**) □ 墙上有一张世界地图。 **Qiáng shang yǒu yì zhāng shìjiè dìtú.** *There's a map of the world on the wall.*
  墙壁 **qiángbì** [comp: 墙 wall + 壁 wall] *n* wall

强 **qiǎng** *v* make an effort
  强迫 **qiǎngpò** [comp: 强 force + 迫 compel] *v* force, coerce □ 你能把马领到水边, 但是不能强迫马喝水。 **Nǐ néng bǎ mǎ lǐng dào shuǐbian, dànshì bùnéng qiǎngpò mǎ hēshuǐ.** *You can lead a horse to the water, but you can't force it to drink.*

抢 **qiǎng** Trad 搶 *v* **1** seize, grab □ 他的玩具手枪被一个大孩子抢走了。 **Tā de wánjù shǒuqiāng bèi yí ge dà háizi qiǎngzǒu le.** *His toy pistol was snatched away by a big boy.* **2** rob, loot
  抢劫 **qiǎngjié** *v* rob
    抢劫银行 **qiǎngjié yínháng** rob a bank
  抢救 **qiǎngjiù** *v* rescue, salvage
    抢救病人 **qiǎngjiù bìngrén** rescue a patient, give emergency treatment to a patient

悄 **qiāo** *adj* quiet
  悄悄 **qiāoqiāo** *adv* quietly, on the quiet □ 他悄悄对我说: "别在这里买, 太贵了。" **Tā qiāoqiāo de duì wǒ shuō: "Bié zài zhèli mǎi, tài guì le."** *He whispered to me, "Don't buy it here, it's too expensive."*

敲 **qiāo** *v* knock, rap □ 有人敲门。 **Yǒu rén qiāo mén.** *Someone is knocking at the door.*

锹 **qiāo** Trad 鍬 *n* spade
  铁锹 **tiěqiāo** spade (把 **bǎ**)

桥 **qiáo** Trad 橋 *n* bridge (座 **zuò**) □ 这座石桥历史很久。 **Zhè zuò shíqiáo lìshǐ hěn jiǔ.** *This stone bridge has a long history.* □ 长江上有很多大桥。 **Chángjiāng shang yǒu hěn duō dà qiáo.** *There are many big bridges across the Yangtze River.*
  过桥 **guò qiáo** cross a bridge
  桥梁 **qiáoliáng** *n* big bridge (座 **zuò**) □ 他的专业是桥梁建造。 **Tā de zhuānyè shì qiáoliáng jiànzào.** *His special field is bridge construction.*

乔 **qiáo** Trad 喬 disguise
  乔装 **qiáozhuāng** *v* disguise

乔装成一个海盗 qiáozhuāng chéng yí ge hǎidào disguise oneself as a pirate

侨 **qiáo** Trad 僑 *v* sojourn, live abroad
侨胞 **qiáobāo** *n* countrymen residing overseas

瞧 **qiáo** *v* Same as 看 **kàn** *v* 1. Used only as a colloquialism.

巧 **qiáo** I *adv* coincidental □ 真巧，我正要找他，他来了。*Zhēn qiǎo, wǒ zhèngyào zhǎo tā, tā láile. What a happy coincidence; he came just when I wanted to see him.* □ 你要买的书最后一本刚卖走，很不巧。*Nǐ yào mǎi de shū zuì hòu yì běn gāng màizǒu, hěn bù qiǎo. Unfortunately, the last copy of the book you want has just been sold.* II *adj* skilled, clever □ 他们的儿子手巧，女儿嘴巧。*Tāmen de érzi shǒu qiǎo, nǚ ér zuǐ qiǎo. Their son is clever with his hands and their daughter has the gift of the gab.*
巧妙 **qiǎomiào** [comp: 巧 skilled + 妙 wonderful] *adj* ingenious, very clever □ 这台机器设计得很巧妙。*Zhè tái jīqì shèjì de hěn qiǎomiào. This machine is ingeniously designed.* □ 她的回答很巧妙。*Tā de huídá hěn qiǎomiào. She gave a clever answer.*

翘 **qiào** Trad 翹 *v* stick up, bend upward

俏 **qiào** *adj* pretty and cute

切 **qiē** *v* cut, slice □ 爸爸把西瓜切成四块。*Bàba bǎ xīguā qiē chéng sì kuài. Dad cut the watermelon into four pieces.*

茄 **qié** *n* eggplant
茄子 **qiézi** eggplant (只 **zhī**)

且 **qiě** *conj* moreover (See 而且 **érqiě**.)

怯 **qiè** *adj* timid (See 胆怯 **dǎnqiè**.)

切 **qiè** *v* be close to, tally with
切实 **qièshí** *adj* 1 feasible, practical 2 earnest
切实可行的办法 qièshí kěxíng de bànfǎ practical measure

窃 **qiè** Trad 竊 *v* steal, pilfer
窃取 **qièqǔ** *v* steal, grab
窃听 **qiètīng** *v* eavesdrop, bug
窃听器 qiètīngqì listening-in device, bug

钦 **qīn** *v* admire
钦佩 **qīnpèi** [comp: 钦 admire + 佩 admire] *v* admire, esteem
令人钦佩 lìngrén qīnpèi admirable

亲 **qīn** Trad 親 I *n* blood relation II *adj* close, intimate
亲爱 **qīn'ài** [comp: 亲 intimate + 爱 love] *adj* dear, beloved, darling □ 我亲爱的祖母去年去世了，我难受了好久。*Wǒ qīn'ài de zǔmǔ qùnián qùshì le, wǒ nánshòule hǎojiǔ. My dear grandmother died last year; I was sad for a long time.*

NOTE: Although 亲爱 **qīn'ài** is glossed as *dear*, the Chinese reserve 亲爱(的) **qīn'ài (de)** for the very few people who are really dear and close to their hearts.

亲笔 **qīnbǐ** *adv* (written) in one's own handwriting
亲密 **qīnmì** [comp: 亲 close + 密 intimate] *adj* intimate, close
亲戚 **qīnqi** *n* relative, relation □ 他爸爸妈妈兄弟姐妹很多，所以他亲戚很多。*Tā bàba māma xiōngdì jiěmèi hěn duō, suǒyǐ tā qīnqi hěnduō. His parents have many siblings, so he has many relatives.*
亲戚朋友 qīnqi péngyou relatives and friends
走亲戚 zǒu qīnqi visit a relative
亲切 **qīnqiè** *adj* cordial □ 过圣诞节的时候，朋友们给我发来电子贺卡，表示亲切的问候。*Guò shèngdànjié de shíhou, péngyǒumen gěi wǒ fālai diànzǐ hèkǎ, biǎoshì qīnqiè de wènhòu. At Christmas, my friends sent me e-cards, conveying cordial greetings.*
亲热 **qīnrè** [comp: 亲 intimate + 热 warm] *adj* affectionate, warm-hearted
亲人 **qīnrén** [modif: 亲 blood relation + 人 person] *n* family member □ 我在故乡已经没有亲人了。*Wǒ zài gùxiāng yǐjing méiyǒu qīnrén le. I haven't got any family member in my hometown.*
亲身 **qīnshēn** *adj* personal, firsthand
亲身经历 qīnshēn jīnglì personal experience
亲生 **qīnshēng** *adj* one's biological (parents or children)
她的亲生父亲 tāde qīnshēng fùqin her biological father
亲手 **qīnshǒu** *adv* with one's own hands, by oneself, personally
亲眼 **qīnyǎn** *adv* with one's own eyes
亲友 **qīnyǒu** [comp: 亲 relatives + 友 friends] *n* relatives and friends
走亲访友 zǒu qīn fǎng yǒu visit relatives and friends
亲自 **qīnzì** *adv* by oneself, personally □ 李校长亲自来征求对教学的意见。*Lǐ xiàozhǎng qīnzì lái zhēngqiú duì jiàoxué de yìjiàn. Mr Li, the principal, came himself to ask for our comments on teaching.*

侵 **qīn** *v* invade, intrude, encroach
侵略 **qīnlüè** *v* invade (by force) □ 侵略别国在国际上是不允许的。*Qīnlüè bié guó zài guójì shang shì bù yǔnxǔ de. Invading another country is not permitted internationally.*
侵入 **qīnrù** [comp: 侵 invade + 入 enter] *v* intrude into, make incursions into
侵蚀 **qīnshí** *v* corrode, erode
侵占 **qīnzhàn** [comp: 侵 intrude + 占 occupy] *v* invade and occupy

琴 **qín** *n* (stringed) musical instrument
钢琴 gāngqín piano (架 **jià**)
提琴 tíqín violin (把 **bǎ**)

勤 **qín** *adj* diligent, hard-working
勤奋 **qínfèn** *adj* diligent, applying oneself to
勤俭 **qínjiǎn** [comp: 勤 diligent + 俭 frugal] *adj* diligent and frugal □ 勤俭致富。*Qínjiǎn zhìfù. Industry and frugality leads to wealth.*
勤恳 **qínkěn** [comp: 勤 diligent + 恳 sincere] *adj* diligent and conscientious
勤劳 **qínláo** *adj* hard-working, industrious

芹 **qín** celery
芹菜 qíncài celery

禽 **qín** *n* bird, fowl

青 **qīng** *adj* green □ 在新西兰草地一年到头都是青青的。*Zài Xīnxīlán cǎodì yì-nián-dào-tóu dōu shì qīngqīng de. In New Zealand the grass is green all year round.*

青菜 **qīngcài** *n* Chinese cabbage (棵 **kē**)

青春 **qīngchūn** [modif: 青 green + 春 spring] *n* the quality of being young, youth
青春期 qīngchūnqī puberty
永葆青春 yǒngbǎo qīngchūn have eternal youth

青年 **qīngnián** [modif: 青 green + 年 year] *n* young person, young people, youth (especially male) (位 **wèi**, 个 **gè**) □ 那位青年是我姐姐的男朋友。**Nà wèi qīngnián shì wǒ jiějie de nánpéngyou.** *That young man is my elder sister's boyfriend.* □ 青年工人往往没有多少经验。**Qīngnián gōngrén wǎngwǎng méiyǒu duōshǎo jīngyàn.** *Young workers often don't have much experience.*

青蛙 **qīngwā** [modif: 青 green + 蛙 frog] *n* frog (只 **zhī**) □ 青蛙能够跳得很高。**Qīngwā nénggòu tiào de hěn gāo.** *A frog can jump high.*

青 **qīng** **I** *adj* **1** clear (water), clean □ 过去这条河的水很清，能看到河底的小石头。**Guòqù zhè tiáo hé de shuǐ hěn qīng, néng kàndào hédǐ de xiǎo shítou.** *In the past this river had very clear water and you could see the little stones on the riverbed.* **2** (of matters) clear, easy to understand □ 这件事没有人能说得清。**Zhè jiàn shì méiyǒu rén néng shuō de qīng.** *Nobody can give a clear account of this matter.* **II** *v* make clear

清查 **qīngchá** [comp: 清 clear + 查 check] *v* check thoroughly

清晨 **qīngchén** *n* early morning

清除 **qīngchú** [comp: 清 clear + 除 remove] *v* remove, clear away
清除垃圾邮件 qīngchú lājī yóujiàn delete junk mail

清楚 **qīngchu** [comp: 清 clear + 楚 clear-cut] *adj* clear (of speech or image) □ 你的意思很清楚，我明白。**Nǐ de yìsi hěn qīngchu, wǒ míngbai.** *Your meaning is clear. I understand it.* □ 老师，黑板上的字我看不清楚。**Lǎoshī, hēibǎn shang de zì wǒ kàn bu qīngchu.** *Teacher, I can't see the words on the blackboard clearly.* □ 我说得清清楚楚，你怎么会误会呢？**Wǒ shuōde qīng-qīng-chǔ-chǔ, nǐ zěnme huì wùhuì ne?** *I said it very clearly. How could you misunderstand it?*

清洁 **qīngjié** [comp: 清 clear + 洁 clear] *v* clean, clear up
清洁工 qīngjiégōng cleaner

清理 **qīnglǐ** [comp: 清 clear + 理 tidy up] *v* sort out, clear out
清理办公桌 qīnglǐ bàngōngzhuō clear out a desk

清晰 **qīngxī** [comp: 清 clear + 晰 clear] *adj* very clear, distinct

清新 **qīngxīn** [comp: 清 clear + 新 new] *adj* pure and fresh, refreshing
清新的空气 qīngxīn de kōngqì fresh air

清醒 **qīngxǐng** [comp: 清 clear + 醒 awake] *adj* clear-headed, sober

轻 **qīng** Trad 輕 *adj* **1** light (of weight) (antonym 重 **zhòng**) □ 油比水轻。**Yóu bǐ shuǐ qīng.** *Oil is lighter than water.* **2** low, soft (of voice) □ 她说话很轻，要仔细听，才能听清楚。**Tā shuōhuà hěn qīng, yào zǐxì tīng, cái néng tīng qīngchu.** *She speaks softly. Only if you listen attentively can you hear her clearly.* **3** of a low degree □ 对他的处分太轻了。**Duì tā de chǔfèn tài qīng le.** *The disciplinary action against him was not severe enough.*

轻便 **qīngbiàn** [comp: 轻 light + 便 convenient] *adj* lightweight and handy, portable

轻工业 **qīnggōngyè** *n* light industry

轻快 **qīngkuài** *adj* **1** light-hearted, lively **2** light-footed, brisk

轻视 **qīngshì** *v* think … unimportant, underestimate, belittle

轻松 **qīngsōng** [comp: 轻 light + 松 loose] *adj* (of a job) easy, not requiring much effort, relaxed □ 这个工作很轻松，当然工资不高。**Zhège gōngzuò hěn qīngsōng, dāngrán gōngzī bù gāo.** *This job is easy and requires no real effort; of course it is poorly paid.* □ 上个周末我过得非常轻松愉快。**Shàng ge zhōumò wǒ guò de fēicháng qīngsōng yúkuài.** *Last weekend I had a very relaxed and pleasant time.*

轻微 **qīngwéi** [comp: 轻 light + 微 tiny] *adj* slight, trifling
只有轻微的损失 zhǐyǒu qīngwéi de sǔnshī only slightly damaged

轻易 **qīngyì** [comp: 轻 light + 易 esay] *adv* **1** easily, demanding little effort **2** without much consideration, rashly
轻易下结论 qīngyì xià jiélùn reach a hasty conclusion

轻音乐 **qīng yīnyuè** *n* light music

氢 **qīng** *n* hydrogen (H)
氢气 qīngqì hydrogen

倾 **qīng** *v* incline, lean

倾听 **qīngtīng** [comp: 倾 lean + 听 listen] *v* listen attentively

倾向 **qīngxiàng** *n* tendency, inclination

倾销 **qīngxiāo** *v* dump (goods)
反倾销法 fǎn qīngxiāo fǎ anti-dumping regulation

倾斜 **qīngxié** *v* tilt, incline

蜻 **qīng** as in 蜻蜓 **qīngtíng**
蜻蜓 qīngtíng *n* dragonfly (只 **zhī**)

情 **qíng** *n* **1** circumstance **2** feeling, sentiment

情报 **qíngbào** [modif: 情 situation + 报 report] *n* intelligence, information □ 这个记者搜集了大量商业情报。**Zhège jìzhě sōují le dàliàng shāngyè qíngbào.** *This journalist has collected a great deal of commercial intelligence.*

情感 **qínggǎn** *n* emotion, feeling

情节 **qíngjié** *n* plot (of a story, movie, etc.)

情景 **qíngjǐng** [comp: 情 situation + 景 scene] *n* scene, occasion □ 旅馆大楼在半夜着火了，人们从楼上跳下，真是可怕的情景。**Lǚguǎn dàlóu zài bànyè zháohuǒ le, rénmen cóng lóushang tiàoxia, zhēn shì kěpà de qíngjǐng.** *When the hotel caught fire at midnight, people jumped from the upper floors. It was indeed a frightening scene.*

情况 **qíngkuàng** [comp: 情 circumstance + 况 situation] *n* situation, circumstance □ 他生病住院了，情况很严重。**Tā shēng bìng zhùyuàn le, qíngkuàng hěn yánzhòng.** *He's been hospitalized. His condition is very serious.* □ 我不大了解这个国家的情况。**Wǒ bú dà liáojiě zhège guójiā de qíngkuàng.** *I don't quite know the situation this country is in.*

情理 **qínglǐ** [comp: 情 emotion + 理 reason] *n* accepted code of conduct, reason
不近情理 bù jìn qínglǐ violate the accepted code of conduct, unreasonable

情形 **qíngxíng** [comp: 情 situation + 形 shape] *n* circumstances, situation □ 两列火车马上要相撞, 情形十分紧张。 **Liǎng liè huǒchē mǎshàng yào xiāngzhuàng, qíngxíng shífēn jǐnzhāng.** *The two trains were about to collide. It was an extremely nerve-racking situation.*

情绪 **qíngxù** [comp: 情 emotion + 绪 mood] *n* mood, feelings □ 天气会影响人们的情绪。 **Tiānqì huì yǐngxiǎng rénmen de qíngxù.** *The weather can affect people's moods.* □ 他看来情绪不好, 你知道为什么吗? **Tā kànlai qíngxù bù hǎo, nǐ zhīdào wèishénme ma?** *He seems to be in a bad mood. Do you know why?*

情愿 **qíngyuàn** [comp: 情 emotion + 愿 willing] *v* would rather, prefer □ 我情愿多花些钱, 也要买到称心的东西。 **Wǒ qíngyuàn duō huā xiē qián, yě yāo mǎidào chènxīn de dōngxi.** *I'd rather spend more money in order to get things that satisfy me.*

NOTE: 情愿 **qíngyuàn** is usually used together with 也 **yě**, as shown in the example sentence. 也 **yě** may be replaced by 都 **dōu**, e.g. □ 我情愿多花些钱, 都要买到称心的东西。 **Wǒ qíngyuàn duō huā xiē qián, dōu yāomǎi dào chènxīn de dōngxi.** *I'd rather spend more money in order to get things that satisfy me.*

晴 **qíng** *adj* (of weather) fine, clear □ 今天上午晴, 中午以后开始下雨了。 **Jīntiān shàngwǔ qíng, zhōngwǔ yǐhòu kāishǐ xià yǔ le.** *It was fine this morning. It began raining in the afternoon.* □ 晴天比雨天舒服。 **Qíngtiān bǐ yǔtiān shūfu.** *A fine day is more comfortable than a rainy day.*

晴朗 **qínglǎng** *adj* fine, sunny

晴天 **qíngtiān** *n* fine day

请 **qǐng** Trad 請 *v* 1 invite □ 今天晚上我请你吃饭。 **Jīntiān wǎnshang wǒ qǐng nǐ chīfàn.** *I'll invite you to dinner tonight.* 2 ask, request □ 学生请老师再说一遍。 **Xuésheng qǐng lǎoshī zài shuō yí biàn.** *The students asked the teacher to repeat it.*

NOTE: 请 **qǐng** is used to start a polite request, equivalent to *Please ...*, e.g. □ 请您别在这里吸烟。 **Qǐng nín bié zài zhèli xīyān.** *Please don't smoke here.* □ 请坐! **Qǐng zuò!** *Sit down, please!* □ 请喝茶。 **Qǐng hē chá.** *Have some tea, please!*

请假 **qǐngjià** *v* ask for leave

请病假 **qǐng bìngjià** ask for sick leave

请事假 **qǐng shìjià** ask for leave of absence

请柬 **qǐngjiǎn** *n* letter of invitation, invitation card (份 **fèn**)

请教 **qǐngjiào** [v+obj: 请 ask for + 教 teaching] *v* ask fro advice, consult

NOTE: 请教 **qǐngjiào** is a polite word, used when you want to ask for advice or information, e.g. □ 我能不能请教您一个问题? **Wǒ néngbunéng qǐng jiào nín yí ge wèntí?** *Could I ask you a question, please?* □ 请教, 这个汉字是什么意思? **Qǐngjiào, zhège Hànzì shì shénme yìsi?** *Would you please tell me the meaning of this Chinese character?*

请客 **qǐngkè** [v+obj: 请 invite + 客 guest] *v* 1 invite to dinner □ 张先生这个星期六在家里请客。 **Zhāng**

xiānsheng zhège Xīngqīliù zài jiāli qǐngkè. *This Saturday Mr Zhang will give a dinner party at home.* 2 treat (someone to something) □ 这次出去玩, 车票、门票都是我请客。 **Zhè cì chūqu wán, chēpiào, ménpiào duō shì wǒ qǐngkè.** *On this date, I'll pay for bus fares and admission tickets.*

请客送礼 **qǐngkè sònglǐ** invite to dinner and give gift to, bribe by gifts and dinner parties

请求 **qǐngqiú** [comp: 请 request + 求 beseech] **I** *v* request, ask for □ 我请求你原谅我的错误。 **Wǒ qǐngqiú nǐ yuánliàng wǒ de cuòwù.** *I ask for your forgiveness of my mistake.* **II** *n* request □ 你们的请求已交委员会考虑。 **Nǐmen de qǐngqiú yǐ jiāo wěiyuánhuì kǎolǜ.** *Your request has been submitted to the committee for consideration.*

请示 **qǐngshì** [v+obj: 请 request + 示 instruction] *v* ask (a person of superior position) for instruction

请帖 **qǐngtiě** *n* letter of invitation, invitation card (份 **fèn**)

请⋯ **qǐng wèn**... Excuse me, ... □ 请问, 您是上海来的张先生吗? **Qǐng wèn, nín shì Shànghǎi lái de Zhāng xiānsheng ma?** *Excuse me, are you Mr Zhang from Shanghai?*

NOTE: When you want some information from someone, start your query with 请问⋯ **qǐng wèn...** , e.g. □ 请问, 去火车站怎么走? **Qǐng wèn, qù huǒchēzhàn zěnme zǒu?** *Excuse me, could you show me the way to the railway station?*

顷 **qǐng** Trad 頃 *n* a unit of area (= 6.6667 hectares)

庆 **qìng** Trad 慶 *v* celebrate

庆贺 **qìnghè** [comp: 庆 celebrate + 贺 congratulate] *v* congratulate, celebrate

庆祝 **qìngzhù** [comp: 庆 celebrate + 祝 good wishes] *v* celebrate □ 英国大使馆昨天举行宴会, 庆祝女王生日。 **Yīngguó dàshǐguǎn zuótiān jǔxíng yànhuì, qìngzhù nǚwáng shēngrì.** *The British embassy gave a dinner party yesterday to celebrate the Queen's birthday.* □ 下个月他们的女儿大学毕业。他们打算好好庆祝一下。 **Xià ge yuè tāmen de nǚ'ér dàxué bìyè, tāmen dǎsuàn hǎohǎo qìngzhù yíxià.** *Their daughter will graduate from university next month. They plan to celebrate lavishly.*

穷 **qióng** Trad 窮 *adj* poor, poverty-stricken □ 她家里比较穷。 **Tā jiāli bǐjiào qióng.** *Her family is rather poor.* □ 国家再穷也应该花足够的钱办教育。 **Guójiā zài qióng yě yīnggāi huā zúgòu de qián bàn jiàoyù.** *No matter how poor a country is, sufficient funds should be spent on education.*

穷苦 **qióngkǔ** [comp: 穷 poor + 苦 miserable] *adj* poor, poverty-stricken

穷人 **qióngrén** poor person, the poor

秋 **qiū** *n* fall, autumn □ 北京香山的秋景很美。 **Běijīng Xiāngshān de qiū jǐng hěn měi.** *The autumn scenery on Fragrance Hill in Beijing is very beautiful.*

秋收 **qiūshōu** *n* autumn harvest

秋天 **qiūtiān** [modif: 秋 autumn + 天 day] *n* fall, autumn □ 秋天不冷不热, 十分舒服。 **Qiūtiān bù lěng bú rè, shífēn shūfu.** *Autumn is neither hot nor cold; it's very comfortable.*

丘 **qiū** *n* mound, low and small hill
丘陵 **qiūlíng** *n* hills, hilly land

求 **qiú** *v* beseech, beg, humbly ask for □ 你只有求他帮忙。 **Nǐ zhǐyǒu qiú tā bāngmáng.** *You can only ask him for help.* □ 我求你再考虑考虑。 **Wǒ qiú nǐ zài kǎolǜ kǎolǜ.** *I beg you to give it further consideration.*
求婚 **qiúhūn** [v+obj: 求 request + 婚 marriage] *v* propose marriage, make a marriage offer

球 **qiú** *n* **1** ball (只 **zhī**) □ 花园里有一只球, 是谁的? **Huāyuán li yǒu yì zhī qiú, shì shéi de?** *There's a ball in the garden. Whose is it?* **2** ball game (场 **chǎng**) □ 我们每星期六下午打一场球。 **Wǒmen měi Xīngqīliù xiàwǔ dǎ yì chǎng qiú.** *We have a ball game every Saturday afternoon.*
比球 **bǐ qiú** have a (ball game) match
棒球 **bàngqiú** baseball
打球 **dǎ qiú** play basketball or volleyball
看球 **kàn qiú** watch a ball game
篮球 **lánqiú** basketball
排球 **páiqiú** volleyball
踢球 **tī qiú** play soccer
足球 **zúqiú** soccer
球场 **qiúchǎng** *n* sports ground (especially where ball games are played)
球队 **qiúduì** *n* (ball game) team
球迷 **qiúmí** *n* (ball game) fan
足球迷 **zúqiúmí** soccer fan
球员 **qiúyuán** (ball game) player

曲 **qū** *adj* crooked, bent
曲线 **qūxiàn** *n* curve
曲线图 **qūxiàntú** line graph, graph
曲折 **qūzhé** *adj* tortuous, winding

区 **qū** Trad 區 *n* district □ 中国的城市一般分成几个区。 **Zhōngguó de chéngshì yìbān fēnchéng jǐ ge qū.** *A city in China is usually divided into several districts.*
商业区 **shāngyèqū** commercial area, business district
工业区 **gōngyèqū** industrial zone, industrial district
区别 **qūbié** **I** *v* set apart, differentiate □ 你能区别美国英语和英国英语吗? **Nǐ néng qūbié Měiguó Yīngyǔ hé Yīngguó Yīngyǔ ma?** *Can you tell American English from British English?* **II** *n* difference □ 这两个词的意义没有多大区别。 **Zhè liǎng ge cí de yìyì méiyǒu duōdà qūbié.** *There is not much difference in the meaning of the two words.*
区分 **qūfēn** **I** *v* put in different categories, differentiate **II** *n* differentiation
区域 **qūyù** *n* region, area

区 **qū** Trad 驅 *v* drive
驱车前往 **qūchē qiánwǎng** drive (in a car) to
驱逐 **qūzhú** *v* drive out, banish
驱逐出境 **qūzhú chūjìng** deport, deportation
驱逐舰 **qūzhújiàn** [modif: 驱逐 drive out + 舰 warship] *n* destroyer

趋 **qū** Trad 趨 *v* tend (to become)
趋势 **qūshì** *n* tendency
令人担忧的趋势 **lìngrén dānyōu de qūshì** a worrying tendency
趋向 **qūxiàng** *v* tend to, incline to

屈 **qū** *v* bend, bow
屈服 **qūfú** [comp: 屈 bend + 服 obey] *v* yield (to), knuckle under

渠 **qú** *n* **1** ditch, canal **2** medium, channel
灌溉渠 **guàngàiqú** irrigation channel
渠道 **qúdào** [comp: 渠 ditch + 道 way] *n* **1** irrigation ditch **2** medium of communication, channel

曲 **qǔ** *n* melody, tune
曲调 **qǔdiào** [comp: 曲 tune + 调 tune] *n* tune, melody
曲子 **qǔzi** *n* song, melody
熟悉的曲子 **shúxi de qǔzi** familiar tune

取 **qǔ** *v* fetch, collect □ 我要找一个自动取款机取点钱。 **Wǒ yào zhǎo yí ge zìdòng qǔkuǎnjī qǔ diǎn qián.** *I'm looking for an ATM to withdraw some money.*
取款 **qǔkuǎn** withdraw money
取代 **qǔdài** *v* replace, substitute for
取得 **qǔdé** [comp: 取 obtain + 得 get] *v* obtain, achieve □ 我们去年取得很大成绩。 **Wǒmen qùnián qǔdé hěn dà chéngjì.** *We made great achievements last year.*
取消 **qǔxiāo** *v* cancel, call off □ 明天的会议已经取消了。 **Míngtiān de huìyì yǐjīng qǔxiāo le.** *The meeting for tomorrow has been called off.*

娶 **qǔ** *v* (of a man) marry
娶媳妇 **qǔ xífù** (of a man) marry, take a wife

NOTE: See note on 嫁 **jià**.

去 **qù** *v* leave for, go to (antonym 来 **lái**) □ 你什么时候去中国? **Nǐ shénme shíhou qù Zhōngguó?** *When are you going to China?* □ 他下星期到美国去。 **Tā xià xīngqī dào Měiguó qù.** *He's going to America next week.*

NOTE: 到 **dào** and 到…去 **dào...qù** have the same meaning and are normally interchangeable.

去年 **qùnián** [modif: 去 what has gone + 年 year] *n* last year □ 她去年才开始学中文。 **Tā qùnián cái kāishǐ xué Zhōngwén.** *She began learning Chinese only last year.*
去世 **qùshì** [v+obj: 去 leave + 世 the world] *v* die, pass away □ 他的祖父在上个月去世了。 **Tā de zǔfù zài shànggè yuè qùshì le.** *His grandfather passed away last month.*

NOTE: 去世 **qùshì** must be used when you want to show respect and/or love to the deceased. For instance, the normal word for *die*, 死 **sǐ**, would be totally inappropriate in the example sentence.

趣 **qù** *n* interest
趣味 **qùwèi** [comp: 趣 interest + 味 taste] *n* **1** interest, delight **2** taste, preference
低级趣味 **dījí qùwèi** vulgar taste

圈 **quān** *n* circle, ring □ 运动会的旗子上有五个圈。 **Yùndònghuì de qízi shang yǒu wǔ ge quān.** *There are five circles on the flag of the Games.*
圈套 **quāntào** *n* snare, trap
设下圈套 **shèxià quāntào** set a trap, lay a snare
落入圈套 **luòrù quāntào** be caught in a trap, be snared
圈子 **quānzi** *n* circle, ring

权 quán Trad 權 *n* **1** authority, power **2** right, privilege

权利 quánlì [comp: 权 power + 利 benefit] *n* right □ 你要享受权利, 就要尽一定的义务。**Nǐ yào xiǎngshòu quánlì, jiùyào jìn yídìng de yìwù.** *If you want to enjoy rights, you will have to fulfil certain obligations.*

权力 quánlì [comp: 权 power + 力 strength] *n* authority, power □ 校长有权力解雇教师吗? **Xiàozhǎng yǒu quánlì jiěgù jiàoshī ma?** *Does a principal have the authority to dismiss a teacher?*

权威 quánwēi [comp: 权 power + 威 awe] *n* authority, authoritativeness
国际法权威 **guójìfǎ quánwēi** an authority in international law

权限 quánxiàn [modif: 权 power + 限 limit] *n* limits of one's authority, extent of one's authority
超出他的权限 **chāochū tā de quánxiàn** exceed the limit of his authority

权益 quányì [comp: 权 rights + 益 benefits] *n* rights, rights and interests

全 quán *adj* whole, complete □ 过圣诞节那天, 全家人一块儿吃午饭。**Guò shèngdànjié nàtiān, quánjiārén yíkuàir chī wǔfàn.** *On Christmas Day, the whole family has lunch together.* □ 你的病还没全好, 怎么能上班呢? **Nǐ de bìng hái méi quán hǎo, zěnme néng shàngbān ne?** *You haven't fully recovered. How can you go to work?* □ 他说的不全是真话。**Tā shuō de bù quán shì zhēnhuà.** *He did not tell the whole truth.*
全国 **quánguó** the whole country
全世界 **quánshìjiè** the entire world

全部 quánbù [modif: 全 whole + 部 part] *n* all, without exception □ 我爸爸全部的时间都放在工作上。**Wǒ bàba quánbù de shíjiān dōu fàng zài gōngzuò shang.** *My father devotes all his time to work.*

全都 quándōu *adv* all, without exception

全会 quánhuì *n* plenary session, plenary meeting
中共中央十六届二中全会 **Zhōnggòng Zhōngyāng shíliù jiè èr-zhōng quánhuì** the second plenary meeting of the 16th Central Committee of the Chinese Communist Party

全集 quánjí *n* completed works (of an author)

全局 quánjú *n* overall situation

全力 quánlì *adv* with all of one's strength, making every effort
全力以赴 **quánlì yǐfù** spare no efforts, go all out

全面 quánmiàn [modif: 全 all + 面 side] *adj* all-round, comprehensive □ 对这个问题, 我们要做全面的考虑。**Duì zhège wèntí, wǒmen yào zuò quánmiàn de kǎolǜ.** *We will give thorough consideration to this issue.*

全民 quánmín *n* the entire people (of a country)

全体 quántǐ [modif: 全 whole + 体 body] *n* all, each and every one (of a group of people) □ 她代表全体学生向老师表示感谢。**Tā dàibiǎo quántǐ xuésheng xiàng lǎoshī biǎoshì gǎnxiè.** *On behalf of all the students she expressed gratitude to the teacher.*

全心全意 quánxīn quányì *idiom* wholeheartedly

拳 quán *n* fist
拳头 **quántou** [suffix: 拳 fist + 头 nominal suffix] *n* fist

泉 quán *n* spring (a small brook)
矿泉 **kuàngquán** mineral water

温泉 **wēnquán** hot spring

犬 quǎn *n* dog
警犬 **jǐngquǎn** police dog

劝 quàn Trad 勸 *v* **1** try to talk ... into (or out of) doing something, advise **2** encourage □ 他劝我不要把钱都存在那家银行。**Tā quàn wǒ bú yào bǎ qián dōu cún zài nà jiā yínháng.** *He advised me not to put all my money in that bank.* □ 我劝你改善和她的关系。**Wǒ quàn nǐ gǎishàn hé tā de guānxi.** *I encourage you to improve your relationship with her.*

劝告 quàngào [comp: 劝 advise + 告 tell] **I** *v* exhort, advise □ 医生劝告他不要吸烟了。**Yīshēng quàngào tā búyào xīyān le.** *His doctor advised him to give up smoking.* **II** *n* advice □ 你不听我的劝告, 以后要后悔的。**Nǐ bùtīng wǒde quàngào, yǐhòu yào hòuhuǐ de.** *You will live to regret it if you don't take my advice.*

劝说 quànshuō *v* persuade, advise

劝阻 quànzǔ [comp: advise + prevent] *v* dissuade from, advise ... not to
劝阻无效 **quànzǔ wúxiào** try in vain to dissuade someone from doing something

券 quàn *n* ticket, certificate
入场券 **rùchǎngquàn** admission ticket

缺 quē *v* **1** lack, be short of □ 要买笔记本电脑, 我还缺三百块钱。**Yào mǎi bǐjìběn diànnǎo, wǒ hái quē sānbǎi kuài qián.** *I'm short of 300 yuan for the purchase of a notebook computer.*
缺人手 **quē rénshǒu** shorthanded
2 be incomplete, be absent

缺点 quēdiǎn [v+obj: 缺 lack + 点 point] *n* shortcoming, defect □ 你要克服粗心的缺点。**Nǐ yào kèfú cūxīn de quēdiǎn.** *You should overcome the shortcoming of carelessness.* □ 这种新产品还有一些缺点, 需要改进。**Zhè zhǒng xīn chǎnpǐn háiyǒu yìxiē quēdiǎn, xūyào gǎijìn.** *This new product still has some defects and needs improvement.*

缺乏 quēfá *v* be deficient in, lack □ 他知识丰富, 但是缺乏实际经验。**Tā zhīshi fēngfù, dànshì quēfá shíjì jīngyàn.** *He has very rich knowledge but lacks practical experience.* □ 人们往往缺乏道德勇气。**Rénmen wǎngwǎng quēfá dàodé yǒngqì.** *People often lack moral courage.*

缺口 quēkǒu *n* breach, indenture

缺少 quēshǎo *v* be short of, lack □ 我们缺少一名球员, 你愿意参加比赛吗? **Wǒmen quēshǎo yì míng qiúyuán, nǐ yuànyì cānjiā bǐsài ma?** *We're still short of one player. Are you willing to participate in the game?*

NOTE: 缺乏 **quēfá** and 缺少 **quēshǎo** are synonyms, but 缺乏 **quēfá** has abstract nouns as objects, while 缺少 **quēshǎo** takes as objects nouns denoting concrete persons or things.

缺席 quēxí *v* be absent from (a meeting, a class, etc)

缺陷 quēxiàn *n* defect, shortcoming

瘸 qué *v* be lame
瘸子 **quézi** lame person, cripple

却 què Trad 卻 *adv* unexpectedly, contrary to what may be normally expected, but, yet □ 今天是星期天, 他却起得比平时还早。**Jīntiān shì Xīngqītiā**

tā què qǐ de bǐ píngshí hái zǎo. *It's Sunday today, but he got up earlier than on weekdays.* □ 他很有钱，却并不幸福。**Tā hěn yǒuqián, què bìng bú xìngfú.** *He is rich, but he is not happy.*

鹊 què Trad 鵲 *n* magpie
喜鹊 xǐquè magpie (只 zhī)

榷 què *v* discuss
商榷 shāngquè discuss

雀 què *n* finch
麻雀 máquè sparrow (只 zhī)

确 què Trad 確 **I** *adj* true, authentic **II** *adv* firmly
确保 quèbǎo [modif: 确 firmly + 保 guarantee] *v* ensure, guarantee
确定 quèdìng [modif: 确 firmly + 定 definite] *v* confirm, fix, determine □ 他出国的日期已经确定。**Tā chūguó de rìqī yǐjīng quèdìng.** *His date of departure overseas has been fixed.* □ 谁当总经理还没有确定。**Shéi dāng zǒngjīnglǐ hái méiyǒu quèdìng.** *Who the general manager will be is not yet confirmed.*
确立 quèlì *v* establish
确切 quèqiè *adj* precise, specific
确认 quèrèn [modif: 确 firmly + 认 acknowledge] *v* affirm, confirm
确实 quèshí [comp: 确 true + 实 substantial] *adj* verified to be true, indeed □ 这个消息不确实。**Zhège xiāoxi bú quèshí.** *This news is not true.* □ 你确实错了。**Nǐ quèshí cuò le.** *You're indeed wrong.*
确信 quèxìn [modif: 确 firmly + 信 believe] *v* firmly believe, be convinced
确凿 quèzáo *adj* conclusive, irrefutable

裙 qún *n* skirt
裙子 qúnzi [suffix: 裙 skirt + 子 nominal suffix] *n* skirt (条 tiáo) □ 你穿白裙子很好看。**Nǐ chuān bái qúnzi hěn hǎokàn.** *You look good in a white skirt.*

群 qún *measure wd* a crowd of, a group of (for people or animals)
一群狗 yì qún gǒu a pack of dogs
一群鸟 yì qún niǎo a flock of birds
一群牛 yì qún niú a herd of cattle
一群小学生 yì qún xiǎoxuésheng a group of primary schoolchildren
一群羊 yì qún yáng a flock of sheep
群岛 qúndǎo [modif: 群 group + 岛 island] *n* archipelago
群体 qúntǐ *n* (social) group
弱势群体 ruòshì qúntǐ weak social group
群众 qúnzhòng [comp: 群 crowd + 众 multitude] *n* the masses (people), the general public □ 在群众的帮助下，警察很快抓到了强盗。**Zài qúnzhòng de bāngzhù xià, jǐngchá hěn kuài zhuādàole qiángdào.** *With the help of the general public, the police soon caught the robber.*

R

然 rán *conj* however
然而 rán'ér *conj* Same as 但是 dànshì. Usually used in written Chinese.
然后 ránhòu [idiom] *conj* afterwards, ... and then
先…然后… xiān...ránhòu... first ... and then... □ 他每天早上先跑步，然后吃早饭。**Tā měitiān zǎoshang xiān pǎobù, ránhòu chī zǎofàn.** *Every morning he first jogs and then has breakfast.*

燃 rán *v* burn
燃料 ránliào [modif: 燃 burning + 料 material] *n* fuel
燃烧 ránshāo [comp: 燃 burn + 烧 burn] *v* burn □ 森林大火燃烧了三天三夜。**Sēnlín dàhuǒ ránshāole sān tiān sān yè.** *The forest fire raged three days and nights.*

染 rǎn *v* dye □ 有些年轻人喜欢染头发。**Yǒuxiē niánqīngrén xǐhuan rǎn tóufa.** *Some young people like to dye their hair.*
染料 rǎnliào [modif: 染 dye + 料 material] *n* dyestuff

壤 rǎng *n* soil (See 土壤 tǔrǎng)

嚷 rǎng *v* yell, shout □ 别嚷了，有话好好说。**Bié rǎng le, yǒu huà hǎohǎo shuō.** *Stop yelling. Speak nicely if you have something to say.*

让 ràng Trad 讓 *v* **1** let, give way □ 你应该让那辆车先行。**Nǐ yīnggāi ràng nà liàng chē xiānxíng.** *You should let that vehicle go first.* (→ *You should give way to that vehicle*) □ 让我想一想。**Ràng wǒ xiǎng yi xiǎng.** *Let me think.* □ 妈不让我告诉你这件事。**Mā bú ràng wǒ gàosu nǐ zhè jiàn shì.** *Mom didn't allow me to tell you this.* **2** allow, make □ 他的话让我明白了许多道理。**Tā de huà ràng wǒ míngbaile xǔduō dàolǐ.** *What he said made me understand many things.* (→ *What he said enlightened me.*)

饶 ráo Trad 饒 *v* have mercy on, forgive □ 饶饶我吧! **Ráo ráo wǒ ba!** *Please spare me! Please don't kill (harm) me!*

扰 rǎo Trad 擾 *v* harass (See 打扰 dǎrǎo.)

绕 rào Trad 繞 *v* make a detour, bypass □ 前面施工，车辆绕道。**Qiánmiàn shīgōng, chēliàng rào dào.** *Road works ahead. Vehicles must detour.*

惹 rě *v* cause (something undesirable), invite (trouble etc.) □ 别惹麻烦了。**Bié rě máfan le.** *Don't ask for trouble.* □ 你和这种人交朋友会惹爸爸生气。**Nǐ hé zhè zhǒng rén jiāo péngyou huì rě bàba shēngqì.** *It will make daddy angry if you make friends with such people.*

热 rè Trad 熱 *adj* **1** hot (antonym 冷 lěng) □ 香港的夏天很热。**Xiānggǎng de xiàtiān hěn rè.** *Summer in Hong Kong is very hot.* □ 我想喝一杯热水，不要冷水。**Wǒ xiǎng hē yì bēi rè shuǐ, bú yào lěng shuǐ.** *I want to drink a glass of hot water, not cold water.* □ 你怎么能肯定当冠军? 脑子发热吧? **Nǐ zěnme néng kěndìng dāng guànjūn? Nǎozi fā rè ba?** *How can you be so sure that you will definitely be the champion? It's going to your head, isn't it?* **2** ardent, passionate
热爱 rè'ài [modif: 热 hot + 爱 love] *v* ardently love,

be in deep love with □ 我热爱我的祖国。**Wǒ rè'ài wǒ de zǔguó.** *I love my motherland.*

热潮 **rècháo** [modif: 热 hot + 潮 tide] *n* upsurge, craze

热带 **rèdài** [modif: 热 hot + 带 zone] *n* the tropics, the tropical zone

热量 **rèliàng** [modif: 热 heat + 量 amount] *n* quantity of heat

热烈 **rèliè** [comp: 热 hot + 烈 intense] *adj* warm, ardent □ 热烈欢迎新同学！**Rèliè huānyíng xīn tóngxué!** *A warm welcome to the new students!*

热闹 **rènao** [comp: 热 hot + 闹 noisy] *adj* noisy and exciting in a pleasant way, boisterous, bustling, lively (of a scene or occasion) □ 中国人过年非常热闹。**Zhōngguórén guònián fēicháng rènao.** *When the Chinese celebrate their New Year's Day, it is a noisy and exciting occasion.* □ 周末的市场十分热闹。**Zhōumò de shìchǎng shífēn rènao.** *The shopping mall bustles with activities on weekends.*

热情 **rèqíng** [modif: 热 hot + 情 emotion] *adj* enthusiastic, warmhearted □ 她对人很热情。**Tā duì rén hěn rèqíng.** *She's warmhearted towards others.* □ 他常常热情地帮助朋友。**Tā chángcháng rèqíng de bāngzhù péngyou.** *He often helps his friends enthusiastically.* □ 他热情的态度让我很感动。**Tā rèqíng de tàidu ràng wǒ hěn gǎndòng.** *His enthusiasm moved me greatly.*

热水瓶 **rèshuǐpíng** [modif: 热 hot + 水 water + 瓶 bottle, flask] *n* thermos, thermos flask (只 **zhī**) □ 有了热水瓶很方便，什么时候都可以喝上热水。**Yǒule rèshuǐpíng hěn fāngbiàn, shénme shíhou dōu kěyǐ hēshang rè shuǐ.** *A thermos flask is very handy. You can have hot water any time.*

热心 **rèxīn** [modif: 热 hot + 心 heart] *adj* warmhearted, enthusiastic
对… 热心 duì...rèxīn be warmhearted towards, be enthusiastic about □ 他对朋友很热心。**Tā duì péngyou hěn rèxīn.** *He is warmhearted towards friends.*

人 **rén** *n* human being, person □ 你认识这个人吗？**Nǐ rènshi zhège rén ma?** *Do you know this person?* □ 人和动物有什么区别？**Rén hé dòngwù yǒu shénme qūbié?** *What are the differences between humans and animals?*

人才 **réncái** [modif: 人 human + 才 talent] *n* talented person, person of ability □ 他自以为是个人才。**Tā zì yǐwéi shì ge réncái.** *He thinks himself quite talented.* □ 我们公司需要电脑人才。**Wǒmen gōngsī xūyào diànnǎo réncái.** *Our company needs people with computer skills.*
人才市场 réncái shìchǎng personnel market, job fair
人才外流 réncái wàiliú brain drain

人道主义 **réndàozhǔyì** *n* humanitarianism
人道主义援助 réndàozhǔyì yuánzhù humanitarian aid

人格 **réngé** [modif: 人 personal + 格 quality] *n* personality, moral quality
以我的人格担保 yǐ wǒ de réngé dānbǎo give (you) my personal guarantee

人工 **réngōng** **I** *adj* artificial, man-made
人工智能 réngōng zhìnéng artificial intelligence
II *n* manpower, man-day

人家 **rénjia** *pron* **1** other people □ 人家能做到的, 我也能做到。**Rénjia néng zuòdao de, wǒ yě néng zuòdao.** *What others can achieve, I can too.* **2** he, she, they

(used to refer to another person or other people) □ 人家不愿意, 你别勉强。**Rénjia bú yuànyì, nǐ bié miǎnqiáng.** *If they aren't willing, don't force them to do it.* **3** I, me (used to refer to oneself, used only among intimate friends or family members)

人间 **rénjiān** *n* the earth, the human world
人间天堂 rénjiān tiāntáng paradise on earth

人均 **rénjūn** *n* average, per capita

人口 **rénkǒu** [comp: 人 human + 口 mouth] *n* population (human) □ 你们国家有多少人口？**Nǐmen guójiā yǒu duōshǎo rénkǒu?** *What is the population of your country?* □ 很多发展中国家都在控制人口增长。**Hěn duō fāzhǎnzhōng guójiā dōu zài kòngzhì rénkǒu zēngzhǎng.** *Many developing countries are controlling population increase.*

NOTE: It is interesting that the Chinese word for *population* is made up of 人 rén (human) and 口 kǒu (the mouth). It suggests that feeding people (mouths) has been the primary concern in China.

人类 **rénlèi** [modif: 人 human + 类 kind] *n* humankind, mankind □ 人类应该保护自然环境。**Rénlèi yīnggāi bǎohù zìrán huánjìng.** *Mankind shoul protect the natural environment.*

人类学 **rénlèixué** *n* anthropology

人力 **rénlì** [modif: 人 human + 力 power] *n* manpower
人力资源 rénlì zīyuán human resource

人们 **rénmen** [suffix: 人 person, people + 们 suffix indicating plural number] *n* people, the public □ 春节那几天, 人们都比较客气, 避免争吵。**Chūnjié nà jǐ tiān, rénmen dōu bǐjiào kèqi, bìmiǎn zhēngchǎo.** *During the Chinese New Year, people are polite to each other so as to avoid quarrels.* □ 人们都认为发展经济很重要。**Rénmen dǒu rènwéi fāzhǎn jīngjì hěn zhòngyào.** *People think it is important to develop the economy.*

人民 **rénmín** [comp: 人 human beings + 民 the people] *n* the people (of a state) □ 人民是国家的主人。**Rénmín shì guójiā de zhǔrén.** *The people are the masters of a country.* □ 政府应该为人民服务。**Zhèngfǔ yīnggāi wèi rénmín fúwù.** *The government should serve the people.*

人民币 **Rénmínbì** [modif: 人民 the people + 币 currency, banknote] *n* the Chinese currency, Renminbi (RMB) □ 我想用美元换人民币。**Wǒ xiǎng yòng Měiyuán huàn Rénmínbì.** *I want to change som U.S. dollars to Renminbi.*

人情 **rénqíng** [modif: 人 human + 情 emotions] *n* common sense, reason
不近人情 bú jìn rénqíng unreasonable (in dealing with interpersonal matters)
2 human feelings
讲人情 jiǎng rénqíng resort to feeings (instead of regulations, law, etc.)
3 gift, favor
送人情 sòng rénqíng give a gift (in order to gain favors)

人权 **rénquán** *n* human rights

人蛇 **rénshé** [modif: 人 human + 蛇 snake] *n* illeg (especially smuggled) immigrant

人参 **rénshēn** *n* ginseng

人生 **rénshēng** *n* (one's entire) life □ 人生苦短。 **Rénshēng kǔ duǎn.** *It's sad that life is so short.*

人事 **rénshì** [modif: 人 people + 事 matters] *n* human resources matters

人事部门 **rénshì bùmén** human resources department, personnel department

人寿 **rénshòu** [modif: 人 human + 寿 lifespan] *n* human lifespan

人寿保险 **rénshòu bǎoxiǎn** life insurance

人体 **réntǐ** *n* human body

人体解剖学 **réntǐ jiěpōuxué** human anatomy, anatomy

人为 **rénwéi** *adj* man-made, artificial

人物 **rénwù** *n* well-known and important person, figure, personage (位 **wèi**) □ 这位大学校长是世界著名人物。 **Zhè wèi dàxué xiàozhǎng shì shìjiè zhùmíng rénwù.** *This university president is a famous figure in the world.*

人心 **rénxīn** [modif: 人 human + 心 the heart] *n* popular feelings, the will of the people

人性 **rénxìng** *n* human nature □ 人性善，还是人性恶？ **Rénxìng shàn, háishi rénxìng è?** *Is human nature good or evil?*

人员 **rényuán** [comp: 人 human + 员 staff] *n* personnel, staff □ 我校有教学人员五十六名，其他人员十八名。 **Wǒ xiào yǒu jiàoxué rényuán wǔshí liù míng, qítā rényuán shíbā míng.** *This school has a teaching staff of 56 people and 18 other staff members.*

人造 **rénzào** [modif: 人 man + 造 make] *adj* man-made, artificial □ 第一颗人造卫星是哪一年上天的？ **Dì-yī kē rénzào wèixīng shì nǎ yì nián shàngtiān de?** *In which year was the first man-made satellite launched?*

人质 **rénzhì** *n* hostage

扣留人质 **kòuliú rénzhì** hold a hostage

仁 **rén** I *n* benevolence, humanity II *adj* benevolent, humane

仁慈 **réncí** [comp: 仁 benevolent + 慈 kind] *adj* benevolent, merciful

忍 **rěn** *v* endure, tolerate, put up with □ 你刚来，有的地方不习惯，还得忍一点。 **Nǐ gāng lái, yǒude dìfang bù xíguàn, hái děi rěn yìdiǎn.** *You're new here, so there may be things you're not used to and will have to put up with for a while.*

忍耐 **rěnnài** [comp: 忍 endure + 耐 endure] *v* bear, put up with, exercise patience □ 没有办法，只能忍耐。 **Méiyǒu bànfǎ, zhǐ néng rěnnài.** *There's nothing we can do, we can only put up with it.*

忍受 **rěnshòu** *v* tolerate, stand

忍心 **rěnxīn** *v* have the heart to (do), be hard-hearted

NOTE: 忍心 **rěnxīn** is usually used in its negative form of 不忍心 **bùrěn xīn**, which means *not have the heart to (do)*, e.g. □ 我不忍心把这个可怕的消息告诉她。 **Wǒ bù rěnxīn bǎ zhè ge kěpà de xiāoxi gàosu tā.** *I don't have the heart to tell her this terrible news.*

忍住 **rěnzhù** *v* endure, bear

忍不住 **rěn bu zhù** unable to bear, cannot help □ 她在电话里听到妈妈的声音，忍不住哭起来。 **Tā zài diànhuà li tīngdao māma de shēngyīn, rěnbuzhù kū qǐlai.** *Hearing mom's voice on the phone, she couldn't help crying.*

忍得住 **rěn de zhù** can endure, can bear

韧 **rèn** Trad 韌 *adj* strong and pliable, tenacious

认 **rèn** Trad 認 *v* 1 recognize □ 两年不见，我几乎认不出你了！ **Liǎng nián bú jiàn, wǒ jīhū rèn bu chū nǐ le!** *I haven't seen you for two years, and I can hardly recognize you.* 2 identify □ 你认一下，这里这么多自行车，哪辆是你的？ **Nǐ rèn yíxià, zhèli zhème duō zìxíngchē, nǎ liàng shì nǐ de?** *Among so many bicycles here, can you identify which one is yours?*

认得 **rènde** *v* Same as 认识 **rènshi**

认定 **rèndìng** *v* be firmly convinced, maintain, decide on

认可 **rènkě** *v* approve

质量认可书 **zhìliàng rènkě shū** certificate of quality approval

认识 **rènshi** [comp: 认 recognize + 识 know] *v* know, understand □ 我不认识这个人。 **Wǒ bú rènshi zhège rén.** *I don't know this person.* (or *I've never met this person before.*) □ 认识你，很高兴。 **Rènshi nǐ, hěn gāoxìng.** *I'm glad to make your acquaintance.* □ 你认识这个汉字吗？ **Nǐ rènshi zhège Hànzì ma?** *Do you know this Chinese character?*

认为 **rènwéi** *v* think, consider (normally followed by a clause) □ 我认为你说得不对。 **Wǒ rènwéi nǐ shuōde bú duì.** *I think what you said is incorrect.* □ 我不这么认为。 **Wǒ bú zhème rènwéi.** *I don't think so.*

认真 **rènzhēn** [v+compl: 认 consider + 真 real] *adj* earnest, conscientious, serious □ 他是个认真的学生。 **Tā shì ge rènzhēn de xuésheng.** *He's a conscientious student.* □ 他是在开玩笑，你不要太认真。 **Tā shì zài kāiwánxiào, nǐ bú yào tài rènzhēn.** *He's joking. Don't take it too seriously.* □ 老老实实做人，认认真真做事。 **Lǎo-lǎo-shí-shí zuòrén, rèn-rèn-zhēn-zhēn zuòshì.** *Be an honest person and a conscientious worker.*

任 **rèn** I *conj* no matter II *v* 1 appoint, take up 2 give free rein to

任何 **rènhé** [comp: 任 no matter + 何 what] *pron* any, whatever □ 你任何时候都可以来找我。 **Nǐ rènhé shíhou dōu kěyǐ lái zhǎo wǒ.** *You can come and see me anytime.* □ 在任何情况下，都要遵守法律。 **Zài rènhé qíngkuàng xia, dōu yào zūnshǒu fǎlǜ.** *One should abide by the law under any circumstances.*

任何人 **rènhé rén** anyone □ 任何人都不可以那样做。 **Rènhé rén dōu bù kěyǐ nàyàng zuò.** *No one is allowed to do that.*

任何事 **rènhé shì** any matter, anything, everything □ 他做任何事都挺认真。 **Tā zuò rènhé shì dōu tǐng rènzhēn.** *He does everything conscientiously.*

任命 **rènmìng** *v* appoint (to a position of importance)

任命他为副总裁 **rènmìng tā wéi fùzǒngcái** appoint him Vice-CEO

任务 **rènwù** [comp: 任 mission + 务 work] *n* assignment, mission □ 李经理要派你一个重要任务。 **Lǐ jīnglǐ yào pài nǐ yí ge zhòngyào rènwù.** *Mr Li, the manager, will give you an important assignment.* □ 这个任务很难，不可能在一个月内完成。 **Zhège rènwù hěn nán, bù kěnéng zài yí ge yuè nèi wánchéng.** *This*

is a difficult mission which cannot be accomplished in a month.

任性 **rènxìng** *adj* willful, headstrong

任意 **rènyì** *adv* randomly, at random

饪 **rèn** Trad 飪 *v* cook (See 烹饪 **pēngrèn**)

刃 **rèn** *n* the edge of a knife, blade

扔 **rēng** *v* throw, toss □ 不要乱扔垃圾。**Bú yào luàn rēng lājī.** *Do not discard rubbish everywhere.* (→ *Don't litter.*)

仍 **réng** *adv* Same as 仍然 **réngrán**

仍旧 **réngjiù** *adv* Same as 仍然 **réngrán**

仍然 **réngrán** *adv* still, as before □ 他有这么多钱, 仍然不满足。**Tā yǒu zhème duō qián, réngrán bù mǎnzú.** *He has so much money but he is still not satisfied.* □ 我睡了十几个小时, 仍然觉得累。**Wǒ shuìle shí jǐ ge xiǎoshí, réngrán juéde lèi.** *I slept for over ten hours but still feel tired.*

日 **rì** *n* date, day
三月二十四日 Sānyuè èrshí sì rì the twenty-fourth of March
九月一日 Jiǔyuè yí rì the first of September

NOTE: In writing, 日 **rì** is used for dates as shown above. However, in speech it is more common to say 号 **hào**. For example, to say *the twenty-fourth of March* 三月二十四号 Sānyuè èrshí sì hào is more natural than 三月二十四日 Sānyuè èrshi sì rì.

日报 **rìbào** *n* daily newspaper, daily

日本 **Rìběn** *n* Japan □ 日本在中国东边。**Rìběn zài Zhōngguó dōngbian.** *Japan lies to the east of China.* □ 你去过日本吗? **Nǐ qùguo Rìběn ma?** *Have you ever been to Japan?*

日常 **rìcháng** [comp: 日 daily + 常 usual] *adj* daily, routine □ 他不希望有规律的日常生活被打乱。**Tā bù xīwàng yǒu guīlǜ de rìcháng shēnghuó bèi dǎluàn.** *He does not want his regular everyday life to be upset.* □ 这是我的日常工作, 一点都不麻烦。**Zhè shì wǒ de rìcháng gōngzuò, yìdiǎn dōu bù máfan.** *It is part of my routine work. There is no trouble at all.*

日程 **rìchéng** [modif: 日 daily + 程 journey] *n* daily schedule, schedule □ 我们开一个会, 安排一下工作日程。**Wǒmen kāi yí ge huì, ānpái yíxià gōngzuò rìchéng.** *Let's have a meeting to plan our work schedule.* □ 今天的日程排得很满。**Jīntiān de rìchéng pái de hěn mǎn.** *We have a full schedule today.*
议事日程 yìshì rìchéng agenda

日程表 **rìchéngbiǎo** *n* timetable (for a schedule)

日光 **rìguāng** *n* sunlight

日记 **rìjì** [modif: 日 daily + 记 record] *n* diary (本 **běn**, 篇 **piān**)
日记本 rìjìběn diary
记日记 jì rìjì keep a diary □ 我从十五岁生日那天开始记日记。**Wǒ cóng shíwǔ suì shēngrì nà tiān kāishǐ jì rìjì.** *I have been keeping a diary since my fifteenth birthday.*

日期 **rìqī** [comp: 日 day + 期 fixed time] *n* date (especially of an event) □ 你知道考试日期吗? **Nǐ zhīdào kǎoshì rìqī ma?** *Do you know the date of the exam?* □ 请你查一下这批饼干的过期日期。**Qǐng nǐ chá yíxià**

zhè pī bǐnggān de guòqī rìqī. *Please check the "use by" date of this batch of biscuits.*

日文 **Rìwén** [modif: 日 Japanese + 文 writing] *n* the Japanese language (especially the writing)

日夜 **rìyè** *adv* day and night, round the clock
日夜服务 rìyè fúwù round-the-clock service

日益 **rìyì** *adv* day by day, increasingly

日用品 **rìyòngpǐn** [modif: 日 daily + 用 use + 品 article] *n* daily necessities

日语 **Rìyǔ** [modif: 日 Japan + 语 speech] *n* the Japanese language □ 日语和汉语很不一样。**Rìyǔ hé Hànyǔ hěn bù yíyàng.** *Japanese is very different from Chinese.* □ 你们学校教日语吗? **Nǐmen xuéxiào jiāo Rìyǔ ma?** *Does your school teach Japanese?*

日元 **Rìyuán** [modif: 日 Japan + 元 dollar] *n* Japanese currency, yen □ 十万美元是一大笔钱, 十万日元不算一大笔钱。**Shíwàn Měiyuán shì yí dà bǐ qián, shí wàn Rìyuán bú suàn yí dà bǐ qián.** *While a hundred thousand American dollars is a big sum of money, a hundred thousand Japanese yen is not.*

日子 **rìzi** [suffix: 日 day + 子 nominal suffix] *n* **1** day, date □ 今天这个日子对我来说特别重要。**Jīntiān zhège rìzi duì wǒ lái shuō tèbié zhòngyào.** *Today is particularly important to me.* □ 今天是什么日子? 为什么街上那么多人? **Jīntiān shì shénme rìzi? Wèishénme jiē shang nàme duō rén?** *What day is today? Why are there so many people in the street?* **2** life □ 我们家的日子比过去好多了。**Wǒmen jiā de rìzi bǐ guòqù hǎo duō le.** *The life of my family is much better than before.* (→ *My family is better off now.*) □ 我只想安安静静地过日子。**Wǒ zhǐ xiǎng ān-ān-jìng-jìng de guò rìzi.** *I only want to live a quiet and peaceful life.*

融 **róng** *v* **1** melt, thaw **2** be in harmony, blend, fuse

融化 **rónghuà** *v* melt, thaw

融洽 **róngqià** *adj* harmonious, very friendly

荣 **róng** Trad 榮 **I** *adj* glorious, flourishing **II** *n* glory, honor

荣誉 **róngyù** [modif: 荣 glorious + 誉 reputation] *n* honor, great credit
荣誉称号 róngyù chēnghào title of honor

容 **róng** *v* **1** tolerate **2** hold, accommodate

容积 **róngjī** *n* amount of space, volume

容量 **róngliàng** [modif: 容 accommodating + 量 amount] *n* the amount that something can hold, capacity

容纳 **róngnà** *v* have a capacity of, hold, contain

容器 **róngqì** *n* container, vessel

容忍 **róngrěn** [comp: 容 tolerate + 忍 endure] *v* tolerate

容许 **róngxǔ** [comp: 容 tolerate + 许 permit] *v* permit, allow

容易 **róngyì** [comp: 容 tolerate + 易 easy] *adj* **1** easy, not difficult (antonym 难 **nán**) □ 这件事很容易。**Zhè jiàn shì hěn róngyì.** *This is easy to do.* □ 这么容易的问题, 你都不会回答? **Zhème róngyì de wèntí, nǐ dōu bú huì huídá?** *You even can't answer such an easy question?* **2** having a tendency to, likely □ 年轻人容易受朋友的影响。**Niánqīngrén róngyì shòu péngyou de yǐngxiǎng.** *Young people are susceptible to their friends' influence.* □ 刚到一个新地方, 容易生病。**Gāngdào yí ge xīn dìfang, róngyì shēngbìng.**

You're likely to fall ill when you first arrive in a new land.

溶 **róng** *v* dissolve, melt
溶化 **rónghuà** *v* dissolve
溶解 **róngjiě** *v* dissolve, melt
溶液 **róngyè** [modif: 溶 dissolve + 液 liquid] *n* solution

熔 **róng** *v* melt, smelt

绒 **róng** Trad 絨 *n* fine hair, down
鸭绒被 **yāróngbèi** duckdown quilt

柔 **róu** *adj* soft, gentle
柔和 **róuhé** [comp: 柔 soft + 和 mild] *adj* soft and mild, gentle
柔和的口气 **róuhé de kǒuqì** a gentle and soothing voice
柔软 **róuruǎn** [comp: 柔 soft + 软 soft] *adj* soft, lithe

揉 **róu** *v* rub, knead
揉面 **róumiàn** knead dough

肉 **ròu** *n* flesh, meat □ 在我们这儿肉比鱼便宜。**Zài wǒmen zhèr ròu bǐ yú piányi.** *Pork is cheaper than fish.*
鸡肉 **jīròu** chicken meat
牛肉 **niúròu** beef
羊肉 **yángròu** mutton
鱼肉 **yúròu** fish meat
猪肉 **zhūròu** pork

NOTE: The most popular meat in China is pork. Unspecified, 肉 **ròu** often refers to *pork*.

如 **rú** I *v* 1 be like, be similar to 2 according to 3 for example, such as II *conj* Same as 如果 **rúguǒ**. Used only in writing.
如此 **rúcǐ** *pron* so, such as
如此说来 **rúcǐ shuōlái** in that case, then, so

NOTE: See note on 如何 **rúhé**.

如果 **rúguǒ** *conj* if, in the event that □ 如果明天下雨，我们就不去海边游泳。**Rúguǒ míngtiān xià yǔ, wǒmen jiù bú qù hǎibian yóuyǒng.** *If it rains tomorrow, we won't go to the seaside to swim.*

NOTE: 如果 **rúguǒ** is usually used with 就 **jiù**.

如何 **rúhé** *pron* how, what □ 你以为如何? **Nǐ yǐwéi rúhé?** *What do you think?*

NOTE: 如何 **rúhé** is one of the few remnants of Classical Chinese still used in Modern Chinese, but it is usually used in writing only. The same is true with 如此 **rúcǐ**, 如今 **rújīn** and 如同 **rútóng**.

如今 **rújīn** *pron* today, now

NOTE: See note on 如何 **rúhé**.

如同 **rútóng** *v* be like, as

NOTE: See note on 如何 **rúhé**.

如意 **rúyì** [v+obj: 如 according to + 意 (one's) will] *adj* as one wishes
称心如意 **chènxīn rúyì** to one's heart's content
万事如意 **wànshì rúyì** best of luck for everything
□ 祝你万事如意! **Zhù nǐ wànshì rúyì!** *I wish you the best of luck!*

辱 **rǔ** *v* insult (See 侮辱 **wǔrǔ**)

乳 **rǔ** *n* 1 breast 2 milk
乳房 **rǔfáng** [modif: 乳 milk + 房 room] *n* female breast, udder
乳牛 **rǔniú** *n* dairy cattle, cow (头 **tóu**)
乳制品 **rǔzhìpǐn** *n* dairy product

入 **rù** *v* 1 enter, go in □ 病从口入。**Bìng cóng kǒu rù.** *Disease enters the body by the mouth.* (→ *Bad food causes disease.*) 2 join, become a member of
入境 **rùjìng** [v+obj: 入 enter + 境 border] *v* enter a country
入口 **rùkǒu** [modif: 入 entry + 口 mouth] *n* entry, entrance
入侵 **rùqīn** *v* invade, make inroads
入手 **rùshǒu** *v* start with, proceed
入学 **rùxué** [v+obj: 入 enter + 学 school] *v* start school

软 **ruǎn** Trad 軟 *adj* 1 soft, supple (antonym 硬 **yìng**) □ 这张床太软。**Zhè zhāng chuáng tài ruǎn.** *This bed is too soft.* 2 weak, feeble
软件 **ruǎnjiàn** [modif: 软 soft + 件 article] *n* computer software, software □ 他除了买这台新电脑以外，还买了一些软件。**Tā chúle mǎi zhè tái xīn diànnǎo yǐwài, hái mǎile yìxiē ruǎnjiàn.** *In addition to the new computer he also bought some software.* □ 他们设计了一个软件非常成功。**Tāmen shèjìle yí ge ruǎnjiàn fēicháng chénggōng.** *They have designed a very successful software.*
软盘 **ruǎnpán** *n* floppy disk
软驱 **ruǎnqū** *n* floppy drive
软弱 **ruǎn ruò** [comp: 软 soft + 弱 weak] *adj* weak, feeble □ 她性格软弱，常常受人欺负。**Tā xìnggé ruǎnruò, chángcháng shòu rén qīfu.** *She has a weak character, and is often subject to bullying.*

锐 **ruì** Trad 銳 *adj* sharp
锐利 **ruìlì** [comp: 锐 sharp + 利 sharp] *adj* sharp, pointed

瑞 **ruì** *adj* auspicious
瑞雪 **ruìxuě** *n* timely snow

润 **rùn** Trad 潤 *v* moisten, enrich (See 利润 **lìrùn**)

弱 **ruò** *adj* weak, feeble (antonym 强 **qiáng**) □ 他年老体弱，不能在田里干活了。**Tā nián-lǎo-tǐ-ruò, bù néng zài tián li gànhuó le.** *He is old and feeble, and is unable to work in the fields.* □ 我使用电脑的能力比较弱，可是我的语言能力很强。**Wǒ shǐyòng diànnǎo de nénglì bǐjiào ruò, kěshì wǒ de yǔyán nénglì hěn qiáng.** *I'm rather weak in computer skills, but strong in languages.*
弱势群体 **ruòshì qúntǐ** *n* weak social group, the disadvantaged

若 **ruò** *conj* if
若干 **ruògān** *num* a certain number

S

撒 **sā** v cast, spread out
撒渔网 sā yúwǎng spread out a fishing net
撒谎 **sāhuǎng** v Same as 说谎 **shuōhuǎng**

洒 **sǎ** Trad 灑 v sprinkle, spray □ 这片稻田有害虫，要洒一点儿药。**Zhè piàn dàotián yǒu hàichóng, yào sǎ yìdiǎnr yào.** *This paddy field is infested. You need to spray some pesticide on it.*

萨 **sà** Trad 薩 as in 菩萨 **Púsà**

腮 **sāi** n cheek

塞 **sāi** v plug, stuff
把很多衣服塞进旅行袋 bǎ hěn duō yīfu sāijìn lǚxíngdài stuff lots of clothes in the duffel bag

赛 **sài** Trad 賽 v compete (See 比赛 **bǐsài**, 竞赛 **jìngsài**.)

三 **sān** num three, 3
十三 shísān thirteen
三十 sānshí thirty

叁 **sān** num three

伞 **sǎn** Trad 傘 n umbrella (把 **bǎ**) □ 今天可能会下雨，带着伞吧。**Jīntiān kěnéng huì xià yǔ, dàizhe sǎn ba.** *It may rain today. Take your umbrella with you.* □ 我的伞又丢了。**Wǒ de sǎn yòu diū le.** *I've lost my umbrella again.*

散 **sǎn** adj loose
散文 sǎnwén n prose, essay (篇 **piān**)

散 **sàn** v 1 disperse, scatter 2 disseminate, distribute
散步 sànbù [modif: 散 random + 步 step] v take a short leisurely walk, stroll □ 这位老人常常在公园里散步。**Zhè wèi lǎorén chángcháng zài gōngyuán li sànbù.** *This old man often takes a walk in the park.* □ 他俩沿着小河散步，直到天快黑了。**Tā liǎ yánzhe xiǎo hé sànbù, zhídào tiān kuài hēi le.** *The two of them took a walk along the stream till it was almost dark.*
散布 sànbù v disseminate, spread
散布谣言 sànbù yáoyán spread rumors
散发 sànfā v distribute, give out
散发广告纸 sànfā guǎnggào zhǐ pass out fliers

丧 **sāng** Trad 喪 n funeral
奔丧 bēnsāng travel to attend a funeral
丧事 sāngshì n funeral arrangements
办丧事 bàn sāngshì make funeral arrangements

桑 **sāng** n mulberry
桑树 sāngshù mulberry tree (棵 **kē**)
桑叶 sāngyè mulberry leaf (张 **zhāng**)
桑拿浴 sāngnàyù n sauna

NOTE: This is a case of a semi-transliteration. 桑拿 represents the sound of *sauna* and 浴 means *bath*.

嗓 **sǎng** n throat
嗓子 sǎngzi [suffix: 嗓 throat + 子 nominal suffix] n 1 throat □ 我嗓子疼。**Wǒ sǎngzi téng.** *I have a sore throat.* 2 voice □ 她嗓子很尖。**Tā sǎngzi hěn jiān.** *She has a high-pitched voice.* (→ *Her voice is very shrill.*)

丧 **sàng** Trad 喪 v lose
丧失 **sàngshī** [comp: 丧 lose + 失 lose] v lose, forfeit

骚 **sāo** Trad 騷 v disturb, upset
骚动 sāodòng [comp: 骚 disturb + 动 move] I v disturb, cause a commotion II n social disturbance, commotion
骚乱 sāoluàn [comp: 骚 disturb + 乱 chaos] I v riot II n riot, disturbance
平息骚乱 píngxī sāoluàn put down a riot

嫂 **sǎo** n elder brother's wife
嫂子 sǎozi [suffix: 嫂 elder brother's wife + 子 nominal suffix] n elder brother's wife, sister-in-law □ 他父母去世以后，嫂子对他非常关心。**Tā fùmǔ qùshì yǐhòu, sǎozi duì tā fēicháng guānxīn.** *After his parents' death, his sister-in-law was very concerned for him.*

NOTE: One's younger brother's wife is 弟妹 **dìmèi**.

扫 **sǎo** Trad 掃 v sweep □ 秋天我得常常扫院子里的落叶。**Qiūtiān wǒ děi chángcháng sǎo yuànzi li de luòyè.** *In autumn, I have to often sweep away the fallen leaves in my courtyard.*
扫地 sǎo dì sweep the floor
扫除 sǎochú v clean (a room, a courtyard, etc.)

扫 **sào** as in 扫帚 **sàozhou**
扫帚 sàozhou n broom (把 **bǎ**)

色 **sè** n 1 color □ 那座白色的大楼就是医院。**Nà zuò báisè de dàlóu jiù shì yīyuàn.** *That white building is the hospital.* 2 sex
色彩 sècǎi n color, hue
色彩丰富 sècǎi fēngfù a riot of colors
色狼 sèláng [modif: 色 sex + 狼 wolf] n a lascivious man, sexual molester
色盲 sèmáng n color blindness, achromatopsia
色情 sèqíng [comp: 色 sex + 情 emotion] n pornography
色欲 sèyù [modif: 色 sex + 欲 desire] n lust, sexual lust

森 **sēn** n forest
森林 sēnlín [comp: 森 forest + 林 woods] n forest □ 防止火灾，保护森林。**Fángzhǐ huǒzāi, bǎohù sēnlín.** *Prevent fires, protect the forest.*

杀 **shā** Trad 殺 v kill □ 你敢杀鸡吗？**Nǐ gǎn shā jī ma?** *Do you dare to kill chickens?*
杀害 shāhài [comp: 杀 kill + 害 harm] v kill, murder

刹 **shā** as in 刹车 **shāchē**
刹车 shāchē I n brake II v apply brakes, brake
急刹车 jíshāchē brake suddenly

沙 **shā** n sand, grit
沙发 shāfā n upholstered chair, sofa, couch □ 他买了一对单人沙发和一个双人沙发。**Tā mǎile yí duì dānrén shāfā hé yí ge shuāngrén shāfā.** *He bought a pair of upholstered chairs and a two-seat sofa.*
沙漠 shāmò [modif: 沙 sand + 漠 desert] n desert □ 沙漠里最需要的是水。**Shāmò li zuì xūyào de shì shuǐ.** *In a desert, what is most needed is water.*
沙滩 shātān n sandy beach
沙土 shātǔ n sandy soil
沙眼 shāyǎn n trachoma

沙子 **shāzi** [suffix: 沙 sand + 子 nominal suffix] *n* sand, grit (粒 **lì**) □ 我右眼里恐怕有一粒沙子, 难受极了。 **Wǒ yòuyǎn li kǒngpà yǒu yí lì shāzi, nánshòu jíle.** *I'm afraid there is a grain of sand in my right eye. It's so irritating!*

砂 **shā** *n* grit, sand

纱 **shā** Trad 紗 *n* yarn
棉纱 **miánshā** cotton yarn

傻 **shǎ** *adj* foolish, stupid (antonym 聪明 **cōngmíng**) □ 你别看他模样傻, 其实一点儿也不傻。 **Nǐ bié kàn tā móyàng shǎ, qíshí yìdiǎnr yě bù shǎ.** *He may look stupid, but he is actually not at all stupid.* □ 你怎么会相信他? 真太傻了! **Nǐ zěnme huì xiāngxìn tā? Zhēn tài shǎ le!** *How could you have believed him? It was really foolish!*

傻子 **shǎzi** [suffix: 傻 foolish + 子 nominal suffix] *n* fool, idiot

厦 **shà** *n* a tall building, mansion
高楼大厦 **gāolóu dàshà** tall buildings and great mansions

啥 **shà** *pron* what
有啥吃啥 **yǒu shà chī shà** eat whatever you've got

NOTE: 啥 **shà** is a dialectal word, used on very casual occasions.

筛 **shāi** *v* sieve, sift
筛子 **shāizi** sieve

晒 **shài** Trad 曬 *v* dry in the sun, bask
晒太阳 **shài tàiyang** sunbathe □ 有的人喜欢在夏天晒太阳, 这对皮肤有害。 **Yǒude rén xǐhuan zài xiàtiān shài tàiyang, zhè duì pífu yǒuhài.** *In summer some people like to sunbathe, which is harmful to the skin.*

山 **shān** *n* mountain, hill (座 **zuò**) □ 这座山真高啊! **Zhè zuò shān zhēn gāo a!** *How high this mountain is!* □ 这个美丽的小城, 前面是大河, 背后是青山。 **Zhège měilì de xiǎochéng, qiánmian shì dà hé, bèihòu shì qīng shān.** *In front of this beautiful town is a big river and behind it are green hills.*
爬山 **páshān** mountain climbing, mountaineering □ 星期六我们去爬山吧! **Xīngqīliù wǒmen qù páshān ba!** *Let's go mountain climbing this Saturday.*
山地 **shāndì** *n* hilly area, mountainous region
山地车 **shāndìchē** mountain bike (辆 **liàng**)
山峰 **shānfēng** *n* mountain peak (座 **zuò**)
山冈 **shāngāng** *n* low hill (座 **zuò**)
山沟 **shāngōu** *n* gully, ravine (条 **tiáo**)
山谷 **shāngǔ** *n* valley (条 **tiáo**)
山河 **shānhé** *n* mountains and rivers, land (of a country)
大好山河 **dàhǎo shānhé** the beautiful land (of a country)
山脚 **shānjiǎo** [modif: 山 mountain/hill + 脚 foot] *n* the foot of a hill (mountain)
在山脚下 **zài shānjiǎo xià** at the foot of the hill (mountain)
山岭 **shānlǐng** *n* mountain ridge
山脉 **shānmài** [modif: 山 mountain + 脉 veins and arteries] *n* mountain range (条 **tiáo**) □ 世界上最大的

山脉—喜马拉雅山脉—是在中国。 **Shìjiè shang zuì dà de shānmài—Xǐmǎlāyǎ shānmài—shì zài Zhōngguó.** *The biggest mountain range in the world—the Himalayas—is in China.*

山水 **shānshuǐ** [comp: 山 hill, mountain + 水 water] landscape □ 新西兰的山水很美。 **Xīnxīlán de shānshuǐ hěn měi.** *The landscape of New Zealand is beautiful.*
游山玩水 **yóu-shān-wán-shuǐ** enjoy the landscape, go sightseeing □ 他有钱, 又有时间, 所以经常出国游山玩水。 **Tā yǒu qián, yòu yǒu shíjiān, suǒyǐ jīngcháng chūguó yóu-shān-wán-shuǐ.** *He's rich and he's got the time, so he often goes sightseeing overseas.*
山头 **shāntóu** *n* hilltop (座 **zuò**)
山腰 **shānyāo** *n* halfway up the mountain, mountainside

衫 **shān** *n* shirt (See 衬衫 **chènshān**.)

珊 **shān** *n* as in 珊瑚 **shānhú**
珊瑚 **shānhú** *n* coral

删 **shān** *v* delete (words)

闪 **shǎn** Trad 閃 *v* 1 flash, sparkle 2 glitter, twinkle
闪电 **shǎndiàn** *n* lightning □ 昨天夜里又打雷, 又闪电, 真吓人。 **Zuótiān yèli yòu dǎléi, yòu shǎndiàn, zhēn xiàrén.** *Last night thunder boomed and lightning flashed. It was really frightening.*
闪盘 **shǎnpán** *n* (computing) flash memory disk
闪烁 **shǎnshuò** *v* twinkle, glitter
闪耀 **shǎnyào** *v* shine

扇 **shàn** *n* fan (See 电扇 **diànshàn**.)

善 **shàn** *adj* good, kind, friendly
善良 **shànliáng** [comp: 善 good + 良 good] *adj* kind-hearted, good-hearted
善于 **shànyú** *v* be good at □ 他善于理解, 不善于表达。 **Tā shànyú lǐjiě, bú shànyú biǎodá.** *He is good at understanding, but not good at expressing himself.*

擅 **shàn** I *v* be good at II *adv* (doing things) without authorization
擅长 **shàncháng** *adj* expert in, having a special skill
擅长谈判 **shàncháng tánpàn** be especially good at negotiation, be an expert negotiator
擅自 **shànzì** *adv* without permission, without authorization

伤 **shāng** Trad 傷 I *v* wound, injure, hurt □ 他踢球的时候伤了脚。 **Tā tīqiú de shíhou shāngle jiǎo.** *He injured his foot playing football.* □ 你这么做会伤他的感情。 **Nǐ zhènme zuò huì shāng tā de gǎnqíng.** *Doing that will hurt his feelings.* II *n* wound, injury □ 你的伤不重, 很快就会好的。 **Nǐ de shāng bú zhòng, hěn kuài jiù huì hǎo de.** *Your injury is not serious and will heal soon.*
受伤 **shòushāng** be wounded, be injured
伤疤 **shāngbā** *n* scar
伤风 **shāngfēng** *v* catch a cold
伤害 **shānghài** [comp: 伤 injure + 害 harm] *v* harm, hurt □ 她无意说的那句话, 大大伤害了他的感情。 **Tā wúyì shuōde nà jù huà, dàdà shānghàile tā de gǎnqíng.** *That casual remark of hers hurt him badly.*
伤痕 **shānghén** *n* bruise, scar

伤口 shāngkǒu [modif: 伤 wound + 口 mouth, opening] *n* wound, cut

伤脑筋 shāng nǎojīn [v+obj: 伤 wound + 脑筋 the brains] **I** *v* be vexed, be frustrated **II** *adj* troublesome, vexing

伤脑筋的问题 shāng nǎojīn de wèntí a very difficult problem, a thorny problem

伤心 shāngxīn [v+obj: 伤 wound + 心 the heart] *adj* heartbreaking, heartbroken □ 听到这个伤心的消息, 玛丽忍不住哭了。**Tīngdao zhège shāngxīn de xiāoxi, Mǎlì rén bu zhù kū le.** *Hearing this heartbreaking news, Mary couldn't help weeping.* □ 当她三岁的儿子死了, 她伤心得不想活。**Dāng tā sān suì de érzi sǐ le, tā shāngxīn de bù xiǎng huó.** *When her three-year-old son died, she was so heartbroken that she did not want to live.*

伤员 shāngyuán *n* wounded soldier (名 míng)

商 shāng **I** *v* discuss, consult **II** *n* commerce, business

商标 shāngbiāo [modif: 商 commercial + 标 mark] *n* trademark

商场 shāngchǎng [modif: 商 commerce + 场 place] *n* **1** shopping center, mall (家 jiā, 座 zuò) □ 这座商场有近一百家大大小小的商店。**Zhè zuò shāngchǎng yǒu jìn yìbǎi jiā dà-dà-xiǎo-xiǎo de shāngdiàn.** *This shopping center has nearly a hundred shops, big and small.* **2** department store □ 这家商场地处市中心, 停车不方便。**Zhè jiā shāngchǎng dìchù shìzhōngxīn, tíng chē bù fāngbiàn.** *This department store is in the city center. Parking is inconvenient.*

商店 shāngdiàn *n* shop, store (家 jiā) □ 这家商店是卖什么的? **Zhè jiā shāngdiàn shì mài shénme de?** *What does this store sell?* □ 我常去那家商店买东西。**Wǒ cháng qù nàjiā shāngdiàn mǎi dōngxi.** *I often shop at that store.*

开商店 kāi shāngdiàn open a shop, keep a shop

商量 shāngliang [comp: 商 discuss + 量 weigh] *v* discuss, consult □ 有重要的事, 先和好朋友商量再决定。**Yǒu zhòngyào de shì, xiān hé hǎo péngyou shāngliang zài juédìng.** *When an important matter arises, discuss it with good friends before making a decision.* □ 我想和你商量一件事, 听听你的意见。**Wǒ xiǎng hé nǐ shāngliang yí jiàn shì, tīngtīng nǐ de yìjiàn.** *There is something I'd like to consult you over and hear your advice.*

商品 shāngpǐn [modif: 商 commerce + 品 article] *n* commodity (件 jiàn, 种 zhǒng) □ 我们卖出的商品都有质量保证。**Wǒmen màichū de shāngpǐn dōu yǒu zhìliàng bǎozhèng.** *All the goods we sell have a quality guarantee.* □ 商品的价格是由什么决定的? **Shāngpǐn de jiàgé shì yóu shénme juédìng de?** *What determines the price of commodities?*

商榷 shāngquè *v* discuss politely, deliberate

商人 shāngrén [modif: 商 commerce + 人 person] *n* merchant, business person

商讨 shāngtǎo [comp: 商 discuss + 讨 discuss] *v* exchange views in order to reach a consensus

商业 shāngyè [modif: 商 commerce + 业 industry] *n* commerce, business □ 这个城市商业十分发达。**Zhège chéngshì shāngyè shífēn fādá.** *Commerce is very well developed in this city.*

商业管理 shāngyè guǎnlǐ [modif: 商业 business + 管理 administration] business administration

商业管理硕士 shāngyè guǎnlǐ shuòshì Master of Business Administration (MBA)

商业区 shāngyèqū *n* business district

商业中心区 shāngyè zhōngxīnqū central business district (CBD)

商议 shāngyì *v* discuss, confer

赏 shǎng Trad 賞 *v* **1** admire, enjoy **2** reward, grant

赏罚分明 shǎngfá fēnmíng *idiom* rewarding merit and punishing mistake fairly, exercise discipline judiciously

赏识 shǎngshí [comp: 赏 admire + 识 recognize] *v* recognize and admire the talent of (people), appreciate the worth of (people)

上 shàng **I** *n* on top of, on, above (antonym 下 xià) □ 山上有一座白房子。**Shān shang yǒu yí zuò bái fángzi.** *There's a white house on the hill.* **II** *adj* previous, last

上星期 shàng xīngqī last week

上一课 shàng yí kè the previous class (lesson)

NOTE: 上 **shàng** is often used after a noun to form words of location. While its basic meaning is *on top*, 上 **shàng** may have various, often semi-idiomatic meanings, e.g.

报纸上 bàozhǐ shang in the newspaper

地上 dì shang on the ground

工作上 gōngzuò shang in work

会上 huì shang at the meeting

世界上 shìjiè shang in the world

手上 shǒu shang in hand, in the hands of

上边 shàngbian [modif: 上 top, upper + 边 side] *n* above, high up (antonym 下边 xiàbian) □ 从那座大楼的上边可以看见飞机场。**Cóng nà zuò dàlóu de shàngbian kěyǐ kànjiàn fēijīchǎng.** *From the top of that high building, one can see the airport.*

上层 shàngcéng [modif: 上 upper + 层 layer] *n* upper stratum (of a society)

上层社会 shàngcéng shèhuì upper social class

上等 shàngděng *adj* (of products) superior, first-rate

上帝 Shàngdì [modif: 上 top + 帝 emperor] *n* God

上级 shàngjí [modif: 上 top, upper + 级 step, grade] *n* higher authorities, superior □ 上级发来通知, 六月三十日停课。**Shàngjí fālai tōngzhī, Liùyuè sānshí rì tíng kè.** *The authorities have advised that school be closed on June thirtieth.* □ 你是我的上级, 我当然要完成你分配的任务。**Nǐ shì wǒ de shàngjí, wǒ dāngrán yào wánchéng nǐ fēnpèi de rènwù.** *You're my superior, so of course I will complete the task you assigned.*

上空 shàngkōng *n* overhead, in the sky

上面 shàngmian *n* Same as 上边 shàngbian

上升 shàngshēng [comp: 上 up + 升 ascend] *v* rise □ 到了晚上, 病人的体温上升了。**Dào le wǎnshang, bìngrén de tǐwēn shàngshēng le.** *When evening came, the patient's temperature rose.*

上述 shàngshù *n* above-mentioned

上诉 shàngsù *v* appeal (to a higher court)

上午 shàngwǔ [modif: 上 upper half + 午 noon] *n* morning (usually from 8 a.m. to noon) (antonym 下午 xiàwǔ) □ 我们上午上三节课。**Wǒmen shàngwǔ shàng sān jié kè.** *We have three classes in the morning.* □ 他一直睡到第二天上午十点左右。**Tā yìzhí**

shuìdao dì-èr tiān shàngwǔ shí diǎn zuǒyòu. *He slept until about ten o'clock the next morning.*

NOTE: 上午 **shàngwǔ** does not mean the whole morning. It denotes the part of morning from about eight or nine o'clock to noon. The period before eight or nine o'clock is 早晨 **zǎochén** or 早上 **zǎoshang.**

上下 **shàngxià** *n* from top to bottom, up and down

上旬 **shàngxún** *n* the first 10 days of a month

上衣 **shàngyī** [modif: 上 upper + 衣 clothing] *n* upper garment, jacket (件 **jiàn**) □ 你这件上衣很好看, 在哪儿买的? **Nǐ zhè jiàn shàngyī hěn hǎokàn, zài nǎr mǎi de?** *Your jacket looks good. Where did you buy it?*

上游 **shàngyóu** *n* upper reaches (of a river)

上载 **shàng zài** *v* upload

上涨 **shàngzhǎng** *v* (of rivers, prices) rise, go up

上 2 **shàng** *v* 1 go upwards, ascend
上楼 **shàng lóu** go upstairs □ 我坐电梯上楼。**Wǒ zuò diàntī shàng lóu.** *I take the lift upstairs.*
上来 **shànglai** come up □ 楼上有空房间, 快上来吧! **Lóu shang yǒu kòng fángjiān, kuài shànglai ba!** *There's a vacant room upstairs, please come up!*
上去 **shàngqu** go up □ 他们在楼上等你, 快上去吧! **Tāmen zài lóu shang děng nǐ, kuài shàngqu ba!** *They're waiting for you upstairs. Please go upstairs.*
2 get on (a vehicle), go aboard (a plane, ship) □ 火车来了, 准备上车吧! **Huǒchē lái le, zhǔnbèi shàng chē ba!** *The train is coming. Let's get ready to board.*
上车 **shàng chē** get into a vehicle
上船 **shàng chuán** board a ship
上飞机 **shàng fēijī** get on the plane
3 attend (school), go to (work)
上大学 **shàng dàxué** go to university
上班 **shàngbān** *v* go to work □ 我母亲每天九点上班, 五点下班。**Wǒ mǔqin měi tiān jiǔ diǎn shàngbān, wǔ diǎn xiàbān.** *Every day my mother goes to work at nine and finishes at five.*
上报 **shàngbào** *v* 1 report to a higher body 2 appear in the newspapers
上当 **shàngdàng** *v* be fooled, be duped □ 他太老实了, 容易上当受骗。**Tā tài lǎoshi le, róngyì shàngdàng shòupiàn.** *He is too straightforward and easily duped.* □ 你怎么又上她的当了? **Nǐ zěnme yòu shàng tā de dàng le?** *How is it that you got fooled by her again?*
上课 **shàngkè** *v* go to class, have classes □ 明天放假, 不上课。**Míngtiān fàngjià, bú shàngkè.** *Tomorrow's a holiday. There will be no classes.*
上任 **shàngrèn** *v* assume office, take up a post
上市 **shàngshì** *v* be available on the market
上市公司 **shàngshì gōngsī** listed company
上台 **shàngtái** *v* 1 go on stage 2 come to power
上网 **shàngwǎng** [v+obj: 上 get on + 网 Internet] *v* get on the Internet, surf the Internet □ 他一般吃了晚饭, 就上网半小时看看新闻。**Tā yìbān chīle wǎnfàn jiù shàngwǎng bàn xiǎoshí kànkan xīnwén.** *After supper he usually gets on the Internet for half an hour to read the news.* □ 这几天我忙得没有时间上网。**Zhè jǐ tiān wǒ máng de méiyǒu shíjiān shàngwǎng.** *These days I'm so busy that I haven't got the time to get on the Internet.*
上学 **shàngxué** *v* go to school □ 你弟弟上学了吗? **Nǐ dìdi shàngxué le ma?** *Has your younger brother start-*

ed school yet? □ 我骑自行车上学。**Wǒ qí zìxíngchē shàngxué.** *I go to school by bike.*

尚 **shàng** *v* worship, revere

裳 **shàng** *n* clothing (See 衣裳 **yīshang**)

烧 **shāo** Trad 燒 *v* 1 burn □ 市政府禁止烧垃圾。**Shìzhèngfǔ jìnzhǐ shāo lājī.** *The city government bans the burning of rubbish.* 2 cook □ 今天我给你们烧个鱼。**Jīntiān wǒ gěi nǐmen shāo ge yú.** *Today I'll cook you a fish.* 3 have a fever □ 这孩子烧得厉害, 得马上送医院! **Zhè háizi shāo de lìhai, děi mǎshàng sòng yīyuàn!** *The child is running a very high fever. He must be sent to the hospital right now!*

烧饼 **shāobǐng** *n* sesame seed cake (块 **kuài**)

烧毁 **shāohuǐ** [comp: 烧 burn + 毁 destroy] *v* burn up

捎 **shāo** *v* take (something) along for (someone)
捎个话儿 **shāo gè huàr** take an (oral) message, relay a message

梢 **shāo** *n* the thin tip of a long-shaped object
树梢儿 **shùshāor** treetops

稍 **shāo** *adv* Same as 稍微 **shāowéi.** Often used in written Chinese.

稍微 **shāowéi** [comp: 稍 slight + 微 tiny] *adv* slightly, just a little bit □ 你能不能把电视机的声音开得稍微大一点? **Nǐ néng bu néng bǎ diànshìjī de shēngyin kāi de shāowéi dà yìdiǎn?** *Could you turn the TV up a bit?* □ 我稍微有点儿头疼, 休息一会儿就会好的。**Wǒ shāowéi yǒu diǎnr tóuténg, xiūxi yíhuìr jiù huì hǎo de.** *I've a slight headache. I'll be all right after a short rest.*

勺 **sháo** *n* spoon
勺子 **sháozi** [suffix: 勺 ladle + 子 nominal suffix] *n* ladle, spoon (把 **bǎ**) □ 她用勺子把汤分给大家。**Tā yòng sháozi bǎ tāng fēn gei dàjiā.** *She gave soup to everyone with a ladle.*

少 **shǎo** I *adj* small in amount, few, little (antonym 多 **duō**) □ 新西兰人少地多。**Xīnxīlán rén shǎo dì duō.** *New Zealand has a small population and much land.* II *adv* not often, seldom □ 我们虽然在同一个学校, 但是很少见面。**Wǒmen suīrán zài tóng yí ge xuéxiào, dànshì hěn shǎo jiànmiàn.** *Although we're in the same school, we seldom see each other.* III *v* be short, be missing □ 原来我有一百元, 现在怎么少了二十元? **Yuánlái wǒ yǒu yìbǎi yuán, xiànzài zěnme shǎole èrshí yuán?** *I originally had one hundred dollars. How is it that I have twenty dollars less now?* □ 要和他们比赛, 我们还少一个人。**Yào hé tāmen bǐsài, wǒmen hái shǎo yí ge rén.** *We're still short of one person if we want to compete with them.*

少量 **shǎoliàng** *n* small amount, little, few

少数 **shǎoshù** [modif: 少 few, little + 数 number] *n* minority (antonym 多数 **duōshù**) □ 少数服从多数, 这是民主的一条基本原则。**Shǎoshù fúcóng duōshù, zhè shì mínzhǔ de yì tiáo jīběn yuánzé.** *The minority should submit to the majority—this is a fundamental principle of democracy.*

少数民族 **shǎoshù mínzú** minority nationality (non-Han ethnic group in China)

少 **shào** *adj* young
少年 **shàonián** [modif: 少 young + 年 age] *n*

young man (from around 10 to 16 years old), adolescent □ 自古少年出英雄。**Zìgǔ shàonián chū yīngxióng.** *Ever since ancient times, heroes have emerged from the young.*

NOTES: (1) A young woman of around 10 to 16 years old is called 少女 **shàonǚ**. (2) The word 青少年 **qīngshàonián** is often used to mean *young people* collectively.

少女 **shàonǚ** [modif: 少 young + 女 female] *n* teenage girl
少先队 **Shàoxiānduì** *n* the Young Pioneers

NOTE: 少先队 **Shàoxiānduì** is the shortened form of 少年先锋队 **Shàonián Xiānfēngduì**.

绍 **shào** Trad 紹 *v* connect (See 介绍 **jièshào**.)

哨 **shào** *n* 1 sentry 2 whistle
哨兵 **shàobīng** *n* sentry, armed guard (名 **míng**)
哨子 **shàozi** *n* whistle
吹哨子 chuī shàozi blow a whistle

奢 **shē** *adj* excessive, luxurious
奢侈 **shēchǐ** [comp: 奢 excessive + 侈 wasteful] *adj* luxurious □ 他们有钱以后生活非常奢侈。**Tāmen yǒuqián yǐhòu shēnghuó fēicháng shēchǐ.** *They lived in luxury after becoming rich.*
奢侈品 shēchǐpǐn luxury item

舌 **shé** *n* tongue
舌头 **shétou** [suffix: 舌 the tongue + 头 nominal suffix] *n* the tongue □ 医生：你舌头伸出来，我看看。**Yīshēng: Nǐ shétou shēn chūlai, wǒ kànkan.** *Doctor: Stick out your tongue and I'll have a look.* (→ *Show me your tongue.*)

蛇 **shé** *n* snake (条 **tiáo**) □ 她最怕蛇。**Tā zuì pà shé.** *She finds snakes the most frightening [of all animals].*

舍 **shě** *v* give up
舍不得 **shěbude** *v* unwilling to give up, hate to part with □ 我在伯伯、伯母家渡过了愉快的暑假，真舍不得跟他们告别。**Wǒ zài bóbo, bómǔ jiā dùguòle yúkuài de shǔjià, zhēn shěbude gēn tāmen gàobié.** *After spending a happy summer vacation with my uncle and aunt, I could hardly tear myself away from them.*
舍得 **shěde** *v* be willing to part with, not grudge □ 她为了孩子，舍得花钱花时间。**Tā wèile háizi, shěde huā qián huā shíjiān.** *She is willing to spend time and money on her children.*

设 **shè** Trad 設 *v* equip, set up
设备 **shèbèi** *n* equipment, installation (件 **jiàn**, 套 **tào**) □ 这座医院设备良好。**Zhè zuò yīyuàn shèbèi liánghǎo.** *This hospital is well equipped.* □ 这套实验室设备是从国外进口的。**Zhè tào shíyànshì shèbèi shì cóng guówài jìnkǒu de.** *This set of laboratory equipment was imported from overseas.*
设法 **shèfǎ** *v* try to find a way, attempt to
设计 **shèjì** [comp: 设 plan + 计 calculate] **I** *v* design □ 工程师正在设计一种不用汽油的汽车。**Gōngchéngshī zhèngzài shèjì yì zhǒng bú yòng qìyóu de qìchē.** *Engineers are designing a car that does not use petrol.* **II** *n* design, plan □ 我有一个叔叔，是搞建筑设计的。**Wǒ yǒu yí ge shūshu, shì gǎo jiànzhù shèjì de.** *I have an uncle who is engaged in architectural design.*

设立 **shèlì** *v* establish, set up
设施 **shèshī** *n* facilities, equipment
设想 **shèxiǎng** *v* conceive, envision
不堪设想的后果 bùkān shèxiǎng de hòuguǒ inconceivable consequences
设置 **shèzhì** *v* set up, establish

社 **shè** *n* association
社会 **shèhuì** [comp: 社 god of the earth + 会 gathering] *n* society □ 我们每个人都应该关心社会。**Wǒmen měi ge rén dōu yīnggāi guānxīn shèhuì.** *Each of us should be concerned for society.* □ 今天的中国是个什么样的社会？**Jīntiān de Zhōngguó shì ge shénmeyàng de shèhuì?** *What kind of society is China today?*
社会上 shèhuì shang in society, the general public
社会学 **shèhuìxué** *n* sociology
社会主义 **shèhuì zhǔyì** *n* socialism
社交 **shèjiāo** [modif: 社 social + 交 association] *n* social life, social intercourse
社论 **shèlùn** *n* editorial (篇 **piān**)

舍 **shè** *n* hut, shed (See 宿舍 **sùshè**.)

摄 **shè** Trad 攝 *v* photograph, shoot (movies, etc)
摄像 **shèxiàng** *v* make a video recording
摄像机 **shèxiàngjī** camcorder
摄氏 **shèshì** *n* Celsius, centigrade
摄氏温度计 shèshì wēndùjì centigrade thermometer

NOTE: China uses Celsius (摄氏 **shèshì**), not Fahrenheit (华氏 **huáshì**). In everyday speech, people usually do not mention 摄氏 **shèshì**. So if a Chinese person says 今天最高气温二十八度, **Jīntiān zuìgāo qìwēn èrshíbā dù**, it automatically means *The highest temperature today will be 28 degrees Celsius.*

摄影 **shèyǐng** [v+obj: 摄 take + 影 shadow] *n* photography □ 这个电影的摄影十分成功。**Zhège diànyǐng de shèyǐng shífēn chénggōng.** *The cinematography of this film is a spectacular success.*
摄影家 **shèyǐngjiā** accomplished photographer
摄影师 **shèyǐngshī** photographer
摄影作品 shèyǐng zuòpǐn a work of photography

射 **shè** *v* shoot (a gun, an arrow etc.)
射击 **shèjī** *v* shoot, fire

涉 **shè** *v* involve
涉及 **shèjí** *v* involve, touch on, have something to do with

谁 **shéi** Trad 誰 *pron* Same as 谁 **shuí**. Used colloquially.

身 **shēn** **I** *n* human body □ 他身高175公分。**Tā shēn gāo yìbǎi qīshíwǔ gōngfēn.** *He is 175 centimeters tall.* **II** *measure wd* (for clothes)
一身新衣服 yì shēn xīn yīfu a suit of new clothes
身边 **shēnbiān** *n* close by one's side, on one's person □ 我身边没有她的地址，我发电子邮件告诉你。**Wǒ shēnbiān méiyǒu tā de dìzhǐ, wǒ fā diànzǐ yóujiàn gàosu nǐ.** *I don't have her address with me. I'll send it to you by email.* □ 他出去身边总带着手机。**Tā chūqu shēnbiān zǒng dàizhe shǒujī.** *He never goes anywhere without his cell phone.*
身材 **shēncái** *n* stature, figure
身材苗条 shēncái miáotiáo with a slender figure

身分(份) **shēnfen** *n* social status, identity
　身分不明 shēnfen bùmíng unknown identity
身分证 **shēnfenzhèng** *n* I.D. card
身体 **shēntǐ** [comp: 身 body + 体 physical] *n* **1** human body □ 少年儿童正处在长身体的时期。**Shàonián értóng zhèng chǔ zài zhǎng shēntǐ de shíqī.** *Children and adolescents are at a stage of physical development.* **2** health □ 我爸爸年纪大了，但是身体还很好。**Wǒ bàba niánjì dà le, dànshì shēntǐ hái hěn hǎo.** *My father is getting old, but is still in good health.* □ 你要注意身体。**Nǐ yào zhùyì shēntǐ.** *You should pay attention to your health.*

NOTE: Although its original meaning is the *body*, 身体 **shēntǐ** is often used in colloquial Chinese to mean *health*. Friends often ask about each other's health in greeting: □ 你身体好吗？**Nǐ shēntǐ hǎo ma?** *How's your health?* □ 你最近身体怎么样？**Nǐ zuìjìn shēntǐ zěnmeyàng?** *How's your health been recently?*

深 **shēn** *adj* **1** deep (antonym 浅 **qiǎn**) □ 这条河深吗？**Zhè tiáo hé shēn ma?** *Is this river deep?* **2** difficult to understand, profound □ 这本书太深了，我看不懂。**Zhè běn shū tài shēn le, wǒ kàn bu dǒng.** *This book is too difficult. I can't understand it.*
深奥 **shēn'ào** *adj* profound, abstruse
深沉 **shēnchén** [comp: 深 deep + 沉 heavy] *adj* deep, heavy
　深沉的爱 shēnchén de ài deep love
深处 **shēnchù** [modif: 深 deep + 处 place] *n* depths, recesses
　内心深处 nèixīn shēnchù one's innermost heart, one's most private feelings and thoughts
深度 **shēndù** [modif: 深 depth + 度 degree] *n* depth, how deep something is
深厚 **shēnhòu** [comp: 深 deep + 厚 thick] *adj* deep, profound □ 他对故乡有深厚的感情。**Tā duì gùxiāng yǒu shēnhòu de gǎnqíng.** *He has deep feelings for his hometown.*
深化 **shēnhuà** [suffix: 深 deep + 化 verb suffix] *v* deepen
深刻 **shēnkè** [modif: 深 deep + 刻 carve] *adj* incisive, insightful, profound □ 这位老人经历十分丰富，对人性有深刻的认识。**Zhè wèi lǎorén jīnglì shífēn fēngfù, duì rénxìng yǒu shēnkè de rènshi.** *This old man has had very rich experiences and has an incisive understanding of human nature.*
深浅 **shēnqiǎn** *n* **1** Same as 深度 **shēndù 2** proper limit for speech or action, propriety
深切 **shēnqiè** *adj* heartfelt, earnest
深情 **shēnqíng** *n* deep feelings
深入 **shēnrù** [modif: 深 deep + 入 enter, penetrate] *v* enter deeply into □ 这一政策深入人心。**Zhè yí zhèngcè shēnrù rénxīn.** *This policy enters deeply into people's hearts. (→ This policy is extremely popular.)*
深入浅出 **shēn-rù-qiǎn-chū** *idiom* explain complicated theories or phenomena in simple, easy-to-understand language.
深信 **shēnxìn** [modif: 深 deeply + 信 believe] *v* firmly believe, be deeply convinced
深远 **shēnyuán** [comp: 深 deep + 远 far away] *adj* profound and lasting, far-reaching

深重 **shēnzhòng** [comp: 深 deep + 重 heavy] *adj* extremely serious, extremely grave
申 **shēn** *v* explain, state
申报 **shēnbào** [comp: 申 state + 报 report] *v* **1** declare (at customs) □（在海关）我没有什么东西要申报。**(Zài hǎiguān) Wǒ méiyǒu shénme dōngxi yào shēnbào.** *(At customs) I've nothing to declare.* **2** submit an official report
申请 **shēnqǐng** [comp: 申 state + 请 request] *v* apply for (a visa, job, permit, etc.)
申请表 shēnqǐngbiǎo application form
申请人 shēnqǐngrén applicant
申请书 shēnqǐngshū letter of application
申述 **shēnshù** [comp: 申 state + 述 narrate] *v* give an official explanation
伸 **shēn** *v* stretch out, extend □ 火车开的时候，你千万不要把头伸出车窗。**Huǒchē kāi de shíhou, nǐ qiānwàn bú yào bǎ tóu shēnchū chēchuāng.** *Never stick your head out of the window when the train is moving.*
伸展 **shēnzhǎn** *v* extend, stretch
绅 **shēn** Trad 紳 as in 绅士 **shēnshì**
绅士 **shēnshì** *n* gentleman, gentry
呻 **shēn** as in 呻吟 **shēnyín**
呻吟 **shēnyín** *v* groan, moan
神 **shén** **I** *n* god, supernatural being □ 你相信神吗？**Nǐ xiāngxìn shén ma?** *Do you believe in gods?*
　财神爷 cáishényé the god of money, Mammon
II *adj* magical, wondrous
神话 **shénhuà** [modif: 神 god + 话 story] *n* mythology, myth
神经 **shénjīng** *n* **1** nerve □ 我牙神经疼。**Wǒ yá shénjīng téng.** *My tooth nerve hurts.* **2** the mind, mental state □ 他神经有毛病。**Tā shénjīng yǒu máobìng.** *There is something wrong with his mind.*
神经病 shénjīngbìng neuropathy, mental disorder, crazy

NOTE: The formal word for *mental disorder* is 精神病 **jīngshénbìng** but 神经病 **shénjīngbìng** may be used in everyday Chinese.

神秘 **shénmì** [comp: 神 god, supernatural + 秘 secret] *adj* mysterious □ 有些西方人觉得汉字很神秘。**Yǒuxiē xīfāngrén juéde Hànzì hěn shénmì.** *Some Westerners find Chinese characters quite mysterious.*
神奇 **shénqí** [comp: 神 magical + 奇 strange] *adj* miraculous, mystical
神气 **shénqì** *adj* **1** arrogant and cocky **2** spirited and vigorous
神情 **shénqíng** *n* (facial) expression, look
神色 **shénsè** *n* appearance, expression □ 那个人神色可疑。**Nàge rén shénsè kěyí.** *That man looks suspicious.*
神圣 **shénshèng** [comp: 神 god + 圣 sacred] *adj* sacred, holy
神态 **shéntài** *n* bearing, appearance
神仙 **shénxiān** *n* immortal, celestial being (位 **wèi**)
什 **shén** *pron* what
什么 **shénme** *pron* what □ 什么是语法？**Shénme shì yǔfǎ?** *What is grammar?* □ 你要什么？**Nǐ yào shénme?** *What do you want?* □ 你要什么菜？**Nǐ yào**

shénme cài? Which dish do you want? (or What would you like to order?)

什么的 **shénmede** pron and so on, and so forth □ 他们要了很多菜, 有鱼、肉、蔬菜, 什么的。**Tāmen yàole hěn duō cài, yǒu yú, ròu, shūcài, shénmede.** They ordered lots of dishes, fish, meat, vegetables and so on.

审 **shěn** v 1 examine   2 interrogate

审查 **shěnchá** [comp: 审 examine + 查 investigate] v examine, investigate

审定 **shěndìng** [comp: 审 examine + 定 decide] v examine and approve (a proposal, a plan, etc.)

审计 **shěnjì** v audit

审计员 **shěnjìyuán** auditor

审理 **shěnlǐ** v try (a legal case), handle (a legal case)

审美 **shěnměi** n appreciation of what is beautiful

审判 **shěnpàn** [comp: 审 interrogate + 判 sentence] v bring to trial, try

审批 **shěnpī** [comp: 审 examine + 批 approve] v examine and approve

审问 **shěnwèn** v Same as 审讯 **shěnxùn**

审讯 **shěnxùn** v interrogate (by the police)

审议 **shěnyì** [comp: 审 examine + 议 discuss] v deliberate, consider

婶 **shěn** n wife of one's father's younger brother

婶母 **shěnmǔ** wife of one's father's younger brother

婶婶 **shěnshen** Same as 婶母 **shěnmǔ**. Used as a form of address

肾 **shèn** n kidney

肾炎 **shènyán** n nephritis

甚 **shèn** adv much, very much

甚至 **shènzhì** adv even, so much so □ 她到过中国很多地方, 甚至西藏也去过。**Tā dàoguo Zhōngguó hěn duō dìfang, shènzhì Xīzàng yě qù guo.** She has been to many places in China, even to Tibet.

慎 **shèn** adj cautious

慎重 **shènzhòng** [comp: 慎 cautious + 重 attach importance to] adj very cautious, discreet

渗 **shèn** v seep, ooze

渗透 **shèntòu** [v+compl: 渗 seep + 透 thorough] v seep into, permeate

升 **shēng** v rise, go up □ 昨天股票升了百分之零点五。**Zuótiān gǔpiào shēngle bǎifēn zhī líng diǎn wǔ.** Shares rose by half a percent yesterday.

生 I **shēng** I v 1 give birth to, grow □ 他妻子上星期生了一个女儿。**Tā qīzi shàng xīngqī shēng le yí ge nǚ'ér.** His wife gave birth to a girl baby last week.   2 be born □ 她生在北京。**Tā shēng zài Běijīng.** She was born in Beijing. □ 生在福中不知福。**Shēng zài fú zhōng bùzhī fú.** Though born in luck, one doesn't appreciate how lucky he is.   3 live, grow II adj alive, living

生病 **shēngbìng** v fall ill

生产 **shēngchǎn** [comp: 生 grow + 产 produce] v produce, manufacture □ 这家工厂去年生产一万辆汽车。**Zhè jiā gōngchǎng qùnián shēngchǎn yíwàn liàng qìchē.** This factory manufactured 10,000 automobiles last year.

生产力 **shēngchǎnlì** n productive force

生产率 **shēngchǎnlù** n productivity

生存 **shēngcún** [comp: 生 live + 存 exist] I v survive, be alive □ 由于过分开发, 野生动物在这里

无法生存。**Yóuyú guòfèn kāifā, yěshēng dòngwù zài zhèlǐ wúfǎ shēngcún.** Owing to excessive development wildlife cannot survive here. II n survival

生动 **shēngdòng** [comp: 生 lively + 动 move] adj vivid, lively □ 她在信里生动有趣地描写了旅行经历。**Tā zài xìn li shēngdòng yǒuqù de miáoxiěle lǚxíng jīnglì.** In her letter she gives vivid and interesting accounts of her travel experiences.

生活 **shēnghuó** [comp: 生 living + 活 alive] I n life □ 这位老人的生活很困难。**Zhè wèi lǎorén de shēnghuó hěn kùnnan.** This old man's life is difficult. (→ This old man lives a hard life.) □ 请您介绍一下中国大学生的生活。**Qǐng nín jièshào yíxià Zhōngguó dàxuéshēng de shēnghuó.** Please tell us something about the life of Chinese university students.

日常生活 **rìcháng shēnghuó** daily life

II v live, lead (a life) □ 我小时候生活得很愉快。**Wǒ xiǎoshíhou shēnghuó de hěn yúkuài.** I lived a happy life in childhood. (→ I had a happy childhood.)

生活费 **shēnghuófèi** [modif: 生活 living + 费 expenditure] n living allowance, stipend

生活费用 **shēnghuó fèiyòng** [modif: 生活 living + 费用 costs] n cost of living

生活水平 **shēnghuó shuǐpíng** [modif: 生活 living + 水平 level] n living standards

提高生活水平 **tígāo shēnghuó shuǐpíng** raise living standards

生机 **shēngjī** n 1 chance of survival, lease of life

一线生机 **yíxiàn shēngjī** a slim chance of survival   2 vitality

生机勃勃 **shēngjī bóbó** full of vigor and vitality

生理 **shēnglǐ** [modif: 生 life + 理 theory] n the physical aspect of human life

生理上 **shēnglǐ shàng** physical, physically

生理学 **shēnglǐxué** physiology

生命 **shēngmìng** [comp: 生 living + 命 life] n life (条 **tiáo**) □ 他的生命在危险中。**Tā de shēngmìng zài wēixiǎn zhōng.** His life is in danger. □ 这只小猫也是一条小生命, 不能眼看它死去。**Zhè zhī xiǎo māo yě shì yì tiáo xiǎo shēngmìng, bù néng yǎnkàn tā sǐqu.** This kitten is also a life. We can't let it die without doing anything.

生命科学 **shēngmìng kēxué** life science

生命力 **shēngmìnglì** n life force

生怕 **shēngpà** conj for fear of, so as not to

生气 **shēngqì** v get angry, be offended □ 别对他生气, 他不是故意的。**Bié duì tā shēngqì, tā bú shì gùyì de.** Don't get angry with him. He did not mean it. □ 你为了什么事生气? **Nǐ wèile shénme shì shēngqì?** What are you angry about?

生前 **shēngqián** n (of a dead person) during his/her lifetime

生日 **shēngrì** [modif: 生 birth + 日 day] n birthday □ 你的生日是哪一天? **Nǐ de shēngrì shì nǎ yì tiān?** Which date is your birthday? (→ When is your birthday?) □ 我忘了今天是我妻子的生日! **Wǒ wàngle jīntiān shì wǒ qīzi de shēngrì!** I forgot it's my wife's birthday today. □ 祝你生日快乐! **Zhù nǐ shēngrì kuàilè!** I wish you a happy birthday!

过生日 **guò shēngrì** celebrate a birthday □ 你今年打算怎么过生日? **Nǐ jīnnián dǎsuàn zěnme guò shēngrì?** How are you going to celebrate your birthday this year

生日贺卡 shēngrì hékǎ birthday card
生日礼物 shēngrì lǐwù birthday present
生态 **shēngtài** [modif: 生 life + 态 condition] *n* ecology
生态学家 shēngtàixuéjiā ecologist
生态旅游 shēngtài lǚyóu ecotourism
生物 **shēngwù** [modif: 生 living + 物 thing] *n* living things □ 生物一般分为动物和植物两大类。 **Shēngwù yìbān fēnwéi dòngwù hé zhíwù liǎng dà lèi.** *Living things are generally categorized into animals and plants.*
生物学 shēngwùxué biology
生物化学 shēngwù huàxué chemical biology, biochemistry
生效 **shēngxiào** *v* come into effect, become effective
生意 **shēngyi** *n* business, trade □ 他每天上网做生意。 **Tā měi tiān shàngwǎng zuò shēngyi.** *He does trading over the Internet every day.* □ 最近生意很不好。 **Zuìjìn shēngyi hěn bù hǎo.** *Business has been slack lately.*
生育 **shēngyù** *v* give birth to, bear
生长 **shēngzhǎng** [comp: 生 living + 长 growing] *v* grow, grow up □ 我生长在一个大城市里。 **Wǒ shēngzhǎng zài yí ge dà chéngshì li.** *I grew up in a big city.* □ 这种植物在河边生长得很好。 **Zhè zhǒng zhíwù zài hébiān shēngzhǎng de hěn hǎo.** *This kind of plant grows well by the river.*
生殖 **shēngzhí** *v* reproduce
生殖系统 shēngzhí xìtǒng reproductive system
生2 **shēng** *adj* 1 raw, not cooked □ 我不敢吃生鱼。 **Wǒ bù gǎn chī shēng yú.** *I don't dare to eat raw fish.* 2 unripe □ 苹果还太生, 要等一段时间才能吃。 **Píngguǒ hái tài shēng, yào děng yí duàn shíjiān cái néng chī.** *The apples are not ripe yet. It will be some time before they are edible.* 3 unfamiliar
生词 **shēngcí** [modif: 生 unfamiliar + 词 word] *n* new words and phrases (in a language lesson) □ 这些生词你都记住了吗? **Zhèxiē shēngcí nǐ dōu jìzhù le ma?** *Have you committed these new words to memory?* □ 这个句子里有一个生词, 我不认识, 也不会念。 **Zhège jùzi li yǒu yí ge shēngcí, wǒ bú rènshi, yě bú huì niàn.** *There's a new word in this sentence. I don't know it, nor do I know how to say it.*
记生词 jì shēngcí memorize new words
生人 **shēngrén** *n* stranger
生疏 **shēngshū** *adj* unfamiliar
人地生疏 réndìshēngshū unfamiliar with the place and the people, be a stranger in a place
甥 **shēng** *n* one's sister's child (See 外甥 **wàishēng**)
牲 **shēng** *n* domesticated animal
牲畜 **shēngchù** *n* livestock, domestic animal (头 **tóu**)
牲口 **shēngkou** *n* pack animal, draught animal (e.g. horse, buffalo, donkey) (头 **tóu**)
声 **shēng** Trad 聲 *n* sound, noise, voice □ 机器声太大, 我听不清你说什么。 **Jīqì shēng tài dà, wǒ tīng bu qīng nǐ shuō shénme.** *The noise from the machine is too loud; I can't hear what you're saying.*
声调 **shēngdiào** [modif: 声 voice + 调 tone] *n* tone of a Chinese character □ 汉语的声调确实比较难学。 **Hànyǔ de shēngdiào quèshí bǐjiào nánxué.** *The tones of Chinese are really rather difficult to learn.* □ "这个

字是哪个声调?" "这个字读第二声。" **"Zhège zì shì nǎge shēngdiào?" "Zhège zì dú dì-èr shēng."** *"Which tone should this character be read with?" (or "Which tone does this character have?") "This character is read with the second tone."*
声明 **shēngmíng** I *n* formal statement □ 外交部就这一事件发表了声明。 **Wàijiāobù jiù zhè yī shìjiàn fābiǎole shēngmíng.** *The Ministry of Foreign Affairs issued a statement on this incident.* II *v* make a statement, publicly declare □ 我声明, 他做的任何事情都与我无关。 **Wǒ shēngmíng, tā zuò de rènhé shìqing dōu yǔ wǒ wú guān.** *I declare that whatever he does has nothing to do with me.*
声势 **shēngshì** [comp: 声 sounds + 势 power] *n* power and influence, momentum
声音 **shēngyīn** [comp: 声 voice + 音 sound] *n* voice, sound □ 我听见有人在楼下说话的声音。 **Wǒ tīngjiàn yǒurén zài lóuxià shuōhuà de shēngyīn.** *I heard the sounds of people talking downstairs.* □ 她的声音很好听。 **Tā de shēngyīn hěn hǎotīng.** *Her voice is pleasant.* □ 请你们说话声音轻一点。 **Qǐng nǐmen shuōhuà shēngyīn qīng yìdiǎn.** *Please talk softly. (or Please don't talk so loudly.)*
声誉 **shēngyù** *n* reputation, prestige
绳 **shéng** Trad 繩 *n* string, rope
绳子 **shéngzi** rope, cord (根 **gēn**, 条 **tiáo**) □ 你拉一下这根绳子, 窗子就会开。 **Nǐ lā yíxià zhè gēn shéngzi, chuāngzi jiù huì kāi.** *Pull this cord and the window will open.*
省1 **shěng** *n* province □ 中国一共有多少个省? **Zhōngguó yígòng yǒu duōshǎo ge shěng?** *How many provinces are there in China?*
省会 shěnghuì provincial capital
省长 shěngzhǎng governor of a province
省2 **shěng** *v* 1 save, economize □ 发电子邮件, 既省钱, 又省时间。 **Fā diànzǐ yóujiàn, jì shěng qián, yòu shěng shíjiān.** *Sending e-mail saves money and time.* □ 他用钱很省。 **Tā yòng qián hěn shěng.** *He is very frugal with money.* 2 leave out, omit
省得 **shěngde** *conj* in case, so as not to
省略 **shěnglüè** *v* omit, leave out
省略号 **shěnglüèhào** *n* (punctuation mark to indicate ellipsis ...), ellipsis
胜 **shèng** Trad 勝 *v* triumph (over), be victorious, defeat □ 上海队胜了北京队。 **Shànghǎi duì shèngle Běijīng duì.** *The Shanghai team defeated the Beijing team.*
胜利 **shènglì** [comp: 胜 triumph + 利 gain benefit] I *v* win victory □ 我们胜利了! **Wǒmen shènglì le!** *We've won!* II *n* victory □ 我们的胜利来得不容易。 **Wǒmen de shènglì lái de bù róngyì.** *Our victory was hard-won.*
剩 **shèng** *v* be left over, have as surplus □ 我原来有五百块钱, 用了四百块, 还剩一百块。 **Wǒ yuánlái yǒu wǔbǎi kuài qián, yòngle sìbǎi kuài, hái shèng yìbǎi kuài.** *I originally had five hundred dollars; I've used four hundred dollars and now have one hundred dollars left.*
剩菜 **shèng cài** [modif: 剩 left + 菜 vegetable, dish] *n* leftovers
剩余 **shèngyú** I *n* surplus, remainder II *v* Same as 剩 **shèng**

盛 **shèng** *adj* **1** flourishing, prosperous **2** magnificent, grand **3** popular, common

盛产 **shènchǎn** *v* produce an abundance of, abound in

盛大 **shèngdà** [comp: 盛 grand + 大 huge] *adj* grand, magnificent
　盛大的典礼 shèngdà de diǎnlǐ a grand and elaborate ceremony

盛开 **shèngkāi** *v* bloom luxuriantly

盛情 **shèngqíng** *n* great kindness, lavish hospitality

盛行 **shèngxíng** *v* be in vogue, be very popular

圣 **shèng** Trad 聖 *adj* sacred, holy

圣诞节 **shèngdànjié** [modif: 圣 holy + 诞 birth + 节 festival] *n* Christmas
　圣诞夜 shèngdànyè Christmas eve

失 **shī** **I** *v* **1** lose **2** err, make mistakes **II** *n* slip, mishap, mistake

失败 **shībài** [comp: 失 lose + 败 be defeated] **I** *v* be defeated, lose, fail (antonym 胜利 shènglì, 成功 chénggōng) □ 他们的计划失败了。 **Tāmen de jìhuà shībài le.** *Their plan failed.* **II** *n* defeat, loss, failure □ 失败是成功之母。 **Shībài shì chénggōng zhī mǔ.** *Failure is the mother of success.*

失眠 **shīmián** [v+obj: 失 lose + 眠 sleep] **I** *n* insomnia **II** *v* suffer from insomnia □ 她昨天夜里又失眠了。 **Tā zuótiān yèlǐ yòu shīmián le.** *She suffered from insomnia again last night.*

失去 **shīqù** [comp: 失 lose + 去 go away] *v* lose (something valuable) □ 她渐渐对孩子失去耐心。 **Tā jiànjiàn duì háizi shīqù nàixīn.** *She is running out of patience with the kids.*

失事 **shīshì** *v* have an accident □ 飞机失事了。 **Fēijī shīshì le.** *The airplane (The flight) had an accident.*

失望 **shīwàng** [v+obj: 失 lose + 望 hope] *adj* disappointed □ 你们没有完成上个月的生产计划，我非常失望。 **Nǐmen méiyǒu wánchéng shàng ge yuè de shēngchǎn jìhuà, wǒ fēicháng shīwàng.** *I am bitterly disappointed that you failed to complete last month's production plan.*
　对…失望 duì…shīwàng be disappointed with … □ 我知道，我哥哥和嫂子对他们的孩子很失望。 **Wǒ zhīdào, wǒ gēge hé sǎozi duì tāmende háizi hěn shīwàng.** *I know my brother and his wife are disappointed with their children.*

失误 **shīwù** [comp: 失 lose + 误 make a mistake] **I** *v* make a mistake, muff **II** *n* fault, error, miscalculation

失效 **shīxiào** [v+obj: 失 lose + 效 effect] *v* (of documents) become invalid, expire, (of medicines) cease to be effective □ 你的护照已经失效了。 **Nǐde hùzhào yǐjīng shīxiào le.** *Your passport has expired.*

失学 **shīxué** [v+obj: 失 lose + 学 schooling] *v* be unable to go to school, be deprived of education

失业 **shīyè** [v+obj: 失 lose + 业 occupation, employment] *v* lose one's job, become unemployed □ 经济情况不好，失业的人越来越多。 **Jīngjì qíngkuàng bù hǎo, shīyè de rén yuèláiyuè duō.** *As the economy is weak, more and more people lose their jobs.* □ 我万一失业了，就再进大学念书。 **Wǒ wànyī shīyè le, jiù zài jìn dàxué niànshū.** *If I lose my job, I will go back to university to study.*

失约 **shīyuē** [v+obj: 失 lose + 约 appointment] *v* fail to keep an appointment

失踪 **shīzōng** [v+obj: 失 lose + 踪 foot print] *v* be missing, disappear
　失踪人员 shīzōng rényuán missing person

师 **shī** Trad 師 *n* master, teacher
　师范 shīfàn teachers' education

师范学院 **shīfàn xuéyuàn** *n* teachers' college, college of education

师傅 **shīfu** [comp: 师 teacher + 傅 tutor] *n* master worker (位 wèi) □ 这位师傅技术很高。 **Zhè wèi shīfu jìshù hěn gāo.** *This master worker is highly skilled.* □ 这个机器坏了，要请一位师傅来看看。 **Zhège jīqì huàile, yào qǐng yí wèi shīfu lái kànkan.** *This machine is not working properly. We need to ask a master worker to come and have a look.*

NOTE: 师傅 **shīfu** is also a polite form of address for *a worker*. For example, an electrician or mechanic can be addressed as 师傅 **shīfu** or, if his family name is 李 **Lǐ**, 李师傅 **Lǐ shīfu**.

师长 **shīzhǎng** *n* **1** teacher **2** division commander (in the army)

诗 **shī** *n* poem, poetry (首 shǒu) □ 现在写诗、读诗的人越来越少了。 **Xiànzài xiě shī, dú shī de rén yuèláiyuè shǎo le.** *Nowadays fewer and fewer people write or read poems.*

诗歌 **shīgē** *n* poem, poetry (首 shǒu)

诗人 **shīrén** *n* poet (名 míng)

施 **shī** *v* carry out, execute
　施肥 shīféi apply fertilizer

施工 **shīgōng** [v+obj: 施 execute + 工 work] *v* (construction work) be underway, be in progress □ 新教学大楼什么时候开始施工？ **Xīn jiàoxué dàlóu shénme shíhou kāishǐ shīgōng?** *When will construction of the new classroom building be underway?* □ 前面施工，绕道通行。 **Qiánmiàn shīgōng, rào dào tōngxíng.** *Road works ahead. Detour.*

施加 **shījiā** *v* exert, bring to bear on
　对…施加压力 duì…shījiā yālì put pressure on …

施行 **shīxíng** *v* (of regulations, laws, etc.) put into force, implement, enforce

施展 **shīzhǎn** *v* put out to good use, give free play to

狮 **shī** Trad 獅 *n* lion
　狮子 shīzi lion (头 tóu) □ 动物园里有两头非洲来的狮子。 **Dòngwùyuán li yǒu liǎng tóu Fēizhōu lái de shīzi.** *In the zoo there are two lions from Africa.*

湿 **shī** Trad 濕 *adj* damp, wet (antonym 干 gān) □ 昨夜下过雨，早上路面还湿着。 **Zuóyè xiàguo yǔ, zǎoshang lùmiàn hái shīzhe.** *It rained last night, so the roads were wet this morning.*

湿度 **shīdù** [modif: 湿 wet + 度 degree] *n* humidity, moisture

湿润 **shīrùn** [comp: 湿 wet + 润 moist] *adj* moist

尸 **shī** Trad 屍 *n* dead body, corpse
　尸体 shītǐ dead body, corpse (具 jù)

十 **shí** *num* ten
　十五 shíwǔ fifteen
　五十 wǔshí fifty

十分 **shífēn** [modif: 十 ten + 分 point] *adv* one hundred percent, totally, fully □ 我十分满意。 **Wǒ shífēn mǎnyì.** *I'm totally satisfied.* □ 我十分理解你们的心

情。**Wǒ shífēn lǐjiě nǐmen de xīnqíng.** *I understand your feelings completely.*

十全十美 **shíquán shíměi** *idiom* perfect in every way

十足 **shízú** *adv* 100 percent, out-and-out

拾 1 **shí** *num* ten

拾 2 **shí** *v* pick up (from the ground)

石 **shí** *n* stone, rock

石灰 **shíhuī** *n* lime
石灰石 shíhuīshí limestone

石头 **shítou** [suffix: 石 stone, rock + 头 nominal suffix] *n* stone, rock (块 **kuài**) □ 这座山上石头太多, 不适合种树。**Zhè zuò shān shang shítou tài duō, bú shìhé zhòng shù.** *This hill is too rocky. It is not suitable for tree planting.* □ 摸着石头过河。**Mōzhe shítou guò hé.** *Cross a river by feeling for stones.* (→ *Make decisions as you go along, act without a premeditated plan.*)

石油 **shíyóu** [modif: 石 stone + 油 oil] *n* petroleum, oil □ 必须在石油用尽以前, 开发出新的能源。**Bìxū zài shíyóu yòngjìn yǐqián, kāifāchū xīn de néngyuán.** *New sources of energy must be developed before petroleum is exhausted.*

蚀 **shí** *v* lose
蚀本 **shíběn** [v+obj: 蚀 lose + 本 capital] *v* lose one's capital (in business ventures)

识 **shí** Trad 識 *v* know (See 认识 **rènshi**, 知识 **zhīshi**.)

识别 **shíbié** *v* distinguish, identify, recognize
识别敌友 shíbié dí yǒu tell enemies from friends

识字 **shízì** [v+obj: 识 recognize + 字 characters] *v* learn to to read, become literate

时 **shí** Trad 時 *n* Same as 点钟 **diǎnzhōng**. Used only in writing.

时常 **shícháng** *adv* often, frequently

时代 **shídài** [comp: 时 time + 代 generation] *n* a historical period, epoch, age □ 人类从石器时代到电脑时代, 花了几千年的时间。**Rénlèi cóng shíqì shídài dào diànnǎo shídài, huāle jǐ qiān nián de shíjiān.** *It took mankind thousands of years to move from the Stone Age to the Computer Age.*

时而 **shí'ér** *adv* occasionally, sometimes

时光 **shíguāng** *n* time

时候 **shíhou** [comp: 时 time + 候 a certain point in time] *n* a certain point in time, (the time) when □ 飞机什么时候开? **Fēijī shénme shíhou kāi?** *When will the plane depart?* □ 他来的时候, 我正在打电话。**Tā lái de shíhou, wǒ zhèngzài dǎ diànhuà.** *I was on the phone when he came.*

时机 **shíjī** *n* opportunity, opportune moment

时间 **shíjiān** [comp: 时 time + 间 moment] *n* a period of time □ 时间不够, 我没做完那道练习。**Shíjiān bú gòu, wǒ méi zuòwán nà dào liànxí.** *As there wasn't enough time, I did not finish that exercise.* □ 我没有时间写信。**Wǒ méiyǒu shíjiān xiě xìn.** *I don't have time to write letters.*

时节 **shíjié** *n* occasion, season
荷花盛开的时节 héhuā shèngkāi de shíjié the season when lotus flowers are in full bloom

时刻 **shíkè** [comp: 时 time + 刻 a point] *n* at a particular point in time □ 在关键时刻, 可以看出一个人的本性。**Zài guānjiàn shíkè, kěyǐ kànchū yí ge rén de běnxìng.** *At critical moments, a person shows his true colors.*

时刻表 **shíkèbiǎo** (railway, coach, etc.) timetable

时髦 **shímáo** *adj* fashionable, in vogue

时期 **shíqī** [comp: 时 time + 期 period] *n* period of time, stage □ 他在少年时期受到良好的教育。**Tā zài shàonián shíqī shòudao liánghǎo de jiàoyù.** *He received a very good education during his adolescence.*

时时 **shíshí** *adv* constantly, at all times

时事 **shíshì** *n* current affairs, current events

时装 **shízhuāng** [modif: 时 current + 装 garments] *n* the latest fashion
时装表演 shízhuāng biǎoyǎn fashion show
时装设计 shízhuāng shèjì fashion design

实 **shí** Trad 實 **I** *adj* real, true **II** *n* reality, fact

实话 **shíhuà** [modif: 实 true + 话 words] *n* true fact, truth
实话实说 shíhuà shíshuō tell the truth

实惠 **shíhuì I** *n* real benefit **II** *adj* substantial

实际 **shíjì I** *n* reality, actual situation □ 这项政策脱离实际。**Zhè xiàng zhèngcè tuōlí shíjì.** *This policy is out of touch with reality.* □ 我们的停车场停不了这么多的车, 这是一个实际问题。**Wǒmen de tíngchēchǎng tíng bu liǎo zhème duō de chē, zhè shì yíge shíjì wèntí.** *It is a real problem that our car park is too small to accommodate so many cars.* **II** *adj* practical, realistic □ 我们订计划要实际一点。**Wǒmen dìng jìhuà yào shíjì yìdiǎn.** *We should be practical when drawing up a plan.*

实践 **shíjiàn** [comp: 实 fruit, fruition + 践 implement] **I** *v* put into practice, apply □ 懂了这个道理, 就要实践。**Dǒngle zhège dàolǐ, jiù yào shíjiàn.** *After you've understood this principle, you should put it into practice.* **II** *n* practice □ 实践出真知。**Shíjiàn chū zhēnzhī.** *Practice leads to genuine knowledge.* □ 多年的实践证明这一理论是正确的。**Duō nián de shíjiàn zhèngmíng zhè yì lǐlùn shì zhèngquè de.** *Years of practical application have proved this theory correct.*

实况 **shíkuàng** [modif: 实 true + 况 situation] *n* what is really happening
实况转播 shíkuàng zhuǎnbō live broadcast

实力 **shílì** [modif: 实 true + 力 strength] *n* actual strength, strength
军事实力 jūnshì shílì military strength

实施 **shíshī** *v* put into effect, carry out

实事求是 **shíshìqiúshì** *idiom* find out truth from the facts, be realistic

实体 **shítǐ** *n* 1 entity 2 substance

实物 **shíwù** *n* real object
实物交易 shíwù jiāoyì barter

实习 **shíxí** *n* practice, fieldwork

实现 **shíxiàn** [comp: 实 fruit, fruition + 现 materialize] *v* materialize, realize □ 我一定要实现这个计划。**Wǒ yídìng yào shíxiàn zhège jìhuà.** *I must realize this plan.* □ 他终于实现了自己的理想。**Tā zhōngyú shíxiànle zìjǐ de lǐxiǎng.** *He finally realized his aspirations.*

实行 **shíxíng** *v* put into practice, take effect, implement, carry out, institute □ 有的大学实行一年三学期的制度。**Yǒude dàxué shíxíng yì nián sān xuéqī de zhìdù.** *Some universities implement the system of*

three terms a year. □ 他的新年决心实行了多久? **Tā de xīnnián juéxīn shíxíngle duōjiǔ?** *How long did he put his New Year's resolutions into practice?* □ 中国从上世纪八十年代开始实行 "改革开放" 政策。**Zhōngguó cóng shàng shìjì bāshí niándài kāishǐ shíxíng "gǎigé kāifàng" zhèngcè.** *In the 80s of the last century China began to implement the policies of "reform and opening-up."*

实验 **shíyàn** [modif: 实 practical + 验 testing] *n* experiment, test (项 **xiàng**, 次 **cì**) □ 学化学一定要做实验。**Xué huàxué yídìng yào zuò shíyàn.** *To study chemistry, one must do experiments.* □ 有人反对用动物做实验。**Yǒurén fǎnduì yòng dòngwù zuò shíyàn.** *Some people oppose experiments on animals.*

实验室 **shíyànshì** [modif: 实验 experiment + 室 room] *n* laboratory

实验员 **shíyànyuán** [suffix: 实验 experiment + 员 nominal suffix] *n* laboratory technician

实业 **shíyè** *n* industry and commerce, industry

实业家 **shíyèjiā** entrepreneur, industrialist

实用 **shíyòng** [modif: 实 practical + 用 use] *adj* practical (for use), useful, handy □ 这套工作服穿着不好看, 但是十分实用。**Zhè tào gōngzuòfú chuānzhe bù hǎokàn, dànshì shífèn shíyòng.** *This set of work clothes does not look beautiful, but it is very practical.* □ 这本词典非常实用。**Zhè běn cídiǎn fēicháng shíyòng.** *This dictionary is very useful.*

实在 **shízài** I *adj* honest, truthful □ 他说的话你听了可能不高兴, 但却很实在。**Tā shuō de huà nǐ tīngle kěnéng bù gāoxìng, dàn què hěn shízài.** *What he said may have made you unhappy, but it was truthful.* II *adv* indeed, really □ 我记不起你的名字了, 实在抱歉。**Wǒ jì bu qǐ nǐ de míngzi le, shízài hěn bàoqiàn.** *I'm really sorry I can't remember your name.*

实质 **shízhì** *n* substance, essence

实质上 **shízhìshang** in essence, practically, virtually

食 **shí** *n* food, meal □ 食, 色, 性也。(孔子) **Shí, sè, xìng yě. (Kǒngzǐ)** *The need for food and sex is human nature. (Confucius)*

食品 **shípǐn** [modif: 食 food + 品 article] *n* foodstuff (as commodities) (件 **jiàn**) □ 新西兰生产的食品质量很高。**Xīnxīlán shēngchǎn de shípǐn zhìliàng hěn gāo.** *The foodstuffs produced in New Zealand are of very high quality.*

食品工业 **shípǐn gōngyè** food industry
食品加工 **shípǐn jiāgōng** food processing
食品商店 **shípǐn shāngdiàn** provision shop, grocery

食堂 **shítáng** [modif: 食 food + 堂 hall] *n* dining hall □ 吃饭的时候, 食堂里人很多。**Chīfàn de shíhou, shítáng lǐ rén hěn duō.** *At mealtimes, there're many people in the dining hall.*

食物 **shíwù** [modif: 食 food + 物 things] *n* food □ 空气、水和食物都是绝对必要的。**Kōngqì, shuǐ hé shíwù dōu shì juéduì bìyào de.** *Air, water and food are absolutely indispensable.*

食用 **shíyòng** *adj* used as food, edible

食欲 **shíyù** [modif: 食 food + 欲 desire] *n* appetite
没有食欲 **méiyǒu shíyù** have no appetite

史 **shǐ** *n* history
史料 **shǐliào** *n* historical data, historical materials

屎 **shǐ** *n* excrement

使 **shǐ** *v* 1 make, enable □ 岁月使人老。**Suìyuè shǐ rén lǎo.** *Time makes one old.* □ 这次旅行使我学到很多知识。**Zhè cì lǚxíng shǐ wǒ xuédào hěn duō zhīshi.** *This trip enabled me to gain a great deal of knowledge.* 2 make use of, apply

使得 **shǐdé** *v* Same as 使 **shǐ** 1

使劲 **shǐjìn** [v+obj: 使 apply + 劲 strength] *v* exert all one's strength

使命 **shǐmìng** *n* mission
不辱使命 **bùrǔ shǐmìng** mission accomplished

使用 **shǐyòng** [comp: 使 use + 用 use] *v* use, apply □ 你会使用这台电脑吗? **Nǐ huì shǐyòng zhè tái diànnǎo ma?** *Do you know how to use this computer?* □ 这辆车是公司的, 只有办公事才能使用。**Zhè liàng chē shì gōngsī de, zhǐyǒu bàn gōngshì cái néng shǐyòng.** *This car belongs to the company; you can use it on company business only.*

驶 **shǐ** *v* sail, drive

始 **shǐ** *v* begin, start
始终 **shǐzhōng** [comp: 始 beginning + 终 end] *adv* from beginning to end, throughout, ever □ 他始终爱着初恋的情人。**Tā shǐzhōng àizhe chūliàn de qíngrén.** *He loved his first love all his life.* □ 我始终不明白她为什么这么恨那个地方。**Wǒ shǐzhōng bù míngbai tā wèishénme zhème hèn nàge dìfang.** *I have never ever understood why she should hate that place so much.*

示 **shì** *v* show, indicate
示范 **shìfàn** [v+obj: 示 show + 范 example] *v* set an example, demonstrate

教学示范 **jiàoxué shìfàn** teaching demonstration
示弱 **shìruò** [v+obj: 示 show + 弱 weakness] *v* show signs of weakness
示威 **shìwēi** [v+obj: 示 show + 威 power] *v* put on show of force, demonstrate

抗议示威 **kàngyì shìwēi** protest demonstration
示意图 **shìyìtú** *n* sketch map

士 **shì** *n* 1 scholar, gentleman (See 博士 **bóshì**, 护士 **hùshì**, 女士 **nǚshì**, 硕士 **shuòshì**, 学士 **xuéshì**, 战士 **zhànshi**.) 2 non-commisioned officer

士兵 **shìbīng** *n* rank-and-file soldier, private

誓 **shì** *v* vow, pledge
发誓 **fāshì** vow, swear, take an oath
誓言 **shìyán** [modif: 誓 vow + 言 words] *n* oath, pledge

氏 **shì** *n* family name

侍 **shì** *v* wait on, serve
侍女 **shìnǚ** maid
侍候 **shìhòu** *v* wait on, look after

释 **shì** Trad 釋 *v* 1 explain (See 解释 **jiěshì**) 2 let go, be relieved of
释放 **shìfàng** [comp: 释 let go + 放 release] *v* release, set free

世 **shì** *n* 1 the world 2 lifetime 3 generation, era
世代 **shìdài** [comp: 世 generation + 代 generation] *n* generations

世代经商 **shìdài jīngshāng** have been businessmen for generations
世纪 **shìjì** [modif: 世 generation + 纪 age] *n* century □ 公元两千年, 世界迎来了一个新世纪——二十一世纪。**Gōngyuán liǎngqiān nián, shìjiè yínglÁile yí ge xīn**

shìjì—èrshíyī shìjì. *In the year AD 2000, the world greeted a new century—the twenty-first century.*

世界 **shìjiè** [comp: 世 world + 界 boundary] *n* the world □ 世界每天都在变。**Shìjiè měitiān duō zài biàn.** *The world is changing every day.*

世界上 **shìjiè shang** in the world □ 世界上的事情都很复杂。**Shìjiè shang de shìqing dōu hěn fùzá.** *Everything in the world is complicated.*

世界博览会 **Shìjiè Bólǎnhuì** the World Exposition

世界贸易组织 **Shìjiè Màoyì Zǔzhī** the World Trade Organization (WTO)

世界卫生组织 **Shìjiè Wèishēng Zǔzhī** the World Health Organization (WHO)

世界观 **shìjièguān** *n* the way one looks at the world, world outlook, ideology

市 **shì** *n* **1** municipality, city □ 下午我要到市里去。**Xiàwǔ wǒ yào dào shìli qù.** *I'm going to the city this afternoon.* **2** market

市场 **shìchǎng** [modif: 市 market + 场 ground] *n* marketplace, market □ 她在市场上买了一只活鸡，两条活鱼。**Tā zài shìchǎng shang mǎile yì zhī huó jī, liǎng tiáo huó yú.** *She bought a live chicken and two live fish from the market.* □ 市场上需要什么，他们就生产什么。**Shìchǎng shang xūyào shénme, tāmen jiù shēngchǎn shénme.** *They produce whatever the market needs.*

市场经济 **shìchǎng jīngjì** market economy

菜市场 **cài shìchǎng** vegetable market, food market

市价 **shìjià** *n* market price

市民 **shìmín** *n* resident of a city, townsfolk

市长 **shìzhǎng** [modif: 市 city + 长 chief] *n* mayor

式 **shì** *n* form, pattern

式样 **shìyàng** *n* style, type

事 **shì** *n* **1** affair, matter (件 **jiàn**) □ 这件事很重要，一定要办好。**Zhè jiàn shì hěn zhòngyào, yídìng yào bànhǎo.** *This is an important matter and must be done well.* □ 大家都很关心这件事。**Dàjiā dōu hěn guānxīn zhè jiàn shì.** *Everybody is concerned over this matter.* **2** job, work

找个事做 **zhǎo ge shì zuò** try to find something to do, try to find a job

3 accident, something bad

事变 **shìbiàn** *n* military or political incident of historical significance

事故 **shìgù** *n* accident, mishap (件 **jiàn**) □ 昨天工厂发生了一件严重事故。**Zuótiān gōngchǎng fāshēngle yí jiàn yánzhòng shìgù.** *A serious accident took place in the factory yesterday.* □ 有关部门正在调查事故的原因。**Yǒuguān bùmén zhèngzài diàochá shìgù de yuányīn.** *The departments concerned are investigating the cause of the accident.*

事故现场 **shìgù xiànchǎng** scene of an accident

工伤事故 **gōngshāng shìgù** industrial accident

交通事故 **jiāotōng shìgù** traffic accident, road accident

事迹 **shìjì** *n* deed, achievement

英雄事迹 **yīngxióng shìjì** heroic deeds

事件 **shìjiàn** *n* (historic) event, incident □ 九一一是个可怕的事件。**Jiǔ-yāo-yāo shì ge kěpà de shìjiàn.** *9/11 was a terrible event.*

NOTE: 一 is pronounced as **yāo** here. See note on 一 **yī** for more information.

事例 **shìlì** *n* example, case

事情 **shìqing** *n* Same as 事 **shì**

NOTES: (1) In many cases, 事 **shì** may be replaced by 事情 **shìqing**, e.g. □ 这件事情很重要，一定要办好。**Zhè jiàn shìqing hěn zhòngyào, yídìng yào bànhǎo.** *This is an important matter and must be done well.* □ 大家都很关心这件事情。**Dàjiā dōu hěn guānxīn zhè jiàn shìqing.** *Everybody is concerned over this matter.*

找个事情做 **zhǎo ge shìqing zuò** try to find something to do, try to find a job.

(2) 事 **shì** or 事情 **shìqing** is a noun that can be applied widely, denoting *any affair, matter or business to be done or considered.* Here are more examples □ 我今天晚上没有事情做。**Wǒ jīntiān wǎnshang méiyǒu shìqing zuò.** *I've nothing to do this evening.* □ 我跟你说一件事。**Wǒ gēn nǐ shuō yí jiàn shì.** *I want to tell you something.* □ 他们在路上出事了。**Tāmen zài lùshang chūshì le.** *They had an accident on the way.*

事实 **shìshí** [comp: 事 thing + 实 truth] *n* fact (件 **jiàn**) □ 我的报告是根据事实写的。**Wǒ de bàogào shì gēnjù shìshí xiě de.** *My report is based on facts.* □ 你应该先调查事实，再作结论。**Nǐ yīnggāi xiān diàochá shìshí, zài zuò jiélùn.** *You should check the facts before drawing a conclusion.*

事实上 **shìshí shang** in fact, as a matter of fact

事态 **shìtài** *n* state of affairs, situation

事先 **shìxiān** *adv* beforehand, in advance □ 他上星期去中国工作了，事先没有告诉任何人。**Tā shàng xīngqī qù Zhōngguó gōngzuò le, shìxiān méiyǒu gàosu rènhé rén.** *He went to work in China last week. He had not told anybody beforehand.*

事务 **shìwù** *n* matters to attend to, work

事务工作 **shìwù gōngzuò** routine work

事项 **shìxiàng** *n* item, matter

注意事项 **zhùyì shìxiàng** points for attention

事业 **shìyè** [comp: 事 work + 业 cause] *n* **1** career □ 要事业，还是要家庭？她决定不了。**Yào shìyè, háishì yào jiātíng? Tā juédìng bù liǎo.** *She can't make up her mind whether to pursue a career or have a family.* **2** cause, undertaking □ 他为世界和平事业作出了巨大贡献。**Tā wèi shìjiè hépíng shìyè zuòchūle jùdà gòngxiàn.** *He made tremendous contributions to the cause of world peace.*

视 **shì** Trad 視 *v* watch

视察 **shìchá** [comp: 视 view + 察 check] *v* (of a high-ranking official) inspect, observe

视觉 **shìjué** [modif: 视 vision + 觉 sense] *n* the sense of sight

视力 **shìlì** [modif: 视 vision + 力 power] *n* eyesight, sight

视力测验 **shìlì cèyàn** eyesight test

视频光盘 **shìpín guāngpán** video compact disc, VCD

视线 **shìxiàn** [modif: 视 vision + 线 line] *n* line of sight

挡住了视线 **dǎngzhù le shìxiàn** block one's view

视野 **shìyě** *n* field of vision

是 **shì** *v* **1** be, yes □ "你们的中文老师是不是北京人？" "是的。" **"Nǐmen de Zhōngwén lǎoshī shì bu shì Běijīngrén?" "Shìde."** *"Is your Chinese teacher from Beijing?" "Yes."* □ "这本书是你的吗？" "不是，

不是我的。" **"Zhè běn shū shì nǐ de ma?" "Bú shì, bú shì wǒ de."** *Is this book yours?" "No."* **2** (indicating existence of), (there) be □ 小学旁边是一座公园。**Xiǎoxué pángbian shì yí zuò gōngyuán.** *There is a park by the primary school.* □ 张教授的办公室里到处是书。**Zhāng jiàoshòu de bàngōngshì li dàochù shì shū.** *There are books everywhere in Professor Zhang's office.* □ 电脑旁边是一台电话。**Diànnǎo pángbian shì yì tái diànhuà.** *Beside the computer is a telephone.* **3** (used to emphasize the words following it) □ 那家饭店的菜是不错。**Nà jiā fàndiàn de cài shì búcuò.** *That restaurant's food is indeed quite good.* □ 他这么做是出于好心。**Tā zhème zuò shì chūyú hǎoxīn.** *He did it out of kindness.* □ 那个电话是谁打来的? **Nàge diànhuà shì shéi dǎ lai de?** *Who rang?*

是非 **shìfēi** [comp: 是 yes + 非 no] *n* **1** right and wrong, truth and falsehood
明辨是非 **míngbiàn shìfēi** distinguish clearly between right and wrong
2 trouble, quarrel
搬弄是非 **bānnòng shìfēi** sow discord, tell tales

饰 **shì** Trad 飾 *v* decorate (See 装饰 **zhuāngshì**.)

室 **shì** *n* room (See 办公室 **bàngōngshì**, 教室 **jiàoshì**, 浴室 **yùshì**.)

柿 **shì** *n* persimmon (See 西红柿 **xīhóngshì**.)

适 **shì** Trad 適 *v* suit, fit
适当 **shìdàng** [comp: 适 suitable + 当 ought to] *adj* appropriate, suitable □ 我会在适当的时候批评他。**Wǒ huì zài shìdàng de shíhou pīpíng tā.** *I will criticize him at an appropriate moment.* □ 在中国送钟给老年人当礼物，是不适当的，因为 "送钟" 和 "送终" 同音。**Zài Zhōngguó sòng zhōng gěi lǎoniánrén dāng lǐwù, shì bú shìdàng de, yīnwèi "sòngzhōng" hé "sòngzhōng" tóngyīn.** *In China it is not appropriate to give an old person a clock as a gift because "give a clock" (sòng zhōng) is pronounced the same as "pay last tribute" (sòng zhōng).*
适合 **shìhé** [comp: 适 suit + 合 be harmonious] *v* suit, fit □ 他善于交际，适合做生意。**Tā shànyú jiāojì, shìhé zuò shēngyi.** *He is good at social dealings, and is suited to be a businessman.*
适宜 **shìyí** *adj* suitable, appropriate
适应 **shìyìng** *v* adapt to □ 你已经适应新环境了吗? **Nǐ yǐjīng shìyìng xīn huánjìng le ma?** *Have you been able to adapt to your new situation?* □ 她以前是教书的，现在当翻译，一时还不适应。**Tā yǐqián shì jiāoshū de, xiànzài dāng fānyì, yìshí hái bú shìyìng.** *She used to teach. Now she works as an interpreter and has not quite adapted to it.*
适用 **shìyòng** [v+obj: 适 suit + 用 use, application] *adj* applicable, suitable □ 你的方法很先进，但是在这里不适用。**Nǐ de fāngfǎ hěn xiānjìn, dànshì zài zhèlǐ bú shìyòng.** *Your method is very advanced, but it cannot be applied here.*

逝 **shì** *v* pass, leave
逝世 **shìshì** [v+obj: 逝 leave + 世 the world] pass away, die

NOTE: See note on 去世 **qùshì**.

试 **shì** Trad 試 *v* test, try □ 你的办法不行，试试我的办法。**Nǐ de bànfǎ bù xíng, shìshì wǒ de bànfǎ.** *Your method didn't work. Try my method.* □ 这种新药，病人试过没有? **Zhè zhǒng xīnyào, bìngrén shìguo méiyǒu?** *Has the patient tried this new drug?*
试试/试一下 **shìshì/shì yíxià** have a try
试卷 **shìjuàn** *n* examination paper, test paper (份 **fèn**)
试行 **shìxíng** *v* try out
试验 **shìyàn** [comp: 试 test + 验 test] *v* test, experiment (项 **xiàng**, 次 **cì**) □ 研究人员正在动物身上试验这种新药。**Yánjiū rényuán zhèngzài dòngwù shēnshang shìyàn zhè zhǒng xīn yào.** *Researchers are testing this new medicine on animals.*
试用 **shìyòng** [comp: 试 try + 用 use] *v* try out, be on probation
试用人员 **shìyòng rényuán** staff on probation
试用期 **shìyòngqī** probation period

势 **shì** Trad 勢 *n* **1** power, force **2** situation, circumstances
势必 **shìbì** *adv* be bound to, be sure to
势力 **shìlì** *n* (social) force

匙 **shì** *n* spoon (See 钥匙 **yàoshi**.)

收 **shōu** *v* **1** receive, accept
收到 **shōudao** receive □ 我昨天收到一封信。**Wǒ zuótiān shōudao yì fēng xìn.** *I received a letter yesterday.*
收下 **shōuxia** accept □ 请你收下这件小礼物。**Qǐng nǐ shōuxia zhè jiàn xiǎo lǐwù.** *Please accept this small gift.*
2 collect (fee), charge □ 这种服务是要收费的。**Zhè zhǒng fúwù shì yào shōufèi de.** *This service will incur a fee.*
收藏 **shōucáng** *v* collect (antiques, collectibles, etc.)
收藏中国明代花瓶 **shōucáng Zhōngguó Míngdài huāpíng** collect Chinese Ming vases
收成 **shōucheng** *n* harvest (of crops)
收复 **shōufù** *v* recover (lost territory)
收购 **shōugòu** [comp: 收 collect + 购 purchase] *v* purchase, buy
收购价格 **shōugòu jiàgé** purchasing price
收回 **shōuhuí** *v* take back, recall
收回贷款 **shōuhuí dàikuǎn** recall a loan, call in a loan
收获 **shōuhuò** [comp: 收 collect + 获 gain] **I** *v* gather in crops, harvest □ 今年这位农民收获了五千公斤小麦。**Jīnnián zhè wèi nóngmín shōuhuòle wǔqiān gōngjīn xiǎomài.** *This year the farmer harvested five thousand kilograms of wheat.* **II** *n* gain (of work), achievement, reward □ 这次试验取得了大量数据，收获很大。**Zhè cì shìyàn qǔdéle dàliàng shùjù, shōuhuò hěn dà.** *A large amount of data has been obtained from the test, which is a big achievement.*
收集 **shōují** [comp: 收 collect + 集 gather] *v* collect, gather □ 他想把世界各国的邮票都收集到。**Tā xiǎng bǎ shìjiè ge guó de yóupiào dōu shōují dào.** *He wants to collect stamps from all the countries in the world.*
收买 **shōumǎi** *v* buy over, buy in
收入 **shōurù** [comp: 收 collect + 入 entry] **I** *v* earn, receive □ 我不想告诉他我去年收入多少钱。**Wǒ bù xiǎng gàosu tā wǒ qùnián shōurù duōshǎo qián.** *I*

didn't want to tell him how much I earned last year. **II** *n* income □ 去年这个国家的人平均收入是增加了，还是减少了？**Qùnián zhège guójiā de rén píngjūn shōurù shì zēngjiā le, háishì jiǎnshǎo le?** *Did this country's per capita income increase or decrease last year?*

收拾 **shōushi** [comp: 收 gather in + 拾 pick up] *v* put in order, tidy up □ 桌子上的书和报纸太多，我要收拾一下。**Zhuōzi shang de shū hé bàozhǐ tài duō, wǒ yào shōushi yíxià.** *There are too many newspapers and books on the table. I'll tidy it up.* □ 她做完饭，总要收拾一下厨房。**Tā zuòwán fàn, zǒngyào shōushi yíxià chúfáng.** *She will always tidy up the kitchen after cooking.*

收缩 **shōusuō** *v* contract, shrink

收益 **shōuyì** *n* profit, earnings

收音机 **shōuyīnjī** [modif: 收音 receive sound + 机 machine] *n* radio (台 **tái**, 架 **jià**) □ 这台收音机还是我爷爷买的。**Zhè tái shōuyīnjī háishì wǒ yéye mǎide.** *This radio was bought by my grandpa.*

手 **shǒu** *n* hand (只 **zhī**, 双 **shuāng**) □ 我的手不干净，要洗一下才能吃饭。**Wǒ de shǒu bù gānjing, yào xǐ yíxià cái néng chīfàn.** *My hands are not clean. I have to wash them before I eat.*

手上 **shǒu shang** in the hand □ 他手上拿着一本书。**Tā shǒu shang názhe yì běn shū.** *He's holding a book in his hand.*

右手 **yòushǒu** the right hand

左手 **zuǒshǒu** the left hand

手表 **shǒubiǎo** [modif: 手 hand + 表 watch] *n* wristwatch (块 **kuài**) □ 我的手表慢了，你的手表几点？**Wǒ de shǒubiǎo màn le, nǐ de shǒubiǎo jǐ diǎn?** *My watch is slow. What time is it by your watch?*

NOTE: In everyday usage, 手表 **shǒubiǎo** is often shortened to 表 **biǎo**: □ 我的表慢了，你的表几点？**Wǒ de biǎo màn le, nǐ de biǎo jǐ diǎn?** *My watch is slow. What time is it by your watch?*

手电筒 **shǒudiàntǒng** *n* flashlight, torch (只 **zhī**)

手段 **shǒuduàn** *n* means, measure □ 我不赞成使用不合理的手段来达到目的。**Wǒ bú zànchéng shǐyòng bù hélǐ de shǒuduàn lái dádào mùdì.** *I don't endorse the use of unjustifiable means to achieve one's ends.*

手法 **shǒufǎ** *n* trick, gimmick

手工 **shǒugōng** [modif: 手 hand + 工 work] *adj* done by hand, made by hand, manual □ 这件丝绸衬衫是手工做的，所以比较贵。**Zhè jiàn sīchóu chènshān shì shǒugōng zuòde, suǒyǐ bǐjiào guì.** *This silk shirt was handmade, so it is rather expensive.*

手工业 **shǒugōngyè** handicraft industry

手工艺品 **shǒugōngyìpǐn** handicraft item

手机 **shǒujī** [modif: 手 hand + 机 machine] *n* cell phone, mobile telephone (只 **zhī**) □ 上飞机以前，要关上手机。**Shàng fēijī yǐqián, yào guānshang shǒujī.** *Switch off your cell phone before boarding a plane.* □ 他又换了一只手机。**Tā yòu huànle yì zhī shǒujī.** *He changed his cell phone again.*

手巾 **shǒujin** *n* face towel, towel (条 **tiáo**)

手绢 **shǒujuàn** *n* handkerchief (块 **kuài**) □ 手绢要每天换。**Shǒujuàn yào měi tiān huàn.** *Handkerchiefs should be changed daily.* (→ *You have to use a clean handkerchief every day.*)

手枪 **shǒuqiāng** [modif: 手 hand + 枪 gun] *n* pistol (把 **bǎ**)

手势 **shǒushì** *n* gesture, signal, sign

打手势 **dǎ shǒushì** make a gesture

手术 **shǒushù** *n* operation □ 外科主任亲自做这个手术。**Wàikē zhǔrèn qīnzì zuò zhè ge shǒushù.** *The chief surgeon will perform the operation himself.*

手术间 **shǒushùjiān** operating room, surgery room

做手术 **zuò shǒushù** perform an operation, operate

手套 **shǒutào** [modif: 手 hand + 套 covering] *n* glove (只 **zhī**, 副 **fù**) □ 今天真冷，我戴了手套、帽子，还觉得冷！**Jīntiān zhēn lěng, wǒ dàile shǒutào, màozi, hái juéde lěng!** *It's really cold today. I'm wearing gloves and a hat, but still feel cold!*

手续 **shǒuxù** *n* formalities, procedures □ 买卖房子，要办法律手续。**Mǎimài fángzi, yào bàn fǎlǜ shǒuxù.** *You will have to complete the legal formalities when you buy or sell a house.*

办手续 **bàn shǒuxù** go through the formalities

手艺 **shǒuyì** [modif: 手 hand + 艺 art] *n* craftsmanship, workmanship

手指 **shǒuzhǐ** *n* finger, thumb □ 她的手指又细又长。**Tā de shǒuzhǐ yòu xì, yòu cháng.** *Her fingers are slender and long.*

NOTE: In Chinese the thumb 拇指 **mǔzhǐ**, or 大拇指 **dàmǔzhǐ** is considered just one of the fingers. So it is correct to say: 我有十个手指。**Wǒ yǒu shí ge shǒuzhǐ.** *I have ten fingers.*

手镯 **shǒuzhuó** *n* bracelet

守 **shǒu** *v* **1** observe, abide by **2** guard, defend

守财奴 **shǒucáinú** [modif: 守财 guard wealth + 奴 slave] *n* miser

守法 **shǒufǎ** [v+obj: 守 observe + 法 law] *v* observe the law

守卫 **shǒuwèi** [comp: 守 guard + 卫 defend] *v* guard, defend

首 1 **shǒu I** *n* the head **II** *adj* first

首创 **shǒuchuàng** [modif: 首 first + 创 create] *v* initiate, pioneer

首创精神 **shǒuchuàng jīngshén** pioneering spirit

首都 **shǒudū** [modif: 首 the head, first + 都 metropolis] *n* capital city □ 中国的首都是北京。**Zhōngguó de shǒudū shì Běijīng.** *China's capital city is Beijing.*

首领 **shǒulǐng** [comp: 首 the head + 领 the neck] *n* leader, chieftain, chief

首脑 **shǒunǎo** [comp: 首 the head + 脑 brain] *n* head

首脑会议 **shǒunǎo huìyì** summit meeting, summit

首席 **shǒuxí** [modif: 首 first + 席 chair] *adj* chief, principal

首席小提琴手 **shǒuxí xiǎotíqínshǒu** the first violinist (of an orchestra)

首席执行官 **shǒuxí zhíxíngguān** chief executive officer (CEO)

首先 **shǒuxiān** [comp: 首 first + 先 before] *adv* first, first of all □ 首先，请允许我自我介绍一下。**Shǒuxiān, qǐng yǔnxǔ wǒ zìwǒ jièshào yíxià.** *First of all, allow me to introduce myself.*

首相 **shǒuxiàng** [modif: 首 first + 相 minister] *n* prime minister

英国首相 Yīngguó shǒuxiàng the British Prime Minister

首要 **shǒuyào** [comp: 首 first + 要 important] *adj* of primary importance

首长 **shǒuzhǎng** [comp: 首 head + 长 head] *n* senior official, ranking officer

首 2 **shǒu** *measure wd* (for songs and poems)
一首歌 yì shǒu gē a song

寿 **shòu** Trad 壽 *n* life, lifespan
长寿 chángshòu longevity □ 祝您老人家健康长寿! **Zhù nín lǎorénjia jiànkāng chángshòu!** (to an elderly person) *Wish you good health and longevity!*

寿命 **shòumìng** [comp: 寿 life 命 life] *n* lifespan

寿星 **shòuxing** birthday boy, birthday girl

受 **shòu** *v* 1 receive, accept □ 每个人都有受教育的权利。**Měi ge rén dōu yǒu shòu jiàoyù de quánlì.** *Everyone has the right to receive an education.* □ 他因为上班迟到而受批评了。**Tā yīnwèi chídào ér shòu pīpíng le.** *He was criticized for being late for work.* 2 suffer, be subject to
受苦 shòukǔ suffer from hardship

受罚 **shòufá** [v+obj: 受 suffer + 罚 penalty] *v* be punished, be penalized □ 拖延付款要受罚。**Tuōyán fùkuǎn yào shòufá.** *Late payment will be penalized.*

受理 **shòulǐ** *v* (of law courts or lawyers) accept and handle a case

受聘 **shòupìn** [v+obj: 受 receive + 聘 invitation for employment] *v* be appointed for a position
受聘担任首席法律顾问 shòupìn dānrèn shǒuxí fǎlù gùwèn be appointed as chief legal advisor

受伤 **shòushāng** [v+obj: 受 suffer + 伤 wound] *v* be wounded, be injured

授 **shòu** *v* give, award
授予 **shòuyǔ** *v* confer, award
授予学位 shòuyǔ xuéwèi confer an academic degree

瘦 **shòu** *adj* thin, lean □ 她比以前瘦多了。**Tā bǐ yǐqián shòu duō le.** *She is much thinner than before.* □ 别以为越瘦越好看。**Bié yǐwéi yuè shòu yuè hǎokàn.** *Do not think that the thinner you are, the more beautiful you become.*

瘦肉 **shòuròu** [modif: 瘦 lean + 肉 meat] *n* lean meat □ 她只吃瘦肉，不吃肥肉。**Tā zhǐ chī shòuròu, bù chī féiròu.** *She eats only lean meat, and does not eat fatty meat.*

瘦子 **shòuzi** [suffix: 瘦 thin + 子 nominal suffix] *n* lean or thin person (antonym 胖子 **pàngzi**)

售 **shòu** *v* sell
售货员 **shòuhuòyuán** [suffix: 售 sell + 货 goods + 员 nominal suffix] *n* shop assistant, sales clerk □ 售货员帮我挑选皮鞋。**Shòuhuòyuán bāng wǒ tiāoxuǎn píxié.** *The shop assistant helped me choose a pair of shoes.*

兽 **shòu** Trad 獸 *n* beast, animal
人面兽心 rénmiàn shòuxīn a human face with a beast's heart—a beast in human shape

兽医 **shòuyī** [modif: 兽 animal + 医 medicine] *n* 1 veterinary science 2 veterinary surgeon, veterinarian

殊 **shū** *adj* different (See 特殊 **tèshū**)

书 **shū** Trad 書 I *n* 1 book (本 **běn**) □ 这本书很有意思，你看过没有？**Zhè běn shū hěn yǒu yìsi, nǐ kànguo méiyǒu?** *This book is very interesting. Have you*

read it? □ 她常常去图书馆借书。**Tā chángcháng qù túshūguǎn jiè shū.** *She often goes to the library to borrow books.* 2 style of calligraphy 3 letter II *v* write
看书 kàn shū read, do reading □ 我喜欢看书。**Wǒ xǐhuan kàn shū.** *I like reading.*

书包 **shūbāo** [modif: 书 book + 包 bag] *n* schoolbag (只 **zhī**) □ 小学生的书包为什么这么重？**Xiǎoxuéshēng de shūbāo wèishénme zhème zhòng?** *Why are children's schoolbags so heavy?*

书本 **shūběn** *n* book

书呆子 **shūdāizi** [modif: 书 book + 呆子 fool] *n* bookworm, nerd

书店 **shūdiàn** [modif: 书 book + 店 store, shop] *n* bookstore, bookshop (家 **jiā**) □ 你们这里哪家书店最好？**Nǐmen zhèli nǎ jiā shūdiàn zuì hǎo?** *Which is the best bookshop here?*

书法 **shūfǎ** *n* calligraphy
书法家 shūfǎjiā calligrapher

书籍 **shūjí** *n* books (collectively)

书记 **shūjì** *n* secretary of the Chinese Communist Party organizations

书架 **shūjià** [modif: 书 book + 架 shelf] *n* bookshelf □ 王老师的办公室有一个大书架。**Wáng lǎoshī de bàngōngshì yǒu yí ge dà shūjià.** *There is a big bookshelf in Teacher Wang's office.*

书刊 **shūkān** *n* books and periodicals

书面 **shūmiàn** *adj* in written form, written (antonym 口头 **kǒutóu**)
书面邀请 shūmiàn yāoqǐng written invitation

书目 **shūmù** *n* booklist, (book) catalogue
参考书目 cānkǎo shūmù list of reference books, bibliography

书评 **shūpíng** [modif: 书 book + 评 comment] *n* book review

书市 **shūshì** [modif: 书 book + 市 market] *n* book fair, book market

书写 **shūxiě** *v* write

书信 **shūxìn** [comp: 书 letter + 信 letter] *n* letter

书展 **shūzhǎn** [modif: 书 book + 展 display] *n* book fair

NOTE: 书展 **shūzhǎn** is the shortening of 图书展销 **túshū zhǎnxiāo**.

叔 **shū** *n* father's younger brother
叔叔 **shūshu** *n* father's younger brother, uncle □ 我叔叔是设计电脑软件的。**Wǒ shūshu shì shèjì diànnǎo ruǎnjiàn de.** *My father's younger brother designs computer software.*

NOTE: 叔叔 **shūshu** is a form of address used by a child for a man around his/her father's age. It is common to put a family name before 叔叔 **shūshu** e.g. 张叔叔 **Zhāng shūshu**. Also see note on 阿姨 **āyí**.

梳 **shū** *n* comb
梳子 shūzi comb (把 **bǎ**)

舒 **shū** I *adj* relaxing, leisurely II *v* stretch, unfold
舒畅 **shúchàng** [comp: 舒 relaxing + 畅 uninhibited] *adj* free from worry
心情舒畅 xīnqíng shūchàng feel carefree

舒服 **shūfu** [comp: 舒 relaxing + 服 conceding] *adj*

comfortable □ 这把椅子很舒服, 你坐下去就不想起来了。 **Zhè bǎ yǐzi hěn shūfu, nǐ zuò xiàqu jiù bù xiǎng qǐlái le.** *This chair is very comfortable. Sit on it and you don't want to get up.* □ 他们不是非常有钱, 但是生活过得挺舒服。 **Tāmen bú shì fēicháng yǒu qián, dànshì shēnghuó guò de tǐng shūfu.** *They are not wealthy, but they live comfortably.*

不舒服 bù shūfu (of a person) not very well, be under the weather □ 我今天不舒服, 想早点回家。 **Wǒ jīntiān bù shūfu, xiǎng zǎo diǎn huíjiā.** *I'm unwell today. I want to go home early.*

舒适 shūshì *adj* comfortable, cosy

疏 shū **I** *adj* **1** sparse, scattered **2** (of relationships) not intimate, distant **II** *v* neglect, overlook

疏忽 shūhu [comp: 疏 neglect + 忽 overlook] **I** *v* neglect, overlook **II** *n* oversight, omission

疏漏 shūlòu [comp: 疏 overlook + 漏 miss] *n* careless omission, slip

疏远 shūyuǎn [comp: 疏 distant + 远 distant] *adj* (of relationships) not close, estranged

蔬 shū *n* vegetable

蔬菜 shūcài vegetable, greens □ 多吃蔬菜, 少吃肉, 对健康有利。 **Duō chī shūcài, shǎo chī ròu, duì jiànkāng yǒulì.** *Eating lots of vegetables and little meat is good for your health.*

输 1 shū Trad 輸 *v* lose (a game, a bet) (antonym 赢 yíng) □ 上回我们队输了, 这回一定要赢! **Shàng huí wǒmen duì shū le, zhè huí yídìng yào yíng!** *Our team lost the game the last time; this time we must win!* □ 客队输了两个球。 **Kèduì shūle liǎng ge qiú.** *The visiting team lost two points.*

输 2 shū Trad 輸 *v* transport

输出 shūchū *v* export

输送 shūsòng *v* transport, convey

输血 shūxuè *n* blood transfusion

熟 shú *adj* **1** ripe, cooked □ 苹果还没有熟, 很酸。 **Píngguǒ hái méiyǒu shú, hěn suān.** *The apples are not yet ripe. They're sour.* □ 肉熟了就可以吃饭。 **Ròu shúle jiù kěyǐ chīfàn.** *We can have our meal when the meat is done.* **2** familiar with, well acquainted □ 这个城市我不熟。 **Zhège chéngshì wǒ bù shú.** *I don't know this city very well.*

熟练 shúliàn [comp: 熟 familiar with + 练 practiced] *adj* skilful, skilled □ 我们工厂缺乏熟练工人。 **Wǒmen gōngchǎng quēfá shúliàn gōngrén.** *Our factory is short of skilled workers.*

熟悉 shúxī [comp: 熟 familiar with + 悉 knowing] *adj* familiar with, well acquainted with □ 他和熟悉的人在一起的时候话很多。 **Tā hé shúxī de rén zài yìqǐ de shíhou huà hěn duō.** *He is talkative in the company of the people he knows well.* □ 我对这个地方不熟悉。 **Wǒ duì zhège dìfang bù shúxī.** *I am not familiar with this place.*

数 shǔ Trad 數 *v* count □ 我来数一下, 这里有多少人, 一、二、三、… **Wǒ lái shǔ yíxià, zhèlǐ yǒu duōshǎo rén, yī, èr, sān…** *Let me count to see how many people are here. One, two, three …*

暑 shǔ *n* heat, hot season

暑假 shǔjià [modif: 暑 summer + 假 holiday, vacation] *n* summer holiday, summer vacation □ 你暑假有什么打算? **Nǐ shǔjià yǒu shénme dǎsuàn?** *What is your plan for the summer holiday?*

薯 shǔ *n* potato, yam

署 shǔ *n* government office

属 shǔ Trad 屬 *v* **1** belong to **2** be born in the year of …

属相 shǔxiang *n* (lunar calendar) the traditional twelve animals that mark the cycle of years □ "你知道中国的十二属相吗?" "知道, 是鼠、牛、虎、兔、龙、蛇、马、羊、猴、鸡、狗和猪。" **"Nǐ zhīdào Zhōngguó de shí'èr shǔxiang ma?" "Zhīdào, shì shǔ, niú, hǔ, tù, lóng, shé, mǎ, yáng, hóu, jī, gǒu he zhū."** *"Do you know the twelve animals of the Chinese Zodiac?" "Yes. They are rat, ox, tiger, rabbit (or hare), dragon, snake, horse, sheep (or goat), monkey, rooster (or phoenix), dog and pig (or boar)."*

属于 shǔyú *v* belong to □ 这些书不是我个人的, 而是属于学校图书馆。 **Zhèxiē shū bú shì wǒ gèrén de, érshì shǔyú xuéxiào túshūguǎn.** *These books are not mine, they belong to the school library.* □ 这块森林属于一家跨国公司。 **Zhè kuài sēnlín shǔyú yì jiā kuàguó gōngsī.** *This forest belongs to a multinational company.*

鼠 shǔ *n* rat, mouse

老鼠 lǎoshǔ rat, mouse (只 zhī)

术 shù Trad 術 *n* craft, skill

术语 shùyǔ *n* technical term, terminology

束 shù *n* knot

束缚 shùfù [comp: 束 knot + 缚 bind] *v* bind up, fetter

述 shù *v* narrate

述评 shùpíng [comp: 述 narrate + 评 comment] *n* commentary, review

树 shù Trad 樹 **I** *n* tree (棵 kē) □ 这棵树又高又大, 树下很凉快。 **Zhè kē shù yòu gāo yòu dà, shù xia hěn liángkuai.** *This tree is big and tall; it's cool under it.* □ 我爸爸在花园里种了两棵树。 **Wǒ bàba zài huāyuán li zhòngle liǎng kē shù.** *My father planted two trees in the garden.* **II** *v* set up

树干 shùgàn *n* tree trunk

树立 shùlì *v* set up, establish

树林 shùlín [comp: 树 tree + 林 wood] *n* woods □ 在树林里有很多种鸟。 **Zài shùlín li yǒu hěn duō zhǒng niǎo.** *There are many kinds of birds in the woods.*

树木 shùmù *n* trees (collectively)

树皮 shùpí [modif: 树 tree + 皮 skin] *n* bark

数 shù Trad 數 **I** *n* number, figure □ 说这种语言的人数在不断减少。 **Shuō zhè zhǒng yǔyán de rénshù zài búduàn jiǎnshǎo.** *The number of speakers of this language is on the decline.* **II** *adj* a few, several

数额 shù'é *n* amount, quota

数据 shùjù [comp: 数 number + 据 evidence] *n* data □ "你能肯定这些数据是准确的吗?" "能肯定。" **"Nǐ néng kěndìng zhèxiē shùjù shì zhǔnquè de ma?" "Néng kěndìng."** *"Are you sure these data are accurate?" "Positive."*

数据库 shùjùkù data base

数目 shùmù *n* number, figure

确切的数目 quèqiè de shùmù precise number

数量 shùliàng [comp: 数 number + 量 quantity] *n* quantity, amount □ 电视节目的数量在增加, 但质量怎么样呢? **Diànshì jiémù de shùliàng zài zēngjiā, dàn**

zhìliàng zěnmeyàng ne? *The quantity of TV programs is increasing, but how about their quality?*

数学 **shùxué** [modif: 数 number + 学 knowledge, study of] *n* mathematics □ 我看，数学和语文是学校里最重要的两门课。**Wǒ kàn, shùxué hé yǔwén shì xuéxiào li zuì zhòngyào de liǎng mén kè.** *In my view, mathematics and language are the two most important subjects in schools.* □ 我们明天考数学。**Wǒmen míngtiān kǎo shùxué.** *We're having a mathematics examination tomorrow.*
数学家 **shùxuéjiā** mathematician

数字 **shùzì** [modif: 数 number + 字 written word] *n* **1** numeral, digit (in writing) □ 我认为写中文的时候，一般应该写中文数字，如 "一"、"二"、"三"。**Wǒ rènwéi xiě Zhōngwén de shíhou, yìbān yīnggāi xiě Zhōngwén shùzì, rú "yī", "èr", "sān".** *I think when we're writing Chinese, we should generally use Chinese numerals, such as "一," "二" and "三."* **2** figure, number □ 每个月都节省一点钱，几年以后就是一笔不小的数字。**Měi ge yuè dōu jiéshěng yìdiǎn qián, jǐ nián yǐhòu jiùshì yìbǐ bù xiǎo de shùzì.** *If you save some money every month, years later you will have quite a large sum.*
数字相机 **shùzì xiàngjī** digital camera
数字摄像机 **shùzì shèxiàngjī** digital camcorder

竖 **shù** *adj* vertical
竖立 **shùlì** *v* erect, set upright

刷 **shuā** *v* brush □ 我每天睡觉前刷牙。**Wǒ měitiān shuìjiào qián shuā yá.** *I brush my teeth before going to bed every night.*

耍 **shuǎ** *v* play

摔 **shuāi** *v* **1** fall, fumble □ 她从自行车上摔下来，擦破了手。**Tā cóng zìxíngchē shang shuāi xiàlai, cāpòle shǒu.** *She fell off the bicycle and scraped her hand.* **2** fall and break, cause to fall and break □ 我不小心把茶杯摔了。**Wǒ bù xiǎoxīn bǎ chábēi shuāi le.** *I accidentally broke the teacup.*

衰 **shuāi** *v* decline, decay
衰老 **shuāilǎo** [comp: 衰 decline + 老 old] *adj* old and in declining health
衰弱 **shuāiruò** [comp: 衰 declining + 弱 weak] *adj* feeble, very weak
衰退 **shuāituì** [comp: 衰 declining + 退 regressive] *v* become weaker, decline
经济衰退 **jīngjì shuāituì** economic recession

甩 **shuǎi** *v* swing, throw

帅 **shuài** Trad 帥 **I** *n* commander in chief
元帅 **yuánshuài** marshal
II *adj* beautiful, handsome

率 **shuài** *v* lead, command
率领 **shuàilǐng** [comp: 率 lead + 领 lead] *v* lead, command (troops)

拴 **shuān** *v* tie, fasten

双 **shuāng** Trad 雙 *measure wd* **1** two, double **2** a pair of (shoes, chopsticks, etc.)
一双鞋 **yì shuāng xié** a pair of shoes
两双筷子 **liǎng shuāng kuàizi** two pairs of chopsticks
双胞胎 **shuāngbāotāi** *n* twins
双方 **shuāngfāng** [modif: 双 both + 方 side, party] *n* both sides, both parties □ 双方同意加强合作。**Shuāngfāng tóngyì jiāqiáng hézuò.** *Both parties agree to strengthen their cooperation.*
双人床 **shuāngrénchuáng** [modif: 双 two people + 床 bed] *n* double bed

霜 **shuāng** *n* frost, frostlike powder

爽 **shuǎng** *adj* **1** crisp, freshing **2** straightforward, open-hearted
爽快 **shuǎngkuài** *adj* **1** refreshed **2** straightforward, frank **3** readily, without hesitation

谁 **shuí** Trad 誰 *pron* **1** who, whom □ 谁是你们的中文老师？**Shuí shì nǐmen de Zhōngwén lǎoshī?** *Who's your Chinese teacher?* □ 你找谁？**Nǐ zhǎo shuí?** *Who are you looking for?* **2** everyone, anybody, whoever, no matter who □ 谁都希望生活过得幸福。**Shuí dōu xīwàng shēnghuó guò de xìngfú.** *Everybody hopes to live a happy life.* □ 谁也不能保证永远不犯错误。**Shuí yě bù néng bǎozhèng yǒngyuǎn bú fàn cuòwù.** *Nobody can guarantee that he will never make a mistake.*

水 **shuǐ** *n* water □ 我口渴，要喝水。**Wǒ kǒu kě, yào hē shuǐ.** *I'm thirsty. I want to drink some water.*
自来水 **zìláishuǐ** running water, tap water □ 这里的自来水能喝吗？**Zhèlǐ de zìláishuǐ néng hē ma?** *Is the tap water here drinkable?*
开水 **kāishuǐ** boiled water
水产 **shuǐchǎn** *n* aquatic product
水产品 **shuǐchǎnpǐn** aquatic product
水稻 **shuǐdào** [modif: 水 water + 稻 paddy rice] *n* paddy rice, rice □ 这些年，水稻产量有了相当大的提高。**Zhèxiē nián shuǐdào chǎnliàng yǒule xiāngdāng dà de tígāo.** *The yield of paddy rice has increased considerably in recent years.*
水电 **shuǐdiàn** *n* Same as 水力发电 **shuǐlì fādiàn**
水电供应 **shuǐdiàn gōngyìng** water and electricity supply
水电站 **shuǐdiànzhàn** *n* Same as 水力发电站 **shuǐlì fādiànzhàn**
水分 **shuǐfèn** *n* moisture content
水果 **shuǐguǒ** [modif: 水 water + 果 fruit] *n* fruit □ 水果人人都爱吃。**Shuǐguǒ rénrén dōu ài chī.** *Everybody loves to eat fruit.* □ 我要去商店买一些水果。**Wǒ yào qù shāngdiàn mǎi yìxiē shuǐguǒ.** *I'll go to the store to buy some fruit.*
水果刀 **shuǐguǒ dāo** penknife
水果店 **shuǐguǒ diàn** fruit shop, fruiterer
水库 **shuǐkù** [modif: 水 water + 库 warehouse] *n* reservoir
水利 **shuǐlì** [modif: 水 water + 利 benefit] *n* water conservancy, irrigation works
水利工程 **shuǐlì gōngchéng** water conservancy project
水力 **shuǐlì** [modif: 水 water + 力 power] *n* waterpower, hydraulic power
水力发电 **shuǐlì fādiàn** *n* hydraulic electricity
水力发电站 **shuǐlì fādiànzhàn** hydroelectric station, hydropower station
水泥 **shuǐní** [comp: 水 water + 泥 mud] *n* cement □ 我要买两袋优质水泥，多少钱？**Wǒ yào mǎi liǎng dài yōuzhì shuǐní, duōshǎo qián?** *I want two sacks of quality cement. How much is it?*

水平 shuǐpíng *n* **1** level, standard □ 政府努力提高人民的生活水平。**Zhèngfǔ nǔlì tígāo rénmín de shēnghuó shuǐpíng.** *The government is working hard to raise the people's standard of living.* **2** proficiency (in language) □ 我的中文水平不高，请您多多帮助。**Wǒ de Zhōngwén shuǐpíng bù gāo, qǐng nín duōduō bāngzhù.** *My proficiency in Chinese is not very high. Please help me.*

生活水平 shēnghuó shuǐpíng living standard

提高生活水平 tígāo shēnghuó shuǐpíng raise the standard of living

文化水平 wénhuà shuǐpíng cultural level, educational experience □ 这位老人的文化水平不高，但是说的话总是有道理。**Zhè wèi lǎorén de wénhuà shuǐpíng bù gāo, dànshì shuō de huà zǒngshì hěn yǒu dàolǐ.** *This old person is not very well educated, but what he says always has a lot of truth in it.*

水土 shuǐtǔ *n* water and soil

水土流失 shuǐtǔ liúshī soil erosion

水银 shuǐyín [modif: 水 water + 银 silver] *n* mercury

水源 shuǐyuán [modif: 水 water + 源 source] *n* source of a river, headwater

水灾 shuǐzāi [modif: 水 water + 灾 disaster] *n* disastrous flooding, inundation

水蒸气 shuǐzhēngqì *n* water vapor, steam

水准 shuǐzhǔn *n* Same as 水平 **shuǐpíng**

税 shuì *n* tax, duty □ 每个公民都有交税的义务。**Měi ge gōngmín dōu yǒu jiāo shuì de yìwù.** *Every citizen has an obligation to pay taxes.*

税务局 shuìwùjú tax bureau, Inland Revenue Service

关税 guānshuì tariff, customs duty

税率 shuìlǜ *n* tax rate

税收 shuìshōu *n* tax revenue

睡 shuì *v* sleep □ 爸爸睡了，你明天再跟他说吧。**Bàba shuì le, nǐ míngtiān zài gēn tā shuō ba.** *Daddy's sleeping. Talk to him tomorrow.* □ 我一般夜里睡得挺好，可是昨天没睡好，因为心里有事。**Wǒ yìbān yèli shuì de tǐng hǎo, kěshì zuótiān méi shuì hǎo, yīnwèi xīnli yǒushì.** *I usually sleep well at night, but I did not sleep well last night as I had something on my mind.*

睡觉 shuìjiào [comp: 睡 sleep + 觉 sleep] *v* sleep, go to bed □ "你每天什么时候睡觉？" "十点钟以后。" **"Nǐ měitiān shénme shíhou shuìjiào?" "Shí diǎnzhōng yǐhòu."** *"When do you go to bed every day?" "After ten o'clock."* □ 这么晚了，你还不睡觉？**Zhème wǎn le, nǐ hái bú shuìjiào?** *It's so late. You're not going to bed?*

NOTES: (1) 睡 **shuì** and 睡觉 **shuìjiào** are often interchangeable. (2) 觉 is pronounced **jiào** in 睡觉 **shuìjiào**, but **jué** in 觉得 **juéde**.

睡眠 shuìmián [comp: 睡 sleep + 眠 sleep] *n* sleep

睡眠不足 shuìmián bùzú sleep deficiency

睡衣 shuìyī [modif: 睡 sleep + 衣 clothing] *n* pajamas, dressing gown

睡着 shuìzháo *v* fall asleep □ 昨天我十点上床，到十二点左右才睡着。**Zuótiān wǒ shí diǎnzhōng shàngchuáng, dào shí'èr diǎn zuǒyòu cái shuì zháo.** *I went to bed at ten yesterday and didn't fall asleep until about twelve o'clock.*

顺 shùn Trad 順 **I** *adj* smooth **II** *v* **1** arrange, plan **2** do at one's convenience

顺便 shùnbiàn [comp: 顺 do at one's convenience + 便 convenient] *adv* in passing, incidentally □ 你回家的路上，顺便给我买一份晚报，好吗？**Nǐ huíjiā de lùshang, shùnbiàn gěi wǒ mǎi yífèn wǎnbào, hǎo ma?** *Could you buy me an evening paper on your way home?* □ 顺便说一句，下个月我要请两天假。**Shùnbiàn shuō yíjù, xià ge yuè wǒ yào qǐng liǎngtiān jià.** *Incidentally, I'm going to ask for a couple of days' leave next month.*

顺利 shùnlì [comp: 顺 smooth + 利 smooth] *adj* smooth, without a hitch, successful □ 我们的计划执行得很顺利。**Wǒmen de jìhuà zhíxíng de hěn shùnlì.** *Our plan has been carried out smoothly.* □ 他一生都很顺利。**Tā yìshēng dōu hěn shùnlì.** *All his life has been plain sailing.* (→ *He has had an easy life.*)

顺手 shùnshǒu *adj* **1** smooth, without hitches **2** convenient, without much trouble

顺序 shùnxù *n* sequence, order

说 shuō Trad 説 *v* **1** say, speak □ 他说什么？**Tā shuō shénme?** *What did he say?* □ 他说今天晚上没有时间。**Tā shuō jīntiān wǎnshang méiyǒu shíjiān.** *He said he did not have time this evening.* **2** explain, tell □ 你说说，这个菜怎么做？**Nǐ shuōshuo, zhège cài zěnme zuò?** *Will you tell me how to cook this dish?* □ 她很聪明，老师一说她就懂。**Tā hěn cōngmíng, lǎoshī yì shuō tā jiù dǒng.** *She is very bright. As soon as the teacher has explained, she understands.*

说笑话 shuō xiàohua tell a joke

说法 shuōfǎ *n* **1** wording **2** statement, version

说服 shuōfú [v+comp: 说 speak + 服 obey] *v* **1** persuade □ 妈妈说服了爸爸提前退休。**Māma shuōfú le bàba tí qián tuìxiū.** *Mom has persuaded Dad to have an early retirement.* **2** convince □ 他说的话没有道理，我没有被说服。**Tā shuōde huà méiyǒu dàoli, wǒ méiyǒu bèi shuōfú.** *What he said was not reasonable; I was not convinced.*

说谎 shuōhuǎng [v+obj: 说 tell + 谎 a lie] *v* tell lies, lie

说理 shuōlǐ *v* reason things out, argue

说明 shuōmíng [v+comp: 说 say + 明 clear] **I** *v* **1** explain □ 我来说明一下，为什么我最近有时候迟到。**Wǒ lái shuōmíng yíxià, wèishénme wǒ zuìjìn yǒu shíhou chídào.** *Let me explain why I've been sometimes late recently.* **2** prove, show □ 你考试取得了好成绩，这说明你学习很努力。**Nǐ kǎoshì qǔdéle hǎo chéngjì, zhè shuōmíng nǐ xuéxí hěn nǔlì.** *You got a good grade at the examination. This shows you studied very hard.* **II** *n* explanation, manual □ 这个电脑怎么用，我要看一下说明。**Zhège diànnǎo zěnme yòng, wǒ yào kàn yíxià shuōmíng.** *As to how to use this computer, I need to read the manual.*

说情 shuōqíng *v* plead for mercy (for someone)

烁 shuò Trad 爍 *v* glitter (See 闪烁 **shǎnshuò**)

硕 shuò Trad 碩 *adj* large, big

硕士 shuòshì [modif: 硕 big + 士 scholar] *n* holder of a master's degree

硕士学位 shuòshì xuéwèi master's degree, masterate

司 sī v take charge of
司法 sīfǎ [v+obj: 司 take charge of + 法 law] n administration of justice, judicature
　司法机关 sīfǎ jīguān judicial office, judicial system
司机 sījī [v+obj: 司 take charge + 机 machine] n (professional) automobile driver, train driver □ 出租汽车司机态度很友好。**Chūzū qìchē sījī tàidu hěn yóuhǎo.** *The taxi driver is very friendly.*
司令 sīlìng n commander, commanding officer
司令部 sīlìngbù n (military) headquarters

斯 sī pron this

NOTE: This character was used in Classical Chinese to mean *this*. In Modern Chinese it is normally used just to transliterate foreign names, e.g. 查尔斯 **Chá'ěrsī** for the English name *Charles*.

撕 sī v tear (a piece of paper)
　撕得粉碎 sī dé fěnsuì tear into tiny pieces, tear up

私 sī adj private
私人 sīrén [modif: 私 private + 人 person] I adj 1 private, personal □ 私人财产受到法律保护。**Sīrén cáichǎn shòudào fǎlǜ bǎohù.** *Private property is protected by the law.* II n personal relationship □ 我和他只是同事, 没有私人关系。**Wǒ hé tā zhǐshì tóngshì, méiyǒu sīrén guānxi.** *He and I are colleagues only, we do not have any personal relationship.*
私营 sīyíng [modif: 私 privately + 营 operate] adj privately operated, private owned
私有 sīyǒu [modif: 私 privately + 有 own] adj privately owned, private
私自 sīzì adv without permission, secretly
　私自决定 sīzì juédìng make a decision all by oneself and without permission from the authorities

思 sī v think
思潮 sīcháo [modif: 思 thought + 潮 tide] n trend of thought, ideological trend
思考 sīkǎo [comp: 思 think + 考 examine] v ponder over, think seriously
思念 sīniàn [comp: 思 think + 念 miss] v miss, think of longingly
思前想后 sīqián xiǎnghòu idiom ponder over, weigh pros and cons
思索 sīsuǒ [comp: 思 think + 索 search] v think hard, beat one's brains
思维 sīwéi n thought, thinking, the process of thinking
思想 sīxiǎng [comp: 思 think + 想 think] n thought, thinking □ 人们的思想是什么决定的? **Rénmen de sīxiǎng shì shénme juédìng de?** *What determines people's thoughts?* □ 这个孩子怎么会有这种思想呢? **Zhège háizi zěnme huì yǒu zhè zhǒng sīxiǎng ne?** *How did the child have this kind of thinking?*
　思想家 sīxiǎngjiā thinker
思绪 sīxù n train of thought, thinking

丝 sī Trad 絲 n 1 silk 2 threadlike things
丝绸 sīchóu [comp: 丝 silk + 绸 silk cloth] n silk, silk cloth □ 我要买一些丝绸产品, 带回去送朋友。**Wǒ yào mǎi yìxiē sīchóu chǎnpǐn, dài huíqu sòng péngyou.** *I want to buy some silk products to take home as gifts for friends.*

丝毫 sīháo n the slightest, in the least
　没有丝毫变化 méiyǒu sīháo biànhuà without the slightest change, haven't changed in the least

NOTE: 丝毫 **sīháo** is usually used alongside with a negative word, as is shown in the example.

死 sǐ v die (antonym 活 **huó**) □ 我家的狗昨天死了。**Wǒ jiā de gǒu zuótiān sǐ le.** *Our family dog died yesterday.* □ 人总有一死, 谁都不能避免。**Rén zǒng yǒu yì sǐ, shuí dōu bù néng bìmiǎn.** *People eventually die. No one can avoid this.*

NOTE: See note on 去世 **qùshì**.

死亡 sǐwáng n death
　死亡证 sǐwáng zhèng death certificate
死刑 sǐxíng n death sentence

四 sì num four □ 四海为家。**Sì hǎi wéi jiā.** *Make the four seas one's home.* (→ *Make one's home wherever one is.*)
　四十四 sìshí sì forty-four
四处 sìchù adv here and there, in all directions, everywhere
四方 sìfāng n the four directions of east, west, north and south, all sides
四季 sìjì n the four seasons, all the year round
　四季如春 sìjì rú chūn (warm and pleasant) like spring all the year round
四面八方 sìmiàn bāfāng idiom in all directions, from all over
四肢 sìzhī n the four limbs, arms and legs
　四肢发达 sìzhī fādá physically strong
四周 sìzhōu adv all around, on all sides

肆 sì num four

饲 sì v Trad 飼 raise (animals)
饲料 sìliào n (animal) feed, fodder
饲养 sìyǎng [comp: 饲 raise + 养 raise, keep] v raise (animals) □ 这位农民饲养了一百多头猪。**Zhè wèi nóngmín sìyǎng le yìbǎi duō tóu zhū.** *This farmer raises over 100 pigs.*

伺 sì v watch, await
伺机 sìjī [v+obj: 伺 await + 机 chance] v wait for one's chances

似 sì v seem
似乎 sìhū adv it seems, as if □ 他们似乎对我们公司的产品很有兴趣。**Tāmen sìhū duì wǒmen gōngsī de chǎnpǐn hěn yǒu xìngqù.** *They seem to be interested in our company's products.* □ 他听了我的话, 似乎不大高兴。**Tā tīngle wǒ de huà, sìhū bú dà gāoxìng.** *He seemed unhappy after hearing what I had to say.* □ 我似乎在哪儿见到过他。**Wǒ sìhū zài nǎr jiàndaoguo tā.** *I seem to have met him before somewhere.*
似是而非 sìshì'érfēi idiom sound right but is actually wrong
　似是而非的理论 sìshì'érfēi de lǐlùn a plausibly deceptive theory, a specious theory

寺 sì n monastery, temple
　清真寺 qīngzhēnsì mosque

松 sōng Trad 鬆 I adj lax, weak (antonym 紧 **jǐn**) □ 这个学校对学生的要求太松。**Zhège xuéxiào**

duì xuésheng de yāoqiú tài sōng. *This school demands too little of the students.* (→ *This school does not set a high standard for students.*) **II** *v* loosen, slacken □ 带子太紧了，要松一下。**Dàizi tài jǐn le, yào sōng yíxià.** *The belt is too tight. It needs to be loosened.*

松 2 **sōng** *n* pine
松树 **sōngshù** pine tree (棵 **kē**)

耸 **sǒng** Trad 聳 *v* 1 alarm, alert 2 rise up
耸耸肩膀 **sǒngsǒng jiānbǎng** shrug one's shoulders
耸人听闻 **sǒngrén tīngwén** *idiom* exaggerate (news) in order to sensationalize

颂 **sòng** Trad 頌 *v* praise, extol
颂扬 **sòngyáng** *v* sing praises of, eulogize

讼 **sòng** Trad 訟 *v* file a lawsuit (See 诉讼 **sùsòng**)

送 **sòng** *v* 1 give as a gift □ 去年圣诞节，爸爸送给他一辆自行车。**Qùnián shèngdànjié, bàba sòng gei tā yí liàng zìxíngchē.** *Last Christmas his father gave him a bike.* 2 deliver □ 我们可以把你买的电脑送到你家。**Wǒmen kěyǐ bǎ nǐ mǎi de diànnǎo sòngdào nǐ jiā.** *We can deliver the computer you've bought to your home.* 3 accompany, take, escort □ 天太晚了，我开车送你回家吧。**Tiān tài wǎn le, wǒ kāi chē sòng nǐ huíjiā ba.** *It's too late. Let me drive you home.*
送礼 **sònglǐ** *v* present a gift to
送大礼 **sòng dà lǐ** give an expensive gift
送行 **sòngxíng** *v* see off
到机场送行 **dào jīchǎng sòngxíng** see ... off at the airport

诵 **sòng** Trad 誦 *v* chant, recite (See 背诵 **bèisòng**.)

艘 **sōu** *measure wd* (used with nouns denoting boats and ships)
一艘渔轮 **yì sōu yúlún** a fishing boat

搜 **sōu** *v* search
搜查 **sōuchá** [comp: 搜 search + 查 check] *v* search, ransack
搜查证 **sōucházhèng** search warrant
搜集 **sōují** [comp: 搜 search + 集 gather] *v* collect, gather
搜集资料 **sōují zīliào** collect data, data-gathering
搜索 **sōusuǒ** *v* search
搜索队 **sōusuǒduì** search party
搜索引擎 **sōusuǒ yǐnqíng** search engine

嗽 **sòu** *n* cough (See 咳嗽 **késou**.)

苏 **sū** Trad 蘇 *v* revive
苏打 **sūdǎ** *n* soda
苏醒 **sūxǐng** [comp: 苏 revive + 醒 awake] *v* regain consciousness, come to

俗 **sú** *n* custom, convention
俗话 **súhuà** *n* traditional saying, saying

诉 **sù** Trad 訴 *v* tell (See 告诉 **gàosu**.)
诉讼 **sùsòng** *v* lawsuit, litigation
对…提出诉讼 **duì...tíchū sùsòng** file a lawsuit against

肃 **sù** Trad 肅 **I** *adj* solemn (See 严肃 **yánsù**.) **II** *v* clean up, eliminate
肃清 **sùqīng** *v* eliminate, clean up

速 **sù** *n* speed
速度 **sùdù** [modif: 速 speed + 度 degree] *n* speed, velocity □ 以这样的速度，我们可以在两小时之内到达目的地。**Yǐ zhèyàng de sùdù, wǒmen kěyǐ zài liǎng xiǎoshí zhīnèi dàodá mùdìdì.** *At this speed, we can reach our destination in two hours.* □ 你开车超过了限定的速度。**Nǐ kāichē chāoguòle xiàndìng de sùdù.** *You have exceeded the speed limit.*

素 **sù** *adj* 1 plain, simple 2 vegetarian
吃素 **chīsù** eat vegetarian food only, be a vegetarian
素菜 **sùcài** *n* vegetarian dish, vegetarian food
素食 **sùshí** *n* vegetarian food
素食主义 **sùshí zhǔyì** vegetarianism
素食主义者 **sùshí zhǔyìzhě** vegetarian (a person)
素质 **sùzhì** *n* (of a person) true quality, basic nature

宿 **sù** *v* stay overnight
宿舍 **sùshè** [modif: 宿 stay overnight + 舍 lodge] *n* hostel, dormitory □ 我的书忘在宿舍里了! **Wǒ de shū wàng zài sùshè li le!** *I've left my book in the dormitory.*
学生宿舍 **xuésheng sùshè** students' hostel (dormitory)

塑 **sù** *v* mold
塑料 **sùliào** *n* plastic □ 这种桌椅是用塑料做的，又轻又便宜。**Zhè zhǒng zhuōyǐ shì yòng sùliào zuò de, yòu qīng yòu piányi.** *These tables and chairs are made of plastic; they are light and inexpensive.*
塑造 **sùzào** [comp: 塑 mold + 造 make] *v* sculpture, portray

酸 **suān** *adj* sour □ 我不喜欢吃酸的东西。**Wǒ bù xǐhuan chī suān de dōngxi.** *I don't like to eat sour food.* □ 这种酒太酸了一点儿。**Zhè zhǒng jiǔ tài suānle yìdiǎnr.** *This wine is a bit too sour.*

算 **suàn** *v* 1 calculate □ 我算一下这个星期花了多少钱。**Wǒ suàn yíxià zhège xīngqī huāle duōshǎo qián.** *Let me calculate how much money I've spent this week.* □ 完成这项工程需要多少人工，你算过没有? **Wánchéng zhè xiàng gōngchéng xūyào duōshǎo réngōng, nǐ suànguo méiyǒu?** *Have you calculated how many man-hours will be needed to finish this project?* 2 regard, consider □ 今天不算冷，昨天才冷呢! **Jīntiān bú suàn lěng, zuótiān cái lěng ne!** *Today can't be considered cold. Yesterday was really cold.*
算了 **suànle** *v* forget about it, let it pass
算盘 **suànpán** *n* abacus (把 **bǎ**)
算是 **suànshì** *adv* at last
算术 **suànshù** [modif: 算 calculation + 术 art] *n* arithmetic
算数 **suànshù** *v* count □ 我说话是算数的。**Wǒ shuōhuà shì suàn shù de.** *Whatever I say counts.* (→ *I mean what I say.*)

蒜 **suàn** *n* garlic
大蒜 **dàsuàn** garlic

虽 **suī** Trad 雖 *conj* although
虽然 **suīrán** *conj* although, though □ 虽然已经是秋天了，这两天天气还是很热。**Suīrán yǐjīng shì qiūtiān le, zhè liǎng tiān tiānqì háishì hěn rè.** *Although it's already autumn, it's still hot these days.* □ 他虽然赚了很多钱，但是还不满足。**Tā suīrán zhuànle hěn duō qián, dàn hái bù mǎnzú.** *Although he's earned a lot of money, he is still dissatisfied.*
虽说 **suīshuō** Same as 虽然 **suīrán**, used colloquially

随 suí Trad 隨 *v* let (somebody do as he pleases), as you wish □ 这件事和我没有关系, 随你处理。**Zhè jiàn shì hé wǒ méiyǒu guānxi, suí nǐ chǔlǐ.** *This matter is none of my business. You can deal with it any way you like.*

随便 suíbiàn *adj* casual, informal □ 中饭我们随便一点, 晚上我请你到饭店去好好吃一顿。**Zhōngfàn wǒmen suíbiàn chī yìdiǎn, wǎnshang wǒ qǐng nǐ dào fàndiàn qu hǎohǎo chī yí dùn.** *For lunch we'll have a casual meal. In the evening I'll take you to a restaurant for a square meal.*

NOTE: 随便 **suíbiàn** is often used in casual conversation to mean *like as you wish*, *anything you like*, or *I have no objection whatsoever.* e.g. □ "你喝红茶还是绿茶?" "随便。" **"Nǐ hē hóngchá háishì lǜchá?" "Suíbiàn."** *"Do you want to drink black tea or green tea?" "Anything's fine with me."*

随后 suíhòu *adv* immediately afterwards
随即 suíjí *adv* immediately, soon after
随时 suíshí *adv* whenever, at any moment □ 你有问题, 可以随时给我打电话。**Nǐ yǒu wèntí, kěyǐ suíshí gěi wǒ dǎ diànhuà.** *If you have a problem, you can call me anytime.*
随时随地 suíshí suídì *idiom* anytime and anywhere, ever
随手 suíshǒu *adv* 1 immediately □ 请随手关门。**Qǐng suíshǒu guānmén.** *Please close the door after you.* 2 casually, without much thought
随手乱放 suíshǒu luàn fàng put ... somewhere casually and without much thought
随意 suíyì I *adv* as one pleases, casually II *adj* random
随意抽样 suíyì chōuyàng random sampling
随着 suízhe *prep* along with, in the wake of

岁 suì Trad 歲 *measure wd* year (of age) □ 我小弟弟今年八岁。**Wǒ xiǎo dìdi jīnnián bā suì.** *My younger brother is eight years old.*

NOTE: See 年纪 **niánjì**.

岁数 suìshu *n* years of age □ 你今年多大岁数? **Nǐ jīnnián duōdà suìshu?** *How old are you?*
上了岁数的人 shàngle suìshu de rén elderly person
岁月 suìyuè *n* years
碎 suì *adj* broken, fragmentary □ 车窗的玻璃被一块石头打碎了。**Chēchuāng de bōli bèi yí kuài shítou dǎ suì le.** *The car window was shattered by a stone.*
穗 suì *n* the ear of grain
麦穗 màisuì ear of wheat, wheat head
隧 suì *n* tunnel
隧道 suìdào *n* tunnel
孙 sūn Trad 孫 *n* grandchild
孙女 sūnnǚ *n* granddaughter
孙子 sūnzi *n* grandson
笋 sǔn *n* bamboo shoot
竹笋 zhúsǔn bamboo shoot
损 sǔn Trad 損 *v* damage
损害 sǔnhài [comp: 损 damage + 害 harm] *v* harm, damage, injure □ 你不能做损害他人利益的事。

Nǐ bùnéng zuò sǔnhài tārén lìyì de shì. *You mustn't do anything that will harm other people's interest.*
损耗 sǔnhào [comp: 损 damage + 耗 consume] I *v* undergo wear and tear, deplete II *n* loss
损坏 sǔnhuài [v+compl: 损 damage + 坏 out of order] *v* damage as to render unusable, damage
损坏公物 sǔnhuài gōngwù damage public property
损人利己 sǔnrénlìjǐ *idiom* harm others to benefit oneself
损伤 sǔnshāng [comp: 损 damage + 伤 injure] *v* damage, harm, hurt
损失 sǔnshī [comp: 损 damage + 失 loss] I *v* lose, suffer from damage and/or loss □ 由于他的错误决定, 公司损失了五十万元。**Yóuyú tā de cuòwù juédìng, gōngsī sǔnshīle wǔshíwàn yuán.** *Owing to his wrong decision, the company lost half a million yuan.* II *n* loss, damage □ 这次水灾造成巨大损失。**Zhè cì shuǐzāi zàochéng jùdà sǔnshī.** *This flooding caused huge losses.*

唆 suō *v* instigate, abet
唆使 suōshǐ [comp: 唆 instigate + 使 make] *v* abet, instigate
缩 suō Trad 縮 *v* shrink □ 棉布下水以后会缩。**Miánbù xiàshuǐ yǐhòu huì suō.** *Cotton cloth will shrink in the wash.*
缩短 suōduǎn [v+compl: 缩 shrink + 短 short] *v* shorten, cut down □ 由于使用了新型飞机, 这段航程的时间缩短了一小时。**Yóuyú shǐyòng le xīnxíng fēijī, zhè duàn hángchéng de shíjiān suōduǎn le yì xiǎoshí.** *Thanks to the use of a new model airplane, the flight time is shortened by one hour.*
缩小 suōxiǎo [v+compl: 缩 shrink + 小 small] *v* reduce in size, shrink

所1 suǒ *measure wd* (for houses or institutions housed in a building)
一所医院 yì suǒ yīyuàn a hospital
两所大学 liǎng suǒ dàxué two universities
所2 suǒ I *n* place II *particle* indicating passive voice
所得 suǒdé *n* income, earnings
所得税 suǒdéshuì income tax
所谓 suǒwèi *adj* what is called, so-called □ 他所谓的 "理由" 完全站不住脚。**Tā suǒwèi de "lǐyóu" wánquán zhàn bu zhù jiǎo.** *His so-called "reason" does not have a leg to stand on.*
所以 suǒyǐ *conj* therefore, so □ 我上星期病了, 所以没有来上班。**Wǒ shàng xīngqī bìng le, suǒyǐ méiyǒu lái shàngbān.** *I was sick last week, so I did not come to work.* □ 因为家里有事, 所以她今天没来上班。**Yīnwèi jiā li yǒu shì, suǒyǐ tā jīntiān méi lái shàngbàn.** *There was an emergency in her family, therefore she did not come to work today.*
所有 suǒyǒu [idiom] *adj* all □ 所有的朋友都反对他的计划。**Suǒyǒu de péngyu dōu fǎnduì tā de jìhuà.** *All his friends opposed his plan.*

NOTES: 所有 **suǒyǒu** is (1) used only as an attribute, (2) always followed by 的 **de** and (3) often used together with 都 **dōu**.

所有制 suǒyǒuzhì *n* ownership
所在 suǒzài *n* place, location

索 **suǒ** *v* search, search for

索赔 **suǒpéi** [v+obj: 索 search for + 赔 compensation] *v* claim indemnity

索取 **suǒqǔ** [comp: 索 search + 取 take] *v* ask for, exact

索取报名单 **suǒqǔ bàomíngdān** ask for an application form

索性 **suǒxìng** *adv* might as well, simply

锁 **suǒ** Trad 鎖 **I** *n* lock □ 门打不开, 恐怕是锁坏了。**Mén dǎbukāi, kǒngpà shi suǒ huài le.** *The door can't be opened. I'm afraid something is wrong with the lock.* **II** *v* lock □ 离开以前一定要把办公室的门锁上。**Líkāi yǐqián yídìng yào bǎ bàngōngshì de mén suǒ shàng.** *Before you leave, make sure you lock the office door.*

嗦 **suo** as in 罗嗦 **luósuo**

T

他 **tā** *pron* he, him □ "他是谁?" "他是我的同学。" **"Tā shì shéi?" "Tā shì wǒ de tóngxué."** *"Who's he?" "He's my classmate."* □ 我不喜欢他。**Wǒ bù xǐhuan tā.** *I don't like him.* □ 他的朋友都叫他小王。**Tā de péngyou dōu jiào tā Xiǎo Wáng.** *His friends all call him Xiao Wang.*

他们 **tāmen** [suffix: 他 he, him + 们 suffix denoting a plural number] *pron* they, them □ 他们有困难, 我们要帮助他们。**Tāmen yǒu kùnnan, wǒmen yào bāngzhù tāmen.** *As they're in difficulty, we should help them.* □ 这是他们的问题, 我们没有办法。**Zhè shì tāmen de wèntí, wǒmen méiyǒu bànfǎ.** *This is their problem. There's nothing we can do.*

他人 **tārén** *pron* another person, other people

它 **tā** *pron* it □ 它是我的小狗。**Tā shì wǒ de xiǎo gǒu.** *It's my puppy.*

它们 **tāmen** [suffix: 它 it + 们 suffix denoting a plural number] *pron* (non-human) they, them (plural form of 它 **tā**)

她 **tā** *pron* she, her □ 她是我班上的女同学。**Tā shì wǒ bānshang de nǚ tóngxué.** *She's a girl student from my class.*

她们 **tāmen** [suffix: 她 she, her + 们 suffix denoting a plural number] *pron* (female) they, them

塌 **tā** *v* collapse, cave in

踏 **tā** as in 踏实 **tāshi**

踏实 **tāshi** *adj* **1** reliable **2** free from anxiety, reassured

塔 **tǎ** *n* pagoda, tower (座 **zuò**) □ 在中国几乎每一个城市都有一座古塔。**Zài Zhōngguó jīhū měi yí ge chéngshì dōu yǒu yí zuò gǔ tǎ.** *In China almost every town has an ancient tower.*

踏 **tà** *v* step on, tread □ 脚踏实地。**Jiǎo tà shídì.** *The feet step on firm ground.* (→ be earnest and down-to-earth)

蹋 **tà** *v* as in 糟蹋 **zāota**

台 **tái** Trad 檯 **I** *n* table, desk (张 **zhāng**) □ 董事长坐在一张大写字台后面。**Dǒngshìzhǎng zuò zai**

yì zhāng dà xiězìtái hòumiàn. *The chairman of the board sat behind a large desk.* **II** *measure wd* (for machines, big instruments, etc.)

一台机器 **yì tái jīqì** a machine

台风 **táifēng** *n* typhoon (场 **cháng**)

台阶 **táijiē** *n* flight of steps, steps

台湾 **Táiwān** *n* Taiwan

抬 **tái** Trad 擡 *v* lift, raise □ 来, 咱们俩把桌子抬到外边去。**Lái, zánmen liǎ bǎ zhuōzi táidao wàibian qù.** *Come on, let's move the table outside.* □ 这几个小姑娘怎么抬得动这台电脑呢? **Zhè jǐ ge xiǎogūniang zěnme tái de dòng zhè tái diànnǎo ne?** *How could these little girls carry this computer?*

抬高 (物价) **táigāo (wùjià)** raise (prices)

泰 **tài** *adj* peaceful □ 国泰民安。**Guó tài mín ān.** *The country is prosperous and the people live in peace.*

泰然 **tàirán** *adj* calm, composed

泰然自若 **tàirán zìruò** behave with great composure

太 **tài** *adv* **1** excessively, too □ 今天我太累了, 不去游泳了。**Jīntiān wǒ tài lèi le, bú qù yóuyǒng le.** *Today I'm too tired to go swimming.* □ 这个房间太小, 坐不下二十个人。**Zhège fángjiān tài xiǎo, zuò bu xià èrshí ge rén.** *This room is too small. It can't seat twenty people.* **2** extremely, really □ 太好了! **Tài hǎo le!** *That's wonderful!* □ 你们现在抬高物价, 太不讲道理了。**Nǐmen xiànzài táigāo wùjià, tài bù jiǎng dàolǐ le.** *It is extremely unreasonable of you to raise prices now.*

太空 **tàikōng** *n* outer space

太平 **tàipíng** *adj* peaceful and orderly

太平间 **tàipíngjiān** [modif: 太平 peace + 间 room] *n* mortuary

太平洋 **Tàipíngyáng** *n* the Pacific Ocean

太太 **tàitai** *n* **1** Mrs, Madam □ 王先生和王太太常常在家里请客吃饭。**Wáng xiānsheng hé Wáng tàitai chángcháng zài jiā li qǐngkè chīfàn.** *Mr and Mrs Wang often give dinner parties in their home.* **2** wife □ 您太太刚才打电话来。**Nín tàitai gāngcái dǎ diànhuà lai.** *Your wife called just now.* □ 今天是我太太生日, 我要早一点回家。**Jīntiān shì wǒ tàitai shēngrì, wǒ yào zǎo yìdiǎn huíjiā.** *Today's my wife's birthday. I need to go home earlier.*

NOTES: (1) While *Mrs* is used in English-speaking countries regardless of class or social status, its counterpart 太太 **tàitai** is only used in middle-class or upper-class circles. Similarly, 太太 **tàitai** meaning *wife* is also only used in such circles. (2) Although Chinese women often retain their family names after marriage, 太太 **tàitai** as a form of address must be prefixed by the husband's family name: 王太太 **Wáng tàitai** *Mrs Wang (the wife of Mr Wang).*

太阳 **tàiyang** [modif: 太 big, super + 阳 open, overt, masculine] *n* the sun, sunshine □ 今天的太阳真好。**Jīntiān de tàiyang zhēn hǎo.** *The sunshine's beautiful today.*

NOTES: (1) Put together, 太 **tài** (meaning *big, great* in Classical Chinese) and 阳 **yáng** (meaning the Yang of ancient Chinese thought) mean the ultimate Yang, as the sun is the ultimate symbol of Yang. The ultimate symbol

of Yin is the moon 月 yuè. (2) In 太阳 tàiyang, 阳 yang is pronounced in the neutral tone.

太阳能 **tàiyángnéng** *n* solar energy

态 **tài** Trad 態 *n* stance
态度 **tàidu** [comp: 态 stance + 度 appearance, bearing] *n* attitude, approach □ 这位服务员的服务态度不好。**Zhè wèi fúwùyuán de fúwù tàidu bù hǎo.** *This attendant's work attitude is not good.* □ 这孩子说话态度不好, 常惹人生气。**Zhè háizi shuōhuà tàidu bù hǎo, cháng rě rén shēngqì.** *This child's manner of speaking is bad, and is often offensive.*

NOTE: Though 态度 **tàidu** is glossed as *attitude* or *approach*, it is more commonly used in Chinese than its equivalents in English.

汰 **tài** *v* eliminate (See 淘汰 **táotài**)

摊 **tān** Trad 攤 *n* trader's stand, stall □ 路两边摆了很多摊子, 有卖吃的, 也有卖工艺品的。**Lù liǎngbian bǎile hěn duō tānzi, yǒu mài chī de, yě yǒu mài gōngyìpǐn de.** *There are many stands on the two sides of the street; some sell food and others sell small handicraft articles.*

滩 **tān** Trad 灘 *n* beach, shoal (See 沙滩 **shātān**)

瘫 **tān** Trad 癱 *v* be paralyzed
瘫痪 **tānhuàn** I *v* be paralyzed II *n* paralysis
全身瘫痪 quánshēn tānhuàn complete paralysis

贪 **tān** *v* 1 be greedy 2 be corrupt, practice graft
贪官 tānguān corrupt official
3 covet, hanker after
贪婪 **tānlán** *adj* greedy, avaricious
贪图 **tāntú** [comp: 贪 be greedy + 图 intend] *v* hanker after, covet
贪污 **tānwū** [comp: 贪 corrupt + 污 filthy] I *v* embezzle, be involved in corruption
贪污公款 tānwū gōngkuǎn embezzle public funds
II *n* graft, corruption
贪污犯 tānwūfàn embezzler, grafter
贪心 **tānxīn** [modif: 贪 greedy + 心 heart] *n* greed, avarice
贪嘴 **tānzuǐ** [modif: 贪 greedy + mouth 嘴] *adj* greedy for food

坛 **tán** Trad 壇 *n* altar
天坛 Tiāntán the Temple of Heaven (in Beijing)

潭 **tán** *n* deep pool

痰 **tán** *n* phlegm, sputum
吐痰 tǔtán spit

谈 **tán** Trad 談 *v* talk, discuss □ 我想跟你谈一件事。**Wǒ xiǎng gēn nǐ tán yí jiàn shì.** *I'd like to discuss something with you.*
谈一下 tán yíxià talk briefly about, give a brief talk about □ 请你谈一下去中国旅行的情况。**Qǐng nǐ tán yíxià qù Zhōngguó lǚxíng de qíngkuàng.** *Please give a brief talk about your trip to China.*
谈话 **tánhuà** [comp: 谈 talk + 话 talk] *v* have a (serious, formal) talk □ 校长找我谈话。**Xiàozhǎng zhǎo wǒ tánhuà.** *The principal summoned me for a talk.*

谈论 **tánlùn** [comp: 谈 talk + 论 comment] *v* talk about
谈判 **tánpàn** I *v* negotiate, hold talks □ 双方正在为签订一项合同谈判。**Shuāngfāng zhèngzài wèi qiāndìng yí xiàng hétóng tánpàn.** *The two sides are negotiating the signing of a contract.* II *n* negotiation (项 xiàng) □ 这项谈判在进行了三个星期以后终于取得双方满意的结果。**Zhè xiàng tánpàn zài jìnxíngle sān ge xīngqī yǐhòu zhōngyú qǔdé shuāngfāng mǎnyì de jiéguǒ.** *After three weeks the negotiations finally reached a conclusion that satisfied both parties.*
谈天 **tántiān** [v+obj: 谈 talk about + 天 the heaven] *v* talk about everything under the sun, shoot the breeze, chitchat □ 上班的时候, 不能谈天。**Shàngbān de shíhou, bù néng tántiān.** *You are not supposed to chat during working hours.*

毯 **tǎn** *n* carpet, rug, blanket
地毯 dìtǎn carpet, rug
挂毯 guàtǎn tapestry
毯子 **tǎnzi** [suffix: 毯 blanket + 子 nominal suffix] *n* blanket (条 tiáo) □ 中国人一般不用毯子, 而用被子。**Zhōngguórén yìbān bú yòng tǎnzi, ér yòng bèizi.** *The Chinese usually do not use blankets, but they use quilts.*

坦 **tǎn** *adj* 1 candid, frank 2 level, smooth
平坦 píngtǎn (of land) level, flat
坦白 **tǎnbái** *v* 1 confess to (crimes or wrongdoing) 2 be frank, be candid
坦白地说 tǎnbáide shuō to be frank with you, to tell the truth
坦克 **tǎnkè** *n* tank (military vehicle)

炭 **tàn** *n* charcoal

碳 **tàn** *n* carbon (C)
二氧化碳 èryǎnghuàtàn carbon dioxide

叹 **tàn** Trad 嘆 *v* sigh
叹气 **tànqì** [v+obj: 叹 sigh + 气 air] *v* heave a sigh

探 **tàn** *v* 1 explore 2 spy 3 visit
探测 **tàncè** [comp: 探 explore + 测 test] *v* survey, probe
探亲 **tànqīn** [v+obj: 探 visit + 亲 parents] *v* visit one's parents, visit relatives
探索 **tànsuǒ** [comp: 探 explore + 索 search] *v* explore, seek, search for □ 这些年他都在探索人生的意义。**Zhèxiē nián tā dōu zài tànsuǒ rénshēng de yìyì.** *All these years he has been searching for the meaning of life.* □ 医生们正在探索医治这种疾病的方法。**Yīshēngmen zhèngzài tànsuǒ yīzhì zhè zhǒng jíbìng de fāngfǎ.** *Doctors are searching for a way to cure this disease.*
探讨 **tàntǎo** [comp: 探 explore + 讨 discuss] *v* explore and discuss, inquire into
探讨…的可行性 tàntǎo...de kěxíngxìng explore the feasibility of ...
探望 **tànwàng** [comp: 探 visit + 望 see] *v* go to see, visit
探望病人 tànwàng bìngrén visit someone who is sick, visit a patient
探险 **tànxiǎn** [v+obj: 探 explore + 险 danger] *v* venture into, explore
探险队 tànxiǎnduì exploration team

探险家 tànxiǎnjiā explorer

汤 tāng Trad 湯 *n* soup (碗 **wǎn**) □ 妈妈做的汤真好喝。**Māma zuò de tāng zhēn hǎohē.** *The soup mom prepared is really delicious.*
喝汤 hē tāng eat soup

汤匙 tāngchí *n* tablespoon (把 **bǎ**)

汤圆 tāngyuán *n* stuffed dumpling made of glutinous rice

堂 táng I *n* **1** main room, hall (See 食堂 **shítáng**.) **2** relationship between cousins of the same paternal grandfather
堂兄弟 tángxiōngdì male children of one's father's brothers
II *measure wd* (for a period of lessons)
上午有三堂课 shàngwǔ yǒu sān táng kè three classes in the morning

膛 táng *n* chest

唐 táng *n* the Tang Dynasty (AD 618–907)
唐人街 tángrénjiē *n* Chinatown

塘 táng *n* dyke, embankment

糖 táng *n* sugar, candy (块 **kuài**) □ "你的咖啡里要放糖吗？""要，请放一块糖。"**"Nǐ de kāfēi li yào fàng táng ma?" "Yào, qǐng fàng yí kuài táng."** *"Do you want sugar in your coffee?" "Yes, a lump of sugar, please."*
糖果 tángguǒ *n* candy, sweets □ 小孩儿一般都喜欢吃糖果。**Xiǎo háir yìbān dòu xǐhuan chī tángguǒ.** *Children usually love candy.*

倘 tǎng *conj* if, in case
倘若 tǎngruò if, in case

躺 tǎng *v* lie □ 她喜欢躺在床上看书。**Tā xǐhuan tǎng zài chuángshang kànshū.** *She likes to lie on the bed and read.* □ 你既然醒了，就起床吧，别躺在床上了。**Nǐ jìrán xǐngle, jiù qǐchuáng ba, bié tǎng zài chuángshang le.** *Now that you've awake, you should get up. Don't lie in bed.*

趟 tàng *measure wd* (for trips) □ 我去了两趟，都没找到他。**Wǒ qùle liǎng tàng, dōu méi zhǎodao tā.** *I made two trips but did not find him.*

烫 tàng Trad 燙 *adj* boiling hot, scalding hot, burning hot □ 这碗汤太烫了，没法喝。**Zhè wǎn tāng tài tàng le, méifǎ hē.** *This bowl of soup is too hot to eat.*

涛 tāo *n* big waves

滔 tāo *v* inundate, flood
滔滔不绝 tāotāo bùjué *adj* talking on and on in a flow of eloquence

掏 tāo *v* pull out, draw out
掏耳朵 tāo ěrduo pick one's ears

陶 táo *n* pottery
陶瓷 táocí [comp: 陶 pottery + 瓷 porcelain] *n* pottery and porcelain, ceramics

萄 táo *n* as in 葡萄 **pútao**

淘 táo *v* wash in a pan or basket
淘金 táojīn pan for gold
淘气 táoqì *adj* naughty, mischievous
淘气鬼 táoqìguǐ a naughty child, an imp
淘汰 táotài *v* eliminate through competition

淘汰赛 táotàisài (in sports) elimination series

桃 táo *n* peach
桃花 táohuā peach blossom
桃树 táoshù peach tree
桃子 táozi peach (只 **zhī**)

逃 táo *v* **1** flee, run away (from danger, punishment, etc.) □ 警察来的时候，强盗已经逃走了。**Jǐngchá lái de shíhou, qiángdào yǐjīng táozǒu le.** *By the time the policemen arrived, the robbers had fled.* **2** evade, escape
逃避 táobì [comp: 逃 flee + 避 avoid] *v* evade, shirk
逃避责任 táobì zérèn evade responsibility
逃跑 táopǎo [comp: 逃 flea + 跑 run] *v* run way, take flight
逃税 táoshuì [v+obj: 逃 run away from + 税 taxes] **I** *v* evade paying taxes □ 有不少公司冒险逃税。**Yǒu bùshǎo gōngsī màoxiǎn táoshuì.** *Some companies risk evading tax payments.* **II** *n* tax evasion □ 逃税是要进监狱的。**Táoshuì shì yào jìn jiānyù de.** *Tax evasion is punishable by imprisonment.*
逃学 táoxué [v+obj: 逃 flea + 学 school] *v* play truant
逃走 táozǒu Same as 逃跑 **táopǎo**

讨 tǎo Trad 討 *v* ask for, demand
讨好 tǎohǎo *v* **1** fawn on, toady to **2** be rewarded with good results
吃力不讨好 chīlì bù tǎohǎo work hard only to get negative results, do a thankless job
讨价还价 tǎojià huánjià *v* haggle over prices, bargain
讨论 tǎolùn [comp: 讨 explore + 论 discuss] **I** *v* discuss, talk over □ 老师们在讨论明年的工作。**Lǎoshīmen zài tǎolùn míngnián de gōngzuò.** *The teachers are discussing next year's work.* □ 我们要讨论一下才能作出决定。**Wǒmen yào tǎolùn yíxià cái néng zuòchū juédìng.** *We must have a discussion before we can make a decision.* **II** *n* discussion (次 **cì**) □ 这次讨论对我们很有用。**Zhè cì tǎolùn duì wǒmen hěn yǒuyòng.** *This discussion is useful to us.*
讨厌 tǎoyàn [v+obj: 讨 ask for + 厌 boredom, vexation] **I** *adj* vexing, disgusting □ 这种电视广告讨厌得很。**Zhè zhǒng diànshì guǎnggào tǎoyàn de hěn.** *This kind of TV commercial is disgusting.* □ 我讨厌连续下雨的天气。**Wǒ tǎoyàn liánxù xiàyǔ de tiānqì.** *I hate incessant rain.*
讨债 tǎozhài [v+obj: 讨 ask for + 债 debt] *v* press for repayment of a debt

套 tào *measure wd* set, suit, suite (for a collection of things)
一套衣服 yí tào yīfu a suit of clothes
两套家具 liǎng tào jiājù two sets of furniture

特 tè *adv* particularly, especially
特别 tèbié [comp: 特 special + 别 other, unusual] **I** *adj* special □ 他病得很重，住在特别病房。**Tā bìng de hěn zhòng, zhù zài tèbié bìngfáng.** *He's seriously ill and stays in the special ward.* **II** *adv* especially □ 我特别喜欢吃新西兰的苹果。**Wǒ tèbié xǐhuan chī Xīnxīlán de píngguǒ.** *I especially like New Zealand apples.*
特别行政区 tèbié xíngzhèngqū special administrative region
特产 tèchǎn [modif: 特 special + 产 product, produce] *n* special local product or produce
特此 tècǐ *adv* hereby

特点 tèdiǎn [modif: 特 special + 点 point] *n* special features, characteristics □ 中国文化有什么特点? **Zhōngguó wénhuà yǒu shénme tèdiǎn?** *What are the special features of Chinese culture?*

特定 tèdìng [comp: 特 special + 定 definite] *adj* specific, specified, special

特定的条件 tèdìngde tiáojiàn special condition

特快 tèkuài [modif: 特 special + 快 fast] *adj* express

特快火车 tèkuài huǒchē express train

特快专递 tèkuài zhuān dì express delivery

特区 tèqū *n* special zone

特权 tèquán [modif: 特 special + 权 rights] *n* privilege

特色 tèsè [modif: 特 special + 色 color] *n* distinguishing feature

特殊 tèshū [comp: 特 special + 殊 different] *adj* special, unusual, exceptional □ 你只有在特殊情况下才能采取这一措施。**Nǐ zhǐyǒu zài tèshū qíngkuàng xia cái néng cǎiqǔ zhè yí cuòshī.** *Only under special circumstances can you take this step.* □ 每个公民都必须遵守法律，没有人可以特殊。**Měi ge gōngmín dōu bìxū zūnshǒu fǎlǜ, méiyǒu rén kěyǐ tèshū.** *Every citizen must obey the law and nobody can be an exception.*

特殊教育 tèshū jiàoyù special education

特务 tèwù [modif: 特 special + 务 task] *n* special agent, spy

特意 tèyì [modif: 特 special + 意 intendtion] *adv* for a special purpose, specially

特征 tèzhēng [modif: 特 special + 征 feature] *n* salient feature

藤 téng *n* vine, rattan

藤椅 téngyǐ rattan chair

葡萄藤 pútaoténg grape vine

腾 téng *v* gallop, jump

疼 téng *v* **1** ache, hurt

头疼 tóu téng headache, have a headache □ 我头疼，得躺一会儿。**Wǒ tóu téng, děi tǎng yíhuìr.** *I have a headache. I have to lie down for a while.* **2** love dearly, dote on □ 我小时候，我奶奶可疼我了。**Wǒ xiǎoshíhou, wǒ nǎinai kě téng wǒ le.** *When I was a child, my granny really doted on me dearly.*

NOTE: 疼 **téng** in the sense of *ache, hurt* is a colloquial word. You can use 痛 **tòng** instead of 疼 **téng** to mean *ache, hurt.*

疼痛 téngtòng [comp: 疼 pain + 痛 pain] *adj* pain, ache, soreness

全身疼痛 quánshēn téngtòng aches and pains all over

梯 tī *n* ladder, steps (See 电梯 **diàntī**, 楼梯 **lóutī**.)

踢 tī *v* kick

踢球 tī qiú play soccer □ 一些男孩儿在操场上踢球。**Yìxiē nánháir zài cāochǎng shang tīqiú.** *Some boys are playing soccer on the sports ground.*

踢足球 tī zúqiú play soccer

提 tí *v* **1** carry in the hand (with the arm down) □ 我可以提这个小皮箱上飞机吗? **Wǒ kěyǐ tí zhège xiǎo píxiāng shàng fēijī ma?** *Can I carry this small bag on board the plane?* **2** mention, raise □ 你见到他

的时候，别提这件事。**Nǐ jiàndao tā de shíhou, bié tí zhè jiàn shì.** *Don't mention this matter when you see him.*

提建议 tí jiànyì put forward a proposal, make a suggestion

提问题 tí wèntí raise a question

提案 tí'àn *n* proposal (份 **fèn**)

提拔 tíbá *v* promote (to a higher position)

提拔为部门经理 tíbá wéi bùmén jīnglǐ be promoted to branch manager

提包 tíbāo *n* handbag, shopping bag (只 **zhī**)

提倡 tíchàng [comp: 提 put forward + 倡 advocate] *v* advocate, recommend □ 政府提倡一对夫妻只生一个孩子。**Zhèngfǔ tíchàng yí duì fūqī zhǐ shēng yí ge háizi.** *The government recommends that every couple have only one child.*

提纲 tígāng *n* outline

提高 tígāo [v+compl: 提 raise + 高 high] *v* raise, advance, improve □ 我要提高自己的中文水平。**Wǒ yào tígāo zìjǐ de Zhōngwén shuǐpíng.** *I want to raise my proficiency in Chinese.* □ 我们不断提高产品的质量。**Wǒmen búduàn tígāo chǎnpǐn de zhìliàng.** *We work constantly to improve the quality of our products.*

提供 tígōng [comp: 提 put forward + 供 supply] *v* provide, supply □ 我们提供售后服务。**Wǒmen tígōng shòuhòu fúwù.** *We provide after-sales service.* □ 这项研究为决定政策提供了有力的数据。**Zhè xiàng yánjiū wèi juédìng zhèngcè tígōngle yǒulì de shùjù.** *This research provided solid data for policy-making.*

提交 tíjiāo [comp: 提 put forward to + 交 submit] *v* submit to, refer to

提炼 tíliàn *v* extract and purify, refine

提名 tímíng [v+obj: 提 put forward + 名 name] *v* nominate (for a/an position/election)

提前 tíqián [v+obj: 提 put forward + 前 forward] *v* put ahead of schedule, advance, bring forward □ 长途汽车提前半小时到达。**Chángtú qìchē tíqián bàn xiǎoshí dàodá.** *The coach arrived half an hour ahead of the schedule.* □ 你知道吗? 考试提前两天举行。**Nǐ zhīdào ma? Kǎoshì tíqián liǎng tiān jǔxíng.** *Do you know that the examination will be held two days earlier?*

提取 tíqǔ *v* withdraw, collect

提取存款 tíqǔ cúnkuǎn withdraw money from a bank account

提取行李 tíqǔ xíngli collect luggage

提升 tíshēng *v* promote (to a higher position)

提示 tíshì *v* hint, tip □ 给我一个提示, 好吗? **Gěi wǒ yí ge tíshì, hǎoma?** *Can you give me a hint?*

提问 tíwèn *v* put questions to

提醒 tíxǐng *v* remind, call attention to

提要 tíyào *n* abstract, synopsis

提议 tíyì **I** *v* propose □ 我提议为主人的健康干杯! **Wǒ tíyì wéi zhǔrén de jiànkāng gānbēi!** *May I propose a toast to the health of our host?* **II** *n* proposal

提早 tízǎo *v* Same as 提前 **tíqián**

题 tí Trad 題 *n* **1** topic, title **2** question, problem

题材 tícái [comp: 题 topic + 材 material] *n* subject matter, theme

题目 tímù *n* **1** question for an examination, school exercises, etc. (道 **dào**) □ 这次测验一共有十道题目。**Zhè cì cèyàn yígòng yǒu shí dào tímù.** *There will be ten questions in this test.* □ 这道数学题目太难了，我

不会做。**Zhè dào shùxué tímù tài nán le, wǒ bú huì zuò.** *This math problem is too difficult for me.* **2** title, subject □ 他要给文章取一个好题目。**Tā yào gěi wénzhāng qǔ yí ge hǎo tímù.** *He will give his essay a good title.*

蒂 **tí** *n* hoof

体 **tǐ** Trad 體 **I** *n* **1** body **2** substance **II** *v* personally do or experience

体操 **tǐcāo** *n* gymnastics

体会 **tǐhuì** **I** *v* learn, realize, gain intimate knowledge through personal experience □ 他当了一年爸爸，体会到当父母是多么不容易。**Tā dāngle yì nián bàba, tǐhuì dào dāng fùmǔ shì duōme bù róngyì.** *After being a father for a year, he realized how difficult parenting was.* **II** *n* personal understanding □ 请你谈谈你在中国工作的体会。**Qǐng nǐ tántan nǐ zài Zhōngguó gōngzuò de tǐhuì.** *Please tell us what you have learned from working in China.*

体积 **tǐjī** *n* volume (mathematics) □ 这个箱子体积不大，为什么这么重？**Zhège xiāngzi tǐjī bú dà, wèishénme zhème zhòng?** *This box is not big. Why is it so heavy?*

体力 **tǐlì** [modif: 体 physical + 力 strength] *n* physical strength

体谅 **tǐliàng** *v* show understanding towards, be sympathetic to, make allowance for
体谅他人的难处 **tǐliang tārén de nánchu** understand and sympathize with other people's difficulties, empathize

体面 **tǐmiàn** **I** *adj* respectable, decent **II** *n* dignity, face

体贴 **tǐtiē** *v* give every consideration to, give loving care to

体温 **tǐwēn** [modif: 体 body + 温 temperature] *n* body temperature, temperature

体现 **tǐxiàn** *v* give expression to, embody

体验 **tǐyàn** **I** *n* personal experience **II** *v* learn through one's personal experience

体育 **tǐyù** [modif: 体 physical + 育 education] *n* physical education, sports □ 体育和学习，哪个更重要？**Tǐyù hé xuéxí, nǎge gèng zhòngyào?** *Sports or study, which is more important?*

体育场 **tǐyùchǎng** [modif: 体育 sports + 场 ground] *n* stadium, sports field □ 体育场里正在举行一场精彩的足球比赛。**Tǐyùchǎng li zhèngzài jǔxíng yì chǎng jīngcǎi de zúqiú bǐsài.** *A thrilling football match is going on in the stadium.*

体育馆 **tǐyùguǎn** [modif: 体育 sports + 馆 building] *n* gymnasium □ 这个体育馆有多少座位？**Zhège tǐyùguǎn yǒu duōshǎo zuòwèi?** *How many seats are there in this gymnasium?*

体育课 **tǐyù kè** *n* physical education (PE) lesson □ 今天下午上体育课，我不能穿皮鞋。**Jīntiān xiàwǔ shàng tǐyù kè, wǒ bù néng chuān píxié.** *I'm having a PE class this afternoon, so I can't wear leather shoes today.*

体制 **tǐzhì** *n* (organizational) system, structure

体质 **tǐzhì** [modif: 体 physical + 质 nature] *n* physique, constitution

体重 **tǐzhòng** *n* (body) weight □ 我体重一百公斤。**Wǒ tǐzhòng yìbǎi gōngjīn.** *I weigh 100 kilograms.*

易 **tì** *adj* be on the alert (See 警惕 jǐngtì)

剃 **tì** *v* shave
剃胡子 **tì húzi** shave one's beard

涕 **tì** *n* **1** tears **2** snivel (See 鼻涕 bíti)

屉 **tì** *n* drawer (See 抽屉 chōutì)

替 **tì** *v* **1** replace, substitute □ 万一他生病了, 谁来替他呢？**Wànyī tā shēngbìng le, shuí lái tì tā ne?** *If he falls ill, who will replace him?* **2** Same as 给 gěi *prep*

替代 **tìdài** [comp: 替 substitute + 代 replace] *v* substitute for, replace

替换 **tìhuàn** [comp: 替 substitute + 换 change] *v* replace, displace

天 **tiān** *n* **1** sky, heaven □ 秋天, 天特别蓝。**Qiūtiān, tiān tèbié lán.** *In autumn, the sky is especially blue.* **2** day □ 我在朋友家住了三天。**Wǒ zài péngyou jiā zhùle sān tiān.** *I stayed with my friend for three days.* □ 这位老人下雨天一般不出去。**Zhè wèi lǎorén xià yǔ tiān yìbān bù chūqu.** *This old man normally does not go out on rainy days.* **3** weather □ 农民还是靠天吃饭。**Nóngmín háishi kào tiān chīfàn.** *Farmers still depend on the weather to make a living.*
老天爷 **Lǎotiānyé** Heavens (a colloquial term that denotes "God" or "Nature") □ 老天爷再不下雨, 就要闹灾了。**Lǎotiānyé zài bú xià yǔ jiù yào nào zāi le.** *If it does not rain, there'll be disaster.*

天才 **tiāncái** [modif: 天 heavenly + 才 talent] *n* genius □ 他们的儿子非常聪明，但是并不是天才。**Tāmen de érzi fēicháng cōngming, dànshì bìng bù shì tiāncái.** *Their son is very smart, but he isn't a genius.*

天地 **tiāndì** [comp: 天 heaven + 地 earth] *n* field of activity, scope of operation

天空 **tiānkōng** [comp: 天 sky + 空 empty] *n* sky

天气 **tiānqì** [comp: 天 weather + 气 weather] *n* weather □ 天气变化很大。**Tiānqì biànhuà hěn dà.** *The weather changes dramatically.* □ 明天的天气怎么样？**Míngtiān de tiānqì zěnmeyàng?** *How will the weather be tomorrow?*

天然 **tiānrán** *adj* natural
天然气 **tiānránqì** natural gas

天色 **tiānsè** *n* time of the day □ 天色还早。**Tiānsè hái zǎo.** *It's still early.*

天上 **tiānshang** *n* in the sky

天生 **tiānshēng** *adj* inherent, natural

天堂 **tiāntáng** [modif: 天 heaven + 堂 hall] *n* paradise

天天 **tiāntiān** *n* every day
天天向上 **tiāntiān xiàngshàng** make progress every day

天文 **tiānwén** *n* astronomy
天文台 **tiānwéntái** astronomical observatory
天文学家 **tiānwénxuéjiā** astronomer

天下 **tiān xià** *n* under heaven, in the world, on earth

天线 **tiānxiàn** *n* antenna

天知道! **Tiān zhīdào!** *idiom* Only God knows!

天真 **tiānzhēn** [comp: 天 natural + 真 genuine] *adj* **1** simple and unaffected, ingenuous □ 和天真的孩子说话, 是一种享受。**Hé tiānzhēn de háizi shuōhuà, shì yì zhǒng xiǎngshòu.** *Talking with innocent children is an enjoyment.* **2** naïve, gullible □ 你怎么会相信这种广告。太天真了! **Nǐ zěnme huì xiāngxìn zhè zhǒng**

guǎnggào? Tài tiānzhēn le! *How could you believe such advertisements? You're too naïve!*

天主教 **tiānzhǔjiào** *n* the Catholic Church, Catholicism

  天主教徒 Tiānzhǔjiàotú member of the Catholic Church, Catholic

添 **tiān** *v* add □ 你这么忙，我不想给你添麻烦。**Nǐ zhème máng, wǒ bù xiǎng gěi nǐ tiān máfan.** *You're so busy. I don't want to trouble you.*

田 **tián** *n* farmland (especially paddy fields), fields □ 他在田里干活。**Tā zài tián li gànhuó.** *He was working in the fields.*

  种田 zhòngtián grow crops, farm □ 在中国光靠种田，很难富。**Zài Zhōngguó guāng kào zhòngtián, hěn nán fù.** *In China, it's difficult to get rich simply by growing crops.*

田地 **tiándì** [comp: 田 farmland + 地 land] *n* farmland, field

田野 **tiányě** [comp: 田 fields, farmland + 野 old country] *n* farmland and open country □ 城里人有时候喜欢到田野走走。**Chénglǐrén yǒushíhou xǐhuan dào tiányě zǒuzǒu.** *City people like to take an occasional stroll in the open country.*

填 **tián** *v* fill in (a form, blanks as in an exercise) □ 进入一个国家要填表，离开一个国家也要填表。**Jìnrù yí ge guójiā yào tián biǎo, líkāi yí ge guójiā yě yào tián biǎo.** *To enter a country you need to fill in a form, and to leave a country you need to fill in a form as well.*

填补 **tiánbǔ** [comp: 填 fill in + 补 patch up] *v* fill, fill up

填写 **tiánxiě** [comp: 填 fill in + 写 write] *v* fill out (a document)

挑 **tiāo** *v* take one's pick, choose, select □ 商店里这么多鞋子，你还挑不到一双喜欢的？**Shāngdiàn li zhème duō xiézi, nǐ hái tiāo bu dào yì shuāng xǐhuan de?** *There are so many shoes in the store, and you still can't choose a pair you like?*

  东挑西拣 dōng-tiāo-xī-jiǎn choose this and pick that, spend a long time choosing, be very choosy

挑选 **tiāoxuǎn** [comp: 挑 take one's pick + 选 select] *v* select □ 董事会要从经理中挑选出一名总经理。**Dǒngshìhuì yào cóng jīnglǐ zhong tiāoxuǎnchu yì míng zǒngjīnglǐ.** *The board of directors will select a chief executive officer from the executives.* □ 有时候可以挑选的东西太多，很难决定。**Yǒushíhou kěyǐ tiāoxuǎn de dōngxi tài duō, hěn nán juédìng.** *Sometimes when there are too many things to choose from, it's difficult to decide.*

条 **tiáo** Trad 條 **I** *measure wd* (for things with a long, narrow shape)

  一条河 yì tiáo hé a river

  两条鱼 liǎng tiáo yú two fish

II *n* 1 strip 2 item, article

条件 **tiáojiàn** [comp: 条 item, piece + 件 item, piece] *n* 1 condition □ 这个地区的自然条件不好。**Zhège dìqū de zìrán tiáojiàn bù hǎo.** *The natural conditions of this region are rather poor.*

  生活条件 shēnghuó tiáojiàn living conditions □ 他们那里的生活条件比较差。**Tāmen nàlǐ de shēnghuó tiáojiàn bǐjiào chà.** *Their living conditions are rather poor.*

工作条件 gōngzuò tiáojiàn working conditions □ 工人们要求改善工作条件。**Gōngrénmen yāoqiú gǎishàn gōngzuò tiáojiàn.** *Workers demand that their working conditions be improved.*

2 requirement, prerequisite □ 她找对象的条件非常高。**Tā zhǎo duìxiàng de tiáojiàn fēicháng gāo.** *She has very high requirements of a fiancé.* □ 对方的条件太高，我们无法合作。**Duìfāng de tiáojiàn tài gāo, wǒmen wúfǎ hézuò.** *The other party's requirements are too high for us to work with them.* □ 参加比赛有一个条件，参加比赛的人必须小于十八岁。**Cānjiā bǐsài yǒu yí ge tiáojiàn, cānjiā bǐsài de rén bìxū xiǎoyú shíbā suì.** *There is a requirement for participation in the competition: the participant must be under eighteen years.*

条款 **tiáokuǎn** *n* clause (in a contract, an agreement etc.) (项 **xiàng**)

条理 **tiáolǐ** *n* orderliness

  有条理 yǒu tiáolǐ well-organized

条例 **tiáolì** *n* regulation, rule

条文 **tiáowén** *n* clause, article, item

条约 **tiáoyuē** [comp: 条 article (of a treaty) + 约 agreement] *n* treaty, pact (份 **fèn**) □ 两国将签订条约，以加强合作。**Liǎng guó jiāng qiāndìng tiáoyuē, yǐ jiāqiáng hézuò.** *The two countries will sign a treaty in order to strengthen cooperation.*

条子 **tiáozi** *n* informal note (张 **zhāng**)

  给他留一张条子 gěi tā liú yì zhāng tiáozi leave a brief note for him

调 **tiáo** Trad 調 *v* 1 adjust 2 mediate 3 provoke, tease

调和 **tiáohé** *v* 1 mediate, reconcile 2 compromise

调剂 **tiáojì** *v* adjust, regulate

调节 **tiáojié** *v* regulate, moderate

  调节器 tiáojiéqì regulator, conditioner

调解 **tiáojiě** [comp: 调 adjust + 解 solve] *v* mediate, make peace

  调解纠纷 tiáojiě jiūfēn mediate disputes

调皮 **tiáopí** *adj* naughty, mischievous

调整 **tiáozhěng** [comp: 调 adjust + 整 rectify] *v* adjust, rectify □ 教育部打算调整中小学的师生比例。**Jiàoyùbù dǎsuàn tiáozhěng zhōng-xiǎoxué de shīshēng bǐlì.** *The Ministry of Education plans to adjust the teacher-student ratio in schools.*

挑 **tiāo** *v* 1 poke, pick up 2 stir up, instigate

挑拨 **tiǎobō** [comp: 挑 poke + 拨 stir] *v* instigate, sow discord

  挑拨同事之间的关系 tiǎobō tóngshì zhījiān de guānxi sow discord among colleagues

挑衅 **tiǎoxìn** **I** *v* provoke **II** *n* provocation

  故意挑衅 gùyì tiǎoxìn deliberate provocation

挑战 **tiǎozhàn** *v* challenge to battle, challenge to a contest, throw down the gauntlet

跳 **tiào** *v* jump, leap, hop □ 他跳得很高，所以篮球打得好。**Tā tiào de hěn gāo, suǒyǐ lánqiú dǎ de hǎo.** *He can jump high, so he plays basketball well.*

跳动 **tiàodòng** [comp: 跳 jump + 动 move] *v* move up and down, beat

跳高 **tiào gāo** *n* high jump

  撑杆跳高 chēnggǎn tiàogāo pole vault, pole jump

跳绳 **tiào shéng** *n* rope-skipping, rope-jumping

跳水 **tiào shuǐ** *n* diving

跳板跳水 tiàobǎn tiàoshuǐ springboard diving

跳台跳水 tiàotái tiàoshuǐ platform diving

跳远 tiào yuǎn *n* long jump

三级跳远 sānjí tiàoyuǎn hop, step and jump, triple jump

跳舞 tiàowǔ [comp: 跳 jump + 舞 dance] *v* dance □ 我可以请您跳舞吗? **Wǒ kěyǐ qǐng nín tiàowǔ ma?** *May I have a dance with you?* □ 她跳舞跳得很美。 **Tā tiàowǔ tiào de hěn měi.** *She dances beautifully.*

跳跃 tiàoyuè *v* jump, leap

跳蚤 tiàozǎo *n* flea (只 zhī)

贴 tiē Trad 貼 *v* paste, stick □ 他回到办公室，发现门上贴了一张便条。 **Tā huídào bàngōngshì, fāxiàn mén shang tiēle yì zhāng biàntiáo.** *When he came back to the office he found a note stuck on the door.*

帖 tiě *n* invitation card

请帖 qǐngtiě invitation card

铁 tiě Trad 鐵 *n* iron □ 花园里的那条长椅是铁做的。 **Huāyuán li de nà tiáo chángyǐ shì tiě zuò de.** *The bench in the garden is made of iron.*

铁道 tiědào *n* Same as 铁路 tiělù

铁路 tiělù [modif: 铁 iron + 路 road] *n* railway (条 tiáo) □ 这条铁路伸进大山脉。 **Zhè tiáo tiělù shēnjìn dà shānmài.** *This railway extends all the way to the great mountain range.*

厅 tīng Trad 廳 *n* hall (See 餐厅 cāntīng.)

听 tīng Trad 聽 *v* 1 listen □ 他每天早上都听广播。 **Tā měi tiān zǎoshang dōu tīng guǎngbō.** *He listens to the radio early every morning.*

听见 tīngjiàn hear □ 我听见有人在花园里叫我。 **Wǒ tīngjiàn yǒu rén zài huāyuán li jiào wǒ.** *I heard somebody calling me in the garden.*

2 heed, obey □ 你不听他的话，会后悔的。 **Nǐ bù tīng tā de huà, huì hòuhuǐ de.** *You will be sorry if you don't heed his advice (or warning).*

听话 tīnghuà *v* heed, be obedient □ 中国家长喜欢听话的孩子。 **Zhōngguó jiāzhǎng xǐhuan tīnghuà de háizi.** *Chinese parents like obedient children.*

听讲 tīngjiǎng *v* listen to a talk (or lecture)

听取 tīngqǔ *v* hear (one's subordinate's report, complaint, etc.)

听说 tīngshuō *v* hear of, it is said □ 听说张先生一家搬走了。 **Tīngshuō Zhāng xiānsheng yìjiā bānzǒu le.** *I've heard that Mr Zhang's family has moved.*

听写 tīngxiě *n* dictation, do dictation

听众 tīngzhòng [modif: 听 listen + 众 crowd] *n* audience (of a radio, a concert, etc.)

NOTE: See note on 观众 guānzhòng.

亭 tíng *n* pavilion, kiosk

亭子 tíngzi pavilion, kiosk

停 tíng *v* stop, park (a vehicle) □ 路上车辆太多了，我们停停开开，花了一个小时才回到家。 **Lùshang chēliàng tài duō le, wǒmen tíng tíng kāi kāi, huāle yí ge xiǎoshí cái huídào jiā.** *Traffic was heavy. We were continually stopping and it took us one hour to arrive home.* □ 我可以把车停在这里吗? **Wǒ kěyǐ ba qìchē tíng zai zhèlǐ ma?** *May I park my car here?*

停下来 tíng xiàlai come to a stop □ 前面是红灯，车子要停下来。 **Qiánmiàn shì hóngdēng, chēzi yào tíng**

xiàlai. *It's a red light in front. The car must stop.*

2 stay over

停泊 tíngbó *v* (of ships) lie at anchor, anchor

停车 tíngchē [v+obj: 停 park + 车 car] *v* stop a car, park a car

停车场 tíngchēchǎng parking lot, car park

停顿 tíngdùn *v* pause

停留 tíngliú *v* stop and stay for a short while, stop over

停职 tíngzhí [v+obj: 停 halt + 职 job] *v* suspend from one's duties (as a disciplinary action)

停止 tíngzhǐ [comp: 停 stop + 止 end] *v* stop, cease □ 那家公司停止营业了，那他们欠我们的钱怎么办呢? **Nà jiā gōngsī tíngzhǐ yíngyè le, nà tāmen qiàn wǒmen de qián zěnme bàn ne?** *That company has gone out of business. Then what about the money they owe us?* □ 请你们立即停止这种影响他人的行为。 **Qǐng nǐmen lìjí tíngzhǐ zhè zhǒng yǐngxiǎng tārén de xíngwéi.** *Stop such disruptive behavior immediately, please.*

停滞 tíngzhì *v* stagnate, be at a standstill

庭 tíng *n* front courtyard

庭院 tíngyuàn *n* courtyard and garden

艇 tǐng *n* light boat (艘 sōu)

救生艇 jiùshēngtǐng lifeboat

挺 tǐng I *adv* very □ 她学习挺认真。 **Tā xuéxí tǐng rènzhēn.** *She studies conscientiously.* II *adj* tall, upright, erect

NOTE: 挺 tǐng and 很 hěn share the same meaning, but 挺 tǐng is a colloquial word.

挺拔 tǐngbá *adj* tall and straight

挺立 tǐnglì *v* stand upright

通 tōng I *v* 1 (of roads, railways) lead to, go to □ 这条路通到哪里? **Zhè tiáo lù tōngdào nǎlǐ?** *Where does this road lead?* □ 条条大路通罗马。 **Tiáotiáo dàlù tōng Luómǎ.** *All roads lead to Rome.* 2 go through without blockage □ 下水道不通了。 **Xiàshuǐdào bùtōng le.** *The sewer is blocked up.* 3 understand, comprehend 4 notify, give notice II *adj* 1 (of language) grammatical, logical □ 这句话不通，但是我说不出错在哪里。 **Zhè jù huà bù tōng, dànshì wǒ shuō bu chū cuò zài nǎlǐ.** *This sentence is not quite right, but I can't identify where the mistake is.* 2 in general use

通报 tōngbào I *v* (of government offices) circulate a notice II *n* circular, bulletin

通常 tōngcháng *adj* general, usual

通道 tōngdào *n* thoroughfare, passageway

通风 tōngfēng *n* ventilation

通风口 tōngfēngkǒu ventilation opening

通风系统 tōngfēng xì tǒng ventilation system

通告 tōnggào I *v* give public notice, announce II *n* public notice, announcement

通过 tōngguò [comp: 通 go through + 过 pass] I *v* pass through □ 从我家到机场，要通过城里。 **Cóng wǒ jiā dào jīchǎng, yào tōngguò chénglǐ.** *Going from my home to the airport, one has to pass through the city center.* II *prep* through, as a result of □ 通过这次访问，我更了解中国了。 **Tōngguò zhè cì fǎngwèn, wǒ gèng liǎojiě Zhōngguó le.** *As a result of this visit, I understand China better.*

通航 **tōngháng** *v* be open to navigation or air traffic

通红 **tōnghóng** *adj* very red

通货膨胀 **tōnghuò péngzhàng** *n* inflation 抑制通货膨胀 yìzhì tōnghuò péngzhàng check inflation

通奸 **tōngjiān** *v* commit adultery

通商 **tōngshāng** *v* (of countries) have trade relations

通顺 **tōngshùn** *adj* (of writing) coherent and smooth

通俗 **tōngsú** *adj* easily understood and accepted by common folks, popular 通俗读物 tōngsúdúwù light reading, popular literature

通信 **tōngxìn** *v* exchange letters with, correspond

通行 **tōngxíng** *v* pass through 通行证 tōngxíngzhèng pass, permit

通讯 **tōngxùn** [v+obj: 通 communicate + 讯 message] *n* communication □ 这几年通讯技术迅速发展, 传真、电子邮件、手机等越来越普及。 **Zhè jǐ nián tōngxùn jìshù xùnsù fāzhǎn, chuánzhēn, diànzǐ yóujiàn, shǒujī děng yuèlaiyuè pǔjí.** *In recent years communication technology has seen rapid development. Fax, e-mail, cell phones and so on are becoming more and more widely used.*

通讯社 **tōngxùn shè** *n* news service

通用 **tōngyòng** *v* be in general use

通知 **tōngzhī** I *v* notify, inform □ 科长通知我们, 明天上午开会。 **Kēzhǎng tōngzhī wǒmen, míngtiān shàngwǔ kāihuì.** *The section head has informed us that there will be a meeting tomorrow morning.* □ 代表团什么时候来, 请及时通知。 **Dàibiǎotuán shénme shíhou lái, qǐng jíshí tōngzhī.** *Please let us know promptly when the delegation will come.* II *n* notice □ 市政府在报上发了一个通知。 **Shì zhèngfǔ zài bào shang fāle yí ge tōngzhī.** *The city government has published a notice in the paper.*

童 **tóng** *n* child
童年 **tóngnián** *n* childhood

同 **tóng** I *adv* together, in common II *prep* with, along with □ 同你在一起, 我感到很愉快。 **Tóng nǐ zài yìqǐ, wǒ gǎndao hěn yúkuài.** *I find it a pleasure to be with you.* □ 我们正在同那家公司商量合办食品加工厂的计划。 **Wǒmen zhèngzài tóng nà jiā gōngsī shāngliang hébàn shípǐn jiāgōngchǎng de jìhuà.** *We are discussing a plan with that company to open a food-processing plant.* III *adj* same, alike IV *conj* and □ 这件事已经分别通知了教育局长同卫生局长。 **Zhè jiàn shì yǐjīng fēnbié tōngzhī le jiàoyù júzhǎng tóng wèishēng júzhǎng.** *The director of the education bureau and the director of the public health bureau respectively have been informed of this matter.*

同伴 **tóngbàn** *n* companion

同胞 **tongbao** *n* fellow countryman, compatriot

同步 **tóngbù** [modif: 同 same + 步 steps] *adj* at the same time, synchronic, simultaneous 同步卫星 tóngbùwèixīng synchronous satellite

同等 **tóngděng** [modif: 同 same + 等 grade, degree] *adj* of the same rank (status, grade, etc.)

同行 **tóngháng** [modif: 同 same + 行 trade] *adj* of the same trade or occupation □ 同行是冤家。 **Tóngháng shì yuānjia.** *People of the same trade hate each other.*

同类 **tónglèi** [modif: 同 same + 类 kind] *adj* of the same category (kind)

同盟 **tóngméng** *n* alliance, league

同情 **tóngqíng** [modif: 同 same + 情 emotion] I *v* sympathize with □ 我很同情这位在交通事故中失去儿子的母亲。 **Wǒ hěn tóngqíng zhè wèi zài jiāotōng shìgù zhong shīqù érzi de mǔqin.** *I sympathize with the mother who lost her son in the traffic accident.* II *n* sympathy □ 他的痛苦经历, 引起了我的同情。 **Tā de tòngkǔ jīnglì, yǐnqǐle wǒ de tóngqíng.** *His painful experience aroused my sympathy.*

同时 **tóngshí** [modif: 同 same + 时 time] *adv* at the same time, simultaneously □ 我和她同时开始学中文。 **Wǒ hé tā tóngshí kāishǐ xué Zhōngwén.** *She and I began to learn Chinese at the same time.* □ 我再找找那本书, 同时希望你也回家找找。 **Wǒ zài zhǎozhǎo nà běn shū, tóngshí xīwàng nǐ yě huíjiā zhǎozhǎo.** *I'll go on looking for the book; at the same time, I hope you'll search for it at home.*

同事 **tóngshì** [modif: 同 same + 事 job] *n* colleague, co-worker □ 同事之间要建立合作关系。 **Tóng shì zhījiān yào jiànlì hézuò guānxi.** *Colleagues should build a cooperative relationship among themselves.*

同屋 **tóngwū** [modif: 同 same + 屋 room] *n* roommate, flatmate □ 他是我的同学, 也是我的同屋。 **Tā shì wǒ de tóngxué, yě shì wǒ de tóngwū.** *He is my classmate, and my roommate as well.*

同性恋 **tóngxìngliàn** [modif: 同 same + 性 gender + 恋 love] *n* 1 homosexuality, homosexual love 2 (a person) homosexual, gay, lesbian

同学 **tóngxué** [modif: 同 together + 学 study] *n* classmate, schoolmate □ 我的朋友大多是我的同学。 **Wǒ de péngyou dàduō shì wǒ de tóngxué.** *Most of my friends are my schoolmates.* 老同学 lǎotóngxué former schoolmate □ 他利用老同学的关系, 取得了那份合同。 **Tā lìyòng lǎotóngxué de guānxi, qǔdéle nà fèn hétóng.** *He got the contract through the connection of an old schoolmate.*

NOTE: In Chinese schools, teachers address students as 同学们 **tóngxuémen**, e.g. □ 同学们, 我们现在上课了。 **Tóngxuémen, wǒmen xiànzài shàngkè le.** *Class, we're starting class now.*

同样 **tóngyàng** [modif: 同 same + 样 way] *adj* same, similar □ 他和妻子有同样的爱好, 同样的理想。 **Tā hé qīzi yǒu tóngyàng de àihào, tóngyàng de lǐxiǎng** *He and his wife share the same hobby and the same dream.*

同一 **tóngyī** *adj* identical, same

同意 **tóngyì** [modif: 同 same + 意 opinion] *v* agree, approve (antonym 反对 **fǎnduì**) □ 我不同意你说的话。 **Wǒ bù tóngyì nǐ shuō de huà.** *I don't agree with what you said.* □ 我不反对你的计划, 但是不同意立即执行。 **Wǒ bù fǎnduì nǐ de jìhuà, dànshì bù tóngyì lìjí zhíxíng.** *I don't oppose your plan, but I don't agree to its immediate implementation.*

同志 **tóngzhì** [comp: 同 same + 志 aspiration] *n* comrade

NOTE: 同志 **tóngzhì** used to be the most common form of

address in China before 1980. Now it is seldom used. 同志 tóngzhì is almost never used between a Chinese and a foreigner. The common forms of address in China today are 先生 xiānsheng (to men) and 小姐 xiǎojiě (to women, especially young women). In some places 同志 tóngzhì has acquired the meaning for *a fellow homosexual*.

铜 **tóng** Trad 銅 *n* copper, bronze □ 铜是一种重要金属。**Tóng shì yì zhǒng zhòngyào jīnshǔ.** *Copper is an important metal.*

筒 **tǒng** *n* section of thick bamboo
竹筒 zhútǒng a thick bamboo tube

捅 **tǒng** *v* poke, stab

桶 **tǒng** *n* bucket, pail (只 zhī) □ 他提了一桶水去洗汽车。**Tā tíle yì tǒng shuǐ qù xǐ qìchē.** *He carried a bucket of water over to wash his car.*

统 **tǒng** Trad 統 *adv* together
统称 tǒngchēng *v* generally be known as
统筹 tǒngchóu *v* plan as a whole
统计 tǒngjì [modif: 统 together + 计 calculate] **I** *v* add up **II** *n* statistics
统一 tǒngyī **I** *v* unify, integrate □ 关于这个问题，我们需要统一认识。**Guānyú zhège wèntí, wǒmen xūyào tǒngyī rènshi.** *We need to reach a common understanding on this issue.* **II** *adj* unified □ 这些国家已经形成一个统一的市场。**Zhèxiē guójiā yǐjīng xíngchéng yí ge tǒngyī de shìchǎng.** *These countries have already formed a common market.*
统治 tǒngzhì [comp: 统 lead + 治 govern] *v* rule □ 这个党统治已经很多年了。**Zhège dǎng tǒngzhì yǐjīng hěn duō nián le.** *This party has ruled the country for many years.*
统治阶级 tǒngzhì jiējí ruling class

痛 **tòng** *v* Same as 疼 téng *v* 1
痛苦 tòngkǔ [comp: 痛 painful + 苦 bitter] *adj* painful, tortuous □ 他不想回忆那段痛苦的生活。**Tā bù xiǎng huíyì nà duàn tòngkǔ de shēnghuó.** *He does not want to recall that painful period of his life.*
痛快 tòngkuài [comp: 痛 to one's heart's content + 快 delight] *adj* overjoyed, very delighted □ 我在会上说了一直想说的话，心里很痛快。**Wǒ zài huìshang shuōle yìzhí xiǎng shuō de huà, xīnli hěn tòngkuai.** *At the meeting I said what I'd been wanting to say, and felt extremely pleased.* □ 上星期日我们玩得真痛快。**Shàng Xīngqīrì wǒmen wán de zhēn tòngkuai.** *We had a terrific time last Sunday.*

偷 **tōu** *v* steal, pilfer □ 我的钱包让人偷了! **Wǒ de qiánbāo ràng rén tōu le!** *My wallet's been stolen!* □ 在有些国家偷东西的人会被砍断手。**Zài yǒuxiē guójiā tōu dōngxi de rén huì bèi kǎnduàn shǒu.** *In some countries, those who steal have their hands chopped off.*
偷窃 tōuqiè *v* steal, pilfer
偷税 tōushuì [v+obj: 偷 steal + 税 tax] *v* evade taxes
偷偷 tōutōu *adv* stealthily, on the quiet □ 我看见一个人偷偷走进校长办公室。**Wǒ kànjiàn yí ge rén tōutōu zǒujìn xiàozhǎng bàngōngshì.** *I saw a figure walking stealthily into the principal's office. (→ I saw someone sneak into the principal's office.)* □ 孩子偷偷告诉我，他

哥哥就躲在门背后。**Háizi tōutōu gàosu wǒ, tā gēge jiù duǒ zài mén bèihòu.** *The child furtively told me that his brother was hiding behind the door.*

头 **tóu** Trad 頭 **I** *n* 1 the head □ 我头疼。**Wǒ tóu téng.** *My head aches. (→ I have a headache.)* 2 head, chief, leader □ 你们的头儿呢? 我要找他说话。**Nímen de tóur ne? Wǒ yào zhǎo tā shuōhuà.** *Who's your head? (or Who's in charge here?) I want to talk to him.* **II** *adj* first, first few □ 我刚来的头几个星期, 几乎天天下雨。**Wǒ gāng lái de tóu jǐge xīngqī, jīhū tiāntiān xiàyǔ.** *The first few weeks after I arrived, it rained almost every day.* **III** *measure wd* (for cattle or sheep)
一头牛 yì tóu niú a head of cattle (*or* buffalo/cow)
两头羊 liǎng tóu yáng two sheep
头发 tóufa [modif: 头 head + 发 hair] *n* hair (on the human head) (根 gēn) □ 爸爸的头发渐渐白了。**Bàba de tóufa jiànjiàn bái le.** *Daddy's hair is turning gray.*
头脑 tóunǎo [comp: 头 head + 脑 brain] *n* brains □ 她很有头脑。**Tā hěn yǒu tóunǎo.** *She's got plenty of brains.* □ 这个人头脑不清楚。**Zhè ge rén tóunǎo bù qīngchu.** *This guy is muddle-headed.*
头脑简单 tóunǎo jiǎndān simple-minded

投 **tóu** *v* 1 throw, toss 2 join
投标 tóubiāo *v* make a bid, lodge a tender
投产 tóuchǎn *v* go into production
投放 tóufàng [comp: 投 throw + 放 put] *v* 1 throw in, put in 2 put (goods, funds) on the market
投机¹ **tóujī** **I** *v* 1 engage in speculation
货币投机 huòbì tóujī currency speculation 2 be opportunistic **II** *adj* opportunistic
投机分子 tóujīfènzǐ opportunist
投机² **tóujī** *adj* agreeable, of the same mind
谈得很投机 tán de hěn tóujī have a most agreeable conversation
投票 tóupiào *v* cast a vote, vote
投入 tóurù [v+obj: 投 throw + 入 enter] *v* put into, invest □ 他们在孩子的教育上投入很多钱。**Tāmen zài háizi de jiàoyù shang tóurù hěn duō qián.** *They put lots of money into their children's education.*
投诉 tóusù **I** *v* complain formally **II** *n* formal complaint □ 公共汽车公司收到很多投诉, 说汽车不准时。**Gōnggòng qìchē gōngsī shōu dào hěn duō tóusù, shuō qìchē bù zhǔnshí.** *The bus company has received lots of complaints about the buses not being punctual.*
投降 tóuxiáng *v* surrender, capitulate
投掷 tóuzhì [comp: 投 throw + 掷 throw] *v* throw, hurl
投资 tóuzī [v+obj: 投 put + 资 capital] **I** *v* invest 投资在一家合资企业 tóu zī zài yì jiā hézī qǐyè invest in a joint venture **II** *n* investment
投资的回报 tóuzī de huíbào return on an investment

透 **tòu** **I** *v* penetrate, pass through □ 月光透进房间。**Yuèguāng tòujìn fángjiān.** *Moonlight came into the room.* **II** *adj* thorough □ 王老师把这个语法问题讲得很透。**Wáng lǎoshī bǎ zhège yǔfǎ wèntí jiǎng de hěn tòu.** *Teacher Wang explained this grammar point thoroughly.*
透明 **tòumíng** [comp: 透 thorough + 明 clear, bright] *adj* transparent
透明度 tòumíngdù transparency

凸 **tū** *adj* protruding (antonym 凹 **āo**)

秃 **tū** *adj* bald, bare

突 1 **tū** *adj* protruding

突出 **tūchū** [comp: 突 protrude + 出 out] **I** *v* give prominence, highlight, emphasize □ 他在这篇文章中突出了市场调查的重要性。**Tā zài zhè piān wénzhāng zhong tūchūle shìchǎng diàochá de zhòngyàoxìng.** *In this article he emphasizes the importance of market research.* **II** *adj* prominent, conspicuous □ 火车上只有他一个外国人，显得很突出。**Huǒchē shang zhǐyǒu tā yí ge wàiguórén, xiǎnde hěn tūchū.** *He is the only foreigner on the train and is very conspicuous.*

突 2 **tū** *adv* suddenly, unexpectedly

突击 **tūjī** [modif: 突 sudden + 击 attack] **I** *n* sudden attack **II** *v* make a sudden attack

突破 **tūpò** [modif: 突 sudden + 破 break] **I** *n* breakthrough **II** *v* achieve a breakthrough

突然 **tūrán** [suffix: 突 sudden + 然 adjectival suffix] *adj* sudden, abrupt, unexpected □ 他没有给我打电话，也没有写信，昨天晚上突然来了。**Tā méiyǒu gěi wǒ dǎ diànhuà, yě méiyǒu xiě xìn, zuótiān wǎnshang tūrán lái le.** *He hadn't rung or written to me, but suddenly showed up yesterday evening.* □ 突然发生这件事，我真不知道怎么办。**Tūrán fāshēng zhè jiàn shì, wó zhēn bù zhīdào zěnme bàn.** *I really don't know what to do about this sudden incident.*

图 **tú** Trad 圖 *n* **1** picture **2** chart, diagram (张 **zhāng**) □ 他画了一张图，说明这种药不同成分的比例。**Tā huàle yì zhāng tú, shuōmíng zhè zhǒng yào bùtóng chéngfèn de bǐlì.** *He drew a chart to show the proportion of the various ingredients in this medicine.*

图案 **tú'àn** *n* pattern, design

图表 **túbiǎo** [comp: 图 picture + 表 form] *n* chart, diagram, graph (张 **zhāng**)

图画 **túhuà** [comp: 图 picture + 画 picture] *n* picture, painting, drawing (张 **zhāng**)

图片 **túpiàn** [comp: 图 picture + 片 card] *n* picture, photograph

图书 **túshū** [modif: 图 pictures + 书 book] *n* books

图书馆 **túshūguǎn** [modif: 图书 books + 馆 building] *n* library (座 **zuò**) □ 我们学校的图书馆没有多少中文书。**Wǒmen xuéxiào de túshūguǎn méiyǒu duōshǎo Zhōngwén shū.** *The library in our school doesn't have many Chinese books.* □ 图书馆里不准吃东西。**Túshūguǎn li bù zhǔn chī dōngxi.** *Eating in the library is not allowed.* (→ *No food in the library.*)

图像 **túxiàng** [comp: 图 picture + 像 image] *n* picture, image

图形 **túxíng** [comp: 图 picture + 形 shape] *n* graph

图纸 **túzhǐ** [modif: 图 picture + 纸 paper] *n* blueprint

徒 **tú** *n* apprentice

徒弟 **túdì** [comp: 徒 apprentice + 弟 younger brother] *n* apprentice, pupil

屠 **tú** *v* slaughter

屠夫 **túfū** [comp: 屠 slaughter + 夫 man] *n* butcher

屠杀 **túshā** [comp: 屠 slaughter + 杀 kill] *n* massacre

涂 **tú** Trad 塗 *v* smear, spread on □ 她在面包上涂了一层黄油。**Tā zài miànbāo shang túle yì céng huángyóu.** *She spread butter on the bread.*

途 **tú** *n* way, route

途径 **tújìng** [comp: 途 way + 径 footpath] *n* way, channel

土 **tǔ** *n* soil, earth □ 你鞋上怎么全是土？**Nǐ xié shang zěnme quán shì tǔ?** *How come your shoes are covered with dirt?*

土地 **tǔdì** [comp: 土 soil + 地 land] *n* land □ 对农民来说，最重要的资源是土地。**Duì nóngmín lái shuō, zuì zhòngyào de zīyuán shì tǔdì.** *To farmers, the most important resource is land.*

土豆 **tǔdòu** [modif: 土 soil + 豆 bean] *n* potato (只 **zhī**, 块 **kuài**) □ "土豆烧牛肉" 是一道有名的西菜。"**Tǔdòu shāo niúròu**" **shì yí dào yǒumíng de xīcài.** *"Beef and potato stew" (or Hungarian goulash) is a famous Western dish.*

土壤 **tǔrǎng** *n* soil

肥沃的土壤 **féiwò de tǔrǎng** fertile soil

吐 **tǔ** *v* spit, exhale □ 她吓得半天才吐出一口气。**Tā xià de bàntiān cái tǔ chū yì kǒu qì.** *She was so terrified that she held her breath.*

吐 **tù** *v* vomit, throw up □ 他酒喝得太多，吐了。**Tā jiǔ hē de tài duō, tù le.** *He vomited because he drank too much.* □ 我想吐。**Wǒ xiǎng tù.** *I want to vomit* (→ *I feel sick*).

兔 **tù** *n* rabbit, hare

兔子 **tùzi** rabbit, hare (只 **zhī**) □ 我小时候养过两只兔子。**Wǒ xiǎoshíhou yǎngguo liǎng zhī tùzi.** *When I was a child I once kept two rabbits.*

团 **tuán** Trad 團 **I** *n* **1** (military) regiment, group, team □ 你打算参加旅行团，还是自己一个人去中国？**Nǐ dǎsuàn cānjiā lǚxíngtuán, háishi zìjǐ yígerén qù Zhōngguó?** *Do you plan to tour China in a tour group or all by yourself?*

代表团 **dàibiǎotuán** delegation

歌舞团 **gēwǔtuán** song and dance troupe

旅行团 **lǚxíngtuán** tour group

II *v* unite, get together

团结 **tuánjié** [comp: 团 rally around + 结 tie up] *v* unite, be in solidarity with □ 这一家的兄弟姐妹很团结。**Zhè yì jiā de xiōng-dì-jiě-mèi hěn tuánjié.** *The siblings in this family are united.* □ 团结就是力量。**Tuánjié jiù shì lìliàng.** *Unity is strength.*

团聚 **tuánjù** *v* reunite

和老同学团聚 **hé lǎo tóngxué tuánjù** reunite with old classmates

团体 **tuántǐ** *n* organization, group

团员 **tuányuán** *n* **1** member of a delegation, group, etc. **2** member of the Chinese Communist Youth League

团圆 **tuányuán** *v* reunite with family members

团长 **tuánzhǎng** *n* **1** head of a delegation **2** (in the army) regiment commander

推 **tuī** *v* **1** push, shove □ 你要推这个门，不要拉。**Nǐ yào tuī zhège mén, bú yào lā.** *You should push this door, not pull it.* □ 他推着自行车上坡。**Tā tuīzhe zìxíngchē shàng pō.** *He pushed the bicycle up the slope.* **2** shirk, shift **3** infer, reason **4** put off, defer

推测 **tuīcè** *v* infer, suppose

推迟 **tuīchí** [v+compl: 推 push + 迟 late] *v* postpone □ 旅行团出发的日期要推迟三天。**Lǚxíngtuán chūfā de rìqī yào tuīchí sān tiān.** *The date of the tourist group departure will be postponed for three days.*

推动 tuīdòng [v+obj: 推 push + 动 move] *v* push forward, promote □ 中国迅速的经济发展推动了中文教学。 **Zhōngguó xùnsù de jīngjì fāzhǎn tuīdòngle Zhōngwén jiàoxué.** *China's rapid economic development has promoted teaching and learning of the Chinese language.*

推翻 tuīfān [v+compl: 推 push + 翻 turn over] *v* overturn, overthrow

推广 tuīguǎng [v+compl: 推 push + 广 wide] *v* popularize, spread □ 中国大力推广普通话，已经取得了成功。 **Zhōngguó dàlì tuīguǎng Pǔtōnghuà, yǐjīng qǔdéle chénggōng.** *China's tremendous efforts to popularize Putonghua have been successful.*

推荐 tuījiàn [comp: 推 push + 荐 recommend] *v* recommend □ 王老师给我推荐一本汉英词典。 **Wáng lǎoshī gěi wǒ tuījiàn yì běn Hànyīng cídiǎn.** *Teacher Wang recommended me a Chinese-English dictionary.* □ 你能不能给我推荐一位会说英语的牙医？ **Nǐ néng bu néng gěi wǒ tuījiàn yí wèi huì shuō Yīngyǔ de yáyī?** *Could you recommend me a dentist who speaks English?*

推进 tuījìn [v+compl: 推 push + 进 go forward] *v* promote, advance

推理 tuīlǐ I *v* infer, reason II *n* reasoning by way of inference, inference

推论 tuīlùn I *v* infer, deduce II *n* conclusion based on inference

推算 tuīsuàn I *v* work out (with figures), calculate II *n* calculation

推销 tuīxiāo [v+obj: 推 push + 销 sale] *v* promote (sale), market

推销新产品 tuīxiāo xīnchǎnpǐn promote a new product

推行 tuīxíng *v* carry out, pursue, implement

推选 tuīxuǎn *v* elect, choose

腿 tuǐ *n* leg (条 tiáo) □ 他腿长, 跑得快。 **Tā tuǐ cháng, pǎo de kuài.** *He's got long legs and runs fast.*

退 tuì *v* move back, retreat □ 请你退到黄线后面。 **Qǐng nǐ tuìdao huángxiàn hòumiàn.** *Please step back behind the yellow line.*

退步 tuìbù [v+obj: 退 move backward + 步 step] *v* retrogress, fall behind □ 我一个多月没有说中文, 口语退步了。 **Wǒ yí ge duō yuè méiyǒu shuō Zhōngwén, kǒuyǔ tuìbù le.** *Not having used it for a month, my spoken Chinese has deteriorated.*

退还 tuìhuán *v* return

退还礼物 tuìhuán lǐwù return a gift

退款 tuìkuǎn *v* refund, ask for refund □ 你对商品不满意, 可以退款。 **Nǐ duì shāngpǐn bù mǎnyì, kěyǐ tuìkuǎn.** *If you are not satisfied with your purchase, you can ask for a refund.*

退休 tuìxiū [comp: 退 retreat + 休 leisure] I *v* retire □ 张校长决定在年底退休。 **Zhāng xiàozhǎng juédìng zài niándǐ tuìxiū.** *Mr Zhang, the Principal, has decided to retire at the end of the year.* II *n* retirement □ 退休以后, 他和妻子要作环球旅行。 **Tuìxiū yǐhòu, tā hé qīzi yào zuò huánqiú lǚxíng.** *After retirement, he and his wife will travel around the world.*

退休金 tuìxiūjīn *n* pension

吞 tūn *v* swallow

屯 tún *n* village

托 tuō *v* entrust, ask □ 你进城吗？ 我托你办一件事, 行吗？ **Nǐ jìnchéng ma? Wǒ tuō nǐ bàn yí jiàn shì, xíng ma?** *Are you going to town? May I ask you to do something?*

托儿所 tuō'érsuǒ *n* nursery, child-care center (所 suǒ)

拖 tuō *v* drag on, defer, procrastinate □ 这件事不能再拖了, 得马上决定。 **Zhè jiàn shì bù néng zài tuō le, děi mǎshàng juédìng.** *We cannot defer any longer but have to make an immediate decision on this matter.*

拖延 tuōyán [comp: 拖 drag + 延 postpone] *v* delay, put off

脱 tuō *v* 1 take off (clothes, shoes, etc.)

脱衣服 tuō yīfu take off clothes □ 这个小孩儿会自己脱衣服吗？ **Zhège xiǎoháir huì zìjǐ tuō yīfu ma?** *Can the child take off his clothes by himself? (→ Can this child undress himself?)*

脱帽子 tuō màozi take off one's hat

脱鞋 tuō xié take off one's shoes

2 get out of

脱离 tuōlí [comp: 脱 get out of + 离 leave] *v* break away from, sever □ 此人已与本公司脱离一切关系。 **Cǐ rén yǐ yú běn gōngsī tuōlí yíqiè guānxi.** *This person has severed all ties with this company.*

脱落 tuōluò *v* drop, come off

驼 tuó *n* camel

椭 tuǒ as in 椭圆 tuǒyuán

椭圆 tuǒyuán *n* oval

椭圆形 tuǒyuánxíng oval shape

妥 tuǒ *adj* appropriate, proper

妥当 tuǒdàng *adj* appropriate, proper

妥善 tuǒshàn [comp: 妥 appropriate + 善 good] *adj* appropriate and satisfactory

妥协 tuǒxié I *v* compromise II *n* compromise □ 双方达成妥协。 **Shuāngfāng dáchéng tuǒxié.** *The two sides have reached a compromise.*

拓 tuò *v* open up (See 开拓 kāituò)

唾 tuò *n* saliva

唾沫 tuòmo saliva, spittle

W

挖 wā *v* dig, scoop, excavate

挖掘 wājué *v* dig, excavate, unearth

哇 wā *particle* Same as 啊 a II

蛙 wā *n* frog (See 青蛙 qīngwā.)

娃 wá *n* baby, child

娃娃 wáwa baby, child (个 gè)

瓦 wǎ *n* tile (片 piàn)

瓦解 wǎjiě *v* disintegrate, collapse

袜 wà Trad 襪 *n* sock, stocking

袜子 wàzi stocking, sock (只 zhī, 双 shuāng) □ 我的袜子破了。 **Wǒ de wàzi pò le.** *My socks have holes.*

穿袜子 chuān wàzi put on socks, wear socks □ 你不穿袜子就穿鞋, 不舒服吧？ **Nǐ bù chuān wàzi jiù chuān**

xié, bù shūfu ba? *Don't you feel uncomfortable wearing shoes without socks?*

脱袜子 tuō wàzi take off socks

歪 **wāi** *adj* not straight, askew, crooked □ 这幅画挂歪了。**Zhè fú huà guà wāi le.** *The picture hangs askew.*

歪曲 **wāiqū** [comp: 歪 askew + 曲 bend] *v* distort, misinterpret □ 我不是那个意思, 你歪曲了我的话。**Wǒ bú shì nàge yìsi, nǐ wāiqūle wǒde huà.** *That's not what I meant; you've distorted my remarks.*

外 **wài** *n* outside (antonym 里 lǐ) □ 墙外是一条安静的小街。**Qiáng wài shì yì tiáo ānjìng de xiǎo jiē.** *Beyond the wall is a quiet by-street.*

外边 **wàibian** [modif: 外 outside + 边 side] *n* outside (antonym 里边 lǐbian) □ 外边凉快, 我们到外边去吧。**Wàibian liángkuai, wǒmen dào wàibian qù ba.** *It's cool outside. Let's go outside.* □ 外边下雨呢, 带着伞吧! **Wàibian xià yǔ ne, dàizhe sǎn ba!** *It's raining outside. Bring an umbrella with you.*

外表 **wàibiǎo** *n* outward appearance, exterior

外宾 **wàibīn** *n* foreign guest, foreign visitor (位 wèi)

外部 **wàibù** *n* exterior, what is external

外出 **wàichū** *v* go outside, leave town

外地 **wàidì** [modif: 外 outside + 地 place] *n* parts of the country other than where one is (antonym 本地 běndì) □ 他经常到外地去开会。**Tā jīngcháng dào wàidì qù kāihuì.** *He often travels to other parts of the country to attend conferences.*

外地人 **wàidìrén** one who is from other parts of the country, not a native □ 她的丈夫是外地人。**Tāde zhàngfu shì wàidìrén.** *Her husband is from another part of the country.*

外观 **wàiguān** *n* exterior, surface, outward appearance

外国 **wàiguó** [modif: 外 outside + 国 country] *n* foreign country □ 你去过外国吗? **Nǐ qùguo wàiguó ma?** *Have you ever been abroad?*

外国货 **wàiguóhuò** foreign products, foreign goods

外国人 **wàiguórén** foreigner

外行 **wàiháng** **I** *adj* lay, not trained **II** *n* layman

外汇 **wàihuì** *n* foreign exchange

外汇储备 **wàihuì chǔbèi** foreign currency reserve

外汇兑换率 **wàihuì duìhuànlù** exchange rate

外交 **wàijiāo** [modif: 外 external + 交 deal with] *n* foreign affairs, diplomacy

外交部 **Wàijiāo bù** Ministry of Foreign Affairs

外交官 **wàijiāo guān** diplomat

外界 **wàijiè** *n* the external world

外科 **wàikē** [modif: 外 external + 科 department] *n* department of external medicine, surgery

外科医生 **wàikē yīshēng** surgeon

外力 **wàilì** *n* external force

外流 **wàiliú** *n* outflow

人才外流 **réncái wàiliú** brain drain

外面 **wàimiàn** *n* Same as 外边 **wàibian**

外婆 **wàipó** *n* (maternal) granndma

外甥 **wàishēng** *n* one's sister's son

外甥女 **wàishēngnǚ** *n* one's sister's daughter

外事 **wàishì** *n* foreign affairs

外事处 **wàishìchù** foreign affairs office

外头 **wàitou** *n* outside, outdoors

外文 **wàiwén** [modif: 外 foreign + 文 writing] *n* foreign language (especially its writing) (门 mén)

□ 这封信是用外文写的, 我看不懂。**Zhè fēng xìn shì yòng wàiwén xiě de, wǒ kàn bu dǒng.** *This letter is written in a foreign language. I can't read it.* □ 这本书已经翻译成多种外文。**Zhè běn shū yǐjīng fānyì chéng duō zhǒng wàiwén.** *This book has been translated into many foreign languages.*

外向型 **wàixiàngxíng** *adj* export-oriented

外向型经济 **wàixiàngxíng jīngjì** export-oriented economy

外形 **wàixíng** *n* appearance, external form

外衣 **wàiyī** *n* coat, outer clothing

外语 **wàiyǔ** [modif: 外 foreign + 语 language] *n* foreign language (门 mén) □ 懂一门外语很有用。**Dǒng yì mén wàiyǔ hěn yǒuyòng.** *Knowing a foreign language is useful.* □ 他本国语都没学好, 还学什么外语? **Tā běnguóyǔ dōu méi xuéhǎo, hái xué shénme wàiyǔ?** *He hasn't even learned his mother tongue properly. How can he learn a foreign language?*

外资 **wàizī** *n* foreign capital, foreign investment

外祖父 **wàizǔfù** *n* (maternal) grandfather

外祖母 **wàizǔmǔ** *n* (maternal) grandmother

豌 **wān** as in 豌豆 **wāndòu**

豌豆 **wāndòu** *n* pea

弯 **wān** Trad 彎 *adj* curved, tortuous □ 你这条线划得不直, 划弯了。**Nǐ zhè tiáo xiàn huà de bù zhí, huà wān le.** *You did not draw this line straight; it's curved.*

弯曲 **wānqū** [comp: 弯 curved + 曲 bent] *adj* curved, zigzagging

湾 **wān** Trad 灣 *n* bay, gulf (See 台湾 **Táiwān**.)

顽 **wán** *adj* naughty, stubborn

顽固 **wángù** *adj* **1** stubborn, pig-headed **2** difficult to cure □ 这种皮肤病很顽固。**Zhè zhǒng pífūbìng hěn wángù.** *This skin disease is difficult to cure.*

顽皮 **wánpí** *adj* naughty, impish

顽强 **wánqiáng** [comp: 顽 stubborn + 强 strong] *adj* indomitable, tenacious

丸 **wán** *n* bolus, pill (粒 lì, 颗 kē)

完 **wán** *v* finish, end □ 电影什么时候完? **Diànyǐng shénme shíhou wán?** *When will the movie end?*

吃完 **chīwán** finish eating, eat up □ 我吃完饭就去开会。**Wǒ chīwán fàn jiù qù kāihuì.** *I'm going to a meeting as soon as I finish my meal.*

看完 **kànwán** finish reading/watching □ 我昨天看完电视已经十二点了。**Wǒ zuótiān kànwán diànshì yǐjīng shí'èr diǎn le.** *It was already twelve o'clock when I finished watching TV last night.*

用完 **yòngwán** use up □ 我的钱用完了, 我要到银行去取钱。**Wǒ de qián yòngwán le, wǒ yào dào yínháng qù qǔ qián.** *I've used up my money. I'll go to the bank to get some cash.*

做完 **zuòwán** finish doing □ 你什么时候可以做完作业? **Nǐ shénme shíhou kěyǐ zuòwán zuòyè?** *When can you finish your homework?*

完备 **wánbèi** [comp: 完 finished + 备 provided] *adj* perfect, complete

完毕 **wánbì** *v* complete, finish

完成 **wánchéng** [comp: 完 finish + 成 accomplish] *v* accomplish, fulfill □ 这个计划在明年六月完成。**Zhège jìhuà zài míngnián liùyuè wánchéng.** *This plan*

will be fulfilled in June next year. □ 我们完成这个任务
后要好好庆祝一下。**Wǒmen wánchéng zhège rènwù
hòu yào hǎohǎo qìngzhù yíxià.** *We will have a good
celebration after we have accomplished this task.*

完蛋 wándàn *v* be done for, be finished

完全 wánquán [comp: 完 finished + 全 all] *adj*
complete □ 你提供的材料不完全。**Nǐ tígōng de cáiliào
bù wánquán.** *The data you have supplied are not complete.* □ 你完全不懂我的意思。**Nǐ wánquán bù dǒng
wǒ de yìsi.** *You completely fail to see my point.*

完善 wánshàn *v* make perfect, perfect

完整 wánzhěng [comp: 完 complete + 整 whole]
adj complete, integrated □ 这一套书一共有二十册, 现
在只有十八册, 不完整了。**Zhè yí tào shū yígòng yǒu
èrshí cè, xiànzài zhǐyǒu shíbā cè, bù wánzhěng le.** *This
set of books has twenty volumes altogether. Now we
have only eighteen volumes so the set is incomplete.*
□ 请你用一个完整的句子来回答。**Qǐng nǐ yòng yí
ge wánzhěng de jùzi lái huídá.** *Please answer in a
complete sentence.*

玩 **wán** *v* have fun, play
玩具 **wánjù** *n* toy (个 **gè**)
玩弄 **wánnòng** *v* play with
玩儿 **wánr** [suffix: 玩 play + 儿 suffix] *v* play, have
fun □ 我们一块儿到公园去玩儿吧。**Wǒmen yíkuàir
dào gōngyuán qù wánr ba.** *Let's go to the park to
have fun!*

NOTE: Though 玩儿 **wánr** is often glossed as *to play*, its
basic meaning is *to have fun* or *to have a good time*. It
can refer to many kinds of activities and therefore has
a very wide application. More examples: □ 我们常常到
小明家去玩儿。**Wǒmen chángcháng dào Xiǎo Míng jiā qu
wánr.** *We often go to Xiao Ming's home to have a good
time. (e.g. singing, dancing, playing cards, playing
games or just chatting.)* □ 上星期天我们在海边玩儿得
真高兴! **Shàng Xīngqītiān wǒmen zài hǎibiān wánr de zhēn
gāoxìng.** *We had a wonderful time by the seaside last
Sunday.* □ 我想去香港玩儿。**Wǒ xiǎng qù Xiānggǎng
wánr.** *I want to have a holiday in Hong Kong.*

玩笑 **wánxiào** *n* joke, jest
开玩笑 **kāi wánxiào** play a prank, crack a joke, pull
someone's leg □ 他喜欢跟别人开玩笑, 有时候太过分
了。**Tā xǐhuan gēn bié rén kāi wánxiào, yǒushi tài guò
fènle.** *He likes to play jokes on people, sometimes he
would go too far.* □ 别开玩笑了, 我是说真的。**Bié kāi
wánxiào le, wǒ shì shuō zhēn de.** *It is no joke; I mean
what I say.*

玩意儿 **wányìr** *n* **1** plaything **2** stuff, thing

NOTE: 玩意儿 **wányìr** is normally used with some contempt to suggest "insignificance" or "unworthiness",
similar to 东西 **dōngxi**. The expletives 什么玩意儿?
Shénme wányìr? and 他是个什么玩意儿? **Tā shì ge shénme
wányìr?** may be roughly translated respectively into
What trash! and *Who does he think himself is?*

挽 **wǎn** *v* salvage, draw, pull
挽救 **wǎnjiù** *v* rescue, save
晚 **wǎn** **I** *adj* late, not on time □ 对不起, 我来晚了。
Duìbuqǐ, wǒ lái wǎn le. *I'm sorry I'm late.* □ 时间太

晚了, 我得走了。**Shíjiān tài wǎn le, wǒ děi zǒu le.** *It's
very late; I've got to go.* **II** *n* evening, night

晚报 **wǎnbào** *n* evening paper (份 **fèn**)

晚餐 **wǎncān** *n* Same as 晚饭 **wǎnfàn**, used formally.

晚饭 **wǎnfàn** [modif: 晚 supper + 饭 meal] *n*
evening meal, dinner, supper (顿 **dùn**) □ 你们家一般
什么时候吃晚饭? **Nǐmen jiā yìbān shénme shíhou chī
wǎnfàn?** *When do you usually have supper at home?*
做晚饭 zuò wǎnfàn prepare supper

晚会 **wǎnhuì** [modif: 晚 evening + 会 assembly] *n*
evening party, an evening of entertainment □ 很多
重要的人要来参加今天的晚会。**Hěn duō zhòngyào de
rén yào lái cānjiā jīntiān de wǎnhuì.** *Many important
people will attend today's evening party.*

晚年 **wǎnnián** [modif: 晚 late + 年 years] *n* old age
□ 他的晚年生活很幸福。**Tāde wǎnnián shēnghuó hěn
xìngfú.** *He had a happy old age.*

晚上 **wǎnshang** *n* evening □ 你今天晚上打算做什么?
Nǐ jīntiān wǎnshang dǎsuàn zuò shénme? *What do
you plan to do this evening?* □ 他往往晚上还要工作两
三个小时。**Tā wǎngwǎng wǎnshang háiyào gōngzuò
liǎng-sān ge xiǎoshí.** *He usually has to work two or
three hours in the evening.*
今天晚上 (今晚) jīntiān wǎnshang (jīnwǎn) this
evening
昨天晚上 (昨晚) zuótiān wǎnshang (zuówǎn) yesterday evening

惋 **wǎn** *v* be sorry for, sigh
惋惜 **wǎnxī** [comp: 惋 sympathize with + 惜 pity]
v feel sorry (for someone or about something)
为浪费人才而惋惜 wéi làngfèi réncái ér wǎnxī feel
sorry about the waste of talents

碗 **wǎn** *n* bowl (只 **zhī**) □ 中国人吃饭一般用碗, 大碗
放菜, 小碗放米饭。**Zhōngguórén chīfàn yìbān yòng
wǎn, dà wǎn fàng cài, xiǎo wǎn fàng mǐfàn.** *Chinese
people usually use bowls for meals: big bowls for
dishes and small ones for cooked rice.*
…碗饭 ...wǎnfàn ... bowl(s) of rice □ "你一顿吃几
碗饭?" "两碗饭。" **"Nǐ yí dùn chī jǐ wǎn fàn?" "Liǎng
wǎn fàn."** *"How many bowls of rice do you have for
one meal?" "Two."*
菜碗 càiwǎn a dish bowl, big bowl
饭碗 fànwǎn rice bowl, livelihood, job

万 **wàn** Trad 萬 **I** *num* ten thousand
一万两千三百 (12,300) yíwàn liǎngqiān sānbǎi
twelve thousand and three hundred
二十万 (200,000) èr shí wàn two hundred thousand
II *n* a very large number **III** *adv* (negative sense)
absolutely

NOTE: 万 **wàn** (ten thousand) is an important number in
Chinese. While English has four basic digits (one, ten,
hundred and thousand) Chinese has five (个 **gè** *one*, 十
shí *ten*, 百 **bǎi** *hundred*, 千 **qiān** *thousand*, 万 **wàn** *ten
thousand*). The Chinese use 万 **wàn** to mean *ten thousand*. Therefore *a hundred thousand* is 十万 **shí wàn**. In
Chinese-speaking communities in Southeast Asia, some
people use 十千 **shíqiān** for *ten thousand*, e.g. 三十千
sānshíqiān 30,000. This is, however, not acceptable in
standard Chinese.

万分 **wànfēn** *adv* extremely

万岁 wànsuì *interj* Long Live □ 祖国万岁! **Zǔguó wànsuì!** *Long live the motherland!*

万万 wànwàn *adv* under no circumstances, never ever □ 万万不可掉以轻心。**Wànwàn bù kě diàoyǐqīngxīn.** *Under no circumstances should you relax your vigilance.*

万一 wànyī I *conj* in the unlikely event of, in case □ 万一飞机失事, 不要惊慌。**Wànyī fēijī shīshì, búyào jīnghuāng.** *In case of an air accident, do not panic.* II *n* a possible but unlikely event, contingency 对付万一的情况 **duìfu wànyī de qíngkuàng** cope with a contingency

万维网 wànwéiwǎng [modif: 万 ten thousand + 维 dimension + 网 net] *n* World Wide Web (WWW)

汪 **wāng** *adj* (of water) vast
汪洋 wāngyáng *n* vast expanse of water

王 1 **wáng** *n* king
王国 wángguó *n* kingdom
丹麦王国 Dānmài wángguó the Kingdom of Denmark

王 2 **Wáng** *n* (a family name)

亡 **wáng** *v* perish, die

枉 **wǎng** *v* treat unfairly, wrong (See 冤枉 yuānwang)

网 **wǎng** Trad 網 *n* net, network
网吧 wǎngbā [modif: 网 net, network + 吧 bar] *n* Internet café (座 zuò, 家 jiā) □ 这家网吧吸引很多年轻人。**Zhè jiā wǎngbā xīyǐn hěn dūo niánqīngrén.** *This Internet café attracts many young people.* □ 他不在家, 就在网吧。**Tā bú zài jiā, jiù zài wǎngbā.** *If he is not at home, then he must be at the Internet café.*
网络 wǎngluò [modif: 网 net + 络 net, network] *n* Internet
网络电话 wǎngluò diànhuà Internet phone
网络警察 (网警) wǎngluò jǐngchá (wǎngjǐng) Internet police
网球 wǎngqiú [modif: 网 net + 球 ball] n tennis □ 我们来打一场网球吧。**Wǒmen lái dǎ yì chǎng wǎngqiú ba.** *Let's have a game of tennis.*
网球场 wǎngqiúchǎng tennis court
网页 wǎngyè [modif: 网 web + 页 page] *n* web page
网站 wǎngzhàn [modif: 网 net, network + 站 station] *n* website □ 欢迎您访问我的个人网站。**Huānyíng nín fǎngwèn wǒ de gèrén wǎngzhàn.** *You are welcome to visit my personal website.*

往 **wǎng** I *prep* towards, in the direction of □ 你往前走, 到红绿灯的地方, 往左拐, 就可以到火车站。**Nǐ wǎng qián zǒu, dào hónglǜdēng de dìfang, wǎng zuǒ guǎi, jiù kěyǐ dào huǒchēzhàn.** *Walk straight on, and turn left at the traffic lights. Then you'll reach the railway station.* II *v* go III *adj* previous, past
往常 wǎngcháng *adv* habitually in the past, used to
往返 wǎngfǎn *v* journey to and from, make a round trip
往后 wǎnghòu *adv* from now on
往后的日子 wǎnghòu de rìzi the days to come
往来 wǎnglái I *v* come and go II *n* contact, dealings
业务往来 yèwù wǎnglái business dealings
往年 wǎngnián *n* (in) former years
往日 wǎngrì *n* in former times, in the past

往事 wǎngshì *n* past events, the past
回忆往事 huíyì wǎngshì recollect past events, reflect upon the past
往往 wǎngwǎng *adv* very often, usually

旺 **wàng** *adj* flourishing

妄 **wàng** *adj* preposterous
妄图 wàngtú *v* try in vain
妄想 wàngxiǎng I *v* attempt in vain II *n* vain hope

忘 **wàng** *v* forget, overlook □ 别忘了寄这封信。**Bié wàng le jì zhè fēng xìn.** *Don't forget to post this letter.* □ 他叫什么名字? 我忘了。**Tā jiào shénme míngzi? Wǒ wàng le.** *What's his name? I've forgotten it.*
忘记 wàngjì *v* forget, overlook
忘却 wàngquè *v* forget

望 **wàng** *v* look at, gaze into the distance □ 举头望明月。**Jǔ tóu wàng míngyuè.** *I look up to gaze at the bright moon.* (a line from a poem by Tang dynasty poet Li Bai)
望远镜 wàngyuǎnjìng *n* telescope, binoculars

危 **wēi** I *adj* perilous II *adv* by force
危害 wēihài [comp: 危 endanger + 害 damage] I *v* harm severely, jeopardize □ 降低农产品价格会危害农民的利益。**Jiàngdī nóngchǎnpǐn jiàgé huì wēihài nóngmín de lìyì.** *Lowering the prices of agricultural produce will severely harm the farmer's interest.* II *n* severe harm, damage □ 森林面积的减少给环境造成很大危害。**Sēnlín miànjī de jiǎnshǎo gěi huánjìng zàochéng hěn dà wēihài.** *The reduction of forest areas causes great damage to the environment.*
危机 wēijī [comp: 危 perilous + 机 situation] *n* crisis □ 要解决危机, 先要了解危机是怎么发生的。**Yào jiějué wēijī, xiān yào liáojiě wēijī shì zěnme fāshēng de.** *In order to resolve a crisis, one should first of all learn how it came into being.*
危急 wēijí [comp: 危 dangerous + 急 urgent] *adj* in acute danger, critical, perilous
危险 wēixiǎn [comp: 危 perilous + 险 risky] I *adj* dangerous, risky □ 下雪天开车比较危险。**Xià xuě tiān kāichē bǐjiào wēixiǎn.** *It's dangerous to drive in snow.* II *n* danger, risk □ 我不怕危险。**Wǒ bú pà wēixiǎn.** *I'm not afraid of danger.* □ 病人已经脱离危险。**Bìngrén yǐjīng tuōlí wēixiǎn.** *The patient is out of danger.*

威 **wēi** *n* awesome force
威风 wēifēng *n* power and prestige, manner or style showing power and prestige
耍威风 shuǎ wēifēng throw one's weight around
威力 wēilì *n* formidable force, power
威望 wēiwàng *n* enormous prestige
威胁 wēixié I *v* threaten □ 森林面积越来越小, 威胁到野生动物的生存。**Sēnlín miànjī yuèláiyuè xiǎo, wēixié dào yěshēng dòngwù de shēngcún.** *Forests are getting smaller and smaller, which threatens the survival of wild animals.* II *n* threat
构成威胁 gòuchéng wēixié pose a threat
威信 wēixìn *n* popular trust, prestige
在同事中享有很高威信 zài tóngshì zhōng xiǎngyǒu hěn gāo wēixìn enjoy high prestige among colleagues

微 **wēi** *adj* tiny, of extremely small amounts, minute

微不足道 wēi bùzú dào *idiom* negligibly small, extremely tiny

微观 wēiguān *adj* microcosmic, micro- (antonym 宏观 hóngguān)

微小 wēixiǎo *adj* tiny, of very small amounts

微笑 wēixiào [modif: 微 small + 笑 smile, laugh] *v* smile □ 她微笑着说, "谢谢你了。" **Tā wēixiàozhe shuō, "Xièxie nǐ le."** *She said, smiling, "Thank you."*

桅 wéi as in 桅杆 wéigān
桅杆 wéigān *n* mast

围 wéi Trad 圍 *v* enclose, surround □ 他建了一道墙, 把自己的房子围起来。**Tā jiànle yí dào qiáng, bǎ zìjǐ de fángzi wéi qǐlai.** *He built a wall to enclose his home.*

围攻 wéigōng *v* besiege, lay siege to

围巾 wéijīn *n* scarf (条 tiáo)

围棋 wéiqí *n* weiqi (a Chinese chess game, also known as *go*)
下围棋 xiàwéiqí play *weiqi*

围绕 wéirào [comp: 围 enclose + 绕 around] *v* 1 move around, encircle □ 地球围绕太阳转。**Dìqiú wéirào tàiyang zhuàn.** *The earth moves around the sun.* 2 center on, focus on □ 请大家围绕这个问题谈, 不要离题。**Qǐng dàjiā wéirào zhè ge wèntí tán, bú yào lítí.** *Please focus on this question. Do not digress.*

唯 wéi *adv* only

NOTE: In some cases, 唯 is also written as 惟 **wéi**.

唯独 wéidú *adv* only, alone

唯物论 wéiwùlùn *n* materialism

唯心论 wéixīnlùn *n* idealism

唯一 wéiyī [comp: 唯 only + 一 one] *adj* the only one, sole □ 他唯一的爱好是打麻将, 一有空就打。**Tā wéiyī de àihào shì dǎ májiàng, yì yǒukòng jiù dǎ.** *His only hobby is playing mahjong. He plays mahjong whenever he has time.*

维 wéi Trad 維 *v* preserve, safeguard

维护 wéihù [comp: 维 preserve + 护 protect] *v* safeguard, defend □ 为了维护国家安全, 必须要有一支强大的军队。**Wèile wéihù guójiā ānquán, bìxū yào yǒu yì zhī qiángdà de jūnduì.** *To ensure national security, we must maintain strong armed forces.*

维生素 wéishēngsù *n* vitamin

维修 wéixiū [comp: 维 preserve + 修 repair] *v* keep in good repair, maintain (a machine, a house, etc.)

违 wéi Trad 違 *v* disobey, violate

违背 wéibèi [comp: 违 disobey + 背 in opposition to] *v* go against, violate □ 你们这样做, 违背了总公司的意愿。**Nǐmen zhèyàng zuò, wéibèile zǒnggōngsī de yìyuàn.** *What you've done goes against the will of the headquarters.*

违法 wéifǎ [v+obj: 违 disobey + 法 law] *v* violate the law, break the law (antonym 守法 shǒufǎ)

违反 wéifǎn [comp: 违 disobey + 反 counter] *v* run counter to, violate □ 婚外恋违反道德标准。**Hūnwàiliàn wéifǎn dàodé biāozhǔn.** *Extramarital affairs violate the moral code.*

违犯 wéifàn *v* break (the law, regulations, etc.)
违犯财务规定 wéifàn cáiwù guīdìng breach financial regulations

为 wéi Trad 為 *v* 1 be, become 2 do, act

为难 wéinán *v* 1 make things difficult for □ 我不想为难你。**Wǒ bùxiǎng wéinán nǐ.** *I don't want to make things difficult for you.* 2 feel awkward
为难的事情 wéinán de shìqing something one finds difficult to cope with, some perplexing matter

为期 wéiqī *adv* (to be completed) by a definite date
为期不远 wéi qī bù yuǎn will take place soon
为期一星期 wéiqī yì xīngqī will last a week

为首 wéishǒu *v* be headed by
以董事长为首的代表团 yǐ dǒngshìzhǎng wéishǒu de dàibiǎotuán a delegation headed by the chairman of the Board of Trustees

为止 wéizhǐ *v* up to, till
到…为止 dào...wéizhǐ up to, until

尾 wěi *n* tail, end
尾巴 wěiba *n* tail (条 tiáo) □ 狗摇尾巴, 是表示高兴。**Gǒu yáo wěiba, shì biǎoshì gāoxìng.** *When a dog wags its tail, it indicates its happiness.*

委 wěi *v* entrust

委托 wěituō [comp: 委 entrust + 托 entrust] *v* entrust □ 公司委托律师正式回答用户的投诉。**Gōngsī wěituō lǜshī zhèngshì huídá yònghù de tóusù.** *The company has entrusted its lawyer to give a formal reply to the consumers' complaint.*

委员会 wěiyuánhuì *n* committee (个 gè) □ 这个委员会的任务是制定教育政策。**Zhège wěiyuánhuì de rènwù shì zhìdìng jiàoyù zhèngcè.** *This committee's mission is to set policies on education.*

伟 wěi Trad 偉 *adj* big

伟大 wěidà [comp: 伟 big + 大 big] *adj* great □ 孙中山是中国历史上的一位伟大人物。**Sūn Zhōngshān shì Zhōngguó lìshǐ shang de yí wèi wěidà rénwù.** *Dr Sun Yat-sen is a great man in Chinese history.*

伪 wěi *adj* false

伪造 wěizào *v* forge, counterfeit
一份伪造的文件 yí fèn wěizào de wénjiàn a forged document

卫 wèi Trad 衛 *v* defend, protect

卫生 wèishēng [v+obj: 卫 defend + 生 life] *n* hygiene, sanitation □ 保持个人卫生和公共卫生, 有利于人民的身体健康。**Bǎochí gèrén wèishēng hé gōnggòng wèishēng, yǒulì yú rénmín de shēntǐ jiànkāng.** *Maintaining good personal hygiene and public sanitation is beneficial to the health of the citizens.*
个人卫生 gèrén wèishēng hygiene, personal hygiene
公共卫生 gōnggòng wèishēng sanitation, public sanitation
环境卫生 huánjìng wèishēng environmental sanitation

卫生间 wèishēngjiān *n* bathroom, (private) toilet

卫生局 wèishēngjú *n* (government) health department

卫星 wèixīng [modif: 卫 encircling + 星 star] *n* satellite □ 月球是地球的卫星。**Yuèqiú shì dìqiú de wèixīng.** *The moon is a satellite of the earth.*
卫星电视 wèixīng diànshì satellite TV
人造卫星 rénzào wèixīng man-made satellite

为 wèi Trad 為 *prep* (do, work) for the benefit of, in the interest of □ 我为人人, 人人为我。**Wǒ wèi rénrén, rénrén wèi wǒ.** *I work for everybody as everybody works for me.* (→ *One for all and all for one.*)

□ 你是为钱工作吗? **Nǐ shì wèi qián gōngzuò ma?** *Do you work for money?*

为何 wèihé *adv* what for, why

为了 wèile *prep* for the purpose of □ 他这样辛辛苦苦地工作, 都是为了孩子。**Tā zhèyàng xīn-xīn-kǔ-kǔ de gōngzuò, dōu shì wèile háizi.** *He works so hard, all for his children.* □ 为了健康, 他不吸烟不喝酒, 每天锻炼身体。**Wèile jiànkāng, tā bù xīyān bù hē jiǔ, měi tiān duànliàn shēntǐ.** *In order to keep fit he does not smoke or drink, and exercises every day.*

NOTE: Both 为 **wèi** and 为了 **wèile** can be used as prepositions and have similar meanings, but 为了 **wèile** is more commonly used in everyday Chinese.

为什么 wèishénme [v+obj: 为 for + 什么 what] *adv* why, what for □ 你昨天为什么没有来上课? **Nǐ zuótiān wèishénme méiyǒu lái shàngkè?** *Why didn't you come to school yesterday?*

未 wèi *adv* have not, did not □ 他未婚以前, 住在学校宿舍里。**Tā wèi hūn yǐqián, zhù zài xuéxiào sùshè li.** *He lived in the school hostel before he got married.* □ 该生未经批准不来上课, 将受处分。**Gāishēng wèi jīng pīzhǔn bù lái shàngkè, jiāng shòu chǔfèn.** *This student was absent from class without permission and will be disciplined.*

NOTE: 未 **wèi** is only used in rather formal, written styles. In everyday Chinese, 没有 **méiyǒu** is used instead.

未必 wèibì *adv* not necessarily, may not

未来 wèilái *n* future □ 少年儿童是国家的未来。**Shàonián értóng shì guójiā de wèilái.** *The youth and children are the future of a nation.* □ 我们对未来有信心。**Wǒmen duì wèilái yǒu xìnxīn.** *We have confidence in the future.*

未免 wèimiǎn *adv* rather, a bit too

位 wèi I *measure wd* ([polite] used for people) 一位老师 yí **wèi lǎoshī** a teacher □ 那位先生是谁? **Nà wèi xiānsheng shì shuí?** *Who is that gentleman?* II *n* position, location

位于 wèiyú *v* be situated in, be located in

位置 wèizhi [comp: 位 seat + 置 locate] *n* 1 place, location □ 没有人能确定沉船的位置。**Méiyǒu rén néng quèdìng chénchuán de wèizhi.** *Nobody can determine the location of the sunken ship.* 2 (abstract) position □ 人力资源经理是公司里一个极其重要的位置。**Rénlì zīyuán jīnglǐ shì gōngsī li yí ge jíqí zhòngyào de wèizhi.** *The human resources manager holds an extremely important position in a company.*

味 wèi *n* taste, flavor

味道 wèidao *n* taste □ 这个菜味道好极了。**Zhège cài wèidao hǎo jíle.** *This dish is very delicious indeed.* □ 我觉得这个菜味道太淡, 我喜欢味道浓一点的菜。**Wǒ juéde zhège cài wèidao tài dàn, wǒ xǐhuan wèidao nóng yìdiǎn de cài.** *I find this dish too bland. I like strongly-flavored dishes.*

味精 wèijīng *n* monosodium glutamate (MSG), gourmet powder

胃 wèi *n* stomach □ 我胃疼。**Wǒ wèi téng.** *I have a stomachache.* □ 她的胃不太好, 多吃一点儿就不舒服。**Tā de wèi bú tài hǎo, duō chī yìdiǎnr jiù bù shūfu.** *She has a weak stomach. If she eats a little too much she feels uncomfortable.*

谓 wèi *v* be called (See 所谓 **suǒwèi**.)

慰 wèi *v* console

慰问 wèiwèn [comp: 慰 console + 问 ask] *v* express sympathy and solicitude for

畏 wèi *v* fear

畏惧 wèijù [comp: 畏 fear + 惧 dread] *v* fear, dread

喂 1 wèi *interj* 1 hey □ 喂, 你的票呢? **Wèi, nǐ de piào ne?** *Hey, where's your ticket?* 2 hello, hi □ 喂, 这里是大华公司, 您找谁? **Wèi, zhèlǐ shì Dàhuá Gōngsī, nín zhǎo shuí?** *Hello, this is Dahua Company. Who would you like to speak to?*

NOTE: In telephone conversations 喂 **wèi** is equivalent to *hello*. In other contexts, 喂 **wèi** is a rude way of getting people's attention. It is more polite to say 对不起 **duìbuqǐ**, e.g. □ 对不起, 先生, 您的票呢? **Duìbuqǐ, xiānsheng, nín de piào ne?** *Excuse me, sir, where's your ticket?*

喂 2 wèi *v* feed □ 她夜里起来给孩子喂奶。**Tā yèli qǐlai gěi háizi wèi nǎi.** *Every night she gets up to feed her baby.*

温 wēn I *adj* warm II *v* 1 warm up 2 review (one's lessons)

温带 wēndài [modif: 温 warm + 带 zone] *n* temperate zone □ 中国和美国部分领土都在北温带。**Zhōngguó hé Měiguó bùfen lǐngtǔ dōu zài běi wēndài.** *Most of the territories of China and the U.S. are in the North Temperate Zone.*

温度 wēndù [modif: 温 warmth + 度 degree] *n* temperature (atmospheric) □ 今天温度比较低, 但是没有风, 所以不觉得怎么冷。**Jīntiān wēndù bǐjiào dī, dànshì méiyǒu fēng, suǒyǐ bù juéde zěnme lěng.** *The temperature is rather low today, but it is not windy, so you don't feel very cold.*

NOTES: (1) 温度 **wēndù** generally refers to *atmospheric temperature* only. For *body temperature* the expression is 体温 **tǐwēn**, e.g. □ 人的正常体温是多少? **Rénde zhèngcháng tǐwēn shì duōshǎo?** *What is the normal temperature of a human being?* When a person has a fever, however, 热度 **rèdù** is used to refer to his/her temperature, e.g. □ 他今天热度还很高。**Tā jīntiān rèdù hái hěn gāo.** *He is still running a fever.* (2) The Chinese use the centigrade system, which is called 摄氏 **shèshì**, e.g. □ 今天最高温度摄氏二十八度。**Jīntiān zuì gāo wēndù shèshì èrshí bā dù.** *Today's maximum temperature is 28 degrees centigrade.* In everyday usage, however, people usually omit 摄氏 **shèshì**.

温度计 wēndùjì [modif: 温度 temperature + 计 meter] *n* thermometer

温和 wēnhé [comp: 温 warm + 和 mild] *adj* 1 (of climate) temperate, without extreme temperatures 温和的气候 **wēnhé de qìhòu** mild, intemperate climate 2 (of people) gentle, mild 语气温和 yǔqì **wēnhé** mild tone

温暖 **wēnnuǎn** [comp: 温 warm + 暖 warm] *adj* warm

温柔 **wēnróu** [comp: 温 warm + 柔 soft] *adj* (of people) gentle and soft, soothing

瘟 **wēn** *n* plague

瘟疫 **wēnyì** [comp: 瘟 plague + 疫 epidemic] *n* epidemic, pandemic (场 **cháng**)

文 **wén** *n* 1 writing, script 2 culture

文化 **wénhuà** *n* culture □ 语言中有很多文化知识。 *Yǔyán zhong yǒu hěn duō wénhuà zhīshi. A language contains a great deal of cultural knowledge.* □ 我对中国文化知道得不多。 *Wǒ duì Zhōngguó wénhuà zhīdào de bù duō. I don't know much about Chinese culture.*

文化部 Wénhuàbù the Ministry of Culture

文件 **wénjiàn** *n* 1 document (份 **fèn**) 2 (computer) file □ 这个文件你保留在电脑里了吗？ *Zhège wénjiàn nǐ bǎoliú zài diànnǎo li le ma? Have you saved this file in the computer?*

文盲 **wénmáng** [modif: 文 writing + 盲 blind] *n* illiterate person

文明 **wénmíng** [comp: 文 culture + 明 enlightenment] I *n* civilization, culture □ 各种文明各有优点，各有缺点。 *Gè zhǒng wénmíng gè yǒu yōudiǎn, gè yǒu quēdiǎn. Each of the civilizations has its merits and shortcomings.* II *adj* civilized □ 在文明社会不应该存在这种现象。 *Zài wénmíng shèhuì bù yīnggāi cúnzài zhè zhǒng xiànxiàng. Such a phenomenon should not exist in a civilized society.*

文凭 **wénpíng** *n* diploma, certificate of academic achievements (张 **zhāng**)

文人 **wénrén** [modif: 文 cultural + 人 person] *n* man of letters, literati

文物 **wénwù** [modif: 文 cultural + 物 object] *n* cultural relic, historical relic

文物商店 wénwù shāngdiàn antique shop

文献 **wénxiàn** *n* document, literature

文学 **wénxué** *n* literature □ 我姐姐在大学念英国文学。 *Wǒ jiějie zài dàxué niàn Yīngguó wénxué. My elder sister studies English literature in university.*

文学家 wénxué jiā (great) writer

文雅 **wényǎ** [comp: 文 cultured + 雅 elegant] *adj* refined and elegant

文言 **wényán** *n* Classical Chinese

文言文 wényánwén Classical Chinese writing

NOTE: Before the 20th century mainstream Chinese writing was done in 文言 **wényán** Classical Chinese, which was based on ancient Chinese and divorced from everyday speech of the time. A literate revolution took place in early 20th century, which succeeded in replacing 文言 **wényán** with 白话 **báihuà**, plain speech, vernacular.

文艺 **wényì** [comp: 文 literature + 艺 art] *n* literature and art, performing arts □ 我妈妈喜欢文艺，我爸爸喜欢体育。 *Wǒ māma xǐhuan wényì, wǒ bàba xǐhuan tǐyù. My mother likes literature and arts while my father likes sports.*

文艺晚会 wényì wǎnhuì an evening of entertainment, soirée

文章 **wénzhāng** [comp: 文 writing + 章 chapter] *n* essay, article (篇 **piān**) □ 昨天晚报上有一篇很有意思的文章。 *Zuótiān wǎnbào shang yǒu yì piān hěn yǒu yìsi de wénzhāng. There was an interesting article in yesterday's evening paper.* □ 他文章写得又快又好。 *Tā wénzhāng xiě de yòu kuài yòu hǎo. He writes good essays, and he writes them quickly.*

文字 **wénzì** [comp: 文 writing + 字 script] *n* written language, script, character □ 这本小说已经翻译成六种文字了。 *Zhè běn xiǎoshuō yǐjīng fānyì chéng liù zhǒng wénzì le. This novel has been translated into six languages.*

文字处理 wénzì chǔlǐ word processing

纹 **wén** Trad 紋 *n* ripple (See 皱纹 **zhòuwén**)

蚊 **wén** *n* mosquito

蚊子 **wénzi** mosquito (只 **zhī**) □ 这里夏天有蚊子吗？ *Zhèlǐ xiàtiān yǒu wénzi ma? Are there mosquitoes here in summer?*

闻 **wén** Trad 聞 *n* what is heard

闻名 **wénmíng** *adj* well-known

吻 **wěn** I *v* kiss □ 每天晚上儿子睡觉前，她都要吻吻他。 *Měitiān wǎnshang érzi shuìjiào qián, tā dōu yào wěn wěn tā. Before her son went to sleep every evening, she would kiss him.* II *n* kiss

稳 **wěn** Trad 穩 *adj* steady, stable □ 等车停稳了再下车。 *Děng chē tíng wěnle zài xià chē. Do not get off the car (or bus) before it comes to a complete stop.*

稳当 **wěndang** *adj* reliable, safe

一个稳当的办法 yí ge wěndang de bànfǎ a reliable method

稳定 **wěndìng** [comp: 稳 stable + 定 fixed] *adj* stable □ 现在的形势十分稳定。 *Xiànzài de xíngshì shífēn wěndìng. The present situation is very stable.*

稳妥 **wěntuǒ** [comp: 稳 stable + 妥 appropriate] *adj* safe and appropriate

问 **wèn** Trad 問 *v* 1 ask (a question), inquire □ 我可以问你一个问题吗？ *Wǒ kěyǐ wèn nǐ yí ge wèntí ma? May I ask you a question?* 2 ask after, send regards

问答 **wèndá** *n* questions and answers

问答题 wèndátí (in tests, exercises, etc.) question requiring an answer in writing (not a multiple-choice question)

问好 **wèn hǎo** *v* ask after, give greetings to □ 请代问您父母亲好。 *Qǐng dài wèn nín fùmǔqin hǎo. Please give my regards to your parents.*

问候 **wènhòu** *v* give regards to, send regards to, ask after □ 见到王老师，替我问候他。 *Jiàndào Wáng lǎoshī, tì wǒ wènhòu tā. When you see Teacher Wang, please give him my regards.* □ 我在信里问候她全家。 *Wǒ zài xìnli wènhòu tā quán jiā. In the letter I sent my regards to her family.*

问路 **wèn lù** *v* ask the way □ 你会用中文问路吗？ *Nǐ huì yòng Zhōngwén wènlù ma? Can you ask the way in Chinese?*

问世 **wènshì** *v* be published, come into being

问题 **wèntí** [comp: 问 inquiry + 题 question] *n* 1 question (道 **dào**, for school examinations only) □ "有什么问题吗？" "有，我有一个问题。" *"Yǒu shénme wèntí ma?" "Yǒu, wǒ yǒu yí ge wèntí." "Do you have any questions?" "Yes, I do."* □ 考试的五道问题，你答对了三道，答错了两道。 *Kǎoshì de wǔ dào wèntí, nǐ dá*

duìle sān dào, dá cuòle liǎng dào. *Of the five questions in the examination, you answered three correctly and two incorrectly.* **2** problem □ 出问题了! **Chū wèntí le!** *Something's gone wrong!*
没有问题 méiyǒu wèntí no problem

翁 **wēng** *n* old man

嗡 **wēng** *onomatopoeia* buzz

窝 **wō** *n* nest, lair
鸟窝 niǎowō bird's nest
窝囊 **wōnang** **I** *v* feel vexed and annoyed
受窝囊气 shòu wōnangqì be subject to petty annoyances
II *adj* (of people) useless, good-for-nothing

我 **wǒ** *pron* I, me □ 我叫张明, 我是中国人。**Wǒ jiào Zhāng Ming, wǒ shì Zhōngguórén.** *My name is Zhang Ming. I'm Chinese.*
我们 **wǒmen** [suffix: 我 I, me + 们 suffix denoting a plural number] *pron* we, us □ 我们是学中文的学生。**Wǒmen shì xué Zhóngwén de xuésheng.** *We're students of Chinese.*

卧 **wò** *v* lie
卧床休息 wòchuáng xiūxi lie in bed and rest
卧室 **wòshì** *n* bedroom (间 **jiān**)

沃 **wò** *adj* (of land) fertile

握 **wò** *v* hold, grasp
握手 **wòshǒu** [v+obj: 握 hold + 手 hand] *v* shake hands □ 他和新认识的朋友握手。**Tā hé xīn rènshi de péngyou wòshǒu.** *He shook hands with his new friends.*

乌 **wū** *adj* black, dark
乌鸦 wūyā *n* crow (只 **zhī**)
乌云 wūyún *n* dark clouds

呜 **wū** *v* toot, hoot
呜咽 wūyè *v* sob

污 **wū** **I** *n* filth **II** *v* smear, defile
污蔑 wūmiè *v* slander
污染 **wūrǎn** [comp: 污 to soil + 染 to dye] **I** *v* pollute □ 这家化工厂严重污染环境, 必须关闭。**Zhè jiā huàgōngchǎng yánzhòng wūrǎn huánjìng, bìxū guānbì.** *This chemical plant is seriously polluting the environment and must be closed down.* **II** *n* pollution □ 工业污染影响了生活质量。**Gōngyè wūrǎn yǐngxiǎngle shēnghuó zhìliàng.** *Industrial pollution affects the quality of life.*

巫 **wū** *n* witch
巫术 wūshù witchcraft
巫婆 **wūpó** *n* witch

诬 **wū** Trad 誣 *v* accuse falsely
诬告 **wūgào** *v* file a false charge against
诬蔑 **wūmiè** [comp: 诬 accuse falsely + 蔑 contempt] **I** *v* slander, vilify **II** *n* slander
诬陷 **wūxiàn** *v* frame
诬陷好人 wūxiàn hǎorén frame an innocent person

屋 **wū** *n* house, room
屋子 **wūzi** [suffix: 屋 house, room + 子 nominal suffix] *n* room (间 **jiān**) □ 这个房子有几间屋子? **Zhège fángzi yǒu jǐ jiān wūzi?** *How many rooms are there in the house?*

NOTE: 屋子 **wūzi** in the sense of *room* is only used in north China. To southern Chinese 屋子 **wūzi** may mean *house*. To avoid ambiguity, it is better to use the word 房间 **fángjiān** for *room.*

无 **wú** Trad 無 **I** *n* nothing, nil
从无到有 cóng wú dào yǒu grow out of nothing
II *v* have no (antonym 有 **yǒu**) □ 我们无法解决这个问题。**Wǒmen wú fǎ jiějué zhège wèntí.** *We have no way to solve this problem.*
无比 **wúbǐ** *adj* matchless, unparalleled
无偿 **wúcháng** [v+obj: 无 have no + 偿 compensation] *adj* free, gratis
无偿服务 wúcháng fúwù voluntary service
无耻 **wúchǐ** [modif: 无 have no + 耻 shame] *adj* shameless, brazen
无从 **wúcóng** *adv* having no way (of doing something), being in no position to
无从说起 wúcóng shuōqǐ don't know where to begin
无法 **wúfǎ** *modal v* unable to
无非 **wúfēi** *adv* nothing but, no more than □ 他无非是为了钱。**Tā wúfēi shì wèile qián.** *He wants nothing but money.*
无话可说 **wú huà kě shuō** *idiom* have nothing to say
无可奉告 **wú kě fènggào** *idiom* No comment
无可奈何 **wú kě nàihé** *idiom* have no alternative (but)
无理 **wúlǐ** [modif: 无 have no + 理 reason] *adj* unreasonable, unjustifiable
无理取闹 **wúlǐ qǔnào** make trouble without any justification, provoke deliberately
无聊 **wúliáo** *adj* **1** bored **2** silly, meaningless
无论 **wúlùn** *conj* Same as 不管 **bùguǎn**. Tends to be used in writing.
无论如何 **wúlùn rúhé** *idiom* no matter what, at any rate
无能为力 **wú néng wéi lì** *idiom* be totally powerless
无情 **wúqíng** [modif: 无 have no + 情 feeling, sentiment] *adj* ruthless, heartless
无情无义 **wú qíng wú yì** *idiom* cold-hearted and merciless
无穷 **wúqióng** *adj* infinite, boundless
无绳电话 **wú shéng diànhuà** *n* cordless telephone
无数 **wúshù** [modif: 无 no + 数 number] *adj* innumerable, countless □ 无数事实证明, 那种社会制度是行不通的。**Wúshù shìshí zhèngmíng, nà zhǒng shèhuì zhìdù shì xíngbutōng de.** *Innumerable facts have proven that kind of social system does not work.*
无所谓 **wú suǒwèi** *v* doesn't matter □ 他同意不同意, 我所谓; 反正我已经决定。**Tā tóngyì bù tóngyì, wúsuǒwèi fǎnzheng wǒ yǐjing juédìng.** *It doesn't matter whether he approves or not—I've made up my mind anyway.*
无所作为 **wú suǒ zuòwéi** *idiom* make no effort, be in a state of inertia
无微不至 **wú wēi bù zhì** *idiom* meticulous, sparing no effort, paying attention to every detail
无微不至的照顾 wú wēi bù zhì de zhàogù meticulous care and attention
无限 **wúxiàn** *adj* infinite, limitless
无线电 **wúxiàndiàn** *n* (wireless) radio
无线因特网 **wúxiàn yīntèwǎng** wireless Internet

无效 **wúxiào** *adj* invalid □ 你的签证已经无效了。**Nǐde qiānzhèng yǐjing wúxiào le.** *Your visa is now invalid.*

无疑 **wúyí** [modif: 无 have no + 疑 doubt] *adv* undoubtedly, beyond any doubt

无意 **wúyì** [modif: 无 have no + 意 intention] *adj* unintentional
无意之中发现 wúyì zhīzhōng fāxiàn discover by chance

五 **wǔ** *num* five □ 五五二十五。**Wǔ wǔ èrshíwǔ.** *Five times five is twenty-five.*
五星红旗 wǔ xīng hóng qí the five-star red flag (the Chinese national flag)

五 **wǔ** *num* five

午 **wǔ** *n* noon
午饭 **wǔfàn** [modif: 午 noon + 饭 meal] *n* lunch (顿 **dùn**) □ 我在学校吃午饭。**Wǒ zài xuéxiào chī wǔfàn.** *I have lunch in school.* □ 工人有一小时的午饭时间。**Gōngrén yǒu yì xiǎoshí de wǔfàn shíjiān.** *The workers have a one-hour lunch break.*
午间 **wǔjiān** *n* lunchtime
午间休息 wǔjiān xiūxi lunchtime break

武 **wǔ** *n* military
武力 **wǔlì** [modif: 武 military + 力 force] *n* military force
武力解决 wǔlì jiějué deal with (a situation) by force
武器 **wǔqì** [modif: 武 military + 器 artifact] *n* weapon (件 **jiàn**) □ 不准带任何武器上飞机。**Bù zhǔn dài rènhé wǔqì shàng fēijī.** *It is forbidden to bring a weapon of any kind on board the plane.*
大规模杀伤武器 dàguīmó shāshāng wǔqì weapon of mass destruction (WMD)
武术 **wǔshù** [modif: 武 martial + 术 arts] *n* martial arts □ 他在中国学了三年武术。**Tā zài Zhōngguó xuéle sān nián wǔshù.** *He studied martial arts in China for three years.*
武术大师 wǔshù dàshī martial arts master
武术馆 wǔshù guǎn martial arts school
武装 **wǔzhuāng** **I** *v* arm, equip
武装到牙齿 wǔzhuāng dào yáchǐ be armed to the teeth
II *n* arms
解除武装 jiěchú wǔzhuāng lay down arms, be disarmed

侮 **wǔ** *v* insult
侮辱 **wǔrǔ** [comp: 侮 insult + 辱 insult] **I** *v* insult, humiliate □ 我不能容忍别人侮辱我的父母。**Wǒ bùnéng róngrěn biérén wǔrǔ wǒde fùmǔ.** *I can't tolerate someone insulting my parents.* **II** *n* insult □ 你这么说，是对我的侮辱。**Nǐ zhème shuō, shì duì wǒde wǔrǔ.** *What you said was an insult to me.*

舞 **wǔ** *n* dance
舞弊 **wǔbì** **I** *n* fraud, fraudulent practice
舞弊案 wǔbì àn a case of fraud
II *v* commit a fraud □ 一名年轻人因利用计算机舞弊而被逮捕。**Yì míng niánqīngrén yīn lìyòng jìsuànjī wǔbì ér bèi dàibǔ.** *A young man was arrested for computer fraud.*
舞蹈 **wǔdǎo** *n* dance
舞会 **wǔhuì** *n* ball
化装舞会 huàzhuāng wǔhuì fancydress party

舞台 **wǔtái** [modif: 舞 dance + 台 table] *n* stage, theater
舞厅 **wǔtīng** *n* dance hall
迪斯科舞厅 dísīkē wǔtīng discothèque, disco

悟 **wù** *v* meet (people)

勿 **wù** *adv* do not, don't □ 请勿吸烟。**Qǐngwù xīyān.** *Please do not smoke.* (→ *No smoking. Smoke-free.*)

物 **wù** *n* **1** things, objects **2** material
物价 **wùjià** [modif: 物 thing + 价 price] *n* price, commodity price □ 最近的物价比较稳定。**Zuìjìn de wùjià bǐjiào wěndìng.** *Prices have been quite stable recently.*
物理 **wùlǐ** [modif: 物 things, objects + 理 pattern, rule] *n* physics □ 我弟弟物理、数学都挺好。**Wǒ dìdi wùlǐ, shùxué dōu tǐng hǎo.** *My younger brother is good at physics and mathematics.*
物力 **wùlì** [modif: 物 material + 力 strength] *n* material resources
物品 **wùpǐn** *n* article, goods
物体 **wùtǐ** *n* object, substance
物业 **wùyè** *n* real estate, property
物业管理 wùyè guǎnlǐ property management
物资 **wùzī** *n* goods and materials, supplies

务 **wù** Trad 務 **I** *v* work, to spend one's efforts on **II** *adv* must, be sure to
务必 **wùbì** *adv* must, be sure to

雾 **wù** Trad 霧 *n* fog, mist □ 今天早上有大雾，很多人迟到。**Jīntiān zǎoshang yǒu dà wù, hěn duō rén chídào.** *Many people were late for work this morning because of the heavy fog.* □ 有雾天气，开车要特别小心。**Yǒu wù tiānqì, kāichē yào tèbié xiǎoxīn.** *You should be particularly careful when driving in foggy weather.*

悟 **wù** *v* realize
悟出了道理 wùchūle dàoli come to see the light, begin to understand
顿悟 dùnwù epiphany

误 **wù** Trad 誤 *adj* erroneous
误差 **wùchā** *n* (in physics) error
误会 **wùhuì** [modif: 误 mistaken + 会 understanding] **I** *v* misunderstand, misconstrue □ 你误会了我的意思。**Nǐ wùhuìle wǒ de yìsi.** *You've misconstrued my meaning.* **II** *n* misunderstanding □ 我没有说清楚，造成了误会，很抱歉。**Wǒ méiyǒu shuō qīngchu, zàochéngle wùhuì, hěn bàoqiàn.** *I did not make it clear, which has caused a misunderstanding. I apologize.*
误解 **wùjiě** *v* misunderstand □ 你误解了我的意思。**Nǐ wùjiěle wǒde yìsi.** *You misunderstood my meaning.*

恶 **wù** *v* loathe (See 厌恶 **yànwù**)

X

西 xī *n* west, western □ 河东是一座小城, 河西是一大片农场。**Hé dōng shì yí zuò xiǎo chéng, hé xī shì yí dà piàn nóngchǎng.** *East of the river is a small town, and on the west is a big farm.*

西北 xīběi [comp: 西 west + 北 north] *n* northwest, the Northwest □ 中国正在努力开发大西北。**Zhōngguó zhèngzài nǔlì kāifā dà xīběi.** *China is making efforts to develop her northwest region.*

西边 xībian [modif: 西 west + 边 side] *n* west side, to the west, in the west □ 太阳在西边下山。**Tàiyang zài xībian xiàshān.** *The sun sets in the west.*

西餐 xīcān [modif: 西 West + 餐 meal] *n* Western-style meal □ 走, 我请你吃西餐。**Zuǒ, wǒ qǐng nǐ chī xīcān.** *Let's go. I'll treat you to a Western-style meal.*

西餐馆 xīcānguǎn *n* Western-style restaurant

西方 xīfāng [modif: 西 West + 方 direction, part] *n* the West, Occident □ 西方文明有什么重要特点? **Xīfāng wénmíng yǒu shénme zhòngyào tèdiǎn?** *What are the major characteristics of Western civilization?*

西服 xīfú [modif: 西 Western + 服 clothing] *n* Western-style clothes, men's suit

西瓜 xīguā *n* watermelon (只 zhī) □ 中国人夏天最喜欢吃西瓜。**Zhōngguórén xiàtiān zuì xǐhuan chī xīguā.** *The Chinese people's favorite fruit in summer is the watermelon.*

西红柿 xīhóngshì [modif: 西 Western + 红 red + 柿 persimmon] *n* tomato (只 zhī) □ 我要买一公斤西红柿。**Wǒ yào mǎi yì gōngjīn xīhóngshì.** *I want to buy a kilogram of tomatoes.*

西南 xīnán [comp: 西 west + 南 south] *n* southwest, the Southwest □ 中国西南地方有很多少数民族。**Zhōngguó xīnán dìfang yǒu hěn duō shǎoshù mínzú.** *There are many national minorities in China's southwestern region.*

西面 xīmiàn Same as 西边 **xībian**

西医 xīyī *n* 1 Western medicine 2 doctor trained in Western medicine (位 **wèi**)
中西医结合治疗 Zhōngxīyī jiéhé zhìliáo treat (patients) with a combination of Chinese and Western medicine

晰 xī *adj* clear, distinct (See 清晰 **qīngxī**)

锡 xī *n* (metal) tin (Sn)

吸 xī *v* 1 inhale, suck 2 absorb, suck up
吸毒 xīdú [v+obj: 吸 inhale + 毒 poison] I *v* take drugs II *n* drug-taking, substance abuse

吸取 xīqǔ [comp: 吸 absorb + 取 take] *v* absorb, draw in
吸取教训 xīqǔ jiàoxun learn a lesson (from past experience)

吸收 xīshōu [comp: 吸 suck + 收 receive] *v* suck up, absorb □ 我们要吸收别人的好经验。**Wǒmen yào xīshōu biérén de hǎo jīngyàn.** *We should draw from other people's positive experiences.*

吸烟 xīyān [v+obj: 吸 inhale + 烟 cigarette] I *v* smoke II *n* smoking □ 这里不准吸烟。**Zhèli bù zhǔn xīyān.** *Smoking is not allowed here.*

吸引 xīyǐn [comp: 吸 suck + 引 guide] *v* attract □ 我们想吸引更多的旅游者来我国游览。**Wǒmen xiǎng xīyǐn gèng duō de lǚyóuzhě lái wǒguó yóulǎn.** *We want to attract more tourists to our country.*

吸引力 xīyǐnlì *n* attraction
有吸引力 yǒu xīyǐnlì attractive

希 xī *v* wish, hope
希望 xīwàng [comp: 希 wish + 望 look forward to] I *v* hope, wish □ 我希望你常给我打电话。**Wó xīwàng nǐ cháng gěi wǒ dǎ diànhuà.** *I hope you'll ring me often.* □ 希望你旅行愉快! **Xīwàng nǐ lǚxíng yúkuài!** *I wish you a happy journey.* (→ *Bon voyage!*) II *n* hope □ 孩子是父母的希望。**Háizi shì fùmǔ de xīwàng** *Children are their parents' hope.*

稀 xī *adj* 1 rare, scarce 2 watery
稀饭 xīfàn *n* rice porridge

稀少 xīshǎo [comp: 稀 rare + 少 few, little] *adj* scarce, few and far between
人烟稀少 rényān xīshǎo sparsely populated

稀有 xīyǒu *adj* rare
稀有金属 xīyǒujīnshǔ a rare metal

夕 xī *n* dusk, twilight
夕阳 xīyáng the setting sun

惜 xī *v* 1 cherish, treasure (See 珍惜 **zhēnxī**) 2 have pity on (See 可惜 **kěxī**)

牺 xī Trad 犠 *n* sacrifice
牺牲 xīshēng I *v* sacrifice, give up □ 他们为子女牺牲了大量时间和金钱。**Tāmen wèi zǐnǔ xīshēngle dàliàng shíjiān hé jīnqián.** *They gave up a great deal of time and money for their children.* II *n* sacrifice □ 她为家庭作出了巨大牺牲。**Tā wèi jiātíng zuòchule jùdà xīshēng.** *She made great sacrifices for the family.*

悉 xī *v* know (See 熟悉 **shúxi**.)

溪 xī *n* small stream
小溪 xiǎoxī a small stream

膝 xī *n* knee
膝盖 xīgài knee

息 xī *v* cease (See 消息 **xiāoxi**, 休息 **xiūxi**.)

熄 xī *v* extinguish (fire)
熄灭 xīmiè *v* (of fire) die out, be extinguished

媳 xí daughter-in-law
媳妇 xífù *n* daughter-in-law
儿媳妇 érxífù daughter-in-law

NOTE: In some dialects, 媳妇 **xífù** may also refer to *a wife*, e.g. 娶媳妇 **qǔ xífu** *to get a wife, (for men) to get married.*

袭 xí Trad 襲 *v* attack, raid
袭击 xíjī *v* (of troops) attack, raid
突然袭击 tūrán xíjī sudden attack, launch a sudden attack

习 xí Trad 習 I *v* practice, exercise II *n* custom, habit
习惯 xíguàn [comp: 习 be familiar with + 惯 be accustomed to] I *n* habit □ 他有一个坏习惯, 我希望他改掉。**Tā yǒu yí ge huài xíguàn, wǒ xīwàng tā gǎidiào.** *He has a bad habit. I hope he'll get rid of it.* II *v* be accustomed to, be used to □ 很多中国人不习惯吃西餐。**Hěn duō Zhōngguórén bù xíguàn chī xīcān.** *Many Chinese are not used to eating Western-style meals.*

习惯上 xíguàn shang habitually

习俗 xísú [comp: 习 practice + 俗 custom] *n* accepted custom, custom

习题 xítí *n* exercises (in school work)

席 **xí** *n* seat

来宾席 láibīnxí visitors' seats

席位 xíwèi *n* seat

洗 **xǐ** *v* wash, bathe □ 吃饭前要洗手。**Chīfàn qián yào xǐ shǒu.** *You should wash your hands before having a meal.*

洗尘 xǐchén [v+obj: 洗 wash off + 尘 dust] *v* give a welcome dinner

洗涤 xǐdí *v* wash, cleanse

洗涤剂 xǐdíjì detergent

洗手间 xǐshǒujiān *n* toilet, restroom, washroom □ 请问，洗手间在哪里? **Qǐngwèn, xǐshǒujiān zài nǎli?** *Excuse me, where's the washroom?*

NOTE: 洗手间 **xǐshǒujiān** is a common euphemism for *toilet*. The formal word for *toilet* is 厕所 **cèsuǒ**, e.g. 男厕所 **nán cèsuǒ** (Men's room, Gents'), 女厕所 **nǔ cèsuǒ** (Ladies' room, Ladies').

洗衣机 xǐyījī [modif: 洗衣 wash clothes + 机 machine] *n* washing machine (台 tái) □ 洗衣机又坏了，得买一台新的了。**Xǐyījī yòu huàile, děi mǎi yì tái xīnde le.** *The washing machine broke down again. We've got to buy a new one.*

洗澡 xǐzǎo [comp: 洗 wash + 澡 bath, take a bath] *v* take a bath, take a shower □ 有人每天早上洗澡，有人每天晚上洗澡。**Yǒurén měi tiān zǎoshang xǐzǎo, yǒurén měi tiān wǎnshang xǐzǎo.** *Some people take a bath early every morning, and others in the evening.* □ 他习惯临睡前洗一个热水澡。**Tā xíguàn línshuì qián xǐ yí ge rèshuǐ zǎo.** *He is used to taking a hot bath just before going to bed.*

洗澡间 xǐzǎojiān bathroom, shower room (Same as 浴室 **yùshì**.)

喜 **xǐ** I *v* be fond of II *adj* happy, glad

喜爱 xǐ'ài [comp: 喜 be fond of + 爱 love] *v* be fond of, love

喜欢 xǐhuan [comp: 喜 be fond of + 欢 pleasure] *v* like, be fond of □ 你喜欢不喜欢中国音乐? **Nǐ xǐhuan bu xǐhuan Zhōngguó yīnyuè?** *Do you like Chinese music?* □ 他喜欢一边喝啤酒，一边看体育节目。**Tā xǐhuan yìbiān hē píjiǔ, yìbiān kàn tǐyù jiémù.** *He likes to drink beer while watching sports programs.*

喜鹊 xǐque *n* magpie (只 **zhī**)

NOTE: In Chinese folklore, 喜鹊 **xǐque** the magpie is an auspicious bird, the harbinger of good tidings, hence 喜鹊 **xǐque**.

喜事 xǐshì [modif: 喜 happy + 事 event] *n* happy event (especially a wedding)

办喜事 bànxǐshì arrange a wedding

喜讯 xǐxùn [modif: 喜 happy + 讯 news] *n* good news, good tidings

喜悦 xǐyuè [comp: 喜 happy + 悦 joy] *adj* happy, joyful

隙 **xì** *n* narrow gap (See 空隙 **kòngxì**)

戏 **xì** Trad 戲 *n* drama, play (出 **chū**) □ 今天晚上我们去看戏。**Jīntiān wǎnshang wǒmen qù kàn xì.** *We're going to watch a play this evening.*

戏剧 xìjù *n* drama

系 **xì** *n* department (of a university) □ 这座大学有十二个系，最大的是电脑系。**Zhè zuò dàxué yǒu shí'èr ge xì, zuì dà de shì diànnǎo xì.** *This university has twelve departments; the biggest is the Computing Science Department.*

系主任 xì zhǔrèn chair of a (university) department

系列 xìliè *n* series

一系列 yíxìliè a series of

系统 xìtǒng *n* a group of items serving a common purpose, system (套 tào) □ 系统中只要有一个地方出毛病，整套系统就不能正常工作。**Xìtǒng zhōng zhǐyào yǒu yí ge dìfang chū máobìng, zhěngtào xìtǒng jiù bù néng zhèngcháng gōngzuò.** *If only one part of a system goes wrong, the entire system will not be able to function properly.*

细 **xì** Trad 細 *adj* 1 thin, slender (of objects shaped like a strip) (antonym 粗 **cū**) □ 中国的面条又细又长, 是我最喜欢吃的东西。**Zhōngguó de miàntiáo yòu xì yòu cháng, shì wǒ zuì xǐhuan chī de dōngxi.** *Chinese noodles are thin and long; they are my favorite food.* 2 small, tiny

细沙 xìshā fine sand

3 meticulous □ 他把计划的各个方面都考虑得很细。**Tā bǎ jìhuà de gè ge fāngmiàn dōu kǎolǜ de hěn xì.** *He considered every single aspect of the plan very carefully.*

细胞 xìbāo *n* (in biology) cell

细节 xìjié *n* details □ 这件事的细节我不清楚。**Zhè jiàn shì de xìjié wǒ bù qīngchu.** *I'm not clear about the details of this matter.*

细菌 xìjūn [modif: 细 tiny + 菌 bacterium] *n* bacterium, germ □ 科学家还没有找到引起这种病的细菌。**Kēxuéjiā hái méiyǒu zhǎodào yǐnqǐ zhè zhǒng bìng de xìjūn.** *Scientists have not identified the bacterium that causes this disease.*

细小 xìxiǎo [comp: 细 tiny + 小 small] *adj* tiny

细心 xìxīn [modif: 细 meticulous + 心 the heart] *adj* very careful, meticulous □ 她做完数学练习后总要细心地检查一遍。**Tā zuòwán shùxué liànxí hòu zǒngyào xìxīn de jiǎnchá yíbiàn.** *After finishing her mathematics exercises she checks every question very carefully.*

细致 xìzhì *adj* careful, meticulous

瞎 **xiā** *adj* blind

虾 **xiā** Trad 蝦 *n* prawn, shrimp (只 **zhī**)

峡 **xiá** *n* gorge

峡谷 xiágǔ *n* gorge, canyon

狭 **xiá** *adj* narrow

狭隘 xiá'ài *adj* narrow

狭窄 xiázhǎi *adj* narrow, narrow and limited

心胸狭窄 xīnxiōng xiázhǎi narrow-minded, intolerant

霞 **xiá** *n* rosy clouds, morning or evening glow

辖 **xiá** Trad 轄 *v* govern (See 管辖 **guǎnxiá**)

下 ¹ **xià I** *prep* below, under, underneath (antonym 上 **shàng**) □ 树下很凉快。**Shù xià hěn liángkuài.** *It's cool under the tree.* 山下 **shānxia** at the foot of a mountain or hills **II** *v* **1** go/come down (antonym 上 **shàng**) **2** leave off, finish **3** issue, deliver **III** *adj* low, inferior

下班 **xiàbān** *v* get off work □ 我下班以后要去买菜。**Wǒ xiàbān yǐhòu yào qù mǎi cài.** *I'll go and do grocery shopping after work.*

下边 **xiàbian** [modif: 下 below, underneath + 边 side] *n* below, under (antonym 上边 **shàngbian**) □ 椅子下边有几本书, 是谁的? **Yǐzi xiàbian yǒu jǐ běn shū, shì shéi de?** *There are some books under the chair. Whose are they?*

下车 **xiàchē** *v* get off a vehicle □ 到了, 下车吧! **Dào le, xiàchē ba!** *Here we are. Let's get off the car (or bus).*

下达 **xiàdá** *v* make known to lower levels

下岗 **xiàgǎng** [v+obj: 下 leave + 岗 post, job] *v* be laid off, be unemployed □ 张师傅下岗好几年了, 生活很困难。**Zhāng shīfu xiàgǎng hǎo jǐ nián le, shēnghuó hěn kùnnan.** *Master worker Zhang was laid off several years ago and has been living a hard life.* 下岗工人 **xiàgǎng gōngrén** a worker who has been laid off, an unemployed worker

下级 **xiàjí** [modif: 下 lower + 级 grade] *n* lower level, subordinate

下降 **xiàjiàng** *v* fall, descend

下课 **xiàkè** finish class □ 你们每天几点钟下课? **Nǐmen měi tiān jǐ diǎnzhōng xiàkè?** *When do you finish school everyday?*

下来 **xiàlái** *v* come down □ 晚饭做好了, 快下来吃吧! **Wǎnfàn zuòhǎo le, kuài xiàlai chī ba!** *Supper is ready. Come down and eat!*

下列 **xiàliè** [modif: 下 below, underneath + 列 listed] *adj* listed below

下令 **xiàlìng** [v+obj: 下 issue + 令 order] *v* issue an order

下落 **xiàluò** *n* what has happened (to someone), whereabouts 打听…的下落 dǎting...de xiàluò inquire about (someone's) whereabouts, try to find what has happened to (someone)

下面 **xiàmiàn** Same as 下边 **xiàbian**

下去 **xiàqu** *v* go down □ 时间不早了, 我们(从山上)下去吧。**Shíjiān bù zǎo le, wǒmen (cóng shānshang) xiàqu ba.** *It's quite late. Let's go down [the hill].*

下台 **xiàtái** [v+obj: 下 leave + 台 stage] *v* **1** step down from the stage **2** lose a position, fall from power (antonym 上台 **shàngtái**)

下午 **xiàwǔ** [modif: 下 lower half + 午 noon] *n* afternoon (antonym 上午 **shàngwǔ**) □ 上午多云, 下午天晴了。**Shàngwǔ duō yún, xiàwǔ tiān qíng le.** *It was cloudy in the morning, but it cleared up in the afternoon.*

下乡 **xiàxiāng** *v* go to the countryside

下旬 **xiàxún** *n* the last ten days of a month

下游 **xiàyóu** *n* lower reaches (of a river)

下载 **xià zài** [modif: 下 down, downward + 载 carry] *v* download

下 ² **xià** *measure wd* (used with certain verbs to indicate the number of times the action is done) □ 我试了几下, 都不行。**Wǒ shìle jǐ xià, dōu bù xíng.** *I tried several times, but it didn't work.*

吓 **xià** *Trad* 嚇 *v* **1** frighten, scare □ 我不是吓你, 你父亲的病极其严重。**Wǒ bú shì xià nǐ, nǐ fùqin de bìng jíqí yánzhòng.** *I don't want to frighten you, but your father's illness is extremely severe.* **2** be frightened, be scared □ 她看到强盗手里拿着刀, 吓得叫起来。**Tā kàndao qiángdào shǒuli názhe dāo, xià de jiàojiào qǐlai.** *When she saw the robber holding a knife in hand, she was so frightened that she screamed.*

吓人 **xiàrén** [v+obj: 吓 frighten + 人 people] *adj* frightening, terrible

夏 **xià** *n* summer

夏天 **xiàtiān** [modif: 夏 summer + 天 days] *n* summer □ 北京的夏天热吗? **Běijīng de xiàtiān rè ma?** *Is summer in Beijing hot?* □ 我们夏天常常到海边去游泳。**Wǒmen xiàtiān chángcháng dào hǎibiān qù yóuyǒng.** *We often go swimming by the seaside in summer.*

掀 **xiān** *v* lift, lift up 掀起 **xiānqǐ** *v* set off, start

先 **xiān** *adv* first (in time sequence) (antonym 后 **hòu**) □ 您先请。**Nín xiān qǐng.** *After you.* 先…再… xiān...zài... first ... and then ... □ 他早上先跑步, 再吃早饭。**Tā zǎoshang xiān pǎobù, zài chī zǎofàn.** *Early in the morning he first jogs and then has breakfast.*

先锋 **xiānfēng** *n* pioneer

先后 **xiānhòu** [comp: 先 before + 后 later] *adv* one after another, successively □ 他们四个孩子大学毕业后先后离家。**Tāmen sì ge háizi dàxué bìyè hòu xiānhòu lí jiā.** *After graduation from university their four children left home one after another.* □ 他的祖父和祖母在去年先后去世。**Tā de zǔfù hé zǔmǔ zài qùnián xiānhòu qùshì.** *His grandfather and grandmother died one after another last year.*

先进 **xiānjìn** [modif: 先 in advance + 进 go forward] *adj* advanced □ 这种照相机使用最先进的技术。**Zhè zhǒng zhàoxiàngjī shǐyòng zuì xiānjìn de jìshù.** *This camera uses the most advanced technology.*

先前 **xiānqián** *adv* previously

先生 **xiānsheng** [modif: 先 first, before + 生 born] *n* **1** teacher **2** Mister (Mr) □ 王先生, 这位是 张先生。**Wáng xiānsheng, zhè wèi shì Zhāng xiānsheng.** *Mr Wang, this is Mr Zhang.* **3** sir, gentleman □ 先生, 有事吗? **Xiānsheng, yǒu shì ma?** *Is there anything I can do for you, sir?* □ 有一位先生要见你。**Yǒu yí wèi xiānsheng yào jiàn nǐ.** *There's a gentleman wanting to see you.* **4** husband □ 您先生在哪儿工作? **Nín xiānsheng zài nǎr gōngzuò?** *Where does your husband work?*

先行 **xiānxíng** *v* go ahead, precede

鲜 **xiān** *Trad* 鮮 *adj* **1** fresh □ 她买了几根鲜黄瓜回家做凉菜。**Tā mǎile jǐ gēn xiān huánggua huíjiā zuò liángcài.** *She bought several fresh cucumbers and brought them home to prepare a cold dish.* **2** bright, brightly-colored **3** delicious □ 这鱼汤真鲜! **Zhè yútāng zhēn xiān!** *The fish soup is really delicious!*

鲜红 **xiānhóng** *n* bright red, scarlet

鲜花 **xiānhuā** [modif: 鲜 fresh + 花 flower] *n* fresh flower, flower (朵 **duǒ**) □ 他采了路边的一朵鲜花, 送给女朋友。**Tā cǎile lùbiān de yì duǒ xiānhuā, sòng gei**

nǚpéngyou. *He picked a fresh flower by the roadside and gave it to his girlfriend.*

鲜明 xiānmíng [comp: 鲜 bright + 明 bright] *adj* bright, clear, distinct

鲜血 xiānxuè *n* blood

鲜艳 xiānyàn [comp: 鲜 bright + 艳 fresh and attractive] *adj* gaily-colored

纤 xiān Trad 纖 *n* fiber
纤维 xiānwéi *n* fiber □ 有了化学纤维, 衣服便宜多了。 Yǒule huàxué xiānwéi, yīfu piányi duōle. *With [the invention of] chemical fiber, clothes have become much cheaper.*

仙 xiān *n* fairy, immortal
仙女 xiānnǚ *n* fairy maiden

仙人 xiānrén *n* immortal, celestial

贤 xián Trad 賢 *adj* virtuous
贤惠 xiánhuì [comp: 贤 virtuous + 惠 kind] *adj* (of women) kind and wise, virtuous

衔 xián Trad 啣 **I** *v* 1 hold in the mouth 2 join, link up **II** *n* rank, title
军衔 jūnxián military rank

衔接 xiánjiē *v* link up, join

弦 xián *n* string (of a musical instrument), bow-string

咸 xián Trad 鹹 *adj* salty □ 你盐放多了, 这个菜太咸。 Nǐ yán fàngduōle, zhège cài tài xián. *You've put too much salt in the dish; it's too salty.*

闲 xián Trad 閑 *adj* idle, unoccupied □ 有的人挺忙, 有的人闲着: 分工不合理。 Yǒude rén tǐng máng, yǒude rén xiánzhe: fēngōng bù hélǐ. *While some are very busy, others are idle. The division of labor is irrational.*

清闲 qīngxián leisurely, carefree

闲话 xiánhuà [modif: 闲 idle + 话 talk] *n* chat, gossip

闲人 xiánrén [modif: 闲 idle + 人 person] idler, uninvolved person □ 闲人免入。 Xiánrén miǎn rù. *No Admittance.*

闲事 xiánshì *n* matter that does not concern you □ 你别管闲事。 Nǐ bié guǎn xiánshì. *It's none of your business.*

嫌 xián **I** *v* dislike, complain **II** *n* suspicion
避嫌 bìxián avoid suspicion

嫌疑 xiányí [comp: 嫌 suspicion + 疑 doubt] *n* suspicion

显 xiǎn Trad 顯 *v* appear, look
显得 xiǎnde *v* appear to be, seem to be □ 他穿了黑衣服显得更瘦。 Tā chuānle hēi yīfu xiǎnde gèng shòu. *Dressed in a black suit, he appeared all the thinner.*

显然 xiǎnrán *adv* clearly, obviously □ 这道题目显然答错了。 Zhè dào tímù xiǎnrán dá cuò le. *The answer to this question is obviously wrong.* □ 他的计划显然不可行。 Tā de jìhuà xiǎnrán bù kě xíng. *It's obvious that his plan is not feasible.*

显示 xiǎnshì [comp: 显 display + 示 show] *v* show, manifest

显著 xiǎnzhù *adj* remarkable, outstanding, notable □ 今年我们公司在开发新产品方面取得了显著成就。 Jīnnián wǒmen gōngsī zài kāifā xīn chǎnpǐn fāngmiàn qǔdéle xiǎnzhù chéngjiù. *This year our company has made notable achievements in developing new products.*

险 xiǎn Trad 險 *adj* dangerous (See 危险 wēixiǎn.)

县 xiàn Trad 縣 *n* (rural) county □ 中国有两千左右个县。 Zhōngguó yǒu liǎngqiān zuǒyòu ge xiàn. *China has around 2,000 counties.*

县城 xiànchéng *n* county town, county seat

县长 xiànzhǎng *n* mayor of a county

现 xiàn Trad 現 *n* now, at present
现场 xiànchǎng *n* 1 (crime, accident, disaster, etc.) scene 2 on the site, on the spot
事故现场 shìgù xiànchǎng accident scene

现成 xiànchéng *adj* ready-made

现代 xiàndài [modif: 现 present + 代 generation] *n* modern times, the contemporary age □ 我祖父不喜欢现代音乐。 Wǒ zǔfù bù xǐhuan xiàndài yīnyuè. *My grandfather does not like modern music.* □ 在这座古庙前, 盖了这么一个现代建筑, 很不合适。 Zài zhè zuò gǔ miào qián, gàile zhème yí ge xiàndài jiànzhù, hěn bù héshì. *It is inappropriate to put up such a modern building in front of this ancient temple.*

现代化 xiàndàihuà **I** *v* modernize □ 我们的教学手段应该现代化。 Wǒmen de jiàoxué shǒuduàn yīnggāi xiàndàihuà. *Our means of teaching and learning should be modernized.* **II** *n* modernization □ 办公设备的现代化提高了工作效率。 Bàngōng shèbèi de xiàndàihuà tígāole gōngzuò xiàolǜ. *The modernization of office equipment has increased work efficiency.*

现金 xiànjīn *n* cash □ 我们只收现金。 Wǒmen zhǐ shōu xiànjīn. *Cash only, please.*

现钱 xiànqián Same as 现金 xiànjīn

现实 xiànshí [comp: 现 present + 实 real] **I** *n* what is real, reality, actuality □ 现实往往不那么美好。 Xiànshí wǎngwǎng bú nàme měihǎo. *The reality is often not so perfect.* **II** *adj* realistic □ 这个计划不太现实。 Zhège jìhuà bú tài xiànshí. *This plan is not very realistic.*

现象 xiànxiàng *n* phenomenon □ 有些自然现象还不能解释。 Yǒuxiē zìrán xiànxiàng hái bù néng jiěshì. *Some natural phenomena still cannot be explained.*

现行 xiànxíng *adj* currently in effect, in effect
现行法令 xiànxíngfǎlìng decrees in effect, current laws

现在 xiànzài [comp: 现 present + 在 being] *n* the present time, now □ 我现在没有时间, 晚上再打电话给他。 Wǒ xiànzài méiyǒu shíjiān, wǎnshang zài dǎ diànhuà gěi tā. *I don't have time now, I'll ring him this evening.* □ 现在几点钟? Xiànzài jǐ diǎn zhōng? *What time is it?*

现状 xiànzhuàng [modif: 现 now + 状 situation] *n* current situation

陷 xiàn *v* 1 get bogged down 2 get trapped, be framed

陷害 xiànhài [comp: 陷 get bogged down + 害 harm] *v* make a trumped-up charge against, frame

陷入 xiànrù *v* get trapped, be caught in

馅 xiàn *n* filling, stuffing
馅儿 xiànr filling, stuffing

线 xiàn Trad 線 *n* string, thread, wire (根 gēn) □ 这根线太短, 有没有长一点的? Zhè gēn xiàn tài duǎn, yǒu méi yǒu cháng yìdiǎn de? *This string is too short. Do you have a longer one?*

线路 xiànlù *n* circuit, route

线索 xiànsuǒ *n* clue, lead (in a police case)

发现线索 fāxiàn xiànsuǒ discover a clue, find a lead

限 xiàn *v* limit
限度 **xiàndù** *n* limitation, limit
超过限度 chāoguò xiàndù exceed the limit
限期 **xiànqī I** *n* time limit, deadline **II** *v* set a time limit, impose a deadline
限期完成 xiànqī wánchéng must be done (finished, completed, etc.) by the deadline
限于 **xiànyú** *v* be confined to, be limited to
限于时间关系 xiànyú shíjiān guānxi owing to the time limitation
限制 **xiànzhì** [comp: 限 limit + 制 control] *v* limit, restrict, confine □ 为了减肥, 她限制自己一天吃两顿饭。**Wèile jiǎnféi, tā xiànzhì zìjǐ yì tiān chī liǎng dùn fàn.** *To reduce weight she restricted herself to two meals a day.* □ 政府限制进口汽车的数量。**Zhèngfǔ xiànzhì jìnkǒu qìchē de shùliàng.** *The government restricts the number of imported cars.*

宪 xiàn Trad 憲 *n* statute
宪兵 **xiànbīng** *n* military police
宪法 **xiànfǎ** *n* constitution □ 根据宪法, 公民享有言论自由。**Gēnjù xiànfǎ, gōngmín xiǎngyǒu yánlùn zìyóu.** *According to the Constitution, citizens enjoy freedom of speech.*

羡 xiàn *v* admire, envy
羡慕 **xiànmù** [comp: 羡 envy + 慕 envy] *v* envy □ 她的家庭这么美满, 真让人羡慕。**Tā de jiātíng zhème měimǎn, zhēn ràng rén xiànmù!** *Her perfectly happy family really makes one envious.* □ 我很羡慕记忆力好的人。**Wǒ hěn xiànmù jìyìlì hǎo de rén.** *I envy those who have a good memory.*

献 xiàn Trad 獻 *v* offer, dedicate
献身 **xiànshēn** [v+obj: 献 offer + 身 one's body] *v* give one's life for, devote oneself to

乡 xiāng Trad 鄉 *n* rural town □ 乡比县小, 比村大。**Xiāng bǐ xiàn xiǎo, bǐ cūn dà.** *A rural town is smaller than a county, but bigger than a village.*
乡村 **xiāngcūn** [comp: 乡 rural town + 村 village] *n* rural area, countryside
乡下 **xiāngxia** *n* countryside, rural area □ 他的爷爷奶奶住在乡下。**Tā de yéye nǎinai zhù zài xiāngxia.** *His grandpa and grandma live in the country.*
乡镇 **xiāngzhèn** [comp: 乡 rural town + 镇 township] *n* townships and villages
乡镇企业 xiāngzhèn qǐyè township and village enterprise, rural industry

相 xiāng *adv* each other, mutually
相比 **xiāngbǐ** *v* compare
相差 **xiāngchà** *v* differ, differ from
相当 **xiāngdāng I** *adj* suitable, appropriate □ 我在翻译的时候, 常常想不出一个相当的词。**Wǒ zài fānyì de shíhou, chángcháng xiǎng bu chū yí ge xiāngdāng de cí.** *When I do translation I often cannot find a suitable word.* **II** *adv* fairly, rather, quite □ 他中文说得相当不错。**Tā Zhōngwén shuō de xiāngdāng búcuò.** *He speaks Chinese rather well.*
相等 **xiāngděng** *v* be equal
相对 **xiāngduì I** *adv* relatively, comparatively (antonym 绝对 **juéduì**)
相对来说 xiāngduì láishuō relatively speaking
相对论 xiāngduìlùn the theory of relativity
相反 **xiāngfǎn** *adj* opposite, contrary (antonym 相

同 **xiāngtōng**) □ 不同的意见, 甚至相反的意见都要听。**Bùtóng de yìjiàn, shènzhì xiāngfǎn de yìjiàn dōu yào tīng.** *We should hear out different, even opposing, opinions.* □ 相反相成。**Xiāng fǎn xiāng chéng.** *Two opposing things may also complement each other.*
相符 **xiāngfú** *v* conform to, agree with, tally with
与事实相符 yǔ shìshí xiāngfú conform with the facts
相关 **xiāngguān** *v* be related to, be interrelated
相互 **xiānghù** *adj* mutual, each other □ 一对年轻人必须相互了解才能考虑婚姻。**Yíduì niánqīngrén bìxū xiānghù liǎojiě cái néng kǎolǜ hūnyīn.** *A young man and a young woman must know each other well before contemplating marriage.*
相继 **xiāngjì** *adv* in succession, one after another
相交 **xiāngjiāo** *v* intersect
相识 **xiāngshí** *v* be acquainted with, come to know
老相识 lǎoxiāngshí someone you have known for a long time, an old acquaintance
相似 **xiāngsì** *adj* similar to, be alike □ 你提出的方案和我的想法很相似。**Nǐ tíchū de fāng'àn hé wǒ de xiǎngfǎ hěn xiāngsì.** *Your plan is similar to my ideas.* □ 他们姐妹俩长得很相似, 但是脾气性格不一样。**Tāmen jiě-mèi liǎ zhǎng de hěn xiāngsì, dànshì píqi xìnggé bù yíyàng.** *The two sisters resemble each other, but have different temperaments.*
相通 **xiāngtōng I** *v* be linked with each other **II** *adj* mutually comprehensible, compatible with
相同 **xiāngtóng** *adj* identical, same □ 相同的年龄, 相同的经历使他们有很多共同语言。**Xiāngtóng de niánlíng, xiāngtóng de jīnglì shǐ tāmen yǒu hěn duō gòngtóng yǔyán.** *The same age and the same experiences give them lots of common language.*
相信 **xiāngxìn** [modif: 相 each other + 信 trust] *v* believe, believe in □ 我不相信他会做这种事。**Wǒ bù xiāngxìn tā huì zuò zhè zhǒng shì.** *I don't believe that he would do such a thing.* □ 你相信鬼故事吗? **Nǐ xiāngxìn guǐ gùshi ma?** *Do you believe ghost stories?*
相应 **xiāngyìng** *adj* corresponding, relevant
相应措施 xiāngyìng cuòshī appropriate measures

镶 xiāng Trad 鑲 *v* **1** set into, set **2** mount

香 xiāng *adj* **1** fragrant, sweet-smelling, aromatic □ 这花真香! **Zhè huā zhēn xiāng!** *How sweet this flower smells!* □ 我闻到烤肉的香味。**Wǒ wéndào kǎoròu de xiāngwèi.** *I smell the delicious aroma of roast beef.* **2** savoury, appetizing
香肠 **xiāngcháng** [modif: 香 savory + 肠 intestine] *n* sausage (根 **gēn**) □ 中国的香肠和西方的香肠味道不一样。**Zhōngguó de xiāngcháng hé xīfāng de xiāngcháng wèidao bù yíyàng.** *Chinese sausages and Western sausages taste very different.*
香港 **Xiānggǎng** [modif: 香 fragrant + 港 harbor] *n* Hong Kong □ 香港是买东西的好地方。**Xiānggǎng shì mǎi dōngxi de hǎo dìfang.** *Hong Kong is a good place for shopping.*
香蕉 **xiāngjiāo** [modif: 香 fragrant + 蕉 banana] *n* banana (根 **gēn**) □ 这些香蕉还没有熟, 过两天再吃吧。**Zhèxiē xiāngjiāo hái měiyǒu shú, guò liǎngtiān zài chī ba.** *These bananas are not ripe yet. Let's wait a few days before eating them.* □ 你饿了, 就吃一根香蕉。

Nǐ è le, jiù chī yì gēn xiāngjiāo. *Have a banana first if you're hungry.*

香味 **xiāngwèi** *n* sweet smell, fragrance

香烟 **xiāngyān** [modif: 香 fragrant + 烟 smoke] *n* cigarette (支 **zhī**)

香皂 **xiāngzào** [modif: 香 fragrant + 皂 soap] *n* toilet soap, bath soap (块 **kuài**) □ 这块香皂很好闻。**Zhè kuài xiāngzào hěn hǎowén.** *This soap smells nice.*

箱 **xiāng** *n* box, chest, trunk
箱子 **xiāngzi** [suffix: 箱 trunk + 子 nominal suffix] *n* trunk, chest, box, suitcase (只 **zhī**) □ 这个箱子是她奶奶传给她的。**Zhège xiāngzi shì tā nǎinai chuán gěi tā de.** *This trunk was passed down to her from her grandmother.*

厢 **xiāng** *n* wing (of a house), wing room
车厢 chēxiāng (train) carriage

详 **xiáng** Trad 詳 *adj* detailed
详细 **xiángxì** [comp: 详 in detail + 细 tiny] *adj* in detail, detailed □ 我只知道大概的情况，详细情况不清楚。**Wǒ zhǐ zhīdào dàgài de qíngkuàng, xiángxì qíngkuàng bù qīngchu.** *I only know the general situation and am not clear about the details.* □ 他详细说明了全部经过。**Tā xiángxì shuōmíngle quánbù jīngguò.** *He told the whole story in detail.*

祥 **xiáng** *adj* auspicious (See 吉祥 **jíxiáng**)

翔 **xiáng** *v* circle in the air, fly (See 飞翔 **fēixiáng**)

享 **xiǎng** *v* enjoy
享福 **xiǎngfú** [v+obj: 享 enjoy + 福 happiness, blessing] *v* enjoy a happy life, live a blessed life
享乐 **xiǎnglè** [v+obj: 享 enjoy + 乐 pleasure] *v* indulge in material comfort
享乐主义 xiǎnglè zhǔyì hedonism
享受 **xiǎngshòu** [comp: 享 enjoy + 受 experience] **I** *v* enjoy □ 在有些方面现代人享受的比古代皇帝还多。**Zài yǒuxiē fāngmiàn xiàndàirén xiǎngshòu de bǐ gǔdài huángdì hái duō.** *In some respects modern man enjoys more things than an emperor did in ancient times.* □ 忙了半个月，今天可以享受一下清闲了。**Mángle bàn ge yuè, jīntiān kěyǐ xiǎngshòu yíxià qīngxián le.** *After half a month's busy work, I can enjoy carefree leisure today.* **II** *n* enjoyment, pleasure
精神享受 jīngshén xiǎngshòu spiritual pleasure
享有 **xiǎngyǒu** *v* enjoy (rights, prestige, etc.)

响 **xiǎng** Trad 響 **I** *adj* loud, noisy □ 教室里在考试，你们说话声音别这么响。**Jiàoshì li zài kǎoshì, nǐmen shuōhuà shēngyīn bié zhème xiǎng.** *There's an examination in progress in the classroom. Don't talk so loudly.* **II** *n* sound, noise
响亮 **xiǎngliàng** *adj* loud and clear, resounding
响声 **xiǎngshēng** *n* sound (especially loud sounds)
响应 **xiǎngyìng** *v* respond, answer

想 **xiǎng** *v* 1 think □ 这个问题我要想想。**Zhège wèntí wǒ yào xiǎngxiang.** *I need to think over this problem.* □ 我想这个手续不会太麻烦。**Wǒ xiǎng zhè shǒuxù bú huì tài máfan.** *I don't think this procedure will be very complicated.*
想一下 xiǎng yíxià think for a while, give ... some thought □ 明天晚上跟不跟他一块儿去看电影? 让我想一下。**Míngtiān wǎnshang gēn bu gēn tā yíkuàir qù kàn diànyǐng? Ràng wǒ xiǎng yíxià.** *Shall I go to the movie with him tomorrow evening? Let me think it over.*
2 think back, recall **3** miss, remember with longing
想办法 **xiǎng bànfǎ** *v* think of a way (to do something) □ 没关系，我来想办法。**Méiguānxi, wǒ lái xiǎng bànfǎ.** *It's OK. I'll think of a way.*
想法 **xiǎngfa** [modif: 想 thinking + 法 way, method] *n* what one thinks, idea, opinion □ 你有什么想法, 尽管谈。**Nǐ yǒu shénme xiǎngfa, jìnguǎn tán.** *Feel free to say whatever you have in mind.* □ 老师想了解一下学生对开口语课的想法。**Lǎoshī xiǎng liǎojiě yíxià xuésheng duì kāi kǒuyǔ kè de xiǎngfa.** *The teacher wants to find out what the students think of introducing an oral Chinese class.*
想方设法 **xiǎng fāng shè fǎ** *idiom* try every means, do all one can
想念 **xiǎngniàn** [comp: 想 think + 念 miss (someone)] *v* miss, remember with longing □ 祖母去世两年了，我还非常想念她。**Zǔmǔ qùshì liǎng nián le, wǒ hái fēicháng xiǎngniàn tā.** *It's over two years since Granny died, but I still miss her very much.*
想像 **xiǎngxiàng** [v+obj: 想 think + 象 image] *v* imagine □ 小女孩常常想像自己是一位美丽的舞蹈演员。**Xiǎonǚhái chángcháng xiǎngxiàng zìjǐ shì yí wèi měilì de wǔdǎo yǎnyuán.** *The little girl often imagines herself to be a beautiful dancer.* □ 我不能想像, 没有音乐, 怎么生活。**Wǒ bù néng xiǎngxiàng, méiyǒu yīnyuè, zěnme shēnghuó.** *I cannot imagine how one can live without music.*
想像力 xiǎngxiànglì imaginative power

相 **xiàng** as in 相声 **xiàngsheng**
相声 **xiàngsheng** *n* comic dialogue, comic cross-talk

巷 **xiàng** *n* narrow street, alley (条 **tiáo**)
一条深巷 yìtiáo shēn xiàng a long alley

项 1 **xiàng** Trad 項 *n* the neck
项链 **xiàngliàn** *n* necklace (条 **tiáo**)
戴一条珍珠项链 dài yì tiáo zhēnzhū xiàngliàn wear a pearl necklace

项 2 **xiàng** Trad 項 *measure wd* item of something (for things that are composed of items or things considered to be components)
一项任务 yí xiàng rènwù a mission
项目 **xiàngmù** [comp: 项 item + 目 item] *n* item □ 他负责一个重要的研究项目。**Tā fùzé yíge zhòngyào de yánjiū xiàngmù.** *He is in charge of an important research project.*

象 1 **xiàng** *n* elephant (头 **tóu**, 只 **zhī**) □ 小孩子都喜欢大象。**Xiǎoháizi dōu xǐhuan dàxiàng.** *Children are all fond of elephants.*

NOTE: Chinese often fondly refer to elephants as 大象 **dàxiàng**.

象棋 **xiàngqí** *n* chess (副 **fù**, 盘 **pán**)
国际象棋 guójì xiàngqí Western chess
中国象棋 Zhōngguó xiàngqí Chinese chess
下一盘象棋 xià yì pán xiàngqí play a game of chess

象 2 **xiàng** Same as 像 **xiàng I** *v*
象征 **xiàngzhēng** **I** *n* symbol **II** *v* symbolize

像 **xiàng I** *v* resemble, take after, be like □ 她很像妈妈。**Tā hěn xiàng māma.** *She takes after her*

mother. □ 他的脾气一点也不像他爸爸。**Tā de píqì yìdiǎn yě bú xiàng tā bàba.** *His temperment is not at all like his father's.* **II** *n* likeness of (a human being), portrait (幅 **fú**) □ 墙上挂着祖父的像。**Qiáng shang guàzhe zǔfù de xiàng.** *On the wall hangs a portrait of their grandfather.*

像样 **xiàngyàng** *adj* presentable, up to the standard

橡 **xiàng** *n* rubber, rubber tree, oak, oak tree
橡胶 **xiàngjiāo** *n* rubber
橡胶树 **xiàngjiāoshù** rubber tree
橡皮 **xiàngpí** *n* eraser (a piece of rubber) (块 **kuài**)

向 **xiàng** **I** *v* face □ 这个房间有两个窗子，一个向南，一个向东。**Zhège fángjiān yǒu liǎng ge chuāngzi, yí ge xiàng nán, yí ge xiàng dōng.** *There are two windows in the room. One faces south and the other faces east.* **II** *prep* in the direction of, towards □ 中国的长江，黄河都向东流。**Zhōngguó de Chángjiāng, Huánghé dōu xiàng dōng liú.** *China's Yangtze River and Yellow River flow to the east.* **III** *adv* all along, always
向导 **xiàngdǎo** *n* guide
旅游向导 lǚyóu xiàngdǎo tourist guide
向来 **xiànglái** *adv* always, all along
向往 **xiàngwǎng** *v* yearn for, look forward to

消 **xiāo** *v* 1 vanish, disappear 2 dispel, remove
消除 **xiāochú** [comp: 消 remove + 除 get rid of] *v* clear up, dispel □ 我跟他好好谈了一次，消除了我们之间的误会。**Wǒ gēn tā hǎohǎo tánle yícì, xiāochúle wǒmen zhījiān de wùhuì.** *I had a good talk with him and cleared up the misunderstanding between us.*
消毒 **xiāodú** [v+obj: 消 dispel + 毒 toxin] *v* disinfect, sterilize
消费 **xiāofèi** *v* consume □ 生活水平提高了，人们消费的商品就越来越多。**Shēnghuó shuǐpíng tígāole, rénmen xiāofèi de shāngpǐn jiù yuèláiyuè duō.** *As people's living standard rises, they consume more and more goods.*
消费品 xiāofèipǐn consumer commodities, consumer goods
消费者 xiāofèizhě consumer
消化 **xiāohuà** *v* digest □ 我中饭还没有消化呢，不想吃晚饭。**Wǒ zhōngfàn hái méiyǒu xiāohuà ne, bù xiǎng chī wǎnfàn.** *I still haven't digested my lunch. I don't want to eat supper.* □ 今天老师讲了这么多，我还没有完全消化。**Jīntiān lǎoshī jiǎngle zhème duō, wǒ hái méiyǒu wánquán xiāohuà.** *The teacher gave us so much information today, I haven't entirely digested it.*
消化不良 xiāohuà bùliáng indigestion
消化系统 xiāohuà xìtǒng digestive system
消极 **xiāojí** *adj* lacking enthusiasm, passive (antonym 积极 **jījí**)
消灭 **xiāomiè** [comp: 消 dispel + 灭 exterminate] *v* eliminate, wipe out □ 这种害虫在本地区基本消灭。**Zhè zhǒng hàichóng zài běn dìqū jīběn xiāomiè.** *This pest has been mainly exterminated in this region.*
消失 **xiāoshī** [comp: 消 vanish + 失 lose] *v* disappear, vanish □ 太阳出来以后，雾渐渐消失了。**Tàiyang chūlai yǐhòu, wù jiànjiàn xiāoshī le.** *As the sun came out, the fog dissipated.*
消息 **xiāoxi** [comp: 消 information + 息 news] *n* news (条 **tiáo**) □ 今天报上有什么消息？**Jīntiān bàoshang yǒu shénme xiāoxi?** *What's the news in today's paper?* □ 我告诉你一个好消息。**Wǒ gàosu nǐ**

yí ge hǎo xiāoxi. *I'll tell you a piece of good news.* □ 一有关于他的消息，请马上告诉我。**Yì yǒu guānyú tā de xiāoxi, qǐng mǎshàng gàosu wǒ.** *Please let me know as soon as you've got news about him.*

宵 **xiāo** *n* night (See 元宵 **yuánxiāo**)

销 **xiāo** Trad 銷 *v* 1 sell, market
畅销书 chàngxiāoshū bestseller (book)
2 cancel, annual
销毁 **xiāohuǐ** [comp: 销 annual + 毁 destroy] *v* destroy (especially by burning)
销毁罪证 xiāohuǐ zuìzhèng destroy incriminating evidence
销路 **xiāolù** [modif: 销 sell + 路 route] *n* market, sale
销路很好 xiāolù hěn hǎo (of a commodity) have a good market
销售 **xiāoshòu** [comp: 销 sell + 售 sell] *n* sale, market □ 你们销售这家汽车制造厂的零件吗？**Nǐmen xiāoshòu zhè jiā qìchē zhìzàochǎng de língjiàn ma?** *Do you sell parts from this auto manufacturer?*
销售部 xiāoshòubù sales department
销售额 xiāoshòu'é revenue from sales, sales takings
销售量 xiāoshòuliàng sales volume

削 **xiāo** *v* peel with a knife
削苹果 xiāo píngguǒ peel an apple

淆 **xiáo** *v* confuse (See 混淆 **hùnxiáo**)

小 **xiǎo** *adj* 1 small, little (antonym 大 **dà**) □ 这双鞋太小了，有没有大一点儿的？**Zhè shuāng xié tài xiǎo le, yǒu méiyǒu dà yìdiǎnr de?** *This pair of shoes is too small. Do you have a bigger size?* 2 being a child, young □ 我小时候，放暑假的时候，常常住在奶奶家。**Wǒ xiǎo shíhou, fàng shǔjià de shíhou, chángcháng zhù zai nǎinai jiā.** *When I was a child, I often stayed with granny during the summer holidays.* □ 我姓李，您就叫我小李吧。**Wǒ xìng Lǐ, nín jiù jiào wǒ Xiǎo Lǐ ba.** *My family name is Li. You can call me Xiao Li.*
小孩儿 xiǎoháir young child, child

NOTE: "小 **xiǎo** + family name," like 小李 **Xiǎo Lǐ**, is a casual, friendly form of address to a person younger than oneself. See note on 老 **lǎo** for forms of address like 老李 **Lǎo Lǐ**.

小便 **xiǎobiàn** [modif: 小 small, minor + 便 convenience] **I** *n* urine
小便池 xiǎobiànchí urinal
II *v* urinate
小费 **xiǎofèi** [modif: 小 small + 费 fee] *n* tip, gratuity □ 你们在餐厅留下小费了吗？**Nǐmen zài cāntīng liúxia xiǎofèi le ma?** *Have you left a tip in the restaurant?*
小伙子 **xiǎohuǒzi** *n* young man, lad □ 这些农村来的小伙子又老实又肯干。**Zhèxiē nóngcūn lái de xiǎohuǒzi yòu lǎoshí yòu kěngàn.** *These country lads are honest and hardworking.*

NOTE: See note on 姑娘 **gūniang**.

小姐 **xiǎojiě** [comp: 小 young + 姐 elder sister] *n* 1 young lady □ 有一位小姐要见您。**Yǒu yí wèi xiǎojiě**

yào jiàn nǐ. *There's a young lady wanting to see you.* **2** Miss □ 王先生, 王太太和他们的女儿王小姐都在美国旅行。 **Wáng xiānsheng, Wáng tàitai hé tāmen de nǚ'ér Wáng xiǎojiě dōu zài Měiguó lǚxíng.** *Mr and Mrs Wang, with their daughter Miss Wang, are all traveling in the United States.*

NOTE: 小姐 **xiǎojiě** is a common form of address to a young (or not so young) woman. If her family name is not known, just use 小姐 **xiǎojiě**. 小姐 **xiǎojiě** is also the form of address for *a waitress* or *female attendant*, e.g. □ 小姐, 请给我一杯水。 **Xiǎojiě, qǐng gěi wǒ yì bēi shuǐ.** *Miss, please give me a glass of water.*

小康 **xiǎokāng** *adj* fairly prosperous, well-off, well-to-do
小康社会 xiǎokāng shèhuì a well-off society

小麦 **xiǎomài** *n* wheat □ 在中国北方粮食以小麦为主。 **Zài Zhōngguó běifāng liángshí yǐ xiǎomài wéi zhǔ.** *In northern China, wheat is the main cereal crop.*

小米 **xiǎomǐ** *n* millet

小朋友 **xiǎopéngyou** *n* (a friendly form of address or reference) child □ 小朋友, 你们校长办公室在哪里? **Xiǎopéngyou, nǐmen xiàozhǎng bàngōngshì zài nǎlǐ?** *Where's your headmaster's office, children?*

小气 **xiǎoqì** *adj* stingy, miserly

小区 **xiǎoqū** *n* residential community, neighborhood

小时 **xiǎoshí** [modif: 小 small + 时 time] *n* hour □ 我等你等了一个半小时了。 **Wǒ děng nǐ děngle yí ge bàn xiǎoshí le.** *I've been waiting for you for an hour and a half.*
半小时 bàn xiǎoshí half an hour

小时工 **xiǎoshígōng** *n* (domestic) worker paid on an hourly basis

小数 **xiǎoshù** *n* decimal

小说 **xiǎoshuō** [modif: 小 small + 说 talk] *n* novel (本 **běn**, 篇 **piān**) □ 这本小说的作者有丰富的生活经历。 **Zhè běn xiǎoshuō de zuòzhě yǒu fēngfù de shēnghuó jīnglì.** *The author of this novel has had rich life experiences.* □ 这篇小说语言优美, 但是没有多大意思。 **Zhè piān xiǎoshuō yǔyán yōuměi, dànshì méiyǒu duō dà yìsi.** *The language of this story is beautiful but it is not very meaningful.*
小说家 xiǎoshuōjiā (accomplished) novelist
爱情小说 àiqíng xiǎoshuō romance novel
长篇小说 chángpiān xiǎoshuō novel
短篇小说 duǎnpiān xiǎoshuō short story, story
历史小说 lìshǐ xiǎoshuō historical novel

小提琴 **xiǎotíqín** *n* violin
小提琴手 xiǎotíqínshǒu violinist
拉小提琴 lā xiǎotíqín play the violin

小偷 **xiǎotōu** [modif: 小 small, petty + 偷 thief] *n* thief, pickpocket □ 抓小偷! 抓小偷! **Zhuō xiǎotōu! Zhuō xiǎotōu!** *Stop thief! Stop thief!*

小心 **xiǎoxīn** [modif: 小 small + 心 the heart] *adj* careful, cautious □ 他说话, 做事都很小心。 **Tā shuōhuà, zuòshì dōu hěn xiǎoxīn.** *He is cautious in speech and action.* □ 今天有雾, 开车要特别小心。 **Jīntiān yǒu wù, kāichē yào tèbié xiǎoxīn.** *It's foggy today. You need to be particularly careful while driving.*

小型 **xiǎoxíng** *adj* small-sized

小学 **xiǎoxué** [modif: 小 small + 学 school] *n* primary school (座 **zuò**, 所 **suǒ**) □ 这座小学操场太小, 孩子没地方玩。 **Zhè zuò xiǎoxué cāochǎng tài xiǎo, háizi méi dìfang wán.** *This primary school's sports ground is too small and the children have nowhere to play.*
小学生 xiǎoxuéshēng primary school student, pupil

小子 **xiǎozi** *n* son, boy

小组 **xiǎozǔ** *n* small group

晓 **xiǎo** Trad 曉 *v* know
晓得 **xiǎode** *v* Same as 知道 **zhīdào**. Only used in colloquial Chinese.

孝 **xiào** *n* filial piety
孝顺 **xiàoshùn** [comp: 孝 filial piety + 顺 obedience] *v* perform one's filial duties faithfully, be obedient and considerate of one's parents □ 他很孝顺父母。 **Tā hěn xiàoshùn fùmǔ.** *He is obedient and considerate of his parents.*

效 **xiào** *n* effect
效果 **xiàoguǒ** [comp: 效 effect + 果 result] *n* effect, result □ 对孩子太严格, 往往效果不好。 **Duì háizi tài yángé, wǎngwǎng xiàoguǒ bù hǎo.** *Being too strict with children often gives poor results.* □ 这种新方法效果怎么样? **Zhè zhǒng xīn fāngfǎ xiàoguǒ zěnmeyàng?** *How effective is this new method?*
效力 **xiàolì** *n* desired effects, intended results
效率 **xiàolǜ** [modif: 效 effect + 率 rate] *n* efficiency □ 我们必须不断提高工作效率。 **Wǒmen bìxū búduàn tígāo gōngzuò xiàolǜ.** *We must constantly improve work efficiency.*
效益 **xiàoyì** *n* beneficial (economic) results, economic benefits

校 **xiào** *n* school
校徽 **xiàohuī** *n* school badge
校园 **xiàoyuán** *n* school ground, campus
校长 **xiàozhǎng** [modif: 校 school + 长 chief] *n* headmaster, principal, university president, university vice chancellor □ 这位校长得到大多数教师的拥护。 **Zhèwèi xiàozhǎng dédào dàduōshù jiàoshī de yōnghù.** *This principal enjoys the support of most of the teachers.* □ 在中文里, 小学、中学、大学的负责人都叫 "校长"。 **Zài Zhōngwén li, xiǎoxué, zhōngxué, dàxué de fùzérén dōu jiào "xiàozhǎng".** *In Chinese, people in charge of primary schools, high schools or universities are all called "xiaozhang."*

NOTES: (1) While in Chinese the chief of any school is called 校长 **xiàozhǎng**, different terms are required in English. (2) In an English-system university, the vice-chancellor is its chief executive officer. *Vice-chancellor* should therefore be translated as 校长 **xiàozhǎng** while *chancellor*, being largely an honorary position, should be 名誉校长 **míngyù xiàozhǎng**.

笑 **xiào** *v* **1** laugh, smile (antonym 哭 **kū**) □ 他笑着和我握手。 **Tā xiàozhe hé wǒ wòshǒu.** *He shook my hand, smiling.* □ 你笑什么? **Nǐ xiào shénme?** *What are you laughing at?* □ 笑一笑, 十年少。 **Xiào yi xiào, shí nián shào.** *Laugh and you'll be ten years younger.* (→ *Laughter is the best medicine.*)
大笑 dàxiào laugh
2 laugh at, make fun of

笑话 **xiàohua** [modif: 笑 laughing + 话 talk] **I** *n* joke □ 我来讲个笑话。 **Wǒ lái jiǎng ge xiàohua.** *I'll tell you*

a joke. □ 他很会讲笑话。**Tā hěn huì jiǎng xiàohua.** *He is good at telling jokes.* **II** *v* laugh at □ 我中文讲得不好，你们别笑话我。**Wǒ Zhōngwén jiǎng de bù hǎo, nǐmen bié xiàohua wǒ.** *I don't speak Chinese very well. Please don't laugh at me.*

笑容 **xiàoróng** *n* smiling expression, smile
笑容满面 **xiàoróng mǎnmiàn** be all smiles

肖 **xiào** *v* resemble, be like
肖像 **xiàoxiàng** *n* portrait (幅 **fú**)

啸 **xiào** *v* howl, roar

此 **xiē** *measure wd* some, a few, a little □ 午饭我吃了一些面包。**Wǔfàn wǒ chīle yìxiē miànbāo.** *I had some bread for lunch.*
好些 **hǎoxiē** quite a few, lots of □ 昨天晚上他和老朋友谈了很久，喝了好些酒。**Zuótiān wǎnshang tā hé lǎo péngyou tánle hěn jiǔ, hēle hǎoxiē jiǔ.** *Yesterday evening he chatted with his old friends for a long time and drank lots of wine.*

歇 **xiē** *v* take a rest □ 我走不动了，歇会儿吧。**Wǒ zǒu bu dòng le, xiē huìr ba.** *I can't walk any further. Let's take a break.*

协 **xié** Trad 協 *v* **1** join **2** assist
协定 **xiédìng** [comp: 协 joint + 定 decision] *n* agreement, treaty □ 两家公司签订了技术合作的协定。**Liǎng jiā gōngsī qiāndìngle jìshù hézuò de xiédìng.** *The two companies signed an agreement on technological cooperation.*
协会 **xiéhuì** *n* association (an organization)
环境保护者协会 **huánjìng bǎohùzhě xiéhuì** Environmentalists Association
协力 **xiélì** [v+obj: 协 join+ 力 strength] *v* join in a common effort, work together
协商 **xiéshāng** *v* discuss and seek advice, consult
协调 **xiétiáo** *v* coordinate, harmonize
协议 **xiéyì** *n* agreement (a document)
协议书 **xiéyìshū** agreement (a document) (份 **fèn**)
达成协议 **dáchéng xiéyì** reach an agreement
协助 **xiézhù** [comp 协 assist + 助 help] *n* assistance □ 由于当地居民的协助，警方很快逮捕了罪犯。**Yóuyú dāngdì jūmín de xiézhù, jǐngfāng hěn kuài dàibǔle zuìfàn.** *Thanks to the asssitance by local residents, the police arrested the criminal in no time.*
协作 **xiézuò** [v: 协 join + 作 work] *v* cooperate

胁 **xié** Trad 脅 *v* threaten (See 威胁 **wēixié**)

斜 **xié** *adj* oblique, slanting **II** □ 他斜穿过马路。**Tā xié chuānguo mǎlù.** *He crossed the street diagonally.*

挟 **xié** *v* hold under the arm
挟持 **xiéchí** *v* **1** seize by force **2** detain under duress

携 **xié** *v* **1** carry, take along with **2** take by the hand
携带 **xiédài** *v* carry, take along □ 以下物品不准携带上机：… **Yǐxià wùpǐn bùzhǔn xiédài shàngjī:** ... *It is forbidden to carry the following objects on the plane:* ...
携手 **xiéshǒu** *adv* hand in hand
携手并进 **xiéshǒu bìngjìn** go forward hand in hand, advance side by side

邪 **xié** *adj* evil, heretical
邪教 **xiéjiào** [modif: 邪 evil + 教 religion] *n* religious cult, cult

鞋 **xié** *n* shoe (只 **zhī**, 双 **shuāng**) □ 他总是穿一双黑鞋。**Tā zǒngshi chuān yì shuāng hēi xié.** *He always wears a pair of black shoes.*
凉鞋 **liáng xié** sandals
皮鞋 **pí xié** leather shoes
拖鞋 **tuō xié** slippers
雨鞋 **yǔ xié** rubber boots
运动鞋 **yùndòng xié** sports shoes
鞋带 **xiédài** *n* shoelace, shoestring (根 **gēn**, 副 **fù**)
系鞋带 **jì xiédài** tie shoelace

谐 **xié** Trad 諧 *adj* harmonious (See 和谐 **héxié**)

血 **xiě** *n* Same as 血 **xuè**. Used only in colloquial Chinese.

写 **xiě** Trad 寫 *v* write, write with a pen □ 这个汉字怎么写？**Zhège Hànzì zěnme xiě?** *How do you write this Chinese character?* □ 他在写一篇经济学论文。**Tā zài xiě yì piān jīngjìxué lùnwén.** *He is writing a thesis on economics.* □ 我经常用电脑，不大写字。**Wǒ jīngcháng yòng diànnǎo, búdà xiě zì.** *I often use computers and seldom write with a pen.*
写作 **xiězuò** *v* write as a professional writer, compose essays

泻 **xiè** *v* flow swiftly
腹泻 **fùxiè** have diarrhea

卸 **xiè** *v* **1** unload **2** remove, strip (See 装卸 **zhuāngxiè**)

泄 **xiè** *v* allow air or liquid to escape, let out, leak
泄露 **xièlòu** [comp: 泄 leak + 露 expose] *v* leak (information)
泄气 **xièqì** [v+obj: 泄 let out + 气 air] *v* lose heart, be discouraged

谢 **xiè** Trad 謝 *v* **1** thank **2** decline
谢谢 **xièxie** *v* thank □ "谢谢你。" "不客气。" **"Xièxie nǐ." "Bú kèqi."** *"Thank you." "You're welcome."* □ 你给我这么大帮助，我不知道怎样谢谢你才好。**Nǐ gěi wǒ zhème dà bāngzhù, wǒ bù zhīdào zěnyàng xièxie nǐ cái hǎo.** *You've given me so much help. I don't know how to thank you.*

NOTE: There are many ways of replying to 谢谢你 **xièxie nǐ**, e.g. □ 不客气。**Bú kèqi.** *You don't have to be so polite.* □ 不用谢。**Bú yòng xiè.** *You don't have to thank me.* □ 没关系。**Méi guānxi.** *It doesn't matter.*

谢绝 **xièjué** *v* decline (an invitation, an offer, etc.), refuse politely

械 **xiè** *n* tool (See 机械 **jīxiè**.)

屑 **xiè** *n* butts, scraps
面包屑 **miànbāo xiè** crumbs (of bread)

心 **xīn** *n* **1** the heart □ 这个人心真好！**Zhège rén xīn zhēn hǎo!** *This person is really kindhearted.*
用心 **yòngxīn** apply oneself to □ 你学习不太用心。**Nǐ xuéxí bú tài yòngxīn.** *You don't really apply yourself to studying.*
放心 **fàngxīn** feel relieved, be assured, at ease □ 你一个人去爬山，我不放心。**Nǐ yí ge rén qù páshān, wǒ bú fàngxīn.** *I'd be worried if you go mountain-climbing all by yourself.*
开心 **kāixīn** be joyous
痛心 **tòngxīn** pained, agonized

伤心 shāngxīn heartbroken
2 mind, feeling **3** core, center
心爱 xīn'ài *adj* beloved, treasured
心得 xīndé *n* what one has learned from work, study, etc, gain in understanding
心理 xīnlǐ [comp: 心 the heart + 理 theory] *n* mentality, psychology □ 夫妻常常吵架, 会对孩子的心理造成不良影响。 **Fūqī chángcháng chǎojià, huì duì háizi de xīnlǐ zàochéng bùliáng yíngxiǎng.** *Frequent quarrels between husband and wife will have undesirable effects on their child's mental well-being.*
心理分析 xīnlǐ fēnxi psychoanalysis
心理学 xīnlǐxué (the science of) psychology
心理咨询 xīnlǐ zīxún psychological consultation
心里 xīnli *adv* in the heart, in the mind
心里有事 xīnliyǒushì have something on one's mind
心灵 xīnlíng **I** *n* soul, spirit
心灵深处 xīnlíng shēnchù deep down in one's heart
II *adj* quick-witted, agile-minded, bright
心灵手巧 xīnlíng shǒuqiǎo intelligent and capable, clever and deft
心目 xīnmù [comp: 心 the heart + 目 the eyes] *n* mental view, eyes
在他的心目中 zài tāde xīnmùzhōng in his eyes, in his opinion and judgment
心情 xīnqíng [comp: 心 the heart + 情 emotion] *n* state of mind, mood □ 她孩子又生病了, 她心情怎么会好? **Tā háizi yòu shēngbìng le, tā xīnqíng zěnme huì hǎo?** *Her child has fallen ill again. How can she be in a good mood?*
心事 xīnshì [modif: 心 the heart + 事 matter] *n* worry, something on one's mind □ 你好像有什么心事, 怎么啦? **Nǐ hǎoxiàng yǒu shénme xīnshì, zěnme la?** *You seem to be worrying about something, what is it?*
心思 xīnsi [comp: 心 heart + 思 thought] *n* **1** idea, thought **2** state of mind, mood
没有心思出去玩儿 méiyǒu xīnsi chūqu wánr not in a mood to go out
心疼 xīnténg *v* **1** love dearly **2** feel sorry
心头 xīntóu *n* mind, heart
牢记心头 láojì xīntóu bear firmly in mind
心血 xīnxuè [comp: 心 the heart + 血 blood] *n* painstaking effort
付出很大心血 fùchū hěn dà xīnxuè put a great deal of painstaking efforts
心血来潮 xīnxuè láicháo *idiom* be seized by an impulse, have a brainstorm
心眼儿 xīnyǎnr *n* heart, mind, intention
没安什么好心眼儿 méi ān shénme hǎo xīnyǎnr do not mean well, have some bad intention
心意 xīnyì [modif: 心 the heart + 意 meaning] *n* regard, warm feelings, good intention □ 您的心意我领了, 但是礼物不能收。 **Nín de xīnyì wǒ lǐng le, dànshì lǐwù bùnéng shōu.** *I appreciate your kindness, but I can't take your gift.*
心愿 xīnyuàn *n* wish, aspiration
心脏 xīnzàng [modif: 心 the heart + 脏 human organ] *n* the heart (as a medical term) □ 经过检查, 医生确定他有心脏病。 **Jīngguò jiǎnchá, yīshēng quèdìng tā yǒu xīnzàng bìng.** *After an examination, the doctor confirmed that he had heart trouble.*

心直口快 xīnzhí kǒukuài *adj* frank and outspoken
欣 xīn *adj* joyful
欣赏 xīnshǎng *v* admire, appreciate □ 秋天, 人们到北京附近的香山欣赏美丽的红叶。 **Qiūtiān, rénmen dào Běijīng fùjìn de xiāng shān xīnshǎng měilì de hóng yè.** *In fall, people go to the Fragrance Hill near Beijing to admire the beautiful red leaves.*
欣欣向荣 xīnxīn xiàng róng *idiom* flourishing, prosperous
辛 xīn *adj* **1** spicy hot **2** laborious, hard
辛苦 xīnkǔ [comp: 辛 hard + 苦 bitter] **I** *adj* **1** hard and toilsome (job) □ 这个工作很辛苦。 **Zhège gōngzuò hěn xīnkǔ.** *This is a tough job.* □ 你们辛苦了。 **Nǐmen xīnkǔ le.** *You've been working hard.*
2 harsh, difficult (life) □ 很多农民的生活很辛苦。 **Hěn duō nóngmín de shēnghuó hěn xīnkǔ.** *Many peasants live a hard life.* **II** *v* (used to request somebody's service) □ 辛苦你把这几只箱子搬到楼上去。 **Xīnkǔ nǐ bǎ zhè jǐ zhī xiāngzi bān dào lóu shang qù.** *Would you please carry these suitcases upstairs?*

NOTE: "你们辛苦了!" **"Nǐmen xīnkǔ le!"** is used by a superior to express appreciation of hard work done by subordinate(s). When somebody has done you a service, you can say: "辛苦你了!" **"Xīnkǔ nǐ le!"**

辛勤 xīnqín *adj* industrious
锌 xīn *n* zinc (Zn)
新 xīn **I** *adj* new (antonym 旧 jiù) □ 你觉得我这件新衣服怎么样? **Nǐ juéde wǒ zhè jiàn xīn yīfu zěnmeyàng?** *What do you think of my new dress?* □ 旧的不去, 新的不来。 **Jiù de bú qù, xīn de bù lái.** *If old stuff doesn't go away, new stuff won't come.* (→ *If you don't discard old things, you won't be able to use new things.*) **II** *adv* newly, recently
新陈代谢 xīnchéndàixiè *idiom* metabolism
新房 xīnfáng [modif: 新 new + 房 room] *n* bridal bedroom
新近 xīnjìn *adv* recently, lately
新加坡 Xīnjiāpō *n* Singapore □ 大多数新加坡人会说华语。 **Dàduōshù Xīnjiāpōrén huì shuō Huáyǔ.** *Most Singaporeans can speak Chinese.*
新郎 xīnláng [modif: 新 new + 郎 young man] *n* bridegroom
新年 xīnnián [modif: 新 new + 年 year] *n* New Year □ 新年好! **Xīnnián hǎo!** *Happy New Year!* □ 祝您新年快乐! **Zhù nín xīnnián kuàilè!** *I wish you a happy New Year!*
新年贺卡 xīnnián hèkǎ New Year card
新娘 xīnniáng [modif: 新 new + 娘 young woman] *n* bride
新生 xīnshēng *n* **1** newborn
新生儿 xīnshēng'ér newborn baby
2 new student
新生报到 xīnshēng bàodào new students registration
3 new life, a new leaf (in one's life)
开始新生 kāishǐ xīnshēng turn over a new leaf
新式 xīnshì *n* new type, new style
新闻 xīnwén [modif: 新 new + 闻 what is heard] *n* news (of current affairs) (条 tiáo) □ 你是怎么样得到新闻的—读报纸, 听广播, 还是看电视? **Nǐ shì zěnmeyàng**

dédào xīnwén de—dú bàozhǐ, tīng guǎngbō, háishì kàn diànshì? *How do you get the news—by reading newspapers, listening to radio or watching television?* □ 他每天一边吃晚饭，一边看电视新闻。**Tā měi tiān yìbiān chī wǎnfàn, yìbiān kàn diànshì xīnwén.** *Every day he watches news on TV while having his supper.*

新西兰 Xīnxīlán *n* New Zealand □ 每年很多外国人到新西兰去旅游。**Měi nián hěn duō wàiguórén dào Xīnxīlán qù lǚyóu.** *Every year many foreigners go to New Zealand on holiday.*

新鲜 xīnxiān [comp: 新 new + 鲜 fresh] *adj* fresh □ 我们每天都要吃新鲜蔬菜。**Wǒmen měi tiān dōu yào chī xīnxiān shūcài.** *We should eat fresh vegetables every day.* □ 这条鱼不新鲜了。**Zhè tiáo yú bù xīnxiān le.** *This fish is no longer fresh.*

新兴 xīnxīng [modif: 新 new + 兴 emerging] *adj* new and fast developing, burgeoning
新兴产业 xīnxīng chǎnyè fast growing industry, sunrise industry

新型 xīnxíng *n* new type, new pattern

新颖 xīnyǐng *adj* new and original

薪 xīn 1 firewood 2 salary
高薪养廉 gāoxīn yǎnglián the policy of high salary for civil servants in order to cultivate a clean government

薪金 xīnjīn Same as 薪水 **xīnshui**

薪水 xīnshui [comp: 薪 firewood + 水 water] *n* salary, wages

信 1 xìn I *v* believe, trust □ 我不信他一天能干这么多活。**Wǒ bú xìn tā yì tiān néng gàn zhème duō huó.** *I don't believe he could have done so much work in a day.* II *n* trust

信贷 xìndài *n* (in banking) credit

信赖 xìnlài I *v* trust, have faith in
可以信赖的 kěyǐ xìnlài de trustworthy, reliable

信念 xìnniàn *n* faith, conviction

信任 xìnrèn [comp: 信 trust + 任 entrust] I *v* trust, have confidence in □ 你既然请他做这么重要的工作，一定很信任他。**Nǐ jìrán qǐng tā zuò zhème zhòngyào de gōngzuò, yídìng hěn xìnrèn tā.** *Since you've asked him to do such an important job, you must really trust him.* II *n* trust, confidence □ 他得到董事会的信任，到外地去开展业务。**Tā dédào dǒngshìhuì de xìnrèn, dào wàidì qù kāizhǎn yèwù.** *He earned the trust of the board and has gone to other parts of the country to develop the company business.*

信心 xìnxīn [modif: 信 believe + 心 the heart] *n* confidence, faith □ 我对公司的前途充满信心。**Wǒ duì gōngsī de qiántú chōngmǎn xìnxīn.** *I have full confidence in the company's future.* □ 他对自己缺乏信心。**Tā duì zìjǐ quēfá xìnxīn.** *He lacks self-confidence.*

信用 xìnyòng *n* 1 trustworthiness
讲信用 jiǎngxìnyòng keep one's word, be trustworthy 2 credit
信用卡 xìnyòngkǎ credit card

信誉 xìnyù *n* reputation, prestige

信 2 xìn *n* 1 letter, mail □ 现在人们很少写信。**Xiànzài rénmen hěn shǎo xiě xìn.** *People don't often write letters now.*
寄信 jì xìn post a letter
介绍信 jièshàoxìn letter of recommendation, reference

收到信 shōudào xìn receive a letter
祝贺信 zhùhèxìn letter of congratulation 2 sign, evidence

信封 xìnfēng *n* envelope

信号 xìnhào *n* signal

信件 xìnjiàn *n* letters, mail

信息 xìnxī [comp: 信 message + 息 news, tiding] *n* information □ 这台电脑处理信息十分迅速。**Zhè tái diànnǎo chǔlǐ xìnxī shífēn xùnsù.** *This computer processes information rapidly.* □ 你有关于他的信息吗？**Nǐ yǒu guānyú tā de xìnxī ma?** *Do you have any information about him?*

信息产业 xìnxī chǎnyè *n* information industry

衅 xìn *n* quarrel, dispute
挑衅 tiǎoxìn provoke

兴 xīng Trad 興 I *v* 1 promote 2 start, begin II *adj* flourishing

兴办 xīngbàn [comp: 兴 promote + 办 manage] *v* set up, initiate

兴奋 xīngfèn [comp: 兴 flourishing + 奋 excited] *adj* excited, overjoyed □ 她们得了冠军，兴奋得跳了起来。**Tāmen déle guànjūn, xīngfèn de tiàole qǐlai.** *When they won the championship, they were so overjoyed that they jumped.* □ 不要在兴奋的时候，做任何决定。**Bú yào zài xīngfèn de shíhou, zuò rènhé juédìng.** *Don't make decisions when you are excited.*

兴奋剂 xīngfènjì *n* stimulant

兴建 xīngjiàn *v* build, construct

兴起 xīngqǐ *v* start and become popular, rise

兴旺 xīngwàng *adj* prosperous, thriving

星 xīng *n* star (颗 kē)
行星 xíngxīng planet □ 太阳系有九大行星。**Tàiyangxì yǒu jiǔ dà xíngxīng.** *There are nine planets in the solar system.*

NOTE: In everyday Chinese 星星 **xīngxing** is normally used instead of 星 xīng, e.g. □ 今天晚上的星星真亮。**Jīntiān wǎnshang de xīngxing zhēn liàng.** *Tonight the stars are really bright.*

星期 xīngqī *n* week (个 gè) □ 一年有五十二个星期。**Yì nián yǒu wǔshí èr ge xīngqī.** *There're fifty-two weeks in a year.*
星期一 Xīngqīyī Monday
星期二 Xīngqī'èr Tuesday
星期三 Xīngqīsān Wednesday
星期四 Xīngqīsì Thursday
星期五 Xīngqīwǔ Friday
星期六 Xīngqīliù Saturday
星期日/星期天 Xīngqīrì/ Xīngqītiān Sunday
上星期 shàng xīngqī last week
下星期 xià xīngqī next week

腥 xīng *n* fishy smell

行 1 xíng I *v* travel, go □ 三人行，必有我师。(孔子) **Sān rén xíng, bì yǒu wǒ shī. (Kǒngzǐ)** *When three people are walking together, at least one of them can be my teacher. (→ One can always find someone good enough to be one's teacher.)* 2 practice, carry out II *n* 1 trip, travel 2 act, behavior

行程 xíngchéng *n* route, distance traveled

行动 xíngdòng [comp: 行 travel, go + 动 move] I *v*

move around □ 老人行动不便, 不愿多外出。**Lǎorén xíngdòng búbiàn, bú yuàn duō wàichū.** *The old man has difficulty moving about and is reluctant to go out very often.* **II** *n* action, behavior □ 不但要听他说什么, 而且要看他的行动。**Búdàn yào tīng tā shuō shénme, érqiě yào kàn tā de xíngdòng.** *We should not only listen to what he says but also look at what he does.*

行贿 **xínghuì** [v+obj: 行 practice + 贿 bribery] *v* offer a bribe, bribe

行径 **xíngjìng** [modif: 行 practice + 径 path] *n* disgraceful conduct, deviant behavior

行军 **xíng jūn** *v* (of troops) march

行李 **xíngli** *n* luggage, baggage (件 **jiàn**) □ 你有几件行李? **Nǐ yǒu jǐ jiàn xíngli?** *How many pieces of luggage do you have?* □ 你的行李超重了, 要付一百元。**Nǐ de xíngli chāozhòng le, yào fù yìbǎi yuán.** *Your luggage is overweight. You need to pay 100 yuan.*

行人 **xíngrén** [modif: 行 travel, go + 人 person] *n* pedestrian
　　行人道 **xíngréndào** sidewalk
　　行人横道线 **xíngrén héngdàoxiàn** pedestrian crossing

行使 **xíngshǐ** *v* exercise (rights, power, etc.)
　　行使公民权利 **xíngshǐ gōngmín quánlì** exercise one's civil rights

行驶 **xíngshǐ** *v* (of a vehicle or ship) travel

行为 **xíngwéi** *n* behavior, conduct, act □ 他的行为不符合教师的身份。**Tāde xíngwéi bù fúhé jiàoshī de shēnfèn.** *His behavior does not befit his status as a teacher.*

行星 **xíngxīng** [modif: 行 traveling + 星 star] *n* planet

行政 **xíngzhèng** [v+obj: 行 exercise + 政 governance] *n* administration
　　行政部门 **xíngzhèng bùmén** administrative department
　　行政命令 **xíngzhèng mìnglìng** executive order

行 2 **xíng I** *v* all right, OK, (that) will do □ "我可以用一下你的词典吗?" "行。" **"Wǒ kěyǐ yòng yíxià nǐ de cídiǎn ma?" "Xíng."** *"May I use your dictionary?" "OK."* □ 学中文不学汉字不行。**Xué Zhōngwén bù xué Hànzì bù xíng.** *It won't do to learn Chinese without learning Chinese characters.* **II** *adj* competent, capable □ 你又赢了, 真行! **Nǐ yòu yíng le, zhēn xíng!** *You've won again. You're really great!* □ 我踢足球不行, 打篮球还可以。**Wǒ tī zúqiú bù xíng, dǎ lánqiú hái kěyǐ.** *I'm not good at soccer but I'm not too bad at basketball.*

刑 **xíng** *adj* penal, criminal
　　刑场 **xíngchǎng** *n* execution ground

刑罚 **xíngfá** *n* torture
　　上刑罚 **shàngxíng fá** torture

刑法 **xíngfá** *n* penal code, criminal law

刑事 **xíngshì** [modif: 刑 penal + 事 affair] *adj* criminal, penal
　　刑事犯 **xíngshìfàn** criminal offender, convict
　　刑事案件 **xíngshì ànjiàn** criminal case

形 **xíng** *n* form, shape
　　形成 **xíngchéng** [v+obj: 形 form + 成 become] *v* take shape, form □ 习惯形成以后, 就很难改变。**Xíguàn xíngchéng yǐhòu, jiù hěn nán gǎibiàn.** *After a habit is formed, it is difficult to break it.*

形容 **xíngróng** *v* describe □ 我形容不出来那个小偷长的样子。**Wǒ xíngróng bu chūlái nà ge xiǎotōu zhǎng de yàngzi.** *I can't describe what the thief looks like.*

形式 **xíngshì** [comp: 形 shape + 式 manner] *n* form, shape (antonym 内容 **nèiróng**) □ 道歉是必要的, 用什么形式还要考虑。**Dàoqiàn shì bìyào de, yòng shénme xíngshì háiyào kǎolǜ.** *While an apology is necessary, we need to think over the form it should take.*

形势 **xíngshì** [comp: 形 shape + 势 force] *n* situation □ 目前的形势对我们有利。**Mùqián de xíngshì duì wǒmen yǒulì.** *The present situation is in our favor.*

形态 **xíngtài** *n* form, pattern

形象 **xíngxiàng** [comp: 形 shape + 象 image] *n* image □ 公司要注意公共关系, 改善社会形象。**Gōngsī yào zhùyì gōnggòng guānxi, gǎishàn shèhuì xíngxiàng.** *The company should pay attention to public relations and improve its public image.*

形状 **xíngzhuàng** [comp: 形 shape + 状 shape] *n* appearance, shape, form □ 这座山的形状像一只猴子, 因此人们就叫它猴山。**Zhè zuò shān de xíngzhuàng xiàng yì zhī hóuzi, yīncǐ rénmen jiù jiào tā hóushān.** *The hill has the shape of a monkey and is therefore called Monkey Hill.*

型 **xíng** *n* model, type
　　型号 **xínghào** *n* model (of a car, airplane, etc.)

醒 **xǐng** *v* wake, wake up □ 我今天很早就醒了。**Wǒ jīntiān hěn zǎo jiù xǐng le.** *I woke up very early this morning.*
　　睡醒 **shuìxǐng** have enough sleep □ 睡醒了没有? **Shuìxǐngle méiyǒu?** *Have you had enough sleep?*
　　叫醒 **jiàoxǐng** wake somebody up □ 你明天早上五点钟叫醒我, 好吗? **Nǐ míngtiān zǎoshang wǔ diǎnzhōng jiàoxǐng wǒ, hǎo ma?** *Could you wake me up tomorrow morning at five?*

兴 **xīng** Trad 興 *adj* joyful
　　兴趣 **xìngqù** [comp: 兴 joy + 趣 interest] *n* interest □ 这孩子对动物很感兴趣。**Zhè háizi duì dòngwù hěn gǎn xìngqù.** *This child is very interested in animals.* □ 我对别人的私事没有兴趣。**Wǒ duì biéren de sīshì méiyǒu xìngqù.** *I'm not interested in other people's private matters.*
　　对…感兴趣 **duì...gǎn xìngqù** be interested in ...
　　对…有兴趣 **duì...yǒu xìngqù** be interested in ...
　　对…不感兴趣 **duì...bù gǎn xìngqù** be uninterested in ...
　　对…没有兴趣 **duì...méiyǒu xìngqù** be uninterested in ...

杏 **xìng** *n* apricot
　　杏花 **xìnghuā** apricot blossom (朵 **duǒ**)
　　杏树 **xìngshù** apricot tree
　　杏子 **xìngzi** apricot (个 **gè**)

性 **xìng** *n* 1 nature, character
　　本性 **běnxìng** (of a human being) innate quality, character
　　2 sex, gender
　　男性 **nánxìng** male

性别 **xìngbié** *n* gender, sex

性病 **xìngbìng** *n* sexually transmitted disease (STD)

性格 **xìnggé** *n* person's character, disposition □ 她性格很坚强。**Tā xìnggé hěn jiānqiáng.** *She has a strong character.*

性工作者 **xìng gōngzuòzhě** *n* sex worker

性交 **xìngjiāo** *n* sexual intercourse

性命 **xìngmìng** *n* (human) life □ 这是性命交关的是啊!
Zhè shì xìngmìngjiāoguān de shì a! *This is a matter of life and death.*

性能 **xìngnéng** *n* function, performance
性能良好 xìngnéng liánghǎo (of a machine) perform well, with satisfactory performance

性情 **xìngqíng** *n* temperament
性情温和 xìngqíng wēnhé with a gentle, mild temperament

性骚扰 **xìng sāorǎo** *n* sexual harassment

性质 **xìngzhì** [comp: 性 nature + 质 substance] *n* nature (of a matter, an event, etc.), basic quality □ 这一事件的性质是新旧力量之间的一场政治斗争。
Zhè yí shìjiàn de xìngzhì shì xīn jiù lìliang zhījiān de yì chǎng zhèngzhì dòuzhēng. *This incident is in nature a political struggle between the new and old forces.*

幸 **xìng** *n* good fortune
幸福 **xìngfú** [comp: 幸 good fortune + 福 happiness] *adj* happy, fortunate □ 多么幸福的家庭!
Duōme xìngfú de jiātíng! *What a happy family!* □ 她实现了自己的理想, 感到很幸福。**Tā shíxiàn le zìjǐ de lǐxiǎng, gǎndao hěn xìngfú.** *She feels happy as she has realized her aspiration.*

NOTE: 幸福 **xìngfú** is used in a sublime sense, denoting *a profound and almost perfect happiness.* So it has a much more limited use than its English equivalents *happy* or *fortunate.* The usual Chinese word for *happy,* as in "I'm happy to hear the news," is 高兴 **gāoxìng**, e.g. □ 听到这个消息, 我很高兴。**Tīngdào zhège xiāoxi, wǒ hěn gāoxìng.** *I'm happy to hear this news.*

幸好 **xìnghǎo** *adv* fortunately, luckily
幸亏 **xìngkuī** *adv* fortunately, luckily
幸运 **xìngyùn** *adj* fortunate, lucky

姓 **xìng** *n* family name □ 中国人最常用的三个姓是李、王、张。**Zhōngguórén zuì chángyòng de sān ge xìng shì Lǐ, Wáng, Zhāng.** *The three most common family names of the Chinese are Li, Wang and Zhang.*
贵姓 guìxìng your family name (polite usage, normally in a question) □ "您贵姓?" "我姓王。" **"Nín guìxìng?" "Wǒ xìng Wáng."** *"What's your family name?" "Wang."*

NOTE: The character 姓 **xìng** has 女 **nǚ**, meaning *female,* in it—an indication that the Chinese once had a matriarchal society.

姓名 **xìngmíng** [comp: 姓 family name + 名 given name] *n* full name □ 请你在这里写上自己的姓名。**Qǐng nǐ zài zhèli xiěshang zìjǐ de xìngmíng.** *Please write down your full name here.*

兄 **xiōng** *n* elder brother
兄弟 **xiōngdì** [comp: 兄 elder brother + 弟 younger brother] *n* brother(s) □ 他们兄弟之间关系很好, 一人有事, 大家帮忙。**Tāmen xiōngdì zhījiān guānxi hěn hǎo, yì rén yǒu shì, dàjiā bāngmáng.** *The brothers have a very good relationship—when one of them is in difficulty, the others will come to help him.*

胸 **xiōng** *n* chest, thorax □ 医生, 我胸口疼。**Yīshēng, wǒ xiōngkǒu téng.** *Doctor, I have a pain in the chest.*

胸怀 **xiōnghuái** **I** *n* mind, heart
胸怀宽广 xiōnghuái kuānguǎng be broad-minded **II** *v* cherish, harbor
胸怀大志 xiōnghuái dàzhì cherish great ambition

胸膛 **xiōngtáng** *n* chest (of the human body)

凶 **xiōng** Trad 兇 *adj* ferocious, fierce □ 有话好好说, 别这么凶。**Yǒu huà hǎohǎo shuō, bié zhème xiōng.** *If you've got something to say, say it nicely; don't be so ferocious.*

凶恶 **xiōng'è** [comp: 凶 ferocious + 恶 bad, evil] *adj* ferocious, fierce □ 癌是人类的凶恶敌人。**Ái shì rénlèi de xiōng'è dírén.** *Cancer is a ferocious enemy of humankind.*

凶狠 **xiōnghěn** [comp: 凶 ferocious + 狠 ruthless] *adj* fierce and malicious

凶猛 **xiōngměng** [comp: 凶 ferocious + 猛 fierce] *adj* ferocious, violent

汹 **xiōng** Trad 洶 as in 汹涌 **xiōngyǒng**
汹涌 **xiōngyǒng** *adj* turbulent

雄 **xióng** *adj* **1** male (of animals) (antonym 雌 **cí**) □ 雄狮子比雌狮子大得多。**Xióng shīzi bǐ cí shīzi dà de duō.** *Male lions are much bigger than female ones* **2** grand, imposing

雄厚 **xiónghòu** [comp: 雄 grand + 厚 thick] *adj* abundant, rich
资金雄厚 zījīnxiónghòu with abundant funds, very well-financed

雄伟 **xióngwěi** [comp: 雄 grand + 伟 great] *adj* grand, magnificent □ 这个城市有很多雄伟的建筑。**Zhège chéngshì yǒu hěn duō xióngwěi de jiànzhù.** *This city boasts many grand buildings.*

雄壮 **xióngzhuàng** [comp: 雄 grand + 壮 strong] *adj* full of power and grandeur, magnificent

熊 **xióng** *n* bear (只 **zhī**)
熊猫 **xióngmāo** [comp: 熊 bear + 猫 cat] *n* panda, giant panda (只 **zhī**) □ 熊猫只吃竹子。**Xióngmāo zhǐ chī zhúzi.** *Pandas eat only bamboo.*

修 **xiū** *v* **1** Same as 修理 **xiūlǐ** **2** build, construct (a building, bridge, road, etc.) □ 这条江上还要修一座大桥。**Zhè tiáo jiāng shang háiyào xiū yí zuò dà qiáo.** *A big bridge will be built across this river.* **3** study, cultivate

修订 **xiūdìng** *v* revise
修订版 xiūdìngbǎn revised edition

修复 **xiūfù** *v* restore (a work of art)

修改 **xiūgǎi** [comp: 修 repair + 改 alter] *v* amend, revise □ 这份报告要修改一下, 再送董事会。**Zhè fèn bàogào yào xiūgǎi yíxià, zài sòng dǒngshìhuì.** *This report needs some revision before it is submitted to the board of directors.*

修建 **xiūjiàn** [comp: 修 build + 建 build] *v* build, construct

修理 **xiūlǐ** *v* repair, fix □ 自行车坏了, 你会修理吗? **Zìxíngchē huài le, nǐ huì xiūlǐ ma?** *The bike is broken. Can you fix it?* □ 这台机器很旧了, 不值得再修理了。**Zhè tái jīqì hěn jiù le, bù zhídé zài xiūlǐ le.** *This machine is very old and is not worth repairing any more.*

修养 **xiūyǎng** *n* **1** accomplishment, training
文化修养 wénhuà xiūyǎng cultural accomplishment **2** self-cultivation, good behavior and manners

修正 **xiūzhèng** *v* amend, revise

修筑 xiūzhù v build, construct

羞 xiū v be shy, be bashful
羞耻 xiūchǐ n sense of shame
羞耻心 xiūchǐ xīn sense of shame
不知羞耻 bùzhī xiūchǐ have no sense of shame, shameless

休 xiū I n leisure II v stop, cease, rest
休息 xiūxi [comp: 休 leisure + 息 pause] v rest, take a rest, have a day off □ 我们工作了两个小时了，休息一会儿吧。**Wǒmen gōngzuòle liǎng ge xiǎoshí le, xiūxi yíhuìr ba.** We've been working for over two hours. Let's take a break. □ 我感到很疲劳，需要休息几天。**Wǒ gǎndao hěn píláo, xūyào xiūxi jǐ tiān.** I feel worn out. I need a few days' rest.
休闲 xiūxián [comp: 休 leisure + 闲 idle] n leisure
休闲服 xiūxiánfú casual clothes
休养 xiūyǎng v recuperate, convalesce

朽 xiǔ v decay
不朽 bùxiǔ immortal

嗅 xiù v smell, sniff

秀 xiù adj elegant
秀丽 xiùlì [comp: 秀 elegant + 丽 beautiful] adj elegantly beautiful

锈 xiù Trad 鏽 n rust

绣 xiù Trad 繡 v embroider

袖 xiù n sleeve
袖子 xiùzi sleeve

须 xū Trad 須 modal v must
须知 xūzhī n (important) notice, essential information
考生须知 kǎoshēng xūzhī important notice to examinees

虚 xū adj 1 void 2 of frail health 3 false 4 modest
虚假 xūjiǎ adj false, sham
虚拟 xūnǐ adj invented, fictitious
虚拟现实 xūnǐ xiànshí virtual reality
虚弱 xūruò adj debilitated, weak
虚伪 xūwěi I adj hypocritical II n hypocrisy
虚伪的人 xūwěi de rén hypocrite
虚心 xūxīn [modif: 虚 empty + 心 the heart] adj open-minded and modest □ 我们虚心地请您提意见。**Wǒmen xūxīn de qǐng nín tí yìjian.** We sincerely request your comments. □ 他很不虚心，总是认为自己了不起。**Tā hěn bù xūxīn, zǒngshi rènwéi zìjǐ liǎobuqǐ.** He is very arrogant, always thinking himself terrific.

墟 xū n ruins (See 废墟 fèixū)

需 xū v need
需求 xūqiú n demand, requirement
需要 xūyào [comp: 需 need + 要 want] v need, be in need of □ 我需要一本中文词典。**Wǒ xūyào yì běn Zhōngwén cídiǎn.** I need a Chinese dictionary. □ "你有什么需要，可以跟我说。" "谢谢，没有什么需要。" **"Nǐ yǒu shénme xūyào, kěyǐ gēn wǒ shuō." "Xièxie, méiyǒu shénme xūyào."** "If there's anything you need, let me know." "Thank you, but there's nothing I need."

许 xǔ Trad 許 I v 1 promise 2 allow II adj approximate, rough

许多 xǔduō [comp: 许 approximate + 多 many, much] adj many, much □ 妈妈买回来许多好吃的东西。**Māma mǎi huílai xǔduō hǎochī de dōngxi.** Mom bought lots of delicious food.
许可 xǔkě v permit, allow

序 xù n 1 sequence, order 2 preface
序言 xùyán n preface

续 xù Trad 續 v continue (See 继续 jìxù, 连续 liánxù, 陆续 lùxù, 手续 shǒuxù.)

绪 xù Trad 緒 n mood (See 情绪 qíngxù.)

絮 xù as in 絮叨 xùdao
絮叨 xùdao I adj garrulous, long-winded II v talk too much, be a chatterbox

畜 xù v keep domesticated animals
畜产品 xùchǎnpǐn n animal products
畜牧 xùmù v raise livestock
畜牧业 xùmùyè animal husbandry

蓄 xù v save up
蓄电池 xùdiànchí n battery

酗 xù as in 酗酒 xùjiǔ
酗酒 xùjiǔ v drink excessively, get drunk

叙 xù v 1 chat 2 narrate
叙述 xùshù v narrate, recount
叙谈 xùtán v chat □ 让我们好好叙谈叙谈。**Ràng wǒmen hǎohǎo xùtán xùtán.** Let's have a nice chat.

宣 xuān v declare, announce
宣布 xuānbù v declare, announce □ 校长在大会上宣布了对他的处分。**Xiàozhǎng zài dàhuì shang xuānbùle duì tā de chǔfèn.** At the assembly the principal announced the disciplinary action to be taken against him.
宣称 xuānchēng v assert, profess
宣传 xuānchuán [comp: 宣 announce + 传 spread] I v 1 disseminate, publicize □ 卫生部正在大力宣传吸烟的害处。**Wèishēngbù zhèngzài dàlì xuānchuán xīyān de hàichu.** The Ministry of Health is making efforts to disseminate information on the harm that smoking does. 2 propagandize II n 1 dissemination 2 propaganda □ 这完全是宣传，不能相信。**Zhè wánquán shì xuānchuán, bù néng xiāngxìn.** This is propaganda, pure and simple. You mustn't believe it.
宣读 xuāndú v read out in public
宣告 xuāngào v declare, proclaim
宣誓 xuānshì v swear an oath
宣誓仪式 xuānshì yíshì swearing-in ceremony
宣言 xuānyán n declaration, manifesto
宣言书 xuānyánshū declaration (份 fèn)
宣扬 xuānyáng v publicize, promote

喧 xuān adj noisy
喧闹 xuānnào [comp: 喧 noisy + 闹 noisy] adj noisy and full of activities, very noisy

悬 xuán Trad 懸 v hang, suspend
悬案 xuán'àn n unsettled case, cold case
悬挂 xuánguà v hang
悬念 xuánniàn n suspense
悬崖 xuányá n overhanging cliff, precipice
悬崖勒马 xuányá lèmǎ rein in at the brink of the precipice (→ avoid an imminent danger at the last moment)

旋 xuán v circle, spin
旋律 xuánlǜ n melody

旋转 **xuánzhuǎn** [comp: 旋 spin + 转 turn] *v* revolve, spin

选 **xuǎn** Trad 選 *v* 1 Same as 选举 **xuǎnjǔ** 2 select, choose □ 不同牌子的电视机都差不多，很难选。 **Bùtóng páizi de diànshìjī dōu chàbuduō, hěn nán xuǎn.** *TV sets of different brands are more or less the same; it is difficult to select one.*

选拔 **xuǎnbá** *v* select, choose

选定 **xuǎndìng** *v* select, decide on

选购 **xuǎngòu** [comp: 选 select + 购 buy] *v* choose and buy
选购年货 **xuǎngòu niánhuò** shop for the Chinese New Year

选举 **xuǎnjǔ** [comp: 选 select + 举 recommend] **I** *v* elect, vote □ 我们下午选举班长。**Wǒmen xiàwǔ xuǎnjǔ bānzhǎng.** *We're going to elect a class monitor this afternoon.* **II** *n* election, voting □ 参加大会的代表必须由选举产生。**Cānjiā dàhuì de dàibiǎo bìxū yóu xuǎnjǔ chǎnshēng.** *The delegates to the congress must be chosen by election.*

选民 **xuǎnmín** *n* voter, electorate

选手 **xuǎnshǒu** *n* (of sports) selected contestant, player, athlete, competing athlete

选用 **xuǎnyòng** *v* select for use

选择 **xuǎnzé** [comp: 选 select + 择 choose] **I** *v* select, choose □ 人生的道路要自己选择。**Rénshēng de dàolù yào zìjǐ xuǎnzé.** *One should decide for oneself what kind of life to lead.* **II** *n* choice □ 我们除此以外，别无选择。**Wǒmen chú cǐ yǐwài, bié wú xuǎnzé.** *We have no choice but to do this.*

削 **xuē** *v* cut, pare
削减 **xuējiǎn** [comp: 削 cut + 减 decrease] *v* cut down, reduce

削弱 **xuēruò** *v* weaken

靴 **xuē** *n* boots
靴子 **xuēzi** boots (只 **zhī**, 双 **shuāng**)

穴 **xué** *n* cave

学 **xué** Trad 學 **I** *v* learn, study □ "你在大学学什么？""学电脑。" **"Nǐ zài dàxué xué shénme?" "Xué diànnǎo."** *"What do you study at university?" "Computer science."* □ 活到老，学到老。**Huó dào lǎo, xué dào lǎo.** *One should keep on learning as long as one lives.* **II** *n* 1 learning, knowledge 2 school, course of study

学费 **xué fèi** [modif: 学 study + 费 fee] *n* tuition, tuition fee □ 你们学校国际学生的学费是多少？ **Nǐmen xuéxiào guójì xuésheng de xué fèi shì duōshǎo?** *How much is the tuition fee for international students in your school?*

学会 **xuéhuì** [v+compl: 学 learn + 会 can] *v* learn (to do something), master

学科 **xuékē** [modif: 学 study + 科 classification] *n* subject for study, discipline

学年 **xuénián** [modif: 学 study + 年 year] *n* academic year □ 在中国，新学年从九月一日开始。**Zài Zhōngguó, xīnxué nián cóng jiǔyuè yí rì kāishǐ.** *In China, a new academic year starts on September 1.*

学派 **xuépài** *n* school of thought

学期 **xuéqī** [modif: 学 study + 期 period] *n* semester, term □ 中国的学校一般分上学期和下学期两个学期。**Zhōngguó de xuéxiào yìbān fēn shàng xuéqī he**

xià xuéqī liǎng ge xuéqī. *Chinese schools generally have two terms: the first term and the second term.*

学生 **xuésheng** [modif: 学 study + 生 scholar] *n* student, pupil (个 **gè**, 名 **míng**) □ "这个班有多少学生？""三十二个。" **"Zhège bān yǒu duōshǎo xuésheng?" "Sānshí'èr ge."** *"How many students are there in this class?" "Thirty-two."*

学时 **xuéshí** [modif: 学 learning + 时 hour] *n* class hour, period

学术 **xuéshù** *n* learning, scholarship
学术会议 **xuéshù huìyì** (scholarly or scientific) conference, symposium

学说 **xuéshuō** *n* theory, doctrine

学位 **xuéwèi** [modif: 学 study + 位 position] *n* academic degree
学士学位 **xuéshì xuéwèi** bachelor degree
硕士学位 **shuòshì xuéwèi** master's degree, masterate
博士学位 **bóshì xuéwèi** PhD degree, doctorate

学问 **xuéwen** [comp: 学 study + 问 ask] *n* learning, knowledge □ 这位老教授很有学问。**Zhè wèi lǎo jiàoshòu hěn yǒu xuéwen.** *This old professor has a great deal of learning.*

学习 **xuéxí** [comp: 学 learn + 习 practice] **I** *v* study, learn □ 年轻的时候，应该多学习些知识。**Niánqīng de shíhou, yīnggāi duō xuéxí xiē zhīshi.** *One should acquire more knowledge when young.* □ 学生不但从书本中学习，而且在社会上学习。**Xuésheng búdàn cóng shūběn zhong xuéxí, érqiě zài shèhuì shang xuéxí.** *A student learns not only from books but also from society.*
向…学习 **xiàng...xuéxí** learn from ..., emulate ... □ 你工作很认真，我要向你学习。**Nǐ gōngzuò hěn rènzhēn, wǒ yào xiàng nǐ xuéxí.** *You work conscientiously. I must emulate you.* **II** *n* study □ 学生应该把学习放在第一位。**Xuésheng yīnggāi bǎ xuéxí fàng zai dì-yī wèi.** *Students should give priority to their studies.*

学校 **xuéxiào** [modif: 学 study + 校 school] *n* school (座 **zuò**) □ 王老师每天八点前就到学校来了。**Wáng lǎoshī měi tiān bā diǎn qián jiù dào xuéxiào lái le.** *Teacher Wang comes to school before eight o'clock every day.* □ 市政府去年新建了两座学校。**Shì zhèngfǔ qùnián xīn jiànle liǎng zuò xuéxiào.** *The city government built two schools last year.*

学院 **xuéyuàn** [comp: 学 study + 院 place (for certain activities)] *n* college, institute □ 在中国有些高等学校叫"学院"，例如"教育学院"。**Zài Zhōngguó yǒuxiē gāoděng xuéxiào jiào "xuéyuàn", lìrú "jiàoyù xuéyuàn".** *In China some institutions of higher learning are called "college," for example "college of education."*

学者 **xuézhě** [suffix: 学 study + 者 nominal suffix, person] *n* scholar

学制 **xuézhì** *n* 1 educational system 2 term of study

雪 **xuě** *n* snow
下雪 **xià xuě** to snow □ "香港冬天下雪吗？""不下。" **"Xiānggǎng dōngtiān xià xuě ma?" "Bú xià."** *In Hong Kong, does it snow in winter?" "No."*

雪白 **xuě bái** *adj* snow-white

雪花 **xuěhuā** [modif: 雪 snow + 花 flower] *n* snowflake (片 **piàn**)

血 **xuè** *n* blood □ 流了一点血, 不要紧。**Liúle yìdiǎn xuè, bú yàojǐn.** *It's just a little bleeding, nothing serious.*
输血 shūxuè blood transfusion □ 病人需要马上输血。**Bìngrén xūyào mǎshàng shūxuè.** *The patient needs blood transfusion immediately.*
血管 **xuèguǎn** [modif: 血 bold + 管 tube] *n* blood vessel
动脉血管 dòngmài xuèguǎn artery
静脉血管 jìngmài xuèguǎn vein
血汗 **xuèhàn** [comp: 血 blood + 汗 sweat] *n* blood and sweat, sweat and toil
血汗工厂 xuèhàn gōngchǎng sweatshop
血库 **xuèkù** [modif: 血 blood + 库 warehouse] *n* blood bank
血型 **xuèxíng** [modif: 血 blood + 型 type] *n* blood type □ "你是什么血型?" "我是O型。" **"Nǐ shì shénme xuèxíng?" "Wǒ shì O xíng."** *"What's your blood type?" "Type O."*
血压 **xuèyā** [modif: 血 blood + 压 pressure] *n* blood pressure
高血压 gāoxuèyā high blood pressure, hypertension
低血压 dīxuèyā low blood pressure, hypotension
血液 **xuèyè** [modif: 血 blood + 液 liquid] *n* blood (as a technical term) □ 你要化验血液。**Nǐ yào huàyàn xuèyè.** *You should have your blood tested.*

熏 **xūn** *v* treat with smoke, smoke
熏鱼 xūnyú smoked fish

循 **xún** *v* abide by, follow
循环 xúnhuán *v* circulate
血液循环 xuèyè xúnhuán blood circulation
循序渐进 xúnxù jiànjìn *idiom* proceed step by step in an orderly way

寻 **xún** Trad 尋 *v* seek, search
寻求 xúnqiú *v* seek, go in quest of
寻找 **xúnzhǎo** [comp: 寻 seek + 找 look for] *v* look for, seek □ 他家的猫不见了, 他们正在到处寻找。**Tā jiā de māo bú jiàn le, tāmen zhèngzài dàochù xúnzhǎo.** *Their cat has disappeared, and they are looking for it everywhere.*

旬 **xún** *n* a period of ten days in a month
上旬 shàngxún the first ten days in a month
中旬 zhōngxún the second ten days in a month
下旬 xiàxún the last ten days in a month

询 **xún** Trad 詢 *v* inquire (See 咨询 **zīxún**)
询问 **xúnwèn** [comp: 询 inquire + 问 ask] *v* inquire, ask about □ 你可以到电话询问报名细节。**Nǐ kěyǐ dào diànhuà xúnwèn bàomíng xìjié.** *You may call to ask for details about the application (for a place in a school).*

巡 **xún** *v* patrol
巡逻 xúnluó *v* patrol, go on patrol
巡逻艇 xúnluótǐng patrol boat

讯 **xùn** *n* message (See 通讯 **tōngxùn**.)

迅 **xùn** *adj* rapid
迅速 **xùnsù** [comp: 迅 rapid, speedy + 速 swift] *adj* rapid, speedy, swift □ 这件事很急, 要迅速处理。**Zhè jiàn shì hěn jí, yào xùnsù chǔlǐ.** *This is an urgent matter, and should be dealt with without delay.*

训 **xùn** *v* train
军训 jūnxùn military training

训练 **xùnliàn** [comp: 训 train + 练 practice] *v* train □ 全国运动会快开了, 运动员正在紧张训练。**Quánguó yùndònghuì kuài kāi le, yùndàngyuán zhèngzài jǐnzhāng xùnliàn.** *The national games will be held soon. Athletes are engaged in intense training.*

逊 **xùn** Trad 遜 *adj* modest (See 谦逊 **qiānxùn**)

Y

压 **yā** Trad 壓 *v* press, push down □ 这纸盒不能压。**Zhè zhǐhé bù néng yā.** *This paper box mustn't be crushed.*
压价 **yājià** [v+obj: 压 push down + 价 price] *v* undersell with reduced prices
压力 **yālì** [comp: 压 press + 力 force] *n* pressure □ 他的父母一定要他上名牌大学, 他觉得压力很大。**Tā de fùmǔ yídìng yào tā shàng míngpái dàxué, tā juéde yālì hěn dà.** *He is under tremendous pressure as his parents insist on him going to a famous university.*
压迫 **yāpò** [comp: 压 press + 迫 force, compel]
I *v* oppress □ 在有些国家, 妇女仍然受到压迫。**Zài yǒuxiē guójiā, fùnǚ réngrán shòudao yāpò.** *In some countries, women still suffer from oppression.*
II *n* oppression □ 有压迫, 就有反抗。**Yǒu yāpò, jiùyǒu fǎnkàng.** *Where there is oppression, there is resistance.*
压缩 **yāsuō** [v+compl: 压 press + 缩 shrink] *v* compress, condense
空气压缩机 kōngqì yāsuōjī air compressor
压抑 **yāyì** [comp: 压 press + 抑 suppress] *v* suppress, bottle up
压抑自己的愤怒 yāyì zìjǐ de fènnù bottle up one's anger
压制 **yāzhì** *v* repress, stifle

呀 **yā** *interj* oh, ah (expressing surprise) □ 呀, 这不是约翰吗, 没想到在这里见到你! **Yā, zhè bú shì Yuēhàn ma, méi xiǎngdao zài zhèlǐ jiàndao nǐ!** *Oh, isn't it John? Fancy seeing you here!* □ 呀, 你还会说上海话! **Yā, nǐ hái huì shuō Shànghǎi huà!** *Oh, you also speak the Shanghai dialect!*

鸦 **yā** *n* crow (See 乌鸦 **wūyā**)
鸦片 **yāpiàn** *n* opium
抽鸦片 chōu yāpiàn smoke opium

鸭 **yā** Trad 鴨 *n* duck
鸭子 yāzi duck (只 **zhī**)

押 **yā** *v* 1 escort (goods, criminal) 2 pawn, pledge as security

牙 **yá** *n* tooth, teeth (颗 **kē**) □ 我牙疼。**Wǒ yá téng.** *I have a toothache.*
牙齿 **yáchǐ** [comp: 牙 tooth + 齿 tooth] *n* tooth, teeth (颗 **kē**)
牙膏 **yágāo** [modif: 牙 tooth + 膏 paste, cream] *n* toothpaste (管 **guǎn**) □ 有这么多种牙膏, 不知道该选哪一种。**Yǒu zhème duō zhǒng yágāo, bù zhīdào gāi xuǎn nǎ yì zhǒng.** *There are so many brands of toothpaste, I don't known which one to choose.*
牙科 **yákē** *n* dentistry
牙科医生 yákē yīshēng dentist (位 **wèi**)

牙刷 **yáshuā** [modif: 牙 tooth + 刷 brush] *n* toothbrush (把 **bǎ**) □ 我忘了带牙刷，要买一把。**Wǒ wàngle dài yáshuā, yào mǎi yì bǎ.** *I forgot to bring my toothbrush. I need to buy one.*

牙医 **yáyī** *n* Same as 牙科医生 **yákē yīshēng**

芽 **yá** *n* sprout, bud
发芽 **fāyá** germinate, to bud, to sprout

崖 **yá** *n* cliff (See 悬崖 **xuányá**)

雅 **yǎ** *adj* elegant, cultured (See 文雅 **wényǎ**)
雅思 **Yǎsī** *n* International English Language Testing System (IELTS)

哑 **yǎ** Trad 啞 *adj* dumb, mute
哑巴 **yǎba** *n* mute person, mute

哑语 **yǎyǔ** *n* sign language

亚 **yà** *adj* second
亚军 **yàjūn** *n* (in sports) second place, runner-up

亚洲 **Yàzhōu** [modif: 亚 Asia + 洲 continent] *n* Asia □ 亚洲是世界上最大的一个洲。**Yàzhōu shì shìjiè shang zuì dà de yí ge zhōu.** *Asia is the largest continent in the world.*

讶 **yà** *v* be surprised (See 惊讶 **jīngyà**)

轧 **yà** Trad 軋 *v* run over, roll

呀 **ya** *particle* Same as 啊 **ā** 2 *particle* (Used after a, e, i, o, u) □ 这个苹果真大呀！**Zhège píngguǒ zhēn dà ya!** *How big this apple is!*

淹 **yān** *v* submerge, inundate
淹没 **yānmò** *v* submerge, flood

烟 **yān** *n* 1 smoke 2 Same as 香烟 **xiāngyān** □ 请勿吸烟。**Qǐng wù xīyān.** *No smoking.*
禁烟区 **jìnyānqū** smoke-free area, "No Smoking" area

烟草 **yāncǎo** *n* tabacco

烟囱 **yāncōng** *n* chimney

烟雾 **yānwù** *n* mist, smoke, smog

严 **yán** Trad 嚴 *adj* strict, severe
严格 **yángé** I *adj* strict, stringent, rigorous □ 在中国的传统中，一位严格的老师才是好老师。**Zài Zhōngguó de chuántǒng zhong, yí wèi yángé de lǎoshī cái shì hǎo lǎoshī.** *In the Chinese tradition, only a strict teacher was a good one.* II *v* make ... strict, make ... stringent □ 工厂决定严格产品质量检查制度。**Gōngchǎng juédìng yángé chǎnpǐn zhìliàng jiǎnchá zhìdù.** *The factory has decided to make the product quality control system more stringent.*

严寒 **yánhán** *n* severe cold

严禁 **yánjìn** *v* strictly forbid □ 此处严禁停车。**Cǐchù yánjìn tíngchē.** *Parking is strictly forbidden here.*

严厉 **yánlì** [comp: 严 severe + 厉 harsh] *adj* stern, severe
严厉的警告 **yánlì de jǐnggào** a stern warning

严密 **yánmì** *adj* tight, watertight

严肃 **yánsù** [comp: 严 severe + 肃 solemn] *adj* serious, solemn □ 李校长为什么总是这么严肃？**Lǐ xiàozhǎng wèishénme zǒngshì zhème yánsù?** *Why does Mr Li, the principal, always look so serious?*

严重 **yánzhòng** [comp: 严 severe + 重 weighty] *adj* serious, critical □ 这是一个严重的问题，必须认真对付。**Zhè shì yí ge yánzhòng de wèntí, bìxū rènzhēn duìfu.** *This is a serious problem and must be dealt with earnestly.* □ 她的病情很严重。**Tā de bìngqíng hěn yánzhòng.** *She is critically ill.*

岩 **yán** *n* rock
岩石 **yánshí** rock (块 **kuài**)

炎 **yán** *adj* scorching
炎热 **yánrè** *adj* scorching hot

延 **yán** *v* extend, delay, postpone
延长 **yáncháng** [v+compl: 延 extend + 长 long] *v* prolong, extend □ 会议延长两天。**Huìyì yáncháng liǎng tiān.** *The conference was extended two more days.*

延缓 **yánhuǎn** *v* put off, delay

延期 **yánqī** [v+obj: 延 extend + 期 date] *v* postpone, defer □ 会议延期一周举行。**Huìyì yánqī yìzhōu jǔxíng.** *The meeting (conference) will be postponed for a week.*

延伸 **yánshēn** [comp: 延 extend + 伸 reach] *v* stretch, extend

延续 **yánxù** [comp: 延 extend + 续 continue] *v* 1 continue, go on 2 last

言 **yán** I *n* speech II *v* talk, say
言论 **yánlùn** *n* remark, expression of opinion
言论自由 **yánlùn zìyóu** freedom of speech

言语 **yányǔ** *v* speak, reply

沿 **yán** *prep* along □ 沿街有很多小商店。**Yán jiē yǒu hěn duō xiǎo shāngdiàn.** *There are numerous small shops along the street.* □ 你沿着公园一直走，就到市中心了。**Nǐ yánzhe gōngyuán yì zhí zǒu, jiù dào shìzhōngxīn le.** *Walk along the park and you will get to the city center.*

沿儿 **yánr** *n* edge, border

沿岸 **yán'àn** *n* bank, coast

沿海 **yánhǎi** *n* coast
沿海城市 **yánhǎi chéngshì** coastal city

沿途 **yántú** *n* (places) on the way
沿途的见闻 **yántú de jiànwén** what one sees and learns on the way

研 **yán** *v* study, research
研究 **yánjiū** [comp: 研 research + 究 investigate] I *v* research, study, consider carefully □ 科学家们正在研究一种新药。**Kēxuéjiāmen zhèngzài yánjiū yì zhǒng xīn yào.** *Scientists are researching a new medicine.* □ 公司已经研究了你的计划，认为是可行的。**Gōngsī yǐjīng yánjiūle nǐ de jìhuà, rènwéi shì kěxíng de.** *The company has considered your plan carefully and believes it is feasible.* II *n* research, study (项 **xiàng**) □ 这项研究得到政府的资助。**Zhè xiàng yánjiū dédào zhèngfǔ de zīzhù.** *This research was funded by the government.*
做气候变化的研究 **zuò qìhou biànhuà de yánjiū** do research on climate change

研究生 **yánjiūshēng** [modif: 研究 research + 生 student] *n* graduate student, post-graduate student
研究生院 **yánjiūshēng yuàn** graduate school (of a university)

研究所 **yánjiūsuǒ** [modif: 研究 research + 所 place] *n* research institute, research unit

NOTE: The difference between 研究所 **yánjiūsuǒ** and 研究院 **yánjiūyuàn** is that the former is usually smaller in scale.

研究院 **yánjiūyuàn** [modif: 研究 research + 院 institute] *n* research institute

NOTE: See note on 研究所 **yánjiūsuǒ**.

研制 **yánzhì** [comp: 研 research + 制 make] *n* research and development, R & D

盐 **yán** Trad 鹽 *n* salt □ 我吃得比较淡, 你菜里少放点盐。 **Wǒ chī de bǐjiào dàn, nǐ cài li shǎo fàng diǎn yán.** *I prefer my food to be bland. Please don't put too much salt in the dish.*

颜 **yán** Trad 顔 *n* complexion, color
颜色 **yánsè** [comp: 颜 complexion + 色 color] *n* color □ "你最喜欢什么颜色?" "蓝颜色。" **"Nǐ zuì xǐhuan shénme yánsè?" "Lán yánsè."** *"What's your favorite color?" "Blue."* □ 我们有各种颜色的墙纸。 **Wǒmen yǒu gè zhǒng yánsè de qiángzhǐ.** *We have wallpaper in various colors.*

掩 **yǎn** *v* cover, cover up
掩盖 **yǎngài** [comp: 掩 cover up + 盖 lid, cover] *v* cover, cover up □ 漂亮的统计数字掩盖不了事实真相。 **Piàoliang de tǒngjì shùzì yǎngài bùliǎo shìshí zhēnxiàng.** *Attractive statistics cannot cover up the truth of the matter.*
掩护 **yǎnhù** [comp: 掩 cover + 护 protect] *v* cover, shield
掩饰 **yǎnshì** *v* cover up, gloss over, conceal
掩饰错误 yǎnshì cuòwù gloss over a mistake

眼 **yǎn** *n* eye
左眼 zuǒyǎn the left eye
右眼 yòuyǎn the right eye
眼光 **yǎnguāng** *n* eye, way of looking at things, point of view
很有审美眼光 hěn yǒu shěnměi yǎnguāng have an eye for what is beautiful
用老眼光看新问题 yòng lǎo yǎnguāng kàn xīn wèntí look at a new problem from an old point of view
眼镜 **yǎnjìng** [modif: 眼 eye + 镜 mirror] *n* glasses, spectacles (副 **fù**) □ 那位戴眼镜的先生是谁? **Nà wèi dài yǎnjìng de xiānsheng shì shuí?** *Who is the gentleman wearing glasses over there?*
太阳眼镜 tàiyang yǎnjìng sunglasses
眼镜店 **yǎnjìngdiàn** *n* optician's shop
眼镜盒 **yǎnjìnghé** *n* glasses case
眼睛 **yǎnjing** [comp: 眼 eye + 睛 eyeball] *n* eye □ 打电脑的时间太长, 我的眼睛累了。 **Dǎ diànnǎo de shíjiān tài cháng, wǒ de yǎnjing lèi le.** *I've been working on the computer for too long; my eyes are tired.*
眼看 **yǎnkàn** *adv* soon, in a moment
眼科 **yǎnkē** *n* department of ophthalmology
眼科医生 yǎnkē yīshēng ophthalmologist
眼泪 **yǎnlèi** [modif: 眼 eye + 泪 tear] *n* tear (滴 **dī**)
流下一滴眼泪 liúxia yì dī yǎnlèi shed a drop of tear □ 她用手绢擦眼泪。 **Tā yòng shǒujuàn cā yǎnlèi.** *She wiped the tears away with her handkerchief.*
眼力 **yǎnlì** [modif: 眼 eye + 力 power] *n* **1** eyesight
眼力好 yǎnlì hǎo good eyesight
2 discerning power, judgment
有眼力 yǒu yǎnlì be discerning
眼前 **yǎnqián** *adv* **1** before one's eyes □ 那件交通事故就发生在他眼前。 **Nà jiàn jiāotōng shìgù jiù fāshēng zài tā yǎnqián.** *The road accident happened right in front of him.* **2** at present, at this moment □ 眼前我们有些困难, 但很快能克服的。 **Yǎnqián wǒmen yǒuxiē kùnnan, dàn hěn kuài néng kèfú de.** *At present we have some difficulties, but they can be overcome very soon.*
眼色 **yǎnsè** [modif: 眼 eye + 色 color] *n* meaningful glance
交换眼色 jiāohuàn yǎnsè exchange meaningful glances
眼神 **yǎnshén** [modif: 眼 eye + 神 spirit] *n* expression in one's eyes
眼下 **yǎnxià** *adv* at the moment, now

演 **yǎn** **I** *v* act, perform, show □ 他很会演戏。 **Tā hěn huì yǎn xì.** *He is good at acting.* **II** *n* show (a film) □ 今天电影院演什么电影? **Jīntiān diànyǐngyuàn yǎn shénme diànyǐng?** *What movies are being shown at the cinema today?*
演变 **yǎnbiàn** *v* evolve, unfold
演出 **yǎnchū** **I** *v* put on a theatrical performance, perform □ 这次音乐会有两位有名的歌唱家演出。 **Zhè cì yīnyuèhuì yǒu liǎng wèi yǒumíng de gēchàngjiā yǎnchū.** *Two well-known singers will perform at the concert.* □ 他们将在全国各大城市演出。 **Tāmen jiāng zài quánguó gè dà chéngshì yǎnchū.** *They will perform in big cities throughout the country.* **II** *n* theatrical performance □ 他们的演出精彩极了! **Tāmen de yǎnchū jīngcǎi jíle.** *How wonderful their performance was!* □ 昨天晚上的演出让人失望。 **Zuótiān wǎnshang de yǎnchū ràng rén shīwàng.** *The performance last night was disappointing.*
演说 **yǎnshuō** [comp: 演 perform + 说 speak] *v* deliver a formal speech
演算 **yǎnsuàn** *v* perform mathematical calculations
演习 **yǎnxí** *n* exercise, drill
军事演习 jūnshì yǎnxí military exercise
演员 **yǎnyuán** [modif: 演 act + 员 person] *n* actor, actress, performer □ 在中国要当演员一定要会说标准的普通话。 **Zài Zhōngguó yào dāng yǎnyuán yídìng yào huì shuō biāozhǔn de Pǔtōnghuà.** *In China if one wants to be an actor one must be able to speak standard Putonghua.*
演奏 **yǎnzòu** *v* give an instrument performance

衍 **yǎn** *v* spread out (See 敷衍 **fūyan**)

厌 **yàn** Trad 厭 *v* detest, loathe
厌恶 **yànwù** [comp: 厌 detest + 恶 loathe] *v* detest, be disgusted with

艳 **yàn** *adj* fresh and attractive (See 鲜艳 **xiānyàn**)

燕 **yàn** *n* (bird) swallow
燕子 yànzi swallow (只 **zhī**)

雁 **yàn** *n* wild goose
大雁 dàyàn wild goose

焰 **yàn** *n* flame (See 火焰 **huǒyàn**)

咽 **yàn** *v* swallow □ 我要喝一点水, 才能把药片咽下去。 **Wǒ yào hē yìdiǎn shuǐ, cái néng bǎ yàopiàn yàn xiàqu.** *I must drink a bit of water to be able to swallow the pill.*

宴 **yàn** **I** *n* feast **II** *v* entertain
宴会 **yànhuì** [modif: 宴 feast + 会 meet] *n* banquet, feast □ 他们回国以前, 举行了告别宴会。 **Tāmen huíguó yǐqián, jǔxíng le gàobié yànhuì.** *Before returning*

to their country, they gave a farewell banquet. □ 明天晚上我要去参加朋友的结婚宴会。**Míngtiān wǎnshang wǒ yào qù cānjiā péngyou de jiéhūn yànhuì.** *Tomorrow night I'll be attending a friend's wedding banquet.*

参加宴会 cānjiā yànhuì attend a banquet

告别宴会 gàobié yànhuì farewell banquet

欢迎宴会 huānyíng yànhuì welcome banquet

结婚宴会 jiéhūn yànhuì wedding banquet

宴请 **yànqǐng** v entertain with a feast

宴席 **yànxí** n banquet, feast

验 **yàn** Trad 驗 v examine

验光 **yànguāng** [v+obj: 验 examine + 光 eyesight] n optometry

验光师 yànguāngshī optometrist

验收 **yànshōu** [comp: 验 examine + 收 accept] v check and accept, check upon delivery

验证 **yànzhèng** [comp: 验 examine + 证 verify] v test to verify

央 **yāng** n center (See 中央 **zhōngyāng**)

秧 **yāng** n seedling

插秧 chāyāng transplant rice seedlings

秧苗 **yāngmiáo** n rice seedling

殃 **yāng** n calamity (See 遭殃 **zāoyāng**)

羊 **yáng** n sheep, goat, lamb (头 tóu) □ 春天是生小羊的时候。**Chūntiān shì shēng xiǎoyáng de shíhou.** *Spring is the lambing season.*

山羊 shānyáng goat

小羊 xiǎoyáng lamb

羊毛 **yángmáo** n wool

羊皮 **yángpí** n sheepskin

羊肉 **yángròu** n mutton

阳 **yáng** Trad 陽 n what is open, overt, masculine, the sun

阳光 **yángguāng** [modif: 阳 the sun + 光 light] n sunshine, sunlight □ 这里的阳光太强了。**Zhèli de yángguāng tài qiáng le.** *The sunshine here is too intense.*

阳性 **yángxìng** adj (of medical test) positive (antonym 阴性 **yīngxìng**)

扬 **yáng** Trad 揚 v raise, make known (See 表扬 **biǎoyáng**, 发扬 **fāyáng**.)

杨 **yáng** n poplar

杨树 yángshù poplar tree (棵 kē)

洋 **yáng** n ocean (See 大洋洲 **Dàyángzhōu**, 海洋 **hǎiyáng**.)

养 **yǎng** Trad 養 v 1 provide for, support □ 爸爸妈妈辛辛苦苦地工作, 把我养大。**Bàba māma xīn-xīn-kǔ-kǔ de gōngzuò, bǎ wǒ yǎng dà.** *Dad and mom worked hard to provide for me.* 2 raise, keep as pet □ 我一直想养一只狗。**Wǒ yìzhí xiǎng yǎng yì zhī gǒu.** *I have always wanted to have a dog.* 3 form, cultivate 4 recuperate one's health

养成 **yǎngchéng** v form (a habit)

养成每天锻炼的好习惯 yǎngchéng měitiān duànliàn de hǎo xíguàn form the good habit of doing exercises every day

养分 **yǎngfèn** n nutrient

养活 **yǎnghuo** [v+compl: 养 provide for + 活 alive] v provide for, support, sustain

养料 **yǎngliào** n nourishment, nutriment

养育 **yǎngyù** [comp: 养 provide for + 育 educate] v bring up (a child), rear

养殖 **yǎngzhí** n breed or cultivate (aquatic products, plants, etc.)

水产养殖场 shuǐchǎn yǎngzhíchǎng aquatic farm

氧 **yǎng** n oxygen (O₂)

氧气 yǎngqì oxygen

氧化 **yǎnghuà** v oxidize, oxidate

痒 **yǎng** v itch, tickle

发痒 fāyǎng itch □ 我背上发痒。**Wǒ bēishang fāyǎng.** *My back itches.*

仰 **yǎng** v face upward

仰望 **yǎngwàng** [comp: 仰 face upward + 望 look] v 1 look up to 2 revere

样 **yàng** Trad 樣 I measure wd kind, category, type □ 他做了几样菜, 招待朋友。**Tā zuòle jǐ yàng cài, zhāodài péngyou.** *He prepared several dishes to entertain his friends.* II n appearance, looks

样子 **yàngzi** n appearance, manner □ 几年不见, 你还是以前的样子。**Jǐ nián bú jiàn, nǐ hái shì yǐqián de yàngzi.** *It's been years since I last saw you and you still look the same as before.*

要 **yāo** as in 要求 yāoqiú

要求 **yāoqiú** I v ask, demand, require □ 老师要求我们每天都读课文。**Lǎoshī yāoqiú wǒmen měi tiān dōu dú kèwén.** *The teacher requires us to read the texts every day.* □ 市场要求我们不断开发新产品。**Shìchǎng yāoqiú wǒmen búduàn kāifā xīn chǎnpǐn.** *The market demands that we constantly develop new products.* II n demand, requirement □ 我想提两个要求, 可以吗? **Wǒ xiǎng tí liǎng ge yāoqiú, kěyǐ ma?** *May I ask for two requirements?* □ 我们尽量满足顾客的要求。**Wǒmen jìnliàng mǎnzú gùkè de yāoqiú.** *We try our best to satisfy our clients' demands.*

腰 **yāo** n waist, small of the back □ 她胖得没有腰。**Tā pàng de méiyǒu yāo.** *She is so fat that she has no waist.*

妖 **yāo** n evil spirit

妖怪 **yāoguài** n monster, bogey man

邀 **yāo** v invite

邀请 **yāoqǐng** [comp: 邀 invite + 请 ask] I v invite □ 他邀请很多朋友来参加他的二十一岁生日宴会。**Tā yāoqǐng hěn duō péngyou lái cānjiā tā de èrshíyī suì shēngrì yànhuì.** *He invited many friends to his twenty-first birthday dinner party.* II n invitation □ 我昨天发出了邀请, 他们大约明天会收到。**Wǒ zuótiān fāchūle yāoqǐng, tāmen dàyuē míngtiān huì shōudao.** *I sent the invitation yesterday, and they'll probably receive it tomorrow.*

邀请信 yāoqǐngxìn letter of invitation

摇 **yáo** v shake, wave □ 点头表示同意, 摇头表示不同意。**Diǎn tóu biǎoshì tóngyì, yáo tóu biǎoshì bù tóngyì.** *Nodding the head indicates agreement and shaking the head signals disagreement.*

摇头丸 **yáotóuwán** n Ecstasy pill (an addictive drug)

谣 **yáo** Trad 謠 n 1 rumor 2 ballad, rhyme

民谣 mínyáo folk ballad, ballad

谣言 **yáoyán** [modif: 谣 rumor + 言 word] n malicious rumor, rumor □ 我不信谣言, 也不传谣言。**Wǒ bú xìn yáoyán, yě bù chuán yáoyán.** *I don't believe rumors, nor do I spread them.*

遥 **yáo** *adj* faraway
遥远 **yáoyuǎn** [comp: 遥 faraway + 远 distant]
adj faraway, remote

窑 **yáo** *n* kiln
砖窑 zhuānyáo brick kiln (座 **zuò**)

咬 **yǎo** *v* bite □ 我给蚊子咬了一口。**Wǒ gěi wénzi
yǎole yì kǒu.** *I was bitten by a mosquito.*

药 **yào** Trad 藥 *n* medicine, drug □ 这种药你一
天吃两次, 每次吃一片。**Zhè zhǒng yào nǐ yì tiān
chī liǎng cì, měi cì chī yí piàn.** *You should take this
medicine twice a day, one pill each time.* □ 现在还没
有药治这种病。**Xiànzài hái méiyǒu yào zhì zhè zhǒng
bìng.** *At present there is no medicine to cure this
disease.*
草药 cǎoyào herbal medicine
吃药 chī yào take medicine
西药 xīyào Western medicine
中药 Zhōngyào traditional Chinese medicine
药方 **yàofāng** *n* prescription
药房 **yàofáng** [modif: 药 medicine + 房 house]
pharmacist's, pharmacy
药片 **yàopiàn** [modif: 药 medicine + 片 flake] *n* pill
药水 **yàoshuǐ** [modif: 药 medicine + 水 water] *n*
liquid medicine

耀 **yào** *v* shine, dazzle (See 照耀 **zhàoyào**)

要 **yào** I *v* 1 want, would like □ 我要一间安静的
房间。**Wǒ yào yì jiān ānjìng de fángjiān.** *I want
a quiet room.* 2 ask (somebody to do something)
□ 我哥哥要我问你好。**Wǒ gēge yào wǒ wèn nǐ hǎo.**
My brother asked me to give you his regards. II *adj*
important
要人 **yàorén** important person, VIP
III *modal v* should, must □ 你想学好中文, 就要多听, 多
讲。**Nǐ xiǎng xuéhǎo Zhōngwén, jiù yào duō tīng, duō
jiǎng.** *If you want to learn Chinese well, you should
listen more and speak more.* IV *conj* suppose, if
要点 **yàodiǎn** [modif: 要 important + 点 point] *n*
key point, major point
要好 **yàohǎo** *adj* on very good terms, very close
□ 他们以前是很要好的朋友。**Tāmen yǐqián shì hěn
yàohǎo de péngyou.** *They used to be very close
friends.*
要紧 **yàojǐn** *adj* important, urgent, serious □ 考试
的时候, 最要紧的是看清考题。**Kǎoshì de shíhou, zuì
yàojǐn de shì kànqīng kǎotí.** *The most important
thing at examinations is to understand the question
clearly.*
不要紧 búyàojǐn it doesn't matter □ "对不起。" "不要
紧。" **"Duìbuqǐ." "Búyàojǐn."** *"I'm sorry." "It doesn't
matter."*
要领 **yàolǐng** *n* main points, gist
要么 **yàome** *conj* either ... (or) □ 你要么现在就去, 要
么别去了。**Nǐ yàome xiànzài jiù qù, yàome jiù bié
qù le.** *You either go right now, or don't go.*
要命 **yàomìng** *adv* extremely □ 我这两天忙得要命。
Wǒ zhè liǎng tiān máng de yàomìng. *I'm extremely
busy these days.*
要是 **yàoshì** *conj* if □ 要是你明天不能来, 请给我打电
话。**Yàoshì nǐ míngtiān bù néng lái, qǐng gěi wǒ dǎ ge
diànhuà.** *If you're not able to come tomorrow, please
give me a call.*

NOTE: Both 如果 **rúguǒ** and 要是 **yàoshì** mean *if*. While 如果
rúguǒ is for general use, 要是 **yàoshì** is a colloquialism.

要素 **yàosù** *n* essential element

钥 **yào** Trad 鑰 as in 钥匙 **yàoshi**
钥匙 **yàoshi** *n* key (把 **bǎ**) □ 钥匙一定要放好。
Yàoshi yídìng yào fànghǎo. *You must keep the keys in
a safe place.*

爷 **yé** Trad 爺 *n* paternal grandfather
爷爷 **yéye** *n* Same as 祖父 **zǔfù**. Used in colloquial Chinese.

也 **yě** *adv* 1 also, too □ 我喜欢打球, 也喜欢游泳。
Wǒ xǐhuan dǎ qiú, yě xǐhuan yóuyǒng. *I like ball
games, and I also like swimming.* □ 你想去北京学习,
我也想去北京学习。**Nǐ xiǎng qù Běijīng xuéxí, wǒ yě
xiǎng qù Běijīng xuéxí.** *You want to study in Beijing,
so do I.* 2 neither, nor □ 你没有看过这个电影, 我也没
看过这个电影。**Nǐ méiyǒu kànguo zhège diànyǐng, wǒ
yě méi kànguo zhège diànyǐng.** *You haven't seen this
movie, nor have I.*
也许 **yěxǔ** *adv* perhaps, maybe □ 天上有大块的云, 也
许会下雨。**Tiān shang yǒu dà kuài de yún, yěxǔ huì
xiàyǔ.** *It's very cloudy. Perhaps it'll rain.* □ "他今天
会给我们发电子邮件吗?" "也许。" **"Tā jīntiān huì gěi
wǒmen fā diànzǐ yóujiàn ma?" "Yěxǔ."** *"Will he send
us an e-mail today?" "Perhaps."*

NOTE: See note on 恐怕 **kǒngpà**.

野 **yě** I *n* open country II *adj* wild
野蛮 **yěmán** [comp: 野 wild + 蛮 rough] *adj*
savage, barbaric
野生 **yěshēng** [modif: 野 wild + 生 living] *adj* wild
(animal or plant)
野生动物 yěshēng dòngwù wildlife
野兽 **yěshòu** [modif: 野 wild + 兽 beast] *n* wild beast
野外 **yěwài** *n* open country, field
野外作业 yěwài zuòyè field work
野心 **yěxīn** [modif: 野 wild + 心 heart] *n* wild
ambition

冶 **yě** *v* smelt
冶炼 yěliàn smelt
冶金 **yějīn** *n* metallurgy

业 **yè** Trad 業 *n* industry
业务 **yèwù** [comp: 业 occupation + 务 business]
n 1 professional work, vocational work □ 她业务
水平很强。**Tā yèwù shuǐpíng hěn qiáng.** *She is very
efficient professionally.* 2 business □ 公司的业务开
展很顺利。**Gōngsī de yèwù kāizhǎn hěn shùnlì.** *The
business of the company has developed smoothly.*
业余 **yèyú** I *n* spare time □ 你业余做什么? **Nǐ yèyú zuò
shénme?** *What do you do in your spare time?* II *adj*
amateur □ 他是一位中学老师, 也是业余音乐家。**Tā shì
yí wèi zhōngxué lǎoshī, yě shì yèyú yīnyuèjiā.** *He is a
high school teacher and also an amateur musician.*

叶 **yè** Trad 葉 *n* leaf
叶子 **yèzi** leaf (片 **piàn**) □ 秋天, 叶子都黄了。
Qiūtiān, yèzi dōu huáng le. *In autumn, leaves turn
yellow.*

页 **yè** Trad 頁 *n* page □ 这本词典有三百多页。**Zhè
běn cídiǎn yǒu sānbǎi duō yè.** *This dictionary has*

over three hundred pages. □ 请把书翻到二十页。**Qǐng bǎ shū fān dào èrshí yè.** *Please turn to page twenty of your book.*

夜 **yè** *n* night, evening □ 他昨夜十一点钟才回家。**Tā zuó yè shíyī diǎnzhōng cái huíjiā.** *Last night he did not return home until eleven o'clock.* (→ *Last night he returned home as late as eleven o'clock.*)

半夜 **bànyè** midnight

夜班 **yèbān** *n* night shift

上夜班 **shàng yèbān** be on a night shift

夜车 **yèchē** *n* night train

夜里 **yèli** *n* at night □ 这条大街夜里也车辆不断。**Zhè tiáo dàjiē yèli yě chēliàng bú duàn.** *There is constant traffic on this main street even at night.* □ 这个人喜欢白天睡觉，夜里工作，是个"夜猫子"。**Zhège rén xǐhuan báitiān shuìjiào, yèli gōngzuò, shì ge "yè māozi".** *This person likes sleeping in the day and working at night, just like an owl.*

夜晚 **yèwǎn** *n* Same as 夜里 **yèli**

液 **yè** *n* liquid, fluid

液体 **yètǐ** *n* liquid

一 **yī** *num* one □ 一万一千一百十一 **yíwàn yìqiān yìbǎi shíyī** *eleven thousand, one hundred and eleven 11,111*

NOTE: (1) 一 undergoes tone changes (tone sandhi). When standing alone, 一 is pronounced with the first tone, i.e. **yī**. When followed by a sound in the fourth tone, 一 changes to the second tone, e.g. 一定 **yídìng**. 一 is pronounced in the fourth tone in all other circumstances, e.g. 一般 **yìbān**, 一同 **yìtóng**, 一起 **yìqǐ**. Pay attention to the various tones of 一 here and in the following words. (2) When saying a number (e.g. a telephone number) people pronounce 一 as **yāo** for clarity, e.g. □ 我的电话号码是五八一三九。**Wǒ de diànhuà hàomǎ shì wǔ-bā-yāo-sān-jiǔ.** *My telephone number is 58139.*

一般 **yìbān** *adj* 1 generally speaking, normal □ 每星期一上午我们一般都开会。**Měi Xīngqīyī shàngwǔ wǒmen yìbān dōu kāihuì.** *We usually have a meeting every Monday morning.* 2 average, commonplace □ 他的学习成绩一般。**Tā de xuéxí chéngjì yìbān.** *His school record is average.* 3 same as, as ... as □ 哥哥长得和爸爸一般高了。**Gēge zhǎng de hé bàba yìbān gāo le.** *My elder brother is now as tall as Daddy.*

一半 **yíbàn** *n* half, one half □ 他一半时间念书，一半时间做工。**Tā yíbàn shíjiān niànshū, yíbàn shíjiān zuògōng.** *He spends half his time studying and the other half working.*

一辈子 **yíbèizi** *n* one's entire life

一边 **yìbiān** *n* one side □ 在这场争论中，我站在你们一边。**Zài zhè chǎng zhēnglùn zhōng, wǒ zhàn zài nǐmen yìbiān.** *In this debate I am on your side.*

一边…一边… **yìbiān...yìbiān...** *conj* while ..., at the same time □ 不少大学生一边学习一边工作。**Bùshǎo dàxuéshēng yìbiān xuéxí yìbiān gōngzuò.** *Quite a few university students study and work at the same time.*

NOTE: 一边…一边… **yìbiān...yìbiān...** links two verbs to indicate that the two actions denoted by the verbs take place simultaneously. Another example: □ 他常常一边做

作业一边听音乐。**Tā chángcháng yìbiān zuò zuòyè yìbiān tīng yīnyuè.** *He often does his homework while listening to music.* When the verbs are monosyllabic, 边…边… **biān...biān...** may be used instead of 一边…一边… **yìbiān...**, e.g. □ 孩子们走边唱。**Háizimen biān zǒu biān chàng.** *The children sang while walking.* □ 我们边吃边谈吧。**Wǒmen biān chī biān tán ba.** *Let's carry on the conversation while eating.*

一旦 **yídàn** *conj* once, in case □ 一旦有她的消息，马上告诉我。**Yídàn yǒu tāde xiāoxi, mǎshàng gàosu wǒ.** *Once you've got news about her, let me know immediately.*

一道 **yídào** *adv* Same as 一起 **yìqǐ**

一点儿 **yìdiǎnr** *n* a tiny amount, a bit □ 那个菜不好吃，我只吃了一点儿。**Nàge cài bù hǎo chī, wǒ zhǐ chīle yìdiǎnr.** *That dish is not tasty. I ate only a tiny bit of it.*

一定 **yídìng** I *adj* 1 fixed, specified □ 他吃饭没有一定的时间。**Tā chīfàn méiyǒu yídìng de shíjiān.** *He has no fixed mealtimes.* 2 to a certain degree, fair, limited □ 你的中文已经达到了一定水平。**Nǐ de Zhōngwén yǐjīng dádàole yídìng shuǐpíng.** *You've already reached a certain level of proficiency in Chinese.* II *adv* certainly, definitely □ 我们的目标一定能达到。**Wǒmen de mùbiāo yídìng néng dádào.** *We can certainly reach our goal.*

一度 **yídù** *adv* for a time, on one occasion □ 他一度得过忧郁症。**Tā yídù dé guò yōuyùzhèng.** *He once suffered from depression.*

一帆风顺 **yìfān fēng shun** *idiom* plain sailing

一方面…一方面… **yìfāngmiàn...yìfāngmiàn...** *conj* on the one hand ... on the other hand ... □ 我们一方面要发展经济，一方面要保护环境。**Wǒmen yìfāngmiàn yào fāzhǎn jīngjì, yìfāngmiàn yào bǎohù huánjìng.** *We should on the one hand develop the economy and on the other hand protect the environment.*

一概 **yígài** *adv* all, without exception

一概而论 **yígài ér lùn** *idiom* lump everything together, make sweeping generalization

一共 **yígòng** *adv* in all, total, altogether □ 你们学校一共有多少学生？**Nǐmen xuéxiào yígòng yǒu duōshǎo xuésheng?** *How many students are there altogether in your school?* (→ *What is the total number of students in your school?*) □ 我们去年一共学了五百二十个汉字。**Wǒmen qùnián yígòng xuéle wǔbǎi èrshí ge Hànzì.** *Last year we learned 520 Chinese characters in total.*

一贯 **yíguàn** *adv* all along, always

一会儿 **yíhuìr** *adv* in a very short time, in a moment □ 不用麻烦倒茶，我一会儿就走。**Bú yòng máfan dào chá, wǒ yíhuìr jiù zǒu.** *Please don't bother making tea. I'll be leaving in a moment.* □ 他只休息了一会儿，就又干起来了。**Tā zhǐ xiūxile yíhuìr, jiù yòu gàn qǐlai le.** *He took only a brief break and started working again.* □ 昨天的电视我只看了一会儿。**Zuótiān de diànshì wǒ zhǐ kànle yíhuìr.** *Yesterday I watched TV for a very short time only.*

一会儿…一会儿 **yíhuìr…yíhuìr** *conj* one moment ... the next (moment) □ 她一会儿哭，一会儿笑，到底怎么啦？**Tā yíhuìr kū, yíhuìr xiào, dàodǐ zěnme la?** *One moment she was crying, and the next she was laughing—what's happened to her?*

一···就··· **yī...jiù...** *conj* as soon as, no sooner ... than ... □ 妈妈一回家, 就做晚饭。**Māma yì huíjiā, jiù zuò wǎnfàn.** *Mom cooks supper as soon as she gets back home.* □ 我一上火车, 车就开了。**Wǒ yí shàng huǒchē, chē jiù kāi le.** *No sooner did I board the train then it started.*

一口气 **yìkǒuqì** *adv* (do something) in one breath, without a break □ 他一口气开了三百英里。**Tā yìkǒuqì kāile sānbǎi yīnglǐ.** *He drove 300 miles without a break.*

一块儿 **yíkuàir** *adv* Same as 一起 **yìqǐ**. Tends to be used in colloquial Chinese.

一连 **yìlián** *adv* in a row, successively □ 他一连输了三盘棋。**Tā yìlián shū le sān pán qí.** *He lost three games of chess in a row.*

一路平安 **yìlù píng'ān** *idiom* have a good journey

一路顺风 **yìlù shùnfēng** *idiom* Have a good trip!

一律 **yílù** *adv* all, without exception

一毛不拔 **yìmáo bù bá** *idiom* unwilling to give even a hair, very stingy

一旁 **yìpáng** *n* one side

一面···一面 **yímiàn...yímiàn** *conj* at the same time, while □ 一面开车一面打手机 **yímiàn kāichē yímiàn dǎshǒu jī** *drive while talking on the cell phone*

一齐 **yìqí** *adv* Same as 一起 **yìqǐ**

一起 **yìqǐ** *adv* together □ 我们一起去吃饭吧。**Wǒmen yìqǐ qù chīfàn ba.** *Let's have a meal together.* □ 他们夫妻俩在同一公司工作, 常常一起上班, 一起回家。**Tāmen fūqī liǎ zài tóng yì gōngsī gōngzuò, chángcháng yìqǐ shàngbān, yìqǐ huíjiā.** *That couple work in the same company, so they often go to work together and come home together.*

一切 **yíqiè** **I** *adj* all, every and each without exception □ 一切工作都做完了, 才能放假。**Yíqiè gōngzuò dōu zuòwánle, cái néng fàngjià.** *You can have your holiday only after all the work is done.* □ 出国的一切手续都办完, 要多长时间? **Chūguó de yíqiè shǒuxù dōu bànwán yào duō cháng shíjiān?** *How long will it take to go through all the formalities for going abroad?* **II** *pron* all, everything □ 我了解她的一切。**Wǒ liáojiě tā de yíqiè.** *I know everything about her.* □ 他做的一切都是为了赚更多的钱。**Tā zuò de yíqiè dōushì wèile zhuàn gèng duō de qián.** *Everything he does, he does it to make more money.*

一生 **yìshēng** *n* all one's life, lifetime □ 这位老人一生都住在这个山区。**Zhè wèi lǎorén yìshēng dōu zhù zài zhège shānqū.** *This old man has lived in this mountainous area all his life.*

一时 **yìshí** *adv* for the time being, momentarily □ 这个字我认识, 但是一时记不起来了。**Zhège zì wǒ rènshi, dànshì yìshí jì bu qǐlái le.** *I do know the word, but I just don't remember at this moment.*

一手 **yìshǒu** *adv* single-handedly, all by oneself

一同 **yìtóng** *adv* Same as 一起 **yìqǐ**

一系列 **yíxìliè** *n* a series of

一下 **yíxià** *adv* (used after a verb to indicate the action is done briefly or casually) for a short while □ 请您等一下, 王先生马上就来。**Qǐng nín děng yíxià, Wáng xiānsheng mǎshàng jiù lái.** *Please wait for a while. Mr Wang will be here in a moment.* □ 我看一下电视就去洗澡。**Wǒ kàn yíxià diànshì, jiù qù xǐzǎo.** *I'll watch TV for a short while before taking a bath.*

NOTE: It is very common in spoken Chinese to use 一下 **yíxià** after a verb, especially as an informal request. Some Northern Chinese speakers use 一下儿 **yíxiàr** instead of 一下 **yíxià**. More examples: □ 请您来一下儿。**Qǐng nín lái yíxiàr.** *Please come over for a while.* □ 我们在这儿停一下儿吧。**Wǒmen zài zhèr tíng yíxiàr ba.** *Let's stop here for a while.* □ 让我想一下儿再回答。**Ràng wǒ xiǎng yíxiàr zài huídá.** *Let me think for a while before I answer.*

一下子 **yíxiàzi** *adv* all at once, all of a sudden □ 这么多事一下子做不完, 明天再做吧。**Zhème duō shì yíxiàzi zuò bu wán, míngtiān zài zuò ba.** *We can't finish so many things at once. Let's continue tomorrow.*

一向 **yíxiàng** *adv* all along, always

一些 **yìxiē** *measure wd* a small amount of, a bit of □ 请你在我的茶里放一些糖。**Qǐng nǐ zài wǒ de chá li fàng yìxiē táng.** *Please put a little sugar in my tea.* □ 我这里有一些书, 你看看还有没有用。**Wǒ zhèli yǒu yìxiē shū, nǐ kànkan hái yǒu méiyǒu yòng.** *I have a few books here. Have a look to see if they are still useful.*

一心 **yìxīn** *adv* single-mindedly, wholeheartedly □ 她一心想当电影明星。**Tā yìxīnxiǎng dāng diànyǐng míngxīng.** *She has a single-minded determination to be a movie star.*

一样 **yíyàng** *adj* same, identical □ "一下" 和 "一下儿" 是一样的。**"Yíxià" hé "yíxiàr" shì yíyàng de.** *"Yixia" and "Yixiar" are the same (i.e. have the same meaning).* □ 你今天去, 明天去, 都一样。**Nǐ jīntiān qù, míngtiān qù, dōu yíyàng.** *It's all the same whether you go today or tomorrow.*

一再 **yízài** *adv* time and again, repeatedly

一直 **yìzhí** *adv* always, all the time □ 我一直住在这个城市。**Wǒ yìzhí zhù zài zhège chéngshì.** *I've always been living in this city.* □ 他一直很关心你, 常打听你的消息。**Tā yìzhí hěn guānxīn nǐ, cháng dǎtīng nǐ de xiāoxi.** *He is always concerned for you and frequently asks after you.*

一致 **yízhì** *adj* unanimous, identical □ 会上没有取得一致的意见。**Huìshang méiyǒu qǔdé yízhì de yìjiàn.** *No consensus of opinion was reached at the meeting.* □ 双方提出的数据是一致的。**Shuāngfāng tíchū de shùjù shì yízhì de.** *The two parties presented identical data.*

壹 **yī** *n* one

衣 **yī** *n* clothing

衣服 **yīfu** [comp: 衣 clothing + 服 clothing] *n* clothes, pieces of clothing (件 **jiàn**) □ 她每年花很多钱买衣服。**Tā měi nián huā hěn duō qián mǎi yīfu.** *She spends lots of money every year buying clothes.* □ 她很会穿衣服。**Tā hěn huì chuān yīfu.** *She has good dress sense.*

NOTE: 衣服 **yīfu** may denote *clothes* or *pieces of clothing*. 一件衣服 **yí jiàn yīfu** may be *a jacket, a coat, a dress* or *a sweater*, but not *a pair of trousers*, which is 一条裤子 **yì tiáo kùzi**.

衣裳 **yīshang** *n* Same as 衣服 **yīfu**

伊 **yī** *pron* she, her, he, his

伊斯兰教 **Yīsīlánjiào** *n* Islam

医 yī Trad 醫 I v heal, cure □ 他的病还能医吗? **Tāde bìng hái néng yī ma?** *Can his illness be treated?* II n medicine

医疗 yīliáo [comp: 医 treat + 疗 cure] n medical care
公费医疗 gōngfèi yīliáo public health service

医生 yīshēng [modif: 医 medicine + 生 scholar] n medical doctor (位 **wèi**) □ 你要听医生的话。**Nǐ yào tīng yīshēng de huà.** *You should follow the doctor's advice.* □ 我们的家庭医生是张医生。**Wǒmen de jiātíng yīshēng shì Zhāng yīshēng.** *Our family physician is Dr Zhang.*

医务室 yīwùshì [modif: 医 medical + 务 affair + 室 room] n clinic (in a school, factory, etc.) □ 我们学校的医务室只有一位护士。**Wǒmen xuéxiào de yīwùshì zhǐyǒu yí wèi hùshi.** *There is only a nurse in our school clinic.*

医学 yīxué [modif: 医 medical + 学 study] n medical science, medicine □ 医学正在经历一场革命。**Yīxué zhèngzài jīnglì yì chǎng gémìng.** *Medical science is experiencing a revolution.*

医学院 yīxuéyuàn n medical school

医药 yīyào [comp: 医 medical care + 药 medicine, drug] n medicine
医药费 yīyàofèi medical expenses

医院 yīyuàn [modif: 医 medicine + 院 place (for certain activities)] n hospital (座 **zuò**) □ 马上送医院! **Mǎshàng sòng yīyuàn!** *Take him to the hospital right now!* □ 请问, 最近的医院在哪儿? **Qǐng wèn, zuì jìn de yīyuàn zài nǎr?** *Excuse me, where is the nearest hospital?*
送⋯去医院 sòng...qù yīyuàn take ... to the hospital
住(医)院 zhù (yī) yuàn be hospitalized □ 他病得很重, 得住医院。**Tā bìng de hěn zhòng, děi zhù yīyuàn.** *He's seriously ill and has to be hospitalized.*

医治 yīzhì v treat (a patient)

依 yī v 1 rely on 2 according to
依次 yīcì adv in order, successively
依旧 yījiù adv as before, still
依据 yījù I v be based on
依据最新资料 yījù zuìxīn zīliào based on the latest data
II n basis, foundation
没有依据的指控 méiyǒu yījù de zhǐkòng unfounded allegation
依靠 yīkào [comp: 依 rely on + 靠 lean on] v rely on, depend on □ 公司的成功依靠全体职工的努力。**Gōngsī de chénggōng yào yīkào quántǐ zhígōng de nǔlì.** *The success of the company depends on the efforts of all staff.*
依赖 yīlài [comp: 依 rely on + 赖 rely on] v rely on, be dependent on
依然 yīrán adv still, as before
依照 yīzhào prep according to, based on

姨 yí n one's mother's sister (See 阿姨 āyí)

仪 yí Trad 儀 n instrument, appearance
仪表 yíbiǎo n 1 appearance, bearing
仪表堂堂 yíbiǎo tángtáng look dignified, with imposing presence
2 gauge, meter
仪器 yíqì [comp: 仪 instrument + 器 utensil] n instrument (件 **jiàn**) □ 做这个试验需要很多仪器。Zuò zhège shìyàn xūyào hěn duō yíqì. *This test requires many instruments.*

仪式 yíshì n ceremony
举行仪式 jǔxíng yíshì hold a ceremony

宜 yí adj suitable (See 便宜 **piányi**.)

移 yí v move, shift □ 窗前的阳光太强, 我要把桌子往上移。**Chuāngqián de yángguāng tài qiáng, wǒ yào bǎ zhuōzi wǎng biānshang yí.** *The sunshine is too strong by the window. I want to move my desk to the side.*
移动 yídòng [comp: 移 move + 动 move] v move, shift □ 强冷空气正在向东移动。**Qiáng lěng kōngqì zhèngzài xiàng dōng yídòng.** *Strong cold air is moving eastward.*
移动电话 yídòng diànhuà mobile telephone
移民 yímín I v immigrate, emigrate II n immigrant, emigrant, immigration
移民局 Yímínjú Immigration Services
新移民 xīn yímín new immigrant

疑 yí v doubt, disbelief
疑惑 yíhuò [comp: 疑 doubt + 惑 doubt] v feel uncertain, wonder
疑问 yíwèn [comp: 疑 doubt + 问 inquire] n doubt □ 这个计划一定要实现, 这是毫无疑问的。**Zhège jìhuà yídìng yào shíxiàn, zhè shì háowú yíwèn de.** *It is beyond any doubt that this plan will materialize.*
疑心 yíxīn n Same as 怀疑 **huáiyí**

遗 yí Trad 遺 v 1 leave behind as legacy, inheritance 2 bequeath, hand down 3 lose, omit
遗产 yíchǎn [modif: 遗 leave behind + 产 property] n inheritance, legacy
遗传 yíchuán [comp: 遗 leave behind + 传 transmit] v pass to the next generation, be hereditary
遗传病 yíchuánbìng hereditary disease
遗憾 yíhàn I v regret □ 部长非常遗憾, 不能接受你们的邀请。**Bùzhǎng fēicháng yíhàn, bù néng jiēshòu nǐmen de yāoqǐng.** *The Minister regrets he is unable to accept your invitation.* II adj regretful □ 我错过了那场音乐会, 真是很遗憾。**Wǒ cuòguole nà chǎng yīnyuèhuì, zhēn shì hěn yíhàn.** *It is a pity that I missed the concert.*
遗留 yíliú v leave behind, hand down
遗失 yíshī v lose, be lost □ 那份遗失的文件找到了。**Nà fèn yíshī de wénjiàn zhǎodào le.** *The lost document was recovered.*
遗体 yítǐ n body of a dead person, remains
向遗体告别 xiàng yítǐ gàobié pay last tribute to a dead person
遗址 yízhǐ n remains (of a building), ruins

已 yǐ adj Same as 已经 **yǐjīng**. Used in written Chinese.
已经 yǐjīng adv already □ 我已经学了三年中文了。**Wǒ yǐjīng xuéle sān nián Zhōngwén le.** *I have already studied Chinese for three years.* □ 她已经三十五岁了, 还没有结婚。**Tā yǐjīng sānshíwǔ suì le, hái méiyǒu jiéhūn.** *She is already thirty-five years old and is not married yet.*

乙 yǐ I n the second of the ten Heavenly Stems II adj second

以 1 yǐ prep 1 with, in the manner of □ 我们要以高标准严格要求自己。**Wǒmen yào yǐ gāo biāozhǔn yángé yāoqiú zìjǐ.** *We should set high standards for*

ourselves. **2** for, because of □ 这个地方以风景优美
著名。**Zhège dìfang yǐ fēngjǐng yōuměi zhùmíng.** *This
place is famous for its beautiful scenery.*

以 2 **yǐ** *conj* in order to, so as to □ 应该推广新技
术以提高工作效率。**Yīnggāi tuīguǎng xīn jìshù yǐ
tígāo gōngzuò xiàolǜ.** *We should promote new technology so as to increase efficiency.*

以便 yǐbiàn *conj* so that, in order that □ 请你尽早通知
我们，以便及时做好准备。**Qǐng nǐ jǐn zǎo tōngzhī wǒ-
men, yǐbiàn jíshí zuò hǎo zhǔnbèi.** *Please let us know
as soon as possible so that we can get ready in time.*

以后 yǐhòu *n* after, later (antonym 以前 yǐqián) □ 做
完作业以后，要检查一下。**Zuòwán zuòyè yǐhòu, yào
jiǎnchá yíxià.** *After you've done an assignment, you
should check it [for mistakes].* □ 这个问题我们以后再
谈。**Zhège wèntí wǒmen yǐhòu zài tán.** *We'll discuss
this problem later.*

以及 yǐjí *conj* Same as 和 **hé 2** *conj*, used in formal
Chinese.

以来 yǐlái *n* since, in the past ... □ 今年以来，天气一
直不正常。**Jīnnián yǐlái, tiānqì yìzhí bú zhèngcháng.**
*Since the beginning of this year the weather has been
quite abnormal.* □ 三个月以来，你的中文口语有了很大
进步。**Sān ge yuè yǐlái, nǐ de Zhōngwén kǒuyǔ yǒule
hěn dà jìnbù.** *In the past three months you have made
good progress in spoken Chinese.*

以免 yǐmiǎn *conj* in order to avoid, so as not to

以内 yǐnèi *n* within, during □ 三天以内我一定把报告
交给你。**Sān tiān yǐnèi wǒ yídìng bǎ bàogào jiāo gei
nǐ.** *I will definitely submit my report to you in three
days.*

以前 yǐqián *n* before, some time ago (antonym 以
后 yǐhòu) □ 回答问题以前，先要想一下。**Huídá wèntí
yǐqián, xiān yào xiǎng yíxià.** *Before you answer a
question, you should think first.* □ 他不久以前身体不大
好。**Tā bùjiǔ yǐqián shēntǐ bú dà hǎo.** *He was in poor
health not long ago.*

不久以前 **bùjiǔ yǐqián** not long ago

以上 yǐshàng *n* over, more than □ 中国人口百分
之六十以上住在农村。**Zhōngguó rénkǒu bǎifēn zhī
liùshí yǐshàng zhù zài nóngcūn.** *Over sixty percent of
China's population lives in rural areas.*

以身作则 yǐshēn zuòzé *idiom* set a good example
(for others to follow)

以外 yǐwài *n* beyond, outside, other than □ 八小时以
外你可以做自己喜欢做的事。**Bā xiǎoshí yǐwài nǐ kěyǐ
zuò zìjǐ xǐhuan zuò de shì.** *You can do what you enjoy
doing outside the eight working hours.*

以往 yǐwǎng *n* formerly, in the past

以为 yǐwéi *v* think (usually incorrectly) □ 呀，你还
在工作? 我以为你已经回家了。**Yǎ, nǐ háizài gōngzuò?
Wǒ yǐwéi nǐ yǐjīng huíjiā le.** *Oh, you're still working. I thought you'd gone home.* □ 我一直以为他是日
本人，现在才知道他是中国人。**Wǒ yìzhí yǐwéi tā shì
Rìběnrén, xiànzài cái zhīdào tā shì Zhōngguórén.** *I
always thought he was Japanese; only now I know he
is Chinese.*

以下 yǐxià *n* below, less than □ 他们的年收入在一万
元以下。**Tāmen de nián shōurù zài yíwàn yuán yǐxià.**
Their annual income is less than 10,000 yuan.

以至 yǐzhì *conj* **1** up to **2** so as to, so ... that

以至于 yǐzhìyú *conj* Same as 以至 **yǐzhì**

椅 yǐ *n* chair
椅子 **yǐzi** chair (把 **bǎ**) □ 房间里有一张桌子和四把
椅子。**Fángjiān li yǒu yì zhāng zhuōzi hé sì bǎ yǐzi.**
There is a table and four chairs in the room.

倚 yǐ *v* lean on or against, rest on or against

蚁 yǐ *n* ant (See 蚂蚁 **mǎyǐ**)

亿 yì Trad 億 *num* one hundred million □ 中国有十
三亿人口。**Zhōngguó yǒu shísān yì rénkǒu.** *China
has a population of 1.3 billion.*
十亿 **shíyì** billion

亿万 yìwàn *num* millions upon millions, an astronomical number of
亿万富翁 **yìwàn fùwēng** billionaire, super-rich

艺 yì Trad 藝 *n* art
艺术 **yìshù** [modif: 艺 art + 术 craft, skill] *n* art
□ 我不大懂现代艺术。**Wǒ bú dà dǒng xiàndài yìshù.**
I don't quite understand modern art. □ 他是搞艺术
的。**Tā shì gǎo yìshù de.** *He is engaged in art.* (→ *He
is an artist.*)
艺术家 **yìshùjiā** *n* (accomplished, recognized) artist
艺术作品 **yìshù zuòpǐn** *n* a work of art

忆 yì Trad 憶 *v* recall (See 回忆 **huíyì**, 记忆 **jìyì**.)

异 yì Trad 異 *adj* different, unusual
异常 **yìcháng** [v+obj: 异 differ from + 常 the
usual] *adj* abnormal, unusual □ 环境遭到破坏，造成
天气异常。**Huánjìng zāodào pòhuài, zàochéng tiānqì
yìcháng.** *As the environment is damaged, abnormal
weather results.*

毅 yì *adj* firm, resolute
毅力 **yìlì** [modif: 毅 resolute + 力 strength] *n*
indomitable will, strong willpower
毅然 **yìrán** *adv* resolutely

抑 yì *v* repress (See 压抑 **yāyì**)

役 yì *n* military campaign (See 战役 **zhànyì**)

疫 yì *n* epidemic (See 瘟疫 **wēnyì**)

亦 yì *adv* also

译 yì Trad 譯 *v* translate, interpret
译员 **yìyuán** *n* interpreter, translator (位 **wèi**, 名
míng)

易 yì **I** *adj* easy (See 容易 **róngyì**) **II** *v* exchange
(See 贸易 **màoyì**)

益 yì *n* benefit (See 利益 **lìyì**.)

谊 yì Trad 誼 *n* friendship (See 友谊 **yǒuyì**.)

意 yì *n* **1** idea, meaning **2** expectation, wish
意见 **yìjiàn** [comp: 意 idea + 见 viewpoint] *n* **1**
opinion, view (条 **tiáo**) □ 对这个问题你有什么意见?
Duì zhège wèntí nǐ yǒu shénme yìjiàn? *What is your
opinion on this issue?* □ 在这个问题上我们已经取得
了一致的意见。**Zài zhège wèntí shang wǒmen yǐjīng
qǔdéle yízhì de yìjiàn.** *We have reached consensus on
this issue.* **2** complaint, objection □ 我对他处理这
件事的方法很有意见。**Wǒ duì tā chǔlǐ zhè jiàn shì de
fāngfǎ hěn yǒu yìjiàn.** *I have objections to the way he*

dealt with this matter. □ 他只想到自己，我对他有意见。 **Tā zhǐ xiǎngdao zìjǐ, wǒ duì tā yǒu yìjiàn.** *My complaint against him is that he thinks only about himself.* 提意见 tí yìjiàn make a comment (on an issue, a proposal etc.), make a complaint

意料 **yìliào** *v* expect, anticipate
意料之中 yìliào zhīzhōng in line with expectations
出乎意料 chūhū yìliào out of expectations, not anticipated

意识 **yìshí** I *n* consciousness II *v* be conscious of, be aware of

意思 **yìsi** [comp: 意 meaning + 思 thought] *n* meaning □ 这个字是什么意思? **Zhège zì shì shénme yìsi?** *What's the meaning of this character?* □ 这句话的意思不清楚。 **Zhè jù huà de yìsi bù qīngchu.** *The meaning of this sentence is not clear.* □ 他的意思是你最好别去。 **Tā de yìsi shì nǐ zuìhǎo bié qù.** *What he meant is that you'd better not go.*

意图 **yìtú** *n* intention
了解他们的意图 liǎojiě tāmende yìtú find out their intentions

意外 **yìwài** I *adj* unexpected, unforeseen □ 这个消息很意外。 **Zhège xiāoxi hěn yìwài.** *This is unexpected news.* □ 她平时常常迟到，今天这么早就来了，让人感到意外。 **Tā píngshí chángcháng chídào, jīntiān zhème zǎo jiù lái le, ràng rén gǎndao yìwài.** *She is usually late for work, but she came so early today. It's quite unexpected.* II *n* mishap, accident □ 我们要采取安全措施，以防止意外。 **Wǒmen yào cǎiqǔ ānquán cuòshī, yǐ fángzhǐ yìwài.** *We should take safety measures to prevent accidents.*

意味着 **yìwèizhe** *v* mean, imply

意向 **yìxiàng** *n* intent, purpose
意向书 yìxiàngshū letter of intent, agreement of intent

意义 **yìyì** [comp: 意 meaning + 义 meaning] *n* significance □ 这件事有很大的历史意义。 **Zhè jiàn shì yǒu hěn dà de lìshǐ yìyì.** *This event has great historical significance.* □ 生活的意义是什么? **Shēnghuó de yìyì shì shénme?** *What is the meaning of life?*

意愿 **yìyuàn** [comp: 意 meaning + 愿 wish] *n* will, wish

意志 **yìzhì** [comp: 意 will + 志 aspiration] *n* will, willpower □ 这位运动员意志坚强，受了伤还每天锻炼。 **Zhè wèi yùndòngyuán yìzhì jiānqiáng, shòule shāng hái měi tiān duànliàn.** *This athlete is strong-willed. He trains every day despite his injury.*

义 **yì** Trad 義 I *adj* righteous II *n* righteousness, justice

义务 **yìwù** *n* duty, obligation □ 交税是每一个公民的义务。 **Jiāo shuì shì měi yí ge gōngmín de yìwù.** *Paying taxes is the duty of every citizen.* □ 先生，我们没有义务为您提供这种服务。 **Xiānsheng, wǒmen méiyǒu yìwù wèi nín tígōng zhè zhǒng fúwù.** *We are not obligated to provide you with this service, sir.*

义务工作(义工) **yìwù gōngzuò (yìgōng)** *n* voluntary work, voluntary worker

义务教育 **yìwù jiàoyù** *n* compulsory education

议 **yì** Trad 議 *v* discuss, exchange views
议案 **yì'àn** *n* proposal, motion (份 **fèn**)

议程 **yìchéng** [modif: 议 discussion + 程 procedure] *n* agenda

议定书 **yìdìngshū** *n* protocol (a diplomatic document) (份 **fèn**)

议会 **yìhuì** [modif: 议 discussion + 会 conference] *n* parliament

议论 **yìlùn** [comp: 议 discuss + 论 comment] *v* comment, discuss, talk □ 我从来不在背后议论别人。 **Wǒ cónglái bú zài bèihòu yìlùn biéren.** *I never talk about people behind their backs.* □ 我看你别议论政治了，挺危险的。 **Wǒ kàn nǐ bié yìlùn zhèngzhì le, tǐng wēixiǎn de.** *I suggest you stop commenting on politics. It is rather dangerous.*

议员 **yìyuán** *n* member of parliament (MP)

翼 **yì** *n* wing

因 **yīn** *conj* because
因此 **yīncǐ** *conj* therefore, so □ 这种产品质量极好，因此价格比较高。 **Zhè zhǒng chǎnpǐn zhìliàng jí hǎo, yīncǐ jiàgé bǐjiào gāo.** *This product is of excellent quality and is therefore rather expensive.*

因而 **yīn'ér** *conj* Same as 因此 **yīncǐ**

因素 **yīnsù** *n* factor, element □ 坚强的意志是事业成功的因素。 **Jiānqiáng de yìzhì shì shìyè chénggōng de yīnsù.** *A strong will is an important factor for a successful career.* □ 目前的这种情况，是由很多因素造成的。 **Mùqián de zhè zhǒng qíngkuàng, shì yóu hěn duō yīnsù zàochéng de.** *The present situation was brought about by many factors.*

因特网 **yīntèwǎng** [modif: 因特 Internet + 网 net] *n* Internet

因为 **yīnwèi** *conj* because □ 因为没有时间，所以我很少去看朋友。 **Yīnwèi méiyǒu shíjiān, suǒyǐ wǒ hěn shǎo qù kàn péngyou.** *I seldom go visiting friends because I don't have the time.* □ 因为大多数人都反对，所以这个计划放弃了。 **Yīnwèi dàduōshù rén dōu fǎnduì, suǒyǐ zhège jìhuà fàngqì le.** *Because the majority opposed the plan, it was abandoned.*

NOTE: 因为 **yīnwèi** is usually followed by 所以 **suǒyǐ**: 因为 ⋯所以⋯ **yīnwèi…suǒyǐ…** *because ... therefore*

阴 **yīn** Trad 陰 *adj* 1 cloudy, overcast □ 昨天上午天晴，下午阴天，晚上下雨。 **Zuótiān shàngwǔ tiānqíng, xiàwǔ yīntiān, wǎnshang xiàyǔ.** *Yesterday it was fine in the morning, cloudy in the afternoon and it rained in the evening.* **2** hidden

阴暗 **yīn'àn** *adj* gloomy
生活中的阴暗面 shēnghuó zhōngde yīn'ànmiàn the seamy side of life

阴谋 **yīnmóu** [modif: 阴 hidden + 谋 plot] *n* conspiracy
揭露一项国际阴谋 jiēlù yí xiàng guójì yīnmóu uncover an international conspiracy

阴天 **yīntiān** cloudy day

阴性 **yīnxìng** *adj* (of medical test) negative (antonym 阳性 **yángxìng**)

姻 **yīn** *n* marriage (See 婚姻 **hūnyīn**.)

音 **yīn** *n* sound
音响 **yīnxiǎng** *n* sound, acoustics
音响设备 yīnxiǎng shèbèi sound system
音响效果 yīnxiǎng xiàoguǒ acoustic effects
音像 **yīnxiàng** *n* audio-video

音乐 **yīnyuè** [comp: 音 sound + 乐 music] *n* music □ 星期天我常常跟朋友一块儿听音乐。**Xīngqītiān wǒ chángcháng gēn péngyou yíkuàir tīng yīnyuè.** *I often listen to music with my friends on Sundays.* □ 你喜欢什么样的音乐? **Nǐ xǐhuan shénmeyàng de yīnyuè?** *What kind of music do you like?*

古典音乐 gǔdiǎn yīnyuè classical music
流行音乐 liúxíng yīnyuè pop music
轻音乐 qīng yīnyuè light music, easy listening
音乐会 **yīnyuè huì** concert (场 **cháng**)
音乐会门票 yīnyuèhuì ménpiào concert ticket
露天音乐会 lùtiān yīnyuèhuì open-air concert
音乐家 **yīnyuè jiā** musician
音乐学院 **yīnyuè xuéyuàn** (music) conservatory

银 **yín** Trad 銀 **I** *n* silver □ 银是一种贵金属。**Yín shì yì zhǒng guì jīnshǔ.** *Silver is a precious metal.* **II** *adj* relating to money or currency
银行 **yínháng** [modif: 银 silver, money + 行 firm] *n* bank (家 **jiā**) □ 他打算到银行去借钱。**Tā dǎsuàn dào yínháng qù jiè qián.** *He plans to ask for a loan from the bank.* □ 这里的银行几点钟开始营业? **Zhèli de yínháng jǐ diǎnzhōng kāishǐ yíngyè?** *What time do the banks here open for business?*

银行家 yínhángjiā banker
储备银行 chǔbèi yínháng reserve bank
商业银行 shāngyè yínháng commercial bank
投资银行 tóuzī yínháng investment bank
银幕 **yínmù** [modif: 银 silver + 幕 screen] *n* projection screen, screen

淫 **yín** *adj* 1 pornographic 2 excessive
淫秽 **yínhuì** *adj* pornographic, obscene

引 **yín** *v* lead, provoke
引导 **yǐndǎo** *v* guide, lead
引进 **yǐnjìn** [comp: 引 lead + 进 enter] *v* introduce, import □ 从国外引进技术和资金, 很有必要。**Cóng guówài yǐnjìn jìshù hé zījīn, hěn yǒu bìyào.** *It is very necessary to introduce technology and capital from abroad.*
引起 **yǐnqǐ** *v* give rise to, lead to, cause, arouse □ 连续三天大雨, 引起了水灾。**Liánxù sān tiān dà yǔ, yǐnqǐle shuǐzāi.** *Three days of incessant heavy rain caused flooding.*
引人注目 **yǐnrén zhùmù** *idiom* eye-catching, conspicuous
引入 **yǐnrù** [v+compl: 引 lead + 入 enter] *v* lead into, introduce
引用 **yǐnyòng** *v* quote, cite
引诱 **yǐnyòu** *v* lure, seduce

隐 **yǐn** Trad 隱 *v* hide, conceal
隐蔽 **yǐnbì** [comp: 隐 hide + 蔽 hide] *v* take cover, conceal
隐藏 **yǐncáng** *v* hide
隐藏的地方 yǐncáng de dìfāng hideaway
隐瞒 **yǐnmán** *v* conceal (facts)
隐瞒真相 yǐnmán zhēnxiàng cover up the truth
隐约 **yǐnyuē** *adj* 1 indistinct, faint 2 vague

饮 **yǐn** Trad 飲 *v* drink
饮料 **yǐnliào** [modif: 饮 drink + 料 stuff] *n* drink, beverage □ "你要什么饮料?" "我要一杯橘子水, 谢谢。" **"Nǐ yào shénme yǐnliào?" "Wǒ yào yì bēi júzishuǐ, xièxie."** *"What drink would you like to have." "A glass of orange juice, thank you."*
饮食 **yǐnshí** *n* food and drink

饮食业 yǐnshíyè catering industry, catering
饮用水 **yǐnyòngshuǐ** *n* drinking water
非饮用水 fēi yǐnyòngshuǐ non-drinking water

印 **yìn** *v* print □ 这张照片, 我想印三份。**Zhè zhāng zhàopiàn, wǒ xiǎng yìn sān fèn.** *I want three prints of this photo.*
影印 yǐngyìn photocopy
影印机 yǐngyìnjī photocopier
印染 **yìnrǎn** [comp: 印 print + 染 dye] *v* print and dye (textiles)
印刷 **yìnshuā** [comp: 印 print + 刷 brush] *v* print (books, pamphlets, etc.) □ 本店印刷各类文件。**Běn diàn yìnshuā gè lèi wénjiàn.** *This shop prints all kinds of documents.*
印刷厂 yìnshuāchǎng *n* print shop, printing press
印刷机 yìnshuājī *n* printing machine, press
印刷品 yìnshuāpǐn *n* printed matter
印象 **yìnxiàng** [comp: 印 print + 象 image] *n* impression
给…留下印象 gěi...liúxià yìnxiàng leave an impression on ... □ 这个展览会给我留下深刻印象。**Zhège zhǎnlǎnhuì gěi wǒ liúxià shēnkè yìnxiàng.** *This exhibition has left a deep impression on me.*

应 **yīng** Trad 應 *modal v* Same as 应该 **yīnggāi**
应当 **yīngdāng** *modal v* Same as 应该 **yīnggāi**
应该 **yīnggāi** *modal v* should, ought to □ 你的朋友有困难的时候, 你应该帮助他们。**Nǐ de péngyou yǒu kùnnan de shíhou, nǐ yīnggāi bāngzhù tāmen.** *When your friends are in difficulty, you should help them.* □ 你应该早一点告诉我。**Nǐ yīnggāi zǎo yìdiǎn gàosu wǒ.** *You should have told me earlier.* □ 不用谢, 这是我应该做的。**Búyòng xiè, zhè shì wǒ yīnggāi zuò de.** *Don't mention it. This is what I should do.*

英 **yīng** *adj* outstanding
英国 **Yīngguó** *n* England, Britain, the UK □ 英国一年中夏天最好。**Yīngguó yì nián zhōng xiàtiān zuì hǎo.** *In England, summer is the best season of the year.*
英俊 **yīngjùn** *adj* (of men) handsome, attractive
英俊青年 yīngjùn qīngnián handsome young man
英明 **yīngmíng** *adj* wise, brilliant
英文 **Yīngwén** [modif: 英 English + 文 writing] *n* the English language (especially the writing)
英雄 **yīngxióng** *n* hero □ 是英雄创造历史, 还是历史产生英雄? **Shì yīngxióng chuàngzào lìshǐ, háishì lìshǐ chǎnshēng yīngxióng?** *Do heroes create history or does history produce heroes?*
英勇 **yīngyǒng** *adj* heroic
英语 **Yīngyǔ** [modif: 英 English + 语 language] *n* the English language □ 你用英语说吧, 大家都听得懂。**Nǐ yòng Yīngyǔ shuō ba, dàjiā dōu tīng de dǒng.** *You can say it in English. Everybody here understands it.* □ 英语是世界上最通用的国际语言。**Yīngyǔ shì shìjiè shang zuì tōngyòng de guójì yǔyán.** *English is the world's most widely used international language.*

婴 **yīng** Trad 嬰 *n* baby
婴儿 yīng'ér baby (个 **gè**)

樱 **yīng** *n* oriental cherry
樱花 yīnghuā cherry blossom

鹰 **yīng** *n* eagle
老鹰 lǎoyīng eagle (只 **zhī**)
秃鹰 tūyīng bald eagle

迎 **yíng** *v* meet, receive, welcome
迎接 **yíngjiē** [comp: 迎 meet + 接 receive] *v*
meet, greet □ 今天下午我们要去机场迎接外国客人。
**Jīntiān xiàwǔ wǒmen yào qù jīchǎng yíngjiē wàiguó
kèren.** *This afternoon we are going to the airport to
meet visitors from overseas.*

营 **yíng** Trad 營 **I** *v* operate **II** *n* (military)
battalion
营长 **yíngzhǎng** battalion commander
营养 **yíngyǎng** *n* nutrition, nourishment □ 这种水
果营养特别丰富。**Zhè zhǒng shuǐguǒ yíngyǎng tèbié
fēngfù.** *This fruit is particularly rich in nutrition.*
营业 **yíngyè** *v* (of a commercial or service establish-
ment) do business □ 本店营业范围广泛。**Běn diàn
yíngyè fànwéi guǎngfàn.** *This shop has an extensive
range of business interests.*
营业员 **yíngyèyuán** *n* shop assistant, salesperson
营业时间 **yíngyè shíjiān** *n* business hours

盈 **yíng** *n* surplus
盈利 **yínglì** **I** *v* make profit, reap profit **II** *n*
profit

蝇 **yíng** Trad 蠅 *n* fly (See 苍蝇 **cāngyíng**.)

赢 **yíng** Trad 贏 *v* win (a game), beat (a rival)
□ 昨天的球赛谁赢了? **Zuótiān de qiúsài shéi yíng
le?** *Who won the ball game yesterday?* □ 他买彩票赢
了一千块钱。**Tā mǎi cǎipiào yíngle yìqiān kuài qián.**
He won 1,000 yuan in the lottery.

影 **yǐng** *n* **1** shadow
影子 **yǐngzi** shadow
2 image, reflection
影片 **yǐngpiàn** *n* movie, film (部 **bù**)
影响 **yǐngxiǎng** [comp: 影 shadow + 响 sound]
I *v* influence, affect □ 经济发展慢, 影响了生活水平
的提高。**Jīngjì fāzhǎn màn, yǐngxiǎngle shēnghuó
shuǐpíng de tígāo.** *Slow economic development
affects the improvement of living standards.* □ 她今
年常常生病, 影响了工作和学习。**Tā jīnnián
chángcháng shēngbìng, yǐngxiǎngle gōngzuò hé xuéxí.**
*She has been sick quite often this year. This has af-
fected her work and study.* **II** *n* influence □ 中学生
受谁的影响大—父母, 还是朋友? **Zhōngxuéshēng shòu
shuí de yǐngxiǎng dà—fùmǔ, háishi péngyou?** *Who
has more influence on high school students—parents
or friends?*

颖 **yǐng** *adj* clever (See 新颖 **xīnyǐng**)

应 **yìng** Trad 應 *v* respond
应酬 **yìngchou** *v* engage in social activities,
entertain
应付 **yìngfu** *v* **1** cope with □ 顾客多的时候, 一个售货
员应付不了。**Gùkè duō de shíhou, yí ge shòuhuòyuán
yìngfu bùliǎo.** *When there're many cusomers, one
sales clerk can't cope.* **2** do perfunctorily
应邀 **yìngyāo** *adj* at the invitation of, on invitation
应用 **yìngyòng** *v* apply □ 这项新技术还不能应用在工
业上。**Zhè xiàng xīn jìshù hái bù néng yìngyòng zài
gōngyè shang.** *This new technology cannot be applied
in industry yet.*
应用科学 **yìngyòng kēxué** *n* applied science

映 **yìng** *v* reflect (See 反映 **fǎnyìng**.)

硬 **yìng** *adj* (of substance) hard, tough (antonym
软 **ruǎn**) □ 这种材料非常硬。**Zhè zhǒng cáiliào
fēicháng yìng.** *This material is very hard.*
硬件 **yìngjiàn** *n* (in computing) hardware

拥 **yōng** Trad 擁 *v* **1** embrace **2** crowd, swarm
3 own, possess
拥抱 **yōngbào** [comp: 拥 embrace + 抱 hold in
arms] *v* embrace, hug □ 中国人一般不习惯和人拥
抱。**Zhōngguórén yìbān bù xíguàn hé rén yōngbào.**
The Chinese are generally unaccustomed to hugging.
拥挤 **yōngjǐ** **I** *v* push, push and shove □ 不要拥挤, 前
面有小孩子! **Búyào yōngjǐ, qiánmiàn yǒu xiǎoháizi!**
Don't push, there're kids before me! **II** *adj* crowded
□ 现在这个时候公共汽车很拥挤, 我们还是叫出租汽车
吧。**Xiànzài zhège shíhou gōnggòng qìchē hěn yōngjǐ,
wǒmen háishi jiào chūzū qìchē ba.** *The buses are
crowded at this moment, let's call a taxi.*
拥有 **yōngyǒu** *v* possess, own

佣 **yōng** *n* servant
女佣 **nǚyōng** woman servant
佣人 **yōngrén** *n* servant

庸 **yōng** *adj* **1** mediocre **2** second-rate, inferior
平庸 **píngyōng** mediocre, commonplace
庸俗 **yōngsú** *adj* vulgar

永 **yǒng** *adv* forever
永久 **yǒngjiǔ** *adj* perpetual, everlasting
永远 **yǒngyuǎn** [comp: 永 forever + 远 remote] *adv*
forever □ 我们永远是朋友。**Wǒmen yǒngyuǎn shì
péngyou.** *We'll be friends forever.* □ 他永远不会做对
家庭有害的事。**Tā yǒngyuǎn bú huì zuò duì jiātíng
yǒuhài de shì.** *He would never do anything that may
harm his family.*

咏 **yǒng** *v* sing (See 歌咏 **gēyǒng**)

泳 **yǒng** *v* swim (See 游泳 **yóuyǒng**)

勇 **yǒng** *adj* courageous, bold, brave
勇敢 **yǒnggǎn** [comp: 勇 bold + 敢 daring] *adj*
brave, bold, fearless □ 他勇敢地从大火中救出两个孩
子。**Tā yǒnggǎn de cóng dà huǒ zhōng jiùchū liǎng ge
háizi.** *He bravely saved two children from the fire.*
勇气 **yǒngqì** [modif: 勇 courage + 气 quality] *n*
courage □ 你要有勇气承认错误。**Nǐ yào yǒu yǒngqì
chéngrèn cuòwù.** *You should have the courage to
admit your mistake.*
勇士 **yǒngshì** *n* heroic warrior, hero
勇于 **yǒngyú** *v* have the courage to
勇于认错 **yǒngyú rèncuò** have the courage to admit
one's mistake

涌 **yǒng** *v* gush, surge
涌现 **yǒngxiàn** *v* emerge in large numbers

用 **yòng** **I** *v* use, (do something) with □ 我可以
用一下你的自行车吗? **Wǒ kěyǐ yòng yíxià nǐ de
zìxíngchē ma?** *May I use your bicycle?* □ 我会用电脑
写汉字。**Wǒ huì yòng diànnǎo xiě Hànzì.** *I can use a
computer to write Chinese characters.* **2** need **II** *n*
use, usefulness
用不着 **yòngbuzháo** *idiom* **1** there is no need to
□ 这点小事, 用不着请别人帮忙。**Zhè diǎn xiǎo shì,
yòngbuzháo qǐng biéren bāngmáng.** *This is a trivial
matter and there is no need to ask for help.* **2** useless
□ 用不着的书别放在书架上。**Yòngbuzháo de shū bié**

fàng zài shūjià shang. *Don't put useless books on the bookshelf.*

用处 yòngchu [modif: 用 use + 处 place] *n* use □ 这东西用处不大，就别买了。**Zhè dōngxi yòngchu bú dà, jiù bié mǎi le.** *This isn't of much use. Let's not buy it.*

用法 yòngfǎ [modif: 用 use + 法 method] *n* the way to use, use, usage

用功 yònggōng [v+obj: 用 use + 功 efforts] *adj* hardworking, diligent (student) □ 她学习非常用功。**Tā xuéxí fēicháng yònggōng.** *She studies diligently.* □ 这学期我没有好好学习，下学期要用功点。**Zhè xuéqī wǒ méiyǒu hǎohǎo xuéxí, xià xuéqī yào yònggōng diǎn.** *I did not work hard in my studies this semester. I will work harder in the next semester.*

用户 yònghù [modif: 用 use + 户 household] *n* user (of a product), consumer

用具 yòngjù *n* utensil, appliance

用力 yònglì [v+obj: 用 use + 力 strength] *v* exert oneself (physically) □ 他用力把桌子推到一边。**Tā yònglì bǎ zhuōzi tuīdao yìbiān.** *He made an effort to push the desk to the side.*

用人 yòngrén *n* Same as 佣人 **yōngrén**

用途 yòngtú *n* use, function □ 这种新型汽车用途很广。**Zhè zhǒng xīnxíng qìchē yòngtú hěn guǎng.** *This new model of automobile has a wide range of uses.*

用意 yòngyì *n* intention, purpose

幽 yōu *adj* **1** quiet, serene **2** dim, secluded
幽暗 **yōu'àn** *adj* dim, gloomy

幽静 yōujìng [comp: 幽 serene + 静 quiet] *adj* quiet and secluded, serene

幽默 yōumò *n* humor □ 他很有幽默感。**Tā hěn yǒu yōumògǎn.** *He's got a good sense of humor.*

悠 yōu *adj* remote
悠久 **yōujiǔ** [comp: 悠 remote + 久 long] *adj* very long, long-standing, time-honored □ 中国历史悠久，人口众多。**Zhōngguó lìshǐ yōujiǔ, rénkǒu zhòngduō.** *China has a long history and a large population.*

优 yōu Trad 優 *adj* excellent, superior
优点 **yōudiǎn** [modif: 优 superior + 点 point] *n* strong point, merit (antonym 缺点 **quēdiǎn**) □ 每个人都有优点和缺点。**Měi ge rén dōu yǒu yōudiǎn hé quēdiǎn.** *Everybody has their strong points and weak points.* □ 这个产品有什么优点? **Zhège chǎnpǐn yǒu shénme yōudiǎn?** *What are the merits of this new product?*

优惠 yōuhuì *adj* preferential, favorable
优惠价 **yōuhuìjià** preferential price

优良 yōuliáng [comp: 优 excellent + 良 good] *adj* fine, good □ 政府正在推广小麦优良品种。**Zhèngfǔ zhèngzài tuīguǎng xiǎomài yōuliáng pǐnzhǒng.** *The government is promoting a fine variety of wheat.* □ 她的儿子年年考试成绩优良。**Tā de érzi niánnián kǎoshì chéngjì yōuliáng.** *Her son gets good examination results every year.*

优美 yōuměi [comp: 优 excellent + 美 beautiful] *adj* beautiful, graceful □ 这里优美的风景吸引大批游览者。**Zhèli yōuměi de fēngjǐng xīyǐn dàpī yóulǎnzhě.** *The beautiful landscape here attracts large numbers of tourists.*

优胜 yōushèng *adj* winning
优胜者 **yōushèngzhě** winner

优势 yōushì [modif: 优 superior + 势 power] *n* superiority, advantage □ 这个国家人力资源丰富，是发展经济的优势。**Zhège guójiā rénlì zīyuán fēngfù, shì fāzhǎn jīngjì de yōushì.** *Rich human resources are an advantage the country has in economic development.*

优先 yōuxiān [comp: 优 superior + 先 first] *adj* taking precedence, having priority

优秀 yōuxiù [comp: 优 excellent + 秀 elegant] *adj* outstanding, excellent □ 这位青年是我们公司的优秀人才。**Zhè wèi qīngnián shì wǒmen gōngsī de yōuxiù réncái.** *This young man is an outstanding talent of our company.*

优异 yōuyì [comp: 优 excellent + 异 unique] *adj* outstanding, exceptional

优越 yōuyuè *adj* superior □ 别以为自己比别人优越。**Bié yǐwéi zìjǐ bǐ biéren yōuyuè.** *Don't think you're superior to others (→ None of your "Holier-than-thou" attitude.)*

优越感 **yōuyuègǎn** superiority complex

优质 yōuzhì [modif: 优 excellent + 质 quality] *n* superior quality, excellent quality

忧 yōu Trad 憂 **I** *v* worry **II** *n* sorrow, anxiety
忧虑 **yōulǜ** [comp: 忧 worry + 虑 concern] *v* feel anxious, worry

忧郁 yōuyù [comp: 忧 worried + 郁 gloomy] *adj* melancholy, heavy-hearted

尤 yóu *adv* especially
尤其 **yóuqí** *adv* especially □ 新西兰的天气很舒服，尤其是夏天。**Xīnxīlán de tiānqì hěn shūfu, yóuqí shì xiàtiān.** *The weather in New Zealand is very pleasant, especially in summer.* □ 我喜欢吃中国菜，尤其喜欢吃广东菜。**Wǒ xǐhuan chī Zhōngguó cài, yóuqí xǐhuan chī Guǎngdōng cài.** *I love Chinese food, especially Cantonese food.*

由 yóu *prep* **1** (introducing the agent of an action) by □ 技术问题由你们解决。**Jìshù wèntí yóu nǐmen jiějué.** *Technical problems will be solved by you.* (→ *You are responsible for solving technical problems.*) **2** (introducing manner or cause of an action) with □ 很多交通事故都是由车速太快造成的。**Hěn duō jiāotōng shìgù dōu shì yóu chēsù tài kuài zàochéng de.** *Many road accidents are caused by speeding.*

由此可见 yóu cǐ kě jiàn *idiom* it can be seen that, this shows

由于 yóuyú **I** *prep* because of, owing to, due to □ 由于家庭她不得不放弃事业。**Yóuyú jiātíng tā bùdébù fàngqì shìyè.** *She had no choice but to give up her career because of her family.* **II** *conj* because □ 由于丈夫身体不好，她不能出国工作。**Yóuyú zhàngfu shēntǐ bù hǎo, tā bù néng chūguó gōngzuò.** *She was not able to go abroad to work because her husband was in poor health.*

油 yóu **I** *n* oil □ 油比水轻。**Yóu bǐ shuǐ qīng.** *Oil is lighter than water.* **II** *adj* greasy (food) □ 这个菜太油了，我不能吃。**Zhège cài tài yóu le, wǒ bù néng chī.** *This dish is too greasy. I can't eat it.*

食油 **shíyóu** edible oil, cooking oil
石油 **shíyóu** petroleum, oil

油画 yóuhuà [modif: 油 oil + 画 painting] *n* oil painting (幅 **fú**)

油料 yóuliào [modif: 油 oil + 料 material] *n* oil material
油料作物 **yóuliàozuòwù** oil-bearing crops

油田 **yóutián** [modif: 油 oil + 画 painting] *n* oilfield

铀 **yóu** *n* uranium (U)

邮 **yóu** Trad 郵 *n* mail, post
邮包 **yóubāo** *n* mailbag

邮购 **yóugòu** *n* mail order □ 这些书都可以邮购。**Zhè xiē shū dōu kěyǐ yóugòu.** *All these books are available by mail order.*

邮寄 **yóujì** *v* mail, post □ 邮寄支票给您。**Yóujì zhīpiào gěi nín.** *Mail you a check.*

邮局 **yóujú** [modif: 邮 post + 局 office] *n* post office □ 请问, 附近有没有邮局? **Qǐng wèn, fùjìn yǒu méiyǒu yóujú?** *Excuse me, is there a post office nearby?* □ 由于电脑的广泛使用, 邮局已经没有以前那么重要了。**Yóuyú diànnǎo de guǎngfàn shǐyòng, yóujú yǐjīng méiyǒu yǐqián nàme zhòngyào le.** *Thanks to the extensive use of the computer, the post office is no longer as important as before.*

邮票 **yóupiào** [modif: 邮 post + 票 ticket] *n* postal stamp (张 **zhāng**) □ 这封信寄到台湾, 要多少邮票? **Zhè fēng xìn jìdao Táiwān, yào duōshǎo yóupiào?** *How much is the postage for this letter to Taiwan?* □ 我买十块钱邮票。**Wǒ mǎi shí kuài qián yóupiào.** *I want to buy ten yuan worth of stamps.*

邮政 **yóuzhèng** *n* mail service, postal service

犹 **yóu** Trad 猶 *prep* like, as
犹如 **yóurú** *prep* just like, just as

犹豫 **yóuyù** *adj* hesitant, wavering, procrastinating □ 去不去国外找工作, 我还有点犹豫。**Qù bu qù guówài zhǎo gōngzuò, wǒ hái yǒudiǎn yóuyù.** *I'm still wavering over going abroad to look for a job.* □ 不能犹豫了, 得马上决定。**Bù néng yóuyù le, děi mǎshàng juédìng.** *You can't hesitate any more. You've got to decide right now.*

游 **yóu** *v* **1** play **2** tour
游击 **yóujī** *v* be engaged in guerrilla warfare
游击战 **yóujīzhàn** guerrilla warfare

游客 **yóukè** [modif: 游 tour + 客 guest] *n* tourist, visitor (to a tourist attraction) □ 游客止步。**Yóukè zhǐbù.** *(in a tourist attraction) No admittance to visitors. No visitors*

游览 **yóulǎn** [comp: 游 play + 览 see] *v* go sightseeing, tour for pleasure □ 每年很多人去香港游览。**Měi nián hěn duō rén qù Xiānggǎng yóulǎn.** *Every year many people go to Hong Kong on holiday.*
游览者 **yóulǎnzhě** tourist

游人 **yóurén** *n* tourist, visitor (to a tourist attraction)

游戏 **yóuxì** [modif: 游 play + 戏 have fun] *n* game □ 我们来做游戏! **Wǒmen lái zuò yóuxì!** *Let's play a game!*
(电脑) 游戏机 (diànnǎo) **yóuxìjī** (computer) play station, (electronic game) console
(儿童) 游戏室 (értóng) **yóuxìshì** (kids') playing room
电子游戏 diànzǐ yóuxì video game, electronic game

游行 **yóuxíng** *n* **1** (celebratory) parade **2** (protest) demonstration
举行游行 jǔxíng yóuxíng hold a parade, hold demonstrations

游泳 **yóuyǒng** [comp: 游 swim + 泳 swim] *v* swim □ 他游泳游得很好。**Tā yóuyǒng yóu de hěn hǎo.** *He swims very well.* □ 我一星期游两次泳。**Wǒ yì xīngqī yóu liǎng cì yǒng.** *I swim twice a week.*

蛙式游泳 (蛙泳) **wāshì yóuyǒng (wāyǒng)** breaststroke
自由式游泳 (自由泳) **zìyóushì yóuyǒng (zìyóuyǒng)** freestyle

游泳池 **yóuyǒngchí** *n* swimming pool
室内游泳池 shìnèi **yóuyǒngchí** indoor swimming pool (座 **zuò**)

游泳裤 **yóuyǒngkù** *n* swimming trunks (条 **tiáo**)

游泳衣 **yóuyǒngyī** *n* swimsuit (件 **jiàn**)

友 **yǒu** *n* friend
友爱 **yǒu'ài** [modif: 友 friend + 爱 affection] *n* friendly affection

友好 **yǒuhǎo** [comp: 友 friendly + 好 amiable] *adj* friendly □ 她对所有的人都很友好。**Tā duì suǒyǒu de rén dōu hěn yǒuhǎo.** *She is friendly to everyone.* □ 你这么做不大友好。**Nǐ zhème zuò bú dà yǒuhǎo.** *It's not friendly of you to do so.* □ 他寄来贺卡是友好的表示。**Tā jì lai hèkǎ shì yǒuhǎo de biǎoshì.** *His sending a card is a friendly gesture.*

友情 **yǒuqíng** [modif: 友 friendly + 情 feelings] *n* friendly sentiments

友人 **yǒurén** *n* friend

友谊 **yǒuyì** [comp: 友 friendly + 谊 congeniality] *n* friendship □ 我希望我们能发展我们之间的友谊。**Wǒ xīwàng wǒmen néng fāzhǎn wǒmen zhī jiān de yǒuyì.** *I hope we will be able to develop the friendship between us.* □ 友谊天长地久。**Yǒuyì tiān-cháng-dì-jiǔ** *Our friendship will last forever.*

有 **yǒu** *v* **1** possess, have □ 他们有一座房子, 一辆汽车, 在银行里还有一些钱。**Tāmen yǒu yí zuò fángzi, yí liàng qìchē, zài yínháng li háiyǒu yìxiē qián.** *They have a house, a car and some money in the bank.* **2** exist, there is (are) □ 世界上有多少国家? **Shìjiè shang yǒu duōshǎo guójiā?** *How many countries are there in the world?* □ 我们学校有三个电脑室。**Wǒmen xuéxiào yǒu sān ge diànnǎoshì.** *There are three computer labs in our school.*

没有 **méiyǒu** do not possess, have no, do not exist, there is no □ 我没有汽车。**Wǒ méiyǒu qìchē.** *I don't have a car.* □ 教室里没有人。**Jiàoshì li méiyǒu rén.** *There is nobody in the classroom.*

有待 **yǒudài** *v* remain, await □ 很多问题有待解决。**Hěn duō wèntí yǒudài jiějué.** *Many problems remain to be solved.*

有的 **yǒude** *pron* some □ 有的人喜欢体育, 有的人喜欢艺术, 也有的人什么也不喜欢。**Yǒude rén xǐhuan tǐyù, yǒude rén xǐhuan yìshù, yě yǒude rén shénme yě bù xǐhuan.** *Some people are fond of sports, others are fond of the arts and still others are not fond of anything.*

有的是 **yǒudeshì** *v* be plenty of, be abundant, not in short supply □ 大学毕业生有的是。**Dàxué bìyèshēng yǒudeshì.** *There are plenty of university graduates.*

有(一)点儿 **yǒu(yì)diǎn** *adv* slightly, a little, somewhat □ 我今天有点儿累了, 明天再谈吧。**Wǒ jīntiān yǒudiǎnr lèi le, míngtiān zài tán ba.** *I'm a bit tired today. Let's talk tomorrow.* □ 他这么回答, 她有一点失望。**Tā zhème huídá, tā yǒuyìdiǎn shīwàng.** *She is somewhat disappointed at his reply.*

NOTE: 有点 **yǒudiǎn**, 有点儿 **yǒudiǎnr**, 有一点 **yǒuyìdiǎn**, 有一点儿 **yǒuyìdiǎnr** mean the same thing. 有点儿 **yǒudiǎnr**

and 有一点儿 **yǒuyìdiǎnr** are only used in colloquial Chinese.

有关 **yǒuguān** *v* have bearing on, have something to do with, be related to (antonym 无关 **wúguān**) □ 这件事与你有关。**Zhè jiàn shì yú nǐ yǒuguān.** *This matter has something to do with you.* (→ *This matter concerns you.*) □ 一个人的性格和事业成功与否有关。**Yí ge rén de xìnggé hé shìyè chénggōng yúfǒu yǒuguān.** *A person's disposition has a bearing on whether his career is successful or not.*

有害 **yǒuhài** [v+obj: 有 have + 害 harm] *adj* harmful (antonym 有益 **yǒuyì**, 有利 **yǒulì**)

有机 **yǒujī** *adj* organic

有力 **yǒulì** [v+obj: 有 have + 力 force] *adj* forceful, powerful, strong □ 我们要采取有力措施节水节电。**Wǒmen yào cǎiqǔ yǒulì cuòshī jié shuǐ jié diàn.** *We should take strong measures to save water and electricity.*

有利 **yǒulì** [v+obj: 有 have + 利 benefit] *adj* favorable, advantageous (antonym 不利 **búlì**, 有害 **yǒuhài**) □ 我们要在那里发展业务有有利条件，也有不利条件。**Wǒmen yào zài nàlǐ fāzhǎn yèwù yǒu yǒulì tiáojiàn, yě yǒu búlì tiáojiàn.** *There are both favorable and unfavorable conditions for developing our business there.*

有名 **yǒumíng** [v+obj: 有 have + 名 name, fame] *adj* famous, well-known □ 这座大学很有名。**Zhè zuò dàxué hěn yǒumíng.** *This is a famous university.* □ 这是一本很有名的小说。**Zhè shì yì běn hěn yǒumíng de xiǎoshuō.** *This is a well-known novel.*

有钱 **yǒuqián** [v+obj: 有 have + 钱 money] *adj* rich, wealthy □ 他爸爸很有钱, 但是他从来不乱花钱。**Tā bàba hěn yǒuqián, dànshì tā cónglai bú luàn huā qián.** *His father is very wealthy, but he is quite frugal.* □ 她想找一个有钱人结婚。**Tā xiǎng zhǎo yí ge yǒu qián rén jiéhūn.** *She wants to find a rich man to marry.*

NOTE: See note on 富 **fù**.

有趣 **yǒuqù** [v+obj: 有 have + 趣 fun] *adj* interesting, amusing □ 我给你讲一个有趣的故事。**Wǒ gěi nǐ jiǎng yí ge yǒuqù de gùshi.** *I'll tell you an interesting story.* □ 他在旅行的时候, 遇到很多有趣的事。**Tā zài lǚxíng de shíhou, yùdao hěn duō yǒuqù de shì.** *He had many interesting experiences during his tour.*

有时 **yǒushí** *adv* Same as 有时候 **yǒushíhou**

有时候 **yǒushíhou** *adv* sometimes □ 爸爸有时候忙, 有时候不那么忙。**Bàba yǒushíhou máng, yǒushíhou bú nàme máng.** *Sometimes my father is busy, sometimes he isn't so busy.* □ 他工作一般都很认真, 但有时候也会马虎。**Tā gōngzuò yìbān dōu hěn rènzhēn, dàn yǒushíhou yě huì mǎhu.** *He is generally a conscientious worker, but he can be careless sometimes.*

有效 **yǒuxiào** [v+obj: 有 have + 效 effect] *adj* 1 effective, efficacious □ 王老师教我们记生词的办法很有效。**Wáng lǎoshī jiāo wǒmen jì shēngcí de bànfǎ hěn yǒuxiào.** *Teacher Wang taught us an effective method of memorizing new words.* 2 valid □ 我的护照还有效。**Wǒ de hùzhào hái yǒuxiào.** *My passport is still valid.*

有效期 **yǒuxiàoqī** *n* term of validity, expiration date

有些 **yǒuxiē** *pron* Same as 有的 **yǒude**

有氧运动 **yǒuyǎng yùndòng** *n* aerobic exercise

有意 **yǒuyì** [v+obj: 有 have + 意 intention] *v* 1 have a mind to, be inclined 2 Same as 故意 **gùyì**

有意思 **yǒu yìsi** [v+obj: 有 have + 意思 meaning] *adj* meaningful, interesting □ 这本书很有意思, 每个人都应该看。**Zhè běn shū hěn yǒu yìsi, měi ge rén dōu yīnggāi kàn.** *This book is very meaningful. Everybody should read it.* □ 董事长讲话的最后几句很有意思。**Dǒngshìzhǎng jiǎnghuà de zuì hòu jǐ jù hěn yǒu yìsi.** *The last few sentences in the Chairman's speech are rather meaningful.*

没有意思 **méiyǒu yìsi** uninteresting, meaningless □ 那个电影没有意思。**Nàge diànyǐng méiyǒu yìsi.** *That movie isn't interesting.*

有益 **yǒuyì** [v+obj: 有 have + 益 benefit] *adj* beneficial (antonym 有害 **yǒuhài**)

有用 **yǒuyòng** [v+obj: 有 have + 用 use] *adj* useful □ 我相信中文会越来越有用。**Wǒ xiāngxìn Zhōngwén huì yuèlaiyuè yǒuyòng.** *I believe the Chinese language will be more and more useful.* □ 这本词典很有用。**Zhè běn cídiǎn hěn yǒuyòng.** *This dictionary is very useful.*

没有用 **méiyǒu yòng** useless □ 这本书太旧了, 没有什么用了。**Zhè běn shū tài jiù le, méiyǒu shénme yòng le.** *This book is too outdated, and is not of much use.*

诱 **yòu** *v* induce, seduce

诱惑 **yòuhuò** [comp: 诱 induce + 惑 confuse] *v* entice, seduce

右 **yòu** *n* the right side (antonym 左 **zuǒ**)

右边 **yòubian** [modif: 右 right + 边 side] *n* the right side, the right-hand side □ 超级市场的右边是一个停车场。**Chāojí shìchǎng de yòubian shì yí ge tíngchēchǎng.** *On the right side of the supermarket is a parking lot.* □ 你右边的那座房子就是图书馆。**Nǐ yòubian de nà zuò fángzi jiù shì túshūguǎn.** *The building on your right is the library.*

幼 **yòu** *adj* very young

幼儿 **yòu'ér** [modif: 幼 very young + 儿 child] *n* young child between 2 and 6 years old

幼儿园 **yòu'éryuán** [modif: 幼儿 young child + 园 garden] *n* kindergarten

幼稚 **yòuzhì** *adj* naïve, childish

又 **yòu** *adv* 1 again □ 电脑昨天刚修好, 今天又坏了。**Diànnǎo zuótiān gāng xiūhǎo, jīntiān yòu huài le.** *The computer was fixed yesterday, but it broke down again today.* □ 晴了半天, 又下雨了。**Qíngle bàntiān, yòu xià yǔ le.** *After just half a day's fine weather, it rained again.* 2 moreover, additionally □ 这个菜味道好, 营养又丰富。**Zhège cài wèidao hǎo, yíngyǎng yòu fēngfù.** *This dish is tasty and also very nutritious.* □ 吸烟很花钱, 又对身体有害。**Xīyān hěn huāqián, yòu duì shēntǐ yǒuhài.** *Smoking is costly and, moreover, harmful to your health.*

又…又… **yòu...yòu...** ... and also ..., both ... and ... □ 他们的小女儿又聪明又可爱。**Tāmen de xiǎo nǚ'ér yòu cōngming yòu kě'ài.** *Their young daughter is both bright and lovely.*

NOTE: See note on 再 **zài**.

愚 **yú** *adj* foolish

愚蠢 **yúchǔn** [comp: 愚 foolish + 蠢 stupid] *adj* foolish, stupid

愚昧 yúmèi [comp: 愚 foolish + 昧 ignorant] *adj* ignorant and foolish

舆 yú *n* chariot
舆论 **yúlùn** *n* public opinion

余 yú Trad 餘 *v* spare (See 其余 **qíyú**, 业余 **yèyú**.)

鱼 yú Trad 魚 *n* fish (条 **tiáo**) □ 河里有鱼吗？ **Hé li yǒu yú ma?** *Is there any fish in the river?*

渔 yú *n* fishing □ 授人以鱼，不如授之以渔。(老子) **Shòu rén yǐ yú, bùrú shuò zhī yǐ yú. (Lǎozǐ)** *Giving someone a fish is not so good as teaching him how to fish. (Laozi)*
渔船 **yúchuán** *n* fishing boat (艘 **sōu**)
渔民 **yúmín** *n* fisherman
渔网 **yúwǎng** *n* fishing net (张 **zhāng**)
渔业 **yúyè** *n* fishery

娱 yú *v* amuse, give pleasure to
娱乐 **yúlè** [comp: 娱 amuse + 乐 amuse] **I** *v* entertain, amuse **II** *n* entertainment, amusement
娱乐活动 **yúlè huódòng** recreation, recreational activities

愉 yú *n* pleasure
愉快 **yúkuài** [comp: 愉 pleasant + 快 delightful] *adj* 1 pleasant, joyful □ 祝你假期愉快！**Zhù nǐ jiàqī yúkuài!** *I wish you a joyful holiday.* □ 和你一起工作是很愉快的。**Hé nǐ yìqǐ gōngzuò shì hěn yúkuài de.** *Working with you is very pleasant.* □ 我永远不会忘记那段愉快的经历。**Wǒ yǒngyuǎn bú huì wàngji nà duàn yúkuài de jīnglì.** *I will never forget that pleasant experience.* 2 pleased, happy □ 听到这句话，我很不愉快。**Tīngdào zhè jù huà, wǒ hěn bù yúkuài.** *I feel displeased to hear this.*

于 yú Trad 於 *prep* in, at (only used in written Chinese) □ 他生于一九七零年。**Tā shēng yú yì-jiǔ-qī-líng nián.** *He was born in 1970.*
于是 **yúshì** *conj* as a result, hence □ 他爸爸在上海找到了工作，于是全家搬到上海去了。**Tā bàba zài Shànghǎi zhǎodao le gōngzuò, yúshì quán jiā bāndao Shànghǎi qú le.** *His father found a job in Shanghai; as a result the family moved to Shanghai.*

予 yǔ *v* give
予以 **yǔyǐ** give

宇 yǔ *n* 1 space 2 building
宇宙 **yǔzhòu** [comp: 宇 space + 宙 time] *n* the universe

与 yǔ Trad 與 Same as 和 **hé** and 跟 **gēn**. Only used in written Chinese.
与此同时 **yǔ cǐ tóngshí** *idiom* at the same time
与其…不如 **yǔqí…bùrú** *conj* would rather … than
与其坐着谈，不如起而行 **yǔqí zuòzhe tán, bùrú qǐ ér xíng** would rather get up and do something than sit here talking

NOTE: Pay attention to the different word orders of 与其…不如 **yǔqí…bùrú** and *would rather … than*; while it is 与其A不如B in Chinese, in English it is *would rather B than A.*

屿 yǔ Trad 嶼 *n* islet (See 岛屿 **dǎoyǔ**)

雨 yǔ *n* rain □ 这里夏天多雨。**Zhèli xiàtiān duō yǔ.** *It often rains here in summer.*

下雨 **xià yǔ** to rain □ 我看马上要下雨了。**Wǒ kàn mǎshàng yào xià yǔ le.** *It seems to me that it's going to rain soon.*
雨天 **yǔtiān** rainy day
雨水 **yǔshuǐ** *n* rainwater, rainfall
雨衣 **yǔyī** *n* raincoat

羽 yǔ *n* feather
羽毛 **yǔmáo** *n* feather (根 **gēn**)
羽毛球 **yǔmáoqiú** [modif: 羽毛 feather + 球 ball] *n* badminton, shuttlecock (只 **zhī**) □ 我常常跟朋友在体育馆打羽毛球。**Wǒ chángcháng gēn péngyou zài tǐyùguǎn dǎ yǔmáoqiú.** *I often play badminton with my friends in the gym.*
羽绒 **yǔróng** [comp: 羽 feather + 绒 down] *n* eiderdown
羽绒衣 **yǔróngyī** eiderdown clothes, eiderdown coat

语 yǔ Trad 語 **I** *n* language, words **II** *v* speak, say
语调 **yǔdiào** [modif: 语 speech + 调 tune] *n* intonation □ 中文的声调不容易掌握，语调也很难。**Zhōngwén de shēngdiào bù róngyì zhǎngwò, yǔdiào yě hěn nán.** *While it is not easy to have a good command of Chinese tones, Chinese intonation is also difficult.*
语法 **yǔfǎ** [modif: 语 language + 法 law, rule] *n* grammar □ 我不大懂汉语语法，我想学一点儿。**Wǒ bú dà dǒng Hànyǔ yǔfǎ, wǒ xiǎng xué yìdiǎnr.** *I don't quite understand Chinese grammar; I want to learn a bit.*
语气 **yǔqì** [modif: 语 speech + 气 quality] *n* tone, manner of speaking □ 同样一句话，语气不同，听了感觉就不同。**Tóngyàng yí jù huà, yǔqì bùtóng, tīngle gǎnjué jiù bùtóng.** *Saying the same sentence in different tones of the voice produces different feelings in the hearer.*
语文 **yǔwén** *n* speech and writing, language
语言 **yǔyán** [comp: 语 language + 言 speech] *n* language (门 **mén**, 种 **zhǒng**) □ 要了解一个民族，就要学它的语言。**Yào liǎojiě yí ge mínzú, jiù yào xué tā de yǔyán.** *If you want to understand an ethnic group, you should study its language.* □ 学一门语言，就是多一个观察世界的窗户。**Xué yì mén yǔyán, jiù shì duō yí ge guānchá shìjiè de chuānghu.** *To learn a language is to have one more window from which to look at the world.*

与 yù Trad 與 *v* take part, participate
与会 **yùhuì** *v* be present at a meeting (conference)

域 yù *n* territory (See 领域 **lǐngyù**)

郁 yù Trad 鬱 *adj* gloomy (See 忧郁 **yōuyù**)

吁 yù Trad 籲 *v* appeal (See 呼吁 **hūyù**)

玉 yù *n* jade
玉手镯 **yùshǒuzhuó** jade bracelet
玉米 **yùmǐ** [modif: 玉 jade + 米 rice] *n* corn, maize (根 **gēn**) □ 肚子饿了，先吃一根玉米吧。**Dùzi è le, xiān chī yì gēn yùmǐ ba.** *If you're hungry, eat some corn first.*

育 yù *v* educate, nurture (See 教育 **jiàoyù**, 体育 **tǐyù**, 体育场 **tǐyùchǎng**, 体育馆 **tǐyùguǎn**.)

浴 yù *v* bathe
浴室 **yùshì** [modif: 浴 bathe + 室 room] *n* bath-

room (间 **jiān**) □ 这套房子很大, 有两间浴室。**Zhè tào fángzi hěn dà, yǒu liǎng jiān yùshì.** *This is a big flat with two bathrooms.*

遇 **yù** *v* encounter
遇到 **yùdào** *v* encounter, come across □ 我在国外旅行的时候, 遇到不少好心人。**Wǒ zài guówài lǚxíng de shíhou, yùdào bùshǎo hǎoxīnrén.** *When I traveled overseas, I came across many kindhearted people.* □ 在工作中总会遇到困难。**Zài gōngzuò zhōng zǒng huì yùdào kùnnan.** *One is bound to encounter difficulties in work.*
遇见 **yùjiàn** *v* meet (someone) unexpectedly, come across □ 我昨天在超级市场遇见一个老同学。**Wǒ zuótiān zài chāojí shìchǎng yùjiàn yí ge lǎo tóngxué.** *I ran into an old classmate of mine in the supermarket yesterday.*

喻 **yù** *v* explain (See 比喻 **bǐyù**)

愈 **yù** I *v* recover from illness
大病处愈 **dàbìng chù yù** have just recovered from a serious illness
II *adv* more

欲 **yù** *n* desire
食欲 **shíyù** desire for food, appetite
性欲 **xìngyù** sex desire
欲望 **yùwàng** [comp: 欲 desire + 望 hope] *n* desire
求知的欲望 **qiúzhī de yùwàng** desire to have more knowledge, hunger for knowledge

预 **yù** Trad 預 *adv* in advance
预报 **yùbào** [modif: 预 in advance + 报 report] *n* forecast, prediction □ 你听过今天的天气预报吗? **Nǐ tīngguo jīntiān de tiānqì yùbào ma?** *Have you listened to the weather forecast for today?*
预备 **yùbèi** [modif: 预 in advance + 备 prepare] *v* prepare, get ready □ 他们在春节前一个星期, 就开始预备春节时的饭菜了。**Tāmen zài chūnjié qián yí ge xīngqī, jiù kāishǐ yùbèi chūnjié shí de fàncài le.** *They began preparing the food for the Spring Festival a week before.*
预备会议 **yùbèi huìyì** preparatory meeting
预备学校 **yùbèi xuéxiào** preparatory school
预测 **yùcè** [modif: 预 in advance + 测 test] *v* forecast, predict
预定 **yùdìng** *v* schedule, fix in advance □ 代表团预定下周一到达。**Dàibiǎotuán yùdìng xià zhōuyī dàodá.** *The delegation is scheduled to arrive next Monday.*
预订 **yùdìng** *v* book, place an order □ 我已经在餐馆预订了席位。**Wǒ yǐjing zài cānguǎn yùdìngle xíwèi.** *I've booked seats in the restaurant.*
预防 **yùfáng** [modif: 预 in advance + 防 defend] *v* take precautionary measures to prevent, prevent □ 预防重于治疗。**Yùfáng zhòngyú zhìliáo.** *Prevention (of disease) is more important than treatment.*
预告 **yùgào** [modif: 预 in advance + 告 announce] *v* announce in advance
预计 **yùjì** [modif: 预 in advance + 计 calculate] *v* project □ 今年的销售额预计将达到一亿元。**Jīnnián de xiāoshòu'é yùjì jiāng dádào yī yì yuán.** *Sales for this year is projected to reach 100 million dollars.*
预见 **yùjiàn** [modif: 预 in advance + 见 see] *v* foresee □ 我早就预见了这个结果。**Wǒ zǎojiù yùjiàn le zhège jiéguǒ.** *I foresaw this result long ago.*

预期 **yùqī** [comp: 预 in advance + 期 expect] *v* expect, anticipate
预赛 **yùsài** *v* trial match, preliminary contest
预算 **yùsuàn** *n* budget
预习 **yùxí** [modif: 预 preparatory + 习 study] *v* prepare lessons before class, preview □ 明天上语法课, 我要想预习一下。**Míngtiān shàng yǔfǎ kè, wǒ yào xiǎng yùxí yíxià.** *Tomorrow there'll be a grammar lesson, and I'll prepare for it.*
预先 **yùxiān** *adv* in advance, beforehand
预言 **yùyán** I *v* predict II *n* prediction, prophecy
古代圣人的预言 **gǔdài shèngrén de yùyán** prophecy made by ancient sages
预约 **yùyuē** *v* make an appointment

狱 **yù** Trad 獄 *n* prison (See 监狱 **jiānyù**)

誉 **yù** Trad 譽 *n* honor (See 荣誉 **róngyù**)

裕 **yù** *adj* abundant (See 宽裕 **kuānyù**)

寓 **yù** I *v* imply II reside
公寓 **gōngyù** apartment, apartment building
寓言 **yùyán** *n* fable

豫 **yù** *n* comfort (See 犹豫 **yóuyù**.)

冤 **yuān** *n* injustice, wrong
冤枉 **yuānwang** *v* treat unfairly, wrong □ 别冤枉好人。**Bié yuānwang hǎorén.** *Don't wrong innocent people.*

猿 **yuán** *n* ape
猿人 **yuánrén** *n* apeman
北京猿人 **Běijīng Yuánrén** Peking man

缘 **yuán** *n* reason
缘故 **yuángù** *n* reason, cause

元 1 **yuán** *adj* first, primary
元旦 **yuándàn** [modif: 元 first + 旦 dawn] *n* the New Year's Day
元件 **yuánjiàn** *n* component part, component
元首 **yuánshǒu** [modif: 元 first + 首 head] *n* head of state □ 中华人民共和国主席是中国元首。**Zhōnghuá Rénmín Gònghéguó zhǔxí shì Zhōngguó yuánshǒu.** *The President of the People's Republic of China is China's head of state.*
元素 **yuánsù** *n* (chemical) element
元宵 **yuánxiāo** [modif: 元 first + 宵 night] *n* 1 元宵节 **Yuánxiāojié**, the Lantern Festival (the 15th of the first month in the Chinese lunar calendar, when the full moon appears for the first time in a year.) 2 the traditional sweet dumpling for the Lantern Festival

元 2 **yuán** *measure wd* (the basic unit of Chinese currency 1 元 **yuán** = 10 角 **jiǎo**/毛 **máo** = 100 分 **fēn**), yuan, dollar
美元 **Měiyuán** U.S. dollar
日元 **Rìyuán** Japanese yen

NOTE: 元 **yuán** is the formal word for the basic unit of Chinese currency. In spoken Chinese 块 **kuài** is more common. For instance, the sum of 50 yuan is usually written as 五十元 **wǔshí yuán**, but spoken of as 五十块 **wǔshí kuài** or 五十块钱 **wǔshí kuài qián**.

员 yuán Trad 員 *n* member (See 党员 **dǎngyuán**, 服务员 **fúwùyuán**, 官员 **guānyuán**, 技术员 **jìshùyuán**, 教员 **jiàoyuán**, 人员 **rényuán**, 售货员 **shòuhuòyuán**, 委员会 **wěiyuánhuì**, 演员 **yǎnyuán**, 运动员 **yùndòngyuán**.)

园 yuán Trad 園 *n* garden (See 动物园 **dòngwùyuán**, 公园 **gōngyuán**, 花园 **huāyuán**.)

原 yuán *adj* original, former

原材料 **yuáncáiliào** *n* raw material

原告 **yuángào** *n* plaintiff, prosecutor

原来 **yuánlái** *adj* original, former □ 她原来的计划是去英国工作一段时间。**Tā yuánlái de jìhuà shì qù Yīngguó gōngzuò yí duàn shíjiān.** *Her original plan was to go to England and work there for a period of time.* □ 古建筑遭到破坏，不能恢复原来的样子。**Gǔ jiànzhù zāodao pòhuài, bù néng huīfù yuánlái de yàngzi.** *The ancient building is damaged and cannot be restored to its former appearance.*

原理 **yuánlǐ** *n* principle, tenet

生物学原理 **shēngwùxué yuánlǐ** principles of biology

原谅 **yuánliàng** *v* pardon, excuse, forgive □ 我今天上午没有能到飞机场去接你，请多原谅。**Wǒ jīntiān shàngwǔ méiyǒu néng dào fēijīchǎng qù jiē nǐ, qǐng duō yuánliàng.** *Please forgive me for not having been able to meet you at the airport this morning.* □ 你这么做，我不能原谅。**Nǐ zhème zuò, wǒ bù néng yuánliàng.** *I can't forgive you for such behavior.*

原料 **yuánliào** [modif: 原 original + 料 material] *n* raw material □ 原料价格又涨了。**Yuánliào jiàgé yòu zhǎng le.** *The price of raw materials has risen again.*

原始 **yuánshǐ** [comp: 原 original + 始 beginning] *adj* primitive

原因 **yuányīn** [modif: 原 origin + 因 cause] *n* cause, reason □ 出了问题，一定要找出原因。**Chūle wèntí, yídìng yào zhǎochū yuányīn.** *When something has gone wrong we must identify the cause.*

原油 **yuányóu** *n* crude oil

原则 **yuánzé** *n* principle □ 不管发生什么，我都不会放弃原则。**Bùguǎn fāshēng shénme, wǒ dōu bú huì fàngqì yuánzé.** *I will not abandon my principles, no matter what.* □ 有时候坚持原则是不容易的。**Yǒushíhou jiānchí yuánzé shì bù róngyì de.** *Sometimes it is not easy to adhere to one's principles.*

原子 **yuánzǐ** [suffix: 原 origin + 子 nominal suffix] *n* atom

原子弹 **yuánzǐdàn** atomic bomb

原子能 **yuánzǐnéng** atomic energy

源 yuán *n* source, fountainhead

源泉 **yuánquán** *n* source, fountainhead

圆 yuán Trad 圓 *adj* round, circular □ 在古代，人们不知道地球是圆的。**Zài gǔdài rénmen bù zhīdào dìqiú shì yuán de.** *In ancient times people did not know that the earth was round.*

圆满 **yuánmǎn** [comp: 圆 round + 满 full] *adj* totally satisfactory, perfect

援 yuán *v* help

援助 **yuánzhù** [comp: 援 help + 助 help] *v* aid, support

远 yuǎn Trad 遠 *adj* far, distant, remote (antonym 近 **jìn**) □ "这里离火车站有多远？" "大概两公里。" **"Zhèlǐ lí huǒchēzhàn yǒu duō yuǎn?" "Dàgài liǎng gōnglǐ."** *"How far is it from here to the railway station?" "About two kilometers."*

离…远… **lí...yuǎn... ...** is far from ... □ 我家离学校不远。**Wǒ jiā lí xuéxiào bù yuǎn.** *My home is not far from school.*

远方 **yuǎnfāng** *n* distant place

远景 **yuǎnjǐng** *n* distant view, prospect

院 yuàn *n* courtyard

院子 **yuànzi** [suffix: 院 courtyard + 子 nominal suffix] *n* courtyard, compound □ 下午四点钟以后很多孩子在院子里玩。**Xiàwǔ sì diǎnzhōng yǐhòu hěn duō háizi zài yuànzi li wán.** *After four o'clock many children will play in the courtyard.*

愿 yuàn Trad 願 *v* wish, hope

愿望 **yuànwàng** [comp: 愿 wish + 望 hope] *n* wish, aspiration, desire □ 我的愿望终于实现了。**Wǒ de yuànwàng zōngyú shíxiàn le.** *My wish came true at last!* □ 谁也不能满足他的愿望。**Shuí yě bù néng mǎnzú tā de yuànwàng.** *Nobody can satisfy his desire.*

愿意 **yuànyì** [comp: 愿 wish + 意 desire] **I** *modal v* be willing, will □ 我愿意帮助你。**Wǒ yuànyì bāngzhù nǐ.** *I'm willing to help you.* □ 你愿意去就去，你不愿意去就别去。**Nǐ yuànyì qù jiù qù, nǐ bú yuànyì qù jiù bié qù.** *If you're willing to go, you can go; if you're not willing to go, you don't have to go.* **II** *v* wish, want □ 父母都愿意自己的孩子幸福。**Fùmǔ dōu yuànyì zìjǐ de háizi xìngfú.** *All parents want their children to be happy.*

怨 yuàn *v* resent, complain (See 埋怨 **mányuàn**.)

约 yuē Trad 約 *adv* Same as 大约 **dàyuē**. Used in written Chinese.

约会 **yuēhuì** [v+obj: 约 arrange + 会 meeting] *n* (social) appointment, engagement, date □ 她今天打扮得这么漂亮，看来有约会。**Tā jīntiān dǎbàn de zhème piàoliang, kànlai yǒu yuēhuì.** *She dressed up beautifully today, she probably has a date.*

约束 **yuēshù** *v* restrain, bind

月 yuè *n* **1** month □ 我在那里住了八个月。**Wǒ zài nàli zhùle bā ge yuè.** *I stayed there for eight months.* **2** the moon □ 明月当空。**Míng yuè dāng kōng.** *The bright moon shines in the sky.*

一月 **yīyuè** January

十二月 **shí'èryuè** December

月份 **yuèfèn** *n* month

四月份 **sìyuèfèn** April

月光 **yuèguāng** *n* moonlight

月亮 **yuèliang** *n* the moon □ 今天晚上的月亮真好！**Jīntiān wǎnshang de yuèliang zhēn hǎo!** *What a fine moon it is tonight!*

月球 **yuèqiú** *n* the Moon (as a scientific term)

乐 yuè Trad 樂 *n* music

乐队 **yuèduì** [modif: 乐 music + 队 team] *n* band, orchestra

乐器 **yuèqì** [modif: 乐 music + 器 implement] *n* musical instrument

乐曲 **yuèqǔ** *n* melody

越 yuè **I** *adv* even more **II** *v* get over, jump

越过 **yuèguò** *v* cross, surmount

越来越… **yuèlaiyuè...** *adv* more and more □ 学中文的人越来越多。**Xué Zhōngwén de rén yuèlaiyuè duō.** *More and more people are learning Chinese.* □ 这孩子长得越来越象他爸爸了。**Zhè háizi zhǎngde yuèlaiyuè**

xiàng tā bàba le. This child is becoming more and more like his father.

越…越… **yuè…yuè…** *adv* the more … the more …
□ 我越学越对中文感兴趣。**Wǒ yuè xué yuè duì Zhōngwén gǎn xìngqù.** *The more I study the more interested I am in Chinese.* □ 你真是越活越年轻了。**Nǐ zhēn shì yuè huó yuè niánqīng le.** *You seem to get younger and younger.* □ 天气越热，她越怕上街。**Tiānqì yuè rè, tā yuè pà shàngjiē.** *The hotter the weather, the more she dislikes to go shopping.* □ 学生越用功，老师越高兴。**Xuésheng yuè yònggōng, lǎoshī yuè gāoxìng.** *The harder students study, the more delighted their teachers.*

悦 **yuè** *adj* pleased (See 喜悦 **xǐyuè**)

阅 **yuè** Trad 閱 *v* read
阅读 **yuèdú** [comp: 阅 read + 读 read] *v* read seriously □ 总经理每天花很多时间阅读各部门的报告。**Zǒngjīnglǐ měi tiān huā hěn duō shíjiān yuèdú gè bùmén de bàogào.** *The general manager spends a lot of time every day reading reports submitted by various departments.*
阅览室 **yuèlǎnshì** [modif: 阅览 read, browse + 室 room] *n* reading room (间 **jiān**) □ 阅览室里的图书杂志不能带出室外。**Yuèlǎnshì li de túshū zázhì bù néng dàichū shìwài.** *You are not allowed to take books and periodicals out of the reading room.*

跃 **yuè** Trad 躍 *v* leap
跃进 **yuèjìn** *v* leap forward

粤 **yuè** *n* a shortened form for 广东 **Guǎngdōng**
粤语 Yuèyǔ the Guangdong dialect, Cantonese

匀 **yún** *v* divide evenly, even up

云 **yún** Trad 雲 *n* cloud □ 蓝天白云，好看极了! **Lán tiān bái yún, hǎokàn jíle!** *White clouds in the blue sky, how beautiful!*
多云 **duōyún** cloudy □ 今天多云。**Jīntiān duōyún.** *It's cloudy today.*
云彩 **yúncai** *n* clouds

允 **yǔn** *v* allow
允许 **yǔnxǔ** [comp: 允 allow + 许 permit] *v* allow, permit □ 这里不允许停车。**Zhèli bù yǔnxǔ tíng chē.** *Parking is not allowed here.* □ 我们不允许任何反社会行为。**Wǒmen bù yǔnxǔ rènhé fǎn shèhuì xíngwéi.** *We do not allow any anti-social behavior.*

运 1 **yùn** Trad 運 *v* transport, carry □ 中国主要靠火车运货。**Zhōngguó zhǔyào kào huǒchē yùn huò.** *China mainly uses trains to transport goods.*
运动 **yùndòng** [comp: 运 move + 动 move] **I** *v* do physical exercises □ 你经常运动吗? **Nǐ jīngcháng yùndòng ma?** *Do you exercise often?* **II** *n* physical exercises □ "你每天做什么运动?" "我有时候打球，有时候跑步。" **"Nǐ měitiān zuò shénme yùndòng?" "Wǒ yǒushíhou dǎ qiú, yǒushíhou pǎobù."** *"What physical exercises do you do every day?" "Sometimes I play ball games and sometimes I jog."* □ 生命在于运动。**Shēngmìng zài yú yùndòng.** *Life lies in physical exercise.*
运动会 **yùndònghuì** [modif: 运动 sports + 会 meeting] *n* sports meet, games □ 这个中学每年十月举行运动会。**Zhège zhōngxué měi nián Shíyuè jǔxíng yùndònghuì.** *This high school holds a sports meet every October.*

奥林匹克运动会 **Àolínpǐkè yùndònghuì** the Olympic Games
运动鞋 **yùndòngxié** [modif: 运动 sport + 鞋 shoe] *n* sport shoes
运动员 **yùndòngyuán** [modif: 运动 sports + 员 person] *n* athlete, sportsman, sportswoman □ 我叔叔年轻的时候是一名长跑运动员。**Wǒ shūshu niánqīng de shíhou shì yì míng chángpǎo yùndòngyuán.** *In his younger days, my uncle was a long-distance runner.*
运输 **yùnshū** [comp: 运 transport + 输 transport] **I** *v* transport, carry □ 你们用什么把煤运输到港口? **Nǐmen yòng shénme bǎ méi yùnshū dào gǎngkǒu?** *How do you transport coal to the port?* **II** *n* transportation □ 修建了这条铁路，运输问题就基本解决了。**Xiūjiànle zhè tiáo tiělù, yùnshū wèntí jiù jīběn jiějué le.** *When this railway is built, transportation problems will be basically solved.*
运送 **yùnsòng** *v* transport, ship
运算 **yùnsuàn** *v* operate (a mathematical problem)
运行 **yùnxíng** *v* move, be in motion
运用 **yùnyòng** *v* use, apply, put into use □ 我们现在运用电脑控制生产过程。**Wǒmen xiànzài yùnyòng diànnǎo kòngzhì shēngchǎn guòchéng.** *Now we use computers to control the production process.*
运转 **yùnzhuǎn** *v* revolve, turn around

运 2 **yùn** Trad 運 *n* fortune, luck
运气 **yùnqì** *n* good luck □ 他运气真好，又中彩票了! **Tā yùnqì zhēn hǎo, yòu zhòng cǎipiàole!** *He is really luck—he has won the lottery again!*

蕴 **yùn** Trad 蘊 *v* hold in store
蕴藏 **yùncáng** *v* hold in store, contain
石油蕴藏量 shíyóu yùncángliàng oil reserves

酝 **yùn** Trad 醞 *v* brew, make wine
酝酿 **yùnniàng** *v* **1** brew, ferment **2** deliberate, prepare mentally

晕 **yùn** Trad 暈 *adj* dizzy, giddy □ 坐了十小时飞机，我有点头晕。**Zuòle shí xiǎoshí fēijī, wǒ yǒu diǎn tóuyùn.** *After ten hours of flight, I feel dizzy.*

韵 **yùn** *n* rhyme
韵母 **yùnmǔ** *n* vowel

孕 **yùn** *n* pregnancy (See 怀孕 **huáiyùn**)

Z

砸 **zá** *v* smash, break

杂 **zá** Trad 雜 *adj* **1** miscellaneous, sundry **2** mixed, mingled, disorderly
杂费 **záfèi** [modif: 杂 miscellaneous + 费 fee, expense] sundry charges
杂技 **zájì** [modif: 杂 miscellaneous + 技 skills] *n* acrobatics □ 听说中国的杂技很有名。**Tīngshuō Zhōngguó de zájì hěn yǒumíng.** *I've heard people say that Chinese acrobatics are very famous.*
杂技团 zájìtuán acrobatic troupe
杂技演员 zájì yǎnyuán acrobat
杂交 **zájiāo** *v* hybridize, cross
杂乱 **záluàn** [comp: 杂 disorderly + 乱 disorderly] *adj* disorderly, in a jumble

杂事 **záshì** [modif: 杂 miscellaneous + 事 matters]
n miscellaneous matters, odd jobs □ 我还有些杂事要办完才能回家。**Wǒ hái yǒu xiē zá shì yào bànwán cái néng huí jiā.** *I still have some miscellaneous things to deal with before I can go home.*

杂文 **záwén** *n* essay of social commentary

杂志 **zázhì** [modif: 杂 miscellaneous + 志 record]
n magazine (本 **běn**, 种 **zhǒng**) □ 他订了两种杂志。**Tā dìngle liǎng zhǒng zázhì.** *He subscribes to two magazines.*

杂质 **zázhì** *n* (in chemistry) foreign substance

咋 **zǎ** *adv* how, why (a Northern dialectal word)

栽 **zāi** *v* plant
栽培 **zāipéi** [comp: 栽 plant + 培 cultivate] *v* cultivate and grow

灾 **zāi** Trad 災 *n* disaster, calamity □ 中国每年都有地方受灾。**Zhōngguó měi nián dōu yǒu dìfang shòu zāi.** *Every year there are places in China that are hit by calamities.*
旱灾 **hànzāi** drought
火灾 **huǒzāi** fire
水灾 **shuǐzāi** flooding, floods

灾害 **zāihài** [comp: 灾 disaster + 害 damage] *n* disaster, calamity □ 由于各种灾害, 全国每年损失几十亿元。**Yóuyú gè zhǒng zāihài, quánguó měi nián sǔnshī jǐ shí yì yuán.** *Owing to disasters of all kinds the country loses billions of dollars every year.*
自然灾害 **zìrán zāihài** natural disaster

灾荒 **zāihuāng** *n* famine caused by a natural disaster

灾难 **zāinàn** *n* great suffering caused by a natural disaster, calamity (场 **cháng**)
灾难性后果 **zāinànxìng hòuguǒ** disastrous consequences

宰 **zǎi** *v* slaughter

载 **zài** *v* carry, be loaded with
载重 **zàizhòng** *n* load, carrying capacity

再 **zài** *adv* again, once more □ 我没听清楚, 请您再说一遍。**Wǒ méi tīng qīngchu, qǐng nín zài shuō yí biàn.** *I did not hear it clearly. Please say it again.* □ 你的电脑修好了, 要是再坏, 我就没有办法了。**Nǐ de diànnǎo xiūhǎo le, yàoshì zài huài, wǒ jiù méiyǒu bànfǎ le.** *Your computer has been repaired. If it breaks down again, there'll be nothing I can do.*

NOTE: 再 **zài** and 又 **yòu** are both glossed as *again*, but they have different usage: 又 **yòu** is used in the context of a past situation while 再 **zài** is used for a future situation. Here is a pair of examples: □ 她昨天又迟到了。**Tā zuótiān yòu chídào le.** *She was late (for work, school, etc.) again yesterday.* □ 明天你不要再迟到了。**Míngtiān nǐ bú yào zài chídào le.** *Please do not be late again tomorrow.*

再见 **zàijiàn** [modif: 再 again + 见 see] *v* see you again, goodbye □ "我回家了, 再见!" "再见, 明天见。" **"Wǒ huíjiā le, zàijiàn!" "Zàijiàn, míngtiān jiàn."** *"I'm going home, goodbye!" "Bye! See you tomorrow."*

再三 **zàisān** [comp: 再 again + 三 three (times)] *adv* over and over again □ 她再三要求, 才让她参加了考试。**Tā zàisān yāoqiú, cái ràng tā cānjiā le kǎoshì.**

It was only after her repeated requests that she was allowed to sit for the examination.

再说 **zàishuō** *adv* **1** what's more, besides **2** later, some other time

在 1 **zài** **I** *prep* in, on, at □ 在新加坡很多人会说中文。**Zài Xīnjiāpō hěn duō rén huì shuō Zhōngwén.** *In Singapore many people speak Chinese.* □ 我在两年以前开始学中文。**Wǒ zài liǎngnián yǐqián kāishǐ xué Zhōngwén.** *I began to learn Chinese two years ago.*
在…里 **zài...li** in □ 他在房间里休息。**Tā zài fángjiān li xiūxi.** *He's taking a rest in the room.*
在…上 **zài...shang** on □ 在桌子上有两本书。**Zài zhuōzi shang yǒu liǎng běn shū.** *There are two books on the desk.*
在…下 **zài...xia** under ... □ 在床下有一双鞋。**Zài chuáng xia yǒu yì shuāng xié.** *There's a pair of shoes under the bed.*
在…之间 **zài...zhī jiān** between □ 我要在这两棵树之间种一些花。**Wǒ yào zài zhè liǎng kē shù zhī jiān zhòng yìxiē huā.** *I'm going to plant some flowers between the two trees.*
II *v* be in □ "你爸爸在家吗?" "他不在家。" **"Nǐ bàba zài jiā ma?" "Tā bú zài jiā."** *"Is your father home?" "No, he isn't."* □ "小明在哪里?" "他在操场上。" **"Xiǎo Míng zài nǎlǐ?" "Tā zài cāochàng shang."** *"Where's Xiao Ming?" "He's on the sports ground."*

在乎 **zàihu** *v* care, care about □ 她不在乎别人的闲话。**Tā bùzàihu biéren de xiánhuà.** *She doesn't care about people's gossip.*

NOTE: 在乎 **zàihu** is normally used in a negative sentence, or a question. The same is true with 在意 **zàiyì**.

在意 **zàiyì** *v* take notice of, mind, care □ 我抽烟, 你在意吗? **Wǒ chōuyān, nǐ zàiyì ma?** *Do you mind if I smoke?*

NOTE: See note on 在乎 **zàihu**.

在于 **zàiyú** *v* lie in, rest with
在座 **zàizuò** *v* be present (at a meeting)

在 2 **zài** *adv* (used to indicate an action in progress) □ "你在做什么?" "我在找东西。" **"Nǐ zài zuò shénme?" "Wǒ zài zhǎo dōngxi."** *"What are you doing?" "I'm looking for something."*

咱 **zán** *pron* Same as 咱们 **zánmen**
咱们 **zánmen** [suffix: 咱 we, us + 们 suffix denoting a plural number] *pron* we, us (including the person or persons spoken to) □ 你在学中文, 我也在学中文, 咱们都在学中文。**Nǐ zài xué Zhōngwén, wǒ yě zài xué Zhōngwén, zánmen dōu zài xué Zhōngwén.** *You're learning Chinese, I'm learning Chinese. We're both learning Chinese.* □ 咱们去吃饭吧! **Zánmen qù chīfàn ba!** *Let's go and have our meal.*

NOTE: 咱们 **zánmen** is only used in colloquial Chinese, and has a Northern dialect flavor. You can always just use 我们 **wǒmen**, even to include the person(s) spoken to. The following examples are perfectly acceptable: □ 你在学中文, 我也在学中文, 我们都在学中文。**Nǐ zài xué Zhōngwén, wǒ yě zài xué Zhōngwén, wǒmen dōu zài xué**

Zhōngwén. *You're learning Chinese. I'm learning Chinese. We're both learning Chinese.* □ 我们去吃饭吧! **Wǒmen qù chīfàn ba!** *Let's go and have a meal.*

攒 **zǎn** Trad 攢　*v* save (money)
　攒钱 **zǎnqián** save money

暂 **zàn** Trad 暫　*adj* temporary
　暂且 **zànqiě** *adv* for the time being, for the moment
暂时 **zànshí** [comp: 暂 temporary + 时 time] *adv* temporarily, for the time being □ 你暂时在这里住一下, 大房间一空出来就可以搬进去。**Nǐ zànshí zài zhèlǐ zhù yíxià, dà fángjiān yí kòng chūlai jiù kěyǐ bān jìnqu.** *Please stay here for the time being. You can move to the bigger room as soon as it is vacated.*

赞 **zàn** Trad 賛　*v* 1 support, favor 2 praise, commend
赞成 **zànchéng** *v* approve of, support, be in favor of □ 我不赞成他代表我们公司去参加会议。**Wǒ bú zànchéng tā dàibiǎo wǒmen gōngsī qù cānjiā huìyì.** *I don't approve of him being our company representative at the conference.* □ 赞成的, 请举手! **Zànchéng de, qǐng jǔshǒu!** *Those in favor, please raise your hands.*
赞美 **zànměi** [comp: 赞 praise + 美 beautify] *v* eulogize, praise highly
赞赏 **zànshǎng** [comp: 赞 praise + 赏 admire] *v* appreciate, admire
赞叹 **zàntàn** [comp: 赞 praise + 叹 sigh] *v* gasp in admiration
赞同 **zàntóng** [comp: 赞 praise + 同 agree] *v* endorse, approve of
赞扬 **zànyáng** *v* praise publicly
赞助 **zànzhù** [comp: 赞 praise + 助 help] *v* support, sponsor

脏 **zāng** Trad 髒　*adj* dirty (antonym 干净 **gānjìng**) □ 这些衣服脏了, 要洗一下。**Zhèxiē yīfu zāng le, yào xǐ yíxià.** *These clothes are dirty and need washing.*

脏 **zàng** Trad 臟　*n* internal organs (See 心脏 **xīnzàng**.)

葬 **zàng** *v* bury (a human body)
葬礼 **zànglǐ** [modif: 葬 burial + 礼 rite] *n* funeral

遭 **zāo** *v* meet with (misfortune)
　遭到 **zāodào** *v* suffer, encounter, meet with □ 公用电话常常遭到破坏。**Gōngyòng diànhuà chángcháng zāodào pòhuài.** *Public telephones are often vandalized.*
遭受 **zāoshòu** *v* suffer, be subjected to □ 去年这个地区连续遭受自然灾害。**Qùnián zhège dìqū liánxù zāoshòu zìrán zāihài.** *Last year this area suffered repeated natural disasters.*
遭殃 **zāoyāng** [v+obj: 遭 suffer + 殃 disaster] *v* suffer disasters, be subject to terrible suffering
遭遇 **zāoyù** [comp: 遭 encounter + 遇 meet] *v* encounter, meet with

糟 **zāo** *adj* messy, wretched
糟糕 **zāogāo** [modif: 糟 messy + 糕 cake] I *adj* in a mess, terrible, very bad □ 我这次考试很糟糕。**Wǒ zhè cì kǎoshì hěn zāogāo.** *I did very poorly in the exam.* □ 情况很糟糕。**Qíngkuàng hěn zāogāo.** *The situation is in a shambles.* II *interj* How terrible! What

bad luck! □ 真糟糕, 我的钥匙丢了。**Zhēn zāogāo, wǒ de yàoshi diū le.** *How terrible! I've lost my keys!*
糟蹋 **zāota** *v* 1 ruin, waste, spoil 2 abuse, violate

凿 **záo** *v* chisel

枣 **zǎo** *n* date (a fruit)
　枣树 **zǎoshù** date tree
　枣子 **zǎozi** date (颗 **kē**)
　蜜枣 **mìzǎo** candied date

早 **zǎo** I *adj* early □ 现在才三点钟, 还早呢! **Xiànzài cái sān diǎnzhōng, hái zǎo ne!** *It's only three o'clock. It's still early!* □ 李先生每天很早上班, 很晚下班。**Lǐ xiānsheng měi tiān hěn zǎo shàngbān, hěn wǎn xiàbān.** *Every day Mr Li goes to work early and comes off work late.* II good morning (See note below)

NOTE: A common greeting among the Chinese when they meet in the morning is 早 **zǎo** or 你早 **Nǐ zǎo.**

早晨 **zǎochén** [modif: 早 early + 晨 early morning] *n* early morning (approximately 6–9 a.m.) □ 他早晨六点半起床。**Tā zǎochén liù diǎn bàn qǐchuáng.** *He gets up at half past six in the morning.* □ 很多人喜欢在早晨锻炼身体。**Hěn duō rén xǐhuan zài zǎochén duànliàn shēntǐ.** *Many people like to exercise in the early morning.*
早点 **zǎodiǎn** Same as 早饭 **zǎofàn**
早饭 **zǎofàn** [modif: 早 early + 饭 meal] *n* breakfast (顿 **dùn**) □ 我今天起得太晚了, 没有时间吃早饭。**Wǒ jīntiān qǐ de tài wǎn le, méiyǒu shíjiān chī zǎofàn.** *I got up too late today and didn't have time for breakfast.*
早期 **zǎoqī** *n* early stage, early phase
早日 **zǎorì** *n* at an early date, soon □ 祝你早日康复! **Zhù nǐ zǎorì kāngfù!** *I hope you'll recover soon. (→ I wish you a speedy recovery.)*
早上 **zǎoshang** *n* Same as 早晨 **zǎochén**
早晚 **zǎowǎn** [comp: 早 morning + 晚 evening] I *n* morning and evening II *adv* sooner or later
早已 **zǎoyǐ** *adv* long ago, for a long time □ 杨先生早已从我们公司退休。**Yáng xiānsheng zǎoyǐ cóng wǒmen gōngsī tuìxiū.** *Mr Wang retired from the company long ago.*

澡 **zǎo** *n* bath (See 洗澡 **xǐzǎo**.)

躁 **zào** *adj* rash, impetuous (See 急躁 **jízào**.)

噪 **zào** *adj* noisy
　噪音 **zàoyīn** *n* noise
　噪音污染 **zàoyīnwūrǎn** noise pollution, white pollution

燥 **zào** *adj* dry (See 干燥 **gānzào**.)

皂 **zào** *n* soap (See 香皂 **xiāngzào**.)

造 **zào** *v* 1 make, build □ 中国人在公元一世纪就会造纸。**Zhōngguórén zài gōngyuán yí shìjì jiù huì zào zhǐ.** *The Chinese knew how to make paper as early as in the first century.* 2 invent, fabricate
造成 **zàochéng** *v* result in, give rise to □ 不幸的童年造成他性格上的很多缺点。**Búxìng de tóngnián zàochéng tā xìnggé shang de hěn duō quēdiǎn.** *An unhappy childhood gave rise to many faults in his character.*

造反 **zàofǎn** *v* rise in rebellion, rebel

造价 **zàojià** *n* cost (of building or manufacturing)

造句 **zàojù** **I** *v* make sentences
用所给的词语造句 yòng suǒ gěi de cíyǔ zàojù make sentences with the given words **II** *n* sentence-making

造型 **zàoxíng** *n* modelling

灶 **zào** *n* stove

则 **zé** Trad 則 *conj* in that case, then □ 不进则退。 **Bú jìn zé tuì.** *If you don't make progress, then you'll fall behind.* □ 如果一切顺利, 则工厂可在明年开工。 **Rúguǒ yíqiè shùnlì, zé gōngchǎng kě zài míngnián kāigōng.** *If everything goes well, then the factory can start production next year.*

NOTE: 则 zé is only used in formal Chinese. In everyday Chinese, use 那 **nà** or 那么 **nàme** instead. See note on 那么 **nàme**.

责 **zé** Trad 責 **I** *n* duty **II** *v* scold
责备 **zébèi** *v* reproach, blame
责备的口气 zébèi de kǒuqì a reproachful tone
责怪 **zéguài** [comp: 责 scold + 怪 blame] *v* blame □ 出了差错, 他总是责怪别人。 **Chūle chācuò, tā zǒngshì zéguài biéren.** *When something goes wrong, he would blame others.*
责任 **zérèn** *n* 1 responsibility, duty □ 教育孩子是父母的责任。 **Jiàoyù háizi shì fùmǔ de zérèn.** *It is the parents' responsibility to educate their children.* 2 responsibility for a fault or mistake □ 这次交通事故责任主要在开快车的那一方。 **Zhè cì jiāotōng shìgù zérèn zhǔyào zài kāi kuàichē de nà yì fāng.** *The person who was speeding is mainly to blame for this traffic accident.*
责任感 **zérèngǎn** *n* sense of responsibility □ 这个男人缺点很多, 但是责任感很强, 很顾家。 **Zhège nánrén quēdiǎn hěn duō, dànshì zérèngǎn hěn qiáng, hěn gù jiā.** *This man may have many shortcomings, but he has a strong sense of responsibility and cares for his family.*

择 **zé** Trad 擇 *v* choose (See 选择 xuǎnzé.)

泽 **zé** Trad 澤 *n* pool, pond (See 沼泽 zhǎozé)

贼 **zéi** Trad 賊 *n* thief

怎 **zěn** *adv* how, why
怎么 **zěnme** *adv* 1 how, in what manner □ 这个汉字怎么写? **Zhège Hànzì zěnme xiě?** *How do you write this Chinese character?* □ 对不起, 请问去北京大学怎么走? **Duìbuqǐ, qǐng wèn qù Běijīng Dàxué zěnme zǒu?** *Excuse me, could you please tell me how to get to Beijing University?* 2 no matter how (used with 都 **dōu** or 也 **yě**) □ 是这把钥匙吗? 我怎么都开不开这个门。 **Shì zhè bǎ yàoshi ma? Wǒ zěnme dōu kāi bu kāi zhège mén.** *Is this the right key? No matter how I tried, I couldn't open the door.* □ 他怎么也找不到那本书。 **Tā zěnme yě zhǎo bu dào nà běn shū.** *No matter how hard he tried, he couldn't find the book.* 3 why, how come □ 你怎么又迟到了? **Nǐ zěnme yòu chídào le?** *Why are you late again?* □ 她今天怎么这么高兴?

Tā jīntiān zěnme zhème gāoxìng? *Why is she so happy today?* 4 how can ... □ 这么多作业, 我今天怎么做得完? **Zhème duō zuòyè, wǒ jīntiān zěnme zuò de wán?** *How can I finish so many assignments today?* □ 你说这种话, 妈妈怎么会不生气? **Nǐ shuō zhè zhǒng huà, māma zěnme huì bù shēngqì?** *How would mom not feel angry, when you had said such things?*
怎么办 **zěnmebàn** *adv* what's to be done? □ 要是飞机票卖完了, 怎么办? **Yàoshì fēijīpiào màiwán le, zěnme bàn?** *What should we do if the air tickets are sold out?*
怎么了 **zěnmele** *adv* what happened? □ 怎么了, 她怎么哭了? **Zěnmele, tā zěnme kū le?** *What happened? Why is she crying?*
怎么样 **zěnmeyàng** *adv* 1 Same as 怎么 **zěnme** 1 2 how □ 你今天觉得怎么样? **Nǐ jīntiān juéde zěnmeyàng?** *How are you feeling today?* □ 他使用电脑的能力怎么样? **Tā shǐyòng diànnǎo de nénglì zěnmeyàng?** *How competent is he in using the computer?* 3 how's that? is it OK? □ 我们每个人讲一个故事, 怎么样? **Wǒmen měi ge rén jiǎng yí ge gùshi, zěnmeyàng?** *We each tell a story, how about that?* □ 我晚上开车来接你怎么样? **Wǒ wǎnshang kāichē lái jiē nǐ, zénmeyàng?** *I'll pick you up this evening. Is it OK?*
怎样 **zěnyàng** *adv* Same as 怎么样 **zěnmeyàng**. Used in writing.

增 **zēng** *v* add, increase
增产 **zēngchǎn** *v* increase production
增加 **zēngjiā** [comp: 增 increase + 加 add] *v* increase □ 去年他家的收入增加了两千元。 **Qùnián tā jiā de shōurù zēngjiāle liǎngqiān yuán.** *Last year his family income increased by 2,000 yuan.*
增进 **zēngjìn** [comp: 增 increase + 进 go forward] *v* promote, enhance
增强 **zēngqiáng** *v* strengthen
增设 **zēngshè** *v* add (a new office, a new department, etc.), introduce (a new course of study)
增添 **zēngtiān** *v* provide (additional equipment, evidence, etc.)
增添人员和设备 zēngtiān rényuán hé shèbèi provide more personnel and euqipment
增援 **zēngyuán** **I** *n* (military) reinforcements **II** *v* send reinforcements
增长 **zēngzhǎng** [comp: 增 increase + 长 grow] *v* increase, grow □ 旅行增长知识。 **Lǚxíng zēngzhǎng zhīshi.** *Traveling increases one's knowledge.* □ 大学生人数在五年中增长百分之三十以上。 **Dàxuéshēng rénshù zài wǔ nián zhong zēngzhǎng bǎifēn zhi sānshí yǐ shàng.** *In the past five years the number of university students has grown by more than thirty percent.*

赠 **zèng** *v* present a gift
赠送 **zèngsòng** *v* present as a gift
向主人赠送礼物 xiàng zhǔrén zèngsòng lǐwù present a gift to the host
赠阅 **zèngyuè** *v* give (a book, a publication) as a complimentary copy

扎 **zhā** *v* prick, stab
扎实 **zhāshi** *adj* solid, sturdy

渣 **zhā** *n* dregs, residue
煤渣 méizhā coal cinders
渣滓 **zhāzǐ** *n* sediment, dregs, residue

闸 **zhá** *n* floodgate
闸门 **zhámén** *n* 1 sluice gate 2 throttle valve

眨 zhǎ v blink, wink
向我眨了眨眼 xiàng wǒ zhǎ le zhǎ yǎn winked at me

炸 zhà v explode, burst
炸弹 zhàdàn [modif: 炸 exploding + 弹 bullet] n bomb (枚 **méi**)
扔炸弹 rēng zhàdàn drop a bomb
炸药 zhàyào n dynamite, explosives
引爆炸药 yǐnbào zhàyào set off an explosive

诈 zhà v cheat, swindle
诈骗 zhàpiàn [comp: 诈 cheat + 骗 deceive] v defraud, swindle
诈骗犯 zhàpiànfàn swindler

榨 zhà v press, extract
榨菜 zhàcài n hot pickled mustard tuber

摘 zhāi v pick, pluck □ 星期天跟我们一起去果园摘苹果吧。**Xīngqītiān gēn wǒmen yìqǐ qù guǒyuán zhāi píngguǒ ba.** Do go to the orchard with us on Sunday to pick apples.
摘要 zhāiyào [v+obj: 摘 pick + 要 what is important] **I** n abstract, summary
论文摘要 lùnwén zhāiyào abstract of an academic or scholarly paper
II v make a summary

宅 zhái n residence, house. (See 住宅 zhùzhái)

窄 zhǎi adj narrow (antonym 宽 kuān) □ 这条街太窄，汽车开不进去。**Zhè tiáo jiē tài zhǎi, qìchē kāi bu jìnqu.** This street is too narrow for a car to enter.

债 zhài n debt □ 借了债，就要还。**Jièle zhài, jiùyào huán.** If you owe a debt, you'll have to repay it.
还债 huánzhài to pay off a debt, to settle a debt
借债 jièzhài to borrow money, to ask for a loan
欠债 qiànzhài to owe a debt □ 她为了读完大学，欠了一大笔债。**Tā wèile dú wán dàxué, qiànle yí dà bǐzhài.** To finish her college education, she incurs a huge debt.
要债 yào zhài to demand repayment of a debt
债务 zhàiwù n debt, liabilities
债务人 zhàiwùrén debtor
债主 zhàizhǔ n creditor

寨 zhài n stockade, stockaded village

瞻 zhān v look up or forward
瞻仰 zhānyǎng v look at with reverence

沾 zhān v be stained with
沾光 zhānguāng v benefit from association, sponge off

展 zhǎn v display
展出 zhǎnchū [v+comp: 展 show + 出 out] v be on show, put on display □ 这两天商场展出最新夏装。**Zhè liǎngtiān shāngchǎng zhǎnchū zuì xīn xiàzhuāng.** These days the latest summer wear is on display in the shopping center.
展开 zhǎnkāi v carry out, launch □ 政府将要展开交通安全的活动。**Zhèngfǔ jiāngyào zhǎnkāi jiāotōng ānquán de huódòng.** The government will carry out activities to promote traffic safety.
展览 zhǎnlǎn [modif: 展 display + 览 view] **I** v put on display, exhibit □ 这个画儿画得真好，可以去展览。**Zhège huàr huà de zhēn hǎo, kěyǐ qù zhǎnlǎn.** This picture is done so well that it can be put on display.

II n exhibition, show □ 我上个星期参观了一个很有意思的展览。**Wǒ shàngge xīngqī cānguānle yí ge hěn yǒu yìsi de zhǎnlǎn.** Last week I visited a very interesting exhibition.
展览会 zhǎnlǎnhuì Same as 展览 II n
展示 zhǎnshì v display, show
展望 zhǎnwàng **I** v look into the distance, look into the future
展望未来 zhǎnwàngwèilái foresee the future, predict the future
II n general view regarding future developments
展现 zhǎnxiàn v present before one's eyes
展销 zhǎnxiāo v show and advertise (products)
汽车展销会 qìchē zhǎnxiāohuì automobile fair, auto fair

盏 zhǎn Trad 盞 measure wd (for lamps)

斩 zhǎn Trad 斬 v chop, cut
斩草除根 zhǎn cǎo chú gēn idiom cut the weeds and dig up the roots (→ destroy root and branch, remove the root of trouble completely)

崭 zhǎn Trad 嶄 as in 崭新 zhǎnxīn
崭新 zhǎnxīn adj brand-new

占 zhàn v occupy □ 你一个人不能占两个座位。**Nǐ yí ge rén bù néng zhàn liǎng ge zuòwèi.** You're only one person and can't take two seats.
占领 zhànlǐng v occupy, seize
占领军 zhànlǐngjūn occupation troops
占便宜 zhàn piányi v gain additional advantage at others' expenses
占有 zhànyǒu v possess, own
占有有利地位 zhànyǒu yǒulì dìwèi occupy an advantageous position

战 zhàn Trad 戰 n 1 war, warfare 2 fight, battle
战场 zhànchǎng n battleground, battlefield
战斗 zhàndòu v combat, fight
战略 zhànlüè n military strategy, strategy
战胜 zhànshèng [v+compl: 战 fight + 胜 victorious] v triumph over, defeat □ 人不可能战胜自然。**Rén bù kěnéng zhànshèng zìrán.** It is impossible for man to triumph over nature.
战士 zhànshì [modif: 战 fighting + 士 person] n soldier, fighter □ 不管天冷天热，战士们坚持军事训练。**Bùguǎn tiān-lěng-tiān-rè, zhànshìmen jiānchí jūnshì xùnliàn.** The soldiers persist in military training in spite of the weather conditions.
战术 zhànshù n military tactics
战线 zhànxiàn n battle line
战役 zhànyì n military campaign
战友 zhànyǒu n army buddy
战争 zhànzhēng [comp: 战 fight + 争 strife] n war □ 在二十一世纪，人类能避免大规模战争吗？**Zài èrshíyī shìjì, rénlèi néng bìmiǎn dà guīmó zhànzhēng ma?** Can mankind avoid large-scale wars in the twenty-first century?

站 1 zhàn v stand □ 房间里有些人站着，有些人坐着。**Fángjiān li yǒuxiē rén zhànzhe, yǒuxiē rén zuòzhe.** In the room some people are standing, and others are seated. □ 站在高山上，可以看得很远。**Zhàn zài gāoshān shang, kěyǐ kàn de hěn yuǎn.** Standing on a high mountain, one can see very far.
站起来 zhàn qǐlai stand up □ 老师走进教室，学生们都

站起来。**Lǎoshī zǒujìn jiàoshi, xuéshēngmen dōu zhàn qǐlai.** *When the teacher came into the classroom, all the students stood up.*

站岗 **zhàngǎng** v stand guard, be on sentry duty

站 2 **zhàn** n station, stop □ 我要一辆出租汽车去火车站。**Wǒ yào yí liàng chūzū qìchē qù huǒchē zhàn.** *I need a taxi to go to the railway station.*
出租汽车站 chūzū qìchē zhàn taxi stand
火车站 huǒchē zhàn railway station
汽车站 qìchē zhàn coach/bus station, bus stop
站长 **zhànzhǎng** n railway/coach stationmaster

张 1 **zhāng** Trad 張 v open, spread
张望 **zhāngwàng** v look around

张 2 **zhāng** Trad 張 *measure wd* (for paper, bed, table etc.)
一张纸 yì zhāng zhǐ a piece of paper
两张床 liǎng zhāng chuáng two beds
三张桌子 sān zhāng zhuōzi three tables/desks

张 3 **Zhāng** Trad 張 n a common family name
张先生/太太/小姐 Zhāng xiānsheng/tàitai/xiǎojiě Mr/Mrs/Miss Zhang

章 **zhāng** n chapter
章程 **zhāngchéng** n regulations (for an organization)

彰 **zhāng** v clear, evident (See 表彰 **biǎozhāng**)

掌 **zhǎng** n hand, palm
了如指掌 liǎo rú zhǐzhǎng know ... like the back of one's hand
掌管 **zhǎngguǎn** v be in charge of
掌上电脑 **zhǎngshàng diànnǎo** n palm-top, hand-held computer
掌声 **zhǎngshēng** n clapping, applause
掌握 **zhǎngwò** [comp: 掌 be in charge + 握 take ... in one's hands] v have a good command of, know well □ 要掌握一门外语是不容易的。**Yào zhǎngwò yì mén wàiyǔ shì bù róngyi de.** *It is not easy to gain a good command of a foreign language.*

长 1 **zhǎng** Trad 長 v 1 grow □ 孩子长高了。**Háizi zhǎnggāo le.** *The child has grown taller.* □ 孩子长大成人，父母也老了。**Háizi zhǎngdà chéngrén, fùmǔ yě lǎo le.** *The parents will be old when their children are grown up.* 2 grow to be, look □ 他们的女儿长得很漂亮。**Tāmen de nǚ'ér zhǎng de hěn piàoliang.** *Their daughter is very pretty.* □ 今年的庄稼长得真好。**Jīnnián de zhuāngjia zhǎng de zhēn hǎo.** *The crops this year are really good.*

长 2 **zhǎng** Trad 長 n chief (See 校长 **xiàozhǎng**)

涨 **zhǎng** Trad 漲 v rise, go up □ 水涨船高。**Shuǐ zhǎng chuán gāo.** *When the river rises the boat goes up.* (→ *When the general situation improves, particular things improve.*) □ 上周股票涨了很多。**Shàng zhōu gǔpiào zhǎngle hěn duō.** *Last week shares rose greatly.*
涨价 **zhǎngjià** v (of prices) rise

帐 1 **zhàng** Trad 帳 n curtain, canopy
帐篷 **zhàngpeng** n tent
搭帐篷 dā zhàngpeng pitch a tent

帐 2 **zhàng** Trad 賬 n account
查帐 chá zhàng examine an account, audit
算帐 suàn zhàng compute income and expense, settle accounts

NOTE: 帐 **zhàng** *account* is also written as 账, e.g. 查账, 算账.

帐单 (账单) **zhàngdān** n bill
付电话帐单 fù diànhuà zhàngdān pay the phone bill
帐目 (账目) **zhàngmù** n items of an account
帐目不清 zhàngmù bùqīng accounts not in order

胀 **zhàng** Trad 脹 v swell

障 **zhàng** v hinder, obstruct
障碍 **zhàng'ài** n obstacle, barrier
排除障碍 páichú zhàng'ài clear an obstacle

丈 **zhàng** n 1 senior 2 husband
丈夫 **zhàngfu** n husband (antonym 妻子 **qīzi**) □ 你认识她的丈夫吗？**Nǐ rènshi tā de zhàngfu ma?** *Do you know her husband?*

招 **zhāo** v beckon, attract
招待 **zhāodài** v receive or entertain (a guest) □ 他们用好酒好菜招待客人。**Tāmen yòng hǎo jiǔ hǎo cài zhāodài kèren.** *They entertained their guests with good wine and good food.*
招待会 **zhāodàihuì** n reception (a social function)
记者招待会 jìzhě zhāodàihuì press conference
招呼 **zhāohu** [comp: 招 beckon + 呼 call] v call, shout at □ 马路对面有人在招呼我。**Mǎlù duìmiàn yǒurén zài zhāohu wǒ.** *There's someone calling me on the other side of the road.*
打招呼 dǎ zhāohu 1 greet □ 他进屋就跟大家打招呼。**Tā jìn wū jiù gēn dàjiā dǎ zhāohu.** *He greeted everybody when he came into the room.* 2 inform casually, tell □ 他也没跟我打招呼就把我的自行车骑走了。**Tā méi gēn wǒ dǎ zhāohu jiù bǎ wǒ de zìxíngchē qízǒu le.** *He rode off on my bicycle without telling me.*
招聘 **zhāopìn** [comp: 招 attract + 聘 invite for service] v advertise for a position, recruit (employees) □ 我们学校正在招聘一名中文老师。**Wǒmen xuéxiào zhèngzài zhāopìn yì míng Zhōngwén lǎoshī.** *Our school is advertising for a Chinese teacher.*
招聘广告 zhāopìn guǎnggào advertisement for employment
招生 **zhāoshēng** v enrol new students, recruit students
招生办公室 zhāoshēng bàngōngshì (college and university) enrolment office
招收 **zhāoshōu** v recruit
招收工人 zhāoshōu gōngrén recruit workers
招收学生 zhāoshōu xuéshēng enroll new students
招手 **zhāoshǒu** v wave (one's hand), beckon

朝 **zhāo** n early morning
朝气 **zhāoqì** [modif: 朝 early morning + 气 atmosphere] n youthful spirit
朝气蓬勃 zhāoqì péngbó full of youthful spirit, full of vigor and vitality
朝夕 **zhāoxī** [comp: 朝 early morning + 夕 late afternoon] n morning and evening, daily
朝夕相处 zhāoxī xiāngchǔ be together from morning till night

着 **zháo** v catch □ 着火了！着火了！**Zháohuǒ le! Zháohuǒ le!** *Fire! Fire!*
着急 **zháojí** v be anxious, be worried □ 已经十二点了，女儿还没有回家，妈妈很着急。**Yǐjīng shí'èr diǎn**

le, nǚ'ér hái méiyǒu huíjiā, māma hěn zháojí. *It was almost twelve o'clock and her daughter was still not home. The mother felt very worried.* □ 你着急有什么用呢？慢慢想办法吧。**Nǐ zháojí yǒu shénme yòng ne? Mànman xiǎng bànfǎ ba.** *What's the use of being worried? Let's think of a plan.*

着凉 zháoliáng *v* catch a cold

找 zhǎo *v* look for, search for □ "你在找什么？" "我在找我的手表。" **"Nǐ zài zhǎo shénme?" "Wǒ zài zhǎo wǒ de shǒubiǎo."** *"What are you looking for?" "I'm looking for my watch."* □ 你真的关心她，就帮她找个对象吧。**Nǐ zhēn de guānxīn tā, jiù bāng tā zhǎo ge duìxiàng ba.** *If you are really concerned for her, help her to find a fiancé.*

找到 zhǎodào *v* find □ 我姐姐在香港找到了一个好工作。**Wǒ jiějie zài Xiānggǎng zhǎodàole yí ge hǎo gōngzuò.** *My elder sister has found a good job in Hong Kong.*

沼 zhǎo *n* pond
沼泽 **zhǎozé** *n* swamp, marsh
沼泽地 **zhǎozédì** swamp, marshland

召 zhào *v* summon
召集 **zhàojí** *v* call, convene
召集紧急会议 **zhàojí jǐnjí huìyì** convene an emergency meeting
召开 zhàokāi [comp: 召 summon + 开 open] *v* convene (a conference) □ 下星期校长要召开全体教师会议，讨论明年工作安排。**Xià xīngqī xiàozhǎng yào zhàokāi quántǐ jiàoshī huìyì, tǎolùn míngnián gōngzuò ānpái.** *Next week the [high school] principal will convene a meeting of all teaching staff to discuss next year's work.*

照 1 zhào *v* 1 take a photo □ 麻烦您给我们照一张相。**Máfan nín gěi wǒmen zhào yí zhāng xiàng.** *Would you please take a photo of us?* □ 这儿风景不错，我想照一张相。**Zhèr fēngjǐng bú cuò, wǒ xiǎng zhào yì zhāng xiàng.** *The scenery is good here. I'd like to have a picture taken.* 2 look in a mirror □ 他们的小男孩从来不照镜子，小女孩老是照镜子。**Tāmen de xiǎo nánhái cónglái bú zhào jìngzi, xiǎo nǚhái lǎoshì zhào jìngzi.** *Their little boy never looks in the mirror but their little girl always looks in the mirror.* 3 shine, light up □ 冬天的太阳照在脸上，暖暖的，很舒服。**Dōngtiān de tàiyang zhào zài liǎnshang, nuǎnnuǎn de, hěn shūfu.** *In winter when the sun shines on your face you feel warm and comfortable.*

照顾 zhàogu [comp: 照 look after + 顾 attend to] *v* look after, care for □ 她每个星期六到老人院去照顾老人。**Tā měi ge Xīngqīliù dào lǎorényuàn qù zhàogu lǎorén.** *Every Saturday afternoon she goes to a senior citizens' home to look after the senior citizens there.* □ 我在阿姨家过暑假的时候，她一家对我照顾得很好。**Wǒ zài āyí jiā guò shǔjià de shíhou, tā yìjiā duì wǒ zhàogu de hěn hǎo.** *When I stayed with my aunt's family for the summer holidays, they took good care of me.*

照会 zhàohuì *n* (diplomatic) note
照料 zhàoliào *v* take care of, attend to
照料日常事务 **zhàoliào rìcháng shìwù** take care of day-to-day affairs
照明 zhàomíng *n* lighting, illumination
照明设备 **zhàomíng shèbèi** lighting equipment

照片 zhàopiàn *n* photograph, picture, snapshot (张 **zhāng**) □ 申请签证，要交三张照片。**Shēnqǐng qiānzhèng, yào jiāo sān zhāng zhàopiàn.** *To apply for a visa, you need to submit three photos.* □ 老人常常看着老照片，回忆过去的生活。**Lǎorén chángcháng kànzhe lǎo zhàopiàn, huíyì guòqù de shēnghuó.** *The old man (or woman) often looks at old photos, recalling life in the past.*

照射 zhàoshè *v* shine on, light up
照相 zhàoxiàng [v+obj: 照 illuminate + 相 photograph] *v* take a picture □ 请你给我们照个相。**Qǐng nǐ gěi wǒmen zhào ge xiàng.** *Please take a picture of us.* □ 人们喜欢站在那幅画前照相。**Rénmen xǐhuan zhàn zài nà fú huà qián zhàoxiàng.** *People like to take photos standing in front of that painting.*

照相馆 zhàoxiàngguǎn *n* photographic studio
照相机 zhàoxiàngjī *n* camera (架 **jià**, 台 **tái**) □ 明天出去玩，别忘了带照相机！**Míngtiān chūqu wán, bié wàngle dài zhàoxiàngjī!** *Don't forget to bring a camera with you on your outing tomorrow!*
数码照相机 **shùmǎ zhàoxiàngjī** digital camera
照耀 zhàoyào *v* shine, illuminate
照应 zhàoyìng *v* look after, take care of

照 2 zhào *prep* according to, in the manner of □ 我们还是照以前的方法付款。**Wǒmen háishì zhào yǐqián de fāngfǎ fùkuǎn.** *We will pay in the same way as before.* □ 照我说的去办，肯定不会错。**Zhào wǒ shuōde qù bàn, kěndìng bú huì cuò.** *Do as I say and you will definitely not go wrong.*

照常 zhàocháng [v+obj: 照 according to + 常 usual] *adv* as usual □ 本店春节照常营业。**Běn diàn chūnjié zhàocháng yíngyè.** *Business as usual during the Spring Festival.*
照例 zhàolì *adv* as usual, as a rule
照样 zhàoyàng *adv* in the same old way

罩 zhào *v* cover, overspread

兆 zhào *n* sign, omen
预兆 **yùzhào** omen, presage

遮 zhē *v* hide from view

折 zhē as in 折腾 **zhēteng**
折腾 **zhēteng** *v* 1 do over and over again 2 cause suffering

折 zhé I *v* convert to, amount to □ 一美元折多少日元？**Yì Měiyuán zhé duōshǎo Rìyuán?** *How many Japanese yen does an American dollar amount to?* II *n* discount, reduction (in price) □ 这些书现在打八折。**Zhèxiē shū xiànzài dǎ bā zhé.** *These books are under a twenty percent discount now.*
折合 zhéhé *v* convert to, amount to
折磨 zhémo I *v* cause much mental or physical suffering II *n* suffering
受病痛的折磨 **shòu bìngtòng de zhémo** suffer terribly from the disease

折 zhé *adj* wise
哲学 zhéxué *n* philosophy □ 我对东方哲学感兴趣。**Wǒ duì dōngfāng zhéxué gǎn xìngqù.** *I am interested in Eastern philosophy.*
哲学家 **zhéxuéjiā** philosopher

者 zhě *suffix* (a nominal suffix denoting a person or people) (See 读者 **dúzhě**, 记者 **jìzhě**, 作者 **zuòzhě**.)

这 zhè Trad 這 *pron* this □ 这是什么? **Zhè shì shénme?** *What's this?* □ 这也不行, 那也不行, 你到底要我怎么办? **Zhè yě bù xíng, nà yě bù xíng, nǐ dàodǐ yào wǒ zěnmebàn?** *This won't do and that won't do either. What do you expect me to do?*

这个 zhège [modif: 这 this + 个 one] *pron* this one, this □ 这个太大, 给我小一点儿的。 **Zhège tài dà, gěi wǒ xiǎo yìdiǎnr de.** *This one is too big. Give me a smaller one.* □ 你为了这个生气, 值得吗? **Nǐ wèile zhège shēngqì, zhídé ma?** *Is it worth getting angry over this?*

这会儿 zhèhuìr *n* now, this time

这里 zhèli *n* this place, here □ 你在这里住了几年了? **Nǐ zài zhèli zhùle jǐ nián le?** *How long have you been living here?* □ 我刚来的时候, 不习惯这里的天气。 **Wǒ gāng lái de shíhou, bù xíguàn zhèli de tiānqì.** *When I first came, I wasn't used to the weather here.*

NOTE: In spoken Chinese 这里 **zhèli** can be replaced by 这儿 **zhèr**.

这么 zhème *adv* like this, in this manner, so □ 这件衣服这么贵, 我没想到。 **Zhè jiàn yīfu zhème guì, wǒ méi xiǎngdào.** *I did not expect this dress to be so expensive.* □ 你这么快就把文章写好了, 佩服佩服! **Nǐ zhème kuài jiù bǎ wénzhāng xiě hǎo le, pèifu pèifu!** *It is simply admirable that you wrote the article so fast!*

这么着 zhèmezhe *adv* like this, so

这些 zhèxiē *pron* these □ 这些书你都看过吗? **Zhèxiē shū nǐ dōu kànguo ma?** *Have you read all these books?*

这样 zhèyàng *adj* 1 such □ 他就是这样的一个人, 根本靠不住。 **Tā jiùshì zhèyàng de yí ge rén, gēnběn kào bu zhù.** *He is just such a person. (→ That's just typical of him.) He is not reliable at all.* 2 Same as 这么 **zhème**. Used only in writing.

这样一来 zhèyàng yìlái *adv* consequently

蔗 zhè *n* sugarcane (See 甘蔗 **gānzhe**)

着 zhe *particle* (used after a verb to indicate the action or state is going on) □ 门开着, 灯亮着, 可是房间里没有人。 **Mén kāizhe, dēng liàngzhe, kěshì fángjiān li méiyǒu rén.** *The door was open and the light was on but there was no one in the room.*

这 zhèi Trad 這 *pron.* Same as 这 **zhè**. Used colloquially.

珍 zhēn *adj* valuable

珍贵 zhēnguì [comp: 珍 valuable + 贵 precious] *adj* precious, valuable □ 这些文物有两千年的历史, 多么珍贵啊! **Zhè xiē wénwù yǒu liǎngqiān nián de lìshǐ, duōme zhēnguì a!** *These cultural relics are 2,000 years old; how precious they are!*

珍惜 zhēnxī [comp: 珍 valuable + 惜 cherish] *v* cherish dearly, value highly

珍珠 zhēnzhū [modif: 珍 valuable + 珠 bead] *n* pearl (颗 **kē**)

珍珠项链 zhēnzhū xiàngliàn pearl necklace

真 zhēn *adj* true, real (antonym 假 **jiǎ**) □ 这个电影是根据真人真事编写的。 **Zhège diànyǐng shì gēnjù zhēn rén zhēn shì biānxiě de.** *This movie is based on a real-life story.* □ 中国真大呀! **Zhōngguó zhēn dà ya!** *China is really big!* □ 我真不愿意去参加那个晚会。 **Wǒ zhēn bú yuànyì qù cānjiā nàge wǎnhuì.** *I really don't want to attend that evening party.*

真诚 zhēnchéng [comp: 真 true + 诚 sincere] *adj* sincere, genuine

真话 zhēnhuà truth □ 这家报纸很少说真话。 **Zhè jiā bàozhǐ hěn shǎo shuō zhēnhuà.** *This newspaper rarely tells the truth.*

真空 zhēnkōng [modif: 真 truly + 空 empty] vacuum

真理 zhēnlǐ [modif: 真 true + 理 reasoning, principle] *n* truth □ 真理往往掌握在少数人手里。 **Zhēnlǐ wǎngwǎng zhǎngwò zài shǎoshù rén shǒuli.** *Truth is very often in the hands of the minority.*

真实 zhēnshí [comp: 真 real + 实 substance] *adj* true, real, authentic □ 到底发生了什么? 没有人知道真实的情况。 **Dàodǐ fāshēngle shénme? Méiyǒu rén zhīdào zhēnshí de qíngkuàng.** *What on earth happened? Nobody knows the true situation.*

真相 zhēnxiàng *n* the real situation, actual facts

真心 zhēnxīn [modif: 真 true + 心 heart] *n* sincerity

真正 zhēnzhèng [comp: 真 neat + 正 orderly] *adj* true, real, genuine □ 真正的友谊是天长地久的。 **Zhēnzhèng de yǒuyì shì tiān-cháng-dì-jiǔ de.** *Genuine friendship is everlasting.* □ 他在农村各地旅行了一年多, 才真正了解中国。 **Tā zài nóngcūn gèdì lǚxíng yì nián duō, cái zhēnzhèng liǎojiě Zhōngguó.** *It was only after he traveled in various parts of rural China for over a year that he really came to understand China.*

针 zhēn *n* 1 needle (根 **gēn**) □ 我要一根缝衣针。 **Wǒ yào yì gēn féngyī zhēn.** *I want a sewing needle.* 2 injection □ 护士给他打了一针。 **Hùshi gěi tā dǎ le yì zhēn.** *The nurse gave him an injection.*

打针 dǎzhēn give an injection, get an injection □ 她打针吃药半个月病才好。 **Tā dǎzhēn chīyào bàn ge yuè bìng cái hǎo.** *She had injections and took medicine for half a month before she recovered.*

针对 zhēnduì *v* aim at, be aimed at □ 这次反吸烟运动主要针对青少年。 **Zhè cì fǎn xīyān yùndòng zhǔyào zhēnduì qīngshàonián.** *This anti-smoking campaign is mainly aimed at teenagers.* □ 厂长的话是针对经常迟到的工人说的。 **Chǎngzhǎng de huà shì zhēnduì jīngcháng chídào de gōngrén shuō de.** *The factory manager's words are directed at workers who often come late for work.*

针灸 zhēnjiǔ [comp: 针 needle + 灸 moxibustion] I *n* acupuncture and moxibustion □ 他学中文的目的是为了研究针灸。 **Tā xué Zhōngwén de mùdì shì wèile yánjiū zhēnjiǔ.** *His purpose in learning Chinese is to study acupuncture and moxibustion.* II *v* give or receive acupuncture and moxibustion treatment □ 他针灸了几次, 肩就不疼了。 **Tā zhēnjiǔle jǐ cì, jiān jiù bù téng le.** *After a few sessions of acupuncture and moxibustion, his shoulder no longer hurts.*

贞 zhēn Trad 貞 *adj* loyal, faithful

侦 zhēn Trad 偵 *v* detect

侦察 zhēnchá *v* reconnoiter, scout

侦察卫星 zhēnchá wèixīng reconnaissance (spy) satellite

侦探 zhēntàn *n* detective

私人侦探 sīrén zhēntàn private detective, private eye

诊 zhēn Trad 診 *v* examine (a patient)

诊断 zhěnduàn I *v* diagnose

诊断为良性肿瘤 zhěnduàn wéi liángxìng zhǒngliú diagnosed as a benign tumor **II** *n* diagnosis
做出诊断 zuòchū zhěnduàn make a diagnosis

枕 zhěn *n* pillow
枕头 zhěntou pillow (只 **zhī**)

阵 1 zhèn Trad 陣 *n* column or row of troops
阵地 zhèndì *n* (military) position
阵容 zhènróng *n* layout of troops
阵线 zhènxiàn *n* (military) front
阵营 zhènyíng *n* military camp

阵 2 zhèn Trad 陣 *measure wd* (for an action or event that lasts for some time) □ 雨下了一阵停了。 **Yǔ xiàle yí zhèn tíng le.** *The rain stopped after a while.* □ 刮了一阵大风, 院子里满是落叶。 **Guāle yí zhèn dà fēng, yuànzi li mǎnshì luòyè.** *A strong wind blew for a while and the courtyard was full of fallen leaves.*
阵雨 zhènyǔ shower

振 zhèn *v* arouse to action
振动 zhèndòng *v* vibrate
振奋 zhènfèn *v* stimulate, excite
令人振奋的消息 lìngrén zhènfèn de xiāoxi exciting news
振兴 zhènxīng *v* promote, develop

镇 zhèn **I** *n* rural town **II** *v* suppress
镇定 zhèndìng *adj* composed, calm
镇定剂 zhèndìng jì sedative (a medicine)
镇静 zhènjìng *adj* calm, composed □ 遇到危险, 千万要保持镇静。 **Yùdào wēixiǎn, qiānwàn yào bǎochí zhènjìng.** *Be sure to keep calm when in danger.*
镇痛 zhèntòng [v+obj: 镇 calm + 痛 pain] **I** *v* ease pain **II** *n* analgesia
镇痛药 zhèntòngyào analgesic medicine, pain-killer
镇压 zhènyā [comp: 镇 suppress + 压 press] *v* suppress, put down

震 zhèn *v* shake
地震 dìzhèn earthquake
震荡 zhèndàng [v+compl: 震 shake + 荡 sway] *v* vibrate
震动 zhèndòng [v+compl: 震 shake + 动 move] *v* shake, quake
震惊 zhènjīng [v+compl: 震 shake + 惊 be surprised] *v* be greatly surprised, be shocked

正 zhēng as in 正月 zhēngyuè
正月 zhēngyuè *n* the first month of the lunar year

蒸 zhēng *v* steam □ 馒头刚蒸好, 快来吃吧! **Mántou gāng zhēng hǎo, kuài lái chība!** *The steamed buns are just ready, come and eat them!*
蒸发 zhēngfā [comp: 蒸 steam + 发 give off] *v* evaporate
蒸汽 zhēngqì *n* steam
蒸汽机 zhēngqì jī [modif: 蒸气 steam + 机 machine] *n* steam engine
蒸气浴 zhēngqì yù [modif: 蒸气 steam + 浴 bath] *n* sauna

挣 zhēng as in 挣扎 zhēngzhá
挣扎 zhēngzhá *v* struggle desperately

征 zhēng Trad 徵 *v* solicit
征求 zhēngqiú [comp: 征 solicit + 求 request] *v* solicit, ask for □ 老师征求学生对教学的意见。 **Lǎoshī zhēngqiú xuésheng duì jiàoxué de yìjiàn.** *The teachers solicit students' comments on their teaching.*

争 zhēng *v* **1** strive **2** argue □ 别争了, 争到明天也争不出结果来。 **Bié zhēng le, zhēng dào míngtiān yě zhēng bu chū jiéguǒ lai.** *Stop arguing. Even if you argue till tomorrow there will be no conclusion.*
争论 zhēnglùn [comp: 争 argue + 论 comment] *v* dispute, debate □ 他喜欢和朋友争论哲学问题。 **Tā xǐhuan hé péngyou zhēnglùn zhéxué wèntí.** *He likes to debate philosophical issues with his friends.*
争气 zhēngqì *v* work hard to win honor
为父母争气 wèi fùmǔ zhēngqì work hard to win honor for one's parents
争取 zhēngqǔ [comp: 争 strive + 取 obtain] *v* strive for, fight for □ 我们争取提前完成计划。 **Wǒmen zhēngqǔ tíqián wánchéng jìhuà.** *We strive to fulfill the plan ahead of schedule.*
争议 zhēngyì *n* dispute
有争议的问题 yǒu zhēngyì de wèntí issue in dispute, a controversial matter

筝 zhēng *n* **1** a musical instrument, zheng **2** kite
风筝 fēngzheng kite

睁 zhēng *v* open (the eyes) □ 奇怪, 这个人怎么睁着眼睛睡觉? **Qíguài, zhège rén zěnme zhēngzhe yǎnjing shuìjiào?** *Strange, how is it that this person sleeps with his eyes open?* □ 对这种行为, 不能睁一只眼, 闭一只眼。 **Duì zhè zhǒng xíngwéi, bù néng zhēng yì zhī yǎn, bì yì zhī yǎn.** *We must not turn a blind eye to such behavior.*

整 1 zhěng *adj* whole, full, entire □ 她昨天整夜没睡。 **Tā zuótiān zhěngyè méi shuì.** *She didn't sleep the entire night.* □ 他整天都在写那份报告。 **Tā zhěngtiān dōu zài xiě nà fèn bàogào.** *He spent the whole day writing that report.* □ 雨下了整整两天两夜。 **Yǔ xiàle zhěngzhěng liǎng tiān liǎng yè.** *It rained incessantly for two days and two nights.*
整个 zhěngge *adj* whole, entire □ 整个工程都是他负责。 **Zhěngge gōngchéng dōu shì tā fùzé.** *He is in charge of the entire project.*
整数 zhěngshù *n* (in maths) whole number, integer
整体 zhěngtǐ *n* whole, entirety, (something) as a whole
从整体上说 cóng zhěngtǐ shàng shuō on the whole
整天 zhěngtiān *n* the whole day, all the time
整天抱怨 zhěngtiān bàoyuàn grumble all the time
整整 zhěngzhěng *adj* whole, full
整整一个星期 zhěngzhěng yí ge xīngqī a full week, the entire week

整 2 zhěng **I** *adj* in good order, neat, tidy **II** *v* put in order
整顿 zhěngdùn *v* put in order, improve, re-organize
整顿纪律 zhěngdùn jìlǜ enforce discipline
整洁 zhěngjié [comp: 整 tidy + 洁 clean] *adj* clean and tidy
整理 zhěnglǐ [comp: 整 put in order + 理 tidy up] *v* put in order, tidy up □ 客人来前, 整理一下房间。 **Kèren lái qián, zhěnglǐ yíxià fángjiān.** *Tidy up the rooms before guests arrive.*
整齐 zhěngqí [comp: 整 neat + 齐 orderly] *adj* in good order, neat and tidy (antonym 乱 **luàn**)
整整齐齐 zhěng-zhěng-qí-qí (an emphatic form of 整齐 zhěngqí) □ 十几双鞋排得整整齐齐。 **Shí jǐ shuāng xié páide zhěng-zhěng-qí-qí.** *Over a dozen pairs of shoes were arranged in a very orderly way.*

正 zhèng I *adj* 1 straight, upright (antonym 歪 **wāi**, 斜 **xié**) □ 帮我看看，这幅画挂得正不正? **Bāng wǒ kànkan, zhè fú huà guà de zhèng bu zhèng?** *Have a look to see if this picture is hung straight.* 2 standard, normal, regular II *adv* Same as 正在 **zhèngzài**

正常 zhèngcháng [comp: 正 straight + 常 usual] *adj* normal, regular (antonym 反常 **fǎncháng**) □ 这几天，车间里一切正常。**Zhè jǐ tiān, chējiān li yíqiè zhèngcháng.** *Everything is normal in the workshop these days.* □ 在正常的情况下，他一周给父母发一份电子邮件。**Zài zhèngcháng de qíngkuàng xià, tā yì zhōu gěi fùmǔ fā yí fèn diànzǐ yóujiàn.** *Under normal circumstances he sends his parents an e-mail once a week.*

正当 zhèngdāng *conj* just when, just as

正当 zhèngdàng *adj* proper, legitimate
正当权益 zhèngdàng quányì legitimate rights and interests

正规 zhèngguī *adj* regular, standard

正好 zhènghǎo [modif: 正 just + 好 good] I *adj* just right □ 我穿这双鞋正好。**Wǒ chuān zhè shuāng xié zhènghǎo.** *These shoes are just the right size for me.* □ 你来得正好，我正要找你呢。**Nǐ lái de zhènghǎo, wǒ zhèngyào zhǎo nǐ ne.** *You've come at the right moment; I was just looking for you.* II *adv* chance to, by coincidence □ 我正好那天下午没课，可以陪她进城。**Wǒ zhènghǎo nà tiān xiàwǔ méi kè, kěyǐ péi tā jìnchéng.** *It happened that I did not have class that afternoon, so I could go to town with her.*

正经 zhèngjing *adj* 1 decent, proper 2 serious, not frivolous
一本正经 yì běn zhèngjing in all seriousness, sanctimonious

正面 zhèngmiàn I *n* facade, the obverse side (antonym 反面 **fǎnmiàn**) II *adj* positive (antonym 负面 **fùmiàn**, 反面 **fǎnmiàn**)

正派 zhèngpài *adj* upright, decent
正派人 zhèngpàirén a decent person

正巧 zhèngqiǎo *adv* as it happens, just at the right moment

正确 zhèngquè [comp: 正 proper + 确 true] *adj* correct, accurate (antonym 错误 **cuòwù**) □ 你的回答不正确。**Nǐ de huídá bú zhèngquè.** *Your answer is not correct.* □ 你要听各方面的意见，才能形成正确的观点。**Nǐ yào tīng gè fāngmiàn de yìjiàn, cáinéng xíngchéng zhèngquè de guāndiǎn.** *You can form the correct viewpoint only after hearing out opinions from all sides.*

正式 zhèngshì [modif: 正 formal + 式 manner] *adj* formal, official □ 公司正式通知职工，明年一月起工资提高百分之十。**Gōngsī zhèngshì tōngzhī zhígōng, míngnián Yíyuè qǐ gōngzī tígāo bǎifēn zhī shí.** *The company has formally informed the staff that they will get a ten-percent raise starting next January.*

正在 zhèngzài *adv* (used before a verb to indicate the action is in progress) □ 他正在看电视。**Tā zhèngzài kàn diànshì.** *He's watching TV.*

正在…呢 zhèngzài...ne Same as 正在 **zhèngzài** but with a casual, friendly tone

证 zhèng Trad 證 *n* proof, certificate
身分证 shēnfen zhèng ID card
学生证 xuéshengzhèng student ID card

证件 zhèngjiàn [modif: 证 proof + 件 article] *n* paper or document proving one's identity, e.g a passport, an ID card □ 在国外旅行，一定要保管好自己的证件。**Zài guówài lǚxíng, yí dìng yào bǎoguǎn hǎo zìjǐ de zhèngjiàn.** *When you're traveling in a foreign country, you must take very good care of your personal papers.*

证据 zhèngjù *n* evidence, proof □ 说话要有证据。**Shuōhuà yào yǒu zhèngjù.** *When you make a claim, you must have evidence.*

证明 zhèngmíng [v+comp: 证 prove + 明 clear] I *v* prove, testify □ 事实证明，他的想法行不通。**Shìshí zhèngmíng, tā de xiǎngfǎ xíng bu tōng.** *Facts have proven that his ideas do not work.* II *n* certificate □ 你要请医生开一张病假证明。**Nǐ yào qǐng yīshēng kāi yì zhāng bìngjià zhèngmíng.** *You should ask your doctor to issue a certificate for medical leave.*
出证明 chū zhèngmíng issue a certificate
出生证明 chūshēng zhèngmíng birth certificate

证书 zhèngshū *n* certificate (份 **fèn**, 张 **zhāng**)
毕业证书 bìyè zhèngshū diploma
结婚证书 jiéhūn zhèngshū marriage license, marriage certificate

政 zhèng *n* governance, government

政变 zhèngbiàn [modif: 政 government + 变 change] *n* coup d'etat

政策 zhèngcè [modif: 政 government + 策 policy] *n* government policy □ 政府的移民政策可能会变化。**Zhèngfǔ de yímín zhèngcè kěnéng huì biànhuà.** *The government immigration policy may change.*

政党 zhèngdǎng *n* political party

政府 zhèngfǔ [modif: 政 governance + 府 building] *n* government □ 政府有关部门正在研究这个问题。**Zhèngfǔ yǒuguān bùmén zhèngzài yánjiū zhège wèntí.** *The government departments concerned are studying this issue.*

政权 zhèngquán [modif: 政 political + 权 power] *n* 1 political power 2 government, regime □ 军人发动政变，建立了新政权。**Jūnrén fādòng zhèngbiàn, jiànlì le xīn zhèngquán.** *Soldiers launched a coup d'etat, and established a new government.*

政治 zhèngzhì [comp: 政 governance + 治 administering] *n* politics, governance □ 我对这个国家的政治情况不了解。**Wǒ duì zhège guójiā de zhèngzhì qíngkuàng liǎojiě bù duō.** *I don't know much about the political situation in this country.* □ 现代政治一定是民主的政治。**Xiàndài zhèngzhì yídìng shì mínzhǔ de zhèngzhì.** *Modern governance must be democratic.*

症 zhèng *n* disease
急症 jízhèng acute disease, (medical) emergency
急症室 jízhèng shì emergency room (ER)

症状 zhèngzhuàng *n* symptom

挣 zhèng *v* work to earn (money)
挣钱养活全家 zhèngqián yǎnghuo quánjiā work to earn money so as to provide for the family

郑 zhèng Trad 鄭 as in 郑重 **zhèngzhòng**

郑重 zhèngzhòng *adj* solemn, serious

之 zhī *particle* Same as 的 **de**. Used in written Chinese or certain set expressions.

之后 zhī hòu *n* after, behind □ 他退休之后，要搬到故乡去住。**Tā tuìxiū zhī hòu, yào bāndào gùxiāng qù zhù.** *After his retirement he will move to his hometown.*

之间 zhī jiān *n* between □ 两座大楼之间有一座小公园。 **Liǎng zuò dàlóu zhī jiān yǒu yí zuò xiǎo gōngyuán.** *There is a small park between the two buildings.* □ 我们之间存在着一些误会。 **Wǒmen zhī jiān cúnzàizhe yìxiē wùhuì.** *There is some misunderstanding between us.*

之前 zhī qián *n* before □ 你要在六月之前给我回信。 **Nǐ yào zài Liùyuè zhī qián gěi wǒ huíxìn.** *You should give me a reply before June.*

之外 zhī wài *n* outside, apart from □ 地球之外，还有其他地方有生命吗？ **Dìqiú zhī wài, háiyǒu qítā dìfang yǒu shēngmìng ma?** *Apart from Earth, is there life anywhere else?*

之下 zhī xià *n* below, under □ 三层楼之下是一个大餐厅。 **Sān-céng-lóu zhī xià shì yí ge dà cāntīng.** *Below the third floor is a large restaurant.*

之一 zhī yī *n* one of □ 杭州是中国名胜之一。 **Hángzhōu shì Zhōngguó míngshèng zhī yī.** *Hangzhou is one of China's tourist attractions.*

之中 zhī zhōng *n* between, among □ 她的朋友之中，没有人会说中文。 **Tā de péngyou zhī zhōng, méiyou rén huì shuō Zhōngwén.** *There is none among her friends who speaks Chinese.*

芝 zhī as in 芝麻 **zhīma**
芝麻 zhīma *n* sesame (粒 **lì**)

支 1 zhī I *v* 1 prop up, sustain 2 send away II *n* branch

支部 zhībù [comp: 支 branch + 部 part] *n* branch (of a political party)

支撑 zhīchēng [comp: 支 prop up + 撑 prop up] *v* prop up, shore up

支持 zhīchí [comp: 支 prop up, support + 持 hold] *v* support □ 同事之间要相互合作，相互支持。 **Tóngshì zhī jiān yào xiānghù hézuò, xiānghù zhīchí.** *Colleagues should cooperate and support each other.*

支出 zhīchū I *v* pay, expend II *n* expenditure, expenses

支付 zhīfù *v* pay □ 我可以用信用卡支付吗？ **Wǒ kěyǐ yòng xìnyòngkǎ zhīfù ma?** *Can I pay by credit card?*

支流 zhīliú [modif: 支 branch + 流 flow] *n* tributary

支配 zhīpèi *v* 1 allocate, arrange 合理支配有限的资金 hélǐ zhīpèi yǒuxiàn de zījīn rationally allocate limited funds 2 control, determine

支票 zhīpiào *n* (in banking) check, cheque (张 **zhāng**) 兑现支票 duìxiàn zhīpiào cash a check

支援 zhīyuán [comp: 支 prop up, support + 援 aid] I *v* support, aid □ 全国支援受灾地区。 **Quánguó zhīyuán shòuzāi dìqū.** *The whole country aided the disaster-stricken region.* II *n* aid, support □ 感谢你们给我们的宝贵支援。 **Gǎnxiè nǐmen gěi wǒmen de bǎoguì zhīyuán.** *Our thanks for your precious aid.*

支柱 zhīzhù [comp: 支 prop + 柱 column] *n* mainstay, pillar

支 2 zhī *measure wd* (for stick-like things) 一支笔 yì zhī bǐ a pen

枝 zhī *n* twig, branch (根 **gēn**)

肢 zhī *n* limb 上肢 shàngzhī upper limbs 下肢 xiàzhī lower limbs

只 zhī Trad 隻 *measure wd* (for animals, utensils, objects normally occurring in pairs, etc.) 一只手 yì zhī shǒu a hand 两只狗 liǎng zhī gǒu two dogs

知 zhī *v* know, be aware of
知道 zhīdào *v* know □ 我不知道这件事。 **Wǒ bù zhīdào zhè jiàn shì.** *I don't know about this matter.* □ 你知道这家公司的传真号码吗？ **Nǐ zhīdào zhè jiā gōngsī de chuánzhēn hàomǎ ma?** *Do you know the fax number of this company?*

知觉 zhījué [comp: 知 know + 觉 be aware] *n* consciousness, senses

知识 zhīshi *n* knowledge □ 旅行使人学到知识。 **Lǚxíng shǐ rén xuédao zhīshi.** *Traveling enables one to learn knowledge.* □ 他这一方面的知识很丰富。 **Tā zhè yì fāngmiàn de zhīshi hěn fēngfù.** *He has rich knowledge in this aspect.*

知识经济 zhīshi jīngjì knowledge economy

蜘 zhī as in 蜘蛛 **zhīzhū**
蜘蛛 zhīzhū *n* spider (只 **zhī**)
蜘蛛网 zhīzhūwǎng spider web

脂 zhī *n* fat, grease
脂肪 zhīfáng *n* fat

汁 zhī *n* juice
果汁 guǒzhī fruit juice

织 zhī Trad 織 *v* weave (See 纺织 **fǎngzhī**, 组织 **zǔzhī**.)

执 zhī Trad 執 *v* 1 grasp, persist 2 take charge, manage

执法 zhīfǎ [v+obj: 执 manage + 法 law] *v* enforce the law

执行 zhīxíng *v* carry out, implement, execute □ 坚决执行上级交给我们的任务。 **Jiānjué zhīxíng shàngjí jiāo gei wǒmen de rènwù.** *We will resolutely carry out the mission entrusted to us by the higher authorities.* □ 这个计划很难执行。 **Zhège jìhuà hěn nán zhíxíng.** *This plan is difficult to implement.*

执行总公司的指示 zhíxíng zǒnggōngsī de zhǐshì carry out instructions from the company HQ

执照 zhīzhào *n* license, permit 驾驶执照 jiàshǐ zhízhào driver's license 营业执照 yíngyè zhízhào business permit

执政 zhīzhèng [v+obj: 执 manage + 政 government] *v* (of a political party) govern, be in power 执政党 zhízhèngdǎng ruling party

直 zhí *adj* straight (antonym 弯 **wān**), direct □ 用尺划一条直线。 **Yòng chǐ huà yì tiáo zhí xiàn.** *Draw a straight line using a ruler.* □ 这班航机直飞香港，中间不停。 **Zhè bān hángjī zhí fēi Xiānggǎng, zhōngjiān bù tíng.** *This airliner flies direct to Hong Kong without any stopover.*

直达 zhídá *adv* nonstop, through □ 这次航班直达纽约。 **Zhècì hángbān zhídá Niǔyuē.** *This flight goes nonstop to New York.*

直到 zhídào [modif: 直 straight + 到 arrive] *prep* until, till □ 孩子们在花园里玩，直到天黑。 **Háizimen zài huāyuán li wán, zhídào tiānhēi.** *The children played in the garden till it was dark.* □ 他一直住在家乡，直到念完中学。 **Tā yìzhí zhù zai jiāxiāng, zhídào niànwán zhōngxué.** *He lived in his hometown until he had finished high school.*

直接 zhíjiē [modif: 直 direct + 接 join] *adj* direct □ 你可以直接找房东，不用通过中间人。 **Nǐ kěyǐ zhíjiē zhǎo fángdōng, bú yòng tōngguò zhōngjiānrén.** *You*

can make direct contact with the landlord without going through the middleman.

直径 **zhíjìng** *n* diameter

直辖市 **zhíxiáshì** *n* metropolis under the direct jurisdiction of the central government (the metropolises of Beijing, Shanghai, Tianjin and Chongqing)

直线 **zhíxiàn** *n* straight line (条 **tiáo**)

直至 **zhízhì** *conj* until

值 **zhí** I *n* value II *v* 1 be worth □ 这辆旧车大约还值两千元。**Zhè liàng jiùchē dàyuē hái zhí liǎngqiān yuán.** *This old car probably is still worth 2,000 yuan.* 2 be on duty

值班 **zhíbān** *v* be on duty

值得 **zhíde** *v* be worth □ 为了这件小事生气, 不值得。**Wèile zhè jiàn xiǎoshì shēngqì, bù zhíde.** *Such a small matter is not worth getting angry over.* □ 这本词典虽然不便宜, 还是值得买。**Zhè běn cídiǎn suīrán bù piányi, háishí zhíde mǎi.** *Although this dictionary is not cheap, it is worth buying.*

植 **zhí** *v* plant, grow

植物 **zhíwù** [modif: 植 plant + 物 thing] *n* plant, flora □ 这种植物很少见, 应该受到保护。**Zhè zhǒng zhíwù hěn shǎojiàn, yīnggāi shòudào bǎohù.** *This plant is rare and should be protected.*

植物学 **zhíwùxué** [modif: 植物 plant + 学 study] *n* botany

植物学家 **zhíwùxuéjiā** botanist

植物园 **zhíwùyuán** [modif: 植物 plant + 园 garden] *n* botanical garden

殖 **zhí** *v* breed

殖民 **zhímín** *v* colonize

殖民地 **zhímíndì** colony

殖民主义 **zhímín zhǔyì** colonialism

侄 **zhí** *n* one's brother's child

侄女 **zhínǚ** *n* one's brother's daughter

侄子 **zhízi** *n* one's brother's son

职 **zhí** Trad 職 *n* job, profession, office

职称 **zhíchēng** *n* professional title

职工 **zhígōng** [comp: 职 clerk + 工 worker] *n* staff (of a factory, a company, an enterprise, etc.), employee(s) □ 我们公司总共有一千八百五十名职工。**Wǒmen gōngsī zǒnggòng yǒu yìqiān bābǎi wǔshí míng zhígōng.** *Our company has 1,850 employees in total.*

职能 **zhínéng** *n* function

职权 **zhíquán** *n* authority of office

职务 **zhíwù** *n* official duties and obligations, post

职业 **zhíyè** [comp: 职 job + 业 occupation] *n* occupation, profession, vocation □ 他的职业是医生, 也是一位业余作家。**Tā de zhíyè shì yīshēng, yě shì yí wèi yèyú zuòjiā.** *He is a doctor by profession but he is also a writer in his spare time.*

职业病 **zhíyèbìng** *n* occupational disease

职业介绍所 **zhíyè jièshàosuǒ** *n* employment agency

职员 **zhíyuán** *n* office worker, clerk (名 **míng**)

止 **zhǐ** *v* stop (pain, cough, thirst, etc.) □ 这个止痛药有没有副作用? **Zhège zhǐtòngyào yǒu méiyǒu fùzuòyòng?** *Does this painkiller have any side effects?*

只 **zhǐ** Trad 祇 *adv* only □ 我只有一个弟弟, 没有哥哥, 也没有姐妹。**Wǒ zhǐ yǒu yí ge dìdi, méiyǒu gēge, yě méiyǒu jiě-mèi.** *I've only got a younger brother. I don't have an elder brother or any sister.* □ 她只喝

水, 不喝酒。**Tā zhǐ hē shuǐ, bù hē jiǔ.** *She only drinks water and does not drink wine.*

只得 **zhǐděi** *v* have got to, have to
只得照他说的做 **zhǐděi zhào tā shuōde zuò** have got no choice but do as he told

只顾 **zhǐgù** *v* care only about, be absorbed in
只顾赚钱 **zhǐgù zhuànqián** only care about making money

只管 **zhǐguǎn** *v* do as you wish, do not hesitate to □ 有事只管来找我。**Yǒushì zhǐguǎn lái zhǎo wǒ.** *Do not hesitate to come to me if you've any problems.*

只好 **zhǐhǎo** *adv* have no choice but □ 他自行车坏了, 只好走路去上学。**Tā zìxíngchē huài le, zhǐhǎo zǒu lù qù shàngxué.** *His bicycle has broken down, so he has to walk to school.* □ 飞机票全卖完了, 我们只好坐火车去。**Fēijī piào quán màiwánle, wǒmen zhǐhǎo zuò huǒchē qù.** *As air tickets were sold out we had no choice but go by train.*

只是 **zhǐshì** *adv* only, just □ 她只是想学几句旅游中文。**Tā zhǐshì xiǎng xué jǐ jù lǚyóu Zhōngwén.** *She only wants to learn some tourist Chinese.* □ 他在饭店打工, 只是因为一时找不到更合适的工作。**Tā zài fàndiàn dǎgōng, zhǐshì yīnwèi yìshí zhǎo bu dào gèng héshì de gōngzuò.** *He worked in a restaurant only because he could not find a more suitable job at that time.* □ 我很想认真了解中国的历史, 只是没有时间。**Wǒ hěn xiǎng rènzhēn liǎojiě Zhōngguó de lìshǐ, zhǐshì méiyǒu shíjiān.** *I'd like to learn Chinese history earnestly, it's just that I don't have the time.* □ 她很想去听音乐会, 只是买不起门票。**Tā hěn xiǎng qù tīng yīnyuèhuì, zhǐshì mǎi bu qǐ ménpiào.** *She wants to go to the concert badly, but unfortunately she can't afford the ticket.*

只要 **zhǐyào** *conj* so long as, provided that, if only □ 只要身体好, 就能享受生活。**Zhǐyào shēntǐ hǎo, jiù néng xiǎngshòu shēnghuó.** *As long as you are in good health, you can enjoy life.* □ 只要打一个电话, 饭店就会马上把菜送来。**Zhǐyào dǎ yí ge diànhuà, fàndiàn jiù huì mǎshàng bǎ cài sònglai.** *You only need to give the restaurant a call and they will deliver your order immediately.*

只有 **zhǐyǒu** I *adv* can only, have no choice but □ 既然答应帮助他, 只有尽力而为了。**Jìrán dāying bāngzhù tā, zhǐyǒu jìn lì ér wéi le.** *Now that I've promised to help him, I can only do my best.* II *conj* only, only if □ 只有认真地学, 才能学好中文。**Zhǐyǒu rènzhēn de xué, cáinéng xuéhǎo Zhōngwén.** *Only if you study in earnest, can you gain a good command of Chinese.* □ 只有经理亲自道歉, 顾客才会满意。**Zhǐyǒu jīnglǐ qīnzì dàoqiàn, gùkè cáihuì mǎnyì.** *Only if the manager himself apologizes, will the customer be satisfied.*

指 I **zhǐ** I *n* finger
手指 **shǒuzhǐ** finger (根 **gēn**, 个 **gè**)
II *v* 1 point at, point to □ 你不知道那东西叫什么, 就用手指。**Nǐ bù zhīdào nà dōngxi jiào shénme, jiù yòng shǒu zhǐ.** *If you don't know what it's called, just point at it with your finger.* □ 他指着自己的鼻子说, "就是我。" **Tā zhǐzhe zìjǐ de bízi shuō, "Jiù shì wǒ."** *Pointing at his own nose, he said, "It's me." 2 refer to, allude to, mean □ 他说有人些工作不负责, 不知道是指谁。**Tā shuō yǒuxiē rén gōngzuò bú fùzé, bù zhīdào shì zhǐ shuí.** *I don't know to whom he was referring*

when he said some people were not responsible in their work.

指头〈**手指头**〉**zhǐtou (shǒuzhítou)** *n* Same as 手指 **shǒuzhǐ**

指标 zhǐbiāo *n* target, quota

指出 zhǐchū [v+obj: 指 point + 出 out] *v* point out □ 老师指出了我发音中的问题。**Lǎoshī zhǐchūle wǒ fāyīn zhōng de wèntí.** *The teacher pointed out the problems in my pronunciation.* □ 这篇文章指出, 社会必须照顾弱者。**Zhè piān wénzhāng zhǐchū, shèhuì bìxū zhàogù ruòzhě.** *This article points out that society must take care of the weak.*

指甲 zhǐjia *n* fingernail
  修指甲 xiū zhǐjia do fingernails, manicure fingernails

指 2 zhǐ *v* **1** guide, refer to **2** reply on, count on
  指导 zhǐdǎo [comp: 指 point + 导 guide] *v* guide, direct, supervise □ 工程师指导技术员修理机器。**Gōngchéngshī zhǐdǎo jìshùyuán xiūlǐ jīqì.** *The engineer supervised technicians in repairing the machine.*

指导员 zhǐdǎoyuán *n* political instructor (in the Chinese People's Liberation Army)

指导思想 zhǐdǎo sīxiǎng *n* guiding principle

指定 zhǐdìng *v* appoint, designate
  指定法律代表 zhǐdìng fǎlǜ dàibiǎo appoint a legal representative

指挥 zhǐhuī *v* command, direct, conduct
  指挥部 zhǐhuībù headquarters

指令 zhǐlìng *n* instruction, order

指明 zhǐmíng *v* point out, show clearly

指南针 zhǐnánzhēn *n* compass

指示 zhǐshì **I** *v* **1** instruct **2** indicate **II** *n* **1** instruction **2** indication

指数 zhǐshù *n* index
  琼斯指数 Dào Qióngsī zhǐshù Dow Jones Index

指望 zhǐwàng *v* count on, expect □ 别指望他会来帮助你。**Bié zhǐwàng tā huì lái bāngzhù nǐ.** *Don't count on his help.*

指针 zhǐzhēn *n* (needle) indicator, pointer

纸 zhǐ Trad 紙 *n* paper (张 **zhāng**) □ 请给我几张纸。**Qǐng gěi wǒ jǐ zhāng zhǐ.** *Please give me some paper.* □ 纸是古代中国人发明的。**Zhǐ shì gǔdài Zhōngguórén fāmíng de.** *Paper was invented by the ancient Chinese.*

纸张 zhǐzhāng *n* paper

址 zhǐ *n* location (See 地址 **dìzhǐ**)

旨 zhǐ *n* purpose (See 宗旨 **zōngzhǐ**)

挚 zhì *adj* sincere (See 诚挚 **chéngzhì**)

至 zhì *prep* to, until (only used in written Chinese) □ 银行营业时间是上午九时至下午五时。**Yínháng yíngyè shíjiān shì shàngwǔ jiǔ shí zhì xiàwǔ wǔ shí.** *The business hours of the bank are from nine in the morning till five in the afternoon.*

至多 zhìduō *adv* at most, maximum

至今 zhìjīn [v+obj: 至 to, until + 今 today] *adv* till now, to this day, so far □ 至今已有七十多人报名学习中文。**Zhìjīn yǐ yǒu qīshí duō rén bàomíng xuéxí Zhōngwén.** *So far over seventy people have applied to study Chinese.* □ 我至今还不明白她为什么突然离家。

Wǒ zhìjīn hái bù míngbai tā wèishénme tūrán líjiā. *To this day I still do not understand why she left home all of a sudden.*

至少 zhìshǎo *adv* at least, minimum □ 我今年学了至少三百个汉字。**Wǒ jīnnián xuéle zhìshǎo sānbǎi ge Hànzì.** *I have learned at least 300 Chinese characters this year.* □ 孩子至少懂得了为什么不应该说假话。**Háizi zhìshǎo dǒngdele wèishénme bù yīnggāi shuō jiǎhuà.** *At least the child has understood why one should not tell lies.*

至于 zhìyú *conj* as to, as for

志 1 zhì Trad 誌 *n* record (See 杂志 **zázhì**.)

志 2 zhì *n* will, aspiration
  志气 zhìqì *n* aspiration, ambition
  有志气 yǒu zhìqì have lofty aspirations

志愿 zhìyuàn **I** *v* volunteer
  志愿者 zhìyuànzhě volunteer (a person)
II *n* wish, ideal

致 zhì *v* **1** send, extend **2** devote (time, efforts, etc)

致词 zhìcí *v* make a (short formal) speech

致富 zhìfù *v* become rich
  勤劳致富 qínláo zhìfù become rich by working hard

致敬 zhìjìng *v* salute

治 zhì *v* **1** treat (disease) □ 医生的责任是治病救人。**Yīshēng de zérèn shì zhì bìng jiù rén.** *It is the responsibility of a doctor to treat diseases and save lives.* □ 他的病恐怕治不好了。**Tā de bìng kǒngpà zhì bu hǎo le.** *I'm afraid his disease cannot be cured.*
2 rule, govern

治安 zhì'ān *n* public order, public security □ 新加坡的治安情况很不错。**Xīnjiāpō de zhì'ān qíngkuàng hěn búcuò.** *The public security situation in Singapore is not bad.* (→ *Singapore is orderly and has low crime rates.*)

治理 zhìlǐ *v* govern, administrate

治疗 zhìliáo **I** *v* treat (a patient, a disease) **II** *n* medical treatment □ 治疗无效。**Zhìliáo wúxiào.** *Medical treatment failed*

制 zhì Trad 製 *v* **1** make, work out **2** control, restrict

制裁 zhìcái *n* sanction
  制裁那个国家 zhìcái nàge guójiā establish sanction against that country

制定 zhìdìng [comp: 制 work out + 定 decide] *v* lay down, draw up □ 他们在每年年底制定第二年的计划。**Tāmen zài měi nián niándǐ zhìdìng dì-èr nián de jìhuà.** *They draw up the plan for the next year at the end of a year.*

制度 zhìdù *n* system □ 目前的教育制度存在很多问题。**Mùqián de jiàoyù zhìdù cúnzài hěn duō wèntí.** *There are many problems in the current educational system.*

制服 zhìfú *n* uniform (件 **jiàn**, 套 **tào**)

制品 zhìpǐn *n* products
  乳制品 rǔzhìpǐn dairy product

制约 zhìyuē *v* constrain, restrain
  受条件的制约 shòu tiáojiàn de zhìyuē constrained by one's circumstances

制造 zhìzào [comp: 制 make + 造 make] *v* make, manufacture □ "中国制造" 的商品越来越多。**"Zhōngguó zhìzào" de shāngpǐn yuèláiyuè duō.** *There are*

more and more goods labeled "Made in China." □ 五年以前这家工厂制造自行车，现在制造摩托车。**Wǔ nián yǐqián zhè jiā gōngchǎng zhìzào zìxíngchē, xiànzài zhìzào mótuōchē.** *Five years ago this factory made bicycles, and now it manufactures motorcycles.*
制造业 zhìzàoyè manufacturing industry
制止 **zhìzhǐ** *v* stop, curb

帜 **zhì** Trad 幟 *n* banner (See 旗帜 **qízhì**)

质 **zhì** Trad 質 *n* nature, character
质变 **zhìbiàn** *n* qualitative change (antonym 量变 **liàngbiàn**)
质量 **zhìliàng** *n* quality (antonym 数量 **shùliàng**) □ 这个牌子的汽车质量好，价格又便宜。**Zhège páizi de qìchē zhìliàng hǎo, jiàgé yòu piányi.** *Cars of this make are of good quality and inexpensive.* □ 你觉得这种产品的质量如何？**Nǐ juéde zhè zhǒng chǎnpǐn de zhìliàng rúhé?** *How do you find the quality of this product?*
质朴 **zhìpǔ** *adj* unaffected, ingenuous

秩 **zhì** *n* order, rank
秩序 **zhìxù** [comp: 秩 order + 序 order] *n* order, proper sequence □ 运动场内秩序良好。**Yùndòngchǎng nèi zhìxù liánghǎo.** *In the stadium the audience maintains good order.*

置 **zhì** *v* place, put (See 布置 **bùzhì**)

掷 **zhì** Trad 擲 *v* throw, hurl

智 **zhì** *adj* wise, intelligent
智者 zhìzhě wise man
智慧 **zhìhuì** *n* wisdom, intelligence
智力 **zhìlì** [modif: 智 intelligent + 力 power] *n* intelligence, intellect
智力发达 zhìlì fādá highly intelligent
智谋 **zhìmóu** [comp: 智 intelligence + 谋 scheme] *n* tactic, clever scheme
智能 **zhìnéng** [modif: 智 intelligent + 能 ability] *n* intelligence and capability
人工智能 réngōng zhìnéng artificial intelligence
智商 **zhìshāng** *n* intelligence quotient (IQ)

稚 **zhì** *adj* childish (See 幼稚 **yòuzhì**)

滞 **zhì** *v* stagnate (See 停滞 **tíngzhì**)

终 **zhōng** Trad 終 *n* end, finish
终点 **zhōngdiǎn** *n* end point, destination
终端 **zhōngduān** [modif: 终 end + 端 extreme] *n* terminal
终究 **zhōngjiū** *adv* after all, in the end
终年 **zhōngnián** *adv* all the year round, throughout the year
终身 **zhōngshēn** *adj* all one's life, lifelong □ 王医生把终身献给了医疗事业。**Wáng yīshēng bǎ zhōngshēn xiàngěile yīliáo shìyè.** *Dr Wang gave all his life to medicine.*
终生大事 zhōngshēng dàshì marriage
终于 **zhōngyú** *adv* finally, at last □ 他终于实现了自己的愿望。**Tā zhōngyú shíxiànle zìjǐ de yuànwàng.** *He finally realized his aspirations.* □ 我终于找到了他的家。**Wǒ zhōngyú zhǎodàole tā de jiā.** *I finally found his home.*
终止 **zhōngzhǐ** *v* terminate, end

中 **zhōng** I *n* center, middle
东南西北中 dōng, nán, xī, běi, zhōng the east, the south, the west, the north and the center II *adj* 1 middle, medium 2 Chinese
中餐 **zhōngcān** [modif: 中 Chinese + 餐 meal] *n* Chinese cuisine, Chinese food □ 我们用中餐招待客人。**Wǒmen yòng zhōngcān zhāodài kèren.** *We entertain guests with Chinese food.*
中餐馆 zhōngcānguǎn Chinese restaurant
中餐厅 zhōngcāntīng Chinese restaurant (in a hotel, etc.)
中国 **Zhōngguó** [modif: 中 middle, central + 国 kingdom, country] *n* China □ 中国历史长，人口多。**Zhōngguó lìshǐ cháng, rénkǒu duō.** *China has a long history and a large population.*
中华 **Zhōnghuá** *n* China, Chinese □ 中华文明对东亚各国有很大影响。**Zhōnghuá wénmíng duì Dōng-Yà gè guó yǒu hěn dà yǐngxiǎng.** *Chinese civilization has had great influence on countries in East Asia.*

NOTE: Both 中国 **Zhōngguó** and 中华 **Zhōnghuá** may refer to *China*, but 中华 **Zhōngghuá** has historical and cultural connotations

中间 **zhōngjiān** I *n* center, middle □ 花园的中间有一棵大树。**Huāyuán de zhōngjiān yǒu yì kē dà shù.** *In the center of the garden there is a very big tree.* II *prep* among □ 我的朋友中间，他体育最好。**Wǒ de péngyou zhōngjiān, tā tǐyù zuì hǎo.** *Among my friends he is the best athlete.*
中立 **zhōnglì** *adj* neutral
中立国 zhōnglìguó a neutral state
中年 **zhōngnián** *n* middle age
中年人 zhōngniánrén middle-aged person
中秋节 **Zhōngqiūjié** *n* Mid-Autumn Festival (the fifteenth day of the eighth lunar month)
中途 **zhōngtú** *n* halfway, mid-way
中文 **Zhōngwén** [modif: 中 China + 文 writing] *n* the Chinese language (especially the writing) □ 世界上有十几亿人用中文。**Shìjiè shang yǒu shí jǐ yì rén yòng Zhōngwén.** *Over a billion people in the world use Chinese.*

NOTE: See note on 汉语 **Hànyǔ**.

中午 **zhōngwǔ** [modif: 中 middle + 午 noon] *n* noon □ 我们中午休息一个小时。**Wǒmen zhōngwǔ xiūxi yí ge xiǎoshí.** *We have a one-hour break at noon.*
中心 **zhōngxīn** [modif: 中 central + 心 heart] *n* central part, center □ 城市的中心是一座大公园。**Chéngshì de zhōngxīn shì yí zuò dà gōngyuán.** *There is a big park in the center of the city.* □ 他讲话的中心思想是必须保证产品的质量。**Tā jiǎnghuà de zhōngxīn sīxiǎng shì bìxū bǎozhèng chǎnpǐn de zhìliàng.** *The central idea of his speech is that product quality must be guaranteed.*
市中心 shìzhōngxīn city center
研究中心 yánjiū zhōngxīn research center
中型 **zhōngxíng** *adj* medium-sized
中学 **zhōngxué** [modif: 中 middle + 学 school] *n* secondary school, high school, middle school (座 **zuò**, 所 **suǒ**) □ 这座城市有十多所中学。**Zhè zuò chéng-**

shì yǒu shí duō suǒ zhōngxué. *This city has over ten secondary schools.* □ 在中国，中学分初中、高中两部分。**Zài Zhōngguó, zhōngxué fēn chūzhōng, gāozhōng liǎng bùfen.** *In China, high schools are divided into junior high and senior high.*

中药 **zhōngyào** [modif: 中 Chinese + 药 medicine, drug] *n* traditional Chinese medicine (e.g. herbs) □ 很多常见的植物都是有用的中药。**Hěn duō chángjiàn de zhíwù dōu shì yǒuyòng de zhōngyào.** *Many common plants are useful traditional Chinese medicine.*

中医 **zhōngyī** [modif: 中 Chinese + 医 medicine, medical science] *n* **1** traditional Chinese medicine (TCM) □ 中医和古代哲学思想有关。**Zhōngyī hé gǔdài zhéxué sīxiǎng yǒuguān.** *Traditional Chinese medicine is related to ancient Chinese philosophical thought.* **2** traditional Chinese medical doctor □ 你这个病可以请一位中医看看。**Nǐ zhège bìng kěyǐ qǐng yí wèi zhōngyī kànkan.** *You can consult a traditional Chinese doctor on your illness.*

中游 **zhōngyóu** *n* middle-reaches (of a river)

忠 **zhōng** *adj* loyal

忠诚 **zhōngchéng** [comp: 忠 loyal + 诚 sincere] *adj* loyal, faithful

忠实 **zhōngshí** *adj* loyal and faithful

忠于 **zhōngyú** *v* be loyal to
忠于祖国 **zhōngyú zǔguó** be loyal to one's motherland

忠贞 **zhōngzhēn** *adj* loyal (to one's country, spouse, etc.)

衷 **zhōng** *n* innermost feelings
言不由衷 **yánbùyóuzhōng** speak insincerely

衷心 **zhōngxīn** *adj* sincere, whole-hearted

钟 **zhōng** Trad 鐘 *n* clock (座 **zuò**) □ 这座钟慢了三分钟。**Zhè zuò zhōng mànle sān fēnzhōng.** *This clock is three minutes slow.*

钟表 **zhōngbiǎo** [comp: 钟 clock + 表 watch] *n* clocks and watches, time-piece
钟表店 **zhōngbiǎodiàn** watchmaker's shop

钟点 **zhōngdiǎn** *n* time, hour

钟点工 **zhōngdiǎngōng** Same as 小时工 **xiǎoshígōng**

钟楼 **zhōnglóu** *n* clock tower

钟头 **zhōngtóu** *n* Same as 小时 **xiǎoshí**. Used in spoken Chinese.

肿 **zhǒng** Trad 腫 *n* swell
肿瘤 **zhǒngliú** *n* tumor
恶性肿瘤 **èxìng zhǒngliú** malignant tumor, cancer
良性肿瘤 **liángxìng zhǒngliú** benign tumor

种 **zhǒng** Trad 種 **I** *measure wd* kind, sort, type □ 这里有三种酒，你想喝哪一种？**Zhèli yǒu sān zhǒng jiǔ, nǐ xiǎng hē nǎ yì zhǒng?** *Here are three kinds of wine. Which one would you like to drink?* □ 你最喜欢吃哪种水果？**Nǐ zuì xǐhuan chī nǎ zhǒng shuǐguǒ?** *What kind of fruit do you like best?*
各种各样 **gè zhǒng gè yàng** all sorts of, all kinds of
II *n* **1** seed, breed **2** racial group

种类 **zhǒnglèi** *n* kind, category

种种 **zhǒngzhǒng** *adj* all sorts of

种子 **zhǒngzi** [suffix: 种 seed + 子 nominal suffix] *n* seed □ 这家公司向农民提供各类优质种子。**Zhè jiā gōngsī xiàng nóngmín tígōng gè lèi yōuzhì zhǒngzi.** *This company provides farmers with all kinds of high quality seeds.*

种族 **zhǒngzú** *n* race
种族主义 **zhǒngzúzhǔyì** racism

种 **zhòng** Trad 種 *v* plant □ 爸爸在我家小花园里种了一些花。**Bàba zài wǒ jiā xiǎo huāyuán li zhòngle yìxiē huā.** *Dad planted some flowers in our little garden.*

种地 **zhòngdì** *v* grow crops, farm

种植 **zhòngzhí** *v* grow (crops)

重 **zhòng** *adj* **1** heavy (antonym 轻 **qīng**) □ 这个机器太重了，我们两个人搬不动。**Zhège jīqì tài zhòng le, wǒmen liǎng ge rén bān bu dòng.** *This machine is too heavy for the two of us to move.* □ 他把钱看得太重。**Tā bǎ qián kànde tài zhòng.** *He attaches too much importance to money.* **2** considerable in value or quantity

重大 **zhòngdà** [comp: 重 weighty + 大 big] *adj* major, great □ 去年国际上有哪些重大事件？**Qùnián guójì shang yǒu nǎxiē zhòngdà shìjiàn?** *What were the major international events last year?* □ 他在决定政策方面起重大作用。**Tā zài juédìng zhèngcè fāngmiàn qǐ zhòngdà zuòyòng.** *He played a major role in policy making.*

重点 **zhòngdiǎn** [comp: 重 weighty + 点 point] *n* main point, focal point, emphasis □ 中文一年级的学习重点应该是发音和口语。**Zhōngwén yì niánjí de xuéxí zhòngdiǎn yīnggāi shì fāyīn hé kǒuyǔ.** *The emphasis in first-year Chinese studies should be on pronunciation and spoken Chinese.* □ 我今年要把重点放在学习语法上。**Wǒ jīnnián yào bǎ zhòngdiǎn fàng zai xuéxí yǔfǎ shang.** *This year I will focus on the study of Chinese grammar.*

重工业 **zhònggōngyè** *n* heavy industry

重量 **zhòngliàng** [modif: 重 heavy + 量 amount] *n* weight □ 称一下这件行李的重量。**Chēng yíxià zhè jiàn xíngli de zhòngliàng.** *Weigh this piece of luggage to see how heavy it is.*

重视 **zhòngshì** [modif: 重 weighty + 视 view] *v* attach importance to, value □ 老年人一般比较重视身体健康。**Lǎoniánrén yìbān bǐjiào zhòngshì shēntǐ jiànkāng.** *Old people generally value good health.* □ 中国人一般重视子女的教育—主要是知识教育。**Zhōngguórén yìbān zhòngshì zǐnǚ de jiàoyù—zhǔyào shì zhīshi jiàoyù.** *Generally speaking, Chinese people attach much importance to their children's education—mainly knowledge education.*

重心 **zhòngxīn** *n* **1** center of gravity **2** focus, point of emphasis

重型 **zhòngxíng** *adj* heavy-duty

重要 **zhòngyào** [comp: 重 heavy + 要 (in this context) important] *adj* important □ 这件事非常重要，你别忘了！**Zhè jiàn shì fēicháng zhòngyào, nǐ bié wàng le!** *This matter is very important. Don't you forget it!* □ 我有一个重要的消息告诉你。**Wǒ yǒu yí ge zhòngyào de xiāoxi gàosu nǐ.** *I have important news to tell you.*

众 **zhòng** Trad 衆 **I** *n* crowd **II** *adj* numerous

众多 **zhòngduō** [comp: 众 numerous + 多 many] *adj* numerous

众人 **zhòngrén** *n* all the people, everybody

众议院 **Zhòngyìyuàn** *n* (U.S.) House of Representatives

舟 **zhōu** *n* boat

周 I **zhōu** I *n* 1 week □ "你们学校寒假放几周?" "三周。" **"Nǐmen xuéxiào hánjià fàng jǐ zhōu?" "Sān zhōu."** *"How many weeks of winter holiday does your school have?" "Three weeks."* 2 circumference, cycle II *adv* all around, all over

NOTES: (1) 周 **zhōu** and 星期 **xīngqī** both mean *week*, but 周 **zhōu** is usually used in writing only. Normally 星期 **xīngqī** is the word to use. (2) 周 **zhōu** is not used with any measure words.

周到 zhōudào [modif: 周 circumference, all sides + 到 reach] *adj* thorough, thoughtful □ 这个旅馆的服务很周到。**Zhège lǚguǎn de fúwù hěn zhōudào.** *This hotel provides thoughtful service.* □ 你们都准备好了,想得真周到。**Nǐmen dōu zhǔnbèi hǎole, xiǎngde zhēn zhōudào.** *It is really thoughtful of you to get everything ready.* □ 你接受新工作以前,要考虑得周到一点。**Nǐ jiēshòu xīn gōngzuò yǐqián, yào kǎolǜ de zhōudào yìdiǎn.** *You should think very carefully before you accept a new job.*

周密 zhōumì *adj* careful and thorough, attentive to every detail

周末 zhōumò [modif: 周 week + 末 end] *n* weekend □ 这个周末我要进城买衣服和鞋子。**Zhège zhōumò wǒ yào jìnchéng mǎi yīfu hé xiézi.** *This weekend I'll go to town to buy clothes and shoes.* □ "上个周末你过得好吗?" "过得很愉快。" **"Shàng ge zhōumò nǐ guòde hǎo ma?" "Guò de hěn yúkuài."** *"Did you have a good time last weekend?" "Yes, I had a very pleasant time."*

周年 zhōunián *n* anniversary
结婚十周年 jiéhūn shí zhōunián the tenth anniversary of one's wedding

周期 zhōuqī *n* cycle, period

周围 zhōuwéi [comp: 周 circuit + 围 encircle] *n* surrounding area, all around □ 新西兰周围都是大海。**Xīnxīlán zhōuwéi dōu shì dàhǎi.** *All around New Zealand is the sea.*

周折 zhōuzhé *n* twists and turns, setbacks

周转 zhōuzhuǎn *n* (of funds) flow, cash flow
周转不灵 zhōuzhuǎnbùlíng not have enough cash for business operation, have cashflow problems

周 2 **Zhōu** *n* a common family name
周先生/太太/小姐 Zhōu xiānsheng/tàitai/xiǎojiě Mr/Mrs/Miss Zhou

州 zhōu *n* 1 administrative district in ancient China 2 state (in the U.S.)
纽约州 Niǔyuēzhōu the State of New York

洲 zhōu *n* 1 island in a river 2 continent (See 大洋洲 Dàyángzhōu, 欧洲 Ōuzhōu, 亚洲 Yàzhōu.)

粥 zhōu *n* porridge, gruel
小米粥 xiǎomǐzhōu millet gruel
喝了半碗粥 hēle bàn wǎn zhōu ate half a bowl of gruel

皱 zhòu Trad 皺 *v* wrinkle, crease
皱纹 zhòuwén [comp: 皱 wrinkle + 纹 line] *n* wrinkle (on skin), lines

昼 zhòu *n* daytime
昼夜 zhòuyè [comp: 昼 day + 夜 night] *n* day and night, round the clock
昼夜服务 zhòuyè fúwù round-the-clock (7/24) service

宙 zhòu *n* time (See 宇宙 yǔzhòu)

骤 zhòu *n* trot (See 步骤 bùzhòu)

猪 zhū *n* pig (头 tóu) □ 这家农民养了十头猪。**Zhè jiā nóngmín yǎngle shí tóu zhū.** *This peasant household keeps ten pigs.* □ 中国人一般吃猪肉, 不大吃牛肉、羊肉。**Zhōngguórén yìbān chī zhūròu, bú dà chī niúròu, yángròu.** *The Chinese normally eat pork and don't eat much beef or mutton.*

诸 zhū *adj* all, various
诸位 zhūwèi *pron* everybody, all of you

朱 zhū *n* 1 red 2 a common family name

珠 zhū *n* pearl (See 珍珠 zhēnzhū)

株 zhū *measure wd* (for plants and small trees)

竹 zhú *n* bamboo
竹子 zhúzi bamboo (棵 kē) □ 院子里的一角种了几棵竹子。**Yuànzi li de yì jiǎo zhòngle jǐ kē zhúzi.** *There is some bamboo planted in a corner of the courtyard.* □ 古代中国人特别喜爱竹子。**Gǔdài Zhōngguórén tèbié xǐ'ài zhúzi.** *The ancient Chinese were particularly fond of bamboo.*

逐 zhú *adv* one after another, one by one
逐步 zhúbù [modif: 逐 successive + 步 step] *adv* step by step, progressively, gradually □ 我们的中文水平在逐步提高。**Wǒmen de Zhōngwén shuǐpíng zài zhúbù tígāo.** *Our Chinese proficiency is progressively improving.*
逐渐 zhújiàn [comp: 逐 successive, one by one + 渐 gradual] *adv* gradually, step by step □ 地球正在逐渐变暖。**Dìqiú zhèngzài zhújiàn biàn nuǎn.** *The Earth is gradually warming up.* □ 他逐渐能听懂中文广播了。**Tā zhújiàn néng tīngdǒng Zhōngwén guǎngbō le.** *Gradually he could understand Chinese broadcasts.*
逐年 zhúnián *adv* one year after another, year by year

烛 zhú Trad 燭 *n* candle (See 蜡烛 làzhú)

主 zhǔ I *n* 1 master, owner 2 host II *adj* dominant, principal

主办 zhǔbàn *v* host (a conference, an event, etc.) □ 这个展览会由城市博物馆主办。**Zhège zhǎnlǎnhuì yóu chéngshì bówùguǎn zhǔbàn.** *This exhibition is hosted by the city museum.*

主编 zhǔbiān [modif: 主 principal + 编 editor] *n* editor-in-chief, editor

主持 zhǔchí *v* be in charge of, host (a TV program), chair (a meeting)
节目主持人 jiémù zhǔchírén host/hostess of a TV/radio show

主导 zhǔdǎo *adj* guiding, dominant

主动 zhǔdòng [modif: 主 self + 动 act] *adj* of one's own accord, taking the initiative □ 他主动提出帮助我们。**Tā zhǔdòng tíchū bāngzhù wǒmen.** *He offered to help us without being asked.* □ 在谈恋爱的时候, 一般是小伙子主动一点。**Zài tán liàn'ài de shíhou, yìbān shì xiǎohuǒzi zhǔdòng yìdiǎn.** *Normally young men take the initiative in courtship.*

主观 zhǔguān [modif: 主 subjective + 观 view] *adj* subjective □ 你这种说法只是建立在你个人的经历上,

所以比较主观。**Nǐ zhè zhǒng shuōfǎ zhǐshì jiànlì zài nǐ gérén de jīnglì shang, suǒyǐ bǐjiào zhǔguān.** *Your arguments are rather subjective because they are based only on your personal experiences.*

主管 zhǔguǎn I *v* be in charge, be responsible for □ 这位副校长主管财务工作。**Zhè wei fùxiàozhǎng zhǔguǎn cáiwù gōngzuò.** *This deputy principal is responsible for the finance of the school.* **II** *n* person in charge

主力 zhǔlì [modif: 主 principal + 力 force] *n* main force

主流 zhǔliú *n* mainstream

主权 zhǔquán *n* sovereign rights, sovereignty

主人 zhǔrén [modif: 主 principal + 人 person] *n* **1** host (antonym 客人 **kèren**) □ 客人都来了, 主人呢? **Kèren dōu lái le, zhǔrén ne?** *The guests have all arrived, but where is the host?* **2** owner, proprietor □ 我是这辆车的主人, 你们为什么把车拖走? **Wǒ shì zhè liàng chē de zhǔrén, nìmen wèishénme bǎ chē tuōzǒu?** *I'm the owner of this car. Why did you tow it away?*

主人翁 zhǔrénwēng *n* master (of one's country, a society, etc.)

主任 zhǔrèn [modif: 主 principal + 任 appointed] *n* chairman (of a committee), director (of a department) □ 这个委员会的主任由一位教授担任。**Zhège wěiyuánhuì de zhǔrèn yóu yí wèi jiàoshòu dānrèn.** *The chair of this committee was held by a professor.* 办公室主任 **bàngōngshì zhǔrèn** office manager 车间主任 **chējiān zhǔrèn** head of a workshop (in a factory)

主任医生 zhǔrèn yīshēng *n* chief physician, chief surgeon

主食 zhǔshí *n* staple food

主题 zhǔtí *n* theme (电影的) 主题歌 (diànyǐng de) **zhǔtígē** theme song (of a movie)

主体 zhǔtǐ *n* main body

主席 zhǔxí [modif: 主 principal + 席 seat] *n* chairman, chairperson 大会主席 **dàhuì zhǔxí** chairperson of an assembly

主要 zhǔyào [comp: 主 advocate + 要 (in this context) important] *adj* major, chief, main □ 这不是主要的问题, 可以以后再讨论。**Zhè bú shì zhǔyào de wèntí, kěyǐ yǐhòu zài tǎolùn.** *This is not a major issue. We can discuss it later.* □ 纠正错误是主要的, 谁该负责以后再说。**Jiūzhèng cuòwù shì zhǔyào de, shuí gāi fùzé yǐhòu zài shuō.** *Rectifying the mistake is the main thing. The question of who is to blame can wait till later.*

主义 zhǔyì *n* doctrine, -ism

主意 zhǔyi [comp: 主 major + 意 idea] *n* definite view, idea □ 这件事我没有什么主意, 你看呢? **Zhè jiàn shì wǒ méiyǒu shénme zhǔyi, nǐ kàn ne?** *I don't have any definite views on this matter. What do you think?* □ 他打定主意要去北京学中文。**Tā dǎdìng zhǔyi yào qù Běijīng xué Zhōngwén.** *He has made up his mind to go to Beijing to learn Chinese.*

主张 zhǔzhāng I *v* advocate, stand for □ 我主张立即恢复谈判。**Wǒ zhǔzhāng lìjí huīfù tánpàn.** *I advocate resuming negotiations immediately.* □ 她不主张借钱买车。**Tā bù zhǔzhāng jiè qián mǎi chē.** *She does not favor borrowing money to buy a car.* **II** *n* proposition, idea, what one stands for □ 你的主张很有道理, 但是

恐怕很难实行。**Nǐ de zhǔzhāng hěn yǒu dàolǐ, dànshì kǒngpà hěn nán shíxíng.** *Your idea is very reasonable but I'm afraid it's difficult to implement.*

煮 zhǔ *v* boil, cook □ 这块牛肉至少要煮一小时才能吃。**Zhè kuài niúròu zhìshǎo yào zhǔ yì xiǎoshí cáinéng chī.** *This piece of beef should be boiled for at least one hour before it is edible.*

嘱 zhǔ Trad 囑 *v* advise

嘱咐 zhǔfu [comp: 嘱 advice + 附 tell] *v* exhort, tell (somebody to do something) earnestly, advise □ 老人去世前, 嘱咐子女要互相爱护, 互相照顾。**Lǎorén qùshì qián, zhǔfu zǐnǚ yào hùxiāng àihu, hùxiāng zhàogu.** *Before his death the old man exhorted his children to love and care for each other.*

嘱托 zhǔtuō *v* entrust

住 zhù *v* reside, stay □ "你住在哪里?" "我住在学校附近。" **"Nǐ zhù zài nǎlǐ?" "Wǒ zhù zài xuéxiào fùjìn."** *"Where do you live?" "I live near the school."*

住房 zhùfáng *n* housing, accommodation

住所 zhùsuǒ *n* where one lives, lodge, residence

住院 zhùyuàn [v+obj: 住 live in + 院 hospital] *v* be hospitalized

住宅 zhùzhái *n* residence, home 住宅区 **zhùzháiqū** residential quarters

助 zhù *v* assist, help

助理 zhùlǐ *n* assistant 助理局长 **zhùlǐ júzhǎng** assistant director of the bureau 局长助理 **júzhǎng zhùlǐ** assistant to the director of the bureau

助手 zhùshǒu [modif: 助 assist + 手 hand] *n* assistant

助长 zhùzhǎng *v* encourage, promote

注 zhù *v* **1** add, pour **2** fix, focus on **3** register, record **4** annotate, explain

注册 zhùcè *v* register 注册商标 **zhùcè shāngbiāo** registered trademark

注解 zhùjiě I *v* annotate, explain with notes **II** *n* explanatory note, note

注目 zhùmù *v* fix one's eyes on 引人注目 **yǐnrén zhùmù** eye-catching

注射 zhùshè [comp: 注 pour + 射 shoot] *v* inject

注释 zhùshì *n* Same as 注解 **zhùjiě**

注视 zhùshì *v* look attentively, gaze at

注意 zhùyì *v* pay attention to, take notice of □ 说话的时候, 要注意语法。**Shuōhuà de shíhou, yào zhùyì yǔfǎ.** *One should pay attention to grammar when speaking.* □ 请大家注意! 明天张老师要开一个重要的会, 所以上不课。**Qǐng dàjiā zhùyì! Míngtiān Zhāng lǎoshī yào kāi yí ge zhòngyào de huì, suǒyǐ bú shàngkè.** *Attention, please! Tomorrow Teacher Zhang will be attending an important meeting, so there will be no class.*

注重 zhùzhòng *v* **1** emphasize, stress **2** pay great attention to, attach importance to 注重售后服务 **zhùzhòng shòuhòufúwù** pay much attention to after-sale service

驻 zhù Trad 駐 *v* stay 驻扎 **zhùzhá** *v* (of troops) be stationed

蛀 zhù *v* (of insects) eat into, bore through 蛀虫 **zhùchóng** *n* bookworm, termite

祝 zhù *v* express good wishes, wish □ 祝你生日快乐! **Zhù nǐ shēngrì kuàilè!** *I wish you a happy birthday!*

祝福 **zhùfú** v give one's blessing to, wish somebody happiness

祝贺 **zhùhè** [comp: 祝 wish well + 贺 congratulate] v congratulate □ 祝贺你大学毕业! **Zhùhè nǐ dàxué bìyè!** *Congratulations on your graduation!*

祝愿 **zhùyuàn** I v wish □ 祝愿你们生活美满幸福。 **Zhùyuàn nǐmen shēnghuó měimǎn xìngfú.** *(to newly-weds) Wish you perfect happiness.* II n good wishes

著 **zhù** v write

著名 **zhùmíng** adj famous, well-known □ 我们的中文老师是一位著名的小说家。 **Wǒmen de Zhōngwén lǎoshī shì yí wèi zhùmíng de xiǎoshuōjiā.** *Our Chinese teacher is a famous novelist.*

著作 **zhùzuò** [v+obj: 著 write + 作 (literary) work] n writings, (literary) work □ 他的著作被翻译为十多种语言。 **Tā de zhùzuò bèi fānyìwéi shí duō zhǒng yǔyán.** *His works have been translated into a dozen foreign languages.*

筑 **zhù** Trad 築 v build, construct (See 建筑 jiànzhù.)

柱 **zhù** n pillar, column
柱子 zhùzi pillar, column (根 gēn)

铸 **zhù** v cast
铸造 zhùzào cast, foundry

抓 **zhuā** v grab, seize □ 他抓住小偷的胳膊。 **Tā zhuāzhù xiǎotōu de gēbo.** *He grabbed the thief by the arm.*

抓紧 **zhuājǐn** [v+obj: 抓 grab + 紧 tight] v grasp firmly □ 你要抓紧时间, 在下星期一前写完报告。 **Nǐ yào zhuājǐn shíjiān, zài xià Xīngqīyī qián xiě wán bàogào.** *You should make the best use of your time and write up the report before next Monday.*

爪 **zhuǎ** n paw, claw
爪子 zhuǎzi paw, claw (只 zhī)

拽 **zhuài** v fling, throw

专 **zhuān** Trad 專 adj special, specific

专长 **zhuāncháng** n special skill, specialist field, expertise

专程 **zhuānchéng** adv (make a trip) specially for

专家 **zhuānjiā** [modif: 专 specialist + 家 expert] n expert, specialist □ 他是计算机专家, 关于计算机的事他没有不知道的。 **Tā shì jìsuànjī zhuānjiā, guānyú jìsuànjī de shì tā méiyǒu bù zhīdào de.** *He is a computer expert and knows everything there is to know about computers.*

专科 **zhuānkē** n school (or college) for vocational training
专科学校 zhuānkē xuéxiào school (or college) for vocational training

专利 **zhuānlì** n patent
申请专利 shēnqǐng zhuānlì apply for a patent

专门 **zhuānmén** adj specialized, specialist □ 他发表过很多语言学专门著作。 **Tā fābiǎoguo hěn duō yǔyánxué zhuānmén zhùzuò.** *He has published many specialized works on linguistics.*

专心 **zhuānxīn** [modif: 专 concentrate + 心 the heart] adj concentrate on, be absorbed in □ 妹妹正在专心地做数学练习。 **Mèimei zhèngzài zhuānxīn de zuò shùxué liànxí.** *My younger sister is absorbed in doing her mathematics exercises.* □ 他做事不专心, 所以一事无成。 **Tā zuòshì bù zhuānxīn, suǒyǐ yí shì wú**

chéng. *He does everything half-heartedly and, as a result, has accomplished nothing.*

专业 **zhuānyè** [modif: 专 specialist + 业 profession] n specialist field of study, specialty □ 他的专业是中国农村经济。 **Tā de zhuānyè shì Zhōngguó nóngcūn jīngjì.** *His specialist field is Chinese rural economics.*

专用 **zhuānyòng** v use for a special purpose
专款专用 zhuānkuǎn zhuānyòng earmark a fund for a specific purpose

专政 **zhuānzhèng** n dictatorship

专制 **zhuānzhì** n autocracy

砖 **zhuān** Trad 磚 n brick
砖头 zhuāntóu brick (块 kuài)

转 **zhuǎn** Trad 轉 v 1 turn, change □ 今天下午雨转晴。 **Jīntiān xiàwǔ yǔ zhuǎn qíng.** *This afternoon it'll change from a rainy day to a fine day.* 2 pass on, forward □ 我已经把他的电子邮件转给他姐姐了。 **Wǒ yǐjīng bǎ tā de diànzǐ yóujiàn zhuǎn gei tā jiějie le.** *I have forwarded his e-mail message to his sister.*

转变 **zhuǎnbiàn** [comp: 转 turn + 变 change] v change, transform (usually for the better) □ 他从一个小偷转变成一个对社会有用的公民。 **Tā cóng yí ge xiǎotōu zhuǎnbiàn chéng yí ge duì shèhuì yǒuyòng de gōngmín.** *He has transformed from a thief to a useful member of society.* □ 她的态度转变了—从怀疑到信任。 **Tā de tàidù zhuǎnbiàn le—cóng huáiyí dào xìnrèn.** *Her attitude changed—from doubt to trust.*

转播 **zhuǎnbō** [comp: 转 pass on + 播 broadcast] v relay a radio or TV broadcast

转车 **zhuǎnchē** [v+obj: 转 change + 车 vehicle] v transfer to another train (or bus)

转达 **zhuǎndá** v pass on (a piece of information)

转动 **zhuǎndòng** v turn around, turn

转告 **zhuǎngào** [modif: 转 transfer + 告 tell] v pass along (word) □ 请你把这个消息转告全班同学。 **Qǐng nǐ bǎ zhège xiāoxi zhuǎngào quán bān tóngxué.** *Please pass on the news to all your classmates.*

转化 **zhuǎnhuà** v transform

转换 **zhuǎnhuàn** v transform, change

转基因 **zhuǎn jīyīn** n genetic modification, GM
转基因食品 zhuǎnjīyīn shípǐn transgenic food

转交 **zhuǎnjiāo** v pass on (something) □ 小王要我把这本书转交给你。 **Xiǎo wáng yào wǒ bǎ zhè běn shū zhuǎnjiāo gěi nǐ.** *Xiao Wang asked me to pass this book on to you.*

转让 **zhuǎnràng** v transfer (a property, rights, etc.)

转入 **zhuǎnrù** v switch over, turn to

转弯 **zhuǎnwān** v turn a corner, turn
向左转弯 xiàngzuǒ zhuǎnwān turn left

转向 **zhuǎnxiàng** v change direction

转学 **zhuǎnxué** [v+obj: 转 change + 学 school] v transfer to another school

转折 **zhuǎnzhé** n a turn in the course of events

转移 **zhuǎnyí** [comp: 转 transfer + 移 move] v shift, transfer

传 **zhuàn** Trad 傳 n biography
自传 zìzhuàn autobiography

传记 **zhuànjì** n biography

赚 **zhuàn** Trad 賺 v make money, make a profit □ 现在赚钱不容易。 **Xiànzài zhuàn qián bù róngyì.** *It is not easy to make any money now.* □ 这家小小的西餐馆去年赚了五万多。 **Zhè jiā xiǎoxiǎo de xīcānguǎn**

qùnián zhuànle wǔwàn duō. *This small Western-style restaurant made a profit of over 50,000 yuan last year.*

庄 **zhuāng** Trad 莊 **I** *n* village **II** *adj* serious, grave

庄稼 **zhuāngjia** *n* crop □ 光种庄稼, 很难富起来。 **Guāng zhòng zhuāngjia, hěn nán fù qǐlai.** *It is difficult to get rich raising crops only.*

庄稼地 **zhuāngjiadì** *n* farmland

庄稼人 **zhuāngjiarén** *n* farmer (especially one that grows crops)

庄严 **zhuāngyán** [comp: 庄 grave + 严 grave] *adj* solemn, imposing

庄重 **zhuāngzhòng** [comp: 庄 grave + 重 heavy] *adj* serious, solemn

妆 **zhuāng** Trad 妝 *v* apply make-up (See 化妆 **huàzhuāng**, 化妆品 **huàzhuāngpǐn**)

装 **zhuāng** Trad 裝 **I** *v* **1** pretend □ 她不想跟他说话, 所以装着没看见。 **Tā bù xiǎng gēn tā shuōhuà, suǒyǐ zhuāngzhe méi kànjiàn.** *She did not want to talk to him, so she pretended not to see him.* □ 不懂就是不懂, 你干吗装懂? **Bù dǒng jiù shì bù dǒng, nǐ gànmá zhuāng dǒng?** *It's all right if you don't understand. Why do you pretend to understand?* **2** load and unload **3** fit, install **II** *n* clothing

装备 **zhuāngbèi 1** *v* equip **2** *n* equipment

军事装备 jūnshì zhuāngbèi armament

装配 **zhuāngpèi** *v* assemble (parts)

装配线 zhuāngpèixiàn assembly line

装饰 **zhuāngshì I** *v* decorate □ 他们用中国工艺品装饰客厅。 **Tāmen yòng Zhōngguó gōngyìpǐn zhuāngshì kètīng.** *They decorated their living room with Chinese handicrafts.* **II** *n* decoration

装饰品 zhuāngshìpǐn article for decoration, ornament

装卸 **zhuāngxiè** *v* load and unload

装置 **zhuāngzhì I** *v* install **II** *n* installation, device

节能装置 jiénéng zhuāngzhì energy-saving device

壮 **zhuāng** Trad 壯 *adj* **1** robust, sturdy **2** magnificent

壮大 **zhuàngdà** *v* grow in strength

壮观 **zhuàngguān** [modif: 壮 magnificent + 观 view] *n* magnificent sight

壮丽 **zhuànglì** [comp: 壮 magnificent + 丽 beautiful] *adj* beautiful and magnificent

壮烈 **zhuàngliè** *adj* heroic

壮志 **zhuàngzhì** *n* high aspirations

状 **zhuàng** Trad 狀 *n* form, shape

状况 **zhuàngkuàng** [comp: 状 shape (of things) + 况 situation] *n* shape (of things), situation, condition □ 目前全国的经济状况很好。 **Mùqián quánguó de jīngjì zhuàngkuàng hěn hǎo.** *At present the national economy is in good shape.* □ 你爷爷的身体状况怎么样? **Nǐ yéye de shēntǐ zhuàngkuàng zěnmeyàng?** *How is your grandpa's health?*

状态 **zhuàngtài** [comp: 状 shape (of things) + 态 condition] *n* state (of affairs), appearance □ 运动员的精神状态非常重要。 **Yùndòngyuán de jīngshén zhuàngtài fēicháng zhòngyào.** *It is important for an athlete to be in a good mental state.*

撞 **zhuàng** *v* bump against, collide □ 两辆汽车相撞, 造成重大交通事故。 **Liǎng liàng qìchē xiāng zhuàng, zàochéng zhòngdà jiāotōng shìgù.** *The two cars collided and caused a major road accident.*

幢 **zhuàng** *measure wd* (for houses) 一幢大楼 yí zhuàng dàlóu a big (multi-storied) building

追 **zhuī** *v* **1** chase, run after □ 孩子们在操场上你追我, 我追你。 **Háizimen zài cāochǎng shang nǐ zhuī wǒ, wǒ zhuī nǐ.** *Children chased one another on the playing ground.* **2** look into, get to the roots of

追查 **zhuīchá** [comp: 追 chase + 查 investigate] *v* trace, investigate

追查谣言 zhuīchá yáoyán try to find out the source of a rumor

追悼 **zhuīdào** *v* mourn over (the death of somebody)

追悼会 zhuīdàohuì memorial service, memorial meeting

追赶 **zhuīgǎn** [comp: 追 chase + 赶 chase] *v* run after, pursue

追究 **zhuījiū** *v* get to the roots, investigate the origin

追究责任 zhuījiū zérèn investigate to find out who is responsible for an accident

追求 **zhuīqiú** [comp: 追 chase + 求 seek] *v* pursue, seek □ 人人追求幸福。 **Rénren zhuīqiú xìngfú.** *Everyone pursues happiness.*

追上 **zhuīshang** *v* catch up with, catch □ 我追不上他。 **Wǒ zhuī bu shang tā.** *I can't catch up with him.*

追问 **zhuīwèn** [comp: 追 chase + 问 ask] *v* inquire in great details

缀 **zhuì** *v* sew, stitch (See 点缀 **diǎnzhui**)

准 **zhǔn** Trad 準 **I** *adj* accurate, exact □ 电子手表一般都很准。 **Diànzǐ shǒubiǎo yìbān dōu hěn zhǔn.** *Electronic watches are usually quite accurate.* **II** *v* permit, allow **III** *n* norm, standard

准备 **zhǔnbèi I** *v* prepare □ 明天考试, 你们准备好了吗? **Míngtiān kǎoshì, nǐmen zhǔnbèi hǎo le ma?** *There'll be an examination tomorrow. Are you well prepared?* □ 他正在准备在下午会议上的发言。 **Tā zhèngzài zhǔnbèi zài xiàwǔ huìyì shang de fāyán.** *He is preparing the speech to be delivered at this afternoon's meeting.*

准备好 zhǔnbèi hǎo be well prepared

II *n* preparation □ 老师上课前要做很多准备。 **Lǎoshī shàngkè qián yào zuò hěn duō zhǔnbèi.** *The teacher needs to do a lot of preparation before class.*

准确 **zhǔnquè** [comp: 准 accurate + 确 verified] *adj* accurate, exact □ 发音不准确, 有时候会闹笑话。 **Fāyīn bù zhǔnquè, yǒushíhou huì nào xiàohua.** *Inaccurate pronunciation can sometimes have comical effects.* □ 你的计算不够准确。 **Nǐ de jìsuàn bú gòu zhǔnquè.** *Your calculation is not accurate enough.*

准时 **zhùnshí** *adj* punctual, on time □ 这里的火车非常准时。 **Zhèlǐ de huǒchē fēicháng zhǔnshí.** *The trains here are very punctual.* □ 我从小养成了准时的习惯。 **Wǒ cóngxiǎo yǎngchéng le zhǔnshí de xíguàn.** *In my childhood I formed the habit of being punctual.* □ 他每天准时九点钟到达办公室。 **Tā měitiān zhǔnshí jiǔ diǎnzhōng dàodá bàngōngshì.** *Every day he arrives at his office punctually at nine o'clock.*

准许 **zhǔnxǔ** [comp: 准 permit + 许 allow] *v* permit, allow

准则 **zhǔnzé** *n* norm, standard

行为准则 xíngwéi zhǔnzé code of conduct

捉 **zhuō** v catch, capture □ 你怎么捉得住猫? **Nǐ zěnme zhuō de zhu māo?** *How can you catch a cat?*

拙 **zhuō** adj clumsy (See 笨拙 **bènzhuō**)

桌 **zhuō** n table
桌子 **zhuōzi** table, desk (张 **zhāng**) □ 桌子上有几本书和一个杯子。**Zhuōzi shang yǒu jǐ běn shū hé yí ge bēizi.** *There are some books and a cup on the table.*

卓 **zhuó** adj outstanding
卓越 **zhuóyuè** adj brilliant, exceptional

啄 **zhuó** v peck
啄木鸟 **zhuómùniǎo** woodpecker

酌 **zhuó** v 1 weigh and consider 2 drink (wine)
酌情 **zhuóqíng** v take the circumstances into consideration
酌情处理 **zhuóqíng chǔlǐ** settle a matter as one sees fit

着 **zhuó** v apply, use
着手 **zhuóshǒu** [v+obj: 着 apply + 手 hand] v begin, set out
着想 **zhuóxiǎng** v consider (somebody's interest) □ 我是为你着想。**Wǒ shì wéi nǐ zhuóxiǎng.** *I'm considering your interest.* (→ *I'm doing this for your good.*)

浊 **zhuó** Trad 濁 adj turbid, muddy (See 浑浊 **húnzhuó**)

镯 **zhuó** n bracelet (See 手镯 **shǒuzhuó**)

姿 **zī** n looks, appearance
姿势 **zīshì** n posture
姿态 **zītài** n 1 posture 2 attitude, pose
保持低姿态 **bǎochí dīzītài** keep a low profile

咨 **zī** n consult
咨询 **zīxún** [comp: 咨 consult + 询 inquire] v seek advice, consult

资 **zī** Trad 資 n money, capital
资本 **zīběn** [comp: 资 capital + 本 principal] n capital □ 他开工厂的资本是从银行借来的。**Tā kāi gōngchǎng de zīběn shì cóng yínháng jièlai de.** *The capital with which he opened his factory was borrowed from the bank.*
资本家 **zīběnjiā** n capitalist
资本主义 **zīběn zhǔyì** n capitalism
资产 **zīchǎn** n asset, property
资产阶级 **zīchǎnjiējí** n bourgeoisie
资格 **zīgé** n qualification □ 她通过考试，终于取得了教师资格。**Tā tōngguò kǎoshì, zhōngyú qǔdé le jiàoshī zīgé.** *She passed the exams and got her teaching qualification.*
资金 **zījīn** [comp: 资 capital + 金 gold, fund] v fund □ 学校向教育局申请建造教室的资金。**Xuéxiào xiàng jiàoyùjú shēnqǐng jiànzào jiàoshì de zījīn.** *The school applied to the education bureau for funds to build new classrooms.*
资料 **zīliào** [comp: 资 capital + 料 material] n 1 material, data □ 王老师从北京带回来很多中文教学的参考资料。**Wáng lǎoshī cóng Běijīng dài huílai hěn duō Zhōngwén jiàoxué de cānkǎo zīliào.** *Teacher Wang brought back from Beijing a great deal of reference materials for teaching and learning Chinese.* 2 means (of production) □ 生产资料公有，是社会主义的特点。**Shēngchǎn zīliào gōngyǒu, shì shèhuì zhǔyì**

de **tèdiǎn.** *Public ownership of the means of production is a special feature of socialism.*
资源 **zīyuán** [modif: 资 capital + 源 source] n natural resources □ 我们要开发海洋资源。**Wǒmen yào kāifā hǎiyáng zīyuán.** *We will develop the natural resources of seas and oceans.*
资助 **zīzhù** v provide financial support, fund

滋 **zī** v grow
滋味 **zīwèi** n taste, flavor
滋长 **zīzhǎng** v grow, develop

子 **zǐ** n 1 son, child
长子 **zhǎngzǐ** the first son
2 something small and hard
子弹 **zǐdàn** n bullets
子弟 **zǐdì** n sons and younger brothers, children
高干子弟 **gāogàn zǐdì** children of high-ranking officials, "princelings"
子女 **zǐnǚ** n sons and daughters, children
子孙 **zǐsūn** n children and grandchildren, descendant
子孙后代 **zǐsūn hòudài** descendants, posterity

籽 **zǐ** n seed

仔 **zǐ** adj as in 仔细 **zǐxì**
仔细 **zǐxì** adj very careful, paying attention to details □ 考试的时候一定要仔细看清题目。**Kǎoshì de shíhou yídìng yào zǐxì kànqīng tímù.** *At an examination be sure to read the questions very, very carefully.*

紫 **zǐ** adj purple □ 他冻得脸都发紫了。**Tā dòng de liǎn dōu fā zǐ le.** *He was so cold that his face turned purple.*

自 1 **zì** pron self, one's own
自卑 **zìbēi** [modif: 自 self + 卑 abase] v feel oneself inferior
自卑感 **zìbēigǎn** inferiority complex, sense of inferiority
自动 **zìdòng** [modif: 自 self + 动 act] adj automatic □ 这台机器会自动关闭。**Zhè tái jīqì huì zìdòng guānbì.** *This machine will turn off automatically.*
自动扶梯 **zìdòng fútī** escalator
自动化 **zìdònghuà** automatic, automation
自动柜员机 **zìdòng guìyuánjī** n automated teller machine (ATM)

NOTE: ATM can also be called 自动取款机 **zìdòng qǔkuǎnjī** or 自动提款机 **zìdòng tíkuǎnjī**.

自发 **zìfā** adj spontaneous
自费 **zìfèi** [modif: 自 self + 费 cost] adj self-supporting, paid by myself □ 我不明白, 他们怎么有钱送孩子去国外自费留学? **Wǒ bù míngbái, tāmen zěnme yǒu qián sòng háizi qù guówài zìfèi liúxué?** *I don't understand how they could afford to send their child overseas as a self-supporting student.*
自费留学生 **zìfèi liúxuéshēng** self-supporting foreign student, fee-paying foreign student
自豪 **zìháo** [modif: 自 self + 豪 pride] v be very proud of oneself
自己 **zìjǐ** pron self, one's own □ 自己的工作自己做。**Zìjǐ de gōngzuò zìjǐ zuò.** *Each must do their own work.* □ 你不能只想到自己。**Nǐ bù néng zhǐ xiǎngdao zìjǐ.** *You mustn't think of yourself only.*
你自己 **nǐ zìjǐ** yourself

你们自己 nǐmen zìjǐ yourselves
他自己 tā zìjǐ himself
他们自己 tāmen zìjǐ themselves
我自己 wǒ zìjǐ myself
我们自己 wǒmen zìjǐ ourselves

自觉 zìjué [modif: 自 self + 觉 conscious, aware] *adj* being aware of, being conscious of, voluntary, conscientious □ 孩子自觉帮助做家务。**Háizi zìjué bāngzhù zuò jiāwù.** *The child helps with the household chores voluntarily.* □ 他犯这个错误不是自觉的。**Tā fàn zhège cuòwù bú shì zìjué de.** *He made the mistake without being aware of it.* (→ *He unconsciously made the mistake.*)

自来水 zìláishuǐ [modif: 自来 self-coming + 水 water] *n* running water

自满 zìmǎn [modif: 自 self + 满 full] *adj* complacent □ 我们取得了很好的成绩, 但是不能自满。**Wǒmen qǔdé le hěn hǎode chéngjì, dànshì bùnéng zìmǎn.** *We've made good achievements, but we mustn't be complacent.*

自然 zìrán I *n* nature □ 哲学问题之一就是人和自然的关系。**Zhéxué wèntí zhī yī jiù shì rén hé zìrán de guānxi.** *One philosophical issue is the relationship between humankind and nature.*
自然保护区 zìrán bǎohùqū nature reserve
II *adj* natural □ 父母爱子女是自然的。**Fùmǔ ài zǐnǚ shì zìrán de.** *It is only natural that parents love their children.* □ 她说话的样子很不自然。**Tā shuōhuà de yàngzi hěn bú zìrán.** *The way she speaks is quite affected.*

自杀 zìshā [modif: 自 self + 杀 kill] I *v* commit suicide II *n* suicide □ 这件案子是自杀, 还是他杀? **Zhè jiàn ànzi shì zìshā, háishi tāshā?** *Is this a case of suicide or homicide?*

自身 zìshēn *n* self, oneself

自私 zìsī [comp: 自 self + 私 private] *adj* selfish, egoistic □ 独生子女往往比较自私, 对不对? **Dúshēngzǐ nǚ wǎngwǎng bǐjiào zìsī, duì bùduì?** *Is it true that an only child tends to be selfish?*

自私自利 zìsī zìlì *idiom* selfish, self-seeking

自卫 zìwèi *n* self-defense

自我 zìwǒ *n* oneself

自相矛盾 zìxiāng máodùn *idiom* self-contradictory

自信 zìxìn *adj* self-confident
缺乏自信 quēfá zìxìn lacking in self-confidence

自行 zìxíng *adv* by oneself

自行车 zìxíngchē [modif: 自 self + 行 walking + 车 vehicle] *n* bicycle (辆 **liàng**) □ 我会骑自行车, 但是不会修自行车。**Wǒ huì qí zìxíngchē, dànshì bú huì xiū zìxíngchē.** *I can ride a bicycle, but I can't fix it.*

自学 zìxué [modif: 自 self + 学 study] *v* study independently, teach oneself □ 他自学日语三年, 已经能看懂日文书了。**Tā zìxué Rìyǔ sān nián, yǐjīng néng kàndǒng Rìwén shū le.** *He taught himself Japanese for three years and is now able to read Japanese books.* □ 我佩服自学成才的人。**Wǒ pèifu zìxué chéngcái de rén.** *I admire those who have made themselves useful through self-study.*

自由 zìyóu I *n* freedom, liberty □ 那个国家缺乏新闻自由, 受到人们的普遍批评。**Nàge guójiā quēfá xīnwén zìyóu, shòudao rénmen de pǔbiàn pīpíng.** *That country lacks freedom of the press and is widely criticized.* □ 他不愿意结婚, 因为他喜欢自由。**Tā bú yuànyì jiéhūn, yīnwèi tā xǐhuan zìyóu.** *He is unwilling*

to marry because he enjoys his freedom. II *adj* free, unrestrained □ 他觉得和父母住在一起不自由。**Tā juéde hé fùmǔ zhù zài yìqǐ bú zìyóu.** *Living with his parents, he does not feel free.*

自愿 zìyuàn [modif: 自 self + 愿 willing] *v* volunteer, of one's own accord

自治 zìzhì *n* autonomy

自治区 zìzhìqū *n* autonomous region
广西壮族自治区 Guǎngxī Zhuàngzú Zìzhìqū Guangxi Zhuang Autonomous Region

自主 zìzhǔ *v* act on one's own, keep the initiative in one's own hands

自助餐 zìzhùcān [modif: 自助 self-help + 餐 meal] *n* buffet dinner

自 2 zì *prep* Same as 从 **cóng**. Only used in written Chinese.

自从 zìcóng [comp: 自 from + 从 from] *prep* from, since □ 自从2001年9月11日, 世界各地的飞机场都加强了行李检查。**Zìcóng èr-líng-líng-yī nián Jiǔyuè shíyī rì, shìjiè gèdì de fēijīchǎng dōu jiāqiáng xíngli jiǎnchá.** *Since September 11, 2001, airports all over the world have strengthened their luggage check system.* □ 自从认识他以来, 我渐渐对他产生了好感。**Zìcóng rènshi tā yǐlái, wǒ jiànjiàn duì tā chǎnshēngle hǎogǎn.** *Since I came to know him, I have gradually grown fond of him.*

自古 zìgǔ *adv* since ancient times

自始至终 zì shǐ zhì zhōng *idiom* from start to finish

字 zì *n* Chinese character, sinogram □ 中国字很有意思。**Zhōngguó zì hěn yǒu yìsi.** *Chinese characters are very interesting.* □ 这个字是什么意思? 怎么念? **Zhège zì shì shénme yìsi? Zěnme niàn?** *What is the meaning of this Chinese character? How is it pronounced?*
汉字 Hànzì Chinese character

字典 zìdiǎn *n* dictionary (本 **běn**)

字母 zìmǔ *n* letter (of an alphabet)
字母表 zìmǔbiǎo alphabet

子 zi *particle* (a nominal suffix) (See 杯子 **bēizi**, 被子 **bèizi**, 本子 **běnzi**, 鼻子 **bízi**, 脖子 **bózi**, 叉子 **chāzi**, 虫子 **chóngzi**, 村子 **cūnzi**, 刀子 **dāozi**, 电子 **diànzi**, 儿子 **érzi**, 房子 **fángzi**, 个子 **gèzi**, 孩子 **háizi**, 盒子 **hézi**, 猴子 **hóuzi**, 胡子 **húzi**, 饺子 **jiǎozi**, 橘子 **júzi**, 句子 **jùzi**, 裤子 **kùzi**, 筷子 **kuàizi**, 例子 **lìzi**, 帽子 **màozi**, 脑子 **nǎozi**, 牌子 **páizi**, 盘子 **pánzi**, 妻子 **qīzi**, 旗子 **qízi**, 裙子 **qúnzi**, 日子 **rìzi**, 嗓子 **sǎngzi**, 嫂子 **sǎozi**, 沙子 **shāzi**, 勺子 **sháozi**, 绳子 **shéngzi**, 狮子 **shīzi**, 毯子 **tǎnzi**, 兔子 **tùzi**, 袜子 **wàzi**, 蚊子 **wénzi**, 屋子 **wūzi**, 箱子 **xiāngzi**, 小伙子 **xiǎohuǒzi**, 样子 **yàngzi**, 叶子 **yèzi**, 一下子 **yíxiàzi**, 椅子 **yǐzi**, 院子 **yuànzi**, 种子 **zhǒngzi**, 竹子 **zhúzi**, 桌子 **zhuōzi**.)

宗 zōng *n* ancestor
宗教 zōngjiào *n* religion
宗教信仰 zōngjiào xìnyǎng religious belief
宗派 zōngpài *n* faction, sect
宗旨 zōngzhǐ *n* primary purpose, aim

棕 zōng *n* palm, palm fiber
棕色 zōngsè *n* brown

综 zōng *adj* comprehensive
综合 zōnghé *adj* comprehensive, synthetical

踪 zōng *n* footprint
跟踪 gēnzōng follow the tracks of, shadow (somebody)

踪迹 zōngjì [comp: 踪 footprint + 迹 trace] *n* trace, track

总 zǒng Trad 總 **I** *adj* **1** overall, total
总开关 zǒngkāiguān switch
2 chief, head
总书记 Zǒngshūjì Secretary-General
II *adv* **1** always, invariably □ 他总觉得自己正确。 **Tā zǒng juéde zìjǐ zhèngquè.** *He always thinks himself correct.* □ 你为什么总这么晚起床? **Nǐ wèishénme zǒng zhème wǎn qǐchuáng?** *Why do you always get up so late?* **2** anyway, after all

总得 zǒngděi [comp: 总 anyway + 得 have to] *modal v* have got to, have to, must □ 我们总得想个办法。 **Wǒmen zǒngděi xiǎng gè bànfǎ.** *We've got to find a way put.*

总的来说 zǒngdeláishuō *idiom* generally speaking, on the whole

总督 zǒngdū *n* governor-general, governor

总额 zǒng'é [modif: 总 total + 额 sum] *n* total (a sum of fund)

总而言之 zǒng'éryánzhī *idiom* Same as 总之 **zǒngzhī**

总共 zǒnggòng [comp: 总 total + 共 altogether] *adv* in all, altogether

总和 zǒnghé [modif: 总 total + 和 sum] *n* sum total

总计 zǒngjì *n* grand total

总结 zǒngjié [modif: 总 general + 结 conclude, conclusion] **I** *v* sum up, do a review of one's past work or life experiences □ 每年年底, 公司都要总结一年的工作。 **Měi nián niándǐ, gōngsī dōuyào zǒngjié yì nián de gōngzuò.** *At the end of every year the company does a general review of the work done.* **II** *n* summary, a general view of one's past work or life experiences □ 这个计划已经完成, 我们应该做一个总结了。 **Zhège jìhuà yǐjīng wánchéng, wǒmen yīnggāi zuò yí ge zǒngjié le.** *Now that this plan is fulfilled, we should do a general review.*

总理 zǒnglǐ [modif: 总 general + 理 administer] *n* premier, prime minister □ 中国的国务院总理是政府首脑。 **Zhōngguó de guówùyuàn zǒnglǐ shì zhèngfǔ shǒunǎo.** *The premier of the Chinese State Council is China's head of government.*

总是 zǒngshì *adv* Same as 总 **II** *adv* 1

总数 zǒngshù [modif: 总 total + 数 number] *n* sum total

总司令 zǒngsīlìng [modif: 总 general + 司令 commander] *n* commander-in-chief

总算 zǒngsuàn *adv* at long last, finally □ 今天总算是星期五了。 **Jīntiān zǒngsuàn shì xīngqīwǔ le.** *At long last, it's Friday today.*

总统 zǒngtǒng [modif: 总 general + 统 rule, command] *n* president (of a country) □ 美国每四年举行总统选举。 **Měiguó měi sì nián jǔxíng zǒngtǒng xuǎnjǔ.** *The U.S.A. holds its presidential election every four years.*

总务 zǒngwù *n* general affairs
总务科 zǒngwùkē general affairs section

总之 zǒngzhī *adv* in a word, in short □ 总之, 你的计划是不可行的。 **Zǒngzhī, nǐde jìhuà shì bùkě xíng de.** *Your plan, in short, is not feasible.*

纵 zòng *adv* **1** from north to south **2** vertical, lengthwise

纵横 zònghéng *adj* in length and breadth

走 zǒu *v* **1** walk □ 我家离学校很近, 我每天走到学校。 **Wǒ jiā lí xuéxiào hěn jìn, wǒ měi tiān zǒudao xuéxiào.** *My home is close to the school. I walk to school every day.* **2** leave □ 时间不早了, 我们得走了。 **Shíjiān bù zǎo le, wǒmen děi zǒu le.** *It's quite late. We've got to go.* **3** visit
走亲戚 zǒu qīnqi visit a relative
4 escape, leak out

走道 zǒudào [modif: 走 walk + 道 way] *n* sidewalk, footpath

走访 zǒufǎng [comp: 走 visit + 访 visit] *v* visit and interview, interview

走狗 zǒugǒu *n* running dog, flunkey

走廊 zǒuláng [modif: 走 walk + 廊 corridor, porch] *n* corridor, hallway

走漏 zǒulòu *v* leak (information)

走私 zǒusī *v* smuggle
走私犯 zǒusīfàn smuggler

走弯路 zǒuwānlù [v+obj: 走 walk + 弯路 roundabout route] *v* take a roundabout course

走向 zǒuxiàng *n* **1** alignment **2** trend
明年市场的走向 míngnián shìchǎng de zǒuxiàng the market trend next year

奏 zòu *v* play music (See 演奏 **yǎnzòu**)

揍 zòu *v* beat, hit
挨揍 áizòu get a thrashing

租 zū **I** *v* rent, hire □ 在这座大楼租一个办公室, 要多少钱? **Zài zhè zuò dàlóu zū yí ge bàngōngshì, yào duōshǎoqián?** *How much is it to rent an office in this building?* **II** *n* rent (money)
房租 fángzū (housing) rent
租金 zūjīn [modif: 租 rent + 金 gold] *n* rent

足 zú **I** *n* foot **II** *adj* sufficient, enough
足球 zúqiú [modif: 足 foot + 球 ball] *n* soccer □ 我爸爸年轻的时候, 常常踢足球, 现在还爱看足球比赛。 **Wǒ bàba niánqīng de shíhou, chángcháng tī zúqiú, xiànzài hái ài kàn zúqiú bǐsài.** *My father often played soccer when he was young, and now he still enjoys watching soccer games.*
踢足球 tī zúqiú play soccer

足以 zúyǐ *adj* enough, sufficient

族 zú *n* clan, nationality (See 民族 **mínzú**.)

阻 zǔ *v* **1** resist, prevent **2** hinder, block
阻碍 zǔ'ài [comp: 阻 hinder + 碍 hinder] *v* hinder, obstruct

阻挡 zǔdǎng [comp: 阻 stop + 挡 block] *v* block, stop

阻拦 zǔlán [comp: 阻 stop + 拦 obstruct] *v* bar the way, stop

阻力 zǔlì [modif: 阻 resist + 力 strength, force] *n* resistance, obstacle

阻扰 zǔrǎo [comp: 阻 hinder + 扰 trouble] *v* obstruct, stand in the way

NOTE: 阻扰 **zǔrǎo** may also be 阻挠 **zǔnáo**. They are interchangeable.

阻止 zǔzhǐ [comp: 阻 stop + 止 stop] *v* stop, hold back

祖 zǔ *n* ancestor
祖父 zǔfù [modif: 祖 ancestor + 父 father] *n*

grandfather □ 我祖父七十多岁了, 还每天锻炼身体。 **Wǒ zǔfù qīshí duō suì le, hái měitiān duànliàn shēntǐ.** *My grandfather is over seventy and still does physical exercise every day.*

祖国 **zǔguó** [modif: 祖 ancestor + 国 country] *n* motherland, fatherland □ 我爱祖国。**Wǒ ài zǔguó.** *I love my motherland.* □ 他虽然住在国外, 但深深地关心祖国。**Tā suīrán zhù zai guówài, dàn shēnshēn de guānxīn zǔguó.** *Although living in a foreign country, he is still deeply concerned for his motherland.*

祖母 **zǔmǔ** [modif: 祖 ancestor + 母 mother] *n* grandmother □ 我祖母一个人住, 我们常去看她。**Wǒ zǔmǔ yígerén zhù, wǒmen cháng qù kàn tā.** *My grandmother lives by herself. We often go to see her.*

祖先 **zǔxiān** [comp: 祖 ancestor + 先 first] *n* ancestor, ancestry

组 **zǔ** Trad 組 **I** *n* group □ 老师把全班分为三个组, 练习口语。**Lǎoshī bǎ quán bān fēn wéi sān ge zǔ, liànxí kǒuyǔ.** *The teacher divided the class into three groups for oral Chinese practice.* **II** *v* form, organize

组成 **zǔchéng** *v* make up, compose □ 这个专家组由五名世界级科学家组成。**Zhège zhuānjiāzǔ yóu wǔ míng shìjiè jí kēxuéjiā zǔchéng.** *This expert panel is made up of five world-class scientists.*

组合 **zǔhé** *v* compose, combine

组织 **zǔzhī** [comp: 组 to group + 织 to weave] **I** *v* organize □ 学校正在组织去北京旅游。**Xuéxiào zhèngzài zǔzhī qù Běijīng lǚyóu.** *The school is organizing a trip to Beijing.* **II** *n* organization □ 我父亲不参加任何组织。**Wǒ fùqin bù cānjiā rènhé zǔzhī.** *My father did not join any organization.*

钻 **zuān** Trad 鑽 *n* drill

钻研 **zuānyán** [comp: 钻 drill, bore into + 研 study, research] *v* study in great depth, study intensively □ 这位科学家有时候钻研一个问题而忘了吃饭。**Zhè wèi kēxuéjiā yǒushíhou zuānyán yí ge wèntí ér wàngle chīfàn.** *Sometimes this scientist studies a problem so intensively that he forgets his meals.*

钻 **zuàn** Trad 鑽 *n* diamond

钻石 **zuànshí** diamiond (粒 **lì**, 颗 **kē**) 一枚三克拉的钻石戒指 yìméi sān kèlā de zuànshí jièzhi a 3-carat diamond ring

嘴 **zuǐ** *n* mouth □ 不要用嘴呼吸, 要用鼻子呼吸。**Bú yào yòng zuǐ hūxī, yào yòng bízi hūxī.** *Breathe through the nose, not through the mouth.*

嘴巴 **zuǐba** *n* mouth 张开嘴巴 zhāngkāi zuǐba open one's mouth

嘴唇 **zuǐchún** *n* lip

最 **zuì** *adv* most (used before an adjective or a verb to indicate the superlative degree) □ 中国是世界上人口最多的国家。**Zhōngguó shì shìjiè shang rénkǒu zuì duō de guójiā.** *China is the most populous country in the world.* □ 我最讨厌电视广告。**Wǒ zuì tǎoyàn diànshì guǎnggào.** *I detest TV commercials most.*

最初 **zuìchū** *adv* in the initial stage, initially □ 最初我不习惯那里的生活。**Zuìchū wǒ bù xíguàn nàli de shēnghuó.** *Initially I was not used to the life there.*

最好 **zuìhǎo** [modif: 最 most + 好 good] **I** *adj* best, top-rate **II** *adv* had better □ 你最好常去看望奶奶。**Nǐ zuìhào cháng qù kànwàng nǎinai.** *You'd better visit your grandma often.*

最后 **zuìhòu** *adv* in the final stage, finally □ 笑得最后, 才笑得最好。**Xiào de zuìhòu, cái xiào de zuìhǎo.** *He who laughs last laughs best.* □ 最后他同意了我们的观点。**Zuìhòu tā tóngyìle wǒmen de guāndiǎn.** *Finally, he accepted our views.*

最近 **zuìjìn** *adv* recently, in recent times □ 我最近特别忙。**Wǒ zuìjìn tèbié máng.** *I'm particularly busy these days.* □ 你最近看过什么好电影吗? **Nǐ zuìjìn kànguo shénme hǎo diànyǐng ma?** *Have you seen any good movies lately?*

罪 **zuì** *n* crime, offense □ 被告不承认自己有罪。**Bèigào bù chéngrèn zìjǐ yǒuzuì.** *The defendant did not admit to any offense. (→ The defendant pleaded not guilty.)*

罪恶 **zuì'è** [comp: 罪 crime + 恶 evil] *n* crime, evil

罪犯 **zuìfàn** *n* criminal, convict □ 警察在案发第二天就抓到了罪犯。**Jǐngchá zài àn fā dì-èr tiān jiù zhuā dào le zuìfàn.** *The police caught the criminal the day after the crime.*

罪名 **zuìmíng** [modif: 罪 crime + 名 name] *n* charge, accusation 逃税的罪名 táoshuì de zuìmíng tax evasion charge

罪行 **zuìxíng** [modif: 罪 crime + 行 act] *n* crime, offense

罪状 **zuìzhuàng** *n* facts about a crime, indictment

醉 **zuì** *v* get drunk, be intoxicated □ 我没醉, 我还能喝。**Wǒ méi zuì, wǒ hái néng hē.** *I'm not drunk. I can drink more.* □ 他昨天晚上喝醉了, 今天头疼。**Tā zuótiān wǎnshang hē zuì le, jīntiān tóuténg.** *He was drunk last night and this morning he has a headache.*

尊 **zūn** *v* respect, esteem

尊敬 **zūnjìng** [comp: 尊 respect + 敬 respect] *v* respect, honor □ 中国的传统是尊敬老人。**Zhōngguó de chuántǒng shì zūnjìng lǎorén.** *A tradition of the Chinese is to respect the aged.*

尊严 **zūnyán** *n* dignity, honor

尊重 **zūnzhòng** [comp: 尊 respect + 重 value] *v* respect, esteem □ 我们非常尊重这位经验丰富的老教师。**Wǒmen fēicháng zūnzhòng zhè wèi jīngyàn fēngfù de lǎo jiàoshī.** *We hold this very experienced old teacher in high esteem.*

遵 **zūn** *v* obey

遵守 **zūnshǒu** [comp: 遵 obey + 守 abide by] *v* observe, abide by □ 你既然在这个学校学习, 就要遵守学校的各项规定。**Nǐ jìrán zài zhège xuéxiào xuéxí, jiù yào zūnshǒu xuéxiào de gè xiàng guīdìng.** *Since you are studying in this school, you should observe its regulations.*

遵循 **zūnxún** *v* follow faithfully, adhere to

遵照 **zūnzhào** *v* act in accordance with

昨 **zuó** *n* yesterday

昨天 **zuótiān** [modif: 昨 past + 天 day] *n* yesterday □ 你昨天晚上去哪里了? **Nǐ zuótiān wǎnshang qù nǎli le?** *Where were you yesterday evening?*

琢 **zuó** as in 琢磨 **zuómo** 琢磨 **zuómo** *v* turn over in one's mind, ponder

左 **zuǒ** *n* the left side □ 我弟弟用左手吃饭, 写字。**Wǒ dìdi yòng zuǒshǒu chīfàn, xiězì.** *My younger brother eats and writes with the left hand.*

左边 **zuǒbian** [modif: 左 left + 边 side] *n* the left side, the left-hand side □ 坐在李先生左边的那位小姐

是谁? **Zuò zai Lǐ xiānsheng zuǒbian de nà wèi xiǎojiě shì shuí?** *Who is the young lady sitting on the left of Mr Li?*

左右 **zuǒyòu** [comp: 左 left + 右 right] *adv* approximately, nearly, about □ 今天最高温度二十度左右。**Jīntiān zuìgāo wēndù èrshí dù zuǒyòu.** *Today's maximum temperature is about twenty degrees.*

做 **zuò** *v* 1 do □ 这件事我不会做。**Zhè jiàn shì wǒ bú huì zuò.** *I don't know how to do this.* "你会做这个作业吗?" "会, 我已经做好了。" "**Nǐ huì zuò zhège zuòyè ma?**" "**Huì, wǒ yǐjīng zuòhǎo le.**" *"Can you do this assignment?" "Yes, I can. I've already done it."* 2 make □ 这张桌子是我爸爸做的。**Zhè zhāng zhuōzi shì wǒ bàba zuò de.** *This table was made by my father.* □ 中国酒是用米做的。**Zhōngguó jiǔ shì yòng mǐ zuò de.** *Chinese wine is made from rice.*

做工 **zuògōng** do manual work, work □ 今年夏天你要去哪里做工? **Jīnnián xiàtiān nǐ yào qù nǎlǐ zuògōng?** *Where are you going to work this summer?*

做法 **zuòfǎ** [modif: 做 do + 法 method] *n* way of doing things, method, practice □ 他这种做法不讲原则, 我不赞成。**Tā zhè zhǒng zuòfǎ bù jiǎng yuánzé, wǒ bú zànchéng.** *This kind of practice of his is unprincipled and I don't approve of it.*

做饭 **zuòfàn** [v+obj: 做 make + 饭 meal] cook, prepare a meal □ "你们家里谁做饭?" "我, 经常是我做饭。" "**Nǐmen jiāli shuí zuòfàn?**" "**Wǒ, jīngcháng shì wǒ zuòfàn.**" *"Who does the cooking in your family?" "I do. I usually do the cooking."*

做客 **zuòkè** *v* be a guest, visit □ 在春节的时候, 我们到亲戚家做客。**Zài chūnjié de shíhou, wǒmen dào qīnqi jiā zuòkè.** *In Spring Festival we visit our relatives.*

做梦 **zuòmèng** [v+obj: 做 make + 梦 dream] *v* dream □ 我昨天夜里做了一个奇怪的梦。**Wǒ zuótiān yèli zuò le yí ge qíguài de mèng.** *I had a strange dream last night.*

做主 **zuòzhǔ** *v* be one's own master

作 **zuò** *v* Same as 做 zuò

NOTE: 做 zuò and 作 zuò have the same pronunciation and often the same meaning, but 做 zuò is much more commonly used while 作 zuò occurs only in certain set expressions.

作案 **zuò'àn** *v* commit a crime

作废 **zuòfèi** *v* become invalid

作风 **zuòfēng** *n* way of behavior, way of working, style

独断独行的领导作风 **dúduàndúxíng de lǐngdǎo zuòfēng** autocratic style of leadership

作家 **zuòjiā** [modif: 作 create + 家 expert] *n* writer (especially of literary works, e.g. novels, stories) □ 在过去, 作家是很受人尊敬的。**Zài guòqu, zuòjiā shì hěn shòu rén zūnjìng de.** *In the past writers were very much respected.*

作家协会 **Zuòjiā Xiéhuì** Writers' Association

作品 **zuòpǐn** [modif: 作 create + 品 article] *n* literary or artistic work □ 这位作家又有新作品了。**Zhè wèi zuòjiā yòu yǒu xīn zuòpǐn le.** *This writer has written another work.*

作为 **zuòwéi** *prep* as, in the capacity of

作文 **zuòwén** [modif: 作 create + 文 writing] *n* (student's) composition □ 她的作文经常得到老师的表扬。**Tā de zuòwén jīngcháng dédào lǎoshī de biǎoyáng.** *Her compositions are often commended by the teacher.*

作物 **zuòwù** *n* crop

作业 **zuòyè** *n* school assignment, homework □ 中国的中小学生每天要做很多作业。**Zhōngguó de zhōng-xiǎo xuésheng měi tiān yào zuò hěn duō zuòyè.** *School children in China have lots of homework to do every day.*

作用 **zuòyòng** [comp: 作 work + 用 use] *n* function, role □ 他在这次谈判中起了很大作用。**Tā zài zhè cì tánpàn zhōng qǐle hěn dà zuòyòng.** *He played a major role in the negotiations.*

在…中起作用 **zài...zhōng qǐ zuòyòng** play a role in ..., perform a function in ...

作者 **zuòzhě** [suffix: 作 create + 者 nominal suffix] *n* author □ 这本书的作者是一位女作家。**Zhè běn shū de zuòzhě shì yí wèi nǚzuòjiā.** *The author of this book is a woman writer.*

坐 **zuò** *v* sit □ 请坐! **Qǐng zuò!** *Sit down, please!* □ 她正坐在窗边看书。**Tā zhèng zuò zài chuāngbiān kànshū.** *She's sitting by the window, reading.*

座 **zuò** I *measure wd* (for large and solid objects, such as a large building)

一座大楼 **yí zuò dàlóu** a big building

一座山 **yí zuò shān** a mountain, a hill

一座工厂 **yí zuò gōngchǎng** a factory

一座大学 **yí zuò dàxué** a university

一座桥 **yí zuò qiáo** a bridge

一座城市 **yí zuò chéngshì** a city

II *n* seat

座儿 **zuòr** *n* seat

座谈 **zuòtán** [comp: 座 seat + 谈 talk] *v* have an informal discussion, have an informal meeting □ 校长今天下午和一年级学生座谈。**Xiàozhǎng jīntiān xiàwǔ hé yì niánjí xuésheng zuòtán.** *The principal will have an informal discussion with first-year students this afternoon.*

座谈会 **zuòtánhuì** an informal discussion, forum

座位 **zuòwèi** [comp: 座 seat + 位 seat] *n* seat □ 请你给我留一个座位, 我马上就到。**Qǐng nǐ gěi wǒ liú yí ge zuòwèi, wǒ mǎshàng jiù dào.** *Please save a seat for me. I'll be there soon.* □ 这个座位有人吗? **Zhège zuòwèi yǒu rén ma?** *Is this seat taken?*

座右铭 **zuòyòumíng** *n* motto □ "为社会做贡献" 是我的座右铭。**"Wéi shèhuì zuò gòngxiàn" shì wǒ de zuòyòumíng.** *"Contribute to the society" is my motto.*

Appendices

1 Common Chinese Family Names

李 Lǐ	梁 Liáng	苏 Sū	范 Fán	顾 Kù
王 Wáng	宋 Sòng	卢 Lú	方 Fāng	侯 Hóu
张 Zhāng	郑 Zhèng	蒋 Jiǎng	石 Shí	邵 Shào
刘 Liú	谢 Xiè	蔡 Cài	姚 Yáo	孟 Mèng
陈 Chén	韩 Hán	贾 Jiǎ	谭 Tán	龙 Lóng
杨 Yáng	唐 Táng	丁 Dīng	廖 Liào	万 Wàn
赵 Zhào	冯 Féng	魏 Wèi	邹 Zōu	段 Duàn
黄 Huáng	于 Yú	薛 Xuē	熊 Xióng	雷 Léi
周 Zhōu	董 Dǒng	叶 Yè	金 Jīn	钱 Qián
吴 Wú	肖 Xiāo	阎 Yán	陆 Lù	汤 Tāng
徐 Xú	程 Chéng	余 Yú	郝 Hào	尹 Yīn
孙 Sūn	曹 Cáo	潘 Pān	孔 Kǒng	黎 Lí
胡 Hú	袁 Yuán	杜 Dù	白 Bái	易 Yì
朱 Zhū	邓 Dèng	戴 Dài	崔 Cuī	常 Cháng
高 Gāo	许 Xǔ	夏 Xià	康 Kāng	武 Wǔ
林 Lín	傅 Fù	钟 Zhōng	毛 Máo	乔 Qiáo
何 Hé	沈 Shěn	汪 Wāng	邱 Qiū	贺 Hè
郭 Guō	曾 Zèng	田 Tián	秦 Qín	赖 Làn
马 Mǎ	彭 Péng	任 Rèn	江 Jiāng	龚 Gōng
罗 Luó	吕 Lǚ	姜 Jiāng	史 Shǐ	文 Wén

2 Common English Names with Chinese Transcriptions
100 Common Surnames

Adams 亚当斯 **Yàdāngsī**
Alexander 亚历山大 **Yàlìshāndà**
Allen 艾伦 **Àilún**
Anderson 安德森 **Āndésēn**
Bailey 贝利 **Bèilì**
Baker 贝克 **Bèikè**
Barnes 巴恩斯 **Bā'ēnsī**
Bell 贝尔 **Bèi'ěr**
Bennett 本内特 **Běnnèitè**
Brooks 布鲁克斯 **Bùlǔkèsī**
Brown 布朗 **Bùlǎng**
Bryant 布赖恩特 **Bùlàiēntè**
Butler 巴特勒 **Bātèlè**
Campbell 坎贝尔 **Kǎnbèi'ěr**
Carter 卡特 **Kǎtè**
Clark 克拉克 **Kèlākè**
Coleman 科尔曼 **Kē'ěrmàn**
Collins 柯林斯 **Kēlínsī**

Cook 库克 **Kùkè**
Cooper 库伯 **Kùbó**
Cox 考克斯 **Kǎokèsī**
Davis 戴维斯 **Dàiwéisī**
Diaz 迪亚士 **Díyàshì**
Edwards 爱德华兹 **Àidéhuázī**
Evans 伊万斯 **Yīwànsī**
Flores 弗洛雷斯 **Fúluòléisī**
Garcia 加西亚 **Jiāxīyà**
Gonzales 贡萨勒斯 **Gòngsàlèsī**
Gonzalez 贡萨勒斯 **Gòngsàlèsī**
Gray 格雷 **Géléi**
Green 格林 **Gélín**
Griffin 格里芬 **Gélǐfēn**
Hall 霍尔 **Huò'ěr**
Harris 哈里斯 **Hālǐsī**

Hayes 海斯 **Hǎisī**
Henderson 亨德森 **Hēngdésēn**
Hernandez 赫南德斯 **Hènándésī**
Hill 希尔 **Xī'ěr**
Howard 霍华德 **Huòhuádé**
Hughes 休斯 **Xiūsī**
Hunt 亨特 **Hēngtè**
Jackson 杰克逊 **Jiékèxùn**
James 詹姆斯 **Zhānmǔsī**
Jenkins 詹金斯 **Zhānjīnsī**
Johnson 约翰逊 **Yuēhànxùn**
Jones 琼斯 **Qióngsī**
Kelly 凯利 **Kǎilì**
King 金 **Jīn**
Lee 李 **Lǐ**
Lewis 刘易斯 **Liúyìsī**
Long 郎 **Láng**

Lopez 洛佩斯 **Luòpèisī**
Martin 马丁 **Mǎdīng**
Martinez 马蒂内斯
Mǎdìnèisī
Miller 米勒 **Mǐlè**
Mitchell 米切尔 **Mǐqiē'ěr**
Moore 摩尔 **Mó'ěr**
Morgan 摩根 **Mógēn**
Morris 莫里斯 **Mòlǐsī**
Murphy 墨菲 **Mòfēi**
Nelson 纳尔逊 **Nà'ěrxùn**
Parker 帕克(派克) **Pàkè**
(**Pàikè**)
Patterson 帕特森 **Pàtèsēn**
Perez 佩雷斯 **Pèiléisī**
Perry 佩里 **Pèilǐ**
Peterson 彼得森 **Bǐdésēn**
Phillips 菲利普斯 **Fēilìpǔsī**
Powell 鲍威尔 **Bàowēi'ěr**

Price 普赖斯 **Pǔlàisī**
Ramirez 拉米雷斯 **Lāmǐléisī**
Reed 里德 **Lǐdé**
Richardson 里查森 **Lǐchásēn**
Rivera 里韦拉 **Lǐwéilā**
Roberts 罗伯茨 **Luóbócí**
Robinson 罗宾逊
Luóbīnxùn
Rodriguez 罗德里古埃斯
Luódélǐgǔ'āisī
Rogers 罗杰斯 **Luójiésī**
Ross 罗斯 **Luósī**
Russell 拉塞尔(罗素)
Lāsāi'ěr (Luósù)
Sanchez 桑切兹 **Sāngqiēzī**
Sanders 山德斯 **Shāndésī**
Scott 斯科特 **Sīkētè**
Simmons 西蒙斯 **Xīméngsī**
Smith 史密斯 **Shǐmìsī**

Stewart 斯图尔特 **Sītú'ěrtè**
Taylor 泰勒 **Tàilè**
Thomas 托马斯 **Tuōmǎsī**
Thompson 汤普森
Tāngpǔsēn
Torres 托雷斯 **Tuōléisī**
Turner 特纳 **Tènà**
Walker 沃克 **Wòkè**
Ward 沃德 **Wòdé**
Washington 华盛顿
Huáshèngdùn
Watson 沃森(华生)
Wòsēn (Huáshēng)
White 怀特 **Huáitè**
Williams 威廉斯 **Wēiliánsī**
Wilson 威尔逊 **Wēi'ěrsùn**
Wood 伍德 **Wǔdé**
Wright 莱特 **Láitè**
Young 扬 **Yáng**

100 Common Male Given Names

Aaron 艾伦 **Àilún**
Adam 亚当 **Yàdāng**
Adrian 埃德里安 **āidélǐ'ān**
Aidan 艾旦 **Àidàn**
Alex 亚力克斯 **Yàlìkèsī**
Alexander 亚历山大
Yàlìshāndà
Andrew 安德鲁 **Āndélǔ**
Angel 安吉儿 **Ānjí'ér**
Anthony 安东尼 **Āndōngní**
Antonio 安东尼奥
Āndōngní'ào
Austin 奥斯丁 **Àosīdīng**
Benjamin 本杰明
Běnjiémíng
Blake 布莱克 **Bùláikè**
Brandon 布兰顿 **Bùlándùn**
Brian 布赖恩 **Bùlài'ēn**
Bryan 布赖恩 **Bùlài'ēn**
Bryce 布赖斯 **Bùlàisī**
Caleb 加勒布 **Jiālèbù**
Cameron 克迈伦 **Kèmàilún**
Carlos 卡罗斯 **Kǎluósī**
Carson 卡森 **Kǎsēn**
Charles 查尔斯 **Chá'ěrsī**
Chase 蔡斯 **Càisī**
Christian 克里斯琴 **Kèlǐsīqín**

Christopher 克里斯托佛
Kèlǐsītuōfó
Cody 科迪 **Kēdí**
Cole 科尔 **Kē'ěr**
Connor 康纳 **Kāngnà**
Dakota 达科他 **Dákētā**
Dalton 道尔顿 **Dào'ěrdùn**
Daniel 丹尼尔 **Dānníěr**
David 戴维 **Dàiwéi**
Devin 德文 **Déwén**
Dylan 戴伦 **Dàilún**
Eduardo 埃杜阿多
Āidù'ā'duō
Edward 爱德华 **Àidéhuá**
Elijah 艾利加 **Àilìjiā**
Eric 埃里克 **Āilǐkè**
Ethan 伊森 **Yīsēn**
Evan 伊万 **Yīwàn**
Gabriel 加百列 **Jiābǎiliè**
Gavin 加文 **Jiāwén**
George 乔治 **Qiáozhì**
Henry 亨利 **Hēnglì**
Hunter 亨特 **Hēngtè**
Ian 伊安 **Yī'ān**
Isaac 艾萨克 **Áisàkè**
Isaiah 埃塞亚 **Āisāyà**
Jack 杰克 **Jiékè**

Jackson 杰克逊 **Jiékèxùn**
Jacob 雅各布 **Yǎgèbù**
James 詹姆斯 **Zhānmǔsī**
Jared 贾雷德 **Jiǎléidé**
Jason 贾森 **Jiǎsēn**
Jeremiah 杰里迈亚
Jiélǐmàiyà
Jesus 杰苏斯 **Jiésūsī**
John 约翰 **Yuēhàn**
Jonathan 乔纳森 **Qiáonàsēn**
Jordan 乔丹 **Qiáodān**
Jose 约瑟 **Yuēsè**
Joseph 约瑟夫 **Yuēsèfū**
Joshua 乔舒亚 **Qiáoshūyà**
Juan 贾安 **Jiǎ'ān**
Julian 朱利安 **Zhūlì'ān**
Justin 贾斯廷 **Jiǎsītíng**
Kevin 凯文 **Kǎiwén**
Kyle 凯尔 **Kǎi'ěr**
Logan 洛根 **Luògēn**
Luca 卢卡斯 **Lúkǎsī**
Luis 路易斯 **Lùyìsī**
Luke 卢克 **Lúkè**
Marcus 马库斯 **Mǎkùsī**
Mason 梅森 **Méisēn**
Matthew 马修 **Mǎxiū**
Michael 迈克尔 **Màikè'ěr**

Miguel 米古埃尔 **Mǐgǔ'āi'ěr**
Nathan 内森 **Nèisēn**
Nathaniel 纳撒尼尔
　　Nàsāní'ěr
Nicholas 尼古拉斯 **Nígǔlāsī**
Noah 诺亚 **Nuòyà**
Oscar 奥斯卡 **Àosīkǎ**
Patrick 帕特里克 **Pàtèlǐkè**
Richard 理查德 **Lǐchádé**

Robert 罗伯特 **Luóbótè**
Ryan 瑞恩 **Ruìēn**
Samuel 塞姆尔 **Sāimǔ'ěr**
Sean 肖恩 **Xiào'ēn**
Sebastian 萨巴斯蒂安
　　Sàbāsīdì'ān
Seth 塞思 **Sāisī**
Spencer 斯潘塞 **Sīpānsāi**
Steven 施蒂文 **Shīdìwén**

Thomas 托马斯 **Tuōmǎsī**
Timothy 提摩西 **Tímóxī**
Trevor 特雷弗 **Tèléifú**
Tristan 特里斯登 **Tèlǐsīdēng**
Tyler 泰勒 **Tàilè**
William 威廉 **Wēilián**
Wyatt 怀亚特 **Huáiyàtè**
Xavier 泽维尔 **Zéwéi'ěr**
Zachary 扎查理 **Zhāchálǐ**

100 Common Female Given Names

Abigail 阿比盖尔 **Ābǐgài'ěr**
Alexandra 亚历山德拉
　　Yàlìshāndélā
Alexandria 亚历山德丽亚
　　Yàlìshāndélìyà
Alexia 亚利克西亚
　　Yàlìkèxīyà
Alexis 亚历克西亚
　　Yàlìkèxīyà
Allison 阿莉森 **Ālìsēn**
Alyssa 阿丽萨 **Ālìsà**
Amanda 阿曼达 **Āmàndá**
Amber 安伯 **Ānbó**
Ana 安娜 **Ān'nà**
Andrea 安德烈 **Āndéliè**
Angela 安吉拉 **Ānjílā**
Angelica 安吉利卡 **Ānjílìkǎ**
Anna 安娜 **Ān'nà**
Ashley 艾什利 **Àishílì**
Audrey 奥德丽 **Àodélì**
Bailey 贝利 **Bèilì**
Brittany 布里特尼 **Bùlǐtèní**
Brooke 布鲁克 **Bùlǔkè**
Caitlin 凯特琳 **Kǎitèlín**
Caroline 卡罗琳 **Kǎluólín**
Catherine 凯莎琳 **Kǎishālín**
Chloe 克洛伊 **Kèluòyī**
Christina 克里斯蒂安娜
　　Kèlǐsīdì'ānnà
Courtney 考特尼 **Kǎotèní**
Danielle 丹尼艾勒
　　Dān'ní'àilè
Destiny 黛丝提妮 **Dàisītíní**
Elizabeth 伊利萨白 **Yīlìsàbái**
Emily 埃米利 **Āimǐlì**
Emma 埃玛 **Āimǎ**

Erin 俄林 **É'lín**
Faith 菲思 **Fēisī**
Gabriella 加布里埃拉
　　Jiābùlǐ'āilā
Gabrielle 加布里埃尔
　　Jiābùlǐāi'ěr
Grace 格雷斯 **Géléisī**
Hailey 海莉 **Hǎilì**
Haley 海莉 **Hǎilì**
Hannah 汉纳 **Hàn'nà**
Hilda 希尔达 **Xī'ěrdá**
Isabel 伊萨贝尔 **Yīsàbèi'ěr**
Isabella 伊萨贝拉 **Yīsàbèilā**
Isabelle 伊萨贝勒 **Yīsàbèilè**
Jacqueline 杰奎琳 **Jiékuílín**
Jane 简 **Jiǎn**
Jasmine 杰斯敏 **Jiésīmǐn**
Jenna 詹娜 **Zhān'nà**
Jennifer 詹妮弗 **Zhān'nīfú**
Jessica 杰西卡 **Jiéxīkǎ**
Joan 琼 **Qióng**
Jocelyn 乔瑟琳 **Qiáosèlín**
Jordan 乔丹 **Qiáodān**
Joyce 乔伊斯 **Qiáoyīsī**
Judith 朱蒂丝 **Zhūdìsī**
Julia 朱丽娅 **Zhūlìyà**
Karen 卡伦 **Kǎlún**
Katherine 凯莎琳 **Kǎishālín**
Kay 凯 **Kǎi**
Kayla 凯拉 **Kǎilā**
Kelly 凯丽 **Kǎilì**
Kimberly 金博莉 **Jīnbólì**
Linda 琳达 **Líndá**
Lauren 劳伦 **Láolún**
Mackenzie 麦肯希 **Màikěnxī**
Madeline 马德琳 **Mǎdélín**

Madison 麦迪逊 **Màidíxùn**
Marcia 玛西娅 **Mǎxīyà**
Maria 玛丽亚 **Mǎlìyà**
Mariah 玛丽亚 **Mǎlìyà**
Marissa 马丽萨 **Mǎlìsà**
Mary 玛丽 **Mǎlì**
Megan 梅根 **Méigēn**
Melanie 梅兰妮 **Méilánnī**
Melissa 梅里萨 **Méilǐsà**
Michelle 米歇尔 **Mǐxiē'ěr**
Miranda 米兰达 **Mǐlándá**
Natalie 纳塔利 **Nàtǎlì**
Nicole 尼科尔 **Níkē'ěr**
Olivia 奥列维亚 **Àolièwéiyà**
Paige 佩奇 **Pèiqí**
Pamela 潘美拉 **Pānměilā**
Rachel 雷切尔 **Léiqiē'ěr**
Rebecca 丽贝卡 **Lìbèikǎ**
Riley 赖利 **Làilì**
Samantha 萨曼莎 **Sàmànshā**
Sara 萨拉 **Sàlā**
Sarah 萨拉 **Sàlā**
Savannah 萨瓦纳 **Sàwǎnà**
Shelby 谢尔比 **Xiè'ěrbǐ**
Sierra 西埃拉 **Xī'āilā**
Sophia 索菲亚 **Suǒfēiyà**
Stephanie 斯蒂芬妮
　　Sīdìfēnnī
Susan 苏珊 **Sūshān**
Sydney 西德尼 **Xīdéní**
Taylor 泰勒 **Tàilè**
Tracy 翠西 **Cuìxī**
Vanessa 瓦内萨 **Wǎnèisà**
Victoria 维多利亚
　　Wéiduōlìyà
Zoe 佐薇 **Zuǒwēi**

3 Chinese Place Names

China is administratively divided into provinces, autonomous regions, municipalities under direct jurisdiction of the central government and special administrative regions. Under each province and autonomous region major cities are listed, with the first city listed being the capital of the province or autonomous region.

Provinces (省 shěng)

Anhui 安徽 **Ānhuī**
  Hefei 合肥 **Héféi**
  Bangbu 蚌埠 **Bàngbù**
  Huainan 淮南 **Huáinán**

Fujian/Fukien 福建 **Fújiàn**
  Fuzhou/Foochow 福州 **Fúzhōu**
  Xiamen/Amoy 厦门 **Xiàmén**
  Zhangzhou 漳州 **Zhāngzhōu**

Gansu 甘肃 **Gānsù**
  Lanzhou 兰州 **Lánzhōu**
  Tianshui 天水 **Tiānshuǐ**
  Dunhuang 敦煌 **Dūnhuáng**

Guangdong 广东 **Guǎngdōng**
  Guangzhou 广州 **Guǎngzhōu**
  Zhuhai 珠海 **Zhūhǎi**
  Zhanjiang 湛江 **Zhànjiāng**

Guizhou 贵州 **Guìzhōu**
  Guiyang 贵阳 **Guìyáng**
  Liupanshui 六盘水 **Liùpánshuǐ**
  Zunyi 遵义 **Zūnyì**

Hainan 海南 **Hǎinán**
  Haikou 海口 **Hǎikǒu**
  Sanya 三亚 **Sānyà**

Hebei 河北 **Héběi**
  Shijiazhuang 石家庄 **Shíjiāzhuāng**
  Baoding 保定 **Bǎodìng**
  Tangshan 唐山 **Tángshān**

Heilongjiang 黑龙江 **Hēilóngjiāng**
  Harbin 哈尔滨 **Hāěrbīn**
  Qiqihar 齐齐哈尔 **Qíqíhāěr**
  Daqing 大庆 **Dàqìng**

Henan 河南 **Hénán**
  Zhengzhou 郑州 **Zhèngzhōu**
  Kaifeng 开封 **Kāifēng**
  Luoyang 洛阳 **Luòyáng**

Hubei 湖北 **Húběi**
  Wuhan 武汉 **Wǔhàn**
  Xiangfan 襄樊 **Xiāngfán**
  Yichang 宜昌 **Yíchāng**

Hunan 湖南 **Húnán**
  Changsha 长沙 **Chángshā**
  Zhuzhou 株洲 **Zhūzhōu**
  Hengyang 衡阳 **Héngyáng**

Jiangsu 江苏 **Jiāngsū**
  Nanjing 南京 **Nánjīng**
  Wuxi 无锡 **Wúxī**
  Suzhou 苏州 **Sūzhōu**

Jiangxi 江西 **Jiāngxī**
  Nanchang 南昌 **Nánchāng**
  Jiujiang 九江 **Jiǔjiāng**
  Jingdezhen 景德镇 **Jìngdézhèn**

Jilin 吉林 **Jílín**
  Changchun 长春 **Chángchūn**
  Jilin 吉林 **Jílín**
  Siping 四平 **Sìpíng**

Liaoning 辽宁 **Liáoníng**
  Shenyang 沈阳 **Shěnyáng**
  Dalian 大连 **Dàlián**
  Jinzhou 锦州 **Jìnzhōu**

Qinghai/Tsinghai 青海 **Qīnghǎi**
  Xining 西宁 **Xīníng**

Shaanxi 陕西 **Shǎnxī**
  Xi'an 西安 **Xī'ān**
  Xianyang 咸阳 **Xiányáng**
  Baoji 宝鸡 **Bǎojī**

Shandong 山东 **Shāndōng**
  Jinan 济南 **Jìnán**
  Qingdao/Tsingtao 青岛 **Qīngdǎo**
  Yantai 烟台 **Yāntái**

Shanxi 山西 **Shānxī**
  Taiyuan 太原 **Tàiyuán**
  Changzhi 长治 **Chángzhì**
  Datong 大同 **Dàtóng**

Sichuan/Szechuan 四川 **Sìchuān**
  Chengdu 成都 **Chéngdū**
  Mianyang 绵阳 **Miányáng**
  Leshan 乐山 **Lèshān**

Yunnan 云南 **Yúnnán**
  Kunming 昆明 **Kūnmíng**
  Dali 大理 **Dàlǐ**
  Jinghong 景洪 **Jǐnghóng**

Zhejiang 浙江 **Zhèjiāng**
  Hangzhou 杭州 **Hángzhōu**
  Ningbo 宁波 **Níngbō**
  Wenzhou 温州 **Wēnzhōu**

(Taiwan 台湾 **Táiwān**
  Taipei 台北 **Táiběi**
  Kaoshiung 高雄 **Gāoxióng**
  Taichung 台中 **Táizhōng**)

Autonomous Regions (自治区 zìzhìqū)

Guangxi Zhuang Autonomous Region
广西壮族自治区 **Guǎngxī Zhuàngzú zìzhìqū**
  Nanning 南宁 **Nánníng**
  Guilin 桂林 **Guìlín**
  Liuzhou 柳州 **Liǔzhōu**

Inner Mongolia Autonomous Region
内蒙古自治区 **Nèiménggǔ zìzhìqū**
  Hohhot 呼和浩特 **Hūhéhàotè**
  Baotou 包头 **Bāotóu**
  Chifeng 赤峰 **Chìfēng**

Ningxia Hui Autonomous Region
宁夏回族自治区 **Níngxià Huízú Zìzhìqū**
  Yinchuan 银川 **Yínchuān**

Tibet Autonomous Region 西藏自治区
Xīzàng Zìzhìqū
  Lhasa 拉萨 **Lāsà**
  Xigaze/Shigatse 日喀则 **Rìkāzé**

Xinjiang Uygur Autonomous Region
新疆维吾尔自治区 **Xīnjiāng Wéiwúěr Zìzhìqū**
  Ūrūmqi/Urumchi 乌鲁木齐 **Wūlǔmùqí**

Municipalities under direct jurisdiction of the central government (直辖市 zhíxiáshì)

Beijing municipality 北京市 **Běijīng shì** (the capital of the People's Republic of China)
Chongqing/Chungking municipality 重庆市 **Chóngqìng shì**
Shanghai municipality 上海市 **Shànghǎi shì**
Tianjin/Tientsin municipality 天津市 **Tiānjīn shì**

Special administrative regions (特别行政区 tèbié xíngzhèngqū)

Hong Kong 香港 **Xiānggǎng**
Macao/Macau 澳门 **Àomén**